The Nonprofit Handbook: Management

NONPROFIT LAW, FINANCE, AND MANAGEMENT SERIES

The Nonprofit Handbook: Management

Second Edition

Edited by
Tracy Daniel Connors

JOHN WILEY & SONS, INC.

NEW YORK / CHICHESTER / WEINHEIM / BRISBANE / SINGAPORE / TORONTO

Library of Congress Cataloging in Publication Data:

ISBN 0-471-17967-1

Printed in the United States of America

10 9 8 7 6 5 4 3 2 1

For my daughters . . . who provide daily inspiration, support, and counsel . . .

Karen Danielle Connors Henson
Miriam Faith Connors McCarns

SUBSCRIPTION NOTICE

This Wiley product is updated on a periodic basis with supplements to reflect important changes in the subject matter. If you purchased this product directly from John Wiley & Sons, Inc., we have already recorded your subscription for this update service.

If, however, you purchased this product from a bookstore and wish to receive (1) the current update at no additional charge, and (2) future updates and revised or related volumes billed separately with a 30-day examination review, please send your name, company name (if applicable), address, and the title of the product to:

> Supplement Department
> John Wiley & Sons, Inc.
> One Wiley Drive
> Somerset, NJ 08875
> 1-800-225-5945

For customers outside the United States, please contact the Wiley office nearest you:

Professional & Reference Division
John Wiley & Sons Canada, Ltd.
22 Worcester Road
Rexdale, Ontario M9W 1L1
CANADA
(416) 675-3580
1-800-567-4797
Fax (416) 675-6599

Jacaranda Wiley Ltd.
PRT Division
P.O. Box 174
North Ryde, NSW 2113
AUSTRALIA
(02) 805-1100
Fax (02) 805-1597

John Wiley & Sons, Ltd.
Baffins Lane
Chichester
West Sussex, P019 1UD
UNITED KINGDOM
(44) (243) 779777

John Wiley & Sons (SEA) Pte. Ltd.
37 Jalan Pemimpin
Block B # 05-04
Union Industrial Building
SINGAPORE 2057
(65) 258-1157

▼ About the Editor

Tracy Daniel Connors is president of the BelleAire Institute in Bowie, Maryland, a management communications and publishing organization. During the past twenty years, Mr. Connors has acted as editor of six of the best-selling, most comprehensive handbooks for leaders and managers of nonprofit organizations. He has served in a variety of management positions in business, government, and nonprofit organizations. A Captain in the Naval Reserve, he has been recalled to active duty frequently since 1985, as director of Congressional and Public Affairs for the Space and Naval Warfare Systems Command and the Naval Sea Systems Command in Washington, D.C., and as Deputy Director of the Navy's Command Excellence and Leader Development Program. Other recent Navy assignments have included duties on the staff of the Chief of Naval Operations, where he served as the first Total Quality Leadership Public Affairs Officer, at Naval District Washington, and the Naval Criminal Investigation Service. Other positions have included Director of Satellite Learning Services for the U.S. Chamber of Commerce; Congressional Administrative Assistant; corporate communications manager for a major electronics corporation; vice president of a national publishing corporation; and as an officer, board member, or professional staff director of numerous nonprofit organizations. A consultant for nonprofit organizations with a special focus on organizational excellence, he is an adjunct faculty member at the Bowie State University Graduate School in Quality Management. He attended Jacksonville University, graduated from the University of Florida, and earned a Master of Arts Degree from the University of Rhode Island. Mr. Connors is the editor of *The Volunteer Management Handbook*, *The Nonprofit Management Handbook: Operating Policies & Procedures*, *The Nonprofit Organization Handbook*, *Financial Management for Nonprofit Organizations*, *The Dictionary of Mass Media and Communication*, and *Flavors of the Fjords: The Norwegian Holiday Cookbook*.

▼ Contributors

Evelyn Alemanni, MBA, is the president of ALL.EA and has been involved in corporate communications for over 20 years. Her work in helping community organizations present their causes effectively is the basis for her contribution to the *The Nonprofit Handbook*.

Pamela G. Arrington, PhD, is director of academic affairs for the Maryland Higher Education Commission and is a volunteer trainer for United Way. Prior to her present position, she was an associate professor in Behavioral Sciences at Bowie State University, Maryland. In recent years, Dr. Arrington has served as a consultant to the Department of Defense Task Force on Human Resource Management: Workforce 2000.

Jody Blazek, CPA, is a partner in Blazek & Vetterling LLP, a Houston CPA firm focused on non-profit organizations. Her concentration in nonprofits began in 1966 at KPMG Peat Marwick and, during the seventies, she gained management experience as the chief financial officer of the Menil Foundation. Ms. Blazek is highly regarded as a lecturer on nonprofit topics and is the author of three books in the Wiley Nonprofit Series: *Tax Planning and Compliance for Tax-Exempt Organizations, Financial Planning for Nonprofit Organizations,* and *Private Foundations: Law and Tax Compliance,* co-authored with Bruce Hopkins for release in 1997.

Jeanne H. Bradner is a nationally known author, speaker, trainer, and consultant in nonprofit management, leadership development, and volunteer management. Among her current clients are the Illinois Commission on Community Service. Bradner is the author of *The Board Members, A Beneficial Bestiary* (Conversation Press, 1995), *Passionate Volunteerism* (Conversation Press, 1993), a contributor to *The Volunteer Management Handbook,* and served for six and a half years as Director of the Illinois Governor's Office of Voluntary Action.

Jeffrey L. Brudney, MA, PhD, is a professor of Political Science and director of the Doctor of Public Administration Program at the University of Georgia. He serves on the editorial boards of leading journals in nonprofit sector studies. His book, *Fostering Volunteer Programs in the Public Sector,* received the John Grenzebach Award for Outstanding Research in Philanthropy for Education.

Joseph E. Champoux, PhD, is a professor of Management at The University of New Mexico. Dr. Champoux serves as a consultant to several public and private organizations. His consulting activities include the design of attitude surveys, organization assessments, management training and development programs, and training in total quality management.

James M. Greenfield, ACFRE, FAHP, is senior vice president, Development and Community Relations, at Hoag Memorial Hospital Presbyterian in Newport Beach, California. He is a longtime active member of the National Association of Fund Raising Executives (NSFRE) and the Association for Healthcare Philanthropy (AHP), and is currently on NSFRE's foundation board. He has written several books including *Fund-Raising: Evaluating and Managing the Fund Development Process, Fund Raising Fundamentals: A Guide to Annual Giving for Professionals and Volunteers,* and *Fund-Raising Cost Effectiveness: A Self-Assessment Workbook.*

Bruce R. Hopkins, JD, LLM, is a practicing lawyer with Polsinelli, White, Vardeman & Shalton in Kansas City, Missouri, where he specializes in the representation of nonprofit organizations. He has served as Chair of the Committee on Exempt Organizations, American Bar Association; and President, Planned Giving Study Group of Greater Washington, D.C. Mr. Hopkins is the series editor of John Wiley & Sons' nonprofit law, finance and management series, and author of several books in that series.

Eugene M. Johnson, DBA, MBA, is a professor of Marketing at the University of Rhode Island. He has served as a consultant for a large number of businesses and nonprofit organizations and is a frequent lecturer. Dr. Johnson has done extensive research on services marketing and sales management and has published articles in *Nonprofit World, Banking, Journal of Services Marketing,* as well as in a number of other publications.

Ray Katz, MBA, studied total quality management with Dr. W. Edwards Deming, and worked with a number of nonprofits, including CARE and United Way of New York City. He is currently a partner with *i-site web design.*

William A. Kleintop, PhD, is an assistant professor of Public Administration in the Center for Public Service at Seton Hall University, where he teaches in the areas of information technology, organizational behavior and human resources management, strategic information planning, and information technology implementation. He also has experience serving on the boards of community-based nonprofit organizations.

Richard F. Larkin, CPA, MBA, is a technical director of the Not-for-Profit Industry Services Group of Price Waterhouse LLP. He is extensively involved in the development of accounting standards for not-for-profit organizations, was the chairman of the AICPA's Not-for-Profit Audit Guide task force, and is a member of the AICPA Not-for-Profit Organizations Committee and FASB Not-for-Profit Accounting Issues task force. He is the co-author of *Financial and Accounting Guide for Not-for-Profit Organizations, Fifth Edition,* published by John Wiley & Sons, Inc.

D. Kerry Laycock, MS, is an organizational consultant serving industry, government, and nonprofit organizations. His practice is devoted to improving organizational effectiveness through planning, employee involvement, and quality management.

Pamela J. Leland, PhD, is an assistant professor in the Center for Public Service at Seton Hall University, where she teaches and conducts research in areas of nonprofit management and public policy. In addition to her current work on charitable tax exemption, Dr. Leland has published on the subjects of housing, homelessness, social policy, and postindustrialism. She has a PhD in Urban Affairs and Public Policy from the University of Delaware.

Suzanne J. Lulewicz is the owner of SJL Associates, an education consulting firm providing education, training, and management consulting services to nonprofit organizations. Specializing in designing training and leadership programs with coaching interventions, Ms. Lulewicz consults to help improve effectiveness in the workplace while maintaining a collaborative operating environment. Ms. Lulewicz has worked with nonprofits as a staff member, vice president of education, director of curriculum, and as a volunteer leader.

Charles C. Manz, PhD, is an international scholar and consultant on the topics of leadership and self-managing teams. Dr. Manz was a Marvin Bower Fellow at Harvard University, and is currently professor of management at Arizona State University. He will be the Charles and Janet Nirenberg Professor of Business Leadership at the University of Massachusetts, Amherst, beginning in the fall of 1997.

Mark Michaels, MPA is president of People Technologies, a management consulting firm providing services in organizational development, personnel management, and training to profit and nonprofit service organizations. Mr. Michaels also teaches courses in nonprofit management and performance management at Benedictine University, Lisle, Illinois.

Jill O. Muehrcke is the founding editor of *Nonprofit World,* a bi-monthly journal for executives of nonprofit organizations, established in 1983 (published by the Society for Nonprofit Organizations, Madison, Wisconsin). She has written books on a variety of topics and has served as a national seminar and workshop leader. An honors graduate from the University of Washington at Seattle, she is listed in *Who's Who of America* and is an associate editor of the Civic Practices Network (CPN), Brandeis University, Waltham, Massachusetts. She is also the founder and owner of the publishing firm JP Publications.

Edward L. Naro is director of the Quality Management Center at TASC Inc., an applied information technology company. Mr. Naro provides total quality and change management implementation support and training within TASC and to a diverse base of government and commercial sector clients. Before joining TASC, Mr. Naro completed 26 years of Naval Service. As a Naval Aviator, Captain Naro's service included assignments as Commanding Officer of a Navy Aviation Squadron, Director of Management and Assessment in the Navy's Office of Civilian Personnel Management, and Director of the Navy Occupational Development and Analysis Center (NODAC), where he successfully implemented TQM in his own organization and assisted other organizations in their implementation efforts. Mr. Naro received his BA in Political Science from the University of Mississippi in 1965. He is a graduate of U.S. Naval War College, class of 1976, and is a graduate of the National War College, class of 1985.

Ruthie G. Reynolds, PhD, CPA, JD, is a professor of Accounting in the School of Business at Morehouse College in Atlanta, GA. She has conducted research in nonprofit accounting and management and has published articles in *Nonprofit World*, *The Woman CPA*, and *The ABC Theological Journal*. In addition, she has conducted seminars and workshops for accountants, board members, and administrators of nonprofit agencies throughout the world.

Howard J. Sartori, PE, is a president of Sartori Associates, Washington, DC, an information technology consulting firm providing turn-key planning, design, installation, training, and networking. Additional assignment included Director of Internet Technology, U.S. Navy. Awards for his Internet work include the President's Legion of Merit Medal, and the Government Agency of the Year Award from *Government Computer News*, for developing the Navy Internet and software kit.

Henry P. Sims, Jr., PhD, is an international scholar and consultant on the topics of leadership and self-managing teams. Dr. Sims is currently professor of Management and Organizations at the Maryland Business School.

Sara H. Skolnick, BBA, CAE, has over 25 years of experience in leadership positions of church, school, and community nonprofit organizations. For the past 15 years, she has held senior management positions in nonprofit associations. Most recently, she was Executive Director of the American Society of Association Executives and has led workshops on cost reduction and control and professional development. She is currently Chief Operating Officer of System Science Consultants and gives advice and counsel on the full range of management topics to religious, trade, and professional nonprofit associations.

Barbara Burgess Soltz is president of AMI Management, Inc., in Cleveland, Ohio. Formerly she was a fund-raising and board development consultant with the firm of Staley/Robeson. She is a doctoral candidate in higher education administration at Kent State University, Ohio.

Richard L. Thompson, APR, is deputy director for public affairs at the Naval Research Laboratory in Washington, D.C.; following duties as Director, Congressional and Media Relations, and Space and Naval Warfare Systems Command. In addition, he is a Washington-based business-to-business, business-to-government, and government-to-business marketing, communications, and public relations consultant specializing in contingency and special event planning for the nonprofit, profit, and government business sectors. Mr. Thompson is a practitioner accredited by the Public Relations Society of America and has conducted contingency public affairs for more than 23 years as an active duty and reserve U.S. Navy public affairs officer, and as a senior counselor at a high technology advertising and public relations agency.

Robbin Zeff, PhD (robbin@zeff.com), is president of *THE ZEFF GROUP*, a consulting firm in Arlington, Virginia, which specializes in Internet strategic planning, Internet conferences and organizational training programs. The Zeff Group is considered one of the leaders in the emerging field of cyberfund-raising—consulting nonprofits on how to maximize their revenue-generating potential on the Internet. Ms. Zeff is the author of *The Nonprofit Guide to the Internet* (John Wiley & Sons, 1996) which demonstrates with extensive examples and case studies the importance of nonprofits going on-line. She holds a PhD in Folklore and American Studies from Indiana University.

Lawrence Zimmerman, LLB is a practicing lawyer in Washington, D.C., where he is a member of the law firm of Sanders, Schnabel, Brandenburg & Zimmerman, P.C. Mr. Zimmerman specializes in the representation of management in virtually all aspects of labor and employment law. He counsels nonprofit organizations and business enterprises concerning employer policies and employee relations, and on such matters as employment discrimination, wrongful termination, compliance with wage-hour laws, and the like. In the case of unionized employers, he provides counsel on collective bargaining, grievance handling, and arbitration proceedings. Mr. Zimmerman is a graduate of Yale College and Yale Law School.

Sally A. Zinno is an administrator, consultant and teacher with over 20 years of planning and hands-on management experience in museums and nonprofit institutions. She has directed the administrative and financial operations at the Delaware Art Museum and the Harvard University Art Museums. She was the senior administrative officer at the Boston Museum of Science at a time when it doubled its operating budget, staff, physical plant, and the number of people it served. Ms. Zinno is currently the Chair of both the American Association of Museums' Management Committee and the Council of Standing Professional Committees. She teaches a graduate level course in administration as part of Harvard University's Museum Certificate Program and Financial Management in George Washington University's Museum Studies Degree Program.

▼ Preface

It has been nearly twenty years since I had the privilege of leading a team of national subject matter experts to compile the first nonprofit management handbook, *The Non-profit Organization Handbook* (McGraw-Hill, 1979). The breakthrough nature of that work lay in its recognition that regardless of the specific public purpose served by a nonprofit organization, all had much in common when it came to management. Specifically, there were seven areas of management and leadership which taken together established that there was an emerging body of professional knowledge and new career fields in something called nonprofit management. The management and leadership areas in which nonprofits have such strong commonality include: organization and corporate principles; leadership, management, and control; volunteer administration; sources of revenue; communication and public relations; financial management and administration; and legal and regulatory issues.

Management of nonprofit organizations is steadily becoming more professional. Information is shared through a growing number of associations and periodicals, enabling sector leaders to adapt these policies and procedures to fulfill the various missions of their organizations. Approaches that work are sorted out from those that generally do not. This process, however, is often sporadic or subject to chance. The need for a convenient, comprehensive guide to the daily operation and management of nonprofit organizations gave rise to the *Nonprofit Management Handbook* (Wiley, 1993). The primary objective of the *Handbook* was to compile the best of these proven approaches in an accessible, readily adaptable format.

The first edition of the *Handbook* was completed at the beginning of the nineties and introduced a new management tool called quality management. While we covered the seven areas of management and leadership, we led off with strong emphasis on quality management techniques and approaches. The first edition served as a comprehensive reference guide to the policies (guidelines, directives, rules, and courses of action) and procedures (established methods and proven best practices) now shared by a great majority of small- and medium-sized nonprofit organizations. This, the second edition, builds on that solid foundation, even as it expands and develops other key areas of management for nonprofit organizations.

Operational policies and procedures are not static, and cannot be adopted and arbitrarily applied to a particular organization. If they are to be effective, they must be carefully adapted to the needs and realities of a specific organization. Second, internal and external environments change, just as the organization itself changes. Operational policies and procedures, once adapted and employed, must be reviewed regularly to ensure that they continue to fulfill the functions for which they were intended.

The dynamic evolving nature of nonprofit management policies and procedures requires constant review, assessment, renewal, and change. Outdated policies and procedures may become impediments to progress and the organization's ability to fulfill its mission. But how and where do we implement changes? In what direction should we move the organization? How do we organize for constant change and also bring about constant improvement in our services, products, and processes? How do we know what we can and should do to fulfill our public services mission in the face of dwindling resources and a more competitive environment?

Timely rational change is a major benefit gained by those organizations adopting continuous quality improvement techniques and philosophies. Therefore, a major objective of both editions of the *Handbook* is to provide the foundation that nonprofit organizations need to implement quality management. Our contributors offers general guidance regarding the basic principles of quality as they apply to nonprofit organizations. In addition, they provide a framework for assessment, evaluation, and decision making for leaders and managers grappling with the challenges of achieving excellence.

Nonprofit organizations (or nonprofits, for short) are interested in quality because they see the relevance of successful industry quality models. This is the view of Dr. Curt Reimann, recently retired former director of the Malcolm Baldrige National Quality Award (NQA) Program of the U.S. Department of Commerce, National Institute of Standards and Technology. "They feel there is a very close correspondence—even perhaps one-to-one correspondence—between the things that promote business effectiveness, and those that can be used to promote the effectiveness of the nonprofit organization." Whether government or business, profit or nonprofit, manufacturing or service, Reimann believes quality principles are applicable to all organizations.

Nonprofit organizations, like their corporate counterparts, are affected by global systems of economics and production. Organizations from all sectors of our economy are trying to establish quality as their "organizational culture." Nonprofits, like business and government, must adopt and apply the principles and best practices of quality and continuous improvement, if they are to meet growing public service needs in the face of scarce resources. Because every element of our society is being forced to move in this new direction, QM is not a trend likely to fade away when organizational leaders change or when press coverage wanes, as it inevitably will. Quality must become the basic culture within nonprofit organizations, just as it must become the way all U.S. organizations do business if they expect to be successful.

While some nonprofits have continued with business as usual, most have acquired a fundamental awareness of important quality management principles and the benefits of process improvement. Many nonprofits, usually under heavy pressure (competition, funding constraints, or changing demographics), have used quality management tools to improve processes and sharpen customer/client focus. They have not always done so eagerly.

While "picking the low hanging fruit" of improved efficiencies through processes analysis, for example, is relatively easy, further progress invariably requires more effort and the investment of time and money to use more of the tools effectively. Even more challenging for many is the development of the requisite organizational environment or culture that must be evolved if the fullest benefits of quality management are to be realized. It is neither quick nor easy. It is, however, increasingly necessary as a survival strategy for many organizations in all three sectors, certainly including the nonprofit sector.

Today, a growing number of nonprofits have learned to apply fundamental quality management tools and approaches. A few however, proverbially reported that they "tried it and don't like it" or "been there, done that." They said that quality management hasn't worked for them. If we take them at face value, we could conclude that quality management is just the latest fad, another "flavor of the month," that will be succeeded in time. Based on personal experience supported by that of our contributors which follows, I urge you to be slow to accept such negative reports at face value. Try to keep some fundamental questions in mind, including:

- Was it really "quality management" or just the use of this popular name applied to some other type of "quick fix" initiative which failed? Simply calling something by a name does not necessarily make it so.
- Was the disappointment due to inadequate training, or application of the wrong tools, or faulty leadership?
- Could it be a strategy by the organization to blame management or leadership disappointments on another cause; or even to convince competitors or "sister nonprofits" not to implement quality management, perhaps not wanting to make the investment and the resulting "changes in the way we do business" themselves?

For most nonprofits today, the question is not truly one of whether to implement quality management, but how soon, to what extent, and with which strategies. These are important questions to which our contributors offer many important answers.

There may be a bit of substance to the disappointment expressed by some nonprofit leaders with the results of what they thought was a quality management implementation program. Perhaps they used the tools haphazardly—without a system—Dr. Deming might conclude. The tools, techniques, and approaches of quality management achieve their strongest beneficial values to the organization when they are used in a coherent program and used interactively. Otherwise, some benefits may be gained, but often the process is frustrating and the benefits short-lived.

American organizations in all sectors of our economy struggle constantly to improve—to respond to the demand of operating environments that grow more competitive and challenging every day. Senior leaders have a variety of tools available to them ranging from strategic planning and process improvement, to new approaches to leadership and improved communications. Tried independently, these may produce improvements in the organization, usually after great investments of time and money. However, these improvements achieved at great cost are all too often temporary and often fail. Most organizations once achieving excellence, find it hard to sustain.

This new work could be subtitled "The Self-Renewing Organization." The contributors share their vision of a new type of organization, one not only able to achieve, but also able to sustain high standards of excellence, including the ability to thrive under competitive pressures. They have tried to provide the insights American leaders need to understand how strategic planning, process improvement, and a culture and organizational environment supportive of change through intrinsically motivating (transformational) leadership can and must work together to help ensure that hard-won gains in productivity, effectiveness, mission readiness, and profitability are sustained. Taken together, they provide for the first time, tools to create a new self-renewing organization, one able to achieve and sustain high standards of excellence—the organizational fulfillment of quality management.

These seasoned leaders outline the proven principles of process improvement, strategic planning, and inspirational leadership. More importantly, they explain how leaders can use these tools interactively to produce a new kind of organization, one able to achieve and sustain high levels of mission effectiveness and environmental efficiency, even while undergoing constant change and transformation—to become self-renewing organizations able to reach and maintain world-class levels of excellence.

The new model, for example, explains how strategic planning contributes to customer-focused mission effectiveness, while process improvement approaches enhance overall organizational efficiency. Employed independently, none can realize its full potential benefits to the organization. Employed aggressively, chaotic change becomes the only constant, potentially threatening organizational cohesiveness. Motivational leadership techniques, however, help establish the communication, coordination, and the organizational culture needed in which leaders become "change agents," and whose members know that change is both required and safe.

Following explanation of the fundamental and proven principles of quality management, strategic planning, and motivational leadership for nonprofit organizations, the book moves forward to explain and demonstrate how leaders can and must use these techniques and tools interactively to obtain the full measure of benefits each offers to an organization. In addition, throughout the work where applicable, other sections provide further tips on organizational self renewal in related areas of nonprofit organization policies, procedures, and management.

The Nonprofit Handbook: Management, Second Edition has been divided into four parts:

   I. Interactive Strategic Planning, Quality Management, and Leadership
  II. Human Resources
 III. Communication, Fund Raising, and Information Management
  IV. Accounting, Finance, and Legal Issues

The Contributors challenge American leaders to an exciting new understanding of the interactive dynamic between strategic planning, process improvement, and leadership. We have tried to integrate in one work and a new model these complementary and mutually interdependent approaches. American leaders can now better appreciate and understand how these elements work together to ensure not only organizational survival, but sustained excellence.

The *Handbook* provides:

- Drafts of policies, procedures, and statements specifically for nonprofits.
- Management, quality, and continuous improvement practices.
- Established models for use by staff and volunteer managers.
- Accepted techniques, explained and illustrated.
- Sample plans, forms, records, and reports specifically for nonprofits.
- Explanations of what we mean by "new" and "self-renewing" organizations and why it is important that organizations stay new.
- The essential requirements necessary for an organization to achieve a self-renewing state—reaching mission effectiveness and environmental efficiency.
- An explanation of the elements of strategic planning useful to any organization.
- The basics of quality management and process improvement, stressing those elements which make the strongest contribution to organizational efficiency.
- Real-world experiences—what really works in quality management. Now that American organizations have enough experience with quality

management, what can we learn that will help us understand what works and what doesn't. What must the typical leader of an American organization really know about the basic essentials of quality management.

- Important understanding of the relationship between efficiency (process improvement), strategic planning (customer focus/mission readiness), and environment (culture characterized by intrinsically motivating leadership). They outline why these three components—each with its requirements and techniques—must be understood and linked in mutually supportive approaches, strategies, and practices in order to fully realize the potential each has to promote individual and organizational excellence.
- An outline of training required, as well as other organizational investments.
- Defines and explains the typical barriers existing in most organizations that prevent them from achieving and sustaining excellence and self-renewal, including recommending proven strategies to help overcome "aging" behaviors and cultures.
- Explains how, when constant change is the norm, it can be effectively managed—the techniques, strategies, and processes.
- And, integrates these concepts and techniques wherever applicable into other functional areas of nonprofit organization management.

One of the major challenges to effective development and implementation of quality management is getting the organization's leaders to recognize the crucial role played by leadership. Effective leadership demands personal involvement and knowledge of quality principles and best practices. Our contributors have stressed and outlined the new and different roles for leaders in the emerging quality organization. Quality concepts in this handbook are presented in ways that will facilitate their adaptation by nonprofit leaders to meet the specific needs in their organization.

Leaders of nonprofit organizations should treat the implementation of quality as an important new tool to take on important challenges facing their organization. "Don't treat quality as an 'off-line' program or thing—'we won't be able to do anything in quality until we all go off and get training in quality, put up signs on the wall, and charts.' Instead, tackle quality improvement within the framework of things you are trying to do well, now," Reimann recommends.

Some "generic" management information will appear in the *Handbook* when needed for continuity, to ensure the work's utility, or to outline significant differences between nonprofit, business, or government management practices. The emphasis, however, will be on policies and procedures that are specific to the effective management of nonprofit, voluntary action organizations, particularly those which focus on or support quality and continuous improvement initiatives and programs.

The *Handbook* is designed for daily use as a guide for nonprofit leaders and managers who are seeking to implement those plans and policies required to bring about excellence or quality transformation within their organization and to develop their own policy and practices manual, to draft policy statements, update management procedures, and establish more effective management systems.

Our national quality of life, from healthcare and culture, to recreation and religion, depends on whether leaders of nonprofit organizations can achieve—and sustain—levels of quality and excellence in the future that by today's standards would be considered extraordinary. We have prepared this handbook to provide what we believe represents the best of current management and leadership approaches to help ensure success in meeting the pressing demands of today. We have tried also to include the basic knowledge and understanding needed to fashion the winning quality management initiatives and culture required to conquer the challenges we know are our future.

Our contributors represent a wide variety of professional backgrounds. They were selected for their demonstrated knowledge of specialized subject areas and for their day-to-day, real world experience with nonprofits. Their specialized expertise is the cornerstone of this work. While editors have worked closely with our contributors, reviewing and editing their manuscripts, each chapter is the work and viewpoint of the contributor.

Making an "enormous difference" has always been the challenge of the dedicated men and women, volunteer and professional, who lead our nonprofit, public service organizations. We have tried in this handbook to present the most successful policies and procedures, and to explain and recommend those principles and practices of quality management that nonprofit leaders need as tools to meet successfully the challenging demands of an uncertain future.

Tracy D. Connors
Fogland Point
Tiverton, Rhode Island

▼ Acknowledgments

The contributors to this handbook deserve our deepest appreciation. In the same spirit of service, dedication, and sharing that characterizes the leaders of our nonprofit organizations, they have devoted countless hours to their respective chapters. We thank these dedicated professionals for their willingness to share their experience and knowledge to help leaders, staff, and members of nonprofit organizations provide a better quality of life for us all.

Others whose efforts on behalf of this handbook deserve special thanks and recognition, include:

Jody Blazek
Daniel Brandenburg, Esq.
Dr. Jeffrey Brudney
Charles Cammack
Dr. Joseph Champoux
Faith R. Connors
James Greenfield
Edward Naro
Howard Sartori
Richard Thompson
Larry Zimmerman, Esq.
Sally Zinno

The sound guidance and judgment sustained by Marla Bobowick throughout the process was invaluable and deeply appreciated. I would also like to thank Robin Sarantos, Assistant Managing Editor, for helping to coordinate this project. In addition, Martha Cooley and Bryan Patrick provided highly professional administrative and editorial support.

▼ Contents

Interactive Strategic Planning, Quality Management, and Leadership

1 The Self-Renewing Organization

TRACY D. CONNORS
The BelleAire Institute, Inc.

Man's job is to govern the future, not simply be a victim of the wind blowing this way and that way. I know, the best plans are upset. But, without a plan there is no chance. Best efforts will not do it!

W. Edwards Deming

1.1 To Govern Our Future

Without ever having met you, I know we have at least one thing in common. Way back when we were just sprouts, someone important to us, someone dear to us, who cared about us and what we would become, gave us one of life's great lessons. "Do your best," they told us. It was, and is, good advice. It was one of many terribly important, even vital, lessons in life and living that we learned as children. Simple, straightforward, not terribly complicated, but important, and true—then as children, and even more so now that we are adults.

Since I already know you remembered that good advice from your childhood and are doing your best, we can go on to some other important questions:

Do you take joy in your work?
If not, do you understand why not?
If you're already doing your best, but there is not enough joy in your work,
    what else should you be doing to add this vital feeling, to help you "govern"
    your future?

Robert Fulghum tells us that "all I really need to know about how to live and what to do and how to be I learned in kindergarten."[1] Share everything, he reminds us. "Play fair. Don't hit people. Put things back where you found them. Clean up your own mess. Don't take things that aren't yours. Say you're sorry when you hurt somebody. Warm cookies and cold milk are good for you. Live a balanced life—learn some and think some and draw and paint and sing and dance and play and work every day some. When you go out into the world, watch out for traffic, hold hands, and stick together. Be aware of wonder. . . . And then remember the Dick-and-Jane books and the first word you learned—the biggest word of all—LOOK."

He pointed out that everything you need to know is in there somewhere, from the Golden Rule to ecology, politics, equality, and sane living.

We should consider the lessons we learned the earliest as among the most important in our lives. Just because we learned them as kids doesn't mean they were trivial. Just because they were basic doesn't mean they were uncomplicated, or even easy to put into practice. "Playing fair," can be a real challenge in a highly competitive environment. The same is true for "sharing everything." If I share, will they share back, or use my share against me?

Similarly, we should remember that basic truths about quality management can be straightforward and uncomplicated—and yet be critically important. To understand and apply quality management does not require extensive training in quantitative analysis or statistical theory. It does require a fundamental understanding of how quality is defined, its functional areas, and its basic definitions as they are applied to levels of quality achievement.

"Man's job is to govern the future," Dr. W. Edwards Deming pointed out, "not simply be a victim of the wind blowing this way and that way." The international authority on quality told hundreds of senior federal government leaders several years ago: "I know, the best plans are upset. But, without a plan there is no chance. Best efforts will not do it. Is anyone here not putting forth his best efforts? Let him stand." This was followed by silence, then a great deal of laughter.

"I've been inquiring for years, trying to find him who is not putting forth his best efforts," Deming said, with tongue firmly in cheek. "No one has stood up yet. That is our problem! Everyone is putting forth his best efforts—without knowledge, without understanding what his job is, just doing his best. He will not take joy in his work without understanding what his job is. He cannot do his work without understanding why, who depends on him. Man is entitled to joy in his work."

With apologies to Mr. Fulghum, doing our best is not enough. For us to govern the future, we must do those things that give us *knowledge*, that bring us to a better understanding of what our jobs really are and how they contribute to the aims of the organization—to the customer-focused mission.

1.2   *What Happened to Quality Management*

American organizations in all sectors of our economy struggle constantly to improve, to respond to the demands of operating environments that grow more competitive and challenging every day. Senior leaders have a variety of tools available to them ranging

---

[1] Fulghum, Robert. 1988. *All I Really Need to Know I Learned in Kindergarten.* New York: Villard Books, p. 6.

from strategic planning and process improvement to new approaches to leadership and improved communications. Tried independently, these may produce modest improvements in the organization, usually after great investments of time and money. However, these improvements, achieved at great cost, are all too often temporary. Most organizations, once having achieved excellence, find it hard to sustain.

American leaders are coming to a better understanding that strategic planning, quality management, and intrinsically motivating leadership can and must work together to help ensure that hard-won gains in productivity, effectiveness, mission readiness, and profitability are sustained.

There can be no "prescription handbook." Like the proverbial lunch, there is no free "prescription" for quality management. "No one can come to your organization and "install" something and tell you, "Here, if you do this, this and this, quality is going to emerge everywhere.' That's just mischievous," notes Dr. Curt Reimann, former director of the Malcolm Baldrige National Quality Award. There is no "instant pudding" for quality. But there is the ability and the need to share those techniques, approaches, principles and best practices which work—even as we point the way to what lies beyond quality management.

Process improvement focused on enhanced product quality and customer satisfaction, the "secret" behind Japan's come-from-behind international success, was "discovered" by American business leaders in the early 1980s. Soon it was being called Total Quality Management (TQM). Advocates credit its use for major successes in productivity and profitability by some of our organizations. Some critics now say that it's not all that it was cracked up to be. Touted as the management miracle that would reestablish America as an international competitor, Total Quality Management (TQM) became a growth industry for gurus and management consultants offering "salvation" to harried American business leaders. TQM spawned a fervent new breed of manager who talked the language of "empowerment" and "profound knowledge."

A new national quality award—the Malcolm Baldrige National Quality Award—was established to mirror a similar award—the Deming Prize—awarded in Japan. Hundreds of thousands of companies sought the criteria, and hundreds applied for consideration. Winning the Baldrige award was good for morale—and business. Many organizations did achieve almost miraculous results. Clearly, customer focus and improved product and services quality were the foundation on which many American organizations rebuilt market share and consumer confidence, and achieved higher levels of productivity and competitiveness.

However, disturbing information began to emerge. Many companies that had won the Baldrige award appeared to backslide. Others announced their commitment to quality with great public fanfare, anointed a guru, and fired up various quality programs. Then, quietly, over ensuing months, they abandoned many of their quality programs, having private doubts as to why they had not measured up to their potential. A few articles appeared in the business press badmouthing "quality" as not working, or as so much managerial snake oil. The journalistic hounds, sensing blood, are poised for the hunt. Is quality management about to become the latest "fox" to be hunted down and dispatched as another victim of "pack journalism?"

What happened to the initial promise held out for quality management? Why hasn't it seemed to measure up to the expectations held by so many? Why do some organizations report success with its principles, and others have mixed results? What works in quality management, and what does not? How can we avoid the pot holes, minefields, and swamps which have damaged or mired many good organizations—private and nonprofit?

More importantly, since the need for significantly improved productivity and profitability has never been greater, what will emerge from the now-cloudy crystal ball that was called "quality management"?

In this edition of the *Nonprofit Handbook: Management* our contributors not only outline the proven principles of quality management, strategic planning, and leadership, but they explain how they should interact to produce a new kind of organization, one which can achieve and sustain excellence—in other words, become self-renewing.

Quality management is not rocket science. Its principles and techniques are as basic and straightforward as the lessons we learned as kids.

In fact, "quality management" as advocated by some gurus is incomplete, focused almost exclusively on achieving more efficiency. We should remember those hardworking folks of yesteryear who manufactured carburetors also did their best. They added "barrels" and many other improvements. Yet, they aren't with us any more. While they were improving their carburetors (process improvement), some other folks took a better look at technology and what the customer really wanted (strategic management and customer focus). They came up with the fuel injection system. The rest, as they say, is history. Of course, that's no consolation to those who worked so hard to make the best carburetor in the world. They are now "history," too!

1.3 Governing Our Future and that of Our Organizations

Governing our future and putting joy in our work will take more than simply *improving our processes*—more than focusing on ever-greater efficiencies. We have to *know where we're going*, to define our strategic vision, mission, and guiding principles. We have to have a way as individuals and as organizations to *see where we're going*, even as we try to *get better at what we do*.

As Dr. Deming so wisely said, we have to have a *plan*, a "vision"—a desired future state—of what we desire for ourselves and our organization, and a direction in which to travel. We need some "strategy."

The plan tells us what direction in which to move, and strategy gives us answers about what means we can use to get there. Moving from here to there, however, requires change, *doing some things differently*. When we were little kids, change was fun. We liked to take new routes home from school, to color the sun in the right-hand corner of the picture instead of the left. Before too long, however, we learned that change can be uncomfortable. In most of our organizations, change can be threatening to our power, our authority, our position. Change, we learned, is suspect, perhaps even dangerous. Our path up the organization hierarchy was through "management." And, managers allocated and coordinated. Most importantly, they controlled. Typically, they resist change unless it is their idea and to their personal advantage.

The essence of management is in its most vital function: dealing with the increased complexity in large organizations. Effective management enables our increasingly complex, far-flung organizations to avoid chaos, by helping impose order and consistency in key functions and operations. Management techniques taught in our business schools stress controlling, planning, budgeting—setting goals and objectives for the future (usually a not-too-distant future). Detailed steps are determined to achieve targets, followed by the process of allocating resources—funds and people—to accomplish plans.

Management emphasizes those capabilities and processes needed to achieve the plan—organizing and staffing, creating an organizational structure; crafting job descriptions and qualifications; communicating the plan down the "chain of command"; delegating responsibilities for implementing the plan; and then putting those systems in place that are needed to monitor implementation.

Accomplishing the plan is ensured by controlling and problem solving—comparing results against the plan in great detail—reports, meetings, inspections. Deviations from the plan are identified, then replanning and reorganization focus on solving the problem.

The essence of leadership, on the other hand, is coping with change. Leadership has become much more important to all organizations, particularly major U.S. corporations. The "world" has become much more volatile and competitive. Technological change on the order of exponential, international competition, rapidly fluctuating economic and political developments, and changing demographics are having a major impact on all our organizations because they are all connected in some way to the "global marketplace."

The lesson we should take to heart about these global developments is that *change is not only necessary, it is inevitable—change is the only constant.* In addition, major change is increasingly necessary for any organization, large or small, if it is to survive and compete successfully in an always-evolving environment. The world outside our organizations keeps changing. Clients and customers are more powerful—and demanding. Suppliers are more numerous, dispersed, and in the midst of changing themselves. The consumer-public is more fickle and less likely to maintain its support for our public purpose. More change inevitably requires and demands more effective leaders.

Until recently and in "normal" times, most of our organizations did a relatively good job of managing and administering their product lines, services, and people—in "peacetime." However, the overall climate and environments in which most of our organizations must operate more closely resembles that of "war"—from international competition to galloping technological change in the face of diminishing budgets. A wartime organization cannot be successful relying exclusively on management. A war-footing organization needs competent, effective leadership *at all levels.* Over 200 years of our country's military history have taught us repeatedly that soldiers and sailors cannot be managed in battle—*they must be led.* The same can be said for any of us and about almost any of our organizations. Management is important, but effective leaders are required— change agents—at all levels.

The primary function of leadership is to bring about change, not simply to react to forces and pressures as they occur. Intentionally determining and then setting the direction of that change or changes then, is fundamental to effective leadership—and effective leaders are "change agents."

"Quality management" as typically defined, by itself, is incomplete, which may account for many disappointments as it was deployed. The primary emphasis for most organizations is placed on process improvement and efficiency. While efficiencies and resources conservation offer us the means to better our best efforts, governing our future requires that we know where we are going, how to get there, and how to create a climate for "safe change" in our organizations for ourselves and those for whom we are responsible. It requires strategic quality leadership.

Expressed as "great lessons," if we wish to govern our future and that of our organizations, we must:

- Know where we're going, why we are going, and how we plan to get there;
- Improve constantly in everything we do; and,
- Make it safe to change for ourselves and those for whom we are responsible.

1.4   Palingenesis: Birth Over Again

Birth, growth, maturation, decline, and death—the cycle is ancient and universal. It is the subject of countless fables and myths from distant times. Finding out where the organization must go and how it should get there, constantly studying ways to improve its processes, changing outmoded concepts and approaches to ensure regeneration and growth—the life cycle never ends. If it did, death would be the inevitable result. Only one thing holds death at bay—birth. Only birth can conquer death, not the old approaches (archaism) repeated, but some things new.

As with our bodies, *long-term organizational survival depends on a continuous recurrence of birth to nullify the unremitting partial deaths our organizations suffer from competition, technological advances, and market saturation.* From victories, the seeds of ruin can spring. Victorious countries continue to prepare for the last war. Organizations continue product lines or services long past their prime. Even organizations that have worked hard to become "quality-managed" organizations can and have fallen back from hard-gained high ground. When corporate death closes in, usually there is no salvation except dismemberment (acquisition), and rebirth as a reinvigorated component of another organization.

What is required to stave off inevitable decline or death is birth over again, regeneration, *palingenesis.*

Strategic planning is essential, but not enough. Continuous improvement of all processes is essential, but can be conducted by those blind to other life-sustaining essentials. Leaders can bring about change so disruptive or misguided that it destroys even as it breaks free from the outmoded past.

Palingenesis requires a fertile culture and environment in which promising concepts and ideas can be conceived and nurtured to maturity. Even as their processes are honed to ensure they make their strongest contribution to renewed organizational strength, their replacements are taking shape, form, and function behind them.

Old . . . new . . . These are two of the first words we ever learned. Mostly, we learned that *new* is good; *old* is bad. *New* has potential, has a future; *old* is worthless, junk, irrelevant. At the time, we didn't realize that *new* and *old* are simply at opposite ends of a continuum matrix of two factors: *condition* and *time* (Exhibit 1.1 The New Vector).

"In mint condition," sums up the highest condition of new—newly minted; shiny, fresh, valuable. At this end "new" means fresh, recent, vigorous, changed for the better, or reinvented. The opposite end of the condition continuum brings to mind associations of stale, no longer needed, outmoded, antique, obsolete, disposable—near death.

"With it," "in step," and "relevant" are terms we associate with things that are current, modern, and in sync with the times. To be "dated," is to be totally out of sync. To be dated is to be considered irrelevant—extraneous and immaterial.

Organizational "newness" can also be understood in terms of *condition* and *surroundings* or *ambient* as seen in Exhibit 1.2. For example, an organization's status or "condition" can be seen as its readiness to fulfill the *mission(s)* for which it exists. If an organization lacks purpose, or is not meeting its public purpose, it is tottering on the

EXHIBIT 1.1 The New Vector

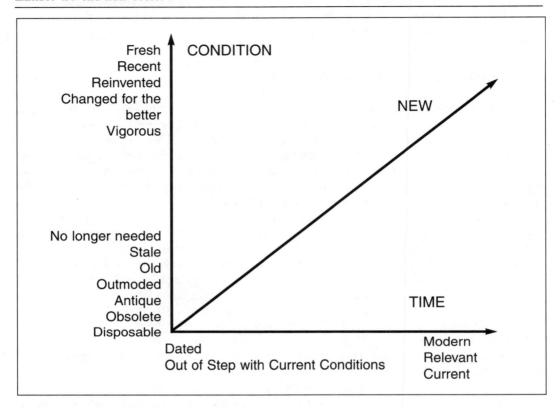

lowest rung of mission-readiness. However, an organization that is customer focused and driven, and is meeting its public purposes, is fulfilling its mission.

Time and surroundings are closely linked as well. The complex circumstances and ambient in which an organization operates are constantly changing—they are time driven. Those organizations that are in synchronous rhythm with their operating environment(s) are seen to be relevant, modern, coping, fresh, and aware. If they are not, they are tuned out, unaware, and out of touch.

1.5 The Self-Renewing Organization Equation

Organizations that are vigorously proactive in meeting their public purposes, that stay mission-driven and customer focused, and have synchronized their operations within their surroundings are prime candidates for excellence. Their effective use of strategic planning is the key factor in whether they get there—and whether they stay there.

Organizations that can achieve and sustain excellence are rare. Some organizations have worked hard to achieve excellence only to see their hard-fought gains erode as the organization fell back from the pinnacle. They could not sustain their "newness."

For any organization to achieve and sustain excellence—to be self-renewing—it must understand and exploit the dynamic interdependent relationship between effectiveness, efficiency, and environment—the Excellence Equation:

$$\mathbf{N}(ew) = \mathbf{E}(nvironment) \times \mathbf{E}(ffectiveness) \times \mathbf{E}(fficiency)$$

Self-renewing organizations have learned that they must operate at high levels of competence in both the Condition (Mission/Effectiveness) and Time (Environment/Efficiency) dimensions (Exhibit 1.2). In addition, they must create and sustain the enabling organizational environment needed to motivate, empower, and support the people on whom the services and customer satisfaction—results—depend.

Self-renewing organizations are effective (Exhibit 1.3). They use strategic planning to define and accomplish their customer-focused mission. They know they serve valid purposes. They *know* they are needed—and why. They know their public purpose is valid, and they continually adjust it, tune it to environmental conditions to achieve business results. Effective organizations use:

- *Customer focus and satisfaction* as the foundation for setting priorities and focusing improvement activities. Results and trends in this area offer a means to determine the appropriate direction for improvement activities and initiatives. Effective organizations listen to and learn from their customers on a continuous basis, then use that intelligence to determine their current and near-term requirements and expectations.
- *Strategic planning* to strengthen their customer-related, operational, and financial performance, to improve customer satisfaction. Planning is essential to help organization leaders use customer and operational

EXHIBIT 1.2 Self-Renewing Organizations In Accord with Mission and Context

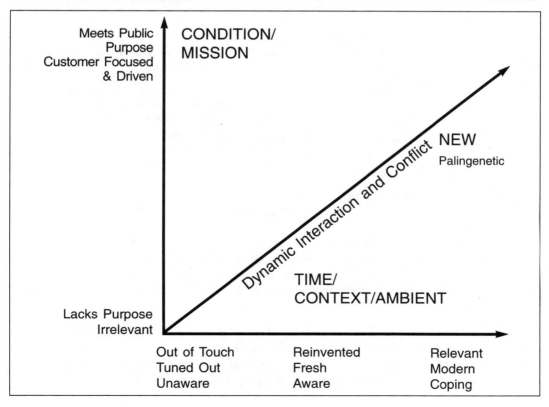

EXHIBIT 1.3 The Interactive Dynamic Between the Excellence Factors of Self-Renewing Organizations

Effectiveness (know and accomplish their customer-focused mission/serve valid purpose);
Efficiency (perform well and economically, with reduced waste of time, energy, and materials); and,
Environment (use Transformational Leadership to establish and maintain an organizational culture able to adapt to changing conditions, manage change effectively, transition to new states, and turn in new directions, in short, to constantly evolve).

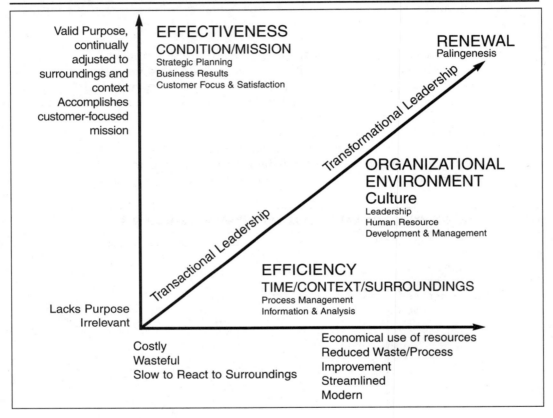

requirements as inputs to setting strategic directions. Strategic planning guides ongoing decision making, resource allocating, and organization-wide management.

- *Business results* as the focus for all processes and process improvement activities to assess its progress toward achieving the superior value of its offerings as viewed by customers and the marketplace, and toward superior organization performance as reflected in productivity and effectiveness.

Self-renewing organizations are efficient. They perform well and economically, with reduced waste of time, energy, and materials (at least in comparison with their competition). Their use of process improvement, information and analysis techniques, and approaches to reduce waste, to streamline their operations, and to make economical use of all resources is laudable. They constantly reassess their processes, products, and services to ensure they meet customer needs while consuming the least amount of resources (money, time, and personnel). Efficient organizations use:

- *Process management* techniques to design and improve their customer/client service design, translating customer requirements into design requirements, and into efficient and effective delivery processes. Efficient organizations also maintain process performance systems to ensure they are performing according to their design, and improved to achieve even better performance.
- *Information and analysis* to support overall organizational mission goals and to serve as the primary basis for key decision making.

Self-renewing organizations create and sustain a transformational organizational environment in both leadership and human resource development and management. They adapt to changing environmental conditions, managing change effectively, constantly transitioning to new states, and turning as necessary in new directions. They are constantly evolving. We hear the popular phrase, "they reinvented themselves." Organizations having a transformational environment use:

- *Leadership* to set strategic directions and to build and maintain a leadership system fostering high performance, individual development, and organizational learning—a leadership that takes into account all stakeholders, customers, employees, staff, volunteers, suppliers, partners, the public, and the community. Leadership in the self-renewing organization uses communications and dedicated commitment as key elements to realize the organization's values, expectations, and directions. Through transformational leadership, the organization's culture becomes one in which the self-fulfilled individual knows that change is not only "safe," but necessary to maintain effectiveness and efficiency.
- *Human resource development and management* practices directed toward the creation of a high-performance workplace, directly linking human resource planning with the organization's strategic directions. Key human resource plans are derived from the organization's strategic plans. The organization's job design, compensation, and recognition approaches enable and encourage all staff and volunteers to contribute effectively, operating within high-performance empowered (increasingly self-directed) work units or teams. In the self-renewing organization, employee and volunteer well-being, satisfaction, and growth potential are based upon a more holistic view of them as key stakeholders.

Self-renewing organizations are effective, efficient, and changing. We may find it increasingly difficult to point out future examples of organizations at the lower end of the "in accord with mission and context" curve in Exhibit 1.2. Those that lack purpose, are irrelevant, costly, wasteful, and slow to react to their environment, are prime candidates for extinction.

Self-renewing organizations gain enthusiasm from their base of intrinsically motivated leadership, reinforcing their desire to excel at ever-higher levels of achievement and comparison with other organizations with reputations for excellence.

Self-renewing, palingenetic organizations have the visionary discipline in their senior leaders to plan and implement long-range strategies; an enlightened commitment to train, nourish, and foster intrinsically motivated "change agent" leaders at all levels of the organization; and the dedication to develop in their team-oriented work groups the tools and approaches needed to continuously improve all major organization processes.

Self-renewing organizations know where they are going, they constantly strive for excellence and improvement in all areas, and their leaders bring about non-threatening change.

A self-renewing organization is the kind of organization we would all like to be a part of; it's the kind of organization we know would offer us the best opportunity for personal development and to make a meaningful contribution.

When we use the Excellence Equation, we establish a straightforward, easily understood "cognitive map" by which to understand the three fundamental elements necessary for organizations to achieve and sustain excellence. Further, when we equate *effectiveness*, *efficiency*, and *environment* to those seven functional categories that contribute most directly to their fulfillment, we have the advantage of understanding their relationship to each of the three elements of excellence.

In addition, by adapting for nonprofit organizations the Malcolm Baldrige Award/President's Quality Award criteria as the national definitions for these seven functional categories, we now have basic descriptions and characteristics of quality performance and achievement in each of these areas—and with these, the ability to benchmark our own organizations against established national criteria and standards. When we determine where our organizations stand in relation to national standards, we then have the ability to outline plans and strategies to help us overcome the "delta" between the next higher level of quality and the level at which we are now performing.

The Excellence Equation is deliberately simplistic. It is my hope that in explaining and outlining the approach to excellence in this way, I can encourage others in their efforts to achieve higher levels of quality—and to improve their ability to do so. In the nonprofit sector, success in quality management by thousands of nonprofit organizations translates to an overall improvement of our national quality of life.

In addition, I intended the Excellence Equation approach to understanding quality management as a way to encourage a deeper appreciation that *sustained excellence is the goal we should be seeking*—in our organizations and in our lives—and that it requires the effective application of all three elements of the Excellence Equation. I'm not sure that the Excellence Equation can be considered a "great lesson," despite its simplicity. I do hope, however, that it will make a contribution to our collective ability to govern our future and that of our organizations—that it will help us better determine:

- Where we're going, why we are going, and how we plan to get there;
- How to improve constantly in everything we do; and,
- How to make it safe to change, to reach, to grow—for ourselves and those for whom we are responsible.

Once again, *The Excellence Equation for self-renewing organizations is as follows*:

$$\mathbf{N}(\text{ew}) = \mathbf{E}(\text{nvironment}) \times \mathbf{E}(\text{ffectiveness}) \times \mathbf{E}(\text{fficiency})$$

When we correlate the equation to the national quality functional areas, we see that:

Effectiveness includes:
    Strategic Planning and Development
    Customer Focus and Satisfaction
    Business Results
Efficiency includes:
    Process Management
    Information and Analysis
Environment includes:
    Leadership
    Human Resource Development and Management

(i) Description of Categories

The following discussion is adapted for nonprofit organizations from the President's Quality Award criteria and guidelines. Each of the seven functional areas of quality is explained and defined for nonprofit organizations. It is doubtful that any single nonprofit organization is currently able to assess itself as having reached these extraordinarily challenging levels of quality and excellence. However, it does illustrate the current "ideal" level of achievement and integration between functional areas toward which nonprofit organizations should be reaching. The extent to which these levels are achieved and sustained over time is the measure of the organization's overall health, viability, and likelihood of being able to survive in our challenging, competitive, fast-changing environment.

1.6 Effectiveness

(A) STRATEGIC PLANNING

The strategic planning functional area (see Exhibit 1.4) addresses strategic and business planning and deployment of plans, with a strong focus on client/customer and operational performance requirements. For self-renewing organization (SRO) leaders, the emphasis here is that customer-driven quality and operational performance excellence are key strategic business issues that need to be an integral part of organization planning. Specifically:

- Customer-driven quality is a strategic view of quality. The focus is on the drivers of customer satisfaction—a key factor in organizational success.
- Operational performance improvement contributes to short-term and longer-term productivity growth and cost/price competitiveness. The focus on building operational capability—including speed, responsiveness, and flexibility—represents an investment in strengthening competitive fitness.

An important role for SRO leaders is to ensure an effective focus for daily work, aligning it with the organization's strategic directions.

In particular, planning is needed to:

- Understand that key customer and operational requirements should serve as input to setting strategic directions; this will help ensure that ongoing process improvements will be aligned with the organization's strategic directions;

EXHIBIT 1.4 Strategic Planning Characteristics of Self-Renewing Organizations

- Sound, systematic, well-documented, effective process used throughout organization to develop business strategies, business plans, key business drivers for overall operational, financial performance
- All appropriate staff, clients, customers, volunteers, suppliers/partners participate fully in planning process
- Strategy development considers organization's vision, customer-driven values and expectations; includes risk analysis, organization capabilities, supplier/partner capabilities
- Strategies, business plans translated into actionable key business drivers used for deployment throughout organization, to key suppliers/partners; managers, staff, volunteers are held accountable for attaining major targets throughout organization; staff know how their work unit contributes to overall business success
- Systematic procedure used to continuously evaluate strategic planning, plan deployment processes; improvements in processes made on ongoing basis
- Specific business drivers derived from strategic directions translated into actionable plan throughout organization; includes key performance requirements, operational performance measures, productivity improvement, cycle time reduction, waste reduction: work unit, supplier/partner plans fully aligned
- Top priority given to deployment of plans, improvement targets as evidenced by extensive resource commitment to ensuring plan success
- Outstanding product/service quality, operational performance projected for key business areas when compared with key benchmarks

---

- Optimize the use of resources and ensure bridging between short-term and longer-term requirements that may entail capital expenditures, training, and so on;
- Ensure that deployment will be effective—that there are mechanisms to transmit requirements and achieve alignment on three basic levels, including the organization-executive level, the key process level, and the work-unit/individual-job level.

(B) STRATEGY DEVELOPMENT

Self-renewing organizations develop their view of the future, set strategic directions, and translate these directions into actionable key business drivers, including customer satisfaction. Effective leadership in fulfilling these functions is critical and determines the organization's operational effectiveness.

Every organization is impacted by key influences, challenges, and requirements that can affect its future opportunities and directions. Leaders of SROs take as long a view as possible, emphasizing the importance of a thorough and realistic context for the development of a customer/client and market-focused strategy to guide ongoing decision making, resource allocation, and organization-wide management.

Strategy and plans are translated into actionable key business drivers, which serve as the basis for operationalizing and deploying plan requirements. This translation often includes a determination of those activities the organization should perform itself and those for which it might seek partners.

The SRO places a high priority on evaluating and improving its strategic planning and plan deployment processes. This can involve input from work units regarding key deployment factors—effective translation and communications of strategy and plans, adequacy of resources, and identification of key new needs by clients/customers.

SRO leaders are focused on developing a competitive strategy and on operationalizing this strategy. Operationalizing the strategy in the form of key public service/business drivers requires clear and measurable performance objectives. These objectives serve to guide the design and management of key processes. The objectives often serve to align organizational systems (e.g., communications, compensation, recognition) with performance objectives.

SRO leaders place high priority on the organization's key business drivers and how these drivers are translated into an action plan. This includes spelling out key performance requirements, alignment of work unit, supplier, and/or partner plans, how productivity, cycle time, and waste reduction are addressed, and the principal resources committed to the accomplishment of plans.

(C) CUSTOMER FOCUS AND SATISFACTION

Customer focus and satisfaction is the functional area dealing with the need to understand in detail the voices of customers and the marketplace (Exhibit 1.5). Much of the information needed to gain this understanding comes from measuring results and trends. Such results and trends provide hard, quantifiable information on customers' views and their marketplace behaviors. This knowledge then serves as a useful foundation on which SRO leaders can establish priorities and focus improvement activities. Subsequent results and trends offer the means to determine whether priorities and improvement activities are appropriately directed.

A quality-focused organization determines current *and* emerging customer requirements and expectations. This is not a onetime process. Many factors may affect customer/client preferences, needs, and loyalty, making it necessary to listen and learn on a continuous basis.

The SRO has established a process to determine current and near-term requirements and expectations of clients/customers. This includes the completeness of the client/customer pool, including recognition of segments and customers of competitors. There is sensitivity to specific product and service requirements and their relative importance to client/customer groups. Validity of the data should be confirmed by use of other data and information such as complaints.

The SRO addresses future requirements and expectations of customers—its key listening and learning strategies. Such strategies depend significantly upon the nature of the organization's services or products, the competitive environment, and relationships with clients/customers. The listening and learning strategies selected should provide timely and useful information for decision making. The strategy should take into account the organization's competitive strategy. For example, if the organization customizes its services, the listening and learning strategy needs to be backed by a responsive, capable information system—one that rapidly gathers information about customers, and makes this information available where needed throughout the organization. Increasingly, internet technologies will be used in this process, creating an organizational *intranet*.

Evaluating and improving processes to determine customer requirements and expectations is important. Such an evaluation/improvement process could entail a variety of approaches—formal and informal—that seek to stay in close touch with customers and

---

EXHIBIT 1.5 Customer Focus and Satisfaction Characteristics of Self-Renewing Organizations

- Comprehensive, documented system for determining current, near-term customer requirements/expectations used throughout organization
- Methods used to obtain knowledge of customer requirements/expectations elicit comprehensive set of quality features for products/services, relative importance of these features; other key data (e.g., complaints) used to support determination of features' importance
- Future customer requirements/expectations addressed throughout organization; listening/learning strategies used to determine future requirements/expectations
- System, processes for determining customer requirements/ expectations evaluated, improved on ongoing basis
- Information readily accessible to all customers to enable them to seek assistance, comment, complain
- Most processes/transactions that bring employees in contact with customers identified throughout organization
- Service standards aimed at exceeding customer expectations; deployed to all employees needing such information, tracked throughout organization
- Effective feedback systems provide knowledge from customers about products/services, recent transactions
- Formal, informal feedback/complaints received by all organization units resolved effectively, promptly; complaint management process ensures effective recovery of customer confidence, meets customer requirements for effective resolution, eliminates causes of complaints
- Organization consistently follows up with customers on products/services, and transactions to determine satisfaction, resolve problems, seek feedback for improvement, build relationships
- Customer service standards, including access and complaint management, reviewed and revised on ongoing basis
- Data from customer feedback systems aggregated, evaluated, used throughout organization to improve customer relationship management
- Feedback systems providing knowledge about customers improved on ongoing basis
- Comprehensive set of approaches used to determine customer satisfaction with products/services, their delivery throughout organization
- Comparisons of customer satisfaction for similar providers determined for major products/services, some other products/services
- Methods for determining customer satisfaction and customer satisfaction relative to similar providers evaluated, improved on ongoing basis
- Key customer satisfaction results sustained at very high level, consistent improvement each year for last five years
- Key customer dissatisfaction results sustained at very low levels for last five years
- Customer satisfaction comparisons with similar providers are outstanding

---

with issues that bear upon customer preference. The purpose of these evaluations is to find reliable and cost-effective means to understand customer requirements and expectations on a continuous basis.

The SRO provides effective management of its responses and follow-ups with customers. Relationship management provides a potentially important means for organizations to gain understanding about, and to manage, customer expectations. Also, frontline staff or volunteers will provide vital information relating to building partnerships and other longer-term relationships with clients/customers. In addition, the SRO provides easy access for customers specifically for purposes of seeking information or assistance and/or to comment and complain.

Complaints are promptly and effectively resolved, including recovery of customer confidence. In addition, the organization learns from complaints and ensures that production/delivery process employees receive information needed to eliminate the causes of complaints.

The SRO follows up with customers regarding products, services, and recent transactions to determine satisfaction, to resolve problems, and to gather information for improvement or for new services.

The SRO evaluates and improves its customer response management with several types of improvements, including improving service standards, such as complaint resolution time and resolution effectiveness, and improving the use of customer feedback to improve production/delivery processes, training, and hiring.

Satisfaction relative to competitors is determined. Such information can be derived from organization-based comparative studies or studies made by independent organizations. The purpose of this comparison is to develop information that can be used for improving performance.

The SRO evaluates and improves the processes and measurement scales that it uses to determine customer satisfaction *and* satisfaction relative to competitors. This evaluation/improvement process draws upon other indicators such as customer dissatisfaction indicators (e.g., complaints). The evaluation also considers how well customer satisfaction information and data are used throughout the organization. Use of the evaluation by the leadership can be enhanced if data are presented in an actionable form meeting two key conditions: (1) survey responses tying directly to key business processes; and (2) survey responses translated into cost/revenue implications.

Customer satisfaction and *customer dissatisfaction* are not the same thing; they require different measures. Customer satisfaction measures can include information on customer retention and other appropriate evidence of current and recent-past satisfaction with the organization's products and/or services, such as customer awards.

Customer dissatisfaction measures and/or indicators depend upon the nature of the organization's services or products. For example, an organization's survey methods might include a scale that uses ratings such as "very dissatisfied" or "somewhat dissatisfied."

The reason for including measures of both satisfaction and dissatisfaction is that they usually provide different information. The factors in high levels of satisfaction may not be the same as those that relate to high levels of dissatisfaction. In addition, the effect of individual instances of dissatisfaction on overall satisfaction could vary widely depending upon the effectiveness of the organization's resolution ("recovery") of a problem.

Customer satisfaction relative to similar providers should be measured and known where possible.

(D) BUSINESS RESULTS

Business results is the term used to describe another vitally important leadership responsibility in the SRO—ensuring a results focus for all processes and process improvement activities (Exhibit 1.6). The objective of this unrelenting focus is to maintain a dual purpose—superior value of offerings as viewed by customers and the public, and superior organizational performance as reflected in productivity and effectiveness indicators. The

EXHIBIT 1.6 Business Results Characteristics of Self-Renewing Organizations

- Key measures of service or product quality demonstrate exceptional results over past five years
- Current levels of service/product quality are comparable to recognized leaders for similar products/services
- Key measures of operational/financial performance demonstrate exceptional results over the past five years
- Current levels of operational/financial performance are comparable to recognized leaders for similar activities
- Quality performance of major suppliers improving over past five years; performance comparable to recognized leaders

initiatives included within business results provide real-time information (measures of progress or effectiveness) for evaluation and improvement of processes, aligned with overall business strategy.

SRO leaders monitor current levels and trends in product and service quality using key measures and/or indicators of such quality. They select measures and/or indicators that relate to requirements of importance to the client/customer and to the public (marketplace).

Correlation between quality and customer indicators is a critical management tool— a device for focusing on key quality requirements. In addition, the correlation process may reveal emerging or changing market segments, changing importance of requirements, or even potential obsolescence of products and/or services.

Comparative information is developed to enable results reported to be evaluated against competitors or other relevant markers of performance.

Some information addresses factors that best reflect overall organization operational performance. Such factors are of two types: generic—common to all organizations; and business-specific. Generic factors include financial indicators, cycle time, and productivity, as reflected in use of labor, materials, energy, capital, and assets. Generic factors also include human resource indicators such as safety, absenteeism, and turnover. Productivity, cycle time, or other operational indicators should reflect aggregate organization performance.

Business- or organization-specific effectiveness indicators vary greatly throughout the sector. However, typical examples include rates of invention, environmental quality, percent of acceptance of recently introduced products or services, and shifts toward new segments.

Supplier performance results are important considerations. These address current levels and trends in key measures and/or indicators of supplier performance. Suppliers are external providers of materials and services, "upstream" and/or "downstream" from the organization. The focus should be on the most critical requirements from the point of view of the organization—the buyer of the products and services. Data reported and assessed should reflect results by whatever means they occur—via improvements by suppliers within the supply base, through selection of better performing suppliers, or both.

Measures and indicators of supplier performance should relate to all key requirements—quality, delivery, and price. SRO leaders also develop and use comparative information so that results reported can be evaluated against competitors or other relevant markers of performance.

1.7 *Efficiency*

(A) PROCESS MANAGEMENT

Effective process management is a critical function for all SROs, requiring effective design, a prevention orientation, evaluation and continuous improvement, linkage to suppliers, and overall high performance (Exhibit 1.7).

Virtually all organizations design and introduce products or services. Some do so with great frequency, others once in the proverbial "blue moon." How the organization goes about designing and introducing products and services says a lot about its health and future prospects in a highly competitive world.

For the SRO, a major focus in this functional area is the rapid and effective integration of production and delivery *early* in the design phase. This integration helps minimize

---

EXHIBIT 1.7 Process Management Characteristics of Self-Renewing Organizations

- New, improved products/services, processes are designed to exceed customer expectations
- Measurement systems are designed to track process performance throughout organization
- Customer/quality requirements reviewed by appropriate organizational units, suppliers, and partners to ensure integration/coordination/capability
- Initial designs reviewed, validated based on variety of performance, capability considerations throughout organization
- Key designs/processes evaluated to meet customer, quality, and operational performance requirements
- Key production, delivery processes managed throughout organization to meet design plans; measurement plan and measurements used to maintain process performance
- Appropriate analytic methods and measurements used throughout organization to identify, solve problems that disrupt production, delivery processes; corrections systematically verified
- Key production, delivery processes improved throughout organization to achieve better quality, cycle time, operational performance; wide range of techniques used, including process simplification, process research/testing, benchmarking, customer information, alternate technology
- Key support service processes designed and managed throughout organization to meet customer, quality, operational performance requirements; measurements used to maintain process performance
- Support design parameters addressed early in process by appropriate organizational units to ensure integration/coordination/capability
- Appropriate analytic methods used throughout organization to identify, solve problems that disrupt support service processes; corrections systematically verified
- Key support service processes improved throughout organization to achieve better quality, cycle time, operational performance requirements; wide range of techniques used, including process simplification, process research/testing, benchmarking, customer information, alternate technology
- Quality requirements defined throughout organization for expected supplier performance; performance feedback systematically communicated to suppliers
- Quality is primary consideration when selecting suppliers
- Systematic approaches used throughout organization to evaluate and improve supplier performance; supplier abilities, procurement process, inspection/audit costs considered

---

downstream problems for clients or customers and reduces or eliminates the need for design changes that will be costly to the organization.

Leaders of SROs pay close attention to three important aspects of this process, including:

- The translation of customer requirements into design requirements for products and services;
- How these product and service design requirements are translated into efficient and effective production/delivery processes; and,
- How all requirements associated with products, services, and production/delivery processes are addressed early in the design process by all appropriate organization units to ensure integration and coordination. Effective design must take into account all stakeholders in the value chain.

The design of products, services, and processes should meet customer requirements. However, truly effective design must also consider cycle time and productivity of production and delivery processes. This usually includes detailed mapping of service processes to achieve efficiency as well as to meet customer requirements.

Prior to full-scale operation, any product, service, production, or delivery process design should be reviewed and tested in detail. This ensures that all parts of the production/delivery system are capable of performing according to design. This stage is a crucial one. Potentially negative customer reactions and high costs to the organization are virtually assured if preoperation changes are significant.

Following initial process design, the process of designing the process should itself be evaluated and improved to progressively better quality and cycle time. This means that SROs extract lessons learned to build capabilities for future designs. Their evaluation might take into account delays and problems experienced during design, feedback from those involved, and post-operation problems that might have been averted through better design. Evaluation and improvement should strive for a continuous flow of work in the key design and delivery processes.

Another important function is that of monitoring and evaluating process performance to ensure that processes perform according to their design. Leaders require such information as: a description of the key processes and their specific requirements, and how performance relative to these requirements is known and maintained.

A process performance measurement plan requires the identification of critical points in processes for measurement or observation. Implied in this plan is that measurements or observations be made at the earliest points in processes to minimize problems that may result from variations from expected (design) performance. When measurements or observations reveal variations, a remedy—often called corrective action—is required to restore the performance of the process to its design performance.

Depending on the nature of the process, the correction could involve both technical and human factors. Proper correction involves correcting at the source (root cause) of the variation. (Note: in some cases, customers may directly witness or take part in the process, and contribute to or be a determinant of process performance. In such cases, variations among customers must be taken into account in evaluating how well the process is performing. This is especially true of professional and personal services.)

In the SRO, processes are improved to achieve better performance—meaning not only better quality from the customer's perspective but also better operational performance (productivity) from the organization's perspective.

Key support service processes are based upon the requirements of the organization's external customers and of other units within the organization—"internal customers" who use the output of the process. These processes are also measured, evaluated, and improved.

The performance of external providers of goods and services is another functional area that requires effective management. Such management is increasingly built around longer-term partnering relationships, particularly with key suppliers.

Certain basic information on the organization's principal requirements for its key suppliers is required, as is the expected performance and measurements used to assess performance, how the organization determines whether or not its requirements are being met, and how performance information is fed back to suppliers.

Here, SRO leaders evaluate and improve supplier management in three elemental areas, including:

- Improving supplier abilities to meet requirements;
- Improving the organization's own supplier management processes; and,
- Reducing costs associated with the verification of supplier performance.

For many organizations, suppliers are an increasingly important member of the complex team needed to achieve not only high performance and lower-cost objectives, but also strategic objectives. For example, key suppliers might provide unique design, integration, and marketing capabilities. Exploiting these advantages requires joint planning and partner relationships to ensure longer-term planning horizons and customer-supplier teams.

(B) INFORMATION AND ANALYSIS

Information and analysis includes all key information needed to drive the improvement of overall performance (Exhibit 1.8). The objective of this functional area is to bring about the alignment of the organization's information system with its strategic directions. Performance can be improved, if key processes are analyzed and improved. This requires the identification and analysis of key information.

Leaders must ensure that the organization selects and manages key information and data that supports overall business goals. Primary emphasis during this process must be on those actions and initiatives that support process management and performance improvement.

Information and data are selected for use based on their strategic importance; they are managed most effectively when they can be rapidly accessed and updated; in turn, these contribute strongly to their reliability.

Leaders of SROs are concerned with how the organization evaluates and improves its selection, analysis, and management of information and data. They insure an emphasis on alignment with business priorities, support of process management, and feedback from information and data users. Their evaluation should take into account factors such as paths of data use, extent and effectiveness of use, gaps, sharing, and organization of information and data.

Information and data are most frequently selected based on their utility to effectively

EXHIBIT 1.8 Information and Analysis Characteristics of Self-Renewing Organizations

- Criteria for selecting data/information for use in quality, operational performance improvement are integrated and used throughout the organization
- Key data/information relating to key public service/business drivers is used to improve quality and operational performance throughout organization
- Processes and technologies are used throughout the organization to assure that information collected is reliable, consistent, valid, and readily accessible in response to user needs
- Processes are in place to evaluate and improve the information and data system supporting the improvement of organization performance; reviewed on an ongoing basis
- Benchmarking process established based on needs and priorities and aligned with overall organization improvement targets; data used to establish stretch targets and/or support breakthrough approaches throughout organization
- Most areas use benchmark/comparison data, including product and service quality, support service processes, staff, volunteer, supplier-related activities
- Organization evaluates and improves its benchmarking process on an ongoing basis
- Performance, customer/client data aggregated with other key data, analyzed, translated into usable information to support reviews, business decisions, planning throughout the organization
- Performance data aggregated with other key data, analyzed, and related to financial indicators of performance; information used to set priorities for improvement actions throughout organization

manage performance. However, information, data, and information technology often have strategic significance as well. For example, information technology can be used to build and disseminate vital knowledge about customers and markets—creating the ability to operate more successfully.

Data and information related to competitive position and to best practices serve as external drivers of improvement—giving this information both operational and strategic importance. Of course, the organization should not only select and use this information, but it needs to consider how it evaluates and improves the processes it uses to do so.

The basic premises here recognize the fact that:

- Organizations need to "know where they stand" relative to competitors and to best practice performance for similar activities;
- Comparative and benchmarking information provides impetus for significant ("breakthrough") improvement and alerts organizations to competitive threats and new practices; and,
- Organizations need to understand their own processes and the processes of others, before they compare performance levels.

Carefully selected and analyzed benchmarking information may also be very helpful to support business analysis and decisions relating to core competencies, alliances, and outsourcing.

Organization-level analysis is the principal basis for guiding an organization's process management toward business results. Despite the importance of individual facts and data, they do not usually (in the self-renewing organization) provide a sound basis for actions or priorities.

Action should be undertaken only after an understanding has been achieved between cause/effect connections among processes and between processes and business results. Process actions often have many resource implications; results may have many cost and revenue implications as well. Because resources for improvement are limited, and cause/effect connections are often unclear, most organizations face a critical need to provide a sound analytical basis for decisions.

Data and information from all parts of the organization must be aggregated and analyzed to support reviews, business decisions, and planning. SRO leaders ensure the focus remains on two key areas of performance: customers and operational performance. Analyses use both nonfinancial and financial data, connected to provide a basis for action. For many nonprofits, a particularly important analysis objective is that of linking customer data, improvements in product and service quality, and improvements in operational performance to improvement in financial indicators—guiding the selection of improvement efforts and strategies, to achieve revenue growth, and to reduce operating costs.

1.8   *Organizational Environment and Culture*

(A)   LEADERSHIP

This excellence category includes the organization's leadership system, strategic directions, and expectations (Exhibit 1.9).

In any self-renewing organization (SRO), senior leaders fulfill key roles—those that cannot be delegated to others. These vital roles include setting the organization's strategic directions, and building and maintaining a leadership system conducive to high performance, individual development, and organizational learning. Truly effective leaders at all levels of the organization, however, take into account all stakeholders, customers, employees, suppliers, partners, public, and the community.

Major aspects of leadership include creating values and expectations, setting directions, developing and maintaining an effective leadership system, and building the organization's capabilities. Senior leaders need to reflect these values, and the leadership system needs to include teamwork at the executive level.

Senior leaders within the SRO devote significant time and attention to evaluating and improving the effectiveness of the organization and its leadership system. This function of leadership is crucial, due to the fast pace of competition. A major objective is to create organizations that are flexible and responsive—changing easily to adapt to new needs and opportunities. Both leadership and organization are crucial to high performance. Through their roles in strategy development and review of organization performance, the senior leaders adapt leadership (creation and management of change) and the organization (vision, mission, customer focus) to changing opportunities and requirements.

In the SRO, the leadership system is translated into an effective overall organization structure and management system focused on performance.

The SRO's management and work processes support its customer and performance objectives. Senior leaders are alert to identify functional or management barriers that could lead to losing sight of customers or create ineffective or slow decision paths. They take strong measures to ensure alignment of organization units.

The SRO's values, expectations, and directions are "made real" throughout the organization via effective communications. Senior leader communications are necessary for effec-

EXHIBIT 1.9 Leadership Characteristics of Self-Renewing Organizations

- All senior leaders personally, visibly, proactively involved in broad range of quality-related activities; significant time devoted to these activities
- Senior leaders create a vision, quality values, customer focus orientation
- Senior leaders fully participate in setting organization's performance excellence goals through strategic, business planning
- Senior leaders devote extensive time to reviewing organization's customer, operational performance
- Extent to which vision, quality values, customer focus orientation have been adopted is evaluated and improved on ongoing basis
- All senior leaders use a variety of methods to communicate and reinforce vision, quality values, customer focus orientation to staff and volunteers; communication is two-way, clear, open, covers all issues
- Effective strategies involve leaders throughout organization in quality-related activities; roles, responsibilities, accountability clearly defined; extensive cooperation among units encouraged, evident
- Senior leaders, union leaders actively participate in planning, attaining quality goals; mutual support visible throughout organization, reinforced through communications, partnering
- Partnering relationships exist with major customer groups, suppliers, others; number of mutually supportive activities expanding in support of quality, performance goals
- Vision, quality values, customer focus orientation effectively communicated inside, outside organization
- Documented review process of organization's quality, operational improvement plans used throughout organization; results used to implement strategies to improve organizationwide performance
- Quality goals and objectives directly address public health, safety, environmental protection, ethical conduct; accountability for achieving goals, objectives clearly established; improvement efforts throughout organization reflect this commitment; these quality goals, objectives go beyond minimum legal/community standards
- Organization recognized as outstanding citizen in its key communities; senior leaders, staff, volunteers share talents/expertise with community

tive overall communications. Making values, expectations, and directions real demands constant reinforcement and "truth testing," as employees observe whether or not stated values and expectations are actually the basis for organization actions and key decisions.

Senior leaders review organization and work unit performance, and ensure that important work process assessments are included in these reviews. The information they assess addresses important aspects of reviews—types, frequency, content, uses, and who conducts them. Frequency, content, uses and who conducts reviews will vary greatly, depending upon many factors. Most commonly, the review system blends ongoing (real-time) and periodic reviews.

As the President's Quality Award points out: "Reviews offer an effective means to communicate and reinforce what is really important, how performance is measured, and how well business objectives are being met." Important considerations in reviews are the content and organization of information to foster learning and to stimulate action. This means that reviews should include nonfinancial and financial information that together present a clear picture of status and trends relative to the organization's key business drivers. Reviews also provide an effective means to assist units that may not be performing according to expectations.

Public responsibility and *corporate citizenship* are vital to nonprofit organizations—how the organization integrates its public responsibilities and corporate citizenship into its business planning and performance improvement practices.

Nonprofits, like public and private sector organizations, should be concerned about three basic aspects of public responsibility: (1) making risk and legal requirements an integral part of performance improvement; (2) sensitivity in planning products, services, and operations to issues of societal concern, whether or not these issues are currently embodied in law; and (3) making legal and ethical conduct visible in the organization's values and performance improvement processes.

Fulfilling public responsibilities means not only meeting all local, state, and federal laws and regulatory requirements, but also treating these and related requirements as areas for improvement "beyond mere compliance." This means that all SROs should maintain constant awareness of potential public impacts related to their products, services, and operations. Nonprofits, often the target of legal or regulatory action by public regulators or private corporations, must be diligent in *exceeding the average* in each of these categories.

SROs serve as a "corporate citizen" in their key communities. They are productive, reputable, and involved as members of different types of communities and serve as a positive influence upon other organizations. They work within and outside their organization to strengthen community services, education, health care, the environment, and practices of trade and business associations.

(B)   HUMAN RESOURCE DEVELOPMENT AND MANAGEMENT

Human resource development and management (see Exhibit 1.10) is the functional area and focal point within any organization for all important human resource practices—those directed toward the creation and sustainability of a high-performance workplace. A vital objective for SRO leaders is to address human resource development and management in an integrated way—aligning them with the organization's strategic directions.

Strategic directions should address the development of all those involved in achieving the organization's mission and vision—staff and volunteers—within the context of a high-performance workplace. This requires a coordinated organizational strategy.

The overall human resource plan should be derived from the organization's strategic and business planning. Primary directions and resourcing must support its overall strategic directions. Senior leaders within the SRO endeavor to develop a multiyear context and guide for human resource planning, management, and evaluation.

As in any quality-centered organization, the human resource development area uses the *Plan-Do-Check-Act* cycle to evaluate and improve overall planning and management. Employee-related and organization performance data and information is tied to overall evaluation of the organization's strategy and business results.

Care is taken to go beyond broad strategy to the essential details of human resource effectiveness. The evaluation needs to provide the organization's senior leaders with information on strengths and weaknesses in human resource practices and development that might bear upon the organization's abilities to achieve its short-term and longer-term business objectives. For example, the evaluation should take into account the development and progression of all categories and types of staff and volunteers, including those newly joining the organization.

The evaluation should also monitor the extent to which education and training is

EXHIBIT 1.10 Human Resource Development and Management Characteristics of Self-Renewing Organizations

- Systematic, integrated HR plan is deployed throughout organization to develop workforce potential; it is linked to quality, operational performance improvement plans
- HR plan includes redesign to improve flexibility, innovation, rapid response to changing requirements; staff/volunteer development, education, training; changes in reward, recognition, recruitment
- HR planning is integral, fully aligned part of business planning process; systematically evaluated, improved on ongoing basis
- Employee-related data, organization performance data consistently analyzed, used to assess development, well-being of all categories, types of employees; assess linkage of HR practices to key business results
- Reliable, complete HR information is readily available for use in strategic, business planning
- Unions partner in development, implementation of HR plan where appropriate
- Work, job design promote high performance throughout organization by creating opportunities for initiative, self-directed responsibility; fostering flexibility, rapid response to changing requirements; ensuring effective communication across functions/units
- Working environment throughout organization supports increased empowerment, personal responsibility, appropriate risk-taking, creativity, innovation
- Managers throughout organization support employee contributions, teamwork; managers routinely exhibit coaching and facilitating behaviors, share authority
- Variety of formal and/or informal reward or recognition mechanisms used throughout organization for all levels and types of employees; developed in conjunction with employees; emphasis on recognition of teamwork
- Employees throughout organization provided feedback; evaluated, promoted, provided career opportunities based on personal development, contributions to quality, operational performance goals
- Systematic, documented education, training strategy deployed builds organization, employee capabilities
- Education, training consistently address key organization performance objectives and motivation, progression, development of all employees
- Education, training based on systematic needs assessment; employees, managers throughout organization provide input
- Special education, training designed to enhance high-performance work units
- Knowledge, skills consistently reinforced through on-the-job application throughout organization
- Education, training systematically evaluated, improved on ongoing basis using feedback from employees, customers; appropriate measures of effectiveness, extent of education, training used
- Extensive quality, skills training throughout organization; all employees trained in quality awareness; teams, work groups trained in appropriate quality tools, techniques in support of customer service, continuous improvement; cross-functional training commonplace
- Organization consistently maintains safe, healthful work environment; improvement efforts cover requirements, measures for all employee well-being factors (health, safety, ergonomics)
- Extensive services, facilities, activities, opportunities available to all employees to support overall well-being, satisfaction/enhance work experience, development potential
- Variety of measures used to determine employee satisfaction, well-being, motivation throughout organization; data consistently used to improve employee satisfaction, well-being, motivation on an ongoing basis

deployed throughout the organization, and how well education and training support organization performance improvement. The overall evaluation will rely heavily upon well-being and satisfaction factors.

Well-being considerations include the work environment and the work climate and how they are tailored to foster the well-being, satisfaction, and development of all employees. Long-term well-being and productivity (not to mention legal and regulatory requirements), require a safe and healthful work environment.

SRO leaders' approach to enhance staff and volunteer well-being, satisfaction, and growth potential is based upon a more holistic view of the organization's human resources as key stakeholders. They consider a wide variety of mechanisms to build well-being and satisfaction, from development, progression, employability, and external activities, to family or other community service activities.

Many factors might affect employee motivation. Although satisfaction with pay and promotion potential is important, these factors alone are not adequate to assess the overall climate for motivation, morale, and high performance. Therefore, the organization will consider a variety of factors relating to the work environment to determine the key elements of the organization's culture and internal environment. Those factors identified that inhibit motivation will be prioritized and addressed. Additional understanding of these factors is developed through exit interviews with departing staff and volunteers.

In the SRO, job design, compensation, and recognition approaches enable and encourage all employees to contribute effectively, operating within high-performance work units. The latter requires effective work design and reinforcement.

The basic intent of such work design approaches should be to enable staff and volunteers to exercise more discretion and decision making, leading to greater flexibility and more rapid response to the changing requirements of the marketplace—in short, to be empowered with a combination of authority, responsibility, resourcing, and accountability.

Effective job design and flexible work organizations are necessary but in and of themselves may not be sufficient to ensure high performance. Job and organization design needs to be backed by information systems, education, and appropriate training to ensure that information flow supports the job and work designs. Also important is effective communication across functions and work units to ensure focus on customer requirements.

Incentives need to be aligned with work systems. Compensation and recognition should be structured and implemented to reinforce high-performance job design, work organizations, and teamwork. These are important considerations because there should be a consistency between the organization's compensation and recognition system and its work structures and processes. Compensation, benefits, and recognition may need to be based upon demonstrated skills and evaluation by peers in teams and networks.

The SRO develops human resources via education, training, and on-the-job reinforcement of knowledge and skills. A major objective of "development" is meeting the needs of a high-performance workplace operating in a dynamic, highly competitive environment. Education and training need to be ongoing as well.

Education and training serve as key vehicles to build organization and people capabilities. These two capabilities are, in fact, investments the organization makes in its long-term future and the long-term future of people.

SRO leaders pay particular attention to how education and training are designed, delivered, reinforced, and evaluated, with special emphasis upon on-the-job application of knowledge and skills. They recognize the importance of involving all levels and categories of people within the organization—staff, volunteers, managers—in the design of

training, including clear identification of specific needs. This involves job analysis—understanding the types and levels of the skills required and the timeliness of training.

Evaluation of education and training is vital and should take into account the supervisor's evaluation, employee/volunteer self-evaluation, and peer evaluation of value received through education and training relative to needs identified in design. The evaluation process could also address the effectiveness of education and training delivery, impact on work unit performance, and costs of delivery alternatives.

2 ▼ Strategic Planning in the Self-Renewing Organization

D. KERRY LAYCOCK
MS Organizational Consultant

TRACY D. CONNORS
The BelleAire Institute, Inc.

2.1 Overview

Strategic planning is a structured, systematic, top-down process. Its outcomes envision the future and help leaders throughout the organization decide what the organization should do today to ensure tomorrow's success. Strategic planning is a management function and a critical leadership responsibility that helps increase the organization's ability to be successful in the future. Strategic planning clarifies and validates the business of the organization, documents the vision of what it plans to become, and serves as a road map to achieve the vision.

Strategic planning is the process by which the leaders of the organization envision the future and develop the necessary procedures and operations to achieve that future. This vision of the future state of the organization provides both the direction in which the organization should move and the energy to begin that move. The strategic planning process is very different from long-range planning—a simple extrapolation of statistic trends of forecasts—and is more than attempting to anticipate the future and to prepare accordingly. Envisioning involves a belief that important aspects of the future can be influenced and changed by what one does now. Properly implemented, the strategic planning process can help your organization do far more than simply plan for the future; it can help the organization *create its future*.

Strategic planning addresses strategic and business planning (including development of plans), with a strong focus on client/customer and operational performance requirements. For self-renewing organization (SRO) leaders, the emphasis here is that customer-driven quality and operational performance excellence are key strategic business issues that need to be an integral part of organization planning.

Customer-driven quality is a strategic view of quality. The focus here is on the drivers of customer/client satisfaction—a key factor in organizational success.

Operational performance improvement contributes to short-term and longer-term productivity growth and overall competitiveness—sustainable operations and self-sufficiency. The focus on building operational capability—including speed, responsiveness, and flexibility—represents a necessary investment in strengthening competitive fitness for all organizations, including nonprofits.

Strategic planning confers many benefits on the organization, including:

- Giving leaders a better understanding that key customer and public service requirements should serve as input as the organization establishes its strategic directions and so help ensure that ongoing process improvements will be aligned with the organization's strategic directions;
- Optimizing the use of resources and ensuring essential bridging between short-term and longer-term requirements that may require resources (e.g., money, volunteers); and,
- Ensuring that implementation and deployment will be effective—that there are mechanisms to transmit requirements and achieve alignment on three basic levels, including the organization-executive level, the key process level, and the work-unit/individual-job level.

A well-developed and effectively implemented strategic plan:

- Establishes the broad direction and goals of the organization;
- Integrates the goals and activities of component parts of the organization, including field activities, into a coherent, effective, and efficiently functioning whole; and,
- Provides a sense of identity and purpose to clients, customers, volunteers, staff, and leaders at all levels within the organization, enabling them to relate their own efforts and interactions to the organization's broader picture.

Self-renewing organizations develop their view of the future, set strategic directions, and translate these directions into actionable key business drivers, including customer satisfaction. Effective leadership in fulfilling these functions is critical and determines the organization's operational effectiveness. An important role for SRO leaders is to ensure an effective focus for daily work, aligning it with the organization's strategic directions.

Mapping out a "plan" is useless without a well defined purpose. Until recently, nonprofits operated in relatively stable environments. Funding and programming were fairly consistent from year to year. Public opinion was the concern of politicians, not nonprofit leaders. Today, all of that has changed. Human service organizations face burgeoning demands for services. Cultural and human service organizations face increasing public scrutiny. Government seeks to turn over more service delivery to nonprofits but is under intense fiscal and public pressure to reduce spending.

For example, health care providers are faced with increased government intrusion into what services are provided and how they are delivered. Hospitals and child welfare organizations must contend with new populations of sick and addicted children.

Most nonprofit organizations face intense pressure from other organizations and individuals who claim a right or responsibility to define the direction of the organization. For example, humane societies must contend with the often conflicting demands of animal rights advocates, professional breeders, local authorities, and a host of other groups. Arts organizations face a reconsideration of what is art and who decides.

Resources are increasingly difficult to obtain. Government has less to spend, corporations seek to support more programs that have direct business benefits, and foundations are overwhelmed by requests for funding. The degree of sophistication in fund raising has increased, too. The funding environment is extremely competitive.

For more nonprofits, the world is chaotic and threatening. For these reasons, leaders of nonprofit organizations increasingly are turning to strategic planning as a way to enhance organizational effectiveness and adapt to the rapidly changing world.

2.2   Definition of Strategic Planning

Strategic planning as practiced by the self-renewing organization is a sound, systematic, well-documented, effective process used throughout organization to develop business strategies, business plans, and key business drivers for overall operational and financial performance. All appropriate staff, clients, customers, volunteers, suppliers, and partners participate fully in the planning process.

Strategic planning, then, is a comprehensive organizational process of adaptation throughout assessment, decision making, evaluation, and change management. Strategic planning seeks to answer the most basic questions about why the organization exists, what it does, and how it does it. The result of the process is a completed plan that serves as a guide for organizational action for the next three to five years.

It may be an overstatement to say that the process is more important than the product, but, in turbulent times, planning offers a constructive approach to organizational learning. Planning team members often emerge from the process as highly knowledgeable and committed members of the organization. Their ability to contribute to the organization increases enormously. Developing a solid plan contributes to organizational effectiveness by helping members make the right decision now and in the future.

2.3 *Characteristics of Strategic Planning*

Four factors distinguish strategic planning from other planning models and organizational improvement strategies.[1]

1. Strategic planning is fundamentally concerned with *adapting to a changing environment*. This external orientation focuses on recognizing and responding to the forces for change that exist *outside* the organization.
2. Strategic planning is *future-oriented*. During the course of planning, consideration is given to current problems only if these problems present a barrier to getting to a desirable place in the future. Strategic planning is anticipatory rather than reactionary. Planners are more concerned with problems of the future than with those of today.
3. Strategic planning is comprehensive. It encompasses a wide range of factors, both internal and external to the organization. It requires an enormous commitment of time and energy and a willingness to struggle with difficult issues and divergent perspectives.
4. Strategic planning is a consensus-building process. Given the diversity of stakeholder interests that many nonprofits face, strategic planning offers a way to surface those needs and interests and to reach agreement on the future direction that best serves them.

Other characteristics, including:

- The strategy development process considers the organization's vision, customer-driven values and expectations; and includes risk analysis, organization capabilities, and supplier/partner capabilities;
- Strategies and business plans are translated into actionable key business drivers used for deployment throughout the organization, to key suppliers/partners; and leaders, staff, and volunteers are held accountable for achieving major targets throughout the organization;
- Staff and volunteers know how their work unit contributes to overall business success;
- Systematic procedures are used to continuously evaluate strategic planning, the plan's deployment processes; and improvements in processes are made on an ongoing basis;
- Specific business drivers derived from strategic directions are translated into actionable plans throughout the organization, including key performance requirements, operational performance measures, and productivity improvement;
- Top priority is given to deployment of these action plans and improvement targets as evidenced by extensive resource commitment to ensuring plan success; and,

---

[1] Portions of the material contained in this chapter originally appeared in D. K. Laycock, "Are You Ready for Strategic Planning?" *Nonprofit World*, 8 (S) (September–October 1990); 26–27.

- Outstanding product/service quality and operational performance is projected for key business areas when compared with key benchmarks, that is, objectives will be achieved.

2.4 Strategy Development

Every organization is impacted by key influences, challenges, and requirements that can affect its future opportunities and directions. Leaders of SROs take as long a view as possible, emphasizing the importance of a thorough and realistic context for the development of a customer/client and market-focused strategy to guide ongoing decision making, resource allocation, and organizationwide management.

Strategy and plans are translated into actionable key business drivers, which serve as the basis for operationalizing and deploying plan requirements. This translation often includes a determination of those activities the organization should perform itself and those for which it might utilize partners.

The SRO places a high priority on evaluating and improving its strategic planning and plan deployment processes. This can involve input from work units regarding key deployment factors—effective translation and communications of strategy and plans, adequacy of resources, and identification of key new needs by clients/customers.

SRO leaders are focused on developing a competitive strategy and on operationalizing this strategy. Operationalizing the strategy in the form of key public service/business drivers requires clear and measurable performance objectives. These objectives serve to guide the design and management of key processes. The objectives often serve to align organizational systems (e.g., communications, compensation, recognition) with performance objectives.

SRO leaders place high priority on the organization's key business drivers and how these drivers are translated into an action plan. This includes spelling out key performance requirements; alignment of work unit, supplier, and/or partner plans; how productivity, cycle time, and waste reduction are addressed; and the principal resources committed to the accomplishment of plans.

2.5 Planning Parameters

Exhibit 2.1 describes the parameters of the planning process. Planning begins with building a consensus about the desired future. This view should be expansive and not constrained by practicality. In other words, vision describes the world in an ideal state.

For example, the vision of an adoption agency may be a world in which all children are raised as permanent members of loving families. In this world, there are no residential institutions and no foster care.

This perfect world may never exist. The next broad area of investigation is the external environment. This inquiry seeks to answer questions about what is most needed and most likely. Every organization is faced with certain opportunities and challenged by certain barriers.

Besides the external barriers, there are questions of internal capacity. No organization can meet all needs. Which needs are met is often the result of defining what the organization does best.

EXHIBIT 2.1 Strategic Planning Parameters

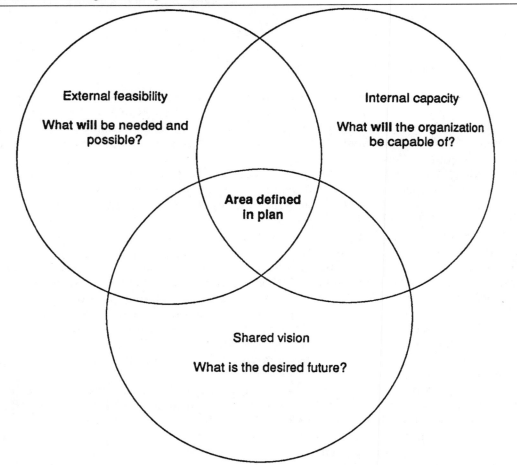

The adoption agency may wish that all children had a permanent, loving home, but may see children with disabilities as the most critical need. In addition, the agency may have a staff that has special strengths in this area and, as a result, may decide to specialize in this one area and leave other children to other organizations. This decision is the agency's strategic position.

Thus, the strategic plan seeks to define the intersection of what is desired, most needed, and most possible. This clarity is critical to the success of nonprofit organizations. As Peter Drucker (1990) has suggested, "Non-profit organizations have no 'bottom line.' " They often consider the public services they provide as righteous, moral, and serving a cause, so they are often less willing to say, if it doesn't produce results, then maybe we should direct our resources elsewhere. "Non-profit organizations need the discipline of organized abandonment perhaps even more than a business does. They need to face up to critical choices" (pp. 10–11). Strategic planning is about the discipline and process of making those choices.

(A) PLANNING FOR QUALITY

Nonprofit organizations have just begun to apply to their operations and services the principles of the quality revolution of manufacturing (Kennedy, 1991). But, unlike manufacturing organizations, nonprofits seldom have a physical product, and measures of quality are not immediately apparent. On an automobile, one can measure fit, form, and function; but it is much more difficult for an organization that serves the homeless to define quality—not impossible, but challenging.

How an organization defines quality depends first on how it defines its mission. If the organization serving the homeless has as its mission the relief of suffering, then the number of beds and of meals served may be counted as indicators of quality. If the mission is the prevention of suffering, then the measures of quality are very different. Serving more people could, in fact, be an indicator of lack of success.

In today's competitive environment, with its growing demands for accountability, it is not enough to "get somewhere." The organization serving the homeless may see doing something, anything, for a group of people so much in need as "getting somewhere." But is it the best use of resources? Does it provide the greatest benefit? Is it what is most needed?

In nonprofit organizations, quality improvement begins with a clear sense of mission and purpose (effectiveness), but it asks another important question that is not mentioned above: How can we do it better (efficiency)? Quality improvement is a multifaceted strategy for improving both organizational effectiveness and efficiency.

(B) ASSESSING READINESS

In recent years, strategic planning has become widely practiced in nonprofit organizations. For the most part, this trend has been very positive, and many would argue that it has had a significant positive impact on the health of nonprofit organizations. But strategic planning is not a panacea, and, in the rush to get involved in planning, many organizations have failed to consider or ensure the appropriateness of the process for their situation.

Understanding the nature and definition of strategic planning, many organizations have failed to consider or ensure the appropriateness of the process for their situation.

Understanding the nature and definition of strategic planning, and asking a number of specific questions, will help define the appropriateness of its application. Exhibit 2.2 describes the assessment process.

(i) Stability
Potential planners must ask whether the organization is stable. In other words, is the organization preparing for the future, or is it attempting to resolve a crisis? If the organization is in crisis, the crisis must be resolved. This is an immediate problem requiring an immediate response.

If the organization faces a major crisis, planning should be delayed until the crisis has passed. All efforts should be focused on stabilizing the organization. Once this is done, the organization may turn to the broader concerns of strategic planning.

(ii) Capability
Potential planners must ask whether the organization is capable of undertaking the work of planning. Planning requires an enormous amount of time and, depending on the

EXHIBIT 2.2 Assessing Readiness for Strategic Planning

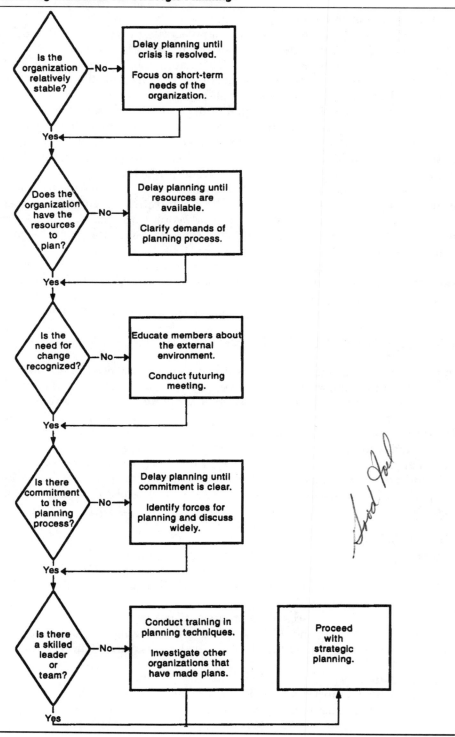

extent of research and the use of an outside consultant, money. Unless these resources are committed up front, the planning process may become an unexpected drain on the organization, particularly in terms of human resources. Burnout and frustration can lead to a hastily completed plan or, worse yet, a failure to complete the plan at all.

Many organizations will include key stakeholders in the planning process. A few stakeholders may be of such importance as to be made members of the planning team. Others will act as resources to the team, to be consulted on specific issues. (Stakeholders are discussed further in section 2.7b.)

Clear role definitions are critical to the success of planning and should be discussed prior to the initiation of planning. Role definitions should be included in a plan-to-plan document.

Because planning is about change, it is an inherently political process (Benveniste, 1989). Choosing the members of the planning team is no small task. As discussed earlier, the group should be representative of the diversity of opinion in the organization.

2.6   The Planning Process: Overview

Exhibit 2.3 outlines the steps in the planning process. Many planning models exist, and the differences are often academic. Nonetheless, some consideration should be given to the needs of the organization and to tailoring the model to fit with those needs. The model in Exhibit 2.3 emphasizes strategic vision and stakeholder interests.

Each component of the planning process will be discussed in detail. Briefly, developing a vision of the desired future involves describing the world as it would be if the organization were successful. Thus, the planning process begins with ultimate ends and works backward to develop means.

The situation analysis attempts to look at external trends, stakeholder issues, internal issues, and organizational performance data, in order to identify potential barriers and means for realizing the desired future. The product of this analysis is a list of critical planning issues.

Mission refers to the development of a clear consensus about the purpose of the organization.

Directions are the basic divisions of resources. Broad organizational goals describe what the organization seeks to accomplish by allocating resources in each of these directions.

Strategies are the means for accomplishing these goals. Objectives describe specifically what each strategy is designed to accomplish. They are measurable outcomes of the strategy implementation and are written in terms of when and how much.

Implementation plans are basic assignments of responsibility and completion dates. They may be expanded into more specific operational plans, but these extend beyond the scope of strategic planning.

Planners should assess and determine whether current operations are strong enough to endure the stress of directing resources, particularly board and staff time, toward planning. It is important that the organization be able to maintain present functions *and* plan for the future.

The board of directors should establish a specific budget allocation for planning. This allocation is to cover the costs of materials, a consultant (if one is used), and research (for example, mailing a survey to members or service users). Organizations that are set up on

EXHIBIT 2.3 The Strategic Planning Process

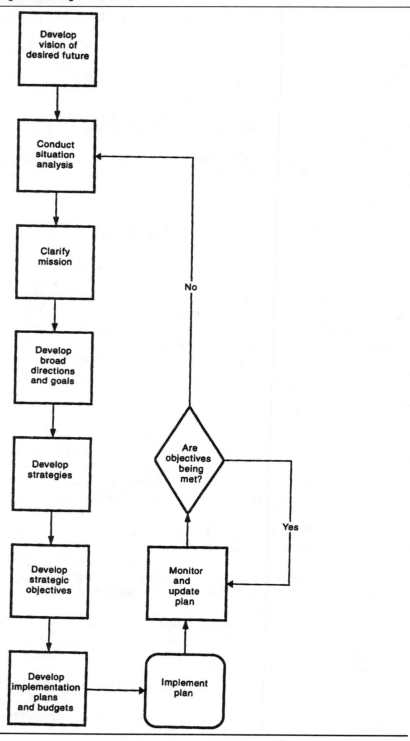

a fund accounting basis will need to allocate staff time to planning. A significant commitment of staff time to planning can have an impact on the organization's overhead ratio.

An organization that lacks the capability to undertake this effort should help members understand the demands of planning and identify additional resources. Planning should be delayed until the organization can ensure that current operations will not be hindered.

(i) Recognized Need for Change

Planners must determine whether there is a recognized need for change. Do members of the organization have some awareness of a changing environment? Is there a leader with compelling ideas or a strong vision? Unless there is a strongly felt need for change, the resistance to change may overpower those attempting to move the organization forward.

If there is not such a need, planners can help the organization explore the external environment, perhaps by developing a futurizing session without a specific commitment to developing a plan. This meeting is designed to explore the future of the organization and develop a consensus about the future and the impact of the organization. (This approach is discussed later in this chapter.)

Whatever approach is chosen, it is essential that formal planning be delayed until there is a strongly felt, compelling need for change.

(ii) Commitment to Planning

The degree of commitment to planning is related to the recognition of the need to change. If the issues are well understood and a course of action is obvious, perhaps strategic planning is not the best use of time.

Experience suggests that there are few issues of this type. They may appear simple on the surface but are, in fact, very complicated. The responses to them require careful consideration of unintentional effects on other aspects of the organization. Frequently, individuals are very clear on an issue, but, as a group, there is a considerable degree of disagreement that must be resolved. Planners must help clarify the divergent views of the issues and assess whether the process is understood and supported by members of the board and staff.

Planning must begin with a clear commitment from the top of the organization. The chairperson or president of the board and the executive director should be involved in the process and act as its advocates. Organizations should be wary of allowing the process to be undertaken by a small, nonrepresentative group of individuals within the organization, without the support of other members. For example, a planning team comprised solely of staff, without board representation or support, or a planning team comprised of a small faction of the board who want to change the organization, would likely fail to get their plan implemented. Perhaps the most extreme example is when the planning is given over to a consultant, with little or no involvement of the organization members.

At best, consultants are often misguided, even though sincere in their interest to help the organization. As worst, they seek to politicize the organization, creating conflict and compromise rather than unity and consensus.

It is important to analyze not just the forces for change, but the forces for planning itself. Is the exercise perceived as valuable, or is planning being done merely to satisfy a major funder, an internal faction, or a key stakeholder?

If there are questions of commitment, planners should attempt to identify and address specific concerns. They should delay planning until the process is better understood and the participants are committed to it: Planners should help identify the driving forces for planning, and initiate discussion within the organization on the politics of planning. If the planning effort is being driven by a funder or other external stakeholder, a scaled-down approach that will satisfy the demand at less cost to the organization should be considered.

Developing a "plan to plan" may help build support for the process. This document provides a concise rationale for undertaking planning, clarifies roles of planning team members, outlines data requirements, and sets a timetable for completion.

(iii) Level of Skill

Planners need to consider the level of skills in the organization. Strategic planning is not as complex as some make it sound. However, it does help to have someone who is familiar with the process, as well as a planning team that has clear roles and responsibilities. Perhaps most important is having someone to lead the process. This person needs both commitment and the organizational skills to pull the team together.

If there is not a clear leader who has sufficient familiarity with the planning process, the organization should consider delaying planning for a short period and should work with the executive director or a key board member to develop leadership for the planning process. A planning orientation for the staff and board can be conducted, and organizations that have completed plans can be investigated as a way to understand the process and commitments necessary.

(A) THE PLANNING TEAM AND MEMBER ROLES

Planning is done by a committee comprised largely of board members, but may include staff, constituents, and a facilitator or consultant. The size of the team is a function of the size of the organization and the scope of planning. For small nonprofits undertaking their first planning effort, a group of about eight people probably would be most efficient.

In nonprofit organizations, strategic planning is largely a board function. The board is responsible for setting the direction of the organization (Houle, 1989; Carver, 1990). The full board should be updated frequently on the progress of the planning team and allowed to have input at any point in the process.

Staff members should be represented on the planning committee; generally, this is the executive director's function. In larger organizations, staff may provide support to the planning committee, help conduct research, and generate financial data.

A key aspect of strategic planning is that it is conducted by members of the organization who know and care most about the organization. Often, nonprofits will turn to an outsider for help in planning. An objective person who has expertise in the planning process can make an enormous contribution. Consultants are expensive, but, in the long run, can save the organization time and money by defining an appropriate process and keeping it on track. The consultant is largely the process expert and the facilitator of meetings. The consultant is not the planner.

Finally, all plans must be periodically monitored and updated. Adjustments in the plan must be made in response to new information, changing conditions, and evaluations of present efforts.

Although Exhibit 2.3 represents the process as having very distinct phases, it is, in actuality, somewhat messier. Experience suggests that groups can become bogged down in defining what is a direction, a goal, a strategy, and an objective. These are not clear lines, and, in general, groups develop a feel for the distinctions only after having wrestled with them for a while. Like the turning of a lens, each level of planning provides greater clarity and specificity. Exhibit 2.4 provides some basic guidelines for constructing each phase of the plan.

2.7 The Planning Process: Assessment

(A) FUTURE VISION

Despite our best efforts, from palm reading to computer modeling, our ability to foretell the future is very limited. The future is uncertain because it has not happened yet, and some people feel threatened by this uncertainty. Strategic planners assume the future is

EXHIBIT 2.4 Elements of the Strategic Plan

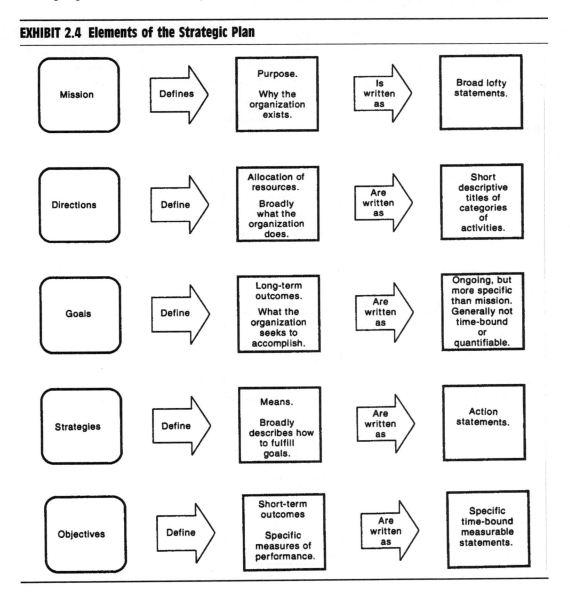

never entirely knowable, and, as such, presents a great opportunity. Strategic planning is about being ready for the future, but it can be more: It can offer a means to move from anticipation to action, thus creating the future.

A vision statement describes the world as we want it to be. It may be possible for the planning team to reach a consensus without employing any specific techniques. A talented writer can capture the discussions of the group in a coherent statement to be shared with others within and outside the organization. These discussions should be held away from the pressure of everyday work. (A Saturday morning retreat often works well.) Exhibit 2.5 describes several areas of investigation for a more structured approach to *futuring*.

(i) Organizational Values Clarification

Formal discussions about vision should begin with a clarification of current organizational (members, staff, management) values, the organization's culture, and the values of its stakeholders. Values and ethics are central to the existence of nonprofit organizations. The American government grants special status to these organizations because they are thought to perform a public good. Current treatment of nonprofits is traceable to early

EXHIBIT 2.5 Future Vision

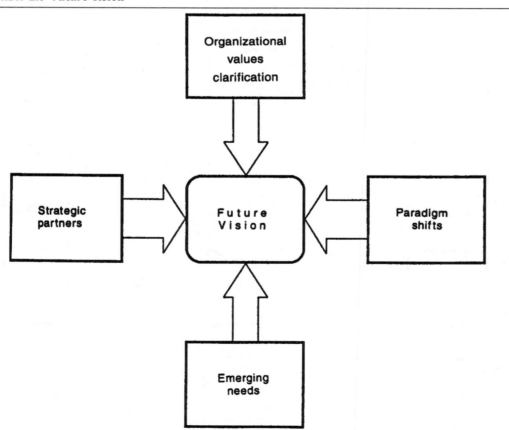

notions of charity and the relationship between church and state (Hall, 1987). Being clear about what is meant by "good" and "public purpose" is extremely important.

Clarifying values is a matter of coming to agreement about the basic beliefs that guide the organization. A values audit is among the first steps in the strategic planning because values directly impact what can or cannot be achieved within and by the organization. It is sometimes useful to analyze critical incidents in the organization's past as a way to surface and test these values.

(ii)   *Paradigm Shifts*

Futurist Joel Barker (1988) popularized the notion of paradigms' sets of rules and assumptions about the way things are. Typically, they are so ingrained that they are unquestioned, perhaps even unspoken. Occasionally, an idea or concept can radically alter the dominant paradigm. Creating a vision requires examining the potential for new or emergent ideas to radically alter the way things are.

For example, until recently, our notion of what is best for developmentally disabled or emotionally impaired people was driven by what might be called the "institutional paradigm": Creating bigger and better institutions was seen as the best way to provide for these people.

About 15 years ago, a new idea began to take hold: Perhaps institutions were inherently harmful to these people. Today, the "community care paradigm" has largely replaced the "institutional paradigm." Governments and organizations that missed the impact of this single idea went on to build more buildings that now stand empty or have been converted to other uses.

In developing a future vision, organizations need to ask: What ideas are being expressed, however wild, that could radically change the way we do business, and in what ways would the organization change?

(iii)   *Emerging Needs*

Identifying emerging needs requires that the organization look at relevant areas of concern and analyze new, unmet needs. At this point in the planning process, needs identification is not intended to yield strategic responses, but rather to justify the continuation of the organization. Child welfare organizations may look to the burgeoning number of "crack"-addicted babies. A community arts agency or fund-raising organization may look to the movement away from federal and state funding of the arts and see a need to develop new sources of financial support. In this case, the vision might be for artists and arts organizations to be supported through private donations.

(iv)   *Strategic Partners*

Developing a future vision may involve identifying strategic partners. No one organization can meet all needs. Identifying collaborators may be necessary to make the vision possible. For example, a community recycling program may see waste haulers, schools, and block clubs as important partners in their cause. A vision to bring them all together could make possible the improvement of the environment.

All of these concepts are brought together in the vision statement, a written statement that describes the future the group hopes to see. In addition, these discussions will have yielded important insights to be explored further in the situation analysis and developed into actual strategies.

(B) SITUATION ANALYSIS

The situation analysis provides the data on which the planning team will make strategic decisions. The key components of the analysis are presented in Exhibit 2.6.

(i) Stakeholder Audit

A stakeholder audit is an analysis of the relationships that exist between an organization and key individuals or groups. Freeman (1984) defines a stakeholder as "any group or individual who can affect or is affected by the achievement of an organization's purpose." Stakeholders may be for or against the organization. They may be customers or suppliers, employees or outside special-interest groups. Stakeholder management assumes that understanding and managing these relationships are essential for organizational success.

Stakeholders will usually fall within one of four categories:

1. Individuals or organizations that control key resources needed by the organization;
2. Individuals or organizations that affect public perception of the organization;
3. Competing organizations; and
4. Individuals or organizations served by the organization.

EXHIBIT 2.6 Situation Analysis

```
                    ┌─────────────────┐
                    │   Stakeholder   │
                    │      audit      │
                    └─────────────────┘
                             │
                             ▼
┌──────────────┐      ┌─────────────┐      ┌──────────────┐
│   Internal   │─────▶│  Critical   │◀─────│ Performance  │
│ strengths and│      │   issues    │      │   measures   │
│  weaknesses  │      └─────────────┘      └──────────────┘
└──────────────┘             ▲
                             │
                    ┌─────────────────┐
                    │    External     │
                    │  opportunities  │
                    │   and threats   │
                    └─────────────────┘
```

The stakeholder audit is a comprehensive look at both strategic partners and competitors. As such, it goes beyond futuring by examining, in depth, the nature of relationships and the opportunities for collaboration. The process is also intended to yield insights into competitive relationships.

The stakeholder audit seeks to answer a number of questions about these relationships, as detailed in Exhibit 2.7 These results are then used as a basis for strategy development.

Nonprofit organizations face significant pressures from outside stakeholder groups. In some cases, these demands are conflicting; in others, stakeholder groups may form coalitions to increase leverage on the organization. Nonprofit stakeholders include: donors, competitors, clients, volunteers, other nonprofits (particularly special-interest or political advocacy groups), and the state and federal governments.

The stakeholder audit can yield important strategic insights. For a rural county humane society, it changed the entire focus of the planning effort. Prior to conducting the audit, the humane society saw itself as serving the community. The audit suggested that the primary stake of the community was to have a place to dump unwanted animals, which seemed contrary to the humane society's purpose. The planning team began to see the disposal of unwanted animals as providing the community with a convenient alternative to spaying and neutering, and perhaps was actually contributing to the problem of unwanted pets.

The humane society realized that its most important stakeholder group was the animals. The society existed to serve them, and, at times, serving them put them in conflict with the community. The second most important stakeholder group consisted of members of the organization who shared a deep concern for the animals and provided financial support to the organization.

This insight brought forth many difficult issues for the organization, including whether to continue to accept all animals and to practice euthanasia. Nonetheless, the insights gained in the stakeholder audit provided focus for the entire planning effort and, in particular, helped clarify the mission. Exhibit 2.8 presents the stakeholder map for the rural county humane society. The strength or influence of each stakeholder group is indicated by the size of its circle; its importance is indicated by its circle's proximity to the organization.

The issues or concerns of the various stakeholders can vary significantly. Even within a constituent group, issues and concerns can vary. For example, funders' concern with fiscal accountability may be reflected in their willingness to provide support to the organization. Business donors may be concerned with how support of the nonprofit reflects on their own organizational image and the exposure they receive.

The planning group may be able to identify the stakes of the various stakeholder

EXHIBIT 2.7 Stakeholder Audit Questions

1. Who are the key stakeholders?
2. What are their stakes, and in what ways do they judge the success of this organization?
3. Who are the most important stakeholders to whom this organization must respond?
4. For those stakeholders that can affect this organization, what is the strength of their influence?
5. For those stakeholders that are affected by this organization, what is their relative importance?
6. How well is this organization responding to these stakeholders?
7. What new strategies must this organization implement?

EXHIBIT 2.8 Stakeholder Map, Rural County Humane Society

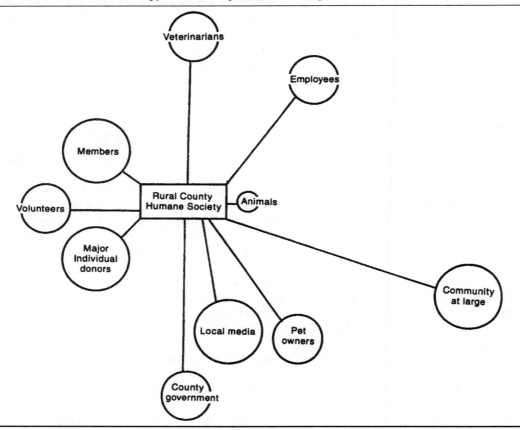

groups without further investigation; often, the stakes are well understood. When a stakeholder group is perceived as important but the planning team is uncertain about what the group's stakes are, a representative of the planning team should seek to clarify them by asking a representative of this stakeholder group.

Assessing how well the organization is performing can generally be accomplished through an educated guess. In most instances, if the criteria can be defined, the evaluation of performance will be relatively simple. Exhibit 2.9 provides an example of the criteria and evaluation of a single stakeholder group.

With a clear indication of who the key stakeholders are and what the issues are, members of the organization will have a better sense of how organizational success is defined. This insight provides a useful starting point for strategy development. In the example shown in Exhibit 2.9, the organization would want to develop strategies for leveraging large corporate gifts for additional matching grants.

(ii) Performance Measures

The stakeholder audit will yield an extensive list of criteria by which to measure the performance of the organization, but the list may not be complete nor will it provide suffi-

EXHIBIT 2.9 Business Donor Stakes

	Performance Assessment		
Criterion	**Good**	**Fair**	**Poor**
Accountability	•		
Donor recognition	•		
Timely reporting		•	
Value to community	•		
Matching grants			•

cient focus. Many organizations are developing critical measures of success, which provide important data for strategic planning and are a key component of continuous quality improvement efforts.

These measures yield significant insight into overall organizational performance and provide a basis for analyzing internal strengths and weaknesses.

Exhibit 2.10 provides an example of critical measures of success for an organization concerned with finding permanent homes for difficult-to-adopt children.

(iii) External Opportunities and Threats

During the course of the stakeholder audit, the planning team will have begun to examine external forces for change. During the assessment of opportunities and threats, the view broadens to encompass all aspects of the organization's external environment.

The process begins with an assessment of external needs. This discussion encompasses the emerging needs discussed in the development of the vision statement, but looks at the issues in the time frame of the plan, generally three to five years.

Next, the organization looks at critical trends that will shape those needs and the organization's ability to meet them. In general, a nonprofit organization will need to investigate six areas, shown in Exhibit 2.11. Although not all-inclusive, the list indicates the common areas in which most nonprofit issues fall. (Organizations with special concerns may identify additional areas.) These issues are then categorized as those presenting an opportunity that may be exploited by the organization, and those representing a threat to the organization's ability to fulfill its mission.

One way to involve more board members and ease the burden on the planning team members is to create small subcommittees to look at each of the relevant areas. In one organization, this was done as a way to not only explore the issues in depth, but to integrate new board members and create an opportunity for board and staff members to work side-by-side. The results were important insights into several key issues, enhanced by the differing perspectives of board and staff, and markedly improved board-staff relations.

EXHIBIT 2.10 Critical Measure of Success

PERMANENCY PLANNING
1. Length of stay in temporary placement.
2. Number of changes in temporary placement.
3. Total number of permanent placements.
4. Number of permanent placements that continue until the child becomes an adult.
5. Average cost of permanently placing a child.

EXHIBIT 2.11 Critical External Trends

AREAS TO BE INVESTIGATED
1. Sources of funding and support.
2. Political (tax, regulation, policy).
3. Volunteerism.
4. Demographics.
5. Technology (computers and other information technology).
6. Competition (for funding and in service-delivery areas).

In the past few years, an enormous volume of research has been conducted on the nonprofit sector (Hodgkinson, Lyman, and Associates, 1989; Powell, 1987; Van Til and Associates, 1990). A short visit to the library can yield a wealth of useful data. Ongoing subscriptions to publications such as *The Chronicle of Philanthropy, Nonprofit World, Nonprofit Management and Leadership,* and *Nonprofit and Voluntary Sector Quarterly* will provide an invaluable knowledge base for planning.

(iv) Internal Strengths and Weaknesses
By this point in the planning process, the internal strengths and weaknesses of the organization should be becoming clear. During this phase, the planning team will seek to assess the capability of the organization in terms of the need to address a threat or pursue an opportunity. Not all opportunities can or should be pursued. Understanding what the organization does well, and what it does not, will help to make these decisions. Exhibit 2.12 lists the areas of concern for internal assessments.

(v) Critical Issues List
The product of the situation analysis is a list of the critical issues that the organization must address in the course of developing the plan. These issues are often stated in the form of questions.

Coming to a consensus on which issues are critical can be a challenge to the planning team. Several issues will emerge clearly; others will overlap or seem uncertain. As a general rule, the final list should not exceed 12 issues. A longer list suggests that the group has failed to achieve sufficient focus and will get bogged down in the process of developing strategic responses.

One technique for generating this list is to have each member of the planning team list his or her top six issues, eliminating the redundancies, summarize the issues on a flip chart, and look at the final list. Often, with just a bit of refinement, a consensus list will have emerged. Another technique is to assign to a single member the task of presenting a draft list to the group. Each member then comments in writing and a second draft is

EXHIBIT 2.12 Internal Assessment

AREAS OF CONCERN
1. Finances.
2. Human resources (staff, board, and volunteer knowledge and skills).
3. Marketing and public relations.
4. Service delivery.
5. Management politics and practices.

EXHIBIT 2.13 Critical Issues List

PRIVATE STATEWIDE ARTS FUND-RAISING ORGANIZATION

1. How can this organization provide support to arts organizations that have lost all state funding and are threatened with closing?
2. How can this organization raise money to support arts organizations without competing against those same organizations?
3. How can this organization enhance public awareness of its activities?
4. Can this organization reduce overhead by sharing facilities with another, noncompeting organization?
5. Can this organization become the arts-funding adviser to small and midsize corporations that have small giving programs?
6. Can this organization expand the amount of funds available to arts organizations rather than redistribute existing monies?

---

created. This procedure continues until the group reaches consensus on the list. Exhibit 2.13 presents an example of a critical issues list for an arts fund-raising organization.

(C) ASSESSMENT SUMMARY

At this point, the assessment phase of planning is complete. The planning team should have a clear vision of the world as it could be, an understanding of key stakeholders and their relationship to the organization, a clear understanding of organizational effectiveness, and a grasp of key trends and of the strengths and weaknesses of the organization. In other words, the team will have defined the areas contained in each of the three circles presented in Exhibit 2.1. The remaining work is to define the area of overlap and create the plan. If the assessment phase has been done well, the actual planning phase should proceed fairly smoothly.

2.8 The Planning Process: Developing the Plan

(A) MISSION STATEMENT

No other aspect of strategic planning is more important than writing the mission statement. All activities of the organization flow from this.

The mission statement provides clarity of purpose and thus directs decision making about what programs to pursue. It is also a guide for action. Because it helps define the manner in which the organization will conduct its activities, it should be understood by all members of the organization.

By communicating purpose to the world, the mission statement helps attract needed resources (money and people). Research suggests that the primary reason individuals donate money and become volunteers is because they identify with the purpose of the organization. Exhibit 2.14 provides a list of questions that the planning team may consider in developing the mission statement.

(i) Writing a Mission Statement
The articulation of an organization's purpose into clear, concise language is achieved through the following steps:

EXHIBIT 2.14 Guide for Writing the Mission Statement

QUESTIONS ABOUT MISSION
1. Whom does this organization serve?
2. What are the basic needs that this organization fills?
3. Broadly speaking, how does this organization meet the needs of those it serves?
4. Is the area served geographically limited? If so, what is the area served?
5. What makes this organization unique?
6. What values does this organization seek to promote?
7. Who are the individuals who make up this organization? How does that affect its purpose?

1. Consensus seeking. The mission statement should reflect a broad consensus of the purpose of the organization. Working in a group, begin by identifying the key concepts or phrases that should be included. As a group, narrow the list by eliminating overlap and providing focus.
2. Generation of individual rough drafts. Allow each group member to generate and share a rough draft statement.
3. Assignment of the first draft. Groups have their limitations. Mission statements generated entirely by a group tend to be wordy, awkward, and sometimes difficult for others to comprehend. Assign the task of creating a first draft to one or two individuals and have them report back to the group at the next meeting. They may wish to begin with someone else's draft. The wordsmiths must incorporate the key concepts and phrases from the group's list into the first draft.
4. Editing. Less is more. Strive for economy of expression. Try to limit the mission statement to fewer than 40 words.
5. Full group review. Present the first draft to the full group for comment. If only minor changes are necessary, the group may settle on a working draft.
6. Repeating the process. If the first draft requires significant revision, send it back for more work by the writers, or reassign the task. Allowing other individuals a turn at writing helps build ownership.
7. Validating the mission. Throughout the planning process, periodically review the mission statement, answering these questions: Are our directions consistent with our mission? If not, is our mission adequate? If the group determines that the mission statement is accurate, all planning should reflect the mission. If the proposed goals consistently fall outside the mission, perhaps the statement is too narrow and needs to be reevaluated. It may be useful to have external stakeholders review the mission statement.

Exhibit 2.15 presents guidelines for the writing of the actual mission statement.

(B) DIRECTIONS AND GOALS

Directions describe the major areas of activity in the organization. Directions can be determined by defining the major categories of the budget or the basic divisions of labor in the organization. The planning process may or may not determine new directions for the organization.

EXHIBIT 2.15 Guidelines for Writing a Mission Statement

QUALITIES OF A GOOD MISSION STATEMENT
- Is clear and concise.
- Is forward-thinking.
- Is a guide to action.
- Defines whom the organization serves.
- Is expressed in broad, nonquantifiable terms.
- Provides inspiration.
- Reflects a broad consensus.
- Is easily understood by people outside the organization.

Goals define in broad terms why the organization directs resources toward these activities. Goals also begin to define the outcomes of the organization.

Taken together, the mission statement, directions, and goals provide a complete picture of the organization's purpose, activities, and desired outcomes. Many planning models do not contain the directions and goals steps, and some might argue that they are unnecessary exercises. Although not mandatory, I believe these steps provide a greater degree of clarity than is possible with a mission statement alone.

Many mission statements are long, obtuse statements that have extensive lists of subpoints. If a camel is a horse designed by a committee, then these mission statements are strategic planning camels.

The approach presented here stresses conciseness and clarity, participation and consensus. Although these pairs are not mutually exclusive, a tension exists between them. Use of this approach and of the guidelines presented in Exhibit 2.15 can help resolve these competing aims. Exhibit 2.16 provides an example of a complete statement of mission, directions, and goals.

EXHIBIT 2.16 Rural County Humane Society—Mission and Goals

Mission: The Society is a community of people who believe that all life should be respected and whose mission is to promote responsible treatment of animals and be an advocate on their behalf.

DIRECTIONS	• Goals
EDUCATION	• Educate the community on responsible pet ownership and the humane treatment of animals. • Reduce pet overpopulation.
DIRECT SERVICES	• Reunite lost pets with their owners as rapidly as possible. • Find homes for homeless animals. • Relieve animal suffering. • Reduce pet overpopulation without euthanasia.
ADMINISTRATION/ FUND RAISING	• Provide the resources necessary to sustain our efforts. • Responsibly manage the allocation of resources and the coordination of the activities of the organization.

EXHIBIT 2.17 Brainstorming

BASIC RULES
1. Criticism of one another's ideas is prohibited.
2. Free-wheeling and wild ideas are encouraged.
3. Quantity of ideas is sought.
4. Combining or modifying ideas is encouraged.

(C) DEVELOPING STRATEGIES

There are no tricks to developing the strategic responses to the issues identified. Many sophisticated approaches to evaluating strategies exist, but few nonprofits will have the time and resources to conduct such research, and the results are not likely to be better than a well-considered approach selected by the group.

Brainstorming is perhaps the most effective approach for generating strategies. A group that has come this far in the planning process should have a deep grasp of the issues and should be able to generate many effective responses. Based on the premise that quantity will lead to quality, brainstorming is designed to generate as many ideas as possible. The key to its success is to defer judgment until the idea generation is exhausted. Exhibit 2.17 lists the basic rules of brainstorming.

(i) Selecting the Right Strategy

There is no way to be certain that the correct strategy has been chosen, but if the issues are well understood and sufficient time has been given to developing possible strategies, the planning team should be in a position to make effective choices. Having a consultant or facilitator who is not a member of the team is important at this point. The planning team is essentially engaged in problem solving and can easily become bogged down. The following process can help keep the group on track:

1. Maintain focus. The facilitator or team leader should clearly state the goal and relevant critical planning issues to be addressed.
2. Refresh the group database. Review the issues and the key points that have been considered up to this point in the process. If resources permit, it is useful to have members of the team create a summary document for each of the planning topics. The discussion may begin with a brief presentation on the issue.
3. Encourage critical thinking and avoid criticism. Help the group learn to work with ideas rather than defend positions. Criticism merely seeks to find fault with others' ideas. Critical thinking looks for strengths and weaknesses and is focused on finding the best solution rather than winning the argument. Criticism makes people defensive of their ideas and less open to others' contributions.
4. Beware of groupthink. Some groups will become overly cautious of offending members and will avoid critical discussions. This reaction is perhaps more dangerous than defensive argumentation. The phenomenon of groupthink has been well studied, and many notorious examples of its effects exist (Zander, 1983). Planning teams may appoint a devil's advocate

or bring in outsiders to help find faults that the group may have missed. Exhibit 2.18 presents the continuum of group decision making, from argumentative criticism to groupthink. Groups should strive for the midpoint: critical thinking.

5. Consider the consequences. The facilitator or team leader should push the group to consider all the possible consequences. An effective technique is to appoint members of the team as temporary representatives of key stakeholders and ask them to react to the strategy under consideration.

6. Summarize and test for consensus. Often, groups will extend the discussion of an issue far beyond the point of agreement. A good facilitator or leader will watch for emerging agreement and attempt to summarize what appears to be the decision. At this point, a show of hands is a useful indicator of how close the group is to agreement.

7. Work for consensus. Voting for the final decision should be avoided if possible. Taking a vote sets up winners and losers and, when it is time to implement the decision, it sets up supporters and dissenters. Working for consensus does not mean achieving unanimous agreement; it simply means that all members of the group can live with the decision.

An example of strategy development is provided by a statewide arts fund-raising organization (Exhibit 2.13), which developed a strategy of targeting growing small and midsize corporations that did not have large corporate giving programs but wanted to make a contribution to the arts and culture. This strategy was chosen because (1) it provides additional money for the arts and does not simply redistribute existing funds; (2)

EXHIBIT 2.18 Group Decision Making—Selecting a Strategy

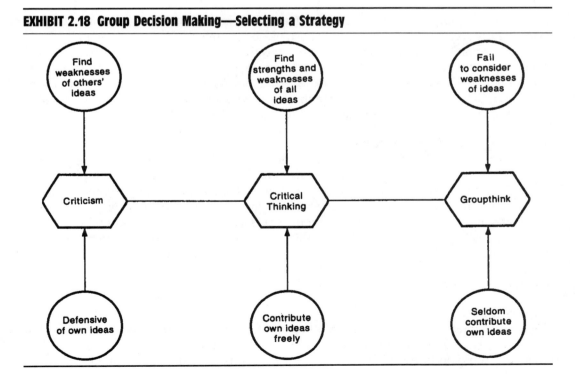

it offers a way to raise money without competing with the arts organizations it serves (most of these arts organizations have not targeted small and midsize corporations); and (3) it offers these corporations a way to tap into arts-funding expertise without having to staff their corporate giving function. In other words, this strategy addresses four of the six critical issues presented in Exhibit 2.13.

(D) DEVELOPING STRATEGIC OBJECTIVES

As stated before, goals describe why resources are being committed to the basic dreams of the organization; they begin to define what the organization seeks to accomplish. Strategies define how the goals will be accomplished. Objectives provide quantitative measures of success; they describe *when* and *how much*.

In the example above, the objective of targeting growing small and midsize corporations was to raise, in three years, $500,000 in new money for the arts in the state. There are some fairly sophisticated approaches to assessing the feasibility of such an objective. If time and money are available to conduct such research, perhaps it is worth doing. If not, the group should set a target that is judged to be challenging but attainable, and should monitor how well the organization is doing. These objectives may be specified in terms of hard numbers, percentages, or specific achievements, and should indicate the expected time for completion.

Adjustments can be made as the organization gains experience. The critical fact is that a target exists. Objectives are the most flexible aspect of the strategic plan and can change as a result of new information or changing conditions.

(E) DEVELOPING IMPLEMENTATION PLANS

It is not the responsibility of the planning team to carry out the strategic plan or even to specify the steps for implementation. Those are better left to the groups or individuals that have expertise or responsibility in the respective areas. Nonetheless, a strategic plan should provide some indication of who will be responsible for implementing major areas of the plan, when implementation is expected, about what it will cost, and if appropriate, how much it will earn for the organization. A planning team cannot present a plan without attention being paid to the availability of resources to carry out the plan.

(i) *Assignment of Responsibility*
It should be clear to readers of a strategic plan who is responsible for carrying out the plan's major aspects. This does not mean that all steps are detailed. It simply means thought has been given to the practicality of the strategy. Exhibit 2.19 provides an example of an implementation planning form that details the necessary information.

Strategies are listed in the first column. The second column indicates who has primary responsibility for implementation; this could be an individual or a committee comprised of board, staff, and volunteers. The third column is divided to show the start and completion dates. The last column is for specifying needed resources such as staff, board, and volunteer time and money.

(ii) *Budgeting*
The implementation of the strategic plan cannot proceed without the necessary financial forecasting and control mechanisms. It is beyond the scope of this chapter to provide a detailed discussion of budgeting, but a few key points should be considered.

EXHIBIT 2.19 Implementation Planning Form

Strategy	Responsibility	Schedule		Resources Needed
		Start	Finish	

Budgets provide a means to determine the amount of financial resources necessary to carry out the plan: to allocate those resources in the appropriate amounts; to control the use of those resources; and to measure performance. In the budget, the entire plan comes together. Assuming that the planning assumptions are correct and the objectives are achievable, the budget will indicate whether the organization can reasonably support the plans it has set forth.

If the implementation plans have sufficiently detailed the needed resources and the objectives have sufficiently detailed the expected earnings, then the creation of a draft budget should be relatively easy. The estimates of earnings can be tested against historically reliable standards, but this is only a marginal indicator and cannot account for changes called for in the plan.

2.9   *The Planning Process: Monitoring and Updating the Plan*

At a minimum, strategic plans should be reviewed and updated annually. Given the volatile environment of most nonprofits, updating should probably occur more often, perhaps even quarterly. In general, quarterly meetings should be for review of progress only, and major considerations of the plan should happen, at most, annually. Ideally, these sessions will not be the only times the plan is taken off the shelf, but they will allow reflection on the experiences to date in implementing the plan. The plan is not only an evaluation tool; it is a guide to action and should be consulted often in the ongoing operations of the organization.

During an update meeting, the planning team should spend three to six hours reviewing the performance of the organization against the specified objectives, considering changes in the situation of the organization, and altering the plan as necessary.

It is important to understand that a need for alterations is not a sign of a poor plan. More likely, it is an indicator of a healthy planning process. Despite the rational formality of the approach presented here, planners should become comfortable with the evolutionary nature of strategic planning. As Henry Mintzberg (1987) has suggested: "Virtually everything that has been written about strategy making depicts it as a deliberate process. First we think, then we act. We formulate, then we implement. The progression seems so perfectly sensible. Why would anyone want to proceed differently? . . . Strategies need not be deliberate, they can emerge" (p. 68).

If the organization is not performing as expected, the updating of the plan proceeds backward through the model. Perhaps the objectives were not realistic and should be scaled back a bit. Perhaps the strategy itself was faulty and should be changed. Perhaps the world has changed in a significant and unexpected way, causing the organization to reconsider everything from mission to strategies. There are no clear guidelines for conducting this assessment. As a rule of thumb, the planning team should question all aspects of the plan and be open to revision of any aspect of the plan that no longer seems appropriate.

2.10   Time Commitment to Planning

There is no simple formula for how long it takes to complete a plan. It depends on the scope of the planning, the number of people on the planning team, the amount of work accomplished between planning meetings, and frankly, the amount of time the organization is willing to devote to the process.

Groups have created effective plans in a single full-day retreat. The focus of these sessions is generally on clarifying mission and perhaps setting long-term organizational goals. Most efforts take longer, however. As a general guideline, planning team members should expect about 32 hours of work. Organizations with large staffs may be able to provide support to the planning team and reduce the actual time commitment of team members.

Planning meetings should be two to six hours in length. Shorter meetings do not allow sufficient time to discuss issues, and longer meetings produce diminishing returns. The recommended interval for planning meetings is ever two weeks. This allows time to accomplish assignments and should prevent the team from losing momentum. Exhibit 2.20 presents an eight-meeting schedule, showing the element(s) of the plan covered at each meeting. This schedule assumes that a considerable amount of work will be done between meetings.

Between-meeting work includes many aspects of the situation analysis and the implementation planning/budgeting process. The latter are largely staff functions (where sufficient staff exists).

2.11   Conclusion

The process we have reviewed in this chapter integrates a variety of strategic quality management concepts, such as environmental scanning and stakeholder management, with mission clarification and planning techniques. This approach also integrates aspects of operational planning and human resource management.

EXHIBIT 2.20 Eight-Meeting Planning Schedule

TEAM MEETINGS

Element of Strategic Plan	1	2	3	4	5	6	7	8
Clarify vision		•						
Situation analysis	•	•						
Clarify mission			•					
Develop directions and goals			•	•				
Develop strategies					•			
Develop objectives						•		
Development implementation plans						•		

Organizations that do not wish to undertake the entire process will find many aspects of the process independently useful. For example, stakeholder management is a critical need for many nonprofits and might represent an appropriate partial use of this approach. Clearly, the more comprehensive and integrated the overall planning effort, the more likely it will be that its full benefits are realized. The most important point presented here is that each organization must understand its own needs for organizational improvement and select an approach that addresses those needs.

Done well, strategic planning can offer substantial improvements in individual and organizational performance. Done poorly, it can be an enormous waste of time and resources, leading to resentment and withdrawal from the organization. Only after the needs of an organization are assessed should the necessary commitment be developed and the approach adapted as necessary. The benefits are worth the investment.

Suggested Readings

Albrecht, K. 1978. *Successful Management By Objectives: An Action Manual.* Englewood Cliffs, NJ: Prentice-Hall.

Barker, J. 1988. *Discovering the Future: The Business of Paradigms,* 2nd ed. Lake Elmoy, MN: ILI Press.

Benveniste, G. 1989. *Mastering the Policies of Planning.* San Francisco: Jossey-Bass.

Carver, I. 1990. *Boards That Make a Difference.* San Francisco: Jossey-Bass.

Drucker, P.F. 1990. *Managing the Nonprofit Organization.* New York: HarperCollins.

Freeman, E. 1984. *Strategic Management: A Stakeholder Approach.* New York: Pitman.

Hall, P.B. 1987. "A Historical Overview of the Private Nonprofit Sector." In W.W. Powell, ed., *The Nonprofit Sector: A Research Handbook.* New Haven: Yale University Press.

Hodgkinson, V.A., Lyman, R.W., and Associates. 1989. *The Future of the Nonprofit Sector.* San Francisco: Jossey-Bass.

Houle, C.O. 1989. *Governing Boards.* San Francisco: Jossey-Bass.

Kennedy, L.W. 1991. *Quarterly Management in the Nonprofit World.* San Francisco: Jossey-Bass.

Locke, E.A., and Latham, G.P. 1984. *Goal Setting: Motivational Techniques That Work.* Englewood Cliffs, NJ: Prentice-Hall.

Mintzberg, H. 1987. "Crafting Strategy." *Harvard Business Review* (July–August); 65:68.

Powell, W.W. ed. 1987. *The Nonprofit Sector: A Research Handbook.* New Haven: Yale University Press.

Van Til, I., and Associates. 1990. *Critical Issues in American Philanthropy.* San Francisco: Jossey-Bass.

Zander. A. 1983. *Making Groups Effective.* San Francisco: Jossey-Bass.

Quality Management Approaches and Their Influence on Nonprofits and the Public Sector

RAY KATZ, MBA
Total Quality Management Consultant

3.1 Universality of Principles

Total Quality Management (TQM), or simply Quality Management (QM), is not a single idea, but a field of study. Experts on the subject disagree about some basic principles. This is not so different from other fields. For example, John Kenneth Galbraith and Milton Friedman are important economists. Both have ideas about the same field—economics. Yet their ideas differ significantly.

Because a TQM program is adapted—tailor-made—for the specific needs of the organization, it cannot be "adopted" from an existing program. Therefore, nonprofits seeking to begin quality programs must decide which ideas about quality make sense to them. This chapter provides an overview of QM experts, their ideas, and the applicability of those ideas to nonprofit organizations attempting to apply those ideas in a new setting, outside the for-profit world.

The term *quality management* has been applied to a variety of theories and practices which, though related, often differ in significant ways. For any organization interested in using QM to improve operations (and everyone should be), understanding the commonalities and differences is critical.

(A) TQM IS NOT A PLAN

One makes plans to implement QM, but it is essentially not a plan, but a group of related principles. For maximum potential to be realized, these fundamental principles must be understood. An effective QM plan cannot be implemented by adopting a predetermined set of steps or using a "generic" or "cookbook" approach.

QM as a philosophy is articulated differently by various experts. Dr. W. Edwards Deming outlined 14 points that summarized his principles of management. Philip B. Crosby summarizes his quality principles as four absolutes. Traditional management assumptions, they would say, are wrong. To change an organization for the better, you need to change not only what you do, but also how you think about management.

(B) TQM APPLIES BROADLY

Because QM is not a series of steps, but principles, it applies broadly. The often-heard comment "our case is different" is rarely true. Like the laws of physics or the rules of mathematics, QM concepts are universal. Many complain that QM was designed for manufacturers and cannot easily be applied to nonprofits, especially social services organizations. Because the history of TQM with nonprofits is relatively short, there are fewer examples to follow. The principles are clear, however, and they are universal and can be applied to any organization. The laws of physics, the rules of mathematics, and the principles of QM apply to manufacturers and nonprofits alike.

(C) AGREEMENT ON BASICS

Most of the major quality "gurus" agree on some basic points. They stress that the focus of an organization must be on the customer. Error prevention is considered a key; correcting errors after the fact is wasteful. Experts also agree that quality goods or services cost less for an organization to produce than inferior ones. Finally, most agree that the economy is at a critical point and that those organizations that do not successfully apply QM may not survive or will continue in an increasingly disadvantaged position.

It is important to be aware of these areas of agreement. The differences, too, are important and understanding them may make the difference between a successful quality program and a failed one. The areas of disagreement are covered later.

(i) Customer Focus

For any organization, the focus of operations must be to satisfy (or preferably *overjoy* or *delight*) customers. Profit-making companies depend upon revenue from paying customers to earn money and stay in business. But for many nonprofits, the main source of revenue may not be a paying customer. Still, providing customer/client/member service is the reason most nonprofits exist, and so they have the same need to focus on customers—internal and external. Furthermore, funding sources (i.e., foundations, individual donors, members, etc.) are also customers. Nonprofits must focus on them as well.

Today, being customer-focused is obvious, but not universally practiced. Many organizations are still task-oriented. People are assigned work designed to complete the steps of an organizational plan, and that plan is rarely based on customer input. There is a tremendous difference between claiming to be customer-focused and really responding to the customer.

(ii) Preventing Errors

Most quality experts agree that day-to-day operations should be studied, changed, and continuously improved to reduce the number of errors produced. Traditional management looks for mistakes (inspection) and then orders that they be fixed. That is a wasteful approach.

As an example, the University of Michigan Hospital, a nonprofit medical facility, realized it had a problem with its admissions process (Flower, 1992). Admitting patients took too long. Hospital officials recognized that this was a problem. They even took it into account in the admissions process. Delivery of a written apology for the delay (along with flowers) was a part of the admissions process!

The delay was costly. It took a great deal of administrative time and resources and irritated the patients. The average admission took more than two hours. Sometimes an admission would take as long as eight hours!

By redesigning the process, the hospital reduced the average wait to less than five minutes. Think about the benefits! Less laborious administration, happier patients, and no more money wasted on the apology card and flowers. In fact, the hospital leadership team estimates it saved about $250,000 in operating costs over two years.

There is wide agreement that error prevention is necessary, but a variety of approaches to go about it.

(iii) Quality Reduces Costs

The traditional wisdom has long been that "you have to pay more for quality; better products and services cost more to produce and buyers must expect to bear that cost." This is no longer the case, according to the quality experts.

Making better products and providing better services are possible when the process used to create them reduces errors and waste. For example, a computer database may be designed to accept only legitimate two-letter state abbreviations. In this case, data entry error is prevented. An even more effective method would have the database automatically enter the correct state abbreviation based on the zip code. In any case, the more difficult it is to make an error, the fewer errors occur. A better system reduces errors made by all data entry operators, regardless of skill level.

The reasons for cost savings include: less rework (i.e., repair or correction); less inspection; and more time for productive activity. Similar savings can be realized in every operation performed by an organization, not just production of an end product or service.

(iv)   Essential to Survival

In tones that might sound alarmist, most quality experts say that QM is becoming a requirement for survival. As customers become more demanding, and as increasingly knowledgeable competitors arise, an organization stuck in the old ways may be unable to compete for revenue.

In the nonprofit world, funding sources from foundations to individual members are becoming increasingly interested in quality issues. This is also true of boards whose members often come from organizations now using QM.

3.2   What the Experts Say

At first glance, the most prominent experts on quality appear to be in general agreement. The differences seem minimal, and often they are.

On the surface, with only a quick reading, QM seems to be a single set of ideas offered up in different "flavors." Some of these differences, however, are fundamental. Let's look at what the experts advocate, and review the differences among them (Exhibit 3.1).

(A)   DEMING

Dr. W. Edwards Deming is highly influential in Japan, and has been since the 1950s when, invited by business leaders there, he gave a series of lectures on statistics and quality theory.

According to Deming, 85 percent of all operational problems are built into the system—that is, the process set up by management to get things done. Because of this, most of the opportunity for improvement lies in analyzing and improving systems, not coaching individual performance. It's *what people do* and how they work *together* that counts.

For people to work together, and to continuously analyze and improve systems, the organizational culture must promote open communication and cooperation. People must be able to identify problems without fear of punishment, so that the problems can be solved. An organization that "shoots the messenger" will always have many hidden problems. Deming asserted the need to "drive out fear" so people are free to do better work. People must feel comfortable working across departments to analyze and improve systems.

Many—perhaps most—managers feel something must be done to motivate employees to work. Deming believed that employees are *internally motivated*, and that they naturally want to do a good job. When employees are sluggish or avoid work, Deming believed that in most cases the organization was responsible. Organizations often *discourage* productive work, and this is reflected in worker attitudes. Some practices that discourage productivity include:

- *Employee evaluations.* Dr. Deming believed evaluations serve no useful purpose and should be abolished. Perhaps this was his most controversial position. A bad evaluation demoralizes a worker. A good evaluation comes with a price—goals for next year are set higher. Eventually, the new goals are

EXHIBIT 3.1 Comparing the Quality Gurus

Expert	Definition of Quality	Program/ Principles	On Motivation	Special Insights
Deming	Determined by the customer	14 Points and "Profound Knowledge" which includes understanding the nature of a process	Tap intrinsic motivation by training people and giving them the freedom to do good work	Major influence on economic success of Japanese companies; Deming Prize for quality created in his honor
Juran	Fitness for use	The Quality Trilogy consisting of Quality Planning, Quality Control, and Quality Improvement	Offer rewards and recognition	Important contributor to revitalization of Japan; champion of managerial breakthrough technique and Pareto analysis
Crosby	Conformance to requirements	4 Absolutes: 1. Quality is conformance to requirements; 2. Prevention is the method of causing quality; 3. Zero defects is the standard; 4. Price of nonconformance is measurement of quality	Motivate by setting a performance standard of "Zero Defects" Offer rewards and recognition	Quality guru with earliest major influence in U.S; bestselling books increase awareness of importance of quality
Tribus	Agrees with Deming	Consistent with Deming	Consistent with Deming	Among his interests, involved with TQM in primary education
Albrecht	Measure of extent to which something meets a need, solves a problem, or adds value.	Total Quality Service: • All quality standards must be customer-referenced • Also focus on internal customers Also has 17-point action plan	Recognition and appreciation	Cites differences in quality for services vs. quality in manufacturing

unreachable. Evaluations force workers to "look out for number one." They discourage teamwork and force people to be defensive rather than creative. Dr. Deming believed that evaluating and improving processes, not individuals, is more useful.

- *Interdepartmental rivalry.* Departments often don't cooperate and communicate, and this is typically a structural problem, not merely a symptom of personality conflicts. The classic example in the for-profit world is distrust between Production and Sales departments. In the nonprofit world, the budget process is often divisive; departments fight over limited funds. In either case, these divisions are caused by a management structure that evaluates departments individually. Instead, management should encourage departments who work together to meet customer needs.

What's wrong with goals for individual departments, and a little internal competition? Let's look at a fundraising department.

The department has a fundraising goal. Each year, the goal must be met or exceeded; falling short may cost some people their jobs. The pressure on the fundraisers may force them into some questionable practices. For example, the direct mail manager may mail too often to the same donors to generate short-run gains in revenue, even though this approach alienates long-term donors and reduces potential future income.

A department that is successful in its own objectives may damage the organization as a whole.

- *Insights rejected or worse.* Most people, in their first job, are innocent of office politics and simply follow their best instincts. They try to do a good job. Often, they are soon discouraged. Here are some examples from real-life nonprofit organizations:
  - A new employee works extra hard and finishes his work in half a day. He asks for additional work, even offering to help people from other departments as time permits. He is warned by his manager not to do this. If he doesn't have enough work to fill the day, she will look bad. She will have trouble justifying hiring him as a full-time employee. The young worker learns that to keep his job, he must either work slower or just look busy when no more work is available.
  - A young woman finds a better way to do something; the change she suggests is a good one. Her boss tells her to go ahead and do it, by herself with no assistance or cooperation. She does and gets good results, but it would have been easier with help. In fact, her boss complains that while making the change, she fell behind in her regular work. The woman learns to keep her ideas to herself. She has discovered that innovation and initiative may be punished.

Deming suggested that the way to improve a system was to reduce variation. He saw the need for consistency in processes, and he offered analytical tools to design consistency into a system. He was a proponent of using statistical methods to control quality. (These tools are often referred to as statistical process control, or SPC.)

Deming believed that an organization can prosper if it provides the proper culture, which supports cooperation, continuously improves processes, and focuses on the customer. The overall effort must be led by management.

(B)   JURAN

Joseph W. Juran, like Deming, influenced Japanese business practices starting in the early 1950s. Both were pioneers of statistical methods to improve quality. Juran summarized his view as a "quality trilogy" consisting of quality planning, control, and leadership.

Perhaps Juran's most important contribution is his "managerial breakthrough" technique. While others were concentrating on stabilizing processes and bringing them into control, Juran emphasized that once a process is "in control," it is time to change the process or design a better one. He shifted the focus from getting things under control to making improvements. (Getting a process under control still must come first, according to Juran and others.) This approach—now decades old—is a clear forerunner of "reengineering," the radical redesign of organizations and processes.

(C)   CROSBY

A controversial figure, largely at odds with Deming and Juran, Philip B. Crosby first came to prominence with his bestseller *Quality Is Free*. He emphasized attitudes rather than processes as the key to quality. Mistakes happen because management tolerates mistakes. Crosby asserts that management should set a standard of zero defects. Perfection is possible with a positive attitude and determination.

For some, this approach is appealing because it asserts the importance of personal responsibility. Furthermore, it frees up managers and employees from any need to learn about statistical process control.

The difference between and emphasis on attitude versus processes is a critical one. Crosby and Deming offer incompatible approaches to quality. In Deming's view, once a person is fully trained, he or she has a certain degree of skill and is either suited to a particular job or not. No matter how positive a person's attitude, or how determined she is to avoid defects, perfection cannot be achieved by an individual's psychology. The entire system within which the person works must be considered.

Crosby also emphasizes prevention of errors and teamwork. He believes that it is important to measure and track the cost of quality. How much does bad quality (defects, rework, etc.) cost an organization?

In another contrast, Deming's view states that the cost of quality is unmeasurable. Although some elements can be calculated, some cannot. What is the cost of a discouraged employee who has no opportunity to contribute? What is the cost of a mistake that drives away a customer, and the customer's friends?

Unlike some others, Crosby offers not just theory and techniques, but a program for quality improvement in an organization. His 14-step program, introduced in *Quality Is Free*, includes such activities as getting management commitment, measuring quality, increasing quality awareness, and holding a "Zero Defects day" to build interest in the effort.

(D)   TRIBUS

Myron Tribus is not known primarily as an innovator, but as a skilled practitioner of QM, who applies a Deming-influenced approach. He publicized a case in which a high school in Alaska applied QM to education. The case is a clear demonstration that QM does not apply only to manufacturing. We will look at this case in more detail later.

(E) ALBRECHT

A prominent author and consultant, Karl Albrecht emphasizes improving quality for service organizations, and service functions within other organizations. His basic assumptions are similar to those of Deming and Juran, but his examples are often more relevant to nonprofits. He created his own charts and tools, but they are similar in many ways to those preferred by Deming, Juran, and others.

Rather than emphasizing processes or statistics, Albrecht talks mostly about how to better understand customers. He promotes various forms of market research, rather than common sense, to deepen knowledge of the needs of customers.

3.3 *How Nonprofits Discovered TQM*

"My case is different" is the excuse used by many nonprofits to ignore QM. It is easy to see how they drew that conclusion. Even today, there are relatively few examples of QM successfully applied at nonprofits. Yet, if QM is a set of principles that apply universally to processes, they must apply to nonprofits as well as the corporate world.

The key distinction of nonprofits from an operational point of view is not their tax status, but that they are usually service organizations. Though there is a long history of understanding manufacturing as a process, providing services is often viewed as an art. Nonprofits usually work with people, not things. Providing services for people cannot easily be reduced to a rigid series of steps to be refined and improved.

Certainly human relations skills are important for nonprofits, yet much of what nonprofits do is indeed systematic, and can be addressed by QM. Furthermore, process improvement is just one piece of the QM approach, which includes understanding customers and providing an organizational culture that enables people to do their best. In any case, examples later in this chapter illustrate how TQM can be used to improve processes in nonprofits, including human services.

For now, we look at how the quality movement developed in the United States and eventually began to be applied to nonprofit organizations.

(A) CROSBY'S PROMOTION OF QUALITY

In the late 1970s, Crosby, a former ITT executive, made the word *quality* an important buzzword for American business. Although the emerging challenge of Japanese businesses had begun to worry U.S. companies, particularly automakers, the book *Quality Is Free* really turned a vague discomfort into a crusade for improvement. "Zero defects" was the key phrase of the movement in the late 1970s and early 1980s. This was also the period when quality circles became popular.

Quality circles provided an opportunity for employees to suggest changes and improvements in how work would be done. Members of the circles often received training in the techniques of problem analysis. Unfortunately, too often they were not given enough authority to do the job, or the organizational culture did not provide the appropriate support to sustain such efforts. Furthermore, such efforts were rarely focused appropriately on customer concerns or organizational objectives. The movement died out, and many decided that "Japanese management" doesn't work here.

Crosby has refined and expanded on his message over the years, and his ideas remain popular, but he is at odds with other leaders of the quality movement. He insists on the importance of attitude (rather than processes), the measurement of the cost of quality (which Deming says is unmeasurable), and has no use for statistical process control.

(B)   DEMING PUBLICITY

As happens so often in the United States, television's influence made itself felt. Dr. Deming, who had been promoting his view of quality to American businesspersons since the 1930s, was seen on a 1980 TV special called *If Japan Can, Why Can't We?* The program was seen by millions, including Ford Motor Company's CEO Donald Petersen. His company had recently suffered record losses, and he was ready to try something new. Thus, Ford became the first highly visible American company to attempt the Deming approach to QM.

Soon Dr. Deming's phone was ringing off the hook. The quality movement continued to grow.

(C)   FORD GIVES LEGITIMACY TO QUALITY MOVEMENT

Ford is a very visible company, and its turnaround from record losses to impressive profits did not go unnoticed. In addition, Ford encouraged its many suppliers to use QM techniques. By the mid-1980s, businesspeople could buy books about Deming's management ideas in their local bookstores. Finally, the ideas themselves were widely available. (Deming's own 1982 book, *Quality Productivity and Competitive Position* was not a bestseller, but it was useful to other American pioneers in QM.) His later books, particularly *Out of the Crisis*, clarified his views and made them available to even more people.

(D)   NONPROFITS GET INVOLVED

Health care and education are critical issues in the United States, and both are often seen as being in a crisis. Pressure for improvement in these areas has been intense, and, not surprisingly, both have become involved in QM.

Nonprofits participated in the National Demonstration Project on Quality Improvement in Health Care. They showed that QM applies to helping people, not just making things. The head of the Juran Institute (set up by Joseph Juran) helped guide the project.

QM has been tried in both grade school and higher education. Myron Tribus documented a project in an Alaskan high school which achieved excellent results, although most educational efforts have been tried only in higher education.

Universities began to incorporate QM, both in managing themselves and as a subject to be taught. The incorporation of TQM into the curriculum at many graduate business schools, starting with Columbia University and Fordham University in the mid-1980s, was perhaps a turning point. Finally, a fairly comprehensive education in TQM was available. Again, as with hospitals, educational institutions involved in QM included nonprofits.

The movement to apply QM in nonprofits came from many directions. Sometimes, nonprofit board members worked for QM companies, and brought the idea to the nonprofit organizations they served. Sometimes, individual leaders of nonprofits discovered QM on their own. In other cases, interaction among sector groups (such as health care and education) brought the subject into focus. Today, QM is well known throughout business and other organizations. (This was not true as recently as the early 1980s.) Tough economic times have required many nonprofits to change, just as record losses forced change at Ford in the 1980s.

3.4   Education

How can QM be applied to education? How can the art of teaching be improved using the ideas of Deming, Juran, and others?

Like any other organization, a school has administrative processes. Administrative functions can easily be viewed as a system. They can be flowcharted, analyzed, and improved. But the education process itself is a greater challenge.

(A)   TRIBUS AND MT. EDGECOMBE HIGH SCHOOL

Hearing that an Alaskan high school had applied Deming principles, Myron Tribus decided to investigate firsthand.

A small rural school, with just over 200 students, Mt. Edgecombe seemed like an unlikely place for such an experiment (Tribus, 1990). One teacher, David Langford, learned about QM from an executive whose company was using it. After reading extensively and discussing the subject with many people, he decided that his school should consider QM. He persuaded others and the experiment began.

Mr. Langford had noticed that students lacked enthusiasm. At the beginning of his course, he decided to adopt a customer focus. He asked questions. Why are we here? What do we want to get from this course? The fact that he took this kind of interest in his students raised the level of enthusiasm. His students found learning exciting again. Teachers and students both learned the principles of QM and worked together to achieve common goals.

The methods of teaching were revised to involve students; information was presented in an interesting way. When school became more than just lectures, it became more involving. Students in biology class not only learned their subject, but also created a simple computerized training program to help others. In business class, the students started a small business, and eventually found themselves so successful that they received a $140,000 order for their product! Every subject is now covered in an interesting and relevant way. With this level of involvement, students really learn. This is clearly more impressive than just memorizing facts to pass a test.

The high school has no grades, but the work is not accepted until it is perfect. Deming opposes performance appraisal, saying that this kind of evaluation creates fear and improves nothing. Mt. Edgecombe High School found that no damage was done by eliminating grades. With the need to compete eliminated, students could help each other to learn. Misconduct among students virtually disappeared.

(B)   WIDE INTEREST IN HIGHER EDUCATION

Starting with business schools, and probably influenced by the business community, universities have become some of QM's greatest supporters. Initially, they discovered that teaching QM could be very profitable—and not just at the Ivy Leagues. Lesser-known schools like the University of Tennessee and Delaware County Community College (PA) have become big names in teaching QM.

But QM is not just a subject to teach. Higher education has had success in applying it within institutions. This is true of both profit and nonprofit colleges. It is seen as a way to keep universities competitive and to improve the quality of education.

Starting from virtually nothing only a few years ago, now many universities support QM newsletters and seminars where experiences are shared. Some very good resources are available for educational organizations interested in quality improvement.

3.5 Health Care

With the same vigor as the educational community, and perhaps with even greater urgency, health care community leaders have developed a strong interest in QM. They, too, have applied QM to their own institutional management, as well as to improving the quality of patient care.

(A) HOSPITAL CORPORATION OF AMERICA

The Hospital Corporation of America (HCA) is a large, profit-making company that manages many hospitals throughout the country (Walton, 1990). It also won the Deming Award for quality. Their approach was summarized by an acronym: FOCUS-PDCA. This meant:

- Find a process to improve.
- Organize a team that knows the process.
- Clarify current knowledge of the process.
- Understand the causes of variation.
- Select the process improvement.
- Plan the improvement and continue data collection.
- Do the improvement, data collection, and analysis.
- Check the results and lessons learned from the team effort.
- Act to hold the gain and to continue to improve the process.

Rather than simply putting together some paper plans, HCA succeeded in making real-world improvement, such as reducing the number of complicated C-section deliveries. (It was found that some of these operations were unnecessary, and a better approach was developed to decide when to perform one and when not to.)

Working on administrative areas also helped cut costs and increase the effectiveness of medical care. For example, studying and improving the storage of medical supplies, so that they could be quickly located, obviously saves valuable time and perhaps lives. HCA worked on improving both administrative and medical processes.

(B) NATIONAL DEMONSTRATION PROJECT

In September 1987, about 100 health care and quality professionals met to inaugurate a National Demonstration Project (NDP) on Quality Improvement in Health Care (Berwick, Godfrey, and Roessner, 1990). The project would attempt to apply QM principles to a variety of health care situations, with the results of 17 teams described in the final report.

The results, overall, were positive, although some teams were unable to complete their work due to an unstable environment—internal changes interrupted their work. The final report cited a number of lessons learned, including: that a great deal of useful (but usually unused) data for quality improvement in health care is normally available; that nonclinical processes (i.e., administration, information systems, etc.) usually need to be addressed first; and involving doctors is difficult but not impossible.

NDP proved that the successes at HCA were not just a fluke. QM *does* apply to health care.

3.6   *Government*

Perhaps the sector of the economy most criticized for poor management is the public sector. We are bombarded with simply amazing reports of mismanagement: people showing up at government offices and told their benefits cannot be restored because the computer insists they are dead, incredible sums of money spent on parts and supplies, and so on.

Often government management has been hamstrung by old ways of doing things, ranging from tight regulation to a very divisive organizational culture. Division of responsibility among areas is very strong, epitomized by the phrase "it's not my department."

In recent years, growing attempts have been made to change all this, applying QM within the public sector.

(A)   MADISON, WISCONSIN

Using statistical methods and teams, Mayor Joseph Sensenbrenner showed that QM could work in municipal government (Mosgaller, 1992). QM principles were applied in a variety of areas, including the Parks Division, Personnel Department, Madison Metro (public transportation), the Police Department, and the Public Health Department. Projects had varying degrees of success, but since the city's commitment to TQM in the early 1980s, numerous improvements were made.

Government poses a special problem for continuity: the change of administrations. Yet, after a new mayor was elected in 1989, the never-ending process of continuous improvement, fortunately, continued.

(B)   "REINVENTING GOVERNMENT"

The pioneering successes of Madison, Wisconsin, were cited in the 1992 book *Reinventing Government*. The book, by David Osborne and Ted Gaebler, cited examples of TQM applied in local governments across the country. Again, using QM principles even in such complex services as law enforcement and public education could result in improvements. Governments can stop being faceless bureaucracies and become public servants. Naturally, this takes time, but the broad range of problems that have been addressed using TQM shows considerable promise.

3.7   *The Future of Quality in the Nonprofit and Public Sectors*

Whether TQM achieves its potential to improve services provided by the nonprofit and public sectors depends on several factors.

First, how many public and private nonprofits make the investment in commitment, training, and resources needed to succeed in QM? The prominence QM has achieved in the for-profit world has spurred interest, and many nonprofits recognize the potential and have committed to the effort.

Next, how successful will those efforts be? Those organizations achieving poor results will probably abandon QM. Fortunately, many, including some cited here, are proving to be skillful implementers of QM methods.

The principles of QM, and their general effectiveness in improving processes, are firmly established. There is nothing unique about nonprofits that would make them exempt from these principles, any more than they could defy the law of gravity or exceed the speed of light. Failure can occur, however, if managers have a poor understanding of these principles or if they are sloppy in application.

It's important that potential practitioners of TQM in any sector learn and continue to reflect on those principles and deepen their understanding. Total Quality Management is a skill, and its skillful application can only result in success.

Suggested Readings

Albrecht, Karl. 1992. *The Only Thing That Matters*. New York: HarperCollins.

Berwick, Donald M., Godfrey, A. Blanton, and Roessner, Jane. 1990. *Curing Health Care: New Strategies for Quality Improvement*. San Francisco, CA: Jossey-Bass.

Crosby, Philip B. 1979. *Quality Is Free*. New York: McGraw Hill.

Deming, W. Edwards. 1982. *Quality, Productivity, and Competitive Position*. Cambridge, MA: Massachusetts Institute of Technology.

Deming, W. Edwards. 1986. *Out of the Crisis*. Cambridge, MA: Massachusetts Institute of Technology.

Dobyns, Lloyd, and Crawford-Mason, Clare. 1991. *Quality or Else: The Revolution in World Business*. Boston, MA: Houghton Mifflin.

Flower, Joe. 1992. "The Practical Zealot: A Conversation with Ellen Gaucher." *Healthcare Forum* (January–February).

Hubbard, Dean L., ed. 1993. *Continuous Quality Improvement: Making the Transition to Education*. Maryville, MO: Prescott.

Juran, Joseph M. 1992. *Juran on Quality by Design*. New York: Free Press.

Mosgaller, Tom. 1992. *The Madison QP Story: A Beginning*. (Paper issued by the City of Madison, WI).

Osborne, David, and Gaebler, Ted. 1992. *Reinventing Government: How the Entrepreneurial Spirit Is Transforming the Public Sector*. Reading, MA: Addison-Wesley.

Tribus, Myron. 1991. *The Applications of Quality Management Principles in Education, at Mt. Edgecombe High School, Sitka, Alaska*. (Paper)

Walton, Mary. 1990. *Deming Management at Work*. New York: G.P. Putnam's Sons.

Implementing Quality Management in Your Organization

EDWARD L. NARO, Director
TASC Quality Management Center

This chapter provides a basic framework and guide for nonprofit organizations that are serious about implementing quality management (QM). It begins with a conceptual framework suitable for implementing QM in any organization. It then outlines a notional approach to implementation that includes a discussion of key implementing strategies to be considered and applied in a way that will satisfy the unique requirements of your organization. At the end of the chapter, you will find a list of suggested readings you might find helpful in planning and executing your implementation effort.

By integrating and acting upon the concepts and strategies discussed in this chapter, you will be able to develop your own tailored approach to implementing QM; one that will help your organization achieve the benefits of increased quality of products and services, increased customer satisfaction, reduced costs, enhanced quality of work life, and an improved competitive position in the marketplace.

4.1 Overview: A Conceptual Framework

(A) QM DEFINED

QM is a leadership philosophy, a set of sound leadership and management principles, and an array of analytical tools, techniques, and methods that are *integrated* into a customer-focused, disciplined approach to improving the quality of products and services through continuous improvement of processes.

(B) QM AND CHANGE MANAGEMENT

QM differs from most, if not all, of the many "enlightened" management approaches that preceded it in that it is far more comprehensive in both scope and application. It deals with and calls for change in virtually all aspects of the workplace (structure, workers, managers, processes, customers, suppliers, environment, etc.). When *truly* implemented in an organization, *QM provides not only tools and techniques for improving an organization's processes, it also provides everyone with philosophies and concepts that fundamentally change the way people think about their work. It redefines the culture of an organization.* For this reason, it is useful to understand at the outset that a significant part of implementing *QM* is really "change management."

In a QM culture, the *analytical* and *behavioral* aspects of an organization are integrated so as to achieve higher levels of quality (increasing levels of customer satisfaction). See Exhibit 4.1. On the analytical side, the organization's leadership emphasizes the *need for change* associated with continuous improvement of processes, that is, process identification, process analysis, statistical process control, customer feedback, and so on. This is often referred to as the "hard stuff."

At the same time, the organization's leadership also emphasizes what is needed to create an environment within the organization that encourages change and makes it *safe for change* to occur, that is, emphasis on teaming, empowerment, getting buy-in, coaching, risk management instead of risk avoidance, and a host of other concepts and techniques often referred to as the "soft stuff."

It is worth noting here, that many people implementing QM find that the soft stuff is really the hard stuff to do! The important point to be made about these two aspects is that both are needed to implement QM successfully. Pressure for continuous change in an environment where change is not viewed as safe will destabilize an organization and generate negative consequences that may even ultimately result in self-destruction of the

EXHIBIT 4.1 Two Fundamental Aspects of QM

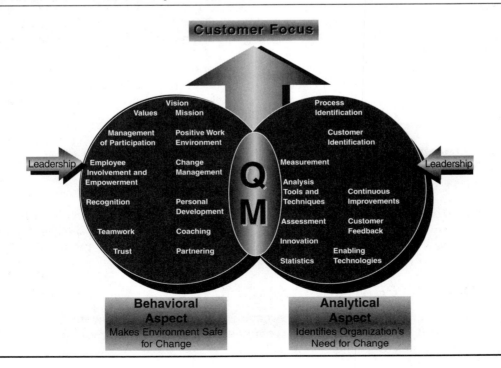

organization. Conversely, creating an environment where continuous change occurs but is not driven by the systematic analyses of process or customer feedback can also result in the loss of organizational performance, because such an environment typically results in change for its own sake and a workforce that is likely to confuse activity with progress.

(C) INTEGRATION OF QM ELEMENTS

Another conceptual way to think about implementing QM is in terms of the ingredients or "Elements of QM." (See Exhibit 4.2.) What is important in this concept is not so much the list of elements (some might choose to show the content of QM as grouped into more or fewer element boxes than depicted here) but rather the fact that in a QM culture, each of the elements of QM relates to and complements each of the other elements. Though each element unto itself can be seen as a good thing to do, all the elements must be integrated if the "force-multiplying" effects QM brings to an organization are to be achieved.

An analogy would be the baking of a cake. A cake is made by combining and cooking a number of ingredients, for example, flour, sugar, baking powder, salt, milk, and butter. But there is more to the taste of a cake than the simple sum of its ingredients. Imagine if in the process of baking a cake, you were to sample all of the ingredients that would be used in the cake, one at a time. You might enjoy the taste of some ingredients (perhaps the spoonful of sugar); others you might even find unpleasant (perhaps the salt, or baking powder). Regardless of which ingredients you did or didn't like, the result of your tasting all of the ingredients, one at a time, would not likely be a comment exclaiming how good your "unintegrated" pieces of the cake taste. It is the integration of the ingre-

EXHIBIT 4.2 Elements of QM

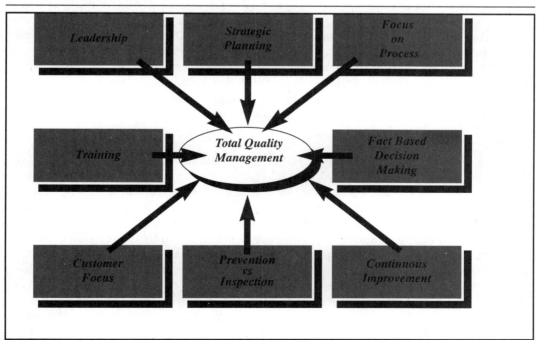

dients and how they complement each other and work together in the baking of the cake as a whole that makes the cake taste better than the mere sum of its parts.

Similarly, it is the integration of the elements of QM in its implementation that makes QM so much more powerful as a leadership and management approach than the mere sum of its elements.

Emphasizing integration of the elements of QM at the very beginning of an implementation effort will speed the implementation while helping everyone in the organization, managers and workers alike, to avoid two pitfalls often encountered during an implementation effort.

The first of these pitfalls is a tendency to focus almost exclusively on one element or a small set of elements with which one feels particularly comfortable. The problem here is that one tends to redefine QM to be only *that* element or subset of elements. Using the cake analogy, the cake is then reduced to the sugar and flour.

The second potential pitfall is to proceed with initiatives in all elements without regard to how they relate to one another. When this happens we see such things as teams created for the sake of having teams rather than for the purpose of contributing to the vision or mission goals and objectives of the organization; we see managers, in the name of "empowerment," delegating responsibility without the commensurate authorities or training necessary to make it possible for those being "empowered" to succeed; and we see QM being implemented for the sake of QM and *not* to move the organization toward a vision of higher levels of customer satisfaction, and improved services and products through improved processes.

To avoid these pitfalls, the leadership of an organization needs to regularly and frequently explain, remind, and be prepared to discuss how the elements of QM are relating to one another and to the vision of the organization. One technique for doing this is to get the senior leaders, managers, and supervisors to start all meetings with a very brief reference to the linkage between some aspect of the corporate vision and one or more related elements of QM. In this way, QM is ever the means and never the end in itself. When you hear large numbers of people in an organization trying to decide if they should be doing QM or their "real" mission work, it's a clue that QM is viewed as an end unto itself as opposed to the means for achieving the mission/vision of the organization. In such an organization, the leadership would be well served to revisit their implementation approach and relink it to the mission/vision strategic planning throughout the organization.

4.2   A Notional Approach for Implementing QM

Many organizations may be similar in a number of important respects, but like snowflakes, no two are exactly alike. For this reason we will look at a notional approach that allows the leadership in any organization to tailor specific strategies into a customized implementation plan best suited to guide their organization in its quality transformation.

Experience has shown that successful QM organizations generally go through three overlapping phases of activities in their quality transformation journey. The three phases which constitute this "notional implementation approach" are: Phase I—Preparation and Planning; Phase II—Implementation; and Phase III—Institutionalization. (See Exhibit 4.3.) Each of these phases contains a number of interrelated actions. Integrating the actions throughout all phases of the implementation effort is needed to ensure complementary

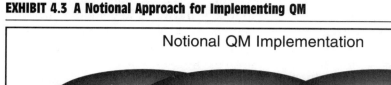

EXHIBIT 4.3 A Notional Approach for Implementing QM

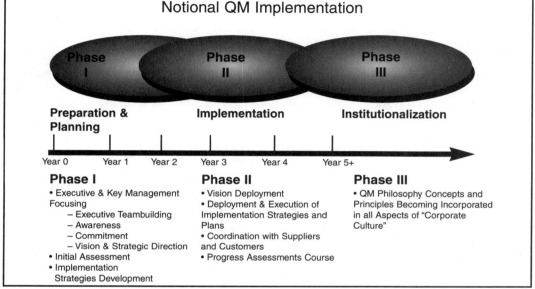

Notional QM Implementation

Phase I — Preparation & Planning

Phase II — Implementation

Phase III — Institutionalization

Year 0 · Year 1 · Year 2 · Year 3 · Year 4 · Year 5+

Phase I
- Executive & Key Management Focusing
  - Executive Teambuilding
  - Awareness
  - Commitment
  - Vision & Strategic Direction
- Initial Assessment
- Implementation Strategies Development

Phase II
- Vision Deployment
- Deployment & Execution of Implementation Strategies and Plans
- Coordination with Suppliers and Customers
- Progress Assessments Course

Phase III
- QM Philosophy Concepts and Principles Becoming Incorporated in all Aspects of "Corporate Culture"

and interdependent aspects of QM are properly sequenced and connected. Planning occurs before execution. Training is provided in time for the needed application. Resources are committed at the time they are required, and policies are developed and communicated in time to support changes occurring in the organization and its processes.

(A) PHASE I—PREPARATION AND PLANNING

Successful implementation of QM requires commitment from the senior leadership of the organization. Without the commitment of an organization's leadership, the organizational transformation to a quality-managed operation is doomed to fail! Thus the overall objective of this phase is to develop executive and key management consensus on a commitment and preliminary plan to implement QM as a means of moving toward attainment of the organization's vision. This first critical step begins with executive and key management focusing.

Executive and key management focusing is achieved through a number of executive workshops. The purpose of these workshops is to: (1) Establish the core executive level team (*team building*); (2) develop consensus within management regarding what QM is (*awareness*); (3) establish executive and key management support required to proceed with implementation (*commitment*); (4) develop consensus on where the organization is going (*vision/goals*); and (5) identify and prioritize significant problems, barriers, and critical processes (*focus*).

As a preliminary step in executive team building, the corporate leader, the senior executives, and key middle manager(s) form into an executive working group (preferably seven to ten people plus a professional facilitator/QM consultant/advisor). Along with team building, initial QM training is provided for the executives and key middle managers. This training should include both awareness and basic tools training that will be necessary for the strategic planning efforts to follow. Including key middle managers in this early activity sets the stage for the eventual establishment of critical linkages between the executive and middle management levels of the organization's QM infrastructure and promotes early buy-in from middle management. The initial output of this working group is the commitment to implement QM.

Following the decision to implement QM, the working group develops a corporate vision (or confirms an existing one). As a part of developing the vision, the working group identifies customers, suppliers, and the organization's key business processes. Using all of this information, the working group next develops a corporate strategic business plan and a set of strategic objectives that will move the organization toward attainment of that vision. This group then becomes the executive steering body for implementation of the corporate strategic plan and the implementation of QM throughout the organization. During the development of the vision and strategic objectives, members of the executive steering body need to collectively and individually provide and get feedback to and from all levels of the organization. *Overt actions by management to solicit input from all levels of the organization and to provide timely feedback on what the executive working group is doing sends a powerful signal that sets the stage for buy-in and heralds the changes to come.*

As the executive steering body begins to develop strategies for implementing QM, its members will need to develop a common understanding of where the organization is as it begins the quality transformation. This will require an initial organizational assessment.

The initial assessment of the organization provides a baseline which serves two important functions. First, it assists the executives and key managers in focusing on the most significant problem areas and barriers to implementation; and second, it provides reference points against which the organization can measure progress in implementing QM.

The initial organizational assessment would normally be chartered by the executive steering body and can include interviews, focus groups, or surveys or some combination of those data collection techniques. The assessment should cover all levels and components within the organization as well as customers and suppliers. If your organization has the resident expertise for conducting organizational assessments you may elect to use internal resources; otherwise, external resources can be employed to collect the information and provide the analysis. If external resources are used, it is prudent to have at least a small number of internal staff members work as part of the assessment team so that assessment techniques can be learned and so that subsequent assessments to measure progress can be related more easily to the initial baseline assessment results.

Information and results from this assessment are fed back to the executive steering body for consideration in developing the implementation strategies and plans. In addition, *and this is critical*, results of the assessment should be fed back to the organization as a whole. Along with the results of the assessment, everyone should be given an opportunity to suggest approaches for dealing with issues raised and then be told how implementation strategies and plans will address the problem areas and opportunities for improvement that were identified in the assessment.

Implementation strategies development. Working with their facilitator/QM advisor, the executive steering body uses their understanding of the concepts and principles of QM, results of the initial organizational assessment, elements of the corporate vision, and objectives in the strategic business plan to identify and develop specific strategies for implementing QM in their organization.

To aid in identifying strategies you may need to develop, Exhibit 4.4. lists those key strategies that would have to be developed by virtually any organization implementing QM. Because initial development of these strategies occurs so early in the transformation, it is reasonable to expect that strategies and plans developed at this point will have to be iterated later in this and subsequent phases.

Strategies developed now will continue evolving as participative management increases, the organization matures, and as the Shewhart "Plan, Do, Check, Act" (PDCA) Cycle is applied to the implementation effort itself. Notwithstanding their evolutionary nature, strategies developed at this point are critical in that they guide the initial implementation planning and resultant early execution. Consistent with the rationale behind the most fundamental concept of QM, "doing the right thing right the first time," a short time wisely spent thinking through these strategies saves many hours and other resource costs during implementation.

The following brief discussions about each of the key implementation strategies listed in Exhibit 4.4, provide examples of the kinds of things you might consider in developing and tailoring these strategies to the needs of your organization. (Because every organization is different, the intent of the discussions with respect to each of the key strategies identified is not meant to be prescriptive, but rather to invite consideration of various approaches that have been effective in other organizations.)

(i) Organizational Acceptance

A logical approach for achieving organizational acceptance of QM begins with consideration of the existing climate and culture of the organization. Exhibit 4.5 arrays examples of representative issues, fears, and perceptions which are found to some degree in most organizations attempting a major quality transformation. Results of your organization's initial self-assessment will probably give you the most useful insights into the greatest areas of resistance to implementation of QM in your organization. For the most part, dealing with these issues requires time and patience, a straightforward acknowledgment of their existance, and a commitment (backed up by overt action) that each level of leadership in the organization will work with subordinate levels to resolve and get past these issues.

While resistance will vary in each organization, a strategy should, at a minimum, include consideration of the components shown below in order to nurture acceptance of QM and achieve lasting organizational improvement.

EXHIBIT 4.4 Key Implementation Strategies to Consider

Organizational Acceptance
Implementation Infrastructure
Strategic Planning
Use of Consultants and Advisors
Focusing on Customers and Suppliers
Getting Everyone Involved
QM Training
Process Improvement
Performance Evaluation and Recognition Systems
Getting Feedback and Measuring Progress

EXHIBIT 4.5 Representative Issues, Fears, and Perceptions: Why People Resist Implementation of QM

Executive Level	Middle Management	Worker Level
Seen it all before—just another fad	Lack of trust of subordinates	Lack of trust of supervisors
Directed from top down background	Fear of metrics as evaluation tool	Fear of statistics
Too Risky—Not while I'm in charge	Fear of loss of authority	Nobody cares what I think
Just "touchy-feely" stuff	Problems beyond my control to fix	Fear of metrics as evaluation tool
Fear of change	Too many meetings already	Afraid to rock the boat
Lack of knowledge about processes	Rice Bowl Syndrome	No recognition for team behavior
Fear of loss of authority	Lack of immediate results	Efficiencies will result in loss of jobs

1. *Leadership by example.* Develop greater levels of trust by insisting that management "walk the talk." QM is about leadership. In this regard, it will be important that typical difficulties associated with implementing QM be shared with all levels so that everyone knows what to expect. Implementation can be explained in a positive light, but it should not be sugar coated. There will be greater support if everyone knows the "good, the bad, and the ugly" up front. It will also be important to be straight about issues beyond the control of the organization, but don't let that become a cop out. Develop workarounds.
2. *Improved communications.* Use techniques such as storyboarding, short speeches, always including Total Quality issues in meetings, wide distribution of QM status reports that ensure feedback on all suggestions for improvement, and establishing subordinate linkages to senior levels of the QM infrastructure.
3. *Management of participation!* Adopt participative management techniques, such as delegating, listening to subordinates, establishing a policy regarding authority to say no to a suggestion, and maximizing the role of all levels in decisions regarding the implementation effort.
4. *Adoption of recognition alternatives.* Reward teamwork and suggestions for improvement. Include smaller but more frequent cash awards for suggestions.
5. *Use pilot initiatives to empower workers* where risk is considered too great to implement a suggestion full scale across the board.
6. *Explain how the transformation is being shaped.* Make it clear that initial implementation policies and plans developed by the Executive Steering Committee (ESC) are subject to review and revision on an iterative basis by the QM infrastructure as it comes into being and as participation in the implementation spreads throughout the organization.

(ii) Implementation Infrastructure

Successful implementation of QM requires a supporting infrastructure. This infrastructure provides a forum for quality improvement focus not found in most hierarchical organizations, where barriers exist between managers and workers. Strategizing implementation of the infrastructure significantly enhances its initial effectiveness. It greatly reduces the amount of time wasted in unproductive meetings where members know they must attend but don't know why. The infrastructure is intended to minimize bureaucracy, to the degree it exists, and to foster similar lines of communication within the organization's existing hierarchical structure. It functions to support the QM implementation effort; enhances communications up, down, and horizontally; manages process improvement teams crossing functional and organizational lines; and identifies and prioritizes opportunities for improvement. The ideal strategy calls for the QM infrastructure to be eventually completely assimilated into, and indistinguishable from, the organization's management structure when the organization transitions into the institutionalization phase and QM becomes the culture of the organization.

The infrastructure consists of an executive-level steering body, referred to here as an Executive Steering Group (ESG); midmanagement-level cross-functional Quality Management Board(s) (QMBs), and Process Action Teams (PATs). (See Exhibit 4.6.) (The names used here are representative and are only intended to convey the design of the infrastructure. Each organization should develop names it is comfortable with for each component, a technique which tends to reduce resistance to change.)

EXHIBIT 4.6 A Notional QM Infrastructure

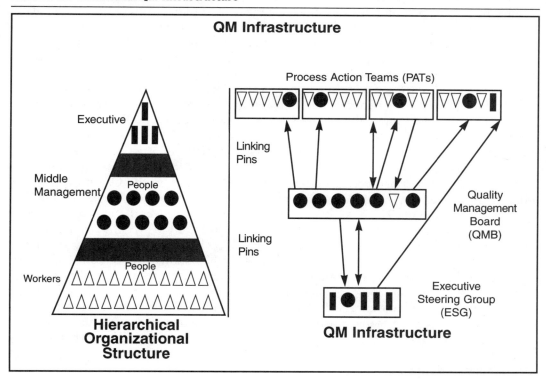

The *Executive Steering Group* (ESG) is made up of the corporate leader, the level of managers reporting directly to the corporate leader, one or more representatives from middle management, and a trained facilitator/quality advisor. It develops and implements the initial QM implementation plan, provides overall policy guidance and direction, commits resources, assigns priorities to major issues, empowers the Quality Management Board(s), and most importantly, removes barriers between functional groupings within the organization.

The *Quality Management Board* (QMB) is made up primarily of middle managers, but includes one or more representatives from the executive and worker level and a facilitator trained in quality management. Chartered by the ESG, they prioritize candidate problems and opportunities for improvement, assign them to process improvement teams, monitor trends, track improvement efforts underway, remove barriers to successful operation of process improvement teams, and approve, direct, or assist in implementation of improvements developed by teams.

The *Process Action Teams* (PATs) are made up of people with a vested interest in the process—stakeholders, subject-matter experts (SMEs), members who own or operate the process of interest (workers, managers, executives, customers, or suppliers), and a trained quality management facilitator. Membership on PATs may cross functional lines and may include members from any level in the organization. These teams use QM tools, techniques, and problem-solving methods to study processes, collect data, perform analysis, and make recommendations for and implement process improvements. In some instances, PATs may be chartered by the ESG or QMB to make decisions to improve processes, and on other occasions, they may be chartered to make recommendations for approval by the QMB or ESG. This chartering process is very important because it empowers the team, ensures there is a champion for the effort, identifies the tasking of the team, and conveys a commitment of the organization to support the work of the team.

Some organizations attempt to start their implementation of QM by immediately setting up one or more "pilot" process teams just to see if this "teaming thing" really works. The process owners or stakeholders may not be involved or commited to success of the team, the mission of the team is usually not clearly defined, and there may be little or no linkage made between the efforts of the team and the mission or vision of the organization. In such instances, the team will likely become frustrated and fail, and the organization will see this "QM stuff" as additional work not related to their "real job." For this reason, and notwithstanding the desire of most leaders to "get on with it," it is important to set the stage with training, a supporting infrastructure, and charters before launching teams.

To maintain necessary vertical linkages between groups in the QM infrastructure, subordinate representation needs to be built into each successively higher echelon, as depicted in Exhibit 4.6. There is often some resistance to this. Middle managers may be reluctant to have a non-manager in their midst at a QMB, or the executive level may feel uncomfortable with a middle manager in the ESG. This resistance usually dissipates quickly after the first several meetings. Experience has shown the bottom-up linkage approach to be effective in maintaining a solid connection between the reality of today and the "vision" of tomorrow. This ensures that legitimate concerns of those working within the processes are addressed at appropriate levels. It also helps avoid disenfranchising various levels of management, who often view the new infrastructure as a threat to their authority and an impediment to getting their jobs accomplished. (This is a natural phenomenon until the cultural transformation makes the QM structure the fundamental way of doing business.)

Acceptance of the new QM infrastructure is significantly enhanced by allowing each group in the infrastructure (ESG, QMBs, and PATs) to *participate* in deciding issues such as membership and naming of the groups. In addition, a consensus-driven, participative approach to chartering the various groups provides immediate examples of empowerment that members of the organization can easily relate to. In this way each group has an opportunity to influence the scope and content of their own charter.

These participative management approaches tend to defuse anxieties associated with change by co-opting and empowering a broad base of the organization. An example of such an approach would be a "catch ball" process for chartering PATs or QMBs. In this process, the QMB provides each new PAT with a "Draft Charter." The PAT then reviews the charter at its first session and comes back to the QMB with any changes needed for them to be successful in accomplishing their tasks.

The process may require one or two iterations, but the result is always a better understanding of what is to be done by all parties. This approach serves three very important objectives. First it helps the PAT come to a common and unambiguous understanding of their reason for being. Second, it often results in a better definition of the problem, a consequence of the fact that the PAT team members are usually closer to the processes involved in the area they are being asked to improve. And third, it facilitates the PAT's ability to take ownership of the task, and to buy in to the process improvement effort.

(iii) Strategic Planning

Strategic planning is a process for developing a future-oriented vision of where the organization is going, and a plan to get it there. It is the overarching component of any successful QM implementation. Conceptually, it is the glue which binds the implementation of QM and attainment of an organizational vision into a cohesive and logical approach. It is critical to the successful implementation of QM in any organization. Strategic planning is used both as the mechanism for planning the implementation of QM and as the model for developing the organization's *Strategic Business Plan*, the ultimate expression of a QM organization's raison d'etre.

The process of developing a strategic plan focuses the leadership on identifying where the organization is going and how to get there. The process of "deploying" the strategic plan (rather than promulgating it) serves yet another purpose. Deploying the strategic plan aligns the entire organization so that it understands and can work together to achieve a common goal. "Deploying" the strategic plan, rather than promulgating it, means cascading the vision and strategic plan down through each successive level in the organization in a series of discussion sessions. In each session, the vision and strategic plan are briefed and then members of the organization are engaged in a dialogue and asked to discuss how they see themselves and what they do fitting into the strategic plan. If the vision and strategic plan for attaining it are not in the minds and hearts of the workforce, if they do not see themselves in it, then publishing the vision and the strategic plan in a notice and posting it around the office will do little more than decorate the walls.

To develop a strategic plan the organization begins by establishing its vision. *Responsibility for ensuring an organization has a vision rests squarely on the shoulders of the leader of the organization.* The process of *developing* the vision can be as simple as the leader knowing where he or she wants to take the organization, or the collaborative product of an executive steering body, or a bottom-up development process involving the entire workforce or some reiterative combination of those choices.

The vision may be divided into one or more parts. There is nothing sacred about the format, since the value of the vision, as is the case with the entire strategic plan, lies in the process of developing and deploying it, not in the piece of paper upon which it is printed. Whatever the format, consider including the following four components:

1. A *Mission Component* that describes the reason for the organization's existence; what product(s) are produced by the organization; or what service(s) are provided by the organization; and in each case the customers for whom they do it.
2. A *Visionary or Inspirational Component* that says what image the organization wants to have at some point in the future (i.e., in 5, 10, 15, or 20 years); and/or what the organization wants to be known for in the same time frame; and/or what will make the organization different from (or better than) all others in the same time frame.
3. A *Core Values and Guiding Principles Component* that states what the organization believes are its core values (what values the organization holds to be sacred and critically important), and guiding principles, which are the translation of those values into action statements that guide all members of the organization in the performance of their jobs.
4. A *Glossary Component* that defines every word in the Visionary Component and thereby removes any ambiguity about what the vision means.

An effective approach to developing a vision is to have the leadership team (an executive steering body) meet in a series of facilitated workshops to brainstorm, prioritize, and come to consensus on answers to each of the following key questions: (1) "Who are we?"; (2) "What do we do?"; (3) "For whom do we do it?", (4) "Why do we do it?"; and (5) "What image do we want the organization to have some number of years from now?" and/or "What will set our organization apart from the competition some number of years from now?"

The prioritized answers to each of these questions provides the information needed to craft the components of an organizational vision. This effort can be expected to take about three full days of in-session contact time. Elapsed time may be longer if the sessions are set up in one-day or half-day increments with time between sessions being allowed for off-line preparation. In some instances, the organization may need to have market research done in advance of the vision development session to ensure that critical market near- and long-term trend information can be considered. Actually crafting the vision statement is most efficiently accomplished by one or two members of the steering body between sessions, with the working group reviewing and adjusting the draft version until a final product is agreed to.

In addition to providing critical input into the vision development process, answering the question "What do we do?" provides a logical starting point for identification of the organization's key business processes. Identifying key business processes is an important early step in translating the vision into a set of goals and objectives that will become the strategic plan. This is an iterative process that requires input from all levels of the organization. Business processes must be identified, assessed, and prioritized in terms of the degree to which they support attainment of the organization's vision. Market research, customer feedback, input from those who operate the processes, results of the organizational assessment, and so on, all feed the process of identifying opportunities and candidate processes for improvement. The list of opportunities and candidates for improvement are then prioritized and linked into a roadmap of objectives that will move the organization to its vision.

At this point in the process, the corporate policy, goals, and objectives (the "Whats") are deployed downward and the specific actions and timelines (the "Hows") are established and fed back upward to the executive steering body. The result is a strategic roadmap to the vision.

The goals and objectives developed in this process are then assigned by the executive steering body to the appropriate cross-functional QMBs that will champion them. Specific process improvement, reengineering, or design efforts required to achieve these objectives are then assigned by the QMBs to Process Action Teams, which are chartered to accomplish the process improvement, reengineering, or design work.

To be of any lasting value, the strategic plan must be dynamic. Specific milestones and metrics need to be tied to the objectives so that progress can be assessed from time to time. Using these metrics, progress in accomplishing the objectives is assessed periodically with feedback from the teams to the QMBs and ultimately to the executive steering body. The overall strategic plan needs to be reassessed and updated periodically (at least annually); however, it should be possible to add, modify, or delete objectives at any session of the steering body without having to wait for the periodic overall reviews of the strategic plan. As the organization moves further into the implementation of QM, the process of updating the strategic plan will generate greater input from the bottom each time the cycle is repeated.

(iv) Use of Consultants/Advisors

Benefits to be obtained from the use of external professional quality management consultants significantly outweigh the costs. Their "hands on" experience and knowledge of quality management concepts, principles, tools, and techniques provide for a faster and smoother organizational transformation. They are able to help organizations in their implementation by providing facilitation, assessment and process analysis, training, and consulting advice in quality management. Over time, an organization's strategy for implementing QM should move it to greater levels of self-sufficiency in the use of consultants. The training strategy, for example, should call for the organization to grow internal facilitators, trainers, and trainers of trainers. Initially, however, it is reasonable to expect you will need external professional consultants to facilitate, train, and advise your executive steering body; to provide awareness and tools training throughout the organization; to provide advanced tools to support such activities as business process reengineering, assessments, customer satisfaction surveys, and so on; and to team-build and regularly facilitate your QM infrastructure (QMBs and PATs) until internal advisors, facilitators, and trainers can be developed.

It is important to select outside consultants with care. The consultants must have the confidence of the leadership of the organization, and must be capable of "telling it like it is" if they are to be successful in helping the organization to implement QM. Changing consultants part way into an implementation effort disrupts progress and will almost certainly result in a significant setback in the implementation and a substantial cost in time and money for the organization.

One or more respected leaders in the organization should be selected to serve, at least part time, as an internal QM coordinator. Care should be taken in selecting a QM Implementation Coordinator because he or she will be dealing with all levels of the organization from the corporate head to the rank and file in the workforce. The coordi-nator will become the glue that binds the mechanics of the implementation activities together for the entire organization. Once identified, this person (or persons) should receive early and intensive quality management training (Awareness, Basic Tools, and Facilitator, and Train-the-Trainer training) to equip them in their role as QM Implemen-tation Coordinator. Working with the external consultant, the QM Implementation Coor-dinator can act as a focal point for establishing a QM resource library, coordinate the scheduling of training sessions, facilitate mechanics of setting up the QM infrastructure, and so on. One caution, here, is the tendency for people in the organization to start thinking that QM emanates from and becomes the responsibility of the QM coordinator. The drive for implementing QM must come from the corporate head of the organization and it must be perceived that way throughout the organization!

The use of internal consultants, assuming the organization has internal professional quality management consultants available, is always a possibility, but it is particularly dif-ficult to be a "prophet in one's own hometown." The changes in management that go on in the implementation of QM deal greatly with peoples' perceptions of "turf" and organi-zational "rice bowls," that impartiality and neutrality play a significant role in making what the consultant advises believable and/or acceptable. For this reason, serious consideration should be given to using outside consultants even if internal consultants are available.

(v)   Focusing on Customers and Suppliers

A strategy for involving customers and suppliers in the quality improvement effort is essential. This is difficult in many organizations, since the concept of "customer" is still often not well established throughout an organization. Employees in a trade association, for example, who view interactions with the members of the association as something to be avoided if at all possible, do not have a clue as to why they are really employed by the association.

Many people working in a typical organization do not have line-of-sight to cus-tomers the organization serves. They are detached and so their lack of any feel for cus-tomer satisfaction is certainly understandable as well as inappropriate. Customers do not often call themselves "customers," and customer satisfaction is not often considered by the rank and file as a prerequisite for organizational continuation or personal advancement. There is frequently little control or influence over suppliers since they tend to be seen as the responsibility of the administrative or office management depart-ment. The suppliers' use is directed by "someone else."

Despite this environment, level of quality remains one of the few differentiating variables available to managers. This makes implementation of QM even more impera-tive if long-term improvement in the quality of services is to be achieved.

The first element of a customer/supplier involvement strategy is the identification of internal and external customers and suppliers. As this difficult process is being under-taken, the organization initiates informal contact with customers and suppliers to inform them of their importance in the organization's QM implementation effort. This allows an opportunity for customers and suppliers to enter a dialogue which lays the groundwork for more comprehensive assessments to follow (assessment formats may include letters, questionnaires, telephone surveys, formal written surveys, personal interviews, or any combination of the above). These discussions set the stage for potential partnering and joint quality improvement efforts later in the implementation effort within a supportive customer/supplier interface infrastructure.

Most QM consultants offer to prepare and conduct assessments of customers and suppliers in such a way as to minimize imposition. In addition, they develop and provide clients with mechanisms for automatically and routinely collecting customer satisfaction information for continuing the assessment into the future. A strategy for involving suppliers and customers also includes joint analysis of the results of these assessments, subsequent development of specific recommendations, and feedback on outcomes.

Recommendations from these joint quality improvement efforts range from immediately implementable "fixes" to referral of problems or opportunities for improvement to joint PATs. As the processes are changed or improved, progress is fed back to the customers and suppliers for their evaluation of the outcomes, incorporating the PDCA cycle. As was the case with the other approaches, the strategy for involving customers and suppliers should be widely communicated to members of the organization. Ensuring everyone understands the rationale behind the selection of process improvement efforts helps to foster organizationwide support for the quality transformation.

A strategy for focusing on customers and suppliers should also take full advantage of the opportunities offered by the emerging *Internet* technologies. Creation and maintenance of a home page that tells the organization's story to literally the whole world is both inexpensive and relatively easy to do. In addition to providing the ideal mechanism for telling your customers what they need to know about you, this technology also offers the near-future possibilities of electronic customer feedback to feed the assessment processes within your organization. Yet another powerful electronic capability is to be found in the use of an *intranet* as a means of communicating with the organization's internal customers. While still an emerging concept, the intranet offers an organization's leadership a powerful tool for improving communications between all levels and across all departments of an organization.

Finally, it is worth considering development of a strategy that will give every rank-and-file member of the organization line-of-sight to the customers. Introduce them at every opportunity. Involve those who actually do the work by asking them to participate in marketing meetings with the customer. If a complaint is received, make it a policy that the employee(s) involved get to respond (in writing if necessary) directly to the customer. Strange as it may seem, this too is a form of empowerment and it lets the employee know they are vital to the success of the organization. Obviously, the same policy should ensure that the employee gets to hear or see praise from a customer they have served well.

(vi) Getting Everyone Involved

An *employee involvement strategy* recognizes that managing participation is a critical aspect of QM and bringing a participative style of management into an organization requires a strategy. It cannot be done by flipping a switch and announcing "we now have participative management." Such an approach results in frustration in an organization and a failed attempt at changing the corporate culture. Employees will not be prepared to assume the greater role they are being given, and managers will not be comfortable with delegating more to subordinates.

The strategy you develop and implement should include team building, developing routine mechanisms to empower employees, training managers in shared decision-making techniques, getting people involved in the problem-solving process, and improving the system of recognition in the organization. Team building at all levels should be an early priority using training and facilitators in support of the QM infrastructure.

Employee empowerment is accomplished over time through delegation of responsibilities and authorities, and implementation of policies/actions that demonstrate trust and confidence in the ability of workers to improve the processes they operate. This means executives, managers, supervisors, and workers have to learn, among other things, the difference between motivators and satisfiers; the difference between behaviors that are motivating and those that are dominating; and the difference between leadership and manipulation. Where salary tends to be a satisfier (or if it is considered too low, perhaps a dissatisfier) it does not typically motivate the employee to want to improve the operation on a daily basis. Expecting to motivate employees by raising their salary will likely have only a short-term impact on performance.

On the other hand, knowing that you can make a difference is a strong motivator. When employees are given to understand they can make a difference for the better, they will be motivated to do so. Unfortunately the reverse is also true. If employees do not believe they can make a difference, they will be demotivated and very much less willing to try.

When managers or supervisors are dominating, the good things they get subordinates to do are viewed as differences made by the manager; hence there is little sense of accomplishment for the worker. The worker is literally robbed of the pride of workmanship he or she needs to develop self-motivation. Similarly, if the employee perceives the supervisor is manipulating him or her (causing the employee to do things through devious and hidden means without open communications), the pride of workmanship or accomplishment is also denied the employee. The strategy for getting everyone involved, therefore, suggests the need for supervisory and management training on principles of leadership and techniques for coaching, as well as example setting from the corporate head all the way down to the rank and file. Such a strategy will increase the desire of members of the workforce to become involved.

While working the leadership and motivation aspects will increase employee desires to become involved, it is the process improvement efforts and participation through the QM infrastructure (QMBs and PATs) that will afford employees the greatest opportunity to become more involved.

By using a strategy of involving employees, we help individuals or focus groups identify problems and opportunities for improvement. This includes employee suggestions, as well as the nomination of problems or opportunities by any group in the organization's formal or informal structure, including the QM infrastructure. The QM infrastructure, in turn, reviews and prioritizes problems and opportunities that have surfaced and assigns PATs as appropriate.

(vii) QM Training

Development of a well-thought-out QM training strategy reduces the cost of implementing QM in an organization. It makes development and subsequent execution of a training plan much less difficult and results in earlier success in process improvement team efforts. Starting a QM implementation effort by "throwing" QM training at everyone (even good QM training) is not effective. Such an approach typically results in false starts and unrealistic expectations. This in turn results in debilitating frustrations, greater resistance to the transformation, and ultimately a failed implementation effort. An organization needs a training strategy that is relevant and that has an immediate application. An example of an approach is shown in Exhibit 4.7.

Where possible, QM awareness and orientation training should be given to every-

EXHIBIT 4.7 Training Strategy

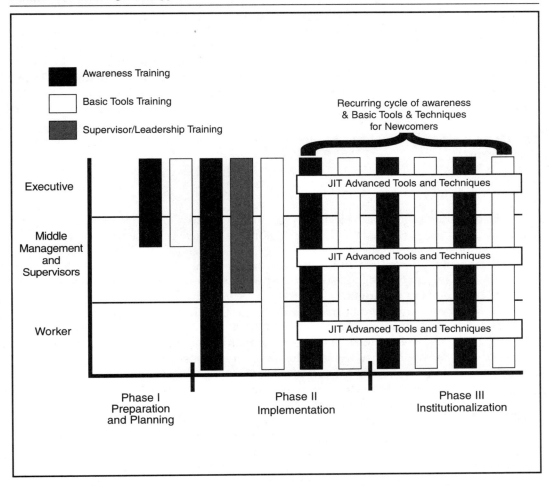

one (workers, managers, and supervisors) at the same time. If the organization is too large to permit this, consider training in vertical cross-sections rather than in horizontal slices of the organization. Even though the implementation strategy calls for executives and key managers to have been involved in prior training necessary for strategy development, it is important for subordinates to see their supervisors hearing the same message. To employees, vertical participation is a visible sign of management's commitment to the QM philosophy and implementation.

There are a number of options available for providing QM training beyond the initial awareness/orientation training. As part of a training strategy, everyone should receive training in basic tools and techniques (to include a process team workshop) between two and six months after the initial awareness training. This training is especially important and should be conducted in smaller groups (20 to 30 people maximum) to ensure the individual attention each person needs. Once again, it is best if classes contain a vertical rather than horizontal cross-section. In these courses, particularly in the workshops, supervisors and managers typically learn a great deal from their subordinates. An advanced QM training strategy should also consider a requirement for *just-in-time* (JIT) training. The more advanced and sophisticated QM training (Quality Function Deployment, Advanced Statistics, Quality Service Gap Analysis, etc.) is only provided to teams as it is needed.

Provision should also be made for training facilitators which are needed to support the QM infrastructure. ESG, QMB, and PAT meetings are far more efficient and productive when they are facilitated. In addition, the requirement for facilitators expands in the later phases of implementation with an increased number of PATs operating. Planning for and training internal facilitators is a cost-effective means of supporting these teams and moving the organization into self-sufficiency. Other considerations in developing a QM training strategy might include the following (depending on the requirements of your organization):

Other Training Strategy Considerations

1. Establishing criteria for selection of in-house QM advisor(s), facilitators, trainers, and team leaders. These positions are critical to implementing and institutionalizing QM.
2. Establishing a requirement for quality assurance measures for QM training courses and materials to ensure time spent in training provides added value to the members attending.
3. Defining a requirement to track and monitor QM training received by individuals. Maximizing utilization of QM skills in selecting people to serve on process teams, as team leaders, as facilitators, or as in-house trainers requires the ability to ascertain who has or needs specific QM training.
4. Establishing a requirement for newcomer QM training. The turnover rate experienced by organizations requires planning for training of new arrivals shortly after they join the organization.
5. Establishing a requirement for "Train-the-Trainer" training. This affords an efficient and cost-effective alternative to continued dependence on outside training resources. In addition to generally being less expensive, such an approach helps an organization to become self-sufficient earlier in the implementation process. This approach makes sense in organizations where the manpower resources and workload will support it.
6. Recognizing the need to incorporate QM training into the organization's overall training plan. This is a key part of the long-term QM training strategy and includes covering advanced subjects such as ServQual, Quality Function Deployment, Concurrent Engineering, and Experimental Design. As part of this effort, organizations might consider incorporating QM training as a formal part of Individual Professional Development Plans as soon as possible once implementation of QM has begun.
7. It is not necessary for all training issues to be resolved in detail at the very beginning of the initial implementation planning effort. What is important at this stage is that the ESC develop a strategic approach and timeline for addressing all of the issues by the time the answers are needed. For example, how QM training will eventually be incorporated into the overall training plan is less important at this point than the decision that QM training *will* be incorporated into the overall training plan.

(viii) Process Improvement

Continuous process improvement is a core element of QM. A strategy for making it a part of the organization's culture begins by identifying the organization's processes and developing a logical approach to prioritizing which ones to work on improving first.

At any given time, such a prioritized list will likely contain a very significant number of candidate process improvement efforts with varying levels of effort required. Since all of the improvement efforts require the expenditure of precious resources (i.e., cost in dollars and peoples' time away from other duties), hard choices need to be made in deciding how many improvement efforts to take on at any given time. For this reason the ESC needs to delegate to the QMBs the responsibility and authority to prioritize and charter process improvement efforts within their area of responsibility. Such an approach allows the organization to eat the "proverbial elephant" one bite at a time. To ensure that the organization does not get bogged down in attempting to proceed with too many process improvement initiatives at one time, the QM infrastructure (ESC, QMBs, and PATs) has to establish and maintain a constant feedback loop on initiatives that are completed, underway, or contemplated.

The use of process improvement teams will be an important part of any strategy for process improvement. The organization's process improvement strategy must involve managers, supervisors, and employees in improving service delivery, solving systemic problems, and correcting errors in all parts of a work process. When people with a *stake* in the decision work together, the quality of the decision increases, commitment to support the change is enhanced, and the likelihood of successful implementation is higher. Below are five points that support the process improvement team concept:

1. Any work process creates information.
2. If you capture that information, study it, and apply data-based decision-making to adjust the work process, you can improve that work process.
3. The people who are in the best position to capture the information (if they don't already know it), are the employees who actually have their hands on the work process and the customer(s) who receive the goods and/or services.
4. To use what employees and customers know in improvement efforts, managers must provide a nonthreatening environment that facilitates communication up, down, and across the organization.
5. Teaming within organizations and across organizational and functional lines is a highly effective way to create such an environment. It is also a very powerful technique for solving problems and improving processes because it:
   a. Takes advantage of the synergism resulting from multiple minds working together to solve a problem; and
   b. Increases commitment to the implementation of the solution or improvement by increasing involvement and ownership.

Teams that work on process improvement have a variety of names depending upon the preferences of the organization establishing them. They are sometimes called Process Action Teams (PATs), Process Improvement Teams (PITs), or Quality Improvement Teams (QITs). Based upon their purpose and makeup, these teams may be grouped into four general categories:

- *Organizational teams* are groups of individuals from a single organizational component (i.e., division, section, or department). The purpose of this type of team is to identify, analyze, and formulate solutions to problems/processes in its area. Solutions are usually recommended to management and they are often implemented by the team members.
- *Cross-functional teams* are composed of representatives from different functional areas of an organization who are involved in a single work process. These teams often cross organizational lines and may include representatives from executive, management, and workforce levels. Cross-functional teams address process concerns/problems and evaluate, analyze, recommend, and/or implement changes. There are generally two types of cross-functional teams:
    1. *Process Improvement/Process Action Teams* focus on one process problem. Once the process is improved, the team disbands.
    2. *Quality Management Teams* function on an ongoing basis, constantly seeking new improvements to a process.
- *Partnering teams* consist of representatives from more than one agency, corporation, or organization who have a direct relationship to or ownership/stake in the process targeted for development or improvement. Members might include managers, process operators, suppliers, and customers who have first-hand knowledge of the operation from beginning to end. They may or may not represent cross-functional areas. When the team has met its challenge, it may disband or continue with follow-on work.

General Objectives of Process Improvement Teams

1. Analyze the way work is performed.
2. Involve employees in process improvement.
3. Develop problem-solving capabilities in employees.
4. Improve communications among employees, and between employees and management.
5. Instill motivation, enthusiasm, and commitment toward improved performance.
6. Identify the customer(s), and improve customer service/customer satisfaction.
7. Provide experience with team building and problem-solving techniques.
8. Enhance the overall functioning of the organization.

(ix) An Approach to Establishing Process Action Teams

In developing effective teams, it is important that the initiator of a team have: (1) a clear goal in mind and (2) a commitment to establishing legitimacy for the team and the results it produces. Below are four steps that are key to initial team development.

Step 1: Identify a *need* or reason for the team's existence. For an organization just beginning the "quality journey" the most effective approach to identifying a need might begin with an examination of the organization's vision/mission, strategic goals, and the objectives that lead to achievement of the vision. Those objectives and the strategic gameplan for accomplishing them will point to improvement efforts where teams are needed. Alternatively, the approach might start with customer satisfaction information which points to problem areas. Additional suggestions for improvement should also be solicited from the workforce.

By linking the need for a team's effort to the vision, goals, and objectives of the organization, customer satisfaction information, or input from the workforce, one establishes that those people who are working on a team are doing the "business" of the organization and not work that is in addition to their "real jobs." Using these approaches, you will find a number of opportunities for improvement. While remaining consistent with your strategic gameplan, focus first on those processes causing the greatest customer concern or organizational irritation. Candidate processes might include those which:

- Require excessive resources (money, time, materials, etc.) with marginal dividends to the organization.
- Create friction within or between functions due to conflicting requirements.
- Cause customer (internal or external) dissatisfaction.
- Need evaluation because they are outdated or do not work.
- Relate to key organization issues or enhance employee job satisfaction.
- Have direct impact on customers (internal and external).
- Have high visibility and importance within the organization.
- Have agreement among all levels of management that the process is important to the organization and needs to be improved.
- Have the support and cooperation of key managers and supervisors.
- Are relatively stable and not slated for restructuring in the near future.
- Have an easily identifiable start and end.
- Are not under study by another Process Action Team.

In selecting early opportunities for improvement you might also consider the following additional criteria:

- *Process analysis experience.* An organization beginning quality improvement should start process analysis efforts by focusing on a highly visible, and relatively uncomplicated process needing improvement.
- *Process analysis results.* Improvements should be recognizable to a substantial and influential portion of the organization's population.
- *Publicity.* Initial team activities should include communicating throughout the organization about the team and its charter. When completed, improvement results should be communicated to demonstrate that quality improvement methods work to benefit the organization.

Successfully developing and narrowing the list of possible needs and opportunities requires a structured decision-making process or technique. Five of the most commonly used techniques, with suggestions on when you might need to use each, are listed in Exhibit 4.8.

Step 2: Identify a *champion* from the senior management level who has both ownership in the process chosen for quality improvement, and authority to provide legitimacy/empowerment to the team's actions.

Step 3: Select *team members* (seven to ten people is the ideal size) based on specified selection criteria that will include members who:

EXHIBIT 4.8 Techniques for Identifying and Prioritizing Improvement Opportunities

- **Brainstorming:** To generate, clarify, and evaluate a sizable list of ideas, problems, or issues.
- **Multivoting:** To accomplish list reduction and prioritization quickly and with a high degree of group agreement.
- **Nominal Group Technique:** To reach consensus within a structured situation.
- **Impact Changeability:** To assess and prioritize problems according to their potential impact on the organization and the ease/difficulty of implementation.
- **Pareto Diagram:** To identify major factors in a subject being analyzed and highlight "the vital few" in contrast to "the trivial many."

- Have a stake in the function/process being reviewed.
- Are operators of the process.
- Are direct recipients/customers of the process.
- Possess expert knowledge in the functions of the process.
- Are suppliers of resources necessary to the process.
- Are interested parties capable of providing fresh ideas/insights.

Step 4: Provide *legitimacy* and *authority* for the team by developing a *Team Charter* as outlined below. Such a charter is normally provided by the Executive Steering Group or Quality Management Board of an organization. In addition to legitimacy, this document provides basic direction for guiding team development and supporting overall operations. Below is a checklist for developing a charter.

Checklist for Developing a Team Charter

- State the precise problem needing resolution—What is wrong?
- Describe how the problem adversely impacts organization quality objectives.
- Identify the process in which the problem appears to reside.
- Specify the initiator (Branch Chief, Director, etc.) of the team.
- Assign an individual that has knowledge and ownership in the process being analyzed to provide day-to-day technical overviews, guidance, and assistance.
- Provide specific details, guidance, and direction about:
  - Desired improvement objectives (time, resources, material, money, etc.).
  - Appropriate parameters related to process examination (i.e., limited to local process operations or extended outside the organization).
  - The owner(s) of the process.
  - Organizational policies related to Process Action Team activity.
  - Unique references and information sources applicable to the process.
- Define methods for selection of Process Action Team leader and members.
- Express initial expectations about process team activity including:
  - Data pertinent to the problem.
  - Policies and procedures for streamlining and improvement.
  - An implementation plan to initiate recommended changes.
  - Expected team duration (days, weeks, months) and specific closing date.

- Frequency of team meetings (initially expressed as "not less than") with follow-on frequency as determined by the team to meet objectives and operating constraints (i.e., time, resources, availability of data).
  - Required actions after process evaluation (briefings, plans, etc.).
- Define parameters concerning findings and implementation of recommendations:
  - Who must review and approve team findings and recommendations?
  - Who will initiate changes and monitor the amount of variation?
  - Who may approve modifications to Process Action Team recommendations?
  - Who has authority to fine-tune process modifications?

(x) Performance Evaluation and Recognition Systems

Improving the systems for performance evaluations and recognition begins with acknowledging those parts of the formal performance evaluations and recognition systems an organization can and cannot change or influence and applying innovative approaches where needed. For example, many performance evaluation and recognition systems do not incentivize group or team behavior. The emphasis is on individual performance measured against "established objectives," which typically do not address quality management concepts. Establishing local mechanisms for formally and informally recognizing team and group efforts can be done almost immediately. Letters, memos, formal approval of recommendations, speeches, personal conversations, and meetings where PATs present their results are all easily instituted. To align performance evaluation systems to the new culture, adding QM concepts such as teamwork contributions for workers or team-building efforts for supervisors starts putting the emphasis on the new behaviors and leadership skills. Similarly, removing "management by a system of quotas" from the performance evaluation system can help make room for establishing real process improvement, customer satisfaction, and business growth objectives.

As the organization matures in its QM implementation, such innovative approaches as self-directed and self-evaluated teams might be considered. Here, organizations organize by process rather than by function. Teams are formed around processes. The teams select their own leader, develop their own quotas, and evaluate their own performance in what is called a 360-degree evaluation process. Using this approach, each team member evaluates all of the other team members' contributions to the team goals. Recognition and awards are shared by the team membership.

(xi) Getting Feedback and Measuring Progress

Early in the preparation and planning phase an internal organizational assessment is used to establish a baseline against which to measure progress in implementing QM throughout the organization. In addition, external customer satisfaction surveys are used to assess the degree to which the organization is meeting the needs of the customer. On at least an annual basis, these assessments should be repeated to measure progress across all fronts. To assist organizations in efforts to assess their progress in implementing QM against a standard, government agencies have the President's Award for Quality and Self Assessment process, and private-sector organizations have the Baldrige Award and Self Assessment process. These two assessment instruments are similar in content and both are extremely helpful in assessing how well an organization is doing on its quality journey. Results from these assessments provide insights for making course corrections with respect to both the QM implementation as well as the overall strategic plan of the organization.

The use of the Internet (and e-mail capabilities associated with it) represents a new wave of assessment and feedback mechanisms that offer relatively low-cost and timely information that organizations can use to structure their process improvement efforts.

(B)   PHASE II—IMPLEMENTATION

To this point, most QM activity has been at the executive and key management level where implementation strategies and plans were being developed. In the *Implementation Phase*, the organization's vision and strategic plan are deployed throughout the organization. Implementation plans developed in the Preparation and Planning Phase are similarly deployed throughout the organization and executed. Implementation strategies and plans that have not been completed or that need to be modified are completed and/or modified as necessary.

Coordination with suppliers and customers occurs with periodic customer/supplier satisfaction assessments being used to measure progress in process improvement initiatives. Organizational assessments are used to measure progress against the original baseline assessment and course corrections are accomplished as required. The ESG focuses on: (1) attainment of the corporate vision; (2) refinement of the strategic plan; (3) assessing progress on executing the strategic plan; (4) assessing corporate progress on implementing QM and making course corrections as required; and (5) guiding new planning efforts as they rise to the corporate level.

Considerable effort is expended training in QM Awareness, Basic Tools, Supervisor and Management Leadership training, and Just-in-Time Advanced Tools Training. Organizational facilitators are selected, trained, and assigned to support QMBs and PATs in the process improvement efforts.

The QM infrastructure is established and empowered. Process improvement initiatives are championed by QMBs and assigned to cross-functional PAT teams. Key business processes are reengineered where enabling technologies and customer requirements call for quantum improvements.

The executive steering body continues leading the implementation effort, but as the remainder of the infrastructure (QMBs and PATs) come on-line, a significant portion of the planning and execution work shifts to the QMBs and their PATs.

Throughout this phase the implementation builds to a critical mass as involvement increases and diversifies across and at all levels in the organization and the new approach starts becoming routinized in parts of the organization.

(C)   PHASE III—INSTITUTIONALIZATION

In this phase, the culture of the organization evolves to reflect the philosophies, concepts, and principles of QM as the norm. The organizational structure and the QM infrastructure are merged into a single team-based organizational structure. Members of the organization do not think of what they are doing as QM. The QM approach is simply the way the work of the organization is done. The vision moves to a point further on the horizon as the organization learns to become self-renewing.

Suggested Readings

These suggested readings include both hardback titles and periodical articles. They are intended to provide an overview of what is being published in the areas related to quality management.

Albrecht, Karl. 1988. *At America's Service: How Corporations Can Revolutionize the Way They Treat Their Customers*. Homewood, IL: Dow-Jones-Irwin.

Albrecht, K. and Zemke, R. 1985. *Service America!: Doing Business in the New Economy*. Homewood, IL: Dow-Jones-Irwin.

Atkinson, Philip E. 1992. *Creating Culture Change: The Key to Successful Total Quality Management*. San Diego: Pfeiffer & Company.

Bass, Bernard M. 1981. *Man, Work, and Organizations*. Boston, MA: Allyn and Bacon.

Bass, Bernard M. 1983. *Organizational Decision-making*. Homewood, IL: R.D. Irwin.

Bass, Bernard M. 1985. *Leadership and Performance Beyond Expectations*. New York: Free Press.

Bass, Bernard M. 1990. *Bass & Stogdill's Handbook of Leadership*. New York: Free Press.

Bennis, Warren. 1976. *The Planning of Change*, 3rd ed. New York: Holt, Rinehart and Winston.

Bennis, Warren G. 1989. *Why Leaders Can't Lead*. San Francisco: Jossey-Bass Publishers.

Bennis, Warren G. 1989. *On Becoming a Leader*. Reading MA: Addison-Wesley.

Bennis, Warren and Nanus Burt. 1985. *Leaders*. New York: Harper & Row.

Berwick, Donald M. 1989. "Sounding Board: Continuous Improvement as an Ideal in Health Care." *New England Journal of Medicine*, January 5. 320 (1): 53–56.

Blumberg, Donald F. 1991. "Improving Productivity in Service Operations on an International Basis." *National Productivity Review* (Spring): 167–179.

Brassard, Michael. 1985. *The Memory Jogger*. Methuen, MA: GOAL/QPC.

Burr, John T. 1990. "The Tools of Quality Part I: Going With the Flow(chart)." *Quality Progress* (June): 64–67.

Byham, William C. and Cox, Jeff. 1988. *Zapp! The Lightning of Empowerment: How to Improve Productivity, Quality, and Employee Satisfaction*. New York: Fawcett Columbine Books.

Connors, Tracy D., ed. 1993. *Nonprofit Management Handbook: Operating Policies and Procedures*. New York: Wiley.

Crosby, Philip, B. 1979. *Quality Is Free*. New York: McGraw-Hill.

Crosby, Philip, B. 1984. *Quality Without Tears*. New York: McGraw Hill.

Crosby, Philip, B. 1989. *The Eternally Successful Organization*. New York: McGraw Hill.

Crosby, Philip, B. 1989. *Let's Talk I*. New York: McGraw Hill.

Deming, W. Edwards. 1981. "Improvement of Quality and Productivity Through Actions by Management." *National Productivity Review* (Winter).

Deming, W. Edwards. 1986. *Out of the Crisis*. Cambridge, MA: MIT Center for Advanced Engineering Study.

Farrow, John. 1987. "Quality Audits: An Invitation to Managers." *Quality Progress* (January).

Feigenbaum, Armand V. 1982. "ROI: How Long Before Quality Improvement Pays Off?" *Quality Progress* (November): 32–37.

Feigenbaum, Armand V. 1983. *Total Quality Control.* New York: McGraw-Hill.

Feigenbaum, A., Juran, Joseph A., and Crosby, Phillip C., 1984. "State of Quality in the U.S. Today." *Quality Progress*, 17, (10): 32–37.

Garvin, David 1984. "What Does 'Product Quality' Really Mean?" *Sloan Management Review* (Fall): p. 25–43.

Gibson, Thomas C. 1990. "Helping Leaders Accept Leadership of Total Quality Management." *Quality Progress*, (November): 45–47.

Gillem, Thomas R. 1988. "Deming's 14 Points and Hospital Quality: Responding to the Customer's Demand for the Best Value Health Care." *Journal of Nursing Quality Assurance* (May).

Gitlow, H. and Gitlow, S. 1987. *Deming Guide to Achieving Quality and Competitive Position.* Englewood Cliffs, NJ: Prentice Hall.

Gitlow, H. and Oppenheim, A. 1989. *Tools and Methods for Improvement of Quality.* Homewood, IL: Irwin.

Gitlow, H., Gitlow, S., Oppenheim, A., and Oppenheim, R. 1990. "Telling the Quality Story. *Quality Progress* (September), 23(9): 41–46.

Gryna, Frank M. 1991. "The Quality Director of the '90s. *Quality Progress*, (May): 51–54.

Guaspari, John; 1987. "The Role of Human Resources in 'Selling' Quality Improvement to Employees." *Management Review*, (March): 76, 20–24.

Hall, Dennis P., Peak, Robert, and Van Buren, Christopher. 1991. "Selling and Telling the Quality Story." *Quality Progress* (August): 24(8), 78–79.

Harrington, H. James. 1987. *The Improvement Process: How America's Leading Companies Improve Quality.* New York: McGraw-Hill.

Harrington, H. James. 1987. *The Improvement Process.* New York: McGraw Hill.

Holpp, Lawrence. 1989. "Ten Reasons Why Total Quality Is Less than Total." *Training* (October) 26, (10): 93–103.

Hodgson, Alan. 1987. "Deming's Never Ending Road to Quality." *Personnel Management*, (July): 40–44.

Holpp, Lawrence. 1989. "Achievement, Motivation, and Kaizen." *Training & Development Journal*, (October), 43, (10): 55–63.

Hradesky, John L. 1988. *Productivity and Quality Improvement: A Practical Guide to Implementing SPC.* New York: McGraw Hill.

Imai, Masaaki. 1986. *KAIZEN: The Key to Japan's Competitive Success.* New York: Random House.

Joiner, Brian and Scholtes, Peter. 1986. "The Quality Manager's New Job." *Quality Progress* (October).

Joiner, Brian L. 1986. *What's Wrong with MBO?* Madison, WI: Joiner Associates Inc.

Juran, J. M. 1981. *Juran on Quality Improvement.* Wilton, CT: Juran Institute, Inc.

Juran, J. M. 1981. "Product Quality—A Prescription for the West: Part 1: Training and Improvement." *Management Review* (June): 9–14.

Juran, J. M. 1981. "Product Quality—A Prescription for the West: Part II Upper Management Leadership and Employee Relations." *Management Review* (July): 57–61.

Juran, J. M. 1986. "A Universal Approach to Managing for Quality: The Quality Trilogy." *Quality Progress* (August): 19–24.

Juran, J. M. 1986. "The Quality Trilogy." *Quality Progress* (August).

Juran, J. M. 1988. *Juran on Planning for Quality.* New York: Free Press (Macmillan, Inc.)

Juran, J. M. 1989. *Juran on Leadership for Quality.* New York: Free Press.

Juran, J. M. 1989. "Quality U.S.A. Status and Prognosis." *Quality Digest* (October), 9 (9): 23–31.

Juran, J.M. 1991. "Strategies for World-Class Quality." *Quality Progress* (March): 81–85.

Kacker, Raghu N. 1988. "Quality Planning for Service Industries." *Quality Progress* (August).

Kanter, Rosabeth M. 1983. *The Change Masters*. New York: Simon & Schuster.

Kanter, Rosabeth M. 1987. "Quality Leadership and Change." *Quality Progress* (February): 45–51.

King, Bob. 1987. "Listening to the Voice of the Customer: Using the Quality Function Deployment System." *National Productivity Review* (Summer): 277–281.

Lawton, Robin L. 1989. "Creating a Customer Centered Culture for Service Quality." *Quality Progress* (May), 2 (5):34–36.

Melan, Eugene H. 1985. "Process Management in Service and Administrative Operations." *Quality Progress* (June).

Metz, E.J. 1984. "Managing Change: Implementing Productivity and Quality Improvements." *National Productivity Review* (Summer): 3(3):303–314.

Moen, R.D., and Nolan, T.W. 1987. "Process Improvement: A Step-by-Step Approach to Analyzing and Improving a Process." *Quality Progress* (September): 20(9):62–68.

Monty, Jean C. 1990. "Service Excellence: The Human Connection." *Quality Progress* (October): 23–24.

Pasmore, W.A. 1989. *Designing Effective Organizations: The Sociotechnical Systems Perspective*. New York: Wiley.

Persico, John Jr. 1989. "Team Up for Quality Improvement." *Quality Progress* (January): 33–37.

Peters, Thomas. 1987. *Thriving on Chaos: Handbook for Management Revolution*. New York: Knopf.

Peters, Thomas with Austin, Nancy. 1985. *A Passion for Excellence*. New York, NJ: Random House.

Peters, Thomas J. and Waterman, Robert H., Jr. 1984. *In Search of Excellence*. New York: Warner Books.

Rosander, A.C. 1991. *Deming's 14 Points Applied to Services*. Milwaukee, WI: Quality Press, American Society for Quality Control.

Scanlon, F. and Hagan, J. T. 1983. "Quality Management for the Service Industry—Part I." *Quality Progress*, 16, (5):18–23.

Scanlon, F. and Hagan, J. T. 1983. "Service Industry Quality Management Part II." *Quality Progress*, 16, (6):30–35.

Scholtes, P.R. 1986. *Getting a New Team Started*. Madison, WI: Joiner Associates.

Scholtes, P.R. 1988. *The Team Handbook: How to Use Teams to Improve Quality*. Madison, WI: Joiner Associates.

Scholtes, P.R., and Hacquebord, H. 1988. "Beginning the Quality Transformation. Part I." *Quality Progress*, 21(8):28–33.

Scholtes, P.R., and Hacquebord, H. 1988. "Beginning the Quality Transformation." *Quality Progress*, 21 (8):44–48.

Scholtes, P.R., and Hacquebord, H. 1988. "Six Strategies for Beginning the Quality Transformation: Part II." *Quality Progress*, 21(8):44–48.

Scholtes, P.R. and Hacquebord, H. 1988. "Six Strategies for Beginning the Quality Transformation, Part II." *Quality Progress* (August).

Shannon, Wayne C. 1991. "Empowerment: The Catchword of the '90s." *Quality Progress* (July): 62.

Smith, Frederick W. 1990. "Our Human Side of Quality." *Quality Progress* (October): 19–21.

Spechler, J.W. 1988. *When America Does it Right: Case Studies in Service Quality*. Norcross, GA: Industrial Engineering and Management Press.

Stein, Bernard. 1991. "Management by Quality Objectives." *Quality Progress* (July): 78.

Sullivan, Laurance P. 1986. "Quality Function Deployment." *Quality Progress* (June).

Townsend, Patrick, L. 1986. *Commit to Quality*. New York: Wiley.

De Fouw, Eugene. 1987. "Training: A Key to Achieving Quality." *Small Business Report* (December) 12 (12):54–59.

Tregoe, Benjamin B., Zimmerman, John W., Smith, Ronald A., and Tobia, Peter M. 1989. *Vision in Action*. New York: Simon & Schuster.

Tribus, M. 1985. *Creating the Quality Service Company*. Cambridge, MA: Center for Advanced Engineering Study, MIT. In selected papers on quality and productivity improvement (pp. 111–124). Washington, DC: American Quality and Productivity Institute.

Uttal, B. 1987. "Companies that Serve You Best." *Fortune* (December 7): 98–116.

Walton, M. 1986. *The Deming Management Method*. New York: Putnam.

Walton, Mary. 1987. "Deming's Parable of the Red Beads." *Across the Board* (February): 43–48.97

5 Leadership and the Self-Renewing Organization

JOSEPH E. CHAMPOUX, Ph.D.
The Robert O. Anderson Schools of Management
The University of New Mexico

5.1 Introduction

Peter Drucker's analysis of high-performing nonprofit organizations pointed to several consistent characteristics (Drucker, 1989, 1990). They have clearly defined missions that are well understood by all paid and volunteer staff. The clear mission focuses behavior on reaching the organization's goals, often by innovative means.

Frances Hesselbein, former National Executive Director of the Girl Scouts, used its strong mission focus to energize Girl Scout Councils around the country to try new programs. Under her leadership, the Girl Scouts developed the Daisy Scout program in response to changing population demographics. More women were working mothers who needed preschool day care. By 1990, the program had 150,000 five-year-old girls who likely will continue with other Girl Scout programs as they get older (Drucker, 1990, Ch. 3).

The characteristics of high-performing nonprofit organizations are similar to the characteristics of self-renewing organizations. Frances Hesselbein combined her leadership qualities with the self-renewing features of the Girl Scouts to transform it into a high-performing nonprofit organization.

This chapter looks at both self-renewing organizations and leadership to show you the combined power of these two sets of ideas. It also has close ties to the previous four chapters of this book. Strategic planning has the tools and methods for assessing your organization's environment and developing a mission. Quality management presses you for a strong client focus and organizational changes for continuous improvement. Reengineering emphasizes massive changes to move an organization to a new configuration such as is needed for a self-renewing organization. You might find a review of those chapters useful after reading this chapter.

5.2 Self-Renewing Organizations

Self-renewing organizations have strong core values that maintain a steady focus for all organization members. They continually adapt to their environments in an unrelenting pursuit of their mission. Self-renewing organizations have the unique qualities of continuous learning, innovation, and growth. These features characterize both individual members and the entire organization.

Exhibit 5.1 summarizes the main features of self-renewing organizations. Although there is little agreement on an exact definition of self-renewing organizations (Garvin, 1993), the following distills their features from many respected sources (Gardner, 1981; Kuhnert, 1993; Lawrence and Dyer, 1983; Senge, 1990; Wheatley, 1994).

Self-renewing organizations have a strong self-identity. They know who they are and what they are all about. They feature strong cultures with well-defined values, customs, and tradition. These organizations react to their environment based on knowledges of who they are and what they are.

EXHIBIT 5.1 Characteristics of Self-Renewing Organizations

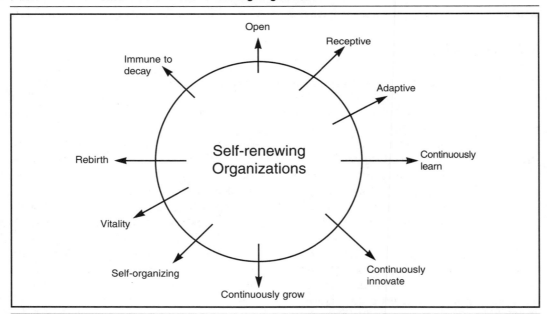

Sources: Developed from Gardner, J. W. 1981. *Self-Renewal; The Individual and the Innovative Society.* New York: W. W. Norton; Lawrence, P. R. and Dyer, D. 1983. *Renewing American Industry.* New York: Free Press; Senge, P. M. 1990. *The Fifth Discipline: The Art and Practice of the Learning Organization.* New York: Doubleday; Wheatley, M. J. 1994. *Leadership and the New Science: Learning about Organizations from an Orderly Universe.* San Francisco: Berrett-Koehler, Inc.

The strong core values of such organizations help sustain a clear focus for everyone in the organization. People have high autonomy but are guided by an unvarying focus on core values and mission. Their focus on a core vision lets them use many routes to reach that vision.

A strong self-identity gives a self-renewing organization high autonomy in its environment although it forges a partnership with its environment. They view their environment as a source of opportunities, not as a source of threats. They have an active exchange with the environment, using it for continual self-renewal. Such organizations aggressively seek feedback from their environment, actively processing such information while remembering who they are and what they are. They use that feedback to shape the future both by changing internal structures and relationships and by changing the environment.

Self-renewing organizations are resilient to environmental disturbances. They do not react with random changes that can disrupt the organization and lead to poor decisions. Leaders in self-renewing organizations understand that human systems do not maintain an endless state of equilibrium. They view change as both inevitable and desirable—as an important source of growth, development, and self-renewal. The result is a flexible and responsive organization that is paradoxically both a partner with and independent of its environment.

Moving self-renewing values into the culture of an organization is often a major organizational change brought about by a strong leader. The next sections describe leadership from several perspectives. You should find those perspectives useful for understanding the leadership requirements of your organization and assessing the leadership qualities of yourself and others in your organization.

5.3   *The Nature of Leadership*

Leadership is a social influence process where the person in a leadership role tries to affect the behavior of another party, a follower or potential follower. The follower must perceive the influence effort as acceptable for it to affect the person's behavior. Power is a central feature of leadership, with leaders getting their power from both their organizational positions and personal qualities.

Leaders can appear at any organizational level. A key position for a leader to affect a self-renewing nonprofit organization is the senior executive position. The position can have almost any title—executive director or manager, for example. This senior position is a key one from which a leader can forge a self-renewing organization.

Leaders and managers do not have the same roles in organizations (Bennis and Nanus, 1985; Kotter, 1990; Yukl, 1994; Zaleznik, 1977, 1990). A simple summary of the differences says: "Leaders change human systems, managers maintain and control them" (Champoux and Goldman, 1993, p. 65). Leaders form visions, inspire others to chase the vision, take risks, gather and use power, and seek opposing views. Managers build commitment to a set of goals, use their knowledge of human motivation to guide the behavior of others, solve problems, and pursue an orderly course of action. Managers typically take fewer risks than leaders and do not try to change an organization's direction. Both leaders and managers play important roles in an organization. They are simply different roles. Leaders seek change; managers keep a steady direction.

5.4 Some Views of Leadership

Research and observation over the past 100 years has produced many different views of leadership. These views offer different perspectives of leadership that give diverse insights about leadership processes. The following describes these views. A later section links them to forming and sustaining a self-renewing organization.

(A) LEADERSHIP TRAITS

Leadership researchers have investigated for almost 100 years the types of traits that distinguish leaders from followers or which followers attribute to their leaders. This research consists of survey assessments, interviews, and observations from experience.

Exhibit 5.2 summarizes the results of much of that work. The first two columns list traits from empirical research as found in rigorous statistical summaries (Bass, 1990; Mann, 1959; House and Baetz, 1979; Kirkpatrick and Locke, 1991). The third column shows the traits that over 60 percent of study participants ascribed to their leaders. That series of studies was done in the 1990s with over 20,000 people from Australia, Asia, Europe, and the United States (Kouzes and Posner, 1995). Column four shows many traits that leadership scholar Warren Bennis has uncovered in his 40-year program of interview-based research (Bennis, 1989, 1993; Bennis and Townsend, 1995). The last column has John W. Gardner's observations on leadership based on his years of public ser-

EXHIBIT 5.2 Comparison of Leadership Traits

Statistical Review 1	Statistical Review 2	Kouzes and Posner	Bennis	Gardner
dominance	cognitive ability	competent	active listener	able to build trust*
energy	desire to lead	forward-looking	articulate	able to motivate
intelligence	drive	honest	consistency	confidence*
self-confidence	honesty/	inspiring	controlled	courage
task-relevant	integrity		personal	decisive
knowledge	knowledge of		ambition	dominance*
	the business		creativity	flexibility
	self-confidence		decisiveness	intelligence*
			dedication	need to achieve
			humility	people skills
			inclusive	responsible
			integrity*	stamina*
			intelligence*	task competence
			magnanimity	understanding
			openness	followers
			persistence	
			self-awareness	
			self-confidence*	
			sense of humor	
			toughness	
			vision*	

vice (Gardner, 1993). The asterisked traits in the last two columns are similar to traits in columns 1–3.

The pattern and consistency of traits in the exhibit is striking. Leaders have vision, energy, and self-confidence. They are competent and bright with knowledge that applies to an organization's business. Leaders have integrity that helps them build trust between themselves and their followers. They can be dominant when they must, such as in moments of decisive action.

The traits in Exhibit 5.2 come from research that is independent of what later sections report. We will see that these traits and related behavior patterns play key roles in leadership processes in self-renewing organizations.

(B)   THE LEADERSHIP MYSTIQUE[1]

The leadership mystique is a view of leadership developed from observing executives who had made major changes in their organizations. That research pointed consistently to three dimensions of leadership: a sense of mission, a capacity for power, and a will to survive and persevere (Jennings, 1960, 1974).

A sense of mission is a vision of a future state for the organization. Leaders passionately hold to their visions. They energetically try to instill that vision in others around them, to move all of them forward toward the vision.

A capacity for power lets the leader get and use the power he or she needs to reach the mission and realize the vision. Such power can come from any source. Some power bases are in the leader as qualities of charisma and expert knowledge. Other bases are in the leader's organizational position (French and Raven, 1959). The latter bases of power can be the authority of a position and the right to reward and sanction behavior.

The will to survive and persevere expresses both the passionate pursuit of a, vision and the intense personal sacrifice that often goes with that pursuit. In Jennings' words, it is ". . . a will to survive and persevere against a discourteous world of sometimes total opposition" (Jennings, 1974, p. 391). The will to survive and persevere clearly plays an important role in facing resistance to organization change.

Frances Hesselbein, former Executive Director of the Girl Scouts of America, moved that organization from a plodding bureaucracy to a responsive, customer-focused organization. During her time as Executive Director, membership increased to 2.3 million, following eight years of declining membership (Byrne, 1990). Her first steps focused on reassessing the mission (or vision) of the Girl Scouts. In her words: "We kept asking ourselves very simple questions. . . . What is our business? Who is the customer? And what does the customer consider value?" (Byrne, 1990, p. 70). Hesselbein is widely credited with successfully changing the Girls Scouts of America by repeatedly focusing on its mission.

---

[1] This section originally appeared in J. E. Champoux and L. D. Goldman, "Building a Total Quality Culture." In T. D. Connors, ed., *Nonprofit Organizations Policies and Procedures Handbook* New York: Wiley, 1993, pp. 65–66 and its *Supplement*, 1996, p. 14. Copyright © 1993 by John Wiley & Sons, Inc. Reprinted by permission of John Wiley & Sons, Inc.

(C)   TRANSFORMATIONAL LEADERSHIP[2]

Transformational leadership theory offers a complementary view to the leadership mystique (Avolio and Bass, 1987; Bass, 1985, 1990; Burns, 1978). This view of leadership features the three dimensions of charisma, individualized consideration, and intellectual stimulation.

Charismatic leaders excite their followers with a new vision of the future for the organization. Such leaders inspire others to transcend their self-interest and work well beyond their expectations of what they can do. Charismatic leaders have the personal qualities of high self-esteem and self-confidence.

Individualized consideration refers to the leader's high commitment to the development of subordinates, based on each person's unique combination of qualities, skills, and abilities. Such leaders thoroughly know their subordinate's abilities, needs, and desires. The leaders delegate decision authority and assign tasks that extend the subordinate beyond his or her current level. They also develop a mentoring relationship with their followers, a relationship that lets the leaders show everyone the type of job performance he or she expects.

Intellectual stimulation is the ability to build awareness of solutions to problems among subordinates and to change their beliefs about the future direction of the organization. This attribute of a transformational leader comes from brilliance and unequaled technical ability. Such leaders' use of intellectual stimulation includes managing images and symbols that show the leaders' vision of the future. Intellectual stimulation is more than stimulating thinking. It includes an emotional element that propels followers toward understanding their role in reaching the desired end-state the leaders envision.

(D)   CHARISMATIC LEADERSHIP[3]

Charismatic leaders attract devoted followers who energetically pursue the leader's vision. Charismatic leaders move their followers to extraordinary heights of performance, profoundly affect their aspirations, build emotional attachment to the leader, and win commitment to the leader's vision. Followers focus on the interest of the organization mission more than on their self-interest. Charismatic leaders win the loyalty of their followers and inspire them to self-sacrifice in the pursuit of a vision (House, 1977; House, Spangler, and Woycke, 1991; Howell and Frost, 1989; Shamir, House, and Arthur, 1993).

Research focused on charismatic leadership has described a constellation of behaviors that distinguish charismatic leaders from other types of leaders and managers (Conger, 1989). Charismatic leaders see well beyond their organization's current situation and develop a view of the future that is different from the present. They develop and widely communicate an inspirational vision—a vision they describe as better in specific ways

---

[2] This section originally appeared in J. E. Champoux and L. D. Goldman, "Building a Total Quality Culture." In T. D. Connors, ed., *Nonprofit Organizations Policies and Procedures Handbook* New York: Wiley, 1993, p. 66 and its *Supplement*, 1996, pp. 14–15. Copyright © 1993 by John Wiley & Sons, Inc. Reprinted by permission of John Wiley & Sons, Inc.

[3] Modified and reprinted by permission from page 337 of *Organizational Behavior: Integrating Individuals, Groups, and Processes* by Joseph E. Champoux. Copyright © 1996 by West Publishing Company. All rights reserved.

from the present. Such leaders form bonds of trust between themselves and their followers. Charismatic leaders empower others in their organizations to carry out the vision.

Looking beyond the present situation includes scanning the environment for new opportunities, predicting changes in the environment, and looking for ways to keep their organization aligned with its outside environment. Charismatic leaders are impatient with present conditions and press their organizations to continuously improve. They push their organizations toward a new state by creating dissatisfaction with the present.

Creating and communicating an inspirational vision is a key behavior of charismatic leaders. To communicate, they use all suitable media with which they feel comfortable. Such media include written documents, speeches, conversations with individual employees, television, and direct electronic communication. Charismatic leaders are especially skilled at framing messages that clearly express and support their vision.

Building trust between the leader and her or his followers is a key part of getting commitment to the leader's vision. Charismatic leaders behave in ways that are consistent with statements about the vision. The leader also tries to forge values supporting the vision into the cultural fabric of the organization. For example, Jan Carlzon, the charismatic former chief executive of Scandinavian Airlines System (SAS), reinforced customer-oriented values when he refused to accept a magazine or newspaper while traveling on SAS before all other passengers were offered one (Carlzon, 1987).

Charismatic leaders are especially skilled at tapping unused motivational energy in their followers. They rely on empowerment, an approach that helps followers develop self-confidence in their ability to fulfill the leader's vision. Such leaders often design experiences to stretch their followers to new levels of performance. By giving them feedback, charismatic leaders help steer followers in the desired direction and inspire them to higher levels of performance.

(E) SUBSTITUTES, NEUTRALIZERS, AND ENHANCERS OF LEADERSHIP BEHAVIOR[4]

Substitutes, neutralizers, and enhancers each operate differently in the relationship between a leader and a follower. Exhibit 5.3 shows the different relationships for substitutes, neutralizers, and enhancers (Howell, Bowen, Dorfman, Kerr, and Podsakoff, 1990; Howell, Dorfman, and Kerr, 1986; Kerr, 1977; Kerr and Jermier, 1978; Podsakoff, MacKenzie, and Fetter, 1993; Podsakoff, Niehoff, MacKenzie, and Williams, 1993).

Substitutes for leadership act in place of the leader, making leader behavior unnecessary. The substitute, not the leader, affects subordinate attitudes and behavior. For example, people doing routine and predictable tasks would find directive leader behavior redundant. The nature of the task, not the leader, guides the person's behavior. Tasks allowing high levels of intrinsic motivation also substitute for motivational influences from the leader.

Neutralizers prevent leader behavior from affecting the attitudes and behavior of subordinates. A neutralizer breaks the connection between leader behavior and subordinate response. A neutralizer has no direct effect on the subordinate. Instead, it is a block between the leader and the subordinate. For example, work groups often develop norms or rules that control the behavior of group members. If those norms are not consistent

---

[4] Modified and reprinted by permission from pages 338–339 of *Organizational Behavior: Integrating Individuals, Groups, and Processes* by Joseph E. Champoux. Copyright © 1996 by West Publishing Company. All rights reserved.

EXHIBIT 5.3 Substitutes, Neutralizers, and Enhancers of Leadership Behavior

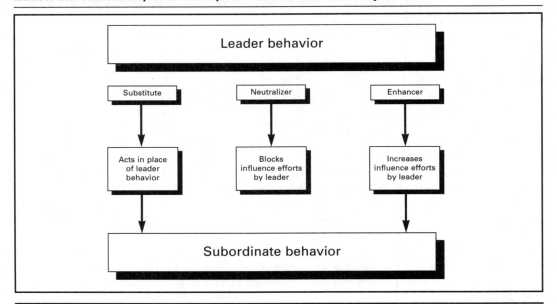

Source: Reprinted by permission from Figure 12-4, page 339 of *Organizational Behavior: Integrating Individuals, Groups, and Processes* by Joseph E. Champoux. Copyright © 1996 by West Publishing Company. All rights reserved.

with what the group leader wants, the norm neutralizes the leader's efforts to influence the group. People with a professional orientation, such as artists and musicians, often turn to their professional peers for recognition and rewards. That orientation can neutralize supportive leader behavior and any efforts at recognition by the leader.

Enhancers strengthen the connection between leader behavior and subordinate satisfaction and performance. If a leader controls rewards for a subordinate's performance, and the subordinate perceives a direct connection between performance and getting the reward, the reward system enhances the leader's influence over the subordinate. Similarly, organization policies that let the leader hire and fire enhance the leader's influence over subordinates.

(F) LEADERSHIP PERCEPTIONS: "WE KNOW A LEADER WHEN WE SEE ONE"[5]

The discussions of leadership in this chapter have focused on the traits and behavior of leaders. Human perceptual processes underlie people's observations of leader traits and behaviors. Researchers have developed two different but related views of leadership perceptions. The first view builds on perceptual categories; the second view describes the process of leadership attribution. Exhibit 5.4 shows both views for easy comparison.

---

[5] Modified and reprinted by permission from pages 339–341 of *Organizational Behavior: Integrating Individuals, Groups, and Processes* by Joseph E. Champoux. Copyright © 1996 by West Publishing Company. All rights reserved.

(i) *Leadership Categorization*

According to the Leadership Categorization view of leadership perception, people observe the behavior of another person and then quickly compare those observations to a cognitive category describing a leader. In exhibit 5.4, (a) shows a simplified version of the Leadership Categorization Process (Lord, 1985; Lord, Foti, and DeVader, 1984; Lord, Foti, and Phillips, 1982; Lord and Maher, 1993).

A person's perceptual process helps filter observations from the person's environment. The person compares his or her perceived observations to a cognitive category that is either a leadership prototype or a leadership exemplar. A leadership prototype is a person's cognitive image of the characteristics, qualities, behaviors, and traits that make up a leader. For example, some people might view leaders as intelligent and industrious while others think of leaders as honest and outgoing (Lord, Foti, and DeVader, 1984). A leadership exemplar is a specific person people regard as a leader, such as Margaret Thatcher, or Martin Luther King, Jr.

A key step in the Leadership Categorization Process is deciding whether the perceived observations match the leadership prototype or exemplar. If they do not match, the observer decides the observed person is not a leader. If they match, she or he decides the observed person is a leader.

EXHIBIT 5.4 Leadership Perceptions

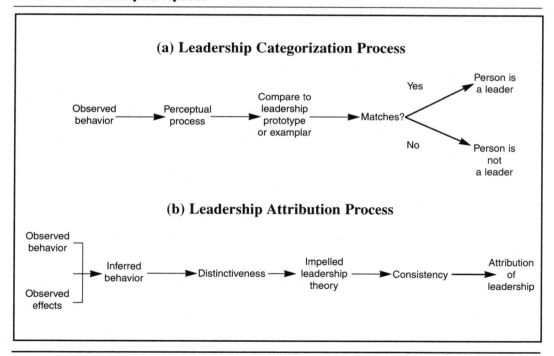

(a) Leadership Categorization Process

Observed behavior → Perceptual process → Compare to leadership prototype or examplar → Matches? → Yes → Person is a leader / No → Person is not a leader

(b) Leadership Attribution Process

Observed behavior / Observed effects → Inferred behavior → Distinctiveness → Impelled leadership theory → Consistency → Attribution of leadership

---

Source: Reprinted by permission from Figure 12-5, page 341 of *Organizational Behavior: Integrating Individuals, Groups, and Processes* by Joseph E. Champoux. Copyright © 1996 by West Publishing Company. All rights reserved.

(ii) Leadership Attributions

Attribution of leadership follows the attribution process shown in Exhibit 5.4(b) (Calder, 1977). Individuals observe the behavior of other people and the effects associated with the behavior. An observer can also infer other behaviors from the observed behavior. For example, an observer might conclude that a talkative person who interacts with many people in a group has much job-related information. The observer made the inference from the talkative and interactive behavior he or she saw.

In the next step in the process, the observer assesses the observed and inferred information for evidence of leadership. A key factor in this step is whether the behavior is specific to one person or is widely shared by other people in a group. An observer accepts only distinctive behavior as evidence of leadership. The observer then compares the distinctive behavior to an implicit leadership theory. Such theories act as perceptual filters and standards of comparison for the leadership qualities a person believes are important for a leader to have. Some people think decisiveness is an important leadership quality. If a leader shows decisiveness, then the person is a leader. The observer now decides whether the behavior is consistent across situations and over time. If the observer sees similar behavior from the same person in different situations and at different times, she or he will build a strong attribution of leadership.

5.5 Leadership and Self-Renewing Organizations

Exhibit 5.5 compares some major characteristics of leadership to the characteristics of self-renewing organizations. They are open, receptive, and adaptive organizations that continuously learn, innovate, and grow. Such features let self-renewing organizations maintain their vitality and protect themselves from decaying.

Leadership is a driving force that can transform an organization into a self-renewing one. Characteristics such as charisma, self-confidence, and building trust can help a leader energize followers to pursue a vision of becoming a self-renewing organization. Perseverance will serve the leader well along the way as he or she meets roadblocks and resistance to the new direction. Empowerment is a leader's important tool to move decision making to the point of contact with clients and get the adaptability of a self-renewing system.

The continual growth and rebirth of a self-renewing organization needs these and other leadership qualities. A leader's knowledge and vision, plus the intellectual stimulation of followers, infuses self-renewing organizations with critical skills to adapt to opportunities in its environment. Seeing beyond the present supports the organization's rebirth and vitality by finding new ways to serve clients.

Peter Drucker's observations on Willowcreek Community Church suggest that it became a self-renewing organization and continues to be one.

Willowcreek Community Church in South Barrington, Illinois, outside Chicago, has become the nation's largest church—some 13,000 parishioners. . . . Bill Hybels, in his early twenties when he founded the church [in 1974], chose the community because it had relatively few churchgoers, though the population was growing fast and churches were plentiful. He went from door to door asking. "Why don't you go to church?" Then he designed a church to answer potential customer's needs: for instance, it offers full services on Wednesday evenings because many working parents need Sunday to spend with

EXHIBIT 5.5 Leadership and Self-Renewing Organizations

Leadership Traits	Leadership Mystique	Transformational Leadership	Charismatic Leadership	Self-Renewing Organizations
builds trust	sense of mission	charisma	sees beyond	open
competence	capacity for	individualized	the present	receptive
dominant	power	consideration	visionary	adaptive
energy	will to survive	intellectual	builds trust	continuously
honest	and persevere	stimulation	empowers	learn
intelligence				continuously
knowledgeable				innovate
self-confidence				continuously
vision				grow
				self-organizing
				vitality
				rebirth
				immune to decay

their children. . . . Hybels continues to listen and react. The pastor's sermon is taped while it is being delivered and instantly reproduced so that parishioners can pick up a cassette when they leave the building because he was told again and again, "I need to listen when I drive home or drive to work so that I can build the message into my life." But he was also told: "The sermon always tells me to change my life but never how to do it." So now every one of Hybels' sermons ends with specific action recommendations. (Drucker, 1989, p. 89)

Mr. Hybels' leadership qualities let him build and maintain Willowcreek Community Church as a self-renewing system.

5.6 Conclusion

Self-renewing organizations have strong core values that focus the behavior of all organization members. They continually adapt to their environments in an unrelenting pursuit of their mission. Self-renewing organizations have the unique qualities of innovation, growth, and continuous learning.

Leadership is an influence process where the leader tries to affect the behavior of a follower or potential follower. Power is a central feature of leadership with leaders getting power from their organizational positions and personal qualities. Leaders and managers play important but different roles in an organization. Leaders seek change. Managers keep a steady direction.

Leadership is the driving force that can transform an organization into a self-renewing one. Charisma, self-confidence, and building trust are characteristics that can help a leader energize followers to pursue a vision of becoming a self-renewing organization. The continual growth of such organizations needs these and other leadership qualities. Knowledge and vision of the leader, plus the intellectual stimulation of followers, infuses self-renewing organizations with critical skills to adapt to opportunities in their environment.

Suggested Readings

Avolio, B. J. and Bass, B. M. 1987. "Transformational Leadership, Charisma and Beyond." In J. G. Hunt, B. R. Baglia, H. P. Dachler, and C. A. Schriesheim eds., *Emerging Leadership Vistas.* Lexington, MA: Lexington Books, pp. 29–49.

Bass, B. M. 1985. *Leadership and Performance Beyond Expectations* New York: Free Press, pp. 42–43.

Bass, B. M. 1990. "From Transactional to Transformational Leadership: Learning to Share the Vision." *Organizational Dynamics* (Winter), 18:19–31.

Bass, B. M. 1990. *Bass & Stogdill's Handbook of Leadership: Theory, Research, and Managerial Applications* (Chs. 4 and 5). New York: Free Press.

Bennis, W. 1989. *Why Leaders Can't Lead: The Unconscious Conspiracy Continues* (Ch. 18). San Francisco: Jossey-Bass.

Bennis, W. 1993. *An Invented Life: Reflections on Leadership and Change.* Reading, MA: Addison-Wesley.

Bennis, W. and Nanus, B. 1985. *Leaders: The Strategies for Taking Charge.* New York: Harper & Row, pp. 21, 23, 40–41, 92–93, 218–226.

Bennis, W. and Townsend R. 1995. *Reinventing Leadership: Strategies to Empower the Organization* (Ch. 2). New York: William Morrow.

Burns, J. M. 1978. *Leadership.* New York: Harper & Row.

Byrne, J. A. 1990. "Profiting from the Nonprofits." *Business Week* (March 26): 66–70, 72, 74.

Calder, B. J. 1977. "An Attribution Theory of Leadership." In B. M. Staw and G. R. Salancik, eds., *New Directions in Organizational Behavior.* Chicago: St. Clair Press, pp. 179–204.

Carlzon, J. 1987. *Moments of Truth.* Cambridge, MA: Ballinger, pp. 94–95.

Champoux, J. E. and Goldman, L. D. 1993. "Building a Total Quality Culture." In T. D. Connors, ed., *Nonprofit Organizations Policies and Procedures Handbook* (Ch. 3). New York: Wiley.

Conger, J. A. 1989. *The Charismatic Leader: Behind the Mystique of Exceptional Leadership.* San Francisco: Jossey-Bass, pp. 9–10.

Drucker, P. E. 1989. "What Business Can Learn from Nonprofits." *Harvard Business Review,* 89(4):88–93.

Drucker, P. E. 1990. *Managing the Non-Profit Organization: Practices and Principles.* New York: HarperCollins.

French, J. and Raven, B. 1959. "The Bases of Social Power." In D. Cartwright, ed., *Studies in Social Power.* Ann Arbor, MI: Institute for Social Research, pp. 150–167.

Gardner, J. W. 1981. *Self-Renewal: The Individual and the Innovative Society.* New York: Norton.

Gardner, J. W. 1993. *On Leadership* (Ch. 5). New York: Free Press.

Garvin, D. A. 1993. "Building a Learning Organization." *Harvard Business Review,* 71(4):78–91.

House, R. J. 1977. "A 1976 Theory of Charismatic Leadership." In J. G. Hunt and L. L. Larson, eds., *Leadership: The Cutting Edge.* Carbondale, IL: Southern Illinois University Press. pp. 189–207.

House, R. J. and Baetz, M. L. 1979. "Leadership: Some Empirical Generalizations and New Research Directions." In B. M. Staw, ed., *Research in Organizational Behavior.* Greenwich, CT: JAI Press, pp. 341–423.

House, R. J., Spangler, W. D., and Woycke, J. 1991. "Personality and Charisma in the U.S. Presidency: A Psychological Theory of Leader Effectiveness." *Administrative Science Quarterly*, 36:364–396.

Howell, J. M. and Frost, P. J. 1989. "A Laboratory Study of Charismatic Leadership." *Organizational Behavior and Human Decision Processes*, 43:243–269.

Howell, J. P., Bowen, D. E., Dorfman, P. W., Kerr, S., and Podsakoff, P. M. 1990. "Substitutes for Leadership: Effective Alternatives to Ineffective Leadership." *Organizational Dynamics*, xx:21–38.

Howell, J. P., Dorfman, P. W., and Kerr, S. 1986. "Moderator Variables in Leadership Research." *Academy of Management Review*, 11:86–102.

Jennings, E. E. 1960. *An Anatomy of Leadership*. New York: Harper & Row.

Jennings, E. E. 1974. "On Rediscovering the Leader." In J. W. McGuire, ed., *Contemporary Management: Issues and Viewpoints*. Englewood Cliffs, NJ: Prentice-Hall, pp. 390–396.

Kerr, S. 1977. "Substitutes for Leadership: Some Implications for Organizational Design." *Organization and Administrative Sciences*, 8:135–146.

Kerr, S. and Jermier, J. M. 1978. "Substitutes for Leadership: Their Meaning and Measurement." *Organizational Behavior and Human Performance*, 22:375–403.

Kirkpatrick, S. A. and Locke, E. A. 1991. "Leadership: Do Traits Matter?" *Academy of Management Executive*, 5:48–60.

Kotter, J. P. 1990. "What Leaders Really Do." *Harvard Business Review*, 90(3):103–111.

Kouzes, J. M. and Posner, B. Z. 1995. *The Leadership Challenge: How to Keep Getting Extraordinary Things Done in Organizations*. San Francisco: Jossey-Bass.

Kuhnert, K. W. 1993. "Leadership Theory in Postmodernist Organizations." In R. T. Golembiewski, ed., *Handbook of Organizational Behavior*. New York: Marcel Dekker, pp. 189–202.

Lawrence, P. R. and Dyer, D. 1983. *Renewing American Industry*. New York: Free Press.

Lord, R. G. 1985. "An Information Processing Approach to Social Perceptions, Leadership and Behavioral Measurement in Organizations." In B. Straw and L. L. Cummings, eds., *Research in Organizational Behavior, Vol. 7*. Greenwich, CT: JAI Press, pp. 87–128.

Lord, R. G. and Maher, K. J. 1993. *Leadership and Information Processing: Linking Perceptions and Performance*. New York: Routledge.

Lord, R. G., Foti, R. J., and DeVader, C. 1984. "A Test of Leadership Categorization Theory: Internal Structure, Information Processing and Leadership Perceptions." *Organizational Behavior and Human Performance*, 34:343–378.

Lord, R., Foti, R., and Phillips, J. S. 1982. "A Theory of Leadership Categorization." In J. G. Hunt, U. Sekaran, and C. A. Schriesheim, eds., *Leadership: Beyond Establishment Views*. Carbondale, IL: Southern Illinois University Press, pp. 122–141.

Mann, R. D. 1959. "A Review of the Relationships between Personality and Performance in Small Groups." *Psychological Bulletin*, 56:241–270.

Podsakoff, P. M., MacKenzie, S. B., and Fetter, R. 1993. "Substitutes for Leadership and the Management of Professionals." *Leadership Quarterly*, 4:1–44.

Podsakoff, P. M., Niehoff, B. P., MacKenzie, S. B., and Williams, M. L. 1993. "Do Substitutes for Leadership Really Substitute for Leadership? An Empirical Examination of Kerr and Jermier's Situational Leadership Model." *Organizational Behavior and Human Decision Processes*, 54:1–44.

Senge, P. M. 1990. *The Fifth Discipline: The Art and Practice of the Learning Organization*. New York: Doubleday.

Shamir, B., House, R. J., and Arthur, M. B. 1993. "The Motivational Effects of Charismatic Leadership: A Self-Concept Based Theory." *Organization Science*, 4:577–594.

Wheatley, M. J. 1994. *Leadership and the New Science: Learning about Organizations from an Orderly Universe*. San Francisco: Berrett-Koehler.

Yukl, G. A. 1994. *Leadership in Organizations*. Englewood Cliffs, NJ: Prentice-Hall, pp. 4–5.

Zaleznik, A. 1977. "Managers and Leaders; Are They Different?" *Harvard Business Review*, 55(3):67–80.

Zaleznik, A. 1990. "The Leadership Gap." *Academy of Management Executive* 4:7–22.

PART II Human Resources

The Board of Directors

6

BARBARA A. BURGESS SOLTZ
President, AMI Management Inc.

6.1 *What the Board Is and What It Does*

Over the years, nonprofit boards have collected a full rack of descriptive tags that characterize styles of operation. One hears about power boards, token boards, working boards, money-raising boards, and hands-on boards. More than anything else, however, how a board operates relates to how well it understands its responsibilities and functions.

This chapter defines and describes the charge of a controlling or governing nonprofit board of directors in two ways. First, it describes the functions and responsibilities of a board generally. Second, it presents a concept of board development that will enable a board to fulfill its responsibilities effectively and, consequently, to evolve and mature.

(A) DEFINITION OF A NONPROFIT BOARD

A nonprofit board of directors is the governing or policy-setting body that bears legal responsibility for the institution it serves. A board also plays a role in maintaining a system of decision-making checks and balances among three organizational branches: the administration, the board, and any constituency that has input into the workings of the organization. A non-profit organization is required to have a voluntary or lay board of directors in order to get a state charter and qualify for Section 501(c)(3) tax status under the Internal Revenue Code.

(B) TYPES OF BOARDS

Boards of directors are sometimes referred to as controlling boards because they are responsible for every major decision an organization makes. An organization can have other boards, such as auxiliary boards or associational boards, but these should not be confused with controlling boards. Auxiliary boards are created by the controlling board to execute a specific responsibility—most often, to raise money. Associational boards usually exist to increase membership and to act as a body that represents the needs and special interests of the general membership. A college alumni association is an example of this type of board.

6.2 *Purposes of a Board*

Whether a nonprofit organization is a social service agency, an educational institution, a health care organization, or a cultural institution, its board will have the same basic charge. Functional differences among boards are more a matter of emphasis than of purpose. Generically, a board has three governing functions (Ingram, 1988):

> To preserve the integrity of the trust;
> To set policy;
> To support and promote the organization.

(A) TO PRESERVE THE INTEGRITY OF THE TRUST

This function has two facets: overseeing the mission and preserving institutional autonomy.

(i) *Overseeing the Mission*

Nonprofit constitutions and governing bylaws usually begin with a statement of the organization's mission or purpose. As overseer of that mission, a board must make certain that everything the nonprofit does is true to it. A board fulfills this purpose by asking hard questions. Because asking questions is perhaps their most important task, members should never hesitate to request information about all facets of the institution's operations. Traditionally, boards involve themselves with financial activity more closely than they do with programs and services, because they are not usually experts in the services their organizations provide. To assess how well the mission is being fulfilled, however, a board must become familiar with *all* areas of the organization. Moreover, extraordinary expertise in the service delivery of the organization is not required in order to determine whether a program is meeting the mandates of the mission. The integrity of the institution rests on more than balanced books or well-managed assets; indeed, the integrity of an organization depends primarily on the fulfillment of its mission and public service.

(ii) *Preserving Institutional Autonomy*

Another aspect of preserving the integrity of the trust relates to preserving institutional independence. A board must weigh carefully decisions that could compromise the organization's ability to steer its own course. Complete independence is nearly impossible today because of strings attached to state and federal assistance. Nevertheless, a board must still reject pressures from special-interest groups that would compromise the organization's mission, or from public agencies or businesses that may try to exert undue influence. It is equally important for a board to protect the organization's autonomy through adoption of a clear policy for accepting gifts and grants that have donor restrictions.

(B) TO SET POLICY

The day-to-day administration of an organization is the charge of a chief administrator, but it is the role of the board to provide an operational framework. Most policy is proposed by administrators and presented to the board for questioning, discussion, and, ultimately, a vote of approval. The degree to which a board becomes involved in policy implementation varies among organizations, depending on the balance of strengths and the level of cooperation between the board and the administrative leadership.

Policy making should be grounded in the mission statement and other governing documents of the organization. It should also be preceded by research and input from those members of the organization who will be affected by the policy. Examples of policy decisions that typically require board approval include:

1. Change of the institution's name;
2. Approval of annual operating budgets;
3. Increases in fees for services;
4. Formal endorsement of fund-raising projects;
5. Staff promotions and salary increases;
6. Changes in program offerings or client services;
7. Endowment decisions;
8. Purchase or sale of property;
9. Risk management decisions.

(C) TO SUPPORT AND PROMOTE THE ORGANIZATION

Outside the boardroom, the directors' role changes from devil's advocate to chief advocate. Directors ask hard questions in the privacy of the boardroom, but in public they put aside their criticisms and promote the organization in every way possible. The board's external functions include bringing positive attention to the institution, supporting it financially, supporting the chief administrator, and introducing the organization to those who may be able to help it. In a word, these functions are ambassadorial.

6.3 *The Differences Between For-Profit and Nonprofit Boards*

Particularly when nonprofit organizations come under criticism, comparisons are frequently made between nonprofit and for-profit boards. Moreover, it is not uncommon for an uninitiated board member to think that a nonprofit board should mold itself in the image of a for-profit board. However, each is a distinctly different entity, and it is important for nonprofit administrators and board members to know the differences.

(A) FUNCTIONAL DIFFERENCES

The most obvious difference between for-profit and nonprofit boards is that for-profit board members usually receive a stipend for their service, and members of nonprofit boards are volunteers. Moreover, for-profit board members normally are chosen for their professional expertise in an area that is directly related to the organization's endeavor; members of nonprofit boards are selected using a different, broader set of criteria, including that of representing a layperson's point of view. This is not to infer that nonprofit board members do not bring expertise to the board. The expertise they bring, however, is often intended to complement the expertise of the staff, not to replicate it.

Typically, nonprofit boards do not include staff or chief executive officers as voting members of the board, as do for-profit boards of directors, although in some states it is legal to do so. Frequently, the chief executive officer is an ex officio member without voting power.

(B) DIFFERENCES IN FOLLOW-THROUGH

Conrad and Glenn (1986) noted several other differences between for-profit and non-profit boards. Decisions of nonprofit boards tend to penetrate the organization more deeply and quickly, and carry more specific ramifications for day-to-day procedures; for-profit boards make decisions that many employees may never hear about. Similarly, nonprofit boards become more involved in the implementation of their decisions; they may even oversee and fund implementation themselves. For-profit boards, on the other hand, merely pass the decision on to the chief executive officer for appropriate delegation and implementation. Perhaps this practice accounts for another difference: for-profit boards generally do not have committees. A nonprofit's major work is often done in and by a variety of committees.

6.4   Ten Responsibilities of a Board

It is in the best interest of an organization to educate its entire staff about board functions and responsibilities. Senior administrators and staff members who interact with their boards should study the ten basic responsibilities of a board, given in this section. It is their job to steer and support the board in fulfilling those responsibilities. Before describing each one, it should be noted that authors who write about nonprofit boards have created myriad lists of board responsibilities. The list given here is a conglomerate of many lists and conventional board wisdom, but owes a special debt to Ingram (1988, 1990).

(A)   SELECT, SUPPORT, AND EVALUATE THE CHIEF ADMINISTRATOR

Because incompetent leadership can threaten an institution's very existence, a board's role in the hiring, evaluation, and termination of a chief administrator is perhaps the most critical responsibility a board has.

(i)   Hiring the Chief Administrator
The process of selection is difficult and time-consuming. The rewards of careful selection, however, are many: a well-chosen leader will oversee efficient operations, facilitate the development of sound programs, and enhance the organization's public relations and fund-raising activities. Even though search committees most often have nonboard members, the final authority to hire a new chief administrator rests with the board. Before voting to hire a candidate, a responsible board will be able to answer all the questions on Exhibit 6.1.

(ii)   Supporting and Evaluating the Chief Administrator
Once a board selects a chief administrator, it owes that individual its whole-hearted support and should refrain from meddling in day-to-day operations. This is not to say, however, that the board cannot express its opinion or disagree with the administra-

EXHIBIT 6.1 Checklist for Hiring a New Chief Administrator

1. Has everyone who will report directly to the new person had a chance to meet and react to the candidate?
   _____

2. Have the candidate's references been thoroughly checked? Did they reveal caveats the board should know about and evaluate?
   _____

3. Has the candidate seen and agreed to a complete, written job description?
   _____

4. Have contract negotiations been thorough? Is the length of the contract clear and have conditions for termination been spelled out?
   _____

5. Have all perquisites of the job been identified in writing and agreed to?
   _____

tor's performance in the appropriate venue. Indeed, if a board member has a concern about the administrator's performance, that member should speak with the administrator directly. If the member is not comfortable with direct conversation, that concern should be discussed with the board chair, who, in turn, will discuss it with the administrator. In general, it is not appropriate to discuss the chief administrator's performance, among directors or anyone else, outside of a meeting at which the board chair is present.

When boards find themselves in disputes over a decision to terminate a chief administrator, they most likely have not conducted formal, annual evaluations. John Nason (1990) has suggested that the process for evaluating the performance of the chief administrator should begin with notification of evaluation and a request for the chief administrator to prepare a self-assessment. At the same time, the board should evaluate itself on how well it has supported the administration. A formal review should be conducted at least once a year and, to guarantee objectivity and candor, a consultant should facilitate the process periodically. Finally, the results of the evaluation should be shared with both the chief administrator and the entire board. When handled with sensitivity, evaluations can be constructive for both the organization and the individual(s) involved.

(iii) Terminating the Chief Administrator

If the hiring and evaluation process are executed well, a board should seldom have to terminate the chief administrator. When termination issues arise, the board should consult legal counsel immediately to review the administrator's contract and to develop a procedural plan for the termination. Hasty, uninformed attempts to terminate often violate the contract or due process, and the organization as well as the board could be sued. Legal counsel minimizes this risk and provides objectivity in a situation that is frequently fraught with subjectivity and highly charged emotions.

(B) REVIEW AND PROTECT THE MISSION OF THE ORGANIZATION

Organizations with financial, operational, and image problems can often trace their troubles to the lack of focus that comes from not having and not communicating a clear institutional mission. Even clear missions need regular review and updating.

(i)   Reviewing the Mission

If a board chair or board committee with planning responsibility does not initiate an annual mission review, the chief administrator should initiate it. The result of a mission review should be a short written statement that answers three questions about the organization (Bryson, 1989): Who are we? What do we do? Why do we do what we do? Every time the board makes a decision, it should ask itself: Is this decision in keeping with what we are all about?

Although a mission statement provides an anchor in policy- and decision-making processes, it is not immutable. Consequently, annual reviews should consider whether changes in internal and external environments are rendering the mission, or parts of it, obsolete.

(ii)   Changing the Mission Statement

If a change in mission seems prudent and justified, the board should begin a revision process that includes representatives from all constituencies of the organization. When the process is complete, the administrator must follow up by making the public aware of the change in mission.

When an organization considers a radical change in mission, the board should consult an attorney specializing in nonprofit law: major changes could impact the organization's state charter or gift endowment—and even, in some cases, place it in jeopardy.

(C)   DRIVE THE ORGANIZATION'S PLANNING EFFORTS

Once a mission has been defined, it is the board's job to motivate and oversee a planning process that results in a vision for the organization. Ongoing planning is necessary for the simple reason that things change. Shifts in demographic trends, changes in national standards of care, the development of new technology, and changes in social needs are all conditions that affect a nonprofit's future. Ideally, and increasingly, it is a necessity that an organization look and plan ahead, anticipating change instead of dealing with it reactively.

It is not a board's role to formulate plans, but it is its responsibility to insist that planning be undertaken. As planning occurs, the board should be kept informed and involved in discussions with the planners. Finally, the board should review formal plans while still in draft form, then vote on final adoption. The administration is responsible for providing the board with all information needed to perform this task effectively.

(D)   SERVE AS FIDUCIARY REPRESENTATIVE OF THE ORGANIZATION

The law is murky about the exact responsibilities of nonprofit board members, but legal precedent supports the ten responsibilities described in this chapter. In general, a board and its individual members are considered agents of a corporation and are liable for the actions of a nonprofit organization. This means that they can be sued collectively, as well as individually, for failure to carry out the duties of the organization. Although many states have passed legislation providing charitable or qualified immunity for directors and officers of nonprofit organizations, there are still areas where liability exists. Consequently, it is important for board members and chief administrators to act at all times in the best interest of the organization and to understand their legal duties. These duties are discussed in detail in a later section of this chapter.

(E) ENSURE THE FINANCIAL SOLVENCY OF THE ORGANIZATION

This responsibility has two facets: overseeing fiscal management and participating in fund raising for the organization.

(i) Overseeing Fiscal Management

In the financial arena, board members routinely approve actions that can have a significant effect on the fiscal health of the organization. While details may be delegated to a board finance committee, the full board will need to approve operating budgets, loans, retrenchment plans, capital expenditures, fee increases, investments, property sales, salary and benefit packages, and funding for new programs and projects. It will also need to make risk management decisions regarding insurance and indemnification.

To tackle this responsibility competently, board members must understand fund accounting and review assiduously the monthly balance sheets, activity and expense statements, and statements of cash flow. In addition, they need to give thorough scrutiny to the auditor's annual report. Because fiscal *mis*management is no stranger to nonprofit organizations, board members have not only the right, but the responsibility, to question any expenditure and financial action the administration takes. The chief financial administrator must provide financial data to the board in a timely fashion and answer all questions. To ensure a system of checks and balances, external accountants and auditors should report directly to the board, not to the chief administrator (Dalsimer, 1991).

(ii) Participating in Fund Raising

In plainest terms, a board has a responsibility to support every fund raising endeavor the institution undertakes. That support comes in two ways: board endorsement of all fund-raising undertakings as the governing body of the organization, and individual financial support from every board member. In other words, fund raising is not merely the responsibility of a development officer, a chief administrator, or a board's fund-raising committee. The commonly heard imperative "Give, get, or get off" may be coarse, but it is grounded in a sound, three-part rationale regarding fund raising: it is an act of leadership that all prospective donors need for guidance in their own giving; it is an act of commitment that all constituents of the organization look to for reassurance of a caring board; and it is an act of faith and confidence in the institution, which all constituencies will use in assessing the health of the organization.

Everyone readily acknowledges that some members are capable of contributing more money than others. This variance gives rise to the question of how much a member should give. The answer is: Members should give as much as they can. It does not matter that, for some, the highest level they can manage is under $100 and, for others, it may be thousands of dollars. No matter what the total, the board should reflect 100 percent participation in the organization's annual giving program every year, in addition to supporting special campaigns authorized by the board. Board members and administrators should note that contributions of time and gifts-in-kind, while welcome and appreciated, should not count as support of the organization's fund-raising programs, for the simple reason that they do not show up as income on fund activity statements.

(F) SERVE AS AMBASSADOR AND SPOKESPERSON FOR THE ORGANIZATION

To carry out this responsibility effectively, the board must be well informed about the organization and willing to promote it at every opportunity. This responsibility calls for circumspection in speaking against the institution in public. It also calls for individual members to take the initiative in finding opportunities to promote the organization and to be visible in supporting events sponsored by the organization, such as fund-raisers and public programs. Board members and administrators alike should recognize the special responsibility and influence that board members have in shaping the public image and awareness of the organization. Some board members will have a natural facility for carrying out this responsibility. Others will have the contacts and connections for doing it, but will need strong direction and support from the staff. It is the staff's responsibility to help channel and choreograph board activities in the public relations and fund-raising arenas. In this sense, the administration should view the board as a special donor constituency and cultivate individual member involvement in the same way as it would a major donor prospect.

(G) EVALUATE THE ORGANIZATION'S PROGRAM REGULARLY

While its members may be laypersons, the board is responsible for making sure that the organization's programs are sound. The chief administrator should provide the board with a rationale and description of each program and service the organization provides. In response, a board should probe and question until it is satisfied that programs are being conducted in keeping with the mission, and in fulfillment of what the organization has promised the public. It is also the duty of a board to determine whether programs are meeting public needs and are being marketed effectively. Specific issues will vary according to the type of service the organization provides. Exhibit 6.2 offers a generic set of questions board members should ask in evaluating their organization's programs.

Just as board members often feel inadequate to the task of reviewing programs because of their lay status, staff members sometimes resist board involvement for the same reason. Both staff and board members need to bear in mind that, regardless of their lay status, board members are legally liable when an organization fails to provide a standard of care.

(H) COMMUNICATE THE COMMUNITY AND THE LAY PERSPECTIVE TO THE ORGANIZATION

There is a special value in board members' perspective as laypeople. By offering their interpretation of the interests and perceptions of the community toward the organization, they provide a valuable perspective that the administration cannot possibly have, and they prevent an organization from viewing itself myopically. A well-chosen board will have broad community representation and expertise not found within the organization.

EXHIBIT 6.2 Questions Board Members Should Ask About Programs and Services

1. Do the programs offered have sufficient depth and diversity to meet the needs of both the current and potential client base? _____

2. What do the consumers of the organization's programs and services say about the organization? _____

3. What other measures of program success or failure (measures of effectiveness) are available? _____

4. How is successful performance rewarded? _____

5. What is the long-range plan for the program and service-delivery areas of the organization? What strategies have been developed to address the program's external threats and opportunities? _____

6. Are new approaches or new research in these programs and services recognized and adopted by the organization? _____

7. Is the institution representing its programs and services accurately in its promotional literature and reports to donors? _____

8. Are there audiences or populations not being served that should be? _____

9. How are fees determined and what is known about how the fees attract or deter new clients? _____

10. Are fee schedules and intake policies fair to all socioeconomic, racial, and ethnic groups? _____

11. How does the organization's service record match that of comparable institutions? _____

12. What is the rationale for a proposed new program and what are the resource requirements attached to it? _____

(I)   IN INTERNAL CONFLICT, SERVE AS A FINAL COURT OF APPEALS

Although it is not the role of the board to become involved in the administration of the organization, situations arise occasionally that cannot be settled by the administration and are brought to the board for resolution. If institutional policy is clear and comprehensive, these situations should be rare. Nevertheless, there will always be disgruntled employees (or volunteers) who will fight institutional policies and there will always be dissatisfied clients who may make extreme demands. Moreover, even the best of administrations is not always right. When a dispute with potential for legal action is brought before a board, it is appropriate for the board to review the situation and decide whether to support or overrule the administration. It must be emphasized, however, that this should be an infrequent event, and a board should remand appeals that are not last-resort. Administrators can avoid board involvement in internal disputes by providing employees with clear, written personnel policy information and by establishing adequate grievance procedures for employees. Clients should receive written clarification of the terms of services provided. When disputes do come before the board, it should seek legal counsel regarding the particulars of its fiduciary and other responsibilities in the case at hand.

(J) SELF-ASSESS PERIODICALLY

With all the scrutiny a board gives an organization, it is only fitting that periodic self-assessment is in order. Too many boards become stagnant and passive—particularly when the administration is effective and there are few crises. Chief administrators often prefer passive boards; they give them freer reign. However, when crises occur and a board is not up-to-date on the administrative action, the administrator is vulnerable to criticism. Depending on the severity of a crisis, the administrator's job could be in jeopardy. Consequently, a chief administrator should eagerly promote an active board that knows and fulfills its responsibilities—one that shows and uses its strengths in times of crisis.

It is incumbent on a board to take a periodic critical look at itself, for the same reason that a mission has to be reviewed: things change. Terms of office end and new members come on board. New members may not be cognizant of the history and policy of the organization, or they may not understand their roles. Self-assessment alerts a board to gaps in understanding about vision, policy, procedure, and responsibility. It also identifies areas of disagreement about the performance of a committee, a chief administrator, or the staff. In addition, it gives a board member an opportunity to express constructive criticism. Finally, self-assessment identifies board members' perceptions of the strengths and weaknesses of the board in all ten areas of its responsibility.

Self-assessment should occur annually. The most common method for doing this is a formal assessment survey instrument that individual members complete confidentially. Surveys can be custom-designed, but both the Association of Governing Boards and Arthur Frantzreb (1988) have available instruments that offer tested reliability and validity. Once a survey has been completed, a meeting should be devoted to analyzing its results and determining how the weaknesses and points of disagreement shall be resolved in ways that strengthen the organization.

6.5 Board Leadership

Although nonprofit bylaws provide for and describe the functions of various board officers (secretary, treasurer, and at least one vice chair), the ultimate effectiveness of a board depends on the leadership of its chair and the relationship of the chief administrator to the board and its committee chairs.

(A) THE BOARD CHAIR

When asked what board chairs do, the most frequent response is: "Preside at meetings." Although correct, the response is far from complete. The hardest work of a board chair is done outside the boardroom and involves two critical roles—organizational spokesperson and board executive.

(i) The Chair as Organizational Spokesperson
In this role, the chair must be prepared to handle inquiries from the media, community representatives, clients, and staff. Fortunately, these inquiries do not always happen in the face of adversity, but, no matter when they occur, the chair must be prepared either to speak or to decline comment. In this role, the chair presides at official functions of the

organization, such as dedications, ground breakings, donor recognition events, and special ceremonies.

(ii)   The Chair as Board Executive

In this role, the chair's chief responsibility is to provide leadership. Pohl (1990) has cited four ways in which a chair leads:

1. Defining objectives;
2. Outlining the year's work;
3. Delegating the responsibility to members;
4. Making members feel as though they are doing the job.

As a leader, a board chair must be adept at facilitating communication among the board, the administration, and committees. It is essential that the chair's relationship with the chief administrator be grounded in mutual respect and trust. In this relationship, they should be able to speak candidly with one another and work through disagreements. It is the job of the chair to inform the chief administrator when board members do not approve of particular administrative actions or decisions. On the other hand, it is the function of the chair to help interpret and clarify for the board the administration's style and actions.

As board executive, a chair must oversee the activity of all board committees. Although it is not feasible for a chair to attend all committee meetings, he or she must stay in touch with committee chairs and diplomatically prod the sluggish ones to follow through on their goals and objectives. Overall, a board chair needs strong motivational talents and leadership skills, including a working knowledge of parliamentary procedure.

(B)   THE CHIEF ADMINISTRATOR

The chief administrator is the paid professional who has ultimate responsibility for running the day-to-day operations of a nonprofit organization. Although its titles may vary—president and executive director are the most common—the position carries specific responsibilities relating to the board: administrator as board informant, and administrator as board adviser.

(i)   Administrator as Board Informant

Although board members sometimes complain that administrators inundate them with materials, the fact is that they could never be too well informed. It is the chief administrator's primary duty to let board members know what is happening, whether the news is bad or good. Contacts should be frequent and should include conversations with the board chair several times a week. Notices of noteworthy activity must be sent to the full board between meetings. The chief administrator also ensures that minutes, financial statements, and reports are distributed well in advance of board meetings, in addition to reports presented at executive committee and full-board meetings. A very important chief administrative duty is to prepare and distribute a comprehensive annual report. The chief administrator also must inform the board about activity at competing organizations and about important trends or issues that could have an impact on the organization or the services it provides. A final responsibility related to keeping board members well informed is providing staffing for board committees and coordinating board committees with their internal counterparts.

(ii) Administrator as Board Adviser

An administrator should proffer to the board opinions about such matters as expansion or retrenchment measures, new policy, changes in programs, or financial decisions. Although an administrator does not tell a board what to do, and a board is in no way bound to adopt offered recommendations, it is important to acknowledge that the administrator probably has the broadest and most professional perspective of most issues facing the organization; the administrator's opinions and advice deserve thorough consideration. On the other hand, in matters where the chief administrator truly feels indecisive, the administrator's responsibility is to acknowledge the indecision and seek the board's guidance.

(C) COMMITTEE CHAIRS

It is frequently observed that the real work of a governing board takes place in committee meetings. If a board's committees are active, this is usually true. How active and effective a committee is rests squarely on its chair and the staff person assigned to work with it. Committee chairs have the same responsibilities for their committees as a board chair has for the full board.

Many committees never accomplish much because they are unclear about their purposes or do not know how to begin carrying them out. A good committee chair will overcome this inertia by taking the initiative to call meetings and by requesting appropriate staffing from the administration. If the chair is inert, two members of the committee may call a meeting without the chair. A designated staff member needs to work closely with the chair to prepare meeting agendas, to gather information and serve as resource persona for the committee, and to make meeting arrangements.

If a committee has been inactive when a new chair is appointed, the chair's first tasks are to review the committee's purpose with its members and to establish goals and objectives. Ideally, these will be integrated and coordinated with the goals and objectives of the whole board and of the other board committees.

All committee work is subject to the approval of the full board, and the chair is responsible for presenting committee reports at full board meetings or executive committee meetings. In making committee recommendations to the board, the chair must include dissenting opinions. Moreover, if the recommendation requires a full-board vote, the dissent must be permitted to present its points of view.

Committee chairs should prepare an annual written report of the committee's activity. Given the leadership skill required of the task, chairing committees provides an excellent training ground for higher positions on a board.

6.6 Committee Functions

There are two types of committees: standing and ad hoc (also known as special committees). Both standing and ad hoc committees may establish subcommittees to deal with issues in a more focused way. Standing committees receive their charge from the bylaws, and function on an ongoing basis. Ad hoc committees, which are created by the board to address special issues that are not ongoing, are dissolved as soon as their charge has been expedited. Pohl (1990) cited five ways to establish committees:

1. A board chair can appoint a committee.
2. A board chair can nominate a committee to be approved by full-board vote.
3. The committee can be nominated from the floor.
4. The committee can be named as part of a motion.
5. The committee can be nominated by ballot.

(A) STANDING COMMITTEES

The number of standing committees a board has varies among boards. There is wisdom in keeping the number of standing committees on the lean side, particularly if the board is not large. A good practice is to have standing committees address ongoing issues, and handle everything else with subcommittees or ad hoc committees. The five standing committees that are prevalent among boards are described in the following subsections.

(i) Executive Committee

Large boards and boards that transact a lot of business between full-board meetings need to have executive committees over which the board chair usually presides. Membership includes board officers and, sometimes, the chairs of standing committees. The responsibilities of an executive committee vary among organizations but usually include: making interim decisions for the board (to be ratified by the full board at its subsequent meeting); overseeing the long-range and strategic planning of the organization; and serving as a sounding board for new programs or policies that should come before the full board eventually. Minutes of executive committee meetings should be sent to the full board of trustees.

(ii) Finance Committee

This committee works closely with an organization's chief financial officer and chief administrator in making recommendations to the full board about asset management, endowment investment, debt management, indemnification, and other aspects of risk management. The committee also oversees monthly financial statements and a proper audit. Members of this committee usually have experience in business and finance and can lend perspective to the institution in investment counseling and in budget planning. Other areas of responsibility that sometimes come within the purview of this committee include: overseeing the buildings and grounds of the organization, personnel policy management, and review of the cost effectiveness of programs.

(iii) Development Committee

This committee, acting in concert with the chief development officer, has the responsibility of planning annual fund-raising programs and capital campaigns. Plans should address major donor cultivation and encourage the involvement of the organization's constituencies in the process. It is important to correct the popular misconception that development committees have the sole responsibility for raising funds. The whole board must participate in helping the organization raise its level of gift and grant income.

(iv) Program Committee

The nature and responsibilities of program committees vary greatly according to the type of service a nonprofit organization provides. Schools will have academic policy committees to review the timeliness, effectiveness, marketability, and cost of the educational programs being offered. Social service agencies' and health care organizations' program committees will review the viability and effectiveness of their programs and services. Community organizations will review how well the programs are meeting the mandates of their funders. Cultural organizations will assess how well their offerings are being received by their publics. Regardless of the type of nonprofit, however, the role of the board's program committee is to become thoroughly familiar with the programs and services offered by the organization and to assess program needs in terms of the institutional mission, financing required, and future trends.

(v) Nominating/Membership Committee

Most organizational bylaws charge a nominating or membership committee with the task of preparing a slate of candidates for membership and board offices. The committee is frequently appointed by the chair of the board, although appointments sometimes require full-board approval. It is an old saw that the nominating committee is the most powerful because it controls the slate and can "pack the court." Normally, terms of board membership are staggered to prevent the nominating committee from making changes that are too radical. Moreover, the committee only has the power to nominate; final appointment to the board usually requires a membership or full-board vote. Nevertheless, because new membership is a key change agent, a nominating or membership committee can indeed influence the future of the board.

Another role of this committee—one that is most often neglected—involves stewardship of members. The purview of stewardship includes assessing the mix of characteristics and constituency representations on the current board and identifying future recruitment needs. Stewardship also involves recruiting new members effectively and educating them about the roles they will be expected to play when they come on the board. The means of fulfilling these responsibilities are discussed later in this chapter.

(B) AD HOC COMMITTEES

Unlike standing committees, ad hoc committees are formed to carry out a specific charge and are dissolved as soon as that charge has been completed. Another difference is that ad hoc committees are more likely to have nonboard membership. For example, if a board chair names a search committee for a chief administrator, the committee may (and should) include members from a cross-section of constituencies, in addition to board members, so that the committee is representative of the organizational community. Another example of a board-initiated ad hoc committee that should include a cross-section of nonboard members is a strategic planning task force.

At the time they are formed, ad hoc committees should receive a specific statement of mission along with a deadline for accomplishing it. They report to the full board in the same manner as standing committees. Examples of charges given to ad hoc committees include: drafting a bylaws revision; planning a fund-raising event, or conducting a feasibility study for a new program. When an organization is running a capital campaign, the board can name a special committee, apart from the development committee, to conduct solicitation of board members.

6.7 Individual Board Member Responsibilities

Even if a board member holds no office and chairs no committee, he or she has important responsibilities to fulfill both in and out of the boardroom.

(A) IN-HOUSE RESPONSIBILITIES

(i) Preparing for Meetings
Adequate preparation involves reviewing the minutes, financial statements, and all reports received prior to meetings, and having a working knowledge of parliamentary procedure.

(ii) Attending Board Meetings Regularly
Each board member has been elected to represent and articulate a valuable point of view in discussions and votes.

(iii) Raising Questions Through the Chair
In the boardroom, constructive dissent should be welcome. If a pending action is unclear to a member or if a member opposes an action, he or she should speak out. If a member feels further information is necessary before a vote is taken, the information should be requested without hesitation.

(iv) Representing the Entire Organization
Board members often face the dilemma of having come from a particular faction of the organization and having to vote against the group's interests. The fiduciary and ethical responsibility of the member is to represent the entire institution—not an individual constituency. Although a board member can and should present any constituency's point of view during discussion, the greater good for the organization should ultimately influence an individual's vote.

(v) Voting Ethically
Conflict of interest occurs when a board member has a relationship to a party who has a stake in a decision the board is about to make. If this is a temporary situation or a one-time conflict, the member can simply abstain from voting on the issue at hand. If the conflict is more permanent, the member must consider resigning from the board. Conflict of interest is discussed in detail later in this chapter.

(B) ROLE OUTSIDE THE BOARDROOM

Outside the boardroom, a board member's job is best characterized as ambassadorial, and, depending on a member's motivation and creativity, the ways and means of carrying out this role are limitless. Minimally, members should attend the organization's functions whenever possible, stay informed about programs and projects sponsored by the organization, and contribute to all fund-raising projects. Apart from fund raising, individual board members have six roles to play outside the boardroom:

1. Taking the initiative to connect corporate funding contacts with the organization;
2. Taking the initiative to make foundation contacts for the organization;

3. Cultivating individual donors for the organization;
4. Helping to promote the organization's services and good reputation.
5. Supporting politicians and legislation favoring the mission of the organization; and
6. Reporting all outside activity on behalf of the organization to the chief administrator or the development officer.

6.8   The Board–Staff Relationship

As long as boards have existed, there has been controversy over where the line of board authority stops and that of administrative authority begins. It is easy to say that a board's job is to make policy and the staff's job is to execute it. However, most organizations do not enjoy a clear-cut distinction in their board-staff functions.

Balance is the key to good board-staff relationships. Conrad and Glenn (1986) used the image of a teeter-totter balancing on a fulcrum, to illustrate the concept of good board-staff relations. When the board is too involved, it weighs operations down and the staff is held up in the air. When the staff is too powerful and not working with the board, the board is held up in the air. When a board and its staff are in balance, the result is a dynamic tension; no one is weighed down nor left in the air; both board and staff are using each other's weight to achieve the desired balance.

There are times when it is appropriate for the board to become more involved in administrative affairs. Times of transition for the organization, times of crisis, and periods when there is no chief administrator in place are examples. As a general guideline, however, it is appropriate for a board to ask questions of its administration; when that board begins to answer its own questions, it is crossing the balance boundary.

6.9   Legal Issues Related to Board Membership

As Tremper and Babcock (1990) have noted, legal liability for nonprofit organizations has been increasing to the point where charitable immunity affords little guarantee that an organization and its board cannot be sued. Boards must prepare themselves to deal with the possibility of legal suits. Risk insurance and indemnification are worthy options that can minimize liability, but the best protection is for the administrators and the board to let their decisions be guided by a sound knowledge of their fiduciary responsibilities. Those responsibilities fall into three categories: the standard of care, the duty of loyalty, and the duty of obedience.

(A)   STANDARD OF CARE

A nonprofit board has a fiduciary responsibility to protect the assets of the organization. An organization's money, people, property, good will, and integrity are all considered assets. When a board member fails to protect them, the law considers the failure to be a breach in the duty of care. Consequently, a board member must always act in good faith and in the best interests of the organization. In making good-faith decisions, the member may rely on information prepared by officers of the organization, by legal counsel, and by a committee of the board. The member can assume, with reasonable certainty, that each source has acted responsibly and competently. However, because different states have varying degrees of protection for directors who delegate decision making to committees, board members and administrators are well-advised to check out the laws in their own state (Kurtz, 1988).

(B) DUTY OF LOYALTY

In the eyes of the law, board members owe the nonprofit organization the loyalty of placing its interests above all others. The preponderance of breach of loyalty suits occurs in two areas: conflict of interest and improper loans to board members.

(i) Conflict of Interest
Conflict of interest occurs in two ways:

- When a board member makes decisions out of self-interest or in the interest of only part of the institution instead of for the common good of the whole organization; and
- When an institution makes a transaction with a business or organization that has a financial connection with a board member or a board member's family.

When financial connections exist, it is incumbent on the board member to refrain from involvement in any decision making that is related to the connection.

To protect an organization from legal repercussions, its board should require board members to sign a written policy statement on conflict of interest when they join the board. Exhibit 6.3 presents a sample statement and questionnaire used by the National Center for Nonprofit Boards. Where it is unclear whether conflict of interest exists, the board can vote to decide, but the safest course of action is to seek legal counsel. Kurtz (1988) has suggested other ways for a board to avoid conflict of interest situations:

1. Select a financially disinterested board;
2. Have a balance of power between the board and the chief administrator;
3. Have a policy that goes further than the law's requirements; and
4. Have an attorney review the policy.

The last point is especially important. The law is becoming increasingly complex about conflict of interest, particularly because many board members serve on more than one board.

(ii) Loans
Loans by the organization to its officers and board members are another source of breach of loyalty. Currently, 30 states ban such loans, but 20 others have at least a limited legal provision for making loans to officers and board members (Kurtz, 1988). A board should be reticent to make loans to employees or directors because, even when they are legal, they are likely to cause the organization negative public and legal scrutiny once they are disclosed.

EXHIBIT 6.3 Policy on Potential Conflicts of Interests

The Board of Directors of the National Center for Nonprofit Boards has adopted the following policy designed to avoid any possible conflict between the personal interests of Board members or staff and the interests of the Center.

The purpose of this policy is to ensure that decisions about Center operations and the use or disposition of Center assets are made solely in terms of the benefits to the Center and are not influenced by any private profit or other personal benefit to the individuals affiliated with the Center who take part in the decision. In addition to actual conflicts of interest, board members and staff are also obliged to avoid actions that could be perceived or interpreted in conflict with the Center's interest.

Conflicts of interest may occur when the Center enters into transactions with not-for-profit organizations as well as those that are undertaken with profit making entities. The best way to deal with this problem is to make known one's connection with organizations doing business with the Center and to refrain from participation in decisions affecting transactions between the Center and the other organization. Such relationships do not necessarily restrict transactions so long as the relationship is clearly divulged and non-involved individuals affiliated with the Center make any necessary decisions.

Policy

1. *Directors.* Any member of the Board of Directors who may be involved in a Center business transaction in which there is a possible conflict of interest shall promptly notify the Chairman of the Board. The Trustee shall refrain from voting on any such transaction, participating in deliberations concerning it, or using personal influence in any way in the matter. The Trustee's presence may not be counted in determining the quorum for any vote with respect to a Center business transaction in which he or she has a possible conflict of interest. Furthermore, the Trustee, or the Chairman in the Director's absence, shall disclose a potential conflict of interest to the other members of the Board before any vote on a Center business transaction and such disclosure shall be recorded in the Board minutes of the meeting at which it is made. Any Center business transaction and such disclosure shall be recorded in the Board minutes of the meeting at which it is made. Any Center business transaction which involves a potential conflict of interest with a member of the Board of Directors shall have terms which are at least as fair and reasonable to the Center as those which would otherwise be available to the Center if it were dealing with an unrelated party.

2. *Staff.* Any staff member who may be involved in a Center business transaction in which there is a possible conflict of interest shall promptly report the possible conflict to the Executive Director. If the possible conflict involves the Executive Director, the possible conflict shall then be reported to the Chairman of the Board.

The Executive Director, or where applicable, Chairman, after receiving information about a possible conflict of interest, shall take such action as is necessary to assure that the transaction is completed in the best interest of the Center without the substantive involvement of the person who has the possible conflict of interest. (This does not mean that the purchase or other transaction must necessarily be diverted, but simply that persons other than the one with the possible conflict shall make the judgments involved and shall control the transaction.)

Each board member and senior staff member shall complete the attached questionnaire on an annual basis.

A written record of any report of possible conflict and of any adjustments made to avoid possible conflicts of interest shall be kept by the Executive Director or, where applicable, Chairman.

3. *Definitions.*

  A. "Involved in a Center business transaction" means initiating, making the principal recommendation for, or approving a purchase or contract; recommending or selecting a vendor or contractor; drafting or negotiating the terms of such a transaction; or

EXHIBIT 6.3 (*Continued*)

authorizing or making payments from Center accounts. That language is intended to include not only transactions for the Center's procurement of goods and services, but also for the disposition of Center property, and the provision of services or space by the Center.

B. A "possible conflict of interest" is deemed to exist where the Director, or staff member, or a close relative, or a member of that person's household, is an officer, director, employee, proprietary, partner, or trustee of, or, when aggregated with close relatives and members of that person's household, holds 1% or more of the issued stock in the organization seeking to do business with the Center. A possible conflict is also considered to exist where such a person is (or expects to be) retained as a paid consultant or contractor by an organization which seeks to do business with the Center, and whenever a transaction will entail a payment of money or anything else of value to the official, member, to a close relative, or to a member of that person's household.

A "possible conflict of interest" exists when an individual affiliated with the Center has an interest in an organization which is in competition with a firm seeking to do business with the Center if the individual's position gives him or her access to proprietary or other privileged information which could benefit the firm in which he or she has an interest.

A "possible conflict of interest" exists when an individual affiliated with the Center is a trustee, director, officer or employee of a not-for-profit organization which is seeking to do business with or have a significant connection with the Center or is engaged in activities which could be said in a business context to be "in competition with" the programs of the Center.

4. This policy statement shall be made available to each trustee and each person appointed to a Center position which regularly involves initiation, review or approval of significant Center contracts or other commitments. Such people will be asked to sign the attached acknowledgment concerning reporting of potential conflicts of interest.

I have read and understand the Center's policy on Potential Conflicts of Interest. I agree to report promptly any such interest which arises in my conduct of Center business and, in other respects, to comply with the policy and its procedures.

_____ (Signed)

_____ (Date)

EXHIBIT 6.3 (*Continued*)

CONFLICT OF INTEREST QUESTIONNAIRE
National Center for Nonprofit Boards

Name _____

Office or Position Held _____

In responding to these questions, please note that a "yes" answer does not imply that the relationship or transaction was necessarily inappropriate.

1. Are you an officer or director of any corporation with which the National Center for Nonprofit board has business dealings?

   Yes_____   No_____

   If the answer to the foregoing question is "yes," please list the names of such corporations, the office held and the approximate dollar-amount of business involved with the National Center for Nonprofit Boards last year.

   _____
   _____
   _____
   _____
   _____
   _____

2. Do you, or does any member of your family, have a financial interest in, or receive any remuneration or income from, any business organization with which the National Center for Nonprofit Boards has business dealings?

   Yes_____   No_____

   If the answer to the foregoing question is "yes," please supply the following information:

   a. Names of the business organizations in which such interest is held and the person(s) by whom such interest is held:

   _____
   _____
   _____
   _____
   _____

   b. Nature and amount of each such financial interest, remuneration or income:

   _____
   _____
   _____
   _____
   _____

3. Did you, or any member of your family receive during the past twelve months any gifts or loans from any source from which the National Center for Nonprofit Boards buys goods or services or with which the National Center for Nonprofit Boards has significant business dealings?

   Yes_____   No_____

EXHIBIT 6.3 *(Continued)*

If the answer to the foregoing question is "yes," list such gifts or loans as follows:

Nature of Source   *Item*   *Approximate Value*

_____

_____

_____

_____

4. Were you involved in any other activity during the past year that might be interpreted as a possible conflict of interest?

Yes_____ No_____

If "yes," please describe:_____

_____

_____

_____

_____

_____

I certify that the foregoing information is true and complete to the best of my knowledge.

_____   _____

Date   Signature

Used by permission from the National Center for Nonprofit Boards, 2000 L St., NW, Suite 411, Washington, DC 20036; 202-452-6262.

(C)   DUTY OF OBEDIENCE

This duty is carried out simply by honoring the stated intentions of an organization's founders and donors. Aside from the ethics involved, organizations have a fiduciary responsibility to spend money received from gifts in a manner consistent with the wishes of the donor. If the donor's intent cannot be honored, or if it is not in the best interest of the organization to honor it, the gift should not be accepted. The best way to avoid litigation in this area is to weigh a donor's gift designation against the organization's mission as well as against the founders' intent. It is also important for the organization to adhere strictly to the organization's governing documents and tax code regulations.

It is not unheard of for nonprofit organizations to be called into court for failure to honor terms of endowment bequests made to them decades ago. Terms of bequests often stipulate that the remains of a trust or endowment revert to another party if its provisions are not met. Would-be inheritors are often alert to an organization's transgressions in this area and will go to court in attempts to gain control of the principal.

6.10   *The Concept of Board Development*

Board members frequently become discouraged because they struggle with board staff involvement issues, because they are not powerhouse fund raisers, or because they do not have an active committee structure in place. In the face of discouragement, it is especially helpful for a board to view itself as an evolving organism and adjust its expectations to its maturational level. It is also helpful for boards to realize that, as with maturing children, change does not occur without growing pains.

(A) MATHIASEN'S STAGES OF BOARD DEVELOPMENT

Karl Mathiasen (1990) has described three developmental stages that nonprofit boards normally go through in the process of becoming a mature board.

(i) The Organizing Board
In this first stage, boards either follow a visionary leader or are steeped in doing the actual hands-on work of the organization. If an organization succeeds at this stage, it will experience strains that will force a board to change. The succeeding board will need to become less of a cheerleading unit for the founder and take a stronger role in governance; the hands-on board may need to turn over its heavy operational involvement to a stronger chief administrator. Either way, transition will lead a successful board into the second stage.

(ii) The Governing Board
At this stage, committee structures usually develop and the board-staff relationship becomes clearer. The board also begins to understand and accept its fund-raising role. Some boards remain in this stage forever, but if the organization grows and achieves widespread recognition, the board will evolve once again.

(iii) The Institutional Board
In this final stage, a board has become larger, has many well-connected members, and focuses primarily on fund raising. The governing activities are handled by a powerful executive committee. Although all boards do not fit these stages exactly. Mathiasen's model can help a board understand where it is in its evolution and lends insight into where the board is headed.

(B) STAGES OF INDIVIDUAL BOARD MEMBER DEVELOPMENT

There are also stages in the involvement of individual board members. Conrad and Glenn's model of board member involvement and contributions (Exhibit 6.4) suggests that, if handled effectively, a board member's activity with the organization is also likely to evolve over time as the member goes through stages of awareness, affiliation, observation, participation, and commitment. It is the administration's job to track the progress and to nurture the development of individual board members.

6.11   Elements of Board Development

There are four major elements in the board development process: self-assessment and selection of board candidates; the recruiting process for new members; orientation of new members; and increased involvement of board members.

EXHIBIT 6.4 Conrad and Glenn's Involvement-Contribution Ratio

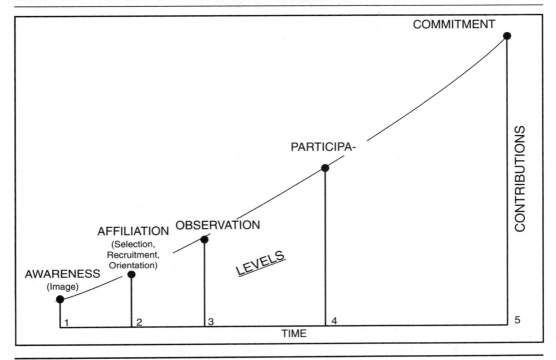

Source: W. R. Conrad and W. E. Glenn, *The Effective Voluntary Board of Directors.* Downers Grove, IL: Voluntary Management Press, 1983, p.197. Reproduced by permission of W. R. Conrad.

(A) SELF-ASSESSMENT AND SELECTION OF BOARD CANDIDATES

As described earlier, the work of the nominating or membership committee sets the future course of the board. It is also the key change agent of the board.

(i) The Board Audit

To carry out its tasks effectively, a nominating committee should conduct an annual board audit to help determine what desired characteristics current board members possess and what special-interest and constituency groups they represent. The literature on nonprofit boards contains many examples of grids or worksheets for conducting audits, but, to tailor an audit to its particular needs, an organization can create its own. Exhibit 6.5 illustrates a sample grid and lists the steps of an audit.

The best way to guarantee that a board will have a composition matching its needs is to view nominations as a long-term process. Last-minute nominations run the risk of selecting weak members or members whose strengths are not needed.

(ii) Identification of Candidates

In the short term, candidates should be very obvious: they will already be close to the organization through committee work and volunteer activity. Planning for the long term, how-

EXHIBIT 6.5 Board Membership Audit Worksheet

Steps:
1. Make a list of characteristics and skills needed in board members, prioritize them and enter them at the top of the grid columns.
2. List the names of current board members in the first column.
3. Assess each board member. Check (✔) the boxes to show characteristics and skills each board member has.
4. Determine when current members' terms expire, and project representation needs for 3 future years, to get a long-range perspective on recruiting.
5. Check (✔) the appropriate boxes to show the characteristics and skills that will have high priority in the new recruits who will replace the outgoing members.

Board Representation Audit

Name	Characteristics and Skills Needed								
Current members:									
New recruits:									
Year 1									
Year 2									
Year 3									

ever, requires early identification of prospective board candidates. The staff and all board members should report suggestions for future candidates to the nominating committee. Civic leaders who might have an interest in the service the nonprofit provides, volunteers serving on auxiliary boards, and donors to similar programs, are all possibilities. Accounting firms and advertising or public relations firms that have a sense of civic duty often encourage their executives to participate in nonprofit organizations and can be a source of skilled board members. Another important resource for identifying board candidates is community leadership programs.

(B) THE RECRUITING PROCESS

It is one thing to identify candidates for board membership; inviting them to serve is another story. There is a correlation between time and success in recruitment: the more time spent recruiting a board member, the better that member will perform on the board. Ideally, the nominating committee should have a long-range plan for board recruitment that includes several years of cultivation of board candidates. The development committee and development officer should work with the nominating committee to make certain that potential board members are being cultivated.

In the shorter term, there are more immediate tactics to consider in effective recruiting. When it gets down to the time to issue the actual invitation to serve, there are eight guidelines for the process:

1. Always recruit in person. Recruitment by letter or telephone sends the message that membership is not very important.
2. Be honest about the current circumstances of the organization. Describe the problems and the weaknesses of the organization as well as its strengths.
3. Clarify expectations about the recruit's financial obligations to the organization.
4. Explain exactly what serving entails. Discuss time commitment, meeting requirements, committee activity, and the need to attend organizational events.
5. Strategize the asking. A senior staff member, preferably the chief administrator, and a board member should do the actual recruiting. Decide where the candidate would be most comfortable.
6. Answer the "Why me?" question. Candidates need to get a sense of why they are wanted. Recruiters should explain specifically what the candidate personally can contribute to the organization.
7. Ask the candidate to think it over. At the invitational meeting, the recruiter should never accept an answer but should, instead, ask the candidate to take at least a week to think over the commitment. Responsible board membership is a serious commitment that is not made spontaneously.
8. Show the recruit around. If a recruit has not seen the organization's facilities or attended events where the fruits of the organization's labors can be seen, the administration should arrange it. It is critical that the candidate have a sense of the organization he or she would represent as a board member. It is the responsibility of the administration to arrange and host on-site visits with candidates.

(C)   ORIENTATION OF NEW MEMBERS

Board members frequently comment: "It seems like I just got the hang of things with this board in time for my term to end." Such remarks indicate that effective orientation has not occurred. With a proper introduction to the issues and procedures of the board, there is no reason why new members cannot begin contributing to the organization from the first day of their term.

Both the staff and fellow board members have roles to play in orienting a new board member. Although there is no one correct way to conduct orientation, there is one desired result—to make the new members feel welcome and acquaint them with the people and the work of the board. Following is a list of approaches to orientation that have served boards well:

1. The buddy system. Assign new board members to experienced board members who will make sure that new members get answers to questions.

EXHIBIT 6.6 Sample Table of Contents for a Board Manual

[In preparation of a board manual, the following sample table of contents provides a generic organizational outline. Content for the manual can be drawn from this chapter and existing documents of the organization.]

**THE ABC NONPROFIT ORGANIZATION
BOARD OF DIRECTORS MANUAL**

Table of Contents

   I. An introduction that explains the scope of the manual.
  II. A description of the purpose and functions of the ABC board.
 III. A description of how the ABC board operates: how members are nominated, their terms of office, how officers are selected, when and where regular meetings occur, and how committees generally operate.
  IV. A statement of attendance expectations for meetings and a description of events at which a board presence is called for—ceremonies, annual dinners, special events, and fund raisers. This section might also include expectations regarding board member visits to the ABC facilities.
   V. A list and explanation of the ten responsibilities of a board.
  VI. A description of the charge of each ABC board committee.
 VII. An explanation of the responsibilities of individual board members, placing special emphasis on the fact that all members have a role to play in the fund-raising area.

Suggested Appendices

The ABC organization's mission statement
Articles of Incorporation and Bylaws of ABC
A copy of the organization's conflict of interest policy
A sample meeting agenda
An explanation of fund accounting
The ABC organization's gift acceptance policy
Current facts about ABC (e.g., number of clients served, special program recognitions, program facts)
A brief history of the ABC organization

---

2. The board manual. Give new members a board manual that outlines all board procedures and policies. Exhibit 6.6 shows a sample table of contents for a board manual.
3. Meeting minutes. Give new members copies of minutes of the previous year's meetings.
4. Social event. Host an introductory event to give the incoming members an opportunity to meet current members in a context outside of the boardroom.
5. Delegation of doable tasks. As soon as new members come on board, give each of them a task that is easy to carry out to help them get invested in the organization from the start.
6. Orientation session. Host a formal orientation session at the facility, to give new members background information on committee issues, to explain board procedures, to answer questions, and to introduce them to staff.

(D)   INCREASED INVOLVEMENT OF BOARD MEMBERS

Board development theory suggests that increasing member awareness and interest requires continuous nurturing. As the model in Exhibit 6.7 indicates, a board can mature, but it is never fully developed. As seasoned members move off the board, the uninitiated come into the cycle, each bringing different perspectives and experience, and each having different nurturing needs.

The chief ingredients in developing a board is good communication between staff and board. Although both the board and staff share the responsibility for good communication, it is the staff's responsibility to facilitate the exchange of information and to anchor efforts to increase member involvement. There are two complementary approaches to increasing board involvement: giving sincere, appropriate recognition to board members, and creating a sense of community. There are also many indirect ways to increase members' understanding of and involvement in fund raising.

EXHIBIT 6.7 The Board Membership Process

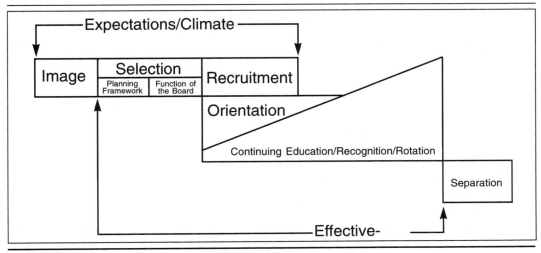

Source: *W. R. Conrad and W. E. Glenn,* The Effective Voluntary Board of Directors *(Downers Grove, IL: Voluntary Management Press, 1983), p. 130. Reproduced by permission of W. R. Conrad.*

(i) Recognition

A critical factor in nurturing the commitment of board members is appropriate recognition of their efforts. For some members, "appropriate" means a simple thank-you note; for others, it means a formal public citation for contributions made to the organization. In all cases, "appropriate" means sincere recognition for real contributions. It is the responsibility of the staff to make sure that board members' contributions are not taken for granted—particularly with those members who are consistently selfless and hardworking. Even among the most dedicated board members, burnout is a very real phenomenon. The staff must make it as easy as possible for these members to do their jobs and should give them all the credit for the results—even if 99 percent of the work was done behind the scenes by the staff.

In addition to staff recognition of board efforts, the board chair should pay attention to giving credit to the work of committees and individual members in full-board meetings. Finally, board members should be given the limelight in public events and media coverage, to strengthen their commitment and sense of identification with the organization.

(ii) Creating a Sense of Community

People generally do not join boards for social reasons. Nevertheless, if people are strangers, they will not work together as well as they will when they know and like one another. Having a sense of fellowship and community with the board is an important factor in getting members to show up for meetings and in influencing how deeply they will dig into their pockets for fund-raising projects. Having an occasional dinner after a meeting, or staging an annual event such as a golf or tennis outing just for board members and spouses or guests, may afford the opportunity for board members to form relationships with one another. Overnight board retreats also serve this purpose.

(iii) Fund Raising

Except for the rare member who has a decided talent for it, board members greatly dislike fund raising. "I hate asking for money" is a standard phrase. If members are enthusiastic about what the money will do for the organization, they are more willing to get involved in raising it. Some members simply need training, to gain confidence in their own ability to ask for gifts. Even the board members who have no hope of becoming good solicitors can develop more positive attitudes about fund raising through indirect involvement with it. The following strategies help to increase the involvement of reluctant board members:

1. Have a board retreat, to consider mission and set goals. This will help members understand the purpose of fund raising.
2. Have the board view and approve a written set of fund-raising policy guidelines. Those who attach a negative connotation to fund raising will feel better about the integrity of the process.
3. Have board members meet major donors. It is inspiring to hear donors discuss why they give.
4. Make sure that members get recognition for whatever they do to help with fund raising, even if their participation does not involve solicitation.
5. Develop a time-line of the history of the organization in a group setting, as part of a special meeting. This helps a board that is becoming more

involved in fund raising to understand how and why it has reached a point where it is important to focus on raising money.

6. As a "toe in the water" tactic, get board members involved in identifying donor prospects.

7. Have board members get close to the activities and the people who are supported by fund raising.

8. Have the board take part in a phonathon with other volunteers, or have them lead pace-setting calling sessions. This will ease tentative solicitors into the process in a pleasant setting where they will have a lot of support.

9. Ask board members to help cultivate prospects by spending time with them. They can take prospects to lunch, visit them in their offices, or ask them to come to the board member's office. The purpose of the meetings is to educate the prospects about the work of the organization—not to solicit.

10. Do things that help board members get to know one another, as a way of increasing their commitment to the group and helping them to accept the fund-raising process more comfortably.

6.12 Dealing with Resistance to Board Development

There are many reasons why board members may resist development. They may have served a long time under a strong chief executive who required nothing of them, and they may like their token status. Boards in transition from a controlling or organizing board status to governing board status may have members who are reluctant to give up their hands-on decision-making power to a stronger chief administrator. Other members might resist change when a previously non-fund-raising board decides it must become active in fund development.

Administrators and board members who are eager to improve their boards' performance need to develop long-term perspectives; change is not easy. The only rapid way to change a board is through crisis. Outside of crisis-motivated change, however, board development is a plodding process that happens through two approaches that have mutually dynamic effects on each other: triage and new membership.

(A) TAKING ADVANTAGE OF CRISIS

The most dramatic changes occur on boards in times of crisis. Even the worst resisters will move when an organization is faced with critical survival issues such as a decision to close its doors, the termination of a chief administrator, the eruption of a scandal, or the threat of a lawsuit. In moments such as these, board members are often forced into making decisions that they would have stalled over had there been no crisis. There is a downside to crisis-motivated change: it is easier to make bad decisions in times of crisis.

(B) THE PRACTICE OF TRIAGE

Like most voluntary groups, boards usually have three factions: those who perform up to or beyond expectations without prodding; those who would perform well if choreographed and educated; and those who will not respond to any intervention by staff and fellow board members. When a board is particularly inert and unresponsive to energizing efforts, it is best to retrench and to work only on the individual members in the second faction. Through personalized attention and the delegation of very clear, time-specific, and doable tasks (followed up, close on the heels of their completion, with recognition from the staff and the board chair), this faction will become more involved. Over time, this strategy will activate the majority of the board and, when this happens, those in the obdurate third faction will cycle off the board.

If a board's bylaws have a section that empowers the board to remove members for nonattendance at meetings, nonperforming members can be removed through those means. This does not usually occur in practice, however; most boards are reluctant to be so direct about "kicking off" a member. Moreover, some of the most ineffective board members seem to be those who attend meetings regularly but are not prepared to contribute to the business at hand.

(C)   NEW MEMBERS AS CHANGE AGENTS

Wise selection of new members is the most effective way to achieve positive change on a board because the minute one active new member arrives, the entire dynamics of the board changes. Because new members have not been mired in ongoing struggles over tough decisions, they arrive with fresh perspectives. Even one new member can change the whole political balance of a board, perhaps allowing the passage of policies that would have failed earlier. Sometimes the arrival of a new member is all that is needed to recharge burnt-out members. Thus, new members are indeed the key change agents for boards.

(D)   FORMATS FOR ADDRESSING CHANGE

There are times outside of crisis when boards recognize the need to change but are not certain how to go about it. In these cases, there are three basic formats for addressing change as a group: conducting a retreat, using a consultant, and conducting a bylaws review.

(i)   Conducting a Retreat

If the majority of board members will commit a day or two of their time to sequestering themselves at a location away from the traffic of normal day-to-day business, a retreat can be a very effective way to get members to look at the board and the performance of individual members in a constructive and introspective fashion. To be effective, retreats should be well-planned and organized around a particular, predetermined charge. The following list suggests situations that may call for a retreat:

1. When a new administrator is hired, a board retreat can focus on clarifying board and administration roles and responsibilities.
2. When there is a major decision to make, such as a change in mission or program, a retreat can afford a board an opportunity to consider the issue thoroughly, in isolation from normal board business.
3. When an organization has a major conflict to resolve, and board and staff are willing to make good-faith attempts to resolve it, a board retreat can provide a time-limited format in which to negotiate a resolution.

4. When an organization is about to undertake a strategic planning process, a board retreat with selected staff members and constituency representatives can provide the means of reviewing the mission and identifying the strategic issues facing the organization.

5. When a board is considering a major fund-raising campaign and needs to get the entire board committed to it, a board retreat offers a forum for discussing the rationale and the case for the campaign.

In addition to being held in an out-of-the-way location, retreats should be facilitated by a person who is not connected with the organization and who will keep the agenda on track without being suspected of favoring a particular point of view. The agenda and format will vary according to the needs and the charge. It is wise to conduct a preliminary survey with open-ended written responses or to require every participant to do pertinent advance reading, to help everyone come to the retreat with a similar point of reference and sense of purpose. Good retreats need 3 to 6 months of planning so that appropriate arrangements can be made and relevant information can be gathered. Board members also need that much notice in order to block such a large chunk of time on their calendars.

(ii) Using a Consultant

Use of a board development consultant is an option that boards and administrators are using with increasing frequency. A consultant can be effective in fostering change within a board or change in the working relationship between the board and the chief administrator. Because consultants work from an external perspective and have a broad base of experience, they often have new ideas to offer when a board seems to be spinning in its tracks. Moreover, because they function outside the political climate of the organization, they can speak candidly to the chief administrator and board members without fear of reprisal or without being accused of harboring a hidden agenda. Finally, because consultants get paid for their point of view, their advice is often accepted by the full board more readily. The following list presents interventions that consultants commonly use to help boards:

1. They advise a new nonprofit organization about how to structure its board and they help prepare its documents.

2. They design board assessment instruments tailored to the circumstances of the organization, as opposed to using standardized instruments.

3. They conduct constituency research and interviews aimed at gathering information needed for the board to make important decisions or to plan strategically.

4. They present organization models and facilitate deliberations over a board restructuring process.

5. They work with individual board committees to forge statements of purpose and identify goals and objectives with action plans for implementation.

6. They facilitate planning and decision-making sessions.

7. They give workshops that address board members' involvement in fund raising and the improvement of members' solicitation skills.

8. They facilitate retreats.

(iii)   Bylaws Review as Change Agent

A bylaws review is an effective means of getting the board to focus on how it functions and to evaluate the individual responsibilities of board members. The advantage of this approach to change is that the decisions made are clear and enforceable by virtue of the revised document. The disadvantages are that a bylaws review will only be able to focus on structural and procedural matters, and that the process does not directly address member performance standards and desired characteristics of a performing member.

6.13   Resources for Continued Board Development

One of the most well-known and well-established resources for information and services related to boards is the Association of Governing Boards of Universities and Colleges (AGB). This organization is a research clearinghouse for postsecondary and independent school trusteeship. It offers board mentoring services, publications on various aspects of boards, and a bimonthly magazine for member institutions.

In response to the proliferation of new nonprofits outside of the education arena, the AGB and Independent Sector secured grant funding for the creation of the National Center for Nonprofit Boards (NCNB) in 1988. This center does for non-educational-related nonprofit boards what the AGB does for college and university boards. Through the NCNB, board members and administrators can find easy access to recent resources and educational materials about board roles and responsibilities. In addition to a newsletter and publications catalogues, NCNB offers board mentoring and retreat facilitation services at reasonable costs. Perhaps most valuable is NCNB's accessibility by telephone; inquiries regarding very specific board problems will either be answered over the telephone or directed to an appropriate source for response.

The increasing academic interest in the workings of the nonprofit sector has given rise to a number of research institutes and graduate programs in nonprofit management. Among the most notable of these are the National Center for Postsecondary Governance and Finance, at the University of Maryland, and the Case Western Reserve University Mandel School for Nonprofit Management. Nonprofit organizations can check with their own local institutions of higher education for library and consulting resources.

In addition to university resources, The Foundation Center in New York City will provide a list of locations of its affiliate libraries around the nation. These libraries have materials on nonprofit board development and management as well as files of materials about local consultants. Independent Sector is another organization that serves as a clearinghouse of information for nonprofit initiatives and offers publications about boards of directors. Following is a list of resource centers for information on nonprofit boards:

The Association of Governing Boards of Universities and Colleges
One Dupont Circle, Suite 400
Washington, DC 20036
Telephone: 202-296-8400

The Foundation Center
7 East 54th Street
New York, NY 10022
Telephone: 212-620-4230

Independent Sector
1828 L Street, NW
Washington, DC 20036
Telephone: 202-223-8100

Mandel School for Nonprofit Management
Case Western Reserve University
11235 Bellflower Road
Cleveland, OH 44106
Telephone: 216-368-2290

National Center for Nonprofit Boards
2000 L Street, NW, Suite 411
Washington, DC 20036
Telephone: 202-452-6262

National Center for Postsecondary Governance and Finance
4114 CSS Building
University of Maryland
College Park, MD 20742-2435
Telephone: 301-405-5582

Suggested Readings

Bryson, J. M. 1989. *Strategic Planning for Public and Nonprofit Organizations*. San
   Francisco: Jossey-Bass.
Conrad, W. R. and Glenn, W. E. 1986. *The Effective Voluntary Board of Directors*. Athens,
   OH: Swallow Press.
Dalsimer, J. P. 1991. "Understanding Nonprofit Financial Statements: A Primer for Board
   Members." Washington, DC: NCNB Governance Series.
Frantzreb, A. C. 1988. *Nonprofit Organization Individual Governing Board Audit*. McLean,
   VA: Arthur Frantzreb.
Ingram, R. T., et al. 1988. *Handbook of College and University Trusteeship*. San Francisco:
   Jossey-Bass.
Ingram, R. T. 1990. "Ten Basic Responsibilities of Nonprofit Boards." Washington, DC:
   NCNB Governance Series.
Kurtz, D. L. 1988. *Board Liability: Guide for Nonprofit Directors*. New York: Moyer Bell Ltd.
Mathiasen, K., III. 1990. "Board Passages: Three Key Stages in a Nonprofit Board's Life
   Cycle." Washington, DC: NCNB Governance Series.
Nason, J. W. 1990. "Board Assessment of the Chief Executive: A Responsibility Essential
   to Good Governance." Washington, DC: NCNB Governance Series.
Paltridge, J. G., White, F., and Ingram, R. T. 1986. "Self-Study Criteria for Governing
   Boards of Independent Colleges and Universities." Washington, DC: AGB.
Pohl, A. N. 1990. *Committees and Boards: How to Be an Effective Participant*. Lincolnwood,
   IL: NTC Publishing Group.
Tremper, C. and Babcock, G. 1990. "The Nonprofit Board's Role in Risk Management:
   More Than Buying Insurance." Washington, DC: NCNB Governance Series.

7 The Board of Directors: Strategic Vision for the Volunteer Corps

JEFFREY L. BRUDNEY, MA, Ph.D.
University of Georgia

7.1 Introduction

In discussions of the responsibilities of boards of directors in nonprofit organizations, providing a strategic vision for the volunteer corps has typically received scant, if any, attention. Apparently, this function—if indeed it has been taken to be a function of the nonprofit board—does not rank high in importance. For example, in Barbara A. Burgess' (1993) chapter on "The Board of Directors" in nonprofit organizations, which appeared in the first edition of this *Handbook* (Connors, 1993), setting a vision for the volunteer corps is not among the responsibilities defined for the board. Two classic books on boards, by Cyril Houle (1989) and John Carver (1990), are, likewise, silent on this issue. Perhaps one might read into these and other treatments of the nonprofit board a concern with volunteers: Authorities concur that the board of directors has ultimate legal, financial, and policy responsibility for the nonprofit organization, and for bringing all aspects of its operations, which would include the volunteer component, to bear on its mission. Yet, this concern has been implicit rather than explicit. The relationship of the nonprofit board of directors to the volunteer program has not been clarified, and the task of establishing and implementing a strategic vision for the volunteer corps has been overlooked.

The self-renewing organization, both as the theme of this edition of *The Nonprofit Handbook: Management,* and as the type of institution necessary to grapple with an increasingly volatile, interdependent, global marketplace, requires a much more sustained and specific focus on volunteers. To survive and thrive in this competitive environment, the self-renewing organization must put each of its resources not just to good, but to superior use. To do so, the board of directors must develop a strategic vision for the volunteer corps. The board must seriously consider, appraise, implement, and support a vision that will galvanize volunteers (and paid staff) toward the attainment of the exciting future members conceive for the organization.

This chapter elaborates how the board of directors of a nonprofit organization can create and sustain a motivating strategic vision for the volunteer corps. It first explains why, despite the manifest importance of volunteers to most nonprofit organizations, the volunteer program does not typically rank high on the list of board priorities. To achieve a strategic vision, this situation must be rectified; the chapter provides effectual methods. The following section describes the strategic vision for the volunteer corps. The vision should articulate the organization's philosophy and purpose for having volunteers and the goals to be pursued into the future. Finally, implementation of the vision for the volunteer corps will require support from the board of directors. To actualize the vision, the board will need to provide for three key elements discussed in the chapter: a basic structure for the volunteer program consisting of leadership positions and a budget, appropriate policies for the program, and risk management and insurance protection for nonpaid personnel. By creating a stimulating vision and affording it the requisite support, the board of directors can be confident that they have brought the self-renewing organization closer to fruition.

7.2 Surmounting Board Inattention to the Volunteer Program

As Susan J. Ellis (1995, p. 1) correctly observes, "While the vast majority of nonprofit organizations involve volunteers in direct service and support roles, the subject of volunteers is rarely raised in the board room." Boards of Directors might give comparatively little attention to volunteers for a variety of reasons. The different reasons or explanations constitute a series of syndromes, which must be overcome in the interest of achieving the self-renewing organization. Although the particular syndrome varies from one nonprofit board to another, the effect is to deter consideration of the volunteer program and, consequently, to limit the opportunity to integrate the program more completely with the rest of the organization and to improve performance. Exhibit 7.1 briefly describes four general board syndromes.

(A) THE "MICROMANAGEMENT" SYNDROME

Probably the greatest reluctance and obstacle to board involvement with the volunteer corps is the seemingly benign desire or intention to stay out of areas of day-to-day organization management. No board wants to be accused of micromanagement, that is, infringing on the legitimate prerogatives of the chief executive officer (the official at the highest level of the organization, usually a paid office) to administer the agency according to its mission and the policy pronouncements of the board. Contemporary treatments strongly encourage the board to "govern" rather than to "manage" the affairs of

---

EXHIBIT 7.1 Board Syndromes that Inhibit Attention to the Volunteer Program

---

- The Micromanagement Syndrome: Nonprofit boards with this syndrome do not devote systematic attention to the volunteer program because this activity strikes board members as meddling in agency management.
- The Discomfort Syndrome: Nonprofit boards with this syndrome do not devote systematic attention to the volunteer program because this activity could expose status differences between board and service volunteers uncomfortable to board members.
- The Overgratitude Syndrome: Nonprofit boards with this syndrome do not devote systematic attention to the volunteer program because this activity could result in a new arrangement in which not all citizen contributions could be accommodated or welcomed.
- The Devaluation Syndrome: Nonprofit boards with this syndrome do not devote systematic attention to the volunteer program because this activity implies and could reveal the value and usefulness of volunteers to the organization.

---

the organization (for example, Burgess, 1993; Carver, 1990; Houle, 1989). Among other major duties, the board is to review and protect the agency mission; act as fiduciary authority for the organization and ensure its financial solvency; and serve as spokesperson and ambassador for the organization externally and represent the viewpoints of community and stakeholders internally. From this perspective, the volunteer component shrinks in significance to a managerial matter in which program purpose, design, and execution can be safely and appropriately left to the discretion of organizational staff.

(B) THE "DISCOMFORT" SYNDROME

The board of directors in nonprofit organizations consists of citizens who are not compensated monetarily for their efforts. So, too, does the service volunteer corps, which is often identified simply as the "volunteer program." While both groups are volunteers, status differences between them are apparent, though usually submerged in the daily crush of organizational activities. Some boards fear that if these differences were to be raised explicitly, however—for example, through the creation of a vision or policies for service volunteers—they would lead to debilitating resentment and conflict among nonpaid personnel. As a result, these boards choose the path of least resistance and avoid matters of governance for the volunteer program.

Board and service volunteer positions have many differences. As discussed above, the board exists to attend to significant matters of organizational mission, policy, finances, and representation; the volunteer program assists in delivering agency services (for example, helping clients) and in maintaining the organization (for example, clerical tasks). The nomination, recruitment, and turnover of the small number of board members tend to be very selective and celebrated; given the heavy demands upon them, nonprofit organizations cannot afford to be nearly as particular in attracting the numerous service volunteers needed, and fanfare is notably absent from their entry into (and exit from) the agency. The actions of the board are highly visible to the organization and often the community; the important work of the volunteer program on behalf of the agency is typically carried out in relative obscurity. Board expert John Carver summarizes that service volunteers play a helping role in the organization, while board members have an "ownership interest rather than a *helpfulness interest*" (1990, p. 16, emphasis in original).

On one level, board and service participants are equally volunteers, who seemingly should be accorded the same respect, appreciation, and recognition in the organization. On another level, though, distinct functions and responsibilities are expected of the two groups, which if fully enacted by the board would reveal status differences among volunteers. Some boards are uncomfortable with this ambiguity and shy away from it. They fear that conscious attention to the volunteer program will expose a "two-tier" or "two-caste" system that could provoke resentment and antagonism among nonpaid participants and, quite possibly, anxiety for themselves. Linda L. Graff (1995, pp. 139–140) describes a tension between "equality or elitism" that confronts the board of directors, consisting of volunteers, should they try to devise organizational policies to apply to other, nonboard (service) volunteers. This tension can be debilitating: Carver warns that "some connotations of volunteerism can *detract* from the board's job, severely reducing its ability to lead" (1990, p. 16, emphasis in original). Concerned about unleashing new problems on the organization, these boards avoid reflective examination of the service-volunteer effort. Their discomfort with one group of volunteers overseeing or dictating to another stymies the creation of a strategic vision for the volunteer program.

(C) THE "OVERGRATITUDE" SYNDROME

The overgratitude syndrome occurs in those nonprofit organizations in which officials view having volunteers as sufficient or the end in itself. The degree to which the skills, talents, abilities, and labor of the volunteers are utilized constructively to meet the needs of clients and the agency is secondary, if considered at all. Organizations lacking a history or culture of volunteer involvement or expertise in volunteer program management can easily fall prey to this syndrome.

Rooted in incorrect stereotypes regarding volunteer participation, overgratitude is manifested in counterproductive organizational behaviors, such as a reluctance to evaluate the performance of volunteers or the program as a whole (evaluation is "threatening"), to sanction or discipline volunteers when appropriate (one cannot "fire" a volunteer), or to insist on adequate record-keeping (it smacks of "bureaucracy" and takes time away from "helping"). The message conveyed is that volunteers come first, and that any participation is valued. In an era in which recruitment of service volunteers has become a major obstacle to an effective program (Brudney, 1990), the spread and influence of this syndrome are understandable. Yet, in such an organizational climate, the board of directors may eschew oversight of the volunteer program: Members would not want to appear to question in any way the nature, extent, or quality of the involvement of service volunteers. Instead, having volunteers is the goal.

(D) THE "DEVALUATION" SYNDROME

At the opposite end of the continuum from this over-gratitude syndrome lies the devaluation syndrome. Instead of appreciating whatever contribution volunteers might make as in the former conception, in nonprofit organizations where the latter has taken hold, the volunteer corps is not viewed as sufficiently important to occupy the time or attention of the board of directors. Here, the volunteer program suffers from "benign neglect" from organization management and the board (Ellis, 1986). Nora Silver asserts, "By their actions, *boards establish an attitude toward volunteerism in their organizations.* Even by doing 'nothing,' they are saying something. In this situation, neutrality is akin to indifference and promotes the message that volunteerism is unimportant in the organization" (1988, p. 116, emphasis in original).

Other observers lament the prevalence of the devaluation syndrome in the nonprofit world. According to Graff (1993, p. 30), "For so long, volunteer programs have gone under-recognized and under-valued. . . . Managers of volunteer programs are often at the bottom of the organizational hierarchy, under-paid, over-worked, and taken for granted. Boards and senior management have lost touch with how important volunteers have become to service delivery and to the community life we all have come to enjoy."

(E) OVERCOMING NEGLECT OF VOLUNTEERS IN THE BOARDROOM

Regardless of the syndrome that may grip a particular nonprofit board of directors, or the organizational culture that gives rise to it, the consequence is the same: Most boards fail to devote attention to service volunteers and the volunteer program commensurate with their actual or potential importance and contribution to the agency (Ellis, 1995). This scenario represents opportunity and capacity squandered.

The nonprofit board of directors bears final responsibility and authority for allocating all organizational assets to their best use, whether paid staff members, revenue or endowment, facilities or production capacity. Volunteers constitute one of these assets. To create a strategic vision for the volunteer corps, the nonprofit board must realize that nonpaid staff are part of this resource mix. The self-renewing organization must learn to mobilize its volunteers to help in meeting the challenges of a turbulent, competitive environment.

Exhibit 7.2 lists a number of steps that boards can take to help internalize this new perspective on volunteers (compare Ellis, 1995). Although the suggestions are eminently practical, for many boards they represent a shift in culture, so that full integration will likely not be immediate.

The board can begin by setting aside time at its meetings to discuss the volunteer program. On a regular basis, too, the board should call for reports from organization staff describing the membership and performance of the volunteer corps. The board can invite representatives of the volunteers to some of its meetings; for example, the volunteer coordinator might appear periodically. Orientation sessions and related materials for board members should treat the volunteer program, dealing with such facets as goals, size, oversight, and responsibilities; joint orientation sessions for board and service volunteers can also be enlightening.

EXHIBIT 7.2 Overcoming Board Syndromes: Steps toward Taking a Strategic View of the Volunteer Program

- Set aside time at board meetings to discuss the volunteer program.
- Call for reports from organization staff describing the membership and performance of the volunteer corps.
- Invite representatives of the volunteers to some board meetings.
- Address the volunteer program in orientation sessions and related materials.
- Visit the organization periodically to observe the activities of volunteers and take part in them.
- Attend recognition events for volunteers.
- Recruit former service volunteers to some positions on the board.

From time to time, the board should visit the agency during working hours to observe the activities of the volunteers, and even take part in them. By attending recognition events for the volunteer program, board members can build greater understanding of the contributions of service volunteers and, simultaneously, convey formal organizational appreciation. When vacancies occur on the board of directors, recruitment might sometimes come from the ranks of those who have formerly assisted the organization as service volunteers. A nonprofit board might engage in a frenetic search for new members who possess extensive background and knowledge on the agency; when seasoned, former volunteers with the desired attributes are often close at hand.

7.3   Creating A Vision for the Volunteer Program

Once the board of directors has begun to embrace this new perspective on volunteers, it is ready to turn its attention to a crucial task: conceiving a vision for the volunteer program. As Brudney (1990, p. 121) elucidates, in designing the program and motivating participants, agency leadership must grapple with the fundamental question, "Why have volunteers?" James C. Fisher and Kathleen M. Cole (1993, p. 6) answer that the vision for the volunteer corps is a "beacon" intended to guide the organization toward its future purpose while simultaneously amplifying the meaning of its present activities.

Board members need not—and, almost certainly, should not—undertake this task alone. Enlisting the input and counsel of agency management, paid staff, volunteers, and especially the volunteer coordinator (see below) will not only yield fruitful ideas and directions but also help to generate acceptance and a sense of ownership of the program (compare McCurley and Lynch, 1989, pp. 20–21). While diverse participation in arriving at a vision is worthwhile, acceptance should not be mistaken for leadership. The vision represents agency policy and aspirations regarding volunteers at the highest level and should, therefore, emanate from deliberation at its apex, the board of directors: "As the board is ultimately legally responsible for the agency program, it is also responsible for the volunteer component. . . . This is one of the tasks that legitimately falls to the board, and the board must assume ultimate responsibility for the volunteer program in the agency" (Silver, 1988, pp. 115–116).

(A)   A FOCUS ON TWO DIMENSIONS

Although the content and format vary dramatically across organizations, typically, a vision communicates a value or ethical dimension for volunteer participation and an instrumental or strategic component. "It articulates an organization's values, communicates its priorities, and inspires behavior that reflects them" (Fisher and Cole, 1993, p. 7).

With regard to the values dimension, the vision should articulate why the organization esteems and seeks volunteers. The rationale often turns on the unique qualities that citizens can bring to an agency. These values include involvement and representation of the community, a more human touch and individual dignity in dealings with clients, more satisfying jobs for paid personnel, commitment to a cause, and credibility with the public and policy makers.

With respect to the instrumental dimension, the vision "will provide a quick and clear understanding of what benefit the agency thinks will be derived from utilization of volunteers, and provide a sense of purpose for the volunteer program." In essence, it should answer *why are we doing this?* (McCurley and Lynch, 1989, p. 19; emphasis in original). One of the most attractive features of volunteer programs is that the answers are manifold and robust. They range from decidedly economic motivations, for example, the potential for cost-savings, increased productivity, and additional labor and expertise, to less tangible, noneconomic motivations, for example, increased client outreach, enhanced agency responsiveness, greater public awareness, and stronger issue and client advocacy (Brudney, 1995, pp. 44–46). In sum, the strategic vision should express both the reasons that the organization values the participation of volunteers and the expectations it holds for their performance.

(B) FROM BOARD SYNDROMES TO STRATEGIC VISION

The process of creating a strategic vision for the volunteer program moves the board beyond the common syndromes discussed above that otherwise inhibit serious attention to the nonpaid component. First, a vision cannot be confused with micromanagement by the board. The vision is a concise statement of the values and ambitions that the board holds for the volunteer program. It is meant to capture what the organizational leadership hopes to accomplish through and with volunteers. The actual follow-through rests with agency staff. As Ellis (1995, pp. 7–8) explains to board members, "the board's role is not to focus on details, but to provide an outline for the staff to fill in. Your dreams set the direction for everyone to follow. . . . The organization's staff will consider the management details . . . but the board sets the framework for volunteer involvement."

Similarly, to provide a motivating vision for volunteer involvement, a nonprofit board of directors cannot be content merely with having and congratulating the present corps of nonpaid participants (the overgratitude syndrome). Nor can a board persist in overlooking the dedicated contributions of these personnel (the devaluation syndrome). Creating a vision requires board members to assess critically the present state of the volunteer program and to weigh this judgment against their aspirations concerning what the program could be, and should be, into the future. Their evaluation is likely to be mixed: Almost certainly the board will encounter negative elements of the program that should not have been condoned, let alone appreciated, as well as positive elements that should not have gone overlooked, let alone demeaned. Based on this appraisal and a survey of the organization environment, the board can chart novel directions for volunteer participation, for example, to introduce citizens with special expertise to complement paid staff, recruit more actively from minority groups (or youth, unemployed, handicapped, etc.), use volunteers to enter new service domains or to take on new projects, give volunteers greater responsibility for fundraising, intensify activity in a particular area, and so forth.

Finally, developing a strategic vision for the volunteer corps is an act of leadership on the part of the nonprofit board of directors. Although board members are volunteers, in formulating a vision for the program they must be forthright in stating their expectations and hopes for the involvement of other (service) volunteers in the organization. By keeping this governance function firmly in mind, the board should be able to surmount any discomfort that may arise with respect to possible status differences among fellow volunteers.

7.4 Supporting and Sustaining the Vision

As challenging as it may be for the nonprofit board of directors to craft a meaningful vision for the volunteer corps, the conception of purpose is not the endpoint in the process. The board must also see to supporting and sustaining the vision. The board has three main responsibilities in this connection: providing a basic structure for the volunteer program, determining policies to govern the program, and furnishing risk management and insurance protection.

(A) PROVIDING A STRUCTURE TO SUPPORT THE VISION

The two main elements necessary to support the vision for the volunteer corps consist of establishing (or approving) positions of leadership for the volunteer program and authorizing a budget for the program commensurate with its goals. Absent such backing from the top, even the most radiant of visions is destined to tarnish and fade. Worse still, failure of the board to provide this follow-through can breed cynicism regarding the credibility of the vision and the place of volunteers in the organization, a result that will surely undermine not only client outcomes but also progress toward higher levels of excellence, which is a hallmark of the self-renewing organization.

(i) Leadership Positions for the Volunteer Program

Experts agree that a successful volunteer program requires a leader, here called the Director of Volunteer Services (DVS) (Fisher and Cole, 1993; Brudney, 1990; Ellis, 1986; McCurley and Lynch, 1989). As detailed in Exhibit 7.3, the DVS position bears a number of leadership responsibilities.

Most important among them, the DVS is responsible for guiding the volunteer program toward fulfillment of the vision. Given this duty, she or he should participate actively with the board in its development and refinement. The charge to the incumbent is to implement the view of the future encapsulated in the vision—to effect the difficult

---

EXHIBIT 7.3 Leadership Responsibilities of the Director of Volunteer Services (DVS)

- Guide the volunteer program toward fulfillment of its vision (for example, communicate the vision, persuade staff to accept it, and inspire them to work toward its achievement).
- Serve as the focal point for contact with the volunteer program for both potential volunteers and employees.
- Represent the volunteers to the organization and facilitate their achievement and satisfaction on the job.
- Act as chief advocate of the volunteer program (for example, express the volunteer perspective, advance useful policies, facilitate collaboration between paid and nonpaid staff).
- Promote the volunteer program in the community through publicity, outreach, and recruitment.
- Promote the volunteer program internally (for example, work with departments and employees to meet their needs for volunteers, expand areas of volunteer participation, prepare job descriptions for nonpaid positions).
- Educate, orient, and train paid and nonpaid staff for volunteer involvement.
- Coordinate, evaluate, and recognize all facets of the volunteer program.

---

translation from rhetorical statement to organizational reality. To do so, she or he will need to communicate the vision throughout the organization; persuade staff, paid and nonpaid alike, to accept it; and inspire them to work toward its achievement (Fisher and Cole, 1993, pp. 8–11). In this manner, the DVS endeavors to align present practice with the volunteer program envisioned for the future. By establishing the position, the board of directors lodges accountability for the volunteer program and its results squarely with the DVS and, thereby, demonstrates its seriousness of purpose.

The DVS is the focal point for contact with the volunteer program for those outside the organization seeking to donate their time as well as those inside who may wish to enlist volunteers or to involve them more productively. The DVS represents the volunteers to other departments and the organization as a whole and promotes their achievement and satisfaction on the job. As the chief advocate of the program, the incumbent works not only to express the volunteer perspective and advance useful policies (see below) but also to allay any apprehensions of employees concerning volunteers and to facilitate collaboration between paid and nonpaid staff.

The DVS is responsible for volunteer recruitment and publicity, a critical function requiring active outreach in the community and highly flexible working hours. The incumbent communicates with department and organizational officials to ascertain workloads and requirements for voluntary assistance and takes the lead in preparing job descriptions for volunteer positions. Assessing agency needs for volunteers, enlarging areas for their involvement, and educating staff to the approach are not a onetime exercise but an ongoing responsibility of the DVS. The DVS interviews and screens applicants for volunteer positions, maintains appropriate records, places volunteers in job assignments, supervises them (or assists employees in this task), and monitors performance. The office coordinates the bewildering variety of schedules, backgrounds, and skills brought by volunteers to the agency. The DVS bears overall responsibility for orientation and training, as well as evaluation and recognition, of volunteers; training for employees, too, regarding volunteers flows through the position. Given the breadth and importance of these responsibilities, other positions of program leadership to support the DVS are likely to prove advisable and necessary (see Ellis, 1986, pp. 45–49).

The board of directors should authorize the DVS position but not infringe upon its prerogatives. The DVS must have the authority and creative license to guide the volunteer program toward the future envisioned. To achieve the strategic vision, the incumbent also needs a budget for the program.

(ii) Budget for the Volunteer Program

Susan Ellis (1995, p. 14) notes that when it comes to fund raising, the board of directors is accustomed to discussions of whether "it takes money to make money." Unfortunately, when it comes to "people raising"—the equally vital task of recruiting, retaining, and invigorating volunteers—the adage is not nearly so well-known or accepted. Because the term "volunteer" connotes free labor, the board and other organizational members are often unaware of the support costs that make a thriving program possible. Although a well-conceived and -managed volunteer program will generate a return in dedicated labor, talents, and caring (and often fund raising) many times greater than the budget invested in the endeavor, it still "takes money to make money." In this case, the investment underwrites the design and delivery of essential program activities. Without an adequate fiscal foundation, progress toward attainment of the strategic vision for the volunteer corps is imperiled.

Some of the more notable expenses incurred in an effective volunteer program include the salary of the DVS (usually a paid position in larger nonprofit organizations) and orientation and relevant training for volunteers and employees (including quality management techniques and skills). Major program components, such as promotion and outreach, recruitment and retention, screening and interviewing, evaluation and recognition, and administration and supplies, add to these costs. Extending organizational liability insurance to cover volunteer personnel is almost always an additional expense (see below). Reimbursement for the work-related expenses of citizen participants can quickly mount with the size of the volunteer contingent.

The board's job is not to prepare the budget for the volunteer program or to undertake a detailed review or audit of expenditures (unless circumstances should warrant). Instead, the obligation of the board is, first, to authorize a budgetary line for the program. The DVS should not have to implore other organizational units with different objectives for funds to sponsor her or his own unit. Absent an independent source of financial support, the incumbent cannot be held accountable to the vision. Secondly, the board should ensure that the amount of funding allocated is commensurate with the scope of the present volunteer effort as well as the future expectations held for it.

In most organizations, the budget is a reflection of priorities. When the nonprofit board of directors grants financial status as well as fiscal accountability to the volunteer corps, it affirms the rightful place of the program among competing agency goals. Conversely, a lack of budget (or leadership positions) dedicated to the volunteers transmits quite a different message to the organization and its members.

(B) DETERMINING POLICIES FOR THE VOLUNTEER PROGRAM

John Carver (1990, p. 30) writes, "To the extent a board wishes to provide strategic leadership, it must clarify policies and expect organizational activities to give them life." No less than in other areas of organizational life, the board should exercise policy leadership with respect to the volunteer program. Inevitably, policies express values and perspectives binding on the organization. The board of directors has the ultimate authority to render these judgments, for this body bears primary responsibility for governance of the agency.

While policies for the volunteer program may strike some as confining, a good policy is actually liberating (Carver, 1990). Well-crafted policies clarify what is, and is not, acceptable in controversial domains of organizational activity where debilitating uncertainty, confusion, and even conflict might otherwise dominate. A clear policy from the board will answer myriad operational questions, thus reducing delays and repeated checks with higher authorities. The policies set by the board of directors can empower the volunteer program: They spell out the boundaries within which participants can move freely and energetically in pursuit of the strategic vision.

(i) Policies for Sharing the Workplace

With regard to volunteers, the initial and most central policy issue facing the board addresses the positions volunteers are to occupy in the agency. What types of functions will volunteers perform, which are reserved for paid staff, and are any protections afforded to either group? Depending upon the organization, its culture and history, employees and volunteers might share the workplace in a number of effective ways. The process by which a suitable arrangement is reached is crucial. The board should take the lead, but seek active participation from agency management, the Director of Volunteer Services, employees, and volunteers (Brudney, 1995, pp. 53–55).

A host of other policy issues await deliberation by the board (Ellis, 1995, pp. 11-12). For example, the board will want to consider and authorize policies governing reimbursement for the job-related expenses of volunteers (What costs are to be covered?). The board will need to set basic requirements for entering volunteer service (interviews, background checks, references) and for meeting standards of appropriate behavior and performance on the job. These standards provide the framework for counterpart policies covering grounds for discipline and termination, a regrettable necessity in volunteer (and employee) programs no matter how worthwhile the endeavor or adroit its leadership. Policies for adjudicating disputes or grievances involving volunteers are another consideration.

(ii) Comparable Policies for Employees and Volunteers

Authorities generally advise organizational leadership to enact policies as comparable as possible for paid and nonpaid personnel (see Brudney, 1995, p. 48). They argue that by setting standards as high for volunteers as for employees, the agency engenders trust and credibility, increased respect and requests for volunteers from paid staff, a healthy work environment, an avoidance of stereotyping (for example, volunteers labeled and resented as "second class" workers and organizational citizens), and high-quality services. These attributes advance dramatically the prospects for achieving the self-renewing organization.

(C) FURNISHING RISK MANAGEMENT AND INSURANCE PROTECTION

Proposing and deliberating organizational policies can be a daunting task, sometimes requiring the board to revisit the rationale for the existence of the agency and the philosophy and purpose that should continue to animate it. Ignoring the need for policies for the volunteer program is far worse, however. Not only does this course mire the board in the dysfunctional syndromes elaborated above (and, in the process, sacrifice the benefits of good policy), but also it courts severe risk management problems. As Graff (1993, p. 130) counsels, "There is no more pressing reason to develop policies for volunteer programs than the role that policies play in an overall risk management system."

In many, if not most, nonprofit organizations, volunteers carry out mainstream activities, often placing them in direct contact with clients. Such responsible and complex work heightens their exposure to risk and hazard on the job. As the final authority, the board of directors is legally responsible for all operations carried out under the auspices of the agency, including the volunteer component; it is this entity that will be served in any potential legal action. The board can be held accountable for the mistakes, accidents, and negligence of volunteers acting on behalf of the organization. Under certain conditions, in fact, individual board members can be held legally liable, for example, for failing to exercise reasonable oversight and diligence over the agency (Graff, 1995, pp. 130–132).

While no person or organization can guarantee that accidents or mishaps will not occur, "policies can reduce an organization's exposure to liability in the event that a law suit is launched . . . there is no better proof that an agency has acted prudently and responsibly in attempting to reduce the likelihood of injury or loss than a full set of current, comprehensive policies and procedures, clearly in place, and consistently communicated to all relevant parties" (Graff, 1995, p. 131). By contrast, a nonprofit board that chooses, instead, to evade its policy responsibility and leave its nonpaid (or paid) staff exposed to needless risks or potential harm will have a difficult time attracting and keeping volunteers, much less motivating and sustaining them toward a strategic vision.

To protect the organization and themselves as individuals from the potential risks and hazards embodied in volunteering and to avert possible legal action, the board of directors should see to the development of a solid plan for risk management (Graff, 1995, pp. 130–132). Given the breadth of information needed, the amount of work entailed, and the far-reaching ramifications of the plan, the board should appoint a committee with wide organizational representation to deal with the issue. Risk management consists of essentially three steps: identification and evaluation of risks, development of strategies for reducing risks, and implementation and reassessment of the risk management plan (Kahn, 1993, pp. 912–913).

(i) Identify and Evaluate Risks

The first step consists of identifying and evaluating potential risks encountered in the volunteer program. Attorney Jeffrey D. Kahn (1993, p. 912) recommends that the risk management committee examine the activities of each volunteer position and list all the ways that the volunteer could cause injury to others, and all the ways in which the volunteer could be personally injured (identification). Next, the committee should evaluate which types of accidents are most likely to result in liability for the organization, which can be expected to occur most often, and which might cause especially great damage (evaluation). This procedure calls for consultation throughout the organization.

(ii) Develop Strategies for Reducing Risks

The second step in risk management is developing strategies for reducing, or possibly avoiding, the risks identified. Policies enacted by the board can be a powerful tool for minimizing the chances that accidents and organizational exposure will occur. For some agency activities, the committee may conclude that the risks are too great and recommend that the board make a policy decision to discontinue them (for example, handling toxic materials, staffing a suicide hotline, or offering medical advice).

In other areas, the committee may determine that the organization can limit accidents and potential risk to reasonable levels through board policies that would authorize rules and procedures for conducting some activities, training for paid staff and volunteers, and screening for certain skills (Kahn, 1993, p. 912). For example, board policies specifying that records checks and further inquiries must be performed before a volunteer is allowed to work with children (or other vulnerable clients) will markedly decrease the chances of an ill-advised job placement. Similarly, board policies requiring general orientation for volunteers as well as training appropriate to particular positions will cut down on mistakes and accidents. A board policy stating that a job description must accompany each volunteer position, which describes the backgrounds and skills necessary for the job as well as the duties and means of supervision, should have the same effect. Policies that clarify how various activities are to be performed (for example, agency vans must be used for all transportation of clients; client counseling is to be performed only by certified personnel, whether paid or nonpaid) also lessen agency risk and potential exposure. Well-designed board policies in the context of risk management not only limit the probability that accidents will occur but also help ensure that volunteer jobs are staffed and functions are performed as effectively as possible (Kahn, 1993, pp. 912–913).

(iii) Implement and Reassess the Risk Management Plan

The third step is to implement and make periodic assessments of the risk management plan. Implementation will proceed more smoothly and gain greater acceptance to the degree that leaders and managers are convinced that the risk management plan will help to decrease the liability of the organization and improve the operation of the volunteer program. Thus, involving representatives from throughout the organization in a risk management committee is a highly recommended strategy. Although the present discussion has centered on the volunteer program, the board should see to risk management for all organization staff, paid and nonpaid; the same three-step procedure can be used for employees (Kahn, 1993, p. 913). Since agencies, activities, and personnel change with the passage of time—possibly raising new or unforeseen hazards and risks—periodic assessment of the risk management plan is desirable.

Even when the board of directors of a nonprofit organization has invested substantial time and effort in formulating and implementing a risk management plan, accidents involving volunteers (or employees) can still occur. These occasions afford a good opportunity to evaluate the plan to see what changes might be warranted to prevent reoccurrence in the future. They also point up the need for liability insurance protection for volunteer workers.

(iv) Provide Insurance Protection

The risk management plan is a complement, not a substitute, for insurance coverage for volunteers. The risk management plan incorporates a sensible series of steps to identify, evaluate, and limit the risks and hazards associated with volunteer service in the organization. The board needs to make sure that the organization's liability insurance embraces volunteers as well as employees for those risks it has judged reasonable and necessary for the effective performance of the agency.

Insurance companies tend to be apprehensive about coverage for volunteers. Evidence that the board of directors has developed a risk management plan can help to persuade carriers of the merits of the agency (Kahn, 1993, pp. 913–914). Moreover, a nonprofit board that can show that it takes the volunteer program seriously enough to create a strategic vision and to bolster it with leadership positions, its own budget, and judicious policies, will, no doubt, encounter much less difficulty in securing the desired coverage for volunteers.

7.5 Conclusion

Nonprofit organizations are continually buffeted by the demands and vagaries of a complex, dynamic environment. At a time in which agencies are pressed to make efficient use of every available resource, most nonprofit boards have not settled on the volunteer program the sustained, comprehensive focus necessary to evaluate how this component might most productively contribute to the future they envision for the organization. Even in those instances where boards have considered the issue, they have not always seen to the support the program would need to become a vital player in this role. This situation represents resources and opportunity foregone.

Creating and supporting a strategic vision for the volunteer corps should rank as a priority in the self-renewing, nonprofit organization. This responsibility rests with the board of directors. Silver maintains that "*the commitment of the administrative leadership of an organization is necessary to raise the volunteer program to priority status.* Without the leadership behind it, a volunteer program—no matter how well organized and potentially viable and valuable—simply will not have the organizational power necessary to progress and develop" (1988, p. 117; emphasis in original). The nonprofit organization, its paid and nonpaid personnel, and, most of all, its clients and constituents, stand to benefit from this act of empowerment on the part of the board of directors.

Suggested Readings

Brudney, J. L. 1990. *Fostering Volunteer Programs in the Public Sector: Planning, Initiating, and Managing Voluntary Activities.* San Francisco: Jossey-Bass.

Brudney, J. L. 1995. "Preparing the Organization for Volunteers." In T. D. Connors, ed., *The Volunteer Management Handbook.* pp. 36–60. New York: Wiley.

Burgess, B. A. 1993. "The Board of Directors." In T. D. Connors, ed., *The Nonprofit Management Handbook: Operating Policies and Procedures.* pp. 195–227. New York: Wiley.

Carver, J. 1990. *Boards that Make A Difference: A New Design for Leadership in Nonprofit and Public Organizations.* San Francisco: Jossey-Bass.

Connors, T. D., ed. 1993. *The Nonprofit Management Handbook: Operating Policies and Procedures.* New York: John Wiley.

Ellis, S. J. 1986. *From the Top Down: The Executive Role in Volunteer Program Success.* Philadelphia: Energize.

Ellis, S. J. 1995. *The Board's Role in Effective Volunteer Involvement.* Washington, DC: National Center for Nonprofit Boards.

Fisher, J. C., and Cole, K. M. 1993. *Leadership and Management of Volunteer Programs: A Guide for Volunteer Administrators.* San Francisco: Jossey-Bass.

Graff, L. L. 1993. "The Key to the Boardroom Door: Policies for Volunteer Programs." *Journal of Volunteer Administration* (Summer), 11 (4):30–36.

Graff, L. L. 1995. "Policies for Volunteer Programs." In T. D. Connors, ed., *The Volunteer Management Handbook.* pp. 125–155. New York: Wiley.

Hodgkinson, V. A. and Weitzman, M. S. 1992. *Giving and Volunteering in the United States: Findings from a National Survey.* Washington, DC: Independent Sector.

Hodgkinson, V. A., Weitzman, M. S., Toppe, C. M., and Noga, S. M. 1992. *Nonprofit Almanac, 1992–1993: Dimensions of the Independent Sector.* San Francisco: Jossey-Bass.

Houle, C. O. 1989. *Governing Boards: Their Nature and Nurture.* San Francisco: Jossey-Bass.

Kahn, J. D. 1993. "Legal Issues in the Involvement of Volunteers." In T. D. Connors, ed., *The Nonprofit Management Handbook: Operating Policies and Procedures*, pp. 907–919. New York: Wiley.

McCurley, S. and Lynch, R. 1989. *Essential Volunteer Management.* Downers Grove, IL: VMSystems and Heritage Arts Publishing.

Silver, N. 1988. *At the Heart: The New Volunteer Challenge to Community Agencies.* Pleasanton, CA: Valley Volunteer Center.

8 Volunteer Management

JEANNE H. BRADNER, Consultant and Author

8.1 The Self-Renewing Volunteer Program

(A) THE CONSTANCY OF CHANGE

John Gardner, co-founder of Independent Sector, said "micromanagement is not the function of leaders. The task of leaders is to have a sense of where the whole system should be going and to institutionalize the problem solving that will get it there. *And the pace of change is such that they will find themselves constantly rebuilding to meet altered circumstances"* (emphasis added). To be effective, to serve the community, to take maximum advantage of volunteer time and talents, yesterday's volunteer programs must be constantly evaluated and reworked in the light of today's needs and today's volunteer force.

(B)   ASSESS AND REASSESS

The Metro Chicago Volunteer Coalition, a voluntary group of leaders of volunteer recruiting and volunteer-involving agencies, came together in 1995 to create a strategic plan for enhancing volunteerism in the Chicago metropolitan area. Through focus groups, open meetings, and surveys, the group discovered that few nonprofits did regular assessments to make sure that the current ways volunteers were involved were still the most meaningful to the agency's mission in the community.

Many volunteer managers become so immersed in micromanagement that it is tempting just to continue doing the volunteer program the way it's always been done. They need to have opportunities to step outside the day-to-day activities to determine, with the aid of other staff, volunteers, and board, the priority areas for involving volunteers. They need to make sure that their program is meeting the needs of their customer: the community they serve.

An organization cannot be self-renewing without realizing that the volunteer program is critical to renewal and community outreach. This is why it is important for the volunteer manager to be part of the agency planning process and for evaluation of the program, the volunteers, and the effects of the program on the community to be performed on a regular basis.

(C)   HAVING A SUCCESSFUL PROGRAM

In 1993, The Points of Light Foundation embarked on a study to determine the factors which facilitate or inhibit the effectiveness of volunteering in nonprofit and public sector human service organizations. They found that successful organizations could differ widely in their approach, but they shared "a commitment to continuous improvement and to challenging current practice in light of changing conditions." Volunteer managers need evaluations as a key to continuous improvement, and they need to be partners in the agencywide planning process to open the door and their imaginations to change and renewal.

(D) THE IMPORTANCE OF VOLUNTEERS TODAY

Volunteers are too important an asset to be taken for granted. They need to be viewed as central to the agency's mission. Volunteers today are of all ages, all races, all ethnic backgrounds and contribute time to agencies that the Independent Sector/Gallup Survey of 1994 estimates to be the equivalent of 8.8 million paid staff!

The opportunities for involving people are manifold: senior citizens, early retirees, families, young professionals, executives, middle management, labor unions, small business, homemakers, religious institutions, college service learning and intern programs, school community service classes, service clubs, fraternal organizations and stipended programs such as Foster Grandparents, Senior Companions, VISTA and AmeriCorps.

(E) THE IMPORTANCE OF BOARD AND CEO SUPPORT OF VOLUNTEERISM

A volunteer program can't be central to the mission of the agency, or self renewing, if it does not have the support of the board and the CEO. Board members, who are volunteers themselves, need to encourage the involvement of the direct service volunteers. A board member should have the assignment of liaison to the volunteer program; consult with the volunteer manager; be a member of the volunteer advisory committee; and represent the board's active interest in the volunteer program. Volunteers should be invited to the board meetings from time to time to share their first-hand experiences in the community.

CEOs need to include reports on the in-kind contributions made by volunteers along with the financial report, and need to regard the manager of the volunteer program as an important part of the Resource Development Department. The value of the time volunteers contribute is great and, in addition, as the Independent Sector survey points out, volunteers give twice as much money to charity as people who do not volunteer.

(F) THE IMPORTANCE OF THE MANAGER OF VOLUNTEERS

Effective volunteer programs need to be led by a skilled manager of volunteer human resources. Various titles are used: Director of Volunteers, Volunteer Manager, and Volunteer Coordinator. But meaningful programs that have a solid impact don't happen without the leadership of a person who can keep one eye on the mission and another on making maximum use of the talents volunteers have to offer while smiling, encouraging, and moving ahead. The following is a slightly tongue-in-cheek want-ad for a skilled volunteer coordinator, but it gives some notion of the skills required:

> WANTED: A manager and developer of resources valued at millions of dollars. Good communication skills, oral and written, are required, as well as thorough knowledge of community needs and services. Applicant must have an understanding of marketing principles to promote exchange of implicit and explicit benefits. Applicant must have the ability to work with people from all racial, economic, ideological, age and social backgrounds. Applicant must have a knowledge of psychology, participatory planning, motivation and human values. Applicant must possess the ability to lead and motivate others, be able to delegate authority, survive ambiguity and be innovative and creative. Applicant must strive for the highest standards in preservation of human dignity, personal privacy, self-determination and social responsibility. (Jeanne Bradner, Volunteer Illinois, Winter 1986)

8.2 The Steps in a Volunteer Program

(A) THE CONTINUUM

The following steps represent a volunteer program continuum:

1. Needs assessments.
2. Mission.
3. Policies.

4. Budget.
5. Risk management.
6. Job descriptions.
7. Recruitment.
8. Interviewing/Screening.
9. Orientation.
10. Training.
11. Guiding/Retraining.
12. Recognition.
13. Evaluation.
14. Reassessment, and then follow steps 1 through 13 once again.

8.3 Needs Assessments

(A) INVOLVING STAFF AND BOARD

Needs assessments serve the purpose of helping the volunteer manager find out what jobs the paid staff needs help with; but, equally important, they allow the staff to be a partner in determining how volunteers will be involved.

Exhibit 8.1 is a very simple needs assessment to circulate to staff. However, even more effective may be conversations at staff meetings, the strategic planning meetings where staff and board articulate their hopes and dreams for the agency and the volunteer manager's own observations of needs. Essential, however, to involving volunteers meaningfully is having staff and board view them as partners .

(B) WINNING STAFF SUPPORT

Staff will resist volunteers if they do not see them as genuinely helpful to them. "They're too much trouble; they won't show up on time; you can't fire them" are ways staff will indicate their unease about volunteers. The volunteer manager must show by word and practice that the volunteers in the agency will be regarded as unpaid staff; that there will be expectations that the volunteer will honor; and that staff will not be expected to continue working with volunteers who are not helpful to them.

CEOs can be helpful by articulating their commitment to the importance of the vol-

---

EXHIBIT 8.1 Staff Needs Assessment

What are some things you would like to see this agency doing for its clients and the community that it is not currently doing?

What parts of your job responsibilities do you wish you could delegate to someone else in order to free up your time for higher priority tasks?

What are those things you would like to have done, but that you don't have the skills and training to do yourself?

Do you have any concerns about involving volunteers in your work?

What assistance would you need before involving volunteers in your work?

---

unteer program; making sure that staff are rewarded for working effectively with volunteers; and stressing to staff the importance of the management experience they gain by working with volunteers.

8.4 *Mission Statement*

(A) THE REASONS FOR A MISSION STATEMENT

A mission statement for the volunteer program helps paid staff, policy volunteers (the board), and direct service volunteers (unpaid staff) understand the importance of the program. Just as the organization mission testifies to why the community needs the agency and what is special about it, the volunteer program mission should state why the volunteer program is important to the agency and what is special about it.

(B) THE IMPORTANCE OF VOLUNTEERS

Think about why volunteers are important to the agency. They:

- Amplify services.
- Represent the community.
- Are credible in the community in volunteer recruitment, fund raising, and advocacy because they are not paid for their work.
- Often are more effective than paid staff with clients because they are working with them voluntarily.

(C) A GOOD AGENCY/VOLUNTEER PARTNERSHIP

Think about the relationship the organization wants to have with volunteers: For example:

- Regard them as unpaid staff.
- Respect them.
- Involve them in ways that are meaningful to them, the agency, and the community.
- Help them grow and learn.
- See them as resources that are as valuable to the agency as money.

(D) A SAMPLE MISSION STATEMENT

Hammer out the wording until you and everyone who reads it can say, "yes, that's why we have a volunteer program; that's why it's important; that's why people will want to be involved." For example: "In this community, many young people need role models to expand their horizons and help them make decisions about their future. Volunteers are integral to the XYZ agency's efforts to meet this need. Part-time, trained volunteers can make a difference in young people's lives. The volunteer human resources are welcomed. They permit the XYZ agency to expand and amplify the services it provides in the community."

8.5   *Policies*

(A)   THE IMPORTANCE OF POLICIES

Policies will be constantly changing to meet new circumstances and will differ among agencies, depending on the agency mission. But it is important to start a program with some statements that reflect the values and principles of the organization, the expectations of volunteers, their expectations of the agency, and the parameters within which they will work. Clear policy guidelines help management make equitable decisions, and set a framework within which people can operate.

Policies are essential to good risk management of a program, and as the manager defines the risks present in the various volunteer jobs in the agency (see Section 8.8), the manager will expand the policy statements to encompass them.

Volunteers should be given a copy of the policies at their orientation and asked to review them and to sign a paper indicating that they have reviewed them.

(B)   AGENCY EXPECTATIONS OF VOLUNTEERS

Policies vary from agency to agency depending on demands and priorities. The following are a few areas to consider. Policies should be no harsher for volunteers than they are for paid staff:

- Professional attitude (e. g., confidentiality, notification of absence).
- Faithfulness to the job description.
- Adherence to agency rules and regulations.
- Participation in training.
- Criminal records checks (when working with vulnerable populations).
- Reference checks.
- A valid drivers' license and car insurance (when driving as an agent of the agency).
- Trial periods.
- Drug-free workplace.
- Dress.
- Use of telephone.
- Health tests, if needed.

(C)   VOLUNTEERS' EXPECTATIONS OF AGENCY

- Orientation and ongoing training.
- Guidance.
- Evaluation.
- Participation in decisions affecting their assignments.
- Equal employment policies.
- Expense reimbursement.
- Insurance.
- To be treated as unpaid staff.
- Suitable assignments.
- Personnel file.

- Grievance procedures.
- To know the reasons a volunteer can be dismissed.

(D) A SAMPLE POLICY

Policies are broad statements of belief and restrictions which serve as guidelines for administration. For example:

It is expected that all volunteers in this agency will keep in confidence any information learned about clients during the performance of their volunteer duties. Failure to do so can be a reason for dismissal of the volunteer.

See Chapter 11 for more information on policies. Many of the policies formulated for paid staff will be equally appropriate for the unpaid volunteer staff.

8.6 *Budget*

Volunteers are very cost effective, but they are not free. A budget will be needed in most agencies for:

Salaried Personnel

- Salary and benefits for a skilled volunteer manager with excellent people skills.
- Salary and benefits for an administrative assistant to keep records and generally assist the manager.
- Professional development (e.g., volunteer management conferences, subscriptions, memberships).

Volunteers

- Reimbursement of volunteers' expenses(e.g., parking and carfare).
- Recognition events (e. g., lunches, dinners, coffees, awards—from coffee mugs to plaques).
- Training.
- Insurance for the volunteers (see risk management, Section 8.8).
- Uniforms, if required.

Operating Expenses

- Printing.
- Administration (e.g., computer, fax, telephone, postage, supplies).
- Space.

8.7 *Job Descriptions*

(A) NEW VOLUNTEER JOBS

When volunteer managers review suggestions made by staff for new positions, they need to analyze whether they are appropriate for volunteers to do. Some of the questions to consider are:

- Is it something that can be done on a part-time basis?
- Is it cost effective to supply the necessary training for a volunteer to do this job?
- Is it something a volunteer would want to do?
- Is it a worthwhile job?

(B) PREPARING THE JOB DESCRIPTION

If you don't know what you want the volunteer to do, how will they know? Therefore, as in all human resource management, the volunteer needs a job description that spells out responsibilities. The job description (see Exhibit 8.2) is the volunteer manager's blueprint to designing a recruitment strategy to find people who are interested and able to do the job (see recruitment, Section 8.9).

(C) THE JOB DESCRIPTION AS RISK MANAGEMENT

The job description is an absolutely essential risk management tool. It clarifies what the volunteer should do and protects the volunteer and the agency. Once the volunteers are recruited and accepted, they and the volunteer manager should sign the job descriptions, demonstrating that they have read and understood it.

EXHIBIT 8.2 Volunteer Job Description and Contract

Job title:

Supervisor: Location:

Objective: (Why is this job necessary; what will it accomplish?)

Responsibilities: (What specifically will the volunteer do?)

Commitment: (Short term; long term; hours)

Qualifications: (What special skills are needed? Can all ages do it? Does the job require any particular educational background?)

Policies: (e.g., confidentiality, criminal records check, code of behavior, prohibited activities)

Training provided:

Benefits: (Transportation, insurance, parking, expenses)

Trial period (probation):

References required:

Other:

Signatures to be added at time of mutual agreement:

Date:

Signature of volunteer:

Signature of supervisor:

8.8   Risk Management

(A)   VOLUNTEER MANAGEMENT AND RISK MANAGEMENT

Good volunteer management is good risk management. Interviewing, screening, orientation, training, guidance, and policies are part of the risk management process.

The volunteer manager should analyze the job descriptions prior to recruitment and determine what risks are involved in the job to the volunteer and to the agency. (See Exhibit 8.3.) The manager should then decide how to manage the risks or reluctantly decide to avoid the risks by not involving volunteers in that particular work.

(B)   PROTECTING THE VOLUNTEERS

Managers of volunteers must remember that volunteers

- Must have a safe working environment.
- Should not be asked to do jobs paid staff would not be asked to do.
- Should not be asked to do jobs paid staff is doing without equal training.

(C)   PROTECTING THE AGENCY

Many states today have legislation limiting the liability of volunteers to acts that are willful and wanton, that is, with a deliberate intent to cause harm. But agencies must be careful to make sure that volunteers are well trained and have clear job descriptions so that the difference between willful and wanton and specified duties is clear. By so doing, the agency is also protecting itself.

For example, a telephone reassurance program for latchkey children states clearly in its job description and policies that volunteers are to have no personal contact with the children beyond the telephone. Clearly, a volunteer who violates this is "willful and wanton" and not acting as an agent of the program.

(D)   INSURANCE THAT COVERS VOLUNTEERS

Agency umbrella liability policies can be expanded to cover both paid staff and volunteers as named insured. In addition, inexpensive liability and excess automobile and

---

EXHIBIT 8.3 Targeted Volunteer Recruitment Analysis

What do I need? (Skills and commitment required. Would the ideal person be motivated by affiliation, achievement, or power?)

Who could do this job? (Flexibly evaluate the times and places the commitment could be fulfilled, the training you will offer, and the diversity of volunteer resources available to you.)

What do they need and want from me? (Training, child care, flexible time commitment, experience, affiliation, achievement, power?)

How can I reach them? (Where do they live, work, go to school, worship?)

What should be my message? (Consider program mission and the motivation of potential volunteer.)

---

accident insurance is available for volunteers. Consult the index for locations where more information on these legal issues can be found.

8.9 *Recruitment*

(A) UNDERSTAND VALUES EXCHANGE

The closer a manager of volunteers can come to meeting the needs of the volunteers while *at the same time* meeting the needs of the program, the more successful he or she will be. Therefore, starting with the development of the recruitment strategy, the successful volunteer recruiter tries to match the needs of the program with the needs of the volunteer. Questions the recruiter must keep in mind continuously are: What can a volunteer get out of the volunteer experience? Who are the people most likely to find satisfaction in the opportunity? How can the program give them a motivational paycheck that will keep them interested?

If the manager worries only about the needs of the program, the volunteers are likely to feel unappreciated and quit. But equally important, if the manager worries only about the needs of the volunteer, the program will suffer. Balancing these needs is essential to good volunteer management.

(B) WHO VOLUNTEERS

Potential volunteers are all around us. The Independent Sector survey *Giving and Volunteering in the United States*, 1994 edition, conducted by the Gallup Organization, shows that 48 percent of those from age 18 and over volunteered an average of two hours a week. While this represented a 5 percent decline since the 1992 survey, the decline was largely in informal volunteering, while formal volunteering in organizations was almost level at 15 billion hours, the equivalent of 8.8 million full-time employees. The value of the time is estimated at $182 billion. In addition, volunteers gave an average of 2.6 percent of their income to charity, while nonvolunteers gave 1.1 percent of their household income.

Among Independent Sector's findings were that memberships in religious organizations and other organizations were a positive indicator of volunteer involvement and charitable giving. Volunteer experiences when young are the most important positive influences on giving and volunteering when older. The largest increase in volunteerism (5%) was among persons who are over 75 and retired. And an important fact to remember for volunteer recruitment is that people are four times more likely to volunteer when they are asked.

(C) FINDING POTENTIAL VOLUNTEERS

Sources from which to recruit volunteers include:

- Volunteer centers, which will try to match prospective volunteers with an agency and job description appropriate to their talents.
- Retired and senior volunteer programs, which involve almost half a million people age 55 and above in volunteer opportunities.
- School, college, and university service learning and community service programs.

- Service clubs, such as Rotary, Kiwanis, and Altrusa.
- City Cares programs, which involve young professionals in projects in major urban areas.
- Corporate, business, and labor volunteer programs.
- Senior centers and retirement homes.
- Religious groups.
- Professional organizations (e.g., accountants, lawyers).
- Executive Service Corps for management volunteers.
- National Retiree volunteer Coalition (groups of retired employees who volunteer under the auspices of their former employer).
- American Association for Retired Persons.
- Alumni groups.
- Sororities and fraternities.
- Stipended programs (e.g., VISTA, AmeriCorps, Foster Grandparents, Senior Companions).
- Open houses.
- Volunteer fairs.

(D) DEVELOPING STRONG AND DIVERSE VOLUNTEER SUPPORT

(i) Ask Them

The Gallup Survey tells us that people of all ages are four times as likely to volunteer if someone asks them . . . particularly someone they know. Fund raisers have known for years that "you don't get if you don't ask," and a person the potential donor respects is the most effective person to do the asking.

In his 1996 book *Designs for Fund-Raising* (so effective that it was reprinted in 1988 by the Fund-Raising Institute), Harold Seymour posits two hypotheses that are equally important for managers of volunteers, who, after all, are also in development work:

1. The most universal and deep-seated fear that people have is xenophobia— fear of the stranger.
2. We all aspire to be sought out and to be worthwhile members of a worthwhile group.

This is why person-to-person recruitment works so well. Because someone who is known to potential volunteers is doing the asking, volunteers are assured that they are not getting involved in something strange or unsavory. Volunteers also know that the group must be worthwhile because the person doing the asking is worthwhile.

(E) PLANNING FOR CULTURAL DIVERSITY

In our society, however, person-to-person asking sometimes breaks down when programs want, as they should, to involve a cross section of the community and need to recruit for ethnic, racial, age, and economic diversity that is not already present in the program. Here setting up an advisory group made up of leaders from the groups the program wishes to involve can be helpful in learning whom and how to target. Sometimes cultural sensitivity training is necessary for both current paid staff and volunteers.

Many programs fail to be as effective as they might because recruiters or volunteer managers have a limited notion of whom to involve. In addition to the diversity mentioned above, think about involving:

- Clients.
- People with disabilities.
- Unemployed people.
- Ex-clients.
- Families of clients.
- Donors.
- Interns.
- Offenders sentenced to community service.
- Displaced homemakers.

When recruiting any groups, however, one must again think of what they need from the program. Clients, people with disabilities, unemployed people, ex-clients, and displaced homemakers, for example, might like to work as volunteers for a limited period of time in exchange for some job training, a personnel file, and a letter of recommendation. Donors might enjoy hands-on experience and some involvement with people rather than always being viewed as writers of checks. Interns might work for a college credit or for experience in the area in which they have concentrated. Offenders, while required to serve, might consciously or unconsciously be looking for something they can care about.

(F) PLANNING FOR DIVERSITY OF COMMITMENT

As managers think about their needs, they are likely to think that those needs can only be met between the hours of 9:00 A.M. and 5:00 P.M. on weekdays. This can seriously limit volunteer resource potential and, more important, the potential to help the community.

Volunteers today can be short term or long term; they can work every Tuesday for a year or more; or they can handle a project that lasts just a few weeks or even just a day. Some might prefer a project they can do at their offices, others will want to do something with their families; some want to work in the evenings, some want to work on the weekends; some want to do something in their area of expertise; some want to develop a new skill; and others want to do something from home.

Although it may not be possible to meet all of these personal desires in any particular program, a wise manager will evaluate whether the job can be done under circumstances different from those envisioned originally.

(G) PLANNING FOR DIVERSITY OF SPECIAL VOLUNTEER NEEDS

Besides understanding the need for cultural diversity and the volunteers' diversity of commitment, managers must understand the special needs that may make it impossible for people to volunteer. Some volunteers may be able to help if the agency can provide child care. A busy program during the day at a Champaign, Illinois, hospital provides baby sitting while young mothers satisfy their needs for affiliation and outreach by working together at the hospital. Families can offer their help on weekend and evening projects if their younger children can be taken care of.

Programs should offer to reimburse volunteer out-of-pocket expenses: car fare, for example. Many volunteers will not turn in their expense lists, but for some, car fare may be the difference between involvement or staying at home. Transportation or parking for volunteers can also be helpful. A hospital parking lot for volunteers at a Connecticut hospital carries a sign "Volunteer Lane."

People with disabilities also have abilities that can benefit programs, but the agency needs to make "reasonable accommodation" for the disability—perhaps supplying a tape recorder for someone who is legally blind or understanding that people with mental retardation are pleased to be involved as volunteers. A program in Chicago involves young adults with mental retardation as ushers in neighborhood theaters.

(H) UNDERSTANDING MOTIVATIONS

Gallup Survey results show that most people volunteer to be helpful and become involved as a direct result of their religious beliefs. However, there are many additional reasons: need to be needed, desire for sociability, interest in a particular area, curiosity about a particular program, job experience, and boredom with a paying job . . . the list can go on and on.

For the purposes of volunteer management, one of the most valuable tools on motivation is the work done by David McClelland and John Atkinson referred to by Marlene Wilson (Volunteer Management Associates, 1976). McClelland and Atkinson conclude that all people are motivated by three things, but most strongly by one more than the others. These motivations are:

1. *Affiliation:* the need to be with other people and enjoy friendship.
2. *Achievement:* the need to accomplish goals and do one's personal best.
3. *Power:* the need to have influence on others.

In 1970, McClelland defined power as having two faces:

1. *Positive power:* socialized power: I win/you win.
2. *Negative Power:* personalized power: I win/you lose.

People motivated by socialized power internalize the *raison d'être* for volunteerism: We can't change the world by ourselves, but if we can involve enough other people in socialized power, we can change the world (or our community or a block). Socialized power people understand that when we improve a community for others, we can also improve it for ourselves. A wise volunteer manager can use affiliation, achievement, and power (negative or positive) to understand volunteers and to match them with the right assignment.

(I) RECRUITMENT TECHNIQUES

To be successful and to protect the agency, client, and volunteer recruitment techniques need to be matched to the challenges, complexities, and risks of the job.

- *Generic* (for mass events and low-risk and unskilled jobs). "Volunteers Wanted" on posters, newsletters, and public service announcement can be effective for assignments that anyone and everyone can do. For example, Hands Across America, a 1986 campaign to raise consciousness about hunger and homelessness by an unbroken line of Americans holding hands, was something in which everyone would be involved. It took no special skills, and the only limitation, for some, was transportation to a site. Therefore, an open invitation was all that was needed.

- *Specific* (for medium- or high-risk and skilled jobs). Targeted recruitment is usually the more effective method since "volunteers wanted" does not work when the recruiter has specific skills in mind, just as "paid staff wanted" would not work when an agency wants to hire someone with the ability to do a specific job.

The recruiter should review the job description and ask: What is the mission of the job (why is it important); what is the commitment (long term, short term, evenings, at home, in the office, or ongoing); what skills would the volunteer need; what will be required of the volunteer; what benefits, psychic and tangible, will the volunteer receive from the assignment; and finally, who might have the necessary skills and be attracted by the mission, commitment, and benefits? (See Exhibit 8.3.)

(J)   OFFERING THE OPPORTUNITY

After this exercise, the volunteer manager will begin to focus on a recruitment strategy; targeting individuals and groups who might be interested in the program. The manager will then ask: "How can I reach them, and what should the message be?"

There are many ways to reach prospective volunteers, but the wise recruiter needs to decide which might be most effective for the job in mind:

- Soliciting names of individuals from current volunteers, board members, and staff and having the most credible person ask them to be involved.
- Contacting volunteer centers or organizations (religious, professional, educational) that include the targeted population.
- Distributing targeted flyers (consider multilingual material).
- Distributing targeted brochures.
- Giving speeches to targeted organizations (most successful when given by a volunteer who is a member of that organization).
- Putting public service announcements on television or radio on stations to which the targeted population listens.
- Placing classified ads in newspapers that prospects might read (include free shoppers and neighborhood papers).

It is important that the promotional message emphasize the need your program hopes to remedy: "Two million people in this state can't read above a fourth-grade level"; "One out of every three children in this country is living in poverty." People want to do worthwhile work, and even though the job may be administrative in nature, prospective volunteers will be more involved if they share the mission that the work is advancing.

The promotional message should also speak to the needs of the people who could potentially be most effective in the job: If they are affiliators, being with others and helping others will be motivating; if they are achievers, concrete accomplishments will be enticing; and if they are power people, a task that has significant impact will attract them. Remember, affiliators are concerned about relationships; achievers look for goals and objectives; and power people demand them. If the program doesn't have them, they will create them or leave!

8.10 Interviewing and Screening Volunteers

(A) THE APPLICATION FORM

Prospective volunteers should fill out an application form. Exhibit 8.4 is a sample, but many agencies use the same form that they use for their paid staff. The application form should include information relevant to the work that is to be done. It should ask for at least two references (not relatives); and it should require the driver's license number and insurance source for volunteers who will drive in the course of their duties. If the volunteer will be working with vulnerable populations, it should ask for permission to do a criminal records check. If health or drug tests are required, it should so state.

A confidentiality agreement may also be required in certain agencies. For example, agencies who work with people with disabilities will require this. Some people who do not understand that volunteers are unpaid staff will suggest that volunteers cannot keep information confidential. That, of course, is nonsense. It is the personal integrity of a person, not a salary, that determines his or her ability to keep a pledge. Agencies for whom confidentiality is important will often state in their policies that a breach of confidentiality is regarded as a reason for dismissal.

(B) THE INTERVIEW

(i) Ask Open-ended Questions
As the volunteer director interviews potential volunteers and works to make sure that the job and the volunteer are a good match, McClelland's affiliation, achievement, and power are extraordinarily helpful. Open-ended questions—What are your goals? What do you hope to get out of your volunteer involvement? What kind of work environment do you like? What job have you had that you enjoyed the most?—can all help the interviewer understand the prospective volunteer and make an effective match.

The volunteer manager should clarify that:

- An interview is necessary to make a proper placement.
- Both volunteer and the program should benefit from the match.
- This is an opportunity for the manager and the prospective volunteer to explore whether the job is appropriate for the volunteer's skills and interest.
- Everyone who is interviewed is not appropriate for the program.

When interviewing, remember that the same rules apply that cover equal employment practices. Questions about race, religion, sexual preference, national origin, age, and marital status should not be asked.

EXHIBIT 8.4 Application for Volunteer Position

Name:

Current address:

Telephone Number: Home: Work:

Current employment:

Volunteer experience, current and past:

Skills:

How did you learn about our program?

Educational background: High school graduate: ___ Some college: ___ College degrees: ___

Have you had any previous experience working with our cause (or population)? Give specifics:

References: (List two people whom we may contact, and include addresses and telephone numbers. These should not be relatives but should be teachers, employers, or other community members)

When (days, hours, seasons) would you prefer to volunteer?

In case of an emergency, whom should we notify?

For high-risk programs, add any of the following that are appropriate:

Since driving is part of the volunteer job for which you are applying, we need your driver's license number and your proof of insurance

License number: Insurance carrier:

State: (Please attach a copy of your certificate)

Since the volunteer job requires working with children, people with disabilities, the dying, or the frail elderly, we will need to do a criminal records check.

Permission granted ___ yes ___ no

All volunteers (and paid staff) are required to sign a confidentiality agreement. By signing on the space below, you agree that you will keep confidential all information you learn about clients or families if you perform volunteer duties for this agency.

Signature _____

(ii)   Tailor Depth of Interview to Risk of Program

Programs that serve vulnerable populations and where the volunteer is directly involved with clients—children, people with disabilities, the homebound, and the dying—will want to explore the motivations of the volunteer for the interest in this particular population; and a second interview, after applications are processed and references checked, may be required.

Although good interviewers listen more than they talk, they know that the interview is the time to review the job description and to pay particular attention to policies that cover agency attitudes and volunteer behavior. It affords an opportunity to listen and observe carefully and to assess volunteers' reactions to these policies. Cover all items appropriate and necessary for the program: confidentiality, contracts, probation, health and drug tests, and criminal records checks.

While it is only fair to ask the same questions and make the same general statements to all prospective volunteers, the less comfortable the interviewer is with the volunteer's reactions to policies, the more the interviewer should emphasize the policies in order to probe the volunteer's attitudes.

Interviews should also cover required training. Some agencies that offer intensive and often-sought-after training (for example, negotiation skills, HIV prevention, or crisis intervention) ask prospective volunteers to commit to six months or more of volunteerism once training is completed.

(iii)   Explore Volunteer's Special Needs

During the interview, managers should be sensitive to accommodations that the agency might make to the volunteer (for example, transportation, parking, car fare, planned leave of absence, flex time, shared jobs, or disability-related accommodations). Exhibit 8.5 is a sample form on which to record interview impressions.

(C)   SCREENING

(i)   The Interview

Preliminary screening starts with the application and the interview. At the end of the interview, one of three things will happen:

1. The manager of volunteers is convinced that the job is not appropriate for the prospective volunteer and suggests another assignment in the agency or refers the volunteer to a local volunteer center or an agency with a more compatible program.
2. The potential volunteer realizes that the job is not appropriate and says so. It is helpful to the manager to say at the end of the interview, "Are you still interested in this job?" This gives the prospective volunteer a graceful exit, if desired.
3. The interview is satisfactory enough that it leads to the next step. . . .

(ii)   The Reference Check

The reference check should be conducted, and Exhibit 8.6 is an easy way to contact the references. If the references are satisfactory, the manager will proceed. If not, the manager will follow suggestion (*i*) 1 above.

EXHIBIT 8.5 Interviewer's Report Form

Name of prospect: Date:

Background relevant to placement:

Does this person have a special reason for wanting to be involved with your population or cause?

Did the person understand your requirements: probation, training, contract, confidentiality, criminal records check, health tests? (Use those appropriate to program and add others.)

Times available for volunteer job:

Strengths of the person:

Weaknesses you perceived:

Special needs:

References checked: ___ Satisfactory   ___ Unsatisfactory

    Date:

(If appropriate, add space for receipt and status of health or drug tests and/or criminal records check.)

Second interview to be scheduled? ___ yes   ___ no

    If "yes," date:

Accept ___ yes   ___ no

Person notified: Date _____

(iii) Special Requirements
The volunteer manager institutes the criminal records check. There are usually two forms this check can take: a check of conviction records based on date of birth and name or a more expensive but surer check based on fingerprints. The latter is recommended for especially sensitive cases, such as screening for possible pedophiles.

If the volunteer is required to have a health test (for example, a tuberculosis test is required for some schools, and drug testing for some correctional facilities), the volunteer should take responsibility for making sure that the manager receives the results.

(iv) Second Interview
In especially sensitive work, a second interview is usually required; and sometimes it is needed in other instances just to verify impressions. If (iii) and (iv) are not satisfactory, the next step is rejection.

(D) REJECTING APPLICANTS

Managers of volunteers should remember that in all personnel work, the most important decision made is whom to hire. This is no less true for volunteer jobs. To involve someone about whom one has real misgivings is not fair to the person and not fair to the program. Refer them to another job, another agency, or a volunteer center. It is good to pay a sincere compliment to the prospective volunteer, such as, "You have wonder-

EXHIBIT 8.6 Volunteer Reference Form

The person named below wishes to become a volunteer in our program. This person has indicated that you would be able to evaluate his/her qualifications. This form is confidential and voluntary; but we would appreciate having it returned as soon as possible.

Name:

How long have you known this person?

In what capacity have you known the person?

In your opinion, is this person responsible?

In your opinion, can this person work well with others?

Are you aware of other volunteer work in which this person is involved? (If so, please name it.)

Please tell us about any special talents you believe this person has.

Additional comments:

Your name: Address:

    Phone:

MANY THANKS FOR YOUR HELP

---

ful writing skills, but as I mentioned to you, our needs are limited in that area. I would like to keep you in mind for the future, but meanwhile, you might call. . . ."

8.11   Orientation

The volunteer has been invited to join the program and has been accepted. The next steps are important to maintain enthusiasm and momentum.

(A)   SIGN A CONTRACT

The simplest form for a contract is the job description, which the volunteer manager shared at the interview. Any additional items agreed upon can be added to the job description (length of probation period, for example), and then it can be dated and signed by the volunteer and the manager. The manager can also make the program policies part of the contract.

The contract can be signed before, during, or after the orientation. The volunteer should be given a copy and the original should go in the office personnel file. (See Exhibit 8.2 for a sample job description and contract.)

(B)   WHAT THE VOLUNTEER NEEDS TO KNOW

Orientation to the program is a process to familiarize volunteers with the broad mission and function of the agency so that the volunteer sees his or her job as an important part of that mission. Orientation can be individual, in small groups, or in large groups. Large-group orientations usually happen when a significant number of volunteers are brought into a program at almost the same time. But whether the orientation is held in a classroom setting with videos and speeches, a small group around a conference table, or individually through appointments with relevant personnel, the agenda must be set to meet the volunteer's needs to know.

Don't bore them with information that may be important to agency operations but is not necessary for them to know to perform their duties. However, do share with them exciting plans for new buildings, new programs, breakthroughs in technology, and recognitions of agency excellence. These make the volunteers feel that they are respected new members of the staff and are learning some things that only "insiders" would know. Exhibit 8.7 is a sample agenda for one person or a large- or small-group orientation.

(C) QUESTIONS

A special packet should be prepared for volunteers. It should include a welcoming letter, an annual report, newsletters, an organizational chart, a list of staff and board, and any other information that might be helpful. If the agency is holding a large-group orientation, make sure that it is lively, friendly, and energetic. Ask only those people who are enthusiastic and mission driven to make presentations. Start with coffee and cookies, have attractive name tags (perhaps permanent ones that the volunteer can use consistently), make sure in advance that audiovisual equipment works, and encourage questions, participation, and evaluation. Send out invitations a month in advance and follow up with phone calls.

8.12 *Training*

Review Section 8.8 concerning risk management. This will point out some of the areas where training is needed in a program. Necessary training varies from job to job.

EXHIBIT 8.7 Sample Orientation Agenda

  I.   Greetings from the boss: the executive director or board president, who acknowledges how integral volunteers are to agency operations.

  II.   A review of the history and organizational structure of the agency. This could be a role for a staff member who has been with the agency a long time, or perhaps the agency has a good video.

  III.   Introductions of staff to volunteer(s).

  IV.   An overview of the population or cause for which the volunteers are working. Experienced and enthusiastic program persons who do not use acronyms and jargon can do this.

  V.   Expectations of volunteers: a review of important policies and behaviors.

  VI.   Volunteer expectations of agency (e.g., benefits, insurance, parking, expenses, training).

  VII.   A presentation from an enthusiastic volunteer about what the agency has meant to him or her.

  VIII.   A tour of the facility.

In-service training is important for volunteers. In-service training also serves as a reflection experience where volunteers can debrief about their experience and share with each other. Some volunteer jobs, like serving on a crisis line, can be quite lonely, and volunteers worry that they are not providing the right answers. Giving them a chance to exchange ideas and problems at an in-service training can be rewarding in terms of improved morale and service.

Frequently it's a good idea to take volunteers to a volunteer management conference or to send them to a workshop on a subject that they are working on. Just as paid staff needs to improve its skills, so do volunteers.

(A) HOW ADULTS LEARN

When working with adults, trainers need to remember that adults, according to Ron and Susan Zemke, learn best:

- When they feel a need for the information or learning experience. Keep in mind that adults have a natural motivation to learn at certain points in their lives—a window of opportunity—when they perceive a need to learn something new or different. If the window of opportunity is missed or delayed, however, the impact of the learning is greatly lessened.
- When the learning experience is problem-centered—when it helps them cope with life-changing events—a new job, a new position, a challenging assignment. The more they perceive that the learning opportunity will address the changes that face them, the more motivated they become to participate.
- When the learning experience builds on the learner's personal goals for the program, and when their own experience is incorporated.
- When their curiosity about the subject is stimulated and the utility of the learning is emphasized—and the experience is designed as low risk for the learner.
- When the learning design promotes information integration. Training designers should expect slower integration of information that conflicts sharply with what learners already hold to be true—forcing them to rethink and reevaluate the old material. Similarly, information is acquired more slowly if it has little conceptual overlay with what is already known.

Adult learners prefer:

- Exercises and cases that have fidelity—that ring true to their life experiences.
- Activities that are realistic and involving, that stimulate thinking, and that have moderate challenge.
- Active to passive learning—exercises, cases, games, and simulations— incorporating reflective elements.
- Planned feedback and recognition—"what we are trying to accomplish and how we're doing."
- Curriculum designs that account for learning-style differences.
- Straightforward how-to content.
- Learning designs that accommodate their continued growth and changing values.

- A safe and comfortable environment.
- Facilitation over lecture presentations.[1]

Frequently, training is done too early, before the adults have an opportunity to know what information they need. That's why it's better to do training in short sessions spread over a period of time rather than heaping all of the information on the volunteers at once.

Adults want to participate in the training. They come with life experiences of their own, so it's important to give them an opportunity to share and problem solve.

(B)   WAYS TO COMMUNICATE INFORMATION

Because people learn in different ways, an entire training should not be a lecture. In fact, the lecture pieces should be short, ten minutes or so at a time, and broken up with some of the following:

- Video.
- Peer presentations.
- Role play.
- Discussions.
- Panels.
- Site visits.
- Case studies.
- Questionnaires.
- Stories.
- Interactive groups.

Interactive groups are effective because after adults hear about concepts, they need to process them, practice them, and experience them.

(C)   ORGANIZE YOUR TRAINING

Trainers need to ask themselves:

- What is the purpose of this training?
- What do I want the volunteers to know and feel when they have completed the training?
- What are the three major concepts I want to get across?
- What variety of techniques can I use to make the training varied, lively, and interesting?
- How will I get the group to know each other (e.g., introductions, icebreakers)?
- How will I get them involved in an interactive way?

---

[1] Adapted in part from Zemke, Ron and Zemke, Susan. 1995. "Adult Learning: What Do We Know for Sure?" *Training* (June): 31–40.

Allow for breaks during the training. Encourage questions. And ask for evaluations at the end so that the next training can be even more successful.

8.13   Guidance/Retention

Effective programs, according to the Points of Light New Paradigm project, "were effective simply (because they) saw volunteers in a different way, a way that was empowering and encompassing."

Managers of volunteers need to provide mission-focused leadership, letting the volunteers know how important they are to making a difference in the community. They need to help volunteers develop their talents; discover new challenges; and feel good about their successes. Volunteer managers need to provide prompt feedback about better ways of attacking problems. They need to solicit the advice of volunteers and involve volunteers as middle managers. After all, if the volunteer manager could do all the work alone, there wouldn't be a need for the volunteers. The manager who does not delegate and does not empower others is performing a disservice to the volunteers and the program.

One hundred percent retention of volunteers is an unrealistic goal. As with paid staff, there are sometimes people who need to be outplaced (yes, volunteers can be dismissed when they consistently do not honor their contract). In addition, new jobs, moves, lifestyle changes, and new interests are bound to take their toll on the volunteer program. However, volunteer managers can do many things to help their volunteers keep their enthusiasm and interest in the program. Some ideas are listed below:

(A)   OPPORTUNITIES FOR EVALUATION

There should be opportunities for mutual evaluation of the volunteer experience. Evaluation can take a very informal tone. Ask "How's it going?" and if the response or body language is negative, invite the volunteer in for a chat. Certainly evaluation is required at the end of a probation period, and managers should provide a chance for discussion about the volunteer commitment at least twice a year. Questions that can be asked are:

- What do you like most about your job?
- What do you like least?
- Was your training sufficient?
- Are there other programs in this agency in which you would like to be involved?
- What can we do to make your time here more fulfilling for you?

In addition, the volunteer manager needs to provide honest feedback on the volunteer's contribution.

(B)   VOLUNTEER VACATIONS AND LEAVES OF ABSENCE

Sometimes good volunteers like to take the winter off, they may become deeply interested in another volunteer assignment, their paying jobs may become overwhelming, or they suffer from burnout. Offer them a volunteer leave of absence or vacation rather than losing them. Keep in touch with them; send them newsletters, an annual report, and a birthday card; and if you don't hear from them, call and invite them back.

(C) VOLUNTEER PROMOTIONS

Few people want to do the same job endlessly, even when they are good at it. Consider offering good volunteers a promotion—perhaps as a manager. Be creative about restructuring your program to make the most of their talents. How about a volunteer as an assistant to the volunteer manager, or as an assistant fund-raiser or marketing person? The possibilities are endless, depending on the talents of the volunteers and the needs of the community.

(D) STAFF MEETINGS

Include volunteers at staff meetings; if this isn't possible, create team meetings. Volunteers need to have a voice in their own assignments, and they can contribute good ideas. Good ideas are not restricted to those who get paid for their work.

(E) PRESENTATIONS

Invite volunteers who are involved in interesting projects to make presentations at a board meeting. The enthusiasm and interest of the unpaid staff person can frequently be more inspirational than that of a paid staff member.

Also, involve volunteers in radio and television interviews. It is tempting for staff to want to take center stage, but volunteers speak engagingly about a program since they are involved only because they want to be.

(F) ADVOCACY OPPORTUNITIES

Invite volunteers to advocate with governmental agencies. Volunteers are often much more credible witnesses, simply because they are not paid to advocate.

(G) VOLUNTEER ADVISORY COUNCIL

Form a volunteer advisory council to discuss the policies and procedures of the program; develop new ideas for volunteer recognition; and assess additional needs for volunteer involvement. Rotate the membership among the volunteers by having terms of office, and always include some members of the board of directors so that policymaking and direct-service volunteers have a chance to interact.

(H) EXPENSE REIMBURSEMENT

Volunteers should be reimbursed for out-of-pocket expenses such as car fare or parking. Volunteers are not free, but a very small budget yields remarkable cost benefit.

(I)   BENEFITS

Volunteers need a cup of coffee or a soda; a safe working environment; and liability, accident, and excess automobile insurance (if they drive as part of their volunteer job description). They also need to be regarded as an important part of the staff.

(J)   PERSONNEL FILE

A volunteer should have a personnel file that contains a record of involvement. This is very useful when the volunteer needs a reference or the manager has to be reminded of good performance to be recognized.

(K)   GRIEVANCE PROCEDURES

It is good for volunteers to know that there is a process for settling grievances—perhaps first with the manager of the program, second with the advisory committee, and finally with the executive director.

(L)   INTERESTING TASKS

Volunteers want to do interesting and meaningful work. Routine tasks have to be done sometime, but vary the work that volunteers are given.

(M)   RESPECTING VOLUNTEERS

No one is "just a volunteer"; volunteers are unpaid staff and deserve respect and work that takes advantage of their skills and interest. If one agency isn't right for them, they should be referred to another.

(N)   PROFESSIONALIZING THE PROGRAM

Volunteer managers are professionals in the area of human resource development. They must respect their own professional development. They must regard their volunteers as professionals, too, and expect professional behavior from them. The more respect volunteers receive, the more they will contribute. Think every day: "There is no job in this agency that the right volunteer can't do."

(O)   VOLUNTEERS AS TRAINERS

Volunteers can be very helpful in training other volunteers, and they will appreciate being tapped for this kind of responsibility.

(P)   VOLUNTEER SOCIALIZATION

Create opportunities for volunteers to celebrate success.

(Q) STAFF APPRECIATION

Recognize and commend staff who work particularly well with volunteers. When staff see that their management skills are recognized, they are much more apt to welcome volunteers as part of their team.

8.14 *Recognition*

Recognition is something that starts the minute a volunteer enters the program, when the program in all that it does recognizes its volunteers as worthy unpaid staff doing significant work in an effective way, and the manager sets high standards and encourages and supports the volunteers.

Recognition is remembering people's names, their birthdays, their needs, and their motivations, and giving them honest compliments for their good work. Recognition can be formal or informal, public or private; it can be tailored to suit the person's individual needs for affiliation, achievement, or power. For example.

- Recognition for people motivated by affiliation:
  Public: Balloons tied to their desks
      A recognition lunch, tea, or dinner and a corsage or coffee mug
      Their pictures on the bulletin board
  Private: A personal note
      A birthday card
      An invitation to have coffee, one on one
- Recognition for people motivated by achievement:
  Public: A report with their byline
      A letter to their boss recognizing their achievements
      A promotion
  Private: A letter from the executive director
      A letter from the chair of the board
- Recognition for people motivated by personalized power:
  Public: Their pictures in a metropolitan newspaper
      An interview on radio or television
      Their picture with the president, governor, or mayor
  Private: A letter from the president, governor, or mayor
- Recognition for people motivated by socialized power:
  Public: Acknowledgment that some important legislation wouldn't have
       passed without their lobbying power
      Acknowledgment that the fund-raising goal wouldn't have been
       reached without their organizational skill
  Private: Observing that they are developing other leaders in the
       organization besides themselves
      Encouragement and respect of peers

Many agencies give annual dinners for their volunteers and find that all volunteers don't attend. That's simply because that kind of recognition doesn't appeal to everyone: It doesn't meet their needs.

Pins, mugs, and certificates are all pleasant ways to recognize volunteers, but there is a great deal of debate about recognition that takes the form of choosing "the best volunteer." Those in favor of choosing an outstanding volunteer say that it is an inspiration to other volunteers and gives them something to strive for. It also can create good media coverage, particularly if the best volunteer is honored by the president, governor, or mayor.

Those opposed to such awards say that it is impossible to choose the best volunteer and that for every volunteer that is happy to be chosen, at least 20 who believe they are just as outstanding feel hurt and unappreciated. They suggest that it is better to choose the "most exciting new idea," the "most interesting project," the "best team"—or, don't worry about the "best"; just celebrate the program and treat everyone equally. If a program does decide to give "best" awards, it should choose an objective committee so that the decision is not attributable to anyone who manages the program or the agency.

8.15   Evaluation

(A)   EVALUATING THE PROGRAM: TYPES OF EVALUATION

(i)   Process Evaluation

Most programs calculate the number of volunteers involved in the program and the number of hours they volunteered. They will also ask themselves if they went through all the proper steps to create the program (see Section 8.2). Good programs will have a mutual evaluation with the volunteers to talk about the quality of their work. These are "process evaluations." They are looking at the *means* through which the program was accomplished. It is essential to measure process, but too many managers stop there, evoking the very natural questions, "that's fine that you did all of those things; but what did the volunteers accomplish; what was improved because of this program?"

(ii)   Outcome-based Evaluation

Outcome-based evaluation answers the most important question: What did the volunteer program accomplish? It is an absolutely essential question so that volunteer managers can assure themselves, their boards, CEOs, funders, and volunteers that something significant happened. But even more important: *It is the way volunteer managers can decide if the result was worth the effort put into the program and, if not, determine how they will change the program to make it even more effective.*

(iii)   What Is Success?

Outcome-based evaluation concentrates on *ends*, not means. Volunteer managers need to ask themselves the following questions at the beginning of the program:

What will be successful outcomes of this program to:

- The agency?
- The volunteers?
- The community?

Successful outcomes for the agency could be:

- The agency's ability to meet client needs successfully will be enhanced by 50 percent.
- There will be a 30 percent increase in funds contributed because of the agency's increased presence in the community.
- Paid staff will undertake a new program (name it) because volunteers have successfully taken over major operations of the current program.
- There is increased CEO, board, and staff commitment to the volunteer program.

Successful outcomes for the volunteers might be:

- Volunteers are excited about the impact they are making.
- Volunteers want to continue in this program.
- Select volunteers are able to serve as middle managers in the program.
- Volunteers have met some of their personal needs by being involved in the program (e.g., experience which has led to a paying job or credit in a college course, knowledge of a particular field).
- Volunteers were involved in this program who might not have been able to be involved in other programs because of flex-time, family volunteering, or other innovations.

Successful outcomes for the community might be:

- Increased percentage of clientele served.
- Percentage of clientele able to do something they were not able to do before program started.
- Community involvement in program (e.g., collaborations with other agencies, involvement of community leaders, involvement of community as volunteers).

(iv) How to Measure Success

Starting simply, the volunteer manager can put in place some useful ways to measure outcomes. In some instances there will be comparable data already available. In others, the wise volunteer manager will need to accumulate some at the beginning of the program. The following are ways to measure:

For the Agency

- Client surveys of satisfaction with the volunteers.
- Fund-raising reports before and after program.
- New program undertaken by staff and its impact on agency's ability to deliver services.
- Board attendance at volunteer recognitions; budget for volunteer program; involvement of volunteer manager in planning before and after program. Staff involvement of volunteers and level of satisfaction with volunteers indicated in staff survey before and after program.

For the Volunteers

- Surveys of volunteer satisfaction
- Volunteer retention.

For the Community

- Client surveys.
- Surveys of community people involved with clients (e.g., parents, teachers).
- Pre- and post-tests of skills attained.
- Survey of community leaders regarding involvement in program.

Community measurements will be different depending on the nature of the program, but the community is the most important measuring stick. They are the agency's prime customer.

If the program rehabilitates housing, it is quite simple to measure the number of houses rehabilitated and the families having better housing. It is more difficult to measure some other programs, such as neighborhood safety or self-esteem building. But surveys and pre- and post-tests can tell a lot about attitudinal changes. These attitudinal results can show more concrete results in the second year of the program. The following are some measurement devices to consider:

- Pre- and post-tests.
- Focus groups.
- Questionnaires.
- Customer satisfaction surveys.
- Tests of a "control group," a group not involved in the program evaluated in contrast to a group that is involved in the program.
- Job placements (for a jobs program).
- One-on-one interviews.

8.16 Conclusion

Volunteers are important resources to meet community needs. They are too important to be taken for granted or patronized. Good volunteer programs demand the best of each person involved. This builds self-esteem and continuing involvement.

Good volunteer programs demand the best of the agency. This builds capacity, collaboration, and community presence.

If programs are to be good for the community, the agency, and the volunteers, they must follow the steps of good human resource management. But having job descriptions, training, and recognition are not enough by themselves. Programs must make sure they are not just continuing to do things the same way because that is the way they have always done them. They must continuously ask themselves: "How can we do it better?"

The need for volunteers changes as the needs of the community changes. The needs of volunteers themselves change as their lives change. The effective leader understands the constancy of change and accepts it has a challenge and an opportunity.

Suggested Readings

Bradner, Jeanne. 1993. *Passionate Volunteerism*. Winnetta, IL: Conversation Press.

Bradner, Jeanne. 1995. "Recruitment, Orientation, and Retention," in T. D. Connors, ed., *The Volunteer Management Handbook*. New York. Wiley.

Bradner, Jeanne and Yallen, Cheryle N. 1996. *The Metro Chicago Volunteer Coalition, Strategic Plan, 1996–1999*, Chicago.

Freedman, Marc. 1994. *Seniors in National and Community Service: A Report Prepared for The Commonwealth Fund's Americans Over 55 At Work Program*. Philadelphia: Public-Private Ventures.

Gardner, John. 1988. *The Changing Nature of Leadership*. Washington, D. C.: Independent Sector.

Independent Sector/The Gallup Organization. 1994. *Giving and Volunteering in the United States, 1994*. Washington, D. C.: Independent Sector.

Points of Light Foundation. 1993. *Changing the Paradigm*. Washington, D. C.: Points of Light.

Seymour, Harold J. 1988. *Designs for Fund-Raising* (2 ed.). Ambler, PA: Fund-Raising Institute.

Wilson, Marlene. 1976. *The Effective Management of Volunteer Programs*. Boulder, CO: Volunteer-Management Associates.

Managing Today's Volunteers in the Training Process

PAMELA G. ARRINGTON, PhD
Maryland Higher Education Commission

9.1 Introduction

The United States has been called a nation of volunteers. At last count, the U.S. had 98 million volunteers who put in 20.5 billion volunteer hours working for charitable causes (Reed, 1991). Donations of both time and money have increased dramatically since 1987: 23 percent more Americans are volunteering their time, and charitable contributions have increased by 20 percent (Reed, 1991).

Furthermore, the number of nonprofit organizations keeps multiplying even with government cutbacks in subsidies to their causes. This chapter discusses how nonprofit organizations can better implement their organizational goals by recruiting and managing today's volunteers in the agencywide training process.

9.2 Contemporary Development Issues

A review of the training and development literature from 1987 to 1996 suggests six major trends that have significant implications for staff development in nonprofit organizations, including:

Continuing education
Performance and accountability
Training and technology
Workforce diversity
Organizational change
Quality and customer-oriented business strategies

These trends run across all areas of human resource development. In "Models for HRD Practice" (McLagan, 1989), human resource development as defined by the American Society for Training and Development includes three areas: training and development, organization development, and career development. All three areas use development as their primary process.

Nonprofit managers must plan for changes in workforce dynamics. More than ever before, the competitiveness of nonprofits will depend on the quality and versatility of their staffs (paid and volunteer). Pressures for workforce productivity will intensify. Managers must ensure high-quality services and products with "leaner" staffs. With advances in technology, the pace of change will continue to accelerate, cycle times for all business processes will be reduced, the useful life of information will shrink, and time will become as valuable a resource as paid staff and volunteers. Workforce structures and designs for nonprofit organizations will change dramatically as they will for all types of organizations. No wonder the fastest growing industry in the United States is continuing education for adult learners.

(A) TRAINING AND DEVELOPMENT

The commitment to a learning climate in organizations is essential to proactive yet responsive management practices. Information is rapidly changing in every discipline. The ability of nonprofit managers to address these challenges will depend on their attention to self-directed learning strategies to maintain a high-performance workforce. Continuous improvement through learning is fundamental for all organizations. Only through learning activities will nonprofits build and maintain their infrastructure capacity for socially responsible systemic decision-making with their organizational vision—to achieve self-renewal. Through planned formal and informal learning, managers enhance their ability as well as their staffs' ability to create, extend, and integrate knowledge in the workplace. The literature continues to emphasize adaptability of the workforce for the next millennium.

The demands of a knowledge-based society continue to escalate. More workers will be asked to do knowledge work, which requires judgment, flexibility, and personal commitment rather than submission to established, inflexible procedures. The challenge for managers and human resources practitioners is creating competent knowledge workers. Managers must seek new partnerships with colleges and universities and other nonprofits as the need for self-directed learning and team learning increases. Outsourcing strategies for training is a current trend in the private and public sectors.

In five years, more than one-third of corporate universities expect to grant degrees in partnership with external universities (Galagan, 1996). The use of such partnerships for outsourcing training and development will assist nonprofit staff seeking the retraining and retooling they require to keep afloat in a fast paced knowledge-based workforce.

The use of volunteers is a proud tradition among nonprofit organizations. This tradition in the nonprofit sector mirrors the current trend in the private sector to use temporary help or contingent workers versus permanent hires. Managers should include contingent workers and volunteers in group learning experiences in collaboration with other staff.

Maintaining the hardworking reputation most nonprofits enjoy in delivering services and products efficiently and effectively will require flexibility coupled with the ability to embrace and incorporate change. Managers will need skills in anticipating changes in the global environment that significantly affect their organizations. In order for nonprofit managers to prepare for the global orientation needed for planning and action in the 1990s and into the next millennium, training and development must be a priority. Nonprofits can pool resources across agencies and participate in training and development. Contracting with training companies and academicians is a viable strategy for needs assessment, design, development, and evaluation of learning programs.

(i) Technology Implications

To date, the literature indicates that technology is not widely used as a deliverer of training and development experiences. Currently, the most widely used technologies are videotapes, audiotapes, and CD-ROM. This practice will change in the near future. A tremendous increase is expected by the year 2000 to include distance learning, just-in-time training via the Internet, and virtual reality. It is expected that the Internet will have one billion users by the year 2000 (Galagan, 1996). This expansion in information technology will enable human resources practitioners and line managers to better meet staff expectations of timely and credible information. A predominant trend in the training and development literature emphasizes the need for just-in-time training directly related to the context of a current work project.

(B) ORGANIZATION DEVELOPMENT

Organizational changes in workplace systems abound:

> Flattened organizations
> Flexible organization designs
> Autonomy for frontline workers
> Blurred boundaries across individual jobs
> Increase in contingent workers
> Increase in telecommuters
> More diversity among new entrants to the workforce
> Fewer new entrants to the workforce in the 1990s

These organizational changes in workplace systems will affect government regulations, recruitment, and retention of employees and business strategies. As organizations accept the reality of a leaner workforce, they grapple with issues of social and ethical responsibilities related to downsizing. With workers struggling to balance work, family, and leisure responsibilities, organizations must consider compensation and benefits such as family-friendly benefits. Current demographics will influence the integration of total quality management principles like employee empowerment and other sociotechnical systems.

Cummings and Worley (1993) define organization transformation as revolutionary changes that can occur at any level in the organization but most often apply to the total system. Such changes are in response to or in anticipation of significant environmental, technological, or internal changes. Transformational changes may dictate an ongoing re-examination of effective management styles, the agency's strategy and culture, as well as internal structures and processes, such as the following:

Systems approach
Performance measures
Emphasis on continuous learning
Self-directed teams
Team accountability
Multiskilled job designs
Participative decision-making
A global mindset

In the area of organization development, attention to planned learning experiences for managers is necessary so that they can better lead their organizations toward fulfill-ment of organizational missions. Since change is probably the one constant in nonprofit organizations for at least the next decade, learning should focus on how to initiate and manage change while ensuring healthy inter- and intraunit relationships.

Managers and professionals within nonprofits responsible for planned learning will need competencies in the following:

Visioning, defined as awareness of organizations' vision/mission, strategy,
    goals, and culture
Management skills
Interpersonal skills, defined as coaching, facilitation, communication,
    questioning, and listening skills
The ability to apply knowledge to utilize different types of software
An understanding of performance support systems

(i) Learning from the Private Sector

Much can be learned from the private sector's lean-and-mean business strategies.

Teaming is one business strategy that is increasingly used with success in the for-profit sector. Instead of employees being responsible for small specialized tasks, organi-zations are investing in cross-training opportunities. This model is applicable in the nonprofit sector as well. It provides opportunities for continuous learning as boundaries between individual jobs become blurred and employees become responsible for work processes from conception to production. With leaner staffs, the teaming approach to management is essential. Small staffs must work interdependently. As nonprofit man-agers begin to employ this strategy, the inclusion of volunteers in the formula will en-sure the transferability of the model to the nonprofit sector.

Technology is an important tool in accomplishing the work of nonprofit organiza-tions. Managers must continue to explore the capabilities of technology in accom-plishing organizational goals. With these new models in hand, managers must continuously involve their superiors and subordinates in group and organizational learning activities so that they, too, are aware of how technology can assist in accomplishing work in a timely and effective way. The integration of technology will enable mangers to train and communicate with a contingent workforce of volunteers and temporary workers.

(ii) Outsourcing as a Strategy

Compounding the need to provide ongoing workplace learning related to accomplishing organizational goals is the global mindset to do so with fewer human, fiscal, and physical resources. This trend has resulted in many organizations employing outsourcing strategies for workplace learning needs. Public and private organizations are pooling resources across companies to accommodate group and organizational learning requirements. Currently, the private sector is outsourcing approximately 30 percent of $30 billion to external providers who design, deliver, and administer training. By the year 2000, this figure is expected to increase to approximately 40 percent.

The implications of this outsourcing trend for management and staff training and development in nonprofits can be seen in the growing collaboration between nonprofits and colleges and universities. One example of this type of collaboration includes sending managers from nonprofit organizations to management courses and seminars at colleges and universities. Many of the lessons on management, organization development and change, and interpersonal relations appropriate for managers of for profit organizations are applicable to nonprofit managers. Another example involves using faculty from colleges and universities to assist with the organizational diagnosis, design, and delivery of workplace learning for nonprofits.

Nonprofit organizations should be encouraged to pool resources and engage faculty from colleges and universities to assist them with the design and delivery of workplace learning around managing change, technology and training, and the high-performance workplace. With multimedia and distance learning technologies, managers and others can participate in specialized lectures without leaving their offices via videotape and software. Using academicians as external consultants often brings an apolitical, systemic, and research-based perspective to problem-solving and decision-making processes. In addition, faculty and advanced-level graduate students can provide expert assistance in the evaluation of existing internal training programs.

Again, the trend to do more with fewer resources emphasizes accountability. Managers are being asked by their boards to document the return on investment for all organizational systems, especially training efforts, which are often viewed as nice to have but not fundamental to organizational goals. Evaluation is a key strategy here. External experts from training companies and colleges and universities can provide unbiased and objective advice with this strategy as well.

Most graduate and professional school programs in adult education, business administration, human resource development, and social work, as well as undergraduate programs in psychology and sociology, require students to complete hands-on field experiences.

Guided by faculty advisors, students in areas commensurate with identified agency needs and goals can be tapped as resources for training and development, organization development, and career development projects. Other examples of specific jobs and expertise matches include faculty and students with expertise in management information systems, public administration, computer science, and so on. Nonprofit managers should establish partnerships with local colleges and universities in accomplishing agency goals.

(iii) *Outsourcing Partnerships*

Today's nonprofits are dependent on the quality and versatility of their human resources. Partnerships with comparable nonprofits and with colleges and universities will increase managers' capacity to provide continuous learning opportunities for their workforce.

In the training and development area, often internal resources are not available for time-consuming assessment processes. Professionals from colleges and universities can be recruited to assist with an organizational diagnosis via a survey feedback project. Too often managers and board members become distanced from their founding missions and from the staff and customers whose professional services they try to facilitate, supervise, or coordinate. The results of the survey feedback project would be invaluable to agency-wide strategic planning efforts. Based on research, faculty and students could develop varied survey instruments, pilot test the instruments, administer the instruments, interview agency staff, analyze the data, and report the findings.

The use of external providers to assess organizational needs offers many advantages in both dollars and time. Long-term cost savings are being documented in the private sector. For example, reductions in internal bureaucracies, paperless operations, and more relational operations versus narrowly compartmentalized operations all provide significant cost savings for organizations.

Outsourcing selected professional services where appropriate should be evaluated. Most academicians possess the research skills and practice required to assist with training and development, organization development, and career development data collection and documentation procedures.

It is important to document the current organizational state of affairs. The agency mission statement is a significant management tool. Only with such documentation can nonprofit managers begin to develop appropriate action plans that will lead to the desired organizational state. Information about the performance gap between the current state and the desired state is a prerequisite for strategic planning. Training and development, organization development interventions, and career development systems should be predicated on these data. Furthermore, the data should be organized at the total system, group, and individual levels. This will allow for organizationwide programming simultaneously with unit and individual programming. All aspects of the organization will understand what the desired goals are and how they can work toward accomplishing the goals. Such steps are necessary for effective change management. Armed with new insights, managers may decide to tighten their focus and reexamine certain programs and services that are no longer viable or commensurate with the agency mission. In some cases, managers may be encouraged to revise or redo mission statements.

In addition, faculty consultants (paid and volunteer) can deliver training in varied subject areas, once these needs have been identified through the assessment process. Subject areas may include training and technology, job analysis, performance appraisals, team building, and stress management, to name a few. With a long-term view, external experts may design specific interventions and train internal staff on how to deliver subsequent interventions.

In both training and development and organization development, the use of technology in training and information systems initiatives will enable small agencies to dramatically increase their infrastructure capabilities. Initial costs will produce important returns on investment via work changes due to advances in technology. Specifically, employees expect timely and credible information. The use of the Internet, for example, enables agencies to efficiently accomplish business goals by enhancing intra- and interunit communications.

Employing appropriate database systems allows nonprofits to reduce time staff on routine administrative paperwork.

Time has become a more valuable resource of organization change in the workplace. Pressures for workforce productivity and high-performance organizations will continue to intensify. In order to systematically offer high-quality services and products, nonprofits must continuously assess business strategies and organizational structures. Such investments enable managers to ready their agencies for change.

(C) CAREER DEVELOPMENT

Career development is the final area where current economic, political, and social trends present challenges for nonprofit managers. Most of the large baby boom cohort are well into their thirties and forties, alert to their midcareer options, bright, well educated, ambitious, and concerned about autonomy, self-development, and balance between worklife, leisure activities, and family life. For most professions, lifelong learning is a mandate. The predominant trend in this area is the move toward administrative staffs with generalist competencies. In the future, workers will need to demonstrate greater versatility.

Professional generalists appear more capable of adapting to change as changes arise. Nonprofit managers can position their agencies for savings by reducing compartmentalized job designs. Emphasis on a division of labor that allows for completion of a whole task should be the goal. Again, borrowing from the private sector's increasing reliance on business strategies such as lateral career moves, cross-training or job rotation, mentoring programs, and tuition reimbursement, nonprofits can customize these techniques as ways of facilitating career development.

Varied functions or operations should be consolidated where possible, versus discrete and specialized jobs. A better sense of what staffs do with their time is required. Efforts at cost control will lead to new workload patterns for staff and volunteers. Managers and human resources practitioners must become skilled at creating staff development opportunities on the job, facilitating self-directed teams, and documenting the benefits of training and development, organization development, and career development interventions.

A key concept in most career development models is the source of learning that occurs through experience—work activities, roles, and contexts. Managers should discuss with their staffs appropriate assignments that match the individual employee's career goals and the agency's needs for current and future workforce competencies and skills. This may include managers' involvement in job design or redesign strategies with staff and human resource planning with agency human resources practitioners. Restructuring the present job may provide job incumbents with fresh goals that are more challenging, meaningful, and psychologically fulfilling. The performance appraisal process is an opportune time to talk about the agency's workforce needs and the individual employee's career plans.

Cross-training among job incumbents focuses on the coordination of the agency's whole work and provides opportunities for interaction with other staff in varied job roles. The goal here is for employees to attain a level of mastery in a variety of job roles that will enable them to satisfactorily perform in a new context or new job. The use of cross-functional teams or lateral transfers introduces variety and growth into an employees's career, particularly for senior personnel who have become functionally over-specialized or suffer from pending skills obsolescence. With the increasing use of technology, the nature of work is constantly changing. Career patterns for nonprofits should be continuously reevaluated and updated because of the dynamic nature of work role behaviors and the context within which they occur (Hall, 1986).

Again, through partnering with other agencies and colleges and universities, nonprofits can facilitate such career activities as:

The use of computerized individual self-assessment and career exploration programs

Outplacement counseling for terminated employees

Participation in career workshops for staff

Training programs for managers on career coaching and counseling skills

While most managers do not routinely possess in-depth skills in career management processes, they can rely on contracting with outside sources to provide these professional services. Managers should encourage their staffs to seek outside assistance with career planning on their own time and at their own expense.

Career development is a strategy to promote planning for anticipated human resources needs as well as a strategy for managing current human resources needs. Some of the tangible and documentable benefits for implementing career development interventions include the following:

Retaining high-quality junior personnel

Improving upward mobility of women and minorities

Reducing professional obsolescence due to advances in technology

Breaking the routine of plateaued workers and related midcareer issues

Demonstrating agency commitment to promotion from within

Increasing the availability of high-quality, promotable talent

Increasing employee commitment

Ensuring that the right person–job fit occurs

Improving workforce productivity

Nonprofit managers must identify agency-specific factors in order to assist any external consultants in developing customized career development programs.

(D) TRENDS SUMMARY

Nonprofit managers face the challenge of ensuring their agencies' future in light of growing trends toward privatization and globalization. A commitment to developing their management skills through learning means they will possess the knowledge and technological skills to lead their agencies into the future while maintaining a proud tradition of effective public service to diverse constituents.

As nonprofits continue to do more with less—integrate technology for routine administrative tasks—their capacity to remain fiscally efficient and effective will depend on recruiting and retaining a quality workforce and ensuring its continuing development. The initiation of training and development, organization development, and career development business strategies can begin at the individual, group, or organizational level. Partnerships with other nonprofits, training companies, and colleges and universities will help nonprofit managers to innovatively lead their agencies toward their desired missions via continuous learning and a quality workforce. The approach of teaming training and development, organization development, and career development will serve nonprofits well as they contemplate current human resources trends and their implications for change.

9.3 Human Resource Development

Nonprofit organizations continue to devote a significant amount of their resources to human resource development for their volunteers and paid staff. Like the public and private sectors, nonprofit organizations depend on human resource development to achieve their organizational goals.

Nadler and Nadler (1989) have defined human resource development as organized learning experiences (intentional/purposeful) provided by employers, within a specified period of time, to bring about the possibility of performance improvement and/or personal growth. Human resource development includes three activity areas: training, education, and development.

Training is defined as organized learning experiences centered around the employee's current position (Nadler, 1988). This training should increase the possibility of the employee's performing current job responsibilities better. Education is defined as learning experiences that prepare the worker to perform future job duties (Nadler, 1984). Developmental experiences are not necessarily job-related but they provide opportunities for professional development and growth.

9.4 Use of Volunteers in the Training Process

One need not be on-site to accomplish a project, if the nonprofit is explicit in its guidelines for the project assignment. The degree of autonomy a nonprofit can afford a volunteer is crucial in the recruitment and retention of highly qualified volunteers. Volunteers who work full-time have little patience with any unwise demands on their time; a challenge for nonprofits is to manage the "knowledge worker" volunteer for productivity. Any assignment given to volunteers needs follow-up.

For example, suppose a nonprofit manager has a volunteer with instructional design skills who needs an assignment. An appropriate project would be to ask the volunteer to design a training program that will prepare volunteers to work on the organization's annual fund-raising campaign (Geber, 1991).

In another example, United Way/United Black Fund Management Services Incorporated recruits professionals with requisite skills to fill predetermined needs for its constituency. Potential volunteers complete a capability profile (see Exhibit 9.1). An annual needs assessment is conducted among United Way/United Black Fund member organizations, as announced in Exhibit 9.2.

Based on the reported member training/consulting needs, volunteers with commensurate areas of expertise are asked to provide professional services to the designated agency. United Way/United Black Fund Management Services Incorporated serves as a broker and makes the person–job match.

Although almost all of the volunteers work full-time, they are eager to participate in the service. Because many are starting their own consulting businesses, they see the service as a way to add up training credits for marketing purposes. Others have strong al-

---

EXHIBIT 9.1 Sample of Volunteer Application

VOLUNTEER APPLICATION

NAME OF CONSULTANT: _____

ADDRESS: _____

TELEPHONE NUMBER—WORK: (___)_____   TELEPHONE NUMBER—HOME: (___)_____

The agencies served by Management Services, Inc. have expressed a number of needs for assistance. These may be categorized into the following key areas: AGENCY POLICY-MAKING, AGENCY ADMINISTRATION & MANAGEMENT, CORPORATE MANAGEMENT, FINANCE, MARKETING AND PUBLIC RELATIONS AND PERSONNEL. Please rank order the areas in which you have knowledge, experience, and demonstrated competence. For the first three choices, provide three references who can verify your expertise in the area noted. (NOTE: PLEASE PROVIDE A RECENT VITA OR RESUME WITH THIS APPLICATION . . . THANK YOU!)

AGENCY POLICY-MAKING _____

____ Board Organization and Structure

____ Policy Development

____ Planning and Goal Setting

____ Resource Allocation

____ Agency Evaluation

CORPORATE MANAGEMENT _____

____ Articles of Incorporation

____ By-Laws

____ Tax-Exempt Status

____ Tax Reporting

MARKETING AND PUBLIC RELATIONS _____

____ Community Analysis: Need for Agency Service

____ Cooperative Relationships with Other Agencies

____ Packaging the Agency's Story

____ Working with the Media

AGENCY ADMINISTRATION & MANAGEMENT _____

____ Decision-Making

____ Time Management

____ Problem Solving

____ Communication

____ Team Building

____ Program Evaluation

FINANCE _____

____ Management: bookkeeping, budget, payroll, indirect cost, cash flow, audit preparation

____ Fund Raising

____ Grantsmanship

PERSONNEL _____

____ Staff Development and Training

____ Wage and Salary

____ Staff Recruitment

____ Staff Performance Appraisal

____ Position Qualifications/Classification

____ Volunteer Recruitment, Training, Management

____ Volunteer/Paid Staff Relations

EXHIBIT 9.1 *(Continued)*

PAGE TWO—VOLUNTEER APPLICATION

REFERENCES

AREA #1	AREA #2	AREA #3
NAME _____	_____	_____
ADDRESS _____	_____	_____
PHONE _____	_____	_____
NAME _____	_____	_____
ADDRESS _____	_____	_____
PHONE _____	_____	_____
NAME _____	_____	_____
ADDRESS _____	_____	_____
PHONE _____	_____	_____

TIME AVAILABLE TO DO VOLUNTEER WORK

TIME OF DAY:	DAY OF WEEK:	TIME OF YEAR:	HOURS PER YEAR:
___ Morning	___ Monday	___ Winter	___ 10
___ Afternoon	___ Tuesday	___ Spring	___ 10–50
___ Evening	___ Wednesday	___ Summer	___ 51–100
	___ Thursday	___ Fall	___ You tell us ___
	___ Friday		
	___ Saturday		
	___ Sunday		

KIND OF VOLUNTEER JOB OF INTEREST (Rank order those of interest)

___ One-to-One Consulting

___ Organizational Diagnosis & Management of Volunteer Trainers Assigned to Case

___ Seminar Presentation (10–20 people)

___ Workshop Presentation (20 + people)

___ Evaluation of MSC Service to Agencies

___ Training of Trainers

___ Special Projects for MSC

WHERE/HOW DID YOU LEARN OF THIS VOLUNTEER OPPORTUNITY?

HAVE YOU BEEN REFERRED TO MSC BY: ___ ASTD

                                           ___ UNITED WAY

                                           ___ UNITED BLACK FUND

WORK HISTORY

Please attach a current resume to this application and respond to the following questions:

- Name of current employer: _____
- Name(s) of employers in past five (5) years
- Educational record:

                         Signed _____

                         Date _____

EXHIBIT 9.2 Cover Letter for Annual Survey of Management Needs

UNITEDWAY·UNITEDBLACK FUND
MANAGEMENT SERVICES INCORPORATED

ANNUAL SURVEY

TO:　　Executive Director of United Way, United Black Fund and other non-profit 501 (C) (3) Agencies of the Washington Metropolitan Area.

FROM:　Myrtle E. Johnson
　　　　Executive Director

DATE:　July 2, 1990

RE:　　Management services available to your agency.

　　Each year we conduct a survey to ascertain the needs of your agency so that we may better assist you in meeting your management objectives. We would greatly appreciate it if you would take a few moments to complete the attached form.

　　On one side, please suggest topics for workshops to be conducted at our facility. On the other side is an Agency Request for Services Application. Please complete it if you want management training, technical assistance, or consultation services provided at your individual agency at no cost. Please return the SURVEY to:

　　　　United Way/United Black Fund
　　　　Management Services Incorporated
　　　　1012 - 14th Street, N.W./Suite 304
　　　　Washington, D.C. 20005

　　Thank you for assisting us. And, if you have questions you may call 347-4024. We look forward to serving you.

MEJ/ah
Attachment

———— 1012 - 14th Street, N.W./Suite 304, Washington D.C. 20005 (202) 347-4024 ————

truistic values and enjoy giving back to their respective communities. Some use the opportunity to gain experience in a new professional endeavor.

Four key steps can be employed to maximize volunteer output in the training process:

- Recruitment and selection;
- Orientation;
- Training;
- Performance appraisals.

As with recruiting and retaining paid staff, there needs to be a person–job match between training roles and responsibilities to be performed and the competencies and skills of human resource practitioners and/or volunteers.

(A) RECRUITMENT AND SELECTION

The recruitment and selection of volunteers is the first step in effectively managing volunteers. Recruitment should involve the same amount of research, time, and strategizing that is required when seeking a million-dollar gift (Alexander, 1991).

Technology can assist in the recruitment and selection of volunteers. Data bases exist in which volunteers have recorded their areas of expertise and agencies have entered their mission, needs, and requests for services. Potential volunteers can go to the local library to identify a person–job match.

Nonprofits must prioritize their training needs around their mission. Once specific training projects are identified as necessary to the organizational mission, then volunteers with commensurate knowledge, skills, and abilities can be recruited, trained, or retrained. The selection, placement, and training of volunteers give everyone an opportunity to advance personal learning and contribute the best of personal talents (Deming, 1989).

Volunteers can be recruited and/or trained to assist nonprofit managers during the needs assessment step. The conduct of a needs assessment should be a very thorough and comprehensive activity. If an agencywide needs assessment is conducted, this part of the training process can be conducted once a year. Volunteers can be recruited and trained to conduct face-to-face interviews; develop questionnaires and accompanying cover letters; collect, organize, and analyze the data; and report the results. These data collection steps are necessary for a thorough and comprehensive needs assessment.

Increasingly, colleges and universities are requiring their students to complete an established number of hours in public service work. Many government-sponsored loans and grants for college students are "forgiven" based on the student's completing a set number of hours of community service.

Most graduate and professional school programs in adult education, human resource development, gerontology, and social work, as well as undergraduate programs in psychology and sociology, require students to complete hands-on field experiences. Graduate programs in areas commensurate with identified agency needs and goals can be tapped as resources for the training process. Other examples include management information, public administration, business management, facility management, and so on. Nonprofit leaders should involve local colleges and universities in the training process as potential resources.

Nonprofit organizations will find college students knowledgeable volunteers who complement their paid staff. Most college students possess the survey research skills required to conduct a needs assessment; at least, nonprofit managers may want to screen for these capabilities. Once identified, involving this group of volunteers in the strategic planning process seems appropriate. Nonprofit managers may invite volunteer professionals and students with a background in computer science to develop computer programming assistance for the needs assessment process. This would include designing and formatting survey instrument/questionnaires so data can be tabulated and analyzed using readily available software packages.

Colleges and universities also offer nonprofit organizations a wealth of human resource development services. Faculty volunteers can function as expert trainers and consultants in various subject areas, once these needs have been identified through the training process. Students can also volunteer as trainers and consultants.

For example, master's-level students in human resource development at Bowie State University in Bowie, Maryland, have served as volunteer consultants in the United Way/United Black Fund Management Services Project. Students' interests and skills were matched with identified organizational needs. Students then developed and delivered seminars, on topics such as stress management and team building, to paid staff and volunteers at Washington (DC) area nonprofits. This was a way to involve volunteers in the training process, particularly the design/development and delivery phases. The training request was the result of predetermined organizational needs.

The library, media, equipment, and facilities at colleges and universities are available to local nonprofits as resources and can be used to enhance their training process and practices. Local college and university departments of education and communications can be tapped to design, develop, and package educational videotapes for use by nonprofits, after course goals and objectives have been agreed on. University experts in the area of adult education can help nonprofits facilitate the writing of course outlines, goals, objectives, and lessons.

In addition, paid staff can avail themselves of credit and noncredit course offerings in subject areas that are critical to the mission of the nonprofit. The possible linkages between colleges and universities and nonprofits are limitless. For example, a needs assessment may reveal knowledge and skill gaps among staff that may be efficiently met through long-term education or development experiences at nearby colleges and universities.

After a needs assessment has been conducted, nonprofit managers can recruit and/or select volunteer trainers who have subject matter expertise and/or experience in the identified organizational need or mission. For example, United Way/United Black Fund Management Services Incorporated volunteer application form (Exhibit 9.1) asks the volunteer to identify the type of position that is of interest. Seminar presentation, workshop presentation, and training of trainers are three of the possible seven choices. More importantly, the volunteer is asked to specify the content area in which he or she would be able to volunteer. The content area is based on annual needs assessment data collected from agencies served by the management services corporation.

Under the United Way Loaned Executive program, volunteer training professionals from the business community become available to nonprofits. Particularly in the fundraising arena, this program has an illustrious history. Senior executives spend up to a year with nonprofits, advising on a myriad of business needs in a consultative role. Training could be one such area. Like the management services corporation, the Washington (DC) Volunteer Clearinghouse provides training and consultation to nonprofits for negotiable fees.

In addition to possible partnership arrangements with colleges and universities, a wish list can be explored with area businesses through a request for service form, as shown in Exhibit 9.3. Nonprofits may want to utilize companies' physical and human resources; they need not call on local business leaders only for monetary contributions. Companies are anxious for their employees to become involved in community service projects. Sometimes, when a business is not initially willing to make substantive cash donations, for whatever reason, it will get involved with the nonprofit in other ways that are beneficial to both. This contact may lead to future contributions once the corporation knows the nonprofit better.

(B) ORIENTATION

Volunteer training should begin with an orientation to the organization. Volunteers should be appraised of the agency mission, financial operation achievements, and long-range goals. United Way/United Black Fund Management Services Incorporated does not provide a structured orientation session for its volunteer consultants, but volunteers are required to come in for a structured interview during which the goals and objectives of the program, as well as the how, when, and where of the delivery of services, are explained. How the consultant's services will be evaluated is also presented. The interview, coupled with handouts such as a workshop survey (Exhibit 9.4), provide the volunteer with an orientation program. In addition, background information about the agency (Exhibit 9.5) is sent to the volunteer, for use in the planning process. The volunteer is encouraged to call and meet with the agency director to collect even more data, in order to affirm the diagnosis specified from the needs assessment conducted earlier. Official agreements are often made between the volunteer consultants and the agency they are servicing (Exhibit 9.6).

(C) PERFORMANCE APPRAISALS

Effectively managing volunteers in the training process includes making the right person–job match. Recruitment and selection, orientation, training, and performance appraisals enable nonprofits to maximize their volunteer productivity.

9.5 *The Training Process*

(A) OVERVIEW

The training process involves four important phases: strategic planning, design and development, delivery, and evaluation. (The strategic planning phase includes conduct of a needs assessment.) These are the elements of the training process phases:

1. Strategic planning
   —Needs assessment
   —Annual training plan
   —Scheduling
   —Budgeting

EXHIBIT 9.3 Sample Request for Service Form

UNITED WAY · UNITED BLACK FUND
MANAGEMENT SERVICES INCORPORATED

AGENCY REQUEST FOR SERVICE

NAME OF AGENCY: _____

MEMBER OF (Check One):   UNITED WAY ___   UNITED BLACK FUND ___   OTHER ___

ADDRESS: _____

TELEPHONE NUMBER: (___)_____

EXECUTIVE DIRECTOR/PRESIDENT OF AGENCY: _____

PRESIDENT/CHAIRPERSON OF AGENCY'S BOARD OF DIRECTORS: _____

NUMBER OF BOARD MEMBERS: _____   NUMBER OF PAID STAFF MEMBERS: _____

NUMBER OF REGULAR VOLUNTEER STAFF MEMBERS: _____

YEAR GROUP WAS FOUNDED: _____

PURPOSE OF THE ORGANIZATION: _____

_____

_____

FUNDING SOURCE(S)—CIRCLE THOSE WHICH APPLY:

SPECIAL EVENTS   SOLICITATION/DONATIONS   GRANTS

FEES FOR SERVICE   MEMBERSHIP FEES   OTHER: _____

ASSISTANCE REQUESTED—PLEASE CHECK THE CATEGORIES:

AGENCY POLICY-MAKING _____

____ board organization and structure

____ policy development

____ planning and goal setting

____ resource allocation

____ agency evaluation

CORPORATE MANAGEMENT _____

____ articles of incorporation

____ by-laws

____ tax-exempt status

____ tax reporting

MARKETING AND PUBLIC RELATIONS _____

____ community analysis: need for agency service

____ cooperative relationships with other agencies

____ packaging the agency's story

____ working with the media

AGENCY ADMINISTRATION & MANAGEMENT _____

____ decision-making

____ time management

____ problem solving

____ communication

____ team building

____ program evaluation

FINANCE _____

____ management: bookkeeping, budget, payroll, indirect cost, cash flow, audit preparation

____ fund raising

____ grantsmanship

EXHIBIT 9.3 *(Continued)*

PAGE TWO—AGENCY REQUEST FOR SERVICE

ASSISTANCE REQUESTED (Continued)

PERSONNEL

____ staff development and training   ____ position qualifications/classification

____ wage and salary   ____ volunteer recruitment, training, management

____ staff recruitment   ____ volunteer/paid staff relations

____ staff performance appraisal

THIS REQUEST IS MADE BY: _____ POSITION: _____

DATE OF REQUEST(S): _____

ADDRESS: _____

TELEPHONE NUMBER(S): _____

---

2. Design and development
   —Job/Task analysis
   —Course objectives and lessons
   —Training of trainers
3. Delivery
   —Trainee preparation
   —Arrangement for training services
   —Conduct of training
   —Record keeping
4. Evaluation
   —Volunteer and paid staff
   —Trainers
   —Assessment of program accomplishments
   —Cost–benefit analyses

(B)   STRATEGIC PLANNING

It is possible for an organization to involve volunteers at all levels of management and decision making. Given the financial situation of most volunteer organizations, more emphasis on planning and evaluation and on the role training plays in those processes is needed. Although the financial situation of nonprofits has preoccupied planning initiatives (Olson, 1984), budget cutbacks provide an opportunity for nonprofit managers to emphasize the need for strategic planning in carrying out the organization's mission. Such a plan may well need to include training in efficiency techniques.

Strategic planning involves the vision of how the organization plans to meet its constituents' needs, based on analyses of both the external and internal environment—local, state, and national economic condition; work force demographics; financial portfolio of the organization; strengths and weaknesses of paid and volunteer staffs; and prioritizing of organizational needs and goals.

The training, education, and development functions for both volunteers and paid staff should be well integrated into any nonprofit strategic plan. All functional area managers should provide input into the training process and practices endorsed by the non-

EXHIBIT 9.4 Sample Workshop Survey Form

UNITED WAY · UNITED BLACK FUND
MANAGEMENT SERVICES INCORPORATED

WORKSHOP SURVEY

Please list below topics/issues you wish to see addressed in a workshop setting:

1) _____

2) _____

3) _____

4) _____

5) _____

6) _____

7) _____

8) _____

PLEASE CHECK AS MANY THAT MAY APPLY!

I prefer a ____ Half-day session.   I prefer ____ Full-day sessions.

I find that ____ Mornings are better for me.   ____ Afternoons are better for me.

The day(s) of the week that works best for me are: ____ Mondays   ____ Tuesdays

____ Wednesdays ____ Thursdays ____ Fridays ____ All with at least two (2) Weeks notice.

NAME: _____ TITLE: _____

AGENCY: _____

ADDRESS: _____

TELEPHONE NO: _____

____ UNITED WAY AGENCY   ____ UNITED BLACK FUND AGENCY   ____ OTHER

1012 - 14th Street, N.W./Suite 304, Washington D.C. 20005 (202) 347-4024

EXHIBIT 9.5 Organizational Policy Statement

UNITED WAY · UNITED BLACK FUND
MANAGEMENT SERVICES INCORPORATED

POLICY STATEMENT

The United Way/United Black Fund Management Services Incorporated was established in the fall of 1981, after months of collaborative planning by the United Way of the National Capital Area, the United Black Fund of Greater Washington, and the Washington Center of the American Society for Training and Development. MSI is designed to respond to management concerns of executives and boards of non-profit agencies. The corporation is supported by the United Way, the United Black Fund, and the American Society for Training and Development.

Consultation services are provided to agencies through the assignment of volunteer consultants. There is no fee for the services, and agencies are placed on a waiting list for service, based upon criteria determined by the MSI Board of Directors.

1. MANAGEMENT ASSISTANCE. MSI recognizes the need for sound, effective management of human service agencies to efficiently provide social services and programs. MSI is designed to strengthen the management core of agencies by providing volunteer consultants from business and industry, government and educational institutions, professional and civic organizations and associations.

   In support of agency autonomy and self-help, MSI encourages agencies to use to the fullest extent possible, their own initiatives for management assistance before requesting assistance from MSI.

2. AGENCY AUTONOMY. Participation in MSI by agencies to not-for-profit agencies located within the MSI service area. Agencies need not be members of the United Way or the United Black Fund.

3. TARGET MARKET. Management assistance is available to not-for-profit agencies located within the MSI service area. Agencies need not be members of the United Way or the United Black Fund.

4. CONFIDENTIALITY. The Management Services Incorporated is separate from the United Way and the United Black Fund; therefore, agencies are encouraged to discuss their problems and seek assistance. Confidentiality is essential to developing and maintaining trust and open communications with agencies. All information pertaining to the agency consultation engagement is considered confidential and will only be released upon the signed authorization of the agency.

5. CONSULTATION. Diagnosis and problem solving are part of the consultation process. Implementation of the recommended solutions is given equal emphasis. Both elements provide agencies with the maximum opportunity to apply new or modified management procedures to the operation of the agency. MSI stresses the importance of the "transfer of skills" to agencies as a result of the consultation engagement.

———— 1012 - 14th Street, N.W./Suite 304, Washington D.C. 20005 (202) 347-4024 ————

EXHIBIT 9.6 Sample of Contract with Volunteer Consultant

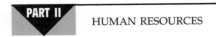

UNITED WAY · UNITED BLACK FUND
MANAGEMENT SERVICES INCORPORATED

VOLUNTEER CONSULTANT CONTRACT

This agreement is made by and between the United Way/United Black Fund Management Services Corporation, hereinafter termed "MSC" and _____ , hereinafter called the volunteer consultant. The contract goes into effect on the _____ day of _____ , 19 _____ .

MSC agrees to assign the volunteer consultant to _____ agency and the Volunteer Consultant agrees to see that the following task(s) are accomplished.

All administrative support, typing, photocopying, etc. will be provided by United Way/United Black Fund Management Services, Inc. immediately upon request from the Volunteer Consultant.

The consultation is to begin by: DATE _____ and to be completed no later than: DATE _____ .

The volunteer consultant agrees that he/she represents the United Way/United Black Fund Management Services Corporation and operates under the direction of the Executive Director during the time that this agreement is in effect. This contract can be terminated by either party with 30 days notice should either feel that it is not in their best interest to continue the relationship.

Date _____

_____
Myrtle E. Johnson
Executive Director

Date _____

_____
Volunteer Consultant

———— 1012 - 14th Street, N.W./Suite 304, Washington D.C. 20005 (202) 347-4024 ————

profit. Their input should be reflected in any organizationwide planning document. Training must be more than a series of random events or activities. Instead, the human resource development program should be based on strategic planning, a systems approach.

Use of a systems approach to training and development enhances the organization's ability to focus training on the prevention of problems. When one is not always in a reactive mode of "putting out fires," energy can be devoted to creative and innovative proactive training. What is good for the human resource development area's strategic plan is good for the organizationwide strategic plan. Indeed, most organizations that adopt quality management principles will make sure training needs, action plans, and evaluation are thoroughly integrated through the organization's strategic plan.

The process ensures that training will be applied to ongoing projects and to projects that are to begin in the near future. If an experience is developmental, then the applicability to the achievement of organizational goals must be evident. The human resource development manager should make the connection explicit.

Key decision makers should gather at least once each year for a planning session. A good brainstorming exercise for this meeting, preferably off-site, is to consider agency problems. For each identified problem and need, solutions should be considered and resources identified. A facilitator will be needed for this planning session. Volunteers with expertise in group dynamics and group process skills should be recruited for this critical planning meeting. The discussion goals for a strategic planning session are:

- Problems and needs;
- Solutions;
- Resources.

Faculty at area colleges and universities can be tapped to identify a facilitator. In addition, during summer months and on weekends, college campuses may provide ideal facilities for a meeting site. Some nonprofit board members may volunteer their homes; vacation or beach homes provide a particularly relaxing setting, away from the agency. In addition, some corporations, like Xerox Corporation, donate space for off-site meetings. The Xerox International Training Center in Leesburg, Virginia, noted for its wooded landscapes complete with wild deer, is an example. More importantly, for actual training programs, such as orientation for new employees and staff retreats for team building, these same resources should be considered. For agencies involved in direct services, it is important to get paid and volunteer staff away from the office occasionally, especially for team-building training.

Agencies need to work these programs into the annual budgeting process—another reason why the human resource development planning process should be integrated into the nonprofit's total strategic planning process. As priorities for the agency are determined, training, education, and development for volunteer and paid staff should be given equal consideration alongside other agency needs.

(C) NEEDS ASSESSMENT

Data collection and analysis are paramount to the planning process. Training outcomes must be based on organization needs or business needs. Key volunteer leadership and executives from the organization, and from similar organizations, must be surveyed.

Performance appraisal data from volunteer and paid staff should be reviewed. Job descriptions should be broken down into key component parts. A job analysis based on job descriptions can be done using a structured staff interview closed-question format. Sample questions may include:

1. Rate yourself in quality of job performance on a scale of 1 to 10.
2. What systems and equipment do you use on the job?.
3. What courses, programs, or training do you think you need, to help you do your job better?
4. What results do you want?
5. What are your strengths?
6. Name any weaknesses you perceive.
7. What are your personal goals?
8. What are your professional goals?
9. Are your personal and professional goals compatible?

Community involvement in the identification of priorities is recommended, and feedback should be incorporated into the planning process. After such a thorough analysis, the human resource development manager can better determine the knowledge, skills, and abilities required of paid and volunteer staff in order to accomplish organizational goals. The value of a comprehensive needs assessment in the training process cannot be overemphasized.

One of the reasons the needs assessment is so necessary to the strategic planning process is that it gives managers, clients, potential participants, paid staff, community leaders, and everyone who has an interest in the success of the organization an opportunity to provide input into the process that determines the training, education, and development experiences needed by paid staff and volunteers to implement organizational goals and objectives.

Training is not always the only answer. Changes in management styles may be necessary, or other organizational development efforts may be more appropriate solutions to problems identified as a result of the strategic planning and needs assessment phase. The benefit of this phase of the training process is the identification of appropriate solutions and resources for confirmed organizational needs. Volunteers with particular skills may need to be recruited. However, orientation must be provided to the newly recruited volunteers: they need to know how their work fits in with the work of the organization.

Returning volunteers need training or retraining programs in order to accomplish certain organizational goals. This type of needs assessment data can only be incorporated into the human resource development planning process if the human resource development manager is an integral player in the organizational planning process. An appropriate human resource development plan can then be implemented, based on the organization's needs, problems, change efforts, development objectives for work performance, personnel strengths and weaknesses, and career opportunities for volunteer and paid staff (Olson, 1984). This kind of goal setting is important for any organization.

Needs assessment data include all of the following:

- Organization needs;
- Organization problems;

- Change efforts;
- Work objectives;
- Personnel strengths;
- Personnel weaknesses;
- Career opportunities.

Needs assessment data are typically collected through the use of face-to-face interviews, confidential questionnaires, agency mission statement, financial statements, personnel records, output records, project costs and projected cost savings, quality improvement goals, logged reports, timeliness of the service rendered, written objectives and standards, and time factors. Needs assessment data should be "hard data," defined as quantifiable, easy to assign dollar values to, objective, and credible in the view of management.

(D)   DESIGN AND DEVELOPMENT

Most national voluntary organizations are large, complex, and highly decentralized (Olson, 1984). Levinson (1987) described training design needs of nonprofit organizations as including: small size, complex interpersonal environments, uncertain and unstable financial environments, a core value of altruism, strong belief in the value of what the organization does, and a large number of minority group members.

The design phase of the training process provides a means for the human resource development manager to gain valuable input and feedback from other managers while developing training programs for the organization. The person responsible for the design and development of the training programs should try to secure input and feedback at each critical step of the training process: the selection of goals and objectives, the selection of instructional strategies, delivery, and evaluation. These are the common training needs for nonprofit organizations:

- Orientation;
- Team building;
- Quality management.

Because of the interdependence of volunteers and paid staff, teamwork between the two groups is of paramount importance. Common technical-skills training includes: fund-raising, donor research and solicitation, efficiency techniques, and computer literacy. Volunteer and paid staff job descriptions should be reviewed as a key step in the training process. Volunteer trainers can be recruited to review job descriptions in order to determine course objectives. Once the training course is written, it is important to prepare the trainers or instructors. Volunteer human resource practitioners can be recruited for all of the roles and responsibilities required of the training process.

Course objectives should always be written in *measurable* terms, such as:

- Tell what the participant will do;
- Can be taught;
- Can be learned;
- Can be measured;
- Should emphasize a behavior to be modified;

- Show linkage to organizational goals;
- Follow job/task analysis;
- Relate to other objectives of the course;
- Specify conditions for learning to occur.

An example of a course objective is:

After completion of a course on desktop publishing software, staff will be able to design and construct a fund-raising brochure using desktop publishing software.

(E) DELIVERY

Geber (1991) has reported that many of today's volunteers are more receptive to the "lean" approach to training. According to research, when delivering training to adult audiences, interactive instructional methodologies should be considered. However, volunteers who work full-time are not particularly receptive to the group process dynamics (games, exercises, role plays, and so on) that most training specialists incorporate into structured learning experiences to illustrate key concepts. Instead, orientation delivered in printed media (handouts, workbooks, and so on) is preferred by this time-conscious audience. This is not to suggest these instructional strategies should not be included in the final training product developed by the volunteers involved in the training process. Volunteers with expertise in educational technology can develop and produce varied educational materials, such as video tapes, to be used in lieu of the traditional classroom format.

Hands-on training techniques are most helpful when trying to keep training activities to a minimum. As much factual information as possible should be delivered in the form of manuals, handouts, handbooks, or other training aids that can be referred to throughout the assigned project. Self-directed learning is a very appropriate, instructional strategy, given the demographics of the typical volunteer.

Trainers should emphasize the need to participate in training activities. How else can the training be related to assigned projects? The trainer and/or human resource development manager must stress the fact that, without certain information presented in the training session, the volunteer will not be able to complete the assigned project in a satisfactory manner. This emphasis on job-related training should motivate the professional volunteer to find time to participate in agency training.

Volunteers are more willing to participate in training that is designed with this target group in mind. Volunteer training should be lean and mean—just the facts, with minimal group dynamic exercises. Team-building activities are important, but many of today's volunteers are not willing to commit time to activities outside of their assigned work project for the organization.

Depending on the skill levels of the volunteers, they may not require an intense training, in order to be effective in assisting paid staff who are responsible for writing and delivering training programs. The quality of instructors is crucial, but Levinson (1987) warns trainers who volunteer their expertise to nonprofits to remember that personal contact is a core nonprofit value and remains the favored mode of communication.

The readiness level of agency personnel is crucial to the training process. Paid and volunteer staff should be recognized for their contributions to the nonprofit's mission. Their participation in training, education, and development programs should be presented as a form of recognition for a job well done as well as an incentive for partici-pation in future projects. Agency employees must be informed of the availability of training programs and materials. Nonprofit managers should ensure that training, edu-cation, and development programs are widely publicized to employees. Other nonprof-its may be invited to participate, to help underwrite some of the costs and to introduce a different set of group experiences when agencies with similar constituents have an op-portunity to compare experiences. Learning experiences must be reinforced back at the office.

Human resource managers need to keep records of staff and volunteers who partic-ipate in agency-related training, education, and development programs. These data should be included in annual performance appraisals and in the annual planning process. it is important to have measures of productivity for meaningful comparisons.

(F) EVALUATION

Evaluation of training, perhaps the most overlooked step of the training process, is crit-ical if nonprofit managers responsible for training participate in the agencywide strate-gic planning process. At this time, nonprofit managers responsible for human resource development need to be able to present program accomplishments in cost-benefit or return-on-investment terms.

The data that were collected to plan and to design and develop training should be revisited in order to assess program accomplishments and outcomes. Evaluation is a cri-terion at each step of the training process. Exhibit 9.7 provides an outline of the key cat-egories and topics.

Nonprofit managers must evaluate the training process. If technical training has occurred—data base management, word processing, financial record keeping—has the

---

EXHIBIT 9.7 Key Evaluation Data

Hard data
Output
Cost savings
Quality improvement
Time savings

Measures of output
Money collected
Forms processed
Clients served
Applications processed
Tasks completed
Productivity
Work backlog

Examples of cost savings
Number of cost reductions
Project cost savings
Program costs
Operating costs
Overhead costs

Examples of cost savings (Continued)
Variable costs
Fixed costs

Examples of quality improvement data
Error rates
Amount of rework
Percent of tasks completed properly
Amount of variance from organizational
    prescribed standards

Time savings possibilities
Time to project completion
Processing time
Supervisory time
Break-in time for new employees
Training time
Meeting schedules
Efficiency
Late reporting
Lost time days

error rate improved? What is the percent of tasks completed properly? Has efficiency improved? Are schedules being met? Has automation shortened task completion time? Did orientation training decrease the amount of break-in time for new employees? Has training resulted in increased output? Is more money being collected? Is the work backlog reduced? Has productivity increased?

Nonprofit managers should ask the above questions in order to assess whether training has affected cost-benefit outcomes. Hard data of this type will show the governing board and senior managers the benefits of training.

The use of data to make decisions is probably the most important factor contributing to a Total Quality effort. The emphasis in continuous process improvement is to make decisions based on objective data (Biech and Danahy, 1991).

Evaluation should be viewed as necessary in order to provide input for planning. Hence, evaluation is another step in an open, continuous training process. Evaluation is a criterion at each step of the training process.

The data collected from the evaluation process provide input for the next planning session. Nonprofit managers should be able to show, in numerical terms, the bottom-line contribution of training, education, and development programs to the achievement of organizational goals. (See Exhibit 9.8.)

The nonprofit human resource development manager must be able to show the above data to nonprofit executive directors and board members. Measurement and evaluation of training are critical. Evaluation begins with the writing of measurable objectives; their written form is another example of the open and continuous nature of the training process.

9.6   Volunteer Recognition/Incentives

Volunteers view volunteer work as a developmental activity through which they can gain skills and knowledge either to benefit them in their current careers or to enable them to try out new careers. Some professionals volunteer as a means to get ahead on their paid jobs. In either case, volunteers are interested in personal and professional growth activities and the satisfaction of doing well.

One of the major activities nonprofits have mastered over the years is volunteer

---

EXHIBIT 9.8 Tasks of Managers Responsible for Human Resource Development

 1. Show how training is tied to organizational goals and priorities;   ____
 2. Identify training outcomes;   ____
 3. Document return on investment and cost of effectiveness of training;   ____
 4. Evaluate training;   ____
 5. Compare training results against training expectations;   ____
 6. Develop data and methods to illustrate bottom-line impact of training;   ____
 7. View training as a strategic investment;   ____
 8. Learn management's current needs and priorities;   ____
 9. Get sufficient resources allocated, to ensure employees are equipped
    to perform duties;   ____
10. Emphasize quality improvement.   ____

recognition. Nonprofits have learned how to express appreciation to volunteers in tangible, concrete terms, such as: "You have contributed your expertise and × number of hours [or weeks] of your time. Because of you, many lives were affected in these ways: . . . ."

Volunteer recognition should begin with the organizational policy statements. Volunteers can be recognized in periodic communications from the board and managers. The use of internal periodicals can also reinforce the need for paid staff to support volunteer staff in a team effort. Peer recognition is important. Some agencies recognize their volunteers at an annual banquet or at regional breakfast meetings. Tokens of appreciation, such as engraved pewter mugs and certificates of recognition, are frequently presented to volunteers.

It is important to ask volunteers what kinds of recognition they appreciate. Depending on their reasons for volunteering, something other than a plaque or volunteer banquet may be appropriate—for example, a new assignment offering more visibility and responsibility, or a letter of appreciation to the volunteer's paid-job supervisor may be a more meaningful form of recognition than a plaque.

Suggested Readings

Alexander, G. D. 1991. "Working with Volunteers." *Fund Raising Management, 12*(2): 62–63.

Anonymous. 1994 "Trends." *Training* (Oct.), *31* (10): 59–64.

Baskett, H. 1993. "The Nanosecond Nineties." *Adult Learning* (July/Aug.).

Beatty, L. 1994. "Pay and Benefits Break Away from Tradition." *Human Resources Magazine* (Nov.), *39*(11): 63–68.

Biech, E., and Danahy, M. 1991. *Diagnostic Tools for Total Quality*. Alexandria, VA: American Society for Training and Development.

Bolt, J. 1993. "Ten Years of Change in Executive Education." *Training and Development* (Aug.), *47*(8): 43–44.

Bramer, W. and Winslow, C. 1994. *Future Work: Putting Knowledge to Work in the Knowledge Economy*. New York: The Free Press.

Burke, W. and Litwin, G. 1992. "A Causal Model of Organizational Performance and Change." *Journal of Management, 18*(3): 523–545.

Carnevale, A. 1994. "Trends in Training on the Job." *Technical and Skills Training* (May/June), *5*(4): 10–16.

Carnevale, A. 1995. *The American Mosaic: An Indepth Report on the Future of Diversity at Work*. New York: McGraw Hill.

Carnevale, A. and Kogod, K., eds. 1995, Summer. *Tools and Activities for a Diverse Workforce*. Alexandria, VA: ASTD.

Carnevale, A. and Stone, S., eds. 1995, Summer. *The American Mosaic: An Indepth Report on the Advantage of Diversity in the U.S. Workforce*. Alexandria, VA: ASTD.

Champy, J. 1995. *Reengineering Management: The Mandate for New Leadership*. New York: Harper Business.

Clark, R. 1994. "Hang Up Your Training Hat." *Training and Development* (Sept.), *48*(9): 61–65.

Conference Board. 1994. *Closing the Human Performance Gap*. New York: Conference Board.

Conger, J. 1993. "The Brave New World of Leadership Training." *Organizational Dynamics* (Winter), *21*(3): 46–58.

Connors, T. 1991. "Avoiding Quality Shock: Can Mere Mortals Achieve Perfection?" *The Observer*, July 15, pp. 3–9.

Cosier, R. and Dalton, D. 1993. "Management Training and Development in a Nonprofit Organization." *Public Personnel Management* (Spring), *22*(1): 37–42.

Cummings, T. and Worley, C. 1993. *Organization and Change*. New York: West Publishing.

Deming, W. E. 1989. *Out of the Crisis*. Cambridge, MA: MIT Center for Advanced Engineering Study.

Dervarics, C. 1993. "Outlook: Jobs, Skills, and Technical Training." *Technical and Skills Training* (February/March), *4*(2): 24–30.

Deutsch, C. 1991. "In Motivation, Nonprofits Are Ahead." *New York Times*. July 14, p. 25.

Dobie, K. 1991. "The New Volunteers." *Vogue*. August, pp. 213–217.

Donaldson, L., and Scannell, E. 1986. *Human Resource Development: The New Trainer's Guide*. Reading, MA: Addison-Wesley.

Eck, A. 1993. "Job-Related Education and Training." *Monthly Labor Review* (Oct.), *116*(10): 21–38.

Filipczak, B. 1994. "Training Consortia: How They Work, How They Don't." *Training* (Aug.). *31*(8): 51–57.

Filipczak, B. 1994. "Looking Past the Numbers." *Training* (Oct.), *31*(10): 67–74.

Franklin, J. 1993. "Industry Output and Employment." *Monthly Labor Review* (Nov.), *116*(11): 41–57.

Frantzreb, R., ed. 1993. *Training and Development Yearbook 1993/1994*. Washington, D.C.: U.S. Department of Labor.

Fullerton, H. Jr. 1993. "Another Look at the Labor Force." *Monthly Labor Review* (Nov.), *116*(11): 31–40.

Galagan, P. 1994. "Think Performance." *Training and Development* (March), *48*(3): 47–51.

Galagan, P. 1994. "The Instructional Designer in a New Age." *Training and Development* (March), *48*(3): 52–53.

Galagan, P. 1994. "Performance Support Systems: A Conversation with Gloria Gery." *Technical and Skills Training* (April), *5*(3): 6–10.

Galagan, P. 1994. "Trends That Will Influence Workplace Learning and Performance in the Next Five Years." *Training and Development* (May), *48*(5): S29–S35.

Galagan, P. 1996. "What Lies Ahead." *Training and Development* (Jan.), *50*(1): 75–79.

Galagan, P. and Carnevale, E. 1994. "The Future of Workplace Learning and Performance." *Training and Development* (May), *48*(5): S36–S47.

Galer, D., and Holliday, A. 1988. "Achieving Quality in Nonprofits (Part 3)." *Nonprofit World* (May/June), *3:* 22–24.

Geber, B. 1991. "Managing Volunteers." *Training* (June), 22–23.

Geber, B. 1993. Retrain to Do What? *Training* (Jan.), *30*(1): 27–34.

Geber, B. 1994. "Re-engineering the Training Department." *Training* (May), *31*(5): 27–34.

Goad, T. 1993. *The Handbook of HRD Technology*. Amherst, MA: HRD Press.

Gordon, E. 1994. "Work Force Education: Training Implications for Business Basic Skills Programs." *Performance and Instruction* (Sept.), *33*(8): 30–34.

Hall, D. and Associates. 1986. *Career Development in Organizations*. San Francisco: Jossey Bass.

Hammonds, K., Kelly, K., and Thurston, K. 1994. "The New World of Work." *Business Week* (Oct. 17), (33394): 76–87.

Hequet, M. 1994. "Should Every Worker Have a Line in the Information Stream?" *Training* (May), *31*(5): 99–102.

Ireland, T. 1991. "Fighting for Financial Support." Paper presented at Technical Trainers Conference, Department of the Navy, Arlington, VA: August.

Johnston, W., and Packer, A. 1987. *Workforce 2000: Work and Workers for the 21st Century.* Indianapolis, IN: Hudson Institute.

Kelley, B. 1994. "High-Tech Hits Recruiting." *Human Resource Executive* (April), *8*(4): 43–45.

Leonard, B. 1995. "Child Care Benefits Shift to Lower-Wage Workers." *Journal of Human Resource Magazine* (Sept. 1), *40*(9): 57–58.

Levinson, D. 1987. "Training and Development for Nonprofits." *Training and Development Journal 41*: 82–82.

Lindsay, J. 1991. Informational interview, Volunteer Clearinghouse, Washington, DC; May.

Martinez, M. 1995. "HRM Update." *HR Magazine* (Nov.), *40*(11): 17–18.

McLagan, P. 1989. "Models for HRD Practice." *Training and Development Journal* (Sept.), *43*(9): 49–64.

Mills, G., Pace, R., and Peterson, B. 1989. *Analysis in Human Resource Training and Organization Development.* Reading, MA: Addison-Wesley.

Moulton, H. and Fickel, A. 1993. *Executive Development: Preparing for the 21st Century.* New York: Oxford University Press.

Nadler, L. (Ed.). 1984. *The Handbook of Human Resource Development.* NY: John Wiley & Sons.

Nadler, L. 1988. *Designing Programs: The Critical Events Model.* Reading, MA: Addison-Wesley.

Nadler, L. and Nadler, Z. 1989. *Developing Human Resources.* Reading, MA: Addison-Wesley.

National Society for Performance and Instruction. 1992. *Workplace Productivity: Performance Technology Success Stories.* Washington, D.C.: NSPI.

Nelson, D. V., and Johnson, M. E. 1991. Informational interview, United Way/United Black Fund Management Services, Washington, DC; May.

O'Connell, S. 1994. "Re-engineering: Way to Do it with Technology." *HRMagazine* (Nov.), *39*(11): 40–46.

Olson, E. A. 1984. "Volunteer Organizations," In L. Nadler (Ed.), *The Handbook of Human Resource Development.* New York: John Wiley & Sons.

O'Reilly, B. 1993. "How Execs Learn Now." *Fortune* (April 5), *127*(7): 52–58.

Reed, J. 1991. "The New Volunteers." *Vogue.* August, pp. 213–217.

Reich, R. 1994. "Jobs: Skills Before Credentials." *Training* (April), *31*(4): 38, 40.

Richman, L. 1994. "The New Work Force Builds Itself." *Fortune* (June 27), *129*(13): 68–76.

Rummler, G. and Brache, A. 1990. *Improving Performance: How to Manage the White Space on the Organizational Chart.* San Francisco: Jossey-Bass.

Schronberger, R. 1994. "Human Resource Management Lessons From a Decade of Total Quality Management and Re-engineering." *California Management Review* (Summer), *36*(4): 109–123.

Silvestri, G. 1993. "Occupational Employment: Wide Variations in Growth." *Monthly Labor Review* (Nov.), *116*(11): 56–86.

Swanson, R. and Torraco, R. 1994. "Technical Training's Challenges and Goals." *Training and Development* (Sept.). *48*(9): 61–65.

Walter, D. 1993. "Enhanced ISD: A Response to Changing Environments for Learning and Performance." *Educational Technology* (Feb.), *33*(2): 12–16.

Walton, J. 1993. "Multimedia-Based Learning: Today and Tomorrow." *Journal of Instruction Delivery Systems* (Spring), *7*(2): 3–8.

Warner, P. 1995. "How Does Your Pay Stack Up?" *HR Magazine* (Nov.), *40*(11): 38–44.

10 ▼ Self-Managed Teams in the Self-Renewing Organization

HENRY P. SIMS, JR., PhD, Professor of Management
and Organization, University of Maryland

CHARLES C. MANZ, PhD, Professor of Management
Arizona State University

The leader looked out at the eyes around the campfire. Slowly, he picked up a stick, and snapped it in a second. Next, he picked up a bunch of sticks together, and attempted to break them. They bent, but did not break. "A stick by itself," he said, "can be broken easily. But if all the sticks stay together, they will not break." Slowly he smiled. "The same is true of us."[1]

10.1 Introduction

Self-leadership is the capacity of individuals to influence their own behavior in the absence of external influences. Fundamentally, self-leadership is an attribute of an individual. That is, each person in an organization has both an opportunity and a responsibility to develop his or her own self-leadership capabilities. Also, leaders have the responsibility of developing and encouraging individual self-leadership. Essentially, developing individual self-leadership is a form of employee empowerment. In fact, much of our previous writing has been concerned with the challenge of how individuals can lead themselves, and how leaders can lead others to become skilled self-leaders.

---

[1]This story is inspired by one told by Kelvin Throop, III in *Analog*, May 1994, p. 81.

But few of us work in isolation. For most of us, our work has some degree of inter-dependence with others. In fact, in today's increasingly complex environment, the op-portunity and requirement for working together is stronger than ever. The "lone wolf" is gone. Much of our work involves working together, and today, working together means teams and teamwork. In this paper, we extrapolate the concept of individual self-leadership to self-managing teams, and how these teams have become a critical factor in sustaining a self-renewing organization.

Empowered teams are the cutting edge of the self-renewing organization. The essence of self-renewal lies in the capacity of each individual and groups of individuals to create a bottom-up culture of renewal. Renewal is possible only through empowerment.

Recent years have brought many challenges for western organizations—intense in-ternational competition, a workforce that now demands more than simply making a liv-ing, and the increasing complexity of technical knowledge and information flows. As a result, companies are pressured to explore more effective ways of using human re-sources. Among the more noteworthy and promising is the concept of empowered teams.

Teams are the focus of this chapter. In fact, in today's contemporary organization, teams are the most common vehicle through which self-leadership is expressed. Em-powerment typically relies on team structures. Thus, teams are a critical element of the organizational self-leadership system. For most organizations, teams are the *springboard* to self-leadership. In this chapter, we address the idea of self-managed and empowered teams, and how these teams can enhance service, quality, productivity, and innovation. And most of all, we emphasize how leaders can encourage self-leadership through em-powered teams. The team becomes the unit of self leadership. Team self-management is the essential building block of a self-renewing organization.

10.2 WHAT IS A TEAM? WHAT DO TEAMS DO?

Work designs based on self-management tend to give employees a high degree of au-tonomy and control over their immediate behavior. Teams are one of the many forms of employee participation that have emerged in the United States. Not all teams are em-powered, however. Indeed, the traditional sports team is seldom a participatory unit. In fact, a team can function well under the thumb of a strong-minded leader—we think of the late Vince Lombardi (coach of the champion Green Bay Packers) as an example of a successful boss-type coach who demanded compliance from his players. His teams were definitely *not* self-managed. But the teams of today's contemporary business sector in the United States are *not* like the Lombardi teams.

In contemporary empowered teams, employees are typically organized into units that complete a whole or distinct part of a product or service. They make decisions on a wide range of issues, often including such traditional management prerogatives as who will perform which task, solving quality problems, settling conflicts between mem-bers on the team, and selecting team leaders. The story of the Fitzgerald Battery Plant of General Motors Corporation is an example of the many activities that self-managed teams have taken on in many work organizations (Exhibit 10.1).

Team designs have varied across companies, and it's difficult to find a single com-monly accepted definition of what the team approach really is. It seems to be more of an overall philosophy and approach to work design rather than a tightly defined set of rules. In fact, part of the essence of teams is to encourage each set of employees to find their own way, their own kind of group self-leadership that best fits their own situation

EXHIBIT 10.1 Team Roles and Responsibilities at Fitzgerald[2]

Here, we describe some of the self-management practices at the Fitzgerald Battery Plant of General Motors Corporation. Our main purpose is to use this concrete, specific example to demonstrate the typical roles and responsibilities of self-managing teams. We derived this information from interviews and observations that we conducted several years after startup. Thus, the plant was at a relatively "mature" stage, rather than a startup stage. Following are some more specific details, in no particular order, that describe how the teams actually handled responsibilities that in other organizations are typically performed by traditional "bosses."

Establish relief and break schedules
Teams had great discretion in establishing their own schedules. Since most of the teams were "buffered" by short-term in-process inventories, breaks could be scheduled at their own discretion. Did teams handle this authority in a responsible way? Yes! Often, breaks are scheduled to facilitate production. For example, a short tool or process change might be undertaken while the team is on their break.

Select and dismiss leader of the group
Teams elected their own team leader, who was a member of the team. Elections were conducted whenever a current leader resigned, or was challenged by another team member. A few teams had the same team leader since the startup of the plant. Other teams had experienced several team leaders over the years. At first, "popular" individuals tended to be elected team leader. However, teams soon found that the leaders who had organizing and planning skills, who also possessed interpersonal and conflict resolution skills, were more effective. So-called "popularity" diminished as a criterion for election to team leader.

In addition, management appointed people to fill the role of "coordinator," which was a leadership role external to the team—that is, the coordinator was not a team member. In other plants, this person might be called a "facilitator" or a "counselor." Each coordinator had responsibility for one to three teams. While the coordinator filled the space in the organizational hierarchy typically occupied by a foreman or general foreman, their behaviors were quite different. Many of the coordinators at Fitzgerald had previously served as team leaders.

Finally, while teams technically had the authority to dismiss a team leader, this was virtually never done. Instead, an ineffective team leader might be encouraged to resign, or might be challenged by another potential leader.

Initiate minor and major equipment and machinery repair
Overall, team members might carry out minor repairs themselves, in order to keep production flowing. Major repairs were carried out by the maintenance department, but were frequently initiated by team members. We recall the statement of a team member in a weekly team meeting: "They better get that bearing replaced this weekend, or that machine will break down next week, and we'll lose a day's production!" Most of all, team members seemed to take an unusual degree of psychological "ownership" in their production equipment. They were very concerned about making the equipment work in the right way.

(Continued)

[2]These roles are taken from Chapter 2, "The Day-to-Day Team Experience: Roles, Behaviors, and Performance of Mature Self-Managing Teams," in C.C. Manz, and H.P. Sims, *Business Without Bosses*, New York, Wiley, 1993. Copyright © 1993 by C. C. Manz and H. P. Sims. Reprinted by permission of John Wiley & Sons, Inc. For readers interested in training, a training case based on the Fitzgerald story is available under the name *The Greenfield Case*, available from *Organization Designing and Development, Inc.*, 2002 Renaissance Blvd., Suite 100, King of Prussia, PA 19406, 212-279-2002.

EXHIBIT 10.1 *(Continued)*

Make specific job assignments within work group

Each team made their own job assignments, and the practices were quite different across teams. One team might rotate jobs every hour, while another team would make assignments strictly on a seniority basis. Overall, teams seemed to find a way to satisfy individual preferences within the team without compromising productivity goals.

Train new members of work group

This was a responsibility that was carried out by all teams. Occasionally, the external coordinator would pitch in or conduct some special training. Of course, other more formal training programs were also conducted for the team members. Training was also important in terms of developing the wide range of skills required for each new member to advance along the pay scale.

Make sure needed production materials are available

In many traditional plants, workers will allow a production material to deplete, in order to take an unauthorized break. At this plant, responsibility to make sure production materials were available was vested in the team itself. Team leaders, in particular, spent a great deal of their time ensuring that proper materials would be available to meet production requirements.

Keep record of hours worked for each group member

Each team member kept a record of their own number of hours worked—the plant had no time clocks. Weekly time records were turned in to their team leader and then to the coordinator. When asked "Don't they cheat?," one team member replied, "Who do they cheat? Other team members! You may be able to get away with it once or twice, but that's all . You can't fool your teammates. "

Make sure spare parts are available

Team members accepted the responsibility for keeping track of minor spare parts that were required to run their own operation.

Perform quality control inspections and compile QC data

For the most part, teams did their own quality inspections and compiled their own quality statistics. One team member might typically be assigned this responsibility. A separate quality control inspector did not exist. However, occasionally, team quality data would be audited by a small central quality control department.

Prepare material and labor budgets

On an annual basis, teams undertook a planning exercise in which they prepared a budget for their team. Budgeting was also done independently, in parallel, by accountants from the office. In general, team budgets were at least as demanding and as stringent as the accounting budgets. Differences were discussed and reconciled in order to arrive at a final budget. Of course, team members required training and appropriate information to carry out this planning exercise.

Prepare daily log of quantity produced and amount of in-process inventory

For the most part, teams compiled their own in-process inventory records, subject to occasional auditing from production scheduling. Teams knew their own production schedule, and kept their own records of how much they produced and the quantity of their in-process inventory.

Recommend engineering changes for equipment, process, and product

As they worked with equipment, teams would occasionally request changes that would lead to significant process or product improvements. One engineer at the division level expressed a preference for placing new or experimental equipment at Fitzgerald. "They make it work!" he exclaimed.

Select new members for group; dismiss members from group

Teams had considerable, but not total, discretion over who would join or leave a group. Most intergroup mobility was facilitated by the coordinator, who would use interpersonal

EXHIBIT 10.1 *(Continued)*

skills to explore new assignments to different groups. Great effort was made to match the preferences of individuals with teams. Employees would move from one team to another for any of several reasons. Some wanted to earn the higher pay rate. Others preferred a different type of work. Others would move because of interpersonal preferences.

Evaluate group members for pay raise
The plant used a "pay for knowledge" system, where an employee was paid according to the tasks he or she was qualified to do, rather than being paid a rate for a particular job that he or she was performing at the moment. To gain the highest pay rate, an employee had to pass performance tests for all tasks on two different teams. These performance tests were conducted by a coordinator, team leader, and senior team member. Thus, part of the evaluation of whether an employee could perform a specific job or not was performed by a teammate.

Conduct safety meetings
Safety meetings were conducted on a scheduled basis—normally by the team leader, or perhaps by a coordinator or other technical person. During the early stages of the startup of the plant, safety performance of the plant was poor. However, the safety record had continuously improved, and during the time of our visits, Fitzgerald's safety performance was in the top quartile of all General Motors plants.

Shut down process/assembly if quality is wrong; stop production to solve process or quality problems
Teams had the authority to stop production without necessarily asking permission from a representative of management. Typically, this authority would be rarely exercised, and almost always to solve a serious quality or process problem Of course, this authority would be used with great discretion, since a shutdown decision might have ramifications for other teams.

Conduct weekly group meetings
Usually, a weekly half-hour meeting was conducted on company time. In addition, shorter ad-hoc meetings would be conducted on almost a daily basis. Also, on occasion, a more lengthy problem-solving meeting might be conducted to work on special production or quality issues.

Review quarterly performance of company, plant, and group
Each quarter, the plant manager met separately with each team, and reviewed company, plant, and team performance with the team. These occasions provided an opportunity for an exchange of communication between the plant manager and team members. The communication exchange went both ways.

Discipline group members for absenteeism or tardiness
Theoretically, this authority was vested within each team, but some teams utilized the authority, others did not. Coordinators said this was the most difficult responsibility to get the team to undertake.

Select new employees for the plant
Employees were selected into the plant through an assessment center process. An evaluation team observed employee candidates during interpersonal exercises and provided ratings and final judgments. The plant evaluation team consisted of one manager, one coordinator, one team leader, and two members of different teams.

Summary
Of course, all of these responsibilities are appropriate to the specific site of The Fitzgerald Battery Plant. Other sites will undoubtedly be different in the specifics of the roles and responsibilities expected of each team. In each case, however, roles and responsibilities must be specified in advance, with a sequenced timetable of implementation, and a substantial degree of flexibility to take advantage of the learning as team implementation proceeds.

and team members. But most of all, the team approach represents an attempt to more fully utilize the organization's human resources—especially those at the lowest levels.

A typical objective of an empowered team system is to simultaneously *improve productivity for the organization as well as the quality of working life for employees*. Sometimes the dignity and freedom workers receive is especially publicized, but the drive toward productivity and competitiveness is always there, whether stated openly or not.

Typically, teams have some common characteristics: a distinct recognizable task that employees can identify with; members with a variety of skills related to the *group* task; discretion over such decisions as work methods, task scheduling, and task assignments; and compensation and performance feedback for the group as a whole.

The team concept has emerged as a distinctly western phenomenon (teams have been used in the United States, Canada, Europe, and Mexico, to name just a few locations) although it's frequently confused with so-called Japanese Management. While both are often associated with the idea of participatory management, each approach is targeted at a quite different population, with distinct cultural values. In our attempts to understand the team system, we have traveled to Japan and read extensively about Japanese management systems. But teams in Japan are quite different from U.S. teams.

Our main conclusion is that we would be better served by attempting to learn from successful experiences with empowered teams in the West rather than looking to the Japanese for innovative organizational philosophies. The rationale and early successes with team designs originated in the United States and Europe, and better fit western cultures. The unique defining characteristic of U.S. teams is that they promote a high degree of initiative, and a sense of responsibility, creativity, and problem solving from within. When teams live up to these ideals, they are uniquely self-reliant.

10.3 Why Teams?

The challenge of competitiveness is upon us. The emergence of the global marketplace has placed a new premium on productivity and quality. Business and nonprofit organizations around the world are struggling to find ways to deal with increasing interdependence, complexity, and uncertainty. In the face of these pressures the team concept is beginning to show proven worth for improving productivity, quality, and employee quality of work life, among other payoffs. It is an approach that is designed to take advantage of the strengths of western culture and history.

Teams have emerged as a potent weapon in the competitiveness wars. In fact, we suspect that the notion of teams has reached the stage of the recurring management "fads" that we often encounter in the United States. Therefore, some team applications are being undertaken simply because "it's the thing to do" with little thought given to how the approach fits with the needs of the organization. We deplore this justification, and strongly believe it's a sure recipe for failure. Nevertheless, there are some solid reasons why teams make good sense. From a management viewpoint, *productivity* and *quality* are typically the main reasons to implement a team system. Teams are a way to undertake "continuous improvement" to enhance productivity. Today, teams are often seen as a critical element within a total quality management (TQM) program. And of course, the real issue is whether teams actually work as well as they're supposed to! (See Exhibit 10.2.)

On occasion, the implementation of teams is motivated by a humanistic ideology. That is, teams are seen as an important way for people to find satisfaction and dignity in their work—in essence, an *enhanced quality employee of work life.* Other reasons are also occasionally cited: better *innovation* and *adaptability,* and also *reduced turnover, absenteeism, and conflict.*

While we are sympathetic with all of these reasons, as researchers and authors we believe that issues of productivity and quality—the important elements of competitiveness—are the more important drivers. In the end, more teams will be adopted only if teams really do work.

For a time—when international competition was not strong, when employees were more accepting of no power and fulfillment—top-down control was sufficient for organizational success. More recently, however, employees have changed—people expect growth, fulfillment, and dignity from their work. Most of all, the emergence of the global marketplace has forced organizations to consider alternative ways of dealing with the competitive challenge. Flexibility, speed, quick response, and short cycle time have become extremely important performance criteria. Many organizations are moving toward flat flexible organizations, including sophisticated structures such as virtual teams.

After more than 15 years of studying teams, we are convinced—teams do work! Moreover, there is something exciting about the challenge of bringing a group of people together to combine their abilities and coordinate their efforts to excel.

EXHIBIT 10.2 Are Teams Effective? The Bottom Line[3]

Do self-managing teams really produce superior results? *BusinessWeek* claims teams can increase productivity by 30 percent or more, and can also substantially improve quality (Horr, 1989). Other examples reported in the press include an ALCOA plant in Cleveland, where a production team came up with a method for making forged wheels for vans that increased output 5 percent and cut scrap in half. At Weyerhaeuser, the forest-product company, a team of legal employees significantly reduced the retrieval time for documents. At Federal Express, a thousand clerical workers, divided into "superteams" of five to ten people, helped the company reduce service problems by 13 percent in 1989. At Rubbermaid, a multidisciplinary team from marketing, engineering, and design developed the "auto office" in 1987, and sales exceeded projections by 50 percent in the first year (Dumaine, 1990).

Corning Glass eliminated one management level at their corporate computer center, substituting a team adviser for three shift supervisors, producing $150K annual savings and *increasing* quality of service. Perceptions of autonomy and responsibility among workers increased because they felt they experienced more meaningful and productive work (Weiss, 1989). In an insurance firm, change to automation led to a shift from functional organizational design to self-managed teams. A twenty-four-month follow-up found improved workstructure, flows, and outcomes (Frederiksen et al., 1984).

Also, in our previous book, *Business Without Bosses,* we describe several organizations that have enjoyed impressive payoffs with teams in both the long and short term. For example, in Exhibit 10.1 we tell a more detailed story of the mature General Motors automobile battery plant organized around teams in which company officials reported productivity savings of 30 to 40 percent when compared with traditionally organized plants. Teams helped Lake Superior Paper Company enjoy possibly the most successful startup in the history of the paper industry. We describe the very beginning adjustments of management to the team approach that a few short months later was credited with

(Continued)

---

[3]This section is adapted from a similar section in Manz and Sims' *Business Without Bosses.* New York, Wiley, 1993. Copyright © 1993 by C. C. Manz and H. P. Sims. Reprinted by permission of John Wiley & Sons, Inc.

EXHIBIT 10.2 *(Continued)*

productivity improvements of 10 percent per year, cost savings of 10 to 20 percent of earnings, and customer service quality levels of over 99 percent.

Considerable data indicates the effectiveness of teams, but perhaps the difficulty of evaluating the team concept in terms of any hard scientific data was best expressed by Miner (1982):

> *The results are often positive. It is hard to predict whether the outcomes will be greater output, better quality, less absenteeism, reduced turnover, fewer accidents, greater job satisfaction, or what, but the introduction of autonomous work groups is often associated with improvements. It is difficult to understand why a particular outcome such as increased productivity occurs in one study and not in another, and why, on some occasions, nothing improves. Furthermore, what actually causes the changes when they do occur is not known. The approach calls for making so many changes at once that it is almost impossible to judge the value of the individual variables. Increased pay, self-selection of work situations, multiskilling, with its resultant job enrichment and decreased contact with authority almost invariably occurs.*

One of the more revealing scientific studies of the bottom-line effect of teams is contained in a paper from Dr. Barry Macy and associates at the Texas Center for Productivity and Quality of Work Life (Texas Tech University) (Macy and Izumi, 1994). Their analysis contrasted the success of various changes involving human resources, work structure, and technology, for example, training, reward systems, work teams. Very strong effects, especially in terms of financial outcomes, were observed with team applications. The Macy study is one of the first rigorous scientific efforts that shows the clear financial effect of the team approach.

In another, more recent study, Lawler, Mohrman, and Ledford, at the Center for Effective Organizations, investigated financial effects of employee involvement programs (which, in many cases, consist of empowered teams). They found significant relationships between usages of employee involvement and firm financial performance.[4]

Are teams *always* successful? Clearly, the answer is no. In our previous book, *Business Without Bosses,* we reported on a team implementation at an insurance company that was clearly a failure. Indeed, we believe that team success depends much on implementation. For example, we continue to hear tales of companies removing a supervisor and precipitously declaring that a work group is "a team." We call this the "team alone" syndrome, where a group of employees suddenly finds itself with much larger responsibility, but without the training and resources to handle this responsibility .

Those close to the self-management movement informally report substantial productivity gains and cost savings that typically range from 30 to 70 percent when compared with traditional systems. Clearly, self-managing teams have the potential to exert substantial effects on the bottom line. Perhaps the notion was captured best by the following quote from Charles Eberle, a former vice president at Procter and Gamble. He speaks with the advantage of years of practical experience.

> *At P & G there are well over two decades of comparisons of results—side by side—between enlightened work systems and those I call traditional. It is absolutely clear that the new work systems work better—a lot better—for example, with 30 to 50 percent lower manufacturing costs. Not only are the tangible, measurable, bottom line indicators such as cost, quality, customer service and reliability better, but also the harder-to-measure attributes such as quickness, decisiveness, toughness, and just plain resourcefulness of these organizations.[5]*

---

[4]See Part III, Section 13 of Lawler (1995).

[5]Interview originally published in *U.S. News and World Report* (Aug. 31, 1981): 66–67.

10.4 The Historical Emergence of Teams—Where Have Teams Been Applied?

According to a recent study by the Center for Effective Organizations at the University of Southern California, 68 percent of the Fortune 1000 companies were using self-managed or high-performance teams in 1993, but they have been applied to only a small percentage of the work force.[6] This data does show a significant increase from 28 percent in 1987, and 47 percent in 1990. In essence, there's a whole lot of experimentation going on out there, but it's touched only a minority of employees. In the early 1980s, Edward Lawler, Director of the U.S.C. Center, estimated that about 150 to 300 work sites were using teams. Clearly, the number of companies using teams has grown considerably. We believe that nearly every major U.S. company is currently trying or considering some form of empowered work teams somewhere in their organization.

Procter & Gamble is generally considered an important U.S. pioneer in seriously applying teams to their operations. Their work began in the early 1960s, although it was not publicized and virtually escaped media attention. P&G saw the team approach as a significant competitive advantage, and up through the 1980s, attempted to deflect attention away from their efforts. The company thought of their knowledge about the team organization as a type of trade secret, and required consultants and employees to sign nondisclosure statements. Other companies have had team-oriented plants for years, but have also considered their team approaches to be proprietary.

Despite their obsession with secrecy, Procter & Gamble's successes with teams received considerable informal "off-the-record" attention from a small group of in-house and external consultants across the country who were inspired by the P&G experiences, and who learned techniques through an informal network. Many of them originally worked at P&G and were attracted away to other companies by lucrative job offers because of their unique knowledge and expertise.

Through the 1970s and 1980s, General Motors was a locus of active experimentation with teams, and was significantly less secretive than Procter & Gamble. Many of the GM team implementations have been very successful, and have served as models for other changes around the country.

General Motors remains an interesting enigma, however—they are a textbook case of how success with teams at one location does not necessarily transfer to another location within a huge corporation. (Further, teams are not the sole answer to the competitiveness challenge.) We suspect the "not-invented-here" syndrome to be rampant at GM. Also, while specific GM manufacturing plants have been on the cutting edge of employee self-management, many would suggest that the corporate level has maintained a more traditional top-down control-based management mentality. Despite the problems of diffusion of their successes with self-management, General Motors should be credited with their leadership in active exploration of the team concept.

Other prominent companies have been active with teams. These include the early work with teams at the Gaines dog food plant in Topeka (incidentally, this is another case where diffusion of a successful change did not occur). Other companies include Cummins Engine, Digital Equipment, Ford, Motorola, Tektronix, General Electric, Honeywell, LTV, Caterpillar, Boeing, Monsanto, AT&T, Texas Instruments, and Xerox, to name just a

[6]See Part I, Section 4 of Lawler (1995).

few. In manufacturing, we now have extensive experience with self-managing teams, starting in the 1960s. Today, teams in manufacturing are a proven system. It's no longer a question of why, but now only a question of fine tuning to specific sites.

In the past few years, the use of teams in the service sector has been the most exciting area of application. Service teams, such as office teams at IDS (now American Express) (Sims et al., 1993), are now well past the experimentation phase, although we still have much to learn.

Perhaps the most promising area of team development in the later part of this decade will be empowered professional and middle-management teams. These include teams like concurrent engineering teams, cross-functional teams, product improvement teams, task force teams, ad hoc teams, and, as discussed later, new venture teams.

Teams in government is the most rapidly changing area of application. Until two or three years ago, there was very little interest in empowered teams in government agencies. Now, however, driven by the "reinventing government" thrust, and the stark reality of government downsizing, experimentation with teams in government seems to be very active indeed. It remains to be seen, however, whether teams in government will attain the same success seen in manufacturing and service.

10.5   *Team Leadership: Roles and Structures*

The key to team success is team leadership. Team leadership comes in all forms, starting with the traditional director, who exercises his or her power through authoritarian behaviors. But in this chapter, we are concentrating most on self-managed or empowered teams. The fundamental question we wish to address is: What type of leadership is most appropriate for empowered teams that are vested with a high degree of power, authority, and self-responsibility? First, consider the four archetypes of leadership that are likely to be found in today's contemporary organizations (Exhibit 10.3).

Before we consider the *behavior* of team leaders, we should first consider the *structure of team leadership*. By structure, we mean the question of how the leader is appointed (and, perhaps unappointed), whether the team leader is a member or co-performer of the team, and the degree of formal authority that is vested to the leader versus the team itself.

As a part of this discussion, we also raise the philosophical issue of whether formal leaders are really necessary. After all, if teams are really to be "self-managed," then why do they need a leader? Occasionally, one hears the term "leaderless teams," which usually means that a team does not have an appointed leader. This is somewhat of a paradox, because, in reality, no team is ever truly "leaderless"—at least no *effective* team is leaderless. Some form of leadership is always necessary for a team to function (for example, team-member self-leadership will exist within the team). In the absence of some form of *formal* external leadership, then, at least some degree of *emergent* leadership will always be present. Thus, so-called "leaderless" teams really do have leadership, but it typically is exercised by leaders that emerge to de facto leadership without being assigned this role by upper management.

In general, we are not in favor of trying to create leaderless teams. Most of the time, particularly in organizations, we believe some type of recognized leadership should be established, especially at the inception of the team. However, a team leader certainly need not be a traditional directive. And, we believe that a high degree of empowerment

EXHIBIT 10.3 The Four Archetypes of Leadership: Strongman, Transactor, Visionary Hero, and SuperLeader

There is an old Norse word, *Laed*, meaning "to determine the course of a ship." We can easily see how our modern word *lead* comes from this ancient expression. And we can even visualize the modern version of a *leader* as the person who guides the course of an organization. But in today's contemporary world, how should this guidance take place?

Fundamentally, leadership means influence—the ability to influence others. But this influence can be carried out in different ways. Here, we present a simplified historical perspective on different approaches to leadership. We focus on four leader *archetypes*: The Strongman, the Transactor, the Visionary Hero, and The SuperLeader.

The *Strongman* pattern of leadership concentrates on command and instruction to influence followers. A strongman's source of power is the coercion that stems from the authority of his or her position. It is a top-down type of leadership that produces a fear-based compliance in followers. The behaviors most frequently used by this leader are instruction, command, assigned goals, threat, intimidation, and reprimand.

The *Transactor* leader enters into an exchange relationship with followers. Rewards are the major source of influence, with the follower entering into a calculating compliance with the wishes of the leader in order to secure rewards that are controlled by the leader. The behaviors most frequently used by this leader are the dispensation of personal and material rewards in return for effort, performance, and loyalty to the leader.

The *Visionary Hero* leader is a source of inspiration to the follower. This leader uses a top-down vision, to inspire and stimulate followers, who make an emotional commitment based on the vision and charisma of the leader. This leader uses behaviors such as communicating a vision, exhortation, inspiration and persuasion, and challenge to the status quo. Other terms that describe the visionary hero are "transformational leader" and "charismatic leader."

The *SuperLeader* is the only leader who focuses primarily on the development of the follower. Sometimes called an "empowering" leader, this leader is "super" because he or she is strengthened through the strengths of followers. This leader leads others to lead themselves. The SuperLeader encourages follower initiative, self-responsibility, self-confidence, self-goal-setting, positive opportunity thinking, and self-problem-solving. Power is more balanced between the leader and followers. SuperLeadership is a perspective that reaches beyond visionary leadership. In the past, the idea of a leader implied that the spotlight was on the leader. This alternative viewpoint places the spotlight on the follower. In return, followers experience commitment and psychological ownership. For the SuperLeader, the essence of leadership is the challenge to lead followers to discover the potentialities that lie within themselves.

of the team itself, rather than primarily relying on the leader, is typically most effective over the long run.

There are various structural alternatives through which team leadership can be expressed. The most common and well known is the traditional external supervisor or foreperson. Typically, this person is appointed by management and has traditional powers that stem from the position itself. This person usually has the authority to make job assignments, give instructions and commands, and allocate some rewards and/or reprimands. Control over the team's activities are mainly vested in this appointed leader rather than the team itself. We think of this person as a "boss." Usually, this person is *not* a team member, and is at least one step removed from actually carrying out the work tasks themselves.

Interestingly, a natural pattern of leadership of an external appointed leader is often to act as a directive leader that directs and commands compliance from the team. Other leadership options, however, are more appropriate. Indeed, even under a traditional system, a supervisor might voluntarily choose to *act* as a SuperLeader, and encourage considerable self-leadership-based empowerment in the group. The main point, however, is that often situations are structured via an external leader appointed by management who retains a high degree of control and decision making that is typical of a formal appointed position.

Other types of structures are possible. For example, leadership may be expressed through an appointed external leader, often called a "facilitator," who is purposefully intended to facilitate empowered workers. Other terms that are sometimes used to label this position are "coordinator," "counselor," or "coach." A facilitator is usually *not* a part of the team—that is, he or she does not actually carry out team tasks, but offers advice and counsel on how the team itself might perform their duties. A facilitator is usually appointed by management, similar to a supervisor, but the expected behavior or "role" of the facilitator is quite different. While a supervisor retains a high degree of control and decision making, a facilitator typically attempts to encourage a team to undertake self-control activities such as self-job assignments, self-goal-setting, and so on. In other words, the expected role and pattern of leadership of an external facilitator is to assist a team to become empowered.

Again, the actual behaviors of this role might vary from person to person. However, generally, we would expect the role of an external facilitator to be consistent with SuperLeader-type behaviors that facilitate and influence team members and the team itself to act more as self-leaders. Directive-type behaviors are quite incompatible with this facilitator role.

There are other types of structures that might be utilized for team leadership, including the internal elected team leader. This type of leader is usually an actual team member, and engages in most of the typical day-to-day activities of the team in addition to leadership responsibilities. This leader frequently comes to his or her position as a result of some type of team election (or, even team leader rotation), and thus might be considered more of an emergent leader. Of course, if there is an election of the team leader, there must be some method of replacement to deal with turnover within the leadership role. This might be accomplished by invoking a specified "term of office," at the end of which the leader may or may not be reelected. Other mechanisms might include a "runoff" to choose between alternate candidates, or a "vote of confidence" in which a leader might be unelected or deposed. (We have found this to be quite unusual. Typically, an elected team leader in difficulty with his or her team will voluntarily step down before an "unelection" is necessary.)

A fellow-worker who is also a team leader will have advantages and obstacles in terms of group norms, interpersonal relationships, and so on that are not shared by external team leaders. For example, *internal* team leaders may be in a better position to contribute to the social well-being (group maintenance) of the group, but may face difficulties in emphasizing task performance because of personal relationships with other group members.

We like to think of an elected team leader as being "empowered from below." That is, this elected leader acts to organize, motivate, and influence the team, but the power and authority to do so comes from the very people the leader is attempting to influence. Note that the team itself may have been "empowered from above" to carry out this and other self-management responsibilities.

Clearly, the leader behaviors of an elected team leader are most consistent with the philosophy of a SuperLeader—that is, a leader who attempts to influence the team to lead itself. Conversely, directive behaviors tend to be highly incompatible with the role of elected team leader. An elected leader who behaves as a directive is likely to incite a rebellion among team members.

To summarize, at least three types of structures might be possible to express team leadership:

- Foreperson or Supervisor.
- Appointed External Facilitator.
- Elected Internal Team Leader.

These structures provide considerable variance in terms of direct control that is vested in the team itself, versus direct control retained by management. In the care of the traditional foreperson or supervisor, virtually all control is retained by management, since most of the power is vested in the supervisor, who represents management. At the other end of the spectrum, a great deal of control is vested in the team itself, which, in turn, "delegates upward" to the elected team leader.

The appointed external facilitator is a role that is somewhere in between in terms of empowerment, although the philosophy and practice typically is moving in the direction of greater team control. A facilitator attempts to move more control into the hands of the team, but in reality, management retains a great deal of control through the power to appoint or remove the facilitator.

In our own experience, we have seen all of these structural forms at one time or another. Of course, the traditional supervisor is the usual baseline or beginning point, and remains the most common structural form of leadership of work groups in the United States today. Nevertheless, we have seen many successful teams that use the elected team leader concept. We believe that for a team to be fully and *truly* empowered, team members should have a significant role in deciding who the team leader should be. However, the use of external facilitators and coordinators is probably the most frequent approach to team empowerment, and indeed can work very well, especially in a transition mode. Also, we have found the use of external facilitators to be most common when management has lingering doubts, or is not 100 percent convinced about team empowerment.

We also wish to note that while the behavior of leaders is *correlated with* the structure of the leadership position, structure and behavior are not necessarily the same. For example, as we mentioned before, a supervisor has a wide range of leadership patterns to select from, ranging from directive to SuperLeader. Facilitators are more likely to behave as SuperLeaders, although we have seen a few that have difficulty in refraining from giving orders and instructions. Also, we would clearly expect elected team leaders to act more like SuperLeaders, or face considerable displeasure from their constituency.

Finally, consider once more the notion of "leaderless" groups. Again, we don't believe there are any truly leaderless groups in formal organizations. Leadership always exists, and the question is how leadership is structured and how leaders behave. The effectiveness of any work group or team is highly dependent of how the leadership function is designed, and we recommend almost any other alternative rather than a "leaderless" group.

10.6   Behaviors of Team Leaders

The role of an external formal leader establishes an apparent paradox or conceptual inconsistency relative to the *ideal* concept of self-managing teams. The leader is charged with the responsibility of leading teams that are philosophically designed to be *self-led*. How can they lead when the team is supposed to lead itself! What is the appropriate role and behaviors for these leaders? Why should such a leader be necessary?

In the organizational hierarchy, this external leader—facilitator or coordinator—has replaced roles traditionally referred to as foreman, general foreman, or supervisor. However, under a self-managing concept, the nature of the authority and responsibility of the leader can become an issue of considerable confusion. To what extent should the leader give direction and evaluate performance yet be a facilitator and communicator? To what degree should he or she directly invoke authority? What are the behaviors that differentiate effective from ineffective facilitators? These questions become particularly challenging when one considers the ideal—that these work teams are supposed to be self-managing. The question "how does one lead employees who are supposed to lead themselves?" establishes a paradox and exemplifies this dilemma.

In our own research about self-managing teams, we have found widespread ambiguity and confusion about the role of appointed external leaders. We believe this issue is commonly a very troublesome point of implementation. While executives and workers who have direct experience with self-managing teams are generally pleased with the results, questions about the role of the external leader continue to be particularly bothersome. For managers who must select, train, counsel, and evaluate these external leaders, the questions are not ones of leisurely theory, but of immediate pragmatic application.

Consider the case of the coordinators at the Fitzgerald Battery Plant. The coordinator behaviors presented are clearly consistent with our earlier definitions of SuperLeadership (Exhibit 10.4).

10.7   The Transition: How Do We Get to Team Leadership?

Let's begin with an assumption that an organization wishes to implement some form of self-managed or empowered work team. Examples of such teams might be: (1) blue-collar manufacturing self-managing teams; (2) white-collar office-worker teams; or (3) cross-

---

EXHIBIT 10.4 What Do Coordinators Do?

In part of our early research on self-managing teams, we investigated team leadership at a manufacturing site with mature self-managing teams. In this section, we describe the results of this elicitation, which was conducted at the Fitzgerald Battery Plant of General Motors Corporation.[7] The particular role that was the target of this elicitation were the coordinators, or external team leaders.

What do "coordinators" do? What are the behaviors and actions of effective

---

[7]See "The Day-to-Day Team Experience: Roles, Behaviors, and Performance of Mature Self-Managing Teams," Chapter 2 in C. C. Manz, and H. P. Sims, Jr., *Business Without Bosses: How Self-Managing Teams Are Building High-Performing Companies.* New York, Wiley, 1993. Copyright © 1993 by C. C. Manz and H. P. Sims. Reprinted by permission of John Wiley & Sons, Inc.

EXHIBIT 10.4 *(Continued)*

coordinators? If employee work teams are supposed to be "participative," or "self-managed," then why are coordinators necessary? There are no formal guidelines regarding what a coordinator actually does, and coordinator behaviors seem to be loosely defined according to social convention rather than according to any structured set of rules and regulations. There is no "job description." At the time of our research, the ambiguities about this position were still an unresolved issue.

The inquiry was intended to answer the question: "What important behaviors can coordinators use in their work?" We asked this question many times, using a focus group technique. A summary of their answers is listed below.

Coordinator Behaviors Identified by Top Management

Try to get a team to solve a problem on its own.
Ask for solutions to problems.
Facilitate a team's attempt to solve conflict within its group.
Tell people (teams and individuals) when they do something well.
Tell the truth even when it may be disagreeable (painful).
Encourage team members to openly discuss problems.
Ask for a solution to a problem rather than proposing (telling) a solution—people promote what they create.
Encourage teams to set performance goals, such as scrap rates, efficiency, quality control index, safety. Provide teams with information they need to "run the business."
Anticipate future problems or situations (planning)
Encourage team self-evaluation.
Train teams in the philosophy of the plant.
Be a resource to a team.

The list provides some interesting insights. First, several of the behaviors, including the behavior obtaining the highest importance ratings, reveal an emphasis on getting teams to manage their own efforts, for example: "Get a team to solve a problem on its own," "Ask for a solution to a problem rather than proposing (telling)," and "Encourage teams to set performance goals."

Another major theme is a focus on some form of communication. Examples include "Tell people when they do something well," "Tell the truth even when it may be disagreeable," "Encourage team members to openly discuss problems," "Communicate plant needs," and "Act as a communication link."

Several behaviors indicated the role of the coordinator as a facilitator rather than a director. This perspective was indicated in such descriptions of behaviors as "Facilitate a team's attempt to solve conflict," "Be a resource to a team," and "Provide teams with information they need to 'run the business.' "

A general view understood in the plant was that teams resented overly *directive* coordinator behavior, for example, a coordinator giving orders to a team regarding solutions to problems.

We concluded that there is a fine line between overdirection and underdirection on the part of coordinators. While team members placed a high value on independence to manage themselves, they also wanted guidance and assistance when needed. It's important for a coordinator to be there, but not with a heavy hand. Consequently, coordinators must make a decision regarding the appropriate level of involvement based on the nature of each unique situation.

Overall, these results show a strong degree of similarity with the notion of SuperLeadership—leading others to lead themselves. Most of all, both sources of data emphasize the potential of unleashing the power of team self-leadership.

functional professional product improvement teams. Whatever the type of team, the transition to teams should always begin with three questions: (1) Where are we now in terms of team capability and team leadership?; (2) Where do we want to get to in terms of team capability and team leadership?; and (3) How long do we want this transition to take?

In this section, we concentrate on the issue of establishing empowered team *leadership*. That is, how do we manage the transition to empowered team leadership? Typically, an organization begins with one of two situations, either (1) a new *startup* (sometimes called a "greenfield"), or (2) a *redesign* of an existing organization (sometimes called a "retrofit" or a "brownfield"). In a startup, the organization begins with essentially a blank slate, with no existing personnel or organization. Conversely, in a redesign, an organization is currently in existence, with personnel currently in place. Often, these personnel may be individuals with considerable seniority and experience. In actual practice, these situations share many issues that must be considered and dealt with as a part of the transition. Let us begin with a startup situation, and we will later extend these ideas to a redesign situation.

10.8   Developing Team Leadership in a Startup Situation

Typically, a startup is the creation of a new organization. In manufacturing, a startup is often called a "greenfield." We will begin with the assumption that this organization has already developed several important elements for the startup such as a mission, strategy, physical location, logistics, a human resources system (including selection of new personnel), a production or service delivery system, a marketing system, and so forth. In addition, we will presume that the organization has made a decision to implement an empowered "team" organization, where the organization structure will mostly consist of small groups of employees who are empowered to carry out many of the day-to-day responsibilities associated with their job duties and responsibilities. The issue we wish to address here is concerned with the design of the leadership of these teams. What kind of leadership do we want? How can we get there?

Actually, we are faced with a rather daunting task. We can select and assemble groups of employees into teams that have logically defined boundaries and at least some initial idea of what their team responsibilities should be. Should we appoint a supervisor or team leader? Should we require the team to elect a team leader?

Also, the question of technical development is important—that is, the employees' need to learn the technical or task performance aspects of the particular process or service they perform. Who will teach these task performance skills to new employees?

We should first recognize that in the beginning there is no formal leadership, and typically very little informal leadership. Management must do something to create this initial form of leadership. At this stage, we recommend that a team leader be *appointed* by management *to a defined term of service*. This term might be six months; it might be a year. We would not recommend an initial term of longer than a year.

At first, this appointed leader frequently needs to behave in ways that are similar to a traditional supervisor. For example, most employees will not be fully trained in the tasks that are necessary to carry out their work. Further, employees are likely to have little experience at group self-leadership. They will probably be used to having others tell them what to do. Unfortunately, their lack of technical experience means that they will likely be highly dependent on their appointed leader in this early stage.

But soon, the team must be weaned of this dependency. Step by step, they must be introduced to team self-leadership. Concurrently, the role and the behavior of the leader must change. At first, the leader provides a significant amount of task instruction, assigned goals, and direct reinforcement for task accomplishment. After all, this is what good "traditional" leaders do. But then, gradually, team members must learn to lead themselves. That is, the leader becomes more concerned with stimulating and reinforcing team self-leadership instead of dealing *directly* with work behavior and team performance. For example, it is not difficult to imagine a team leader encouraging a team to define their own goals.

From a process viewpoint, a leader can: (1) model the specific self-management strategies; (2) provide encouragement and guidance for teams to use them; and (3) provide reinforcement when they are used. A leader could facilitate the use of team goal setting, for example, by displaying it in his or her own behavior, providing guidance (e.g., suggesting that specific and challenging goals are especially effective), asking for and encouraging the *team* to begin using self-goal-setting, and then praising team members when goal-setting behavior is observed.

As time goes by, the focus of goal setting and administration of consequences will logically and significantly change. That is, the team leader becomes more concerned with stimulating and reinforcing self-managing behavior than dealing *directly* with work behavior and performance. For example, eventually the team leader will want to facilitate the team in defining its own goals. There may also be occasions of blatant worker misconduct which necessitate the use of punishment, but we have observed team self-discipline to be a most effective alternative in our own research—a process we suspect a leader would be wise to encourage at a reasonable level. The point is, *the leader's primary task becomes helping the team to manage itself.* External modes of influence should mainly be devoted to developing team self-management capabilities, especially in the early team development stages, and also in providing the external guidance needed when team self-management breaks down.

Finally, the culture that surrounds team leadership is critical to success, especially in the early stages. First, the culture must reward leaders for team development, rather than short-term performance. A focus on short-term performance is dysfunctional because team implementation is sometimes accompanied by an initial temporary drop in performance. Leaders who are rewarded solely for performance will abandon their patient development of team self-leadership and instead return to older supervisory behaviors of instruction and command. While short-term productivity is always a matter of concern, it should not overwhelm the objective of developing team self-leadership capabilities for the long term.

10.9 Developing Team Leadership in a Redesign Situation

The term "redesign" typically means converting an existing organization from a "traditional" to a team system. Sometimes the term "brownfield" is used. In redesign, a critical question arises in terms of the role of existing supervisors. Can supervisors who have been trained to command and direct change their behavior to team leader behaviors?

According to Kim Fisher, who has extensive experience with conversion to teams at Procter & Gamble, many supervisors become extremely frustrated when asked to convert from a supervisory role to a team leader role. Here are the four most common reasons he gives for difficulty in the supervisor transition:[8]

- It is frequently seen as a net loss of power or status.
- The team leader role has not been well defined for them.
- Some are concerned that they will lose their jobs as a result of the transition to teams.
- Many supervisors are asked to manage in a way that is quite different from the way they are managed themselves.

We have encountered similar situations in our own experience. One supervisor in the midst of a transition to a team organization stated that "the atmosphere rewards a high profile (by leaders) and getting personally involved in everything, not in recognizing people who support others."

Some are not very confident about the potential to convert supervisors to facilitators. At the Texas Instruments Malaysia Plant, A. Subramaniam (usually called "Subra") recounts how one manager could not make the transition to teams (Cheney et al., 1993). According to Subra, this manager "completely dominated his team, with his self-centeredness. He never was able to adapt to the give-and-take of the team system and the sharing of authority. He wanted to make all the decisions himself." Eventually this manager left the organization for another. "From a technical viewpoint, we regretted his loss," says Subra. "He was excellent at the technical side, but he was never able to accept the team system. I've talked to him recently, and he's much happier in a traditional management setting."

In the end, however, many can make this transition, and the problems seem to solve themselves once the supervisors are truly in the new role of team leader. Our own viewpoint is this: We do not believe that every supervisor can successfully make this transition (at least not in a reasonable time frame). However, we know of no reliable way of predicting who will make it, and who will not. We have seen the most intense "bull of the woods" foreman become the most passionate advocate of the team system. We believe that every supervisor deserves a chance to change, and most of all, should be given the training and modeling necessary to make the transition. But in the end, some will not succeed. Even those who do successfully make the transition are aware of the challenge. Consider the comments from former supervisors at IDS Corporation who undertook the transition to team facilitator, presented in Exhibit 10.5.

10.10 Teams, Leadership, and the Self-Renewing Organization

When contrasting a traditional organization with a team organization, leadership roles are the most critical element that changes. The main purpose of the team leader is to create a positive atmosphere for exercising team self-management. More specifically, he or she acts as a SuperLeader by stimulating the use of the follower self-leadership. Some

---

[8]For further development of these ideas, see: Kimball Fisher, *Leading Self-Directed Work Teams: A Guide to Developing New Team Leadership Skills*, New York, McGraw-Hill, 1993, p. 48.

EXHIBIT 10.5 On the Transition from Supervisor to Facilitator

Following are quotations taken from supervisors experiencing a transition to team facilitators at the IDS Corporation.[9]

- In the traditional system it was clear that I had the final word, and right now it is not clear. That's different. Another thing that's different is that we have changed the tasks. It's one thing to be self-managing in your old room and doing the same function, but now we've put together 20 other types of jobs that we didn't know anything about, so instead of having one set of goals and objectives, we've got a variety of them.

- It's frustrating because you feel like you should be knowing it, but you don't, and yet we know it's unrealistic for us to think at this point that we can know everything. We make it a learning experience, and it takes a lot of time to do that.

- The thing I've been struggling with is that there's nothing to call my own. Eventually, if they're truly self-managing, it's going to be the team that gets most of the recognition. Now, I get more satisfaction out of helping someone to do something on their own rather than telling them to do it.

- In the traditional structure of supervision, you'd have goals and objectives: It was laid out. I always felt I knew what part of the path I was traveling on. Here as a team facilitator, so far I haven't felt that clarified yet, so I don't quite know where we're going.

- The reorganization of the task and the structure of the task are one dimension, and the management style or the division of authority is a different dimension.

- Weekly, we just feel more and more comfortable with it. The pilot team is working. They're getting work done. Things are going fine. I'm delighted. I think that it's going to make jobs a lot more interesting for people. There will be a lot more buy-in to decisions if it's a group decision than if it's mine.

of the particularly important elements in this role are: (1) the evaluative and reinforcement functions are gradually shifted from external sources to the work team itself; (2) the progress made in a team's self-leadership behavior is encouraged; and (3) increased emphasis is placed on the goals and expectations of team members themselves rather than external sources (e.g., external leaders).

As the leader shifts to this supportive and facilitating perspective, changes will take place in team-member motivation, satisfaction, effort, flexibility of response and, ultimately, performance. Most important, this provides a *process* by which external leaders can develop and enhance, over time, the team self-management. Team leadership can create a foundation for true empowerment.

Our years of studying teams had convinced us of their tremendous potential. We were gratified that finally, at the beginning of the 1990s, the topic of teams had reached the front page. *Fortune* Magazine featured a cover story—"Who Needs a Boss?"—about teams in the May 7, 1990 issue. *BusinessWeek* also featured a cover story about teams in their July 1989 issue. Even Dan Rather spoke about "self-directed" teams.

Although it's taken some time, the topic of teams has clearly reached the stage of

[9]Taken from Chapter 4, "The Early Implementation Phase: Getting Teams Started at the Office," in C. C. Manz, & H. P. Sims, Jr., *Business Without Bosses: How Self-Managing Teams are Building High-Performing Companies*. New York, Wiley, 1993. Copyright © 1993 by C. C. Manz and H. P. Sims. Reprinted by permission of John Wiley & Sons, Inc.

becoming a popular fad with all the accompanying advantages and disadvantages, but we believe they will pass the test of time and prove to be enduring. We think that teams are here to stay, and that they constitute a fundamental change in the way we go about work. We suspect the label and approach will evolve and perhaps pass—like all fads—but the fundamental ways that teams do business will remain with us for a long time—mainly because teams are effective. Teams may represent a whole new management paradigm. Perhaps they reflect a new business era as influential as the industrial revolution and are destined to revolutionize work for decades to come.

Self-managing and empowered teams are a natural extension of self-leadership. Teams are a type of collective or group self-leadership. The SuperLeader makes it happen by initiating, encouraging, and supporting empowered teams. Indeed, teams are a critical ingredient in creating a company of heroes.

Most of all, self-managing teams are the day-to-day mechanism through which the self-renewing organization is actually implemented on the firing line. Teams promote self-renewal by influencing both the effectiveness and the efficiency factors of the self-renewing equation (see Chapter 1). Through myriad small decisions and actions, teams keep the organization focused on both doing things right (efficiency) and doing the right thing (effectiveness). In today's contemporary organizations, teams are the essence of self-renewal.

Suggested Readings

Cheney, A. B., Sims, H. P. Jr., and Manz, C. C. 1993. "Teams and Total Quality Management: An International Application." In C. C. Manz, and H. P. Sims, Jr., *Business Without Bosses: How Self-Managing Teams Are Building High-Performing Companies*. New York: Wiley.

Dumaine, Brian. 1990. "Who Needs a Boss?" *Fortune* (May 7): 52–60.

Frederiksen, Lee W., Riley, Anne W., and Myers, John B. 1984. "Matching Technology and Organizational Structure: A Case in White Collar Productivity Improvement." *Journal of Organizational Behavior Management* (Fall Winter): 59–80.

Horr, John. 1989. "The Payoff from Teamwork." *Business Week* (May 7): 56–62.

Lawler, E. E. III, Morhman, S. A., and Ledford, G. E. Jr. 1995. *Creating High Performance Organizations: Practices and Results of Employee Involvement and Total Quality Management in Fortune 1000 Companies*. San Francisco: Jossey-Bass.

Macy, Barry A. and Izumi, Hiroaki. 1994. "Organizational Change, Design, and Work Innovation: A Meta Analysis of 131 North American Field Studies—1961–1991." *Research in Organizational Change and Development*, vol. 7, JAI Press, pp. 235–313.

Miner, John B. 1982. *Theories of Organizational Structure and Process*. Hinsdale, IL: Dryden, pp. 110–111.

Sims, H. P. Jr., Manz, C. C., and Bateman, B. 1993. "The Early Implementation Phase: Getting Teams Started at the Office." Chapter 4 in C. C. Manz, and H. P. Sims, Jr., *Business Without Bosses: How Self-Managing Teams Are Building High-Performing Companies*. New York: Wiley.

Designing and Implementing Effective Personnel Policies

Lawrence T. Zimmerman, LLB
Sanders, Schnabel, Brandenburg & Zimmerman, P.C.,
Washington, D.C.

11.1 Part I—An Overview of Personnel Administration

(A) THE NEED FOR EFFECTIVE PERSONNEL POLICIES

Nonprofit organizations, whether large or small, have to deal with a broad range of employment-related issues. The size of the organization may dictate the degree of formality by which its policies and procedures are articulated, but a nonprofit organization of any size must have policies and procedures in place. Those policies will serve several purposes. They will enlist the employees as active participants in the effort to attain the goals of the organization. They will announce and shape the working conditions and employee benefits that management believes will attract and keep the workforce that it desires. They will provide guidance for fair and consistent treatment of the organization's employees. And they will reflect management's expectations of appropriate employee performance and management's response to deficient and unacceptable employee performance or conduct.

Today, the management of a nonprofit organization, like its management counterparts in commercial enterprises, must not only deal with morale and performance issues, but must also take into account the array of federal, state, and local laws that affect the employment relationship by providing various statutory protections to employees. Historically, before the advent of laws protecting certain categories of employees from discrimination in employment, the "employment-at-will" doctrine gave employers a largely free hand in terminating employees for good reason, bad reason, or no reason at all. Although the doctrine of employment-at-will still survives in most states, it has been severely eroded in its application, both by the prevalence of antidiscrimination and other laws protective of employee interests and by judicial rulings finding implied contracts of employment with attendant implied "just cause" requirements for dismissal.

The expansion of employee rights and the consequent constraints on employer prerogatives are factors that must be taken into account in formulating and implementing personnel policies. Sound personnel practices have always been founded on sets of rules and procedures of generally uniform application, communicated to the entity's employees in some fashion (but not necessarily in handbook form). The objective was a positive one, to let employees know what was expected of them and accordingly to boost employee morale and performance. An organization's efforts to be fair in its pay, promotion, evaluation, and disciplinary procedures were not always perceived that way by the affected employees, but as long as the "employment-at-will" doctrine was dominant and there was no contract of employment in force, employers were generally not put to the test of defending the propriety of their actions before a court or administrative tribunal. However, as protective laws became the order of the day, and employees became far more aggressive than ever before in litigating asserted violations of their real or perceived rights, the formulation and implementation of personnel policies have now taken on a defensive role as well.

The designing of appropriate personnel policies is only half the battle. If such policies are to be effective, they must be communicated to employees, and communicated in a way to be absorbed and understood by them. Personnel policies that are clearly articulated, enforced without favoritism, and well documented in writing, play a vital role in supporting both management's objectives and the employer's defense.

(B) DEALING WITH APPLICABLE LAW

Despite the limitations that now surround the doctrine of employment-at-will, it is still a concept definitely worth preserving. Most dismissals (or other adverse personnel actions) are not even arguably acts of unlawful discrimination, although they may be perceived as unfair by the affected employee. In such situations the employment-at-will doctrine provides a meaningful measure of insulation from litigation.

That having been said, it remains evident that the leadership of nonprofit organizations should have at least a general knowledge of the laws affecting the employment relationship, and of personnel actions necessary or helpful in avoiding their violation. A brief summary of pertinent aspects of federal law follows, but with the caveat that management should contact legal counsel for the details of the federal employment laws and the body of state and local laws that may apply to the organization's employment relationships.

(i) Laws Prohibiting Discrimination

Federal laws bar discrimination in hiring, firing, promotions, disciplinary actions, compensation, fringe benefits (including coverage under health and retirement plans), and virtually all other aspects of employment, if such discrimination is based on race, color, religion, sex, or national origin (Title VII of the Civil Rights Act), is based on age (the Age Discrimination in Employment Act, the ADEA), and for persons otherwise qualified, is based on disability (the Americans with Disabilities Act, the ADA). State laws generally contain overlapping coverage and may add other protected categories, such as sexual orientation, marital status, political affiliation, and so on. Federal antidiscrimination laws often do not reach employers with fewer than 15 or 20 employees, but smaller entities may well be subjected to such prohibitions by state laws.

The antidiscrimination provisions of such laws include intentional discrimination against a particular employee because of the individual's race, sex, and so on (so-called "disparate treatment"), as well as the use of employment practices or policies which seem neutral on their face but have a disproportionate adverse effect on certain protected groups ("disparate impact"). A reliance on arrest records, for example, would fall in the latter category. A claimant's case may be proven by various means, including racist or sexist comments by a managerial employee, statistical imbalance indicating adverse treatment of persons in the claimant's protected category, an otherwise inexplicable personnel decision or more favorable treatment in similar circumstances of persons outside of the particular protected category, or any other evidence which suggests that the real reason for the employer's action was a discriminatory one. An additional element comes into play in situations involving an employee with a covered disability under the ADA, where the employer may be required to make an effort at a reasonable accommodation to enable the employee to perform his job, so long as it does not create an undue hardship on the employer.

Such employee protections also include prohibitions against a hostile workplace environment, including harassment (sexual, racial, etc.) that is sufficiently severe or pervasive to alter the individual's conditions of employment and create an abusive, intimidating, or unduly offensive working environment. Not all acts that are offensive or disturbing to an individual amount to a hostile environment; their severity and/or frequency are an important element. Unlawful harassment can occur as the result of actions by co-workers as well as by supervisory employees. The employer is liable if it knew or should have known about the harassment and did not take prompt and effective action to stop it.

Although the antidiscrimination laws generally do not prescribe specific personnel policies that must be adopted by employers, certain steps are plainly prudent ones. The organization should be on record as opposing and prohibiting discriminatory policies, through the circulation of a handbook or some document to that effect to its employees. The same holds true regarding sexual harassment or harassment of any kind directed against employees in protected categories. It is extremely important, as a means of underscoring its commitment, for the employer to have a published antiharassment policy (in a handbook or written notice posted or circulated to employees) to make clear that harassment of a co-worker by any employee will not be tolerated, to encourage employees who believe they are being harassed to bring the matter to the attention of management, and to provide that disciplinary action will be taken against offenders where warranted.

Precise and comprehensive record-keeping of personnel actions is vital. Employers should carefully document the basis for all personnel decisions, and should be meticulous in reducing warnings and other disciplinary actions to writing. It is far more difficult to counter claims of discrimination if the employer cannot show by written documentation that its treatment of the alleged discriminatee was in keeping with treatment of other employees under similar circumstances.

(ii) Other Laws Affecting Employment

For the most part federal laws (and generally state laws as well) do not require the employer to offer particular benefits. An employer's decision to grant such benefits as vacation, sick leave, health benefits and the like, is a voluntary one not required by federal law. (However, if certain benefits *are* offered, federal law may apply to assure proper funding, payment, or continuation under certain circumstances, such as the application of the Employee Retirement Income Security Act—ERISA—to various heath and retirement plans.)

Perhaps the major exception to that voluntary approach to benefits is the Family and Medical Leave Act (FMLA), an Act which reaches only comparatively large organizations, those which employ 50 or more employees in the same locality for 20 or more work weeks in a year. This law mandates the granting of unpaid leave for certain health conditions or family-related purposes, and continuation of medical benefits, for up to 12 weeks per year for those employees who have been employed for at least a year and who have worked 1250 hours in the 12-month period before taking such leave. If the employer is subject to the FMLA, any employee handbook that it offers must alert the reader to the application of that Act.

The employer must also comply with the requirements of the Fair Labor Standards Act (FLSA), which mandates the payment of no less than the statutory minimum hourly rate and premium pay of one and one-half times the employees's regular hourly rate of pay for hours worked in excess of 40 in any week. Although many organizations are under the impression that salaried employees are automatically exempt from overtime pay requirements, that is not the case. Salaried employees can be exempt as executives, administrative, or professional employees, but only if (a) they meet certain duties tests, (b) they are salaried at a certain monetary level, and (c) they are truly salaried, which means that deductions from their pay for time off must comply with certain restrictions.

Nonprofit organizations may well be affected by the Drug-Free Workplace Act, which applies to recipients of federal grants of any amount as well as to most recipients of federal contracts above a certain monetary amount. As a condition of receiving such government funding, the organization must certify its compliance with the Act, a certification which requires the organization to have certain drug-related prohibitions and sanctions in place, and to have informed its employees of the organization's policy to maintain a drug-free workplace, the dangers of drug abuse, and any available drug counseling, rehabilitation, or assistance programs. The Act, however, leaves to the employer the option of whether it will engage in drug testing, employee assistance programs, or supervisory training.

The Immigration Reform and Control Act prohibits employers from knowingly hiring or continuing to employ any alien not authorized to work in the United States. Employers must verify every applicant's legal right to work in the United States within 3 working days of hire, on the basis of an acceptable document or documents establishing the identity and employment authorization of the employee (e.g., passport, voter registration card). The Act also prohibits employers from discriminating on the basis of citizenship.

Also, a federal law that should not be overlooked is the National Labor Relations Act, which gives employees the right to join labor unions, to bargain collectively and to engage in other concerted activities, or to refrain from any or all such activities. That Act establishes procedures for employee representation by unions, and establishes various unfair labor practices on the part of employees and unions, among which is a prohibition barring employer discrimination against employees on the basis of their union activities.

(C)   THE PREHIRE STEPS

The application of an effective personnel policy begins with the prehire process, and involves among other things the design of the employment application, the development of an outline of questions to be asked of the applicant for employment by the organization's interviewer, and a decision as to whether to require prehire drug screening. The importance of the text of the employment application should not be underestimated. Apart from its use in eliciting information useful to a hiring decision, the application can also be an important means of announcing prospective conditions of employment and obtaining employee consent to meaningful employment conditions that otherwise might be a source of controversy. The employment application enables the employer to notify the prospective new hire that employment is terminable at will, and that there can be no contract of employment unless authorized by a specified officer of the organization. It can condition employment on preemployment drug screening and/or subsequent substance abuse screening during employment. It can obtain the applicant's acknowledgment of the employer's right to inspect property such as e-mail, desks, lockers, or certain vehicles, and to provide authorization for employer conduct that otherwise might give rise to invasion of privacy or other employee claims. The applicant's signature will signify knowledge and acceptance.

The prehire interview should follow, to the extent practicable, a prearranged outline of initial and follow-up questions. The procedures and questions should not be left to chance. Because substantial areas of interrogation are off-limits as a matter of law, it is important that the interviewer be knowledgeable about such restrictions, and that the interviewer work from a written source. The ADA, in particular, has extensive guidelines delineating lawful and unlawful questions, so as to avoid eliciting in the preemployment stage information regarding present or past disabilities as defined by that Act. Other limitations arise under Title VII, as well as other laws. As a practical matter, the questioning should be confined to matters that are truly job-related.

(D)   THE ORIENTATION PROCEDURE

The orientation period, in particular the initial posthire conference between the new employee and the Executive Director or the employee's immediate supervisor, is a crucial part of any effective personnel policy. Unlike the prehire interview, which may well have emphasized the gathering of information from the applicant, the posthire orientation interview provides the employer with full opportunity to describe its policies, working conditions, benefits, and expectations of performance and behavior. The employer should work from a written check list of the matters to be covered, and the documents to be furnished to the employee. The employee should be provided with an acknowledgment of receipt form referring to each of the documents so provided, and a signed and dated receipt should be obtained.

The documents should include an employee handbook (described below) which will serve as the basic written set of guidelines to the organization's personnel and benefits policy, but there will also be a number of other documents which provide more detailed information and perhaps employee waivers as well. There are likely to be insurance or retirement benefit booklets or summary plan descriptions which will provide substantially more detail than appears in the organization's handbook, together with any enrollment forms. Depending upon the sophistication of the organization's research or other operations, the organization may wish to have the employee sign, as a condition of employment, a waiver of rights to patents or other proprietary materials that may eventually develop from his work-related efforts, and perhaps various confidentiality and non-disclosure agreements. If the organization in its employment application has not incorporated waivers with regard to alcohol or drug testing, or inspection of personal property—or perhaps even if it has—then the time to do this is before the employee starts work rather than when an incident occurs.

The employee should be instructed to read the materials, with special emphasis on the handbook, within a prescribed time, and should be urged to follow up that indoctrination by asking any questions of his supervisor that arise from his reading of the furnished documents. The entirety of the orientation period that follows will be directed, of course, to an ongoing evaluation of the new hire's performance, but it should also be designed to elicit questions from the employee and to provide the opportunity for discussions between the employee and his supervisor.

(E) THE EMPLOYEE HANDBOOK

A written and comprehensive statement of the organization's personnel policies is vital for the reasons described above, but an effort to provide all such information in a single document to be distributed to employees is likely to be self-defeating. A document that is too lengthy, too detailed, or too stilted in its phrasing is likely to go unread, and will accordingly fail as an effective means of communication to the organization's employees. The core of written communication to employees should be an employee handbook which is distributed to every employee (and signed for by each recipient) and which contains matters of importance in an easily read format. The handbook can incorporate by reference other documents where additional detail is provided, such as referring the reader to copies of insurance brochures maintained by the organization. Particularly in larger organizations, there may be a more elaborate policy manual, for use primarily by managers and supervisors but available for reference by employees upon request.

An example of an employee handbook is provided in Part III of this chapter, together with some explanatory notes. Plainly the particulars will differ from organization to organization, but most handbooks will cover the same essential features. They should generally contain (a) a brief statement of the organization's function and objectives; (b) a description and definition of who is covered by the handbook's terms, and to what extent (e.g., full-time or part-time employees, exempt or nonexempt); (c) a statement of employment-at-will and a disclaimer announcing that the handbook does not create any contract of employment; (d) a statement of an equal employment opportunity policy; (e) a statement of an antiharassment policy; (f) a statement in compliance with the Drug-Free Workplace Act; (g) a statement of selection and promotion procedures, including performance reviews and evaluations; (h) a statement of working hours, overtime arrangements, and attendance requirements; (i) a statement of operational policies, including such matters as nondisclosure of confidential information, proprietary rights of the organization, appearance and dress codes, no-smoking policy, and so on; (j) a statement of compensation policies; (k) a statement of employee benefits, including insurance and retirement plans, paid- and unpaid-leave policies; (l) a statement of disciplinary policies, including conditions for termination; (m) a statement of a procedure for resolution of grievances or complaints; and (n) a statement regarding the organization's right in its discretion to modify the stated policies at any time. In addition, those organizations subject to the FMLA must include a statement regarding that Act's application.

(F) DISCIPLINARY PROCEDURES

There are essentially three elements to an effective disciplinary procedure. It starts with the pronouncement by management (generally expressed in the employee handbook) of the types of conduct management finds unacceptable (loosely enough defined so as not to imply that matters not specifically mentioned are necessarily excluded), including a list of examples of the types of misconduct likely to prompt disciplinary action including immediate termination. It requires a firm and consistent application of similar penalties under similar circumstances, and a system of warnings or progressively more severe discipline in matters where it is the pattern of employee conduct (such as poor attendance) and not a particular incident standing alone that management finds unacceptable. And it requires documentation of the misconduct (date, time, participants, witnesses, and nature of the act), of the notification to the employee, and of the penalty imposed.

It is far too easy for supervision to rationalize its failure to call employees to account and to maintain proper records. There is often a laxity in a nonprofit organization's administration of personnel matters, due in part to a reluctance to criticize employees engaged in helping attain the organization's goals and in part to the press of day-to-day operations exacerbated by under staffing. The result is frequently the substitution of casual oral admonitions for deserved written warnings, and the creation of inflated evaluations so as not to hurt the employees's feelings. What emerges is a pattern of employer condonation of unacceptable conduct that makes it all the more difficult to take severe action against offending employees when necessary, and gives rise to claims of disparate treatment when supervision departs from that pattern in the case of a particular offender.

To be effective, disciplinary action must promptly and clearly identify the offensive act and provide a degree of punishment to the offender. For an organization to be consistent in its disciplinary actions, it must maintain sufficient records of the circumstances of the acts of misconduct and the penalties imposed. The organization that ignores those truisms does so at its peril.

(G) CONCLUSION

A few basic guidelines should be kept in mind. A policy should be specific enough to provide guidance for consistent action in similar situations, but it should not be so detailed as to suggest that any action other than a specified one is necessarily excepted from its coverage. Any procedure outlined in the organization's employee handbook or any other statement of personnel policy should be followed. A failure of the organization to follow its own processes or to be consistent in their application undermines the very stability that the policies are intended to offer, and exposes the organization to arguable claims of arbitrary or allegedly discriminatory treatment. Policies and practices do change, however, and the organization should always be on record with the statement that the adopted policies are subject to modification or termination at any time at the discretion of management. Whenever the stated policies are issued or changed, or new policies added, a written and dated statement of the policy should be provided to the employee, and a signed and dated receipt obtained.

As a final word of caution, an organization would be well advised to obtain legal advice before adopting a set of personnel policies, so it can be sure that the proposed document complies with federal, state, and local laws and regulations.

11.2 Part II—The Organization's Statement of Employment Policies and Procedures

The personnel policies of nonprofit organizations will reflect their approach to dealing with their human resources. Their policies should as a general rule be adopted by the Board of Directors, and when amendments are made, they should be adopted through a similar procedure. The organization's *policies* should not be amended frequently, for they are intended to provide a measure of stability to the employer-employee relationship. Items of *procedure* fall into a different category, and for the sake of efficiency, are best left to staff. The staff needs to have the authority and flexibility to amend procedures as circumstances warrant.

Part II is designed to identify most of the basic elements to be covered in a set of personnel policies and procedures and to highlight issues or problems that might arise in connection with their formulation or administration. It is to be read in conjunction with the sample handbook for employees contained in Part III. The objective of providing the text of a sample handbook in this chapter is to illustrate the policy and practice considerations that must be taken into account by management and communicated to employees in such a way as to foresee and answer questions that are likely to arise and to convey the organization's view of what it expects of the people who work for it. An employee handbook is a set of guidelines, and cannot be all-inclusive. In many instances it can and should do nothing more than identify the key elements of a feature of employment and refer the employee to a more informative source document. Separate documents, such as summary plan descriptions of the organization's health plan or retirement plan, are generally readily available. Other features of employment, such as the organization's leave policy for health or family care—an entitlement which is becoming more prevalent as a legal requirement—may simply be too cumbersome to explain in detail in a handbook, and will require reference to a more detailed policy statement or perhaps even government forms or booklets.

There are also aspects of personnel policy to be addressed by a Board of Directors that must be documented and maintained in the organization's files but are extraneous to policies and procedures that need to be communicated directly to the work force at large. Matters such as the authority of the Board, the nature of any contract of employment between the Board and the Executive Director, or the role of volunteers in the organization, are best left to incorporation in the organization's bylaws or separate policy statements.

This Part will address the features in the sample handbook for employees (identified in Part III as "The Nonprofit Organization's Guide to Employment Policies") in the order that the items appear, in order to explain—where the reason is not self-evident—what the provision is designed to accomplish, and why. The sample handbook, it should be kept in mind, purports to be nothing more than a series of examples of policies and procedures which have been adopted arbitrarily by the writer for illustrative purposes. A convention adopted in the sample handbook is generally to treat the Executive Director as not only the chief officer of the organization but also as the employee's supervisor, the keeper of all records, the person to whom all reports are made, and so on. An organization of any size, of course, will have other individuals serving in some of those capacities, and where appropriate those individuals should be substituted. We turn now to a section-by-section analysis of "The Nonprofit Organization's Guide to Employment Policies."

(A) ARTICLE I—INTRODUCTION

A. Welcome to the Nonprofit Organization

Reasons for inclusion:

To welcome each employee.
To state that the handbook is only a general guideline.
To state that amendments may be made from time to time.
To state that amendments can be made at the sole discretion of
    management.
To describe briefly the mission of the organization.

B. Terms of Employment

Reasons for inclusion:

To state that employment is "employment-at-will."
To notify employees that the handbook is not a contract guaranteeing
    employment for any period of time.
To explain who has the authority to make an employment contract and that
    such a contract must be in writing.

Note: An employer will generally want to protect the concept of employment at will, and to do so must avoid creating an implied contract. A handbook without a specific assertion of employment-at-will and a disclaimer making clear that it is not creating a contract of employment runs the risk of being deemed a contract of employment. To be effective any such disclaimer must be stated early and prominently, so as not to be missed by the employee. If an organization chooses to have any written employment contracts, it should be particularly clear in each about the extent to which that contract supersedes the published personnel policies.

C. Classes of Employment

Reasons for inclusion:

To explain who is covered by the handbook's provisions, and, in general, to what extent.

To define the distinction between full-time and part-time employees (and temporary employees), which can result in differing compensation, benefits, or treatment.

To define the distinction between exempt and nonexempt employees, in accordance with the Fair Labor Standards Act (FLSA).

To avoid repetition throughout the document.

Note: The failure to define the limitations on employees who are covered can create the impression that all employees are entitled to all benefits and all have the same standing and rights, and thus mislead employees with regard to eligibility for overtime premiums, compensatory time, and certain benefits.

(B)   ARTICLE II—GENERAL EMPLOYMENT INFORMATION

[Note: Some issues are of such general importance or interest as to warrant highlighting at the beginning of the document.]

A. Equal Employment Policy

Reasons for inclusion:

To state the organization's commitment to equal employment opportunities and non-discrimination in employment.

To state the organization's policy against unlawful harassment.

To explain the procedure for addressing instances of job-related discrimination or harassment.

Note: Courts have exonerated employers from sexual harassment liability where the employer has shown that it has a policy in place and publicized, so that employees are on notice of the employer's commitment and of the availability of a complaint procedure that can bypass any appeal to the alleged harasser. The employer must, of course, actively enforce the policy.

B. Drug-Free Workplace

Reasons for inclusion:

To comply with the Federal Drug-Free Workplace Act of 1988.

To indicate the organizations's commitment to providing a drug-free workplace.

To underscore the organization's prohibition of drug use or possession.

To make clear that violation of the policy will invoke disciplinary sanctions.

Note: The organization may prefer to hand out a copy of its policy at orientation and make only a general reference to it in the handbook.

C. Health and Safety

Reasons for inclusion:

To indicate the organization's commitment to a safe workplace.
To make clear that safety is also an employee responsibility.
To inform employees that they must report injuries and hazardous
conditions.

D. Conflict of Interest

Reasons for inclusion:

To remind employees that the organization is sensitive to and jeopardized
by conflicts of interest or the appearance of such conflicts.
To define conflicts of interest by employees.
To specify actions when such conflict exists.

Note: Board members are covered by the organization's bylaws which are
likely to address conflicts. This provision of the handbook makes clear that
the principle applies to the organization's employees. A nonprofit
organization that distributes funds is well advised to prohibit employees
from serving on the boards of any current or prospective grant-seeking
organizations.

E. Employment of Relatives

Reasons for inclusion:

To forestall problems when Board or staff members press for hiring a relative.
To define a "relative" for such purposes.
To make clear that in any event there cannot be a reporting relationship
between an employee and relative.

Note: An organization may choose to have a policy that encourages the hire
of relatives, despite the possibility of morale or performance problems. Any
policy, however, should preclude any supervisor-employee relationship
between relatives.

F. Ownership of Certain Materials

Reasons for inclusion:

To notify employees of the proprietary rights of the organization.
To make clear that any work-related product developed by the employee is
the organization's and not the employee's property.

Note: Particularly with respect to organizations engaged in scientific or
similar research, the matter of proprietary rights is sufficiently important for
employers to require employees to sign an agreement upon hire as a
condition of employment.

G. Substance Abuse

Reasons for inclusion:

To prohibit both the use and possession of alcohol and unlawful drugs on
the organization's premises or at functions of the organization.

To prohibit working or reporting to work under the influence of alcohol or
drugs.

To notify employees of possible inspection of their possessions on the
organization's premises.

To notify employees of the prospect of drug or alcohol testing.

To provide that refusal to submit to such testing will result in automatic
termination.

Note: The Americans with Disabilities Act does not protect current drug
users, but does treat alcoholism as a disability. Although the organization's
disposition of a person who is actually an alcoholic will have to take the
ADA into account, that does not invalidate the assertion and enforcement of
a substance abuse policy. This section, by notifying employees in advance
that their possessions are subject to inspection, also reduces the risk of
invasion of privacy charges by reducing expectations of privacy at the
outset.

(C)   ARTICLE III—EMPLOYMENT POLICIES

A. Job Creation and Description

Reasons for inclusion:

To make clear that there is a written description for every position, and that
such description is subject to review on a specified periodic basis and
subject to revision where appropriate.

To describe the use of job descriptions and specifications as a guide to
evaluation of performance.

To indicate, where appropriate, the authority and steps for creating a
position.

To encourage the employee's suggestions as to needed modifications.

B. Recruitment and Selection

Reasons for inclusion:

To explain how and when job openings are posted internally.

To explain how, when, and perhaps where, job openings are advertised
externally. To state who has the authority to make recruitment or other
staffing decisions.

Note: Whether or not an organization affirmatively encourages promotion
from within, it should generally let staff know of openings no later than the
time they are advertised to the general public. The failure to do so is likely
to cause dissatisfaction by seeming to deny people the opportunity for
upward mobility. Moreover, informed staff members can be helpful in
identifying likely candidates or sources of candidates.

C. Orientation

Reasons for inclusion:

To ease the process of terminating an employee by specifying a 90-day try-
out period.

To make clear that an employee, both during and after the try-out period, remains subject to an "at-will" employment relationship.

Note: It is important to assure that the employee's survival of a "probationary" period is not interpreted as creating a contract of employment.

D. Performance Reviews

Reasons for inclusion:

To specify the purposes of reviews.
To indicate that informal reviews occur on a continuing basis.
To specify the intervals for written reviews.
To indicate which people are involved in reviews and the factors to be considered in evaluation.
To indicate the steps to be taken when an employee disagrees with an evaluation.

E. Personnel Files

Reasons for inclusion:

To describe what is maintained in the personnel files.
To explain rights of access to such files and under what circumstances.
To urge employees to report changes so as to keep personnel records current.

Note: Some state laws, in varying ways, address access to personnel files. Some states do not require any right of employee access to his or her personnel file; some states entitle employees to receive certified copies of relevant portions of their records; some permit employees to add statements to their files if they disagree with the contents; in some, access must be given "at reasonable intervals."

(D) ARTICLE IV—SCHEDULING POLICIES

A. Working Hours

Reasons for inclusion:

To specify standard working hours and lunch or other break periods.
To remind employees of the organization's right to change working schedules as circumstances dictate.

B. Overtime

Reasons for inclusion:

To clarify eligibility for overtime pay, the procedure for earning it, and the formula for determining its amounts.
To specify the need and procedure for recording time worked.
To state the need for advance approval to work overtime.
To state whether, and to what extent, compensatory time off will be considered or granted.

Note: Nonexempt employees must be paid overtime in accordance with the FLSA. Inasmuch as the FLSA counts as hours worked all hours the employee is "permitted" to work by the employer, underscoring the need to obtain advance written approval provides an important restraint on excessive hours and pay.

C. Attendance at Meetings and Conferences

Reasons for inclusion:

To state that such attendance must be authorized.
To state how time spent in out-of-town engagements, including travel time, is compensated.
To indicate how expenses are reimbursed.

Note: Individuals sometimes have to be told they are not free to attend any meeting of their choosing and in any event should know in advance how they will be paid for authorized attendance. Although the FLSA imposes obligations regarding minimum payments, the organization still needs to determine whether it wishes to exceed those requirements when authorized time away from home extends beyond a normal workday.

(E) ARTICLE V—COMPENSATION AND REIMBURSEMENT POLICIES

A. Pay and Payroll Policies

Reasons for inclusion:

To state the organization's general approach to setting compensation.
To specify the workweek used in pay calculations.
To describe how compensation is related to job descriptions and specifications.
To specify when people will be paid, and what happens when a scheduled payday falls on a weekend or holiday.
To indicate treatment of mandatory and voluntary payroll deductions.
To explain what employees should do if there is a payroll error.
To announce the procedure, if any, for payroll advances.
To clarify the connection between performance and compensation while indicating the role of budgetary constraints.

Note: Because definitions of the standard workday, workweek, and pay period vary widely, an organization needs to provide its own definitions to avoid misunderstanding. Complete and accurate time records are vital. The difficulty in forcing employees to complete time sheets does not relieve the employer of needing such records in order to meet both legal and practical requirements. Having such a provision in the personnel policies underscores the importance of time records.

B. Compensatory Time

Reasons for inclusion:

To state conditions under which compensatory time may or will be granted.

To distinguish between exempt and nonexempt employees.

To provide a procedure for requesting compensatory time.

To state the situations in which the granting of compensatory time is discretionary.

To underscore the need to maintain time records.

C. Travel Expenses

D. Other Expenses

Reasons for inclusion:

To identify the types of job-related expenses for which employees may be reimbursed.

To describe the method by which such expenditures are authorized and reimbursed.

Note: Without a specific authorization policy, employees might incur expenditures for which the organization has neither the funds nor the intention to provide reimbursement.

(F) ARTICLE VI—EMPLOYEE BENEFITS OTHER THAN LEAVE

A. Overview

Reasons for inclusion:

To announce the general coverage of benefit programs.

To state that more detailed information may be contained in other documents.

To make clear that benefits may be changed.

To state that changes can be made at the discretion of the organization.

Note: Because of the rapidly changing nature of benefits plans, highlights but not details of the benefits should be provided in the handbook. The particular carriers and details of policies can be found in separate documents.

B. Mandatory Benefits

Reasons for inclusion:

To list and briefly describe the benefits required by law (FICA, unemployment insurance, worker's compensation and others as required by state law).

To state that those benefits involve costs to the employer.

Note: Employees often regard these programs as automatic and having no cost to the employer. Informing them of this reality can be helpful when budgetary constraints (or tax increases) limit the availability of funds for pay increases.

C. Health Insurance

D. Dental Insurance

E. Long-Term Disability Insurance

F. Life Insurance

G. Retirement Plan

H. Educational Assistance

Reasons for inclusion:

To list and briefly describe the nature and extent of each employee benefit sponsored and/or paid for by the employer in the absence of any legal requirement to do so (generally including such items as health insurance, disability insurance, pension or savings plan, life insurance, dependent care, and educational reimbursement).

To state the basic requirements for eligibility for each benefit.

To state that an employee must enroll in order to obtain coverage.

To state whether the employee only, or the employee and dependents, is eligible for coverage.

To state when coverage, or entitlement to benefits, begins.

To state when benefits cease.

To indicate the extent to which the employer and the employee pay for each benefit, and how the payment formula is determined.

To indicate how and where copies of relevant documents (including summary plan descriptions) can be obtained.

To alert the employee to certain basic limitations and restrictions, such as pre-existing conditions or substantial waiting periods, in health, disability and other plans.

Note: Employees seldom have a clear idea of these costs, so it is important for a management representative to be available to explain the concepts of deductibles, copayments, vesting, and so on. However, the details of coverage are too cumbersome for a handbook and should generally be provided in separate documents. Also, in formulating many of its benefit programs (e.g., health, disability, retirement plans), the organization must take care to comply with the many legal requirements of ERISA.

(G)   ARTICLE VII—PAID AND UNPAID LEAVE

A. Holidays

Reasons for inclusion:

To specify the holidays recognized by the organization as warranting paid leave.

To indicate the categories of employees entitled to such leave.

To state restrictions on entitlement, such as working the day before and the day after the holiday.

To specify procedures for pay or leave when a holiday falls on a weekend.

To indicate any special requirements that may restrict payment or scheduling of leave, such as the need to keep the office open.

To describe pay arrangements if the employee is required to work on a holiday.

Note: Standard holidays vary by state, and sometimes by municipality. They generally are obligations imposed upon the government as employer and not upon private employers, but commonly are voluntarily observed by them. Insistence that employees work the days before and after a holiday in order to receive pay for that holiday is a meaningful spur to attendance.

B. Vacation

Reasons for inclusion:

To indicate the amount of paid vacation to which each category of employee is entitled annually.

To define, where appropriate, the vacation year for vacation credit purposes.

To state the formula for accrual and the requirements for using accrued vacation leave (including any provisions for carrying vacation leave over into another year).

To state any limitations on when a new employee can begin taking vacation.

To indicate whether employees can receive pay instead of paid leave.

To state the amount of advance notice of vacation preference that must be given by the employee.

To describe the arrangements and authority for scheduling vacation leave.

To make clear that operational considerations may override employee preferences.

To explain what happens when vacation periods include holidays, paydays, or periods of illness.

To state whether, and to what extent, vacations can be taken in increments.

Note: Given budgetary and scheduling constraints, nonprofit organizations are well advised to minimize carryover options. Also, because of the importance of having alert employees, it seems generally in the employer's interest to require employees to take their vacations rather than permit a pay substitute. There is no federal law requiring the granting of any vacation leave.

C. Personal Days

Reasons for inclusion:

To indicate the amount of paid personal leave to which each category of employee is entitled annually.

To indicate the formula for accrual and the requirements for use of accrued personal leave (including provisions for carrying personal leave over into another year).

To indicate whether employees can receive pay instead of paid personal leave.

To describe the notification and scheduling requirements concerning personal leave.

Note: Failure to put restrictions on the use of personal days can result in being short-handed at critical times, particularly around holidays and proposal writing time. The presence of personal leave can be an effective vehicle for accommodating religious needs.

D. Sick Leave

Reasons for inclusion:

To state the limited purpose of sick leave and to indicate whether it may be extended to an illness other than the employee's.

To state the amount of paid sick leave to which each category of employee is entitled annually.

To state the formula for accrual and the requirements for use of accrued sick leave (including any carryover provisions for sick leave).

To indicate any provision for receiving pay instead of paid sick leave.

To describe the notification requirements concerning sick leave.

To explain what happens when an employee becomes ill while on another form of paid leave.

To explain, where appropriate, the relationship between sick leave and the organization's disability policies or Family and Medical Leave Act entitlements.

Note: It is important to make clear that sick leave is confined to sickness and is not the equivalent of an unfettered personal leave. Insistence on a doctor's certificate may impose a degree of control over its abuse.

E. Family and Medical Leave

Reasons for inclusion:

To comply with federal or state laws which require the granting of such leave.

To comply with any requirements of such laws for notification to employees.

To describe conditions for eligibility.

To describe the reasons for which such leave can be taken.

To indicate the unpaid nature of such leave and any conditions under which it can be compensated.

To state requirements for advance notice by the employee.

To state requirements for medical certification of illness and/or of fitness to return to work.

To state the benefits that continue, the conditions of their continuance, and job protection and restoration conditions.

Note: Federal law and state laws which require family and medical leave generally apply only to employers with a threshold number of employees (50 in the case of the FMLA) and provide benefits only to these employees who have worked a minimum number of hours (1250 hours in the past 12 months under the FMLA). If not covered by law, an organization is free to adopt any, or none, of those leave provisions.

F. Bereavement Leave

Reasons for inclusion:

To state entitlement to that benefit.

To state limitations on pay and time off.

To identify the relatives whose death may invoke bereavement leave and pay.

G. Jury and Witness Duty Leave

H. Military Leave

Reasons for inclusion:

To indicate other reasons (if any) for which the organization will grant paid or unpaid leave.
To indicate the circumstances under which such leave is granted.
To state whether leave is paid or unpaid.
To indicate job restoration rights upon completion of leave.

Note: Legal requirements affect policies regarding jury and military leave, generally requiring the granting of leave but not pay.

I . Leave of Absence

Reasons for inclusion:

To state the circumstances under which an employee may take leave from work beyond the normal limits of vacation, sick leave, or other types of leave recognized by the employer.
To specify the unpaid nature of (or any compensation for) such leave.
To specify whether health care coverage will continue and under what circumstances.
To indicate which individual(s) have the authority to grant such leave.
To clarify the effects on seniority and various benefits.

J . Emergency Closing

Reasons for inclusion:

To set established rules for reporting (or not reporting) to work in inclement weather.
To condition pay on an official decision to close or not to close the office.
To set pay policy for full-time and part-time employees and/or exempt and nonexempt employees.

(H) ARTICLE VIII—EMPLOYEE RESPONSIBILITIES

A. Disciplinary Procedures

Reasons for inclusion:

To describe a framework of conduct that management finds unacceptable.
To indicate the disciplinary penalties that may be imposed.
To make clear that the severity of some offenses may warrant immediate discharge.
To reaffirm the employment-at-will concept.

Note: A statement of disciplinary procedures should put an employee on notice of conduct regarded as unacceptable, but should avoid mandating a system of progressive discipline. As a practical matter, in most cases there will be one or more warnings before an employee is terminated, but management must reserve the authority to dismiss at once where it regards the offense as a serious one. The text of the provision should not tie management to specific courses of action, but for reasons of fairness and to avoid charges of discrimination, management must be consistent in its enforcement.

B. Smoking

Reasons for inclusion:

To indicate the organization's regulations concerning smoking on its premises or at its functions.

Note: A nonprofit organization may be located in a building designated as smoke-free by its owner or the local government.

C. Use of NPO-Owned Equipment and Supplies

Reasons for inclusion:

To identify the circumstances under which employees may use (or borrow) organization-owned equipment, the process for seeking authorization, and the limits on such use.
To provide for reimbursement for some uses, such as long-distance telephone calls.

D. Political Activities

Reasons for inclusion:

To explain the restrictions on use for political activities of employer-owned equipment and employer-paid time.
To prevent unauthorized political activity or endorsement implicating the organization.

Note: Given the reliance on governmental funds by nonprofit organizations, political involvement is not surprising. Nevertheless, the organization needs to restrict use of its resources for such activities because of its nonprofit status and its receipt of public funds.

E. Confidential Information

Reasons for inclusion:

To impose the requirement of confidentiality on employees.
To protect confidential information from unauthorized disclosure.
To prevent removal of materials from the premises, unless authorized.
To provide for the return of materials upon termination.

F. Attendance

Reasons for inclusion:

To state the job requirements of regular attendance and punctuality.
To require notification in the event of absence or lateness.

G. Personal Appearance

Reasons for inclusion:

To require a well-groomed appearance as a matter of policy.

To remind the employee of the importance to the organization of a
professional image.

H. Collection and Solicitation

Reasons for inclusion:

To prevent disruption during work caused by personal solicitation.
To establish a uniform prohibition of solicitation or distribution of literature,
including union solicitation.
To prohibit all forms of gambling on the organization's premises.

Note: Union solicitation during working time can be prohibited by the
employer under the National Labor Relations Act only if there is a general
rule in effect and enforced that prohibits *all* forms of solicitation or
distribution during working time. The text of the rule must be carefully
tailored to meet the National Labor Relations Board's requirements. The one
exception to the broad rule that has been approved by the NLRB is
solicitation for a United Way campaign or its equivalent.

(I) ARTICLE IX—TERMINATION OF EMPLOYMENT

A. Retirement

Reasons for inclusion:

To urge the employee to give advance notice.

B. Termination for Reasons Other than Retirement

Reasons for inclusion:

To distinguish, where appropriate, between voluntary and involuntary
termination.
To indicate benefits payable at termination, such as payment for accrued but
unused vacations.
To describe the process of exit interviews.
To provide for the employee's return of organization materials.

(J) ARTICLE X—COMPLAINT RESOLUTION

Reasons for inclusion:

To outline the steps to be taken to resolve conflicts or misunderstandings.
To state that there will be no retaliation for following the steps to resolve a
conflict or misunderstanding.
To make clear that seeking resolution of a complaint will not by itself
prevent or delay any announced disciplinary action.
To state who has the authority to make a final decision.

Note: Employees should be encouraged to try to resolve conflicts in the
smallest arenas possible. Most issues can be resolved informally, and there is
little to be gained by an elaborate grievance procedure. If a controversy
escalates to a point where litigation seems likely, then the organization may
want to consider an *ad hoc* resolution procedure such as outside mediation
or arbitration.

We turn now to Part III of this chapter, the sample handbook, as a demonstration of how many of these propositions can be applied. The policies are illustrative only, and by no means should be adopted until an organization has checked with its attorney to assure their compliance with all applicable laws and regulations.

11.3 Part III—The Nonprofit Organization's Guide to Employment Policies

(A) INTRODUCTION

(i) Welcome to The Nonprofit Organization

The mission of The Nonprofit Organization (NPO) is to develop, promote, and support programs that will _____ .

All of us at NPO believe that our goals and those of our employees are closely related. Indeed, the success of NPO, to a great extent, is dependent on the success of our employees in meeting their own goals. We welcome you to NPO and express our sincere hope that your association with NPO will be a mutually rewarding one.

We have prepared this handbook of our employment policies, practices, and benefits to answer many of the questions you might have regarding the conditions of your employment at NPO, the responsibilities that you will have, and the benefits that you will enjoy. The handbook is a general guideline; it is not intended to capture every detail of our policies and procedures.

Please read the handbook carefully and retain it for future reference. From time to time, you may receive updates of individual sections, or of the entire document, should the management of NPO in its sole discretion decide that some or all policies and procedures need changing. If you have any questions about any of the policies, please feel free to discuss them with the Executive Director.

(ii) Terms of Employment

This handbook does not represent a contract of employment between NPO and its employees, and does not assure your employment for any length of time. The employment relationship between NPO and its employees is exclusively an "at-will" relationship. This means that NPO has the right to terminate your employment at any time, with or without reason, with or without notice, and that you have the same right to resign your employment at your option. Only the Executive Director has the authority to enter into an agreement providing employment for a specified period of time and then must do so in writing.

(iii) Classes of Employment

1. This handbook applies to all full-time, part-time, and temporary employees of NPO. *Full-time employees* are those individuals hired to work a scheduled 37.5-hour workweek on a regular basis. They are entitled to full participation in NPO's benefits, as defined in subsequent sections. *Part-time employees* are those hired to work fewer than 37.5 hours a week on a regular basis. They are entitled to full or prorated participation in NPO's benefits, as defined in subsequent sections. *Temporary employees* are those individuals hired by NPO

with the understanding that their employment ceases when a particular assignment has been completed or a particular deadline has been reached. They are not entitled to participate in the NPO's benefits, except to the extent expressly set forth in this handbook.

2. All full-time, part-time, or temporary employees are classified as either exempt or nonexempt employees in accordance with standards established under the federal Fair Labor Standards Act. The categories of exempt and nonexempt determine whether or not the employee is to be paid for overtime work. *Exempt* employees are paid on a salaried basis and are expected to work whatever hours are necessary to perform their duties, and are not paid overtime for working beyond 40 hours in a given week. *Nonexempt* employees may or may not be paid on a salary basis and must be paid overtime at the rate of 1.5 times their regular rate for all work in excess of 40 hours in any workweek. To qualify for overtime pay, the overtime work must be authorized in advance by the Executive Director or the appropriate supervisor. Compensatory leave is not an acceptable substitute for overtime pay. All employees will be informed at the time of hire of their position's classification as exempt or nonexempt.

(B)   GENERAL EMPLOYMENT INFORMATION

(i)   *Equal Employment Policy*

1. NPO is an equal-opportunity employer. All employment decisions are made without regard to race, color, religion, sex, age, national origin, or, in the case of a qualified individual with a disability (as defined by applicable law) without regard to the disability. NPO's policy of equal employment applies to all phases of the employment relationship, including recruitment, advertising, hiring, promotion, demotion, layoff, termination, rates of pay, and all other forms of selection, training, and compensation. NPO's employment decisions are strictly directed toward qualifications and ability to perform available work. Anyone believing that an incident of discrimination has occurred should report this to his supervisor or to the Executive Director.

2. NPO is committed to maintaining a work environment that is free of discrimination. It is a violation of NPO's rules and policies for any management or other employee to harass any person, through verbal or physical conduct of any kind, on the basis of race, color, religion, sex, national origin, age, or physical or mental disability, or to behave in a manner which tends to create an atmosphere of intolerance or intimidation as to such matters.

Consistent with NPO's policy of equal opportunity without regard to sex, NPO prohibits any manager, supervisor, or employee from making sexual advances of a verbal or physical nature, and from engaging in conduct of a sexually oriented nature, including sexually oriented verbal comments, gestures, and physical contacts, toward another employee or applicant for employment. Also, NPO will not base any decision affecting any aspect of the employment relationship, including pay or any condition of employment, upon an individual's initiation of a complaint claiming a violation of the Company's sexual harassment policy.

Any complaint of sexual or other harassment should immediately be brought to the attention of the employee's supervisor or the Executive Director. All complaints of sexual harassment will be investigated promptly and, where warranted, prompt and appropriate remedial action will be taken.

3. NPO forbids retaliation against anyone for reporting, assisting in making a complaint of, or cooperating in an investigation of, an alleged incident of harassment and/or discrimination. NPO's policy is to investigate all such complaints thoroughly and promptly. To the fullest extent practicable, NPO will keep complaints and terms of their resolution confidential. All such relevant documents will, however, be included in and made a part of the appropriate employees's permanent personnel file. If an investigation confirms that harassment or discrimination has occurred, NPO will take appropriate corrective action. Any manager, supervisor, or employee found to have violated our policy is subject to disciplinary action, up to and including discharge.

[Note: If the organization is headquartered in a state which prohibits discrimination on the basis of categories beyond those mentioned here, e.g., sexual orientation, those categories should be added to the section's prohibitions.]

(ii) *Drug-Free Workplace*

NPO adheres to the requirements of the Drug-free Workplace Act of 1988, which prohibits the unlawful use or possession of a controlled substance in the workplace. Use of controlled substances is inappropriate behavior that can subject co-workers, grantees, visitors, and others to unacceptable safety risks and that undermines NPO's operating effectiveness. Employees must comply with the following conditions:

1. Reporting to work, or working under the influence of a controlled substance (except with a physician's prescription), is prohibited. This prohibition extends to the NPO premises and to all other sites where an employee is engaged in NPO business.
2. NPO prohibits the criminal use, manufacture, distribution, dispensation, possession, or sale of a controlled substance on any NPO-affiliated worksite. Such conduct is also prohibited outside scheduled working hours to the extent that NPO regards it as impairing the employee's ability to perform on the job or as threatening the reputation of NPO.
3. Any employee convicted of a violation related to a controlled substance (or pleading no contest to such a change) must notify the Executive Director in writing within five working days of the conviction or plea.
4. Employees wanting information on locally available sources of substance abuse counseling should contact the Executive Director, who will make every reasonable effort to keep the request confidential.
5. Individuals who violate any aspect of this policy will be subject to disciplinary action, up to and including termination. NPO may also require that an employee successfully complete a substance-abuse or rehabilitation program as a condition of further employment.

(iii) Health and Safety

1. NPO is dedicated to providing a safe and healthful environment for employees, grantees, visitors, and others while they are on NPO premises or attending NPO-sponsored programs. All employees are required to follow the safety procedures that have been established, and are expected to report any potentially unsafe or hazardous conditions, or any injuries, to the Executive Director. All employees share responsibility for personal safety and for the security of NPO property. Any suspicious behavior by any visitor or person in the vicinity of the NPO premises or the location of any NPO-sponsored program should be reported to the Executive Director immediately.

2. Employees may be injured in the course of work and therefore may have to be absent from work. If so, they are subject to the provisions of the State's workers' compensation program and receive compensation in accordance with its terms.

(iv) Conflict of Interest

All employees should strive to avoid conflicts of interest as well as the appearance of any such conflict. To avoid any action that could be interpreted as using their positions at NPO unfairly, all employees shall refrain from serving on the board of directors of any organization or institution known to be or likely to become an applicant for NPO funds. Employees shall not accept any fees or other remuneration from any organization or institution in conjunction with a project or program for which NPO funds are being sought or have been granted. If an employee's spouse or other immediate relative has any financial or managerial connection to a project or organization for which NPO funds are being sought or have been granted, that relationship must be disclosed before any proposal concerning that project or organization is reviewed. The employee then may not participate in or be present during any discussion of the project or organization in question.

(v) Employment of Relatives

1. Because the employment of relatives can result in conflicting interests, which impair efficiency, it is the policy of NPO that no immediate relative of an employee or of a member of the NPO Board of Directors shall be employed by NPO as long as the original employee or board member remains with the organization. Immediate relatives include parents, siblings, and children; people in those categories with a "step" or "in-law" relationship; and any other member of the employee's or Board member's immediate household.

2. Should employees marry each other while working for the NPO, they may both remain employed so long as the Executive Director does not perceive any conflict or the appearance of any conflict of interest. However, under no circumstances may an employee supervise an immediate relative. If a conflict or the appearance of conflict should arise, the employees will be given an opportunity to decide which one will leave NPO, and if they fail to make that decision, the NPO may select and terminate one of them with 30 days' notice. The same policy applies in the event a Board member and an employee become married.

(vi) *Ownership of Certain Materials*

All information and material that you write, develop, receive, or compile during the performance of your duties at NPO automatically becomes the property of NPO, whether or not written, developed, or compiled in the office or at home, and whether done during business hours or at other times

(vii) *Substance Abuse*

It is unacceptable for any employee to report for work under the influence of alcohol or drugs, or in any unsafe or unfit condition, or to be in possession of alcohol or drugs on NPO's premises at any time. In order to protect the safety and well-being of the workplace and our employees, NPO officials may inspect any items on NPO's premises, including personal property in an employee's possession. Employees may also be required to submit to any physical tests to determine the presence of alcohol or drugs in their system, and, if an employee fails to submit to such tests, the employee is subject to immediate termination.

(C) EMPLOYMENT POLICIES

(i) *Job Creation and Description*

1. Job descriptions are helpful in providing you with an understanding of the performance and results expected of you in your job. NPO maintains a written description of the responsibilities, qualifications, and salary range for each of its positions. Your position description will be discussed with you upon hiring and during each annual performance review, as both a guide for performance and a means of identifying any needed changes. A copy of each individual's position description is kept in the employee's personnel file.
2. Each position description will be formally reviewed by NPO at least once every three years to determine any need for revision. If you feel that yours might need revision at any other time, you should talk with the Executive Director about possible changes.

(ii) *Recruitment and Selection*

1. NPO's recruitment and selection activities are conducted so as to hire the best qualified candidates. When a position is created or when one becomes vacant, NPO employees will be notified before or at the same time that external recruitment begins in order to give current staff members the opportunity to apply for such positions. If you believe you are qualified, we encourage you to apply for such openings.
2. Within the organization, the Executive Director must approve all employment decisions (including recommendations for hiring, promotion, demotion, and other changes) before any commitments are made or any notification is given to an applicant or a current employee.

(iii) *Orientation*

For each new employee, NPO will provide an orientation period to familiarize the employee with our organization, the work, and the co-workers. The first 90 days of employment is regarded as the orientation period, during which time you can evaluate

NPO and your supervisor can evaluate your performance. This does not imply that employment is guaranteed during or following the orientation period.

(iv) Performance Reviews

We expect you to give your best effort and we encourage outstanding performance. NPO believes in keeping its employees aware of how they are performing, so that employees can be recognized for good performance and informed of areas where improvement is necessary. Accordingly, you can expect that your performance will be evaluated by the Executive Director or your supervisor on a continuing basis. You will receive a written performance evaluation from the Executive Director after your first six months at NPO and at least once a year thereafter. These evaluations will be discussed with you by your supervisor, so that you and your supervisor can work together toward improved job performance. All written performance reviews will be based on your performance in relation to your responsibilities. They will also take into consideration your demeanor, record of attendance, dependability, and demonstrated willingness to cooperate with colleagues in furthering the NPO mission.

Should you disagree with any items on your evaluation or feel that any information is incorrect, you are encouraged to discuss your concerns with the evaluator. If this discussion does not meet your expectations, you are entitled to have your written comments added to your personnel file.

(v) Personnel Files

The NPO retains a personnel file for each employee. This file will contain documentation regarding such aspects of your employment as job descriptions, performance appraisals, beneficiary designation forms, letters of commendation, and disciplinary notices. You may review your own personnel file, upon contacting the Executive Director and scheduling an appointment. To keep your personnel file up-to-date, it is important that you notify the Executive Director or other appropriate staff member of any changes in your name, telephone number, home address, marital status, dependents, beneficiary designations, educational attainments, and any other relevant factors.

(D) SCHEDULING POLICIES

(i) Working Hours

1. The regular workweek for full-time employees is 37.5 hours, based on a daily schedule of 7.5 hours, Monday through Friday. Regular work hours for full-time employees are 9 A.M. to 5:30 P.M., with a one-hour unpaid lunch break, to be taken between 11:30 A.M. and 2:00 P.M. The specific meal time will be scheduled by the Executive Director so as to assure appropriate coverage of the office. Work schedules for part-time and temporary employees will be arranged by the Executive Director.
2. Daily and weekly schedules may be changed from time to time by the Executive Director to meet the changing needs of the organization. Any such changes will be announced as far in advance as possible.

[Note: Some state laws may specify other break periods for nonexempt workers.]

(ii) Overtime

1. Nonexempt employees are eligible for overtime pay for authorized hours worked beyond 40 hours in any workweek. This pay is to be calculated on a weekly basis, at the rate of 1.5 times each individual's normal hourly rate. If you are a nonexempt employee, you will be paid at your normal rate of pay for work between 37.5 and 40 hours in any workweek. Overtime pay begins after the 40th hour. The employee's supervisor must approve *in writing* all overtime hours *before* they are worked. [Note: Some states have more restrictive standards. A state law may require, for example, that a nonexempt employee be paid time-and-one-half for working more than 8 hours in a given day, and double-time for working more than 12 hours. Also, the 40-hour requirement under the FLSA is a legal minimum; an employer may choose to pay an overtime premium starting at any hour short of 40.]

2. For exempt employees, the standard workweek of 37.5 hours represents the minimum number of hours they are expected to work. Exempt employees are not eligible for overtime pay, but in some cases may be credited with accrued compensatory time, as described in Section V.B. of this Guide.

3. All employees are required to keep accurate records of the time they work on a daily basis, on the forms provided. These forms are to be submitted to the Executive Director by noon each Monday.

(iii) Attendance at Meetings and Conferences

The nature of NPO's business will, from time to time, require that staff members attend meetings and conferences outside the office. When such sessions occur during normal working hours, no special provisions are made, except that individuals are reimbursed for expenses as described in Section V. When such sessions extend to time beyond normal working hours, the following guidelines pertain.

1. In compliance with Department of Labor regulations, when a nonexempt employee is required to make a one-day trip, the employee is compensated for the time spent traveling to and from the assigned location (but not the time spent traveling between home and the airport or train station) and the time involved in actually working on the assignment. The time normally spent on meal breaks is not compensable.

2. When a nonexempt employee's travel extends overnight, the only travel time that is compensable is that which overlaps the normal working schedule (even if the travel occurs on a weekend or holiday). When conference or meeting attendance involves work at the other site(s) that extends beyond normal working hours, those hours are compensable in accordance with Section IV.B.

3. When an exempt employee is required to attend a meeting or conference that necessitates being away from home for more than two consecutive nights, the employee accrues four hours of compensatory time for each additional night he or she is required to be away.

(E) COMPENSATION AND REIMBURSEMENT POLICIES

(i) Pay and Payroll Policies

NPO endeavors to pay salaries competitive with those offered by similar nonprofit organizations. This process involves setting a compensation range for each position. Each salary range is reviewed at least once every three years for possible adjustment. Your compensation will be reviewed at least once a year. Factors to be considered include your performance, the NPO budget for the coming year, your responsibilities, and the recommendation of the Executive Director. If your salary is to be changed, the new amount will normally be effective at the beginning of the fiscal year.

1. NPO's pay period is Monday through Sunday. NPO employees are paid by check on a semimonthly basis, usually on the fifteenth and the last day of the month. All required and authorized deductions will be withheld automatically from your paycheck. If the scheduled payday falls on a weekend or an NPO-observed holiday, checks will usually be issued on the day before the weekend or holiday. However, you will not receive a paycheck on time unless the Executive Director has received your completed time sheet by the scheduled deadline. You should review your paycheck for accuracy when you receive it. If you find an error, please report it to the Executive Director immediately.
2. If your paycheck is lost or stolen, notify the Executive Director immediately so that a stop-payment order can be issued. If the check is cashed before such a stop-payment order can be issued, you alone will be responsible for the loss.
3. NPO does not normally provide payroll advances. However, if you have been an employee for at least a year, and if a payday would fall during your scheduled vacation, NPO will advance an amount equivalent to your base salary, less the standard deductions. This amount, in turn, will be deducted from the payroll in question. To receive such an advance, you should complete the required form and return it to the Executive Director at least one week before the start of the vacation.

(ii) Compensatory Time

1. Because nonexempt employees receive overtime pay, they do not accumulate compensatory time. The Executive Director, however, may grant some such leave in addition to overtime pay for extraordinary work on major projects. Exempt employees may be credited with compensatory time for required work on holidays, at conferences, and on significant projects with short deadlines.
2. Each employee is required to keep accurate records of all such time spent in performing such work. An employee who desires to obtain compensatory time must submit a request for such time to the Executive Director. Except as provided in Section IV.3. and Section VII.A.3., the decision of whether to grant any such request is a matter subject to the sole discretion of the Executive Director. Compensatory time must be taken within 30 days of any such approval. No payment is made for approved but unused compensatory time.

(iii) *Travel Expenses*

1. If you are required to use your automobile on NPO business, you will be reimbursed at a mileage rate determined annually, plus expenses for tolls and parking. Reimbursement will not be provided for travel between your home and the office. Air fares will be reimbursed at coach rates. Costs for alternative transportation on ground will be reimbursed at rates not more than the coach fare. If you make travel arrangements for non-NPO reasons, such as traveling by an indirect route or stopping over, you will be responsible for any extra charges. If your air travel involves the accumulation of frequent flyer miles, you may credit them to your account.

2. If NPO business requires that you stay overnight away from home, NPO will reimburse you for the cost of reasonably priced accommodations. Normally, meals away from home will be at your expense. However, when you incur meal costs in direct connection with NPO business, you will be reimbursed according to the NPO schedule.

3. Any out-of-town travel must be authorized in advance by the Executive Director. To secure reimbursement for any travel expense, you must complete a travel expense form and attach the relevant receipts within a month of completing the travel.

(iv) *Other Expenses*

NPO will reimburse you for any fees involved with conferences you are required to attend. Membership fees for professional and social organizations will normally be your responsibility. You will be reimbursed for expenses incurred for NPO-related telephone calls, supplies, postage, copying, and other items authorized by the Executive Director. The procedure for obtaining reimbursement is the same as that for travel expenses.

(F) EMPLOYEE BENEFITS OTHER THAN LEAVE

(i) *Overview*

1. NPO provides a number of benefit programs designed to help you and in many cases your eligible dependents meet the expenses that may arise in connection with such matters as illness, disability, family care, death, and retirement. This section of the Guide highlights features of those benefit programs required by law and those benefit programs which NPO voluntarily has chosen to sponsor. The specific details of these NPO-sponsored benefit programs can be found in the summary plan descriptions available from the Executive Director. All employees are covered by the mandatory programs to the extent provided by law. Only full-time employees and regular part-time employees, to the extent stated, are covered by the voluntary programs.

2. Benefits can and do change from time to time without notice. NPO reserves the right, at its discretion and for any reason, to change or terminate any of the nonmandatory programs or to require employee contributions toward any benefits.

(ii) Mandatory Benefits

1. All NPO employees are covered by Social Security and unemployment insurance, in accordance with the requirements of law. NPO pays the employer share of the Social Security taxes on your behalf, in an amount equal to what you pay, and pays unemployment insurance taxes to the state for your coverage.
2. All NPO employees are covered by workers' compensation insurance, the cost of which is paid for by NPO. If you are disabled because of an injury or disease resulting from the performance of duties within your job, you are likely to be entitled to benefits under workers' compensation. You must immediately report any accident, however slight, to the Executive Director, so that the legal requirements concerning those benefits can be met.

(iii) Health Insurance

1. NPO offers eligible employees (and their dependents) a choice of health insurance coverage between an indemnity plan and a health maintenance organization. NPO pays 80 percent of the cost of individual coverage for a full-time employee, and the employee pays 20 percent. NPO pays 50 percent of the cost of individual coverage for a part-time employee who works a regular schedule of at least 20 hours per week, and the employee pays 50 percent. Other employees are not covered. Health insurance premiums to cover your dependents are your individual responsibility at your own cost, but NPO will handle the transfer of premiums to the carrier. All full-time and part-time employees as designated above become eligible for health insurance coverage on the first day of the month following 30 days of continuous employment; if you have dependents, and want coverage for them, then coverage begins the same day. To obtain coverage, complete the enrollment form provided by the Executive Director. For complete details, including restrictions regarding pre-existing conditions, consult the summary plan description booklet.
2. If you leave NPO (for reasons other than gross misconduct) or if your work schedule is changed so that you are no longer eligible for health insurance coverage, you and your eligible dependents may be eligible to continue to participate for a period of time at your expense. Continuing coverage may be ended, however, under certain circumstances, such as if you fail to make required payments, if NPO drops its plan, or if you join another health plan. Details on this option are available from the Executive Director.

(iv) Dental Insurance

NPO offers dental insurance to its eligible employees and their dependents. NPO pays the entire cost of individual coverage for all full-time employees and pays 50 percent of the cost of individual coverage for all part-time employees who work a regular schedule of at least 20 hours per week. Dental insurance premiums to cover your dependents are your individual responsibility at your expense, but NPO will handle the transfer of premiums to the carrier. For details on coverage, consult the summary plan description booklet. To obtain coverage, complete the enrollment form provided by the Executive Director. Dental insurance benefits cease when you leave NPO.

(v) Long-Term Disability Insurance

NPO offers every full-time employee an option to elect long-term disability insurance coverage. No other employee is eligible. NPO and the employee each pay 50 percent of the cost. This coverage is designed to replace a percentage of weekly income in the event the employee is unable to work because of illness or injury. It is not available for your dependents. Benefits are paid after a 90-day waiting period, and may continue until age 65. Employees are eligible for such coverage on the first day of the month following 30 days of continuous employment. Coverage under this plan terminates when you leave NPO, unless you are receiving disability benefits at the time of termination, in which case the benefits continue as long as your qualifying disability continues. To obtain coverage, complete the enrollment form provided by the Executive Director. For complete details of the program, including its limitations and restrictions, consult the summary plan description booklet.

(vi) Life Insurance

All full-time employees are eligible to participate in NPO's life insurance program, which offers coverage for employees but not for dependents. NPO pays the entire premium for a life insurance benefit of twice your annual salary, to a maximum of $50,000. Additional coverage in the same amount is provided for accidental death or dismemberment. Your coverage will automatically begin on the first day of the month following 30 days of continuous employment, provided that you have completed an enrollment form. Life insurance benefits terminate on the date your employment with NPO ends.

(vii) Retirement Plan

You are eligible to join NPO's retirement plan, as of January 1 or July 1, if you are a full-time or part-time employee who has completed one year of service, work at least 1000 hours per year, and have reached age 21. The plan pays you a defined benefit when you reach retirement age, provided various conditions are met. The full details of the plan are provided in a summary plan description booklet.

(viii) Educational Assistance

NPO is interested in helping full-time employees develop their skills and upgrade their performance. To those ends, NPO offers an educational assistance program to all full-time employees who have completed at least a year of service. NPO will reimburse you an amount equivalent to the state university's charges for up to three academic credits per term for courses (a) which are offered at an accredited postsecondary institution and (b) which are directly or reasonably related to your present position or are part of a degree program which has previously been approved by NPO. Costs will be reimbursed only if (a) you receive approval from the Executive Director before enrolling, (b) you earn a grade of B or better, and (c) you supply the Executive Director with evidence of having successfully completed the course.

(G) PAID AND UNPAID LEAVE

(i) Holidays
1. NPO observes the following holidays: New Year's Day, Martin Luther King, Jr. Day, President's Day, Memorial Day, Independence Day, Labor Day, Columbus

Day, Veterans Day, Thanksgiving Day, and Christmas Day. Holidays falling on a Saturday are normally observed on the preceding Friday, while those falling on a Sunday are normally observed on the following Monday. The Executive Director will post a schedule of the specific dates at the beginning of each January.

2. Full-time employees will be compensated at their regular rate for 7.5 hours for each holiday, provided that they have worked the regularly scheduled workdays immediately preceding and following the holiday. Approved vacation or approved sick leave is regarded as a day worked for the purposes of holiday pay eligibility. Part-time employees who are normally scheduled to work on a day that is observed as a holiday will be compensated at their regular rate for the hours on that holiday during which they would normally have worked, but will not receive holiday pay if they were not normally scheduled to work on that holiday. Temporary employees are not eligible for holiday pay.

3. Nonexempt employees who are required to work on an observed holiday will be paid their regular hourly pay for the hours worked, in addition to normal holiday pay. Exempt employees who are required to work on an observed holiday will be eligible for one hour of compensatory time for every hour worked on the observed holiday (to a maximum of 7.5 hours per holiday).

(ii) Vacation

1. Vacation time provides important opportunities for rest, recreation, and personal activities. NPO grants annual paid vacations to all full-time and part-time employees, in varying amounts according to work schedule and length of service. For the first five years of full-time employment, an employee earns 10 vacation days per calendar year, accrued at the rate of 5/6th of a day per month. Thereafter, a full-time employee receives 15 vacation days a year, accrued at the rate of 1.25 days a month. Part-time employees accrue vacation on the above schedules but prorated to correspond to their average hours worked. Newly hired employees may not take paid vacation leave until they have worked at NPO for six months. At that point, they are eligible to take one half of their first year's vacation.

2. Employees are required to use their earned vacation time or lose it. There will be no payments made in lieu of vacation time, except that an employee leaving NPO will be compensated for any accrued but unused leave at the time of termination. You may not carry more than five vacation days into a subsequent year. If you are working on a time-limited project, all accrued vacation must be taken before the scheduled end of the project.

3. If an NPO-observed holiday falls during your scheduled vacation, you will be granted an alternative vacation day later. An employee who becomes ill during a scheduled vacation may not substitute sick leave days for the period.

4. Scheduled vacations must be approved by the Executive Director. Requests for vacation should be submitted at least two weeks in advance. Although every effort will be made to accommodate the employee's request, work

priorities of NPO and the vacation needs of all employees may at times override individual considerations. Vacations may be taken as individual days or in longer intervals, provided that the periods have been approved in advance by the Executive Director.

(iii) *Personal Days*

1. NPO provides full-time employees with up to three days of personal leave a year to deal with personal business, religious observance, and other matters of personal importance. Personal leave is accrued at the rate of one day for each four months of work per calendar year and may not be taken in units smaller than a half-day. Personal days may not be used to extend a scheduled vacation. Personal days may be taken only after they have been accrued. They may not be carried over into a subsequent calendar year, and there shall be no payment for any personal days that have not been taken by the end of the calendar year.

2. You must give the Executive Director written notice of your intention to take a personal day (although you need not give the reason) at least one week before taking that day off, except in emergency situations. The Executive Director will consider NPO's needs before granting that request; scheduled vacation time has priority. However, every effort will be made to accommodate requests for personal leave to observe holidays of religious significance.

(iv) *Sick Leave*

1. NPO provides sick leave to encourage employees to take care of their health and to help alleviate the financial hardships that might accrue in its absence. Sick leave may be taken only because of the employee's own sickness, and not that of a family member or other person. Full-time employees accrue up to 10 days of paid sick leave per calendar year, at the rate of 5/6th of a day per month. Part-time employees accrue sick leave on a prorated basis. Employees are eligible to take sick leave after having worked at NPO for three months. Any time taken off during the first three months will be treated as unpaid leave. Sick days may not be carried over into a subsequent calendar year, nor are payments made for any accrued but unused sick days at the end of a calendar year.

2. If you are unable to work because of illness, you must notify the Executive Director by 9 A.M. on each day of your inability to work, unless you have been granted an official medical leave. Failure to notify NPO will result in the day's being treated as unpaid leave. At any time, NPO has the right to require a statement from a physician concerning your illness, its expected duration, and your ability to return to work.

3. Your regular pay and benefits continue while you are on approved sick leave. Time off for medical or dental appointments shall be charged to sick leave. Sick leave may not be taken in units smaller than two hours. If you have exhausted your sick leave but are still unable to return to work, you may request that your accrued vacation and personal days and compensatory time be discharged as sick leave. Should all of these be exhausted, you may request an unpaid leave of absence.

(v) *Family and Medical Leave*

[Note: Although the federal Family and Medical Leave Act (FMLA) applies only to those employers which employ 50 employees at work sites within a 75-mile radius for at least 20 weeks in a 12-month period, many states have adopted their versions of such laws, generally applying to employers with fewer employees. The sample used here is based on the FMLA.]

1. Eligible employees are entitled, with certain restrictions, to unpaid family or medical leave for up to a total of 12 weeks in a consecutive 12 month period, in accordance with requirements established by the Family and Medical Leave Act (the FMLA). To be eligible for such leave, an employee must have completed at least 12 months employment with NPO and must have worked at least 1250 hours during the 12 months immediately preceding the leave. No other employee is eligible.

2. Family leave may be taken for the birth of a child of the employee or the placement of a child with the employee for adoption or foster care, and must be taken for the care of the child within 12 months of the birth or placement. Family leave may also be taken in the event of a serious health condition of the employee's child, parent, or spouse.

3. Medical leave may be taken in the event of a serious health condition of the employee which prevents the employee from performing the essential functions of his or her job.

4. A serious health condition is a condition requiring in-patient hospital care, or a period of incapacity of at least 3 days requiring treatment by, or at the direction of, a physician or other health care provider. Any leave granted to an employee for his or her own serious health condition or that of a family member may be taken consecutively, or if medically necessary, on an intermittent basis. The employee must give reasonable advance notice to NPO when the need for leave is foreseeable, and must make a reasonable effort to schedule planned medical treatment as not to unduly disrupt NPO's operations. NPO requires employees to provide verification of the serious health condition by a licensed physician or other health care provider, and may require a "fitness-for-duty" certification as a condition for returning to work.

5. NPO may require the employee first to use paid accrued vacation and personal leave, as well as paid sick leave if the leave involves the employee's own serious health condition, which counts against the 12 weeks of FMLA leave.

6. NPO will continue the employee's health coverage during the leave period under the same conditions that would be provided if the employee were actively employed during that period, with NPO and the employee each responsible for their share of the premiums during that period. The employee will generally be restored to his former position with equivalent benefits, provided that he or she returns to work by the end of the leave period.

7. The FMLA contains numerous requirements, including special provisions if both a husband and wife are employed by the same employer or if an employee is among the most highly paid employees of the organization. Please see the Executive Director for additional details.

(vi) Bereavement Leave

NPO will provide leave for work time missed due to the death and funeral of a member of the immediate family. A member of the immediate family is defined as a spouse, parent, brother, sister or child of the employee. For full-time employees, the maximum is three days with pay; for part-time employees, the maximum is three scheduled workdays with pay. Temporary employees may take up to three days of leave, but without pay. Normally the period covered will start with the day of death and end upon the funeral of the deceased relative. An employee not actively at work at the time of death is not eligible for bereavement pay.

(vii) Jury and Witness Duty Leave

All full-time and part-time employees summoned to jury duty are allowed paid leave at their regular daily rate of pay for up to 15 working days per calendar year, less the amounts paid for each such day of jury service, and are allowed unpaid leave for any additional time required for jury service. Temporary employees are given unpaid leave while serving on a jury. All employees are allowed unpaid leave for answering a summons to appear as a witness in court. To qualify for jury or witness leave, you must give the Executive Director or the Budget Officer a copy of your summons and of your jury discharge notice.

(viii) Military Leave

Military leave permits employees to fulfill their military obligations as members of the U.S. Armed Forces, the National Guard, or the State Militia in accordance with federal and state laws. All full-time and part-time employees called to active duty or to Reserve or National Guard training will be granted leaves of absence without pay in accordance with federal and state laws, and will be granted the right to return to work in accordance with the conditions prescribed by law.

(ix) Leaves of Absence

1. Any full-time or part-time employee who has worked for NPO for at least one year may request an unpaid personal leave for a period of up to 30 calendar days. You must request this leave in writing at least two weeks prior to the planned beginning of the leave. If the leave is precipitated by an emergency, the request must be made by you or an immediate relative within three days of the beginning the leave. Unpaid personal leave may be granted at the discretion of the Executive Director, if in the Executive Director's judgment it does not unduly disrupt NPO operations. Such leave shall not commence until all accrued vacation and personal days have been discharged.

2. If an unpaid leave is granted, NPO will continue paying its share of any premium due for health and life insurance, but paid leave and retirement benefits will not continue to accrue. Reinstatement cannot be guaranteed after an employee takes an unpaid personal leave, but every effort will be made to return the employee to the same or a comparable position. Budgetary constraints, the availability of temporary replacements, and the need to fill positions may affect the reinstatement.

(x) *Emergency Closing*

1. An authorized paid absence may occur when the NPO work schedule must be curtailed because of inclement weather or other emergency conditions. When the Executive Director determines that the NPO must close, employees will be notified in accordance with established procedures. Full-time employees will be paid as if NPO remained open; part-time employees will be paid only if they had been scheduled to work during the closed hours. Temporary employees do not receive compensation.

2. Both exempt and nonexempt employees required to work during the closing will receive an hour of compensatory time for each hour of required work. When NPO remains open, employees who are late to work because of inclement weather or other natural disasters must notify the Executive Director of their difficulties at the start of the workday. At the Executive Director's discretion, they will be permitted to extend their work hours to compensate or they will be required to discharge the time from available vacation, personal, or compensatory leave. When NPO remains open, employees who are absent from work because of inclement weather or other natural disasters must notify the Executive Director at the start of the workday. The missed time will be charged to available vacation, personal, or compensatory leave.

(H) EMPLOYEE RESPONSIBILITIES

(i) *Disciplinary Procedures*

1. As a member of the NPO team, you are expected to accept certain responsibilities and adhere to acceptable principles of conduct. Because your conduct reflects on NPO and [its mission], it is vital that you observe the highest standards of behavior at all times. We believe that one way to help you avoid problems is to make you aware of areas in which problems can occur. Since we cannot cover every conceivable area, consult your supervisor if you are in question as to what is proper or not proper.

2. There are certain actions which can subject you to severe disciplinary action, including discharge. Some of the types of behavior which the NPO considers misconduct, and which constitute reasons for discharge, suspension, or warning, include but are not limited to the following:

    a . Violating NPO's policies against discrimination and sexual harassment.

    b . Soliciting or accepting gratuities or consulting contracts from clients, applicants, or grantees.

    c . Excessive absenteeism or tardiness, including failure to report absences.

    d . Excessive, unnecessary, or unauthorized use of NPO facilities, supplies, or equipment (including the telephone and facsimile machine).

    e . Falsifying employment reports or other records of NPO.

    f . Using abusive, obscene, or threatening language or gestures.

    g . Theft, destruction, or unauthorized removal of NPO property.

    h . Disregarding safety regulations, including no-smoking regulations.

    i . Insubordination, including refusal or failure to perform work as assigned.

> j. Reporting to work intoxicated or under the influence of nonprescribed drugs, or otherwise violating NPO's policy relating to the Drug-Free Workplace Act, or possession of weapons on NPO premises.
> k. Failure to maintain confidentiality of NPO records and information.
> l. Neglect of job duties and responsibilities, including failure to perform work in accordance with recognized standards of performance.
> m. Violation of NPO policies or rules.
>
> 3. Performance, conduct, or demeanor that is unsatisfactory can result in a verbal or written warning, a suspension, or discharge, depending upon the severity of the offense, your previous performance, and other considerations. Accordingly, a single act of misconduct may be regarded, at NPO's discretion, as warranting immediate termination. Where practicable, NPO will attempt to inform the employee of deficiencies in performance and suggest means of improvement before resorting to termination. However, employment relationships with NPO are on an at-will basis, so that NPO retains the right to terminate at any time without cause and without giving any reason for termination.

(ii)   Smoking

To provide a safe and comfortable working environment, several parts of the NPO facility have been designated as no-smoking areas. Smoking is not permitted in those areas. Also, there shall be no smoking during a staff or Board meeting in the meeting room itself, regardless of its designation at other times.

[Note: Some state and local laws might restrict smoking entirely, as might some host institutions or landlords.]

(iii)   Use of NPO-Owned Equipment and Supplies

Employees are expected to use NPO equipment carefully and its supplies prudently. In cases of obvious misuse, an employee may be expected to pay all or part of the replacement cost. NPO's telephones are provided for NPO business. While employees might occasionally have a legitimate need to use an NPO telephone for personal matters, such calls are to be kept to a minimum, both in number and duration. Employees are expected to reimburse NPO for any personal long-distance calls they make on NPO telephones. Employees are expected to reimburse NPO for any personal use of the NPO facsimile machine.

(iv)   Political Activities

In all facilities, employees are prohibited from distributing literature about, or soliciting funds for, any candidate for public office. In any outside work on behalf of a political candidate or party, you may not publicly represent yourself as an agent of NPO providing any express or implied endorsement by NPO. If you choose to run for public office, your political activities may not be conducted in whole or in part from NPO facilities or with NPO materials.

(v)   Confidential Information

In the course of your work at NPO, you may be involved with information regarding the finances and various operations of NPO as well as information concerning co-employees, NPO members, or other individuals or activities. Most of this information is confidential and is not to be disclosed to others, except to such supervisory or other personnel at NPO who have a need to know such information. This is particularly true of information regarding personnel, accounting, research and development. As a general rule, such information is not to be removed from the NPO office, except when expressly authorized by the Executive Director. In the event of the termination of your employment with NPO, you must be sure that all documents are returned to NPO.

(vi) Attendance

NPO relies upon your dependability regarding attendance and punctuality. Your regular on-time attendance is important to our team effort. If for any reason you expect to be absent or late, you must notify your supervisor as early as possible, and in any event no later than the beginning of that workday.

(vii) Personal Appearance

It is important for NPO and its employees to maintain a professional image, particularly in light of the frequent visitors to our office. You are expected to exercise good judgment at all times in your personal appearance and apparel. Your clothing should be appropriate to your job and the operational performances of your department.

(viii) Collections and Solicitation

1. No employee or visitor will be permitted to engage in solicitation on NPO premises for membership, subscriptions, contributions or any other outside activities during working time or with another employee during that employee's working time. Any employee who does so and interferes with his or her own work or the work of others will be subject to discipline, up to and including discharge. Working time is defined as that period of the work day when an employee is on the job or otherwise attending to the duties of their job; it does not include free time such as breaks, lunch period, or before and after work.
2. Voluntary collections are permitted in the case of illness of an employee, an employee leaving the company, marriage of an employee, or death of an employee or someone in the employee's immediate family, but such collections must also be confined to non-working time.
3. There will be no distribution of literature or other printed matter by employees in the working areas of the NPO premises at any time, or in nonworking areas during working time. There will be no distribution of literature on NPO premises at any time by any person not employed by NPO.
4. The sole exception to the rules described above is the annual United Way Campaign, for which NPO may authorize special arrangements for solicitation of voluntary contributions.
5. There will be no gambling allowed on NPO premises at any time.

(I) TERMINATION OF EMPLOYMENT

(i) Retirement

If you plan to retire, you are expected to give NPO at least three months' notice. Doing so will not only permit the organization to make the necessary staffing adjustments but also enable the staff to process the paperwork necessary for a timely payment of any retirement benefits. NPO may make an early retirement offer from time to time. The Executive Director will hold an exit interview with each retiree, just as with all others leaving the organization.

(ii)   Termination for Reasons Other Than Retirement

If you decide to leave NPO, we would appreciate at least two week's notice before the termination date so that staffing patterns can be adjusted and your final pay can be calculated. Each departing employee is normally scheduled for an exit interview. This session is intended to review eligibility for continuation of benefits and complete any required forms, to collect all NPO property in the individual's possession, and to discuss the employees's job-related experiences with NPO.

(J)   COMPLAINT RESOLUTION

For working relationships within the NPO to remain effective, efforts should be made to resolve misunderstandings and conflicts before serious problems develop. If a situation does not seem to be resolving itself, you are encouraged to discuss it with any other individuals involved, and in particular with your immediate supervisor. If such discussion does not resolve the situation, you are welcome to take up the matter with the Executive Director. Normally, you will receive a response from the Executive Director concerning the situation within five working days of your discussion. NPO does not tolerate any retaliation against any employees for following this complaint resolution process. However, the process should not be construed as limiting or delaying the NPO's right to take disciplinary action (up to and including termination) against any employee if the NPO regards such action as appropriate.

12 ▼ Employment Related Benefits

SALLY A. ZINNO, Consultant

12.1 Overview of Employment Related Benefits

A universal goal for self-renewing organizations is attracting and keeping skilled and motivated staff members. In order to achieve that goal, the organization has to provide its employees with a work environment, motivators, and compensation that encourage job satisfaction. A carefully designed employee benefits program is a key contributor to a strong compensation package.

As recently as the late 1970s, nonprofit organizations could use the term "fringe benefits" rather comfortably to describe those goods and services provided to employees in addition to basic salaries and wages. Even the customarily above-average amounts of paid leave were seldom costly, in light of the modest salary levels.

Over the past half-century, however, the amount spent on employment related supplements in the United States has risen at a rate 11 times more rapid than that of salaries and wages. The cost of health insurance premiums alone has been rising at double-digit rates for several years. Today, it is not uncommon for an employer to spend an additional amount, equal to 20 to 35 percent of payroll, to cover benefits. The term "fringe" is clearly no longer appropriate.

At the same time, employees and potential employees have become much more aware of their total compensation including employer paid benefits as well as salary and wages. Before making the decision to accept a position, candidates now want to know what benefits are offered. In order to recruit and maintain quality staff, nonprofit organizations have to provide a package of benefits that allows them to compete with businesses and the larger nonprofits, such as hospitals and universities, which offer benefit packages competitive with the business community.

(A) OBJECTIVES OF COMPENSATION SYSTEMS

The primary objective of a compensation system is to attract and retain employees who meet the organization's needs and help it to achieve its mission. The total compensation package consists of the salaries and wages (see Chapter 14) and the employee benefits which are the services purchased or provided by the employer for the employee. These include mandated coverage such as the employer contribution to Social Security benefits as well as voluntary programs including medical insurance, group life insurance, disability coverage, and a retirement plan as well as paid leave time including holidays, sick days, and vacation.

The organization needs to offer a benefits package which is competitive with external organizations and meets internal needs. Meeting these objectives requires an awareness of two types of equity:

- *External equity*, a condition existing when the compensation is competitive with those of similar organizations; and
- *Internal equity* where individuals feel that differences in compensation within an organization are justified by differences in job requirements, length of service, or both.

The nonprofit manager must address both types of equity while coping with numerous constraints, including:

- The organization's financial resources;
- The internal labor market (including present and proposed positions, their relationships, and the existence of unions);
- The external labor market (particularly the number and compensation patterns of competitors for employees);
- Employment related laws, for example, the Fair Labor Standards Act, the 1964 Civil Rights Act, and relevant state laws; and
- The requirements of the Internal Revenue Code and Regulations ("The IRS Code").

The goal of any benefits program should be simplicity and clarity which results in a process that is easy to administer and simple to explain to employees. The employer should also seek to take advantage of favorable tax treatment.

(B) FINANCIAL CONSIDERATIONS

The cost of employee benefits packages has been among the fastest rising portions of employers' budgets in recent years. Employers are balancing the growing mix of compensation options, the changing needs of an increasingly diverse workforce, and management requirements to contain costs.

(i) The Benefits Budget
In order to design a package that meets these competing demands, the governing board has to determine a target dollar amount for benefits expenses as a percentage of the total

salary cost. For example, an organization may determine that an amount equal to 25 percent of the total annual payroll cost will be allocated to pay for all employee benefits. This target figure then is used by the manager responsible for selecting the benefits and the providers. (See Exhibit 12.1.)

In this example, the 25 percent figure is an average. It does not mean necessarily that each employee will receive 25 percent of his or her salary in benefits. The level of the employee's salary, the eligibility requirements, the options the employee selects and other factors will make the percentage vary for each individual. (See Exhibit 12.2.)

Management will need to consider three cost elements in calculating how much it has to spend on benefits:

- *Costs of benefits mandated by law*: These include (1) Social Security and Medicare, generally listed as Federal Insurance Contribution Act (FICA) deductions; (2) workers compensation; and (3) unemployment. Individual states may also have mandated programs such as temporary disability insurance.
- *Costs of discretionary benefits paid directly by the employer.* These may include coverage such as health, life, and disability insurance and the employer's pension plan contribution.
- *Employees' payment toward benefits.* Some employers may ask employees to contribute an amount for the cost of benefits. Most often, employees contribute toward medical or dental insurance, although some employers' insurance plans allow the employees to pay directly for increased coverage beyond what the employer provides.

The costs for most benefits which are mandated by law are fixed. The employer has to pay the amount specified by the Federal Government for Social Security and Medicare, and the state for unemployment. Insurance companies provide state-defined insurance coverage for workers compensation with costs that vary depending on a number of factors. Although currently, programs are underway to manage the cost for workers compensation by increasing control of the process and the monitoring of those who are being paid through the worker's compensation program.

The employer can take actions to control the cost of discretionary benefits and the employees' contribution. Normally, benefits insurance carriers review and, if necessary, revise prices once each year on the policy anniversary date.

(ii) How Can the Employer Offer the Best Package for the Dollars Available?

The cost for insurance-related benefits is lowest if the organization has an employee base large enough to spread the risks. Large nonprofits go to insurers directly to get competitive bids on their packages.

Many nonprofits that seek insurance on their own may be too small to qualify for

EXHIBIT 12.1 Benefits Budget

Total annual salary costs for the organization:	$1,000,000
Benefits target at 25% of annual salary costs:	$ 250,000

EXHIBIT 12.2 Comparison of Benefit Costs for Two Employees

Example using hypothetical costs:

	Employee A	Employee B
Basic annual salary	$20,000	$50,000
Mandatory benefits		
FICA @ 7.65%	1,530	3,825
Unemployment insurance, workers compensation @3.35%	670	1,675
Other employer paid benefits:		
individual health and life insurance, pension	4,100	6,050
Total benefits and salary	$26,300	$61,550
Benefits as % of salary	31%	23%

rate discounts. As a result, organizations have begun to collaborate in order to achieve the benefits of large group rates. For example, the Greater Philadelphia Cultural Alliance and the American Association of Museums offer their member organizations benefits options with lower negotiated rates than many members could get on their own. State collaboratives such as the Delaware Association of Nonprofit Agencies or the Chamber of Commerce do the same for their members. Such organizations also make it possible for nonprofits to offer their members additional types of benefits which they would not be eligible for at all because they have so few employees. Employers need to seek out such collaboratives among their peer organizations as they create or revise benefits packages.

Some nonprofits work with insurance brokers or insurance consultants who assist them with technical advice. They will also seek the best price through market competition by asking several insurance companies to bid on the organization's insurance package. Usually the competitive process results in lower costs. Brokers can also assist the organization with claims and policy-related issues. The insurance brokers are paid a fee by the insurance company. The fee is most often a small percentage of the insurance premium.

(C) KEY QUESTIONS IN DEVELOPING AND MANAGING THE BENEFITS PROGRAM

Defining and maintaining an effective benefits program is an ongoing process. The employer must develop strategies to respond to a constantly changing environment and a number of issues:

- *Benefits design*—developing packages that meet both the employees' and the employer's needs, particularly in view of changing family patterns and resource constraints.
- *Benefits communication*—involving employees in the selection of options, letting them know the details of their compensation and enlisting their aid in managing costs.
- *Government requirements*—complying with frequently changing state and federal laws
- *Group size*—finding insurance companies that will provide coverage to organizations with a small number of employees.

- *Rising costs*—developing procedures and identifying options to deal with the continuing increase in benefits costs; for example, exploring medical insurance cost savings using higher deductibles and second opinions before costly procedures are done.

An organization regularly has to answer some key questions about needs, options, and constraints whether it is developing a benefits program for the first time or is involved in the continuous process of self-renewal. Some of those questions are:

(i) What Benefit Options Are Available?

The benefits package consists of the coverage mandated by federal and state law, and an ever-growing list of discretionary benefits.

The mandated benefits include:

- *Social Security* retirement and disability payments for those who meet the guidelines (see Section 12.2.a);
- *Medicare insurance* coverage for the elderly and disabled (see Section 12.2.a);
- *Unemployment* benefits (see Section 12.2.a);
- *Workers compensation*, required by the states, provides payments to employees who are unable to work because of a work-related illness or injury;
- *Programs mandated by the individual states*, such as temporary disability insurance.

The employer has a wide range of discretionary benefits available. As a general rule the employer is not required to provide these benefits; however the employer must make a selection based on criteria which meet the employees' needs, the organization's values, the employer's constraints, and community norms. Some of the more popular options available are the following:

- *Accidental Death and Dismemberment Insurance* coverage offers additional payments for accidental death or the loss of a limb, sight, or hearing due to injury. It is often added to the life insurance policy.
- *Employee assistance* provides counseling to employees for serious problems which are interfering with their work performance. Usually services are for substance abuse, however, referrals may be provided for other problems including financial and marital. This does not duplicate medical insurance covered services.
- *Life Insurance* is usually based on the employee's salary level. Under the IRS Code, any premium payment for life insurance coverage in excess of $50,000 is considered income to the employee and is taxable.
- *Long-Term Disability Insurance* provides partial replacement of income during a period of total disability when the employee is unable to work (usually after a defined waiting period).
- *Medical and dental insurance* for the employees and, if the employee chooses, for their eligible dependents. Employers have to explore a variety of insurance coverage packages, managed care options, and employee copayment alternatives so that they can offer their employees the widest choice for the lowest cost.

- *Medical/dental and child care/dependent care accounts* allow the employee to pay for certain medical and dental expenses not covered by their insurance plans, and child care or dependent care expenses with funds which are not taxed. Employees state once per year how much of their expected earnings, up to a defined limit, they want placed in these accounts. If these funds are not used during the year, they revert back to the employer.
- *Retirement plans* provide income after an employee retires. "Defined benefit" plans provide an annual pension usually based on years of service and salary level. "Defined contribution plans" generally offer a lump-sum payment based on the employer's contributions, which are typically a percentage of the eligible employee's annual salary or a matching contribution based on the employee's contribution.
- *403(b) Tax-deferred Annuity Plan* is designed specifically for employees of nonprofit organizations. Current regulations allow them generally to save up to 25 percent of their annual salary up to $9,500 per year exempt from federal income tax. Funds are taxed only when they are withdrawn, usually after retirement. Penalties apply if funds are withdrawn before retirement.
- *Travel accident insurance* covers employees when they are traveling on business.
- *Tuition assistance* plans reimburse employees for some portion of the cost of courses they take in accredited programs. This benefit may be taxable to the employee.

Some employers offer benefits under a *Cafeteria Plan* or Flexible Benefit, which allows each employee to select from among a menu of options those that best meet his or her personal and family needs. Although they offer flexibility, these plans must be carefully structured to qualify for favorable tax treatment.

Paid leave time benefits include sick leave, vacation, paid holidays, family leave to care for a new child or a sick family member, personal leave (the employee does not need to specify the reason), sabbatical, and professional development leave. Employees may also be concerned about the amount of unused leave time that they can accumulate from year to year. Often the employer allows the employee to accumulate up to a defined amount of unused vacation and/or sick leave. Sick leave often is allowed to accumulate until it reaches the number of days required in the waiting period for long-term disability insurance.

Employees are often able to balance family needs and work needs more easily if the employer offers benefits which cost nothing but provide flexibility. These include:

- *Flex time* lets employees adjust their work schedule to meet personal needs while allowing the employer to achieve its goals;
- *Job sharing* has two or more individuals do one job on a regular schedule.

Nonprofit organizations also have a unique opportunity to enhance their employee benefits package with little- or- no-cost options that relate to the services they provide. For example, institutions offering classes can let employees and their families take, at no cost, the classes which are not filled. Membership organizations like museums can provide each employee with a family membership. Day care centers can offer reduced rates to employees. Available seats for events or performances can be offered to employees as well.

Unique benefits such as these enhance the nonprofit's ability to recruit and retain skilled employees and compete with other organizations.

(ii) What Do the Employees Want?

The typical benefits package was developed for a stereotypical family structure that no longer represents the majority of households. An employer cannot hope to know what employees value and what motivates them without asking the employees themselves.

Employee input into the creation and restructuring of a benefits plan can be solicited in several ways:

- Written survey of employees;
- Focus groups where representative employees are asked to define their needs and to react to options; and/or
- Employee participation on a committee that has responsibility for assisting management in the process of selecting benefits.

(iii) How Can the Needs of the Employer and the Employee Be Met at the Same Time?

Answering these questions requires a balancing act. For some, the solution is to provide a flexible plan wherein everyone receives some core benefits such as individual health insurance and has some choice about the others. For others, the best approach is to increase salaries enough to offset higher taxes and let employees make their own purchases. For still others, the preferred approach is to offer a set package and give employees the right to refuse all or some of the items they do not need or want. In all cases, the package that works for an organization is one that considers its unique history and is tailored to the values of the employer and the life style of the employees.

(D) COMMUNICATING WITH EMPLOYEES ABOUT THEIR BENEFITS

Often the success of a benefits program depends on how effectively the organization explains the package to the employees. Benefits descriptions can be vague and the procedures required in order to receive benefits can be complex. The employer has the responsibility to set up a system which both delivers the benefits and provides information in a clear and timely manner. Four communications tools can assist the employer in carrying out these responsibilities:

- *A key person* who acts as the source of information for the employees and a communications link to the benefits provider. This person should be able to answer questions or know who can.
- *Summary Plan Descriptions* are the descriptions of the benefit plans which the plan administrator is required to provide for employees. The employer must ensure that each employee is given an up-to-date description of each insurance benefit program.
- *Benefits update meetings* should be held before any new insurance package is introduced and periodically thereafter. The meetings allow employees to ask questions and comment on the services provided. Presentations need to be made by individuals who know the policies and procedures thoroughly.

Where possible, the employer should ask representatives of the insurance carriers or brokers to make presentations.

• *Personal Statement of Compensation and Benefits*, distributed annually, lists the level of benefit and compensation which the employee is eligible to receive and the actual cost of the benefit to the employer. The statement serves both to summarize the major benefits the employee receives and to share what it actually costs the employer to provide the benefits. Regulations require that this information be provided annually for retirement plans, but it is an advantage to the employer and the employee to include all benefits as in the example below. Some statements, like the example below, include the cost of leave time allowed as well as other benefits. (See Exhibit 12.3.)

12.2   Compensation- and Benefits-Related Laws

Many pieces of legislation touch on compensation in some way, but the framework for compensation in this country was provided in the 1930s by the Social Security Act and the Fair Labor Standards Act, both of which have been amended several times. From the benefits perspective, the major law remains the Employee Retirement Income Security Act of 1974 (ERISA), although the pace of benefits-related legislation has been accelerating in recent years.

EXHIBIT 12.3 Sample Personal Statement of Compensation and Benefits

Dear (employee name):

This confidential report has been prepared to acquaint you with the total compensation including benefits which you receive from your employer. It also indicates the total value of the compensation package including leave time which is 45% above your base salary. The level of benefits the organization provides represents our strong commitment to you and to all of our employees.

This report is issued annually with the aim of keeping you informed about the nature and value of your benefits. Where estimates were required, certain necessary assumptions were made based on the information available. We urge you to review it carefully and keep it as a guide for your personal planning.

	Benefit Level	**Annual Cost**
Salary	$30,000	$30,000
Life Insurance	2 times annual salary, $60,000	100
Long Term Disability	$1,500 per month after 6 months total disability	2,000
Medical Insurance	Individual coverage fully paid by employer	3,500
Dental Insurance	Individual coverage, employer pays 50%	150
Social Security (FICA)	7.65% of annual salary	2,300
Pension	6% of annual salary	1,800
Worker's Compensation	Benefit level defined by a formula if you are disabled due to a work related accident or illness	200
Total cost for your compensation and benefits		$40,050
In addition, your annual leave time including vacation, holiday, and sick leave, if taken, costs		$3,500
Total including leave time		$43,550

(A) SOCIAL SECURITY ACT

(i) *Overview*

The county's most comprehensive piece of social legislation, the Social Security Act created the social security program, the federal–state unemployment insurance system, and various other governmental programs. The social insurance portions are funded through payroll taxes.

(ii) *Major Provisions*

The following comments concern only the programs funded through payroll taxes:

- Employees are exempt from overtime pay obligations if their job meets the requirements for an exempt position. First they must hold bona fide administrative or professional positions or work as outside sales representatives. Second, the exempt level work must be paid on a salaried basis which is defined as the same amount of pay per pay period regardless of the quality or quantity of work performed.
- Retirement benefits (income and Medicare coverage) are funded through provisions of the Federal Insurance Contribution Act (FICA), with each employer and employee paying the same percentage on the salary or wages received.
- Unemployment benefits are funded through a payroll tax paid by the employer. Four states also require that the employee contribute some amount. Because the unemployment program is managed on a state level, amounts and duration of payments vary.

Details on program eligibility, rates, and benefits are too numerous for this chapter.

(iii) *Implications for Nonprofit Organizations*

- Payroll tax amounts must be withheld from employees' wages, supplemented by the employer's share, and deposited in the appropriate account in a timely fashion. Failure to do so results in penalties.
- Employees must be given an accounting of the amount withheld for their FICA share. This must be done on the annual W-2 form given employees for income tax purposes.
- Nonprofits generally may choose, once a year, whether to pay the unemployment amount (1) as a flat tax on the first X dollars of each person's wages or (2) as a dollar-for-dollar reimbursement of amounts paid to former employees collecting benefits. An employer with high turnover would choose the former; an employer with little or no anticipated turnover would choose the latter.
- Given that nearly all nonprofit employees earn less than the social security wage cap, managers need to create budgets with the realization that the two mandatory programs will cost them perhaps an eighth more than each employee's nominal salary.
- Another reality is that the program's old-wage benefits were never intended to provide an adequate income for retirement. Thus, as nonprofits (and their employees) mature, the importance of having some type of pension plan will grow.

(B) FAIR LABOR STANDARDS ACT

(i) Overview

The FLSA established the minimum wage, maximum work hours, child-labor standards, and overtime pay requirements.

(ii) Major provisions

- Employees are exempt from overtime pay requirements if they hold bona fide administrative, managerial, or professional positions or if they work as outside sales representatives. Nonexempt employees *must* be paid at 1.5 times their normal hourly rate when they work more than 40 hours in a given workweek.
- Employees must be paid the federal minimum wage unless the state minimum wage is higher, in which case the latter applies. A student or "learner" wage may also be paid in some circumstances, after the employer has received the appropriate certificate from the Department of Labor.
- Children between the ages of 14 and 16 may be employed if the work is other than mining or manufacturing (which are not areas known for nonprofits) and if the work does not interfere with their education, health, or well-being.
- Independent contractors are exempt from FLSA provisions.

(iii) Implications for Nonprofit Organizations

- State and local governments have the option of granting nonexempt workers compensatory time instead of paying overtime. Private employers do not have a similar right. Also, the government views the workweek as the unit of measurement: Overtime is earned for each week separately. It is not legal to average a 30-hour week and a 50-hour week, declare them two 40-hour weeks, and thereby avoid paying overtime.
- To support decisions about overtime pay, employers must keep sufficiently accurate records of time worked. If these records are incomplete or missing, the *employee's* memory may be deemed sufficient to win a claim.
- The label of "independent contractor" or "consultant" cannot be used to avoid compliance with FICA and FLSA. Among the factors examined are the contractor's economic ties to the employer and the permanency of the relationship. In recent years, the Internal Revenue Service has looked much more closely at the use of such arrangements in the nonprofit sector. They apply a 20-factor test to the situation. The IRS looks at the contractor's ability to perform work according to their own methods without being subject to the control of the employer except for the results.
- The nonprofit sector is not exempt from scrutiny for FLSA violations. In the past few years, libraries have been prosecuted for child-labor violations (too many hours) and even the Salvation Army has been accused of violating the minimum wage provisions.

(C) EMPLOYEE RETIREMENT INCOME SECURITY ACT (ERISA)

(i) Overview

ERISA is the major law governing the establishment, operation, and administration of employee benefit plans, specifically those concerning pensions and welfare (including health care, vacation benefits, dependent care, prepaid legal services, and educational assistance). It also covers the requirements for informing employees of their benefits and rights.

(ii) Major Provisions

ERISA is a lengthy, highly complex piece of legislation. It does not require that any employer offer a pension or welfare benefit plan. Should an employer choose to offer a plan, however, that plan is subject to ERISA. In general:

- The Act covers requirements for reporting and disclosure, participation, vesting (the right to receive a benefit), funding, and fiduciary standards. It also covers tax provisions, presented as amendments to the Internal Revenue Code.
- ERISA is enforced by the Treasury Department (for participation, vesting, and funding matters) and the Labor Department (for reporting, disclosure, and fiduciary matters).

(iii) Implications for Nonprofit Organizations

- Pension and welfare plans cannot be established or operated for the exclusive or disproportionate benefit of highly compensated or "key" employees. (The complexity of the nondiscrimination rules precludes their presentation here.)
- Employers must give employees understandable information about their plans and benefits.
- Employers must file annual IRS reports on forms from the 5500 series.

(D) CONSOLIDATED OMNIBUS BUDGET RECONCILIATION ACT (COBRA)

(i) Overview

Essentially, this Act, referred to as COBRA, amended ERISA and the IRS Code to require that employees and their dependents (current and former), be allowed to continue group health insurance coverage after certain qualifying events occur by reimbursing the employer for the amount of the coverage plus an additional 2 percent as an administrative fee.

(ii) Major Provisions

- An employee who leaves or loses a job (for reasons other than gross misconduct) may continue group health insurance for up to 18 months by electing to continue and making the payments mentioned above. An employee whose hours are reduced to a level below that at which eligibility for coverage begins may continue the coverage in the same way. Someone ruled disabled under the Social Security Act is eligible for 29 months of continuation after job loss or reduction of hours.
- Some dependents are eligible for 36 months of continuation of certain events occur, such as divorce or legal separation from the covered employee.

(iii) Implications for Nonprofit Organizations

- Employers must amend the summary plan descriptions of their health insurance plans to advise employees of their COBRA rights. In addition, there are several notification requirements.

- Employers with fewer than 20 employees are exempt from COBRA but may be liable under COBRA-like state laws.

(E)   OTHER RECENT BENEFITS LEGISLATION

Since ERISA was passed in 1974, the pace of legislative action on compensation and benefits issues has quickened. Four major trends are discernible:

1. An increasing interest in ensuring that taxpayers will not subsidize the wealthy, evidenced in the requirements that benefit plans seeking tax breaks in turn not discriminate in favor of owners or the highly compensated;
2. Changes in regulations concerning the establishment and funding of Individual Retirement Accounts (IRAs) and pension plans for small employers;
3. Expanded requirements to help ensure solvency of pension plans;
4. Increased regulations affecting for-profit employers (such as those concerning employee stock ownership plans (ESOPs)).

Many changes have been designed to expand coverage and benefits; all have increased the system's complexity. This section highlights the major pieces of legislation and summarizes their main features.

(i)   Tax Reform Act of 1976
A worker with a nonworking spouse can set aside $2,250 a year in an IRA.

(ii)   Revenue Act of 1978
The Simplified Employee Pension was created for small employers. It also allowed employers to establish what became known as 401(k) plans, named after their relevant section in the Internal Revenue Code.

(iii)   Economic Recovery Tax Act of 1981
The maximum deductible limit for an IRA was raised to $2,000 and IRAs were extended to all workers, even those covered by an employer-provided pension plan. ERTA also doubled the amount that could be contributed to a simplified employee pension (SEP) or a Keogh plan.

(iv)   Tax Equity and Fiscal Responsibility Act of 1982
This Act restricted the maximum contribution and benefit limits for pension plans, permitted partial rollovers between IRA accounts, and limited the kinds of loans people could get from their pension plans without tax consequences. Keogh plans became subject to the same minimum age and service requirements as other pension plans.

(v)   Deficit Reduction Act of 1984
Intended to close tax loopholes, this Act limited flexible benefit plans ("cafeteria" plans). The only benefits that could be included in a cafeteria plan without tax consequences were those specifically excluded from gross income by the Internal Revenue Code. These included health care benefits, group term life insurance, prepaid group legal services, dependent care, and educational reimbursement.

(vi)   Retirement Equity Act of 1984

Designed to improve women's pension opportunities, this Act lowered the age at which an employee must be allowed to participate in a pension plan and lengthened the acceptable "break in service," the period during which one may leave work without losing pension credits. The law also specified that a worker could not waive survivor benefits or designate a nonspouse beneficiary without the spouse's written consent. (The intention here was to constrain a worker from choosing higher benefits during his or her own lifetime in exchange for coverage as long as either spouse survived.) It also added provisions allowing pension benefits to be paid to a former spouse in certain circumstances in connection with a divorce.

(vii)   Tax Reform Act of 1986

"TRA 86" shortened vesting periods (generally to 5 years); restricted the ability of workers covered by an employer-sponsored pension to make tax-deductible contributions to an IRA; dropped the annual employee deferral in a 401(k) to $7,000 (indexed to $9,500 as of 1996); allowed small employers to defer part of a salary to a SEP; imposed a 10 percent penalty on funds withdrawn from an IRA before a person reaches age 59½; and increased nondiscrimination rules.

(viii)   Omnibus Budget Reconciliation Act of 1986

The Age Discrimination in Employment Act was amended to require employers to continue pension benefit accruals for workers over 65.

(ix)   Omnibus Budget Reconciliation Act of 1987

Pension contributions for employers having defined benefit plans were increased, and restrictions on pension plan terminations were tightened.

(x)   The Unemployment Compensation Amendments of 1992

These modified the rules relating to withholding from pension distributions and tax-free rollovers. For distributions made on or after January 1, 1993, any part of a taxable distribution from a tax-qualified plan or tax-sheltered annuity (other than one required minimum distribution) can be rolled over tax-free to an IRA or other eligible retirement plan, unless the distribution is one of a series of substantially equal installments made over the participant's (or the participant and his beneficiary's) life expectancy or over a period of 10 years or more. An "eligible rollover distribution" which is not transferred directly to an IRA or other eligible retirement plan is subject to 20 percent withholding.

(xi)   The Retirement Protection Act of 1994

This changed the rules relating to funding of defined benefit pension plans in an effort to insure adequate funding of pension benefits.

(F)   FAMILY AND MEDICAL LEAVE ACT

(i)   Overview

FMLA entitles eligible employees to take up to 12 weeks of unpaid, job-protected leave each year for specified family and medical reasons. The law, which went into effect in 1993, contains provisions relating to employer coverage; employee eligibility for the benefits; entitlement to leave, maintenance of health benefits during leave, and job restoration after leave; notice and certification of the need for FMLA leave; and protection for employees who request or take FMLA leave. The law also includes certain employer record-keeping requirements.

(ii) Major Provisions

- Unpaid leave must be granted for any of the following reasons: to care for the employee's child after childbirth or placement for adoption or foster care; to care for the employee's spouse, son or daughter, or parent who has a serious health condition; or for a serious health condition that makes the employee unable to perform the employee's job. At the employee's or employer's option, certain kinds of paid leave may be substituted for unpaid leave.
- Upon return from FMLA leave, most employees must be restored to their original or equivalent positions with equivalent pay, benefits, and other employment terms.
- The law applies to all public agencies and local educational agencies as well as private sector employers who employ 50 or more employees for at least 20 workweeks in a calendar year.

(iii) Implications for Nonprofit Organizations

- Employers must amend their policies and procedures and employee handbooks to reflect the provisions of the law. In addition, the employer is required to notify employees of the provisions of the law.
- Employers with fewer than 50 employees are exempt from FMLA.

12.3 Benefits-Related Resources

Given the rapidly changing nature of employment related benefits, a resource listing needs updating almost as soon as it is printed. Nonetheless, this section presents major types of resources that may be useful to nonprofit organizations.

(A) ASSOCIATIONS AND ORGANIZATIONS

(i) American Law Institute—American Bar Association (ALI—ABA) Committee on Continuing Education

Provides numerous short courses throughout the year to inform both lawyers and managers about changes and proposed changes in the laws and regulation. A number of the courses are related to nonprofits and employee benefits.

ALI-ABA
4025 Chestnut St.
Philadelphia, PA 19104
(215) 243-1630

(ii) Association of Part-Time Professionals

This association publishes information on job sharing and on employers of part-time professionals. Its publication, *Employee Benefits for Part-Timers*, covers ways of prorating benefits. For further information, contact:

Association of Part-Time Professionals
7700 Leesburg Pike
Falls Church, VA 22043
(703) 734-7975

(iii)   Association of Private Pension and Welfare Plans

With members from large and small benefits consulting firms, investment firms, accounting firms, insurers, utilities, law firms, and other businesses, APPWP is a national association that lobbies Congress on benefits issues. It also helps members deal with governmental agencies and elected officials. In addition to an annual conference, it offers members a newsletter and a report on legislation and regulation. For more information, contact:

Association of Private Pension and Welfare Plans
1212 New York Avenue, N.W.
Washington, DC 20005
(202) 289-6700

(iv)   Bureau of National Affairs, Inc.

The BNA sponsors conferences and offers weekly and biweekly summaries of court cases, legislation, arbitration decisions, and other factors affecting benefits. On an affordable level for nonprofit organizations are BNA's many books, including the recently published third edition of Barbara Coleman's *Primer on ERISA*. For more information, contact:

Bureau of National Affairs
1231 25th Street, N.W.
Washington, DC 20037
(202) 452-4276

(v)   Business Group on Health

Such groups can be found variously on state and city levels. They exist to share information and sometimes to lobby. Probably the best known is the Washington Business Group on Health, which produces *Business and Health*, a monthly journal. For more information, check local telephone books.

(vi)   The Conference Board

One of the most widely known providers of information about employment-related issues, the Conference Board bases its reports and conferences on actual practices. Representatives of over 2,500 organizations from business, academia, and government are connected through Conference Board activities. The organization has produced reports on such issues as retiree health care, family issues, and flexible benefits. One regular publication is *Across the Board*. For more information, contact:

The Conference Board
845 Third Avenue
New York, NY 10022
(212) 759-0900

(vii)   Employee Benefit Research Institute

A "nonprofit, nonpartisan, public policy research institution," EBRI sponsors policy forums and produces research reports and other publications on benefits-related issues. Its monthly report, *EBRI Issue Briefs*, examines benefits issues and trends. Of its many publications, one is particularly noteworthy: *Fundamentals of Employee Benefit Programs*, now in its fourth edition. This is an excellent primer on the subject. For further information, contact:

> Employee Benefit Research Institute
> 2121 K Street, N.W., Suite 600
> Washington, DC 20037-2121
> (202) 659-0670

(viii)   Group Health Association of America

A national association representing prepaid health care programs (meaning Health Maintenance Organizations, HMOs), GHAA provides information through publications on industry trends, regulatory trends, and legislative issues. Its library provides research help on matters concerning managed care plans. For more information, contact:

> GHAA Library Services
> 1129 20th Street, N.W.
> Washington, DC 20036
> (202) 778-3268

(ix)   Health Insurance Association of America

A major trade association of commercial health and life insurers, HIAA provides information on cost containment approaches, benefit plan designs, financing insurance, and insurers that write policies for small employers. For more information, contact:

> Consumer Affairs
> Health Insurance Association of America
> 1025 Connecticut Avenue, N.W.
> Washington, DC 20036-3998
> (202) 223-7780

(x)   International Foundation of Employee Benefit Plans

Founded to foster an exchange of information about benefits, the Foundation sponsors conferences at the introductory and advanced levels; programs leading to certification as an employee benefits specialist (CEBS designation); books on such topics as cost containment and ERISA; research reports; the quarterly *Employee Benefits Journal;* and various other publications on legislation, regulations, and benefits. The Foundation also has an extensive library on benefits-related topics. For further information, contact:

> International Foundation of Employee Benefit Plans
> 18700 West Bluemound Road, P. O. Box 69
> Brookfield, WI 53008-0069
> (414) 786-6700

(xi) Practising Law Institute

Among PLI's many courses and conferences are several each year concerning employee benefit plans. The materials for these sessions are published in thick compendia for general purchase. In the 18-title tax law and estate planning series, for example, PLI offers a two-volume set, *Employee Welfare Benefit Plans*. Because the laws and regulations change so rapidly, the PLI publications are valuable for timeliness. For more information, contact:

Practising Law Institute
810 Seventh Avenue
New York, NY 10019
(212) 824-5700

(xii) U.S. Chamber of Commerce

Of this organization's services, two seem particularly useful to nonprofit organizations: (1) the annual survey on employee benefits (quantity discounts available), and (2) the syndicated television show, "It's Your Business." For more information, contact:

Research Center, Economic Policy Division
U. S. Chamber of Commerce
1615 H Street, N.W.
Washington, DC 20062
(301) 468-5128

(xiii) U.S. Government Printing Office

Federal bookstores offer publications on wages and salaries, benefits, and various other human resource issues. Among these are *Handbook for Analyzing Jobs and Employee Benefits in Medium and Large Firms*. For more information, consult local telephone directories for the nearest federal bookstore or write:

Superintendent of Documents
U. S. Government Printing Office
North Capitol and H Streets, N.W.
Washington, DC 20401

(B) PUBLICATIONS AND PUBLISHERS

Specific topics vary with journals and issues. A brief annotation is given for general recommendation of these sources.

(i) Benefits Quarterly

A publication (with refereed articles) of the International Society of Employee Benefit Specialists, through the International Foundation of Employee Benefit Plans.

(ii) Business and Health

A monthly publication of Health Learning Systems, in consultation with the Washington Business Group on Health.

(iii) Compensation & Benefits Management

Quarterly journal of articles and columns directed to those in charge of designing or managing compensation programs; in mid-1980s, won award as outstanding new journal in business/social sciences/humanities category. Address:

> Panel Publishers, Inc.
> 36 W. 44th Street
> New York, NY 10036

(iv) Compensation and Benefits Review

Bimonthly published by the American Management Association. Address:

> American Management Association
> 135 W. 50th Street
> New York, NY 10020

(v) Employee Benefits Journal

Quarterly published by the International Foundation of Employee Benefit Plans; free to members of the IFEPB.

(vi) Employee Benefit Plan Review

Monthly digest of developments concerning employee benefits; summarizes legislation, speeches, consulting firms' studies, court cases, and trends. Address:

> Charles D. Spencer & Associates, Inc.
> 222 West Adams Street
> Chicago, IL 60606

(vii) Pension World

Monthly directed toward pension plan sponsors and investment managers; understandable by people other than actuaries. Address:

> Pension World
> 6255 Barfield Road
> Atlanta, GA 30328

12.4 Benefits-Related Terminology

Although this volume contains an extensive glossary, benefits-related terms are presented here for the reader's convenience. The entries have been selected to provide a basic working vocabulary, but by no means are they the only terms with which a benefits manager would have to be familiar.

Accidental death and dismemberment insurance Coverage is usually added onto the life insurance policy. It offers additional payments for accidental death or the loss of a limb, sight, or hearing due to injury.

Accrual   The accumulation and crediting of benefits to an employee by virtue of his or her participation in a compensation plan. Accrued benefits may be forfeited unless they are vested.

Actuarial equivalent   Amount of equal present value. An amount to be received in the future is the actuarial equivalent of another if they have the same present value, determined by using the same actuarial assumptions (such as rate of return and retirement age). See *present value*.

ADEA   Age Discrimination in Employment Act, which prohibits discrimination in conditions or termination of employment because of age (protecting those over age 40). Mandatory retirement for employees eligible to receive pensions violates ADEA.

Annuity   A contract for the periodic payment of specified or objectively determinable amounts over a specified period or over the recipient's lifetime.

Beneficiary   The person eligible for benefits or payments upon the death of a plan participant.

Bonus   A lump-sum payment to an employee in recognition of some achievement. Because a bonus is not added to the employee's base pay, some employers use this approach to limit compensation and taxation growth as well as to recognize achievement.

Break in service   A year in which an employee is credited with no more than 500 hours of service. If an employee has such a break, he or she may lose credit for service before the break, unless he or she returns to service and works another year. A qualified maternity or paternity leave may not be counted as a break in service but may be treated as a neutral year.

Cafeteria plan   A plan in which participants can choose from among two or more options consisting either of tax-qualified benefits or of a combination of cash and tax-qualified benefits.

Cliff vesting   A schedule for vesting in which accrued benefits become nonforfeitable after a specified period of service, such as five years.

COBRA   Consolidated Omnibus Budget Reconciliation Act of 1985.

CODA   Cash or deferred tax arrangement, as a 401(k) plan.

Coinsurance   Payment by employees for part of the benefit being provided. A common approach is for a health insurer to pay 80 percent of a health service while the employee pays the remaining 20 percent.

Contributory plan   A plan to which contributions are made in part or whole by participants rather than (or in addition to) their employer.

Coordination of benefits   Procedure whereby two insurance companies share information to limit their individual liability for expenses. This may arise when spouses have insurance from different employers or when someone is covered by both Medicare and an employer-provided policy.

Coverage test   Requirement that a plan benefit a minimum number or percentage of employees, with the aim of avoiding discrimination in favor of highly compensated employees.

Deductible   Expense amount that an employee must pay before other sources (insurance company or employer) assume liability for payment. Deductibles are seen as cost-saving measures by employers and insurance companies.

Defined benefit plan   A pension plan that pays a specified benefit at retirement, often keyed to average salary over the last few years of employment and to years of service. Contributions to the plan vary according to the amount needed to provide the projected benefit. In this instance, the employer bears the risk and must set aside enough now to make the payments later.

Defined contribution plan   A pension or profit-sharing plan to which the contributions are specified amounts and the participants have a right to receive benefits contingent on the accumulated value of the total contributions. In other words, the benefits may vary according to the investment expertise of the plan's trustee; the employee, therefore, bears the risk under this plan.

Dependent care assistance programs   A plan whereby the employer helps employees with services for dependents, which the employee needs in order to earn a living. The employer may provide the needed services, pay the service provider directly, or reimburse the employee for the expenses incurred. If the employer gives the money to the employee, the funds are treated as regular compensation and the employee seeks tax relief under Internal Revenue Code Section 21, dependent care tax credit. If the employer provides or subsidizes the benefit, up to $5,000 per year may be excluded from gross income ($2,500 each, for married individuals filing separately).

Direct compensation   Pay received in the form of cash or cash equivalents (generally, wages and salaries).

Discrimination   Favoring of highly compensated employees, owners, or officers by the operation or terms of a plan.

Disqualified person   Someone who has a specified relationship to a plan, such as the fiduciary, the employer, and officers, directors, and highly compensated employees.

Educational assistance program   A plan whereby an employer provides instruction for or pays educational expenses of an employee. The plan must be written and must not discriminate in favor of officers, owners, highly compensated employees, or their dependents.

Employee   One who performs services for compensation and whose working conditions are set by the employer.

Employee assistance   Provides counseling to employees for serious problems which are interfering with their work performance. Usually services are for substance abuse, however, referrals may be provided for other problems including financial and marital. This does not duplicate medical insurance covered services.

Entry date   The date on which an employee must be allowed to participate in a plan. The Internal Revenue Code requires that a tax-qualified plan admit an employee who has satisfied the age and length-of-service requirements no later than the earlier of these dates: (1) the first day of the first plan year beginning after the date on which the employee first satisfied the requirements; or (2) the date six months after the date on which the employee satisfied the requirements. Multiple dates (as many as 366 in a leap year) may be used when employers want to cover employees as soon as possible.

ERISA   The Employee Retirement Income Security Act of 1974 (Public Law 93-403), the law that established the basic requirements for tax-qualified plans. ERISA covers pension and welfare plans, both of which must comply with provisions concerning reporting and disclosure, fiduciary responsibility, and enforcement. The former are also subject to detailed regulations concerning coverage, funding, and vesting. ERISA does not cover federal or state governmental plans for public workers, unemployment insurance, workers' compensation, church plans, excess benefit plans, or plans maintained outside the United States.

ERISA preemption Explicit preemption by ERISA (in Section 514) of state laws concerning employee benefit plans, except those laws regulating insurance, banking, and securities.

Excess benefit plan A plan that provides benefits beyond those in a tax-qualified plan and therefore is not covered by ERISA.

Executive perquisites ("perks") Special benefits made available to top managerial employees. These are becoming more and more likely to represent taxable income to the employee receiving them.

Federal Insurance Contributions Act (FICA) The source of social security withholding requirements.

Forfeiture Loss of benefits caused by leaving employment before all accrued benefits have been vested.

Forward averaging Procedure of computing tax on a lump-sum distribution whereby the tax is determined as if the money were received over a period of years. This application of Internal Revenue Code (IRC) Section 402(e) avoids combining the total distribution with the taxpayer's other income for a tax year, thereby lowering the overall effective tax rate.

401(k) plan A CODA; a profit-sharing or stock bonus plan wherein an employee may choose to be paid in cash or through having the funds placed in a trust under the plan. Under the 1986 Tax Reform Act, tax-exempt organizations, as well as state and local governments, can no longer establish such plans, although any in existence before July 1986 could be continued.

403(b) plan Tax-deferred annuity plan for retirement for employees of tax-exempt IRC Section 501(c)(3) organizations. The same nondiscrimination rules apply here as to Section 401(a) plans, including minimum participation rules. In addition, a Section 403(b) plan can be considered discriminatory in terms of elective deferrals unless *all* employees have an opportunity to make the deferrals. (These deferrals are amounts shielded from current taxation through a salary reduction agreement.) An employee's annual deferral is generally limited to $9,500 (with some possible additions), a limit higher than those for CODAs or SEPs.

Frozen plan A plan in which benefit accrual has stopped but existence continues to distribute assets to participants and beneficiaries.

Graded or stepped vesting A schedule whereby an increasing percentage of accrued benefits become vested, until 100 percent is reached. The 1986 Tax Reform Act replaced earlier forms with seven-year graded vesting: a plan must provide at least 20 percent vesting after three years, 40 percent after four, 60 percent after five, 80 percent after six, and 100 percent after seven years.

Highly compensated employee One who, in the current or previous plan year, (1) was a 5 percent owner; (2) received $85,485 (in 1990) in compensation; (3) received $56,990 (in 1990 compensation) and was in the most highly paid fifth of employees of the organization, or (4) was an officer and received compensation more than 50 percent of the dollar limitation on annual benefits ($51,291 in 1990). (These figures are adjusted annually for inflation.) The 1986 Tax Reform Act created alternative tests for discrimination with regard to the percentage of compensation deferred in a year.

Hour of service   An hour for which an employee is paid or entitled to be paid for performing duties, exercising excused absences, or meriting back pay.

Indirect compensation   Pay received in the form of benefits or services.

Integration   Reduction of pension benefits or contributions to take into account social security benefits to which a participant is entitled. Some pension plans are designed to yield a retiree a certain amount when combined with social security. In such cases, the contribution or benefits will vary according to the amount being paid into or received from social security.

IRA   Individual retirement account, a trust organized and created in the United States for the exclusive benefit of an individual and his or her beneficiaries. The limit on contributions for a tax year is $2,000, except for rollover contributions. An IRA may not be invested in insurance contracts or in "collectibles" (such as stamps or rare coins) and must provide for mandatory distributions. Under Internal Revenue Code Section 408(c), employers and employee associations may establish IRAs for employees. Distributions from both types are taxable in the year paid.

J & S   Joint-and-survivor annuity; upon the participant's retirement, a J & S lasts for his or her lifetime and then provides an annuity for the lifetime of the surviving spouse.

Key employee   One who is an officer of the employer or who meets one of several ownership tests. "Key" and "highly compensated" are not synonymous.

Leased employees   Someone who is not an employee yet provides services usually provided by an employee, but does so under contract with a leasing organization and on basically a full-time basis for over a year.

Life insurance   Is usually based on the employee's salary level. Under the IRS Code, any premium payment for life insurance coverage in excess of $50,000 is considered income to the employee and is taxable.

Long-term disability insurance   Provides partial replacement of income during a period of total disability when the employee is unable to work (usually after a defined waiting period).

Lump-sum distribution   Distribution of the entire balance of an employee's account within the same tax year as a triggering event (retirement, death, disability, termination of service, or reaching age 59½).

Mandated insurance benefit   A benefit that a state requires in an insurance package or plan if the insurer is to operate within the state. The most commonly mandated benefit is mental health care within employee health plans.

Medical and dental care accounts   Allow the employee to pay for certain medical and dental expenses not covered by their insurance plans, with funds which are not taxed. The employee elects how much he or she wants placed in these accounts, up to a defined limit, once per year. Any funds that are not used during the year revert back to the employer.

Minimum accrual standards   Established by ERISA's Section 204, these reinforce the vesting requirements. Section 204 describes three formulas to prevent backloading, or the limiting of generous accrual until later years. Accrued benefits may not be reduced because of increased age or years of service. Also, pension plan assets or liabilities cannot be transferred, merged, or consolidated unless each participant receives benefits at least equal to those to which he or she would have been entitled before the transaction. Still, someone may transfer enough assets to meet this stipulation and then keep the rest, a phenomenon increasing in recent years.

Minimum funding standards   Guidelines for the minimum amount an employer must contribute to a plan, to cover all liabilities and operating costs. A plan is underfunded when the market value of its assets is less than the present value of vested deferred benefits. Sections 301 to 306 of ERISA specify funding requirements for pension plans.

Minimum vesting standards   Requirements for the points at which benefits become nonforfeitable. Benefits derived from employee contributions are fully vested immediately. Employer contributions may meet one of three standards: (1) 100 percent vesting after five years (cliff vesting), (2) seven-year graded vesting, or (3) ten-year cliff vesting under multiemployer, collectively bargained plans.

Money purchase plan   A defined contribution plan.

Normal retirement age   The earlier of (1) the age specified in the plan, or (2) the latest of (a) the participant's 65th birthday, (b) the fifth anniversary of plan participation, for someone who began participating within five years of the plan's stated normal retirement age, or (c) the tenth anniversary of someone's initial plan participation. Term does not refer to the age at which one falls asleep reading a benefits glossary.

Participant   Someone entitled to receive benefits under an ERISA plan. A former employee is a participant if he or she has been vested and has yet to receive all accrued benefits under a plan.

Participation   Taking part, or allowing one to take part, in a plan. Generally, the maximum required waiting period is one year if the employer wants to retain tax qualification; an employer may allow employees to participate immediately. The usual minimum age requirement is 21, although tax-exempt educational institutions may use age 26.

PBGC   The Pension Benefit Guarantee Corporation, an entity operated under the Department of Labor to administer pension plan insurance and termination provisions. The PBGC may terminate a plan experiencing financial difficulty; it might also assert claims against an employer filing for bankruptcy.

Pension plan   A plan providing for definitely determinable retirement benefits over a period of years for participants or their beneficiaries. A tax-qualified plan must be in writing, be established by an employer, be communicated to employees, be a permanent rather than a temporary program, and exist for the exclusive benefit of covered employees and their beneficiaries.

Plan year   Any 12 consecutive months specified in a plan, not necessarily the calendar year or the employer's fiscal year.

Present value   Value in today's terms of money to be received in the future. Because money has a time value, a dollar today is not the same as a dollar received in a year. Present value calculations are used to translate future benefits or income to today's terms for ready comparison and to determine the amount of money one must put aside or invest to yield benefits of a certain amount in the future. Consider, for example, a sweepstakes awarding the winner $1 million to be paid at the rate of $25,000 a year for 40 years. Assuming a 6 percent inflation rate, that award is worth only $542,000 in today's dollars. Clearly, then, there is a substantial difference between a benefit promised in nominal dollars and one promised in current dollars.

Prohibited group   That group in favor of which a tax-qualified plan must not discriminate.

Prohibited transaction   One that is not allowed for a plan. For example, a plan fiduciary may not buy, sell, or exchange property or services with the plan; also, there must be an arm's-length relationship between the employer and the plan.

Prototype plan   A master plan operated by a mutual fund or financial institution and adoptable by an employer upon execution of a participation agreement. (By using such an approach, an employer is saved the trauma of creating legally correct plan language.)

Qualified plan   A plan that meets IRS requirements and therefore receives favorable tax treatment.

REA   Retirement Equity Act of 1984, noteworthy for requiring that married vested participants retiring under a plan must receive joint and survivor benefits (rather than having the employee exhaust all benefits and leave the surviving spouse without income) unless both participant and spouse consent in writing to a different option.

Rollover   Reinvestment in a tax-qualified plan of funds or property received from a nonrequired distribution of another tax-qualified plan. If done within 60 days of the distribution, the transaction is not taxed.

Simplified employee pension plan (SEP)   Essentially, an individual retirement account of annuity established by an employer, often under a model or prototype arrangement with a bank or other financial institution.

Summary plan description (SPD)   Summary of each plan that must be given to all participants and beneficiaries. It must be written in language that the average participant can understand while at the same time covering the plan's provisions—not an easy task. ERISA requires that the plan administrator file the SPD with the Labor Department, and file an update every fifth year thereafter. (Employers adopting a prototype plan avoid this requirement because the operator of the master plan does the filing.) Among the items that must be included are the plan sponsor's name and administrative type; the name and address of the plan administrator; the requirements for eligibility, benefits, and vesting; the source of funding; the procedures for claiming benefits and redress; and the dates of the plan year. Failure to supply a participant or beneficiary with the SPD (or a summary of material modification when a major change is made) within a month of plan adoption or amendment can result in a fine of $100 a day.

Tax-deferred annuity   An investment method used to fund retirement plans of tax-exempt employers or their employees. See *403(b) plans*.

TEFRA   Tax Equity and Fiscal Responsibility Act of 1982, regarded by some as the beginning of the trend toward nondiscrimination rules; this Act applied nondiscrimination rules to group term life insurance plans. When an employer pays the premium for more than $50,000 in group term life insurance for an employee, the amount in excess of the premium for $50,000 of coverage is taxable income to the employee.

Top-heavy   Giving disproportionately more benefits to key employees.

Travel accident insurance   Covers employees when they are traveling on business.

Tuition Assistance   Plans reimburse employees for some portion of the cost of courses they take in accredited programs. This benefit may be taxable to the employee.

Unemployment insurance   Combined federal and state program (administered by each state) that is intended to provide financial security to jobless workers. Program is financed by an employer-paid tax on the first X dollars of each worker's pay; in a few states, a small employee contribution is required as well. Nonprofits may have the option of paying the tax (at a rate determined by employer age and experience) or of paying no tax but reimbursing the system for all unemployment benefits claimed. Such a choice can be made only once a year.

Vesting   Acquiring the right to receive benefits; reaching the point at which benefits become nonforfeitable.

Welfare benefit plan   Any plan or program to provide participants (and beneficiaries) with benefits for health care (medical, surgical, dental, hospital coverage), sickness, accidents, disability, death, unemployment, vacation, training, day care, educational assistance, or prepaid legal services.

Workers' compensation   Employer-paid insurance program regulated by each state and designed to protect employees from financial loss as a consequence of a work-related injury or illness.

Year of service   Any 12-month period during which an employee has at least 1,000 hours of service.

13 ▼ Performance Evaluation

Mark Michaels, MPA
People Technologies

13.1 *The Performance Management System*

(A) PERFORMANCE MANAGEMENT AS SELF-RENEWAL

Why do people go on retreats? They will say it is to renew their spirits, to renew their direction. When they are on a retreat, they spend time looking at where they are and where they are going. Self-renewal is the process of performance evaluation.

This cycle of self-renewal is really a process of scanning for differences between what one is doing, and what needs to be done to survive and, hopefully, grow. We know what needs to be done by looking around us, by assessing expectations of others or of "the system." This is not so much a process of continuous improvement—an example of an effective performance management system—as it is one of continuous *adaptation*. In performance management systems, this process establishes the standards for performance.

Establishing performance management systems in organizations is also an effective intervention for starting self-renewal in the organization. The scanning of needs and establishing of standards awakens the total organization to change. The process of change that results can become an invigorating one, taking the organization out of the doldrums of equilibrium into ongoing adaptability.

Continued success requires that the same process of renewal—of continuous adaptation—is applied to the performance management system as is applied to those who participate in that system. So long as performance management emphasizes standards that were identified in the past, the organization will keep striving for that past, while the rest of the world rushes ahead.

For example, an agency may evaluate case workers based on their caseload levels. At Agency X, Joe maintained a caseload average of 40 clients throughout the past year with a positive turnover of 30 percent. Jill maintained a caseload average of 30 clients with a positive turnover of 50 percent.

Because of the agency's past practices and funding agreements, the agency goal is written as a 40-client caseload with a 30 percent positive turnover rate for each case worker. Which case worker will receive the higher evaluation?—Joe, even though Jill was able to positively discharge 80 percent more clients than Joe.

In this case, the performance management system resembles someone who is driving while looking only in the rear-view mirror. As a result of the evaluation, Joe's future will involve doing what he's always done. Jill's plans for the coming year will include building a larger caseload at the expense of her positive turnover rate.

When performance evaluation is an act of self-renewal, the results will be different. The manager learns to look out of the front windshield. Even though Joe was on target, the manager looks ahead to where Joe and the agency can go. The past tells the manager that Joe can handle a caseload of 40 with a 30 percent turnover rate. So Joe is told, "great job," and is asked, "How can you increase the positive turnover rate for your cases?" Jill is also told "great job" and is then asked, "How can you increase your caseload while maintaining the positive turnover rate?"

The impact of this forward planning does not stop with the caseworkers. Performance management systems are an integral part of the total management system. And when properly used, they are a critical part of the larger, organizationwide adaptation process.

Continuing the caseload example demonstrates this system connection. Successful implementation of forward planning with caseworkers will result in an increase in the organization's caseload capacity. This causes the agency to consider a new set of organizational options.

Assuming that the agency competes for its grant funds, or as part of its move into the managed care environment now permeating the medical and social services field, the increased capacity will make the agency more competitive for grants or managed care contracts. The agency can offer to handle a larger caseload where there are more potential clients, or offer a better capitation rate for its contract. Or it could compete to take over the caseload from a weaker agency nearby. Another option is to move some of the saved funds into a developing program area. The performance management system is directly impacting the strategic direction of the organization.

Both the personal and organizational levels demonstrate a core dynamic that leads to renewal. In science it is called a *positive feedback loop*. In quality management, it is the *plan-do-check-act* cycle. In performance management, it is the *ongoing cycle of planning, evaluating, and planning again*. The cycle, which enables an organization to look at what is needed, try something, and look again, is the focal point of all renewal (Exhibit 13.1).

(B) THE PERFORMANCE MANAGEMENT SYSTEM

As with all systems, the performance management system can be understood in terms of inputs, process, outputs, and feedback. Exhibit 13.2 displays the entire system with its

EXHIBIT 13.1 The Continuous Improvement Cycle

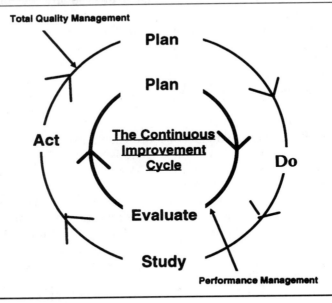

major connections. The exhibit shows that an effective performance management system affects not only personal growth but organizational strategy and the human resource management systems as well.

(i) System Inputs

An effective performance management system starts with information about the organization and individuals within the system.

Organizational inputs are the most critical, yet most frequently forgotten ingredients for a successful performance management system. The organizational inputs are the standards of performance which the organization originally determines are necessary to achieve its goals.

Consultants are frequently asked questions like, "Should we evaluate tardiness on our forms?" The answer must be, "What impact does tardiness have on achieving your strategic plan?" If your agency uses flex-time, evaluating tardiness is absurd.

To define the organizational inputs, ask the question, "What are we going to measure?" For instance, in the case management example above, we determined that Jill was more effective, because we measured outcome quality against caseload. However, if the agency is in a managed care setting where cost effectiveness is critical, than Joe's results may actually prove more effective, especially since it appears that he obtains positive outcomes more quickly.

A number of organizations in both the private and nonprofit sectors use preprinted evaluation forms or checklists. These forms list behaviors such as tardiness, creativity, timeliness of work, and so on. The supervisor evaluates the worker on a scale ranging from poor to excellent.

Executives love the forms because they are an inexpensive way to fulfill a cumber-

EXHIBIT 13.2 The Performance Management System

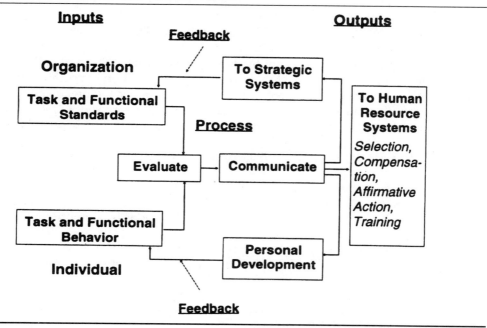

some management chore. Supervisors love them because they are quick and easy to complete. But they do not evaluate what is important to that organization. They also provide no real information about an individual's performance.

Consider having to rate someone's creativity on the job based on a standard evaluation scale. To do the rating, the supervisor must ask what the organization means by the word *creativity* and what it means to meet standards in that organization. The preprinted forms do not include this information.

To be effective, the evaluation form—the organizational standards—must ask two questions:

- Do the standards evaluate what is important to our organization?
- Do the standards define various levels of performance in such a way that two people reading them will come to the same conclusions?

A method for developing performance standards will be described in Section 13.2.

If the organizational inputs define what is wanted, the individual inputs define what is actually happening. That is, the individual inputs are the employee's behavior.

Behavior can be evaluated from two perspectives; task and function. Task performance looks at *what* is done—is the job complete, is the objective reached, what was the average caseload. Functional performance looks at *how* the job is done—is it timely, are there defects, was the individual an effective team member.

According to Schneir and Beatty (July 1979), an effective performance management system will evaluate both task and function. The authors demonstrate their point with an example of a manager who achieved his objective of reduced delivery time by using punitive supervision on subordinates.

Objectively gathering information about an individual's performance is difficult. Our observation skills are hindered by a number of inherent biases. The biases are caused by the way we process information, filtering out more than we take in.

Clear performance standards are the best defense against observation bias. Without such standards, the evaluator must make assumptions based on her or his value system. These assumptions are rarely shared with the subordinate or the organization.

Training evaluators is also critical to reducing bias. Training should include methods of behavior observation, techniques for avoiding typical evaluation biases, and feedback communication skills.

Exhibit 13.3 describes six major biases and some methods for avoiding them.

(ii)   System Process

The act of evaluation is the process of comparing the individual's performance with the standards established by the organization. Clear standards simplify the evaluation process.

Evaluation is like piecing together a puzzle. One half of the puzzle defines the desired behavior. If the second half fits into the puzzle, the employee has demonstrated acceptable behavior.

EXHIBIT 13.3 Performance Assessment Bias

Bias	Precautions
Comparison Error Employees are compared to each other instead of to the performance standards. Results in lowering evaluations of individuals whose work is almost comparable.	Spread out evaluations over the year. Use clear performance standards.
Judging a book by its cover Employees are evaluated based on conditions not related to job performance, such as dress.	Use clear standards. Provide method for evaluator to review historical performance data during evaluation.
Halo effect Total performance is overlooked in favor of recent achievements. Also, there is a tendency to rate an individual higher than deserved because he or she falls within a group of highly rated workers.	Provide method for evaluator to review performance data from entire evaluation period. Spread out evaluations over the year.
Self-emulation Employees who appear or act like the rater receive higher evaluations. Race and sex biases tend to show here.	Review aggregate evaluation data by organization and evaluator, to identify possible trend. Provide diversity sensitivity training to evaluators.
Central tendency, leniency, and strictness Based on the assumption that performance overall will statistically fall on a bell curve. Some evaluators and systems support average evaluations, some evaluators are generally lenient to be supportive, some start strict to allow for movement. In all cases, comparison with standards is ignored.	Use clear performance standards. Train evaluators to observe behavior. Review aggregate evaluation data by evaluator, to identify trend.

A task example: The comptroller is required to make monthly financial reports to the board. During the past year, the comptroller made such reports in 10 out of the 12 months. The pieces do not fit.

A functional example: An employee is expected to resolve client complaints about agency services with little involvement from a supervisor. During the past year, the employee handled 20 complaints, bringing the supervisor in for help only once. The pieces fit.

Communicating the evaluation results to the employee is also considered a part of the process. A well-conducted feedback session is a two-way communication where the evaluator observes the performance from the employee's perspective. The resulting new information often leads to changes in evaluation decisions, causing different pieces of the puzzle to fall in place.

(iii) System Outputs

The most tangible output of a performance management system is a plan of action for a change in employees' behavior. Under our renewal model, this is a personal improvement plan. Plans can be both task oriented, such as increasing caseload, and function oriented, such as improving communication skills.

But a number of other outcomes also develop. These outcomes provide feedback to the organization's strategy and human resource management systems. Attention and action on these items provide for ongoing self-renewal in organizations.

The potential for strategy change is caused by information that develops from a review of one or more evaluations. The anticipated increase in caseloads described above is an example of the system in action.

Performance management systems affect most human resource management systems. Data from one or more evaluations provides the basis for determining training needs. The information is also used in succession planning and to validate the employee selection process. The output provides critical information on the success of affirmative action programming.

If the program is linked to the compensation system, the aggregate results will affect the budgeting and financial status of the organization. Even if the compensation link does not exist, the output can help identify compensation-related turnover problems.

(C) USE AUTOMATION TO ACCESS PERFORMANCE INFORMATION

The performance management system can provide data for continuous improvement activities. The problem becomes how to access the large quantities of data to make optimum use of the system.

Data acquisition is always a problem in continuous improvement programs. Performance management data is no exception. In most cases, the information is stored in an individual's personnel folder, never to be seen again unless there is a discipline problem.

Personnel files are manual human resource information systems (HRISystems). During the past decade, it became possible for the majority of organizations to automate the HRISystem. Many HRISystems now function on personal computers and cost under $1,000.

Automating personnel information into larger, relational databases makes it possible to look for correlations that used to remain hidden in individual personnel folders. Automating the human resource management function is a critical step to being able to effectively use performance management information.

Most HRISystems include fields for performance review data. Unfortunately, the larger systems usually include a checklist type system similar to the preprinted checklist. However, there are also a number of standalone performance systems which help the manager develop job descriptions and performance standards, and then tracks evaluations. The manager can then correlate the data to identify performance problems or opportunities. Both Management By Objectives (MBO) and Behaviorally Anchored Rating Scale Systems are available. The Personnel Software Census (Advanced Personnel Systems) maintains an updated list of available programs.

(D)   TYPES OF PERFORMANCE MANAGEMENT SYSTEMS

Performance management systems fall into four general categories; global, trait-based, effectiveness-based, and behaviorally based.

Global evaluation systems consider the total performance of an individual either against some standard or, more typically, other individuals. The most prevalent form of global evaluation is forced ranking. Here, the supervisor is asked to rank employees from best to poorest.

Forced ranking works when there is a single, clear objective which defines a person's job. For instance, salespeople can be ranked based on sales quantity. In this case, forced ranking can be used for compensation planning.

However, forced ranking is a nightmare if there is any complexity to the job. On an old episode of the TV show, *Cagney and Lacey*, Cagney was asked to force-rank her fellow detectives for pay purposes. Cagney dreaded the task. In the end she had little information to support her position when she ranked her partner second. As with Lacey, the lower-ranked employee has a sense of being the worst performer, even when the performance differences may be very small.

Trait-based evaluations were developed by industrial psychologists during the 1940s. They assume that there is a single list of personality traits which distinguish between good and poor performance on the job, regardless of company. Most of the research over the years disproves the theory. Yet trait-based evaluations, such as the preprinted forms, remain the most common evaluation system in the country.

Effectiveness-based systems measure task performance—does the job get done. The oldest such system is the *work standards* evaluation. Work standards originated in industrial settings, although it now is used in service industries as well. A work standards evaluation establishes an output work level, such as 100 widgets per day or 60 discharges per month. The employee is then evaluated based on achieving or not achieving the standard. Emphasis on work standards has been increasing as part of the transition to managed care for many organizations.

Management by Objectives (MBO) is a work standards system for managers. The manager is given a list of objectives to be reached in the coming evaluation period. Traditionally, the evaluation is based solely on whether the objectives are reached, regardless of what was done to reach them.

A number of management theorists, including Deming, criticize MBO as limiting the continuous improvement process. The feeling is that objectives place constrictions on creativity and the manager's willingness to change directions when necessary. Other criticisms include concern that the manager emphasizes achieving objectives at the expense of day-to-day activities. Others point to problems which develop when the manager is not in complete control of the resources necessary to achieve an objective.

No one has found a suitable replacement for MBO. In fact, MBO methods are now being applied outside of management in such settings as educational development plans, development plans for the disabled, and patient management plans. In management, only the name has changed. Many organizations now practice *action planning*, which is the objectives planning process from MBO systems. To enable more flexibility, the action plan has lost some of its connection to the strategic plan.

The conflict between MBO and continuous improvement can be resolved by assessing how objectives are used. Some objectives establish behavioral limits. An objective to sell 30 widgets this year will be limiting. However, other objectives can break down restraining walls. The objective to build the creative capacity of the work team will be invigorating.

A somewhat different approach is the *Critical Incident Process*. Its purpose is to provide pure feedback to employees on their behavior. The supervisor maintains records of exceptional incidents, both good and bad, and reviews them periodically with the employee. Critical Incident reports can also be used to develop data for behaviorially based systems.

Beginning in the 1960s, as a reaction to the weaknesses of effectiveness-based systems, a number of *behaviorally based* systems were developed. These systems assess functional behavior.

The first major behaviorally based system was the *assessment center*. An assessment center places a worker, usually a manager, into a simulated work situation. The typical environment is the "in-basket" exercise, but simulations are as varied as the creativity of assessors. Trained assessors observe the employee's behavior in the simulation. In some cases, observation is on set criteria, other times the purpose is to provide pure feedback. If the center is used for developmental purposes, the employee will write a developmental plan based on the assessors' report.

Performance Standards (Behaviorally Anchored Rating Scales) improve upon and customize the traditional checklist. Each performance standard scale includes an operational description of a behavior as performed in that organization. For instance, communication skills to be assessed in one job may include written and oral, while only oral communications are required in another position. Evaluation is done by comparing the individual's behavior with examples of acceptable and unacceptable behaviors listed with the description.

Both behaviorally based systems are time consuming, and development is expensive. Both require extensive job analysis, and the assessment center requires exceptional training of assessors.

Supervisors usually complain about the time necessary to evaluate an employee using performance standards. And frequently, the supervisor will learn to skip the standards descriptions, providing inaccurate information to the employee. Various coding schemes have been developed to reduce this problem.

It is possible to mix and match evaluation systems for optimum effect. Schneir and Beatty (September 1979) believe that a mix of effectiveness-based and behaviorally based systems is essential to creating an effective performance management system.

13.2 *Developing the Performance Management System*

(A) DEVELOP YOUR OWN SYSTEM

Developing an effective performance management system is a major organizational undertaking. Implementation will change many of the agency's other systems, including its values and culture. For a small to medium nonprofit, creation of the system can take six months from start to full implementation (Exhibit 13.4). Larger organizations can take even longer.

It is no wonder that purchasing preprinted evaluation forms is the most popular method for implementing the system. It is the quickest and least expensive method. Purchase and copy the form, hand it to the supervisors, and expect results.

Sometimes the supervisors are sent to a public training program on performance evaluation to augment the system. By the time they leave the program they are getting mixed messages about workable systems and program purpose. The result is, an attitude that the form is only a vehicle to enhance communication between the employee and supervisor.

A more enlightened approach is for the human resource manager or a committee to gather forms from other agencies and cut and paste their way to a new form. The theory is that if it works at a successful organization, it should work here. At times training is held in-house to help clarify the performance definitions on the new form. Often such training sessions end in confusion because of disagreements over definitions in the form.

The reason the system works at Agency A but fails in Agency B is that Agency A addressed the critical issue being ignored at Agency B. Agency A took the time to identify the organization's inputs—the performance expectations—for meeting the agency's strategic plans. For the same system to work in Agency B, the second agency must have the same strategic plan and culture.

An effective performance management system is a method for achieving the organization's strategic goals while providing the vehicle for continuous improvement. Implementation requires answering strategic questions specific to the organization. There are no right answers for these questions:

EXHIBIT 13.4 Performance Management System Project Plan (Mixed Systemwide and Individual Performance Standards)

Task	Month					
	1	2	3	4	5	6
Establish system goals	→					
Conduct employee orientation meetings	→					
Train a task force	⟶					
Develop a list of job dimensions	⟶					
Develop performance standards		⟶				
Design an evaluation form		⟶				
Test the pilot system			⟶		⟶	
Evaluate and adjust the system						⟶
Train supervisors						→
Promote the plan to employees						→
Implement the system						→

- *Should compensation be linked to the performance management system?* Linking pay to individual performance can negate team building efforts. Failing to make the link when there are obvious performance differences can hurt morale.
- *Should individual performance standards be established for each position, one set for all positions, or some combination?* A large organizational change may be accomplished by evaluating a broad group of organizationwide values. Maintaining quality and morale in a static environment may require more individualized attention.
- *Should different types of systems be used for different employee levels?* MBO may not be appropriate for nonexempt employees, while work standards have no meaning to managers. The organization may be too small to manage multiple systems.
- *How should we evaluate individuals in terms of their teams?* An individualized performance management system can work against efforts at team building.
- *Should managers, employees, and/or others participate in developing the standards?* Who runs the organization? What are our trust levels? Do we want to build participatory structures?

No two agencies will have the same answers to these questions. Therefore, no two systems will be exactly alike. Developing an effective performance management system is a process unique to each organization.

However, it may not be necessary to hire a consultant to help develop the system. Consultants are hired to design compensation systems to relieve employees from the task of determining salaries of peers. In developing a performance management system, the conflict of interest within staff is much less than with compensation planning. The only two reasons for hiring a consultant are: (1) the organization lacks the expertise to design to system; or (2) no one in the organization has time to coordinate the development of the system.

(B) DEVELOP TASK STANDARDS

Developing task standards is much easier than functional standards. They come directly from the organization's strategic and long-term plans and grant agreements.

Some form of Management by Objectives remains the best method for creating managerial task standards. On paper this starts with the strategic plan and board-produced annual plan. The CEO develops a list of objectives from the board plans to be achieved by staff in the coming year. Objectives are assigned to and become the goals of department heads according to their area of specialty. The same process is used by the department heads to develop work plans for supervisors.

In practice the system is not run in such a top-down fashion. In fact, according to Tosi and Carroll (1970), one of the major benefits of MBO is that it enables participation by the subordinate in the planning process. In practice, the system works in both directions at once. Usually, the CEO develops the work plan in a series of meetings with department heads, who usually are already meeting with their staff. Sometimes the board is the last group to see the plan. This results in a more free-flow negotiation over resources necessary to achieve goals in the coming year.

(The reader is cautioned that an MBO system which is linked to an agency's strategic plan cannot be conducted in a vacuum. Annual management objectives must be agreed to before the budgeting process can begin.)

Either an MBO or a work standards system can be effective at the professional level. A fund raiser may have the goal of increasing revenues by at least 10 percent. A job placement counselor may be required to meet a work standard of maintaining an average caseload of 30 and a goal to increase long-term placements 10 percent in the coming year.

Technical and other nonprofessional positions may work best under a work standards system. In this case, the standards can be incorporated into the job description. The evaluation system then refers to the job description for evaluative information.

Developing work standards is a job analysis process, and can be accomplished through the strategies described in Chapter 14.

Even nonprofessional positions can use a modified version of MBO as part of their evaluation. During the evaluation, the employee and supervisor develop an action plan for personal development. The plan may include such tasks as taking a course at the local college, or spending 30 hours in an upgraded position. The plan is evaluated during the year and at the end of the evaluation period to determine whether the objectives were met and whether those objectives had an impact on reaching the developmental goal.

(C) DEVELOP FUNCTIONAL STANDARDS

Many certifying agencies recognize the effectiveness of performance standards and require their development for individual jobs. Performance standards appear similar to the trait-based checklist. But they overcome the biases built into the trait-based system in three ways:

1. Performance standards use job analysis to clearly define the behavior being evaluated.
2. Performance standards use job analysis to clearly define acceptable and unacceptable performance of the behaviors.
3. Performance standards are unique to a given organization and/or job.

Historically, performance standards were developed by industrial psychologists who came in and observed behavior within a given organization. In the past few years, methods have been developed for nonprofessionals to develop the ranking scales. The process is time consuming, especially if a management or employee task force is involved. But in-house development saves cash resources (there is the cost of the time for task force involvement). It also begins the supervisory training process, and increases organizational acceptance in the implementation phase. As Jeff Adams, the General Manager of a small telephone cooperative in Idaho, explained: "Setting up our performance management system has taken several hundred man-hours. But I wouldn't do it any other way" (Michaels, 1987).

Performance standards are usually developed for behavioral evaluation. However, they also work for task evaluation. A work standard is established to do 30 widgets a day. Then 35 widgets per day exceeds standards and anything above that is exceptional. However, it is not necessary to quantify performance which does not meet standards.

The following sections will describe a participatory process for developing performance standards. It starts with the assumption that only one set of Performance Standards is being developed for the entire organization. Suggestions are added later for developing systems in larger organizations.

(i)   Using In-house Staff to Develop Performance Standards

First the organization must assign responsibility for developing the performance standards. The project can be completed independently by a human resource manager or CEO skilled in job analysis techniques. However, the person can expect a great deal of conflict and negotiation over standards definitions when implementing the system.

The conflict can be reduced by using a task force to develop the performance standards. Using a task force also helps instill a spirit of renewal into the organization. That is because the task force becomes involved in looking at the basic renewal process—where we are and what we need to do now.

The task force can include just managers or managers and workers, depending upon the culture of the organization. The more levels of the organization involved in the process, the greater the acceptance of the final product. But some organizations strongly believe that establishing standards is a managerial function, accepting the necessary trade-offs.

When a task force is used, the CEO, human resource specialist, or an outside consultant serves as the task force facilitator. The facilitator's role is to bring the decision process into the task force. The facilitator must be able to forgo the expert role.

(ii)   The Performance Standards Development Process

Follow these five steps to develop performance standards:

> *Step 1: Create a List of Job Dimensions.* This is a critical policy step because it answers the question, What do we want to measure? Activities essential to the success or culture of the organization that are ignored here will be ignored in employee performance.

Three methods can be used to create the list of job dimensions. The first method recognizes the importance of the list as a policy issue by requesting the list from the Board and/or CEO. The list may be drawn from the organization's mission statement and statement of values. Or it can be developed by facilitating the exercise in the third method at the Board level.

With the second method, the job dimensions can be taken directly from the "Knowledges, Skills, and Abilities" section of a well-written job description for standards for individual positions.

The third method begins by having each task force member independently list from six to 10 activities that are performed by those to be evaluated, which the member believes is critical to successful performance. Instruct the task force to write complete descriptive sentences instead of single words like "communication." The sentences should not include judgmental terms. For instance:

Acceptable: Communicates both orally and in writing with staff and with clients from diverse populations.
Not Acceptable: Effectively trains and motivates clients from diverse backgrounds so that they improve their personal hygiene habits.

In the second example, the adverb "effectively" is judgmental and the verb "improve" implies a successful outcome, making it judgmental as well.

The facilitator then uses the nominal grouping technique to develop consensus around a maximum of ten job dimensions. This technique involves listing the suggestions from all task force members, eliminating duplicates, discussing activities which can be combined, and then achieving a consensus on a prioritization of the list.

Step 2: Develop examples of behavior for each job dimension. Steps 2 through 5 should be done for each dimension independently.

There are also two ways to do Step 2. The first, and more time consuming, is to have supervisors maintain critical incident reports for three to six months. These reports are reviewed by the task force, who assign behavioral characteristics of each report to one or more job dimensions.

The second method is to ask the task force to list behavioral examples associated with the job dimension being discussed. Have the task force members list answers to the following three questions:

1. Think of a person who was an exceptional performer on this dimension. List behaviors that this person shows when performing this activity.
2. Think of a person who was a poor performer on this dimension. List behaviors that this person shows when performing this activity.
3. Think of a person who is not deficient when performing this dimension, but also does not excel. List behaviors that this person shows when performing this activity.

Task force members should be cautioned to think only in terms of the activity under question. An example can be given of an exceptional performer in general who is a poor performer in this one area. Task force members should also be encouraged to be specific with their adjectives. Use of words like "effective," "frequently," and "excellent" are too subjective for this process. Specifics should be used instead, such as "never," "always," and "20 percent. (In Step 5, the facilitator will be required to help the task force replace subjective terms with specific adjectives.)

Step 3: Mix Up the Responses. Mix up the task force responses so that no one knows the behavioral level assigned by the authors. This can be done away from the task force meeting by randomly listing the descriptions on a separate paper for review by the task force members. By performing this task outside of the meeting, the facilitator can remove duplicates and edit out statements which do not relate to the activity in question.

Step 4: Individual Rating of Behaviors. Provide each task force member with the randomized list of behaviors for the dimension under discussion and the Performance Standard Worksheet (Exhibit 13.5). Have each task force member place each behavior into one of the five categories: "unacceptable," "below standards," "meets standards," "exceeds standards," and "exceptional." Collect the results and create a report for the task force showing how many task force members assigned each behavior to each level. For instance, one behavior under a communications-related scale might read: "Uses mixed media when making public presentations." In one case, five task force members placed this under "meets standards" and five placed it under "exceptional."

Step 5: Facilitate Consensus Rating. Bring the task force together to discuss the differences in ratings. Facilitate a consensus rating for each behavior. This usually requires making subjective statements more specific. Sometimes there will actually be a values difference that cannot be resolved. In that case, leave the specific behavior off the scale.

When complete, the performance standard can be edited to look like those in Exhibit 13.6. Then repeat steps 2 through 5 for the remaining essential activities.

Task force members should do as much work as possible away from the task force meetings, saving meeting time for consensus-building discussions. Under this strategy, each standard should take about one hour of meeting time. Otherwise, facilitating consensus on a single standard can take two to three hours.

(iii) Development in Larger Organizations

Some successful evaluation systems consider each position according to its own job description. Hospitals in Illinois are required to develop performance standards for each

---

EXHIBIT 13.5 Sample Worksheet—Performance Standards Development

Performance Standards Development Worksheet

Job Dimension _____

Unacceptable	Below Standards	Meets Standards	Exceeds Standards	Exceptional

EXHIBIT 13.6 Sample Form—Evaluation

Evaluation Form

Employee _____   Position _____

Department _____   Years in position _____

Evaluation date _____

Part 1—Performance Standards

	Communication	Team Work	Job Aptitude	Job Attitude
Standard	The ability to transmit information and instructions both orally and in writing	The ability to participate in building consensus decisions and support team efforts	The ability to perform tasks assigned	The extent to which the employee shows motivation for the job
Unacceptable	Only explains problem once. Memos are difficult to read or understand. ☐	Argues for personal agenda and goals. Only performs personal work, and does not chip in when team goals are not met. ☐	Requires extensive coaching and support to perform tasks considered standard for position. ☐	Complains whenever assigned any task outside of own job description. ☐
Below	Problems explained through extensive questioning. Memos state point but lack supportive detail. ☐	Always takes position of central negative, but supports final decisions. Chips in but acts unsocial within the group. ☐	Asks questions about procedures without first checking available resources such as manual. ☐	Performs additional tasks which meet personal interests without complaint. ☐
Standard	Presentations are clear, needing only minimal clarification. Memos state point, lack detail. ☐	Participates with constructive ideas in team meetings. Backs up other team members' actions when asked. ☐	Performs standard duties without problem. Researches new problems before asking questions. ☐	Performs all tasks assigned without complaint. Shows specific job interest. ☐
Exceeds	Presentations use appropriate and varied media. Written materials are clear. ☐	Takes a facilitative leadership role, but doesn't share leadership. Gets others to help with problem solving and team tasks. ☐	Performs standard and new assignments without supervisory help, except for special circumstances. ☐	Seeks out new tasks that can expand personal growth. ☐
Exceptional	Presentations wow the listeners. Written materials are prepared with desktop publishing. ☐	Participates in and raises team process issues. Jumps in to support other team members, offers social support. ☐	Performs all assignments with ease. Instructs others in methods. Can function as lead person. ☐	Loves work and motivates others through positive spirit. ☐

EXHIBIT 13.6 *(Continued)*

Part 2—Task Evaluation

Step A: List critical tasks as described in the job description or major objectives from last year's evaluation. (Tasks must be described in terms of expected outcomes.)

Step B: Describe the observed outcomes or results for each task.

Step C: Identify differences between A and B.

Task 1:	Task 1:	Task 1:

Task 2:	Task 2:	Task 2:

Task 3:	Task 3:	Task 3:

Task 4:	Task 4:	Task 4:

Task 5:	Task 5:	Task 5:

Task 6:	Task 6:	Task 6:

(Continued)

EXHIBIT 13.6 *(Continued)*

Part 3—Action Plan

INSTRUCTIONS

1. List goals relating to task differences and objectives differences. Goals may be corrective action to complete the task or fulfill the goal, or they may be directed at changes to the task or goal based on the information acquired during the evaluation period.
2. Write specific objectives to be done in the next evaluation period to achieve each goal.
3. Write planned follow-up and completion dates for each goal.

Goals	Objectives	Due Dates

This is to certify that the above evaluation was reviewed by both of us and that we are in agreement with regard to the above action plan as representing the critical actions which we will take during the coming evaluation period.

_____   _____   _____

Supervisor's signature   Employee's signature   Date

---

job description as part of the certification process. For smaller organizations, this is expensive and time consuming. It also can be counterproductive in any size organization which is going through a major change.

It is possible to mix organizationwide and individual performance standard scales in one form. Some agencies list about five agencywide performance standards and then develop specific standards on the department or job description level. This mixed standards method allows for flexibility within the organization, and a chance for employees to receive more personal performance feedback.

One way to develop the mixed system is to teach supervisors how to develop performance standards. Individual supervisors can then sit down with an employee or a group of employees in the same job description and jointly develop the nonstandard performance standards.

Allowing supervisors to develop standards can improve communications between supervisors and subordinates. It also helps move decision making down into the organization. However, the system loses some of its reliability and credibility when the same job is done in different departments and the employees are evaluated on different performance standards.

A second strategy is to use multiple task forces for performance standards development. An organizationwide task force develops organizationwide performance standards. Cross-departmental task forces for agencywide positions can work with departmental task forces for specific departmental positions to develop the job-specific standards. The original task force serves as a steering committee during this process.

(D)   THE EVALUATION FORM

There is no perfect evaluation form. Every organization creates its own to meet its own information needs. If the form is associated with an automated record-keeping system, form design will have to relate to data input requirements.

Assuming that an agency is assessing both task and functional behavior, the form will include at least three major parts. One section will cover task performance. This may be a place to review the previous year's objectives in an MBO system, or it may list specific work task requirements, for a work standards system.

A second section will include the functional performance standards. Usually, the performance standards are boxed together as in Exhibit 13.6. However, some organizations have found it helpful to have supervisors review a checklist of behaviors exhibited by the employee, without knowledge of the rating for those behaviors. The information is then compiled in the human resource office to establish the actual performance level. The method is quicker for the supervisor and it reduces the supervisor's tendency to ignore the behavioral descriptions in favor of the rating scale. But the system can reduce trust between the supervisor and the organization.

The third section will be the action plan for the coming evaluation period. If an MBO system is being used for managers, the action plan will include both organizational objectives and personal development objectives. For others, the form includes just personal development objectives.

Must the employee sign the form? Most forms require that the employee sign the form only to indicate that the form has been shown to and discussed with the employee. Agreement with the evaluation is never required.

Refusing to sign an evaluation form is not insubordination. The employer wants it signed to protect itself from claims that performance information was never shared with the employee. The same protection can be achieved by having a third party witness the employee's refusal and indicate so on the form.

(E)   TESTING AND IMPLEMENTING THE SYSTEM

In the spirit of continuous improvement, a new performance management system should not be implemented until it has been "studied." In this case, testing requires identifying a small group of employees and supervisors, placing them on the system, and assessing the results.

Medium-sized nonprofits can test the system in one department. For smaller organizations, the test may have to be agencywide. However, since in both cases the test should last only about three months, the agencywide test will still only be on a smaller percentage of the organization.

The organization should not link salary increases to performance until after the system is fully tested. If a merit plan is already in effect, pay increases should either be based on evaluations on the older system, or increases should be across the board until the new system is implemented.

It will not be possible to test the effectiveness of the system—whether it improves performance—in the trial period. The system can only be tested for reliability and acceptance.

(i) Reliability

When two people see an apple and call it an apple, there is reliability between their assessments. Similarly, if two supervisors look at the same information, they should make similar decisions about the employee's performance.

Reliability can be tested in several ways. One way is to have both supervisors and employees complete the evaluation form. For them, comparing the results serves as a good starting point for discussion in the performance evaluation meeting.

To show reliability, the HR manager or task force does a statistical analysis comparing the frequency of agreement between supervisor evaluations and employee self-evaluations. The higher the frequency of agreement, the more valid the system.

In like fashion, a supervisor and department head can perform parallel evaluations. Both must have access to the same employee information for this to work. The same statistical analysis can establish reliability.

Reliability fails for two reasons: (1) the evaluator was not properly trained in observation; or (2) the language on the form is not yet clear. Determine which is the real problem by interviewing supervisors and employees.

Reliability issues will most likely result in fine tuning the performance standards.

(ii) Acceptance

Acceptance can be assessed informally through interviews with employees or reviewing evaluation complaints. A more formal approach is to survey employees who have been evaluated approximately one month after their evaluation.

Acceptance and reliability are closely related. If the employees believe the system is fair, they will accept it. If acceptance is rejected, reliability should be looked at more closely. If reliability is high, the organization has other employee issues to deal with, such as trust and compensation levels, before the system will be accepted.

Once the system works, use the following steps to implement the program agency-wide:

1. Before starting the project, inform all employees of the project and solicit volunteers for task forces. During the project keep employees informed of task force actions. Allow observers into task force meetings.
2. Set the date for switchover to the new system.
3. Conduct in-depth supervisory training programs which include a clear explanation of the performance standards, skill development for observing behavior, a strategy for comparing observed behavior with standards, and communication skills, including nondefensive feedback and counseling skills for the evaluation meeting. Employees can be invited into the training sessions as well.

4. Conduct employee meetings to explain the new system. Answer questions and concerns. Describe task force process and testing results, particularly those relating to reliability and acceptance.
5. Switch over to the new system.

13.3　*Managing the Performance Management System*

(A)　GENERAL SYSTEM PROCEDURES

Like a Rolls Royce, the best performance management system is worthless unless it is properly maintained. Policies and procedures similar to the following should be included in the organization's personnel policy and procedure manual and then followed to insure proper maintenance of the system.

Policy 1:

The performance management system is established to provide a vehicle for continuous improvement and growth for our employees. The system is not designed to be punitive. It is intended to act as a critical part of the forward-directed planning process by helping our employees grow through receipt of constructive positive feedback concerning their performance. At the same time, the performance management system provides the agency with information on the current capacity of the organization, enabling us to plan future activities more effectively. The performance management system will be managed in a manner which complies with our affirmative action plan and will not be used to discriminate against any employee on the grounds of race, sex, religion, national origin, or physical or mental handicap.

Starting the policies with a preamble establishes the purposes and limitation of the performance management system. It tells your employees that the system exists for the benefit of both the employee and the organization. It also sets the tone for integration of the system into the organization's efforts toward quality transformation.

Policy 2:

The Performance Management System was developed by a joint committee of employees and managers. This committee shall be responsible for the continuous improvement of the quality of the system. The committee shall establish policies which allows it to continue indefinitely while providing for an orderly change in its membership. The committee shall review on request and periodically review at its own initiative the effectiveness of the performance management system and may propose, from time to time, to add, change, or eliminate agencywide work and performance standards. The committee will also act as the coordinating committee of departmental and cross-departmental committees established to develop standards not in use agencywide.

Instituting a method for system maintenance and change is critical to enabling the ongoing effectiveness of the system. This policy institutes the participatory development process recommended for the development of a performance management system. The committee is a continuous improvement team with a changing membership. The committee changes membership to avoid burnout of committee members, while maintaining its credibility with the rest of the staff.

Procedures

1. The committee shall consist of both management and nonmanagement staff members in equal proportion. A chair will be elected annually by the committee members, with the responsibility of calling meetings, insuring that minutes are kept, and ensuring that employees are kept informed of committee actions.

The use of a joint committee is in keeping with the methodologies of continuous improvement programs. The chair's role has been limited to task maintenance issues to maintain a consensus-making decision process.

2. The human resource director shall serve as facilitator to the committee. The human resource director shall have no vote on the committee and shall not participate in discussions outside of a facilitative capacity, except that the director may answer technical questions on request.

In traditional companies, the human resource director chairs committees like this one. This places their expertise in a powerful position, generally hurting the participatory nature of the program. The committee is seen as the personnel manager's committee, resulting in reduced attendance and involvement. Since the work of the performance management committee affects more than just human resource systems, a broader chair representation is appropriate. Implementation of this procedure and any quality-based program may require that the human resource director receive facilitation skills training.

3. Decisions by the committee concerning changes in the performance management system shall be made by consensus. When consensus is not achieved, a 75 percent supermajority must be achieved to approve a decision.

The decision process is in keeping with continuous improvement programs.

Policy 3:

New and promoted employees will be evaluated and will meet with their supervisor to review the evaluation during the last week of their first six months in their new position. After that time, employees will be evaluated and will meet with their supervisor to review the evaluation annually no later than two weeks following the employee's annual hiring or last promotion date.

It is important that probationary employees be informed of their evaluation before the end of their probationary period. Once the probationary period is over, their employment status is the same as that of regular employees with regard to benefits and rights to employment, even if it is subsequently determined that they failed to pass probation.

Many organizations evaluate their employees on the same date. Such policies insure that the halo effect bias will impact the results. It is also easier for supervisors to pay close attention to evaluations spaced out in time, than when they have to commit a large block of time to many evaluations.

Evaluations should not be allowed to drag on. Untimely evaluations reduce morale in subordinates and damage the credibility of the system.

Procedures:

1. One month before the employee's anniversary date, the Human Resource Department will send both the supervisor and the employee notice of the pending evaluation, a copy of the previous year's evaluation, and a blank draft evaluation form. Upon receipt, the supervisor shall contact the employee to set up a meeting date to begin discussing the evaluation.

Either through an automated HRISystem or some other form of record-keeping, the human resource manager maintains a tickler file of upcoming evaluation dates and due dates. The human resource manager sends out the original forms as stated and follow-up reminders of due date two weeks and one week before the evaluations are due back.

2. The employee and supervisor shall both complete draft evaluation forms. The completed forms will be shared at the first evaluation meeting. A final completed form will be prepared by the supervisor and/or employee and signed by both at the end of or shortly following the evaluation meeting(s).

Employee self-evaluation has proven to be an excellent evaluation tool in many non-profits. Comparing evaluation forms provides an effective format for identifying and discussing performance problems in the evaluation meeting.

3. The supervisor will return the completed evaluation form to the human resource department no later than the due date. (If the completed evaluation form is returned to the human resource management office late, the employee shall receive a pay raise equal to the rate paid for "exceeds standards" for his or her job classification beginning with the pay period following the due date and continuing through one pay period past the time the evaluation is received. [Assumes a connection between the compensation and performance management systems.])

Employees should not be punished for the supervisor's failure to complete the evaluation in a timely manner. Establishing some sort of bonus system for the employee insures that the supervisor will at least complete questionable evaluations in a timely manner. Supervisors who routinely complete late evaluations should have such noted as part of their own evaluation.

Policy 4:

Both the supervisor and employee shall sign the evaluation form signifying that the evaluation was reviewed with the employee and that the action plan on the form was agreed to between the employee and the supervisor. Signing the form does not signify agreement with the evaluation by the employee.

By signing the form committing to the action plan, the employee establishes a contract for performance of work. Should a discharge situation arise, the "contract" can be raised by the employer as an affirmative defense under contract law as well as labor relations law.

Procedures:

1. If the employee refuses to sign the evaluation form because of disagreement with the evaluation, the supervisor shall request that the form be signed by the supervisor in front of a third party. The third party will then place a note on the form with his or her signature stating that he or she witnessed that the employee refused to sign the form.

As mentioned earlier, failure to sign the evaluation form is not insubordination because signing the form protects the interests of the employer while possibly hurting the employee's interests. Usually such insubordination charges do not hold up in arbitration or administrative hearings. The employer's interests can be protected in other ways, such as the one suggested here of using a third-party witness.

2. Evaluations are subject to the agency grievance procedure. (However, the employee pay adjustment will be in accordance with the disputed evaluation unless and until the grievance is decided in the employee's favor. [Assumes compensation is related to the evaluation system.])

A performance management system that contains clear standards will show fewer appeals going through the grievance procedures. It is also easier to document performance under such systems because the arbitrariness and subjectivity have been reduced.

3. If the employee refuses to sign the evaluation form because of a disagreement over the contents of the action plan, the human resource manager shall be called in to act as a mediator between the supervisor and employee. If mediation fails, both the supervisor and the employee shall draw up separate proposed action plans. The plans will be reviewed by the Chief Executive Officer who shall choose between the plans or prepare an alternative plan. The Chief Executive Officer's plan shall be considered the action plan for the coming evaluation period. Failure to comply with the action plan submitted by the Chief Executive Officer shall be treated in the same manner as if the plan had been drawn up and agreed to between the supervisor and the employee.

Supervisors with strong communication skills rarely have problems with the employee's signing of the contract. However, when an employee refuses to sign the action, the action plan does not become a contract. This procedure takes advantage of recent experiments in mediation of MBOs while maintaining ultimate control with management.

(B) SUPERVISORY TRAINING

Effective implementation of the performance management system requires training supervisors on how to use the system. Maintaining the system over time requires an ongoing training program to instruct new supervisors in the procedures, refresh supervisory evaluation skills, and bring supervisors up to date on changes in the system. The training program also provides a separate vehicle for receiving feedback on the system's effectiveness in the field.

Whether it is the initial training program or a refresher, the program should consist of four topics:

1. *Review the current and anticipated changes in the policies and procedures.*
2. *Review the agreed-to definitions of the unclear terms in the performance standards.* This may include a discussion of how the participants are interpreting the standards and a review of grievance procedure decisions.
3. *Skill development in performance observation.* Observing and recording behavior are the most difficult parts of the observation process. Supervisors are being asked to perform a task for which psychologists and social workers attend graduate school. This section should include a review of observation biases and techniques for performance record-keeping (such as critical incident files).
4. *Communication skill development for conducting nondefensive, goal-oriented evaluation meetings.* These skills include providing constructive feedback, active listening, conflict resolution, negotiation, decision making, and counseling.

A sample agenda from successful training sessions is shown in Exhibit 13.7.

(C)   SUPPORTING CONTINUOUS IMPROVEMENT WITH PERFORMANCE MANAGEMENT DATA

The performance management system describes how performance management affects many other areas of the organization. In this role, the system provides vital support for the continuous improvement process.

The performance management program includes data for problem identification. Any trend in aggregate performance statistics is worth investigating. Often the information identifies problems within the human resource management system. For instance, applying a fishbone cause-effect diagram to determine the cause of a performance drop in a job classification where turnover has been constant might reveal a need to change the selection or training programs.

Consult performance data when performing cause-effect analyses on other quality issues as well. If there is a quality problem with a specific service, the problem may be caused by physical conditions. But discovering that there has been a concurrent drop in performance levels adds important information to the analysis.

Acquiring aggregate performance data is not easy. Usually, performance reports are placed in individual personnel files, never to be seen again. Finding the information can require a great deal of clerical work. Automated Human Resource Information Systems are very effective tools for making such data easily accessible without jeopardizing an individual's right to privacy.

(D)   APPLYING CONTINUOUS IMPROVEMENT TO THE PERFORMANCE MANAGEMENT SYSTEM

When ignored, the best performance management system loses its effectiveness after three to five years. Standards change and even become irrelevant. The initial training wears off, resulting in disagreement over performance standard definitions. New super-

EXHIBIT 13.7 Sample Workshop Agenda

Performance Management for Supervisors—Workshop Agenda

8:30	Introductions, Icebreaker Exercise: Characteristics of Successful Evaluation Systems
9:00	Evaluating the Employee
	Observation Skills
	Documentation
	Reducing Bias
10:00	Break
10:15	Evaluation Case Study Exercise
10:45	The Evaluation Meeting—An Overview
11:15	Conducting a Nondefensive Goal-Oriented Evaluation Meeting
	Step 1 Establishing Rapport
11:45	Lunch
1:15	Step 2 Describing Behavior
	Step 3 Problem Solving
	Step 4 Setting Performance Standards
	Step 5 Follow-Up
2:30	Break
2:45	Performance Evaluation Role-Plays
3:30	Procedural Issues
4:30	Wrap-Up and Evaluation

visors remain untrained in using the system. Only by applying continuous improvement principles to the performance management system itself will the system remain vital.

Two performance indicators determine the quality of the performance management system: validity and reliability.

Validity tests the effectiveness of the system. The validity question asks, Is the system improving performance?

Showing validity can be very difficult when performance is defined as the organization's achievement of its mission. Other factors, such as economic conditions, affect the same question. To assess the system's support of the mission, review whether any given performance standard is still an effective contributor to achieving the mission.

It is possible to make a more detailed assessment of individual work and performance standards. The effectiveness of work standards can easily be checked. The manager just looks to see if the rate for exceeding standards goes up following a series of evaluations. If it does, the system works.

The validity of an MBO system is a little more complicated. It requires assessing the continued linkage between objectives and the organization's mission. The most common MBO problems happen when managers fail to take the system seriously and begin writing easily achieved goals. The CEO or human resources manager must track the goals managers establish and intercede when the goals become too simplistic. On the other hand, when goals are out of line with the mission, it may mean that the mission should be changed. Other MBO problem indicators include an increasing failure rate of goal achievement, late evaluations, and goal carryover for specific objectives.

It is easier to test the effectiveness of organizationwide performance standards. The manager looks for organizational outcomes associated with that standard and tracks change in those outcomes. For instance, if there is a standard on client/customer service, look for a decrease in client complaints, and/or an increase in complimentary letters. A management standard on equal employment opportunity can be correlated with re-duced complaints and achieving affirmative action goals.

Failing validity may indicate a need to change or drop a performance standard. If customer service is being evaluated, yet complaints are rising, the organization needs to identify a more effective set of behaviors than those being evaluated.

A standard may also be dropped when it is no longer an essential organizational activity. For instance, once a performance management program is firmly in place, it should not be necessary to evaluate managers on how they conduct their evaluations.

After the system has been running a while, reliability can be tested statistically. The statistical null-hypothesis is that the distribution of evaluation scores is not random. If the scores are random, then the system remains reliable. Any trend development in the data raises a red flag of caution. This is especially true when scores become attracted to any one point—midpoint, low, or high. This means that either rating biases are creeping into the system, or the standards need changing to reflect changing organizational conditions.

For example, the human resources manager notes that there is a strong tendency for supervisors to rate people high on creativity. This could be the result of a lack of un-derstanding of the scale or lack of importance in the scale (reliability). Or the trend may be the result of a recent agencywide training program on creativity. The last possibility validates the standard and the training program, while indicating a potential need to ei-ther drop or improve the standard.

13.4   Conclusion

In the words of Rodney Dangerfield, performance management can't get no respect. The last time performance management was a popular business topic was with the advent of MBO in the 1960s. Since then it has been eclipsed by such management buzzwords as *continuous improvement, reengineering*, and now, *renewal.*

True, most decent management books still laud the value of performance manage-ment. Yet because the topic is not timely, the process is relegated to once-a-year, boring administrative activity, without any real impact. Performance management itself needs renewal.

But take a second look at each of these hot topic management methods. The same process is found at the core of every one of them—the cycle of planning, evaluating, and planning again. They are all methods of performance management.

The issue is not so much one of importance, but of understanding. Whenever you jump into any of the methods, you are establishing a chance for renewal. It will succeed only if you remember that renewal is a process of continuous adaptation, a process of scanning what's needed and adjusting to fulfill that need. In short, it is always the type of performance management that starts with today and looks to the future.

Suggested Readings

Advanced Personnel Systems. 1988. *The Personnel Software Census*, Vol. 1(1), Roseville, CA.

Babcock, Richard and Sorensen, Peter Jr. 1980. *Strategies and Tactics in Management by Objectives*. Champaign, IL; Stipes Publishing.

Baird, Lloyd S., Beatty, Richard W., and Schneier, Craig Eric. 1985. *The Performance Appraisal Sourcebook*. Amherst, MA; Human Resource Development Press.

Deming, W. Edwards. 1986. *Out of the Crisis*. Cambridge; MIT-CAES.

Latham, Gary P. and Wexley, Kenneth N. 1981. *Increasing Productivity Through Performance Appraisal*. Reading, PA: Addison-Wesley.

Michaels, Mark. 1987. "Putting Performance Management to the Test." *Rural Telecommunications* (Fall), 6(4).

Michaels, Mark. 1988. *The Performance Technologies Workbook*. Champaign, IL: People Technologies.

Michaels, Mark. 1990. "CEO Evaluation, The Board's Second Most Crucial Duty." *Nonprofit World*, 8(3).

Sample, John A. 1986. "The Use of Behaviorally Based Scales in Performance Appraisal," *The 1986 Annual: Developing Human Resources*, University Associates.

Schneir, Craig E. and Beatty, Richard W. 1979. "Integrating Behaviorally-based and Effectiveness-based Methods." *The Personnel Administrator* (July), 42.

Schneir, Craig E. and Beatty, Richard W. 1979. "Developing Behaviorally-anchored Rating Scales (BARS)." *Personnel Administrator* (August), 42.

Schneir, Craig E. and Beatty, Richard W. 1979. "Combining BARS and MBO: Using an Appraisal System to Diagnose Performance Problems." *Personnel Administrator* (September), 42.

Tosi, Henry L. and Carroll, Stephen. 1970. "Management by Objectives." *Personnel Administrator* (July–August), 33.

University Associates. 1986. "BARS: Developing Behaviorally Anchored Rating Scales." *The 1986 Annual: Developing Human Resources*, University Associates.

14 Compensation Management

Mark Michaels, MPA
People Technologies

14.1 Components of an Effective Performance-Based System

(A) ELEMENTS OF AN EFFECTIVE COMPENSATION SYSTEM

Effective compensation systems balance the internal worth of positions with compensation that is competitive when compared with rates paid and ranges utilized by other, similar employees. Balancing internal and market worth is the critical task in compensation management. It helps employees feel comfortable with the answers to the questions: "What is my job worth to the organization compared with my co-worker"; and, "What is my job worth to the organization compared with what I can receive elsewhere?"

When employees compare compensation, they generally think only in terms of their wages. Often, upwards of 35 percent of an employee's real compensation in nonprofits is benefits. This high figure developed as nonprofits found it difficult to stay competitive with private-sector wages. To retain employees, nonprofits offered longer vacations, more holidays, more sick leave, and similar noncash benefits. Eventually insurance policies were added. Then state and federal law added additional requirements for some nonprofits like Social Security, and those organizations which had started pension funds found their funds regulated by law. Quietly, the costs added up. Because of the high cost of benefits, as much as 30 percent of a labor-intensive nonprofit's annual operating budget can be spent on employee benefits. This forces the nonprofit executive into managing total compensation instead of just wages.

Total compensation is the total cash value of all compensation received through wages and benefits. Determining the total compensation value requires computing the cash value of three types of costs: program benefits, both mandatory and voluntary, such as insurance, pension, unemployment and workers compensation; pay for time worked; and pay for time not worked such as holidays, vacation, and sick leave.

It is almost impossible to calculate total compensation. But any compensation study must find some way to consider all these factors when attempting to define a fair level of compensation. It is also important that the employees know the value that these benefits add to their compensation program.

Workable compensation systems distinguish among a number of elements. All systems start with positions within organizations. *Positions* are the specific jobs held by employees. For instance, two registered nurses hold two positions, one in department A and one in department B.

A *job classification* is defined as the description of a group of positions which entail similar, but not necessarily identical work. The positions share similar organizational responsibilities. They also share the same group of skills, knowledge, and abilities for successful performance of the work. The two registered nurses described above are in the same job classification, but they are in a different classification than, say, practical nurse.

A *pay classification* or *pay range* is a salary or salary range assigned to a group of job classifications. Registered nurses and human resource assistants may be in the same pay classification. Registered nurses would most likely be in a different pay classification than practical nurses.

The *classification system* is composed of all pay ranges. It, along with the benefits, constitute the complete compensation system.

(B) THE FOUNDATION OF EFFECTIVE PERFORMANCE-BASED COMPENSATION SYSTEMS

To meet both employee and employer needs, a performance-based compensation system must be considered fair by the employee. But it must also produce results for the employer in terms of increased organizational effectiveness. The foundation of such systems includes four cornerstones: (1) job analysis; (2) salaries that are competitive in the market place while maintaining equity within the organization; (3) a valid performance management system; and (4) a policy guaranteeing that the greatest rewards go to the best performers.

Job analysis is the core function of all human resource management processes. For an effective compensation system, job analysis must identify the key contributions that each job makes to an organization's mission plus the critical skills, knowledge, and abilities (KSAs) required to make such contributions. This becomes the data used for comparative analysis when establishing the salaries for the positions.

For instance, a supervisor in a sheltered workshop may be exposed to dangers associated with industrial equipment. At the same location, a social worker may be exposed to dangers associated with infectious diseases. The effective compensation system establishes a way to place a separate dollar value on each of these dangers.

How much is a job worth? Valuing contributions and skills in the organization requires balancing information from two, often conflicting sources. The first source is the marketplace and is called *market worth*. The second, called *internal worth*, is the position's worth relative to other positions within the agency—the pecking order.

The market worth of a skill or position is the amount paid for that commodity by other employers with whom the agency competes when hiring and retaining employees. In some cases, as for social worker, this comparison may be possible based on the whole job. The market worth of social work positions in your community is the average salary for social workers.

Nonprofits compete to recruit and retain social workers primarily within the nonprofit and public sector. As a group, the market worth for social worker is depressed by the tight financial conditions experienced by nonprofit and public organizations. However, to recruit and retain a secretary, the agency competes with both the public and private employment sectors. Current economic conditions can put an agency in the ticklish situation of paying a secretary the same salary as a social worker.

Before the 1970s, most organizations set their salaries as a function of budgetary ability and market conditions. This eventually lead to charges of discrimination against women, because the marketplace paid lower salaries for female-dominated positions than for those held by males. The first response and attempt to remedy the problem was the Equal Pay Act of 1963. The Act requires equal pay for equal work. Two positions whose job descriptions are highly similar are required to be paid the same within the same establishment, or at least be in the same pay range. For instance, men and women in computer programming jobs are placed in the same salary range, and the average salaries for males and females in that position should be equal. Job analysis is used to thwart attempts to evade the law by having two job titles, one filled by men and the other by women, but with virtually the same duties.

Such job analysis studies revealed a second, more insidious form of pay discrimination. It was discovered that an organization may value two different jobs or even skill sets as equal, or skills in a traditionally female position may have greater value over a male-dominated skill set, but the marketplace values them differently because one is a traditionally female job. A frequently cited example is to compare a janitor with a secretary. Since the salaries are set based on market value, the traditionally female jobs are kept as lower-paying positions.

The new finding resulted in demands to consider the internal, organizational worth of the position as part of the compensation formula. The demand for equal pay for comparable worth was born and internal equity became an important part of the compensation process.

To date, the Supreme Court has rejected the comparable worth doctrine under both the Civil Rights Act of 1964 and the Equal Pay Act. However, many state governments have passed comparable worth laws. Some of the laws cover local governments and state grant recipients. Unions, especially the American Federation of State, County, and Municipal Employees (AFSCME), are actively pushing comparable worth both politically and in negotiations. Nonprofits are quickly finding it strategically necessary, if not also motivationally valuable, to include internal worth in their compensation planning process.

The third cornerstone to a solid compensation system is a valid performance management system. To be valid, the performance management system must exhibit both validity and reliability. Validity means that the system measures what it claims to measure. Reliability means that when two or more evaluators review the same performance against the same criteria, their evaluations will be very similar.

An effective performance-based compensation system will never be achieved without the fourth cornerstone: The system must guarantee that the best performers receive the highest awards. The need is logical and simple enough. But putting it in practice has been a nightmare, especially for merit systems.

The problem begins with misuse of the bell curve as the controlling dynamic of the compensation system. Using the bell curve, or what some consultants call midpoint budgeting, assumes that over time the distribution of performance evaluations in an organization will look like the bell-shaped, or standard curve. Since the curve is symmetrical, budgeting for performance increases only requires budgeting as if everyone received an average evaluation. That average would be achieved over time.

However, as with any statistic, the concept of "over time" means over a long time. In any given year the probability exists that the majority of the evaluations will fall on one side of the line or the other. And if the performance management system is invalid, expect that the results will usually fall above the midpoint. When these evaluations are linked to the compensation system, they cause salary increases to go over budget. Profit-making organizations can manage such overages in the short run. But nonprofits running on tight revenues can be devastated in just one year.

Traditional responses to the problem include arbitrarily lowering evaluations to fit the budget, reducing the amount available for the award for above average evaluations during the second half of the year, and stopping pay increases totally at some point in the year. Each response destroys the integrity of the performance management system.

A second problem is "topping out," reaching the top of a pay scale through exceptional performance and then not being able to go higher. At this point the top performer no longer is rewarded for performance, or the policy is manipulated on an individual basis, slowly destroying the integrity of the compensation system.

Many organizations have tried a systemic response to the topping-out problem. When an employee is low in the pay scale, the percent increase for top performance will be higher than for a person higher up on the scale. Employee A, who is currently paid below midpoint receives an excellent evaluation, making her eligible for a 7 percent raise. Employee B's current salary is in the top quartile. With an excellent evaluation, he is only eligible for a 4 percent raise. The policy is justified with the learning curve. As you can imagine, in reality Employee B's motivation quickly deteriorates in future years.

Piecework, commission, and other systems are all able to give the highest compensation to the best performer. Using methods described in Section 14.4, merit systems can also achieve this goal.

(C) PAY-FOR-PERFORMANCE WORKS, SO WHAT'S THE PROBLEM?

Merit pay, the strategy of providing annual pay increases based on a formula which relates the increase to one's annual performance review, is the most pervasive form of performance-based compensation in nonprofit organizations. Yet numerous studies show that employees strongly dislike merit pay systems.

Ask just about any employee upon what she would like her pay based and the answer will be, "my performance." Is this some kind of schizophrenia? Or is it impossible to develop a workable pay-for-performance system?

Actually, neither situation is the case. Many workable pay-for-performance systems are found in for-profit and nonprofit organizations. They have been in existence since the industrial revolution, and probably before. Examples include piecework, commission, profit sharing, gainsharing, and achievement bonuses. These successful programs will be discussed in detail later.

Discussions with employees during consultations in nonprofits and seminars for nonprofits has shown a consistent pattern of problems with merit pay systems. Some of the problems are inherent with the compensation program, others are failures in the performance management system. The most frequently cited problems include:

Compensation System–Based Complaints

- Poorer workers and workers with less seniority can get greater increases.
- Workers can top out on the system (reaching the highest pay level, restricting further increases).
- Merit increases are too small to be worth the effort.
- The difference in increase between top workers and average workers is too small to be worth the extra effort.
- The merit increase fund runs out before the evaluation period.
- Everyone gets the same raise, regardless of evaluation, to fit the budget.

Performance Management System–Based Complaints

- The evaluations are biased.
- The pay increase is based on the rank of the evaluation, even when two are very close together.
- The pay increase comes six months after the evaluation.

With many human resource management issues, the problem is not with the baby, but with the bath water. Strategies exist for resolving the employees' legitimate complaints. Chapter 13 provides answers to performance management systems. This chapter addresses solutions to the compensation-based problems.

To avoid confusion, this chapter will distinguish between merit and performance-based compensation systems. Performance-based compensation systems include all methods for paying employees based upon their work output, including merit pay. Merit pay will be the type of system where annual increases or bonuses are paid based upon an annual performance evaluation review.

14.2 Types of Performance-Based Pay

(A) PIECEWORK

Performance-based pay is one of the oldest bases for compensation. Whether bushels picked per day or widgets built per hour, individuals employed under piecework systems are paid for each piece produced.

Piecework systems are possible when the worker has control over his materials and work process. They require a defined product, such as total assembly of a product or completion of a series of repetitive tasks that form part of a total product. Pure piecework systems are now rare outside of agriculture. They have been banned to protect workers from the sweatshop conditions found in the garment industry early in this century.

An alternative and popular piecework approach is to establish a base salary and a baseline production level. An employee can earn additional income for each piece made above the baseline level. In some systems, the higher one produces, the greater the amount of the award per piece.

Piecework is almost nonexistent in nonprofit management. Piecework acts contrary to good service delivery, and most nonprofits are service providers. Admittedly, some governmental programs pay the nonprofits under a piecework model. The performance-based contract under the Joint Training Partnership Act, is one example.

(B) COMMISSION COMPENSATION

Commission is piecework for salespeople. Commission pays the employee a percentage of the sale price of an item when it is successfully sold. Pure commission systems, which also are not popular in nonprofits, pay only for the percentage of sales, with no other payment. Usually, the employee is allowed to take a draw—borrow from—expected future commissions until her sales level is adequate for sustaining her livelihood.

Most commission systems combine base salary and commission. The base salary is recognition that the employee does not completely control the sales process. In most cases the sale is dependent upon the performance of various support staff. However, the base salary is lower than comparable, noncommission, salaried positions. The salary difference usually runs between 25 and 35 percent. The difference is expected to be made up in commissions.

Commission payments can be manipulated to support desired behaviors. Examples of motivational commission structures include:

- To increase the incidence of repeat clients, because the cost of sales is lower, paying a higher commission for repeat business over new sales.
- To increase sales of one stock over another, increase the commission on the desired stock.
- To increase sales volume per buyer, increase the commission rate for higher sales volume.
- To protect from overselling to one customer, use a graduated commission, decrease the commission rate after reaching the desired sales volume.

Modified commission programs, such as described above, frequently appear in nonprofit environments. Agencies with thrift stores provide commissions to managers dependent upon store volume. Agencies with sheltered workshops commission the employees responsible for selling the workshop goods. Fund raisers often receive a percent of donations and grant income as part of their compensation. Membership recruiters, magazine subscription telemarketers, and advertising sales representatives are also prime candidates for commission programs.

(C) MANAGEMENT BY OBJECTIVES (MBO)

The performance management system, Management by Objectives, is frequently linked to the compensation system for managers. MBO was developed by Peter Drucker. If achieving objectives is viewed as production, MBO becomes a piecework system for managers.

The 1980s saw a decrease in the popularity of MBO compensation systems among the academic and consulting communities. W. Edwards Deming believed that MBO systems block development of a quality-focused organization. As described by Schneir (September 1979), MBO systems encourage achievement of the objectives at the expense of the *process* for achieving the objectives. One manager may achieve his objectives, yet, due to his aggressive approach, lose all his staff at the same time. When the manager's achievement of objectives is linked to compensation, that manager still gets rewarded. Objectives can also make managers inflexible, and even blind to the need for change. Yet, although MBO-based compensation has many critics, it remains one of the most popular systems for performance-based compensation in the United States.

A simple MBO system rewards a worker for meeting objectives established at the beginning of the evaluation period. The objectives are written in clear, quantifiable language. An example of an objective for a development director might be, "Increase donation income 10 percent in six months." With clear objectives, evaluation is very simple.

The administrative structure for an MBO-based compensation system can become complex. As Exhibit 14.1 demonstrates, the final rating defining the percent salary income can be the sum of a number of factors: timeliness in completing the objective, the priority of the objective, and so forth. Points are given for each objective; they are added together with the sum being matched against some external guideline. The guideline

EXHIBIT 14.1 Rating Sheet for Management by Objectives (MBO)

MBO RATING SHEET

Goals	Weight (A)	Complete (B)	Effect (C)	Time (D)	Total
	100%	SCORE 1 to 3	SCORE 3 to 5	SCORE 2 to 5	A(B+C+D)

NOTE: Weightings and scores are for example only. Agencies should set their own standards establishing the importance of each criterion.

reads something like, "For a total score of 50–60, award a 3% raise. For a total score of 61–70, award a 4% raise." And so forth.

(D) ACHIEVEMENT-BASED COMPENSATION PROGRAMS

The fastest growing area of performance-based pay today is the achievement-based compensation system. Achievement-based systems are particularly effective in organizations with few promotional opportunities and in connection with total quality management (TQM) programs.

Achievement-based pay is simple to administer. The agency starts by establishing developmental opportunities for employees. For instance, secretaries can be encouraged to learn computer word processing. Or employees may be encouraged to learn facilitation skills for facilitating TQM teams. When an employee demonstrates learning and effective use of the new skill, the employee is given a predetermined raise as a reward.

One of the earliest of the modern achievement systems was the Dual Career Ladder. The Dual Career Ladder is a response to the Peter Principle, the adage that everyone is promoted to his own level of incompetence. The ladder rewards individuals who want to remain producers by allowing an alternative growth trackladder, to the traditional ladder to management. At the same time, Dual Career Ladders help organizations retain upwardly mobile employees where there are few promotional opportunities.

Exhibit 14.2 shows that the ladder provides two paths for development in the organization. The first is the traditional path to supervision and management. The second

EXHIBIT 14.2 Alternative Paths on a Sample Pair of Dual Career Ladders

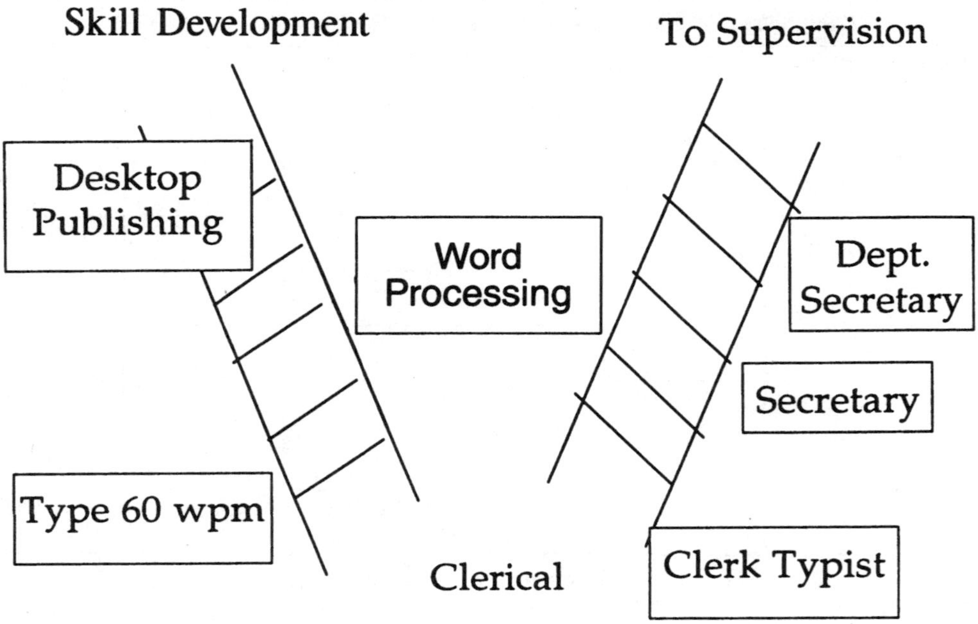

path works like the Boy Scout merit system. The organization identifies additional skills needed within the job category. An employee who is happier as a service provider can go up the second ladder by completing the required development activities. A pay increase is given each step of the way. Of course, this system is possible only in organizations which can set aside the money for such increases.

Many merit pay and MBO systems foster competition between individual employees. This tends to work against the group involvement approach inherent in TQM. Achievement-based systems are jumping in to fill the void.

In places like Ford Motor Company, as well as many hospitals now promoting quality, total quality transformations eventually affect the entire work system. Work redesign leads to a breakdown of departmental differentiation of work and creation of work cells involving the performance of multiple tasks in a team environment. This job expansion requires the development of team membership and technical skills. TQM program companies use the achievement-based system to encourage individual skill development and team collaboration.

(E) MERIT PAY SYSTEMS

Merit pay is the catchall term for compensation systems which base part or all of their annual pay increase on the results of a formal evaluation of individual employee performance.

Merit pay was developed as a reward structure in situations where the task, the work process, or both are not clearly defined and easily assessed. It is this perceived lack of clarity which is the basis for many of the problems with merit pay systems.

To function successfully, merit pay systems minimally require:

- A valid annual (or semiannual) evaluation of the employee's performance.
- A compensation system based on salary ranges instead of flat salaries.
- An objective rule linking allowed salary increases to performance levels. The rule might read something like: "Excellent performers receive 5.5–7% increases, average performers receive 4.5–5.5% increases, below-average performers receive 3–4% increases, and poor performers receive no increases." The percentages may change each year as a function of the budget and market worth.
- Support for the objective rule which assures that the rule will be followed under all circumstances. If financial conditions are allowed to affect the rule, the result is that the compensation system controls the performance system. The opposite is necessary for an effective performance-based compensation program.

(F) GAINSHARING

Gainsharing compensation systems are group rewards programs which provide bonuses based upon group and organizational success. They range from bonuses for successful suggestions to complex profit sharing programs. Gainsharing programs are becoming very popular as part of total quality transformations because they support team identity and achievement of organizational goals.

Gainsharing works in nonprofits, but with a catch. Private companies take a portion of their profits and distribute that portion to the employees. The distribution may be in cash, stock, or increased benefits. Nonprofits have no profits to share.

But nonprofits can share money that is saved through a more efficient delivery of services. If through continuous improvement efforts employees develop techniques that save $5,000 over the budgeted expense, assuming revenues met budget projections, a portion of those funds can be distributed to the employees as a bonus. The result is a win–win scenario for both the employees and the organization.

A typical gainsharing program will start with some sort of problem solving, suggestion, or continuous improvement team system involved in organization problems. The decision-making process will work as follows:

1. The team recommends a change in equipment, procedure, or whatever, which it believes will save the organization some money.
2. Either a steering committee or management reviews and approves the proposal.
3. The steering committee estimates the current budget costs associated with the problem.
4. The proposal is implemented and savings are tracked. After a set time period (usually either a quarter or after a year), the savings are computed. A portion of the savings is distributed to the employees as a bonus.
5. A bonus is paid based only on the initial savings from the change. The organization should experience ongoing savings as a result of the change.

The agency must decide to whom the bonuses are distributed. Some organizations distribute the bonuses to the team that developed and implemented the change. This supports team identity. It can also create competition between the teams, a concept that has actually been institutionalized at places like Motorola.

However, some organizations disagree on the value of interorganizational competition. They value large group identification with organizational goals. Others are too small for multiple teams. These organizations distribute bonuses to the entire staff.

14.3 Compensation Planning with Employee Participation

(A) AN OVERVIEW OF THE COMPENSATION STUDY

Developing an effective compensation system is a complex process requiring a series of steps ranging from initial board policy development to detailed job and quantitative analysis. The project can take from three to six months in small to medium-sized nonprofits. Some of the steps, like conducting a salary survey, must take no less than one month. Other processes, like job analysis, depend more upon the number of employees involved.

Use a qualified consultant skilled in conflict management to guide the process. Even if, as will be suggested here, an employee participation strategy is used, it is still critical to use a consultant. Under the best of circumstances there will be conflict during the project—because it involves individuals' livelihoods and egos.

The project manager is the lightning rod for the project. If that person is an employee and the conflict is even slightly mishandled, it can take years to repair the relationships within the organization. Compensation study problems have seeded the termination of many professional executives who insisted on saving money by doing the work themselves. A good consultant deflects the criticism while effectively managing the project. A poor consultant?—Well, at least you can just blame it on him.

Compensation studies take a great deal of time and effort. As a result, few compensation consultants are willing to perform the work for free. However, local retired executives are sometimes available through the local Chamber of Commerce, larger United Way systems may have consulting resources, and some trade associations offer help to their members at below consulting rates.

Compensation studies include eight basic steps. Listed below are the specific steps with a short description. Each step is described in greater detail throughout the remainder of the chapter.

1. *Establish policy direction.* For the consultant to act effectively, the board must answer four questions: (a) Will we pay employees at, above, or below the market rate?—to guide development of the salary ranges. (b) Against whom do we compete when recruiting and retaining our employees?—to guide development of the salary survey. The answer may differ for employees in various positions. (c) What value do we want to give to market worth versus internal worth? (d) What is the relative value of the factors defining a given job's value (i.e., responsibility, skill, mental effort, physical effort, etc.)? Although consultants have their own answers to some of these questions, using them as policy questions helps achieve board approval of the final proposal.

2. *Conduct a job analysis.* This requires having employees complete self-analysis questionnaires, conducting bench audits (interviews) with a large percent of the employees, and writing the job descriptions.

3. *Conduct a compensation survey.* Send out, receive, and evaluate a salary and benefits survey.

4. *Perform a job evaluation study.* This is the critical process of integrating salary survey and job analysis data to establish tentative midpoint salaries for each job classification. The three primary methods for this task are the factor comparison system, the point factor system, and the whole job system.

5. *Combine positions with similar midpoint salaries into pay classifications.* This task involves a regression analysis of the midpoint wages from step 4.

6. *Adjust the benefit system to meet survey results and internal needs.* It will be necessary to keep your eye on the benefits survey results at all times. Otherwise, wages can be over- or underestimated relative to the total compensation package.

7. *Facilitate employee appeals of the classification decisions.* Employee appeals provide accountability while helping to gain employee support for the project. Communication with and the involvement of employees throughout the project reduces the conflict of a compensation study. However, mistakes are made. And employees become more accepting of the results once they have had a chance to hear the reasoning behind the decisions affecting them.

8. *Implement the plan.*

The agency can perform some of these steps under the guidance of the consultant and save consulting costs. In particular, the agency should be able to conduct the salary survey according to the consultant's survey strategy. Job analysis can also involve agency staff. Doing both tasks helps develop the in-house capacity for managing the system once the consultant is gone.

Whenever the client assists the consultant, the client must be careful to work within the consultant's research model. Each consultant has her own project strategy which may not fit your initial strategy. For instance, your job descriptions may not contain the information the consultant needs for making decisions in the job evaluation process. The consultant will still have to conduct a job analysis, and your time will have been wasted.

Throughout this chapter, we will discuss ways to involve employees in the compensation process. When compensation planning became popular in the 1970s as the result of available federal funds through the Intergovernmental Personal Act, most consultants acted as experts making all compensation decisions as recommendations to their clients. Conflict between management and staff in these agencies was very high, resulting in a high project rejection rate.

During the 1980s, a number of consultants began applying employee participation strategies to compensation planning. The employees did not set individual salaries. But they either rated positions on point factor scales or ranked the positions through factor comparison, providing data from which consultants could work the final compensation figures. Conflict has been reduced significantly when employee involvement is coupled with a strong communication program.

(B)   CONDUCTING A JOB ANALYSIS

Job analysis is the foundation of all human resource management functions, including designing effective compensation plans. It is also the starting point in involving employees in the compensation planning process.

Job analysis involves asking employees to describe their jobs, clarifying the information from the employees through a bench audit, and writing and rewriting job descriptions.

Employees can prepare a written description of their duties using a standardized questionnaire. The questionnaire must be designed to elicit the information that will be needed to rate or rank the job.

People Technologies' Job Analysis Questionnaire (JAQ), Exhibit 14.3, was designed to work with a factor-comparison job evaluation strategy. It has been broken up to elicit information about each of the five factors in the factor comparison exercise. Employees are given one to two weeks to complete the JAQ. It is then reviewed by the supervisor, who is allowed to comment about the information on a separate sheet. This two-step approach helps the consultant quickly identify task and role conflicts and to thoughtfully plan the *bench audit*.

Bench audits are one-on-one interviews and job observations with individual employees. There are three reasons for conducting bench audits. First, they help the analyst clarify vague responses in the JAQ. Responses to the questionnaire differ depending upon the employee's intelligence and attention to detail. It is necessary to complete the form with some employees. In some cases, the employee thinks in terms of broad categories and objectives, providing brief responses. Others are so detail oriented that they add multiple pages to their response. The bench audit allows the job analyst to standardize the information.

Second, some critical job information cannot be described in the questionnaire. Com-

EXHIBIT 14.3 Sample Job Analysis Questionnaire

ABC NONPROFIT JOB ANALYSIS QUESTIONNAIRE

Instructions

This questionnaire is the key ingredient for preparing a new position description for your job, and in assigning your position to an appropriate salary classification.

Developing the position description will include a review of your responses by your supervisor. If necessary, we will discuss any major differences between your responses and your supervisor's review in a meeting with you. The consultant may also meet with you to gather additional information about your job. Later, you will also have the chance to review a draft of the position description and to make comments and suggestions. The final description will be reviewed by you and your supervisor.

The information you provide in this questionnaire will also be important in assigning your position to a pay classification. Those assignments will be based on a number of variables relating to the position's skill level; level of responsibility; level of physical and mental effort required to perform job tasks; and the job's working conditions, as these variables relate to other positions.

The questionnaire will not be used to evaluate your individual job performance. The assignment of positions to the pay classifications will be based on the requirements of the job, regardless of who the occupant is. Performance becomes a factor only when determining your actual salary within the assigned salary range. That issue will continue to be a matter among you, and your supervisor.

As you can see, it is important that you answer the questions as completely as possible. Please consider each question carefully and provide as much information as possible.

This questionnaire must be completed and passed on to your supervisor no later than close of business Friday, _____ , to keep this project on schedule.

Thank you for your cooperation.

Position: _____

Name _____   Rate of Pay _____

Title _____   Date of Hire _____

Immediate supervisor _____

Supervisor's title _____

I. **Job Responsibilities:** Please describe all your job responsibilities. Break broad responsibilities into duties and tasks, but try to avoid getting bogged down in detail. For tasks that are performed more than once per day, please include the average number of times the task is performed each day. (For example: "Type approximately 10 letters each day." "Check through approximately 50 books each day.")

A. Daily responsibilities (responsibilities you must achieve every day)   #Hrs/Day   Rank

B. Weekly responsibilities (responsibilities you must achieve every week)   #Hrs/Wk   Rank

C. Monthly responsibilities (responsibilities you must achieve every month)   #Hrs/Mo   Rank

D. Annual responsibilities (Responsibilities you must achieve annually)   #Hrs/Yr   Rank

(Continued)

EXHIBIT 14.3 *(Continued)*

E. Choose from the above lists the responsibilities that you think are the 10 most important for the successful performance of your job. List them in their order of importance (1 = absolute highest, 10 = 10th highest):

1. _____   6. _____

2. _____   7. _____

3. _____   8. _____

4. _____   9. _____

5. _____   10. _____

II. **Job Relationships**

A. Draw a chart showing how you believe your position really fits into the organization. The chart should show your immediate supervisor(s) at the top, you and your co-workers (by name and title) on the next level, and the names and titles of those you supervise on lower levels.

B. Supervision Received
   1. Describe actions that you can perform and/or decisions you can make without approval from your supervisor.

   2. Describe work problems that you must review with your supervisor before taking action.

   3. For problems not needing a supervisor's review, indicate which of the following you consult or rely on for guidance.

   _____ Established procedures such as:

   _____ Manuals such as:

   _____ Past training by a supervisor such as:

   _____ Past technical training such as:

   _____ Independent research and consultations such as:

   _____ Past professional training such as:

C. Supervision Given
   (If your position does not involve supervising any employee, please proceed to Section D below.)
   Check the appropriate responses to describe the nature of your supervision.

   _____ Recommend applicants for hiring for vacant positions

   _____ Recommend firing subordinates for rule infractions

   _____ Suspend subordinates for rule infractions

   _____ Recommend suspensions for rule infractions

   _____ Give subordinates written and/or oral warnings for rule infractions

   _____ Recommend written and/or oral warnings for rule infractions

   _____ Conduct performance evaluations of subordinate employees

(Continued)

EXHIBIT 14.3 *(Continued)*

D. Fiduciary Responsibilities
Check the appropriate responses to describe your responsibilities, and fill in the approximate amounts.

_____ Receive cash and/or checks on behalf of the agency
Avg. amount per day:
_____ Prepare, authorize, and/or sign agency checks to pay agency expenses
Amount authorized to approve:
_____ Authorize the purchase of materials or equipment on behalf of the agency
Amount authorized to approve without higher approval:
_____ Handle materials of exceptional value, such as rare documents.
Examples: _____

_____
_____

E. Public Contacts
My job involves frequent contact with:

_____ 1. Executives in government, business, or other similar agencies
Purposes:
_____ To establish and maintain public contact
_____ To plan and/or negotiate cooperation, funding, or support
_____ To discuss, plan, or interpret policy
_____ To provide or request a specific service
_____ To ask or answer questions about agency practices
_____ 2. Representatives of outside organizations
Purposes:
_____ To establish and maintain public contact
_____ To plan and/or negotiate cooperation, funding, or support
_____ To discuss, plan, or interpret policy
_____ To provide or request a specific service
_____ To ask or answer questions about agency practices
_____ 3. The general public
Purposes:
_____ To establish and maintain public contact
_____ To plan and/or negotiate cooperation, funding, or support
_____ To discuss, plan, or interpret policy
_____ To provide or request a specific service
_____ To ask or answer questions about agency practices

III. **Working Conditions**

A. Describe the physical conditions under which this job is performed.

B. Describe any unusual psychological demands connected with this job.

(Continued)

EXHIBIT 14.3 *(Continued)*

C. Describe any conditions under which the job is performed which make it unique.

D. Describe fully any health or safety hazards associated with this job.

E. Is any safety training or equipment required?

IV. **Tools**

A. Please describe any equipment that is necessary for completion of your job (automobile, typewriter, computer, etc.).

Equipment	Purpose	% Time Used	Alternative Method
_____	_____	_____	_____
_____	_____	_____	_____
_____	_____	_____	_____
_____	_____	_____	_____
_____	_____	_____	_____

V. **Special Requirements**

A. List any special certifications or licenses required by law for your position.

B. What level of education had you achieved before starting in this position?

C. How many years' experience did you have in your profession before starting in this position?

Certification of Employee

I hereby certify that the answers to the foregoing are my own, and that, to the best of my knowledge, they are complete and correct.

Signed _____   Date _____

Name (please print) _____

Supervisor's Review:

Comments on:
Section I

Section II

Section III

Section IV

Section V

Signed _____   Date _____

Name (please print) _____

munication skill requirements like reading level, complexity of decision making, and working conditions can be difficult to understand from answers to the questionnaire. For example, in one study done by this author for a health district, one job had the simple title of Infectious Disease Investigator. The responses on the questionnaire were brief but accurate regarding report making and accountability. What did not show up was that employees in this position put their lives on the line daily as they visit dangerous housing projects to inform people that they may have contracted AIDS or other dangerous diseases. And the position had taken on case management responsibilities as well.

Third, in addition to information gathering, bench audits increase a sense of ownership and participation in the project for employees. Bench audits show employees that their input is important to the process, that the project is attempting to meet their needs. For this reason, when contracting with a consultant, the proposal should include requiring a minimum number of bench audits. For smaller agencies the number should be high, from 50 to 75 percent of the resulting job classifications (not employees). For larger organizations, no less than 50 percent of the resulting job classifications should receive bench audits.

Specific items to consider during the bench audit which are not well defined in the questionnaire include:

- Examples of how work is assigned to the employee, in written and/or oral form.
- Materials that the employee must read to assess reading grade level requirements.
- Forms and reports the employee completes to assess writing skill levels.
- The complexity of special equipment that the employee uses, including diagnostic equipment, office equipment (like computers and the associated software), manufacturing equipment.
- The working conditions—inside or outside, special dangers and exposure to environmental hazards.
- Physical conditions which require either established limitations relative to physical disabilities or adaptations which make the position accessible to people with disabilities. (Compliance with the Americans with Disabilities Act.)
- Any special conditions which the employee wishes you to consider.

The next job analysis step is writing the job description. Job descriptions are a byproduct of the compensation process. Job evaluation is possible with the information gathered in the JAQ and bench audits. But properly prepared job descriptions are a valuable contribution to all management functions.

Exhibit 14.4 is an outline for a simple job description. For compensation planning purposes, Nature of Work, Required Knowledge, Skills and Abilities, and Required Education and Experience are the critical elements for the job evaluation process. Being certain that there is a clear understanding of the skills and abilities in particular is crucial for compliance with the Americans with Disabilities Act.

Draft job descriptions should be sent to employees and their supervisors for review and comment. This also is part of the participation process. Minor comments can easily be incorporated into the description. Major complaints may require a second bench audit and, possibly, mediating between the employee and the supervisor.

EXHIBIT 14.4 Job Description Outline

Nature of work:
A. The relationship of the position to the overall function of the organization, and the responsibilities incorporated in that job classification.
B. Extent of supervision received and from where.
C. Role in policy development.
D. Special responsibilities, such as for safeguarding funds.
E. Overall strategy for evaluation of performance for the position.

Examples of work
A. Examples of the types of tasks that are performed by members of the job classification covered by the description. Do not include all tasks performed by a given position covered by the description. Not all tasks listed will be performed by all positions covered by the description. Use those tasks that exemplify the knowledge, skills, and abilities listed in the next section.

Required knowledge, skills, and abilities (KSAs)
A. Describe the underlying performance requirements for satisfactory performance of this job.
B. Use a uniform rating system to define the levels of performance.

Required education and experience
A. Define the minimum education and experience levels needed for a person to be able to learn the KSAs for adequate performance of the job. There must be a relationship between this section and the KSAs.
B. Indicate the required licenses, certifications, and similar documents.

Once the job descriptions are finalized, they should be subject to the grievance procedure that is established for the project.

(C) CONDUCTING THE COMPENSATION SURVEY

The goal of the compensation survey is to determine the average and range of wages and benefits paid for comparable positions within your recruitment area. The questions which need to be answered include whom to survey, which positions to use, and the number of organizations to include in the survey.

Whom to survey is determined by the recruitment area for any given job classification in the survey. The organizations surveyed should be those with whom your agency competes when recruiting and retaining employees.

While it may be easy technically to answer the question, the problem can be complicated. The simple answer comes from the person responsible for advertising job openings. That individual knows what region is covered by the publications in which the ads are placed. But that information is not enough.

The reason, disagreement between the board, the employees, and the surveyor can scuttle an entire project. Nonprofit employees are concerned that the survey will only include other, low-paying nonprofits. At the same time, the board is concerned with issues like the impact of including agencies from other communities with a higher cost of living index.

The problem is compounded when different positions are recruited from different recruitment areas. Nonprofessional positions may be recruited locally while the agency may fill top positions with a national search. The survey should be designed to cover the appropriate area. This can mean sending out multiple surveys.

Because of the potential for conflict, the board should consider these issues early in the project planning stages. And all parties should be made aware of the board's decision. The following can serve as a guideline:

1. Conduct a local survey for clerical positions and include for-profit companies.
2. Survey technical and professional positions which are specific to nonprofit services with comparable agencies within your region. Include private-sector employers for technical and professional positions, like accountant, which are also found in the for-profit sector.
3. Survey similar organizations for executive position salaries within your recruitment area (regional or national).

Job classifications included in the survey are called *benchmark positions*. Benchmark positions are chosen for their ease of comparison with positions in other organizations. For instance, the responsibilities, skill, and education for the job classification of Social Work Supervisor may be fairly standard among the surveyed organizations, making it an ideal benchmark position. On the other hand, there may be a great deal of difference in the work of secretaries in one agency, where the title describes department head secretaries, and in a second agency, where the secretaries work in a pool. In this case, comparison is impossible and the position should not be used as a benchmark.

Choose classifications for benchmarking from all levels of the existing salary scale. This way there will be adequate anchors for the job evaluation process.

During analysis of the survey, some of the results may prove useless for the job evaluation process. There may not be enough responses for the one position, or you may discover that there was not a standard description of that classification. For that reason, make sure that the survey includes more positions than may be needed for the job evaluation process.

How many organizations should be surveyed? The more organizations included in and responding to the survey, the more valid the results. Establishing a statistically representative sample is probably too cumbersome a job, since 25 or more organizations would need to respond in each survey. In setting your goal, begin by expecting no more than a 50 percent survey return rate. If major competitors who are known to impact market rates are selected, a minimum survey return of 10 responses may be sufficient. That would require sending out at least 20 surveys.

Effective survey management can insure higher returns and higher survey quality. The following steps can help improve the quality of survey results:

1. Include a brief description of each classification, including major responsibilities, critical job skills, and required education level, in the description. (See Exhibit 14.5 for a sample survey form.)
2. Establish a deadline one month after mailing the surveys for return of the surveys. Include a stamped, return-addressed envelope with the survey. Offer confidentiality of the respondent's form and to send a copy of the aggregate survey results to the respondent upon completion of the study.

EXHIBIT 14.5 Sample Survey of Salary and Benefits

SAMPLE SALARY SURVEY

Occupation, Title, Description	Total No. Employees	Minimum/ Starting Wage/Hr.	Maximum Wage/Hr.	Weighted Avg. (Actual)	Comments
Janitor/Porter/Cleaner Performs general custodial duties, including cleaning floors, facilities, washrooms, and trash removal.					
Receptionist/Telephone Operator Receives visitors, takes incoming phone calls, may handle plant/factory paging system and outgoing calls. In addition, may perform simple clerical/typing duties.					
Secretary Serves as secretary for a department or division, sets up and maintains files and records and takes care of routine office functions without supervision. Meets and screens people, schedules appointments, handles correspondence not requiring a dictated reply, and allocates mail to subordinates.					
Administrative Assistant Serves as an assistant to an executive of the organization with regard to office management, personnel and fiscal management, allocation of work to others, and scheduling of meetings; makes decisions with regard to work flow assignments, and originates correspondence. Required: 4 years college and 4 years experience.					

BENEFITS SURVEY

COMPANY _____ PREPARED BY _____

ADDRESS _____ TELEPHONE (___)_____

CITY _____ STATE _____ ZIP _____ Send results?   YES ___ NO ___

General Information

No. employees:

    F/T hourly ___

    P/T hourly ___

    Salaried   ___

    TOTAL   ___

No. of hours in avg. work week:

    Hourly   ___

    Salaried ___

Are any employees unionized?   YES ___ NO ___

No. of unions: _____   No. employees covered: _____

EXHIBIT 14.5 *(Continued)*

Present agreements from _____ to _____

_____ to _____

Compensation Increase Policies

Do you grant across-the-board COLA increases?	YES ___	NO ___	Month ___
Do you grant market movement increases?	YES ___	NO ___	Month ___
Excluding the above, do you change salary ranges at a scheduled time?	YES ___	NO ___	Month ___

Anticipated percent increase this year? _____ %

Do you grant individual "merit" increases?   YES ___   NO ___

Do you grant automatic longevity increases?   YES ___   NO ___

Paid Vacation: How long does an employee need to work, to earn a particular period of vacation leave?

1 week: ___ years   3 weeks: ___ years   5 weeks: ___ years
2 weeks: ___ years   4 weeks: ___ years

Sick Leave:

Does the organization offer paid sick leave?   YES ___   NO ___

Days per year? _____   Incentive Plan?   YES ___   NO ___

Holidays:

Number of paid holidays offered per year? _____

Birthday as day off?   YES ___   NO ___

Number of floating or personal days off _____

Overtime Pay Policy indicate 1 (regular rate), 1½ (time-and-a-half), 2 (double-time), etc.

Over 8 hrs/day ___   Over 40 hrs/week ___
Saturdays ___   Sundays ___   Holidays ___

Premium Pay Policies:

2nd shift $ _____   3rd shift $ _____   Work environment $ _____

Variable by job title?   YES ___   NO ___

Call-in pay ___   Minimum hours _____   Rate of pay _____

Other Time Off:

Does your company offer paid funeral leave?   YES ___   NO ___

Days for immediate family ___   Days for others ___

Does your company offer paid leave for jury duty?   YES ___   NO ___

Does your company offer flex-time?   YES ___   NO ___

Does your company offer a compressed workweek?   YES ___   NO ___

Insurance Programs: If your company offers different programs for different employees, please report your policies as they cover your _____ employees.

Is weekly disability income insurance offered?   YES ___   NO ___

Duration of Coverage _____ weeks

Employer cost/employee $ _____   Employee contribution $ _____

(Continued

EXHIBIT 14.5 *(Continued)*

Health Insurance:

Company's contribution/employee for:

    Individual coverage: $ _____

    Dependent coverage: $ _____

Employee's contribution for:

    Individual coverage: $ _____

    Dependent coverage: $ _____

Maximum amount covered: $ _____   Deductible $ _____

Does your company offer:

Prescription coverage?   YES ___   NO ___

Dental coverage?   YES ___   NO ___

Optical coverage: YES ___   NO ___

Other: _____

Life Insurance:

Company's contribution/employee $ _____

Employee's contribution for basic amount $ _____

Amount of death benefit $ _____

Pension Plan:

Type: Earnings and service _____   Gain sharing _____   Other _____

Employee contribution: ___ % of cost

Other Benefits:

Tuition refund?   YES ___   NO ___

% of reimbursement _____ %

Other benefits?   YES ___   NO ___

Describe:

3. Call the respondents two weeks after the mailing to insure it was received and to check their intention for participation. This is the most critical step in insuring a high return rate.

4. On the deadline date, call any respondents who indicated that they would participate but have not responded and determine their response date. (Put two weeks extra into the project time schedule to allow for late returns.)

5. Call a sample (20–30%) of the respondents to discuss their survey response. Discuss any comments that they made about any classifications, and review their job descriptions for a sample of the classifications. This will help you determine the validity of their response. If the sample shows that the positions in the response match your survey positions, you can assume that all of the survey responses are valid.

Exhibit 14.5 includes a sample salary and benefits survey form. The form has been set up to simplify inputting the data into an electronic spreadsheet or database. Compensation survey software is available from a number of private sources. If you are working with a consultant, check to see if the consultant has developed software for this purpose and request a copy for use to upgrade your compensation plan in future years.

Exhibit 14.6 shows the results of one survey for the position of Janitor. The important information in the survey is at the bottom. The information includes an actual weighted average salary for all the survey participants, plus information about the range of salaries paid by the respondents for that classification. The survey weighted average salary is computed by averaging the weighted salaries in the individual responses. The individual weighted salaries are averages of actual salaries being paid, not of the midpoints of salary ranges in the reporting organizations. The weighted average is used to establish the preliminary midpoint for that position.

If the agency's policy will be to pay wages comparable to the market, the weighted average will be the preliminary midpoint. But the decision could be to establish wages at the bottom of the range, the first or third quartile, or the top of the range. If so, the amounts are computed from this average and the minimum and maximum salary averages.

To the greatest extent possible, benefit survey results should be reported and analyzed in comparable dollars. For instance, the survey's average monthly contribution to health and life insurance premiums is more important for assessing total compensation than the benefit received. (The information may help you identify other survey participants who are getting greater benefits from their premiums. In that case, contact the agency to find out more information.)

It is very difficult to compute time off in dollar terms. Rather than taking the time to do so, compare the total time off allocations with your agency.

Throughout the process, keep an eye on the relationship between the average cost

EXHIBIT 14.6 Example of Salary Survey Results for One Position

TYPE   Janitor/Porter/Cleaner

Code	No.	Minimum	Maximum	Weighted Average	Comments
000	1	$9,000	$9,000	$9,000	
002	9	5,700	10,280	9,630	
003		4,250	7,700		
013	53	8,030	10,130	9,270	
014					
015					
016	1	8,950	8,950	8,950	
017	10	4,230	7,440	6,300	
018	27	4,250	6,160	5,210	
019					
020	9	4,540	6,140	4,740	
021	15	6,200	10,140	9,360	
022	17	4,000	6,360	5,360	
023	1	3,800	5,500	5,000	
MINIMUM		$3.80	$ 5.50		
AVERAGE		$5.72	$ 7.98	$7.54	
MAXIMUM		$9.00	$10.28		

of benefits and the average wage rates in the survey. If your agency shows generally lower salaries but higher benefits than the survey results, reduce the value of the benchmark midpoints before moving on to job evaluation to compensate for the difference. There will be less conflict when a lower wage is proposed than when attempting to equalize wages while taking away existing benefits.

(D) JOB EVALUATION

(i) Job Evaluation Strategies

The core process for developing salary systems is job evaluation. Job evaluation combines market worth as identified through a salary survey, internal worth as identified through a ranking process, and job analysis information into a dollar value used to establish the midpoint salary for each position. There are three basic strategies for job evaluation; whole job comparison, point factor, and factor comparison. It is very important to distinguish between the three methodologies.

Whole job comparison determines the value of a position relative to all other positions in the organization, without reference to varying factors within that position. It is a ranking process which, in one sense, is an attempt to identify the pecking order within the organization and then establish salaries accordingly.

Whole job comparison must be done by a highly experienced person who is sensitive to the organization's culture, organizational structure, and job analysis issues. It is actually performed by taking completed job descriptions and shuffling them into an order which appears to match the needs of the organizational chart and culture, while conforming as close as possible to salary survey information.

Whole job comparison is no longer a popular evaluation method. The decisions involved are usually based on the expertise of one or two individuals, and are not easily validated.

The point factor system is the most popular evaluation strategy. The point factor process begins by breaking the job evaluation into constituent parts called *factors*. Examples of factors include knowledge, responsibility, and mental effort. The number of factors varies from one system to another, and can range as high as eighteen.

Each job factor for a job classification is compared against an externally developed matrix of points assigned to that factor. For instance, under the factor "Education," the system may give fifty points for a high school diploma, seventy-five points for a two-year college associates' degree, and one hundred points for a four-year college degree.

Points represent dollars within the system. The final midpoint salary awarded to a job classification is derived from the weighted sum of points it receives.

The point/value relationship is usually established in a two-step process. First, the firm determines the weighting of each factor to the whole job. Exhibit 14.7 shows examples of weightings for various point factor schemes. The weighting results in identifying how many points should be assigned to a given factor. For instance, the system may award between five hundred to a thousand points on the responsibility factor scale, while only awarding between fifty and one hundred points on the mental effort scale.

The second step, actually assigning a dollar value for each point, is done externally through regression analysis of large databases of salary surveys.

Consulting firms which specialize in point factor–based evaluation now involve employee groups in the rating process. An employee committee will, individually and then

EXHIBIT 14.7 Factor Comparison and Point Factor Systems: Two Alternative Weighting Systems

Factor	NEMA-NMTA*	XEROX Corporation
Skill	50 %	55 %
Responsibility	20	40
Mental effort	7.5	—
Physical effort	7.5	2.5
Working conditions	15	2.5

National Electrical Manufacturers Association-National Motels Trades Association

collectively, assign points to each job classification based on the matrix information assigned to any given factor.

The factor comparison methodology attempts to combine the strengths of both the whole job and point factor systems. Like the whole job system, factor comparison allows for a ranking of positions based on internal, organizational realities instead of an external standard. Like the point factor system, factor comparison breaks down the job evaluation process to the factor level, allowing more information to be used in making ranking decisions.

Factor comparison enables a comparison of jobs on from four to seven factors. Standard factors used include responsibility, skill, mental effort, physical effort, and working conditions. To insure reliability in the ranking, these or other factors that are used are given specific definitions. An example of such definitions is given in Exhibit 14.8.

Four steps comprise the factor comparison method: (1) Each factor is assigned a weighting relative to the other factors. These may come from other systems such as in Exhibit 14.7 or may be defined by the organization. (2) Job classifications are ranked for each independent factor. (3) Benchmark classifications from the salary survey are assigned dollar values under each factor. The amounts come from multiplying the weighted average salary for the classifications in the salary survey by the percent weight for each factor. (4) Dollar amounts are awarded for each factor in each classification according to its ranking in the factor relative to the benchmark positions.

The factor comparison method can be easily integrated into an employee participation process. The methodology and employee participation process will be described in detail in part three of this section.

(ii) Bringing Employees into the Job Evaluation Process

Both the point factor and factor comparison methods can be adjusted to include employee participation. When properly done, employee participation reduces organizational conflict while increasing client ownership of the compensation study results. When done poorly, employee participation results in politicization of the process while exposing the potential for unfair discrimination in the results.

Three keys to effective employee participation are: (1) selection of task forces from a representative group of employees; (2) group decision by consensus; and (3) the fact that the final salary assignment for job classifications is not made by the task force members.

Most small to medium-sized nonprofits can perform the job evaluation task with one task force. The task force should include from seven to fourteen employees representing

EXHIBIT 14.8 Factor Definition

SKILL: Measures the level of education needed to establish a base of understanding, common language, and professional or technical knowledge for performance of the job. Also measures the amount of experience that must be obtained from working in other positions to develop the knowledge, skills, and abilities necessary for the job, and the complexity of the problem-solving processes used in the job.

MENTAL EFFORT: Measures the amount of judgment and analysis, such as the amount of independent judgment required and how much leeway is available in decision making. Also measures the extent to which creative mental skills are required, such as the need for ingenuity, resourcefulness in adapting, and developing new solutions or methods; mental demands, such as the amount of attention needed (normal vs. continuous or close); and the duration and extent of concentration needed.

PHYSICAL EFFORT: Measures the amount of physical exertion necessary to perform the job, including type of exertion, extent of strain, and duration. Coordination and need for dexterity are also measured.

RESPONSIBILITY: Measures the extent to which supervision is needed: how much supervisor responsibility is in the position; the extent of and purpose for contact with others; the position's role in developing policies and procedures; and the effect of errors on the organization's ability to achieve its purpose. The amount of responsibility for safeguarding funds, valuables, or equipment should be considered. Also described as the amount of accountability in the position.

WORKING CONDITIONS: Measures the extent to which employees in the position are exposed to physical and environmental hazards that may affect their health or safety.

various constituencies within the organization. These numbers are effective for generating consensus-based decision making. The group can be selected from a combination of volunteers and recruits. However, it is not wise to force an individual onto the task force.

The obvious constituencies represented in the group are managers and nonmanagers. Restricting the task force to just managers meets the traditional concept of chain-of-command, but acts contrary to what the organization may be attempting in other areas of its total quality management program. The attempts to use just managers also makes it very difficult to establish a differentiated classification structure for managers. The group does fine ranking nonmanagement positions. But the participants tend to smooth over real differences that exist between their own positions.

Other constituencies can also be represented. Obvious employee groups include clerical, technical, and professional employee groups. If the agency perceives that a problem exists for a particular job classification, it is wise to include that classification in the task force. There must also be a fair representation of minorities and women, especially since most compensation discrimination issues arise from an insensitivity to diversity issues.

The task force participants perform two critical functions in addition to completing the job evaluation process. Even though the consensus-based decision-making process removes the political nature of constituency representation, the participants are seen as representing the interest of their constituencies. This representative process results in more members of the organization feeling that they have had their say in the decisions, even if they did not get the results they wanted. This establishes a sense of fairness to the process. At the same time, the members communicate task force achievements. The employees recognize the project as an organizational decision instead of the decision of a "cold, disinterested, outside consultant."

As part of the organizational process for the task force, the group should agree that decisions will be made by consensus instead of by a vote. Averaging point spreads or voting on rankings brings about strange results. For instance, five task force members may rank Job Classification A at number 3 in a 10-classification list, while five rank the classification seventh. Job Classification B on the same list is ranked at 5 by all participants. If averaging is used, than both jobs are equal. Yet none of the participants believe they are equal, and their constituencies won't believe it either. Consensus discussion resolves this conflict, producing a more credible outcome.

Make it clear at the beginning that the task force will not assign final salaries to any job classification or employee. The task force product is a ranking that establishes a raw midpoint rating job classification. That assignment will be adjusted by the consultant as job classifications are grouped into pay ranges. Final position salaries will be determined based on identifying the position's current salary in relationship to the proposed salary range in a series of cost options for plan implementation.

Task force members are, of course, relieved to know that they are not responsible for determining the final salaries of their peers and friends.

The employee participation strategy provides one other important benefit. After the project is finished, the task force remains available for job evaluations of new positions and requests for classification upgrades. Building such in-house capacity to manage the new compensation system should be a critical consideration for any compensation program.

(iii) Employee Participation in a Factor Comparison Evaluation

The *factor comparison job evaluation method* mixes some of the best strategies from both the whole job and point factor methodologies. As with the whole job method, factor comparison is a ranking of positions. However, whole ranking tends to reinforce an existing pecking order that is usually based on responsibility alone. Factor comparison ranks positions on from four to seven critical factors, including responsibility, working conditions, skill level, and mental and physical effort. Multiple rankings of this nature increase the objective nature of the results in a manner similar to the point factor system.

Employee task forces work through six steps to complete their part in the factor comparison exercise.

Step 1: Task Force Orientation. Task force participants are introduced to the job analysis methodology and information used by the consultant to create job descriptions. Strategies used to differentiate skill, knowledge, and responsibility levels within the job descriptions are clearly explained. The factors being used in the study are clearly defined and explained so that all members have the same information available to them.

Step 2: Individual Ranking. Task force members review job descriptions and job analysis information for each job classification. They then individually rank the job classifications for each of the evaluation factors. By separating factors, jobs like janitor should fall low on skill levels, yet high on the scale defining working conditions. If the factors are defined in a way similar to Exhibit 14.8, it will be impossible for any one job to fall at the top or bottom of all factor scales.

Step 3: Develop Group Consensus Rankings. The consultant shares the individual ranking results on one and then another factor and facilitates a discussion to achieve a consensus ranking of job classifications for each factor. This is the hardest part of the process. A good facilitator will enable group members to share their reasoning. Usually, rankings change when individuals realize that they did not apply the factor descriptions in a consistent manner or that they missed job analysis information. Discussion leads to the group developing a consistent use of the job analysis and factor definition information. It is useful to keep records of any group decisions regarding definitions for later use analyzing new positions once the plan is implemented.

Step 4: Insert Benchmark Values Into Rankings. The consultant converts salary survey information for usable benchmark positions into factor values based on the factor weightings established by the consultant or previously agreed to by the board. For instance, the survey weighted average for Nurse may be $10.45 per hour. The factors may be weighted at Responsibility = 45%, Skill = 45%, Mental Effort = 2.5%, Physical Effort = 2.5%, and Working Conditions = 5% of the total salary. The salary is then broken down so that Responsibility = $4.70, Skill = $4.70, Physical and Mental Effort each equal $.26 and Working Conditions = $.52. These values are then inserted into the task force values as shown in Exhibit 14.9. Some minor adjustments are made when a position which is generally ranked high has a low ranking for the specific factor.

Step 5: Assign Values to Nonbenchmark Positions. The task force fills in the blanks with dollar values for the nonbenchmark positions. At this point the rule is that the values assigned must maintain the ranking previously agreed to. This step establishes the distance between each job classification within the ranking process. When done, the task force has completed its role in the process. However, it is advisable to go back to the task force after Step 6. The task force is given the chance to review the result of their work and consider adjustments.

Step 6: Determine Raw Midpoint Rate. The consultant adds together the values assigned to each position on each factor to determine the total value, or raw midpoint rate, for the position. The raw midpoint rate determines the final ranking of the positions.

After the raw midpoint rate is established, the consultant uses regression analysis to bring job classifications into pay classification or pay ranges. The goal is to bring together, into single pay range, job classifications whose raw midpoint rates are close.

From this process, the consultant should be able to provide a compensation rule by which the agency can assign future positions into pay ranges. The rule will identify the cutoff points for range assignments from raw midpoint rate data. Exhibit 14.10 is an example of the decision rule.

The consultant should make sure that a position is not excluded from a higher pay range just because its raw midpoint rate is just a few cents off the required minimum for the next range. As with all job evaluation processes, there is some subjectivity to the process. Excluding a case of this nature from a higher range will probably be overturned in the grievance process through political pressure anyway.

(iv) Establishing Pay Ranges

Creating competitive salary midpoints represents the critical step toward an effective compensation program. Expanding the system from the midpoints into salary ranges makes it possible to link the compensation and performance management systems.

EXHIBIT 14.9 Benchmark Decision Sheet

SKILL FACTOR

Position	Final Value ($)
Dir. of Dental Health I	_____
Dir. of Nursing	7.32
Dir. of Health Education	_____
Dir. of Envir. Health	_____
Dir. of Communicable Diseases	6.60
Dir. of Nutrition	_____
Dir. of Administration	_____
Program Consultant	_____
Public Health Nurse	5.88
Sanitarian I	_____
Nutritionist	5.45
Sanitarian II	_____
Assoc. Nutritionist	_____
Clinic Nurse I	_____
Communicable Diseases Investigator	_____
Dental Hygienist	4.60
Departmental Secretary	_____
Accounting Clerk	_____
Vision and Hearing Supervisor	_____
Intake Specialist	_____
Dental Assistant	2.13

The final midpoint position relative to market worth is a policy decision that should be decided by the board at the beginning of the project. The position of the midpoint has a major impact on the agency's ability to recruit and retain employees. This decision impacts most other human resource management issues in the organization.

There are three primary choices for the board:

Choice 1: Establish the midpoint above the market value. Establishing above-market pay helps with both recruitment and retention of employees. The higher salaries will result in more qualified applicants. Selecting a more qualified applicant reduces training costs and startup time. Reducing turnover reduces training costs. Larger agencies who recruit from smaller agencies must consider this option, realizing that their employees were trained in smaller, related agencies.

Choice 2: Establish the midpoint below market value. This second choice reduces the quality of applicants since qualified applicants in other agencies will be less likely to apply. At the same time, turnover will be higher as your employees go on to better paying, and usually larger agencies. Organizations selecting this option must expect to offset the application loss and turnover with higher training costs to maintain quality. Smaller agencies with less funding will frequently select this cash-saving strategy and accept the fact that they are a training ground for their employees' upward mobility.

Choice 3: Maintain the midpoint at market value. Assuming that the survey results are valid, the third choice is a half-way point between the two positions. It is most viable politically because employees and board members agree that employees are being recognized for their real worth.

Pay ranges can be any breadth desired. Traditional ranges run 10, 20, 25, or 30 percent above and below the midpoint. In other words, a range may have from a 20 to a 60 percent spread.

Some of the issues raised by the midpoint choices can be offset by the breadth of the salary range. A wide range on a below-average midpoint can help retain current employees. However, the starting salary rate, which is usually held to the first quartile of the range, may need to be extended to enable recruiting more qualified people. That decision would negate the reason for selecting a low midpoint value in the first place.

In like fashion, a wide range on an above-average salary can help bring in less qualified applicants for training while strengthening the retention rate. This may be the ideal situation for agencies with unique services requiring new employee training anyway.

The range spread can also be related to organizational structure. The wider the spread, the more likely one range will overlap another one or more ranges. A problem generally arises when an overlap exists between supervisor and subordinate or when the two positions are on the same career path. Range overlaps should be allowed between subordinate and supervisory positions, if the organization includes limited chances for promotion or there is an achievement-based pay-for-performance system. In such systems, employees choosing not to become supervisors continue to have room and motivation for growth, thereby thwarting the Peter Principle (which suggests that everyone in the agency will rise to their greatest level of incompetence).

The impact of the overlap on promotion can be managed with a personnel policy

EXHIBIT 14.10 Example of Range Assignment Rule

UNADJUSTED SALARY		
Minimum	Maximum	Range Assignment
$20.10	$21.19	1
19.10	20.09	2
18.00	19.09	3
16.90	17.99	4
15.80	16.89	5
14.70	15.79	6
13.60	14.69	7
12.50	13.59	8
11.40	12.49	9
10.30	11.39	10
9.20	10.29	11
8.10	9.19	12
5.90	8.09	13

such as, "The salary for an individual who is promoted will be within the first quartile of the salary range except when the employee's current salary already falls within or above the first quartile of the new position, in which case the employee will receive a raise of between 10 and 20 percent above his or her current salary."

When there is an overlap in career ladder pay ranges, such as between two clerical positions, the confusion will be more frequent. Organizations should try to minimize the overlap in these cases to provide ample motivation for pursuing promotions. This will result in pay conflicts developing only for promotions onto a different career ladder.

Often the final decision factor for range development is project implementation cost. Most compensation programs offer the board a choice of two implementation strategies: Nonprobationary employees who are currently paid below the salary range be brought up to the bottom of the range, or all employees below the midpoint of the range be brought up to the midpoint. The first option presents a problem when long-term employees are brought up to the bottom of the range. Long-term employees know that the midpoint represents the salary of the average performer, so they resent the idea of working with new employees hired in at the same salaries.

Bringing everyone up to midpoint makes the statement that the study is not a judgment on individual performance. But the strategy can be three times as expensive to implement.

When a decision is made to bring people below the range to the bottom, a link is made between range width and implementation costs. Assuming that a number of employees are being paid below the midpoint, the wider the range, the greater number of those employees who will not require upgrading. So the wider the range, the less costly the implementation.

The pay range issue always raises the question of how to handle cases where the study identifies employees who are being paid above the range. The traditional response to the problem is to *red-circle* the employee's pay. This is done in one of three ways:

1. Employees in red-circled positions receive no pay raises until their salary falls within the pay range. This is not a recommended strategy.
2. The red-circled employee's salary remains the same but the individual receives an annual bonus based on the pay-for-performance plan guidelines instead of a salary increase. When the position is vacated, the new hire is brought in at the appropriate rate for the position.
3. The employee receives a pay raise each year based on performance. When the position is vacated, the new hire is brought in at the appropriate rate for the position.

(E) MAINTAINING COMMUNICATION THROUGHOUT THE PROJECT

Nothing is more stress provoking to an employee than to know her salary is being discussed behind closed doors. Images of smoke-filled rooms and political trades, and similar disheartening scenarios immediately come to mind. The more the employee is faced with such images, the more distrustful she will become of the project.

The following communication strategy will reduce tension and conflict throughout the project time line:

1. Hold an employee-orientation meeting at the beginning of the project to discuss the project, employee concerns and fears, and employee expectations of the project results. Explain the project schedule, the nature of decision making, grievance system, and employee participation strategies.
2. Until the task force is organized, send periodic notes to the employees to update them on the study.
3. Use the bench audit process as an additional method for communicating with employees.
4. Share draft job descriptions with the employees before they are carved in stone.
5. Have the task force take and disseminate minutes of their deliberations. Train the task force secretary to screen out sensitive information.
6. Send a note to each employee describing that employee's proposed salary range, including an explanation of where the position will fall into place in the system.
7. Hold employee debriefing sessions to explain results and contact information if questions arise from results. Include public recognition of the task force's work. Answer all questions during the session until employee concerns are exhausted. Use task force members to help with answers.

14.4　*Implementation and Management Issues*

(A)　MAINTAINING SYSTEM INTEGRITY USING THE TASK FORCE

How many nonprofits have experienced this problem: A current employee is given a new task. The employee complains that the new task adds responsibilities and should be compensated with a pay raise. The agency rule restricts raises within a job classification to the annual performance increase. So to placate the employee, the department head gives the employee a new title and starts politicking for the pay raise. If the budget allows it, the new job is created with a new salary. Otherwise, the employee gets disgruntled and refuses to do the new tasks. Once one employee successfully plays the game, the rest join in. Within two years, the compensation system that cost $20,000 has, in practice, been discarded.

This does not have to be the case. A well-implemented system includes procedures which reject insidious job-creep demands while providing employees with an objective strategy for assessing job changes. The same process also helps the organization integrate new positions into job and pay classifications. As a final benefit, the system supports the agency's budgeting proposals for fair wages for positions covered under governmental or other grants.

In larger organizations, these compensation management issues are traditionally left in the hands of the personnel department. However, the employee participation structure used in the compensation study leaves the organization with a well-trained group capable of making objective decisions which support maintenance of the system.

The following procedures for requests for pay classification changes institutionalize the task force process and reduce the politicization of the system.

1. Employees and supervisors may request a change in a job classification, and supervisors may request the establishment of new job classifications. The request is made to the personnel director. Upon making such a request, the employee (for an existing position) or the supervisor requesting a new job classification will complete a Job Analysis Questionnaire (JAQ). The personnel director will review the questionnaire and conduct a bench audit if necessary. If, upon review of the JAQ and bench audit data, the personnel director believes that the position requires changing to a different but existing job classification, such shall be recommended to the executive director. If, upon review of the information, the personnel director determines that a new job classification is needed for the position, a new job description will be written and sent to the executive director for recommendation for approval. If the personnel director determines from the information that a new job classification should not be established, a recommendation of that nature shall be sent to the executive director along with a copy of the JAQ and of the current job description. The decision of the executive director shall be subject to the grievance procedure.

2. Employees may request a change in pay classification after successfully receiving a change to a new job classification. Classifying newly established positions shall follow this same procedure.

3. The Salary Classification Task Force, facilitated by the personnel director, will be responsible for proposing pay classification upgrades and assignment of new job classifications to the executive director.

4. The original membership of the task force was established during the classification study. The task force will develop rules for rotation and replacement of its members.

5. The task force will operate as follows:
   a. The task force will be called to order by the personnel director.
   b. The personnel director will facilitate individual and then joint consensus ranking of the position for each of the five factors used in the study using the original ranking scale developed in the study. The ranking decision will be, "Where does this job classification fit into the existing rankings for this factor?"
   c. When consensus is reached on the rankings, the task force will assign a cash value under each factor for the position through individual and consensus. The value must fall between the cash values for the positions just above and below the position as ranked in that factor.
   d. The personnel director adds together the cash value for each factor, and consults the Rules of Classification Assignment to arrive at the tentative pay classification for that job classification.
   e. The personnel director reports the task force's results to the executive director who will make a recommendation to the board concerning the reclassification request. If the recommendation differs from that of the task force, the task force's decision and a written explanation of the executive director's decision to differ shall accompany the recommendation.

6. If the new pay classification for the job classification is lower than the one from which the job classification was created, the incumbent employee shall remain

in the existing pay range, but new employees shall be hired in on the new range.

7. Reclassification decisions are grieveable through the agency's grievance system.

(B) HANDLING IMPLEMENTATION COMPLAINTS DURING SYSTEM IMPLEMENTATION

Many people will not be happy with the results of the compensation study. In most cases, employees believe they deserve higher salaries. Either because of survey results or the implementation strategy, these expected raises do not materialize. Luckily, if there has been a strong communication program throughout the study, most of these employees will still accept the results.

However, some employees will still believe that their pay is unfair in relation to others in the organization. These are the individuals who will take action against the study, most likely by politicizing their complaint to the board. The problem can be addressed by incorporating a complaint system into the study itself. The complaint process should be clear from the start, with a written description handed to employees during the project orientation meetings.

Complaints are possible at two points; the assignment to a job classification and the assignment to a pay range. Each type can be handled differently.

Complaints about job classifications and job descriptions are generally easy to handle. After the employee has reviewed the first draft job description, the consultant will review requested changes. Usually the consultant will either go ahead and make the changes or meet with the employee to discuss the request. A proposed final description should be sent back to the employee.

The overwhelming majority of job classification complaints are resolved at this stage. For that reason, if the employee is still unhappy with the job description or the assignment to that classification, the employee should be allowed to use the agency's regular grievance system.

Complaints concerning pay classification (range) assignments are a little more complicated. The employee should be notified of the proposed pay range assignment upon completion of the assignment by the task force and consultant. The employee is not notified of any actual salary change at this time, although he is notified of the rules which are proposed for implementing the ranges. This is because the actual salary change will still be based first on bringing the employee's salary into range, and then on performance—as determined by the supervisor and not anyone involved in the study.

If one or more employees in a job classification have a complaint about their pay range, the task force is reconvened to hear the employees' reasoning. At the same time, the task force, through its chair, explains the basis for its reasoning, reviewing the ranking of the position on each factor. This description helps the employee better understand how the decision was arrived at and helps the employee focus his or her explanation into terms that may affect the task force's decision.

Following the meeting, the task force reconsiders its factor rankings for that position based on the new information received. A report of its recommendations, showing either to change or not to change, is made in writing to the executive director with a copy to the employee.

The overwhelming majority of complaints are resolved in the meeting between the employee and the task force. The meetings are usually very productive, and help the task force recognize when groupthink was a part of its decision process. And the employee better recognizes what is being valued by the agency, especially when the factor weightings are explained. But when the issue is still not resolved, the employee should be directed to make use of the agency's grievance policy.

(C) THE ROLE OF THE BOARD IN COMPENSATION MANAGEMENT

The role of the nonprofit board is to develop the strategy of the agency and to insure that the strategy is being implemented. The compensation program, representing as much as 80 percent of the agency's operating budget, is part of the strategic management of the organization. Considering the salaries of individuals, which places board members in the position of performance evaluator, is not a strategic endeavor.

The core strategic compensation issue is to determine the role played by market worth for agency positions. To what extent does the board feel it is necessary to compensate employees at, above, or below the market worth for its positions? Market worth also establishes the issue of whether the market for comparison is the nonprofit industry or both nonprofit and profit-making organizations.

It is generally believed that an agency must pay above-market value if it wants to provide quality services and products. A more strategic view shows that quality can be achieved when paying lower entry-level wages by increasing available training funds. Low wages and little training are, of course, the deathbed of quality.

The corollary strategic issue is the agency's ability to pay. The decision to pay market value instead of going for the cheapest available employee requires increasing revenues or decreasing services. The systemic question is whether the agency's revenues will increase over time as a result of its improved quality as a service provider to offset the increased expenses.

The other major concern is proper implementation of the board-approved compensation system. This represents the board's role in quality control.

The board can perform the control function in two ways. First, as with most other human resource issues, the board acts as the last step in the grievance procedure for most small to medium-sized agencies. The information discussed in the grievance hearing enables the board to determine whether its wishes were actually carried out.

It's second action is to assess the quality of compensation information presented to it. Is the information strategic or operational? Operational information includes issues like individual pay raise requests, job descriptions, performance evaluations, and classification upgrade requests.

Strategic information includes salary comparison with competitors, budget impact statements, tracking of the number and disposition of grievances, career ladders, and pay classification assignment rules. When planning staff pay increases, the board should want to see the money available and the recommended organizationwide range changes. The board should also be looking at wage distributions based on race, sex, and so on to insure that the salaries are being paid out equitably.

14.5   Integrating the Compensation Program into the Performance Management Program

Merit pay fails because the performance management program is not integrated into the compensation program. The result is that the compensation program runs the performance system. The opposite is necessary to make the system work.

The following process, Compensation for Excellence, is a system which resolves the major compensation-based complaints against merit pay. The system is designed to award top performers with the highest pay increases when computed on a cash basis. At the same time, the system insures that funds are available for salary increases throughout the year. The system also insures that individuals at the top of the scale cannot top out. Individuals whose performance lags behind find that while they continue to get pay increases, their position falls in the salary range. And as a side benefit, agencies using this system are able to build their fund balance over a period of years.

The system starts with the agency's determination of the average annual increase to be awarded. In the ideal world, this would be determined solely on the amount by which the midpoints need to be raised to maintain market equity. In reality, the amount will be a trade-off between maintaining market equity with budget considerations. A what-if exercise is performed between this and the budgeting strategy below until the cash value of the increase equals funds available for the increases.

According to *The Performance Technologies Workbook*, the budget for increases in the salary schedule are computed as follows:

1. Determine the percentage increase for the salary system—how much to raise the midpoints of the system. That percent is applied to the midpoints of all ranges.
2. Compute new salary ranges by adding and subtracting the appropriate percent (breadth of range) of each new midpoint amount to establish new minimum and maximum levels for the ranges.
3. Determine the budget for implementing the new ranges by computing the difference between the old and new maximum for each range and multiplying that amount by the number of employees in that salary range, regardless of where they fall in the range. Then add up the cost for each range to identify the total cost for increasing the system.

Example

a. The agency decides to raise the midpoints 5 percent next year.
b. The old midpoint for level 13 is $16,150, with the minimum at $12,920 and the maximum at $19,380.
c. The new midpoint will be ($16,150* 1.05) = $16,957. The new minimum will be ($16,957 * 0.8) = $13,565, and the new maximum will be ($16,957 * 1.2) = $20,348.
d. The amount budgeted for pay raises for this range is ($20,248 – $19,380) = $868, times the number of job positions at this pay classification (3), for a total budgeted amount of $2,604.

4. Do similar calculations for each range, and add up the total budgeted amounts for each range to determine the amount to be budgeted for raises that year.

This budgeting strategy makes it possible for all employees to receive the highest merit increase for their pay classification as possible. At the same time, the procedure results in a positive fund balance at the end of each year, unless everyone receives the top rating. That balance can be carried over to decrease the cost of management of this program in future years, or it can be applied to other agency needs, including improving the cash basis of the agency over time.

The second part of the process defines how individual pay increases are awarded. *The Performance Technologies Workbook* provides the following steps:

1. Individual salary increases are based on individual performance as identified through the organization's performance appraisal policies.
2. Each performance appraisal provides for an overall rating for the employee on a five-point scale ranging from "Excellent" to "Poor" performance. (This can be the average of the ratings on the performance standards, or some computation based on a weighting of the standards.)
3. Individual employee pay raises are computed according to the following schedule:
   a. An employee receiving a top rating receives a raise equal to the dollar amount by which the maximum of his or her range was raised in the budgeting process, regardless of where the employee is currently being paid in his or her pay range.
   b. An employee receiving the middle rating receives a raise equal to the dollar amount by which the midpoint of his or her range was raised in the budgeting process, regardless of where the employee is currently being paid in his or her pay range.
   c. An employee receiving a poor rating receives a raise equal to the dollar amount by which the minimum of his or her range was raised in the budgeting process, regardless of where the employee is currently being paid in his or her pay range. (The organization may choose to give no raise to an employee receiving a poor rating instead. However, it should be noted that the proposed system acts to reduce a person's position in a range if performance is poor, without resulting in employees being paid below the minimum of their range.)
   d. Discretion can be used to compute increases for those employees falling in between top and middle, and middle and poor, if the discretion maintains the procedure in the previous three steps.

Example
Using the example from the budgeting section above:

An employee in this pay classification who receives the top rating would receive a pay increase of ($20,348 − $19,380) = $968, regardless of where the employee presently falls on the range. This will move the top performers into the upper levels of the range, and continue to give them the top pay increases if they maintain top performance.

An employee in this pay classification who receives a middle rating will receive a pay increase of ($16,957 – $16,150) = $807, regardless of where the employee presently falls on the range. This will keep average performers at midpoint, move former top performers whose work is no longer tops slowly back to midpoint, and will move average performers who are at the bottom of the scale eventually to midpoint.

An employee in this pay classification who receives a poor rating will receive a pay increase of ($13,565 – $12,920) = $645, regardless of where the person currently falls in the salary scale. This will keep a poor performer who is on the bottom at the bottom, and move others down toward the bottom of the scale over time.

An employee in this pay classification who receives a rating between top and middle can receive an increase between $968 and $807, and a rating between middle performance and poor can receive an increase between $807 and $645.

The first-year cost of implementing a Compensation for Excellence program can be high. Certainly the agency will not be used to putting aside what appears to be a large chunk of revenue in one year. But the carryover helps future years until, like a self-insurance program, the fund begins to run itself.

14.6   Conclusion

Performance management and self-renewal are intrinsically linked. The effectiveness of a performance management system is enhanced when it is possible to link it to a motivational compensation system. Yet all too often in the past, the compensation system has driven the performance management system as organizations have attempted to cope with increasing demands and tightening budgets.

As this chapter has shown, this does not have to be the case. Linking an effective performance management system with a comprehensive compensation system provides the rewards needed to increase motivation and organizational loyalty.

Compensation management strategies are in flux as the total quality movement raises questions about the old procedures. What seems to be emerging is recognition that employees can participate in developing the system, and that a link between compensation and performance is a critical step in building high-quality organizations—especially if quality is the primary performance standard throughout the organization.

Suggested Readings

Baird, Lloyd S., Beatty, Richard W., and Schneier, Craig Eric. *The Performance Appraisal Sourcebook*. 1985. Amherst, MA: Human Resource Development Press.

Baird, Lloyd S., Beatty, Richard W., and Schneier, Craig Eric. 1988. *The Strategic Human Resource Management Sourcebook*. Amherst, MA: Human Resource Development Press.

Deming, W. Edwards. 1986. *Out of the Crisis*. Cambridge: MIT-CAES.

Jones, John W., Steffy, Brian D., and Bray, Douglas W. 1991. *Applying Psychology in Business: The Handbook for Managers and Human Resource Professionals*. Lexington, MA: Lexington Books.

Latham, Gary P. and Wexley, Kenneth N. 1981. *Increasing Productivity Through Performance Appraisal*. Reading, MA: Addison-Wesley.

Michaels, Mark. 1988. *The Performance Technologies Workbook*. Champaign, IL: People Technologies.

Mtazer, John Jr. 1984. *Creative Personnel Practices: New Ideas for Local Government*. 1984. International City Management Association.

Schneir, Craig E. and Beatty, Richard W. 1979. "Combining BARS and MBO: Using an Appraisal System to Diagnose Performance Problems." *Personnel Administrator* (September), 42.

Werther, William B., Jr. and Davis, Keith. 1985. *Personnel Management and Human Resources*, 2nd ed. New York: McGraw-Hill.

PART III

Communication, Fund Raising, and Information Management

15 ▼ Marketing

Eugene M. Johnson, DBA, MBA
University of Rhode Island

There are no magic formulas for successful marketing. The principles and concepts presented in this chapter, however, will help nonprofit directors and managers plan, organize, and control their marketing activities. The key step for nonprofits are: to recognize the importance of marketing and to develop a marketing plan. Having a plan will help everyone within the organization focus on what is most important—identifying the needs of clients and supporters and determining the best ways to meet those needs.

15.1 *Introduction*

(A) MARKETING AFFECTS EVERYONE

Marketing is an exciting, dynamic discipline that affects everyone's life in many ways. Everyone is a consumer, and many people are part of the marketing process, as salespeople, advertising executives, product managers, wholesalers, retailers, and so forth.

For most of its history, marketing has been viewed as strictly a for-profit business function. This is no longer true. Marketing has become a significant activity for nonprofit organizations with important contributions to make to overall quality improvement. Consider the following:

- A large midwestern hospital conducts inpatient surveys to determine the level of patient satisfaction and to identify suggestions for improved service.
- An art museum uses an "art-mobile" to bring famous works of art to a city's neighborhoods.
- A Roman Catholic religious order employs a national advertising campaign to recruit candidates for the priesthood.
- A public television station features a "900" number during program breaks to request contributions.

These are just a few examples of the many nonprofit organizations that have successfully applied marketing techniques during the past few years. The application of marketing research tools, advertising, personal selling skills, and the like has changed the way many nonprofit organizations operate.

(B) MARKETING INVOLVES EXCHANGE

Most definitions of marketing refer to marketing as an exchange process. From a business standpoint, this process involves at least two parties—buyer and seller. Each party gives up something of value and receives something of value.

Because marketing activities bring about exchanges, marketing is an essential function in an economic system. In a free-enterprise system, resources are allocated by the interaction of supply and demand in the marketplace. Marketing activities and institutions provide the framework and mechanisms for this interaction and for the exchange that is taking place.

Although business aspects of marketing are very important, business-oriented definitions of marketing have been found lacking in recent years. Critics observe that marketing involves a wide range of activities and organizations and should be viewed from a broader perspective. They point out that marketing takes place in many nonprofit organizations, such as hospitals, universities, and social and government agencies. These new applications of marketing are further evidence of its growing importance in our society. Any definition must recognize that marketing is a fundamental human activity and that marketing decisions affect everyone's welfare.

The definition of the American Marketing Association provides a description of marketing in its broader context:

> *Marketing is the process of planning and executing the conception, pricing, promotion, and distribution of ideas, goods, and services to create exchanges that satisfy individual and organizational goals.*

While it includes exchange as a key part, this definition expands the marketing process to include all types of organizations. This has been termed the "broadened" or "generic" view of marketing. The importance and application of marketing to nonprofit organizations and problems are recognized. As in business, a carefully planned, coordinated marketing program can help a nonprofit organization reach its goals, whether they are to attract more members, to increase donations, or provide better client service.

15.2 *Broadening the Scope of Marketing*

(A) EARLY VIEWS OF MARKETING

The earliest forms of marketing started in primitive economic systems. Specialization and division of labor allowed early economies to achieve a production surplus. This necessitated an exchange process. For example, one person's surplus of farm produce might be traded for another's surplus of clothing items. This process of a face-to-face exchange of goods and services is known as bartering. It still characterizes some types of transactions.

The development of monetary systems permitted the emergence of selling, by which goods and services were exchanged for some form of currency. Later, selling on credit further expanded the selling process. For most of history, selling has dominated marketing thought. From the first widespread use of money to the advent of the marketing concept following World War II—a span of several thousands of years—selling was the basic thrust of marketing thought and activity.

Marketing as we know it today began to emerge when marketing support activities were recognized. Staff activities such as advertising, marketing research, and product management were acknowledged to be important segments of the total marketing program. The marketing concept's emphasis on *customer satisfaction* as the organization's prime objective signaled the acceptance of marketing as a major function within a business enterprise. The marketing concept was widely accepted by industry, and customer orientation became the basic premise for most business philosophies.

(B) MARKETING THOUGHT TODAY

Concern for customer satisfaction will certainly remain a critical ingredient of sales and marketing thought. However, since widespread adoption of the marketing concept, several proposals have been suggested that advance or extend the concept of marketing beyond the traditional limits of a business organization. These and earlier changes in sales and marketing are shown in Exhibit 15.1.

(i) Broadening Concept
This view sees marketing as a pervasive societal activity that goes well beyond the selling of toothpaste, soap, or steel. First proposed by Kotler and Levy (1979), the broadening concept views marketing as being an important activity of nonbusiness, as well as

---

EXHIBIT 15.1 Advancement of Marketing Thought

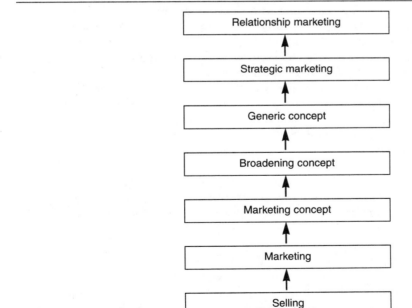

business, organizations. The ideas, philosophies, and concepts espoused by museums, government agencies, labor unions, colleges and universities, hospitals, charitable organizations, and other nonprofit entities can also be marketed. In fact, it has been argued that many worthwhile social projects have failed simply because they were not marketed effectively.

Although some have disagreed with this contention, the broadening concept has been generally accepted by marketing scholars and practitioners. Marketing will continue to play an increasingly larger role in the administration and operation of nonbusiness enterprises.

(ii) Generic Concept

The broadening concept of marketing has been taken even further to include *any* transaction between an organization and its publics. The generic concept of marketing proposes that marketing applies to any social unit that seeks to exchange values with other social units. Products include organizations, persons, places, and ideas, in addition to goods and services. These products are marketed by a wide variety of business, political, social, religious, cultural, and knowledge organizations. Thus, all marketers face the same tasks in all forms of marketing.

A further aspect of generic marketing is the concept of social marketing, which is described as the use of marketing principles and techniques to advance a social cause, idea, or pattern of behavior. Also suggested by this approach to marketing are ethical and social concerns related to marketing practices. This means that both business and nonprofit organizations may be marketing the same cause or social issue. For instance, Anheuser-Busch, Miller Brewing Company, Seagram's, and other firms have begun to point out the dangers of underage drinking and of drinking and driving, in their promotional efforts. At the same time, the primary mission of MADD (Mothers Against Drunk Driving) is to prevent drinking and driving.

As marketing thought has changed to include nonprofit organizations and social concerns, the need for marketing in nonprofit organizations has become very clear. Writing in *Marketing News*, the news magazine of the American Marketing Association, Schwartz (1989) put it this way:

> *High ideals, mission statements, and dedicated volunteers may not be enough for nonprofit organizations in the 1990s.*

> *Faced with pursuing lofty goals and paying the rent in a crowded world of service, charitable, and educational groups, competing for the same dollars, many nonprofit organizations—without marketing plans—soon may be taking unwelcome baths in vats of red ink.*

(iii) Strategic Marketing

In the 1980s, the focus of business management shifted to strategic planning. Limited resources, changes in world markets, intense competitive pressures, and other forces caused senior management to reexamine the role of marketing. Nonprofit managers have also turned to strategic planning, in their effort to adapt to rapidly changing conditions (Laycock, 1990).

Although some executives and scholars have questioned the validity of a marketing orientation, it has been suggested that the shift to strategic planning presents an opportunity for marketing to assert its traditional influence. This thrust, which has been termed strategic marketing, has been described by Day and Wensley (1983):

> *The strategic decision process requires a dialogue between the corporate and business unit levels to develop individual strategies based on the specifics of market segments and competitive positions. Such a dialogue can only be effective if marketing management reasserts its role in providing strategic direction at the product-market level.*

(iv) Relationship Marketing

The 1990s saw the embrace by marketers of still another philosophy. Known as relationship marketing, this view assumes that an organization wants to form long-term relationships with its customers. Therefore, the focus of its efforts is not on creating transactions, but rather on customer satisfaction and retention, based on developing a relationship with the customer over time. The customer is viewed as a partner who will help the organization achieve its goals.

This approach, which requires extensive knowledge of customers and their needs, has been the basis for the business success of MCI, Lands' End, Compaq, Fidelity Funds, and others. It is also appropriate for nonprofit organizations, since they will benefit from the support of donors and clients who have long-term relationships with the organization. This is because relationship marketing provides nonprofits with a strategy that helps them build a mutually beneficial partnership with donors and clients, thus increasing loyalty. In addition, the relationship becomes a tangible benefit which offsets the intangible nature of a nonprofit's activities (McCort, 1994).

(C) IMPLICATIONS FOR NONPROFIT ORGANIZATIONS

The changes in marketing thought emphasize that marketing is applicable to all forms of nonprofit organizations. Effective marketing does not just happen, however. There are no magical formulas or secrets to marketing. Nor will nonprofit managers be able to adapt business marketing concepts and practices to their organizations without some difficulty. Like all management activities, marketing must be planned, organized, and controlled. Further, because marketing is new to most nonprofit organizations, it is even more critical that a carefully thought-out, customer-focused marketing strategy be developed and carried out (Miaoulis, 1985). And it is crucial that nonprofits work very hard to build and maintain long-term relationships with donors and clients.

15.3 Marketing Concept

(A) ORGANIZATIONAL PHILOSOPHY

Most businesses—and some organizations—have adopted what has become known as the marketing concept. This philosophy, or conceptual framework, has given marketing a much more important role in all forms of organizations, for-profit and nonprofit alike.

Kotler and Andreasen (1991) call this the "marketing mindset." They point out that a nonprofit organization's directors and managers must have a clear appreciation of what marketing is and what it can do for the organization. Most importantly, they must put the customer, or client, at the center of everything the organization does.

(B) MAJOR PROPOSITIONS

As applied to a nonprofit organization, the marketing concept is based on three major propositions: client orientation, coordination of all client-related activities, and goal direction.

(i) Client Orientation

As noted above, this is the key to the marketing concept. Nonprofit managers must shift from an internal organizational perspective to the client's viewpoint. Successful marketing in a nonprofit organization requires a complete understanding of an organization's clients—their needs, attitudes, and buying behavior. For instance, a community agency that provides services to the elderly must know exactly what the needs of the elderly in its community are and must develop programs that meet these needs. *A nonprofit organization must never forget that it exists to serve the needs of its clients.*

When a nonprofit organization does not understand or heed the needs of its clients, marketing can be a dismal failure. The U.S. Treasury Department's introduction of the Susan B. Anthony dollar clearly made this point. Despite research studies that suggested little enthusiasm for a small dollar among bankers and business executives and likely rejection by consumers, Treasury Department officials went ahead with their plan to introduce the Anthony dollar. Almost a million dollars was spent to promote and publicize the new dollar, but consumers rejected it. Why? The major reason was that the Anthony dollar was designed poorly and did not meet the needs of businesses and consumers. It was too similar to a quarter in size and appearance. The Treasury Department's promotion effort could not overcome the product's design weakness.

(ii) Coordination

For marketing to be effective in a nonprofit organization, *there must be coordination of all elements of the marketing program.* Because these elements, known as the "marketing mix," constitute an interrelated system, the program must be viewed and planned as a whole. Marketing itself must be closely interrelated with other activities of a nonprofit organization.

To achieve the desired coordination, there must be close cooperation among all components of an organization. For instance, if the executive director of a health care agency commits the agency to participate in a community health education program, the director must be sure that the agency's education committee supports this activity and that the agency has the resources available to participate.

(iii) Goal Direction

The marketing concept stresses that *the only way an organization can achieve its own goals is by satisfying the needs of its clients (customers).* For example, a college wishing to increase the level of funding provided by the business community must demonstrate to business executives that it is meeting the business education needs of the community. This may require the development of special educational programs and activities for local businesses and their employees.

(C) IMPLEMENTING THE MARKETING CONCEPT

Nonprofit directors and managers must shift their focus from an internal organizational perspective to the clients' viewpoint. Exhibit 15.2 suggests how some nonprofit organizations have redefined their orientation to reflect the clients' viewpoint.

A marketing success story illustrates how a coordinated marketing plan based on meeting clearly understood needs will work. Several years ago, the Dallas Museum of Fine Arts was faced with an urgent need to develop an effective marketing program after its goal of expansion was thwarted. The defeat of a bond referendum for a new museum forced the Dallas Museum's administrators to redefine the museum's goals and its relation to the public. They decided to emphasize that "a great city deserves a great art museum." Through a carefully planned marketing program, they informed the people of Dallas that an art museum is more than a place to store art treasures. They stressed the educational values and the economic benefits from tourists attracted by exhibits and special shows. They developed a model showing the key features, and the corresponding benefits for the public, of the proposed building. Museum officials used this model when they met with public groups. These marketing efforts succeeded, and the second bond referendum passed.

(D) INVOLVING SALES AND MARKETING PEOPLE

To develop and implement the required marketing orientation, nonprofit organizations must include sales and marketing managers on their boards and on appropriate committees and teams. According to Fram (1991), board members with sales and marketing backgrounds will help nonprofit organizations view their operations from their customers' viewpoint. They will also help to identify changes in the market for an organization's services, to assess how well an organization is meeting the needs of its clients, and to develop a strategic plan to meet future needs.

Recruiting sales and marketing people for nonprofit boards is not easy. They travel frequently, and board membership may not fit their career needs and life-styles. Aggressive recruiting efforts and strong network building will be required to attract people who have the desired sales and marketing expertise.

EXHIBIT 15.2 Organizational Versus Marketing Orientation

Nonprofit Organization	Organizational Orientation	Marketing Orientation
Urban transit authority	We run a bus system.	We provide transportation services.
Art museum	We display art objects.	We offer artistic experiences.
Child-care center	We take care of children.	We provide security for children and their parents.
Community theater	We put on plays.	We offer entertainment.
Family planning center	We give family-planning information	We offer solutions to family-planning problems.

15.4 Unique Aspects of Nonprofit Marketing

(A) MULTIPLE PUBLICS

The marketing efforts of business organizations are concentrated on the firm's customers. This is not the case with nonprofit organizations, which must market to multiple publics. As defined by Kotler and Andreasen (1991), a public is "a distinct group of people, organizations or both whose actual or potential needs must in some sense be served." Four types of publics are identified for nonprofit organizations by Kotler and Andreasen:

- Input publics (e.g., donors and suppliers) provide resources;
- Internal publics (e.g., staff and volunteers) convert resources into useful goods and services;
- Intermediary publics (e.g., agents and facilitators) deliver goods and services;
- Consuming publics (e.g., clients and local residents) gain satisfaction from the goods and services provided.

From a marketing standpoint, the key publics are supporters and clients. Supporters (donors and volunteers) provide the key resources to a nonprofit organization, through either their monetary contributions or their time and personal expertise. Clients, who are the primary customers of a nonprofit organization, benefit from its services.

In addition to clients and supporters, a specific nonprofit organization's publics will include many other types of people and groups. A brief review of the important publics of a community hospital illustrates this fact. Its publics include:

- Patients and their families and friends;
- Members of the community who aid the hospital through donations, volunteer services, and other forms of support;
- Suppliers of goods and services;
- Doctors, nurses, administrators, and other employees;
- Trustees of the hospital;
- Regulatory agencies;
- The general public.

Because members of each of these publics have different needs and attitudes, marketing concepts must be applied differently.

(B) MULTIPLE OBJECTIVES

Business firms have long-run profitability as their overriding objective. Because they must serve multiple publics, nonprofit organizations have multiple objectives. Sometimes, these objectives may not be consistent with one another. For instance, a community center may wish to provide free family-planning counseling to its clients, but it is limited because a major portion of its funding comes from donors who are opposed to certain forms of birth control.

For many nonprofit organizations, the process of formulating objectives involves compromise and consensus building. This makes marketing more difficult than in business because more time must be spent in involving board members, staff, and volunteers, and convincing them to accept the objectives.

(C) PRODUCTS ARE SERVICES

The products of most nonprofit organizations are services, not tangible goods. A service is an activity performed for another person or organization. Johnson, Scheuing, and Gaida (1986) have identified several characteristics that set services apart from goods and make their marketing more challenging.

(i) Intangibility
Services go out of existence at the very moment they are rendered (e.g., counseling session), although their effects may last for some time. Because of the lack of tangibility, marketers of services find it quite difficult to differentiate their offerings. Their clients see intangible services as abstract and thus difficult to describe and understand.

(ii) Perishability
Services cannot be stored; they have to be produced on demand. Marketers of services, unlike goods marketers, are unable to manufacture for inventory during slow times and draw on inventory during periods of peak demand. Excess capacity not used in services production is lost forever—for example, empty beds in a hospital or vacant seats in a classroom.

(iii) Simultaneity
Services are produced and consumed at the same time, in contrast to goods, which are generally produced, then purchased, and then consumed. As a result, a service performer and service buyer usually have to interact and, accordingly, be in the same place at the same time.

(iv) Heterogeneity
The quality of service performance varies from one service organization to another, from one service performer to another, and from one occasion to another. This variability of service output makes it difficult for a nonprofit service organization to establish and maintain performance standards and thus guarantee quality continuously.

(D) PUBLIC SCRUTINY

Many nonprofit organizations provide vital services for society. Because of this, they are often subsidized by government and are given tax-exempt status by government. Their activities are closely watched by government officials, news media, and the general public.

One particular concern is public criticism of the administrative and marketing costs incurred to raise funds. For instance, a newspaper article reported that a charitable organization raised $9 million. After deducting marketing and administrative expenses, about $650,000—less than 8 cents of every dollar raised—was left to assist the needy.

From a marketing perspective, this type of media coverage is harmful to all nonprofit organizations that rely on contributions for a portion of their funding. The negative publicity and possible government intervention related to this situation increase the public pressure on nonprofit organizations. Accordingly, they must be very careful to conduct their affairs in a way that does not result in public displeasure.

15.5   Markets and Buyer Behavior

(A)   DEFINING A MARKET

Marketers view the term "market" in a very specific way. To them, a market is a group of people or organizations who have a common need or share a common problem. Their common need or problem requires them to seek a product or service to satisfy their need or to resolve their problem.

In some cases, almost everyone is part of the market for a particular nonprofit organization. For example, there are very few people who have not been affected in some way by the dreaded impact of cancer. As a result, the American Cancer Society finds widespread interest in its activities and programs. In contrast, the market for a local church is limited to the people in a community who have similar religious beliefs.

(B)   BUYER BEHAVIOR

Human behavior, especially buyer behavior, and its causes are complex. In attempting to understand and predict buyer behavior, marketers have turned to the behavioral sciences: psychology, sociology, social psychology, and anthropology. Behavioral concepts can help a nonprofit manager understand the "whys" and "hows" of behavior.

For most people, the buying process involves a series of steps, as shown in Exhibit 15.3. The starting point is *need recognition*, which may result from internal or external stimuli. For instance, a mother notices that her teenage daughter is showing signs of behavioral difficulties that may be caused by drug abuse.

After recognizing the need, a buyer begins a *search for purchase alternatives*. This step usually involves a search for information about various ways to satisfy the need. The mother may talk to the high school guidance counselor, a priest, a social worker, and others, to find out more about her daughter's problem. She may also read books, pamphlets, and other published information on teenage drug problems.

Nonprofit organizations may be called on to play an important role in these first two steps of the buying process. They can assist people like this mother in recognizing a problem and identifying alternatives. In fact, the dissemination of information about

---

EXHIBIT 15.3 Buying Process Model

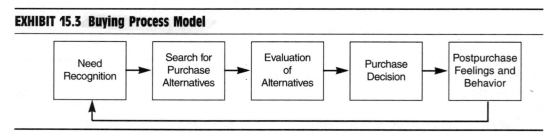

Source: *Eugene M. Johnson,* Fundamentals of Marketing from Product to Profit *(Boston: American Management Association, 1990), p. 21.*

social issues and problems is one of the major marketing tasks of many nonprofit organizations.

Evaluation of alternatives comes next. Again, a nonprofit organization can assist the buyer. Advice on treatment options, costs, and other relevant concerns will be important to the mother. Her actual choice may involve comparing several options; for instance, a community-funded drug abuse center, a church-affiliated drug counseling program, or a health care facility.

An important *purchase decision* like the one this mother must make will require careful deliberation. Even after making the decision, she will have doubts. The final step in the buying process involves *postpurchase feelings and behavior*. Postpurchase doubt, which has been called purchase dissonance, is not unusual. It is important, therefore, for marketers to follow up important purchase decisions in a supportive manner. The model of the buying process also shows how feedback from the decision will affect future buying decisions.

This aspect of buying behavior is especially important to nonprofit organizations. Contributions must be acknowledged promptly, and donors must receive feedback about how their money is used. Nonprofit organizations must also use surveys and other forms of communication to obtain feedback from their clients. They cannot neglect the postpurchase feelings and behavior of their donors and clients.

(C)   NEEDS AND MOTIVES

People act in response to a need or a combination of needs. Behavioral scientists suggest that buyer behavior is multimotivated; a decision to buy is normally the result of a number of different needs or motives, not merely one. What the nonprofit marketer must determine is the priority donors and clients give to their various, sometimes conflicting needs.

Guy and Patton (1988) have studied donor behavior from the perspective of buying motivation and behavior. They concluded that the strongest motivating force for giving to a nonprofit organization is the "very basic, deep-seated need to help others." Their study also assessed the behavioral process that results in a decision to make a contribution. Nonprofit marketers must make sure that potential donors are aware that a need exists, that they have a personal responsibility to help, and that their contribution can help others in need.

(D)   GROUP INFLUENCES ON BEHAVIOR

Buyers do not live in isolation. As social beings, they belong to various groups or social units. These groups may play a significant role in influencing buyer behavior. The various groups include members of a person's social class, peers, family, friends, business associates, members of social clubs, and so forth. How closely a person identifies with a group determines the influence of that group on the person's behavior.

Nonprofit organizations themselves are groups and, therefore, are a factor in determining buyer behavior. People will be influenced to join a nonprofit organization, contribute money, or volunteer their time based on the organization's current membership. They will become clients of the organization if they feel that it reflects their social values. For example, an urban church that wants to increase participation by teenagers in its recreational activities will improve its chance for success if it attracts peer group leaders as participants.

Some nonprofit organizations use famous people to influence buyer behavior. Because they are well-known and serve as role models, professional athletes, motion picture and television performers, and other celebrities will influence the behavior of young people and other consumers. Featuring Chicago Bulls' basketball star Michael Jordan in a TV advertisement to prevent alcohol abuse by teenagers has more impact because he is recognized and admired by teenage viewers.

(E) MARKET SEGMENTATION

In recent years, marketing theorists and practitioners have learned much about buyers' behavior. This new knowledge has led to the emergence of market segmentation as a significant marketing planning and management tool. Market segmentation is the process of dividing a market into separate subsets, or segments, of buyers. The organization can concentrate its marketing efforts on a distinct subset of the market, or it can develop different marketing strategies for each market segment. For instance:

- A college offers classes during the day for its full-time students and at night for its part-time students who work during the day.
- A hospital offers outpatient surgery options for minor operations and traditional inpatient surgery for more serious conditions.
- A nonprofit theater offers matinee performances for senior citizens and school children and evening performances for working people.
- A library provides large-print books for the visually impaired and Saturday morning reading sessions for preschool children.

The most frequently used bases for segmenting consumer markets are demographic, geographic, behavioral, and purchase volume characteristics.

(i) Demographic
A market is subdivided on the basis of age, gender, occupation, income, education, marital status, and other demographic variables. For example, a health-care agency might want to concentrate on services for the elderly.

(ii) Geographic
A market is subdivided into different locations, such as states, counties, urban versus rural areas, and so on. For instance, public libraries in rural areas must often use bookmobiles to take books to their distant clients; urban libraries are more accessible to their clients, who may be within walking distance of a branch.

(iii) Behavioral
A market is subdivided on the basis of life-style, personality, social class, attitudes, and other behavioral characteristics. Organizations that build housing complexes for the elderly use behavioral characteristics to segment the housing market and develop appropriate facilities. Social service agencies that cater to single parents use life-style characteristics to reach those in need of their services.

(iv) *Volume*

A market is subdivided on the basis of usage. Heavy, medium, and light users are studied, to determine whether they have similar demographic or behavioral characteristics. For example, it has been shown that certain segments of the population are most likely to abuse alcohol and other drugs and are therefore the prime target market for rehabilitation programs.

(F) BUSINESS MARKETS

Many nonprofit organizations seek support from businesses, and some may offer services in cooperation with businesses. For example, many large companies have charitable foundations that provide funds for the arts, education, health care, and other types of nonprofit programs. Usually, the support of businesses is driven by the interests of management and the goals of the business. Thus, nonprofit managers and directors must understand how businesses function and make resource allocation decisions.

Business managers are professional decision makers. They are trained to make deliberate, informed decisions. They will give careful consideration to objective factors when deciding whether to support a nonprofit organization. Of particular concern is whether the nonprofit organization's mission and activities are compatible with the mission and goals of the business. Business managers tend to support causes that fit their company's image and are not controversial.

Beginning in the early 1980s, American Express, Kimberly-Clark, Johnson & Johnson, and many other firms turned to cause-related marketing as a promotion approach that provides funding for nonprofit organizations (Williams, 1986; Kelly, 1991). Perhaps the best known is the widely publicized Statue of Liberty restoration effort by American Express. This 1983 campaign is often cited as the genesis of cause-related marketing.

Corporate sponsorship of a fund-raising event can be good for business and for a nonprofit organization. The charity receives a fixed amount of money for the use of its name during the promotion, a fee for coupons redeemed by consumers, or a percentage of the sales of the product or service promoted. The Children's Miracle Network, American Heart Association, and Shelter-Aid are causes that have benefited from corporate marketing programs.

In the 1990s, some companies have taken cause-related marketing to another level (Arnott, 1994). Sometimes called passion branding or social issues marketing, this involves making a major, long-term commitment to a cause. This may involve an alliance with a specific nonprofit, such as Dollar Rent a Car's multiyear agreement to sponsor Special Olympics and Visa's support of local Meals on Wheels chapters. In other cases, the business commits to an issue. Prominent examples include Lady Foot Locker's focus on violence against women, Coors Brewing Company's literacy campaign, and Avon's Breast Cancer Awareness Crusade. In promoting a social issue, a business may work with several nonprofit partners.

Another aspect of business markets that may offer marketing opportunities for nonprofit organizations is the needs of employees. For instance, many businesses are beginning to recognize the growing need for safe, affordable child-care centers at business locations. Other business needs include alcohol and drug abuse counseling, advice on caring for the elderly parents of employees, and continuing education. Each of these needs represents a potential market for nonprofits with experience in these areas.

15.6   *Information for Marketing*

(A)   MARKETING INTELLIGENCE

Marketing intelligence is a broad term used to describe the information-gathering function of marketing. This function may involve informal information gathering, such as conversations with clients in waiting rooms or discussions between nonprofit managers at seminars and conferences. Most often, however, marketing intelligence refers to formal, organized information-gathering activities and subsequent analysis.

The purpose of marketing research and other marketing intelligence activities is to provide information for marketing planning, decision making, and control. For instance, a community service agency carried out a market survey of the attitudes and practices of employers toward hiring people with a mental handicap (Tomes and Hamilton, 1991). The results of the survey were used to develop a marketing program, which involved a job trainer at no cost to the hiring firm, and a promotional program, which emphasized the dependable job performance of employees with a mental handicap.

(B)   MARKETING INFORMATION SYSTEM

A marketing information system (MIS) is a set of procedures and methods that provides an orderly flow of relevant information to marketing decision makers. Two types of information are gathered, processed, and analyzed by an effective MIS: secondary data and primary data.

Secondary data are data that have been or are being collected for another purpose and are already in existence. Frequently available from both outside and inside sources, secondary data save a manager time and money. Data from publications, government reports, university studies, and other published sources often provide the information needed for nonprofit marketing planning. Also needed, however, are data about clients and donors, and other relevant data from sources within the nonprofit organization. In particular, a current database of clients and donors is essential to follow up other marketing activities.

Primary data involve the collection of information by the nonprofit organization for a specific purpose. Primary data are needed to fill the information gaps left by lacking, outdated, or otherwise inadequate secondary data. For example, a Chamber of Commerce knew from its internal records that members were canceling faster than new ones were enrolling. However, there was no information on why the Chamber was losing members. To find out, primary data collection was needed. A survey of members who had canceled led to the development of a marketing program to involve inactive members, provide added benefits to members, and offer after-sale service (Nall and Dimsdale, 1985).

(C)   DATABASE MARKETING

Computer technology, which developed rapidly during the 1970s and 1980s and is expected to continue to grow during the coming decades, has been the driving force behind the emergence of database marketing. Marketers now have the capability to compile and analyze tremendous amounts of information about individual customers. In addition to the increased sophistication of computers and computer software, the growth of database marketing is also the result of the expanded use of credit cards and toll-free telephone services, the increased availability of ZIP codes and census tract information, and the development of advanced statistical and financial analytical methods.

Many successful business marketers (L.L. Bean, American Express, and AT&T, for example) have used their ability to store and quickly analyze vast amounts of customer information effectively. They have moved from relying on mass marketing to the use of more targeted and individualized means to communicate with their customers. The key to their success has been the development of sophisticated customer databases (Petrison, Blattberg, and Wang, 1993).

Nonprofits can also benefit from the development of databases. By compiling information on clients and donors, nonprofits will better understand them on an individual basis. They will be able to target fund raising and other marketing activities to specific needs of their donors and clients. And the effective use of database marketing information by nonprofits will help them create desired long-term relationships. However, this will not happen if nonprofits do not invest their resources in database marketing information and technology.

(D) MARKETING RESEARCH

As part of an organization's marketing information system, marketing research is used to collect, process, and analyze primary data. Because marketing research is concerned with helping mangers find solutions to marketing problems, there are almost as many uses of marketing research as there are problems.

Many nonprofit marketing research studies are concerned with clients and donors—who they are and what they need; their attitudes and behavior patterns; and so forth. Other projects study marketing activities, such as pricing, service policies, advertising, and public relations. Control and reappraisal of marketing costs, such as promotion expenditures and delivery costs, are the subject of other research efforts. Finally, many nonprofit organizations are concerned with overall marketing strategy considerations, such as the organization's image, marketing policies, and objectives.

Marketing researchers use a number of different techniques and tools to obtain the desired information. Among those that might be used by nonprofit organizations are:

- Informed opinion interviews—asking people with special expertise or knowledge to discuss a problem or to suggest other sources of information;
- Focus groups—exploring the feelings and ideas of a small group of people who have similar backgrounds and interests;
- Case studies—reviewing, in depth, a few selected situations in order to identify key factors and relationships;
- Observation—noting objects or actions through the senses, primarily sight and hearing;
- Surveys—obtaining information by asking questions of people (clients or donors, for example) who are affected by marketing activities.

15.7 Marketing Management

(A) ROLE OF THE EXECUTIVE DIRECTOR

The long-term success of any organization is determined by the capabilities of its management. In a nonprofit organization, the Executive Director must assume responsibility for marketing management. When the Executive Director is innovative and customer-driven, a nonprofit organization will prosper and grow ("Profiting from the Nonprofits," 1990).

Frances Hesselbein became Executive Director of the Girl Scouts of America in 1976. She took over an organization that had seen its membership fall for 8 straight years. When she retired 13 years later, the Girl Scouts had grown to a healthy 2.3 million members. She accomplished this growth by using marketing strategies and programs to adapt to changes occurring in girls' interests and motivations.

Hesselbein had market studies conducted to find out how to attract more members and retain the interest of teenage girls. Based on these studies, greater emphasis was placed on girls' growing interests in science, the environment, and business, and less on cooking, sewing, and traditional household skills. Fashion designers developed a modern line of uniforms. Special programs for girls in low-income neighborhoods were developed. The Girl Scout Handbook was revised to reflect changing interests and racial and cultural patterns. Through these and many other activities, Hesselbein changed her nonprofit organization to meet the needs of its customers. Some other innovative, customer-driven Executive Directors are Faye Wattleton of Planned Parenthood, James A. Osborne of the Salvation Army, and Gail L. Warden of the Henry Ford Health Care Corporation ("Profiting from the Nonprofits," 1990).

(B) MARKETING MANAGEMENT IN NONPROFIT ORGANIZATIONS

Management is defined as the process necessary to bring the most return from a particular commitment of an organization's resources (technical, financial, human, and so on) when other alternative commitments are possible. The information on which the commitment is made is always incomplete, and the conditions under which the decision will be carried out are uncertain.

Nonprofit organizations feel special pressure because they have limited resources. Cutbacks in assistance from federal, state, and local governments, changes in tax laws that hurt gift giving, and limited growth in corporate giving have combined to place added financial pressure on directors and managers of nonprofit organizations. They must learn to use marketing concepts and techniques to focus their efforts on the needs of their clients.

An overview of the marketing management process is presented in Exhibit 15.4. As suggested by the marketing concept, marketing management is an integrated, interrelated process. The first, very important step is to analyze the marketing situation. This is part of marketing planning, as are the next three steps shown in Exhibit 15.4. In summary form, the critical marketing management tasks are:

- Planning: analyzing the marketing situation, selecting marketing objectives, identifying target markets, and developing a marketing strategy and programs;
- Organization: developing a marketing structure;
- Control: selecting activities that will make sure that the objectives are achieved.

The description of the marketing management process highlights the importance of marketing planning and suggests that marketing planning is a continuous process. Even the most thorough marketing planner realizes that plans cannot be cast in stone. Flexibility is needed. Changes must be made in marketing plans, in order to meet unantici-

EXHIBIT 15.4 Marketing Management Process

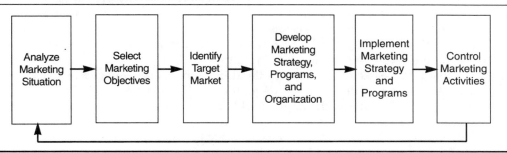

Source: *Eugene M. Johnson, "Marketing Planning for Nonprofit Organizations,"* Nonprofit World, *May–June, 1986, p. 21.* Reprinted by permission of Society for Nonprofit Organizations, 6314 Odana Road, Suite 1, Madison, WI 53719 (1-800-424-7367).

pated market changes, competitive actions, and similar environmental changes. This is why Exhibit 15.4 contains a feedback path from marketing control to the beginning of the marketing management process.

(C) STRATEGIC MARKETING PLANNING

Strategic marketing planning is an essential activity for all nonprofit organizations, regardless of size, location, or function. As shown in Exhibit 15.5, the strategic marketing planning process can be divided into four major steps:

EXHIBIT 15.5 Strategic Marketing Planning Process

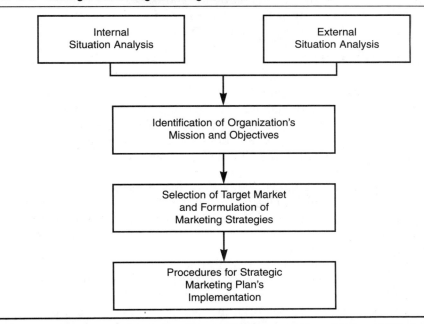

Source: *Eugene M. Johnson, "Marketing Planning for Nonprofit Organizations,"* Nonprofit World, *July–August, 1986, p. 26.* Reprinted by permission of Society for Nonprofit Organizations, 6314 Odana Road, Suite 1, Madison, WI 53719 (1-800-424-7367).

1. *Situation analysis* answers the question "Where are you?" by providing a realistic view of the organization's environment, marketing opportunities, and internal strengths and weaknesses.
2. *Identification of an organization's mission and objectives* provides an answer to a second question: "Where do we want to go?"
3. *Formulation of marketing strategies* is the third step. These strategies answer the question "How do you want to get there?" The answer to this question is dependent primarily on the target market that the organization wishes to serve.
4. Procedures for *implementation of the marketing plan* provide the schedule ("When do you want to arrive?"), organization ("Who is responsible?"), and budget ("How much will it cost?") for carrying out the marketing plan.

15.8   *Marketing Situation Analysis*

(A)   COMPONENTS OF SITUATION ANALYSIS

Situation analysis is an assessment of an organization's present position in its current environment. Before establishing its marketing objectives and plans, a nonprofit organization must have a clear understanding of its present situation. This involves the identification of present and potential problems and opportunities. There are two parts to this analysis:

- External analysis: evaluating an organization's markets and publics, market segments, competitors, environmental trends and issues;
- Internal analysis: evaluating critical measures of an organization's performance, resources, strengths, and weaknesses.

(B)   MARKETING AUDIT

Some organizations use a marketing audit to review their marketing resources and activities and to carry out the situation analysis. Just as a nonprofit organization's financial position is regularly and systematically reviewed, so should its marketing efforts be subjected to regular and systematic evaluation to determine whether the marketing efforts are appropriate and whether they are being properly executed.

A marketing audit is sweeping and comprehensive. Kotler and Andreasen (1991) provide a complete guide to the kinds of questions that a marketing audit should consider, as do Lovelock and Weinberg (1989). The nonprofit organization's environment is studied; its policies, organization, methods, and marketing philosophy are reviewed; its programs for reaching its goals are assessed; and its procedures for determining and controlling its marketing efforts are analyzed.

Even the most successful nonprofit organizations should carry out regular marketing audits. Seldom is any organization so good that it cannot be improved. Also, past success may breed complacency and carelessness. Audits that can be conducted easily and inexpensively on certain aspects of the marketing program should be undertaken frequently. In some situations, a checklist can be used to provide a flexible, inexpensive self-study tool (Van Doren and Smith, 1985).

(C) EXTERNAL ANALYSIS

External situation analysis concentrates on a nonprofit organization's environment. It focuses on external factors that can influence funding and participation.

(i) Clients and Supporters

The external situation analysis should begin with an assessment of an organization's clients. The key questions are:

- Who are they?
- Who should they be?
- What are they "buying"?
- What could cause this situation to change?
- Why do they "buy" or participate?
- When do they "buy" or participate?
- How do they make decisions to "buy" or participate?
- Where do they "buy" or participate?

The next step is to consider the nonprofit organization's supporters. Unlike business organizations, which are mainly concerned with customer analysis, nonprofit organizations depend on others for support. In particular, a nonprofit organization must answer similar questions about its funders and volunteers.

- Who are they?
- What are they supporting?
- What could cause this situation to change?
- Why do they provide support?
- When do they provide support?
- How do they make decisions to provide support?

Based on the analysis of clients and supporters, several key issues will emerge, including:

1. Market size and growth. The primary concern here is to determine how large the market is and what potential growth opportunities exist, based on estimates of (a) the potential number of clients and supporters, and (b) the potential rate of participation and/or support.
2. Client/Supporter decision making. An organization must try to understand how clients and supporters (or potential clients and supporters) make decisions regarding the organization; specifically, how do they decide whether to "buy" service and which organization to "buy" from?
3. Market segments. The organization must identify groups of clients and supporters who are similar in terms of decision making and who might represent specific targets for specialized marketing efforts.

Thorough analysis of clients and supporters will help an organization identify marketing opportunities. This requires taking a broad view of the market and avoiding the limitations of "marketing myopia."

Theodore Levitt (1975), in his classic article "Marketing Myopia," pointed to the shortcomings of major firms and industries that failed to analyze their marketing opportunities correctly. His contention was that top executives in many industries have unnecessarily taken a limited view of the scope of their businesses. They have been product-oriented rather than customer-oriented. Because of their limited views of marketing, executives in these industries, such as dry cleaning, railroads, electric utilities, and motion pictures, missed marketing opportunities based on changing customers' needs.

Levitt's admonishment is just as applicable today as in the past and as applicable to nonprofits as it is to businesses. A public library that fails to provide its clients with videotapes, computer software, and other recently developed techniques for making knowledge and entertainment available will soon lose many clients. In contrast, an organization that successfully changed was the March of Dimes. After polio ceased to be a major health concern, this organization switched to birth defects and prenatal care as causes that needed a focal point.

(ii) Publics
In addition to clients and supporters, a nonprofit organization must assess the impact of its other publics. As noted earlier, a nonprofit organization's publics will include many types of people, organizations, and groups.

Key questions that should be asked are:

- Who are the people and/or entities that have an impact on the organization?
- Which are most influential?
- Why do they have an impact on the organization?
- What are their objectives and the reasons for their concern with the organization?
- In what ways do they affect the organization?
- What could cause this situation to change?
- What impact will changes have on an organization's publics and their relationship with it?

(iii) Competition
In recent years, competition has become an important concern for most nonprofit organizations. Not only must an organization be concerned about competition from other nonprofits, but it is also likely to be facing competitive challenges from business organizations. For example: public hospitals compete with for-profit hospitals for patients, staff, and financial support; private and public colleges compete with profit-oriented trade schools, correspondence programs, and business educational services for students; the United States Postal Service competes with United Parcel Service, Federal Express, and other businesses for customers.

The key questions to be asked as part of the competitive analysis are:

- Who are the major competitors?
- How do they compete?
- What are their strengths and weaknesses that will pose problems and opportunities? These may include:
  - costs and fees;
  - access to clients and supporters;
  - image;

- type of client base;
- personnel;
- marketing budgets and other resources.

(iv) Other External Factors

Nonprofit directors and managers make marketing decisions in a dynamic environment. There are many other external factors over which they have little or no control. Some specific questions that must be considered are:

- What economic factors might influence the attainment of the organization's objectives?
- What national, state, and local regulations affect the organization?
- What are the demographic, social, technological, and other external factors that may affect the organization?

(D) INTERNAL ANALYSIS

The internal situation analysis will help a nonprofit organization identify the internal problems and opportunities that can affect the organization's performance. In particular, what are the organization's marketing strengths and weaknesses? This portion of the situation analysis concentrates on those aspects of the organization that affect its ability to satisfy the clients' needs and influence participation and support.

To assess the marketing performance of their organizations, nonprofit directors and managers must ask themselves questions relating to the following critical areas of performance:

1. **Trends.** What are the significant trends in the organization's programs, services, participation, and support?
2. **Share of market.** How much of the market does the organization have in relation to competitive organizations?
3. **Stability.** Has the organization demonstrated "staying power"?
4. **Efficiency.** Has the organization been cost-effective in its utilization of facilities, personnel, and other resources?
5. **Flexibility.** Has the organization been able to adapt to market and environmental changes?

A second part of the internal situation analysis involves an assessment of the nonprofit organization's marketing efforts (that is, its marketing objectives, programs, personnel, and practices). The organization must examine its physical, financial, personnel, and other resources used to provide services to clients. The two critical questions are:

- What key competitive advantages and disadvantages does the organization have?
- How can the organization maintain its competitive advantages and overcome its competitive disadvantages?

After completing this assessment, marketing planners will have an understanding of what sort of marketing their organization can and cannot do. They will know which of the marketing opportunities can be pursued.

15.9 *Marketing Planning*

The three strategic marketing planning steps are: selecting marketing objectives, identifying the target market, and developing a marketing strategy. The planning steps are then implemented through the preparation of an action plan.

(A) SELECTING MARKETING OBJECTIVES

Objectives provide the direction for a nonprofit organization's activities; they answer the question: "Where do we want to go?"

(i) Marketing Objectives and Mission
A nonprofit organization's marketing objectives must be consistent with its mission. If they are not, marketing activities may work against what the nonprofit wants to accomplish.

For example, a medium-size university located in a resort area wanted to upgrade its image as a quality institution with high academic standards. However, the advertising theme used to promote the university to potential students continued to emphasize "sun and fun." Unfortunately, the advertising efforts conflicted with the university's goal.

(ii) Marketing Objectives and Organizational Goals
It is not easy to coordinate marketing objectives and activities with the goals of a nonprofit organization. Unlike a business, which is dominated by the profit motive, nonprofits tend to have multiple goals, such as survival, growth, and social change. As a result, marketing objectives may require modification to adapt them to the varied goals of a nonprofit organization.

(iii) Guidelines for Setting Marketing Objectives
When formulating marketing objectives, there are several guidelines to follow. Most important, marketing objectives must be specific; an objective must be a precise statement of what is to be accomplished by the organization's marketing efforts. Objectives should be stated in simple, understandable terms, so that everyone involved in marketing knows exactly what is to be done. Further, objectives should be measurable; that is, they should be stated in quantitative terms. Finally, marketing objectives should be related to time, so that everyone knows when the objectives should be achieved. Examples of marketing objectives that meet these criteria include the following:

- Church: "To increase average attendance at the Sunday morning worship service from 130 to 150 by the end of one year."
- Senior citizens' center: "To raise $250,000 for a new recreation facility in two years."
- Private college: "To increase enrollment by 10 percent for next year's fall class."

(B) IDENTIFYING THE TARGET MARKET

After formulating its marketing objectives, a nonprofit organization will choose its target market—the specific group of clients and supporters to whom it wishes to appeal. Selection of a target market depends on a careful review of potential clients' and supporters' needs, attitudes, and buying behavior. This analysis will provide nonprofit marketers with the insights needed to develop an appropriate marketing strategy.

There are two prime marketing strategy options: concentrated marketing and differentiated marketing.

Concentrated marketing, also called targeted marketing or niche marketing, involves focusing on a single, easily defined market segment. This approach is especially appropriate for organizations with limited resources. For instance, a small private college might concentrate its efforts on providing a quality liberal arts education for students from its region of the country.

When a nonprofit organization defines its target market in terms of several market segments, it is employing a differentiated marketing approach. A large state university will offer professional as well as liberal arts courses and programs. It may have several campus locations and will schedule classes at many times of the day and evening. It may offer special courses and seminars to businesses and government agencies for their managers and professional employees.

(C) DEVELOPING A MARKETING STRATEGY

Strategy, the "how" of marketing planning, is the overall design for achieving a nonprofit organization's marketing objectives. Development of a marketing strategy depends on the target market chosen. The nonprofit marketing planner formulates a marketing approach that will best satisfy the needs of the target market.

(i) Creating a Differential Advantage

When developing its marketing strategy, a nonprofit organization must strive to achieve a differential advantage. This is the "something extra" that makes an organization's marketing efforts just a little better than those of its competitors. Consequently, a particular group of clients (the target market) prefers the organization's services.

A differential advantage can be the result of any part of the marketing effort—price, service uniqueness or quality, psychological benefits created by promotion, and so forth. Consider, for example, the prestigious image of certain colleges and universities, such as Harvard, Yale, and Stanford. When people think of the nation's top academic institutions, they usually think of these universities. As a result, these schools have an advantage when recruiting students and faculty or seeking financial support.

(ii) Growth Strategies

Because clients' needs are changing rapidly and competition is increasing for traditional nonprofit services and programs, many nonprofit organizations are searching for growth opportunities. Exhibit 15.6 suggests four growth strategy options: market penetration, market development, service development, and diversification.

Market penetration involves an organization's efforts to increase sales and support of its present services to its present markets. The organization may do so by persuading present clients to use more of its services or by attracting clients and supporters from competitors. Aggressive promotion is the approach used most often by nonprofits to increase their market penetration. For instance, college admissions officers are using direct mail, telemarketing, and personal selling to recruit students. On a smaller scale, a minister, priest, or rabbi can increase attendance at religious services and other activities by visiting members and potential members in their homes.

EXHIBIT 15.6 Growth Strategy Options

	Present Services	New Services
PRESENT MARKETS	Market Penetration	Service Development
NEW MARKETS	Market Development	Diversification

Source: *Eugene M. Johnson, "Marketing Planning for Nonprofit Organizations,"* Nonprofit World, *September–October, 1986, p. 30.* Reprinted by permission of Society for Nonprofit Organizations, 6314 Odana Road, Suite 1, Madison, WI 53719 (1-800-424-7367).

Market development involves selling present services to new markets. This is often done by moving into new geographic markets. Boston's Northeastern University is drawing new students for its specialized, nondegree courses by offering night classes to high-tech engineers and computer scientists in California's Silicon Valley—over 3,000 miles away!

Service development involves creating new services for present markets. In this approach, an organization identifies an unsatisfied need that can be met by introducing a new or modified service. Many hospitals, for instance, are developing community "wellness" programs, designed to prevent illness rather than to provide treatment. These hospitals are serving the same clients but in a different way. Another example of service development by nonprofits is the emergence of Christian schools. Sensing a need for a different approach to education, many fundamentalist churches have established their own elementary and secondary schools. Thus, they provide a new service to their present members.

Diversification involves developing new services for new markets. An example is a community service agency that decides to market its internal management development seminars to other local nonprofit organizations. This approach carries the most risk, because diversification opportunities are difficult to evaluate. A nonprofit organization must be sure it understands the new markets it wants to pursue.

Many churches, especially those in inner cities, have redefined their markets and become more involved in economic development activities. Some of the business activities are used to help fund social programs. For example, Hartford Memorial Baptist Church in Detroit has opened an auto mechanics training center and leases land to new businesses to promote economic development (Miller, 1993).

(D) PREPARING AN ACTION PLAN

Implementing marketing strategies ("How do we get there?") requires the preparation of a marketing action plan. The development of schedules and budgets will answer the questions: "When do we want to arrive?" and "How much will it cost?" Marketing organization and implementation plans are also needed.

(i) Schedule

As noted in the discussion of marketing objectives, a marketing plan must have a time frame, a schedule for achieving the plan's objectives. The plan must also include priorities, or a statement of which objectives are to be given the most attention. Marketing planners develop three types of schedules for marketing plans: short-range plans cover a period of one year or less, medium-range plans cover a period of up to 5 years, and long-range plans are developed for 5 years or more. Long-range plans are the most difficult to prepare because long-range forecasts of rapidly changing markets and environmental conditions are unpredictable.

(ii) Budget

Because marketing resources are limited, especially in nonprofit organizations, budgets are needed to allocate resources to the desired marketing activities. The budgeted amount for an activity should match its importance to the organization's marketing strategy. For instance, as the number of college-age students has declined in recent years, colleges and universities are spending more of their budgets on direct mail and other techniques to attract students. This reflects the increased importance of recruiting to the growth—and even the survival—of many colleges and universities.

The objective and task approach has become the preferred method for budgeting marketing expenditures. This approach begins with the formulation of specific, measurable marketing objectives. Then the marketing activities, or tasks, required to achieve the objectives are determined. The marketing budget will be the total amount of money needed to accomplish the required activities. The strength of this budgeting approach is its close relationship to the nonprofit organization's marketing objectives.

(iii) Organization

A structure must be established to achieve the nonprofit organization's marketing objectives. If the marketing concept is accepted as a philosophy, the organization must focus itself to reflect its commitment to its supporters and clients. The result will be an expanded policy-making role for marketing personnel.

Because the board of directors is the policy-making body for most nonprofit organizations, its members must include people who have marketing knowledge and experience (Fram, 1991). It may be wise to establish a marketing committee and to designate specific staff persons to perform marketing tasks such as market research and promotion. Larger nonprofit organizations have created marketing departments with a director or vice president of marketing charged with overseeing all customer-related activities (Lovelock and Weinberg, 1989).

(iv) Implementation

Finally, the nonprofit marketing planner must transmit marketing objectives, strategies, schedules, and budgets to the people who will carry them out. However, communication of marketing plans involves more than informing people of the plans. Nonprofit managers will have to "sell" people on accepting and implementing the marketing plans. People tend to resist change, even a change that may benefit them. They anticipate that new marketing plans and programs will mean more work for them. Management must convince skeptical members of the nonprofit organization that the success of a plan will help them achieve their personal goals.

15.10 Marketing Mix

A convenient concept for explaining a nonprofit organization's marketing activities and the decisions made by marketing managers is the marketing mix. Just as a cook prepares a mix of ingredients for a favorite recipe, a marketing manager combines marketing activities to form a satisfactory marketing mix.

The major components of the marketing mix (Exhibit 15.7) are:

- Product: the "bundle of satisfactions" provided; the services and ideas marketed to clients and supporters;
- Price: what is charged for the services and ideas provided; a "price" may be money, time, or something else of value;
- Distribution: where and how services are provided; the delivery systems responsible for getting services to clients;
- Promotion: the organization's efforts to inform and persuade clients and supporters; promotional techniques include advertising, personal selling, public relations, and sales promotion.

These four elements are blended together to create a total package that will best satisfy the target market's needs.

(A) PRODUCT

The product component of most nonprofit organizations consists of services, ideas, experiences, and, in some cases, complementary goods. Albrecht and Zemke (1985) called this the service package—"the sum total of the goods, services and experiences offered to the customer." They and others (Lovelock (1991) for example) pointed out that the service package consists of a core service or idea plus a cluster of supplementary goods and services. The core service or idea is the specific benefit the nonprofit customer wants. For example, a church member will seek spiritual inspiration and guidance. Supplementary goods and services support, complement, and add value to the core service. Examples

---

EXHIBIT 15.7 The Marketing Mix

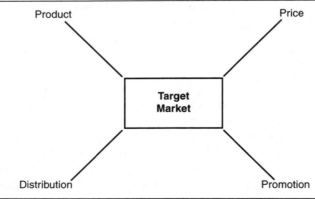

include a church's newsletter, nursery care during services, and recreational activities for young adults. Developing the appropriate service package requires a clear understanding of the nonprofit organization's mission and the needs of its clients and supporters.

(i)   Product Life Cycle

Products, like people and other living things, have life cycles. An important managerial planning and control tool, the product life cycle follows a product from birth (introduction) to death. It provides a conceptual framework for developing marketing strategies and programs for different stages of a product's life. As shown in Exhibit 15.8, the life cycle of a product can be divided into four major stages: introduction, growth, maturity, and decline.

Lovelock and Weinberg (1989), in describing the role of the product life cycle in non-profit marketing management, noted that public and nonprofit organizations are frequently involved with a product for only a portion of its life cycle. For instance, a nonprofit agency may raise public awareness of a social issue, such as the dangers of smoking or the need for environmental protection, during the early stages of the life cycle. As awareness grows, legislation is passed, public agencies become more involved, and responsibility for the issue shifts to them. At the other extreme are services that have reached the decline stage of the life cycle in the private sector and are then taken over by public or nonprofit organizations. Passenger rail service and urban public transit are historical examples.

During the introductory portion of the product life cycle, the marketer's major task is to create demand. Potential clients and supporters must be told about the cause or service, the need must be demonstrated, and they must be persuaded to make a commitment. In the growth stage, these efforts begin to take effect as support for the nonprofit cause or service increases. However, competitors also emerge during the growth stage.

As the product moves into maturity, support begins to level off as competition becomes more intense. Finally, as the decline stage is reached, the nonprofit cause or ser-

EXHIBIT 15.8 Product Life Cycle

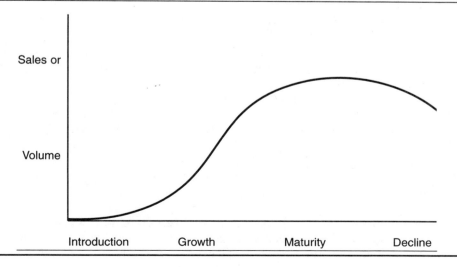

vice will become out-of-date and may be eliminated. Some organizations will shift their cause, as the March of Dimes did; others may alter their services, as the Girl Scouts did.

(ii) New Service Development

The needs of a nonprofit organization's supporters and clients are constantly changing. Responding to these changing needs involves the development of new services. This process should be similar to the new product development procedures used by service businesses (Johnson, Scheuing, and Gaida, 1986).

Ideas for new services can come from a variety of sources. Volunteers and staff members may have insights into emerging needs of clients; client surveys, focus groups, and other forms of market research may provide guidance; secondary sources of information may suggest new service opportunities. For instance, the rapid growth of personal computer sales and use has stimulated many educational institutions to offer new courses and programs to teach people how to use the new technology.

Once an idea for a new service has been suggested, it should be subjected to careful screening and evaluation. This is essential, because taking the idea further will usually require significant time and monetary investments. Most ideas are rejected at this point, for reasons of limited resources, unacceptable market potential, inappropriate fit with the organization's mission and objectives, and potentially strong competition.

If the idea passes the assessment step, the development process begins in earnest. The idea is further tested and refined, and the overall marketing strategy is formulated. Frequently, a new service idea is test marketed: it is introduced to a limited market prior to full-scale introduction. This process is very much like a dress rehearsal before a new theater production opens.

Gail L. Warden, chief executive officer of Detroit's Henry Ford Health Care Corporation, has proposed a new-product strategy to provide more facilities for inner-city people ("Profiting from the Nonprofits," 1990). The "Urban Initiatives Program" may include such innovations as storefront clinics to provide health care at lower costs. Warden has been meeting with community leaders and other constituents to test the new program idea.

(iii) Product Differentiation

Many nonprofit organizations use various marketing techniques to differentiate their service offerings. The development of a unique name, symbol, or design, a process known as branding, is one approach. United Way, March of Dimes, college mascots, like the University of Michigan's wolverine, and American Medical Association are widely recognized examples. Like business brands, these provide a means of identifying and differentiating one service or nonprofit agency from another.

Services may also be modified, or supplementary goods and services may be provided to differentiate one organization's product from others. A church's special services feature unique forms of music; a public TV station offers local cultural shows to compete with network programs; a civic club sponsors a long-distance bike race. Sometimes tangible goods are used to differentiate. T-shirts displaying the nonprofit organization's name and logo, reproductions of a museum's most famous artwork, and souvenir programs are examples.

Finally, the nonprofit organization's clients or supporters may receive added value from the "packaging" of several services. A community theater offers major donors preferred seating and parking, tickets to social events, and other amenities. A museum includes free parking and a guided tour as a part of its program for selected visitors. A university offers married student housing, a campus child-care center, and a family health-care program for its students with families. These and many other examples represent ways in which nonprofit organizations can distinguish themselves through product differentiation.

(B) PRICE

Everything has a price, whether price is called "dues," "fare," "tuition," "admission fee," or something else. All nonprofit organizations must raise revenue to support their activities. More and more, these revenues must come from clients and donors because government sources of funding are becoming restricted.

(i) Fees

Many nonprofit organizations have moved to a membership-based structure. If this is done, it is important that membership fees be reasonably priced for the marketplace (Temper, 1991). This can be accomplished by establishing several categories of membership, with different fees for various levels of participation and support. Other nonprofit organizations choose to charge program or activity fees above and beyond membership fees. For instance, a YMCA may charge its members for swimming lessons.

(ii) Donations

Most nonprofit organizations receive money, time, and personal effort in the form of donations from members, volunteers, and other supporters. The donation is the price paid by the supporter. Sometimes, the level of donation is set—tithing to a church, or a "suggested" donation to a museum when entering. In many other cases, however, the donor sets the level of monetary support and volunteered assistance. To encourage that assistance, it may be wise to provide guidance by suggesting desired levels of support.

(iii) Service Charges

Faced with rising costs and diminished government support, many nonprofit organizations are charging for services that were once free. This brings up the question: "How much can we charge?"

Ellis (1990) has suggested two ways to establish prices for nonprofit services. Both of these approaches require that a nonprofit organization accurately estimate its expenses before establishing a price for an activity or event:

- The recovery of costs approach involves determining what the organization's expenses will be and charging whatever is necessary to recover these expenses.
- The revenue-producing approach covers all expenses and provides additional revenue for the organization.

Ellis feels that the revenue-producing approach makes more sense because excess revenues from one activity and event may be needed to offset losses from others. To establish a reasonable charge, the nonprofit organization must consider demand and competitive market conditions, in addition to costs. Further, like all other marketing decisions, the decisions concerning price should be based on the target market selected and the organization's objectives.

(C) DISTRIBUTION

Business marketing theory and practice stress the importance of establishing an integrated network, known as a channel of distribution, to transfer goods and services from producers to consumers.

(i) Utilities Provided

Taken together, the components of a channel of distribution comprise a delivery system that makes goods and services available to buyers and creates time, place, and possession utilities, as follows:

- Time utility refers to making goods and services available when buyers want them. Examples: Hospital emergency rooms remain open 24 hours a day; colleges offer classes during the evening and weekend hours; community centers remain open late in the evening to provide activities for young adults.
- Place utility refers to making goods and services available where buyers want them. Examples: Storefront clinics and counseling centers provide services in local neighborhoods; emergency hotlines allow people with problems to reach counselors from their homes; colleges have satellite campuses.
- Possession utility refers to the transfer of ownership from the producer to the buyer. Examples: A college student "owns" the professor's time and knowledge during a class; a patient "owns" a doctor's expertise during a visit; a group of teenagers "own" a community center's playground during a game.

(ii) Service Delivery Systems

Because nonprofit organizations deal mainly in ideas and services, goods distribution concepts and strategies must be modified. Lovelock (1991) has suggested that two major questions must be considered, in order to understand service delivery systems:

- Must the customer be in direct physical contact with the service organization or can transactions be completed at arm's length?
- Should a service organization maintain only a single outlet or should it serve customers through multiple outlets at different sites?

Answers to these questions will help a nonprofit organization develop its distribution approach. For example, community medical care can be provided at a single location (hospital) or at several (storefront clinics). A community visiting nurses association can visit the elderly and others who need medical attention but are unable to leave their homes for treatment.

For some nonprofit services and ideas, the contact can be at arm's length through mailings, written materials, or electronic media. For example, a public TV station's contacts with its clients and donors is usually accomplished through its broadcasts. Likewise, many nonprofit organizations use radio, television, and other nonpersonal media to deliver educational messages to the public. The University of Rhode Island, for example, teaches a literature course via e-mail.

(iii) Intermediaries

Although intermediaries, or "middlemen," as they were formerly called, are primarily involved in the marketing of goods, they are also becoming important in service and nonprofit marketing. Intermediaries make the distribution process more efficient by reducing the number of contacts between producers and their customers. They also perform a number of distribution tasks, such as communication and resource allocation. Applying the concept of intermediaries to nonprofit marketing yields several intriguing possibilities. Some nonprofit organizations, such as United Way, can serve as clearinghouses for other agencies. They can raise and distribute funds, provide information about other agencies and their services, and suggest appropriate agencies to potential clients. A social worker can serve as an intermediary, guiding needy clients to specific nonprofit agencies and services. This role can also be played by the clergy, doctors, community action agencies, and others. It is important, therefore, that nonprofit organizations establish and maintain relationships with people and organizations that can serve as intermediaries for them.

(iv) Direct Marketing

By far, the fastest growing form of distribution is direct marketing. As a special kind of delivery system, direct marketing bypasses established distribution channels to deliver goods and services directly from sellers to buyers. The two major forms of direct marketing are direct mail and telemarketing.

Like businesses, many nonprofit organizations have turned to direct marketing for its efficiency as a sales and marketing approach. To date, the major applications have involved fund-raising. Direct mail appeals and telemarketing have become commonplace as fund-raising techniques. Organizations as diverse as the American Cancer Society, college alumni associations, and local chambers of commerce use direct marketing to solicit members and contributions.

In fact, almost all fund raisers use direct marketing, and this approach has become the dominant method for distributing fund-raising requests. Major objectives for direct marketing include generating new donors, reactivating lost donors, increasing responses from recent donors, building awareness, maintaining donor relations, and promoting special events. Both large and small nonprofit organizations have found that direct mail, telemarketing, and other direct marketing techniques are key strategic and tactical components of their fund-raising efforts (Peltier and Schibrowsky, 1995).

Direct marketing has the potential to deliver services to clients. Interactive communication (mail, telephone, or electronic media) can be used to establish direct relationships with targeted clients. For instance, prenatal information and an invitation to visit a prenatal clinic can be sent to young women identified as expectant mothers. Follow-up telephone calls can verify receipt of the information and schedule appointments at a clinic. A video illustrating proper diet, exercise, and personal care programs could be provided.

In an effort to reverse their declines in membership and attendance, some churches have turned to direct mail. This has proven to be an effective way to communicate their messages and inform their target audiences of their activities and services. To make sure their direct mailings succeed, church marketers state specific objectives for their direct mail programs, identify clearly the target audience and develop an appropriate mailing list, prepare compelling messages that will attract people within the target audience, pretest and modify direct mail offerings prior to mailing, and make sure that their mailings are timed properly. When these steps are followed, church marketers have a marketing tool that not only helps them increase participation, but also provides feedback and helps them learn something about their targeted audience (Considine, 1994).

Another direct marketing tool for delivering nonprofit services and ideas is the advanced telephone technology, specifically "800" and "900" numbers and fax services. These relatively new services offer convenient access to a nonprofit organization's staff, information, and expertise. They can be used to provide time and place utility to clients who are unable to visit the organization in person. An example is a university's "answer center" for gardeners and other people who have questions related to their homes, lawns, and gardens.

Finally, nonprofit marketers should consider using e-mail, commercial online services, and the Internet as means of providing access to their services and information. Since over a third of American households now have personal computers (and the number is growing), electronic commerce has become a reality. The Internet, in particular, has become a major source of information, entertainment, and commerce.

Marketers, such as L.L. Bean, have begun to use the Internet and the World Wide Web, its browsing and searching system, as a promotion medium. Nonprofit agencies can do the same. A nonprofit can have a site (known as the home page) that includes a history of the agency, descriptions of programs and services, and other relevant information. For example, a university can provide prospective students and their parents with admissions information on its home page.

(D) PROMOTION

No matter how excellent a nonprofit organization may be, or how worthwhile its purpose and services, or how dedicated its staff and volunteers, all effort will be wasted unless people are informed and reminded about its availability and persuaded to use its services and support its activities. This is the task of promotion, which involves communication with a nonprofit organization's publics.

The three primary goals of promotion are:

1. To inform. As a method of communication, promotion informs people about a nonprofit organization's existence, purpose, services, and capabilities. This is an especially important goal for new agencies, programs, and services. For example, a civic association has decided to offer a late-night basketball program to inner-city youth. To obtain participation in the new program, the association must use promotion to inform the community's young people of the program's availability, time, and location.
2. To persuade. Promotion attempts to influence people to do something— support the Easter Seal Society, don't drink and drive, fight illiteracy. Persuasion becomes an important promotional goal as an agency or service enters the growth stage of its life cycle.
3. To remind. Promotion is often used to keep an idea, service, or nonprofit organization's name in people's minds. This goal is important during the

maturity stage of the life cycle. The Salvation Army, American Red Cross, and United Way are organizations that stress reminder promotion.

To accomplish these goals, advertising, personal selling, sales promotion, and public relations are combined to form the promotional mix. It is especially important that the promotional mix elements be properly coordinated so that they work together to achieve the same goals.

(i) Advertising

This is the dominant form of nonpersonal promotion. Promotional messages are carried to the public by mass communications media—newspapers, television, and outdoor signs.

There are many forms of advertising and many purposes for which advertising may be used. Product and institutional advertising, the two major forms, are described as follows:

- Advertising designed to stimulate sales of a specific product or service, or participation in a specific activity, is called product advertising. Nonprofit organizations use this form of advertising when they feature a specific program or activity—for example, a fund-raising event, a blood donors' day, or a special museum exhibit.
- Institutional advertising promotes a concept, idea, image, or philosophy of a nonprofit organization or cause. Anyone who may have an impact on the advertiser, such as legislators, business leaders, or the general public, can be a target of institutional advertising. Much of the advertising done by nonprofit organizations is institutional advertising—for example, the promotion of values and beliefs by the Mormon Church.

(ii) Personal Selling

In contrast to the impersonal approach of advertising, in personal selling the promotional message is carried by someone who normally communicates with the potential client or supporter face-to-face. As a result, personal selling can be a highly individualized process that involves complex interpersonal relations.

Kotler and Andreasen (1991) observed that almost everyone in a nonprofit organization is likely to have personal contact with persons outside the organization. Salespeople, whose job is to actively influence the behavior of others, will have the most extensive contacts with outsiders. College recruiters, development officers, community organizers, and lobbyists are all contact persons. Service personnel who provide assistance to clients and members of the public will also have personal contacts and must understand the nature of personal selling. Service personnel include receptionists, museum guards, ticket takers, librarians, and the like.

Many observers of service marketing have emphasized the importance of personal contacts to customer satisfaction. Gronroos (1982) suggested that service organizations require a different organizational structure, one that integrates the simultaneous production and marketing of a service. This has been called "interactive marketing." As shown in Exhibit 15.9, the focus is on client–organization interactions.

These points of interaction have been termed the "moments of truth." To make sure that its clients are truly satisfied, a nonprofit organization must manage these moments

EXHIBIT 15.9 Interactive Marketing

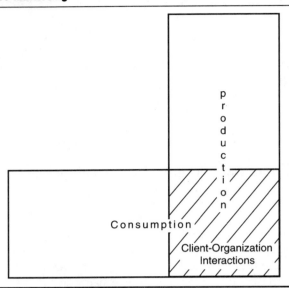

Source: *Adapted from Christian Gronroos,* Strategic Management and Marketing in the Service Sector *(Helsingfors: Swedish School of Economics and Business Administration, 1982), p. 137.*

of truth from start to finish. For instance, the receptionist in a health-care clinic must greet clients warmly; health-care professionals must be friendly and professional; billing and other follow-up activities must be handled effectively. In short, all the contacts with the clinic must make the client feel good about having come there.

Some nonprofit organizations are discovering that they must take personal selling further. They have to continue to provide good service to their clients, but they also have to become more aggressive in their selling efforts. The United States Postal Service is an example. To compete against UPS, Federal Express, and other business competitors, the Postal Service has created a 200-person national sales force to deal with large national and international customers with complex needs and multiple mailing sites (Keenan, 1994).

(iii) *Public Relations*

These promotion activities play an important role in the marketing programs of most nonprofit organizations. Public relations activities and programs are used to create a favorable impression for the organization and its efforts. Further, effective public relations complement a nonprofit organization's other promotion activities by building credibility. As a result, potential supporters and clients will be more receptive to the organization's ideas and services.

Many nonprofit organizations plan, manage, and coordinate their public relations activities through a director of public relations. This manager is responsible for communicating with an organization's various publics. The media and form of public relations will be adapted to each specific public. Some of the techniques used are press releases, speeches by executives, facility tours, annual reports, and community events. The goal of public relations management is to ensure that all contacts with a nonprofit organization's publics support and reinforce the desired image.

Harrison (1991) suggested that the most important public relations development for nonprofits is the concept of issue-oriented public relations. This involves positioning an organization as an authority on an issue and as an important part of the solution to the problem. The key, according to Harrison, is to focus on one or two issues that are "hot." By doing this, a nonprofit organization will create an environment in which people are more inclined to respond to its appeals for funds and volunteers, to attend its events, and to support its cause.

A final critical aspect of public relations is dealing with negative events and unfavorable media coverage. In particular, perceived funds mismanagement and other forms of misconduct threaten the credibility of charitable and other nonprofit organizations (Bailey, 1992). In the early 1990s, two large national nonprofits, the United Way and the NAACP, suffered a major loss of public confidence and financial reversals because of management irregularities. In both organizations, leadership changes were made and strong public relations efforts were undertaken to regain support.

(iv) Sales Promotion

A variety of promotion activities—other than personal selling, advertising, and public relations—can be used to achieve specific short-term objectives. Business examples include samples, premiums, coupons, demonstrations, contests, sweepstakes, and games.

Because they provide services, many nonprofit organizations are limited in their use of sales promotion techniques, but there are some examples. Fund-raising programs sometimes include a contest or sweepstakes to generate interest and excitement. Contributors may receive tokens of appreciation, and large contributors may be given special gifts. Even clients or customers can be stimulated with sales promotion techniques. For instance, a public transit authority rewards its one-millionth passenger; a museum gives a free bumper sticker to the first 5,000 visitors; a college recruiter gives prospective students a pen with the college logo. The possibilities are endless and so, it is hoped, are the results.

Suggested Readings

Albrecht, Karl and Zemke, Ron. 1985. *Service America!* Homewood, IL: Dow Jones-Irwin.

Arnott, Nancy. 1994. "Marketing With a Passion." *Sales & Marketing Management* (January).

Barbeito, Carol L. 1991. "How Researchers Can Make Their Work Relevant to the Needs of Non-Profits." *Chronicle of Philanthropy* (May).

Barna, George. 1992. *Church Marketing*. Ventura, CA: Regal Books.

Coffman, Larry L. 1986. *Public Sector Marketing*. New York: John Wiley & Sons.

Considine, John J. 1994. "Direct Mail: Can it Work for Religious Organizations?" *Journal of Direct Marketing* (Autumn).

Day, George S. and Wensley, Robin. 1983. "Marketing Theory with a Strategic Orientation." *Journal of Marketing* (Fall).

De los Santos, Gilberto. 1986. "Universities Offer Marketing Research Key." *Nonprofit World* (January–February).

DeVos, Karen. 1986. "Manufacturing Support Through Marketing." *Nonprofit World*. (March–April).

Dickson, John P. and Dickson, Sarah S. 1984/1985. Four-part marketing research series. *Nonprofit World* (November–December, 1984 through May–June, 1985).

Drucker, Peter F. 1989. "What Business Can Learn from Nonprofits." *Harvard Business Review* (July–August).

Ellis, Susan J. 1990. "What Should We Charge for Our Services?" *Nonprofit World* (May–June).

Fram, Eugene H. 1991. "Nonprofit Boards Would Profit with Marketers Aboard." *Marketing News*, April 29.

Gronroos, Christian. 1982. *Strategic Management and Marketing in the Service Sector*. Helsingfors: Swedish School of Economics and Business Administration.

Guy, Bonnie S. and Patton, Wesley E. 1988. "The Marketing of Altruistic Causes: Understanding Why People Help." *Journal of Services Marketing* (Winter).

Harrison, Thomas A. 1991. "Six PR Trends That Will Shape Your Future." *Nonprofit World* (March–April).

Johnson, Eugene M., Scheuing, Eberhard E., and Gaida, Kathleen A. 1986. *Profitable Service Marketing*. Homewood, IL: Dow Jones-Irwin.

Keenan, William, Jr. 1994. "Can We Deliver?" *Sales & Marketing Management* (February).

Kelly, Bill. 1991. "Cause-Related Marketing: Doing Well While Doing Good." *Sales & Marketing Management* (March).

Kotler, Philip and Andreasen, Alan. 1991. *Strategic Marketing for Nonprofit Organizations* (4th ed.). Englewood Cliffs, NJ: Prentice-Hall.

Kotler, Philip, Ferrell, O. C., and Lamb, Charles (Eds.). 1987. *Strategic Marketing for Nonprofit Organizations: Cases and Readings*. Englewood Cliffs, NJ: Prentice-Hall.

Kotler, Philip and Levy, Sidney, J. 1979. "Broadening the Concept of Marketing." *Journal of Marketing* (January).

Lancome, Claude. 1985. "Strategic Marketing for Nonprofit Organizations." *Nonprofit World* (July–August).

Lauffer, Armand. 1984. *Strategic Marketing for Not-for-Profit Organizations*. New York: Free Press.

Laycock, D. Kerry. 1990. "Are You Ready for Strategic Planning?" *Nonprofit World* (September–October).

Levitt, Theodore. 1975. "Marketing Myopia" (With Retrospective Commentary). *Harvard Business Review* (September–October).

Lovelock, Christopher H. 1991. *Services Marketing* (2nd ed.). Englewood Cliffs, NJ: Prentice-Hall.

Lovelock, Christopher H. and Weinberg, Charles B. 1989. *Public and Nonprofit Marketing* (2nd ed.). Redwood City, CA: Scientific Press.

McCort, J. Daniel. 1994. "A Framework for Evaluating the Relationship Extent of a Relationship Marketing Strategy: The Case for Nonprofit Organizations." *Journal of Direct Marketing* (Spring).

Miaoulis, George. 1985. "Nonprofits' Marketing Strategies Begin with Customer Satisfaction." *Marketing News*, March 15.

Miller, Krystal. 1993. "More Black Churches Go into Business." *The Wall Street Journal* (January 27).

Muehrcke, Jill (Ed.) 1989. *Marketing: The Society for Nonprofit Organizations' Leadership Series*, Madison, WI: The Society for Nonprofit Organizations.

Nall, Janice R. and Dimsdale, Parks B. 1985. "Civic Group Adopts Marketing Technique." *Marketing News*, June 21.

Peltier, James W. and John A. Schibrowsky. 1995. "The Direct Marketing of Charitable Causes: A Study of U.S. Fundraisers." *Journal of Direct Marketing* (Summer).

Petrison, Lisa A., Robert C. Blattberg, and Paul Wang. 1993. "Database Marketing: Past, Present, and Future." *Journal of Direct Marketing* (Summer).

"Profiting from the Nonprofits." 1990. *Business Week*, March 26.

Riley, Anne Lowry and Millar Bruce. 1992. "United Way: The Fallout After the Fall." *Chronicle of Philanthropy* (March).

Schwartz, Karen. 1989. "Nonprofits' Bottomline: They Mix Lofty Goals and Gutsy Survival Strategies." *Marketing News*, February 13.

Temper, Roy H. 1991. "Donations Versus Dues." *Nonprofit World* (January–February).

Tomes, Anne E. and Hamilton, Barbara. 1991. "The Marketing of a Community Service." *Journal of Marketing Management*. April, 1991.

Van Doren, Doris C. and Smith, Louise W. 1985. "Self-Analysis Can Gauge Marketing Orientation." *Marketing News*, December 6.

Williams, Monci Jo. 1986. "How To Cash in on Do-Good Pitches." *Fortune*, June 9.

16 ▼ Role of Communications in Organizational Transformation and Renewal

SUZANNE J. LULEWICZ

SJL Associates, Inc.

Yet possessing language, we are the only beings who can transmute the material thing and the transitory event into an enduring immateriality.

Douglas (1973)

16.1 Introduction

For all of us, change has become a way of life—change for the better, or change for the worse. However we wish to view it, social, cultural, and economic change is overtaking our abilities to deal with the various dislocations that are occurring in our society, our organizations, and our personal and work lives. As our world becomes smaller, the distinctions among our choices have become more and more ambiguous, even as the consequences of choice become increasingly costly.

The rate of social and technological change that is currently overwhelming us drives the need to implement the information and initiatives presented in this chapter. Organizations, leaders, teams, and individuals must have tools that can help them bring about the innovation and creativity that are the hallmarks of a high-performing and community-building organization, a self-renewing organization that has the vision and mission to address some of the intractable problems facing our society.

These specific tools are needed for a number of reasons. Organizations seem to be plagued by ineffective problem solving and decision making. Senior managers, middle managers, and employees are found not to have the information needed to do an effective job. Work processes that provoke fear and ambiguity and which do not explain how decisions at all levels are made appear to be a consistent presence in many organizations.

Some employees feel a sense of powerlessness in the face of their leaders' lack of responsiveness to their ideas or suggestions. Such leaders often send inconsistent or mixed messages worsened by cold and aloof behavior.

And, finally, there is the presence of unethical conduct in the workplace. This includes not only the more obvious drug abuse, stealing, embezzlement, and violence, but also lying to customers, producing low-quality products, and the development of golden parachutes and other self-serving shelters for today's senior executives, even as they downsize their workforces and increase stockholders' market share.

The tools of visioning and dialogue are important skills all managers and leaders need to develop and use in order to transform their work units and their organizations from those capable of creating human suffering, to those capable of support and self-renewal of the human spirit. They require the time-honored communication skills of good listening, and speaking to others in ways that allow individual responsibility, the sharing of relevant information, the building of trust and openness, respect for and valuing of others' differences, as well as their competencies and organizational roles.

However, what you will also find as you read this chapter is hopefully a new way of using those communications skills, a new way of framing your own organization's goals and future. The use of language in both the visioning and dialogue process can help align those within an organization behind a commitment that identifies the common values of all concerned with the future of the organization. As each of you goes about your workday building and perpetuating your organization's culture, the information here will help you notice the language you and your associates use to talk about departments, systems, products, volunteers, members, customers, and employees. What can you interpret from what you hear?

Does everyone know what the organization is about? Do people treat each other with respect at all levels and in all situations? Do people explain their decision-making process clearly? Do systems help people to do an effective job?

If you've answered *no* to any of these questions, then you need to learn more about the process of visioning and dialogue and how your use of language is pivotal for you to successfully implement change. This chapter is intended to provide you with some concrete ways to deal with potentially destructive cultures and systems that can sap the strength, creativity, innovation, and competitive edge of both yourself and your organization or department.

16.2   New Organizational Context

Organizations that conduct business have been and for the most part continue to be defined by the language of control: control of resources, of budgets, of the market share, of the bottom line, of the corporate image, of employee behavior and productivity. The list could go on and on.

Since the seventeenth century, when Descartes first defined the metaphor of the universe working as a gigantic mechanical clock, the most pervasive symbol of organizational structures has been a machine-driven one. Management science has focused on how one can successfully manage a company's resources, people, and image, the consumers' choice of product, and the myriad resources that help an organization produce a product or service.

In addition, mechanistic and often military metaphors continue to guide twentieth-century organizations toward developing lines of authority that generally keep people from knowing or sharing information. These lines of authority perpetuate and maintain barriers across departmental systems and focus on keeping staff, especially senior staff, from speaking frankly to one another during some of the most crucial times of organizational decision making. While this "divide and conquer" metaphor for leadership is in the process of being transformed, this type of management structure is still more often the political rule rather than the exception. Its tenacity appears to lie in its ability to maintain the survival of leaders and their personal operating agendas just as if they were the organization's own.

However, the discoveries in quantum physics that have brought forward a new way of perceiving reality have affected many areas of study: organizational behavior, business management, psychology, physics, and philosophy. We are in the throes of clarifying, defining, and experimenting with ways organizations need to operate in order to survive and prosper in the reality we are currently creating for ourselves. Margaret Wheatley, in her 1993 book *Leadership and the New Science*, explains that: "Our concept of organizations is moving away from the mechanistic creations that flourished in the age of bureaucracy. We have begun to speak in earnest of more fluid, organic structures, even of boundaryless organizations. We are beginning to recognize organizations as systems, construing them as 'learning organizations' and crediting them with some type of self-renewing capacity."

16.3   *Scientific Basis*

Scientific experimentation in the area of subatomic physics over the past 25 years has highlighted that we perceive reality in a way different from what was traditionally thought, and that as a result of our perceptions of reality we affect that reality. Physicists have found that in this world of subatomic particles, an observer can change, or participate in creating, the outcome. In other words, the unfolding of our reality has as much to do with our participation in it as it has to do with the laws of science.

Quantum theory is the science which encompasses this paradoxical quality of nature. According to physicist Fritjof Capra, author of *The Tao of Physics* (1980), nature does not represent the logic and rationality of known science, but rather represents the "probabilities of interconnections." This "probability of interconnections" reveals to today's scientists the basic oneness of the universe. This probability shows that we cannot break apart the world into independently existing subunits. What was once considered the basic building blocks capable of being objectively measured has now become a complicated web of relations.

The underlying nature of life as described by quantum theory helps point out that it is no longer Descartes' mechanical and controlled clock that moves the universe but rather a "dynamic connectedness."

Wheatley (1993) goes on to describe how the impact of this discovery alters how we view our natural world: "Streams have a different relationship with natural forces. With sparkling confidence they know that their intense yearning for ocean will be fulfilled, that nature creates not only the call, but the answer."

16.4 Role of Language

Language has traditionally been viewed as a tool to identify, articulate, and analyze our organizational structures and strategies. Now, however, we are coming to a realization that the language we speak and the organizations we describe cannot really be separated. To put it in context, in *The Fifth Discipline Fieldbook* (Senge et al., 1994), Fred Kofman states that: "While the speaker creates language, the language also creates the speaker." In other words, when the leader and the members of an organization create the language that describes, quantifies, and qualifies what they do and how they feel about their work, the language they've created will in turn create them as members of that organization.

Another way to say it is if all we see is the color green, we will never be able to talk about those things that are blue. Organizations that consider people a valuable human resource, not easily replaceable, will not see or attempt to construct an organizational reality in which employees are viewed as work units who can be represented and measured on a profit/loss statement.

To reinforce the cultural power of language and how it filters our perception of what is real, the following is an example taken from Richard Bandler and John Grinder's book *The Structure of Magic I* (1975). According to Bandler and Grinder, within any particular language system, part of the richness of experience is associated with the number of distinctions the language can make in areas of sensation. In Maidu, for example, an American Indian language of Northern California, only three words are available to describe the color spectrum. They have a word for red; a word for green-blue; and a word that identifies yellow-orange-brown. The English language with its eight distinctions, has a greater array of choice and perceived distinctions in which to describe the world in color.

What does this discussion have to do with the way members of organizations communicate, strategize, plan, and represent their organizations to their customers and their communities? How we choose to live our lives and express our values and assumptions about the reality that supports and reinforces our social and cultural beliefs is grounded in the very nature of the language that we use. Our words—whether in conversations, discussions, memos, letters, social or business context—express who we are and what we believe. According to Humberto Maturana and Francisco Varela, in their book *The Tree of Knowledge* (1992), every reflection invariably takes place in language. Language is the starting point, our instrument of thinking, and our sticking point. Underlying everything we say is this constant awareness that the phenomenon of knowing cannot be taken as though there were facts or objects out there that we grasp and store in our head.

Communications systems and processes within an organization now become not just a means of sharing information and inspiring motivation, but they become a way for us to transform our organizations, and, as a result, the lives of those who work in them. Even though language may still be a way to perpetuate ambiguity, error, and shortsighted judgment within organizations, it can be, according to Kofman (*The Fifth Discipline Fieldbook*), "a medium through which we create new understandings and new realities as we begin to talk about them. In fact, we don't talk about what we see, we see only what we can talk about."

Thus, language is an extremely powerful form of organizational communications and of organizational transformation or creation. Vision, mission, values, principles, and ethics are all powered by an ability of an organization's members to articulate clearly the things that matter to them—those elements that make up the quality of their lives. What follows are some of the strategic ways communications processes can empower people to make those distinctions.

16.5 Communicating Leadership Through Visioning

Much interest, attention, and education has focused on leaders bringing to life a vision that can be shared by others in an organization. According to Warren Bennis and Burt Nanus in their 1995 book *Leaders: Strategies for Taking Charge*, a vision articulates a view of a "realistic, credible, attractive future for the organization, a condition that is better in some important ways than what now exists." In other words, it is a unique and ideal image of a common future.

Discovering a common purpose and getting others to share in that purpose is evidence of dynamic and strategic leadership. For an organization to have a potential future and provide knowledge, inspiration, energy, and guidance to all who work within it is a vital aspect of organizational transformation and individual self-renewal.

There are a number of ways to begin transforming an organization's future using a visioning process. A dynamic and enthusiastic leader does, however, need to be a lightning rod, giving energy to the visioning process and enabling the organization to move into the future. Enlisting the support of key participants within the organization is critical for the organization to achieve success with its potential future.

A leader can create his or her own personal vision for the organization and set about communicating that vision in order to enlist the members' support. When a leader is the ultimate symbol of the organization, the driving force behind its work, then this option may be the one that can transform the organization most successfully. Charismatic leaders can quite possibly generate the organization's vision and communicate it most intensely and nearly singlehandedly, developing their base of support from those who gravitate to their vision, personality, and message. Leaders such as Martin Luther King, Jr. and John F. Kennedy model the energy of this process.

Another way for a leader to begin the process of visioning is to co-create an organization's vision with selected stakeholders of the organization. This process starts by gathering various leaders of the organization, board members, senior staff, and members of the organization at large for a series of facilitated retreats, meetings, and dialogues, sometimes taking place over an extended period of time, possibly a year. Organizational issues, strategies, products, customers, scenarios, purposes, and goals may all be discussed and viewed in the context of potential futures that could motivate, inspire, and guide the organization's workforce and members through the years ahead. This process is more participative and has a longer timeline than a visioning process determined solely by the leader.

Another process designed to help formulate a vision works along the lines of the "Future Search" process. In his book, *Discovering Common Ground* (1993), Marvin Weisbord describes how Future Search conferences can bring people together to achieve a shared vision. A Future Search conference brings together a large representative group of organizational stakeholders, including customers. Diversity of viewpoints are expected and encouraged and the relationship of the organization to the world outside—customers, workers, and the community—is explored. While the entire event is facilitated, participation among individuals takes places in self-regulated groups, and lasts usually for two to three days. Consensus is sought and action plans are developed.

Whatever process an organization works with, a vision will not instill life in an organization unless others' personal visions share in the organizational one as well. Leaders who have successfully enrolled key members in an organization's visionary future have relied heavily on communication through the oral and written word (newsletters, telephone calls, slogans, memos, letters), graphics (posters, symbols, letterhead), and liberal use of distinctive metaphors, stories, examples, and anecdotes to enlist support.

The essence of any vision, personal or organizational, is that it be concrete, not abstract. A vision not only needs to be communicated in special and one-time-only group presentations, but on a daily basis within the organization's culture—over coffee, in meetings, over lunch, in daily memos and e-mail—and in nonverbal behavior as well. An organization's vision must live and breathe in everyone and be seen in their behavior, their attitudes, their work. It is only through the development of a new culture that a vision is continually renewed and that the organization has a chance to successfully meet its future.

This can happen only if the organization's leaders are successful in communicating their message and enlisting the support of others in their vision. This can happen through a rich series of concrete visualizations and formal and informal communications that, according to authors James Kouzes and Barry Posner (1991), make good use of identifiable metaphors, figures of speech, stories, examples, and anecdotes.

Kouzes and Posner identify a corporate leader who has successfully articulated a symbol to represent his organization's future. The chair of Kollmorgen Corporation often used a visualization of a brilliantly cut three-inch diamond to capture the multifaceted symbol of excellence he wanted the company to represent—excellence in product and service. The CEO estimated that he spent at least 25 percent of his time talking with employees about the company and the culture that he was seeking to perpetuate. Sometimes he presented this diamond symbol to groups in a presentation style; other times he performed a visualization exercise where he asked employees to clearly imagine this diamond as a dynamic and pulsating force and for them to think about what it means to them in relation to their work.

This conscious use of metaphorical expressions gives concrete connection to abstract ideas. Such figures of speech as "I have a dream," "climb every mountain," "reach for the stars," and "turn this ship around," enable those who hear them to connect at a level deeper than a conceptual one and to engage their own personal vision and purpose to it. When communicated through the many channels we use to share life—poetry, storytelling, humor—a vision can capture peoples' imagination and enthusiasm, providing them the power to help implement an organization's future that perpetuates their own values. According to Kouzes and Posner, leaders communicate to others how to behave in the culture through what they call "moments of truth." How leaders spend their time, what questions they ask, how they react to critical incidents, and what they reward make crystal clear what is really expected of people in the organization.

Informal channels of communications within an organization are another important way for a culture to be conveyed and reinforced. With the use of symbols, artifacts, and ceremonies of workday life, leaders who communicate successfully make great efforts to link their organizational issues to the day-to-day culture, history, and tradition of the organization.

Thus, once a clear future for the organization has been articulated, through whatever means chosen, it requires a long and continuous process of keeping the vision alive, dynamic, and in the forefront of everyone's operating behavior. Through information (conversations, e-mail, stories, norms, traditional ways of operating) and more formal means (meetings, seminars, presentations, newsletters, magazines, memos, etc.), the basics of what the vision represents are continually reinforced and brought forward. For the organization to be transformed, all involved in the process must have a personal stake in the organization that will further both the organizational future and their own.

16.6   Transformation Through Metaphor

The language of metaphor is an extremely important dynamic in organizational transformation and change. The generative power of language to shape our world and, in turn, interpret what we shape helps to create the reality in which we exist.

Using metaphors is a wonderful way to communicate directly to the feelings of members. They contain the essence of the meaning, without having to explain or define in ways that could limit the connection for others. It becomes possible to take an abstract idea or concept and propel it forward with excitement, enthusiasm, and energy with concrete and tangible images that make the future possible.

In *The Fifth Discipline Fieldbook* (Senge, et al., 1994), one of its contributors, Rick Ross, comments that all words are symbols and as such are abstractions and that they often have different meanings to different people. "If most people understand this—if they assumed that they did not understand what an individual means by a particular word unless they inquired about it—then everyone would routinely check the meanings behind the words being spoken more often and there would be far less miscommunication." Thus, if language helps to generate reality and there is limited shared meaning of language among members of an organization, then to drive change in which all stakeholders can take part requires the building of a shared vocabulary that all can relate to. Experience has shown that using metaphors may be the best way to do this.

Webster's Dictionary defines a metaphor as a figure of speech in which a term is transferred from the object it ordinarily designates to an object it may designate only by implicit comparison or analogy. It comes from the Greek *meta*, meaning to change and *pherein*, meaning to bear. In other words, metaphor literally means to *bear the change*.

Because we participate more deeply than we imagine in the shaping of the world we perceive, it is important to pay close attention to the language we use. We need to take care to make evident the meaning or lack of meaning others share in a word or phrase.

In her essay on "Language as Action: Linking Metaphors with Organizational Transformation," Susan Bethanis talks about language as a medium of change and of the link between language, thought, and action (Chawla and Renesch, 1995). She identifies the language as a perpetuating medium. The reason for this is that metaphors become embedded in all of the various relationships—supervisor/subordinate, employee/customer, leader/staff, and so on—that make up the organization. Because these metaphors are reinforced over and over again—in discussions, internal written memos, marketing materials—the metaphors become tacit or taken for granted. And when assumptions are not questioned, learning stops.

In their *In Search of Excellence* (1982), Peters and Waterman highlight Peter Vaill's work with high-performance systems. High-performing systems behave in much the same way as other self-fulfilling prophecies. Something works for observable reasons, then a private language and set of symbols emerge; people feel energized because something works, and if they are permitted, will act in a new way. As a result of this acting in a new way, more good things happen until an air of invincibility takes over.

Metaphors can also perpetuate domination and control. According to Susan Bethanis, metaphors are able to infiltrate and create a culture on many levels, social, interpersonal, intrapersonal, and so on. Certainly metaphors, if not continually questioned and compared with our own individual interests and values, can have an overpowering energy, rather than an empowering one.

An example of both the high-performing system and the perpetuation of domination and control can be illustrated with Hitler and his specific use of Germany's traditional Teutonic myths. At every possible opportunity he combined military language and mythic images of historic Germanic stories to capture the hearts and minds of Germans in establishing his vision for the future. The symbols of such figures as Wotan and Siegfried, from Teutonic myth, were used to frame and power his vision of a new Germany.

Metaphors are not merely figures of speech, nor are they merely an unusual way of saying something. According to Bethanis, when we do things with words, it alters our way of being in the world; human beings pay closer attention to the interplay of their own and others' expressions. If we listen carefully, for example, we can better discern what people mean by what they are saying. We can clarify by asking questions. When we speak, we can be more conscious about how words reflect our deeply held assumptions and thoughts.

Metaphors are a spark for new meanings to emerge, says Bethanis. The opportunity exists for assumptions to shift as a result of new understandings.

16.7   The Concept of Dialogue

In addition to the visioning process, there is another extremely important transformational communications process that is available to organizations to influence and further drive the process of change. This is the concept of dialogue.

The physicist David Bohm first defined dialogue by contrasting it with discussion and identifying the important distinctions between the two. According to Bohm (Land and Jarman, 1992), discussion is associated with defending a point of view. Dialogue, on the other hand, is concerned with how information and meaning flows through people. In dialogue, no one is trying to make a point, or defending their current view.

In *The Fifth Discipline* (1990), Senge further explains that Bohm frames discussion in terms of each individual's drive to win. The subject of common interest could very likely be analyzed and broken apart into may different points of perspective by those who are participating in the discussion. However, while another person's view may be accepted in order to strengthen someone else's, the purpose each person has within that team or group is to have their view ultimately prevail.

According to Bohm (Senge, 1990), thought is to a large degree collective and can be viewed in such things as cultural myths and social norms. As a result, we cannot just improve thought individually. We must look on thought "as a systemic phenomena arising from how we interact and discourse with one another." Therefore, Bohm argues that in dialogue a group of people access a larger "pool of common meaning"; that individuals gain insights into how and what makes them think the way they do that simply could not be achieved individually. What happens is that a new way of looking at things begins to emerge as a result of a team developing a common and shared meaning. People no longer oppose each other, seeking to defend their point of view. Rather, the team defines for itself a common and shared ground that is capable of producing continual growth and change.

One of the remarkable requirements of dialogue is a person's ability to suspend his or her individual assumptions, beliefs, or opinions and be able to communicate them freely. This means that if a team of department heads is holding a dialogue around a strategic issue of concern to the entire organization and that there are unspoken assumptions in the organization's culture that certain departments have more strategic value to the organization than others, that belief, and other related operating assumptions connected to it, must surface and be clearly stated for all team members to recognize and respond to it. The reason for this is that if in this dialogue the department heads do not reveal all of their beliefs and opinions about the relationships of the departments to each other and to the organization, these undisclosed assumptions will block any flow of common meaning the team would have been able to achieve. Real generative and creative dialogue could not take place.

In light of Bohm's and Senge's experiments, the team will end up with a group of individuals sharing information and points of view that are incoherent. They are incoherent because as long as beliefs, opinions, and assumptions do not get voiced and heard by all within the team engaging in dialogue, then the team's discourse will not be based on coherent thinking, but rather on patterns of thought driven by emotion, perception, memory, or opinion. There will be no opportunity for team members to actively inquire into the validity of the underlying assumptions. These beliefs are then viewed as fact and not subject to question. They become the accepted status quo. The results of decisions based on incoherent thought can be seen in the fact that we produce outcomes that have uncontrollable consequences that we either did not want in the first place or were trying to avoid.

In addition to this important suspending of assumptions, Bohm identifies two additional requirements needed for dialogue to take place: All participants must regard one another as colleagues; and there must be a facilitator who can maintain the framework and context of dialogue (Senge, 1990).

This need to regard each of the team members as equals or colleagues is critical in order to create a positive and participative environment within the team. It allows the team to build an interactive trust with each other, which is a vital component to the success of dialogue.

The more skilled the participants are at suspending their assumptions within view of the entire team and continuing their mutual quest for clarity and deeper insight, the less will be their need for a facilitator. Deep listening, not only to oneself but to others on the team, is a critical and vital skill participants in a dialogue need to demonstrate. However, pending the development of these skills that self-regulate the context of dialogue, it is the facilitator who helps keep the team on track in sustaining dialogue, without letting it drift off unintentionally into discussion or debate.

(A) ROLE OF DIALOGUE IN ORGANIZATIONAL TRANSFORMATION

In a chapter from *Learning Organizations: Developing Cultures for Tomorrow's Workplace*, called "Mindshift: Strategic Dialogue for Breakthrough Thinking," written by Sherrin Bennett and Juanita Brown, strategic dialogue is described as the process by which organizational stakeholders can begin to develop dramatic and far-reaching initiatives for change in order to transform the way an organization does business (Chawla and Renesch, 1995). According to Bennett and Brown, strategic dialogue is built on an operating principle that the stakeholders in any system already have within them all of the wisdom and creativity to confront even the most difficult of challenges.

Innovation is much more likely to occur under these circumstances because a team skilled in dialogue will be able to surface their own individual opinions and beliefs and continually inquire as to their validity and truth. Innovation comes about as a result of these team members being able to give voice to the beliefs that shape key organizational decisions and the sometimes mutually held assumptions that drive thinking and all action within an organization. The members of a team in a successful dialogue process are able to see the whole picture, and yet create fresh and new insights that would not have been apparent to the team outside of this dialogue framework. Thus, strategic dialogue can lead to creative and innovative potential solutions in response to challenging issues. "In dialogue, the process of change feels like giving birth to new meaning out of which we realize creative possibilities for action" (Bennett and Brown, 1995).

The activity of strategic dialogue can help an organization pursue a generative way of dealing with its strategic issues and concerns because, as Bennett and Brown explain, the process of change within the activity of dialogue reveals the "profound realization that the way we have linked concepts in our mind gives rise to patterns of thought and feeling as well as perception of the world and thus our actions in daily life. If we have difficulties, they are our difficulties and the resolution of them often lies in re-conceiving with one another our pattern of thought itself."

16.8   The Creation of Culture

Much of what we have talked about over the course of this chapter has to do with how communications within an organization can cultivate transformation and innovation to meet the intractable issues and concerns of today's society. The communications processes within organizations that can help further this transformation require skills in internal reflection techniques, knowing how to listen to oneself and others, and the ability to articulate clearly, and for beneficial purposes, guiding metaphors, symbols, stories, and anecdotes that help build organizations, communities, and cultures that can sustain and nourish us, rather than diminish us.

With the scientific concept of this web of dynamic connectedness providing the basic foundation, the communications processes of visioning and dialogue are all about turning our workplaces into communities: Communities that reflect values of commitment, caring, and, indeed, love. Shaffer and Anundsen (1993) state that while offices and factories still continue to display their unique brands of internal, hierarchical politics, a new wave has been sweeping through America's businesses that promises to make a sense of community much more commonplace.

Building a sense of community seems to improve not only the bottom line (increased commitment, better work performance, higher quality customer service, better product, etc.), but also the work environment for employees. Considering that workers are spending the majority of their lives at work, the concept of "treating workers as whole human beings with families, spiritual lives, and values that deserve attention along with their job descriptions, and that the organization itself is inseparable from the environment in which it operates" could be a welcome value and relief—both spiritual and physical—to today's embattled and stressed workers.

Systems thinking, which views the world through the "probabilities of interconnections," and which is framed in all of the preceding concepts we've discussed, can create an operating environment where longed-for feelings of community can flourish. In our world, where cultural change is accelerating and we seem to have lost the traditional anchors—family, religion, marriage, the church, the government—that have helped us maintain our compass bearing as we move through changing and difficult times, this is truly a valuable contribution.

To create a workplace community requires a number of elements to occur or be in place that allow a community to flourish. Shaffer and Anundsen (1993) describe them as follows: an alignment of organizational values, an employee-based structure, teamwork, open communication, mutual support, respect for individuals and individuality, permeable boundaries, and group renewal. All of these values are evident in the work of all of the individuals who have theorized and worked to develop the practical applications of organizational renewal and transformation in what have come to be known as *learning organizations*, and which have been outlined here, though in a very abbreviated form.

Bringing these elements into the workplace is not without its challenges. Shaffer and Anundsen (1993) cite one highly successful organization that exemplified all of the elements of a workplace community but began losing its competitive edge when a recession struck. The employees had focused so much on their interpersonal relationships that they had neglected to take the steps needed to bring in new business. When the financial pinch came, they split into factions, thus damaging community and productivity.

However, it is incumbent upon organizations, as society moves into the twenty-first century, and at a time when family and social connectedness is at an all-time low, to balance the internal dynamics of their culture and group behavior. People need as much attention focused on their needs, expectations, and feelings within the workplace as they often get regarding the quality and quantity of their performance and productivity.

Suggested Readings

Argyris, Chris. 1992. *On Organizational Learning*. Cambridge, MA: Blackwell Business.

Bandler, Richard and Grinder, John. 1975. *The Structure of Magic I: A Book About Language and Therapy*. Palo Alto, CA: Science and Behavior Books, p. 10.

Bandler, Richard and Grinder, John. 1982. *Reframing, Neuro-Linguistic Programming and the Transformation of Meaning*. Moab, UT: Real People Press, p. 10.

Bennis, W. B. and Nanus, B. 1985. *The Strategies for Taking Charge*. New York: Harper Row, p. 89.

Bohl, Don L., ed., 1994. *The Learning Organization in Action*. Organizational Dynamics articles collected and published by the American Management Association.

Bohm, David and Edwards, Mark. 1991. *Changing Consciousness: Exploring the Hidden Source of the Social, Political and Environmental Crises Facing our World*. San Francisco: Harper.

Capra, Fritjof. 1980. *The Tao of Physics*. New York: Bantam Books, p. 57.

Chawla, Sarita and Renesch, John, ed. 1995. *Learning Organizations: Developing Cultures for Tomorrow's Workplace*, Portland, OR: Productivity Press pp. 189–191; 167, 181–182.

Douglas, Kenneth, ed. 1973. *World Masterpieces*, 3rd ed. vol. 2. New York: Norton, p. 1356.

Kouzes, James M. and Posner, Barry Z. 1991. *Credibility*. San Francisco: Jossey-Bass.

Kouzes, James M. and Posner, Barry Z. 1991. *The Leadership Challenge*. San Francisco: Jossey-Bass, pp. 107, 118, 210.

Land, George and Jarman, Beth. 1992. *Breakpoint and Beyond: Mastering the Future—Today*. New York: HarperBusiness, p. 170.

Maturana, Humberto and Varela, Francisco J. (Translated by Robert Paolucci). 1992. *The Tree of Knowledge: The Biological Roots of Human Understanding*. Boston & London: Shambhala, p. 247.

Peters, Tom and Waterman, Robert H. 1982. *In Search of Excellence: Lessons from America's Best-Run Companies*. New York: Warner Books, p. 264.

Senge, Peter M. 1990. *The Fifth Discipline: The Art and Practice of the Learning Organization*. New York: Doubleday, pp. 240, 242–243.

Senge, Peter M., Roberts, Charlotte, Ross, Richard B., Smith, Bryan J., and Kleiner, Art. 1994. *The Fifth Discipline Fieldbook: Strategies and Tools for Building a Learning Organization*. New York: Doubleday, pp. 287, 388.

Shaffer, Carolyn R. and Anundsen, Kristen. 1993. *Creating Community Anywhere: Finding Support and Connection in a Fragmented World*. New York: Perigee Books, Putnam, pp. 113, 116–122.

Wheatley, Margaret J. 1993. *Leadership and the New Science: Learning about Organization from an Orderly Universe*, San Francisco: Berrett-Koehler, pp. 13, 16.

Weisbord, Marvin R. 1993. *Discovering Common Ground*, San Francisco: Berrett-Koehler.

17 Communicating Your Cause

Evelyn Alemanni

ALL.EA

17.1 Introduction

Nothing happens without communication. Whatever the focus of the nonprofit organization—providing day care referrals, sponsoring medical research, preserving and protecting the environment, helping victims of earthquakes and storms—one of the first steps to achieving successful results is effectively communicating the organization's cause. After all, no one can help you if they don't know what you're trying to accomplish. Achieving this through public relations planning and the use of print media is the subject of this chapter.

Section 17.2 introduces the concepts of public relations (PR) as they apply to nonprofit organizations. Guidelines for setting PR objectives are provided. Section 17.3 describes the process of developing a balanced public relations plan that carefully focuses an organization's message.

A group's manager or founder may not always make the best spokesperson. Section 17.4 describes what it takes to be a spokesperson and presents the alternative of using an outside PR agency. Access to the media and the credibility of the person providing information are two keys to successful media coverage. Section 17.5 tells how to develop a media list, how to work with reporters, and how to become a news source. Tools of the trade include faxes, modems, the Internet, and the ability to originate a story concept. Section 17.6 describes tools to assemble and decisions to make before writing for the media.

The time taken to research an issue and write a simple letter to the editor can be capitalized upon to develop newspaper features, articles for monthly magazines, op-ed pieces, and more. Section 17.7 demonstrates the development of a concept and its use in a variety of published pieces.

17.2 Public Relations Introduction

Price, product, promotion, and distribution are the four commonly cited elements of the marketing mix. *Promotion* is the means by which the consuming public is informed, persuaded, and reminded of the organization's goals, activities, purpose, and services. Aspects of promotion include advertising, personal selling, direct mail, and public relations. *Public relations* includes all communications to the organization's audience (or "customers"), including newsletters, press releases, articles in newspapers and magazines, Internet home pages, interviews on radio and television, and events such as press conferences and community events, speeches by executives, and presentations to government agencies and boards. The goal of public relations is to influence public opinion by presenting an accurate and positive image of the organization. The relationship of marketing, promotion, and public relations is illustrated in Exhibit 17.1.

Marketing issues are covered more fully in Chapter 16.

Why bother with public relations? The most important reason is that, compared with traditional advertising, it is an inexpensive means to broadcast an organization's message to a wide audience. An added benefit is that articles written about an organization tend to carry more credibility than paid advertising. To gain the benefits of good PR, an organization must carefully plan its PR strategy and tactics and execute the plan professionally.

You may find further reading on public relations in Chapter 18.

EXHIBIT 17.1 Relationship of Marketing, Promotion, and Public Relations

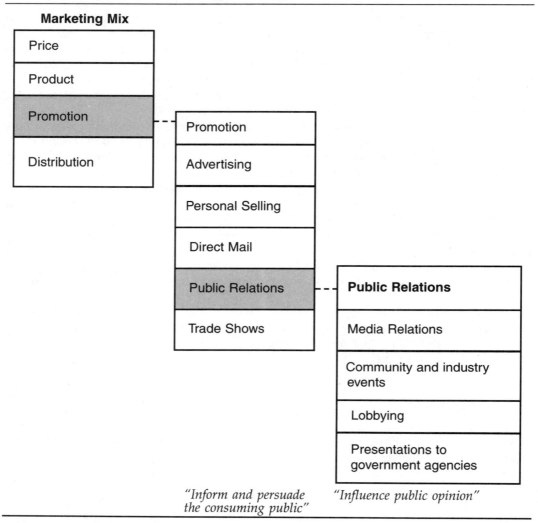

17.3 Public Relations Planning

Because of the long lead time required for some types of publicity, planning and scheduling are as important to the success of a PR plan as actual tactics. PR planning involves defining the goal of the communication, focusing on a specific message or messages, delivering consistent and reliable messages, using the appropriate media for the message, and timing the message. This chapter addresses only a subset of all the possible written communications. However, the same concepts can be applied to PR activities such as community events, speeches by organization executives, and presentations to government boards and agencies.

(A) DEFINING THE GOAL

What do organizations typically try to achieve through their public relations? Typical objectives include:

- Increase awareness of the organization's purpose
- Solicit support and funding
- Establish a reputation in the field
- Enhance visibility in the community
- Increase awareness of projects and programs
- Recognize achievements.

Before any public relations projects are started, the organization and its leaders must agree on the goal(s) of the public relations activities and their expected outcomes.

(B) FOCUSING THE MESSAGE

When an organization communicates with its various publics, one primary goal is to assure that the message is aligned with the organization's objectives and that it supports the organization's mission statement. It is helpful when messages can be focused on one or two main topics.

For example, an organization that provides recycling services (the fictional AAA Recyclers, for instance) has an objective to be recognized as the primary provider of this service in the area it serves. Hence, it would focus any articles and press releases on the service it provides, plans for improving or expanding the service, and success stories.

In a second example, another organization (Recycling Experts) might have a goal of being recognized as an authority in the field of recycling and for its leadership in helping communities to organize recycling programs. Its message would be focused in a way to establish the organization and its management as experts in the field. Public relations for this organization could focus on the background and experience of its staff and volunteers, the specialized knowledge and talents the organization offers, and profiles of communities which have benefited from its services.

In planning a public relations campaign, organizations have a variety of media available to them. This is referred to as the *media mix*. Each type of media offers a unique way to communicate to a specific audience, and each has unique requirements for how information is presented to it.

The media mix presents timing and scheduling considerations: for example, a press release to a newspaper might be published the next day, whereas the same release sent to a national magazine might take six months to be published. Of course, the newspaper remains in use for hours; a magazine could be retained and used for months.

(C) USING A PUBLIC RELATIONS AGENCY

The thought of developing and executing comprehensive public relations strategies and tactics can be intimidating. Sometimes great efficiency can be achieved by working with a firm that can provide guidance in developing the plan, with a view to taking the work in-house at some point or sharing the tasks. The PR agency can assist with other functions as well, including planning community events, writing press releases, writing and placing articles, arranging press tours, and developing the media list.

The benefits of using an outside agency include:

- Experience with PR planning
- Fresh ideas
- Access to media
- Experience writing and placing articles and press releases
- Establishing editorial contacts.
- Ability to focus the message

The disadvantages of an outside agency include:

- Expense
- Takes additional time to coordinate and review the agency's work
- Agency must be thoroughly educated in organization's objectives
- Some publications prefer to work directly with the source
- Adds an extra layer between the organization and its public.

In deciding to use an outside agency, it is important for the organization to carefully interview several prospective firms, interview the firms' clients, and get a specific fee proposal that enumerates the fee, retainer, and deliverables.

(D)   RELATING THE MESSAGE TO THE MARKETING PLAN

A successful public relations plan must be keyed to the organization's marketing plan. This helps ensure that messages and events are targeted to the correct audience and delivered by the most appropriate media. In the example of the recycling organizations cited in the previous paragraphs, one organization would target households and businesses, while the other might target communities and large corporations. Exhibit 17.2 illustrates the differences in planning for the two organizations.

EXHIBIT 17.2 Public Relationship Planning for Two Organizations

	AAA Recyclers	Recycling Experts
Mission	To be considered the primary provider of the service	Recognition as an authority. Help communities establish recycling programs
Audience	Households, businesses	Government Agencies and boards Large corporations
Message	Description of service provided Ease of use Success stories	Description of service provided Management profiles Authority
Media	Newspapers, direct mail, Community events	Newspapers, magazines, industry journals, conferences

(E) RELATING THE MESSAGE TO THE BUSINESS PLAN

Organizations usually operate with both short-term and long-term business plans. The short-term business plan is usually an annual plan that details a sequence of events or programs. This plan can be used as a basis for scheduling public relations events.

(F) SAMPLE PLAN

Exhibit 17.3 shows projects scheduled in the annual business plan for AAA Recyclers. Exhibit 17.4 shows how the public relations activities plan is linked to one of the projects, and Exhibit 17.5 shows the scheduling of public relations events related to the project. Notice that this schedule only indicates when the events will occur, but does not include details on the steps of their development. This is included later in this chapter in Section 17.6.

Notice how the timing of each public relations activity supports the other and, in turn, supports the program by informing the public of its existence and benefits. People may receive a direct mail piece announcing the program, then read about it in a daily newspaper and hear a public service announcement on the radio. Each message builds and reinforces the previous one. Other activities might include a television news piece and a community gardening day when people can get free compost for their yards.

17.4   Choosing a Spokesperson

Although public relations planning and development of the message(s) may be accomplished by a group, the function of delivering the message and executing the plan is best handled by one person who can be the central point of contact for all media representatives. Many organizations communicate to their various publics (audiences) through a single spokesperson, who may be the organization's top manager, a public relations specialist within the organization, or a contact at a public relations agency.

EXHIBIT 17.3 Annual Business Plan—Projects

Project	Jan	Feb	Mar	Apr	May	Jun	Jul	Aug	Sep	Oct	Nov	Dec
Add mixed paper to items collected at curbside		x										
Start composting project—Phase 1						x						
Expand composting citywide											x	

EXHIBIT 17.4 Public Relations Activities in Support of Phase 1 Composting Project

Projects		Description
1	Press release #1	Describe composting program and benefits
2	Press release #2	Announce start of program areas served, how to participate
3	Press release #3	Review success of program, % participation, benefits to community
4	Press release #4	Announce program expansion
5	Article 1—newspaper	"Composting Comes to City"
6	Article 2—magazine	"City Saves by Composting"
7	Article 3—magazine	"Gardens Thrive on Compost"
8	Editorial	Value of composting
9	Radio announcement	Public service announcement of program
10	Direct mail #1	Announces program to area served
11	Direct mail #2	Describes how to participate in program, announces start date
12	Direct mail #3	Announces program to new area served

The benefits of channeling all communications through one person (or group) include the ability to:

- Control the information
- Deliver information consistently
- Disseminate only the appropriate information
- Assure conformance to the PR plan
- Build and nurture media relationships
- Assure prompt and consistent follow-up to media requests for information.

EXHIBIT 17.5 Public Relations Schedule in Support of Phase 1 Composting Project

Project	Jan	Feb	Mar	Apr	May	Jun	Jul
Project start						x	
Press release #1			x				
Press release #2				x			
Press release #3					x		
Article 1—newspaper				x			
Article 2—magazine						x	
Article 3—magazine					x		
Editorial					x	x	
Radio announcement					x	x	
Direct mail #1				x	x		
Direct mail #2					x	x	

The spokesperson should be someone who is well versed in all the organization's goals, mission, and activities, and who can speak enthusiastically, convincingly, knowledgeably, and authoritatively on related areas of interest. It is important that this individual's job be structured to allow sufficient time to respond quickly to media requests and to be proactive in searching out media opportunities.

If a public relations agency is tasked as the point of contact, it should be made clear to the agency that all statements to the media must be approved by a designated individual within the organization.

17.5 Developing Media Relationships

The media is an organization's ally. It needs news items just as much as the organization needs publicity. Time spent developing rapport with media contacts pays off in many ways. When the spokesperson has proven to be a reliable news source, the step of writing a press release can sometimes be skipped in lieu of a quick phone call and fax outlining key points. Also, reporters will come to rely on the organization's spokesperson as a source of news and knowledge in particular areas and will often call for opinions or quotes when working on a story in a related field.

Before writing a single press release or article, it is important to know the target publications. It is helpful to develop a media list (or database) that includes names, addresses, telephone and fax numbers, and contacts at all appropriate media. There may be several contacts at a single publication: for example, at a newspaper, the contacts might include a features editor, a writer assigned to the general topic, the editor of the opinion page, and so on.

The media list should be segregated by media type, for example, local newspapers, national newspapers, trade publications, local radio and television stations. The list can be the foundation for a contacts database that tracks contacts with media, conversations with reporters, and dates when inquiries were received and information was sent. A sample media list is shown in Exhibit 17.6, and a sample database entry for one publication is illustrated in Exhibit 17.7.

Media list compilation can usually be completed within a day or two. (However, a PR agency may already have an acceptable list on file that need only be reviewed.) The best way to start is by simply calling the publication (or TV or radio station) and asking for the information. Be sure to be specific about the information needed. For example, ask for the person who handles stories on the organization's issues (health care, environment, etc.) rather than just any reporter's name. To find out who handles letters to the editor, don't ask for the editor's name; ask for the name of the person in charge of the editorial page. For magazines, a publication called *Standard Rate and Data* (see the Sources and Suggested References at the end of this chapter) lists all magazines published by area of interest and includes the phone number, address, and editor's name, as well as advertising rates. It is available by subscription and at most public libraries.

As is the case with most organizations, people who work in media experience promotions, reassignments, and resignations, so it is wise to update the media list at least twice a year, or more often if necessary.

EXHIBIT 17.6 Media List

Newspapers				
	Phone	**Fax**	**Address**	**Contact**
Blade Citizen	555-1111	555-2222	111 E. Main Oceanside, CA	Mark Reporter (writer) Sam Editor (letters to the editor)
Times	444-1122	444-1234	1023 Boca St. Hillside, CA	Susie Arner (writer) David Letters(letters to the editor)
Magazines				
Communication Today	333-1111	333-1211	42 Washing St. Anytown, CA	Maggie Sterns (features editor) John Wilen (news editor)
TV				
Ch. 8	222-2222	222-2223	101 Front St. San Diego, CA	Mike Senton (news editor) Barbara Johnson (news producer)
Ch. 10	555-4444	555-2341	1212 W. Santa Fe Del Mar, CA	Bob O'Wick (news editor)

(A) ESTABLISHING INTEREST

Before developing a press release or article, it is a good idea to contact a writer or editor at the publication for which the piece is targeted and establish that there is, indeed, interest in the piece. This is generally not as important with newspapers, which are always glad to receive interesting news items. However, it is essential with magazines because of their limited space and long-range scheduling. Before developing an article for a magazine, request a copy of its editorial calendar and authors' guidelines. Contact the editor with the story proposal and determine whether there is any interest before investing the time and energy to develop the story. (Section 17.7 provides more details on contacting editors with story ideas.)

(B) TRACKING PUBLISHED PIECES

Keeping a clipping file of all pieces published about the organization offers several benefits:

- Provides a historical resource
- Demonstrates accomplishments of PR campaign
- Summarizes media that has been most helpful
- Becomes useful for direct mail or background pieces.

The clipping file can include the actual clippings, but it is better to make a photo-copy of each article, because newspaper originals tend to fade and curl. In addition, the clipping file can include related stories, not limited to those specifically about the organization. It is a good idea to index the clippings as shown in Exhibit 17.8. If a database is used to index the clippings, it will be easy to find an article by date, publication, author, or title, and even to generate reports showing which publications provide the most coverage for the organization.

EXHIBIT 17.7 Sample Database Entry

Blade Citizen	Date	Contact	Discussed/ comments	Sent
	3/2	Mark	composting project	press release #1 describing project
	3/5	Mark	composting project	background information on similar sites
	4/10	Mark	story ideas	
	4/12	Mark	met with Mark and his editor to brain-storm ideas for composting story	
	4/15	Mark		names of city officials who have backyard compost piles

(i) Clipping Services

Note that publications do not automatically send tear sheets of articles, and most newspapers are reluctant to do so even when asked. It is up to someone in the organization to locate published articles so they can be included in the clipping file. Organization members, employees, and friends can be tasked with clipping items of interest. For example, all articles on composting could be collected, not just the composting efforts in the area. This keeps the organization networked and informed and will, over time, reflect trends for what is newsworthy.

If the budget permits, a clipping service can be retained. However, such services are expensive (monthly fee plus a charge for each clipping) and clippings can lag by up to two months. The advantage is that clipping services bear the expense of subscribing to and reading a large variety of publications and may find many related stories of interest

EXHIBIT 17.8 Sample Clipping File Index

Date	Article title	Publication	Writer	Comments
3/5/93	Composting Project Announced	Blade Citizen	Mark Reporter	from press release #1
5/1	City Council Composts!	Blade Citizen	Mark Reporter	from brainstorming session
5/15	City Council Composting Project	Times	—	picked up from Blade story
6/1/93	Citywide Composting Saves Space and Benefits Gardens	Composting Monthly	PR agency	written and placed by PR agency

that might otherwise be missed. If a publication is also available on the Internet, you can do a search and download the article.

(ii)   Reprint Services

Many magazines offer to sell reprints of articles. Reprints are very inexpensive relative to the cost of typesetting and producing a brochure and can often serve as part of a press kit (discussed later in this chapter) or a direct mail campaign.

17.6   Writing for the Print Media

Print media bring a message to a wide audience at the lowest possible cost; usually the cost is limited to only the time and effort it takes to generate and place a story. This section summarizes items to be considered before writing begins.

(A)   TOOLS OF THE TRADE

The tools of the trade are simple and easily available: a telephone, a word processor or typewriter, a dictionary, and a few reference books such as *The Associated Press Stylebook and Libel Manual* and Strunk and White's *The Elements of Style*. Everything submitted for publication should be neatly typed and error-free.

(i)   Fax

A facsimile (fax) machine may seem like a luxury, but it is unrivaled for instantaneous communication and invaluable for sending press releases, letters to the editor, editorial materials, and background information in response to a reporter's requests. In many cases, the cost of sending the fax is the same, or less than, the cost of postage, paper, and envelope, with the added benefit that the original material remains in the originator's office. A fax modem in your computer can be even more efficient.

(ii)   Letterhead

As simple as it sounds, all material should be submitted on letterhead. This not only looks professional, but also helps establish credibility. Be sure to include the organization's full name, address, and telephone and fax numbers, as well as the name of the person to contact for more information.

(iii)   Computers

Creating public relations materials on a computer allows easy editing, revisions, and rewriting of materials for a variety of media. In addition, computers can be equipped with fax boards so that information can be faxed directly from the computer without first printing a hard copy. Some fax boards are sold with optical character recognition (OCR) software that allows them to convert incoming faxes into text that can be edited.

(iv)   Modems

Equipping a computer with a modem allows the transfer of text and graphics files over telephone lines. This lets organizations send and receive information as quickly as with a fax, with the added benefit that the information can be merged with other materials already in the computer.

Another use for a modem is to connect to on-line information services and databases like CompuServe or the Internet. This type of service is worthwhile for performing research and communicating with special interest groups without leaving the office.

(B) WHO SHOULD WRITE A STORY?

The responsibility of the media is to inform the public in an objective and timely manner, so why should someone in the organization write a story about its issues? After all, newspapers pay reporters and staff writers to do just that. Of course, it is possible to pick up the telephone, call a few reporters, and try to talk them into writing a story. But chances are good that they have higher priorities and will work on the story idea presented to them only if it is convenient.

Who should develop the material submitted to a reporter? It can be generated in-house, by a PR agency, or by a freelance writer. The decision depends on budget, schedule, and available talents.

(C) CRITERIA FOR A GOOD STORY

For a story (article or letter) to be considered for publication, it must be:

- Factual
- Focused
- Timely
- Well written
- Interesting to an identifiable audience.

When developing material, ask the big question, "Who cares?" The issue may be crucially important to the organization, but when developing material for a particular publication, it must be presented in a manner that makes it significant to the thousands of others who read it. It helps to put things into perspective if the cause is viewed as a commodity or product; the media needs the product to sell its publications. As with all products, good quality, proper care, packaging, and presentation are essential to ensure success in the marketplace. Don't worry if global conflicts are competing with space for headlines; the newspaper still needs stories to fill the local news section!

Another way to generate interest is to link the cause to another event currently in the news. If the cause is an animal rights issue, for example, take advantage of zoo anniversary celebrations, associated worldwide news stories, or a visiting circus or rodeo to tie in and promote the organization's concerns.

(D) BEFORE SUBMITTING MATERIAL FOR PUBLICATION

Before submitting any kind of material to the media, even skilled and experienced writers must find someone to read and critique the material. Because writers are often too close to the material, a review by another person can quickly determine whether the readers' knowledge of the subject has been taken for granted and whether vital information has been omitted. Ask someone to check for the following:

- Ask, "Who cares?" Will readers be able to relate to what has been written? How might they feel about it?

- Are all the facts supported?
- If asked, are names and phone numbers of people who can provide additional information or opposing views available?
- Are spelling and grammar correct?
- Is the story told consistently and concisely?
- Could the story be interpreted in more than one way?
- Are the length and style appropriate to the intended audience and publication?
- Is the author's (or spokesperson's) name, address, phone and fax number, and e-mail address included?

When submitting a story or op-ed piece, include a cover letter that explains the purpose of the piece and its significance to the publication's readers. Be sure to sign the correspondence and keep a copy. It may sound elementary, but sometimes, in the hurry of the moment, these details are easily overlooked. Cover letters are generally not needed for press releases.

17.7 Packaging the Communication

As a story concept is developed, think about the various ways it can be packaged and "recycled." For example, a letter to the editor can be rewritten as a press release, a feature article, and an op-ed piece. A single story, and even a letter to the editor, can be split into various components, each telling a different part of the story. Each type of written communication is described in more detail in the following sections.

(A) LETTERS TO THE EDITOR

A letter to the editor is an opportunity to comment on topics currently in the news. It should generally not be more than 200 to 300 words. To enhance its chances of publication, a letter to the editor should be vivid, persuasive, concise, interesting, timely, well written, and typed. Make one or two points and get to those points without being verbose. Stay focused, and don't ramble or stray from the point.

Be careful to avoid an overly emotional tone. A letter written in anger will read like one. Temper emotions with facts. Imagine reading the letter in one month, or in six months. Is it still clear? Or would it be somewhat embarrassing?

(i) Complex Topics
It is often difficult to condense a complex topic into the 200- to 300-word limit of a letter to the editor. When addressing a complex issue, it is often effective to divide its elements among several writers, not all necessarily affiliated with the organization. Alternatively, one writer can pen a couple of letters to be submitted (with permission, of course) under different signatures. Plan the strategy thoughtfully and carefully to maximize exposure.

For example, a trash incinerator proposed for the Escondido, California area was opposed by a number of community groups and cities on the grounds of environmental damage, excessive construction cost, and irregularities in the contracting process. Each issue had volumes of supporting, and damaging, information, so each issue warranted a separate letter to the editor. Even if all the letters are submitted to the newspaper on the same day, it is unlikely that they will all run on the same day. The effect is one of greater public interest in the issue, and someone who may have missed the editorial page on a particular day will have a greater chance of seeing at least one of the letters.

(ii) Getting More Mileage from Letters

A letter's impact can be stretched by revising it and submitting it to publications whose focus may be slightly different. For example, a letter may be appropriate for a local newspaper, and would make an interesting regional topic if its focus were shifted somewhat. Another version could be submitted to a special interest magazine. If a letter is published by one newspaper and overlooked by others, it can be clipped and sent with an "FYI" to other papers or to specific reporters.

(iii) Letters that Do Not Get Published

Depending on the size of a particular publication, editors receive from 50 to thousands of letters every day. They must screen them all to compile a few letters that represent readers' opinions on all topics currently in the news, not just one issue. When editors sift through the mail bag, these types of letters hit the trash can (or recycle bin) first:

- Letters that are overly eccentric
- Unsigned letters or those without return addresses and phone numbers
- Letters with poor grammar or those that don't make a point
- Letters that don't address a specific, topical issue
- Letters that are too long (although some may be accepted and used as op-ed pieces or guest columns)
- Letters that obviously come from a "letter-writing industry"; that is, a PR agency, a lobbying organization, political action groups, or an organized letter-writing campaign
- Letters that come from out of the newspaper's circulation area.

The letter may not be selected for publication for any number of reasons. Often, there simply is not enough space, and by the time space becomes available, the topic is no longer timely. Sometimes the editor just does not understand the point. If an organization has developed a good working relationship with staff writers, they can sometimes be persuaded to put a word in with the editorial page editor.

(B) OPINION-EDITORIAL (OP-ED) ARTICLES

An *op-ed article*, as its name implies, expresses an opinion and editorializes on an issue while presenting facts. This allows much greater latitude than simply writing an article in a strict reporting style. Some newspapers publish guidelines for unsolicited material written for the op-ed page. Follow these guidelines as closely as possible.

Op-ed articles are run on the editorial (sometimes called the opinion or issues) page of the newspaper. They usually are given the same amount of space and are on the same part of the page in every issue. They will include a byline and possibly the author's photograph and a brief biography.

When deciding to write an op-ed article, first target a specific publication. This is not the type of piece that can be sent to every newspaper on the media list. Because of length, a newspaper will want an assurance that it will be the only one to run the piece. This is also true of feature stories. Publications will expect an "exclusive."

Start by studying the format used by the target publication. Look at the preferred length, and note whether the author's photo and biographical material are included. Outline the topic and key points, then call the editor to discuss them. Explain the author's qualifications for writing the piece.

To save time and trouble, don't write more than an outline until an editor agrees to the idea. Keep an open mind to suggestions for rewriting and repositioning the story. If one editor flatly rejects the idea, contact others on the media list. Ask the editors for feedback on the idea and for ways to make it acceptable for publication.

Consult Section 17.6 for guidelines on writing a good news story. The same rules apply to op-ed pieces. After submitting the article, the editor may want more information, minor rewrites, or approval regarding editorial changes.

Be sure that all supporting information is available, although it need not be submitted with the manuscript. Be sure that the author has time available to make revisions on short notice, and that the author will be open to changes. Exhibit 17.9 shows a letter to the editor that was run as an op-ed piece and inspired an editorial graphic.

(C) WRITING A PRESS RELEASE

A press release is the best way to communicate a news story or event to the media. Basically, a press release should describe what has happened or is going to happen, in addition to answering the usual "who, what, when, where, and why." If it doesn't, then the story is probably not newsworthy. Be careful not to overdo the use of the press release; one per month is adequate.

Always keep the news editor's job in mind when preparing a release. By doing a thorough job of writing the press release, the editor's job is made easier and the chances of getting the story placed are improved. Well-written releases are often used as is. If the story is lengthy, make sure the editor is able to cut from the bottom. This means that the most important information is placed at the beginning of the release. Background information about the organization is usually placed at the end.

Give careful thought and attention to the format, style, and tone of press releases. Consistency among these elements is vital in helping to establish the group's identity and promoting its cause. Remember, newsworthy stories always contain one or more of the following elements: human interest, public interest, information, conflict, timeliness, exclusivity, novelty, tragedy, or humor, to name a few. Look for these elements while preparing the release and use them to best advantage.

Always type press releases on 8½-inch by 11-inch white paper or stationery. If letterhead is used, indicate that the submission is a news release by typing the words "NEWS RELEASE" at the top of the page. Leave fairly wide margins (1½ inches) on all sides, type on one side only, and double-space so the editor has plenty of room to edit the copy.

Clearly indicate the contact person's name and phone number at the top of the page. Be sure this person is available to answer calls; if there's any doubt, include a second contact.

Most releases will be designated "For Immediate Release." If the release is timed correctly, the editor's job is easier. One sure-fire way to kill chances of publication is to make an editor search for a date. Sometimes it is necessary to specify "For Release After Date" or "For Release on Date." Try to avoid time constraints if at all possible. Include the date in a visible place.

EXHIBIT 17.9 Op-ed Piece that Inspired an Editorial Graphic (Los Angeles Times 11/10/91)

Hard Lesson on Landfills

■ The San Diego County Public Works Department's (DPW) most recent list contains 16 sites under consideration for new North County landfills. From our home next to the San Marcos landfill, we have a front row seat to the debacle resulting from the DPW's ineptitude. We want to educate our neighbors near these proposed sites on what to expect.

First, don't be overwhelmed by the flurry of acronyms related to landfills: WTE, CEQA, DPW, DEIR, EIR, SWAT, MRF, RDF, RWQCB, CIWMB, APCD, EHS, LEA, PRP or EPA. Just remember that when a "sensitive receptor" is mentioned, that's you, and if you are concerned about your property values or quality of life, you automatically become a NIMBY (Not in My Back Yard). No application or dues required. Oh, by the way, be sure to stock up on "vector" traps (that's rats in DPW-speak).

When the Environmental Impact Report gets under way, don't get the idea that its intent is to protect the environment. It only identifies what will be destroyed.

Thirteen years ago, when the county promoted the concept of a landfill to the citizens of Elfin Forest, they promised us that it would close the minute it reached capacity, and that a 200-acre park would be created there.

Instead of upholding its part of the "bargain," the county increased the landfill's capacity, blasting and crushing rocks 12 hours per day, for four months in the summer of 1989, forcing residents to stay inside to avoid choking in the dust, while drapes, carpets and sensitive computer equipment were ruined.

The DPW then dropped the big trash bomb, the landfill expansion. After all the assurances about a timely closure, the DPW mounted a sneak attack. Not only did the DPW not solicit community input prior to writing the environmental impact report, they did not announce its availability, except through the newspaper. We had to purchase a copy of the EIR for $25 or go to the local library to read it.

The expansion supposedly adds seven years to the landfill's life. When the DPW's figures are reviewed and analyzed in light of mandatory recycling, the expected life may be closer to 20 years.

If the landfill were the only issue, the story would end here, but the landfill draws other projects, like flies to trash: To scavenge the putrid gases generated by buried garbage, the county built a methane extraction plant. This facility was built next to existing homes, where the roar of its turbine engine can lull us to sleep on otherwise quiet evenings, instead of on the western edge of the landfill, where

it might go unappreciated.

The landfill spawned a proposal for a carcinogen-spewing incinerator with its $125-million, soon-to-be-constructed front end disguised as a recycling facility. Not one to pass up a bargain, the DPW will operate this facility 18 hours a day, six days a week, for a minimum of 24 years. Such a deal! For the next 24 years, trucks will not only bring trash, but, after the landfill closes, they'll be hauling away the shredded remains as well.

In November, 1990, the DPW decided that composting green waste would save landfill space. Yet mismanagement of a simple substance like grass clippings and leaves has resulted in tons of rotting matter, which can be smelled from as far as three miles away.

As the community turned its collective cheek, the next slap in the face came from the Encina Sewer District, which plans a sludge treatment facility on a 70-acre site next to the landfill.

Because Elfin Forest has been so adept at upholding its civic responsibilities, the DPW has chosen to "reward" this weary community with four more sites proposed within 5 miles of the current landfill.

If a landfill is slated for your community, you must do everything you can to educate yourself, keep informed and become part of the siting and monitoring process, because now, with 16 proposed landfill sites, NIMBY takes on a whole new meaning: Next, It Might Be You.

EVELYN ALEMANNI
Escondido

A sample format for a news release is shown in Exhibit 17.10.

A catchy headline can help sell the story; a cutesy or overly clever one can earn it a berth in the round file. Give some thought to the "angle" and play with it a little while. The headline should be in capital letters, centered, and boldfaced if possible.

The first paragraph of the press release should briefly tell the story and must answer the "five Ws"—who, what, when, where, and why. Subsequent paragraphs provide

---

EXHIBIT 17.10 Sample News Release Format

AAA Recyclers
101 Second Ave.
Canterbury, CA 92000
619-555-1211 FAX 619-555-2222

NEWS RELEASE

March 4, 1997
For immediate release.

For further information, contact:
Ms. Spokesperson
AAA Recyclers
619-555-1215 (direct line)

or

Mr. Wordsmith
XXX Public Relations, Inc.
619-555-3333

"HEADLINE"

Paragraph 1. Who, what, when, where, why, how.

Paragraph 2-x. Supporting details. Be sure to add quotations from organization members or executives.

Closing paragraph: One to three sentences that describe the organization and its purpose.

If continued onto an additional page, type "—more"" and indicate page # of #
(for example, page 1 of 2).

At the end of the release, indicate its end by typing:

###

---

background, simplify information, expand on the details, and provide an opportunity to quote members of the organization to clarify its position.

Try to keep the release to a single page, but if that is not possible, number each page and at the bottom of each, except the last, type "—more—." The last page should end with the symbol "###" or "***" to indicate the end of the story.

(D) WRITING A QUERY LETTER

An important communication tool, the query (or pitch) letter provides more creative latitude than a press release. The quality of the writing in the query letter is important, because its main objective is to sell a story idea and convince the editor of the author's ability to do the job.

Whether writing a query letter for a newspaper, a magazine, or to organize thoughts for a phone contact, the elements are exactly the same. Answer the five Ws—who, what, when, where, and why. A strong lead paragraph should resemble the intended lead in the story and pique the editor's interest.

A good query letter must:

- Introduce the story's concept
- Provide a synopsis of the supporting facts
- Document available material, such as photos, illustrations, graphics, related articles, and studies
- Include a list of experts to be interviewed
- State the author's qualifications and writing experience (if none, don't mention it)
- Request to write the article
- Estimate the word count and completion time
- Tie the story to the objectives of the intended publication
- Demonstrate why the story is of interest to the publication's readers.

Think of the pitch letter as a business letter and treat it as such: single-spaced and typewritten, using letterhead or stationery, and leaving approximately 1½-inch margins on all sides. Avoid lengthy paragraphs; several short ones are more attractive and inviting. The easier the letter is to read, the better its chances of getting a response. Do not send original photographs or artwork with a query letter.

Try to keep the letter to a single page, or one-and-a-half at most. The author's name, the date, and phone number should be readily visible. Always include a self-addressed, stamped envelope (SASE) with the correspondence, especially if it is unsolicited; the convenience will be appreciated.

(E) FEATURE ARTICLES

Feature articles are lengthy, timely, focused, in-depth editorial pieces designed to highlight and examine an issue, group, or individual, present opposing viewpoints, educate the reader, and provide detailed information using text, photographs, or illustrations. Whereas the job of hard news reporters is to answer the five Ws mentioned earlier, feature writers have more latitude, in that they invite readers to educate themselves while forming their own opinions about the information presented.

There are countless opportunities for possible feature material. Profile a member of the organization; perhaps it includes an environmental attorney, a geologist, biologist, or city council member. It is interesting to watch individuals who might never have come together under ordinary circumstances become passionately involved in a cause that unites them and their respective talents. Or promote the cause by imparting the knowledge to educate readers. Successfully placing a feature article will serve the organization's cause well and enhance credibility with published clips.

(i) Feature Newspaper Articles
Generally, newspapers do not accept freelance feature articles for publication. Some smaller publications may, but feature articles are usually authored by staff writers. As

with op-ed pieces, it is wise to contact the editor of the newspaper to discuss the concept before writing anything. Whether this contact is made over the phone or through a query letter, the method of preparation is the same. If the idea is well developed and interesting enough to an editor, it is usually assigned to a staff writer.

(ii)   Magazine Articles

Before contacting magazines, it is essential to understand their particular requirements and focus. Call the editorial department (even before sending a query letter) and request writer's guidelines and an editorial calendar to best determine the types of stories that typically appear in that publication. The editorial calendar helps in scheduling when the manuscript must be available.

Carefully scrutinize several issues of the magazine. Pay particular attention to editorial voice, average article length, departments, design and layout, even letters to the editor. If the average length of the articles is 3,000 words, don't try to sell a 7,000-word piece to the editor. Show some knowledge and interest in the publication.

In planning the story, remember that a magazine story takes at least six months from concept to printed piece, so the story must have staying power.

(F)   EDITORIAL CARTOONS

Letters or articles generated by an organization may inspire an editorial cartoon! This is very gratifying and can serve to illustrate points effectively. A reader may overlook a letter about environmental degradation and health risks associated with living near a proposed trash incinerator, but the universal language of a cartoon will engage his or her attention long enough to get the message across.

If a particular angle or some event conjures a strong mental picture, suggest it to an editor as a potential cartoon. Describe it briefly, whether it is written or illustrated with some degree of legibility to convey the idea, and send it via mail or fax. Don't follow up; just trust that your idea was evaluated.

(G)   PRESS KITS

In the course of working with the media (not just the print media), it is helpful to have a current press kit available. A press kit serves as a reference for reporters when they are writing about an organization and is a time saver for updating not only new writers but new employees, volunteers, or customers.

Media kits can range from a simple manila folder with a neatly typed label to a custom-printed presentation packet with pockets for inserts and die cuts for business cards. Regardless of the sophistication of the cover, it's what's inside that counts. The contents can be customized for a particular event and include some or all of the following items:

- Backgrounder
- Two or three recent press releases
- Profile of top executive
- Two or three recent press clippings
- Photos or slides related to the current topic
- Business card of the spokesperson and agency contact

The *backgrounder* is a one- or two-page, double-spaced fact sheet that profiles the organization. It should include information about the organization's purpose, its goals, its executives, the length of time it has been in existence, and brief summaries of current activities and accomplishments.

Press releases can be included to provide additional information about the organization's recent activities.

A one-page summary of a top executive's experience and accomplishments may be supplemented by quotes from the executive. A photo is optional.

Copies of recent articles or reprints of features in magazines are appropriate to use in a press kit. They add credibility and demonstrate that the organization's activities are newsworthy.

If the expense of photographs or slides is prohibitive, add a sheet of paper that states, "Photo available on request. Please contact . . ."

The press kit might also include a page summarizing the kit's contents, a letter of introduction from an executive, a copy of the organization's logo, a calendar of upcoming events, and small brochures.

17.8   Communicating Your Cause on the Internet

Information Superhighway and *Internet* are two buzzwords that have received great exposure recently. Is there any advantage to communicating your cause on the Internet? This section gives you some guidelines for when and why the Internet can help. Although explaining all about the Internet and its use is beyond the scope of this chapter, excellent references are included at the end of this chapter.

(A)   WHAT IS THE INTERNET?

The Internet is a computer-based repository of information. Companies and individuals maintain accounts on it, through which they can offer product information, customer support, company details, and news. In addition to text, graphics of all sorts, audio, and even video clips can be posted on the Internet. The Internet is quickly replacing the postal service for interbusiness communications, and when long distance calls are involved, communicating via the Internet is less expensive than sending a fax.

Through the Internet, you can send and receive messages, post information about your organization, and search for topics related to your cause. You may find it confusing at first, because it offers so many options. Further, the organization and quality of the data that you access is not consistent. However, using the Internet for specific kinds of communication can be cost effective and productive.

(B)   WHAT DO YOU NEED TO USE THE INTERNET?

There are several prerequisites for using the Internet:

- Computer with fast modem (28.8 KB or higher recommended).
- Internet account.
- Browser software.

While slower modems do not inhibit your access to the Internet, they dramatically increase the time it takes to transfer information onto your computer, increasing your connect time and preventing you from using your computer for other purposes (unless you are running OS/2 or another multitasking operating system).

An Internet account lets you connect to the Internet via your computer. You will have an account name, through which people can communicate with you. Most large cities have service providers who will set up your account, which gives you access to the Internet with a local, toll-free call. You will want to check with several vendors, as the service level and price may differ. Compare the monthly access cost with what you are currently paying for long distance and postage to determine if an Internet account makes sense for your organization.

(C)   USING THE INTERNET FOR COMMUNICATION

Many newspaper and magazine editors have their own Internet accounts, so press releases or article inquiries sent via the Internet often get more attention than those sent by mail. Sending Internet messages is also a very fast and efficient way to communicate with large numbers of members or sponsors, or to communicate with various branch offices of your organization.

Posting information about your organization on your own Internet home page is another way to let people know what your organization does, and what's new. You can post a calendar of coming events, for example, and copies of your press releases.

17.9   Enhancing Your Communications with Video

Multimedia presentations are becoming increasingly important to the communications mix. While this chapter focuses on communication with the print media, this section will give you a brief introduction into the possibilities of video communication, and information on how to create presentations inexpensively (usually for just the cost of ¾O video tape) with the help of your local cable television station. Many of the techniques for written communications, such as targeting your audience and planning your message, apply to video communications as well.

(A)   WHY USE CABLE TELEVISION?

Producing quality video presentations is time consuming, and requires expensive equipment and a level of sophistication that most nonprofit organizations don't have in-house. The cost of using an outside video production company is usually prohibitive, starting at well over $500 per finished minute. This is where cable television stations can help. Most cable television providers, must, as an element of their contract with the area they serve, provide community service programming. To do this, they must make their studios and equipment available. In addition, their professional staff members may be available to assist you with filming and editing.

(B)   PREREQUISITES

Most cable stations require that you complete their "producer's training" program before using their studios and equipment. These training programs generally include guidelines on producing a show or public service announcement and use of equipment. There is often a fee for these classes, and they fill up quickly. Plan to call several cable stations and ask detailed questions about their programs and the level of assistance you can expect.

(C) PLANNING

Cable studio and editing suite time is carefully rationed, often in blocks of four hours. Some stations limit the number of hours available to each producer in a month; for example, you may use four hours of studio time and four hours of editing suite time once per month. The waiting lists for studios and equipment are often long, so it is imperative that you schedule your time well in advance. If you can't finish an entire project in one session, it may be four or more weeks before you can schedule another. Be sure to ask your local station how time is allocated.

Because your studio and editing time is limited, it is best to storyboard your program and rehearse it before you arrive at the studio. If you don't need a studio, some stations will allow you to check out video equipment for several days of field use, which gives you more flexibility.

(D) GETTING HELP

If you need technical talent, for example, camera operators, lighting technicians, directors, or video editors, the cable station can usually give you the names of volunteers. These individuals contribute their hours for college credit or industry experience to build a portfolio. If you need acting or voiceover talent, you can contact a local college or amateur theater group.

(E) USING WHAT YOU PRODUCE

Before producing anything, be sure to check with the cable station for its guidelines. For example, some stations require that they be the first to broadcast your work. Others prohibit the use of its studios and equipment for projects that might be considered advertising or "for profit." After the cable station has aired your show, you will be free to make copies of it and submit it to other stations, either public or commercial. Be sure to ask the station first regarding technical requirements, for example, tape size, length, color bars, titles, and so on. For your tape to be played, it is critical that it be in the proper format.

For more information on producing videos, see the books listed in the Suggested Readings section.

17.10 Conclusion

This chapter introduced one aspect of public relations for nonprofit organizations, the development and writing of material for the print media. The principles presented here can be applied to other PR projects, including speeches and presentations, community events, radio and television news stories and interviews, direct mail, and marketing. Most important is to plan the message, keep it consistent, be proactive about telling the organization's story, and stay enthusiastic and motivated.

Suggested Readings

Benedict, L. and Benedict, S. 1992. *The Video Demo Tape*. Newton, MA: Focal Press.

Brody, M. 1992. *Power Presentation*. New York: Wiley.

Cagnon. 1994. *What's on the Internet*. Peachpit.

Cappen, R. J. 1991. *Associated Press Guide to News Writing*. Englewood Cliffs, NJ: Prentice Hall.

Carson. 1992. *Video Editing and Post Production*. Englewood Cliffs, NJ: Prentice Hall.

Doty, D. 1990. *Publicity and Public Relations*. New York: Barrons.

Goldstein, N., ed. 1992. *The Associated Press Stylebook and Libel Manual*. New York: Dell.

Harrison, T. A. 1991. "Six PR Trends That Will Shape Your Future." *Nonprofit World* (March–April).

Lambert, S. and Howe, W. 1993. *Internet Basics*. New York: Random House.

Peoples, D. 1992. *Presentations Plus*. New York: Wiley.

Smith, Jeannette. 1992. *Bacon's Publicity Checker*. Chicago: Bacon's Publishing.

———. 1990. *If You Want Air Time*. Washington, DC: NAB Services.

———. 1991. *The Publicity Kit*. New York: Wiley.

———. 1991. *The UPI Stylebook*. Washington, DC: United Press International.

———. 1993. *Editor & Publisher International Year Book*. New York: Editor & Publisher Co.

———. 1993. *Standard Rate and Data Service*. Wilmette, IL: Standard Rate & Data Service.

Public Relations and the Self-Renewing Organization

TRACY D. CONNORS

BelleAire Institute, Inc.

18.1 Introduction

Effective public relations planning and program implementation have never been more important for nonprofit organizations. Even as competition for space and air time are making it more of a challenge to be heard in and through the mass media, several other significant developments are changing the role of nonprofit organization "communicators" and further emphasizing the vital roles they play in developing and sustaining good relations with the various publics important to nonprofits, internal and external. These include the growing use of long-range, strategic planning by nonprofits and a growing awareness of the major benefits accruing to the organization by planning the public relations program as an important tool to be used in its implementation. And "transformation" initiatives focused on creating an organizational culture characterized by the practices and behaviors of quality management and continuous improvement will not only benefit substantially from the lavish employment of communication resources, but will fail to achieve their full potential unless public relations strategies and techniques are included in implementation planning.

For most nonprofit organizations, the process of gaining and maintaining public understanding and support grows more challenging all the time. The bewildering, headlong change which characterizes the age we live in is almost instantly communicated around the world through a variety of mass media. Economic, social, scientific, political, and moral issues compete for space and attention on our local, regional, and national agendas. Press coverage is characterized by stridency, sensationalism, and cynicism.

Many nonprofits depend on public awareness of their services to provide the various types of support they need to meet public needs. Getting their messages to the right publics and having them understood and acted upon becomes ever more critical. However, this is increasingly difficult since most public communications media are churning with a bewildering variety of information, some designed and intended to influence public thinking and some employed in ways that generate revenue, often using sensationalism and heated controversy to gain viewers or readers.

Being heard and understood over the din is not getting easier. The implications are clear: Nonprofit public relations programs will require careful planning and solid implementation by leaders with specific skills and experience in organizational and mass media communication.

18.2 *Effective Leaders Are Effective Communicators*

Most successful nonprofit organization leaders understand (or think they do) the importance of public support to the organization's ability to fulfill its public purpose. They understand the increasing challenges of planning and implementing an effective public relations program in the face of constant change and the intense competition for the public's attention. They understand and respect the increasing special knowledge needed by those within the organization having the responsibility for internal and external communications. These organizations and their leaders have organized and put into place public relations programs which:

- Reflect solid understanding and appreciation for the vital role of public relations.
  - Every nonprofit has public relations whether it recognizes them or not, and whether or not it does anything about them.
  - The most basic element to any nonprofit public relations program is integrity.
  - Public goodwill is the most important asset that a nonprofit can develop and sustain. Public opinion generated through fact and solid interpretation of needs and benefits is the basis for sympathy—and support—for a cause.
  - Public understanding, awareness, approval, and support must be deserved before they can be earned. Public relations involves far more in organizational planning, consideration, and linkage with other organizational initiatives (e.g., marketing, strategic planning, customer

satisfaction) than simply publishing a newsletter or issuing a press release. The basic foundation for public relations in the nonprofit, as it is for other organizations, is the development and articulation of sound policies and services in the public interest.

- Ensure that public relations initiatives are planned and implemented within an overall long-range framework, including the strategic plan and marketing strategies.

"Excellent communication helps to make organizations excellent, and excellent organizations foster excellent communication," Grunig (1991) emphasizes, "both are part of a holistic system." Internal communication systems are particularly important since they also create structure and culture. While the organization's operating environment affects how a nonprofit's leadership constructs its structure, culture, and communication, these also "affect who has power and how an organization perceives (or enacts) its environment and how it responds to the environment."

Unfortunately, far too many nonprofits still limit their effectiveness or even jeopardize their future by failing to recognize the true extent of public relations planning and initiatives. Many of them believe they have "good PR" when someone gets a news release out announcing an upcoming special event or fund raiser. Others, with more extensive programs, feel good about issuing regular news releases and publishing a newsletter for the membership. Far fewer can report they use most of the tools of the public relations professional, including: news releases, backgrounders, public service announcements, advertising (print or broadcast), articles, editorials, collateral publications (brochures, pamphlets, flyers and other direct marketing pieces), annual reports, speeches, and presentations. (Increasingly, this list would include the establishment and management of the organization's Home Page on the Internet.)

Even those nonprofits with programs producing and using a variety of these tools far too often do so without knowing how or whether in doing so they are complementing and supporting the organization's strategic goals and marketing objectives. Inevitably, many resources are wasted (suboptimized) and opportunities missed to use organizational communications planning and activity to support long-term development and improvement (strategic management). Leaders in these nonprofits should consult and follow the guidance contained in the suggested readings listed at the end of this chapter.

In addition, as growing numbers of organizations begin to focus on the quality management transformation process, public relations roles and responsibilities will expand to include using communication with various publics as a vehicle for changing the organization's characteristics, and ultimately, its culture. An ever stronger focus on public relations planning will be required to support both strategic planning and the institutionalization of quality and continuous improvement.

Clearly, we have enough data and experience to conclude that nonprofit leaders who are determined to ensure their organizations survive and prosper in these changing times will:

- Find the resources to prepare and implement an effective public relations program.
- Recruit qualified volunteers or hire professionals with the requisite training and experience in public relations to plan the program to an appropriate level of detail and sophistication (focus).

- Ensure its senior leaders participate fully in the strategic planning process, including senior leaders in public relations.
- Link public relations planning and initiatives with the organization's strategic plan and marketing strategy.
- Understand the potential inherent in the public relations/communications area to help overcome barriers to organizational change and to bring about changes in individual attitudes, behaviors, and practices.

Leaders of these organizations will ensure their public relations programs:

- Are strategically planned, with measurable objectives.

    Each tool used—news release, flyer, Public Service Announcement (PSA), direct mail letter or brochure—should be systematically developed to support definite public relations end-result objectives derived from the organization's strategic plan. Grunig and Hunt (1984) explain the five impact levels on a scale of difficulty ranging from receipt of the message, to remembering the message and believing it, to changing the attitude with an intention of acting on the message, and finally, to behavior change when the message is acted upon. Most organizations define success in terms of level one, did they receive the message? To achieve behavior change, however, communication goals and planning will need to find ways to reach impact levels far beyond message receipt.
- Assess target audience(s) needs, goals, and capabilities.
- Continually evaluate performance against plan.
- Assess and use complimentarily a variety of media.
- Choose appropriate media for each target audience.
- Link plan implementation with motivation principles.

Tucker and Derelian (1989, p. 14) emphasize the complementary aspects of strategic (long-term) and operational (annual) plans to public relations practitioners. "Operational plans constitute an organization's annual commitment to performance." However, they stress that "operational plans are most effective when designed as the first-year game plan for a long-term strategic direction. ... The strategic planning process helps managers think beyond a year's time to where they would like to see their organization in three or five years."

Clearly, it is vital that public relations leaders be included in the strategic planning process. Their participation offers major contributions to the development of specific communication techniques and media employment that will be essential during the implementation of the strategic plan. In addition, they help ensure the leadership understands what the techniques and media messages should accomplish toward achieving the organization's goals or fulfilling its mission.

In the growing number of nonprofits moving to integrate quality philosophies and practices into the organization, the linkage of public relations with strategic and operational planning is even more critical. The long-term objective of quality management (QM) initiatives is to "change the way the organization does business." Public affairs planning should be reconsidered as an invaluable resource and strategy to bring about, ultimately, a culture change within the organization to quality and continuous improvement. Typical communication objectives such as "informing the public," "improving awareness" and "broadening support," should now be strongly complemented by new QM communication objectives such as "changing attitudes," "modifying behavior," "lowering resistance to change," and "promoting intrinsic motivation."

18.3 New Roles and Responsibilities for Public Affairs

One of the major impacts public relations professionals can expect from QM deployment is a new role and responsibility: helping create and sustain an important change and shift in the characteristics which, taken together, define their organization—its "climate" or "culture." Over the next few years, all our organizations can expect to change their structure and behavior in many fundamental ways. As public relations practitioners, we need to improve our processes and develop innovative new communication strategies, even as we implement QM in our own communication departments and support its deployment within our organizations. "An individual without information cannot take responsibility," notes Jan Carlzon, the former head of SAS, "an individual who is given information cannot help but take responsibility" (Rifkin, 1996).

Quality organizations recognize effective implementation of QM is correlated to a vigorous, consistent, proactive, media-communications-awards-recognition program. In one review of 15 well-known companies implementing quality programs, all emphasized how critical communications is to successful QM deployment—the *importance of constant, lavish communication in every possible media as a key strategy for overcoming inertia within the organization and reinforcing the quality philosophy and message.*

A proactive, multifaceted communications program linked to the long-range/strategic plan is a key to successful long-term implementation of quality management. This is true because to realize its fullest potential and to be sustained, quality management cannot simply be a program, it must become the way the organization's leaders think, act, and do business—the corporate culture of the organization—if it is to be successfully implemented.

A very important distinction should be kept in mind, however, between a typical "public information program," and the "QM communications program." The public relations focus for QM must be on achieving "changes in organizational characteristics/culture" objectives, versus simply "getting the word out." Senior leaders with a solid foundation in QM philosophies will not be looking for hype, but rather communication initiatives which support, complement, and encourage the "new way of business"—new behaviors, approaches, attitudes, processes, and tools.

QM and supportive communications initiatives cannot be a one-shot program, vulnerable to changes in personnel or other political priorities; they should be a continuous process—with a never-ending focus on constant improvement and customer satisfaction. Changing the organization's culture cannot wait until all those who do not believe are gone through attrition, and those who might become believers are brought on board and successfully indoctrinated with the basics of QM. Instead, it must be implemented in a timely way, through a deliberate program of change within the organizational culture. This change, in turn, cannot take place through simply retraining those who are currently in need of training and who would go forth and implement the program.

A much broader group of initiatives must be planned, focused, and implemented— initiatives which use a variety of carefully selected communication media to get the messages in a variety of forms across to the broadest cross-section of the organization and to targeted publics. The objective here is not simply to release information, and there-fore, to merely generate press releases, talking points, speeches, and that type of thing, although these are valid tools in the process. Instead, the objective here is to use the communications media in a focused and deliberate manner to support and help sustain changes in the philosophies and attitudes of leadership and management within the organization's culture. A major objective of an organization's internal communications program, for example, will be to disseminate news reporting successes of quality initia-tives, as well as to serve as a public recognition and reward vehicle for those who have been singled out for their contributions to quality, continuous improvement, successful team initiatives, and the fulfillment of strategic goals.

18.4   *Strategic Change, Quality Management, and Public Relations*

Strategic change is challenging, disruptive, labor intensive, even threatening—in short, it's hard work. Why should you as a leader put your organization through what could be defined as trauma? Simply because the trauma of not doing so will inevitably be *more* challenging, disruptive, labor intensive, and threatening. Effective leaders recognize that the old ways, with the old patterns of iron-fisted managerial control and arbitrary or intuitive decision-making, are not good enough in today's resource-constrained, highly competitive world. Customer demands and expectations of today and tomorrow cannot be met with yesterday's technology, knowledge, and behaviors. Clearly, strategic change through planning is more effective because *it seeks to achieve focused, sustained improve-ment in the organization's performance.*

Organizations that will not or cannot change are probably not going to be able to compete successfully for the various resources they need to survive. Organizations not able to change probably should not survive. Simply changing for the sake of change, however, without having a supportable rationale for doing so is both illogical and risky to the point of being foolhardy.

In the private sector, "reengineering" was the Next Big Thing in management hits. More recently, "reengineering has become a word that stands for restructuring, layoffs, and too-often failed change programs," notes one of its creators, Thomas Davenport. Reengineering treated people inside organizations "as if they were just so many bits and bytes, interchangeable parts to be reengineered." The most profound lesson of business process reengineering was never reengineering, but business processes, Davenport says. "Processes are how we work." Any organization that "ignores its business processes or fails to improve them risks its future." However, organizations can use "many different approaches to process improvement without ever embarking on a high-risk reengineer-ing project" (Davenport, 1995).

While successful organizations realize that they must change, they understand that it must be based on facts and a rational process that is in turn based on customer satis-faction. A good rule of thumb could be Davenport's question: " 'Would I like this man-agement approach applied to me and my job?' If the answer is yes, do it to yourself first. You'll set a great example."

The fundamental purpose of long-range/strategic planning for quality management is to change the way the organization does business. *Integrating quality management prin-ciples and best practices with long-range planning provides the essential strategic framework to optimize system performance.* In this case, the organization itself is an "extended system." The strategic plan provides the foundation and the framework needed to develop and refine the total quality implementation plan. Considered together, they outline the guidance and the steps to be taken to begin the organization's transformation to quality. The nonprofit's public relations program plays a key role in keeping internal and external publics informed. It also plays a key role in bringing about and sustaining culture change, even as it reports on milestones reached. Before outlining specific action required by nonprofit public relations leaders, the following review of strategic planning is provided.

18.5   Strategic Planning and Other Planning

Strategic planning is conducted from the top of the organization, by its senior leaders, to "create and publish a statement of the aims" of the organization. The aims are usually found in the mission and vision statements. Development of these vital statements cannot be delegated to members of the staff, volunteers, or a paid consultant. If the key leaders are not involved in and committed to the process, the resulting plan will have no meaning for them.

Strategic plans are not collections of plans generated at other locations within the organization and passed up or over to serve as guides for what the leaders should do. Rather, each level of management or component of the organization develops its own plans to support and complement the strategic goals developed by senior leadership. "Strategic Plans" developed by aggregating plans from various functions or components within the organization usually focus on financial or fund-raising requirements needed to maintain services in the immediate future. Often, the process for developing and presenting these plans is competitive rather than cooperative and consensual. They often concentrate on how and when things should be done, rather than on what needs to be done or why. For these reasons, this type of planning often leads to suboptimization within the organization's systems, rather than the optimization of the entire system—the organization.

One of the major reasons for strategic planning is to make something happen that is beneficial for the customer and for the long-term survival and development of the organization. The guidance which evolves from the process of strategic planning should energize all members of the organization. It is important that public relations leaders ensure that coverage of that process captures and conveys the energy, excitement, and commitment the strategic planning process represents.

Without the vision, and lacking the focused, organized process of defining that vision, leaders can lead their organizations into major mistakes, even oblivion. It is fine to redefine leadership in "change-agent" terms. However, the changes leaders try to bring about must be on target, or they represent dangerous and wasteful tampering. Strategic planning, coupled with the principles and tools of quality management and continuous improvement, offers leaders a vital process to help them determine *what* should be changed, *why*, and *when*.

Unfortunately, leaders lacking vision generally don't understand the benefits of strategic planning. They tend not to participate in the process. Their organizations suffer as a result. Who will follow leaders who (1) don't know where they are going, (2) won't take the time to find out, and (3) waste resources and betray the trust of stakeholders?

Most organizations undertake some form of long-range planning, usually covering a time span of a few months to a few years. Unfortunately, it is often based on doing the same things being done today. There is no customer focus, no commitment to improve processes. The emerging requirements of the customer and the exponential changing of the external environment are not considered. A status quo or "don't make waves" approach often is used in planning. Obviously, if the organization's customer needs change, or if the mission should reflect this and doesn't, the organization's vision rapidly moves "out of focus."

Strategic planning looks much further into the future than other forms of planning. The focus is maintained by the vision of a new state for the organization, rather than by a need to perpetuate its present state. Transformation cannot be accomplished over night. It requires planners and leaders to bring about implementation as a series of time-phased steps to achieve the transformation.

Have you ever seen a business or financial plan that referred to values, beliefs, or assumptions? One that provided guidance to members throughout the organization as to desired behaviors? Not likely, because typical business or financial plans reinforce existing behaviors, such as short-term results, managing by results, competing for internal resources, and fixing blame.

The strategic plan should incorporate: the vision of the future agreed to by its guiding members; their values-based philosophy; and the guiding principles which outline what is acceptable behavior within the organization. The strategic plan articulates assumptions and beliefs about effective ways to deal with external and internal conditions. It establishes what should be taught and rewarded as the correct way to behave in relation to these conditions. In defining and establishing these values, behaviors, and a desired end state, the strategic plan provides guidelines and a profile for the organization's new culture. It explains for the organization how to do the right thing, not just how to do things right. This, in turn, provides an invaluable tool both for QM assessment and for public affairs initiatives.

The strategic plan as a product is an important leadership and communication tool. However, the process engaged in by senior leadership to produce the plan, while it does not offer a palpable product as a result, is perhaps the most valuable outcome. The process of self-examination, confrontation and resolution of challenging issues, and the developing consensus on strategic priorities among the organization's senior leaders, provides vital direction for the organization and alignment of those leaders who will be largely responsible for implementing the plan. They define the future and set the course, and will use and follow the plan *because they own it.*

Major responsibilities for public affairs leaders in this process include keeping members of internal publics focused on the plan and its implementation progress, and providing a monitoring service for customers. Monitoring activities include: periodic coverage of various important implementation efforts; coverage of any modifications of goals or changes in mission adopted by senior leadership; and, in general, contributing messages emphasizing that strategic planning is a process for continuous improvement—the constant striving to change in ways that enhance the organization's ability to fulfill its mission.

Programmatic change is perhaps the most common approach used in the majority of organizations today. It is beguiling in its apparent simplicity and the fact that it promises quick results with little effort. The strategic change process and approaches we have discussed are more complex, more difficult to develop, and not as easy to define or outline. Programmatic change approaches often give quicker results, but usually yield poorer-than-hoped-for results than strategic change approaches. Small gains that might be realized through programmatic changes are not sustainable over time. The small gains disappear quickly and the cycle of tampering begins anew.

18.6 Linking Public Relations Planning and Initiatives to Strategic Planning

Public relations planning should be linked to strategic planning for many reasons. Those that apply to most organizations include the following:

- It helps define and create the future.
- It provides the framework and a focus for determining and improving communication improvement efforts.
- It suggests subjects and foci for coverage and public affairs activities which support and complement efforts to optimize the organization and its systems.
- It provides a basis and means to assess public affairs programs.
- Members, employees, and publics who know (and share) the organization's vision will help it become reality. Simply having a mental picture of what the organization should "look like" in the future provides invaluable impetus and form to your efforts in creating the conditions that will lead to achieving that vision. Without the vision, your future is far more likely to be determined by others. And why not? Without the vision you and other organizational leaders really don't know where you are going, so one leader's opinion or agenda for prioritizing actions or resources is just as good as another's. Without strategic planning, how do you really know your publics, their needs, and the messages you should be sending and the media you could use most effectively?
- The strategic plan provides the framework and focus for your efforts to improve the public affairs program and its initiatives. The communication goals you establish ultimately should be based on data from the organization's customers. When you begin this process, the data may be sparse or inaccurate, so be prepared to devote the time and resources needed to upgrade this information to the types and level of accuracy you need. For many organizations, one of the new public affairs challenges is that of developing better customer feedback approaches and mechanisms to ensure customer needs and expectations are met. Better customer data equals better organizational mission performance.
- Being a part of the strategic planning process will help you as a leader develop ways to optimize your communication efforts and systems. More importantly, because the process considers the entire organization as a system, optimization benefits apply across all systems, not just those involving internal or external communication.
- Because you know where the organization's leaders "want to go" with the organization, strategic planning helps you order and prioritize your day-to-day decisions and activities. Otherwise, like the Cheshire Cat said to Alice, "If you don't know where you're going, any road will do."

- Your participation in the strategic planning process will help you see the organization as a system itself, not just a collection of unrelated functions. You will better understand the linkages between functions and the different requirements of the organization and its subsystems. This knowledge will be invaluable to you in terms of audiences, messages, and media.
- Those participating with you in strategic planning represent the organization's most important leaders, those with the knowledge, power, and support potential to play major roles in the transformation. Throughout the process, they are constantly learning about the organization and its needs. One person from whom they should be learning is the public affairs leader. You should be alert to opportunities to point out to them important public affairs principles and practices as they relate to the plan and its implementation. Of particular importance is their learning from you the role public affairs has in bringing about culture change within the organization.
- Participation in the strategic planning process provides the information you need to assess your program plans and progress in terms of their contributions to achieving strategic goals. This assessment enables you to make adjustments to stay on track.
- Almost certainly, the majority of strategic goals will relate to satisfying external customer needs. This means that ongoing assessments will be invaluable in revealing ways of improving your external communication program—message changes or refocus, new or changing publics, different media or new media emphases. Obviously, this means that careful attention needs to be given to the proper methods of generating reliable data tracking progress toward strategic goals relating to public affairs objectives. Whatever the goal area or initiative being assessed, from changes in culture to some organizational output or service, the strategic planning process needs the capability to track performance continually, and to provide the correct data needed to make appropriate adjustments (decisions) to reduce variation and conserve limited resources in the pursuit of the organization's vision.

18.7 Toward a QM Culture: New Challenges for Nonprofit Communicators

The following discussion suggests new roles and definitions for public relations functions which are emerging as nonprofits move solidly into the transformation toward quality and continuous improvement. It is presented generically and in the present tense to assist in its adaptation to public relations planning and policy statements supporting the organization's strategic plan.

(A) QM COMMUNICATIONS VISION

Quality management and continuous improvement are the organization's core values, and its primary leadership and management philosophy. We are working together as a team to create an environment and culture committed to continuous improvement in our people, our processes, and our systems through quality management.

(B)   QM PUBLIC AFFAIRS MISSION

The organization's public affairs mission is to implement a multifaceted communications plan and program, the objective of which is to create a self-sustaining culture throughout the organization which supports and advocates continuous quality improvement as the organization's premier value, leadership principle, and "way of doing business."

(C)   QM PUBLIC AFFAIRS GUIDING PRINCIPLES

Communications initiatives will be identified, designed, planned, prioritized, and resourced based on perceived utility and contributions to improved:

Job Performance through QM

- Abilities, traits, and skills needed by QM practitioners.
- Role fulfillment and improved role perceptions, while serving as a member of a QM team.

Job Satisfaction Resulting from QM

- Intrinsic rewards, such as personal growth, pride, integrity, responsibility, accountability, respect, preparedness, and concern for people.
- Extrinsic rewards, such as improved quality of work life, benefits, pay, and allowances.
- Equitability of rewards, such as degree of certainty regarding prompt, fair recognition for personal participation.

(D)   QM ASSUMPTIONS

For the generic public relations plan, QM assumptions include suppositions as to the pivotal truths, facts, and principles influencing and determining the effectiveness of organizational communication strategy. The following should prove useful as a generic foundation while developing guiding principles, objectives, and initiatives:

- QM is more than simply a new management program. It is a philosophy and leadership tool so powerful and useful throughout an organization that it constitutes a new "way of doing business"—*a new organizational culture.*
- Culture is, in essence, the integrated patterns and sum total of the individual *beliefs, values, attitudes,* and *behaviors* of those belonging to the organization— the acquired, collective knowledge that people use to interpret experience and to generate social behavior. Culture is learned, shared, transgenerational (cumulative and passed along from one generation to another), symbolic (using one thing to represent another), patterned (change in one area will bring changes in another area), and adaptive. *A communications plan focused on culture change, should assess these components and characteristics of culture, formulating strategic objectives which take these factors into consideration.*
- These beliefs, values, attitudes, and behaviors were not recently acquired, nor are they easily changed. Some of them, gained over a lifetime, were brought with the individual when he or she joined the organization. Others

were developed after exposure to the organization's prevailing beliefs, operating procedures, "common knowledge," attitudes, and atmosphere—its culture.

- Changing an organization's culture by working to change key behaviors in those currently a part of an organization is a challenge not lightly undertaken, nor done with expectations of "quick fixes." Doing so requires careful planning, broad commitment and alignment by senior leaders, and diligent, patient implementation of the plan.

- Ciampa (1992, p. 58) warns of a "clear danger in the belief that the culture can be altered permanently by any single individual, or, for that matter, by an organization improvement effort . . . this sort of change does not take place in the short term, and certainly not because people will it to happen. The culture of an organization . . . is not something that a single leader creates, nor is it something that managers control and make predictable, like a budget or a project with a starting point and a completion date." He argues instead for a change in the character of the organization, the features and traits of the individual nature of the organization. (These traits are described later in Section 18.9. They also hinge on behaviors and behavior patterns.)

- Changing behavior is a complex process involving consideration of such variables as perception, personality, attitudes, learning, and motivation. Of these variables, *motivation is clearly a key factor in bringing about culture change*, although all must be factored into communications planning.

- An effective QM public affairs plan operating to change motivation can improve its effectiveness by considering and addressing several levels of diverse human needs, often doing so simultaneously through the same "vehicle" being communicated through the same medium. Abraham Maslow's work in defining a "hierarchy of needs" provides a useful, although simplistic model, for illustrating the importance of motivation within any organization. The five levels as translated into work motivation, include: *basic needs* (pay); *security needs* (seniority plans, severance pay, unions); *belonging needs* (formal and informal work groups); *esteem needs* (titles, status symbols, promotions, recognition); and *self-actualization* (self-fulfillment, the culmination of all previous needs levels). The model is simplistic, but useful in underscoring the diverse needs of humans interacting within an organization, and the importance of recognizing and addressing in public relations planning a wide variety of motivating factors—when an important objective is to change the organization's collective characteristics, behavior, or culture.

- Viewing motivation change as a process offers important communication insights in which variables influence various stages in behavior adjustment.

A useful applications-oriented model of expectancy motivational theory is the Porter-Lawler model (Luthans, 1989, p. 247). Of course, it would be difficult to measure the strength of each individual variable. However, it offers a model which is useful in understanding the complex dynamics involved in planning and implementing communications plans in which behavior change is an objective. For example, the following strategic organizational communications assumptions are suggested by the Porter-Lawler motivation model:

- If behavior change is sought to improve *job performance* using QM principles and best practices, then communication (plus other implementation-related initiatives) *should focus on that information which supports and improves individual abilities in performing QM functions, and explains new role perceptions.* This is likely to help improve performance (accomplishment), but not necessarily satisfaction. In QM terms it is roughly the equivalent of reaching only for the "low-hanging fruit," since it argues for early success when "easy" quality improvements are made, followed by a probable flattening of the improvement curve since in-depth, sustained continuous improvement requires not only effective use of the tools and roles of QM, but also the total involvement of satisfied employees.
- When *job satisfaction* is an objective, then communications program efforts also should focus on rewards—intrinsic rewards (particularly important), extrinsic rewards, and perceptions of equitability in reward programs. Improvements in these areas suggest the potential for more positive attitudes regarding job satisfaction, which in turn feeds back into and reinforces the initial effort (motivation) phase of this cyclical process. Public relations audit studies, Grunig (1991) reports, show that employees "are most satisfied with information that helps them make sense of their situation . . . by telling them how their job fits into the organizational mission, about organizational policies and plan, and about relationships with key constituencies in the organization's environment."

18.8   *Objectives of Organizational QM Public Relations Plan*

Objectives of QM public relations include the following:

- Support organizationwide initiatives that assist in implementing QM, including the development and implementation of an organizational QM Communication Plan.
- Inform internal audiences regarding QM development, evolution, application, policies, and opportunities, raising consciousness and awareness in internal audiences regarding:
  - The value of QM to the organization and to them as a better way "of doing business;" and
  - QM and continuous improvement concepts, principles, and best practices.
- Demonstrate commitment to QM at all levels within the organization.
- Publicize and describe QM actions and progress in ways which outline and highlight QM concepts, principles, and best practices in ways which provide measures of general training as well as raising levels of awareness and generating broad support.
- Focus thrust of communications initiatives on achieving behavior change, for one or more of the following reasons:
  - QM approaches ultimately provide more effective, efficient ways of accomplishing more.

- QM benefits everyone by helping achieve better productivity, customer satisfaction, and continuous improvement.
- QM application will enhance professional development and, ultimately, promotion and recognition.
- QM practices improve overall job satisfaction.

18.9 Quality Management Public Relations Coverage Focus

The following is a compilation of specific messages developed for target markets and an indication of the goals they are designed to satisfy.

(A) QM SUCCESS STORY GUIDELINES

The following statements and questions were prepared for public affairs personnel to suggest story coverage areas and focal points which not only report the Who, What, Why, Where, When, & How ("five W's and the H") of QM news, but also offer more detailed information on tools, techniques, principles, and best practices used by QM advocates and practitioners. Of course, the list is far more extensive than needed for any particular story. However, each success is different and results from a unique combination of factors. The following list can assist in determining the most important factors at work in any program or initiative, the factors which should receive the most emphasis in news and story preparation.

The list offers guidance as to:

- *Subjects*: What should we be covering for QM "news"?
- *Significance/Future State*: What focus in our coverage might offer the most benefit to the organization's QM implementation efforts in terms of linking progress stories and coverage with "destination"—the characteristics or environment in a particular area of a total quality organization?
- *Why and How of QM*: What principles and best practices might be highlighted in the coverage as a means of expanding awareness of not the "*what*" happened, but "*why*" and "*how*." This, in turn, helps develop a larger "critical mass" of support and complements ongoing QM training initiatives.

Please take note: QM initiatives often result in savings of money, and these savings can be seen as the most important "news hook." This is not necessarily true! In fact, monetary savings are only one of a number of important, newsworthy results of a successful QM initiative. Since the goal is to help others understand the principles, tools, and practices of QM, in many important respects, the real "news" is not the savings but the processes and approaches through which they were achieved. QM public affairs leaders should be particularly interested in *QM success stories* which highlight such important areas as:

- Teamwork
- Process and product improvements
- Time or other resource savings
- Cross-functional training

- How QM organizations (e.g., QMBs/PATs) function and interact: challenges and solutions
- Organizationwide support for and involvement in QM
- Data collection and assessment approaches
- Recognition and reward strategies and programs
- Customer focus and interaction
- How the organization got started in QM
- Resistance to QM and how it was handled
- Myths of QM ("it won't take much time and we'll get big savings—fast") and how "reality" was created.
- New standards of operations
- Implementation

(B) TOP MANAGEMENT LEADERSHIP AND SUPPORT

- How was senior leadership directly and actively involved in quality-related activities?
- How did senior leadership help to create and communicate the organization's quality vision?
- In what ways did the organization get across the point that its policy is that *QM is the number-one priority*—the key to success—a belief in continuous improvement that permeates the organization?
- What effective strategies were used to involve all leaders, supervisors, and work associates in quality?
- In what ways did the organization's leadership provide significant resources (time, training, dollars) necessary to improve quality throughout the organization?
- How did your organizational environment encourage innovation, pride in work, continuous improvement, and open communication (vertically and horizontally) by which information is shared and cooperation encouraged and supported across departments?
- What may illustrate and underscore the fact that the organization's top leadership holds everyone accountable for improving systems/processes, products/services, and then rewards behavior that reflects quality improvement goals?
- To what extent, in this successful QM initiative, did your leaders play active roles in removing barriers to excellence?

(C) LONG-RANGE/STRATEGIC PLANNING

- Were quality considerations taken into account throughout the planning process? How can that be illustrated or explained?
- Were short- and long-term goals for quality improvement established across your organization as part of the overall strategic planning and budgeting process (goals set in ways that require the organization to "stretch")? How was this done?
- Did operational plans at suborganizational levels provide clear details for strategic plans? Are leaders held accountable for attaining objectives?

- Have formal processes been established throughout the organization to develop quality improvement goals and to update plans periodically?
- What types of quality data, information, analyses (of customer requirements, process capabilities, supplier data, benchmark data) were used in planning for this successful QM initiative?
- To what extent were customer needs/expectations and issues relating to improved supplier relationships incorporated into quality improvement planning?
- Were benchmark data from the best organizations in the field used to help determine potential quality improvements?
- Were key requirements—such as technology, employee training, supplier quality—formally assessed and compared to current status in those areas, and identified needs factored into plans?
- Were planning assumptions made? How did they affect strategic planning?

(D) CUSTOMER FOCUS

The focus should be on the organization's overall customer service systems, knowledge of the customer, responsiveness, and ability to meet requirements and expectations.

- Were various effective/innovative methods used to obtain customer (internal, external) feedback for pertinent functions?
- Did processes requiring improvement based on customer feedback receive priority attention with corrective action plans developed and implemented?
- To what extent does leadership actively seek ways to ensure that all employees are aware of customer needs and expectations and that they understand and fulfill customer service standards?
- Are service goals aimed at exceeding customer expectations? Is progress toward goals tracked and reported to relevant units, and then used to plan improvements?

(E) EMPLOYEE TRAINING AND RECOGNITION

- In what ways or areas does the organization place a high priority on efforts to develop and utilize the full potential of the workforce for quality improvement, and personal and organizational growth? In addition, how does it use rewards, recognition, and incentives to recognize employees who improve quality and productivity?
- Has the organization implemented a systematic, documented training plan, based on a comprehensive needs analysis? To what extent was the effectiveness of quality education and training evaluated and improved on a continuing basis?
- To what extent have training plans been fully integrated into overall strategic and implementation and quality planning? Do key strategies exist for increasing effectiveness and productivity of all employee groups?
- Is everyone trained (or being trained) to support and participate in continuous improvement, with the focus of that training on prevention of problems? Are technical training/skills continuously upgraded?

- Are frequent updates on new developments in quality improvement shared with the entire organization?
- Does the training investment show clear evidence of human resource development priority?
- How do managers personally, regularly, and fairly recognize individuals and teams for measurable contributions?
- Contributing to the QM success story are rewards and recognition broad-based and innovative, and do they encompass all levels of the organization?
- Is there increased emphasis on recognizing teamwork, with an equitable balance achieved between individual and team recognition? Are small successes common to the organization shared and celebrated?
- Are systems improvements recognized?
- To what extent is peer recognition an important part of reward structure?
- Is there favorable, reportable data regarding the percent of employees and teams recognized in different employee categories, by type of recognition?

(F) EMPLOYEE EMPOWERMENT AND TEAMWORK

Regarding the effectiveness and thoroughness of employee involvement in QM:

- What innovative and effective employee involvement approaches were used in the successful QM initiative, and avenues where available for participation in improvement efforts?
- What examples can be cited to illustrate that leadership provided the environment that supported employee involvement, contribution, and teamwork—a positive atmosphere of trust and respect that exists between functions and levels of the organization?
- Was cross-functional team cooperation occurring across the organization to better meet customer needs a significant factor in the success? Did suppliers and customers participate in team activity?
- What indications exist to illustrate participation by all members of the organization—positive suggestion trends, acceptance rates, percent of employees making suggestions, and team participation trends—including the improvement in the overall quality of work life throughout our organization?
- Do employees have strong feelings of empowerment and of team ownership of work processes? Do effective approaches exist to enhance employee authority to act?
- Was success in the QM initiative assisted by an environment in which employees feel ownership of quality improvement, and exhibit personal pride in quality of work?
- In the *quality managed organization*, power, rewards, information, knowledge are steadily moved to the lowest feasible levels. Is this process a factor in this particular initiative?
- Is the organization being "flattened" as a result of employee empowerment?
- What improvements resulting from employee participation are seen in systems, processes, products/services?

- Is a formal survey process used on a regular basis to determine levels of employee satisfaction? Are follow-up actions taken to improve the organizational environment and human resource practices?
- What future plans address objectives, strategies, and goals to sustain momentum and enthusiasm?

(G) MEASUREMENT AND ANALYSIS

It is important to consider the scope, validity, use, and management of data and information that underlie the organization QM system and how the data are used to improve process, products, and services.

- How is quality and timeliness information collected on products and services for external customers and from suppliers, and for all significant products/services for internal customers? Was this data helpful in achieving the QM success?
- How do employees across the organization (1) use measures to identify problems, (2) use quantitative methodologies to identify solutions, and (3) use assessment tools and techniques to verify that remedies produce expected results?

(H) QUALITY ASSURANCE

This concerns the systematic approaches used by the organization for quality control of products and services, and the integration of quality control with continuous quality improvement.

- Is it an organization objective that all products, services, and processes are designed, reviewed, verified, and controlled to meet customer needs/expectations?
- Do methods used to assure quality emphasize prevention, not detection? (Illustrations and examples are helpful.)
- Are comprehensive assessments of quality assurance systems performed at appropriate intervals? Are the findings translated into improvements of systems?
- Are quality assurance systems updated to keep pace with changes in technology, practice, and quality improvement?
- To what extent and how are established methods used to verify quality requirements to be met by all suppliers?
- What examples are there that product and service-related standards are set for all internal support functions?

(I) QUALITY AND PRODUCTIVITY IMPROVEMENT RESULTS

In determining the measurable and verifiable results of organizational QM practices:

- What examples and illustrations exist to document that significant indicators of performance demonstrate exceptional results—superior to the competition in select (all/significant/specified) areas—and that customer satisfaction has shown steady improvement?

- What examples can be offered to illustrate and highlight the excellent results that have been achieved in key dimensions (quality, timeliness, efficiency, effectiveness) across all areas? (The results are clearly and strongly related to the QM approach.)

18.10 Beliefs, Attitudes, and Behavior Comparisons in Quality Management

The following comparisons are offered to suggest the change in individual attitudes and behaviors that organizational communicators should keep in mind as they design and implement their programs. (Obviously, the examples are far too simplistic to illustrate the continuum between them, which is most likely the case in any organization.)

Former Attitudes, Behaviors, and Organizational Environment Characteristics	QM-Enhancing Behaviors and Characteristics
Attitudes	
Bored; little involvement; "checks brain at the door on the way in"	Creative; activity has real meaning, is genuinely needed; activity translates to vision achievement or realization
Behavior	

Individual focus: Looks out for #1	Team Focus
	 • commitment to shared vision/mission
	 • responsibility for team interests and products
	 • leadership
	 • motivation for selves and teams matters
	 • diversity
	 • credibility
	   • competence
	   • objectivity
	   • trustworthiness
	   • coordination

Powerless pawn in large organization	Process owner
Powerless	Empowered • works on critical tasks • discretion/autonomy over tasks • visibility and recognition • strong connective relationships in the organization • improved personal autonomy and responsibility • held accountable for resources used and for results achieved

Regimented work environment	Self-directed work teams
No vision	Shared vision and goal clarity
Uninformed about organization policy	Knowledgeable participant
Extrinsic/environmental reward system	Intrinsic motivation
Problem solving groups	Cross-functional teams
Emphasis on person	Emphasis on process
Focus on traditional management functions: planning, organizing, staffing, evaluation	Management by commitment, focus on team motivation, process improvement, coaching, facilitation.
Leadership at the top	Proactive, transformational leadership at all levels.
Mistrust	Respect for the individual and for diverse talents; individual opinions sought on process improvements; acted upon and respected
Information, communications at the top	Information moved to lower levels
Competition	Collaboration
Environmental focus in which people are held responsible	Environmental focus in which people are positioned and supported for success
Integrity compromised for upward mobility	Integrity supported and encouraged
People are "consumables"	People are our greatest asset, used as the basis and focus for planning and implementation
Pigeonholed, alienated	High level of sharing; shared set of goals; shared values and expectations; teamplayers unite others toward common destiny through sharing information, values, empowering others, developing trust

Suggested Readings

Associated Press. 1980. *The Associated Press Stylebook and Libel Manual*. New York: Author.

Atkinson, Philip E. 1992. *Creating Culture Change: The Key to Successful Total Quality Management*. San Diego: Pfeiffer & Company.

Batten, Joe. 1992. *Building a Total Quality Culture*. Menlo Park, CA: Crisp Publications.

Bivins, Thomas. 1991. *Handbook for Public Relations Writing*. Lincolnwood, IL: NTC Business Books.

Bliss, Edward and Patterson, John M. 1978. *Writing News for Broadcast*. New York: Columbia University Press.

Ciampa, Dan. 1992. *Total Quality: A User's Guide for Implementation*. Reading, MA: Addison-Wesley.

Cutlip, Scott M., Center, Allen H., and Broom, Glen M. 1985. *Effective Public Relations*, 6th ed. Englewood Cliffs, NJ: Prentice-Hall.

Davenport, Thomas H. 1995. "Why Reengineering Failed. The Fad that Forgot People." *Fast Company* (December): 73.

Grunig, James E. 1991. *Excellence in Public Relations & Communication Management*.

Grunig, James E. and Hunt, Todd. 1984. *Managing Public Relations*. New York: Holt, Rinehart & Winston.

Helm, Lewis M., et al. 1981. *Informing the People: A Public Affairs Handbook*. New York, NY: Longman.

Kotter, John P. and Heskett, James L. 1992. *Corporate Culture and Performance*. New York: Free Press.

Luthans, Fred. 1989. *Organizational Behavior*. New York: McGraw-Hill.

Maddalena, Lucille A. 1981. *A Communications Manual for Nonprofit Organizations*. New York: AMACOM.

Montana, Patrick J. 1978. *Marketing in Nonprofit Organizations*. New York: AMACOM.

Nolte, Lawrence E. and Wilcox, Dennis L. 1984. *Effective Publicity: How to Reach the Public*. New York: Wiley.

Oaks, L. Robert. 1977. *Communication By Objective*. South Plainfield, NJ: Groupwork Today, Inc.

Rifkin, Glenn. 1996. "Buckman Labs Is Nothing but Net." *Fast Company*, (June–July): 123.

Schramm, Wilbur. 1973. *Men, Message & Media*. New York: Harper & Row.

Smeyak, G. Paul. 1983. *Broadcast News Writing*. Columbus, OH: Grid Publishing.

Tucker, Kerry and Derelian, Doris. 1989. *Public Relations Writing: A Planned Approach for Creating Results*. Englewood Cliffs, NJ: Prentice-Hall.

▼ Contingency and Emergency Public Affairs

RICHARD L. THOMPSON, APR
Space and Naval Warfare Systems
Command

19.1 Introduction

Many nonprofit organizations, by the nature of their activities, operate in inherently hazardous environments. Other organizations conduct "administrative" functions in an office setting. Regardless of the nature of operations, proper response to a contingency or emergency demands mature judgment and appropriate action taken without hesitation throughout the organization. One vital component of an organization's response in a contingency or emergency is communication with concerned publics.

Public affairs contingencies and emergencies can include an accident involving injury or death. They may also include other occurrences reflecting badly on the organization, such as employee drug abuse incident, fraud, mismanagement, improper hazardous waste disposal, and the like.

The purpose of this chapter is to provide basic overview guidance to assist organization leaders, managers, and their public affairs executives in meeting their public affairs responsibilities in a wide variety of contingencies—incidents, accidents, and other emergencies.

19.2 Public Affairs Practitioner and Staff

During a contingency or emergency, the public affairs practitioner and staff are key elements of the management team providing direct support to the organization leadership. In the event of a crisis, the public affairs staff should employ a variety of internal information systems—such as e-mail, faxes, bulletins, and newsletters—to keep staff and volunteers and their families informed as crisis response proceeds. In a public information capacity, the public affairs staff informs both the internal and external publics of the incident and the organization's actions to control it.

19.3 Public Affairs Contingency Plan

The most effective way to deal with and respond to a contingency or emergency is to have a public affairs plan in place *before* anything happens. This plan should anticipate and prepare for a wide range of contingencies, up to and including destruction of the organization's facility. Your plan should incorporate communications plans to notify the organization structure (both up and down), local support agencies, customers, stockholders, clients, members, and others in the event of any accident, incident, or contingency.

Employees, clients, customers, members, and the public have a legitimate interest in an occurrence which adversely impacts your organization or operations, leading to injury, death, or extensive damage to property. To plan for and to be responsive and forthcoming in such situations:

1. The public affairs director should be a participating member of panels, boards, or teams concerned with the planning for and response to crises and emergencies.
2. Public affairs should be an element for consideration in all contingency and emergency planning.
3. Public affairs actions should be prescribed in all organization contingency or emergency action plans.
4. The senior leadership should promptly notify the public affairs director or designated alternate when any incident, occurrence, or situation develops that has potential for causing reaction on the part of the news media or the general public.
5. Contact the organization's senior public affairs practitioners for advice and counsel in an emergency, or in contingency planning.

Contingency and emergency planning, like public affairs, is a management function that is coordinated and done in conjunction with other departments within the organization. Organizations should plan for contingencies and emergencies the same way they operate on a daily basis, as a team. Therefore, the contingency planning team should include senior members from legal, public affairs, operations, security, finance/supply, human resources, facilities management, administrative services, and other departments depending on your organization.

To aid in preparing the public affairs contingency plan, Exhibit 19.1 provides a useful development checklist:

EXHIBIT 19.1 Public Affairs Contingency Checklist

(1) Who is the first public affairs official to be notified?

(2) Who is notified if that person is not available?

(3) Who is responsible for notifying the public affairs person?

(4) Who of the public affairs staff is to be notified and mobilized. How will that notification be achieved?

(5) Who notifies the public affairs staff?

(6) Who is the organization's primary media spokesperson. What training and background do they have in contingency/crisis public affairs?

(7) Who is the alternate spokesperson?

(8) Who notifies the media? What is the process by which news and information is processed and approved for release?

(9) Who notifies employees?

(10) Where is the press room? Where is the briefing room?

(11) Who will be the secretary in the pressroom?

(12) Who will be the messenger in the pressroom?

(13) Who will gather factual information and relay it to the pressroom?

(14) Who will arrange for food and supplies in the pressroom?

(15) Who will arrange for transportation from the pressroom to the site, if not collocated?

(16) Who will transport the press from the pressroom to the site?

(17) Who in the organization will review and approve information before it is released to the press?

(18) What statements, if any, will be released by the organization?

(19) How will press inquiries to the organization be handled and processed?

(20) Who decides if media can visit the site?

(21) Who will accompany the media on site visits?

(22) Who are the public information officers for area organizations, city, county, state, and so on? How will they be informed?

(23) How will your organization coordinate public information operations with other organizations?

(24) Who can take photos/video for your organization?

(25) Who will maintain a record of press contacts and monitor press coverage?

(26) Who will correct the record should incorrect information be communicated by the media?

Keep a folder with incident/accident instructions, local and organization public affairs telephone numbers, and a list of established local organizational public affairs procedures. Include instruction pages from various organization manuals and current policy references that deal with contingencies.

In addition, preformatted contingency press releases that allow the user to either "fill in the blanks" or mix and match should be included. Update this material periodically. Finally, ensure that the contingency and emergency plans are easily understood so that someone outside the public affairs staff can initiate the plan in the event you are not available.

19.4   Public Affairs Goals During a Contingency or Emergency

Detailed instructions cannot be provided to cover every possible contingency; however, there are certain general actions that are appropriate in most circumstances. Public affairs goals in a contingency or emergency include the following:

1. Safeguard people and protect property.
2. Ensure civil authorities are provided prompt and correct information to enable them to make decisions concerning protection of the public.
3. Retain public confidence in the organization.
4. Respect the rights of organization personnel to privacy and protect their welfare and the dignity of the next of kin.
5. Honor the right of the public to be informed rapidly and accurately of accidents and incidents and the organization's response in emergencies and other contingencies.

It is during a time of crisis that your knowledge of the local media is most valuable. Media relations with members of the general media in your area, and specific trade media in your business sector, should be constant and ongoing. An organization's working relationships with local media, that is, the ability to contact a media representative who is familiar with your organization, gives a public affairs practitioner a significant head start in solving a contingency or emergency communications situation.

19.5   Release of Information

Accurate public affairs assessments are essential elements of an organization's evaluation of and report on a crisis or emergency. Public affairs assessments must be included in incident reports to higher levels of authority within your organization. The rapid release of accurate, factual information concerning an accident, incident, disaster, or other emergency is in the best interest of an organization.

Speed and accuracy are vital; however, a release containing incorrect or speculative information may create panic and confusion. Conversely, an accurate release that is too late to inform the public is of little or no value. While most details are unavailable and a comprehensive picture is illusive in the early stages of a contingency, rapid initial release of known, confirmed facts provides valuable information to the community.

When passed to higher elements of your organization, the initial release also alerts a larger public affairs network to render assistance to the local organization involved. If media representatives are at your location or nearby at the time of accident, full cooperation should be rendered in covering the story consistent with safety, protection of property and information at the site, and other pertinent requirements. Organizations should modify or expand the following public affairs assessments as required to fit their local situation:

1. No media present.
2. Media present; press release follows.

3. No media present; media interest expected.
4. No known press interest.
5. Public concern anticipated; proposed statement and contingency questions and answers to follow.
6. Local media on scene; the following statement was made at (date/time): Summary of statement.

When an accident or significant incident occurs, the public affairs practitioner must be notified immediately. Depending on the situation, the public affairs practitioner must have the authority to recall some or all of the staff, and prepare, properly staff, and disseminate information to the news media. The organization should draft the initial release or forward it to higher authority for release or do so locally; the information is not held pending inquiry. The goal for initial release is one hour from the time the public affairs office is first notified of the occurrence and the time information is prepared for initial release. Within the next hour, the majority of local and other interested news media are informed. This is a goal; situational constraints may cause initial release to take longer. Be right the first time.

During a crisis situation, it is especially important that the organization have only one spokesperson. Establish who that person is in advance; designate an alternate. If too many individuals talk to the media, conflicting or out-of-date information will be presented, resulting in an impression that information management by the organization is poor and, ultimately, not credible. (This impression will have longer-term impact on overall public support—including funding—on which nonprofits depend.) Strongly suggest to the media that if they haven't heard it from the designated spokesperson, they haven't heard it correctly. Then "turn off" the unauthorized spokesperson.

The organization spokesperson is the final point of quality control prior to release of information. It is the spokesperson who must ensure that the following elements are considered and achieved prior to release:

1. Gather and relate accurate information. Consider how the public affairs organization will: discover the facts, keep management informed, notify next of kin (if a fatality or serious injury is involved), and deal with media.
2. Consider legal aspects carefully. Consider how the organization will determine or be affected by legal liabilities, possible violations, and so on, and delegate this responsibility to a qualified authority early in the public affairs contingency process.
3. Provide full, factual, objective, truthful information. Resist inclinations—your own or others'—to slant, distort, manipulate, or fragment the truth. Being discovered in a lie will be much more damaging than anything an unfavorable truth might cause.
4. Gather, verify, and complete all units of information before release to the media. Avoid giving out partial, unchecked facts which could result in repeated media mention with undue emphasis on bad news. Avoid the appearance of noncooperation.
5. Ensure accuracy, thoroughness, and completeness by providing information packages. Press conferences, information sheets, handouts, prepared statements for broadcast appearances, and in the final stages, press kits, will

contribute to effective communication when an emergency requires disseminating information to the media simultaneously.

6. Emphasize perspective by balancing bad news with good. The organization's reputation, earned over the years, should not be forgotten in a crisis.

19.6　Denial and Adverse Information

One way to *create* a public affairs problem for an organization is to deny that a particular event occurred (when it did). If an organization has a contingency or emergency situation, either release the information or respond to media query with approved responses. The goal is to keep a one-day news story just that, a one-day story. Denial or "no comment" on a bad news story will only prolong the issue, and reinforce negative impressions among your publics on whom you depend for support, funding, and volunteers.

19.7　News Releases

Do not eliminate adverse information from a story. Present the facts without opinion and in detail. Your incident/accident story will then be given the treatment it deserves. If you create a situation in which reporters are forced to guess, or even more dangerous, seek out "a source" (an informer), you can expect inquiries from every level within your organization into the incident—including the information release policies of your office.

The initial release should provide as much information as possible on the key points. It is extremely important that information be released to the public as soon as possible; the rapid release of information prevents or dispels rumors that could easily cause public alarm or promote misinformation in news media reports. Newly arriving media representatives can be updated later.

In general, initial and follow-on releases should include:

1. Type of incident, accident, or contingency.
2. Location and time of the incident, accident, or contingency.
3. Persons involved. Initially, release number injured and killed, if known; also, the number of staff and volunteers; don't speculate, if you don't know, say so. Then, find out as soon as possible.
4. If a transportation-related incident or accident, the place of departure and destination. This pertains to vehicles, aircraft, vessels, and so on.
5. Type of equipment or system involved.
6. Pertinent facts about activities or operations at the time of the incident or accident.
7. Investigation. *Never* speculate about the cause or contributing causes of an accident or the responsibility for the mishap. If the situation warrants, ensure that you release information stating that an investigation into the causes is being conducted by the proper authorities and corrective measures are being taken. For example, if there is an environmental waste disposal problem, you should be prepared to tell the public what your organization is doing to clean it up and to prevent future occurrences.

19.8   Release of Information Pertaining to Employees or Volunteers

Whenever possible, the public affairs practitioner must coordinate with the Human Resource Office or other designated organization department prior to releasing information on employees who have been injured or killed in accidents. There are several critical aspects in releasing information that pertains to employees involved in accidents:

1. Information must not be released to news media until confirmation is received that next of kin have been notified. Thereafter, information released to media must agree with that provided to the next of kin. That means, the next of kin are advised of details prior to the media, and that the media are not given any information that is not provided to the next of kin.
2. Following medical care for the injured, the rights and dignity of the persons involved in accidents and their next of kin are of paramount importance. However, the public's right to know takes on new importance in accidents, incidents, and other disasters. Releasing the names of accident victims can relieve the anxiety and concern of relatives and friends of those not injured. Early and ongoing liaison with the human resources office point-of-contact will enable the organization to release names as soon as possible after the accident.
3. Should an accident occur off the organization's property and employees are involved, news media on the scene may be able to obtain identification without consulting the public affairs practitioner. Humanitarian considerations dictate the next of kin be notified of the situation prior to learning of it through the news media. If it is apparent that news media know the identity of accident victims and next of kin have not been notified, the public affairs practitioner should make a professional appeal to the reporters or editors requesting they withhold names of persons involved until notification is made. It is critical to inform the human resources office of the results of this appeal and the personnel whose names are likely to be known by the reporters. Knowing and having an established relationship with local and regional editors prior to the occurrence can make the critical difference between success and failure in this area.

19.9   Helping Family Members Deal with the Media

During times of crisis, your organization's employees, volunteers, and families may become the targets of news media attention as reporters try to localize or place an emotional edge to the story.

It is easy to blame the press for a lack of compassion. But the truth is that many families don't realize that once they are publicly identified, they become targets for other reporters and the general public.

The following are some important things family members should know about dealing with the press.

1. News is an extremely competitive business, with reporters going to great lengths to "get the story" before their competitors.
2. It is the right of the individual to say *no* to an interview request. In the past some reporters have coerced family members into submitting to an interview by emphasizing the public's "right to know" and "freedom of the press," but *your right to privacy always takes precedence.*
3. The individual's home is private property; no one, media or otherwise, has a "right" to enter your home or be on your property unless you grant them that privilege.
4. If the subject under scrutiny does decide to talk with the media, ground rules for that protection should be established before the interview. Responsible professional reporters will work to meet reasonable ground rules. These ground rules are often negotiated or brokered by the public affairs practitioner, who represents and provides counsel to the interviewee. The public affairs practitioner will discuss and seek agreement of the ground rules with the media representative prior to any direct contact with the interviewee. Ground rules can include no photos/video of faces, disguising of voices, nonattribution of comments, and so on.
5. Some suggestions are that family members may not wish to have their full name used, and you should always ensure that the home address is not used. Television pictures of an employee or volunteer's house are usually not a good idea.

19.10   Incidents or Accidents Outside Your Facility

Should an incident or accident occur outside your facility, the public affairs challenge becomes more complex. From a logistics standpoint, the public affairs team must then operate from two locations, the public affairs office and the accident site, with public affairs representatives at both locations. This complicates communications, transportation, and public information clearance procedures. This eventuality should be anticipated and addressed in your planning.

Consistent with organizational, legal, and operational constraints, your organization should give maximum cooperation to news representatives covering incidents and accidents. Immediately following an accident or incident the organization should:

1. Take action to minimize further injury and property damage.
2. Assist in rescue of survivors and treating the injured.
3. Report the incident or accident to higher authority.
4. Preserve the accident scene to assist investigators.
5. Protect organization files and records.
6. Consult with civil authorities if activating public warning or evacuation plans may be appropriate.
7. Rapidly meet the need for public information about the accident or incident.

No two contingencies are identical, but public affairs actions at an off-site location should include:

1. *Define the area:* Upon arrival at the accident scene, the senior public affairs official should request that law enforcement or public safety authorities rope off the entire area to protect the public from injury and property from further disturbance.

2. *Brief the reporters:* The organization should prepare contingency questions and answers to respond to likely news media inquiries at the incident or accident scene. Once statements or contingency answers are approved, the senior public affairs official at the scene should be granted permission to release the preapproved information. In addition, reporters should be briefed on safety hazards (if any) and the need to preserve the site for investigators before they are permitted to enter the cordoned area. The briefing should be done by the public affairs official at the scene who can get information from others present. If a reporter refuses to cooperate with the ground rules, you have the option to request that security personnel deny access to the individual. Keep in mind that you may not physically restrict the movement of the news media at accident sites except on your property.

3. *Admitting reporters to the area:* After the area is cordoned off, news media representatives are briefed, and law enforcement, public safety, and organization officials advise that an area is safe, the senior public affairs official on the scene may grant permission to enter the accident area.

4. *Media identification:* As part of the public affairs office contingency planning, special news media identification badges may be required and should be kept on hand. These may consist of inexpensive plastic badges, armbands, or other similar devices that conform to the organization's security badging system and are ready for immediate issue in the event of an incident or other emergency. Badges can be prepared in advance, with one or more badges marked and set aside for each local newspaper, several for each television station, and so on. The badges can be taken to the accident scene by the public affairs office member assigned that duty by the organization's contingency planning. Wearing the badge signifies to organization and law enforcement personnel that the wearer has been briefed on safety considerations regarding the accident site and the need to preserve the site for investigators. More importantly, the badge system can ease confusion at a busy, crowded site. Wearing such identification by reporters is voluntary in areas outside your property, but can be required of them when at your facility.

As soon as possible following the conclusion of the event, the public affairs practitioner should develop a narrative summary of public affairs actions taken before and following the contingency as a training tool to critique the staff and share lessons learned. The summary should be shared with the rest of the organization. A cassette tape recorder is quite helpful in "taking notes" during fast moving situations.

19.11 Contingency Public Affairs Do's and Don'ts

Do's

1. Get the facts before you talk with the press.
2. Establish who is going to speak for the organization.

3. Get information to the press as quickly as possible and be aware of press deadlines.
4. Issue statements in writing if at all possible.
5. Emphasize the positive.
6. Know to whom you are speaking. Get the reporter's name and get the name and telephone number in telephone interviews. Log all media queries on media query forms.
7. Aid the press in getting the story.
8. Monitor press coverage and correct errors quickly.
9. Say "I don't know" if you don't know.

Don'ts

1. Don't say "No comment."
2. Don't guess or speculate—ever!
3. Don't release damage estimates without double checking for accuracy.
4. Don't release names of victims until notification of next of kin has been made. Then confirm it has been made again.
5. Don't try to mislead or cover up information. Never lie.
6. Don't try to place blame.
7. Don't play favorites with the media. Release information to everyone at the same time.
8. Don't ever make "off the record" comments. There is no such thing.
9. Don't use inflammatory, spectacular terms like "blown to bits," "raging fire," or "torn limb from limb."
10. Don't repeat negative or inaccurate statements in answering questions.
11. Don't panic, cry, or lose control.

19.12   Who Has Release Authority?

Who in your organization has the releasing authority for news? Important news releases are, in effect, announcements by the senior administrator concerning major appointments, policy, or matters of sufficient importance that justify release from the highest level in the organization. This also includes news that may affect organization policy or have a political impact.

Release of information that affects the entire organization may be released by the organization headquarters. The news release and information could be researched and developed by your department or division and provided to the organization headquarters for further staffing and approval prior to release. Depending on the size of the organization, there may be several levels of hierarchy to negotiate prior to reaching headquarters.

Matters concerning an individual organization, such as announcements of limited interest (local achievements, background materials, etc.), may be released at the local level.

If you have any doubt about your authority in a given situation, you should contact public affairs officials at a more senior level of your organization *before you talk to the press.*

19.13   The Mobile Laptop Public Affairs Office

With the rapidly expanding capabilities of laptop computer technology, increased hard drive storage, high-data-rate internal modems, and increasingly user-friendly software, the mobile laptop office has become a reality.

As more powerful laptop computers with large-capacity hard drives and modems bundled with popular software packages continue to drop in price, these systems have become a business essential for the public affairs practitioner and nonprofit executives.

The savvy executive, with some thought and preparation, can load software programs and data that allows the laptop computer to become not only a multipurpose mobile office capable of word processing, desktop publishing, database management, and spreadsheet development, but a powerful communications tool for faxing information to both individuals and groups, and corresponding via e-mail and the Internet.

Due to the rapid evolution of computer technology, I will avoid addressing particular systems except to say that the most recent Windows and Macintosh operating system laptops provide more computing power than the average nonprofit executive will ever use. The same can be said for fax/modem and printer technologies; while faster is better, faster is also more expensive.

The same rule that applies to desktop computers applies to laptop computers. While the circuits, central processing units, and hard drives may be the same from one model to the next, prior to purchasing, pay close attention to the man/machine interface and ergonomics. Of particular importance is determining whether the laptop keyboard (often smaller in size than a desktop computer keyboard) and display are comfortable for you. The best way to determine if you and a laptop are a good ergonomic fit is to perform a number of functions on the keyboard while viewing the screen in varying light conditions. If either your hands or eyes feel strained, then search for another laptop with a better fit.

Other laptop features to look for include random access memory (RAM) expandability, a built-in mouse, built-in video monitor capability that allows you to connect to a 14″, 15″, or 17″ color monitor, and built-in ethernet capability.

Once you find the computer that suits your specific needs, the next task is selecting software and loading data to make it useful.

Regardless of the operating system you use (Windows or Macintosh), there are literally thousands of software products on the market to fill your hard drive. Because you are mobile, it is recommended that you use industry-standard software for word processing, desktop publishing, database management, spreadsheeting, and communications software (for fax/modem and on-line services). WordPerfect, Microsoft Office, Adobe Pagemaker and others are widely accepted, and offer a high degree of cross-platform (Windows to Macintosh and vice versa) compatibility. A personal information manager (PIM) that incorporates a calendar, electronic rolodex, and to-do list is also important.

What would a nonprofit public affairs practitioner require to operate from a remote site on short notice? From a public affairs standpoint, the well-equipped laptop should include some or all of the following information (type of software application is in parenthesis):

1. Executive biographies, history, product and organization fact sheets (word processing or desktop publishing software).
2. Calendar (PIM software).
3. Electronic rolodex (PIM software).

4. To-do list (PIM software).
5. Organization decision makers and key staff members list with names, addresses, fax, telephone, and e-mail (PIM software).
6. Public affairs contingency plan with fill-in-the-blanks contingency press releases (word processing or desktop publishing software).
7. Media list with name, address, telephone, and e-mail (PIM software or database software, tab-separated entry with ability to export to fax/modem transmission software, word processing mail merge for envelope labels, letters/memorandums/press releases, and e-mail).
8. Organization membership list with name, address, telephone, and e-mail (PIM software or database software, tab-separated entry with ability to export to fax/modem transmission software, word processing mail merge for envelope labels, letters/memorandums/press releases, and e-mail).
9. Organization budget and obligations to date in the event you must operate away from your normal office (spreadsheet software).
10. An inventory of supplies required to equip an off-site or remote office (database or spreadsheet software).

Other equipment required should include:

1. Backup operating system and software program diskettes.
2. Backup diskettes of program data.
3. Serial and parallel port printer cables.
4. Electrical extension cord (batteries don't last forever).
5. Spare, charged batteries.
6. RJ-11 duplex adapter (allows you to plug in a phone and a modem into a single wall telephone jack).
7. 25 feet of telephone wire.
8. Blank diskettes.

While operating away from your office, there are normally three options in terms of printing. These include:

1. Use of a printer on-site.
2. Carrying a laptop portable printer.
3. Use of a local fax machine as a printer.

Unless planning to be off-site for an extended period, seriously consider options 1 and 3. "Borrowing" an on-site laser printer when away from your office is a good option, and use of a plain-paper laser fax provides high-quality printing. Consider these options before carrying a three- to four-pound portable printer that often provides less quality or speed.

Communicating via fax/modem is now much easier, with many office, hotel, and pay telephones equipped with data ports. Using a fax/modem allows you to transmit and receive your e-mail messages from your on-line service mail box, or transmit a fax.

Whether operating in borrowed or leased office space, a hotel room, or a pay telephone, with the properly equipped laptop and a fax/modem the mobile-office-savvy public affairs practitioner can communicate efficiently and effectively virtually worldwide.

19.14   Public Information Center Operating Procedures

The guide presented in Exhibit 19.2 is provided to help nonprofit executives prepare Standard Operating Procedures (SOP) for an off-site Public Information Center (PIC). While such a detailed level of planning is not often needed by most nonprofits, when extraordinary circumstances occur, there is little time for advance planning. Response must be rapid, basically a "come as you are" situation. The SOP guidelines which follow should help public affairs personnel understand what will be required in the way of functional organization and services to news media at an off-site scene, which could be a special event, an exercise, or the real thing.

EXHIBIT 19.2 Standard Operating Procedures

---

1. *General.*
    A. Situation
       This SOP assigns responsibilities and provides guidance for the operation of the Public Information Center in support of (name of organization)
    B. Discussion
2. *Mission/Objective.*
   The mission and objective of the (name of organization) Public Information Center includes:
    A. The public affairs mission of . . . is to provide both timely and factual on-the-scene coverage of the exercise to both internal audiences and the general public through international, national, regional, and local news media.
    B. All public affairs actions associated with this service will be consistent with policy guidance provided by (name of organization).
    C. The following will be accomplished by public affairs personnel assigned to . . . :
       (1) a. Increase public understanding of . . . services.
           b. Minimize potential negative reaction by the community through effective community relations programs.
           c. Generate improved public understanding and support for (name of organization).
           (i) Generate broad public awareness and support through active public affairs programs and operations, including:
               • producing radio broadcast service for participants
               • releasing information for print/broadcast media
               • providing comprehensive photographic or video image coverage
               • processing, credentialling, briefing, escorting news media representatives to assist them in collecting and preparing their stories
               • providing timely response to queries received via telephone or directly from news media representatives
       (2) Increase the internal community's understanding of the (organization) and its components. Create positive motivation in participants.
       (3) Highlight the public services, readiness, and capabilities of participating organizations and personnel.
       (4) Provide training for public affairs personnel in joint operations.
3. *Execution.*
    A. Concept of Operations. (Relevant excerpts from contingency public affairs plan)
       Explanation of:
       • public affairs chain of command
       • press briefings
       • audio-visual support (photography/documentation)

EXHIBIT 19.2 *(Continued)*

- rights to privacy
- direct communication guidelines
- tasking

4. *Organization.*

The Public Information Center is functionally organized as follows:
- Director/Chief, Public Information Center
- Deputy Director/Chief, Public Information Center
- Query/Answering Department
- News/Collecting Department
- Photographic Department
- Broadcasting Department
- Program Department
- Administrative Services Department

5. *Tasking.*

A. Director/Chief, Public Information Center
- Serves as exercise spokesman on behalf of the Director (or Chief Executive Officer)
- Maintains overall responsibility for the direction and effective operation of the PIC
- Has release authority

B. Deputy Director/Chief, Public Information Center
- Serves as Chief, PIC in his or her absence; maintains special responsibility for PIC administration, support, personnel, visitors, and social functions
- The following PIC department heads report to the chief of PIC through the Deputy Chief for the proper performance of their duties and the effective management of their departments:

C. Query/Answering Department Head

Responsible for the effective function of the Answering Section, whose responsibilities include:
- Responding to all external calls to PIC
- Logging queries and responses
- Providing immediate responses based on background information, plus new, cleared information incorporated from the Collecting Department
- Preparing and forwarding to the Collecting Department questions for which answers are needed for response to query
- Logging all questions/responses to the News and Broadcasting Departments
- Providing basic briefings for news media representatives, including briefing on current issues for individual media or groups

D. News/Collection Department Head

Responsible for the effective function of the News/Collection Department, whose responsibilities include:
- Collecting and updating newsworthy information from participating organizations or other relevant sources
- Passing gathered information to the Answering Department
- Conducting special investigations to obtain needed answers to queries
- Maintaining a constantly updated operations map
- Producing PIC press releases, background, and photo feature materials.
- Maintaining the Query/Release Log of information released by the Answering Department
- Producing news material distribution lists
- Producing the daily news summary report based on clippings obtained by the Administrative Department

(Continued)

EXHIBIT 19.2 *(Continued)*

    E. Still Photography Department Head
       Responsible for the effective function of the Still Photographic Department, whose responsibilities include:
- Produce quality releasable photographs which document the exercise and provide professional level photographs for use by print media.
- Maintain and operate darkroom facilities needed to support Public Information Center photographic needs.
- Maintain photographic display and provide copies as requested by media
- Maintain log of photos released.

    F. Broadcast/Electronic Media Department Head
       Responsible for the effective function of the Broadcast/Electronic Media Department, whose responsibilities include:
- Producing and broadcasting radio and television/video programs in the area which meet internal information objectives for participating organizations, and community relations objectives in the exercise/broadcast area
- Obtaining or assisting News Media Representatives (NMRs) in obtaining good-quality news-oriented video tape in support of overall public affairs/PIC objectives; providing tape to civilian or military broadcast news organizations for use in exercise coverage

    G. Program Department Head
       Responsible for the effective function of the Program Department, whose responsibilities include:
- Organizing and implementing all aspects of visits to exercise areas by news media representatives
- Training and administering escorts for NMRs
- Coordinating responses to query by visiting media through the Query/Collecting and Answering/News Departments to ensure prompt, accurate responses and/or briefings
- Maintaining constantly updated "current affairs" picture through close liaison with the Answering Department

    H. Administrative Services Department Head
       Responsible for the effective function of the Administrative Services Department, whose responsibilities include:
- Vehicular transportation, including training and scheduling qualified drivers
- PIC internal/external communications, including: telephone, facsimile, and message traffic
- Accommodations for PIC staff
- Personnel
- Secretarial support, including xerographic or other forms of information reproduction
- Maintaining the PIC Log for tracking releases and other written materials passing through
- Manning and administering the Public Information Center Reception and Service Counters with qualified personnel

6. *Release of Information.*
    A. (Release authority)
    B. (Procedures)
    C. (Conditions for release/caveats)

7. *Crisis Management.*
    In the event of a situation with potential to result in media attention (e.g., accident, incident, casualty, demonstration), the following procedures will be followed based on an assessment of the situation by Director/Chief, Public Information Center:

EXHIBIT 19.2 *(Continued)*

A. Public Information (PI) Cell will inform the Public Information Center immediately and maintain a steady flow of updates.

B. Query/Answering and News/Collecting Departments will be fully staffed and prepared to implement an around-the-clock watch schedule, depending on the severity of the situation (e.g., anticipated degree and duration of media interest). The Program Department will be prepared to augment Query and News Departments with personnel as needed to fill out the manning schedule.

C. News and Broadcasting Departments will be prepared to dispatch News Gathering Team(s) to the location of the event. News Gathering Teams will include four p/a personnel representing the collecting, news, photographic, and broadcasting departments, plus a driver. The Administrative Department will prepare and maintain a "Crisis Kit" of equipment/supplies for use by the Public Information Center Crisis News Gathering Team. As necessary, the Public Information Center Crisis News Gathering Team will be augmented and transformed into a Public Information Center subteam either before or after dispatch. The News and Broadcasting Departments will prepare release(s) of information/photographs for release immediately following confirmation of initial reports by the Collecting Unit/Public Information Center Crisis News Gathering Team.

D. Deputy Chief, Public Information Center will have responsibility for the continuation of normal functions and activities during the crisis/contingency situation, based on priorities provided by Chief, Public Information Center.

E. Program Department will be prepared to augment the News Department and will provide qualified public affairs personnel for the Crisis News Gathering Team.

F. Administrative Department will prepare/maintain the Crisis Kit for the News Gathering Team. It will have responsibility for acquiring transportation, ground or air, needed by the News Gathering Team. If necessary, it will limit and control access to the Public Information Center by news media representatives during the crisis management period.

8. *Daily Routine/Schedule.*
   A. Working hours
   B. Daily Meetings/Briefings
   C. Media Update
      Each morning news media representatives will be issued an approved list of day's events, planned news and photo coverage opportunities (including availability of material), and plans for the day's radio broadcast schedule. This information will be developed by department heads, reviewed during the morning staff meeting, and given final approval by Chief, Public Information Center.

9. *News Media.*
   A. News media representatives with known arrival times will be picked up at the airport by an escort officer assigned by the Program Department.
   B. Upon arrival at the Public Information Center, a news media representative will be logged in and accredited by the Administrative Department, including the issuance of the proper press identification (e.g., card, armband).
   C. Upon arrival of the news media representatives at the Public Information Center Administration Desk, a designated public affairs specialist will be notified and will officially welcome the person or group.
   D. Following a brief familiarization tour of the Public Information Center, the news media representatives will be turned over to the Program Department to continue with a pre-planned orientation program or the scheduling of same. A complete briefing on the exercise and current activities will be provided by the Program Department.

(Continued)

EXHIBIT 19.2 *(Continued)*

10. *Communication.*
    A. Computer communications
       • e-mail
       • Internet home page
    B. Faxes/print communications
       • process
       • address
       • distribution
    C. Telephones
       • connections
       • telephone book
       • procedures for use
       • numbers
    D. Mobile Telephones
    E. Telefax
    F. Telephoto
    G. Other
11. *Accommodations.*
    A. To be determined

19.15 Contingency Public Affairs Office Equipment Checklist

The list in Exhibit 19.3 provides a comprehensive supply checklist required to equip a remote public affairs office. This checklist should be used as a "mix and match" to meet the nonprofit organization requirements contingency or remote requirements. Also, don't forget the option of using locally available vendors, public relations/advertising agencies, and other sources to provide some equipment and services required temporarily.

EXHIBIT 19.3 Equipment Checklist

1. *Public Affairs Equipment.*
    Audio cassette tape recorder, hand-held, with lectret condenser microphone
    Video cassette recorder (3/4-in. or 1/2-in. VHS)
    Television receiver/monitor
    Camera kit (35mm SLR), electronic flash unit, lenses (35mm/50mm/70-120mm zoom, or
        comparable), appropriate filters, tripod, case
    Megaphone/hailer
    Handheld communications system
    Automatic broadcast feed unit
    Cellular telephone with spare, fully charged batteries
    Portable lecterns (with built-in microphone/speakers/auxiliary inputs/outputs)
    Media feed "multiboxes"
    Portable mixers, extra microphones, power outlets, cables, and connectors
    VHF/Bearcat frequency scanner
    Radio, multiband, portable
    Slide projector
    Overhead projector
    Screen
    Backdrop for briefings
    Chalkboard/Bulletin board

EXHIBIT 19.3 *(Continued)*

2. *Public Affairs Supplies.*
   Audio cassette tapes (C-30 and C-60)
   Video cassette tapes
   Film, 35mm (Tri-X/Plus-X/Color print/Color slide)
   Nicad batteries for camera and flash unit
   Nicad batteries for tape recorders
   Lettering/sign-making kit
   Photo mailers
   Cardboard photo protector
   News release letterhead
   Media Center sign (with Velcro holder)
   Nicad battery charger
3. *Public Affairs Publications.*
   Dictionary (English/Spanish/French/German)
   Thesaurus (or comparable software program, hard copy/floppy disk)
   Public affairs staff directories
   Ayers *Dictionary of Publications*
   Regulations, instructions, directives (as appropriate)
   Telephone directory
   Maps/charts of area, including road map
4. *Office Furniture.*
   Desks
   Chairs
   Computer desk/printer table
   Filing cabinet, 2-drawer
   Light table
5. *Office Equipment.*
   Laptop microcomputers with hard drive and fax modem
   Backup system and application software
   Backup files of all current work
   Printers with cable connectors
   Surge protector/fused electric cords
   Facsimile/fax machine, portable
   Typewriter, self-correcting electric, with various typewriter balls
   Typewriter, manual
   Telephone answering machine with audio cassette and audio patch cords
   Xerographic copier portable
6. *Office Supplies.*
   Clipboards
   Staplers
   Staple remover
   Scissors
   Rulers (12- and 18-inch)
   Pencil sharpener, electric
   Pencil sharpener, manual
   Hole punchers (2- and 3-hole)
   File basket
   Trash baskets
7. *Office Supplies (Consumables).*
   Staples
   Rubber bands (various sizes)
   Erasers

(Continued)

EXHIBIT 19.3 *(Continued)*

Thumb tacks/push pins
Pens and pencils
    pencils
    ball point pens
    felt tip pens (blue/black/red/green, etc.)
    felt tip markers (blue/black/red) waterproof
Tape
    masking (½-in., 1-in., 2-in. rolls)
    duct tape
    nylon filament tape
    cellophane tape (clear/transparent)
Clips
    paper
    binder
Paper
    bond paper (8½ × 11)
    writing pads
    legal pads
    stenograph pads
    carbon paper
    manifold sets
    pocket pads
    continuous form
        plain white
        organization letterhead
        labels (⅞ by 3½ in.)
        name tags
Envelopes
    business, white
    manila (9½ × 12-in., 6 × 9-in.)
Diskettes, computer
    Floppy diskettes (appropriate for type of laptop)
    hard/protected case labels
Telephone Message pads
    Address labels
    gummed
    continuous form/fan folded
    3 × 5 cards
    Sticking notes (Post it)
    Name tags
    individual, self-sticking
    continuous form
Telecopier paper
Fax paper
Index tabs
File folders
Accordion file folders
Glue sticks
Razor blades, single edge
Ribbons
    typewriter
    computer printer

EXHIBIT 19.3 *(Continued)*

      correction, manual
      electric typewriter
    Correction tape
    Laser printer toner cartridges
8. *Miscellaneous Equipment.*
    Heavy-duty worklight
    Flashlights
    3-cell, 2-cell, penlight
    Extension cords
    100-foot, 50-foot with multiple outlet strips
    Coffee pots 50-cup, including filters, coffee cups, sugar, cream substitute
    Tool box with standard screwdrivers, Phillips screwdrivers, claw hammer, pliers,
      assorted nuts/bolts/nails/screws
9. *Miscellaneous Supplies.*
    Nicad flashlight batteries (D and C sizes with recharger)
    Insect repellent
    Fly swatter
    Broom
10. *Temporary Shelter.*
    Leased office space
    Mobile home on-site (office configuration)
    Tent (large enough to accommodate 20 people plus equipment)

NOTE:
Quantities of each item and actual items required would be determined by local
requirements and expected duration.

20 Fund-Raising Management

James M. Greenfield, ACFRE, FAHP
Hoag Memorial Hospital Presbyterian

20.1 Management of the Fund Development Process

The essential characteristics of a successful fund-raising program is quite easy to define—ask for the gift! Were it that simple, no one would need to know anything more about it. What complicates asking is which solicitation method to use, whom to ask and when, who does the asking, what's the money for, who benefits from its use, how much to request, how much is tax-deductible, how much to spend on asking, and many more crucial questions. Asking for gifts is a much more complex and challenging task than many believe and appreciate.

Fund development has been described as "planned promotion for participation, understanding and support" (Seymour, 1966). But fund raising is not the mission of nonprofit organizations; it is a means to aid them in fulfilling their mission. Nonprofit organizations are dedicated to public benefit and community service, and philanthropy is the means whereby the public is invited to participate. Philanthropy has been defined as "voluntary action for the public good" (Payton, 1988), and the scope of fund-raising practices is composed of the methods most often employed in asking people to volunteer their time and money. It helps to remember always that giving is voluntary. Those valued people we call volunteers must be identified, recruited, trained, supported, rewarded, and thanked many times, just as donors also must be cultivated and treated. Fund raising is an action-oriented contact sport and a team effort. It relies on people and depends on their performance (how their time, talent, effort, and money are used), and relies on their confidence and trust perseverance in helping their chosen nonprofit organization to achieve its mission. Success is best measured not in how many volunteers or donors are involved, nor in how much money was raised, but in how their combined efforts and funds were used to benefit others. Outcomes measurement, an inadequate exercise today, is the true test of both philanthropic practice and the mission of nonprofit organizations.

To be successful, nonprofit organizations must understand the relationship among institutional decisions, as guided by their mission, purposes, goals, and objectives, the quality of the programs and services they offer, and the public's interest and willingness to support their current and future endeavors. Public support is based largely on that same public's confidence in the worth of the organization followed by their trust in its board of directors, in whom their money is invested, to "do the right thing" for the community. The most essential ingredient to successful fund development is a well-founded and well-documented master plan for the nonprofit organization. The organization that has carefully evaluated its present ability, measured its capacity against unmet public needs, and defined how it can address these needs successfully, provides the best reason for the public to join the effort—because it knows and can document its purpose and can explain exactly how it will use their money. Lacking this essential plan, fund raising is only about asking for money and can never achieve much above "pocket change" from those asked to give.

(A) MANAGING PROSPECTS AND DONORS

Every nonprofit organization has friends and supporters, even if it is largely unknown, unpopular, or even unliked. People believe in causes and become advocates for "their" cause. They will join with others to improve the quality of their own and others' lives and to help the cause, be it the environment, animals, or inanimate objects. In all these efforts, they advocate the merits of the cause to others and invite them to join, with the key words being *advocate* and *invite*. Solicitation of their time, talent, energy, and money follows their conviction of the worth, merits, and benefits of the cause itself.

Volunteerism is immensely strong in America and growing worldwide. Research studies by Independent Sector report that one of every two American adults spends 4.2 hours per week in some voluntary capacity (Hodgkinson, 1992). Volunteerism is also a critical factor in gift decisions; individuals who give of their time also give twice as generously ($1,155 compared with $601) than those who do not. And those volunteers who are also regular participants in religious organizations are the most generous of all, with 78 percent making contributions each year.

How much do Americans give and where do they give? Although there is no single source for such data, the American Association of Fund Raising Counsel has collected and reported giving statistics from a variety of sources for more than 40 years. Their most recent annual report (see Exhibit 20.1) reveals that $130 billion in contributions were made in 1994, a modest increase of 3.68 percent over 1993. That sum is greater than the annual operating budgets of any state in the union and most nations around the world. Further (and surprising to some), the majority of these contributions (81%) comes from living individuals plus another 7 percent from bequests. Most people presume contributions to charity come largely from corporations and foundations, but their combined giving amounts to 14 percent of this annual total. These facts should help to offset assertions made by some members of Congress, when considering major cuts in social, welfare, education, and health programs, that contributions from corporations and foundations can "make up the difference." Furthermore, most contributions are made to religious organizations (45%), not to human service organizations (9%), education (13%), health care institutions (9%), or the arts and culture (8%).

EXHIBIT 20.1 Charitable Contributions

Total Giving: $129.88 billion
**Sources of
Contributions**
($ in Billions)

**Corporations
$6.11** (4.7%)

**Bequests
$8.77** (6.8%)

**Foundations
$9.91** (7.6%)

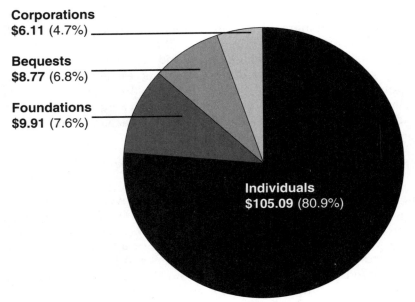

**Individuals
$105.09** (80.9%)

Comparison of 1994 Estimates to 1993 Estimates ($ in billions)

	Original 1993	Revised 1993	1994	% Change Current $	Change Adjusted for Inflation
Sources of Contributions					
Individuals	$102.55	$101.16	$105.09	3.89%	0.77%
Bequests	8.54	8.54	8.77	2.70%	−0.39%
Foundations	9.21	9.53	9.91	4.00%	0.87%
Corporations	5.92	6.05	6.11	1.00%	−2.04%
	$126.22	$125.27	$129.88	3.68%	0.56%

*Note: Totals and percentage changes incorporate computer rounding. Revised figures reflect new data
released by primary sources.*
Source: Giving USA, 1995, p. 12.

People give for a multitude of reasons (see Exhibit 20.2). Corporations give with an
eye toward self-interest goals, and foundations make grants only where projects match
up well with their current purposes and priorities. Matching the priority of needs as well
as the mission, purposes, goals, and objectives of nonprofit organizations with these
three revenue sources is both the art and science of fund development. It is important
to appreciate that to succeed in receiving gifts from any individual, corporation, or foundation is a major accomplishment and never accidental.

EXHIBIT 20.2 Framework for Determining Why People Give

Internal Motivations	External Influences
Personal or "I" Factors	**Rewards**
Acceptance of self or self-esteem	Recognition
Achievement	Personal
Cognitive	Social
Growth	
Guilt reduction or avoidance	**Stimulations**
Meaning or purpose of life	Human needs
Personal gain or benefit	Personal request
Spirituality	Vision
Immortality	Private initiative
Survival	Efficiency and effectiveness
	Tax deductions
Social or "We" Factors	
Status	**Situations**
Affiliation	Personal involvement
Group endeavor	Planning and decision making
Interdependence	Peer pressure
Altruism	Networks
Family and progeny	Family involvement
Power	Culture
	Tradition
Negative or "They" Factors	Role identity
Frustration	Disposable income
Unknown situations	
Insecurity	
Fear and anxiety	
Complexity	

Source: Reprinted with permission from *Principles of Professional Fundraising* by Joseph R. Mixer (San Francisco: Jossey Bass Publishers, 1993), 14.

Because nonprofit organizations are not the same in how they define their mission and purposes, in what "their" community's priority of needs may be, and in how they carry out their programs and services for community benefit, such diversity makes for a multitude of challenges to each entity that is engaged in charitable work. They must define their daily activity with great precision in order to reach exactly the people or issues their mission is dedicated to address, or else their impact or ability to solve problems is limited or misdirected. In most instances around the nation and the world, these public needs are obvious—hunger, housing, health, education, not to mention equal access and equal opportunity for all. In other settings, it is less visible or we are just unaware and, as a result, the voice that brings the message to awaken us is not easily heard.

In order to be heard as well as effective in stimulating a response, communications require both funds and expertise when delivering the desired message repeatedly over multiple channels. Another objective of these communications is to reach and stimulate contributor candidates, whether for their time, talent, energy, financial support, or all of these. Not everyone who receives information or even receives a service provided by a nonprofit organization is able to help. Certainly those who must use a homeless shelter or soup kitchen, or receive funds to attend college or go to summer camp, are grateful for the service they enjoyed, but they are not likely (at the moment) to do much to help the organization advance its mission—or are they? At another time, they may be better able to help. It is important to remember that those whom you serve also may be able to serve you in the future.

Volunteers and donors are more than valuable partners in the daily operations of a nonprofit organization; they are its friends and advocates, its foot soldiers, its "arms and legs," and its "eyes" in the community. The value of their hours of volunteer service alone, estimated to represent half the adult population, if measured by the minimum wage at $4.25, is in the tens of millions. What they permit nonprofit organizations to do is to allocate their limited resources to the most critical areas of day-to-day operations. Volunteers and donors also are the most flexible resource a nonprofit organization may have because they can respond to new directions, address new challenges, and give with greater generosity (any of these or all) when the need arises. Those who are donors, because of the added dimension of financial accountability, deserve additional consideration. Recognition and reward for sharing their personal resources are always appropriate, but more valuable to both donors and their chosen charity is respect. The Donor Bill of Rights has been prepared to guide nonprofit organizations in their relations with their contributors (see Exhibit 20.3). This text should be formally adopted by the board of directors of every nonprofit organization as both its policy and practice with respect to both volunteers and donors.

(B) MANAGING SOLICITATION ACTIVITIES

Given the value of volunteers and donors and their absolute necessity to every nonprofit organization in the successful pursuit of its mission, the methods and techniques that invite public participation should command high attention within each nonprofit organization. Too often, fund raising is viewed only as a source of money rather than a carefully managed resource whose full agenda includes constituency building, friend raising, relationship building, marketing and communications, community relations, solicitation activities, recognition and reward, and more.

The best use of the methods and techniques of solicitation is to see them as a continuum of resource development, financial investment, volunteer and leadership development, and institutional advancement. The day-to-day practice of identifying and inviting new prospects to join with others in ongoing annual and major gift support is conducted in conjunction with educating and involving those donors who have already begun their support so that their combined interest and enthusiasm results in faithful giving over many years. This level of commitment has the potential to provide several annual and major gifts and even a portion of their estate in the future. Appreciate this hypothesis: No individual, corporation, or foundation is likely to make their largest gift to a nonprofit organization *first*; but they may make many such gifts over a lifetime if enjoined in a positive and rewarding relationship by that same nonprofit organization. The fund development process is the guidebook for achieving lifetime relationships.

Successful fund development is a planned mix of donor and volunteer contacts, growth, and commitment, as illustrated in the Pyramid of Giving (see Exhibit 20.4). Actual solicitation methods are identified in three groups or tiers, beginning with annual

EXHIBIT 20.3 A Donor Bill of Rights

A Donor Bill of Rights

PHILANTHROPHY is based on voluntary action for the common good. It is a tradition of giving and sharing that is primary to the quality of life. To assure that philanthropy merits the respect and trust of the general public, and that donors and prospective donors can have full confidence in the not-for-profit organizations and causes they are asked to support, we declare that all donors have these rights:

I.
To be informed of the organization's mission, of the way the organization intends to use donated resources, and of its capacity to use donations effectively for their intended purposes.

II.
To be informed of the identity of those serving on the organization's governing board, and to expect the board to exercise prudent judgment in its stewardship responsibilities.

III.
To have access to the organization's most recent financial statements.

IV.
To be assured their gifts will be used for the purposes for which they were given.

V.
To receive appropriate acknowledgment and recognition.

VI.
To be assured that information about their donations is handled with respect and with confidentiality to the extent provided by law.

VII.
To expect that all relationships with individuals representing organizations of interest to the donor will be professional in nature.

VIII.
To be informed whether those seeking donations are volunteers, employees of the organization, or hired solicitors.

IX.
To have the opportunity for their names to be deleted from the mailing lists that an organization may intend to share.

X.
To feel free to ask questions when making a donation and to receive prompt, truthful, and forthright answers.

DEVELOPED BY
AMERICAN ASSOCIATION OF FUND RAISING COUNSEL (AAFRC)
ASSOCIATION FOR HEALTHCARE PHILANTHROPY (AHP)
COUNCIL FOR ADVANCEMENT AND SUPPORT OF EDUCATION (CASE)
NATIONAL SOCIETY OF FUND RAISING EXECUTIVES (NSFRE)

ENDORSORED BY (INFORMATION)
INDEPENDENT SECTOR
NATIONAL CATHOLIC DEVELOPMENT CONFERENCE (NCDC)
NATIONAL COMMITTEE ON PLANNED GIVING (NCPG)
NATIONAL COUNCIL FOR RESOURCE DEVELOPMENT (NCRD)
UNITED WAY OF AMERICA

---

giving at the bottom of the pyramid. Nearly every nonprofit organization is or should be engaged in one or more forms of annual giving. As these activities mature on their own, they expand their performance and professionalism to higher levels where greater sophistication in major and planned gift solicitation and management are required. Those organizations who are most successful have invested both time and money in building and maintaining the entire pyramid as an organized and structured investment program. A continuous series of cultivation, solicitation, and donor relations activities are well integrated between all three program levels, which concentrates on volunteers and donors as a team, and which is well managed by professional fund-raising executives using principles of coordination, cooperation, and communication.

EXHIBIT 20.4 The Pyramid of Giving

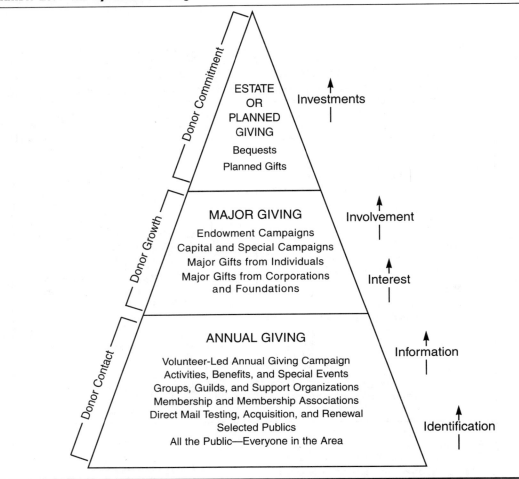

Source: James M. Greenfield, *Fund-Raising Cost Effectiveness: A Self-Assessment Workbook* (New York: John Wiley & Sons, 1996), p. 132. Reprinted by permission of John Wiley & Sons, Inc.

Annual goals and objectives can be established for each area and useful measurement conducted regularly to monitor performance and progress. Nonprofit organizations should expect a seasoned fund development program (3 to 5 years of operation) to be effective in carrying out these multiple tasks. Newcomers must invest in the basics of annual giving and grow their programs into a fully integrated pyramid of independent yet coordinated series of activities. Performance measurement tools are available and can be applied to each area to attest to its utility. It is recommended that each solicitation activity be measured using a uniform performance index (see Exhibit 20.5); a minimum of three years is required to achieve reliable performance levels, depending on internal investment and the organization's own ability to deliver valued benefits to the community. Each solicitation activity also has a different performance level. Most are built upon the previous support achieved

EXHIBIT 20.5 Solicitation Performance Index

Nine-Step Performance Index

1. Participants	= Number of donors responding with gifts
2. Income Received	= Gross contributions received
3. Expenses	= Fund-raising costs (direct, indirect, overhead)
4. Percent Participation	= Divide participants by total solicitations made
5. Average Gift Size	= Divide income received by participants
6. Net Income	= Subtract expenses from income received
7. Average Cost Per Gift	= Divide expenses by participants
8. Cost of Fund-Raising	= Divide expenses by income received; × 100
9. Return	= Divide net income by expenses; × 100

Source: James M. Greenfield, *Fund-Raising Cost Effectiveness* (New York: Wiley, 1996).

by volunteers and donors, as outlined in the pyramid of giving, plus its own experience in managing each individual method. Fund raising, like the nonprofit organization it serves, does not perform the same for every organization. To understand the effectiveness and efficiency of your current solicitation activities, measure each fund-raising program against its own prior performance, *not* against that of other nonprofit organizations.

There are internal and external factors that exert substantial influences over the potential for success in solicitation activities (see Exhibit 20.6). For example, every organization cannot be addressing the most urgent of community needs. Mission statements will differ (education is not health; art and culture are not welfare). The sources of gift support, be they individuals, corporations, or foundations, also have perceptions of issues and causes in need, which differ widely just as does their individual ability to provide quality voluntary assistance and strong financial support. A successful fund development program must be designed to address its most likely constituents, must communicate with them in the most effective and efficient ways possible, must invite their support for the most urgent of priorities, and must employ the best and most talented of volunteers and staff that it can recruit and afford. To know what to do, even how to do it, is easy to explain, but in the end, it is good old hard work that wins the day.

20.2 Revenue Sources

Nonprofit organizations rely on charitable contributions as an essential source of revenue for their annual operations. A generous public will act on factual information and, possessing of confidence and trust, will give their money for good works to benefit others. This revenue enables nonprofit organizations to carry out their mission, purpose, goals, and objectives for public benefit.

Public solicitation is carried out by nonprofit organizations using several fundraising methods and techniques, often in combination. Supervision of these interactive and interdependent activities begins with the board of directors because stewardship, the board's chief responsibility, includes developing revenue along with proper investment and management of funds raised. Policy and procedures for fund-raising begin with the board and flow to guidelines and operating rules for all elements of the fundraising enterprise.

EXHIBIT 20.6 Environmental Audit for Fund-Raising Programs

	SCORE				
Group A: External Environmental Factors	low				high
Clear mission, purposes, goals, and objectives	1	2	3	4	5 ✓
Competition, image, and market position	1	2	3	4	5 ✓
Public confidence in programs and services	1	2	3 ✓	4	5
Board leadership and competency	1	2	3	4	5 ✓
Management leadership and competency	1	2	3	4 ✓	5
Fiscal management and profitability	1	2	3	4 ✓	5
Overall economic conditions	1	2	3	4	5
Overall political and government conditions	1	2	3	4	5
Geographic location (urban or rural)	1	2	3	4 ✓	5
Accepted style of local fund-raising practice	1	2	3	4	5 ✓
Media attention to fund-raising scandals	1	2	3	4	5
Median Scores Sub-Total:					
Group B: Internal Environmental Factors	low				high
Type of nonprofit organization	1	2	3	4	5 ✓
Written long-range and strategic plan	1	2 ✓	3	4	5
Board leadership, background, and attitude	1	2	3	4 ✓	5
Ethics and professionalism	1	2	3	4	5 ✓
Employee wages and benefits	1	2 ✓	3	4	5
Status of debt financing	1	2	3	4	5 ✓
Pressure for cash	1	2	3	4	5
Commitment to develop an endowment	1	2	3	4	5
Volume and variety of fund-raising practices	1	2	3	4	5
Leadership development program	1	2	3	4	5
Volunteer recruitment and training	1	2	3	4	5
Availability of new prospects	1	2	3	4	5
Existing donors for renewal and upgrading	1	2	3	4	5
Access to wealth	1	2	3	4	5
Focus on major gift cultivation and solicitation	1	2	3	4	5
Professional staff and fund-raising counsel	1	2	3	4	5
Appropriate staff, space, budget, and systems	1	2	3	4	5
Operating donor recognition program	1	2	3	4	5
Median Scores Sub-Total:					
Median Scores Grand Total:					

There is great breadth to fund development and, given the importance of each of the several forms of revenue it produces, a comprehensive policies and procedures manual for its successful conduct is highly necessary. These will explain direction and purpose for every phase of solicitation activity. A sample of a board-level policy and procedure manual for management of resource development is provided as the appendix of this chapter and has been written as a comprehensive guide to an overall fund development program.

Fund development is, of necessity, a highly coordinated and cooperative program designed to yield maximum public support for nonprofit organizations. The methods and techniques of fund-raising are segregated into three broad operating areas: annual giving, major giving, and planned giving, with each built, in pyramid fashion, on the others' success. This structure permits each of the individual fund-raising methods in use to concentrate on three common fund-raising objectives: to acquire, to retain, and to maximize donors. Each fund-raising method, again for simplification, will make use of three common solicitation techniques for its communications: mail, telephone, and in-person solicitation. The purpose here is not to instruct the reader in detail on how each method of fund raising performs. Descriptions are adequately explained so that fund-raising policies and procedures, guidelines, and operating rules can be better understood.

A brief description of the three broad operating areas of fund raising follows.

(A) ANNUAL GIVING PROGRAMS

Nearly every nonprofit organization engages in one or more active forms of solicitation each year. These annual programs have two main objectives: to ask for the money needed to support the urgent priorities in the current operating budget, and to find and retain more donors whose continued contributions will fund future programs with reliability. Annual giving serves as the backbone of fund development because it is designed to produce predictable amounts of gift revenues year after year. Sources for annual gifts include associations and societies, corporations, foundations, government, and individuals. Because the majority of gifts (an average of 80 to 85 percent) are made by individuals each year, solicitation programs for most organizations should concentrate on people most of the time. Each annual giving method is designed to acquire new donors while retaining as many prior donors as possible. Management of annual giving requires careful coordination of each separate method, whether during one year or as part of a multiyear effort, and is essential to increasing performance year after year. Directors and managers of nonprofit organizations who fail to understand the need for such coordination also may fail to understand the purpose of annual giving, which is to produce reliable revenue every year. Some may view an annual campaign only as a money-raising activity—a misleading perception that results in accepting quick fixes and easy money ideas for the apparent dollars they promise. These fund raisers fail to appreciate the value of traditional annual giving methods; they have been tested a thousand times and proven to be reliable, cost-effective, and highly profitable because they work to build relationships.

Annual giving, the chief means to build relationships between donors and nonprofit organizations, will not succeed or long survive if thought of only as a money-raising activity. Donors result from annual investments; their value increases in direct proportion to the care and attention they receive over time. This also means that donor relations programs are an active part of every annual giving activity. Such attention will help ensure that each donor's interest and enthusiasm are retained and that his or her commitment to the organization grows and continues to produce faithful contributions for the future.

Nonprofit organizations can elect to use one or more annual giving methods during their operating year. The options include direct mail, for acquisition of first-time donors as well as for renewal of prior donors; telephone and public media channels; membership development; special and benefit events; support group organizations; donor clubs; volunteer solicitation committees; and more. The goal of each option is to achieve multiple gifts from the same donors during each year; one gift every 12 months is not likely to provide all the revenue needed to meet annual operating needs. Churches across

America invite their members to give weekly; they also raise more money than any other type of nonprofit organization. These faithful, committed weekly/monthly/annual donors can and will provide the money needed for operations year after year. These same donors will become the patrons and benefactors of non-profit organizations in the future, provided that the fund development program is designed to this end and not seen only as a money-raising activity within a single year.

A variety of skills are required to manage several annual giving activities at the same time. Coordination and cooperation will help to produce reliable results without causing confusion or "turning off" donors. Written procedures are needed to help guide the conduct of multiple methods of annual solicitation that are performed at the same time with the same audiences. The goals are: to increase the pool of suspects and prospects, to increase the number of donors, to retain most prior donors, to upgrade the gift level of current donors, to invite multiple gifts, to encourage active participation, to encourage volunteerism, to offer opportunities for leadership, and to recognize and reward everyone who steps forward to do more. The preservation of good will among all who become donors is essential; these same committed friends will faithfully support the priorities of the future with their "time, talent, and treasure."

(B) MAJOR GIFT PROGRAMS

When a solid base of annual giving activity is in full operation, nonprofit organizations are better prepared to engage in more complex forms of solicitation for significantly greater gifts, in size and in donor involvement and participation. Few donors will be engaged at this level as compared with annual givers, but their larger gifts will provide a greater majority of the funds required. The fund-raising techniques used in development of major gifts and grants are usually defined within the context of a special or capital campaign, which is possible only after years of successful annual giving activity. Some history of giving is always necessary before these expanded areas can begin to be successful.

Nonprofit organizations must prepare themselves for their own future, because their future plans will address the needs of more sophisticated donors. Long-range and strategic plans explain specific directions to be taken, timetables, steps required, estimated costs, opportunities for major gift support, reasoned outcomes, public benefits expected, and more. Major gifts can be solicited separately from annual giving, even in the absence of new institutional plans, in the same manner that government grants may be applied for once a program area is qualified. However, major gift solicitations always will be more successful when included as part of a visibly promoted, multi-year, institutional effort. This is true because the best sources of leadership, commitment, and enthusiasm are assembled in support of the organization to achieve such overall objectives.

The fund-raising method often employed to meet master plan objectives is a major campaign, usually designed to address only the most urgent of priorities. This means that new and higher levels of funding are essential to the organization's future. The campaign is the method to marshall attention to these priorities, presenting them as relevant, urgent, and to be met *now*. Special donor recognition opportunities are offered as added benefits for large gifts, to encourage donors in their generosity. Simply put, it is much more difficult to amass a winning combination for successful solicitation with a single project standing alone than to offer donors the biggest and best ideas the organization has to offer.

(C) PLANNED GIVING PROGRAMS

Donors can be introduced to the special area of opportunity associated with planned giving at any time during annual giving, major giving, or capital campaign programs. In fact, through these communications the idea-seeds are planted early and lead to financial and estate-planning discussions. Planned giving is, by definition, a means whereby individuals plan to designate a portion of their estate to be delivered later to the nonprofit organizations of their choice. All that is required is a specific instruction written in their will or living trust. Planned gifts are major gifts involving significant assets, which is why they match up well with capital campaigns rather than annual giving programs. The technical complexity of planned giving requires close attention to appropriate policy and procedure by all who would consider this area of fund raising. Planned giving also remains the preferred method to develop the endowment funds that are so essential to financial flexibility and security in every nonprofit organization's future.

Planned giving represents final decisions by donors who choose to make arrangements in advance to maintain their personal support of favorite organizations into the future, even after they are deceased. These decisions are guided by their estate plan, prepared alongside their personal financial plan for their retirement years. Planned gifts can be made now, either with (1) benefits from the transfer retained for the donor's lifetime and the asset transferred to the organization after death, or with (2) final assignment, via a will or living trust, of current assets that will flow to the organization after death. Because of their complex technical nature and the permanent obligations of the nonprofit organizations who accept them, estate planning and planned giving programs must be guided by clear and complete policies and procedures that address fully the fiduciary, legal, and stewardship responsibilities of the nonprofit organization for the life of the donor.

While the balance of this chapter will address fund-raising support, it is helpful to keep in mind three common ingredients. Success in fund raising is always dependent on the interaction of: (1) leadership and voluntary action, (2) cultivation, solicitation, and donor relations, and (3) relationships built between donors and their choices of nonprofit organizations. Policies and procedures, guidelines, and operating rules must be designed to match each nonprofit organization's operating style, taking into account the need to support the professional conduct of fund-raising. Such guidelines are seldom a goal unto themselves, however, especially where they would impede fund development operations. These three ingredients for successful fund-raising are described briefly in the sections that follow.

(D) LEADERSHIP AND VOLUNTARY ACTION

Nothing much happens in fund-raising until voluntary leadership takes charge and provides direction to all other volunteers and staff alike. Leadership, whether it comes from the board or from individuals appointed by the board, is much more than an appointment; it requires dedication, advocacy, personal sacrifice, and serving as an example to others. Among the qualities most often associated with effective fund-raising leaders are: they are rich, have "clout," are generous to lots of causes, are well liked, are true believers in the project, are well-organized, are good speakers, and are fearless (Warner, 1990). Leaders also have to be trained and aided toward a complete understanding of the mission and purpose, goals and objectives, personality and operating style of the nonprofit organization they serve. Professional staff can assist in many ways, but their chief purpose is to assure that each leader succeeds in the task he or she is assigned.

Leadership includes providing guidance and direction to others who volunteer their time and energy to the same cause. Volunteers can be asked to perform every task required for successful fund raising; the trick is to pick the right people for the right task at the right time so that the entire program will run smoothly. Although this idea is forever elusive, constant attention to volunteers' training and encouragement of their active support will help to achieve success every time. Volunteers are the "arms and legs" of fund raising; no fund development program can expect to be successful without a host of men and women committed to the cause and willing to give of their personal "time, talent, and treasure" toward its fulfillment. Each volunteer must be given adequate time to learn an assignment, allowed to experiment with personal ideas measured against proven methods and prior successes, invited to do more rather than less, given opportunities for growth within the organization, asked for a personal gift early, recognized and rewarded for all that is accomplished, and considered for promotion to leadership assignments, including a seat on the board of directors.

(E)   CULTIVATION, SOLICITATION, AND DONOR RELATIONS

Donors and prospects, whether people or institutions, require attention and consideration. Each has potential to assist and, although some can give more money than others, each can give a share of time and a best effort to the cause. Annual giving, by its nature, invites thousands of donors and prospects to participate, and then asks them to do it again. It is not possible to give personal attention to all donors, so the focus must be on those whose prior giving history or potential volunteerism merits added consideration. Annual giving provides the best means to find and develop more qualified candidates. The use of mass communication techniques—for example, mail, telephone, and benefit events—is a bit impersonal, but careful analysis of the results is a means to identify those few-among-many who, by reason of gift size, pattern of support, and commitment, justify more personal attention and further evaluation. Volunteers can help in these final evaluation steps leading to designation of those who will receive more active personal attention, all of which yields cultivation and solicitation of others who will follow.

Volunteer solicitors are pure gold to a fund development program. People who will ask their friends for money for an organization they believe in are indeed beautiful people. It is each organization's duty to train such volunteers in how best to approach others, how to be sensitive when mixing their enthusiasm for the cause with the prospects' potential for present and future support, and how to inform and invite prospects to join worthy programs that will benefit others. Each form of solicitation, whether an impersonal letter, a telephone call, or a personal visit, is an important opportunity for the nonprofit organization to make friends. These initial few friends will invite others to join them and, over time, build a cadre of many friends who can be prepared to help the nonprofit organization realize its annual priorities and fulfill its long-term aspirations.

Relations with donors, as mentioned earlier, remain highly important for reasons other than just the next gift. As with friendships, time and effort are required of both parties to keep up the contact, show an honest interest in one another, share ideas and goals, and work together whenever possible. Formal recognition programs offer privileged communications for donors; they let them "inside" and include them in "family" discussions. Nonprofit organizations have an obligation to design donor communications programs and to include public recognition of those whose faithful service and generous contributions have made all the difference in achieving success.

(F)   BUILDING RELATIONSHIPS

The entire purpose of fund development can be captured in the concept of good relations with a community of friends. Opportunities for friends' involvement and active participation exist alongside expectations that these faithful advocates and generous supporters stand ready to assist the organization in achieving its mission to the rest of society. Here, the true purpose of the fund development "process" come to term: it guides leadership and volunteerism, friend raising and active solicitation, donor relations, and more; it unites *people* with the *purposes* of nonprofit organizations.

Relationships take time—often, lots of time—to develop. Multiple opportunities are included in the objectives of annual giving, major giving, and planned giving programs to nurture each individual who chooses to associate with a cause toward achieving the most satisfactory of outcomes for both parties, which can be repeated over many years.

20.3   *General Areas for Policy and Procedures*

Guidance for daily operations begins at the point of inception of the organization itself. Ownership, legal name, mission and purpose, authority, structure and organization, procedures for dissolution, and more, are all defined in the articles of incorporation. The next document, called the bylaws, states the operating rules and procedures for the organization. The bylaws define in detail the process for the election of officers and directors, and their job descriptions; the procedures for the conduct of all meetings; annual operations, including fiscal activities; the process to amend the bylaws; and much more. In combination, the articles of incorporation and the bylaws establish the board of directors as the supreme authority for ownership and operation of the nonprofit organization. Federal and state authorities, acting on these texts alone, will charter the organization as a voluntary nonprofit public benefit corporation under the law, by which it is forever bound. Out of these government approvals flow privileges of income, sales and property tax exemptions, and a charitable contribution deduction for all of the organization's donors.

Daily operations remain the responsibility of the board of directors. However, because the board's primary duty is to establish policy and supervise operations, day-to-day tasks are assigned to professional staff whom the board hires and directs through the president/CEO, who also evaluates their performance. Once routine operations are defined and implemented, including the accounting and reporting of all revenue received and spent, the board's attention shifts to supervision of daily activities against stated objectives. A mission statement, drawn from the articles of incorporation, completes the written interpretation of the purposes, goals, and objectives of the organization. Operations are guided through defined programs and services provided through the annual budget and, in time, through long-range and strategic plans designed to move the organization forward toward fulfilling the objectives stated in its articles of incorporation and mission statement.

All of these deliberate activities are necessary and must precede public solicitation activity. When complete, they also provide all the information needed to begin a successful fund-raising program. The board of directors appoints a committee on fund development and authorizes it to supervise all fund-raising activity, including setting annual and multiyear goals matched to the organization's plans and priority funding requirements. The objective is to raise, on schedule, the money for priority needs. The annual budget for fund-raising is prepared, reviewed, and approved by the administration and the board. Hiring practices, job descriptions, and evaluation procedures (for programs as well as employees) are used to recruit and supervise professional and support staff hired to conduct fund-raising activities as defined by the committee. Policies and procedures for fund raising, the use of the institutional name in solicitation activities, accounting and reporting for all funds raised and budget expended, honors and recognition accorded to donors—all of these activities are defined, developed, and approved by the committee, administration, and the board. Everyone involved should receive complete information on how each of these activities will be performed and their relationship to all other aspects of the fund development program.

Because fund-raising programs produce cash and other forms of revenue for use by the organization, instructions on their proper disposition are required within the organization's fiscal policy and procedures. Other committees involved in the management of funds raised include the audit, finance, and investment management committees, which ensure accurate accounting for each gift and its appropriate use, investment of funds (including charitable trusts and endowments), and preparation of required audits and public fiscal reports in accordance with accounting standards and in fulfillment of state and federal requirements. Considerable coordination is required to ensure that the board's obligation for fiduciary stewardship of gift revenue is complete. The stewardship includes solicitation practices, fund accounting, budget and expenditures for fund-raising, and public reporting of the results, including benefits delivered back to the annuity.

The concluding segment of this chapter gives an example of guidelines, operating rules, and procedures that must be prepared, to cover all aspects of the fund development program. Given the importance of the funds themselves and their value to the organization, the board of directors assigns its active responsibility for this entire area to the committee on fund development. This committee must define the programs of solicitation in the areas of annual giving, major gifts, and planned giving, and then supervise their conduct each year according to policy procedures. The result is a manual such as is shown in the appendix to the chapter.

In addition, direction for organizations that are related to the parent corporation and that also engage in fund raising to support the mission of the parent is required from the committee on fund development. A related organization may be a subsidiary unit, such as a foundation, that is controlled by the parent or acts as its fund-raising arm. Related organizations may also be separate but affiliated groups whose existence, purpose, and franchises to exist originate from the parent corporation and whose own articles and by-laws establish, as their mission and purpose, the provision of financial and other support to the parent corporation. In each instance, operating rules and procedures are valuable and should include prescriptions (often in the form of bylaws) for the nomination and election of officers and directors, the approval of the fund-raising programs employed, the use of the parent organization's name, the accounting required for all funds raised in its name or expended for appropriate charitable purposes, and any other accounting and legal requirements associated with full and proper operation of related organizations.

When all these procedural necessities are in place and well-understood by all the participants, a program of fund development can proceed with confidence in its own excellent preparation and with the full support of the board of directors. The community of volunteers and active supporters will be secure in a sound design, will be prepared to follow the organization's leadership, and will be willing to work hard to provide the financial support so necessary to its success.

Appendix: A Manual of Fund Development Policy and Procedure for Nonprofit Organizations

CONTENTS

A. AUTHORITY FOR FUND DEVELOPMENT

1. *The Importance of Philanthropy.* The several benefits enjoyed by [name of organization] under the law include active support and voluntary contributions from individuals, corporations, foundations, government, associations, and societies. The relations among all these parties are essential to the mission of this organization, especially its financial stability. Responsibility for preservation and enhancement of philanthropy shall be retained by the Board of Directors and carried out as it shall herein define.

2. *Board of Directors.* The Board holds authority and stewardship responsibility for all methods and techniques of fund-raising activity; for all forms of contributions received; for professional staff, consultants, and vendors hired; for investment and management of all funds raised; and for disbursement of contribution revenues in exclusive support of the mission of this organization.

3. *Board Committee on Fund Development.* This committee of the Board of Directors is charged with leadership and direction of fund raising toward the objectives of: (a) defining and developing programs asking for public support, (b) active solicitation, and (c) maintaining positive relations with donors.

4. *Department of Fund Development.* Under the chief development officer, this department is responsible to the President/CEO and the Committee on Fund Development for day-to-day management of all fund-raising activities. Professional and support staff will provide professional assistance to fund-raising programs, the acknowledgment of all gifts and maintenance of donor records and recognition, deposit and accounting for all gifts received, supervision of the annual budget, and direction of all employees, consultants, and vendors hired.

5. *Related Organizations.* By authority of the Board of Directors, related organizations whose purpose is to develop gift revenue for this organization shall be authorized to use the name and tax-exempt privileges granted this organization, and shall be subject to the policies and procedures of the Committee on Fund Development. Accounting for all income of and expenses incurred by related organizations shall be made to the Office of Fund Development.

6. *The Role of Volunteers.* Active volunteer participation in the fund development program is essential to its success. The roles of volunteers shall be defined as to level of responsibility, period of service, reporting relationships, staff support, and

other details as required. A volunteer recognition program shall also be provided to honor the service given by those who lead and assist this organization.

7. *The Rights of Donors.* The value of past, present, and future donors shall be preserved and respected at all times. The privileges and benefits accorded donors are defined in Honors and Recognition (Section J).

B.   MANAGEMENT OF FUND DEVELOPMENT ACTIVITIES

1. *Priority Established by the Board of Directors.* The priorities for public participation and support shall be established by the Board of Directors and carried out by the Committee on Fund Development through the Department of Fund Development.

2. *Job Description for Director of Fund Development.* The Committee on Fund Development and President/CEO shall define the duties and responsibilities of the Director of Fund Development and shall participate in the hiring and performance evaluation of occupants in this position.

3. *Public Solicitation Programs.* All fund-raising activities shall be approved by the Committee on Fund Development and the President/CEO for approved priorities only. Goals and budgets associated with their achievement shall be prepared in advance of active public solicitation.

4. *Priority and Project Management.* Each fund-raising priority shall be managed as a fund-raising project. The assistance of volunteers, staff, and budget shall be organized to meet project deadlines and objectives. Fund development volunteers, staff, time, and budget shall be authorized only for approved priorities. Overlapping priorities shall be resolved by the Committee on Fund Development.

5. *Procedures for Approval for Gift Solicitation.* All priorities for fund development shall be defined, within procedures established by the President/CEO, for submission to the Board of Directors for approval, including budgetary authorization. Those programs appropriate for fund-raising support shall be so identified, and evaluation shall be performed by the Committee on Fund Development to assess anticipated public support and budget and staff requirements for successful solicitation.

6. *Prospect Reservation.* Prospective candidates deserve considerate treatment at all times. When more than one approved project may qualify for the attention of the same prospect, the prospect reservation procedures shall guide resolution of the timing and period of reservation of each prospect. This procedure will ensure against duplicate solicitations of prospects already assigned to approved projects, which shall have priority.

7. *Use of Consultants and Vendors.* Professional assistance may be retained or purchased to support fund-raising activities. Each such association shall be guided by a written contract or memorandum of agreement, upon recommendation by the Committee on Fund Development and approval of the Board of Directors

C. PUBLIC SOLICITATION PROCEDURES

1. *Correct Legal Name.* All charitable contributions, regardless of value, form, or designated use, shall be made only to this organization, using the proper legal name of this corporation. Questions about methods of giving, timing, assignment, purpose, or use of gifts shall be directed to the Department of Fund Development, as shall all questions about legal forms for gifts, their tax consequences, and donor recognition.

2. *Use of Organization Name for Fund Raising.* The use of the name of this organization for any fund-raising purpose by any other organization or entity shall require prior approval of the Committee on Fund Development, acting on recommendations from the Department of Fund Development.

3. *Commercial Co-ventures and Charitable Sales Promotions.* Joint ventures for public marketing and solicitation with business or commercial organizations shall be defined within applicable state and federal laws and regulations. Each such association shall be guided by a written contract or memorandum of agreement approved by the Board of Directors upon recommendation of the Committee on Fund Development and shall include disclosure by the commercial partner of all income and expenses associated with these promotions. The uses to be made of proceeds from each joint venture shall be in keeping with the mission statement of this organization.

4. *Tax Laws and Public Reporting Requirements.* Voluntary gift support of non-profit organizations is endorsed by federal and state governments, which also permit substantial tax deductions for donors. The Board of Directors will, at all times, comply fully with its obligations to fulfill applicable tax laws and public reporting requirements. Public report documents shall be available within five days of receipt of a written request.

5. *General Fund-Raising Guidelines.* Donors and prospects shall be encouraged to support approved priorities and established programs at all times, in order that the most urgent requirements of this organization may be met to the greatest extent possible. Donor wishes will be considered to the extent possible, so long as their intended use of funds is in keeping with the mission statement. Resolution of donor wishes outside approved priorities and established programs shall be by the Board of Directors upon recommendation of the Committee on Fund Development.

6. *Joint Fund-Raising Programs.* Joint fund-raising activities between programs within this organization shall be encouraged because they provide donors more opportunities to meet approved priorities.

7. *The Calendar for Solicitations.* Each twelve-month period contains limited time available for fund-raising activities. Coordination and cooperation are required in planning each solicitation, to respect the rights of donors and to avoid creating the appearance of confusion and competition among the public. Each fund-raising program requires time for its own fulfillment and must also respect the preferred periods when other programs shall be scheduled. The calendar for solicitation shall

be reviewed and approved by the Committee on Fund Development at the beginning of each fiscal year. Modifications to the calendar will be resolved by the Committee based on recommendations of the Department of Fund Development.

D. FORMS OF CONTRIBUTIONS

1. *Types of Gifts.* Besides *monetary gifts* in the form of cash, checks, money orders, and the like, *nonmonetary gifts* may be accepted, such as: (a) bonds and securities, (b) real property, (c) tangible personal property, (d) gifts-in-kind to be used in the form in which they are given, (e) royalties, copyrights, and trademark rights, and (f) insurance policies naming this organization as beneficiary in whole or in part.

2. *Unrestricted and Restricted Gifts.* Gifts with no stipulation by the donor as to their purpose or use are *unrestricted.* Gifts given and accepted for a specific purpose, as designated by the donor as a condition or so directed by this organization, shall be *temporarily restricted.* Such gifts are only to be used for the purpose intended, and their status is to be disclosed in financial and audit statements in accordance with FASB and AICPA accounting standards and guidelines. Gifts given or so directed by this organization to be *retained* are considered to be endowment and are recorded and reported as *permanently restricted,* with only their investment and interest earnings available for use.

3. *Appraisal Rules and Procedures.* Current Internal Revenue Service (IRS) regulations will be observed when calculating the charitable contribution deduction value of gifts of property, including advice to such donors regarding these regulations and the reporting obligations both parties must observe. A list of qualified professional appraisers will be offered each donor for his or her independent use. Donors are obliged to pay for professional appraisals of their property. The appraised value thus certified will be entered in the donor's gift record and reported in IRS Form 8282 if sold within two years of the date of the gift. Official gift acknowledgment documents will refer only to the appraised value.

4. *Special Handling of Select Gifts.* Commemorative gifts may be received in the form of "in memory of," "in honor of," or "on the occasion of" from any source. Separate gift acknowledgment procedures will reflect the special nature of these select gifts. Unless their use is specified by the donor or the person or family named, they shall be considered unrestricted gifts. Commemorative gifts that qualify for Honors and Recognition also will observe the procedures described in Section J herein.

5. *Temporarily Restricted Funds.* A donor may deliver funds or property as a gift and specify a conditioned use over time, with such funds to be held for a fixed period until the condition is met. Among the conditions may be a specific event, decision, financial transaction, or time-defined future activity. During this interim, the Investment Committee may invest the funds; any earned income is usable by this organization until such time as conditions or maturation are achieved. After the condition has been met and the funds dispersed for the restricted purpose, the use shall be recorded and reported as an unrestricted expense in accordance with FASB and AICPA accounting standards and guidelines.

6. *Gifts in Trust.* This organization may accept gifts in trust, agreeing to hold and manage a donor's principal resources and assets in exchange for life income, after which the principal and future income become the property of the organization for use as designated by the donor. A donor may deliver funds or property in a trust agreement to provide income for his or her lifetime and the lifetime of a spouse or other designated beneficiary, in accordance with the operating procedures of the Planned Giving Program (Section K). Specific details regarding trust documents, tax consequences, and income projections shall be reviewed by legal counsel prior to completion. If this organization acts as trustee, the selection of investment manager and custodian, performance evaluation, and administrative/accounting services shall be directed by the Investment Committee.

7. *Income-Producing Properties.* In instances where income-producing properties are gifted, the Investment Committee shall determine and report to the Board of Directors, in advance of acceptance, several details including unrelated business, income tax implications, environmental analysis and toxic waste potential, operations and maintenance expenses, and salability of the property. If accepted, the Investment Committee shall provide guidance on operations and disposition of the property to resolution.

8. *Legacies and Bequests.* A donor may arrange in a Will or Living Trust that this organization be designated as a beneficiary to receive a direct gift from the Estate. A donor may also arrange, after the death of a named beneficiary, that the principal or some of the surviving Estate shall become the property of this organization. Any restrictions on the use of such income as specified by the donor shall be in keeping with the mission statement. Unless otherwise specified, the Board of Directors, on advice of the Fund Development and Investment Committees, shall consider all other legacy and bequest income as unrestricted endowment.

E. FUND-RAISING METHODS AND TECHNIQUES

1. *Procedures for Setting Goals.* Annual goals and multiyear campaign objectives shall be established by the Committee on Fund Development based on prior years' experience, established priorities of need, and budget appropriated, with approval by the Board of Directors. Fund development staff, time, and budget are reserved only for established priorities approved by the Board of Directors.

2. *Annual Giving Activities.* The several methods and techniques that solicit donors as well as prospects for support each year shall be coordinated by the Committee on Fund Development. A variety of solicitation programs may be offered, including direct mail, memberships, benefit events, telephone and media appeals, personal solicitation, and more.

3. *Procedures for Benefit Events.* Each special and benefit event shall be approved in advance by the Committee on Fund Development, based on the following criteria: (a) appropriate fit to the existing calendar of fund-raising activities, (b) recruitment of an adequate volunteer committee or sponsoring agency or organization, and (c) a budget reflecting income and expense plans projecting a minimum of 50 percent net

proceeds as gift income to this organization. All event funds shall be administered by the Office of Fund Development; so also shall be all contracts and agreements for services required to support any event.

4. *Business, Corporation, and Foundation Relations.* These gift prospects are important resources and deserve careful consideration at all times. Direct contact with any business, corporation, or foundation for any purpose shall be only with prior approval of the Committee on Fund Development. Prospect reservation procedures shall apply at all times.

5. *Special-Project Campaigns.* Separate solicitation programs may be developed to meet urgent priorities or to take advantage of unusual opportunities offered by donors that match well with current fund-raising program objectives. Each such special-project campaign shall be approved by the Committee on Fund Development prior to initiation, based on (a) appropriate fit to the existing calendar of fund-raising activities, (b) recruitment of an adequate volunteer committee or sponsoring agency or organization, and (c) a budget reflecting the expense required to achieve the income potential proposed with a minimum of 75 percent net proceeds as gift income to this organization.

6. *Multiyear and Capital Campaigns.* The Board of Directors may direct that a major fund-raising effort of a multiyear nature be conducted for urgent priorities, in keeping with long-range and strategic plans. Such plans shall be developed by the Committee on Fund Development in concert with the Finance and Investment Committees and with thorough analysis of leadership and volunteer support, gift potential, internal capability, time and expense required, and other preparations.

7. *Planned Giving Programs.* Public solicitation that offers forms of estate planning and planned giving shall be guided by the Planned Giving Policy (Section K) and administered by the Committee on Fund Development. This organization will act as trustee when accepting gifts in the form of charitable remainder trusts, charitable lead trusts, and pooled income funds, in accordance with state and federal regulations, subject to approval of each gift by the Board of Directors.

F. GOVERNMENT GRANTS AND CONTRACTS ADMINISTRATION

1. *Authority and Supervision.* The President/CEO and the Sponsored Research Administrator are authorized agents for all grant and contract agreements. Each grant or contract application shall be approved by the President/CEO and Sponsored Research Administrator prior to submission.

2. *Office of Grants and Contracts.* The Office of Grants and Contracts shall provide resource services including: details on application requirements, budget preparation with appropriate indirect costs and fringe benefits, application preparation and review, final signature approvals, and liaison to government agencies. Completed applications must be delivered to the Grants and Contracts Office at least five working days prior to the submission deadline.

3. *Grants and Contracts Officer.* The Grants and Contracts Officer is responsible for supervision of all grant and contract applications including budget review and approval, and for supervision of accounting for funds received and public reports required by these agreements.

4. *Institutional Review Committee (IRC).* An Institutional Review Committee shall be appointed by the President/CEO to be composed of nine members, three of whom shall be laypersons not employed by this organization. IRC duties include oversight and analysis of all work proposed and performed under grants and contracts as well as such other issues of ethics and professional conduct associated with any activity performed by this organization that is funded by government agencies and other revenue sources.

5. *Manuscripts and Articles.* Manuscripts, articles, and reports based on work performed under a grant or contract awarded this organization, or work identified with this organization by name, shall be reviewed by the Grants and Contracts Officer prior to submission for publication.

6. *Accounting, Reporting, and Audits.* The Chief Financial Officer will establish accounting procedures for administration of all funds received in a grant or contract agreement. Budget changes requested by the Principal Investigator shall be delivered to the Grants and Contracts Officer, who will negotiate with the agency for resolution. Requests for disbursement by the Principal Investigator first shall be directed to the Grants and Contracts Officer, who will verify the fund balance and expense to be in accordance with the approved budget. The Chief Financial Officer will supervise the preparation of all financial statements and public reports, including grant and contract audits, for submission to the granting or contract agency, in accordance with generally accepted accounting principles.

7. *Royalties, Copyrights, and Patents.* All royalties, copyrights, and patentable results from work performed under grant and contract agreements shall adhere to the Royalties, Copyrights, and Patents policy of this organization.

8. *Nongovernment Grants and Contracts.* Funds requested or received from nongovernment sources (e.g., corporations or foundations) that are, in fact, a formal agreement for specific work as defined in the application shall be administered by the Grants and Contracts Office in accordance with its operating policy and procedures, with support from the Fund Development Office as appropriate.

G. GIFT PROCESSING PROCEDURES

1. *Checks and Cash.* All gifts in the form of checks, cash, or credit cards received by any department shall be delivered *on the day they are received* to the Department of Fund Development, which will process the gift. In instances where the use specified by the donor is unclear, these details shall be brought to the immediate attention of the Department of Fund Development by telephone, because acceptance of any gift binds this organization to fulfilling the donor's wishes.

2. *Gifts of Securities.* The transfer of securities certificates or their ownership to the name of this organization is especially sensitive and may only be accomplished as follows: (a) Ask the donor and his or her broker to call the Department of Fund Development for instructions on transfer to our agent, setting up a brokers' account, board authorization action, and other details. In instances where prior securities transfer have occurred with the same broker, the Department of Fund Development will proceed with transfer instructions. (b) Certificates belonging to the donor will be delivered only by certified or registered mail, or by hand. A stock power form, signed by the donor and naming the organization as transferee, will be in a separate envelope using certified or registered mail. Disposition of the securities will be guided by policy from the Investment Committee.

3. *Gifts of Personal Property.* Personal property may be accepted when (a) the property can be sold, or (b) the property can be used in keeping with the mission of this organization. Internal Revenue Service regulations require gifts other than money or publicly traded securities valued in excess of $5,000 to be appraised by a certified professional appraiser, and a copy of the appraisal must accompany the gift. Cost of the appraisal shall be the responsibility of the donor. The gift value shall be the appraised value at the time of the gift. If the property is sold within two years of its receipt, IRS Form 8282 will be completed and submitted to the IRS.

4. *Gifts of Real Estate.* Real estate in the form of a residence, business, commercial building, undeveloped land, etc., may be accepted when (a) the environmental and toxic waste review is completed, and (b) the property can be sold, or (c) the property can be used in keeping with the mission of this organization. A certified appraisal performed within 60 days of the gift date shall be provided by the donor. In most cases, real estate will be sold at current market prices through a broker hired by the organization. Properties with mortgages will not be accepted if the mortgage amounts to 50 percent or more of fair market value established in the appraisal.

5. *Gifts-in-Kind.* Gifts of material or products may be accepted when the form of the gift can be used immediately by the organization.

6. *Employee Gifts and Payroll Deduction.* Employees may make gifts at any time and may use payroll deduction to transfer their funds. Arrangements for the amount of the gift, frequency of deduction, and period when deductions are to begin and conclude are made by the employee, who shall be responsible for instructing the Payroll Office of these details in writing. The Department of Fund Development will provide sample language or a proper pledge card for these purposes.

7. *Fiscal and Calendar Year-End Procedures.* Gifts in any form received near the date ending the fiscal or calendar year may be credited to the proper reporting period if there is evidence that the donor intended to make the gift within this period, and the gift is received and processed within 10 days of the closing date for the fiscal or calendar year-end.

H.   GIFT ACKNOWLEDGMENT PROCEDURES

1. *Official Acknowledgment.* All gifts, regardless of value, form, or designated use, shall be acknowledged by this organization with official correspondence. Acknowledgment represents to the donor this organization's acceptance of the gift along with its restrictions, and may also serve the donor as evidence to certify a possible tax-deductible event.

2. *Additional Acknowledgments.* Additional "thank you" messages by volunteers and staff are encouraged and are dependent on the donor, size of the gift, or purpose, as determined by the Department of Fund Development. Details about the gift will be provided by the Department of Fund Development; copies of additional acknowledgments shall be sent to the Department of Fund Development for retention in the donor file.

3. *Time of Acknowledgment.* Gifts must always be acknowledged as promptly as possible. Gift processing shall have as its first priority the timely acknowledgment of all gifts within 48 hours of receipt.

4. *Donor Records and Recognition.* The Department of Fund Development shall retain all correspondence regarding contributions, gift records, cumulative gift histories, and other data on donors' activity, which shall be confidential information for use only in support of fund-raising activities. All recognition and reward accorded to donors by reason of their frequency, amounts, or cumulative total shall be in accordance with the Honors and Recognition guidelines (Section J).

5. *Gift Substantiation Rules.* IRS requires nonprofit organizations to disclose to donors of $75 or more *at the point of solicitation (invitation)* when the gift is related to a special or benefit event, the amount of the gift value that is *nondeductible* because of material goods (e.g., food and drink) consumed by the donor in exchange for their gift. Further, IRS requires of *all* contributions of $250.00 or more disclosure to the donor of the extent (value) of any benefits, including material goods, due to the donor in exchange for their gift, the value of any such benefits to be reported to the donor as *nondeductible.*

6. *Tax Records and Public Disclosure.* Gift acknowledgment correspondence is useful to donors for tax submission purposes. Donors may request verification of previous gifts for any purpose, which will be documented and released only to donors. Public release of details surrounding individual gifts shall be made only with the express permission of the donor, who shall be appraised of the purpose for such disclosure and given prior approval of the language to be used.

7. *Gift Reports on Results.* Public reports of gift results will not disclose gift amounts for individual donors. Gift reports will tally results by revenue sources, purposes or use, and fund-raising programs employed. Distribution of gift reports shall be limited to those who need to know these results.

I. ACCOUNTING FOR GIFT REVENUE

1. *Fiduciary Responsibility*. Each gift, regardless of value, form, or designated use, shall be accounted for at the time of receipt until used as directed by the donor in support of the mission of this organization. During such time as funds are retained, they shall be actively invested in accordance with procedures of the Finance and Investment Management Committees. The Department of Fund Development shall be responsible for any reports to donors on the use of their funds, to be accomplished in concert with operating managers and the fiscal/accounting department.

2. *Allocation to Restricted Funds*. Gifts received for restricted purposes (either temporarily restricted or permanently restricted) shall be separately accounted for in order to maintain stewardship of these funds as donors direct. The segregation of these funds is to be performed by the fiscal/accounting department, who shall report to donors on their disposition and use by the departments and managers involved, through the Department of Fund Development.

3. *Expenditure Controls*. The uses of gift revenues, especially restricted gifts, shall be fully accounted for, beginning with their deposit to temporarily restricted fund accounts, stewardship, disposition reports, and with expenditures only as directed by the donor in keeping with the mission of this organization.

4. *Allocation to Endowment*. Funds restricted to endowment or so restricted by the Board of Directors shall be invested and accounted for in accord with policies of the Finance and Investment Management Committees.

5. *Investment of Funds*. All gifts received shall be invested until used in accord with donor wishes, using short-term or long-term investment plans as defined by the Finance and Investment Management Committees. Funds restricted to endowment or so restricted by the Board of Directors shall be invested and accounted for as directed by the Finance and Investment Management Committees. Investment earnings shall be used only for the purposes specified by the donors or Board, with amounts as resolved by the Finance and Investment Management Committees.

6. *Accounting Reports*. Regular accounting reports will summarize the disposition of all gift money, illustrating their present disposition by source, purpose or use, and fund-raising program, which shall be prepared monthly and distributed to the Board of Directors and the Finance, Fund Development, and Investment Management Committees. Annual reports will be prepared as a summary of all fiscal-year activity.

7. *Audits and Tax Returns*. The Board of Directors will conduct an audit of all contributions received and held, which shall be conducted in accordance with generally accepted accounting principles. Public reports of financial details shall be prepared as required by federal and state regulations, which shall be available to the public within five days after receipt of a written request.

J. HONORS AND RECOGNITION

1. *Policy Concept.* Formal recognition of distinguished service to this organization, in the forms of gift support and voluntary time and talent, shall receive official consideration by the Board of Directors. The qualifications, review and decision procedures, and methods of recognition to be followed in regard to gift support in its many forms, and as specified in this Section are: (a) the naming of buildings, property, or any space therein; (b) the naming of departments or titled positions, including chairs within this organization; and (c) the conferring of awards or citations on any individual, institution, association, or society for gift support or services rendered.

2. *Guidelines.* The Board of Directors, in concert with the Committee on Fund Development, shall assess each recommendation for honors and recognition. They shall consider the relationship between the honoree's qualifications and the size and scope of the project supported. Consideration in the conferral of honors and recognition will include (a) benefit to this organization, (b) visibility and prominence accorded to the honoree, and (c) use of honors and recognition to further the goals and objectives of this organization in financial gain and in public recognition and respect.

3. *Qualifications.* Individuals or institutions that make large contributions shall be qualified for honors and recognition. A gift of $25,000 or higher qualifies for such consideration and may include a single gift received, total giving over several years, or a pledge amount of fund-raising goal achieved. Each such donor may be offered an appropriate form of recognition to be placed in the area selected or in the main donor recognition area, or a suitable dedication ceremony with a tour of the area identified for recognition included whenever possible. Gifts valued under $25,000 shall be recognized at the discretion of the Committee on Fund Development.

4. *Procedure for Approval.* Recommendations for honors and recognition shall be made to the Board of Directors after review and approval by the Committee on Fund Development, with adequate details on the individual or institution to be honored and the reasons for such action by the Board of Directors.

5. *Naming of Buildings or Space Therein.* All areas of this organization are subject to naming. Such identification will be sensitive to function and location and shall be consistent with internal graphics and signage procedure. Buildings, floors, and areas may be named as donors prefer when the extent of service and contribution merits such recognition.

6. *Naming of Endowed Chairs.* Endowed chairs represent another means to recognize major contributions to this organization. Endowed chairs may be named in honor of a present or former staff member, the donor, or someone the donor wishes to honor, and may be either a memorial or a living tribute to the honoree. A financial goal shall be set for each endowed chair that is approved by this organization, and shall be based on a preliminary budget prepared for the use of a portion of the investment earnings.

7. *Naming of Departments or Title Positions.* Professional, scientific, and service departments and their administrative positions represent another means to honor a donor or someone the donor wishes to honor, or a present or former staff member. Such occasions occur especially when the personal contributions, service, and achievements of the honoree have been intimately associated with that department or its service or functional area.

8. *Awards or Citations.* This organization may establish and may confer at its pleasure such awards or citations on individuals or institutions in recognition for either or both their voluntary service and contributions. These awards or citations may be given at such time and on such occasions as the organization's Board of Directors may determine. Recommendations for conferring an award or citation shall be made as defined in paragraph 9 below.

9. *Process for Recommendation.* Recommendations for honors and recognition are directed to the Committee on Fund Development, who shall confer with the Chairperson of the Board of Directors and the President/CEO before action is taken. In those instances where a present or former employee is nominated or a department or title position is proposed, the President/CEO shall confer with the department head most closely associated with the candidate, or the department head most closely associated with the title position, for advice in advance of forwarding the recommendation to the Board of Directors for their decision. In addition, adequate consultation with the honoree or his or her family or their representative(s) shall be conducted at the same time as other internal consultations, to be concluded to their satisfaction prior to presentation of these recommendations to the Board of Directors for action.

10. *Public Notice.* Honors and recognition decisions represent opportunities for public announcement. Agreement for such public notice shall be requested of each honoree, or his or her family or representative(s), in advance. Honorees shall have the opportunity to notify family and friends, and to invite their participation with the organization in any dedication ceremonies and receptions conducted in connection with the conferring of honors and recognition. Responsibility for coordination of such public notice shall be by the President/CEO and Director of Fund Development.

11. *Forms of Recognition.* Various forms of recognition shall be available in accordance with the wishes of the donor and with the concurrence of the Board of Directors. Details as to form shall be included in recommendations submitted to the Committee on Fund Development. Forms of recognition may be among the following: formal dinners, portraits, dedication ceremonies, receptions, plaques, gifts to donors and honorees, photo sessions, and other forms of recognition.

12. *Graphics Continuity.* Materials, type face, and presentation forms shall be consistent with graphics standards established by this organization. The application of overall visual aids, signage, and graphics utilization shall be in accordance with graphics standards established by this organization.

13. *Renewed Solicitation.* The resolicitation of donors who have been accorded honors and recognitions shall be reviewed in advance by the Committee on Fund Development, and shall be based on submission of a strategic action plan for continued donor relations and the master gift plan defined for each such donor prior to consideration of another gift that may qualify for added honors and recognition.

14. *Donor Communications.* The Office of Fund Development shall monitor relations with all individuals or institutions accorded honors and recognition, in order to provide continued communications with this organization at a level satisfactory to these donors.

K. MANAGEMENT OF PLANNED GIVING PROGRAMS

1. *Programs for Solicitation.* The types of planned gifts to be offered, minimum gift amount, range for percentage payout, assignment as trustee, and administrative services shall all be defined by the Committee on Fund Development and approved by the Board of Directors, and shall include procedures for preparation and review of performance of planned gifts in force.

2. *Acting as Trustee.* This organization will prefer to act as trustee of charitable trusts and pooled income funds with concurrence of the donor(s), and will provide (or arrange to provide) such investment, distribution, income tax, audit, and other administrative services as required of a trustee.

3. *Charitable Trust and Pooled Income Fund Management.* The Board of Directors, acting on recommendations of the Fund Development and Investment Management committees, will administer each charitable trust and pooled income fund in accordance with guidelines established by the trust document or pooled fund agreement, including investment strategies and payout rates. Investment managers will be selected by the Investment Management Committee, who will perform regular evaluations of investment performance and will report these results to the Board of Directors at least annually.

4. *Life Insurance Programs.* All life insurance programs offered as gift opportunities shall be defined by the Fund Development and Investment Management Committees and approved by the Board of Directors. Selection of agents, performance of due diligence, and supervision of policies in force shall be the responsibility of the Investment Management Committee, acting on recommendations from the Committee on Fund Development. Other life insurance gifts may be accepted, provided the policy is fully paid and designates this organization as owner and beneficiary. If partially paid, the donor will be required to submit a written pledge to complete premium payments within eight years and to provide the original policy to this organization.

5. *Commissions Paid for Planned Gifts.* It shall be the policy of this organization not to pay commissions or percentages associated with negotiation and acceptance of any form of planned gift. Further, the standards of professional conduct in this area shall be as published by the National Committee on Planned Giving.

6. *Wills and Bequests: Probate Procedures.* Sample texts shall be provided to all those who express an interest in naming this organization to receive a bequest. Donors who name this organization in their Will or Living Trust will be asked to provide a copy of their document or that section wherein this organization is named. It shall be the policy of this organization to closely follow to conclusion all probate proceedings where this organization is a named beneficiary.

L. INVESTMENT AND ENDOWMENT OPERATIONS

1. *Obligation of the Board of Directors.* All gifts to be invested or funds held as endowment shall be managed with professional assistance at all times with the express approval of the Board of Directors. The objectives in management of such funds shall be to preserve their current value and to generate earnings for current use by this organization. Supervision shall be by the Investment Management Committee, who will establish investment guidelines, conduct performance evaluation, recommend distribution of earnings, and submit regular status reports on all invested funds.

2. *Selecting Professional Management Services.* The Investment Management Committee shall interview and recommend to the Board of Directors such professional managers, custodians, and performance evaluation services for all invested and endowment funds as are required, and shall conduct performance evaluations at least semiannually.

3. *Short-Term Money Management (under two years).* The Investment Management Committee shall recommend to the Board in concert with the Finance Committee how funds to be held for a brief period (under two years) shall be invested and managed, including the selection of professional managers and setting their investment guidelines.

4. *Invested Funds Management (two to five years).* The Investment Management Committee shall recommend to the Board in concert with the Finance Committee how funds that may be held for a period of up to five years shall be invested and managed, including the selection of professional managers and setting their investment guidelines. Funds to be held for more than five years shall observe endowment fund management.

5. *Endowment Fund Management.* Funds restricted to endowment or designated by the Board to observe endowment management shall be invested with professional managers and may include commingling such funds together for maximum benefit. Guidelines for investment shall consider current market conditions, preservation of principal, balanced fund strategies, and the annual income needs of this organization.

6. *Purposes and Uses of Earnings.* Investment earnings shall observe the use designated for any invested or endowment fund at its inception or may otherwise be used at the discretion of the Board of Directors. If a portion of earnings is not consumed or their use is not required, it shall be the policy of this organization to retain and reinvest all such funds.

M. CORPORATE MEMBER: THE SEPARATE FOUNDATION

1. *Corporate Member of the Foundation.* Any organization established in the form of a separate nonprofit corporation in foundation form, whose mission is to assist this parent corporation, shall be as a related organization. The Corporate Member shall be the Board of Directors of this organization, who shall approve the Articles of Incorporation and Bylaws and annually elect the Directors of each such related organization.

2. *Routine Operations and Information Reports.* The routine operations of the foundation shall be guided by its Articles of Incorporation and Bylaws. Information reports shall be made to this organization by the foundation President or other officer who shall be invited to regular meetings of the Board of Directors of the parent corporation. Reports shall include information about its activities in support of this organization, fund-raising programs, and financial results.

3. *Review of Annual Goals and Objectives.* The foundation shall prepare its annual goals and objectives in concert with the priority needs of this organization. These goals shall include projects identified for fund raising, estimated income, and operating budget and staff required, to be submitted to the Board of Directors of this organization for review prior to inception.

4. *Professional Staff Hiring Procedures.* Professional employees of the foundation, including employees of this organization assigned to foundation work, shall include the Chairman of the Board, Chairman of the Fund Development Committee, Chief Financial Officer, and the President/CEO in the interview and selection process. All employees shall observe the policies and procedures of the parent corporation at all times.

5. *Transfer of Funds Raised and Held.* The transfer of funds raised and held by the foundation shall be at the request of the President/CEO or Chief Financial Officer of the parent corporation or their delegates. Recommendations shall include the use or disposition of funds to be transferred for reports to donors. Each transfer shall be approved by the foundation board of directors and reported to the Board of the parent corporation.

6. *Nominations Process for Foundation Directors.* The Bylaws of the foundation specify that the Nominations Committee of the Board of Directors of the parent corporation shall identify, recruit, and nominate candidates for service on the Board of Directors of the foundation.

7. *Honors and Recognition by the Foundation.* Honors and recognition accorded to qualified donors and volunteers shall be conducted in concert with the parent corporation at all times, including the naming of any part of facilities, named positions, and the placement of donor recognition materials in or on buildings owned by the parent corporation. Honors and recognition accorded by the

foundation shall otherwise be guided by the Honors and Recognition policy of the parent corporation (see Section J above).

8. *Annual Meetings and Annual Reports.* The foundation shall conduct its annual meetings and issue its annual reports in concert with the parent corporation at all times. A selection of foundation directors, volunteers, and donors will be invited to attend annual meetings of the parent corporation. Annual reports prepared for the two organizations may be separate or combined, as the two Boards may determine.

9. *Annual Audit Review.* Audits prepared for the foundation shall be conducted in accordance with generally accepted accounting principles. Selection of the firm to conduct the audit shall be made by the parent corporation and the report delivered to the parent corporation. Further, as accounting guidelines may direct, the financial experience of the foundation may also be reported in the consolidated audit of the parent corporation as a related organization.

N.   RELATED ORGANIZATIONS: SUPPORT GROUPS

1. *Authorization to Exist.* Support group organizations may be formed either by this organization or its subsidiary foundation only with the approval of the board of directors of both organizations. The purpose of any such support group shall be in keeping with the mission, purpose, goals, and objectives of the parent corporation. Support groups may not be established as separately incorporated associations except in the form of a subsidiary foundation as defined in Section M above.

2. *Approval of Operating Rules and Procedures.* Support group organizations formed for fund development purposes shall be guided in their activities by written operating rules and procedures, which shall be approved by the parent corporation or its subsidiary foundation. Their operating rules and procedures shall include text reporting their formal affiliation, purposes, members, Board of Directors, election of officers and their duties, powers, committees, meetings, receipt of funds and assets and their disposition, rules of order, limitations on political activities, insignia, amendments, and the like.

3. *Use of the Organization's Name.* Support groups may act only in the name of the parent corporation or its subsidiary foundation, use their name in their communications, solicit contributions only for support of their mission and priorities of need, and otherwise support their purposes, goals, and objectives.

4. *Review of Annual Goals and Objectives.* The annual goals and objectives of each support group organization shall be prepared in coordination and cooperation with the parent corporation or its subsidiary foundation. Preparation of annual goals and objectives shall be defined and approved by the Board of Directors of each support group and reported to the Board of Directors of the parent corporation or its subsidiary foundation for review and approval.

5. *Nominations Process for Officers and Members of the Board of Directors.* A nominations committee shall be appointed by the Board of Directors of each support group who

will conduct elections to its Board of Directors. Composition of each nominations committee will include the Chairman of the Board, Chairman of the Committee on Fund Development, and President/CEO of the parent corporation, along with similar representatives of its subsidiary foundation. Candidates for election shall be approved by the parent corporation and its subsidiary foundation in advance of their election.

6. *Professional Staff Hiring Procedures.* Professional staff hired to assist support group organizations shall be employees of the parent corporation or its subsidiary foundation. Representatives of each support group will be invited to serve on selection committees for the hiring of professional staff whose duties include staff management and support for these organizations.

7. *Control of Funds Raised and Held.* All funds raised and held by support groups shall be in the name of the parent corporation, or its subsidiary foundation, and shall be delivered to it upon receipt or following completion of the activity for which these funds were raised. Regular reports of funds raised and held shall be made to the Committee on Fund Development of the parent corporation or to the Board of Directors of its subsidiary foundation, which funds shall be included in their regular financial statements and annual audit report.

8. *Annual Meetings and Annual Reports.* Support groups shall conduct their annual meetings and prepare their annual reports as their Operating Rules and Procedures specify. Invitations to annual meetings shall include representatives of the parent corporation or its subsidiary foundation, who shall also receive their annual reports.

9. *Annual Audit Review.* Funds raised or held in the name of the parent corporation or its subsidiary foundation are the property of these organizations and shall be included in their financial statements and annual audit report. If support groups manage their own funds, their books and financial statements will be delivered annually to the parent corporation or its subsidiary foundation for review and to provide such information as is required for preparation of the annual audit statement and IRS return. A report of each review will be delivered to the President of each support group.

O. DEPARTMENT OF FUND DEVELOPMENT

1. *Areas of Management Responsibility.* The Department of Fund Development reports to the President/CEO and is changed with management and staff support to the entire fund development program, including all employees, annual budget, donor records, and files. The definition and direction of fund-raising activities, recruitment and training of volunteers, accounting for all funds raised, and public reports shall be with the approval of the Committee on Fund Development and the Board of Directors.

2. *Approved Fund-Raising Programs.* Only those fund-raising programs and activities approved by the Committee on Fund Development shall be performed by this

Department with the use of its employees and their time and with such budget funds as are made available. Any other program must first receive full and formal approval by the Committee prior to its implementation.

3. *Donor Relations and Communications.* This Department is charged with responsibility for the complete supervision of all records, personal relations, and communications with donors, including honors and recognition. This Department shall act as a resource to this organization on its formal obligations to donors at all times.

4. *Support Service.* The organization shall provide this Department with normal and routine support services, such as accounting, financial management, personnel, employee health, engineering, housekeeping, etc., in the same manner as other Departments and assist in completion of its assigned duties, as appropriate.

5. *Job Descriptions and Hiring Practices.* All employees of this Department shall be guided in their daily duties by a written job description prepared for their position, as reviewed and approved by this organization. Salary levels, pay schedules, benefits, performance evaluations, and other matters relating to full- or part-time employment shall be consistent with personnel procedures of this organization, as shall be all hiring practices. Employees shall observe the same policies and procedures that apply to all other employees at all times.

6. *Budgets and Accountability.* Budget preparation and accountability for funds entrusted to the Department shall be performed by management staff of the Department in accordance with routine procedures of this organization. Departmental managers are responsible for the correct expense of all funds provided for operating purposes in accordance with organization policy, and for verifying these details to the finance division as required.

7. *Records and Files.* All records of correspondence, gift transactions, and their related details will be maintained by the Department as sensitive information for such periods of time and in such form as is appropriate. The use and disclosure of any of this information shall be restricted to Department employees and such others who have a need to know in order to carry out their assigned duties. Donor gift histories shall be preserved for the life of the donor. Any record destroyed shall protect the sensitive nature of the contents until destruction is complete.

P. PUBLIC REPORTING REQUIREMENTS

1. *Internal Revenue Service.* Preparation of Internal Revenue Service Form 990 and other IRS documents associated with the conduct of public solicitation and acceptance of gifts of any type and form shall be completed on schedules provided and in accordance with current IRS regulations.

2. *State and Local Agencies.* Such other reports as may be required by state, county, local community, or other agencies shall be completed on schedules provided and in accordance with current regulations. Such permits, licenses, and fees that may be

required along with public disclosure of tax-exempt certificates, audits, financial statements, etc., will be completed in accordance with current regulations.

3. *Public Requests for Information.* Any request in writing, asking for copies of public documents so defined by law, such as reports submitted to the IRS and local authorities, will be completed in accordance with current regulations and will be honored within five working days of receipt of the request.

Q. APPROVALS, REVIEWS, AND AMENDMENTS

1. *Authority of the Board of Directors.* This Manual is authorized by the Board of Directors, acting on recommendation of the Committee on Fund Development. It is designed to provide guidance and direction to all areas of fund development activity of this organization. Its contents shall be followed by all who accept appointment to voluntary and staff positions of this organization.

2. *Periodic Review and Reissue.* A review of this entire Manual will be conducted by the Committee on Fund Development every other year, with results reported to the Board of Directors. The purpose of this review will be to maintain an accurate relationship between the current practices of operating programs and the contents of this Manual. Any section or subsection may be examined at any time, as appropriate, with changes and additions proposed in accordance with the amendment procedures.

3. *Process for Amendment.* Changes to this Manual must be approved by the Board of Directors, who will act only on formal recommendations from the Committee on Fund Development. Proposals for amendment may be submitted in writing, at any time, by any participant in the fund development program who shall utilize existing committees, related organizations, or other appropriate and standing leadership structure for prior reviews and approvals leading to submission by the Committee on Fund Development.

Suggested Readings

Blazek, Jody. 1994. *Tax and Financial Planning for Tax-Exempt Organizations*, 2nd ed. New York: Wiley.

Brakeley, George A., Jr. 1980. *Tested Ways to Successful Fund Raising*. New York: AMACOM.

Burlingame, Dwight F., ed. 1992. *The Responsibilities of Wealth*. Bloomington: Indiana University Press.

―――― and Hulse, Lamont J., ed. 1991. *Taking Fund Raising Seriously*. San Francisco: Jossey-Bass.

Broce, Thomas E. 1986. *Fund Raising: A Guide to Raising Money from Private Sources*, 2nd ed. Norman: University of Oklahoma Press.

Cutlip, Scott M. 1990. *Fund-Raising in the United States: Its Role in American Philanthropy*. New Brunswick, NJ: Rutgers University Press (reprint of a 1965 work).

Drucker, Peter F. 1990. *Managing the Nonprofit Organization: Practices and Principles*. New York: HarperCollins.

Fink, Norman S, and Metzler, Howard C. 1982. *The Costs and Benefits of Deferred Giving*. New York: Columbia University Press.

Grasty, William K. and Sheinkopf, Kenneth G. 1983. *Successful Fund Raising: A Handbook of Proven Strategies and Techniques*. New York: Charles Scribner's Sons.

Gray, Sandra T. 1993. *A Vision for Evaluation*. Washington, DC: Independent Sector.

Greenfield, James M. 1991. *Fund-Raising: Evaluating and Managing the Fund Development Process*. New York: Wiley.

———. 1994. *Fund-Raising Fundamentals: A Guide to Annual Giving for Professionals and Volunteers*. New York: Wiley.

———. 1996. *Fund-Raising Cost-Effectiveness: A Self-Assessment Workbook*. New York: Wiley.

Gross, Malvern J. Jr., Warshauer, William Jr., and Larkin, Robert F. 1994. *Financial and Accounting Guide for Nonprofit Organizations*, 5th ed. New York: Wiley.

Gurin, Maurice G. 1991. *What Volunteers Should Know for Successful Fund Raising*. New York: Stein & Day.

———. 1985. *Confessions of a Fund Raiser: Lessons of an Instructive Career*. Washington, DC: Taft Corporation.

Herman, Robert D. and Associates. 1994. *The Jossey-Bass Handbook of Nonprofit Leadership and Management*. San Francisco: Jossey-Bass.

Hodgkinson, Virginia A. and Associates. 1992. *The Nonprofit Almanac 1992–1993: Dimensions of the Independent Sector*. Washington, DC: Independent Sector.

——— and Weitzman, Murray S. 1992. *Giving and Volunteering in the United States: Findings from a National Survey*. Washington, DC: Independent Sector.

Hopkins, Bruce R. 1993. *The Law of Charitable Giving*. New York: Wiley.

———. 1991. *The Law of Fund-Raising*. New York: Wiley.

———. 1991. *The Law of Tax-Exempt Organizations*, 6th ed. New York: Wiley.

———. 1993. *A Legal Guide to Starting and Managing a Nonprofit Organization*, 2nd ed. New York: Wiley.

Huntsinger, Jerald E. 1985. *Fund Raising Letters: A Comprehensive Study Guide to Raising Money by Direct Response Marketing*. Richmond, VA: Emerson.

Howe, Fisher. 1991. *The Board Member's Guide to Fund Raising*. San Francisco: Jossey-Bass.

Kotler, Philip and Andreasen, Alan R. 1987. *Strategic Marketing for Nonprofit Organizations*, 3d ed. Englewood Cliffs, NJ: Prentice-Hall.

Lautman, Kay and Goldstein, Henry. 1991. *Dear Friend: Mastering the Art of Direct Mail Fund Raising*, 2nd ed. Washington, DC: Taft Group.

Lindahl, Wesley E. 1992. *Strategic Planning for Fund Raising*. San Francisco: Jossey-Bass.

Mixer, Joseph R. 1993. *Principles of Professional Fundraising*. San Francisco: Jossey-Bass.

Murray, Dennis J. 1994. *The Guaranteed Fund-Raising System: A Systems Approach to Planning and Controlling Fund Raising*, 2nd ed. Poughkeepsie, NY: American Institute of Management.

New, Anne L. and Levis, Wilson C. 1991. *Raise More Money for Your Nonprofit Organization: A Guide to Evaluating and Improving Your Fundraising*. New York: Foundation Center.

O'Connell, Brian. 1983. *America's Voluntary Spirit: A Book of Readings*. New York: Foundation Center.

———. 1987. *Philanthropy in Action*. Washington, DC: Independent Sector.

O'Neill, Michael. 1989. *The Third America: The Emergence of the Nonprofit Sector in the United States*. San Francisco: Jossey-Bass.

Payton, Robert L. 1988. *Philanthropy: Voluntary Action for the Public Good*. New York: Macmillan.

Rosso, Henry A. and Associates. 1991. *Achieving Excellence in Fund Raising: A Comprehensive Guide to Principles, Strategies, and Methods*. San Francisco: Jossey-Bass.

Schmaedick, Gerald L. 1993. *Cost-Effectiveness in the Nonprofit Sector* New London, CT: Quorum Books.

Seltzer, Michael. 1987. *Securing Your Organization's Future: A Complete Guide to Fundraising Strategies*. New York: Foundation Center.

Seymour, Harold J. 1966. *Designs for Fund Raising: Principles, Patterns, Techniques*. New York: McGraw-Hill. (Paperback edition: Ambler, PA: Fund Raising Institute, 1988).

Smith, Bucklin and Associates. 1994. *The Complete Guide to Nonprofit Management*. Ed. by Robert H. Wilbur, Susan Kudia Finn, and Carolyn M. Freeland. New York: Wiley.

Von Til, John and Associates. 1990. *Critical Issues in American Philanthropy*. San Francisco: Jossey-Bass.

Warner, Irving R. 1990. *The Art of Fund Raising*, 3rd ed. New York: Harper & Row.

Warwick, Mal. 1990. *Revolution in the Mailbox*. Baltimore, MD: Fund Raising Institute.

——— . 1992. *You Don't Always Get What You Ask For: Using Direct Mail Tests to Raise More Money for Your Organization*. Berkeley, CA: Strathmoor Press.

21 ▼ Resource Assessment for the Self-Renewing Manager

JILL O. MUEHRCKE
Nonprofit World

21.1 Self-Assessment

Too often, nonprofit organizations consider fund raising as a separate function. But fund raising and quality management are integrally related. The elements needed to sustain excellence are the same elements necessary to raise funds.

Effective fund raising requires concerted planning and a broad view. As noted in the "Excellence Equation" (Chapter 1), successful organizations listen to their customers and use that information to map their path. No aspect of fund raising is more important than understanding your customers, who in this case are your potential donors. You need to know everything you can about who they are, why they might give to your organization, and what you can offer in return for their support.

Before you ask for a penny, you must be sure that you are attuned to your environments—both internal and external. You must do a thorough assessment of your organization to be certain you are *ready* for fund raising and to ascertain which fund-raising methods are most appropriate for you. Here are the steps to such a fund-raising assessment.

First, be sure that you have powerful, up-to-date mission and vision statements. Note that your vision statement grows directly from and incorporates aspects of your mission statement. While your mission statement tells what your organization was founded to do, your vision statement explains what you want it to become.

Be certain that everyone in your organization—volunteers, paid staff, and board members—agree on your mission and vision statements. If they don't, arrange to meet with as many board and staff as possible to brainstorm ideas until you all agree on updated mission and vision statements.

Don't begrudge the time spent on this activity. It's a crucial early step in laying your fund-raising foundation. Once you have a clear mission and vision statement that everyone in your organization supports, you can use this statement again and again throughout the fund-raising process. It will help rally people and show them why your organization deserves donations.

21.2   External Assessment and Demographics

The next step is to assess the world outside your door. List your organization's key populations (also known as markets, constituents, audiences, or stakeholders). These are the groups who control your organization's future. They probably include your current and potential donors, volunteers, funders, clients, vendors, and government officials. These people are the foundation on which to build your future.

Survey these key populations, using phone or written questionnaires or focus groups. Ask them to give you their image of your organization, including:

- How the organization is positioned in relation to others offering similar services
- Why the organization is a community asset
- Which programs and services the organization should expand
- Which programs and services the organization should eliminate or cut back
- What new programs or services the organization should pursue

This step will tell you what your key stakeholders think of your organization and why they consider it worthy of support. This is valuable information to pass on to potential donors. You also know what changes to make to meet your constituents' needs. You cannot renew your organization until you know what your stakeholders think about the job you are doing.

21.3   Internal Assessment and Resources

The next step is to assess the world inside your organization. Answer the following questions to help you pinpoint your organization's internal strengths and weaknesses. Then determine ways to turn each weakness into a strength.

- What are the skills of your volunteer and paid staff members? Are staff members committed, knowledgeable, energetic? Or are they overworked, discouraged, spread too thin? Can you think of ways you can change weaknesses to strengths? For example, including staff members in this self-assessment exercise is a good way to turn discouragement into a renewed sense of excitement about the organization's possibilities.
- What are your board members' skills? Are board members active and dedicated? Are they well connected in the community? Do they make friends for your organization wherever they go?
- What is each staff and board member's attitude toward fund raising? If most are eager fund raisers, give yourself extra points for this major strength. If not, begin a campaign to emphasize fund raising as an important board role. Give all board members targets to reach, and hold them accountable. You cannot expect outsiders to give to your organization if your own board is not willing to do so.
- What resources do you have earmarked especially for fund raising? How much staff time is set aside specifically for development efforts? What is your budget for training paid and volunteer staff in fund raising? Do you have any money to hire a fund-raising consultant? If your answer to these questions is *no*, plan to develop these resources.

- What assistance is available to you from other organizations? For example, do you have a national or umbrella office that may have fund-raising resources available? Do you have good relations with other nonprofit organizations in your community or in your field of interest? If they have fund-raising expertise and resources, will they share these with you? Perhaps you have something you could offer them in return.
- Do you have up-to-date information systems, including mailing lists, donor databases, and record-keeping procedures? Is your technology state of the art?
- Do you have a strategic plan for your organization? Does it include fund raising? If you do have a plan in place, use it as your starting point as you begin the fund-raising process. If you don't, plan a board-staff retreat to develop one.
- Is your organization financially strong? Do you have reserve and endowment funds? Do you have sources of revenue from nontraditional, nongovernmental entities? Do you have at least four different sources of income? Does each of these income sources make up *less* than 30 percent of your income? (If one income source makes up more than 40% of your budget, this is a serious danger sign. If one source of income makes up more than 50% of your budget, you are in deep trouble.) If you answered *no* to any of these questions, begin working to turn it into a *yes*.
- Do you use total quality management teams? Such teams are the best way to get all employees working for the organization's goals and striving for constant improvement.
- Do you love what you do? Are you totally committed to your organization's mission and vision? As the organization's leader, you set the tone. Your energy will fuel everyone else's. Your passion is your best fund-raising tool.
- List other strengths and weaknesses of your organization and ideas for turning weaknesses into strengths. Hold a brainstorming session with key staff and board members to get their suggestions, too.

Answering these questions will give you a portrait of your organization's strengths—important information to share with potential donors. These questions will also pinpoint your organization's weaknesses and allow you to turn each weakness into a strength.

21.4 *Program Objectives and Evaluation*

Next, evaluate your programs and services. Decide which you would like to expand— and why. Ask yourself:

- What is the objective of each program? Do you measure the effectiveness of each program? Do you have hard data to show how successful each program is?
- What special procedures or capabilities does your organization have for doing what it does? Examples: unique volunteer training, customized computer software, specialized counseling skills, publishing capabilities.
- What special networks, contacts, and relationships does your organization have in place for getting your products and services to your clients?

Examples: linkages with distributors, contacts with publishers, service contracts with corporate employee assistance programs, collaborations with other nonprofits in your field.

- Do your key constituents identify your organization with your programs? What do they consider to be the strengths and weaknesses of each program? (You will want to refer to the surveys of your stakeholders which you performed earlier.)
- Are all your programs compatible with your mission? If not, decide whether to drop incompatible programs or expand your mission to include them. (It's perfectly all right to expand your mission. In fact, the broader your mission the more flexibility you have to meet people's needs.)
- Do you have a program, service, or product you could sell to other organizations or to the public? For example: Could you turn your expertise on a subject into a book or training session that would help other nonprofits while earning a fee for you?
- What new programs would you like to add? Are they compatible with your mission? Are they needed? Are they wanted?
- What resources (staff, money, collaborative relationships) do you have in place to expand programs or add new ones?

Answering these questions will tell you which programs to emphasize to potential donors (the ones that are working well and are clearly identified with your organization). It will also give you ideas about turning new or existing programs into money-makers.

After evaluating your programs and services, take a look at your organization's visibility. Does at least 80 percent of the community you serve know about your organization—and really understand what you do? Does the media know about your organization and what it does? Do you have a press list for each geographic area you serve? Do you regularly prepare press releases about your activities? Have you ever invited members of the media to attend an event?

If you can't answer *yes* to all these questions, you need to work on building your organization's reputation. Don't think of public relations as a separate function. Combine public relations, advertising, marketing, fund raising, and volunteer activities into a total plan to increase your visibility with your key stakeholders. Such visibility is a key ingredient in raising funds.

As part of this effort, be sure you have up-to-date, descriptive materials about your organization. These materials include brochures, newsletters, a case statement, public service announcements, and marketing pieces. Don't be stingy with these materials; include them in mailings, and give them out to everyone you meet.

After you have completed these steps, you're ready to choose the best methods to use to raise funds. First, list the sources of income your organization currently has. Also note the percent of your budget that comes from each source.

For each of your current fund-raising methods, answer the following questions:

- Last time you used this fund-raising method, how much money did you raise?

- Did this amount meet, exceed, or fall below your expectations?
- How much time did both paid and volunteer staff spend on this fund-raising method?
- How much was the value of the time spent (cost of each volunteer and paid staff hour)?
- By how much did the money you raised exceed the total cost (including staff time)?
- Calculate the percentage of dollars raised per volunteer hour. For example, say you held an event and raised $1,000. Your direct expenses were $100. Volunteers and paid staff spent 30 hours on the event. The value of staff time is $10 per hour for a total of $300. Thus, the event really netted $600 or $20 per hour.

Remember, money isn't the only reason for choosing a fund-raising method. Answer the following nonmonetary questions about each method:

- Did your organization become more visible as a result of this fund-raising method?
- Did you discover new potential donors through this fund-raising method?
- Did you make important contacts and liaisons through this fund-raising method?
- Did this fund-raising method increase staff energy and motivation?

All the above are important ways to renew your organization, form connections, and increase commitment. Some of these benefits may be even more important than raising money!

21.5 Developing Methodology

Your answers to the above questions will reveal which fund-raising methods are most appropriate for your organization. Consider adding other methods, which may be even more effective. These might include: fees, grants for general purposes, grants for specific programs, memberships, direct mail solicitation, direct (person-to-person) solicitation, telemarketing, special events, income earned from marketing products or services, memorials, corporations, cause-related marketing, planned giving, in-kind contributions, and capital or endowment campaigns.

Be open to new types of income generation, such as earned income—an underused but vital component of a nonprofit's tool kit. This method can be as simple as taking a workshop your organization provides and figuring out how to expand its scope and make a profit doing it. Or perhaps your clients tell you they need a certain product or service, which you can develop and sell.

Earned income has many advantages. There are no strings attached to the money you earn. You may use it however you wish. It allows you to be self-sufficient, not dependent on "the kindness of strangers." It strengthens your organization by diversifying your offerings. It forces you to be sensitive to your customers and to monitor the marketplace, which will improve the way you serve your clients. It helps you and others in your organization develop a more business-oriented mindset, which is bound to increase your fund-raising savvy.

While developing new fund-raising methods takes time, it will be well worth the effort. It's crucial to find a good "fit" between your organization and the way you raise funds.

Equally important, you must develop a broad spectrum of different fund-raising methods. Your aim should be to spread your budget among as many different methods as possible, so that you're not dependent on any one or two sources of income.

After following the steps outlined here, you will have created a valuable self-assessment of your organization. Remember that such an assessment is an ongoing process, and you should repeat it at least once a year.

Performing such an assessment regularly will give your organization's key players a clear picture of where your organization is and where it is going. Thus, it will turn everyone in your organization into a fund raiser, because this information is at the heart of every successful funding request.

Finally, a periodic self-assessment is the best way to keep in touch with a changing world, accomplish your customer-focused mission, and forge lasting bonds. No true fund raising can occur without it.

Information Resources Management for Nonprofit Organizations

WILLIAM A. KLEINTOP, PhD
Assistant Professor of Public Administration
Seton Hall University

22.1 Introduction

As a nonprofit manager, your use of computers probably started out simply. The first computer was for word processing, or maybe for managing financial accounts. But over time you realized something more about that computer. It could hold a lot of data about what was going on in the organization. It could be a tool for corresponding with others both inside and outside of the organization. The computer was a place to share ideas and build the quality of services and types of services being provided to the public. Finally, the computer became a tool for running the whole organization.

This chapter is about the mythical computer which came to run the whole organization. *Mythical* is a purposely chosen word. Organizations are run by people, not by machines, electronic or otherwise. The choices related to choosing hardware and software, and their deployment, are management decisions. The computer, however, in its many forms brought a new way of approaching the social systems called *organizations*. The computer brought the capability to both manage and create information. It is both a tool and a service. This chapter is about information resources and how those resources can be used successfully in nonprofit organizations.

Information technology (IT) is a general term referring to technologies used to process information in any format. IT is often used to refer to technologies based upon integrated circuits, commonly referred to as computer chips. In this use, IT includes the desktop and laptop computer, printers, facsimile machines, telephone systems, cars, and even toasters! IT refers not only to computer hardware, but also to the software which generally is of greatest value to nonprofit organizations. For our purposes, we will ignore the use of IT such as is found in toasters and focus on IT as a tool for operating a nonprofit organization.

The key to understanding information technology in nonprofits is understanding what the role of information is in these organizations. When we know the value of information, we can next discuss how, like other resources, information can be managed in nonprofits. From that discussion we can move on to understanding what happens in nonprofit organizations and their use of computers. We will briefly examine different foci of information resources management and outline a process for planning and managing those resources.

A note of caution is appropriate at this point. This chapter is not intended to provide an exhaustive look at information resources management (IRM). It is also not meant to be the compendium of techniques for IRM. Rather, the chapter is meant to introduce the concept for use in nonprofit organizations to allow you, the reader, to assess the value of the technique for nonprofit organizations.

22.2 *Defining Information Resources Management*

In this section we will briefly examine information as a resource to managers. Once information is understood to be a resource, it is subject to being managed as is any resource in organizations. We will look at the rationale for managing information as a resource to conclude this section.

(A) INFORMATION AS A RESOURCE

Recently a nonprofit childcare organization undertook the effort to determine a direction for developing its information technology. The agency has an annual budget of about $3.5 million, and operates 17 separate sites and programs. On advice from the individual asked to facilitate the effort, the management staff created a list of categories of information needed to manage the agency (Exhibit 22.1). The general types of data used

EXHIBIT 22.1 Table of Information and Data for a Nonprofit Childcare Agency

Category of Information	Types of Data
1. Center intake and marketing	Contacts—drop-ins, telephone inquiries, follow-ups, information given and sent, parent questionnaires—at six weeks, annually, etc., competitor analysis, staff time used for activities, staff contacts with parents— newsletters, daily reports
2. Child records	Attendance, pickup and drop-off times, medical information, including regular medical and additional information, emergency contact, authorized escorts, releases—trips, photos, etc., child evaluations and development, subsidy, scholarships, AFDC, TCC, invoicing done at Center level, injury reports, applications, special needs of children, fee agreements, developmental history, anecdotal histories
3. Curriculum	Developmentally appropriate practices for all age groups, enrichment programs, daily class activities and lesson plans, assessments of the program, parents handbook
4. Demographics of centers	Community, staff, families: parents and children, employers, schools
5. Demographics of current donors	Board members, corporations, individuals, foundations
6. Fiscal information	Accounts receivable, accounts payable, payroll, banking, budgeting, purchasing (inventory control), facilities, taxes
7. Food program	Eligibility, meals served to eligible children, training
8. Fund raising	Activities history (all), annual giving campaigns, center activities, donor base needs, parents' employers, who gets what information about the organization
9. Human resources	Benefits, personnel policies, staff training, skills inventory, security and confidentiality, staff incentives and recognition, staffing, AA/EEO, attendance, promotion history, work history, performance appraisals, scheduling, QWL
10. Insurance	Liability, student accident, D&O employee bonds, property, workers compensation
11. Legislative information	Addresses of legislators, legislation supporters, legislation sponsors, names of legislators
12. Licensing, regulations, accreditation	Current status of all centers and programs, accreditation status
13. Program inventories	Supplies and equipment, services provided at each center, staff skills
14. Property	Leases, physical investments (capital equipment), physical conditions of buildings, security, insurance
15. Risk management	Communications with lawyers, lawsuits
16. Telephone system needs	Current usage and capabilities, cost, future needs
17. Training and technical assistance	Topics and workshops, attendance, marketing, materials, library, trainee demographics, trainer demographics, trainer competencies
18. Training and technical assistance—library	Borrower, materials borrowed, number of walk-ins, frequency of materials borrowed

were also assigned to the categories of information. The list became quite extensive, encompassing 18 general areas of information and a multitude of data types.

While the table of information and data types developed by this childcare agency is not what one would expect for a nonprofit providing a dissimilar public service, such as an arts organization, there are similarities. More important than the information presented in the table itself is that information came to be seen by the participants in the process as an all-pervasive and important tool for managing the organization.

Information is usually taken for granted. It shows up on forms all over the organization. There is also vital information for managing activities embedded in the daily occurrences of organizational life. Take, for example, the transaction created when a parent drops a child off for care each morning at a childcare center. A common practice is for the parent to record the time the child is dropped off on a sign-in sheet, along with a signature. Within this simple transaction is a variety of important information—the simple fact that the child is dropped off for care, the day the child is dropped off, and the time of day the child is dropped off. Here you know (1) who your customers are, child as well as parent, (2) when a child is on-site and is the responsibility of the center, and (3) the time of day when staff must be available to care for children and to meet mandated staff-to-children ratios. The first item is important for directing activities of service delivery. Item two is an important security issue for the child and parent. And item three is an important issue associated with productivity in childcare. As a manager, you don't want to have staff being paid when there are not children in care.

Exhibit 22.1 provides evidence of the importance of information for managing a nonprofit organization. When creating the list, management staff verified that information plays a vital role in organizational life. Managers were surprised at the extensiveness of the data and information necessary to run the organization. Practically, the amount of information was too large to be handled as listed. Three portfolios—operations, program and curriculum, and planning and evaluation—were created to better conceptualize the types and interconnections of information used within the organization. This classification was the final step in management's viewing information as having value and being a key resource of the organization.

(B)   THE IMPORTANCE OF MANAGING INFORMATION

We have established that information is an important resource in organizations. Resources must be managed because they are usually scarce. Information in and of itself is not scarce. There is an abundance of it, as indicated in Exhibit 22.1. What is important to managers with respect to information, and that which makes information a scarce resource, is the quality, usability, and value of information. Quality is accuracy and consistency of data, usability is associated with accessibility to data in useful formats, and value is determined by the timeliness, relevance, and completeness of data (van den Hoven, 1995).

"Garbage in, garbage out" is often used in computing to indicate that poor quality inputs result in poor quality outputs. In other words, bad data leads to bad decisions. The goal of information resources management (IRM) is to enhance the quality, usability, and value of information. When this goal is met, the value of information is maximized to all members of the organization. Furthermore, information management is the responsibility of all organization members because they both use and create data which is the basis of information. Thus, IRM must be a coordinated venture requiring the attention of top management.

The goal of IRM is achieved by enacting a comprehensive approach to planning, organizing, budgeting, directing, monitoring and controlling the people, funding, technologies and activities associated with acquiring, storing, processing, and distributing data to meet business needs for the benefit of the entire organization (Lewis, Snyder, and Rainer, 1995, 204). This requires an approach to information management focusing not only on the technologies used but also on the people using the technologies.

22.3 Components of IRM

There are three tasks of managers with respect to the growing importance of IT in organizations (Lewis, et al., 1995, 203). The first is to ensure that IT provides a return on investment, to make sure that "IT pays its way." The second task is to ensure that IT investments are targeted appropriately. Both these tasks are largely strategic information management planning tasks. They require the development of standards for applying IT to organizational issues. Those tasks also require a process for allocating resources to IT beyond those of the normal, annual budgeting task. However, these tasks are insufficient for reaching the potential inherent in the application of information technology to organizational goals.

The third task is of importance as well. That task is for managers to ensure that the potential of IT is reached within the organization. This task requires managers to take the steps necessary to carry out a strategic IT plan and to implement successfully the technologies purchased, developed, and implemented in that effort. This requires managers to be aware of the impact of changes caused by IT in the work processes and to the worklife of human resources. Implementation planning, employee development and training, and leadership are all part of this third task.

These three tasks encompass three important concepts in information resources management. The first is planning, the second is implementing, and the third is evaluating. Exhibit 22.2 presents these components of IRM as three interconnected rings. As with all systems, one aspect of IRM affects the others. The type of IT chosen for use in the organization, part of planning, will determine the training needed for successful implementation. The strategic goals of the organization will determine the basis upon which the investments in IT are evaluated. Choices in other circles have similar effects in this model. Furthermore, feedback from each circle will affect choices made in future rounds of the IRM process. IRM is a continuous process operating in cycles. The time horizon of each discrete cycle is a choice to be made by managers. Because of rapid changes in the development of IT, the timeframe for IRM may be shorter than timeframes for strategic planning.

Each ring also has its set of components. The ring contents represent the activities nonprofit managers need to carry out to successfully manage their organization's information. We will now examine the three tasks and specify how the components affect the outcomes of information resources management in nonprofit organizations.

22.4 Managing Information Strategically—Information Resources Management Planning

Technology today is changing rapidly. The Internet is expanding rapidly, bringing the opportunity for new forms of communication with funders, as well as with clients and

EXHIBIT 22.2 Components of Information Resources Management for Nonprofit Organizations

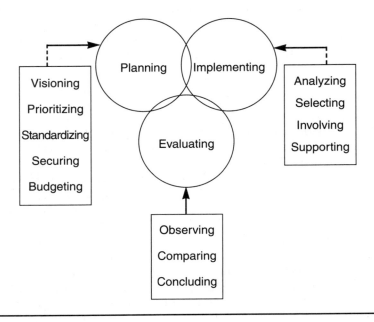

others. New operating systems make old systems obsolete. But to use the new systems to their fullest advantage new hardware and software must be purchased. Choices about which technologies to employ need to be made by managers.

Information needs are also changing, often in unpredictable ways. As federal and state governments change regulations for providing social services, information requirements will change. As donors become more concerned with how their funds are used because of various scandals in the nonprofit sector, information requirements will change. New technologies also create new expectations about organizational goals with which managers must cope (Chaiklin, 1991). "Do we need to upgrade to new computers or can we use are existing computers with new software?; Which functional areas would benefit most from IT investment—finance, service delivery, human resources?" These questions may be answered differently by every organization using IT.

New technologies also allow for the development of new services or products. A nonprofit agency involved with school-age children's projects developed an extensive list of resources for those projects, all stored in a bibliographic database. That database has potential as a revenue source to maintain the agency's work. Specialized directories can be created from that database and sold to customers using IT. Whether the agency wishes to pursue that source of revenue is a strategic decision which should be answered within the IRM planning process.

Information resources management planning, sometimes known as strategic information management planning, means making the choices between technologies, the manner of their implementation, and the use of resources to insure successful implementation within the context of organizational goals and objectives. IRM planning cuts across all aspects of nonprofit organizations embracing service delivery, human resources, finance, marketing, control, and other functional areas. IRM planning culminates in standards to guide the choice of new projects to develop and technologies to acquire. As a result, the IRM plan provides firm guidelines for management decision making about the use of technology. The IRM plan will be the basis for managers to make decisions about which IT investments to fund in any specific annual budget cycle.

These decisions have significance to nonprofit organizations. They involve answering questions such as, should we upgrade our server to a Windows 95 or to Windows 3.11? Or, should we use Windows for Workgroups? Is the applications software we use and plan to use available for Windows 95 or only Windows 3.11? Will vendors be offering software for Windows 95?

These are real questions which must be addressed. In childcare, as with many software applications focused on nonprofits, applications are not readily available for running in Windows 3.11, let alone Windows 95! Critical applications software is only currently available to run in DOS with Windows 3.11 upgrades expected to be available in the near future. Windows 95 may not successfully run the DOS applications. Such compatibility issues must be evaluated and addressed if information technology is to be successfully managed.

IRM planning involves creating a vision of how IT is to be used, prioritizing the investments in IT, standardizing the technologies to ensure integration of hardware and data across all activities of the organization, securing the hardware, software, and data of the organization from loss or damage, and budgeting for the implementation of the plan. We will now examine these components of IRM planning.

(A)   VISIONING

IRM planning is visionary—looking at where the organization is now and where its members want it to be in the future with respect to technology (Dula, 1995). The purpose of IRM planning is to derive a framework to guide the decisions managers must make when choosing among information technology projects to achieve nonprofits' organizational goals. Wilson (1996) called visioning the prerequisite for effective technological planning.

Visioning starts with the strategic plan of the organization. That plan should already provide guidance with respect to where the organization wants to be in the next years and the challenges ahead. What information will you need to run the organization effectively in accordance with that plan? This will require you to develop goals associated with information but relating to the mission of the organization as specified in the strategic plan.

The childcare agency described earlier went through this process. While the agency's strategic plan provided direction, it was not easily translated to information requirements. The management staff participating in IRM planning developed a set of goals for eight areas of need in the organization (Exhibit 22.3). They then defined goals for each area. These goals became the basis for developing the agency's IRM plan.

The process of developing the goals was not easy. Three meetings were needed to complete the list of goals. The process required the participants to think about the information they used as part of their daily work routines, as well as the information needed for strategic planning and by the board of directors. People do not usually think in terms of the information they use in their work. They are more likely to think about the tasks they complete. IRM planning requires one to do both.

EXHIBIT 22.3 Goals for IRM

General Area of Goal	Goals
1. Communicating	• To actively and completely communicate with parents. • To maintain and improve communications among centers, particularly of ideas and information. • To maintain and improve communications between the Central Office and centers. • To enhance communications within centers and programs.
2. Organizational strategy	• To enhance and increase the ability to respond to outside stimuli. • To enhance the organization's ability to seek new sources of information in the environment. • To increase accessibility to socioeconomic data about the communities we serve or about communities we may wish to serve. • To increase knowledge about our current customers and families. • To plan and implement program enhancements, such as new center openings, programs, and to add new offerings within center programs. • To support decision making of the board at a strategic level. • To enhance and expand opportunities for comprehensive resource development for all activities of the organization.
3. Marketing	• To enhance the marketing of our services and goods. • To identify, develop, and market our expertise. • To standardize and produce marketing material.
4. Curriculum	• To bring age-appropriate computer software into the classroom. • To enhance and improve financial reporting. • To transfer successful initiatives from one center to another.
5. Information technology	• To develop a training structure to support information technology use. • To enhance and improve the ability of organizational members to access data needed for operations and planning. • To increase capability to analyze data. • To monitor and evaluate IT needs on an ongoing basis.
6. Operations	• To improve records management. • To maintain and enhance security. • To improve purchasing and inventory management. • To reduce duplicative paper work.
7. Human resources	• To enhance employees' quality of work life (time management, information access, communications). • To support the personnel (staffing) functions of the organization. • To support the training and development of the organization's human resources. • To assess the organization's compliance with equal employment opportunities and Americans with Disabilities Act regulations. • To track, evaluate, and document the relationship between staff turnover and program quality.
8. Evaluation	• To provide ongoing evaluation of the IT planning process, marketing program, and curriculum programs.

(B) PRIORITIZING

The next step in IRM planning is determining the priority of goals. Priorities are important. They determine which IT investments get funded and completed first. Priorities provide the road map to get to the end result of IRM planning (Wilson, 1996).

Prioritizing is often a difficult task. Some goals will stand out clearly as needing top priority. For instance, maintaining the organization's accounting software system usually has a high priority. Smaller nonprofits without much in the way of formal organization structure may have the development of such a system as a top priority. Without money, no work gets done.

Once the "easy" goals are prioritized, the more difficult task of prioritizing the rest of the goals needs to take place. The childcare agency used in this example could not complete the prioritization tasks. There were disagreements among participants about the importance of various goals. This disagreement is quite common as people look at their areas of responsibility and make judgments on priorities based upon their needs. A different technique was used to move from this impasse. In this case, goals were grouped into portfolios—operations, program and curriculum, and planning and evaluation. The classification was not totally discrete. However, the process allowed the participants to then prioritize the portfolios so that IT investment decisions could be made taking into account those priorities. The decisions to invest in IT projects within each portfolio will be judged independently based on the value of that individual project within the general priorities of the portfolios.

(C) STANDARDIZING

Standardizing refers to the setting of basic hardware and software requirements upon which to build the organization's IT infrastructure. The standards should include such basic issues as which kind of hardware platform to use, which operating system should be supported by the organization, and which software and versions should be in use.

Going back to earlier questions, should you choose a Windows 3.11 or a Windows 95 standard for your computers? Is your hardware standard to be the PC or the Apple Macintosh? These choices affect future choices. If you choose a PC platform, you can use various operating systems. If you choose a Macintosh platform your operating system choices are limited. As suggested previously, your operating system limits your choice of applications software. If your preferred childcare management software is only available on a DOS platform, you may not want to migrate to a Windows 95 platform. But if it is available to run under Windows 3.11, you might consider the longer-range implications of using Windows 95.

Rather than make the decisions about what to buy on a purchase-by-purchase basis, choices should be set as part of a planning process, then promulgated throughout the organization as a standard. Each decision to buy hardware or software will not be made independently. Instead, they will be made as part of the larger organizational perspective on technology. Standards have the basic benefit of assuring that the employees will understand and be able to use all of the computers in the organization. One will be able to sit down at any computer and know how to operate it and how to use the software running on it. Standards also make the process of procurement easier and improve the timeliness of decision making because important considerations of purchase were already determined.

Standards should not be limited to hardware and software. Standards should also include the skill levels of the organization's human resources. If you choose to standardize the use of Windows 3.11, all employees should be trained on Windows 3.11 to achieve a specific level of skill. In general, a standard should be developed which specifies which software employees should be able to use and at what skill levels. Job requirements may need to be altered to specify that candidates for open positions in the organization have a specified level of computer skill prior to hiring. Coupled with hardware and software standards, human resources standards for technology will assure that your employees are able to take advantage of the technological tools available to them.

(D) SECURING

Have you ever visited an office using client/server systems when the server is down? You might observe employees talking, walking, doing anything but working. If completing work is a function of the availability of data or application software loaded on the server, work cannot be completed if the server is down. Or, consider the value of a payroll system operating on a computer. If the system goes down, preventing the production and distribution of pay checks, employees will not only be inconvenienced but very unhappy. Planning for these problems seems like a simple idea, but many organizations do not plan for securing their systems.

Securing your systems means taking precautions to assure that the critical functions of the organization which depend upon information technologies continue to be carried out even if those technologies fail. Securing systems also includes providing for the security of the data stored in those systems.

Securing starts with the identification of your mission-critical systems. Those are systems so critical to operations that downtime on the systems cannot be tolerated. In a childcare setting, mission critical systems could include those that track the attendance of children in service for revenue generation purposes, and payroll. Without revenue, the operations of the organization will cease. A lack of paychecks can create significant personnel problems for the organization.

At a minimum, a plan for the purchase and installation of uninterruptible power supplies and surge suppressers and development of a policy for consistently backing up data should result from the discussion of securing data. An uninterruptible power supply (UPS) is an alternative power source which automatically provides power to computer hardware if the normal power source is interrupted. Usually the power is provided by batteries and is only sufficient to keep a computer operating for a short period of time. In that time, the computer systems should be shut down in an orderly manner. Surge suppressers protect computers from unexpected increases in voltage.

Backups require more effort. Critical data can be copied to various media, including tapes and diskettes. Backups should occur daily and weekly with at least one copy of the weekly backup stored someplace other than the agency's office. The offsite storage site should be accessible to more than one employee.

Backup also includes providing alternative processing sites. The identified critical systems should be able to be operated at a site other than the agency's office. If fire, flood, or other disaster should occur, the critical systems must continue to operate. A site, maybe at a vendor or at another agency, should be identified as a backup location. At that location you should be able to operate your systems on compatible computers.

Securing is also about protecting data from accidental or purposeful disclosure. Many nonprofit organizations, especially those providing human services, collect and maintain large stores of client-related data. Much of that data is of a confidential nature and is protected by laws and regulations. IRM planning should account for the kinds of data gathered and specify policies for the protection of that data.

(E) BUDGETING

Budgeting is an annual planning activity. It is important to IRM planning in that budgeting is the process through which the IRM plan is implemented.

Wilson (1996, 27) noted that the ongoing costs involved in information technology are critical because IT is not a onetime "buy and stop strategy." IRM planning must include the understanding that initial costs of hardware and software may be extensive. A proposal to purchase a client/server network, also known as a local area network, for five users may require a $17,000 initial invest. Applications software, accounting, payroll, client tracking, and other software, are additional costs. Other costs include service agreements, especially important if you do not have a technologist in your employment, training, software upgrades, and miscellaneous costs associated with storage media, printer cartridges, and the like.

The IRM plan should differentiate the investment aspects of IT from the ongoing costs of IT. Hardware and software are generally investments with a specified lifetime allowing for depreciation. The IRM plan should contain a statement to be used as part of the annual budget process which stipulates the depreciation period for these assets. The IRM plan should also acknowledge the existence of ongoing costs, particularly those for supporting the use of software. This will have the benefit of making sure that ongoing costs are considered in the evaluation of IT before its purchase.

22.5 *Implementing Information Technology*

The second ring of the IRM model in Exhibit 22.2 is implementing, which refers to both the IRM plan and the task of bringing information technology to the workplace. In this ring, managers must apply the priorities and goals of the IRM plan through the purchase and implementation of information technologies. A manager must be prepared to critically analyze specific work processes, determine which information technologies to apply to meet the goals of those processes, procure and install the hardware and software, and prepare employees to use them in a productive manner. The activities in implementing include analyzing, selecting, involving, and supporting.

(A) ANALYZING

The planning ring (Exhibit 22.2) deals with IT broadly with an organizationwide approach. The implementation ring deals with the specifics of individual systems and work processes. Analysis doesn't end with the IRM plan. Analysis must continue to examine the specific IT which can be applied in the workplace.

What should analyzing do for implementation? The simple answer is to provide a basis for determining which hardware and software systems should be implemented to carry out any particular work process in the organization. Analyzing involves the investigation of work processes, examining what work is done, how it gets done, where it gets done, what resources are needed to get it done, and who does it. The purpose is to identify where IT can benefit the work process by improving the productivity of individuals involved in that process and improving the use of information throughout the organization.

The outcome of analyzing is a list of requirements for a new IT and a set of goals for managing the implementation process. Requirements must completely specify what the new technology is to do—what inputs are needed to produce the desired outputs, what the outputs from the system should look like. The requirements also specify how the inputs are converted to outputs. The list of requirements becomes the blueprint from which the new system can be constructed.

Goals are vital to the effective management of the implementation of a new IT. There are many stories about the time and cost overruns for the introduction of new computer systems. Many of the overrun horrors can be avoided by specifying accurately what is to be achieved by the new IT, when it is to be achieved, and the cost of achievement.

(B) SELECTING

While selecting does involve the choice of hardware and software systems to implement, from a management point of view it is also the outcome of evaluating the proposal to implement a system. Selecting involves three components (Exhibit 22.4).

The first component, alignment, involves ascertaining if the proposed project is in line with the vision and goals of the IRM plan. The IRM plan specifies the technological direction of the organization. Use the plan to decide if a particular proposal for developing an IT makes sense given the formally developed and approved vision and goals. The second component, investment analysis, applies the IRM plan. The plan should specify criteria for evaluating the economic cost and benefit to be achieved by a system, as well as the goals of the organization. The goals are important for value analysis, to be discussed more fully below.

The final component is risk analysis. While a proposal may meet the criteria espoused in the IRM plan, there is still risk to developing that system. Project size, experience with technology, and project structure are part of the risk analysis (Cats-Baril and Thompson, 1996). Each component should be assessed separately than combined qualitatively into one generalized assessment.

The first component is project size. Project size refers to the cost, number of staff and functions involved in the project, and the length of time the project is expected to take to complete. The larger the project size (higher cost, larger number of staff involved, longer timeframe), the more risk that the project will run into implementation problems.

Experience with information technology is very important in assessing risk. The more familiar the organization is with the types of technology being installed—hardware, operating software, applications software, and so on—the less risky the project. If a new local area network is being installed in a nonprofit which previously used one computer for word processing, the risk is high. In this example, risk is high because the staff do not have experience managing network software, routing printer requests, accessing common files, and other network-related functions. While the risk can be overcome by hiring new staff, extensive training, and other interventions, the cost of the project and the likelihood that the benefits projected for the system will be achieved in the short term is low.

EXHIBIT 22.4 Selection Criteria in IRM Implementation

Component	Vital Questions
1. Alignment	Is the proposal aligned with the vision and goals defined in the IRM plan?
2. Investment Analysis	Does the project meet return on investment criteria? Does the project meet the qualitative goals established in the IRM plan?
3. Risk	Is the project too risky?

Finally, project structure refers to your ability as a manager to clearly identify the outcomes of the IT project prior to its start (Cats-Baril and Thompson, 1996). If as a manager you are comfortable that you understand what is involved from the analysis of the project (analyzing stage outcomes), the risk of the project will be low. If the analysis is vague or unclear, risk will be increased.

If the proposed project is aligned with the IRM plan, the investment analysis meets plan criteria, and the risk assessment suggests low risk, the project should get a conditional green light. Two more questions need to be addressed before giving a full green light to the project: Do we have the skills to carry out this project on our own and do we have the funds to carry out this project? For many community-based nonprofits, large IT projects will require the hiring of consultants. Consultants will bring the necessary skills to the project to ensure successful completion. They will increase the costs of implementation. The use of consultants will also increase the amount of management oversight necessary to ensure the project stays on track. Communications between the agency's project team and the consultant must occur regularly to ensure that project goals are achieved on a timely basis.

(C) INVOLVING

Involving requires that employees be part of the process of implementing IT. A large number of research studies have examined the value of participation and involvement in implementing new information technologies. The rationale for employees' involvement lies in the fact that managers are dependent upon subordinates to implement new information technologies and participation prepares individuals to implement decisions (Miller and Monge, 1986).

Increasing the number of opportunities to participate in implementation has three outcomes. Participation increases workers' understanding of a new IT through the dissemination of information about the IT and the reasons for changes. This will reduce uncertainty and anxiety. Participation will also bind end users to the use of the IT when their acts of participation are public, explicit, and irrevocable (Goodman, Griffith, and Fenner, 1990). This will have the affect of increasing individuals' commitment to use of the new system. Participation will also provide management with important information about the work processes and how they will be affected by new IT. Much knowledge about how work is completed, after all, is known and understood by line workers not managers.

Involvement should start at the beginning of any IT process. Ideally it should start with the IRM plan. Large committees often have difficulty completing work so that not every employee can or should be involved. Employees should be represented, however.

Employees should be involved in the process of selecting IT when their work will be directly affected by changes in technology. They should be given the opportunity to provide information about how current work processes are carried out and which technologies would be most useful in attaining the ends of the processes. The most successful implementation efforts occur when employees have input which is accepted, acknowledged, and visibly used by management.

(D) SUPPORTING

A computer manufacturer once touted the ease of using its product with a television commercial showing workers unfamiliar with computers coming into their office one morning with computers on their desks waiting to be unpacked and used. Management chose the easiest system to use so workers would have no fear and need no training. If it was only that easy! To be successful with IT, managers must support the introduction of new information technologies with training and create a general atmosphere of support within the organization which may extend as far as restructuring how work is completed.

Training is one very important, obvious but often overlooked requirement for new computer hardware and software installations. Training relates both to job-specific skills and to the general atmosphere of change which exists when new technologies are introduced. Employees should know how to turn on the hardware, how to boot up the software, and how to apply the software to their jobs. These requirements may require formal training programs, especially if new software is introduced. Training should also be used to specify to employees what behaviors are expected concerning the information technology, how they are expected to perform, and other issues related to productivity (Gattiker, 1990). This form of training shows how the new technology changes the organization's rules and procedures and how these affect work.

IT influences strategy and operations as well as being affected by strategy and operations. This interdependency is shown when organizations attempt to become more effective and efficient by using IT, yet do not reorganize the way work is done to take advantage of the capabilities of IT. Do not install a system to complete work exactly as it is now done! The communications capabilities of IT make it possible to greatly improve the effectiveness and efficiencies of work processes. But to take advantage of these capabilities, work processes need to be examined and altered. Employees' job descriptions may also need to be changed to reflect the new way in which work is being completed.

Overall support by management is important when introducing new IT. Managers support implementation of new information technologies by providing an environment in which subordinates can use the behaviors and skills learned in training (Fossum, 1990). Supportive environments occur when full information is shared about upcoming changes with those being affected by change. By providing full information, managers modify unrealistic expectations held by users (Rice et al., 1990). Employees who perceive management as being supportive are more likely to understand the effect of a new technology on their work and to be more aware of ways of dealing with the uncertainties of its implementation process. This should lead to a group of employees who are more productive with the new technologies than they would be if not so prepared.

22.6   Evaluating the Value of Information Technology

Was the investment in that new server worth it? How do you know? Could we better use our money and time elsewhere? These are the basic questions of evaluating the value of IT. The basic assumptions of evaluation are that both financial and human resources are limited so that decisions to implement specific information technologies must be made wisely.

While the process of evaluation has its own ring on the diagram (Exhibit 22.2), it overlaps with the other rings and begins in the planning ring. Evaluation takes place both before and after implementation.

There are two general methodologies for determining the value of an IT investment. The first is return on investment analysis; the second is value analysis, a qualitative approach to determining the value of an IT investment. Both of these methods are applied before and after implementation of new information technologies. Before implementation, the results of these analyses can be used to choose one IT for investment over others. After implementation, these tools can be used to determine if goals have been achieved and to provide feedback for improving the selection process in the future.

(A)   OBSERVING

Successful evaluation and assessment of IRM requires a set of standards to act as bases of comparisons and to guide collection of data for that comparison. Observing, therefore, begins with planning and requires effort during implementation.

As part of IRM planning, standards for evaluation must be set. Two sets of standards are needed—quantitative and qualitative.

Quantitative standards are needed for assessing the financial return of investments in IT. This is the basis of return on investment analysis. The quantitative standard may be tied to the rate of return on savings, investments, or other instruments designated by the agency. It should be a standard set in consultation with the board of directors which has fiduciary responsibility for the organization.

Qualitative standards are somewhat easier to come by. As part of IRM planning, goals are established and prioritized. These goals, and the priority assigned to them, are the qualitative standards for IT investment and assessment. These are specific standards about the value of IT to the organization. They need to be applied to allocation decisions and post-implementation review of investments.

Observing requires that the quantitative and qualitative standards be applied. When making the choices about which systems to implement, observing requires that the quantitative values for the cost and expected benefits of the technologies under review be set. Observing requires that each IT presented for development justify itself based upon the specific goals established in IRM planning. By comparing the results of observations, choices about IT investments can be made. By comparing expectations with actual outcomes of IT investment, feedback can be attained to improve the investment process.

(B)   COMPARING

As noted previously, there are two methods for comparing outcomes of IT investments—return on investment analysis and value analysis.

Return on Investment Analysis (ROI)

The most widely used method for evaluating IT investments is ROI analysis. Using this method, one compares the lifetime benefits, or savings, of alternative solutions based on a percentage rate that represents the expected return on the cost of implementing a new technology. This approach requires comparing the ROI ratio established within the IRM planning process to the estimates of return developed as part of the implementation process.

The formula for an ROI calculation is:

$$ROI = \left(\frac{Benefits - Costs}{Costs}\right) \times 100$$

where, *benefits* are the improvements expected from the IT in business operations, and *costs* include the initial costs associated with the development and implementation of the IT, including costs associated with converting from one system to another, and training and operating costs, including costs of personnel, supplies, maintenance, and so on.

ROI analysis requires that all costs and benefits be measurable and that a dollar value can be assigned to them. The dollar value provides a common basis so that comparisons can take place with a set standard and with a ratio determined for other IT investments. The largest ROI ratio indicates the best return on the dollars invested in an IT.

The most difficult aspect of using ROI analysis is projecting costs and benefits to use in comparing investments. Costs are often straightforward, except that some effort needs to be made to be all-inclusive in estimating them. Measuring benefits can be straightforward if the costs of existing systems and processes are being supplanted by the new IT. However, many benefits are intangible, making it difficult to accurately determine the return on investment.

Value Analysis

The focus of value analysis is to measure the value of intangible aspects of implementing an IT. There are compelling benefits to investing in IT that defy the assignment of a number or dollar figure. These benefits can't be quantified. To assess them, qualitative standards must be used for comparison. The basic question in value analysis is "How effectively do IT investments help the organization meet its goals?"

Previously, the standards of value analysis were noted to be the goals and priorities established in IRM planning. To conduct value analysis, one must ask if the proposed technology will advance the goals established in the agency's IT portfolios. There should exist direct links between the goals and the IT. If these links aren't there or if they aren't strong, the investment should be questioned.

An example of justifying an IT investment with IRM planning goals can be seen with the development of a program to put computers into childcare classrooms (Exhibit 22.3). Justification, in part, is based upon the organization's goals "To bring age-appropriate computer software into the classroom (a curriculum-related goal)" and "To plan and implement program enhancements, such as new center openings, programs, and add new offerings within center programs (an organizational strategy goal)." Putting computers with age-appropriate software into preschool classrooms is consistent with the curriculum goal. Furthermore, as a new offering within existing childcare centers, the initiative would be consistent with the organizational strategy goal.

After implementation, a similar activity of review should be undertaken. Assuming the investment decision was based upon value analysis, the actual outcomes of the IT's implementation should be reviewed to determine if the IT achieved the goals from the IRM plan upon which it was justified. Unlike ROI analysis, this will be a more difficult task requiring a close examination of what has happened to work processes, client outcomes, and worker outcomes. In our example of the computers-in-the classroom initiative, a postimplementation evaluation would examine whether the software used was age appropriate and consistent with the curriculum in place for those students. That examination would also attempt to determine if the computers as a new offering made a difference in terms of keeping children enrolled and enrolling new children in the program.

(C) CONCLUDING

Once the data has been collected (observing) and the methods applied (comparing), conclusions about the reasonableness of the IT investment must be drawn. There are two tasks associated with concluding the evaluation of IT. The first task involves balancing the results of ROI and value analyses. The second involves using the results to better the process of IRM and better the implementation of information technologies.

Which is more important—the return on investment or the value analysis? This is a question which must be decided by each agency as part of its IRM process. A balance needs to be determined to allow conclusions about the usefulness and reasonableness of the investment in IT. That balance can be assessed by answering these questions:

- *Are the outcomes of the two analyses consistent with each other?* If similar conclusions are reached by both sets of analyses, your job of concluding is fairly straightforward. If dissimilar results are found, further analysis will be required.
- *Are the outcomes consistent with the organizational vision for using information technology?* The IRM planning process should specify a vision for the use of IT. Comparing outcomes with this vision will provide another perspective on the value of the IT to the organization.
- *Is the proposed investment, or the outcomes, consistent with the organization's broad strategy?* Finally, the organization's broad strategy should be brought to bear on the question. IRM assumes that managing information as a resource is a key for achieving organizational goals. If the outcomes from an IT project are consistent with the direction of the organization's broad strategy, that project would appear to have value to the organization.

Feedback is another important reason for concluding the evaluation. Feedback is important for learning from the experience of implementing a new system. Feedback should occur at two levels. The first is to improve the IRM process to benefit future implementations. Better estimates of time, effort, and resources needed will result from applying past experience to new IT efforts. The feedback will also help to clarify and improve the IRM planning process. At the second level, feedback will also be useful for tweaking the IT just implemented to improve its outcomes. The evaluation process may show that the reason expected outcomes were not achieved was because of a training failure. Not only will this information improve future implementations, it can be used to establish a retraining program for employees using the system to improve current outcomes.

22.7 Getting Ready to Use IRM

(A) STRATEGIC PLANNING

Briefly, a strategic plan is the precursor for IRM. Information technology is a tool which is meant to further organizational goals. Information, the resource managed with IRM, is vital to understanding the environments of organizations—internal and external. Unless that information is managed so as to achieve organizational goals, it will be of minimal value. Yes, the bills will be paid and revenue collected. However, the additional value of information, that value from using it to support services and create new services, will not be reached. Without a clear understanding of organizational goals, IRM cannot be beneficial to an organization.

(B) LEADERSHIP AND BOARD INVOLVEMENT

Leadership is important for establishing and institutionalizing the IRM effort in a nonprofit organization. Leadership must occur at two levels—executive management and the board.

Many private, for-profit organizations hire chief information officers (CIOs) to manage information in their organizations. These people are knowledgeable about computers and management. They frequently report directly to the chief executive officer so that IT has a very visible role in the organization. This degree of formal leadership is not often possible for nonprofit organizations which face restrictions in resources. Someone in a leadership role with management responsibilities and interests in IT is important in order for IRM to occur in nonprofits.

This leadership is necessary for communicating the need to change the way work is done, for initiating and facilitating that change, and for taking the responsibility for meeting the IT needs of people within the organization. These activities set the tone for IRM and the use of IT within the organization. They communicate what is needed and what is expected of people within the organization with respect to IT. One individual, preferably the executive director, must take on the responsibility for initiating IRM and seeing that it is carried through.

The governing board must also take a leadership role. The board of a nonprofit organization establishes overall policy for the organization. The board is involved in the strategic planning process and approves the final result of that process. Including the board in IRM efforts, particularly planning, insures the strategy of the organization is taken into account. The board also approves annual budgets for the organization. Gathering board participation for IRM will create board support for the expenditures on IT that will appear in annual budgets.

For smaller nonprofits in particular, board participation may be vital for acquiring the necessary skills and understanding to make the IRM process work. While the necessary skills may not be available among employees, they may be available through the board. Including board members as part of an IRM team, formally and informally, will bring these skills into the process.

(C) INVOLVING STAFF

Previously the importance of involving employees in the implementation aspects of IRM was stressed. That participation is important for communicating to employees about the process of change, its importance, and their role in it. Involvement in the overall IRM process is equally important.

Involvement of employees is important for the IRM process. One person cannot carry out the whole IRM process because of its complexity. One person does not know all of the work processes and information needs of the organization. Involvement of employees helps to incorporate complexity and breadth into the IRM effort. That involvement will also bring the variety of individual skills held by employees to bear in solving problems that have surfaced in the IRM effort. This is one important practical outcome of involvement.

Another vital outcome is getting employees' understanding of and commitment to the IRM process. Information is an organizationwide resource which is the responsibility of all members of the organization. By involving employees, the concept of information as a resource will be communicated and understood. With that understanding will come the commitment to acquire and use information to meet organizational goals.

22.8   Conclusion

Information resources management (IRM) is a set of processes and techniques for managing information in organizations. It is a concept which becomes useful to managers of nonprofit organizations as they come to accept information as a key resource for their work. As a key resource, information must be organized and managed for it to be useful. IRM provides meaning to information so that it can be used to manage nonprofits, plan their activities, and provide their services. This chapter was built on the concept that three processes—planning, implementing, and evaluating—need to be managed to make information valuable to support the work of nonprofit organizations.

IRM can be presented as a way of organizing the whole work of a nonprofit organization. After all, each activity of service creates information so that information is pervasive in the organization. IRM, however, is only a tool. It is a tool to organize investments in IT so that the goals of the nonprofit organization are achieved. It guides investment decisions, draws attention to problems and issues of implementation, and provides for feedback so that future IRM endeavors can be improved.

This chapter has focused on the importance of information as a key resource and on the need to manage information as such. Not all of the issues and techniques will fit all nonprofits. Others not discussed here, such as process reengineering, should also be examined for use. There are many other sources of information and applications in IRM available to you as well. As a nonprofit manager, you need to be familiar with the concepts of information management so that you can organize your agency's use of information. To do so you need to choose the tools that fit you and your agency best. The purpose of this chapter was to help you to organize that effort.

Suggested Readings

Buckland, M. 1991. *Information and Information Systems*. New York: Greenwood Press.

Cats-Baril, W. and Thompson, R. 1996. "Managing Information Technology Projects in the Public Sector." *Public Administration Review*, 55(6); 599–566.

Chaiklin, S. 1991. "Using Computers in Community Educational Programs." In J. Downing, R. Fasano, P. A. Firedland, M. F. McCullough, T. Mizrahi, and

J. J. Shapiro, eds., *Computers for Social Change and Community Organizing*. New York: Haworth Press, pp. 73–87.

Dula, M. D. 1995, May 17. "Planning—Yes [electronic issues thread]." Center for Information Systems Management, University of Texas at Austin. Available WWW: http://cism.bus.utexas.edu/issues/issue48/comment1.html.

Fossum, J.A. 1990. "New Dimensions in the Design and Delivery of Corporate Training Programs." in L. A., Ferman, M. Hoyman, J. Cutcher-Gershenfeld, and E. J. Savoie, eds., *New Developments in Worker Training: A Legacy for the 1990s*. Madison, WI; Industrial Relations Research Association, pp. 129–156.

Gattiker, U.E. 1990. "Computer Skills Acquisition: A Review and Future Directions for Research," *Journal of Management*, 18(2); 547–574.

Goodman, P. S., Griffith, T. L., and Fenner, D. B. 1990. "Understanding Technology and the Individual in an Organizational Context," In P. S. Goodman, L. S. Sproull and Associates, eds., *Technology and Organizations*. San Francisco, Jossey-Bass, pp. 45–86.

Hammer, M. and Champy, J. 1993. *Reengineering the Corporation: A Manifesto for Business Revolution*. New York: HarperBusiness.

Hares, J. and Royle, D. 1994. *Measuring the Value of Information Technology*. Chichester: Wiley.

Lewis, B. R., Snyder, C. A., and Rainer, R. K., Jr. 1995. "An Empirical Assessment of the Information Resource Management Construct." *Journal of Management Information Systems*, 12(1); 199–223.

Linden, R. M. 1994. *Seamless Government: A Practical Guide to Re-engineering in the Public Sector*. San Francisco: Jossey-Bass.

Miller, K. I. and Monge, P. R.. 1986. "Participation, Satisfaction, and Productivity: A Meta-analytic Review." *Academy of Management Journal*, 29; 727–753.

Neuman, S. 1994. *Strategic Information Systems: Competition through Information Technologies*. New York: Macmillan College Publishing.

Osterman, P. 1991. "The Impact of IT on Jobs and Skills." In M. S. Scott Morton, ed., *The Corporation of the 1990s: Information Technology and Organizational Transformation*. New York: Oxford University Press, pp. 220–243.

Rabin, J. and Jackowski, E. M., eds. 1988. *Handbook of Information Resource Management*. New York: Marcel Dekker.

Rice, R. E., Grant, A. E., Schmitz, J., and Torobin, J. 1990. "Individual and Network Influences on the Adoption and Perceived Outcomes of Electronic Messaging," *Social Networks* (12); 27–55.

Scott Morton, M. S., ed. 1991. *The Corporation of the 1990s: Information Technology and Organizational Transformation*. New York: Oxford University Press.

van den Hoven, J. 1995. "IRM: An Enterprisewide View of Data," *Information Systems Management*. 12(3); 69–72.

Wilson, C. 1996. "The Right Approach Assures the Right Choices. Focus on Technology Planning." *Contributions*, 10(3); 21, 24, 27.

23 Navigating the Internet for Nonprofits

ROBBIN ZEFF, PhD
The Zeff Group

23.1   Introduction

As a society we are fully engaged in the technological age. This technological revolution is not only changing the way America does business, but the way the entire world communicates, exchanges information, and purchases goods and services. Computers are a key aspect of communication—locally, nationally, and internationally. If an organization fails to incorporate new technology into daily operations, an organization risks not only being outdated, but also being unable to function in today's computer-centered work and home environment.

The nonprofit community continues to evolve and struggle with the pressing issues facing society today: We must work harder; we must work smarter. On-line (connection to the Internet) access is a tool that will enable your organization to be more efficient and effective. In short, going on-line will make your organization work smarter.

The press today bombards the public with *whiz-bang* articles about the Internet and the activities of the on-line revolution. There is no question that on-line activity is destined to increase. For the nonprofit organization, the decision to go on-line is no longer a matter of "if" but of "when" and "how." While the Internet may drastically change over the next few years, an organization that takes initial steps toward involvement today will ensure success.

The following chapter is divided into eight sections. Section 23.2, "Navigating the Internet," provides a tour of the on-line world. Section 23.3, "Benefits of Going On-line," outlines the advantages of putting an organization on-line. "Preparing the Organization for the Information Superhighway" addresses important questions that the nonprofit must tackle in the initial states of making certain an office is ready to operate and excel in this unique environment. Section 23.5 is a "Technical Audit" that analyzes equipment and software requirements. The next two sections discuss the premier functions of on-line activity—exchanging and gathering information—as they affect and benefit the nonprofit community. Section 23.8, "CyberFund-Raising," explores the huge potential of fund raising on the Internet. Finally, one of the key applications of the Internet is the World Wide Web. "Establishing Your Presence on the World Wide Web" examines the issues involved in developing a strategic plan for your Web presence.

23.2   Navigating the Internet

To best understand the concept of being on-line, and to take full advantage of all it has to offer, it is important to first understand some of the fundamentals.

(A)   THE INTERNET

The Internet is not a thing or a place; rather, it is a cooperative computer networking effort that spans the globe. The underlining principle behind the Internet was born during the cold war when the Department of Defense sought a communication system that would survive a nuclear confrontation. The thinking went that if a communication network in its entirety is innately unreliable in such a situation, then a system needs to be designed where each contributing part of the whole must be able to function independently in the tasks of sending, receiving, and storing information. In this way, each packet of information would travel the network independently like a giant game of hot potato, the packet always staying airborne, so that the dismantling of any computer or computer network would never destroy the traveling information packet's ability to reach its destination. This general concept served as the defining structure behind the development of the communication network of all networks that eventually became known as the Internet.

Today the Internet connects some 45,000 independent computer networks linked worldwide and is growing at a rate of 10 percent per month. This translates into roughly 30 million people using the Internet worldwide. The Internet is not owned by any one person, company, or country, nor is it managed by any one group or organized body. And yet, the computers networked on the Internet communicate via an agreed-upon and consistent protocol of operation.

There are many components to the Internet. One can use the Internet to send electronic mail (called e-mail); move files from one location to another (called ftp for file transfer protocol); or explore the multimedia capabilities of the World Wide Web.

(B)　E-MAIL

E-mail is mail sent over a computer network, like the Internet. Via e-mail, messages can be sent from one computer user to another anywhere in the world, usually within minutes. If a user is not at his or her computer, the mail is stored and can be read at any time. It is so fast and convenient that computer users refer to regular mail as *snail mail*. It is estimated that more than 30 million people worldwide have an e-mail address, making e-mail the most utilized application of the Internet.

E-mail addresses vary considerably. The most common Internet address includes the individual's first initial and up to seven characters of his or her last name. This is followed by the @ symbol, meaning *at*, which is followed by the domain name, the location of the individual's e-mail account. For example, the President of the United States has the e-mail address *president@whitehouse.gov*. Another format for e-mail addresses used by commercial services consists of a series of numbers instead of an individual's name. For example, a sample e-mail address from CompuServe might read 12345.6789@compuserve.com.

(C)　FTP SITES

In addition to short e-mail messages, entire files can be transferred over the Internet. *File Transfer Protocol (ftp)* is a means to transfer files of information from an off-site database or server to a user's computer.

(D)　THE WORLD WIDE WEB

The World Wide Web is the premier feature of the Internet. It offers vast amounts of information in easily accessible text and graphics format. For this reason, it is very appealing. Documents on the Web are viewed through a browser, which is special software that translates the hypertext markup languages (html) used on the Web.

(i)　Understanding a Web Address

The addressing system for the Web is called Uniform Resource Locator (URL) (see Exhibit 23.1). The URL tells the computer what type of protocol is being used, where the

EXHIBIT 23.1 The Anatomy of a Web Address

Http://www2.whitehouse.gov/WH/Welcome.html

  1   2   3   4   5

1. The first letters in a URL address indicate the type of protocol being used. There are various options: *http* indicates the World Wide Web, *FTP* is for files, and *news* is for UseNet newsgroups.
2. Tells the type of service. WWW stands for World Wide Web.
3. This is the location of the site.
4. This indicates the domain type. The White House is a government site.
5. The name of this particular page, indicating it is an HTML document.

site is located, and what type of site is being summoned. For example, the address [http://www2.whitehouse.gov/WH/Welcome.html] would bring the user to the White House Web site. A Web address is made up of several parts. The first tells the browser what type of protocol is being used. In this address it is "http" (hypertext transport protocol), the commonly accepted protocol for transporting hypertext documents on the Web. The "www2" stands for the World Wide Web. "Whitehouse" is the name of the site and the suffix "gov" indicates that this is a government site. The remainder of the address "/WH/Welcome.html" identifies the location of the document on the server and the type of document, that is, the suffix ".html" shows that the document is composed in html (hypertext markup language), the text editing system used on the Web.

(ii)   Home Page

Home page is the name given to the first page of a site. This page welcomes the user to the site and offers basic information concerning what the site has to offer. Exhibit 23.1 is the home page of the White House Web site.

(iii)   Links

The Web consists of tens of thousands of sites connected by links, also known as hypertext links, which allow one to move from site to site. A link is easily visible on the Web because it appears in a different-color text (the most common is blue) and is underlined. A link tells the computer to travel to the address of that site when the user points and clicks on the link.

23.3   Benefits of Going On-Line

The technological revolution is changing not only the way America does business, but also the way the entire world communicates, exchanges information, and purchases goods and services. There are three important reasons why an organization should go on-line. First is the fact that the Internet enhances an organization's ability to communicate with its members, its staff, and the general public. Second, the Internet provides incredible access to information from around the world. Third, the Internet is an exciting new fund-raising medium.

(A)   ABILITY TO COMMUNICATE

The Internet is a remarkably flexible and diverse outreach vehicle that will expand your organization's ability to communicate internally and externally. "It is another tool to help us to get our message across," says Ray Mitchell of Amnesty International. "The big difference is that this tool allows us to reach tens of thousands of people very quickly and for very little cost." Being on-line establishes a 24-hours-a-day, 365-days-a-year location where anyone can access information about an organization directly from that organization. Users who may never have heard of your organization before can directly interact with you at their own convenience.

(B)   ABILITY TO GATHER INFORMATION

Being on-line provides an organization with access to information unconstrained by its physical proximity. Once on-line, one can access or exchange information as easily with a person or site in Paris, Texas as in Paris, France. And without a doubt, being able to provide information quickly will help you better service your clients.

The information available through the Internet includes searchable databases, directories, bibliographies, dictionaries, and resource lists. Most major university library card catalogs are on-line as well as the Library of Congress. Some are text only, but more and more on-line information appears through the Web with its elaborate text and graphic capabilities. Whether one is doing prospect research on a foundation or a corporation, scanning newspaper articles on a particular policy issue, or gathering data on a specific illness, the Internet allows you to do global research from the comfort of your home or office computer with material immediately retrievable and downloadable.

(C) FUND-RAISING POTENTIAL

The Internet has the potential to start a revolution in the area of fund raising. With the number of people connected to the Internet growing at a feverish pace, the Internet provides the nonprofit community with the ability to reach a mass audience for fund-raising purposes quickly and cost effectively.

(D) ORGANIZATIONAL DEVELOPMENT

Putting your organization on-line boosts staff morale by providing training and expertise on new technologies that are taking the business world by storm. Additionally, the ease and convenience of on-line access as well as cost and time saving attributes accentuates job performance and efficiency.

23.4 Preparing Your Organization for the Information Superhighway

Technological change can be scary. But the true phenomenon of the Internet is not so much about technology as it is about building relationships and connecting communities beyond geographical barriers. In fact, the Internet is now being called a "relationship technology." There are three components to preparing your organization for a strong on-line presence.

(A) MENTALLY

Building the technological infrastructure of your organization enhances it in every aspect. A good internal computer system connected to a strong on-line presence does not mean that your organization is losing touch with those it serves. Rather, it is maximizing its available communication tools to better service its constituents. Without a doubt, the Internet will never replace the personal side of organizing and outreach. Instead, the Internet helps amplify outreach. Robert B. Tewes, Webmaster of Taxpayers Against Fraud, finds that "the Internet allows nonprofit organizations, or any organization for that matter, to disseminate their message to a potential audience numbering in the millions." The expansive reach of the Internet to a global audience provides unprecedented exposure for the nonprofit community. Moreover, this outreach vehicle is immediate and inexpensive in relation to the short- and long-term benefits.

(B) FINANCIALLY

Purchasing and maintaining a computer system for your organization is a financial commitment. Computer technology changes rapidly and is not a onetime-only investment. A computer system purchased today will become increasingly out of date with each passing year. Therefore, once you enter the information age and purchase computers, you need to commit to systematically upgrading the system both in terms of hardware and software as the technology dictates.

However, there are many means to help defray the costs of building the technological infrastructure of an organization. Computer companies like to coordinate their philanthropic activities with their business interests. For example, Apple Computers has a long history of donating computers to nonprofit organizations. One should pursue such donations from other hardware manufacturers as well. Software manufacturers have similar programs. There are also organizations in place that work to distribute computer equipment—hardware and software—to the nonprofit community. And volunteer labor to build and maintain a web site can also help defray costs.

(C) ORGANIZATIONALLY

Once you make the decision to put your organization on-line, several key issues must be addressed:

- *Access*—Will everyone in the organization have on-line access? In other words, should every computer be fully equipped for Internet connection? For many organizations, this will be a financial decision based upon equipment availability and equipment purchasing ability. The more people in your organization who communicate on-line and use on-line resources, the more on-line communication will become part of your organizational culture.
- *Training*—Training is key for successful incorporation of on-line activities into your organization. Today, a plethora of Internet workshops are available at local nonprofit training centers, such as the Support Centers of America, to local colleges and computer training centers. Moreover, with computers, as with any skills-building experience, one learns by doing. Whether one is learning a new software program or trying to navigate the Internet, the best way to learn is by practicing. Staff will need time to explore and expand their personal capabilities in cyberspace. This will be time well spent, because a comfortable and knowledgeable Web surfer will be able to navigate the Internet more effectively and efficiently.
- *Use Policy*—The issue of an office Internet use policy may present itself because of the high entertainment value of the World Wide Web and the tendency for people to exchange personal e-mail messages as well as work-related ones. Most organizations have an official or unofficial in-house policy dealing with personal use of office equipment, such as the telephone, fax, computers, and copy machines. In fact, for many nonprofits, the unofficial policy is merely not to abuse the privilege of access and use. For many, a separate Internet policy is unnecessary, for issues of Internet use are covered under the professional office protocol standards already in place.

23.5 *Technical Audit*

The reason on-line activity has grown so rapidly over the past few years is the ease of access and use. Very little is required to go on-line, send e-mail, navigate the Web, or set up your own Web site. The following section describes specifically what you will need to go on-line in terms of hardware, software, and connection services.

(A) HARDWARE

Many computer manufacturers are designing computers with the Internet in mind. With today's computer applications, the faster the computer the better. This means they include speakers and a graphics and sound card as well as high-speed processors and at least 16 MB of RAM or more. In buying an office personal computer, think about the applications for which the computer will be used. This is especially important considering that the average life span of a personal computer is two to three years before it is out of date. The price of computers seems to stay around $2,000–$2,500 with more features being added with each passing year.

(i) Monitor

A color monitor is best to easily recognize links and display graphics. While monitors vary in price, the rule of thumb is the better the monitor, the clearer the presentation. Color monitors start at around $200.

(ii) Modem

Because of exponentially increasing on-line use, major developments are being made to improve modems. As of this printing, 28,000 (28.8) KB baud rate modems are commonly used. The baud rate determines the speed of the modem in reading and transmitting data. Many new computer packages include modems. The price for a 28.8 KB averages around $200.

(iii) Printer

A printer is not required but is useful. It is very convenient to download information and print it for reading at a later time. Some on-line services charge a per-hour fee for usage commonly referred to as connect time. Printing documents can save on connect time, reducing on-line costs. For quality printing, laser printers are becoming the standard. Prices vary considerably, with the price of a personal laser printer usually starting at around $400.

(B) SOFTWARE

The software needed to go on-line ranges from communication software to Internet-specific applications. Many computer packages are now including Internet-related software. This software ranges from modem software to communication software that dials the Internet. A list of such software is provided in the on-line checklist in Exhibit 23.2.

(i) Browser

The most discussed piece of software for the Internet is the browser. A browser is a user or client program which interprets and provides the environment in which the user navigates the Web. It allows the user to access and search on the Internet by inputting different URL addresses. It also prints, saves, places bookmarks, sends e-mail, and performs numerous other tasks. Netscape and Microsoft Internet Explorer are among the most popular browsers.

EXHIBIT 23.2 On-Line Checklist

Hardware:
Computer (minimum 486 and 8 MB)
Monitor (color recommended)
Modem (minimum 14.4 Kbps)
Access provider or on-line service
Phone line

Software:
Communications software—Dialer
    Merit Network's MacPPP 2.0.1 (ftp://ftp.merit.edu/internet.tools/ppp
    InterCon Systems' InterSLIP (ftp://ftp.intercon.com)
Browser software
    Netscape Software (http://home.netscape.com/comprod/mirror/index.html)
    NCSA Mosaic (http://www.ncsa.uiuc.edu/SDG/Software/Mosaic/NCSAMosaicHome.html)
E-mail software
    Pegasus Mail version 2.01 (ftp://ftp.let.rug.nl/pub/pmail/winpm201.zip)
    Eudora Light (http://www.qualcomm.com/quest/light.html)

(C) GETTING CONNECTED

The Internet is the backbone of the on-line world. To get directly connected to the Internet, you can join an Internet Service Provider (ISP) which provides direct dial-up Internet access. ISPs can be found with a local, regional, or national focus in dialup accessibility. There are also independent commercial on-line bulletin board services which, in addition to providing Internet access, offer proprietary services and material unavailable elsewhere; among the largest of these are America On-line and CompuServe. It is through one of these options that one jumps on the on-ramp of the information superhighway.

23.6 *Exchanging Information*

When computers first exploded onto the scene, they were primarily used for processing information—from numbers to words. Now computers influence how we communicate and with whom we communicate. From sending e-mail messages to accessing information from a database located on the other side of the world, on-line technology offers the nonprofit a wealth of capabilities that make an organization more efficient and better informed.

(A) COMMUNICATION DEVICES

The Internet offers your organization a wealth of outreach devices to contact and communicate. These devices include:

- e-mail
- electronic publishing

- mailing lists
- UseNet newsgroups
- Bulletin boards

It is these tools and the audiences they serve to connect that comprise the dynamic communication component of the Internet for nonprofits.

(i) E-mail Database

With over 30 million people actively using e-mail, one of the richest resources of information on the Internet are the users themselves. There is no doubt that e-mail addresses will become as pervasive as phone and fax numbers in the near future. In no time at all, e-mail databases will be as valuable to an organization in its outreach efforts as a mailing list is today.

(ii) Mailing Lists

A mailing list (commonly referred to as a list or a discussion group) is a discussion carried on by a group of people through e-mail. The beauty of a mailing list is that you only have to send your message to the mailing list administrator for the message to be automatically sent to all members of the list. You receive mailing list messages just as you would any e-mail. It is up to you to choose to send a message, reply, or just observe.

Mailing lists are wonderful resources because they allow you to contact and connect with people with similar interests. There are thousands of mailing lists on every topic from bike touring to folklore. Two mailing lists of particular interest to the nonprofit community include:

- Prspct-l—A mailing list about prospect research and donor cultivation. To subscribe, send an email message to *listserv@bucknell.edu*. The message should read, *subscribe prspct-l* followed by your first and last name.
- Talk-amphilrev—A mailing list of general interest to those in the nonprofit area and fund-raising field. To subscribe, send an email message to *majordomo@tab.com*. The message should read, *subscribe talk-amphilrev*.

(iii) Bulletin Boards

A Bulletin board system (BBS) is a single computer or a network of computers that people dial into via a modem. The difference between a bulletin board and the Internet is that with a bulletin board all users must dial into the same designated and stationary server. Some BBSs have a gateway to the Internet so that users can send e-mail via the Internet and connect to the World Wide Web, but most are freestanding entities that are available either at no cost or for an hourly or monthly fee. With the Internet, once the user is connected to the network she or he can go to any location at any time. America On-line, CompuServe, and so on are examples of large and elaborate bulletin boards, but many exist that are only available through one local number.

(iv) UseNet Newsgroups

UseNet is an Internet application organized by topics called newsgroups. Newsgroups are ongoing discussions where participants post messages called articles. A person can visit a newsgroup at any point and jump into the discussion by posting an article. A newsgroup is not live, but rather a board where messages are posted.

Newsgroups are an invaluable resource for quick answers to questions from a community of experts. A newsgroup is an interactive communication model that flows from idea to idea mirroring the dynamic nature of conversation. Newsgroups represent one of the oldest applications on the Internet. They are an open and dynamic channel for the exchange of ideas between people with similar interests. Initially, newsgroups emerged on college campuses to facilitate the exchange of scholarship. Soon the concept was adopted by the general Internet community and used as an informal vehicle to discuss everything from recipes to pet care.

The topic of the newsgroup is reflected in its naming. The name is done in a hierarchical system similar to e-mail and URL addresses. The primary newsgroup for nonprofits is *soc.org.nonprofit*. Newsgroup addresses move from general to specific. Soc.org.nonprofit is a *soc* (for social issues) newsgroup that discusses the topic of *org* (for organizations) specifically related to the *nonprofit* community.

(v)   Electronic Publishing

The Internet presents a dynamic venue to develop and disseminate information, from magazines and newsletters, to press releases and reports. Electronic publishing allows a nonprofit to publish material without the expense of printing and postage. "Unfortunately funds for production and mailing of a print piece are not so readily available as they once were, which sent me in search of alternative ways to keep the information flowing at less cost," says John Bancroft, Senior Editor at the Office of Arid Lands Studies at the University of Arizona. On-line distribution provides the option for an interested party to download the publication as a file instead of receiving a hard copy via the U.S. postal service.

(B)   INTERNET COMMUNICATION IN ACTION

How can you use the Internet as a communication vehicle? Below are just a few of the possibilities:

- *Membership Recruitment*—The Internet is a tremendous outreach vehicle for your organization to present its mission, programs, and services to interested persons, potential members, and contributors. On your Web site, you can ask users to join your organization immediately after you have serviced their information request.
- *Job Announcements*—One can use the Internet to advertise and look for job openings.
- *Volunteer Recruitment*—The Internet is turning into fertile ground for volunteer recruitment and utilization.
- *Advocacy on the Internet*—The Internet offers an organization the ability to inform members and interested persons on how to take action from the statehouse to Capitol Hill by sending e-mailing messages or signing an on-line petition.

23.7   *Gathering Information*

(A)   INFORMATION AS A TOOL

Gathering information on the Internet allows an organization to keep its finger on the pulse of America and the world through a few strokes on a keyboard. The Internet is an incredible resource which makes information easily and quickly accessible. Yet, there is no defined organization or structure to that information. There is no definitive card catalog or list of lists to the Web, no all-encompassing phonebook or directory that serves as a road map to all sites available. Moreover, the Web is constantly growing, changing, and evolving. There are, however, tools and applications that compensate for the lack of internal linear order in the Internet.

(i)   Search Tools
The Internet has a variety of means to search for Web sites available to the user. Most are free, although commercial fee-based versions are quickly emerging. A search tool is a general term used to denote a site or an application that assists shuffling through the massive amount of information accessible through the Web. A search engine is the software that actually conducts the search. There are Web sites that consist solely of a keyword search engine that assists one in locating sites. Such sites include Lycos (http://www.lycos.com) and WebCrawler (http://www.Webcrawler.com). Other sites are indices of sites that have a search engine feature that assist in locating a site listed in the index. The premiere example is Yahoo (http://www.yahoo.com), considered one of the most popular sites on the Web today.

For the most part, these tools are restricted to subject searches using a word or group of words relative to the topic. Many of them use the if-then Boolean search method. The word or group of words is entered into a keyword field and the search engine then searches for uses of the word in site descriptions. Results appear showing the number of hits, or sites found, which make reference to the search word(s), usually with a description of the site. The name of the site most often appears in hypertext so the user can easily link to the site directly. Keywords provide an easy and quick means of searching vast databases. Word matches are found and the file is displayed for the user, similar to a subject search in a library card catalog.

(B)   RESOURCES ON THE INTERNET

Resources on the Internet of interest to the nonprofit field come in a variety of types and formats. Nonprofits are now putting up their own home pages as public awareness and fund-raising vehicles. In terms of fund raising, an organization can find a wealth of fund-raising information on the Web from foundation grants to funding resource centers. In addition, many corporations have Web sites with a wealth of information about their philanthropic and marketing interests. Finally, one can use the Internet as a reference library, looking up magazine articles, government documents, and specific research material. What makes on-line resources so valuable is the immediacy of acquisition and the contemporaneous nature of the material, often not available through other means.

23.8   CyberFund-Raising

Whether sending a solicitation by e-mail or requesting contributions on a home page, cyberfund-raising is a medium with extreme potential. Depending upon approach and intentions, visitors to a nonprofit's site can be asked for donations, membership, action, or opinion on an issue. These activities will bring the individual into the nonprofit's arena and can, in time, promote additional participation and contributions. Whether it is the Sierra Club selling merchandise or advertising wilderness adventures on their Web site or the American Red Cross soliciting donations in response to the latest natural disaster, nonprofits are finding the Internet is a dynamic fund-raising medium that works.

(A)   ELECTRONIC COMMERCE

The true potential of cyberfund raising will not be reached until commerce is readily exchange electronically and the general public becomes secure regarding the exchange of commerce on-line.

Electronic payment methods already occur. Telephone sales, automatic teller machines, electronic fund transfers, and even electronic filing of income tax happens already. What is new in cyberspace is the direct exchange of funds in a sales transaction.

The benefit of using an electronic payment method is that one maintains a fluid progression from information request, to interest in making a donation, to actually making the donation. In fund raising one never wants to lose entrée to that "givable moment" when a donor is ready and willing to make a contribution. Electronic payment methods minimize the potential of a distraction occurring before payment is secured.

(B)   SOLICITING MEMBERSHIP AND MEMBERSHIP DONATIONS

A Web site offers nonprofits the perfect opportunity to attract persons navigating the Internet to the affairs and activities of the organization. The Internet community is extremely diverse and reaches a broad audience whose tastes, interests, and demographics are still unknown. A smartly designed Web site can attract individuals to the organization and promote members and solicit donations.

The age-old saying in fund raising, "If you don't ask, you won't get," holds true in cyberspace as well. A membership and/or contribution form can be put directly on a Web site to facilitate easy participation. With the subtlety of links, you can put a link to a membership or solicitation form on every page of your Web site. When the form is completed, the user can immediately be added to the organization's e-mail database and start receiving material from the organization within minutes.

(C)   FOUNDATION FUND RAISING

The Web is becoming a valuable resource for foundation grant resources. Information on foundations can be found in three types of sites on the Web. The first are sites of key foundation assistance and resource centers such as the Foundation Center [http://www.fndcenter.org/] and the Council on Foundations [http://www.cof.org/]. The second type of site consists of Web sites of foundations. Currently there are over 100 foundations with pages on the Web, many of which include grant applications. And finally, commercial sites are appearing that offer access to fee-based searchable foundation and corporate giving-program databases, such as the Access Point Fund-raising System (http://www.accesspt.com).

(D) CORPORATE PARTNERSHIPS

One of the greatest challenges on the Web right now is getting people to look at your home page. Links with similar nonprofits is one way, but in terms of fund raising, there is another possibility. In cause-related marketing, a company tries to link itself with a nonprofit organization in order to boost its image and sales and at the same time raise money for the organization. Cyberfund-raising offers great potential for such corporate and nonprofit partnerships.

For example, Rhino Chasers microbeer has a partnership with African Wildlife Foundation (AWF). When Rhino Chasers [http://www.rhinochasers.com] put up their Web site, they immediately offered to put up one for AWF [http://www.rhinochasers.com/awf/index.html], donating the costs for the site. This inspired AWF to design its own page and now the two sites assist each other in the flow of visitors.

23.9   Establishing Your Presence on the World Wide Web

Putting up a site on the World Wide Web means more than hanging a billboard on the information superhighway. It means taking charge of your site as an outreach vehicle that meets your organization's goals and objectives for entering and investing in cyberspace.

There are six key elements to formulating a web strategy:

1. Defining your purpose: membership services, fund raising, outreach, publication sales, and so forth.
2. Identifying your audience: who will be using your web site and why.
3. Designing the Web site: what your site will look like and what content it will include.
4. Publicizing your site.
5. Determining success: clarify from the start how you will determine if your site is successfully meeting your goals and objectives.
6. Addressing the issues involved in merging a web site into your organization's operations so that the site is truly an integrated communication vehicle accessed and employed by every arm of your organization.

23.10   Conclusion

This article summarizes the wealth of benefits available to a nonprofit going on-line today. And yet, the dynamic nature of the Internet will present the nonprofit with new options and new possibilities with each passing month. The on-line community is uncharted and infinite. The full potential of going on-line for a nonprofit is yet to be determined. The only way to keep up with the on-line revolution is to be part of it.

Selected Web Resources for the Nonprofit

RESOURCES AND SERVICES FOR NONPROFITS

The Internet includes many sites which are resources or offer services geared specifically towards nonprofits. Because the nonprofit community is so large and varied, the sites are as well.

HandsNet on the Web
Web Address: http://www.igc.apc.org/handsnet/
E-mail Address: hninfo@handsnet.org
Description: National nonprofit network promoting collaboration, information sharing, and advocacy on a broad range of public interest issues among individuals and organizations. Also operates commercial on-line service for nonprofit community.

Independent Sector
Web Address: http://www.indepsec.org/
Description: A national nonprofit coalition of corporate, foundation, and voluntary organization members with national interest and impact in philanthropic and voluntary issues.

The Institute for Global Communications (IGC)
Web Address: http://www.igc.apc.org/
E-mail Address: webweaver@igc.apc.org
Description: IGC provides on-line communication services to the progressive community through: PeaceNet, EcoNet, ConflictNet, LaborNet, and WomensNet

Internet Nonprofit Center
Web Address: http://www.human.com/inc/
E-mail Address: clandesm@panix.com
Description: Website provides information to donors and volunteers about nonprofits.

NonProfit Times
Web Address: http://haven.ios.com/~nptimes/index.html
Description: Monthly publication for nonprofit management.

Putnam Barber's Resources for Nonprofits
Web Address: http://www.eskimo.com/~pbarber/
E-mail Address: pbarber@eskimo.com
Description: Contains news and hyperlinks of resources for nonprofits.

FUND RAISING

A great many fund-raising resources, from foundation and corporate grant-making activities, to sample grant applications can be accessed on the Internet. These sites include: foundations; fund-raising resources; government funding programs; and corporate philanthropic information.

Charities USA
Web Address: http://www.charitiesusa.com/
E-mail Address: request-for-info@ charitiesusa.com
Description: National membership of charitable organizations.

Council on Foundations
Web Address: http://www.cof.org/
E-mail Address: webmaster@cof.org
Description: The Council on Foundations, an association of foundations and corporations, serves the public good by promoting and enhancing effective and responsible philanthropy.

Fortune 500: Industry and Service
Web Address: http://www.cs.utexas.edu/users/paris/corporate.real.html
Description: Directory of Fortune 500 companies.

Foundation Center
Web Address: http://fdncenter.org/
E-mail Address: mfn@fdncenter.org
Description: Library for nonprofits.

Prospect Research Page
Web Address: http://weber.u.washington.edu/~dlamb/research.html
E-mail Address: dlamb@u.washington.edu
Description: Contains hyperlinks to valuable research tools, and resources on the Internet. Includes company and executive information, foundations, search engines, commercial information providers and more.

Prospex Incorporated
Web Address: http://prospex.com/
E-mail Address: info@prospex.com
Description: Prospect research firm.

Waltman Associates
Web Address: http://www.umn.edu/nlhome/g248/bergq003/wa/
E-mail Address: berg003@gold.tc.umn.edu
Description: Company which provides prospect research information and services.

GOVERNMENT AND RELATED SITES

Federal, state, and local governments also provide information, documents, and publications on-line. This allows nonprofit organizations to keep abreast of legislation, issues, and events, as well as gather reports and other publications. Moreover, this makes the organization located outside of a metropolitan area as up-to-date and efficient as the organization housed next to city hall.

Library of Congress
Web Address: http://www.loc.gov/
E-mail Address: lcweb@loc.gov
Description: Information and materials from the collection at the Library of Congress.

State and Local Government on the Net
Web Address: http://www.piperinfo.com/~piper/state/states.html
E-mail Address: piper@piper.info.com
Description: A searchable index of all 50 states, Tribal governments, and Guam.

StateSearch
Web Address: http://www.state.ky.us/nasire/NASIREhome.html
E-mail Address: darnold@ukcc.uky.edu
Description: Clearinghouse of state government information provided by the National Association of State Information Resource Executives.

Thomas-Legislative Information on the Internet
Web Address: http://thomas.loc.gov/
E-mail Address: Thomas@loc.gov
Description: Searchable database of full texts of legislation, bill summaries, the Congressional Record and more. Catalogued by bill number, title, sponsor, year, etc.

US Government Web Pages
Web Address: http://www.igc.apc.org/igc/www.gov.html
E-mail Address: not available
Description: Directory of U.S. Government sites on-line. Includes all branches of government, agencies, departments, services, and more.

EDUCATIONAL AND RELATED SITES

There are many educational sites on the Web. These range from K–12 to college and university level. There is also a good deal of educational programming and training on-line.

EdLinks
Web Address: http://www.marshall/edu/~jmullens/edlinks.html
E-mail Address: jmullens@marshall.edu
Description: A directory of educational links on the Web, both commercial and nonprofit.

EdWeb
Web Address: http://K12.cnidr.org:90/
Description: Resource for information on the role of information technology in education.

InfoList for All Teachers
Web Address: http://www.electriciti.com/~rlakin/
E-mail Address: rlakin@cello.gina.calstate.edu
Description: Digest of information on education.

COMMERCIAL SERVICES

There are many sites on the Web that provide general assistance and help expedite office procedures for a nonprofit organization.

AT&T—Toll-Free 800 Directory
Web Address: http://www.tollfree.att.net/dir800/
Description: AT&T's directory of toll-free numbers.

Commercial Sites Index
Web Address: http://www.directory.net
Description: Directory of commercial services, products, and information on the Internet.

FedEx
Web Address: http://www.fedex.com
Description: Allows visitors to download package-tracking software and learn about company operations.

News York Times
Web Address: http://www.nyt.com
Description: New York Times' news service available free over the Internet.

Pathfinder
Web Address: http://www.pathfinder.com
Description: Time-Warner's site. Access to all of the company's publications.

UPS
Web Address: http://www.ups.com
Description: Offers services and company information.

Wiley Publishing
Web Address: http://www.wiley. com/
Description: Company develops, publishes, and sells products in print and electronic media for the educational, professional, scientific, technical, and consumer markets worldwide.

Glossary

Baud rate The unit of measure used to describe the speed at which a *modem* can transmit information to and from the user's computer.
Bulletin board Also known as bulletin board systems (BBS). A single computer or a network of computers that people dial into via a modem to use the service. Some BBSs are on the Internet, but most are freestanding entities that are available either at no cost or for an hourly or monthly fee.
Browser Software which interprets *HTML* and presents it to the viewer as a Web page.
Byte A measurement for computer file size.

CyberFund-raising Fund raising that is accomplished utilizing on-line methods. In many cases this involves using an electronic commerce provider. In other cases, the Internet is used to solicit the funds and another method is used to make the financial transaction (phone, mail, etc.).
Cyberspace The community of Internet users.

Domain Name System (DNS) A naming system that translates Internet addresses into computer-interpretable IP (Internet Protocol) addresses. IP addresses are a series of numbers. The DNS allows the numbers to be replaced with words.

E-mail Mail sent *on-line* over a *network* from one computer to another as opposed to through the postal service.

FTP File Transfer Protocol is a tool that allows the transfer of files from an off-site database or server to a user's computer.

Hit (1) Refers to a visitor accessing a site, as in the number of hits a site has received. (2) When performing a search using a *search tool*, a hit is the number of successful entries found relating to the chosen topic or *keyword*.

Home page The first and introductory page to a *Web* site. When users travel to a *Web* site, they most often begin at the home page, which offers explanation, instruction, and links to the rest of the site.

HTML (HyperText Markup Language) A computer language, used on the *Web*, which formats text files through the use of special commands. *Browsers* interpret HTML for viewing by the user.

HTTP (HyperText Transport Protocol) The commonly accepted protocol for transporting hypertext documents on the *Web*.

Hyperlink, Hypertext link, or link A connection between two *hypertext* documents. This allows users to travel freely, in any direction, throughout an *HTML* document series or *Web Site*. Often, *hyperlinks* appear as different-colored or underlined text, or as a colored border around an image.

Information superhighway An all encompassing title for *on-line* information access. In general terms it is the *Internet* itself.

Internet At the fundamental level, a global network of computer networks. The Internet has come to mean all activity and interaction which takes place on the network, such as *e-mail*, the *World Wide Web*, and *UseNet* news.

Internet Service Provider (ISP) An organization or business that provides a gateway to the *Internet*. Many of these are commercial ventures. Check local listings for one in your area. Commercial in-line services also provide a gateway to the *Internet* and *Web* and may be contacted for additional information.

Keywords The use of specific words as references (similar to the *Find* command on a word processor) to perform a search. This allows for expansive searches for information in numerous resources.

Kilobyte (KB) A thousand bytes.

Link See hyperlink

Mailing list An e-mail-facilitated group discussion (also known as list).

Megabyte (MB) A million bytes.

Modem Short for *mo*dulator *dem*odulator, which allows conversion of digital data to analog sounds that can be transmitted over ordinary phone lines, which can then be changed back into digital data.

On-line A computer which is connected to *a network*. Similar to a printer being on-line through it's connection to a computer. Computers that are connected to the *Internet* are said to be *on-line* as are people who are connected through their computers.

Protocol An understanding on how to communicate between different computers.

RAM (Random Access Memory) A volatile form of data storage which the CPU uses to store and retrieve information. Volatile memory electronically disappears when power is shut off.

Root Domain The root of a domain that signifies the type of entity. The five main root domains in the United States are .com, .edu, .gov, .org, and .net. Countries also have root domains. The root domain for the United States is .us and the roots domain for the United Kingdom is uk. There are 106 country domains.

Search Engine A device which searches a database of *Web* sites, documents, and other information available through the *Internet*. The search is usually performed based on *keywords*.

SLIP, PPP (Standard Line Internet Protocol, Point-to-Point Internet Protocol) Technology that allows the user to turn a standard telephone line into an access way to a *network* (the *Web*).

Snail mail Term used by *Internet* users for mail sent through the U.S. postal service to denote the swiftness of e-mail.

URL (Uniform Resource Locator) A URL is simply the name of a *Web* or other address which is inputted into a *browser* or other software to retrieve files from that location.

UseNet The Internet's *bulletin board* system of discussion groups, known as newsgroups.

Webmaster The person who manages a *Web* site.

Web Site A location on the *World Wide Web* dedicated to a specific purpose. The *Web* is composed of thousands of sites all *hyperlinked* together. That is where the name *Web* originates.

World Wide Web (the Web, W3, or WWW) The Web is an *Internet* service which has grown to dominate information distribution on the *Internet*, because of its combined text, graphics, audio, and video capabilities as well as ease of use. It is composed of thousands of individual *Web Sites* connected to one another via *hyperlinks*.

Suggested Readings

BOOKS

December, John and Ginsburg, Mark. 1995. *HTML & CGI Unleashed*. Indianapolis, IN: Sams.Net Publishing. Covers the complete life cycle of Web development: planning, analysis, implementation, and gateway programming using Perl, REXX, and C.

December, John and Randall, Neil. 1995. *The World Wide Web Unleashed*. Indianapolis, IN: Sams.Net Publishing. Overview and guide for a general audience.

Eager, Bill et al. 1995. *net.search* Que Corporation. Detailed analysis and instruction of how to perform searches on-line. Offers both a quick and easy and a more thorough scientific approach.

Ellsworth, Jill H. and Ellsworth, Matthew V. 1994. *The Internet Business Book*. New York: Wiley. Includes basic Internet information and specifics for business including: establishing a presence, finding business resources, doing business on-line and more.

Gilster, Paul. 1994. *Finding It on the Internet*. New York: Wiley. Slightly outdated, but still very useful for gaining an understanding of the older model Internet, pre-WWW. Includes Veronica, WAIS, WWW, Archie, and Gopher searches.

Gilster, Paul. 1993. *The Internet Navigator*. New York: Wiley. One of the originals, it contains all the basics necessary to operate on the Internet as well as explanation of more complex operations.

Graham, Ian S. 1995. *The HTML Sourcebook*. New York: Wiley. Programming guide for HTML. More complex, but offers instruction on Web page construction and linking.

Hoffman, Paul E. 1995. *Netscape and the WWW for Dummies*. Foster City, CA: IDG Books Worldwide. Best-selling series of computer know-how books for beginners. Tips for browser and Web use with easy-to-follow instruction.

Swadley, Richards K. 1995. *The Internet Unleashed*, rev. 2nd ed. Indianapolis, IN: Sams.Net Publishing. Expansive collection of information for home, business, and educational use. Includes information the Web and is helpful for beginners and experts.

PERIODICALS

HomeOffice Computing. Dedicated to small business, which makes it distinct from other on-line-focused magazines. Also includes general coverage of Internet activity and growth. Subscriptions: 411 Lafayette St., New York, NY 10003, (800) 288-7812.

InfoActive. Telecommunications monthly for nonprofits. Easy to read and understand and dedicated to the nonprofit community. Published by the Center for Media Education. Subscriptions: InfoActive, 1511 K Street, NW, Suite 518, Washington, DC 20005, (202) 628-2620 (cme@access.digex.net).

Internet Connection. Guide to Government Resources available on-line. Comprehensive guide to all the government has to offer. Subscriptions: (800) 274-4447.

Internet World Magazine. Dedicated to Internet use. It offers informative articles for Internet users, both personal and professional. Subscriptions: P.O. Box 713, Mt. Morris, Illinois 61054, (800)573-3062 (http://www.mecklerweb.com).

NetGuide Magazine: For the Internet and on-line services. For personal and professional use. Subscriptions: 600 Community Dr., Manhasset, New York 11030, (800) 829-0421 (http://techweb.cmp.com/net).

On-line Access Magazine: Devoted to on-line services, bulletin boards, and the Internet. More general information for all types of on-line users. Subscriptions: 5615 W. Cermak Rd., Cicero, Illinois 60650-2290 (e-mail 70324.343@compuserve.com).

Wired: Feature magazine for cyberspace community. Subscriptions: P.O. Box 191826, San Francisco, CA 94119-9866, (800)SO-WIRED (subscriptions@wired.com).

24 Internet World Wide Web Home Page Writer's Guide

Howard J. Sartori, PE

Sartori Associates (howard@sartori.com)

24.1   Introduction

The World Wide Web (WWW) is a rapidly growing information service on the Internet. Organizations can make information about their activities available on the WWW by creating home pages. HyperText Internet applications can improve marketing, sales, and support, as well as provide a view of your organization to the Internet public. Easy-to-use web browsers and software tools facilitate the development of documents written in HyperText markup language (HTML). They have given rise to a proliferation of WWW home pages on the Internet. Home pages provide an efficient and effective means of communication and information distribution.

     The National Information Infrastructure (NII) goal is to increase the ease of access and availability of information. This chapter provides some basic and intermediate guidance for those wishing to establish home pages. Regardless of how or by whom these pages are actually developed, the appearance, accuracy, currency, and relevance of this information will reflect, directly or indirectly, on your organization's image. Included also are some basic guidelines and samples that will serve as a starting point for people without extensive experience in writing home pages, especially in the HyperText markup language.

24.2   Information Security

Because the Internet is a public domain network, access is not restricted. As a result, only certain kinds of information can be placed on the Web. Under no circumstances should the following information be accessible:

Copyrighted information with specific conditions of release/availability
Information quoting individuals without specific cited permission

Just like other publicly released material, all information placed on the Web must have approval from the appropriate release authority. In most organizations, this is typically the organization's public affairs manager. A web server administrator may be designated by the organization. The web server administrator should be responsible for confirming receipt of release authority before information is placed on the Web. All information placed on any Web server, whether directly or indirectly connected to the Internet, is presumed accessible by the public. Therefore, the web server administrator will only process information that has been approved for release.

24.3   Authoring With HTML

HyperText Markup Language (HTML) has been around for a long time. For example, Microsoft Windows™ applications "Help" documents are a form of HTML. HTML is a standardized documentation format that is independent of computer platform and software.

HTML documents are easy to prepare. Navigators or browsers can easily read it after the HyperText transfer protocol (http) transfers the file from a host (WWW server) to the client's computer. HyperText incorporates "tags" that signal the document processor to invoke particular textual attributes, such as font size, underline, bold, and so on. HyperText documents are easy to transmit, because they offer a high degree of compression.

Tags generally turn attributes on and off for the text contained between them. For example in this line

<b>Nonprofit Manual for Writing Home Pages</b>

the <b> and </b> pair of tags signal the document processor to turn the bold attribute on and off. Not all tags have pairs. An example is the separator line <hr>.

HTML has a few basic rules:

HTML tags are not case-sensitive.
HTML processors generally ignore carriage returns (exception is preformatted text).
HTML processors generally ignore white space.

HTML can perform various text functions:

automating features
   numbered lists
   bulleted list
   jump to other sections of the document
format and display
   alignment to left, right, top, etc.
   limited fonts
   in-line images (do not require the user to have a viewer)

The overall template for an HTML document is:

```
<HTML>
  <HEAD>
  <TITLE>Document Title<TITLE>
  <base href . . .>
  </HEAD>
  <BODY>
  . . . The actual textual content is placed in this area . . .
  </BODY>
</HTML>
```

Customized templates can aid in rapidly producing an HTML page.

Small "gif" icons can serve as highway signs informing the user how to navigate throughout the document, what to look out for, and how to take shortcuts back to the first home page or to other locations. Examples are "return to Home Page," and "sound icons."

24.4 Basic Format

A list of specific items that should be included (or linked to) on Web pages are:

Section I. Who, what, where, and why.
   Organization Logo
   Organization Name
   Organization Mission
   Organization Location
   Organization's Point of Contact
   Phonebook (optional)
   Organization Locator (optional)
   Organization Chart (optional)

Section II. Benefits, services, where to go for more information (internal links to your organization's other pages).
   Departments

Services
Impending events

Section III. Supporting or collaborative information from other sources (external links).
Supporting associations or organizations.
Supporting advertisers.
Supporting research sites that document and enhance your mission.

Section IV (optional). Interactive search engine that best supports your mission and clients.
Whereas the preceding information need only be provided on the home page of the Web document, the following items should be placed on *all* Web pages:

Explicit navigational links (especially to first page); for example, succeeding
pages should provide a "return to Home or Section Page" icon
Date of last update
Approved by
Point of contact
Phone number(s) and name(s) for more information

24.5 *Design Topics*

Organize your Internet Web team. Your Web home page is another form of public information. It represents your organization in the same manner as other forms of publications, such as magazines, newsletters, radio, and television. The difference is the media.

Your magazine publication requires cooperation between your public affairs department and your printer. Similarly, your Web home page is a publication that requires cooperation between your public affairs department and your information and telecommunications services personnel. In fact, collaboration between your printed publications producers and Web home page(s) will enhance your organization's name recognition.

(A) DESIGNING FOR YOUR READER

Keep the technology of your reader's equipment in mind. If your audience is elementary and middle-school children, then you might follow these guidelines:

Design for VGA monitor (640 × 480),
Design graphics with no more than 16 colors.
Design fonts with the viewer in mind.
Design margins accordingly, and
Design using the HTML version most likely to be used by your audience.

If your audience is not likely to have high-speed modems, minimize graphics. Make the most out of two colors.
When your audience is made up of "surfers," then your message will be truncated to their first full screen view of your home page without scrolling down the page.

Surfers will look beyond the first full screen view only when you capture their attention with that first impression. When the *first view*—one full screen—is the only likely chance you have to capture the attention of your surfing viewer, balance the graphics with the text and use appropriate fonts and sizes.

Journalistic rules of thumb apply to Internet publishing even more so than with printer or newspaper publications. Get the key story up front. Put the impact in the first view. Put lesser detail further down, usually on secondary pages.

After you have captured your viewer, make quality graphics available on the second or successive pages. Design your first page with typical navigation/browser software in mind. Most navigators/browsers now show the text while the graphics load. Use this time to get your ideas across with high-impact words. This is your first impression on your potential new member or client. Make it count! The graphic you have selected should then amplify, support, or add organization recognition to your first impression.

Warn your user about potential obstacles on the information superhighway. *Obstacles* are events that annoy users because the universal reference locator (URL) is unexpectedly large and can cause unexpected delays, a required viewer software was not loaded in the viewer's system, or the user did not have specific hardware such as a sound card. To assist the viewer navigate,

Show the file size at the end of a URL that would download the file (e.g., 16KB)
Show an icon indicating that the file is a sound file and show the file size
    (sound files are typically large)
Show desktop publication file viewer type (e.g., Adobe Systems' Acrobat)
Show a place where the user may obtain this viewer software, even from your
    Web page

Avoid large graphics files. They can become obstacles on your viewers' information superhighway and cause them to detour around your home page. Keep graphics files less than 20K. Thumbnails (small 100 × 100 pixel graphics) are recommended for graphic files larger than 20 KB. Make the thumbnail a link to the full-size graphic, with the full graphic size (KB) information provided at the end of the URL line.

Multimedia formats can add value to your Web home page, but avoid placing them on the first page. Located on the first page, they become obstacles rather than enhancements. Use a link from the first page with an accompanying high-impact statement such as "Boats offers real-life experiences through multimedia." Numerous software viewers can provide short movie clips, high-resolution graphics, sound, and animation to make your home page(s) unique and attract different audiences. Remember, to effectively use these technologies, include URLs to sources of these software viewers or include them on your Web site.

(B)   PICK YOUR THEME AND STICK TO IT

If your objective is to show that your organization offers the best member services and you want to collect memberships on the Internet, then list your services on the first page, using "teasers" with local links to more information. Put a data input block for registering potential new members at the bottom of the first page. Although collection of a credit card number can be risky, you may do that, or you may use an Internet collection agency. These organizations, such as First Virtual, offer valuable services at a very reasonable cost.

(C)   USE A STANDARD HTML VERSION

Don't necessarily use the newest HTML standards. Although Internet navigator/browser technology is rapidly advancing, Internet users typically don't install the newest software on their equipment. If your home page is elaborate, help your reader know what to expect. Provide a supplement page explaining the technology and versions you are currently using. Offer a URL where users may download new viewer software to enable them to take advantage of your new home page features and functions.

(D)   PROOFREAD YOUR HOME PAGE

Always spell check and proofread any document going onto the Web. This information should be treated just like a journal article. Make sure wording and spelling are correct. The impression readers will have is determined by how professional the document looks. Readers should not find themselves mentally correcting spelling errors; this takes readers' attention away from the point of the document.

24.6   *Enhance Your Home Page*

Enhance your home page to add value to your organization's image through the Internet publication media. Enhancements can attract viewers, and lower your fax, printing, distribution, and overhead costs. Increase readership and membership through the low-cost Internet media, increasingly access where magazines and newspapers are not available. Access is becoming available to sectors of society previously unreachable by traditional publication media.

An organization's home page on the Internet Web often becomes a focal point for a particular industry, special interest group, market, or commercial sector. Internet sites are becoming as much a competitive way of promotion as magazines, billboards, newspapers, or television.

First, register a domain name for your organization. The current annual fee is $50. You will own the domain name and may move it to another Internet service provider as required from time to time. A domain name is important for many reasons:

Name recognition
Presence
Listing on the national registration list (white pages of Internet users)
Short address to your home page
Show your commercial or nonprofit status (e.g., .com or .org)

An example of the use of a domain name will illustrate its value. A normal home page address might be:

www.isp.net/pub/client/your_org/your_org.html

A domain-based (or *virtual*) home page address would be:

www.boats.org

where, if your nonprofit organization name is "Boats Int.," the domain name is "boats.org"

Alternatively, consider a virtual Web site with the URL format *www.boats.org* vs. *www.boats.org/boats*. The first is referred to as a "virtual Web site," while the second is an "associated Web site." The extra expense is about $100 per month, but gives the viewer the impression that you own your site.

Brand your home pages by placing icons or small identifying graphics on each screen. This technique keeps your image constantly in view. Color schemes help add identity to your organization.

Significantly enhance your outreach to the public and draw people to you by adding functions that provide valuable and important information not normally available to your audience. This information can be real-time news, detailed information found only in a library, or brochures provided by your organization. By placing this information on the Web, you will not only enhance your image as a knowledgeable Internet resource, but you will also reduce your mail, tax, and phone costs, as well as personnel time required to process membership and public requests.

Consider setting up password-protected subsections of your home page for national and local chapter boards of directors. These subsections might contain advance news, board meeting minutes, and schedules. You may offer a list server (specialized version of e-mail and beyond the scope of this publication) interactive input from the page for collecting data from your members.

Most organizations now maintain large amounts of data relevant to their membership on PCs or network-based file servers. Consider reformatting these valuable assets into a marketable resource on the Internet. Some organizations consider this information so valuable that they now charge a subscription cost for online access to these valuable assets. Again, the technology is available to support special user-name/password access to this information.

Interactive databases set your Internet site apart from the crowd. Database search-engine software products, though not widely distributed, are now very economical. They give online library search quality to your information resources. In fact, some are quite sophisticated and can return a database of resources to the user to be saved on the viewer's computer for future use.

Another variation of adding an interactive database search engine to your home page is to link to one of the university, public, or commercial search engines. Enhance your link by "framing" your user query so that the answers serve your specific organization objectives. Many search engines are available internationally on the Web. However, each has very specific strengths and weaknesses. Avoid making a hasty choice and thoroughly test the search engine you select to ensure that your organizational objectives are met.

24.7 Apply Information Technology

Several technologies are available to accomplish all of these enhanced services. The cornerstone for many of these services is the Common Gateway Interface (CGI). If you have browsed the FTP sites on the Web to download files, you've probably seen it as a sub-directory of an FTP host. CGI is a collection of software that provides your viewer an interaction between the home page(s) and computer-based resources, usually database or file information already existing on one of your organization's PCs or servers. This type of technology has been largely UNIX-based. However, by the end of 1996 most of these technologies will be ported to Microsoft's NT™ operating system. There is a great deal of development going on in cross-technology Internet/traditional information technology products, which is allowing small organizations to offer what heretofore only large corporations or leased services could offer.

Increase your impact on Internet users by combining technologies. Incorporate responses into your home page(s). Additionally, consider collecting those responses in the form of databases so you can conduct surveys.

Collecting dues, as well as fees for information, has already been discussed.

Use portable file formats such as Adobe Systems' Acrobat to provide desktop-published documents to your membership. Using this format, local chapters can have print-ready material ready to reproduce and distribute locally.

Use your Internet service provider's access log to show your monthly home page readership. This is a valuable, low-cost way to enable your organization to optimize marketing and user services on the Internet. This access log includes:

User addresses
Access by group (e.g., government, commercial, military, country)
Time of access (e.g., surfers vs. real users)
Growth or decline of readership
Access problem, such as restricted communications access to your home page(s)

Consider using an Internet service provider that serves only nonprofit and government organizations, as your organization is nonprofit. Nonprofit ISPs offer lower-cost services, but may require payment on an annual basis.

Some of the technologies required for these enhanced Internet Web home page services are beyond the scope of this publication. Appropriate information technology consultants will be able to assist you in achieving your objectives.

24.8   Technical Implementation

Preparing an HTML document does not necessarily require HTML software. HTML software applications are useful for "starting from scratch" to build sophisticated documents. Experts frequently edit HTML pages with ASCII editors.

As discussed later, the extensions do not necessarily require renaming to a "html" extension when the files are moved to an Internet web browser. Of course, it is helpful to have a navigator, such as Mosaic, to view the results and test both internal and external links. Each time the document is modified, remember to reload the page on the navigator. On a small VGA screen, alternately edit, then minimize the editor, maximize the navigator, and reload the edited document. On a PC, the files will have the extension ".htm" with the exception of the first file, index.html.

The process of putting a completed home page on an Internet Web server may be organized into these steps:

Organize file subdirectories

Write and edit files on a local PC

Test the home page with all the URLs, text presentation, and graphics

Create the subdirectory structure on the Web server (the subdirectory/file
  structure should mirror the structure on the PC)

Transfer the finished files to the Web server using FTP software (FTP software
  with a graphical user interface is a great help; e.g., WS_FTP by John A. Junod,
  ftp.usma.edu)

Rename the index.htm file to index.html

Change attributes (UNIX only) of the Web server directories and files so
  viewers have access

  Telnet to your Web home page account. Then
    chmod 755 dir_name
    chmod 644 file_name

Test the home page from your PC. Debug the errors. A simple method of debugging
is to Telnet to your home page account. Use a Web server editor, Pico on UNIX systems,
to debug your files by editing online. Launch your navigator/browser to view the results. Continue to edit and view the final product by switching between the navigator
and Telnet windows.

When working in a mixed environment (PC work stations and UNIX Web servers),
remember that file names must adhere to DOS/Windows operating system standards
(e.g., eighty-three alphanumeric characters). UNIX supports a much broader file name
standard. It is perfectly acceptable to use the same name structure as in DOS/Windows
PCs. Files don't have to be renamed on the UNIX server, with the exception of index.html.

Shortcuts in URL implementation depend upon the Web server. For example, the
Web server may permit a URL www.boats.org to launch the first page with the name
index.html. (The rest of the files may have "htm" extensions). Consult with your Web
server support staff for additional information.

Subdirectory organization is not critical if the home page is a small publication.
However, if the home page is expected to grow, or perhaps several departments will
contribute, develop a subdirectory structure. Assign corresponding responsibilities.
Common organization graphics and files may be placed in one subdirectory for ease of
use and simplified updating.

Prepare graphics with care. Electronic publishing shops, now commonplace in most
cities, can quickly and cost-effectively prepare your graphics files to meet your specifications, with a high degree of quality. Limit the size of the first page logo/graphic to 1.5
inches high—about 10–20 KB. Make thumbnail files for graphics larger than 20 KB. Test
your graphics with a PC using a video driver with only 16 colors to avoid strange effects on low resolution and VGA color video cards.

24.9 Style Guidelines

HTML has features not available in standard text documents, such as linking and the
use of graphics directly integrated into the text. Use of these features can greatly mag-
nify the impact your organization's information message can have on the viewer. However, just as in standard text, HTML can be used improperly, resulting in confusion and

obscuring the intended content. Style guidelines can be used to help you avoid pitfalls and get the most out of the HTML features.

Style can be broken down into two pieces: structure and layout. *Structure* is concerned with the overall organization of the Web pages making up a WWW document, whereas *layout* looks at how each page is organized.

(A) STRUCTURE OF OVERALL HOME PAGE INCLUDING SUPPORTING PAGES

The single most important question concerning Web page structure is *how long should each logical page be?* As might be expected, there is no clearcut answer to this question. A well-constructed Web page is exactly as long as it needs to be. There are, however, a few guidelines which can help determine just how long it needs to be.

For each logical page:

Organize for your readers' quick scanning.
- Use headings to help readers find the portions of the document that are of immediate interest to them.
- Use lists/link menus for summarizing related items. Similar to a table of contents, a list of topic areas, with each list item being a link to that topic, is a fast and efficient way for readers to obtain the information they are interested in.
- Don't bury important information in text. All important points should be made near the top of the page or at the beginning of a paragraph. Always assume that your reader is very busy and does not have time to read through the full text.

Formulate a complete idea.
- Do not split the logical page just to make it shorter. If five full screens of text are needed to convey your idea, then use five full screens.
- Each page should be able to stand on its own. It must always be remembered that people can enter a page without going through your document's home page. Therefore, if the current page does not stand on its own, the reader will become lost. If that page is stored in the reader's browser without your organization's name, you have lost your chance to gain recognition.

Do not make it too long.
- A few screens is a typical limit for a Web page. After the first or second screen, if there is nothing of interest to "grab" a person, he or she will usually go off to another home page. Therefore, put the most important information at the top of the document.

Provide a supplemental page explaining how to get the most out of your home page.
- List viewers that are required to take advantage of your graphics, multimedia, etc.
- Provide links to permit your readers the opportunity to obtain this (usually free) software.

- List the current HTML version together with a list of navigator/browser software that supports this revision level.
- Give the date that a new HTML version will be implemented, together with a list of the navigator/browser software supporting the new version.

(B)   LAYOUT OF EACH PAGE

The single most important factor for any layout scheme is *consistency*. If HyperText pages are all set up with common features, then readers will learn what the elements of each page are and where to find different elements. Thus, even users not familiar with Web navigation will quickly learn how to move around through documents. Two areas of importance are page elements and navigation.

(i)   Consistent Page Elements
If a heading and a rule line at the top of the page is used, then use that same layout on *all* pages. If second-level headings (<H2>) are used on one page to indicate major topics, then use level two headings for major topics on *all* pages.

(ii)   Consistent Forms of Navigation
Put navigation menus in the same place on every page (usually at the top or bottom of the page), and use the same number of them. If using navigational icons, make sure the same icons are in the same order for *every* page.

(iii)   Composition of Each Document
- *Provide a descriptive title.* Information within the TITLE tag (i.e., <title> . . . . </title> is displayed at the top of the WWW browser (e.g., Mosaic, Netscape). It conveys clearly that this page is related to your organization. The title tag is also important because it is copied into the user's WWW browser menu when he or she selects the "Save Current Page" option. One possibility is to use the same text for both the title and the page heading. However, *do not* use redundant words like "Home Page." Keep the title short and descriptive, because the browser menu dialog box space is often restricted. You want to be easily recognized.
- *Write readable text, whether or not links are used.*
  - Avoid using "by clicking _here_". This makes the reader stop and check to see what is being linked. Instead, use the following idea: make sure the object-you-click is actually some kind of title for what it is when you click there. For example, "information about _blah blah blah_ is now available."
  - Avoid talking about a link; just use normal text, with descriptive text being the link. Construct the HTML page so that it can be read even if you don't have any links. For example, instead of "here are links to _blah_ and _barg_, which are used for", use "_blah_ and _barg_ are used for".
  - The text and vocabulary within a document should stand by itself (i.e., be self-contained). People other than the author may make links to it, so the

document should be able to stand on its own merits. A good test is to imagine yourself reading the text sometime later—does it still make sense?
- *Use graphics sparingly.*
  - Most people will be accessing the Internet using a dial-up modem. If there are many graphics, this implies a longer wait time before seeing the page. Graphics should be kept small, preferably 20 KB or less, providing for a quick display of the page. If you wish to provide a large graphic, then display a thumbnail version which is a link to the larger, higher-resolution graphic. To decide whether or not to view the larger, higher-resolution graphic, the reader should be provided with the size of the graphic (in KB next to the graphic).
  - In addition, make allowance for users who cannot view images due to browser limitations or because graphics viewing is switched off. To do this, use the ALT attribute of the <IMG> tag to automatically substitute appropriate text strings for the graphics in text-only browsers. Use either a descriptive label to substitute for the graphic, or use an empty string ( ) to ignore the graphic altogether.
  - Remember, many readers will choose to link to pages because they are browsing for related information, *not* because of the nifty graphics. It is considered good netiquette to keep the amount of data you're asking others to move across their networks, on your behalf, to a minimum.
- *Use navigational icons.* Typically there might be three icons, one for <back to the previous page>, a second one for <top of current page>, and one for <proceed to the next page>. If graphical icons are used, they should be no larger than 3–5 KB in size and typically are 3–1 KB.
- *Make each footnote a HyperText link.* That way you will see it quickly and can then return to the document to continue reading.
- *Provide the current status.* Indicate if the page (or document) is still being developed, has been finalized, and so forth.
- *Provide additional information.* Show how more information may be obtained (e.g., mail address, more points of contact, etc.).
- *Give a name and/or e-mail address.* This information at the bottom of the page provides a way for comments and suggestions to be sent to the author, and establish authority and responsibility.
- *Provide the date of the last update.* Place this at the bottom of the page. The format for this might be *dd mm yy.*
- *List any disclaimers.* Add disclaimers required by the host organization at the bottom of the page.

(C) HTML LINKS

Like graphics, links should not be overused. There should be a good reason for using links. Each link should serve a purpose, for relevant reasons. Just because the word "coffee" is mentioned somewhere in a page dealing with the Civil War, don't link "coffee" to the coffee home page. If a link has no relevance to the current content, remove it. Otherwise it will just confuse the reader.

(i)   Definitions

Link the *first* occurrence of a word in a document. This way the definition of a word can be explained to readers who do not know the meaning, while not distracting the readers who do understand.

(ii)   Explicit Navigation Links

Often indicated by navigation icons, these links indicate specific paths through documents (e.g., forward, back, up, home). A link should always exist to connect back to the home page from the current page. Because people can always enter a HyperText page from places outside the home page, a link back to the home page helps readers from feeling (or getting) lost.

(iii)   Implicit Navigation Links

In this case, the link text implies, but does not directly indicate, navigation between documents. Link menus (these can be thought of as tables of contents) are the best example of implicit navigation links.

(iv)   Tangents and Related Information

Think of these as footnotes or endnotes. Refer to citations or additional information that is interesting but not directly relevant to the point of the document. Like definitions, a link should only be made for the *first* instance of a tangent.

24.10   A Generic Home Page

LOGO (UPPER LEFT CORNER)   YOUR ORGANIZATION NAME HERE

Organization point of contact name
E-mail address and phone number (optional)
[A few words could be put here briefly describing the organization and giving its location, but use only a few sentences at most. Let the body of your Web document do most of the talking.]
[A separator line goes here.]

ORGANIZATION SPECIFIC INFORMATION

> Organization services of value and benefits
> Most important topics first (the first impression for your viewers)

IMPORTANT ORGANIZATION INFORMATION
[Use links via URLs to amplify information:]

> Organizational chart
> Phonebook
> Organization locator

[Follow with less important topics. Introduce topics as bullets; each bullet is a link to that topic.]

SUPPORTING INFORMATION
[Use links via URLs to external sites that support your organization's mission:]

Federal projects, commissions, agencies
National library resources [use specific URLs that take the reader to a specific place]
Newspapers
Suppliers
Advertisers
State and federal laws
Newsgroups
E-mail list servers

REFERENCE INFORMATION LOCATED AT THE BOTTOM OF THE PAGE

Explicit navigational links (especially to top-level home page as required)
Date of last Web page update
Web page point of contact, with name/phone number for more information

Remember, the home page acts as a title page and table of contents for the information you are making available about your organization. Using this format as a guideline will ensure that your interested Internet viewers will be able to find the information supporting your goals and objectives.

24.11   HTML Style Guides and Software Editor References

There is a massive amount of information on the Web dealing with HTML page style. A good example is http://www.ncsa.uiuc.edu/general/Internet/WWW/HTML. There is a growing number of books dealing with how to construct your own Web pages, as well as the do's and don'ts of producing good HyperText documents. Two books that were useful in the writing of this document are:

HTML Manual of Style, Larry Aronson, Ziff-Davis (ZD) Press, 1994, ISBN 1-56276-300-8

Teach Yourself Web Publishing with HTML in a Week, Laura Lemay, SAMS Publishing. 1995, ISBN 0-672-30667-0

Any text editor can be used to create a Web document. However, editors that insert control characters at the end of lines of pages (which include most commonly used word processing software) must be used with care. These characters are not supported by the HTML, although there is software that can take a document produced from these word processors and reformat it to HTML. If you are a Windows (© Microsoft Corporation) user, then you already have a rudimentary HTML editor called NOTEPAD. It does not put in control characters like other word processors. The problem with this editor is that all HTML tags must be typed in manually. Therefore, you either have to know all the HTML tags or keep a book on HyperText Markup Language close by your side.

Software vendors such as Microsoft produce HTML editors available as freeware on their Internet FTP and WWW sites. Numerous software authors produce freeware or shareware HTML editors. For example:

WebAuthor 2.0
  A very advanced HTML editor/converter which integrates into Microsoft Word
  6.0 © QuarterDeck Corporation
  http://www.quarterdeck.com
HTML Assistant and *HTML Assistant Pro* by Howard Harawitz
  A standalone product.
  Email: harawitz@fox.nstn.ns.ca
  FAX: (902) 835-2600
  ftp.cs.dal.ca/htmlasst/htmlasst.zip

The National Center for Supercomputing Applications has a large number of Internet applications, including HTML editors:

  http://www.ncsa.uiuc.edu/SDG/Software/Mosaic/NCSAMosaicHome.html

Another place to look for information about HTML editors is the World Wide Web. Here can be found links to information concerning editors that function on various operating systems, reviews of HTML editors, and more. A good launching point from which to begin a search for the ultimate HTML editor is:

  http://www2.infoseek.com/Titles?qt=HTML+editors

Another Web site has a listing of many of the known HTML editors. Some vital statistics are given, as well as links to the home pages associated with these editors:

  http://luff.latrobe.edu.au/-medgjw/editors/thelist.html

Major word processor software vendors, such as Microsoft and Corel, also offer HTML supplements.
  Ensure that the HTML editor you select uses reasonably current HTML specifications. Failure to comply with standards can result in erratic or garbled pages to your audience.

24.12   *Definitions*

What differentiates information on the WWW from standard text information sheets is the use of HyperText Markup Language. Some terminology essential for understanding and implementing guidelines for posting information on the WWW follows.

CERN   Centre for European Nuclear Research, Switzerland; the developer of the World Wide Web Project.

Domain name   A level of hierarchy in the Internet address that identifies a particular organization. For instance, whitehouse.gov is the domain name for the U.S. White House within the larger grouping of the U.S. Government (gov).

FTP   File Transfer Protocol. One of the main ways in which files are uploaded and down-loaded from computer servers. The protocol operates on TCP/IP (Internet) networks.

GIF   Graphics Interchange Format, a platform-independent file format developed by CompuServe for a graphic. The graphic has the file extension ".gif".

Home page   The primary starting (entry) point of a WWW document. It is similar to a page produced by combining the title page and table of contents of a hard-copy document. It is important to note that although the home page of a document is the most common access point into a WWW document, it is not the only way. Any WWW document can link to any other WWW document by calling its HTTP (HyperText Transport Protocol) address. Also, *home page* is frequently used interchangeably with the entire group of pages for an organization's "Website."

HTML   HyperText Markup Language, a subset of SGML. Current version is 3.0.

HTTP   HyperText Transfer Protocol, used by the WWW to transfer data from source computers to user computers.

ISP   Internet service provider. A telecommunications company that provides a large bandwidth connection to the national Internet backbone and, through an array of equipment, including gateways, domain name servers, and modems, provides leased-line or dial-up connections to clients. Different from online services (e.g., Prodigy and CompuServe), ISPs provide only a direct connection to the Internet.

JPEG   Joint Photographic Experts Group format, a platform-independent file developed by a standards group that has defined a compression scheme that reduces the size of image files by up to 20 times, at the cost of a slightly reduced image quality. The graphic has the file extension ".jpg"

Link   As its name implies, a link connects one Web page to another Web page. The link typically appears as a word, or words, with blue letters, or underlining. As the cursor touches the link, the cursor takes the form of a hand. Clicking the mouse button causes the Web browser to connect to the page pointed to by the link.

Logical page   Often referred to as a *Web page*, or just *page*, a logical page is the building block of a WWW document; composed of text and possibly graphics and multimedia. Although a Web page usually contains links to other pages, only the information currently being accessed (i.e., viewed) by a Web browser is a part of the current logical page. The term *logical* is used because, unlike a physical piece of paper, a Web page can be as long as needed (less than one physical page to many physical pages in length). When scrolling down a Web page with a browser, the end of the current page is reached when the scroll bar reaches the bottom.

SGML   Standard Generalized Markup Language, superset of HTML.

Tag   An HTML term for the command inserted into ASCII text to apply a particular attribute or format of the text. For example, text may be underlined by "<u>." Generally, the "/" turns the particular attribute off "</u>."

Telnet Both a terminal emulator protocol that is used to log into other machines on Internet, and programs that implement this protocol on various platforms, such as PCs and UNIX.

URL Universal Reference Locator, used to define the address of the WWW page. For example, the address is printed in two different manners. (1) http://www.your-company.domainname.com or simply (2) www.yourcompany.domainname.com. The former merely includes the protocol identifier (http://) required by some browsers, such as Netscape and Mosaic. Other protocol identifiers are ftp:// gopher://, and nntp://. The latter assumes that the user knows the format required by his or her particular WWW viewing software.

Viewer Software, mostly shareware or freeware, that automatically reads file information and converts it to graphics, sound, desktop formats, and so on. Viewers usually work in conjunction with the navigator/browser to enable the automatic features.

Web browser The program running on a PC used to access the WWW. Often referred to as a Web navigator or explorer. This client software browses the Web pages and outputs the information to the computer screen in a readable format. Examples of Web browsers are Internet Explorer and Netscape.

WWW World Wide Web; refers to the technical process by which a computer on an Internet network may access information displayed in a defined format using specific protocols.

WWW document Is similar in information content to any professionally produced document or journal article. It is, however, composed of a home page, logical pages, and links. Instead of flipping through pages to read a section of interest, you simply click on a link, displaying a new Web page containing the information of interest. Like traditional articles and documents produced using paper, a WWW document contains graphics. But, unlike its hard-copy counterpart, a WWW document can also contain multimedia information (i.e., animation and sound).

24.13 Commonly Used HTML Tags

Syntax can have one of two forms: an empty tag, such as <hr> (meaning horizontal separator line), or a nonempty tag like <b> . . . </b>. Nonempty tags enclose some portion of the document contents, either text, graphics, or both. Some nonempty tags include large portions of text. For example, <html> is the first tag of the page, whereas </html> is the last tag of the page. Most nonempty tags apply to paragraph organization, such as adding numbering or bullets. Some of the more common HTML tags are listed here along with their definitions.

<!-- -->	Author comments—not displayed by browser.
<a> . . . </a>: *Anchor Tag*	HTML's HyperText-related tag. Anything placed between the angle brackets becomes a HyperText link to another document. The document being pointed to is specified by using the parameter HREF=*filename* followed by the text that will

	serve as the HyperText link (see the next section's example).
<b> . . . </b>: *Bold Tag*	Produces bold text.
<body> . . . </body>: *Body Tag*	Designates the content of an HTML document, as opposed to the document's title.
 : *Line Break Tag*	Used to break a line within a paragraph. A line break will occur immediately following the word behind which this tag is placed.
<center> . . . </center>: *Center Tag*	Centers the enclosed text on the current line.
<code> . . . </code>: *Code Tag*	Used to print text in computer program-type format.
<dd>: *Description Definition Tag*	Used in conjunction with description lists (i.e., <dl>). Definitions are indented and started on a line separate from the description title (i.e., <dt>).
<dl> . . . </dl>: *Description List Tag*	A list consisting of alternating description titles (i.e., <dt>) and a description (i.e., <dd>). No bullets are used.
<dt>: *Description Title Tag*	Used with a description list (i.e., <dl>). Web browsers generally place the title on a line by itself.
<hl> . . . </h1>: *Level 1 Heading Tag*	Headings have six levels, with H1 being the most prominent and H6 being the least prominent. Headings are displayed in larger and/or bolder fonts than the rest of the document.
<h2> . . . </h2>: *Level 2 Heading Tag*	
<h3> . . . </h3>: *Level 3 Heading Tag*	
<h4> . . . </h4>: *Level 4 Heading Tag*	
<h5> . . . </h5>: *Level 5 Heading Tag*	
<h6> . . . </h6>: *Level 6 Heading Tag*	
<hr>: *Horizontal Rule Tag*	This tag produces a horizontal line.
<html> . . . </html>: HTML Tag	Defines the source file to be of the HTML document type. This tag is optional for most Web browsers.
<head> . . . </head>: *Heading Tag*	Defines that part of the HTML document containing information about the page (e.g., the document title). Never put any of the text of your document into the header.
<I> . . . </I>: *Italics Tag*	Produces italics text.
<img>: *Image Tag*	Used in HTML for specifying in-line graphic images. Within this tag, the graphic source file must be specified using SRC="*filename*" (the filename must be enclosed in quotes). Using ALT="*text*" will replace the image with text if the

	browser does not support graphics or if the graphic mode is turned off.
<li>: *List Item Tag*	The text following this tag is used in producing unordered (i.e., <ul>) and ordered (i.e., <ol>) lists.
<menu> . . . </menu>: *Menu List Tag*	Are similar to ordered and unordered lists (i.e., <ol> and <ul>, respectively) except that usually no numbers or bullets are used. Some browsers may also indent the list or precede each list item with a different symbol (such as a square).
<ol> . . . </ol>: *Ordered List Tag*	The list items (i.e., <li>) will be preceded by a number instead of a bullet (as in the case of an unordered list, <ul>).
<p>: *Paragraph Tag*	Web browsers ignore blank lines in HTML source files. Therefore, the only way to insert a line break for a new paragraph is by using the paragraph tag. This tag is placed at the end of the paragraph.
<pre> . . . </pre>: *Preformatted Tag*	The text within this tag will appear exactly as it is typed. All spaces and line breaks will be reproduced. Other tags cannot be used within this tag.
<title> . . . </title>: *Title Tag*	This is displayed separately from the document and is used primarily for document identification.
<ul> . . . </ul>: *Unordered List Tag*	The list items (i.e., <li>) will be preceded by a bullet. The next section illustrates how an unordered list is produced.

24.14   Sample WWW Home Page

```
<html>
<head>
<title>Boats Association</title>
<!--Boats Association, a non_profit organization dedicated to-->
<!--National Association office; 111 Main St., Town, ST. ZIP, USA-->
<!--E-mail John B. Cool: jcool@boats.org-->
<!--Last update: 27 July 1995-->
</head>
<body>

<center>
<img align=middle src="boats.gif" alt="BOATS Logo">
<h1>Boats Association. International</h1>
```

Executive Director, John B. Cool<p>
</center>

Welcome to <b> Boats Association, International </b>! We are the largest association in the world dedicated to . . . . . <b>Boats provides its members with vital and important services. Contact us via e-mail at <u> jcool@boats.org</u></b> or 800-111-1111<p>

<hr>
<h2>Boats Member Services </h2>
<ul>
   <li><a href="mission.htm">Mission Statement</a>
   <li><a href="org_info.htm">Organizational Information</a>
   </ul>

<hr>
<h2>Projects</h2>
<ul>
   <li><a href="projects.htm#AIT">Afloat Installation Teams</a>
   <li><a href="projects.htm#Depot">Depot Repair Facility</a>
   <li><a href="projects.htm#Rapid">RAPID</a>
   </ul>

<p><center><img src="boatl.gif"alt=""></center>.<p>
<h2>Supporting Information Sources</h2>
<ul>
   <li><a href="http://www.xxx.yyy/nik/">Boat Association Approved Suppliers</a>
   <li><a HREF="http://www.xxx.yyy/">US Weather Service</a>.
   <li><a href="http://www.xxx.yyy">US Coastal Tide Reports</a>
   </ul>

<p><center><img src="rainbow.gif"alt=""></center><p>

<img align=bottom src="form.gif"alt="">
Please address all questions/comments to: <a href="mail to: jcool@boats.org">
<i>jcool@boats.org</i>.</a><p>
<hr>
<i>Last update: 24 May 1995</i>
<i>E-mail: mary@boats.org</i>
</body>

Accounting, Finance, and Legal Issues

25 Accounting

RICHARD F. LARKIN, CPA, MBA
Price Waterhouse LLP

A sound accounting and financial management function is important for every not-for-profit organization. Good financial practices by themselves will not ensure program success, but they will greatly facilitate it. On the other hand, poor financial practices are a certain recipe for organization failure.

Responsibility for sound financial management, as for all other operating functions, rests squarely on the senior executive staff. There may be others involved, such as a trea-

Based on chapters from *Financial and Accounting Guide for Not-for-Profit Organizations, 5th edition* by Malvern J. Gross, Jr., Richard F. Larkin, Roger Bruttemesso, and John J. McNally (Wiley, 1995).

surer/board member, an outside CPA, and paid or volunteer controller and bookkeeping staff. However, the Executive Director controls the process.

Specifically, the Executive Director must determine the kinds of accounting functions the organization needs, hire the senior financial staff, supervise the financial activities on an ongoing basis, ensure that adequate controls are in effect, know when to take action and what action is needed if problems arise, ensure that financial information is received by those who need it (in useful form and on a timely basis), and coordinate the budget process (see Chapter 26).

All of this sounds like it requires a person with a lot of financial savvy; it does. Yet, very often in the not-for-profit sector, senior executives and (most) board members hold the positions they occupy not as a result of extensive training in management or finance, but because of knowledge of a dedication to the program activities of the organization. Thus, these managers (and trustees) have a special responsibility to learn what they need to know to effectively discharge their financial duties.

25.1 Duties of the Chief Executive

(A) FINANCIAL RECORDS

The Executive Director is charged with seeing that the organization's financial records are maintained in an appropriate manner. If the organization is very small, the treasurer will keep the records. If the organization is somewhat larger, a part-time employee—perhaps a secretary—may, among other duties, keep simple records. If the organization is still larger, there may be a full-time bookkeeper, or perhaps even a full-time accounting staff reporting to the Executive Director. Regardless of size, the ultimate responsibility for seeing that adequate and complete financial records are kept is clearly that of the Executive Director. This means that, to some extent, this person must know what is involved in elementary bookkeeping and accounting, although not at the level of a bookkeeper or a CPA.

(B) FINANCIAL STATEMENTS

One of the important responsibilities of the Executive Director is to see that complete and straightforward financial reports are prepared for the board and membership, to tell clearly what has happened during the period. To be meaningful, these statements should have the following characteristics:

1. They should be easily comprehensible so that any person taking the time to study them will understand the financial picture. This characteristic is the one most frequently absent.
2. They should be concise so that the person studying them will not get lost in detail.
3. They should be all-inclusive in scope and should embrace all activities of the organization. If there are two or three funds, the statements should clearly show the relationship among the funds without a lot of confusing detail involving transfers and appropriations.

4. They should have a focal point for comparison so that the person reading them will have some basis for making a judgment. In most instances, this will be a comparison with a budget or with figures from the corresponding period of the previous year.
5. They should be prepared on a timely basis. The longer the delay after the end of the period, the longer the period before corrective action can be taken.

These statements must represent straightforward and candid reporting—that is, the statements must show exactly what has happened. This means that income or assets should not be arbitrarily buried in some subsidiary fund or activity in such a way that the reader is not likely to be aware that the income or assets have been received. It means that if the organization has a number of "funds," the total income and expenses of all funds should be shown in the financial statements in such a manner that no one has to wonder whether all of the activities for the period are included. In short, the statements have to communicate accurately what has happened. If the statement format is confusing and the reader doesn't understand what it is trying to communicate, then it is not accomplishing its principal objective.

It will be noted that the characteristics listed above would apply equally to the statements of almost any type of organization or business. Unfortunately, financial statements for not-for-profit organizations frequently fail to meet these characteristics.

(C) PROTECTING ORGANIZATION ASSETS

Unless the organization is very small, there will be a number of assets requiring safeguarding and, again, it is the responsibility of the Executive Director to be sure that there are both adequate physical controls and accounting controls over these assets.

Physical controls involve making sure that the assets are protected against unauthorized use or theft, and seeing that adequate insurance is provided. Internal accounting controls involve division of duties and record-keeping functions that will ensure control over these assets and adequate reporting of deviations from authorized procedures.

Another responsibility of the Executive Director is to see that the organization's excess cash is properly invested to ensure maximum financial return.

(D) GOVERNMENT REPORTING REQUIREMENTS

The Executive Director is also charged with complying with the various federal and state reporting requirements. Most larger tax-exempt organizations, other than churches, are required to file annual information returns with the Internal Revenue Service, and some are even required to pay federal taxes. In addition, certain organizations must register and file information returns with certain of the state governments even though they are not resident in the state. All of these requirements taken together pose a serious problem for a person who is not familiar with either the laws involved or the reporting forms used. Chapters 29 and 30 discuss these requirements in detail.

25.2 *Understanding Not-For-Profit Accounting*

Many businesspersons, as well as many accountants, approach not-for-profit accounting with a certain amount of trepidation because of a lack of familiarity with such accounting. There is no real reason for this uneasiness because, except for a few troublesome areas, not-for-profit accounting follows many of the same principles followed by commercial enterprises.

One of the principal differences between not-for-profit and commercial organizations is that they have different reasons for their existence. In oversimplified terms, it might be said that the ultimate objective of a commercial organization is to realize net profit for its owners through the performance of some service wanted by other people; the ultimate objective of a not-for-profit organization is to meet some socially desirable need of the community or its members.

So long as the not-for-profit organization has sufficient resources to carry out its objectives, there is no real need or justification for "making a profit" or having an excess of income over expense. Although a prudent board may want to have a "profit" in order to provide for a rainy day or to be able to respond to a new opportunity in the future, the principal objective of the board is to fulfill the functions for which the organization was founded.

Instead of profit, many not-for-profit organizations are concerned with the size of their cash balance. They can continue to exist only so long as they have sufficient cash to provide for their program. Thus, the financial statements of not-for-profit organizations often emphasize the cash position. Commercial organizations are, of course, also concerned with cash, but if they are profitable they will probably be able to finance their cash needs through loans or from investors.

Not-for-profit organizations have a responsibility to account for resources that they have received. This responsibility includes accounting for certain specific funds that have been given for use in a particular project, as well as a general obligation to employ the organization's resources effectively. Emphasis, thus, is placed on accountability and stewardship. To the extent that the organization has received gifts restricted for a specific purpose, it may segregate those resources and report separately on their receipt and disposition. This separate accounting for restricted assets is called fund accounting. As a result, the financial statements of not-for-profit organizations can often be voluminous and complex because each restricted fund grouping may have its own set of financial statements.

There are five areas where the accounting principles followed by not-for-profit organizations often have differed from the accounting principles followed by commercial organizations. The accounting significance of these five areas should not be minimized, but it is also important to note that, once the significance of each is understood, the reader will have a good understanding of the major accounting principles followed by not-for-profit organizations. The five areas are discussed in the sections that follow.

(A) CASH VERSUS ACCRUAL ACCOUNTING

In commercial organizations, the records are almost always kept on an accrual basis. The accrual basis simply means keeping records so that, in addition to recording transactions resulting from the receipt and disbursement of cash, there is also a record of the amounts owed to and by others. In not-for-profit organizations, the cash basis of accounting is frequently used instead. Cash basis accounting means reflecting only transactions where cash has been involved. No attempt is made to record unpaid bills owed or amounts due. Most small not-for-profit organizations use the cash basis, although, more and more, the medium and larger organizations are now using the accrual basis.

The accrual basis usually gives a more accurate picture of an organization's financial condition. Why, then, is the cash basis frequently used for not-for-profit organizations? Principally, because it is simpler to keep records on a cash basis than on an accrual basis. Everyone has had experience keeping a checkbook. This is cash basis accounting. A nonaccountant can learn to keep a checkbook but is not likely to comprehend readily how to keep a double-entry set of books on the accrual basis. Furthermore, the cash basis is often used when the nature of the organization's activities is such that there are no material amounts owed to others, or vice versa, and so there is little meaningful difference between the cash and accrual basis.

Some not-for-profit organizations follow a modified form of cash basis accounting: certain items are recorded on an accrual basis and certain items on a cash basis. Other organizations keep their records on a cash basis but at the end of the year convert to the accrual basis by recording obligations and receivables. The important thing is that the records kept are appropriate to the nature of the organization and its needs.

(B) FUND ACCOUNTING

Although commercial enterprises often do a separate accounting for departments or branches, fund accounting is a term that is not used by most businesspersons. In fund accounting, assets are segregated into categories according to the restrictions that donors place on their use. All completely unrestricted assets are in one fund, all endowment funds in another, all building funds in a third, and so forth. Typically, in reporting, an organization using fund accounting presents separate financial statements for each "fund." Fund accounting is widely used by not-for-profit organizations because it provides stewardship reporting. This concept of separate funds in itself is not particularly difficult, but it does cause problems in presenting financial statements that are straightforward enough to be understood by most readers. Many organizations now use more simplified reporting formats.

(C) TRANSFERS AND APPROPRIATIONS

In not-for-profit organizations, transfers are frequently made between "funds." Unless carefully disclosed, such transfers tend to confuse the reader of the financial statements. Some organizations make "appropriations" for specific future projects (i.e., set aside a part of the fund balance for a designated purpose). Often, these appropriations are shown, incorrectly, as an expense in arriving at the excess of income over expenses. This also tends to confuse. Transfers and appropriations are not accounting terms used by commercial enterprises.

(D) TREATMENT OF FIXED ASSETS

In commercial enterprises, fixed assets are almost always recorded as assets on the balance sheet, and are depreciated over their expected useful lives. In not-for-profit accounting, some fixed assets may not be recorded. Some organizations "write off" or expense the asset when purchased; others record fixed assets purchased at cost and depreciate them over their estimated useful life in the same manner as commercial enterprises.

(E) CONTRIBUTIONS, PLEDGES, AND NONCASH CONTRIBUTIONS

In commercial or business enterprises there is no such thing as a "pledge." If the business is legally owed money, the amount is recorded as an account receivable. A pledge to a not-for-profit organization may or may not be legally enforceable. Some not-for-profit organizations record pledges because they know from experience that they will collect them. Others have not because they feel they have no legally enforceable claim. A related problem is where and how to report both restricted and unrestricted contributions in the financial statements. Recently issued accounting standards will result in more uniformity of practice in this area. For further discussion see Gross, et al. (1995).

Noncash contributions include donations of securities, equipment, supplies, and services. Commercial enterprises seldom are recipients of such "income."

25.3 *Avoiding Financial Problems*

Some people have the mistaken idea that bankruptcy only happens to businesses. Not-for-profits are not immune, and management must work to avoid financial problems that could cause the organization to be unable to carry on its activities. Although final responsibility is the board's, the Executive Director is the person who must watch both the day-to-day and long-term financial pictures. The treasurer, controller, and other financially oriented persons are important resources for management, but they are often either not around every day or do not have the broad perspective of the Executive Director.

The Executive Director must monitor the financial progress of the organization with respect to the budget, both as to whether revenue is keeping up with projections and whether expenses are being kept within limits. In particular, the current and forecasted cash position must be watched carefully for any trend that indicates possible future shortages. This monitoring must occur regularly during the year; the more delicate the organization's financial position, the more frequently a "reading" must be taken.

If problems occur or appear imminent, the Executive Director must alert others in the organization, especially other members of management and key board members, so that a plan of action to deal with the problems can be implemented. It is, however, management's responsibility to decide what needs to be done, and do it, whether more revenue is needed or expenses must be cut, or some other action is required.

Some possible ways to respond to financial problems include:

- Increasing contributions. This is often more easily said than done. It usually requires an up-front outlay of money and/or time, and the results may not be seen for awhile, or at all. An organization in or approaching financial difficulty has an especially hard time convincing donors to support what some may see as a sinking ship.
- Raising service fees. By the laws of supply and demand, this may or may not result in an overall revenue increase. Some "customers" will be lost, especially if the organization serves an economically disadvantaged population.

- Reducing expenses. This is also easier said than done, because many expenses are relatively fixed, at least in the short term. It is not easy for dedicated staff and volunteers to make decisions that may reduce the entity's services.
- Borrowing. This is quick (if a willing lender can be found), but expensive (interest cost). Further, it may merely postpone an ultimate day of reckoning. Borrowing should be undertaken only for long-term projects such as capital assets, where the debt can be repaid over the life of the assets, or as a very temporary short-term measure, when receipts to repay the borrowing are assured in the near future. A grant may be awarded but not yet received, or a firm pledge may have arrived from a reliable donor.
- Considering whether the needs of the organization's service beneficiaries would be better met by other organizations that have greater financial resources. This is a euphemism for one of two actions: merging with another entity, or going out of business and turning the organization's remaining resources and clients over to another service provider. These are never easy choices, but are sometimes the only feasible alternatives. If one of these options is to be chosen, the decision should be made quickly so that the transfer of services will occur smoothly, before cash is totally depleted and operations become disrupted.

25.4 Staffing the Accounting Function In a Small Organization[1]

Obtaining the right kind of accounting staff is important to the smooth running of this function. The Executive Director usually has no training, time, or inclination to do the bookkeeping. Competent professional assistance is needed.

The problem of finding the right bookkeeper is compounded for not-for-profit organizations because, traditionally, such organizations pay low salaries to all of their staff, including the bookkeeper. The salary level frequently results in the organization's getting someone with only minimum qualifications, which appears to be a false economy. A good bookkeeper can help the organization save money and can free the time of other staff and volunteers.

Often, the other staff members in the organization are extremely dedicated individuals who are interested in the particular program of the organization and willing to accept a lower-than-normal salary. Bookkeepers may not be dedicated to the programs of the organization in the same way. They have been hired to provide bookkeeping services and often have no special interest in the program of the organization.

(A) FINDING A BOOKKEEPER

The first step in obtaining a bookkeeper is to determine what bookkeeping services are needed. Depending on the size of the organization, there are a number of possibilities.

---

[1] This section deals only with the bookkeeping problems of relatively small organizations. Larger organizations are not discussed because, to a very large extent, they are run like commercial organizations.

If the organization is very small and fewer than 25 checks are issued per month, a "checkbook" type set of records will likely be all that is required. If so, the treasurer may very well keep the records and not try to find someone to help.

For many organizations, the number of transactions is too large for the treasurer to handle but not large enough to justify a full-time bookkeeper. If the organization has a paid full- or part-time secretary, often some of the bookkeeping duties are delegated to the secretary. Usually, this means keeping the "checkbook" or perhaps a simple cash receipts and cash disbursements ledger. At the end of the month, the treasurer will summarize these cash records and prepare the financial statements.

Another possibility for the small organization is to find a volunteer within the organization who will help keep the records. While this can occasionally be effective, it often turns out to be less than satisfactory. Keeping a set of books is work, and although a volunteer bookkeeper's enthusiasm may be great at the beginning, it tends to diminish in time. The result is that there are often delays, clerical errors, and, eventually, the need to get another bookkeeper.

Another possibility is a part-time bookkeeper. Some of the best potential may be found among parents with school children, who were full-time bookkeepers at one time, or, if the organization wants someone at its office for a full day each week or during hours not suitable for a parent with school children, then perhaps a retired bookkeeper or accountant will be the next best bet.

For larger or growing organizations, there is a point when a full-time bookkeeper is needed.

An advertisement in the newspaper is probably the best approach. Alternatively, an employment agency can be used. The principal advantage is a saving of time and effort. The agency will place the ad in the paper and will do the initial weeding out of the obvious misfits before forwarding the potential candidates to the organization for review. Agencies also know the job market and will probably be in a good position to advise on the "going" salary. They should also be able to help in checking references.

If the organization has outside auditors, they may be able to help. Their advice should be requested and, before actually hiring a bookkeeper, they should talk with the candidates.

(B) ALTERNATIVES TO BOOKKEEPERS

One thing that can be done to reduce the burden on the bookkeeper is to let a bank or a service bureau handle the payroll. This is particularly effective where employees are paid the same amount each payroll period.

Responsibility for bookkeeping, however, cannot be delegated outside the organization. An employee of the organization must continuously monitor and review the work of an outside bookkeeper.

Some banks will handle the complete payroll function. Most will prepare the payroll tax reports. Banks usually have a minimum fee for each payroll. If there are more than about 20 employees, this amount increases. The charge may seem high, but the time saved can be considerable. In addition to the payroll preparation, the bank will keep cumulative records of salary paid to each employee and will prepare the various payroll tax returns, W-2 forms, and similar documents.

Another possibility is to have a service bureau keep all the bookkeeping records. If there is any volume of activity, a service bureau can often keep the records at less cost to an organization than hiring a bookkeeper. For example, some service bureaus will enter information from original documents, such as the check stubs, invoices, and so on. They can then prepare a cash receipts book, cash disbursement book, general ledger, and financial statements, all automatically. The organization only has to provide the basic information.

It is also possible to hire an outside accounting service to perform the actual book-keeping. Many CPAs and public accountants provide bookkeeping services for their clients. Under this arrangement, the accountant has one of the staff do all of the book-keeping but takes the responsibility for reviewing the work and seeing that it is properly done. The accountant usually prepares financial statements monthly or quarterly.

There are still some functions the organization itself usually must perform. The organization will normally still have to prepare its own checks, vouchers, payroll, depositing of receipts, and billings. This means that normally it cannot delegate 100 percent of the bookkeeping to an outside accounting service.

25.5 Providing Internal Control

"Employee admits embezzlement of ten thousand dollars."
"Trusted clerk steals $50,000."

These headlines are all too common, and many tell a similar story—a trusted and respected employee in a position of financial responsibility is overcome by temptation and "borrows" a few dollars until payday to meet some unexpected cash need. When payday comes, some other cash need prevents repayment. Somehow the employee just never catches up, and borrows a few more dollars, and a few more and a few more.

The reader's reaction may be, "Thank goodness, this kind of thing could never happen to my organization. After all, I know everyone and they are all honest, and besides who would think of stealing from a not-for-profit organization?" This is not the point. Very few people who end up as embezzlers start out with this intent. Rather, they find themselves in a position of trust and opportunity and, when personal crises arise, the temptation is too much. Not-for-profit organizations are not exempt, regardless of size. There is always a risk when a person is put in a position to be tempted.

The purpose of this section is to outline some of the practical procedures that a small organization can establish to help minimize this risk and thus safeguard the organization's physical assets. For purposes of this discussion, the emphasis is on smaller organizations (those with one or two persons handling all the bookkeeping). This would include many churches, country clubs, local fund-raising groups, YMCAs, and other agencies. Internal control for larger organizations is not discussed here because controls for such organizations can become very complicated and would require many chapters. The principles, however, are essentially the same.

Internal control is a system of procedures and cross-checking which, in the absence of collusion, minimizes the likelihood of misappropriation of assets or misstatement of the accounts, and maximizes the likelihood of detection if embezzlement occurs. For the most part, internal control does not prevent embezzlement but should ensure that, if committed, it will be promptly discovered. This likelihood of discovery usually persuades most workers not to allow temptation to get the better of them. Internal control also includes a system of checks and balances over all paperwork, to ensure that there was no intentional or unintentional misstatement of financial data.

There are several reasons for having a good system of internal controls. The first, obviously, is to prevent the loss through theft of some of the assets. A second reason, equally important, is to prevent "honest" employees from making a mistake that could ruin their lives.

Aside from this moral responsibility of the employer, there is a responsibility of the board, to the membership and to the general public, to safeguard the assets of the organization. If a large sum were stolen and not recovered, it could jeopardize the program of the organization. Furthermore, even if only a small amount were stolen, it would be embarrassing to the members of the board. In either case, the membership or the public would certainly want to know why internal control procedures had not been followed.

For example, several recent, real, well-publicized situations involving not-for-profit organizations were all at least partly due to the absence of adequate internal controls:

- The chief executive officer of a major charity misused some of the organization's funds for personal benefit. If this person had been subject to adequate oversight and review by the organization's board of directors, the amount of money that could have been misused probably would have been only a small fraction of what the organization eventually lost.
- The chief financial officer of a national organization embezzled money from the organization's bank accounts and covered up the theft by making improper entries in the books. Had this person been subject to adequate control, including proper segregation of duties, enforced by the organization's board and chief executive, the thefts would likely not have happened at all, or, if money had been taken, the loss would have been evident to others more quickly.
- Another chief executive spent the organization's money on personal expenses and on projects that were not subject to adequate review and approval by the board. Had the board been more aware of what was happening, these wasteful expenditures could have been minimized, or possibly avoided altogether.
- A large religious organization entered into contracts which created liabilities that it had no ability to fulfill. The chief executive did this on his own, without proper board supervision and review.
- (Although governments are not the type of not-for-profit mainly discussed in this book, this organization's story could happen in a not-for-profit as well.) The treasurer of a local government invested its cash reserves in extremely speculative investments, which eventually turned sour. The government was forced into bankruptcy. If the governing board had exercised stronger controls over the investment activities of the treasurer, the speculative investments would have been much less likely to have resulted in the large losses that occurred.

This is not in any way to condone or excuse the actions of the individuals who did things they should not have done; however, the fact that they were able to do what they did, over a period of time, without being promptly called to account for their actions, indicates that those in position of responsibility over these individuals were not adequately discharging their responsibilities for guarding the organizations' resources. In fact, the very presence of adequate internal controls might have deterred some of these people from even attempting to do anything improper. Note that we are not talking here about taking $50 from the petty cash fund. Of course a board (or a chief executive) has more important things to do than worry about that (that's the controller's job). These were situations so significant that the very existence of the organizations and their programs were called into question. That is surely a major concern of the very top officials of an organization.

Further, in every case, the ultimate harm to the organization extended far beyond the actual amount of money stolen or wasted. Each situation became a public relations disaster; three ended up in bankruptcy court; some people have gone to jail. When the not-for-profit organizations' donors finally became aware of what had happened, contributions dropped significantly. The loss of contributions can never be measured precisely, of course, but it was doubtless many times the actual amount that triggered the donors' reactions. It can take many years for an organization's finances to recover from such a debacle, if they ever do.

(A)   EFFECTIVE INTERNAL CONTROLS

One of the most effective internal controls is the use of a budget which is compared to actual figures on a monthly basis. If deviations from the budget are carefully followed up by the controller or Executive Director, the likelihood of a large misappropriation taking place without being detected fairly quickly is reduced considerably. This type of overall review of the financial statements is very important, and every member of the board should ask questions about any item that appears out of line either with the budget or with what would have been expected to be the actual figures. Many times, this type of probing for reasons for deviations from the expected has uncovered problems.

A number of other basic internal controls are probably applicable to many, if not most, small not-for-profit organizations; these controls are discussed below. However, it must be emphasized that these are only basic controls and should not be considered all-inclusive. Establishing an effective system of internal control requires knowledge of the particular organization and its operations.

In this discussion, we will be considering the division of duties for a small organization, The Center for World Peace. This organization sponsors seminars and retreats and has a paid staff to run its affairs. The office staff consists of an Executive Director, the Executive Director's secretary, a program director, and a bookkeeper.

The officers of the Center are all volunteers and usually are at the Center only at irregular times. The Executive Director, treasurer, president, and vice president are check signers. With this background, let us now look at each of eleven controls in detail and see how they apply to this organization.

(B)   CONTROLS OVER RECEIPTS

The basic objective in establishing internal control over receipts is to obtain control over the amounts received at the time of receipt. Once this control is established, procedures must be followed to ensure that these amounts get deposited in the organization's bank account. Establishing this control is particularly difficult for small organizations because of the small number of persons usually involved.

1. *Prenumbered receipts should be issued for all money at the time first received. A duplicate copy should be accounted for and a comparison eventually made between the aggregate of the receipts issued and the amount deposited in the bank.*

The purpose of this control is to create a written record of the cash received. The original of the receipt should be given to the person from whom the money was received; the duplicate copy should be kept permanently. Periodically, the aggregate receipts issued should be compared with the amount deposited. The receipts can be issued at the organization's office, or, if door-to-door collections are made, a prenumbered receipt can be issued for each amount received by the collector.

In our illustration, the Center receives cash at its seminars and retreats on weekends, when the bookkeeper and treasurer are not available. One of the participants, designated as the fee collector for that session, collects the fees and issues the receipts. After all of the fees are collected, they are turned over, with the duplicate copy of the receipts (along with all unused receipt forms), to the program director. A summary report of the cash collected is prepared and signed in duplicate. One copy of this report is mailed directly to the treasurer's home in an envelope provided, and the duplicate is turned over to the program director. The program director counts the money, agreeing the total received with the total of the duplicate receipts and with the summary report. The program director puts the money in the safe for the weekend and, on Monday morning, gives the money, the duplicate receipts, and the copy of the summary report to the bookkeeper for depositing. The bookkeeper deposits the money from each program separately, and files the duplicate receipts and summary report for future reference. Once a month, the treasurer compares the copy of each summary report with the deposits shown on the bank statement.

2. *Cash collections should be under the control of two people wherever possible, particularly where it is not practicable to issue receipts.*

In the illustration in the previous paragraph, control was established over cash collections by having the person collecting at each seminar issue receipts and prepare a summary report. The program director also had some control through knowledge of how many persons attended and comparison of the amount collected with the amount that should have been collected. This provided dual control.

There are many instances, however, where cash collections are received when it is not appropriate to give a receipt. Two examples are church "plate" collections during worship services, and coin canisters placed in stores and public places throughout the community for public support. To the extent that only one person handles this money, there is always a risk. The risk is not only that some of it will be misappropriated, but also that someone may erroneously think it has been. This is why it is recommended that two people be involved.

With respect to church plate collections, as soon as the money has been collected, it should be locked up until it can be counted by two people together. Perhaps the head usher and a vestryman will count it after the last service. Once the counting is completed, both should sign a cash collection report. This report should be given to the treasurer for subsequent comparison with the deposit on the bank statement. The cash should be turned over to the bookkeeper for depositing intact.

This procedure will not guard against an usher's dipping a hand into the "plate" before it is initially locked up or counted, but the ushers' duties are usually rotated and the cumulative risk is low. The bookkeeper and treasurer normally have access to such funds on a regular and recurring basis. This is why their function of counting these cash receipts should be controlled by having a second person involved. It is not because they are not trusted; it is to ensure that no one can think of accusing one of them.

Canisters containing cash, which are placed in public places, should be sealed so that the only way to get access to the cash is to break the canister open. Someone could take the entire canister, but if the canister is placed in a conspicuous place—near the cash register, for example—this risk is fairly low. These canisters should be serially numbered so that all canisters can be accounted for. When the canisters are eventually opened, they should be counted by two people using the same procedures as with plate collections.

3. *Two persons should open all mail and make a list of all receipts for each day. This list should subsequently be compared to the bank deposit by someone not handling the money. Receipts in the form of checks should be restrictively endorsed promptly upon receipt.*

Two persons should open the mail; otherwise, there is a risk that the mail opener may misappropriate part of the receipts. This imposes a heavy burden on the small organization with only a few employees, but it is necessary if good internal control is desired.[2] One alternative is to have mail receipts go to a bank lock box and let the bank do the actual opening of the mail.

The purpose of making a list of all checks received is to ensure that a record is made of the amount that was received. This makes it possible for the treasurer to later check to see whether the bookkeeper has deposited all amounts promptly.

Checks should be promptly endorsed because, once endorsed, there is less likelihood of misappropriation. The endorsement should be placed on the check by the person first opening the mail.

In theory, if the check has been made out in the name of the organization, no one can cash it. But experience has shown that a clever enough person can find a way to cash it or deposit it in a "personal" bank account opened for the purpose. On the other hand, once the check is endorsed with the name of the bank and the organization's account number it is very difficult for the embezzler to convert the check to personal use.

In our illustration, the secretary to the Executive Director of the Center, together with the bookkeeper, jointly open all mail and place the rubber-stamp endorsement on the check. They then make a list, in duplicate, of all checks received; one copy of the list goes to the bookkeeper with the checks for depositing. They both sign the original of the list, which goes to the Executive Director. The Executive Director obtains the copy, to see what amounts have been received. At the end of the month, all of these lists are turned over to the treasurer, who then compares each day's lists with the respective credit on the bank statement.

4. *All receipts should be deposited in the bank, intact and on a timely basis.*

The purpose of this control is to ensure that there is a complete record of all receipts and disbursements. If an organization receives "cash" receipts, no part of this cash should be used to pay its bills. The receipts should be deposited, and checks issued to pay expenses. In this way there will be a record of the total receipts and expenses of the organization on the bank statements.

---

[2] Organizations that have their financial statements audited by CPAs will find that the CPA cannot give an unqualified opinion if internal control is considered inadequate.

This procedure does not prevent someone from stealing money but it does mean that a check must be used to get access to the money. This leaves a record of the theft and makes it more difficult for a person to cover up.

(C) CONTROLS OVER DISBURSEMENTS

The basic objective in establishing internal controls over disbursements is to ensure that a record of all disbursements is made and that only authorized persons are in a position to withdraw funds. The risk of misappropriation can be significantly reduced if procedures are established to minimize the possibility that an expenditure can be made without leaving a trail, or that an unauthorized person can withdraw money.

5. *All disbursements should be made by check, and supporting documentation should be kept for each disbursement.*

This control is to ensure that there will be a permanent record of how much and to whom money was paid. No amounts should be paid by cash, with the exception of minor petty cash items. For the same reason, no checks should be made payable to "cash." Checks should always be payable to a specific person, including checks for petty cash reimbursement. This makes it more difficult to fraudulently disburse funds.

At the Center, the bookkeeper is the one who prepares all checks for payment of bills. Before a check is prepared, however, the vendor's invoice must be approved by the Executive Director. If the purchases involved goods that have been received at the Center, the person who received the goods must indicate their receipt, right on the vendor's invoice.

The bookkeeper is not a check signer. If this were the case, this person could fraudulently disburse funds to himself or herself and then cover up the fraud in the books. The check signers are the Executive Director, the treasurer, the president, and the vice president. Normally, the Executive Director signs all checks. Checks of more than $1,000 require two signatures, but these are very infrequent. The Executive director carefully examines all supporting invoices, making sure that someone has signed for receipt of the goods before signing the check. After signing the check, each invoice is marked "paid" so that it won't inadvertently be paid twice. The secretary mails all checks to the vendors as an added control over the bookkeeper. By not letting the bookkeeper have access to the signed checks, the bookkeeper is not in a position to profit from preparing a fraudulent check to a nonexistent vendor.

6. *If the treasurer or check signer is also the bookkeeper, two signatures should be required on all checks.*

The purpose of this control is to ensure that no one person is in a position to disburse funds and then cover up an improper disbursement in the records. In part, this recommendation is designed to protect the organization, and in part, to protect the treasurer.

Two signatures on a check provide additional control only so long as the second check signer also examines the invoices or supporting bills behind the disbursement before signing the check. The real risk of having dual signatures is that both check signers will rely on the other and will review the supporting bills in such a perfunctory manner that there is less control than if only one person signed but assumed full responsibility.

7. *A person other than the bookkeeper should receive bank statements directly from the bank and should reconcile them.*

This control is to prevent the bookkeeper from fraudulently issuing a check for personal use and, as bookkeeper, covering up this disbursement in the books. The bookkeeper may not be a check signer, but experience has shown that banks often do not catch forged check signatures. The bookkeeper usually has access to blank checks and could forge the check signer's signature. If the bookkeeper were to receive the bank statements, the fraudulent and forged cancelled checks could be removed and then destroyed, with the fraud covered up through the books.

In most smaller organizations, the bank statement and cancelled checks should go directly to the treasurer, who should prepare the bank reconciliation.[3] In those situations where the treasurer is also the bookkeeper, the bank statements should go directly to another officer to reconcile. The treasurer should insist on this procedure as a protection from any suspicions of wrongdoing.

In the Center's case, the bank statement and cancelled checks are mailed directly to the treasurer's home each month. After receiving the bank statement, the treasurer usually spends half a day at the Center's offices preparing the complete bank reconciliation and comparing the lists of mail and program receipts received throughout the month to the deposits shown on the bank statement.

(D)   OTHER CONTROLS

8. *Someone other than the bookkeeper should authorize all write-offs of accounts receivable or other assets.*

This control is to ensure that a bookkeeper who has embezzled accounts receivable or some other assets will not also be in a position to cover up the theft by writing-off the receivable or asset. If the bookkeeper is unable to write such amounts off, someone will eventually ask why the "receivable" has not been paid and this should trigger correspondence that would result in the fraud's being discovered.

Generally, write-offs of small receivables should be approved by the treasurer (provided the treasurer is not also the bookkeeper), but if they are large in amount they should be submitted to the board for approval. Before any amount is written off, the treasurer should make certain that all appropriate efforts have been made, including, possibly, legal action. The treasurer must constantly keep in mind the fiduciary responsibility to take all reasonable steps to make collection.

The Center only very rarely has accounts receivable. It does have, however, many pledges receivable. Although the Center would not think of taking legal action to enforce collection, it does record those pledges as though they were receivables. Occasionally, the bookkeeper has to call the treasurer's attention to a delinquent pledge. The treasurer, in turn, usually calls the delinquent pledgor in an effort to evaluate the likelihood of future collection. Once a year, a written report is submitted to the board advising it of delinquent pledges, and requesting formal approval to write them off. The board discusses each such delinquent pledge before giving its approval.

---

[3] In large organizations, the control can be even more effective where the division of duties is such that an employee who is not a check signer *or* bookkeeper can prepare the bank reconciliation. It is possible for check signers to fraudulently make out a check to themselves and then, if they have access to the returned checks, to remove the cancelled check. However, if they don't also have a means of covering up the disbursement, sooner or later the shortage will come out. The person reconciling the bank account is not in a position to permanently "cover up" a shortage, although it could be hidden for several months. For this reason, it is preferable to have neither a check signer nor the bookkeeper prepare the reconciliation.

9. *Marketable securities should be kept in a bank safe deposit box or held by a custodian in an account in the name of the organization.*

This control is to ensure that securities are protected against loss by fire or theft or from bankruptcy of a brokerage house. Safeguarding investments is discussed more fully on pages 617–619.

10. *Fixed asset records should be maintained and an inventory taken periodically.*

These procedures ensure that the organization has a complete record of its assets. The permanent record should contain a description of the asset, cost, date acquired, location, serial number, and similar information. Such information will provide a record of the assets that the employees are responsible for. This is particularly important in not-for-profit organizations where turnover of employees and officers is often high. It also provides fire insurance records.

11. *Excess cash should be maintained in a separate bank or investment account. Withdrawals from this account should require two signatures.*

Where an organization has excess cash that will not be needed for current operations in the immediate future, it should be placed in a separate account to provide an added safeguard. Frequently, this separate account will be an interest-bearing savings account. The bank or investment manager should be advised that the signatures of two officers are required for all withdrawals. Normally, in such situations, withdrawals are infrequent; when they are made, the funds withdrawn are deposited intact in the regular current checking account. In this way, all disbursements are made from the regular checking account.

In this situation, the officers involved in authorizing a withdrawal should not do so without being fully aware of the reasons for the need of these funds. Approval should not be perfunctorily given.

One final recommendation. Fidelity insurance should be carried. The purpose of fidelity insurance is to ensure that, if a loss from embezzlement occurs, the organization will recover the loss. This insurance does not cover theft or burglary by an outside person; it provides protection only against an employee's dishonesty. Having fidelity insurance also acts as a deterrent because the employees know that the insurance company is more likely to press charges against a dishonest employee than would a "soft-hearted" and embarrassed employer.

There is only one "catch" to this type of coverage. The organization has to have good enough records to prove that an embezzlement has taken place. This means that this coverage is not a substitute for other internal controls. If the theft occurs but the employer doesn't know it or if there is no proof of the loss, fidelity insurance will not help.

Sometimes, employees feel that a lack of confidence in them is being expressed if the organization has fidelity insurance. The treasurer should assure them that this is not the case, and that fidelity insurance is similar to fire insurance. All prudent organizations carry such coverage.

Even the smallest organization should be able to apply the internal controls that have been recommended in this section. The board should insist that these and similar controls be established. It has a responsibility to insist that all practical measures be taken to protect the organization's assets. Otherwise, the board would be subject to severe criticism if an embezzlement were to occur.

The controls discussed in this section are basic ones and should not be considered all-inclusive. A complete system of internal control encompasses all of the procedures of the organization. If the organization is large or complex, or if it has peculiar problems or procedures, the board will want to retain the services of a professional to help set up and monitor the effectiveness of internal control. The next section discusses the services that the certified public accountant can provide, including assistance in establishing internal controls.

25.6 Independent Audits

Related to the internal controls discussed in the preceding section is the question of whether the books and records should be audited. Like many other decisions the board has to make, this is a value judgment for which there are no absolute answers. Audits cost time and money, and therefore the values to be derived must be considered carefully.

An audit is a series of procedures followed by an experienced professional accountant to test, on a selective basis, transactions and internal controls in effect, all with a view to forming an opinion on the fairness of the presentation of the financial statements.

Several things should be underscored. Auditors do not examine all transactions. If they were to do so, the cost would be prohibitive. They do look at what they believe is a representative sample of the transactions. In looking at these selected transactions, they are as concerned with the internal control and procedures that were followed as they are with the legitimacy of the transaction itself. If internal controls are good, the extent of the testing can be limited. If controls are weak, the auditors will have to examine many more transactions to be satisfied. In smaller organizations, where internal controls are often less effective, auditors must examine proportionately more transactions.

Another point is that, for the most part, the auditors can only examine and test transactions that have been recorded. If a contribution has been received but not deposited in the bank or recorded in the books, there is little likelihood that it will be discovered. This is why the preceding section emphasized that controls should be established over all receipts at the point of receipt and all disbursements should be made by check. In this way, a record is made and the auditor has a chance of testing the transaction.

The end product of the audit is not a "certificate" that every transaction has been properly recorded, but an expression of an opinion by the auditor on the fairness of the presentation of the financial statements. The auditor does not guarantee accuracy; the bookkeeper may have stolen $100, but unless this $100 is material in relation to the financial statements as a whole, the auditor is not likely to discover it.

(A) WHY HAVE AN AUDIT?

Audits are not free. This means that the board has to evaluate the benefits to be derived from an audit, and its cost. What are the benefits that can be expected from an audit? There are four: credibility of the financial statements; professional assistance in developing meaningful financial statements; professional advice on internal control, administrative efficiency, and other business matters; and assistance in tax reporting and compliance requirements.

Credibility is the principal benefit of having an independent CPA express an opinion on the financial statements. Unfortunately, over the years, there have been many instances where not-for-profit organizations have been mismanaged and the results have been buried in the financial statements in a manner that made it difficult, if not impossible, for the readers of the statements to discern them.

It has been noted that the purpose of financial statements is to communicate in a straightforward manner what has happened. The presence of an auditor's opinion helps in this communication process because an independent expert, after an examination, tells the reader that the financial statements present fairly what has happened. Not-for-profit organizations are competing with other organizations for the money of their members or of the general public. If an organization can tell its financial story accurately and completely and it is accepted at face value, the potential contributor is more likely to feel that the organization is well managed.

Another benefit of having professional help is that the auditor is an expert at preparing financial statements in a format that will be most clear to the reader. All too often, financial statements are poorly organized and hard to understand. The CPA has experience in helping organizations to prepare financial statements in clear and understandable language.

Another benefit is that the CPA will be in a position to advise the board on how to strengthen internal controls and simplify the bookkeeping procedures. The CPA can also assist the board in evaluating the organization's bookkeeper and can help the organization hire someone for this position.

The CPA has had experience in dealing with different types of organizations and is likely to have a number of general business suggestions. Typically, periodic meetings with senior staff or board members will be held to discuss the problems of the organization and business conditions in general. Many boards arrange annual meetings to ask questions and to be sure that the organization has picked the CPA's brain. This meeting also provides the CPA with an opportunity to call any potential problems to the board's attention.

As is discussed in Chapters 29 and 30, most not-for-profit organizations are required to submit some form of report to one or more agencies of a state government and the IRS. These reports are technical in format and, unless the treasurer is an accountant, the assistance of an expert will probably be required. The CPA is an expert, and can either offer advice on how to prepare the returns or can actually prepare them.

(B) FINDING AN AUDITOR

When it comes time to choose a CPA, discussion should include the organization's banker, attorney, and members of the board. The chances are that collectively they will know many CPAs practicing in the locality and will know of their reputations. Officers of other not-for-profit organizations should be consulted. They will probably have had some experience that may be of help. One significant criterion in the selection should be the CPA's familiarity with not-for-profit entities.

As in any professional relationship, the CPA's interest and willingness to serve the organization are among the most important factors to consider when making a selection. It is always difficult to judge which of several CPAs has the greatest interest in helping the organization. In large part, the board will have to make the decision from impressions formed in personal interviews. The appendix at the end of this chapter discusses this subject further.

During this personal interview, the CPA should be asked to take a look at the records, to get a general impression of the amount of time that will be necessary, and thus the fee. For the most part, the judgment should not be swayed significantly by the fee range estimated, unless it is out of line with other CPA fees. Like a doctor or lawyer, the accountant expects to receive a fair fee for services. The organization is largely dependent on the honesty and professional reputation of the accountant to charge a fair fee.

What does it cost to have an audit? This is a difficult question to answer because most CPAs charge on an hourly basis. If the organization's records are in good shape, the time will be less. There is no way to know how much time will be involved without looking at the records and knowing something about the organization.

Sometimes an organization will shop around in an effort to find the CPA that will charge it the least. Because the treasurer is not likely to be in a position to judge the quality of the work, there is a risk in choosing a professional accountant solely on the basis of an estimated fee. Choosing a CPA should be on the basis of reputation, expertise, and willingness to serve the organization.

(C)   REVIEW SERVICES

A possible alternative to an audit, for an organization that does not have to submit audited financial statements to a state, a funding source, or another organization, is to have its financial statements "reviewed" by a CPA. A review requires less time, hence incurs less cost; however, it results in a lesser degree of assurance by the CPA. Instead of saying that the financial statements "present fairly," the CPA does only enough work to be able to say, "I am not aware of any material modifications that should be made in order for the financial statements to be in conformity." This is called "negative assurance" and does not give as much credibility to the financial statements as an audit does. Nevertheless, a review may meet the needs of some smaller organizations.

(D)   AUDIT COMMITTEES

Many smaller organizations do not feel they can afford a CPA and yet want some assurance that accounting matters are being adequately managed, and especially that disbursements have been made for proper purposes. One solution to this is to set up an "audit committee" consisting of several members of the board or of the membership. The committee may meet on a monthly or bimonthly basis and review transactions since the last meeting. It may also review bank reconciliations, marketable securities bought, sold, and on hand, and any other matter that could be "sensitive."

The advantage of an audit committee is that it strengthens internal control significantly, with little cost. This is particularly important where internal control is weak because it is not practical to segregate duties as much as might be desired.

The institution of external audit committees has now become a common practice for not-for-profit organizations. A properly functioning audit committee goes a long way toward demonstrating that the board of trustees has taken prudent steps to perform its administrative and control functions. Thus, with regard to audit committees, the author recommends that:

- Every not-for-profit organization that raises funds from the general public or that receives grants or membership dues should have an active and functioning audit committee.
- For most effective operation, audit committees should be composed of three to five directors, with the majority (including the chairperson) being trustees who are not employees.

- Audit committees should be responsible for recommending the appointment of the independent accountants and for discussion of their work with them.
- Audit committees should be responsible for the review and evaluation of reports prepared by the independent accountants that contain recommendations for improvements in controls. Audit committees should determine whether management has taken appropriate action on these recommendations.
- Audit committees should be delegated the responsibility to review the annual financial statements with the independent accountants.

25.7 *Investments*

Some not-for-profit organizations have an investment program to manage, as a result of receipt of endowment funds and other restricted gifts. Some organizations also have excess cash in their unrestricted general fund, which can be invested. Sometimes all of these investment funds can be very sizable. They are usually invested in publicly traded securities, although occasionally a partial amount is invested in real estate or in mortgages.

Where should an organization go to get good investment advice? The answer is clear: to a professional; to someone who knows the market and is in the business of advising others.

Sometimes, a nonprofit's board, recognizing its fiduciary responsibilities, will tend to be too conservative in its investment policy, and will purchase high-grade, low-interest-bearing bonds. This conservatism can be almost as risky as purchasing a highly volatile stock, as many holders of bonds discovered in recent years when high interest rates depressed bond prices. This is why professional advice is needed.

There are a number of places to go for professional advice. If the total investments are relatively small in size (say, under $100,000), many organizations find that a no-load mutual fund or a bank common stock fund is the answer.[4] In both cases, the organization is purchasing expertise while it pools its funds with those of many other people. Mutual funds offer a convenient way to obtain investment management when the organization has a minimum amount to invest.

Bank-commingled or common stock investment funds are a form of mutual fund. One of the advantages of using a bank fund is that the reputation of the bank is involved and the bank will pay close attention to the investments made. Banks are often more conservative than mutual funds in their investment decisions, but this may be appropriate when one considers the fiduciary responsibility of not-for-profit organizations.

If the investment fund is large in size, the organization may prefer to select a professional to advise on specific stocks and bonds to purchase for its own portfolio. Most brokers are pleased to offer this service. On the other hand, many not-for-profit organizations are reluctant to entrust investment decisions to the brokers who handle the ac-

---

[4] If an organization has under $100,000 to invest, the board should carefully consider the nature of the funds being invested before buying common stocks. If the funds available are to be invested for only a short period of time, or if investment income is essential, then the organization should not be investing in common stocks. Instead, a savings account or money-market instrument is probably more appropriate.

ACCOUNTING, FINANCE, AND LEGAL ISSUES

tual purchasing, because they are "wearing two hats." This can be avoided by going to one of the many available investment advisory services that does not handle the actual purchasing or selling.

Investment professionals can also offer advice on a type of investment that is frequently not given the attention it warrants by not-for-profit organizations—short-term investments. Short-term investments are investments in interest-bearing instruments of that portion of an organization's cash balances which is currently inactive but will be needed to fund programs and activities in the near future.

An ordinary savings account is one type of short-term investment of cash balances that are temporarily not deployed. Often, however, it is possible to improve on the interest rate available in savings accounts, without substantially increasing risk, by purchasing "money-market" instruments. These vary in interest rate, risk, minimum denomination available, time to maturity, and marketability prior to redemption; included are U.S. Treasury Bills, "agencies," certificates of deposit, and repurchase agreements.

Treasury Bills are the most marketable money-market instrument. The smallest denomination currently available is $10,000 and the shortest maturity is 13 weeks.

"Agencies" are federally sponsored debt instruments issued by federal agencies or quasi-governmental organizations. Some are explicitly guaranteed by the full faith and credit of the United States Government but others are not.

Certificates of deposit (CDs) are available directly from commercial or savings banks, or through securities dealers. Only large CDs (over $100,000) are negotiable, and all bear substantial penalties for redemption prior to maturity.

Repurchase agreements are agreements under which a bank or securities dealer agrees to repurchase, at a specific date and at a specific premium, securities sold earlier to an investor. Interest rates on repurchase agreements are often attractive, and a wide range of maturities is usually available.

A list of investment advisory services can usually be found in the classified telephone directory. As with all professionals, the investment adviser's reputation should be carefully checked. The bank's trust department is usually also happy to give advice on investment decisions. The point to emphasize is that investment decisions should be made by professionals in the investment business and not by amateurs (this is as true of investments as it is of medicine!). Even professionals can make errors in judgment, but the risk is lower.

The professional adviser will charge a fee, generally calculated on the basis of a percentage of the monies invested. The larger the investment fund, the lower the rate charged.

The physical safeguarding of an organization's investment securities is as important as making the right decision as to which stocks to buy or sell. This is often overlooked. The board of directors or the finance committee of the board has general responsibility for all investment instruments owned by the organization. Periodic verification of the existence of the securities should be made, either by independent accountants or the board itself. Verification usually involves a physical counting of the securities at the location where they are deposited. Three areas warrant special attention. The first is that stock certificates aren't lost or misplaced through carelessness or poor handling. The second is that they are not lost through misappropriation by an employee. The third is that the stockbroker doesn't lose the certificates or, worse yet, go bankrupt.

If the organization keeps the certificates in its possession, the certificates should be kept in a bank safe deposit box. They should be registered in the name of the organization. The organization should also maintain an investment register that shows the certificate number as well as the cost and other financial information. There should be limited access to the safe deposit box, and it is wise to require the presence of two persons (preferably officers) whenever the box is opened.[5]

An organization must always be concerned that someone having access to stock certificates may be tempted to steal them. Although the certificates may be registered in the organization's name, there is an underworld market for stolen certificates. Furthermore, if the loss is not discovered promptly and the transfer agent advised to "stop transfer," the organization's rights may be jeopardized.

The best control is to have the broker deliver the stock certificate directly to a custodian for safekeeping. When the stock is sold, the custodian is then instructed to deliver the certificate to the broker. In this way, the organization never handles the certificate.

Some organizations leave their certificates in the custody of their broker. This has certain risks. One is that the broker will temporarily lose track of the certificates if the back office falls behind in its paperwork or incorrectly records the certificates.

The other risk is the broker's going bankrupt while holding the stock. Provided the broker has not fraudulently hypothecated the stock, bankruptcy should not result in a loss to an organization. However, there could be considerable delay before the stock is released by a court. On the other hand, if the broker has, without the consent of the organization, pledged the stock for personal borrowings, there is a possibility of actual loss. While the organization might be able to take both civil and criminal action against the broker, this would be of little consolation in bankruptcy. The first $500,000 of such losses, however, would be recovered from the federally chartered Securities Investor Protection Corporation.

While these risks might be relatively small, a not-for-profit organization has a fiduciary responsibility to act with more than ordinary care and judgment. Accordingly, it would be prudent for an organization to have the broker deliver the stock certificates in the organization's name, either to an independent custodian or to the organization.

Appendix: Checklist of Criteria for Selection of a CPA

Not all of these criteria will be relevant in every selection process, and their relative importance will vary for different organizations. The order of the items in the list is not intended to indicate an absolute degree of importance to an organization, but criteria listed in the early part of the list are those that are often considered more important. An organization should set tentative criteria at the start of the proposal process, but should not hesitate to change the criteria or their relative importance if considered desirable. (Criteria that have been disseminated to proposing CPAs should not be changed without notifying the CPAs.)

---

[5] It is also wise for the board to establish an investment committee charged with the responsibility for authorizing all investment transactions. If an outside adviser is retained, this committee should still review the outside adviser's recommendations before they are accepted. It is not wise to delegate authority to an outside adviser to act except in accordance with an investment policy approved by the investment committee.

1. Characteristics of the personnel to be assigned to the engagement:
   - *Experience and expertise in the area of not-for-profit organization accounting and auditing on the part of the personnel who will be assigned to the engagement.* These are the people who will be directly responsible for serving the organization's needs, and it is their abilities on which the quality of that service primarily depends. The not-for-profit environment is different in many ways from that of for-profit organizations; a lack of experience with that environment can be only partly offset by experience with other types of clients, except in the most routine circumstances.
   - *Personal ability of the designated key engagement personnel to relate well to and work effectively with organization staff.* This is a hallmark of any successful professional relationship.
2. *Ability of the CPA to respond quickly, effectively, and competently to the organization's needs.* This is a more general statement of the previous criterion, as well as reflecting other factors such as the ability of the engagement staff to call upon other resources if needed. Such resources might include other personnel within a firm, reference material, and other persons with appropriate knowledge and skills. It also encompasses the overall attitude with which a CPA approaches service to clients.
3. *Experience with similar organizations* (e.g., medium-size symphony orchestras, Red Cross chapters, large trade associations, community colleges). A long list of a CPA's present clients can be considered positive evidence supporting an ability to meet criterion 2, but, especially in a larger firm, many of these clients may not be served by the same personnel as would serve your organization. Such a list is certainly a plus but should not be the only basis for choosing a CPA. An organization may wish to request the proposing CPAs to furnish names of client references who may be contacted.
4. *Reputation.* This includes the two previous criteria, as well as a lot of more intangible factors such as how the CPA is looked upon by others in and outside the not-for-profit industry, his or her commitment to serving organizations in the industry, and involvement by personnel in professional activities. (What an organization sometimes means by this criterion is, will the presence of a particular CPA's or CPA firm's signature on our accounts help our fund-raising efforts? The Answer is, usually, not much.)
5. *Fee.* This should not be the deciding criterion (although it too often is), unless two or more CPAs are perceived as nearly equal in all other respects. A CPA who proposes a fee significantly lower than others' fees is sometimes: (1) not being realistic about the effort required to complete an engagement or (2) "low-balling" to get the work, and will either give a lower quality of service and/or try to raise the fee significantly in future years. When evaluating a proposal of this type, the organization should question the CPA about the basis for the quoted fee.
6. *Proposed approach to the engagement.* What does the CPA believe needs to be done, and how will the engagement be undertaken? A well-thought-out presentation on this subject improves the chances that the CPA meets criteria 1 and 2. The presentation need not be long but should show evidence that the work will be well planned and tailored to the particular

needs and circumstances of the organization. There should also be an indication of the commitment of adequate time to the engagement by more senior personnel.

7. *Closeness of the CPA's office to the organization's headquarters.* (In the case of a multilocation organization; closeness of one or more offices of a firm to the principal operating locations of the organization.) This is really just part of criterion 2. Distance can be a negative factor, but it does not have to be if the CPA can compensate for this.

8. *Size of the CPA's firm and/or local office.* Except for an extremely large and complex organization (which usually does require the services of a large firm), there are no rules on this point. Both larger and smaller firms and individual practitioners can render distinguished service to both larger and smaller organizations, if the conditions of criteria 1 and 2 are well met.

9. *Ability of the CPA to provide other services such as consulting work.* Sometimes this may be important to an organization and sometimes not. An organization should think about this in view of its own current and anticipated future circumstances.

10. *Organization structure of the CPA's firm.* How centralized or decentralized is it? How much authority does the engagement partner have to make decisions? Usually any effect of this factor is far outweighed by criteria 1 and 2, unless a large firm is so centralized that local personnel have little authority.

11. *Continuity of staff assigned to the engagement.* Some amount of staff turnover is inevitable in almost any accounting practice, but excessive turnover is not desirable as it partly defeats the goal of building familiarity with a client. At the same time, some organizations consider orderly slow rotation of personnel desirable as a way of maintaining the CPA's independence and bringing fresh ideas to bear on the engagement.

Other criteria that are not judgment criteria, but rather should be prerequisites for any CPA to be considered for selection:

- Ability to meet reasonable deadlines.
- Willingness to furnish recommendations for proposed improvements in internal controls and management procedures identified during the course of other work.
- Ability to assign the requisite number and experience levels of personnel to work on the engagement.
- Ability to render the desired services in a professional manner.

Suggested Readings

American Institute of Certified Public Accountants, New York:
Accounting Standards Division, "Accounting for Joint Costs of Informational Materials and Activities of Not-for-Profit Organizations that Include a Fund-Raising Appeal," Statement of Position No. 87-2, 1987. (In process of revision)
Accounting Standards Division, "The Application of the Requirements of Accounting Research Bulletins, Opinions of the Accounting Principles Board, and Statements

and Interpretations of the Financial Accounting Standards Board to Not-for-Profit Organizations," Statement of Position No. 94-2, 1994.

Accounting Standards Division, "Reporting of Related Entities by Not-for-Profit Organizations," Statement of Position No. 94-3, 1994.

Committee on Not-for-Profit Organizations, "Audits of Not-for-Profit Organizations Receiving Federal Awards," Statement of Position No. 92-9, 1992.

Committee on Not-for-Profit Organizations, "Not-for-Profit Organizations," 1996.

Health Care Committee, "Health Care Organizations." 1996.

Anthony, R. N. 1978. *Financial Accounting in Nonbusiness Organizations: An Exploratory Study of Conceptual Issues.* Norwalk, CT: Financial Accounting Standards Board.

Anthony, R. N. and Young, D. W. 1984. *Management Control in Nonprofit Organizations,* 3rd ed. Homewood, IL: Richard D. Irwin.

Blazek, J. 1993. *Tax Planning and Compliance for Tax-Exempt Organizations: Forms, Checklists, Procedures,* 2nd ed. New York: Wiley.

Daughtrey, W. H., Jr. and Gross, M. J., Jr. 1978. *Museum Accounting Handbook.* Washington, DC: American Association of Museums.

Evangelical Joint Accounting Committee, "Accounting and Financial Reporting Guide for Christian Ministries," Christian Management Association, Diamond Bar, CA, 1994.

Financial Accounting Standards Board, Norwalk, CT:

Statements of Financial Accounting Concepts:

No. 4, "Objectives of Financial Reporting by Nonbusiness Organizations," 1980;

No. 6, "Elements of Financial Statements," 1985.

Statements of Financial Accounting Standards:

No. 93, "Recognition of Depreciation by Not-for-Profit Organizations," Norwalk, CT, 1987 (amended by No. 99, "Deferral of the Effective Date of Recognition of Depreciation by Not-for-Profit Organizations," 1988).

No. 95, "Statement of Cash Flows," 1987.

No. 116, "Accounting for Contributions Received and Contributions Made," 1993.

No. 117, "Financial Statements of Not-for-Profit Organizations," 1993.

No. 124, "Accounting for Certain Investments Held by Not-for-Profit Organizations." 1995.

Gross, M. J., Larkin, R. F., Bruttomesso, R. S., and McNally, J. J. 1995. *Financial and Accounting Guide for Not-for-Profit Organizations,* 5th ed. New York: Wiley, 1996 Supplement.

Holck, M., Jr. and Holck, M., Sr. 1978. *Complete Handbook of Church Accounting.* Englewood Cliffs, NJ: Prentice-Hall.

Hopkins, B. R. 1992. *The Law of Tax-Exempt Organizations,* 6th ed. New York: Wiley.

Hopkins, B. R. 1991. *The Law of Fund-Raising.* New York: Wiley.

Hummel, J. 1980. *Starting and Running a Nonprofit Organization* Minneapolis: University of Minnesota Press.

Larkin, R. F. 1994. "Accounting Issues Relating to Fundraising." Chapter 2 of *Financial Practices for Effective Fundraising.* San Francisco: Jossey-Bass.

Larkin, R. F. 1996. "Not-for-Profit Organizations." Chapter 29 of the *Accountants' Handbook,* 8th Ed. New York: Wiley.

National Association of College and University Business Officers. 1990. *Financial Accounting and Reporting Manual for Higher Education,* Washington, DC. (In process of revision)

National Association of Independent Schools. 1987. *Business Management for Independent Schools*, 3rd ed. Boston: Author. (In process of revision)

National Health Council, National Assembly for Social Policy and Development, Inc., and United Way of America. 1988. *Standards of Accounting and Financial Reporting for Voluntary Health and Welfare Organizations*, 3rd ed. New York. NHC, NASPD, and UWA. (In process of revision)

Price Waterhouse, New York.

The Audit Committee, the Board of Trustees of Not-for-Profit Organizations and the Independent Accountant, 1992.

Effective Internal Accounting Control for Nonprofit Organizations, 1988.

Not-for-Profit Organizations' Implementation Guide for SFAS Statements 116 and 117, 1993.

Ramanathan, K. V. 1982. *Management Control in Nonprofit Organizations*. New York: Wiley.

United Way of America, Alexandria, Va.:

Accounting and Financial Reporting: A Guide for United Ways and Not-For Profit Human Service Organizations, 2nd ed., 1989.

Budgeting: A Guide for United Ways and Not-for-Profit Human Service Organizations, 1975.

Wacht, R. F. 1984. *Financial Management in Nonprofit Organizations*. Atlanta, GA: Georgia State University.

26 ▼ Budgeting

RUTHIE G. REYNOLDS, PhD, CPA, JD
Morehouse College

26.1 Introduction

As in business enterprises, budgeting is the key to successful nonprofit management. The two most important components of budgeting in business enterprises are *planning* and *controlling*. These components are also part of nonprofit budgeting, but a third component, *programming*, is added. These three components comprise the overall management system.

Budgeting may be defined as the process of projecting future resources to be received and future resources to be used. This process involves the development of a plan of action that will be used to guide the management team in the use of its resources. Quantitative and qualitative data are used in this process.

In addition to planning the use of future resources, budgets are used to plan future programs. Programs are the essence of nonprofit organizations. Unlike business enterprises established for the primary purpose of earning a profit, nonprofit organizations are established to provide services through programs. The control aspect of budgeting allows management to compare actual results of operations with the budget, gaining feedback which is used to evaluate performance.

This chapter discusses the budgeting process. The discussion includes budgeting techniques, types of budget, steps in preparing budgets, and the ethical aspects of budgeting. The relationship of accounting and budgeting will be discussed also. The appendix to this chapter contains sample budgeting forms recommended by United Way of America for human service organizations.

26.2 *Purposes of Budgeting*

The three major components of budgeting summarize the purposes of budgeting: planning, programming, and control.

(A) PLANNING

The planning phase of budgeting is best explained through an organization's mission statement. The mission statement sets forth the vision of the organization and generally is formulated by the founding members. It may, however, be altered or completely replaced over the years.

Economic and social changes are the major reason for changes in mission, goals, and objectives. For example, twenty years ago day care was not a major community issue. Few mothers worked, and family members were available to assist when needed. Today, a greater number of women work outside the home. There are more single-parent homes than ever before, and the number continues to increase. Therefore, day care for children and senior citizens is a major community concern. Accordingly, an agency with a mission that provides day care services may find it necessary to change or amend its goals and objectives in order to deliver services.

The goals set forth the manner in which the mission is to be accomplished, and the objectives are operational statements of goals. The setting of goals and objectives are outlined for the specified period of time. Goals and objectives set forth the future direction of an organization. Usually, specific targets, dates, and methods of reaching targets are spelled out. The period of time covered by a budget is usually an accounting period, 12 months. However, longer or shorter periods are not uncommon. Exhibit 26.1 shows an example of the relationship among the mission, goals, and objectives of a hypothetical human-service organization called American Centers.

Balancing is the key in planning. Strategies must be developed to make the objectives consistent with goals. Furthermore, it is necessary to make sure goals complement the established mission of the organization.

EXHIBIT 26.1 Examples of Mission/Goals/Objectives

American Centers
Statement of Mission, Goals, and Objectives

Mission: To provide program services as needed to the citizens of American City, regardless of their ability to pay.

Goals: To assist the citizens in improving the quality of their lives by providing community services, day care, and recreation.

Objectives: To provide community services through an adult tutoring service; to provide day-care services for 20 children and 10 senior citizens; and to provide after-school and summer recreation activities for children.

Planning requires cooperation among all members of the organization. The administrator, the staff, and the board of directors must work together to ensure successful planning. The management style of the chief administrator has a bearing on this cooperative effort.

Some administrators and managers prefer a management style in which directives are handed down from the top; others favor a management style in which directives are developed from the bottom. The former style is commonly referred to as *imposed budgeting*, and the latter is referred to as *participatory budgeting*. Governmental units and nonprofit organizations, with monetary control and fiscal responsibility as their primary emphasis, have traditionally used imposed budgets. But planning cannot be carried out successfully under imposed budgeting.

Learning from the experiences of business enterprises, nonprofit organizations have begun to embrace participatory budgeting. They realize that cooperation and communication among all members of the operation is necessary. Some of the advantages of participatory budgeting are summarized in Exhibit 26.2.

Participatory budgeting is part of a broader concept called *participatory management*. Both are outgrowths of the behavioral approach to management which hold that employees' ideas and opinions should be solicited and incorporated into the final budget plans. By soliciting the input of the employees, administrators are likely to have better acceptance of the budget because the employees will feel they are working on a team effort.

During the planning phase, administrators should take a new look at the needs and desires of the group or groups to be served. They should look at past performance by comparing budgeted data with actual results. By looking at past performance, changes in approaches and strategies can be made. Information and opinions should be gathered from the communities served. Surveys of community needs are very helpful in this phase of the process.

(B) PROGRAMMING

In nonprofit budgeting, programming refers to the execution of the plans developed in the planning phase. During this phase, programs and the staffing of the program positions are the major considerations.

Programming connects the goals and objectives into programs or activity units. As in the planning phase, balancing is a key element as management attempts to design specific programs within the constraints given. Naturally, resource availability is important; however, management should attempt to concentrate not on the availability of funds, but on the desired results if sufficient resources were made available. In fact, the

---

EXHIBIT 26.2 Advantages of Participatory Budgeting

1. Focuses on teamwork.
2. Solicits input from workers who are most familiar with operations.
3. Improves morale of workers.
4. Encourages acceptance of the budget.
5. Introduces realism into the process.

"desired results approach" is quite beneficial to management because management may use its planned programs in soliciting funding for its operations.

The programming phase begins with a review of the proposed goals and objectives and an evaluation of the existing programs. Old programs are continued, revised, or abandoned. Next, new programs are developed and evaluated as alternatives to existing programs. Finally, the programs that best fit the goals, objectives, and mission of the organization are selected. Programs should be the result of fact-finding, not guesswork.

(C) CONTROL

One means of control is comparing actual performance with planned goals and objectives. It calls for monitoring actual activity to ensure that budgeted activity is accomplished in an efficient and effective manner.

Today, most nonprofit organizations use many of the same budgeting tools as business enterprises. One of the control tools used is *responsibility accounting*. As nonprofit organizations become larger and more complex, responsibility accounting satisfies the need to communicate results up and down the organizational hierarchy. Program managers are held accountable for use of resources and also required to account for performance of the planned activity. This system produces responsibility reports which administrators use to evaluate programs and program managers. These reports may contain quantitative and qualitative data. Responsibility accounting requires that program managers and other subordinate managers accept responsibility for their units.

Another common way to use budgets as a control measure is *variance analysis*. In variance analysis, actual activity is compared to planned (budgeted) activity. The difference between the actual and planned is called a variance. Variances are labeled favorable and unfavorable, depending on whether or not the planned activity was achieved. If the variances are significant, they are investigated and subordinate managers must provide explanations.

The explanation should reflect the cause and source of the variance. A common misconception in variance analysis is that only unfavorable variances should be investigated. In most cases, favorable variances should be investigated with equal attention. For example, a favorable expense variance may be the result of the use of inferior goods or services. A favorable revenue variance may be the result of poor forecasting or poor management. For effective control, all factors underlying the variance, both external and internal, must be isolated.

Another misconception about budget variances is that the manager should be "blamed" for unfavorable variances. This belief is in direct opposition to the purpose of variance analysis: to improve decision making by explaining their causes and sources. Often, managers' explanations justify results.

26.3 Key Participants

Successful budgeting requires the cooperation of many different people. In light of decreasing sources of revenue and increasing demands for services, nonprofit organizations must develop a set of planned programs that will efficiently and effectively utilize the entrusted resources. Accountability is not only expected, it is required.

The major participants in the budgeting process are:

- Board members.
- Administrator or Executive Director.
- Controller.
- Fund raiser.
- Program managers.
- Staff members.
- Volunteers.

The board members set forth the mission, goals, and objectives. In many instances, they comprise the only oversight body for the organization. The administrator or Executive Director acts as a coordinator of the budgeting process and, with the assistance of the staff and controller and within the constraints handed down by the board, develops the revenue and expense estimates. Staff members' input is often solicited as to daily performance expectations, especially if participatory budgeting is followed. The controller, the chief accountant, provides historical data that are used to form a basis for projected data. Volunteers assist in various capacities, ranging from clerical to administrative.

In many organizations, a budget committee is formed to take on the responsibility for overseeing the entire budgeting process. The committee is composed of selected board members, the administrator or Executive Director, the controller, and key program managers. The administrator represents the committee on a day-to-day-basis, acting as the liaison between the groups.

After all revenue and expense estimates are gathered, the information and data are combined into the final budget documents: the operations budget, the cash budget, the capital budget, and the pro forma statement of financial position. The final budget, also known as the master budget or comprehensive budget, is presented to the board for approval. It may also be presented to various funding sources. Budget presentation can be informal or formal, depending on the audience.

26.4 Relationship of Budgeting and Accounting

Budgeting was defined in the introductory section as the process of projecting future sources and uses of resources. Accounting is defined as the financial reporting of the historical events of any entity. Accounting provides for the recording, classifying, summarizing, analyzing, and reporting of past financial transactions. Budgeting is future oriented and accounting is past oriented. In addition, budgeting in a nonprofit organization involves a great deal of qualitative reporting, whereas accounting deals more with quantitative reporting.

In profit-oriented organizations, budgeting and accounting are reported separately. That is not the case in nonprofit organizations. It is not uncommon to see the operations budget as part of the accounting reporting system. For example, some agencies show a comparison of actual operation and budgeted operations as part of their periodic accounting report.

In the traditional sense, accounting provides data for the budgeting process. First, from the planning perspective, historical data provided by the accounting system is the beginning point for forecasting future revenues and expenses. Next, accounting aids in the control phase of budgeting by supplying actual data needed for comparison with budgeted data. Rarely will accounting be the only means of projecting future data or comparing actual data, but it is a very useful and convenient starting point.

26.5 Budgeting Techniques

Numerous techniques have been developed to plan program expenses. Some of the most commonly used approaches in budgeting for nonprofit organizations are:

- Line-item budgeting (LIB)
- Planned-programming-budgeting system (PPBS)
- Zero-base budgeting (ZBB)
- Integrated approach (IA)

All three approaches deal with the estimation of expenses because revenue estimation generally does not call for a specific technique. It is based largely on historical costs.

(A) LINE-ITEM BUDGETING (LIB)

Traditionally, the most common type of budgeting in nonprofit organizations is LIB. The distinguishing characteristic of LIB is its emphasis on the past. Preparers of the budget look at amounts expended for various program activities in the past. The attempt is made to adjust the amounts upward using a predetermined rate.

Inflation and other sources of increases in expenses may be used to adjust each budget line item upward. Top administrators provide these figures. The projected increases are called *increments*. Thus, LIB is often referred to as *incremental budgeting*. The upwardly adjusted figures are used as estimates of the upcoming year's expenses. The incremental adjustment may differ for each line item or it may consistently be applied to some or all line-item amounts.

Exhibit 26.3 shows a line-item budget for a day-care program. The given percentages, representing the increase adjustments, are applied to each line item to arrive at the budgeted amounts for the upcoming year.

The most obvious advantage of LIB is simplicity. Once the percentages are determined, the new budget results from mere mathematical computations. The major disadvantage is that ineffective programs, along with their related costs, are maintained in the budget year-after-year because of a the heavy reliance on historical costs. In spite of the major disadvantages, LIB is still widely used in nonprofit budgeting today. It should be kept in mind that LIB does not have to be totally abandoned. When used in conjunction with other techniques, the benefits are retained while the negatives are minimized.

(B) PLANNED-PROGRAMMING-BUDGETING SYSTEM (PPBS)

PPBS was a product of the 1960s. Its popularity was an outgrowth of its use in the Department of Defense. It was abandoned in the early 1970s when zero-base budgeting was introduced. Although the technique has lost its popularity, many of its elements still linger in the budgeting process of many organizations today.

ACCOUNTING, FINANCE, AND LEGAL ISSUES

EXHIBIT 26.3 Example of Line-Item Budget

American Centers
Line-Item Expense Budget for Day-Care Program
Budget Year 19x2

Expense	Actual 19x1	Percent of Increase	Budget 19x2
Salaries	$155,327	7	$166,200
Employee benefits	7,766	7	8,310
Payroll taxes	15,532	7	16,620
Supplies	62,891	6	66,665
Telephone	2,596	4	2,700
Occupancy	15,472	10	17,020
Total	$259,584		$277,515

Exhibit 26.4 shows the steps in PPBS. The center of focus is the program. This technique is often confused with the programming phase of the budgeting process discussed earlier. As the steps indicate, PPBS is more extensive than the programming phase of the budgeting process. The latter deals exclusively with the establishment of programs needed to meet the goals and objectives of the nonprofit organization.

PPBS deals not only with the establishment of programs, but with the evaluation of those programs in terms of cost effectiveness. The advantages of PPBS are (1) it provides an integrated approach to management control and (2) it is somewhat scientific in that it leads to effective and efficient use of resources. The major disadvantages are: (1) it requires good coordination of efforts which is often difficult to achieve, (2) it is political in nature, and (3) it is costly to implement, both in terms of resources and time.

(C) ZERO-BASE BUDGETING (ZBB)

Zero-base budgeting was popularized in the 1970s during Jimmy Carter's tenure as governor of the State of Georgia. Later, when he became President, he took the technique to the White House where it was implemented in the federal government.

The initial appeal of ZBB was centered around the fact that each program had to justify its existence and costs each year. There was complete disregard for historical costs. As a result, only those programs that were "productive" in satisfying the organization's goals and objectives survived the evaluation process. In a sense, program managers had to "fight" for their programs' existence each time a budget was prepared. Supporters of this technique were quick to point out the fact that it eliminated the ill effects of traditional LIB.

EXHIBIT 26.4 PPBS Steps

1. Define the program.
2. Set program priorities.
3. Allocate cost to programs.
4. Evaluate programs in terms of cost effectiveness.
5. Select most cost-effective programs.

PART IV

The federal government's experience with ZBB, as well as the experiences of many nonprofit organizations, proved to be unfavorable. The major disadvantage of ZBB was the excessive amount of time required to implement the technique. Today, ZBB is not as widely used as it was during the 1970s, but certain aspects of the techniques still have possible benefits in the budgeting process for nonprofit organizations. This is especially true when used in conjunction with other techniques.

Exhibit 26.5 presents the steps in the ZBB. The emphasis in ZBB is on a fresh start each year. Historical costs based on actual performance are disregarded. The process begins with the preparation of decision packages. Each program manager is required to prepare projections of expenses at various levels of effort. These estimates are proposed as alternative ways of accomplishing the goals and objectives of the particular program. Therefore, one program manager's set of decision packages may resemble a complete traditional budget for an entire organization rather than just one program within an organization. This phase results in massive volumes of paperwork.

The greatest time and effort, however, are spent ranking the decision packages. Because ZBB requires handling literally thousands of decision packages each year, rarely is there sufficient time in the normal budgeting cycle to accommodate a proper evaluation. Furthermore, it may be necessary to go through the ranking procedures more than once, or even more than twice, which will place additional time pressure on the preparer. The resulting demands on time and resources can be overwhelming, placing a drain on time to perform program services.

(D) INTEGRATED APPROACH (IA)

Although LIB, ZBB, and PPBS are often thought of as individual budgeting techniques, there is no reason these methods cannot be combined. The integrated approach to budgeting takes the advantages of all budgeting techniques and formulates an approach to budgeting that is tailor-made for the specific organization involved. In reality, this is an ideal approach for nonprofit organizations because the unfavorable attributes of the individual methods can be abandoned while preserving the favorable attributes. Therefore, ZBB may be used for some program expense estimates while LIB or PPBS may be used for others. The obvious benefit of this approach is that the organization gets the best of all worlds.

26.6 The Budget Process

Generally, the first phase of the process is the dissemination of the guidelines that govern the budgeting process. If a nonprofit organization established a budget committee,

---

EXHIBIT 26.5 Zero-Base Budgeting Steps

1. Define the decision center (program or activity).
2. Assume that each line item in each program has a zero balance.
3. Develop decision packages for each decision unit.
4. Rank each decision package, first within the decision unit, then within the organization.
5. Allocate the resources to the decision packages.

---

the committee will be responsible for distributing the guidelines to the appropriate members. This task is usually handled by the committee chairperson or chief administrator.

Guidelines for the budgeting process, formulated by the budget committee or administrator, are passed on to program managers to act as floors and ceilings on program activities. The guidelines set forth all constraints: those on spending, hiring, and government regulations. Other matters covered include budget format, timetable, and feasible assumptions.

Administrators usually estimate revenue, with input from the board and funding sources. Program managers usually estimate the expenses using one or a combination of the techniques mentioned earlier. These figures may go through several revisions before they are accepted. There may be negotiations between the administrator and program managers, and the success of these negotiations is of utmost importance in the overall success of the budgeting process. Even if estimates are in agreement with guidelines, they may be challenged. If so, all or selected budget items may require justification. This procedure strengthens the budgeting process because it increases the probability that only worthy programs survive. The revised data and information are compiled into a single document that has several interrelated parts.

(A) TYPES OF BUDGETS

There are at least four component parts of the final (master) budget: operations budget, cash budget, capital budget, and the pro forma statement of financial position.

(i) Operations Budget

The operations budget is probably the most common in nonprofit organizations. It contains the estimates of revenues from all sources and the estimates of expenses for administration and all programs. This budget projects the financial operating activities of the organization for a specified period of time. The period of time is often one year, but annual budgets are also broken down into monthly estimates.

The appendix contains sample budget forms for human service organizations. The operations budget form is labeled Budget Form 1. There are two major sections of an operations budget: revenues and expenses. On Budget Form 1, the human service revenue is called Public Support and Revenue, and Expenses. The form shows that United Way agencies, which are human-service organizations, receive their support from the sources appearing on lines 1–12.

Sources of revenue differ, depending on the type of nonprofit organization. A human-service organization such as a neighborhood center may receive contributions, legacies, bequests, and grants. In addition to receiving support from the public, most human-service organizations also receive assistance from the federal government, state and local governments, and special interest groups. A governmental agency receives revenue from various types of taxes such as income tax, sales tax, and property tax.

Once a technique has been selected, the budget documents are prepared and presented to the board for approval.

Revenues. The starting point for the estimation of revenues is prior-year sources. It is not unusual for administrators to receive commitments from former supporters prior to the estimating phase. Grant approval or special allocations from related organizations may be received months before the budgeting process begins. It is an advantage for organizations to receive revenue commitments prior to preparing the budget. Government agencies have different types of advantages. In order to meet revenue requirements, increases in taxes and assessments can be imposed. Therefore, revenue estimation for governmental units may occur before expense estimates are finalized.

When services and products are sold to the public by nonprofit organizations, the procedure for estimating revenues to some extent resembles the estimation activity of a profit-making enterprise. The number of service units or products to be sold is estimated, an estimated sale price or rate is applied, and gross revenue is calculated.

Example 1. A neighborhood center may be licensed to provide day care for 20 children. The administrator estimates an average operating capacity of 90 percent throughout the budget year. Assuming that a sliding scale will be used to charge clients and that the average hourly rate is determined to be $5, the estimate of the revenue to be earned by the day-care program is:

$$\text{At 90\% capacity: (20 clients} \times 90\%) = 18 \text{ clients}$$
$$18 \text{ clients} \times 40 \text{ hours} \times 52 \text{ weeks} \times \$5 = \$187,200$$

The day-care service fees are not likely to be the only source of revenue for the program. Additional sources of revenue may include grants and contracts from governmental agencies, as well as contributions.

Other forms of revenue can be estimated, also. Investment income, for example, can be estimated by applying an expected rate of return to the investment amount.

Example 2. An organization has a portfolio of stocks and bonds of $80,000, and its financial advisor estimates an annual return of 9 percent; the revenue estimate from the investment can be determined as follows:

Expected Return of 9%:
$$\text{Investment} \times \text{Expected return} = \text{Estimated investment income}$$
$$\$80,000 \times 9\% = \$7,200$$

Governmental agencies can estimate revenues by applying the tax rate to the tax base.

Example 3. In estimating revenue from property taxes, assume the assessment base is $10 million and the assessment rate is 15 mills per $1:

Assessment Base of $10 million:
$$\text{Assessment base} \times \text{Assessment rate} = \text{Estimated Tax Revenue}$$
$$(\$10,000,000) \times .015 = \$150,000$$

If the governmental agency needs to increase the tax assessments to balance its budgets, it may do so by raising the tax base or the assessment rate. The increase must be approved by the appropriate governmental bodies, but this is an option that no other nonprofit organizations enjoy.

Expenses. Estimated expenses for a human-service organization appear on lines 14–29 of Budget Form 1, which appears in the appendix. A sample program expense budget is present in Exhibit 26.6. The hypothetical organization, American Centers, has three programs. Most of the expenses shown are common to all types of nonprofit organizations. One of the largest expense categories is compensation expense, which is the sum of salaries, employee benefits, and payroll taxes. These expenses appear on lines 14, 15, and 16 on Budget Form 1 and appear as the first three line items in Exhibit 26.6.

EXHIBIT 26.6 Example of Program Expense Budget

American Centers
Program Expense Budget
For the Year Ending December 31, 19X2

	Day-Care Services	Recreation Services	Community Services	Management and General	Total
Salaries	$166,200	$124,000	$7,200	$40,315	$337,715
Employee Benefits	8,310	6,200	360	2,015	16,885
Payroll Taxes	16,620	12,400	720	4,030	33,770
Total Compensation	191,130	142,600	8,280	46,360	388,370
Professional Fees	—	—	—	3,335	3,335
Supplies	66,665	12,500	1,300	7,280	87,745
Telephone	2,700	1,300	400	8,450	12,850
Postage	—	—	—	1,350	1,350
Occupancy	17,020	12,160	2,100	1,475	32,755
Equipment Rental	—	11,600	—	—	11,600
Total	$277,515	$180,160	$12,080	$68,250	$538,005

The estimation of compensation expense requires a personnel budget. Budget Form 5, which lists personnel positions and the related salaries, should be optional only for small agencies. This particular personnel form requires past and present years' data to be presented along with the projected data for budget year.

The personnel budget is usually prepared during the programming phase, when the objectives and goals are defined in terms of programs. Optional Budget Form 5 does not provide for program information; however, the "Account No. Charged" column serves the same purpose. Programs are assigned specific account numbers in the accounting system, to allow each program to be identified individually.

Employee benefits and payroll taxes are usually stated as percentages of salaries. Therefore, if a day-care program's annual salaries expense is estimated at $166,200, the employee benefit expense at 5 percent of salaries, and payroll taxes expense at 10 percent of salaries, compensation expense can be projected as shown in Exhibit 26.7.

Salaries expense and other compensation costs for a particular employee may be assigned to one individual program or they may be prorated to two or more programs based on expected time devoted to each program. Consider the salary and related cost of the chief administrator. In addition to the management of the entire organization, assume the position calls for the administrator to tutor adults in reading, through its community service program. If 30 percent of the administrator's time is expected to be devoted to tutoring, 30 percent of the salary, related employee benefits, and payroll taxes should be allocated to the Community Service Program. The remaining time is prorated to other programs and to the management and general function.

An important aspect of expense budgeting is making estimates as specific as possible. The type and quality of goods and services to be used should be considered. Future price increases should be anticipated, as well as technological changes that may positively or negatively affect future operations.

Equally important in preparing the operations budget is the need to prepare estimates by months in addition to years. Too often, operations budgets are prepared for the

---

EXHIBIT 26.7 Projection of Compensation Expense

American Centers
Estimation of Compensation Expense
Budget Year 19X2

Salaries Expense	$166,200
Employee Benefits (5%)	8,310
Payroll Taxes (10%)	16,620
Total Compensation Expense	$191,130

---

budget year, then divided by 12 months. This approach bears the erroneous assumption that each month will have the same operational level of activity. Nothing could be further from the truth. Rarely will an organization's revenues and expenses be the same each month.

Consider an organization that provides recreational services for youth. Because most students do not attend school during the summer months, recreational services are likely to be in more demand during this time. Thus, the budgets for the summer months of June, July, and August should have provisions for greater operation cost than other months.

Estimating Techniques. To some extent, the type of budgeting technique (LIB, PPBS, ZBB, IA) influences the type of estimating technique. Various approaches are used, and just as in budgeting techniques, a combination of the individual techniques may be used.

A commonly used technique for estimating revenues and expenses for the upcoming budget year is the *market survey*. A nonprofit organization may hire a professional marketing team or may develop its own. The team begins by performing a traditional market survey of the community needs, and then investigates the availability of resources to meet those needs.

Other expense estimation techniques include statistical methods such as regression analysis, probability theory, and modeling. Some preparers have found statistical methods to be reliable; other have not. Generally, the more homogeneous the data and the larger the database, the more reliable the results. Some nonprofit organizations still prefer traditional methods such as informed judgment and analysis of historical data.

(ii) Cash Budget

The cash budget should begin with an estimate of the beginning cash balance for the budget year. Estimated cash receipts are added to the estimated beginning cash balance, resulting in the total cash available for use during the budget year. Cash disbursements expected during the year are estimated and subtracted from the estimated total cash available, resulting in the estimated ending cash balance for the budget year.

The cash budget allows the management team to plan ahead for expected cash shortages. In addition, expected cash overages can be more adequately managed.

Estimated cash receipts may approximate estimated revenues, and estimated cash disbursements may approximate estimated expenses. This is especially true if the organization operates on a cash basis. Cash basis is an accounting method that results in the recognition of revenues when cash is received and the recognition of expenses when cash is paid. In contrast, under accrual-basis accounting, revenues are recognized when earned, and expenses are recognized when incurred. It should be noted that only accrual basis is a generally accepted accounting principle; thus it is required for most nonprofit organizations. Some organizations, however, still may use cash basis.

(iii) Capital Budget
Capital budgeting in the nonprofit sector may be viewed as fixed asset planning. It differs from capital budgeting in business enterprises in that there is no expected dollar rate of return. The capital budget provides for acquisitions and disposition of property, equipment, and other types of fixed assets. If a fixed asset is to be purchased, the specifications and the funding source are outlined in the capital budget. If an asset is to be disposed of, the selling price and replacement information are also included. Therefore, the capital budget may contain as much qualitative data as it does quantitative.

(iv) Pro Forma Statement of Financial Position
The pro forma statement of financial position (referred to as a *pro forma balance sheet* in business enterprises) estimates the financial status of the nonprofit organization at the end of a budget year. All estimated assets and liabilities are presented. The difference between the two categories is the projected fund (equity) balance. The cash balance appearing in the asset category is the same estimated ending cash balance from the cash budget.

26.7   Ethics in Budgeting

Budget committees and administrators should seek fairness in developing and implementing the budget. To be successful, everyone must buy into the budget. If the staff members do not believe the administrator and board are behind the budget, staff acceptance will be low, and the effectiveness of the budget process will be destroyed.

Also, administrators and program managers should seek to avoid what is commonly referred to as budgetary slack, or padding the budget. This is a common problem in nonprofit organizations when it is believed that funding sources will automatically reduce revenue requests by matching them with estimated expenses. Such practice is counterproductive and leads to distrust.

26.8   Conclusion

Budgeting is an important but time-consuming part of management. It is used in planning, programming, and controlling an organization's activities. Coordination plays a key role in the process because of the desirability to gather estimates from all levels of the organization. The participants in the process are the board of directors, the administrator, the controller, and program managers. It is desirable for staff members to take an active role in the budgeting process, too.

Unfortunately, there is no perfect budgeting technique. The recommended approach is referred to as an *integrated* approach, where elements of several commonly used techniques are combined. The benefit of this approach is that it minimizes the disadvantages of individual techniques. Three of these individual techniques, LIB, PPBS, and ZBB, were discussed in this chapter.

Four types of budgets were discussed: the operations budget, the cash budget, the capital budget, and the pro forma statement of financial position. These budgets together form the final or master budget which is used to guide the organization through the process of achieving its goals and objectives.

Appendix

The appendix to this chapter contains a set of simplified budget forms prepared by United Way of America for use by United Way–funded agencies. The forms and chart are presented with the permission of United Way of America, Alexandria, VA.

The set contains:

- Summary Information Form—A two-page outline of the agency's mission, services, budgetary requests, and audit comments.
- Budget Form 1—This is the Support, Revenue, and Expense Form, which, together with the Summary Information Form, can be used as the basic budget forms for those United Way agencies not using functional accounting.
- Budget Form 2—This optional "spread sheet" details the income and expense by function. It provides a total agency picture and unit costs of programs where appropriate.
- Budget Form 3—This is an optional form that describes funds that have restrictions placed on their use by the donor.
- Budget Form 4—This is also an optional form. It describes reserve funds designated by the agency's board.
- Budget Form 5—An optional form that lists the personnel positions and salaries of the agency.

PART IV

ACCOUNTING, FINANCE, AND LEGAL ISSUES

UNITED WAY FINANCIAL REPORTING FORMS

AGENCY:_____

Mailing Address: _____

City, State, Zip: _____

Telephone: (   ) _____

For the Fiscal Year

_____**To**_____

Presented _____ on _____
                                 (Name of Funding Body)   (Date)

This budget was considered and approved for submission at the Board of Directors Meeting on _____
                                                                              (Date)

_____   _____
       Chief Professional Officer   President or Other Authorized Official

AGENCY: DATE:

I. SUMMARY INFORMATION

A. Program Data

1. What is the agency's mission?

_____
_____
_____

2. What programs/services did your agency provide this year?

_____
_____
_____

3. Target population served: (age, sex, special interest, etc.)

_____
_____
_____

4. Number of unduplicated individual units served in United Way area: (3 yrs. ago _____ 2 yrs. ago_____ last yr._____)

_____
_____
_____

5. Geographic area covered:

_____
_____
_____

6. How are agency programs/services assessed for effectiveness?

_____
_____
_____

7. What are the specific objectives?

_____
_____
_____

(Continued on Back)

8. What new or different programs/services does your agency contemplate providing next year?

_____

_____

_____

9. How will these new or different programs/services be financed?

_____

_____

_____

10. What supplementary fund-raising activities does the agency conduct?

Activity	Net$ Results	Area Covered	Month Conducted

B. Financial Highlights

Financial Highlights	Last Year	This Year	Next Year
Total Expenses (BF 1: Line 35)			
Total Support & Revenue—All Sources (BF 1: Line 13)			
Excess (Deficit)			
Allocation From This United Way Direct to Agency Matching Government Grant Total			
Allocation From Other United Ways to Agency			

FOR UNITED WAY USE ONLY

Audit report has been received by the United Way for the year ending _____.

This audit report was: (   ) Unqualified   (   ) Qualified

If Qualified, explain: _____

_____

_____

_____

_____
(Signature of Chairman of Audit Committee)

AGENCY:

Budget Form: 1

Support Revenue & Expenses	Fiscal 19 Last Year Actual	Fiscal 19 This Year Budgeted	Fiscal 19 Next Year Proposed
Public Support & Revenue— All Sources [4000-6999]			
1 0000 **Allocation From This United Way**			
2 4000 Contributions			
3 4200 Special Events			
4 4300 Legacies & Bequests (Unrestricted)			
5 4600 Contributed by Associated Organizations			
6 4700 Allocated by Other United Ways			
7 5000 Fees & Grants From Government Agencies			
8 6000 Membership Dues			
9 6200 Program Services Fees & Net Incidental Revenue			
10 6300 Sales of Materials			
11 6500 Investment Income			
12 6900 Miscellaneous Revenue			
13 TOTAL SUPPORT & REVENUE (Add 1 thru 12)			
Expenses [7000-9999]			
14 7000 Salaries			
15 7100 Employee Benefits			
16 7200 Payroll Taxes, etc.			
17 8000 Professional Fees			
18 8100 Supplies			
19 8200 Telephone			
20 8300 Postage & Shipping			
21 8400 Occupancy			
22 8500 Rental & Maintenance of Equipment			
23 8600 Printing & Publications			
24 8700 Travel			
25 8800 Conferences, Conventions & Meetings			
26 8900 Specific Assistance to Individuals			
27 9000 Membership Dues			
28 9100 Awards & Grants			
29 9400 Miscellaneous			
30 TOTAL EXPENSES (Add 14 thru 29)			
31 9691 Payments to Affiliated Organizations			
32 Board Designations for Specified Activities for Future Years			
33 TOTAL EXPENSES FOR BUDGET PERIOD FOR ALL ACTIVITIES (30 + 31 + 32)			
34 TOTAL EXPENSES FOR ACTIVITIES FINANCED BY RESTRICTED FUNDS			
35 TOTAL EXPENSES FOR ACTIVITIES FINANCED BY UNRESTRICTED FUNDS (33 − 34)			
36 EXCESS (DEFICIT) OF TOTAL SUPPORT & REVENUE OVER EXPENSES (13 − 35)			
37 9500 Depreciation of Buildings & Equipment			
38 9900 Major Property & Equipment Acquisition ($ __1000__ +)			

All Financial Information Rounded to Nearest Dollar

AGENCY:

Proposed Budget for Fiscal 19 ___ By Program & Supporting Functions	Grand Total (2 + 5)	Total Supporting (3 + 4)	Supporting Services		Total Program Services 6 through 12
			Management & General	Fund Raising	
	1	2	3	4	5
Public Support & Revenue— All Sources [4000-6999]					
1 0000 **Allocation From This United Way**					
2 4000 Contributions					
3 4200 Special Events					
4 4300 Legacies & Bequests (Unrestricted)					
5 4600 Contributed by Associated Organizations					
6 4700 Allocated by Other United Ways					
7 5000 Fees & Grants From Government Agencies					
8 6000 Membership Dues					
9 6200 Program Services Fees & Net Incidental Revenue					
10 6300 Sales of Materials					
11 6500 Investment Income					
12 6900 Miscellaneous Revenue					
13 TOTAL SUPPORT & REVENUE (Add 1 thru 12).					
Expenses [7000-9999]					
14 7000 Salaries					
15 7100 Employee Benefits					
16 7200 Payroll Taxes, etc.					
17 8000 Professional Fees					
18 8100 Supplies					
19 8200 Telephone					
20 8300 Postage & Shipping					
21 8400 Occupancy					
22 8500 Rental & Maintenance of Equipment					
23 8600 Printing & Publications					
24 8700 Travel					
25 8800 Conferences, Conventions & Meetings					
26 8900 Specific Assistance to Individuals					
27 9000 Membership Dues					
28 9100 Awards & Grants					
29 9400 Miscellaneous					
30 TOTAL EXPENSES (Add 14 thru 29)					
31 9691 Payments to Affiliated Organizations					
32 Board Designations for Specified Activities for Future Years					
33 TOTAL EXPENSES FOR BUDGET PERIOD FOR ALL ACTIVITIES (30 + 31 + 32)					
34 TOTAL EXPENSES FOR ACTIVITIES FINANCED BY RESTRICTED FUNDS					
35 TOTAL EXPENSES FOR ACTIVITIES FINANCED BY UNRESTRICTED FUNDS (33 − 34)					
36 EXCESS (DEFICIT) OF TOTAL SUPPORT & REVENUE OVER EXPENSES (13 − 35)					
37 9500 Depreciation of Buildings & Equipment					
38 9900 Major Property & Equipment Acquisition ($ ___1000___ +) . . .					

Summary of Program Cost Analysis	
Computation of Per Unit Cost of Agency's Programs	1. Total Program Services Expenses Direct (from Line 33)
	2. Total Supporting Services Expenses (Line 33, Column 2 proportionally distributed)
	3. Payments to Affiliated Organizations (Line 31, Column 1, proportionally distributed)
	4. **TOTAL PROGRAM (1 + 2 + 3)**
	PROGRAM VOLUME & UNIT COST 5. Total Number Program Units
	6. Direct Cost Per Unit (Line 1 - Line 5)
	7. Total Cost Per Unit (Line 4 - Line 5)
	8. Unit Description

All Financial Information Rounded to Nearest Dollar

Budget Form: 2

Program Services						
6	7	8	9	10	11	12

c United Way of America 1982

AGENCY: _____

EXPLANATION OF RESTRICTED FUNDS
(Source Restricted Only—Exclude Board Restricted)

A. Name of Restricted Fund _____ Amount: $ _____

1. Restricted by: _____

2. Source of fund: _____

3. Purpose for which restricted: _____

4. Are investment earnings available for current unrestricted expenses?
   ___Yes ___No   If Yes, what amount: _____

5. Date when restriction became effective: _____

6. Date when restriction expires: _____

B. Name of Restricted Fund _____ Amount: $ _____

1. Restricted by: _____

2. Source of fund: _____

3. Purpose for which restricted: _____

4. Are investment earnings available for current unrestricted expenses?
   ___Yes ___No   If Yes, what amount: _____

5. Date when restriction became effective: _____

6. Date when restriction expires: _____

C. Name of Restricted Fund _____ Amount: $ _____

1. Restricted by: _____

2. Source of fund: _____

3. Purpose for which restricted: _____

4. Are investment earnings available for current unrestricted expenses?
   ___Yes ___No   If Yes, what amount: _____

5. Date when restriction became effective: _____

6. Date when restriction expires: _____

AGENCY: _____ **Optional Budget Form: 4**

EXPLANATION OF BOARD DESIGNATED RESERVES
(For Funds Which Are Not Donor Restricted)

A. Name of Board Designated Reserve:_____ Amount: $_____

  1. Date of board meeting at which designation was made: _____

  2. Source of funds:_____

  3. Purpose for which designated: _____

  _____

  4. Are the investment earnings available for current unrestricted expenses?
  ___Yes ___No   If Yes, what amount: _____

  5. Date when board designation became effective: _____

  6. Date when board designation expires: _____

B. Name of Board Designated Reserve:_____ Amount: $_____

  1. Date of board meeting at which designation was made: _____

  2. Source of funds:_____

  3. Purpose for which designated: _____

  _____

  4. Are the investment earnings available for current unrestricted expenses?
  ___Yes ___No   If Yes, what amount: _____

  5. Date when board designation became effective: _____

  6. Date when board designation expires: _____

C. Name of Board Designated Reserve:_____ Amount: $_____

  1. Date of board meeting at which designation was made: _____

  2. Source of funds:_____

  3. Purpose for which designated: _____

  _____

  4. Are the investment earnings available for current unrestricted expenses?
  ___Yes ___No   If Yes, what amount: _____

  5. Date when board designation became effective: _____

  6. Date when board designation expires: _____

Optional Budget Form: 5

AGENCY:

Account No. Charged	Position Title and/or Employee Name*	Full-Time Equiva-lent**	19___ Last Year Actual	19___ This Year Budgeted	19___ Next Year Proposed
	TOTAL				

*Denotes position vacant.
*Full-time staff will be noted as 1:00:Halftime as 0.50:Quartertime as 0.25, and so on.
All Financial Information Rounded to Nearest Dollar.

Suggested Readings

Adams, Roy M., Denby, Stephanie H, and Zipser, Jacqueline C. 1996. "A Nonprofit Director's Roadmap for Survival." *Trusts & Estates* (March):43–54.

Allen, Michael B. 1995. "The Ethics Audit." *Nonprofit World* (November/December):51–55.

Anthony, Robert N. and Young, David W. 1988. *Management Control in Nonprofit Organizations*, 4th ed. Homewood, IL: Richard D. Irwin.

Apostolou, Nicholas G. and Crumbley, D. Larry. 1992. *Handbook of Governmental Accounting and Finance*, 2nd ed. New York: Wiley.

Barton, Thomas L, Shenkir, William G., and McEldowney, John E. 1996. "The Case of Dr. Grayson: Fraud and Abuse at a Not For Profit." *CPA Journal* (February): 46–50.

Brinckerhoff, Petter C. 1996. "How to Save Money Through Bottoms-Ups Budgeting." *Nonprofit World* (January/February):22–24.

Covaleski, Mark A. 1988. "The Use of Budgetary Symbol in the Political Arena: A Historical Informed Field Study." *Accounting, Organizations and Society* (November 1):1–24.

Deckard, Kevin. 1996. "A Capital Idea: Linking the Operating and Capital Budgets in Rockville, Maryland." *Government Finance Review* (April):49–53.

Deshpande, Satish P. 1996. "Ethical Climate and the Link between Success and Ethical Behavior: An Empirical Investigation of a Non-Profit Organization." *Journal of Business Ethics* (March):315–320.

DioGuardi, Hon. Joseph J. 1995. "Our Unaccountable Federal Government: It Doesn't Add Up." *Accounting Horizons* (June):62–67.

Douglas, Patricia. 1995. *Governmental and Nonprofit Accounting: Theory and Practice*. New York: Dryden Press.

Ensman, Richard G. 1996. "New Approaches to Accountability." *Fund Raising Management* (January):58.

Gray, Sandra T. 1995. "Practicing Ethics to Build Public Confidence." *Association Management* (August):304.

Hayes, Robert D., and Millar, James A. 1990. "Measuring Production Efficiency in a Not-for-Profit Setting." *Accounting Review* (July):505–519.

Herzlinger, Regina E. 1996. "Can Public Trust in Nonprofits and Governments Be Restored?" *Harvard Business Review* (March/April):97–107.

Higuera, Jonathan J. 1996. "An Ounce of Oversight." *Foundation News & Commentary* (March/April):36–38.

Lang, Andrew S. 1996. "Board Primer: Nonprofits Do it Differently." *Association Management* (January):L52–L54.

Leighting, Ben. 1995. "Nonprofit Groups Need to Be Run Like a Business." *Denver Business Journal* (July 14):11B.

Sollenberger, Harold M. and Schneider, Arnold. 1996. *Managerial Accounting*. Cincinnati, OH: South-Western College Publishing, pp. 290, 569–570.

Stevens, Susan K. 1996. "Measuring Financial Health in the 1990s." *Foundation News & Commentary* (March/April):42–45.

Trigg, Rodger, and Nabangi, Fabian K. 1995. "Representation of the Financial Position of Nonprofit Organizations: The Habitat for Humanity Situation." *Financial Accountability & Management* (August):259–269.

United Way of America. 1989. *Accounting and Financial Reporting: A Guide for United Ways and Not-for-Profit Human Service Organizations*, rev. 2nd ed. Alexandria, VA: United Way of America.

———. 1982. *Simplified Budget Forms for United Ways in Smaller Communities*. Alexandria, VA.

———. 1975. *Budgeting: A Guide for United Ways and Not-for-Profit Human Service Organizations*. Alexandria, VA: United Way of America.

Weidner, David. 1996. "Opportunity to Exercise Professional Judgment." *Pennsylvania CPA Journal* (October):18.

Ziebell, Mary T. and Decosta, Don T. 1991. *Management Control System in Nonprofit Organizations*. New York: Harcourt Brace Jovanovich.

27 Unrelated Business Income

JODY BLAZEK, CPA
Blazek & Vetterling LLP

Based on material from *Tax Planning and Compliance for Tax-Exempt Organizations: Forms, Checklists, Procedures*, 2nd ed. by Jody Blazek (Wiley, 1993). Supplemented annually.

Exempt organizations (EOs) receive two types of income: earned and unearned. Unearned income—income for which the EO gives nothing in return—comes from grants, membership fees, and donations. One can think of such income as "one-way-street" money. The motivation for giving the money is gratuitous and/or of a nonprofit character with no expectation of gain on the part of the giver; there is donative intent.

In contrast, an EO furnishes services/goods or invests its capital in return for earned income: an opera is seen, classes are attended, hospital care is provided, or credit counseling is given, for example. The purchasers of the EO's goods and services do intend to receive something in return; they expect the street to be "two-way." An investment company holding the EO's money expects to have to pay reasonable return to the EO for using the funds. In these examples, the EO receives earned income. The important issue this chapter considers is when earned income becomes unrelated business income subject to income tax.

The subject is highly complex due to the nature of nonprofits themselves and the legislative and judicial forum in which the rules are developed.

The purpose of the unrelated business income tax rules is to eliminate the unfair competition that results when an EO conducts the same activity a for-profit taxpaying entity would. Because the rules are based upon apparent legislative madness as well as logic, an understanding of the basic concepts is critical to identifying an activity that results in tax versus one that doesn't. Congress has carved out special exceptions and "modifications" to exempt certain types of business revenue from tax, either because they are considered to be inherent (related) in accomplishing the nonprofit's exempt purposes or because the revenue-generating activity is not conducted in a competition with businesses.

Oversight held hearings and drafted revisions over a four-year period during 1987 to 1990 and still has not proposed tax legislation.

27.1 IRS Scrutiny of Unrelated Business Income (UBI)

Beginning in 1989 with the addition of a new page 5 to Form 990, an exempt organization must disclose its unrelated income. Until page 5, with its "Analysis of Revenue-Producing Activities," was added to the annual EO reporting requirements, UBI was not identified in any special way on Form 990; the income was simply included with related income of the same character. Both the Congressional representatives and the IRS agreed there was insufficient information to propose changes to the existing UBI rules.

Now, EOs filing Internal Revenue Service (IRS) Form 990 (not including Form 990EZ filers whose gross income is less than $100,0000) complete the new page 5 to separate income into three categories:

1. Unrelated income (identified with a business code from Form 990T that describes its nature),
2. Unrelated income identified by the specific Internal Revenue Code section by which the income is excluded from UBI, and
3. Related or exempt function income, along with a description of the relationship of the income-producing activity to the accomplishment of exempt purposes.

27.2 History of the Unrelated Business Income Tax (UBIT)

A historical note helps to understand how the rules have evolved. Before 1950, an EO could conduct any income-producing activity and, in fact, did operate businesses without paying income tax. Using a "destination of income" test, as long as the income earned from the business was totally expended for grants and other exempt activities, any amount of business activity was permissible. One famous tax case involved New York University Law School's operation of a highly successful spaghetti factory.[1] In view of the extensive profits and businesslike manner in which the factory was operated, the IRS tried to impose an income tax on the profits. The courts decided, however, that no tax could be imposed under the then existing tax code as long as the profits were used to operate the school.

In response to pressure from businesses, Congress established the unrelated business income tax (UBIT) with the intention of eliminating the unfair competition charitable businesses represented, but it did not prohibit its receipt. The Congressional committee thought that the:

> tax free status of exemption section 501 organizations enables them to use their profits tax free to expand operations, while their competitors can expand only with profits remaining after taxes. The problem. . . . is primarily that of unfair competition.[2]

The key questions in finding UBI are, then, whether the activity that produces earned income competes with commercial businesses and whether the method of operation is distinguishable from that of businesses. Another way to ask the question is, "Does it serve an exempt purpose and therefore is it related?" The distinction between for-profits and nonprofits has narrowed over the years as organizations have searched for creative ways to pay for program services. Consider what the difference between a museum bookstore and a commercial one is, other than the absence of private ownership. Privately owned for-profit theaters operate alongside nonprofit ones. Magazines owned by nonprofits, such as *National Geographic* and *Harper's*, contain advertising and appear indistinguishable from Condé Nast's *Traveler* or *Life Magazine*. The health-care profession is also full of indistinguishable examples.

27.3 Consequences of Receiving Unrelated Income

There are potentially several unpleasant consequences of earning unrelated income.

- *Payment of unrelated income tax.* Unrelated net income may be taxed at corporate or trust rates with estimated tax payments required. Social clubs, homeowners' associations, and political organizations also pay the UBI tax on their passive investment income in addition to the business income.
- *Exempt status revocation.* Exempt status could be revoked. Separate and apart from the UBI rules, the basic exemption statute under Section 501 of the

---

[1] *C.F. Mueller Co. v. Commissioner*, 190F.2d 120 (3d Cir. 1951).
[2] House of Representatives No. 2319, 81st Cong., 2d Sess. (1950) at 36, 37.

Internal Revenue Code[3] requires that an organization be organized and operated *exclusively* for exempt purposes, although "exclusively" has not been construed to mean 100 percent. Some commentators say any amount of UBI under 50 percent of the EO's gross income is permissible, although many others recommend no more UBI than 15 to 20 percent. The courts have allowed higher amounts; the IRS tends to vote for lower amounts in measuring whether the EO is operating "exclusively" for example purposes rather than for business purposes. An organization can run a business as a secondary purpose, but not as a primary purpose.

In evaluating the amount of unrelated business activity that is permissible, not only the amount of gross revenue but other factors may be taken into consideration. Nonrevenue aspects of the activity, such as staff time devoted or value of donated services, are factors in determining whether UBI is substantial.

A complex of nonexempt activity caused the IRS to revoke the exemption of the *Orange County Agricultural Society*.[4] The unrelated business revenues represented between 29 to 34 percent of the gross revenue; although troublesome, they were not the sole factor in the decision of the Tax Court to uphold the IRS's revocation. The presence of private inurement in doing business with the Society's board of directors influenced the decision.

The IRS condoned a 50–50 revenue ratio in allowing a child welfare organization to maintain its exempt status.[5] "About half" of the exempt's gross receipts were generated by a travel agency operated in its headquarters by a full-time employee. The organization had one other full-time and two part-time exempt-activity employees. Because the activity was intended as a fund raiser, there was no indication of insiders receiving profits from the program, and the program was not operated in such a way as to unduly benefit anyone, the IRS found that "operation of the travel service business was not inconsistent with its exempt status." An EO is permitted to conduct an unrelated business as a substantial part of its total activities so long as the business is not its primary purpose.[6]

- *All income taxes.* Income from all sources will be taxed if exempt status is lost.
- *Private foundation issue.* Private foundations' ownership of unrelated businesses would likely trigger "excess business holdings" tax and cause loss of exemption.

27.4 *Definition of Trade or Business*

To have UBI, the EO must first be found to be engaging in a trade or business. *Trade or business* is defined to include any activity carried on for the production of income from

---

[3] Throughout the chapter, references to "Section" will mean a Section of the Internal Revenue Code, unless otherwise stated.
[4] *Orange County Agricultural Society*, 90.1 USTC ¶ 50.076 (2d Cir. 1990, *aff'd* 55 T.C.M. 1602 (1988)).
[5] Priv. Ltr. Rul. 9521004.
[6] Reg. §1.501(c)(3)-1(e)(1).

the sale of goods or performance of services.[7] This is a very broad, sweeping definition. The language seems pretty straightforward and, as a safe rule-of-thumb, would literally mean that any activity for which the exempt receives revenues constitutes a business. Unfortunately, this is an area where the tax rules are very gray and the statutory history is difficult to follow. The word "income" does not mean receipts or revenue and also doesn't necessarily mean net income. Section 513(c) provides: "Where an activity carried on for profit constitutes an unrelated trade or business, no part of such trade or business shall be excluded from such classification merely because it does not result in profit."

If one delves deeper into the Internal Revenue Code ("the Code") and the Treasury Regulations ("the Regulations"), it becomes more difficult to find what is meant by "trade or business." The Regulations couch the definition in the context of unfair competition with commercial businesses, saying that "when an activity does not possess the characteristics of a trade or business within the meaning of Section 162," the unrelated business income tax (UBIT) will not apply. These Regulations, however, were written before the Section 513(c) profit motive language was added to the Code, and they are the subject of continuing arguments between taxpayers and the IRS. The Tax Court said the §162 test is whether an activity is conducted with "continuity and regularity." A similar, but not identical, test to apply is whether the organization operates the activity in a competitive commercial manner or similar to a profit-making enterprise.[8]

(A) PROFIT MOTIVE TEST

The confusion has produced two tests: profit motive and commerciality. Under the profit motive test, an activity conducted simply to produce some revenue but without an expectation of producing a profit (similar to the hobby loss rules) is not a business.[9] This test is used by the IRS in situations where an EO has more than one unrelated business. Losses from the hobby cannot be offset against profits from other businesses. Likewise, the excess expenses (losses) generated in fundamentally exempt activity, such as an educational publication undertaken without the intention of making a profit, cannot be deducted against the profits from a profit-motivated project.

(B) COMMERCIALITY TEST

The commerciality test looks instead to the type of operation: if the activity is carried on in a manner similar to a commercial business, it constitutes a trade or business.[10] This test poses serious problems for the unsuspecting because there are no statutory or regulatory parameters to follow. A broad range of UBI cases where the scope of sales or service activity was beyond that normally found in the exempt setting have been decided by examining the commercial taint of the activity.

---

[7] Treas. Reg. § 1.513-1(b).

[8] *National Water Well Association, Inc. v. Commissioner*, 92 T.C. 75 (1985).

[9] *West Virginia State Medical Association, aff'd*, 89-2 U.S.T.C. § 9491 (4th Cir. 1989); 91 T.C. 651 (1988), *Commissioner v. Groetzinger*, 480 U.S. 23 (1987).

[10] *Better Business Bureau v. United States*, 326 U.S. 279, 283 (1945); *United States National Water Well Association, Inc. v. Commissioner*, 92 T.C. 7 (1989); *Scripture Press Foundation v. United States*, 285 F.2d 800 (Ct. Cl. 1961), *cert. denied, Greater United Navajo Development Enterprises, Inc. v. Commissioner*, 74 T.C. 69 (1980).

EXHIBIT 27.1 Components of Unrelated Business Income

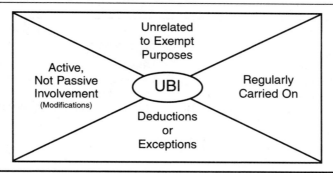

(C) FRAGMENTATION RULE

Further evidence of the overreaching scope of the term "trade or business" is found in the *fragmentation rule*.[11] This rule carves out an activity carried on alongside an exempt one and provides that unrelated business does not lose its identity and taxability when it is earned in a related setting. Take, for example, a museum shop. The shop itself is clearly a trade or business, often established with a profit motive and operated in a commercial manner. Items sold in such shops, however, often include both educational items, such as books and reproductions of art works, and souvenirs. The fragmentation rule requires that all items sold be analyzed to identify the equational, or related, items the profit from which is not taxable and the unrelated souvenir items that do produce taxable income. (See "Special Interest Topic—Museums," Section 27.19 in this chapter, for more information about museums.)

27.5 What is Unrelated Business Income (UBI)?

UBI is defined as the gross income derived from any *unrelated trade or business regularly carried on*, less the *deductions* connected with the carrying on of such trade or business, computed with *modifications* and *exceptions*.[12] These terms are key to identifying UBI. Exhibit 27.1 shows them graphically. All four of the prongs of the circle surrounding the circle must be considered, to determine what earned income is to be classified as UBI.

27.6 Regularly Carried On

A trade or business regularly carried on is considered to compete unfairly with commercial business and is fair game for classification as a taxable business. In determining whether an activity is regularly carried on, the IRS looks at the *frequency and continuity* of an activity when examined by comparison to commercial enterprises. The normal

---

[11] Section 513(c).
[12] Section 512(a)(1).

PART IV

time span of comparable commercial activities can also be determinative.[13] Compare the following:

Irregular	Regular
Sandwich stand at annual county fair.	Cafe open daily.
Annual golf tournament.	Racetrack operated during racing "season."
Nine-day antique show.	Antique store.
Gala Ball held annually.	Monthly dance.
Program ads for annual fund-raising event.	Advertisements in quarterly magazine.

(A) MEANING OF IRREGULAR

Intermittent activities may be deemed "regularly carried on" or commercial unless they are discontinuous or periodic. For example, the revenue from a weekly dance would be more likely to be taxed than the profits from an annual fund-raising event. By the same token, ads sold for a monthly newsletter would more likely be classed as commercial than program ads sold for an annual ball. Where the planning and sales effort of a special event or athletic tournament is conducted over a long span of time, the IRS may argue that the activity itself becomes regularly carried on despite the fact that the event occurs infrequently. (See the NCAA advertising sales discussion following under "Agency Theory," page 669.)

In a 1981 case, the IRS lost in arguing that the engagement of professionals to stage the show and produce a program guide containing advertising caused a patrolmen's fund-raising event profits to be UBI.[14] The fact that the solicitors worked for 16 weeks in preparing and organizing the event made the activity regular in the IRS eyes; the Tax Court disagreed.

(B) SEASON ACTIVITY

Activities conducted during a period traditionally identified as seasonal, such as Christmas, if conducted during the "season," will be considered regular and the income will not qualify to be excluded from UBIT. Christmas card sales during October or November, or Independence Day balloons sold in June/July, would be "regular."

(C) MEANING OF REGULARLY CARRIED ON

Events held once a year have been the subject of argument as to their regularity. In most situations they were deemed "irregularly carried on" and therefore incapable of producing UBI. Congress specifically mentioned "income derived from annual athletic exhibition" in stating that the UBI applies only to business regularly carried on.[15] When the IRS proposed taxing broadcast rights, it argued that preparatory time, not the actual playing time, determines regularity. If an event or program takes the entire year to pro-

---

[13] Treas. Reg. § 1.513-1(c).
[14] *Suffolk County Patrolmens' Benevolent Association, Inc. v. Commissioner*, 77 T.C. 1314 (1981), *acq.* 1984-1 C.B. 2.
[15] S. Rep. 91-552, 91st Cong., 1st Sess. (1969).

duce, this span of time spent negotiating contracts and otherwise working on the event is considered. The development of this concept is reflected in the following rulings:

- Time spent by volunteers in soliciting advertisements or sponsorships will be considered in evaluating the time span of the activity.[16]
- An eight-month concert season program was ruled to be comparable to commercially published seasonal publications and thereby regularly carried on.[17]
- The National College Athletic Association (NCAA) pays an independent for-profit company to produce its "Final Four" program for the annual championship basketball game. The program contains many pages of advertisements sold by the company. NCAA received a $56,000 payment under the contract, which the IRS deemed to be UBTI. The Tax Court determined that the revenues were unrelated to the NCAA's underlying exempt purpose. The Tenth Circuit Court agreed about the unrelatedness of the revenue but deemed it not taxable because it was irregularly carried on. The court refused to attribute the year-round efforts of the company in selling the ads and looked only to the three-week duration of the tournament as determinative. It is very important to note that the IRS strongly disagrees with this decision.[18]

Year-round sales effort for ads in a labor organization's yearbook, in IRS eyes, means the activity is regularly carried on. Because the book was distributed at an annual event, the EO argued that the ad campaign was irregular, based upon the *Suffolk County* decision. Unfortunately for the union, the facts indicated that the yearbook only contained mention of the event and had relevance to the members throughout the year. The fact that "the vast majority of advertisements carry a definitely commercial message" did not help.[19] The IRS is continuing its fight against the *NCAA* and *Suffolk County* court decisions. A recent letter ruling, however, said it would be difficult to conclude that an annual ball, which occurs only once each year, is regularly carried on.[20]

Biannual publication of a business league's directory was also ruled to be a regular activity; the every-other-year publication cycle was regular or normal in commercial settings. The IRS opined that "continuity" did not necessarily mean "continuously," but rather having a connection with similar activities in the past that will be carried forward into the future.[21]

27.7 Substantially Related

"Any business the conduct of which is not substantially related (aside from need to make money) to the performance of an organization's charitable, educational, or other

---

[16] Rev. Rul. 75-201, 1975-1 C.B. 164.

[17] Rev. Rul. 75-200, 1975-1 C.B. 163.

[18] *National College Athletic Association v. Commissioner*, 914 F.2d 1417 (10th Cir. 1990) Also see Priv. Ltr. Rul. 9044071.

[19] Priv. Ltr. Rul. 9304001.

[20] Priv. Ltr. Rul. 9417003 (December 1, 1993).

[21] Priv. Ltr. Rul. 9302035.

purposes or function constituting the basis of its exemption is defined as unrelated," according to the Regulations.[22]

An activity is substantially related only when it has a causal relationship to the achievement of an EO's exempt purpose (that is, the purpose for which the EO was granted exemption according to its Form 1023 or 1024 or subsequent Form 990 filings). The Regulations suggest that the presence of this requirement necessitates an examination of the relationship between the business activities (of producing or distributing goods or performing services) that generate the particular income in question and the accomplishment of the organization's exempt purposes.[23]

The size and extent of the activity itself and its contribution to exempt purposes are determinative. The "nexus" (association, connection, or linkage) between the activity and accomplishment of exempt purposes is examined to find "relatedness." The best way to illustrate the concept is with example.

(A) EXAMPLES OF RELATED ACTIVITY

Related income-producing activities include:

- Admission tickets for performances or lectures;
- Student or member tuition or class fees;
- Symphony society sale of symphonic musical recordings;
- Products made by handicapped workers or trainees;[24]
- Hospital room, drug, and other patient charges;
- Agriculture college sale of produce or student work;
- Sale of educational materials;
- Secretarial and telephone answering service training program for indigent and homeless;[25]
- Operation of diagnostic health devices, such as CAT scans or magnetic imaging machines by a hospital or health-care organization;[26]
- Sale of online bibliographic data from EO's central databases;[27]
- "Public entertainment activities," or agricultural and educational fair or exposition;
- "Qualified conventions and trade shows."[28]
- Producing tapes of endangered ethnic music.

(B) SCHOOL ATHLETIC AND ENTERTAINMENT ACTIVITIES

The IRS precedent for the relatedness of college events goes way back. The rule has continually been that such events foster school spirit and advance the educational purposes of the schools. Revenues produced through sales of admission tickets, event programs,

---

[22] Treas. Reg. § 1.513-1(a).
[23] Treas. Reg. § 1.513-1(d).
[24] Rev. Rul. 73.128, 1973-1, C.B. 222 and Priv. Ltr. Rul. 9152039.
[25] Priv. Ltr. Rul. 9009038.
[26] Tech. Adv. Mem. 8932004.
[27] Priv. Ltr. Rul. 9017028.
[28] Priv. Ltr. Rul. 9210026.

refreshments, and similar items have not normally been treated as UBI. Legislative history underlying the UBI provisions states that "Athletic activities of schools are substantially related to their educational functions. For example, a university would not be taxable on income derived from a basketball tournament sponsored by it, even where the teams were composed of students from other schools."[29]

Payments for radio and television broadcast rights, however, have been controversial. In 1977, the IRS advised TCU, SMU, USC, and the Cotton Bowl Athletic Association that revenue derived by the universities from the telecasting and radio broadcasting of athletic events constituted unrelated trade or business income. In a 1978 ruling, the IRS reversed its position after a challenge by the Cotton Bowl and National College Athletic Association.[30] In 1979, the IRS further expanded its position regarding such events and provided a good outline of the issues:[31]

- Sales of broadcast rights were regularly carried on and the activity looked at as a profit-motivated trade or business activity, with extensive time expended training the teams and preparing for the game.
- The events were regularly carried on (systematic and consistent; not discontinuous or periodic).
- Games, however, were related to the Cotton Bowl's exempt purpose. Income from sale of the game broadcast was a byproduct because it was presented in its original state and provided a simultaneous extension of the exempt-function game to the general public.

A long series of IRS proclamations on the subject was issued in following years concerning the sale of broadcast rights by colleges, all of which ruled that such sales produced related income.[32] See Section 27.8(e) of this chapter for special consideration of corporate sponsorship of such events.

Recently the IRS applied what is now called the "commerciality standard" (see Section 27.4(b) of this chapter) to treat the promotion of rock concerts in a "multipurpose college auditorium" as a taxable unrelated activity. The college was found to emphasize "revenue maximization to the exclusion of other considerations indicating that the trade or business is not operated as an integral part of educational programs and that the activity, therefore, fails the substantially related test." The nature of the entertainment and the audience were not the criteria used to judge the activity's relatedness; instead, it was the manner in which the college selected activities for their profitability that was the determining factor. The facts outlined in the ruling evidencing the businesslike manner of conduct were as follows:[33]

- During the school year, 45 "ticket events" were held, 44 percent of which were rock concerts. Contemporary professional entertainers comprised 40 percent of the concert season.

---

[29] S. Rep. 2375 and H. Rep. 2319, 81st Cong., 2d Sess. 109 (1950).
[30] Priv. Ltr. Rul. 7851004.
[31] Priv. Ltr. Rul. 7930043.
[32] Priv. Ltr. Ruls. 7851005, 7930043, 7940043, 7948113; Rev. Ruls. 80-295 and 80-296; and Priv. Ltr. Rul. 8643091.
[33] Priv. Ltr. Rul. 9147008.

- The facility was managed by a director with more than 30 years' experience in promoting commercial events.
- The school's fine arts department had no involvement in the selection of events to be held at the center and normally did not participate.
- Twenty-six percent of the tickets were sold to nonstudents.
- Tickets were sold through a commercial ticket service.
- Ticket prices for students were not discounted.
- Concerts were generally indistinguishable by price or type of performance from similar events provided by commercial impresarios.
- Compensation to the performers was negotiated and generally the same as compensation paid by for-profit centers.

27.8   Unrelated Activities

Potentially unrelated categories of UBI are numerous, as the following controversial types of income illustrate. The examples don't always follow a logical pattern because courts and the IRS don't always agree and the IRS has not always been consistent in its rulings.

(A)   RENTALS

Rentals of equipment and other personal property (for example, computer or phone systems) to others are specifically listed in Section 512(b)(3) for inclusion in UBI. Such rental presumably is undertaken only to earn revenue and cover costs, with no direct connection to the EO's own exempt purposes; it "exploits" the exempt holding of the property. However, the following situations should be noted:

- Renting to (or sharing with) another EO (or, conceivably, an individual or a for-profit business) is related if the rental expressly serves the landlord's exempt purposes, such as a museum's rental of art works—that would otherwise be kept in its storage—to other institutions to ensure maximum public viewing of the work.
- Mailing list rentals produce UBI except for narrow exceptions allowed to Section 501(c)(3) organizations ("501(c)(3)s").[34] For business leagues and other EOs that are not 501(c)(3)s, revenues from the exchange or rental of mailing lists may produce UBI. The Disabled American Veterans fought a valiant battle in the tax courts to avoid this tax. Twice—in 1982, and again in July 1991—they lost in the Tenth Circuit court their attempts to characterize their mailing list sales as royalty income. But the Sierra Club won. (Refer to "The Royalty Dilemma," Section 27.20(e) of this chapter, for more information.)
- Whether rental charges are at, below, or above cost can be determinative in evaluating relatedness. A full fair market value rental arrangement does not evidence exempt purposes (although the taint can be overcome by other reasons for the rental, such as dissemination of educational information).

---

[34] Section 513(h).

- Real estate revenues may also be excluded from UBI under the passive exceptions, but only if the property is unencumbered (see later discussion of debt-financed property).[35]

(B) SERVICES

Providing services (such as billing, technical assistance, administrative support) to other EOs doesn't serve the exempt purposes of the furnishing EO and is unrelated, according to the IRS. The fact that sharing services creates efficiencies that allow all the EOs involved to save money doesn't necessarily sway the IRS. Only where the services themselves represent substantive programs better accomplished by selling the services to other EOs has the IRS classified the revenue as related. The services themselves must be exempt in nature. Selling computer time to enable another EO to maintain its accounting records would create UBI, but selling computer time to analyze scientific information might be related. Where an organization is created to serve a consortia of organizations with a common building or pooled investment funds, the IRS has generally allowed its exemption where the new organization itself is partly supported by independent donations.

- Certain cooperative service organizations have been specifically exempted, by Congress, to avoid the IRS position that such rendering of services was a taxable business activity. Section 501(e) grants exempt status to cooperative hospital organizations that are formed to provide on a group basis specified services including data processing, purchasing (including the purchase of insurance on a group basis), warehousing, billing and collection, food, clinical, industrial engineering, laboratory, printing, communications, record center, and personnel (including selection, testing, training, and education of personnel services). Note that laundry is not on the list.

Cooperative services organizations established to "hold, commingle, and collectively invest" stocks and securities of educational institutions are also provided a special exempt category under Section 501(f).

Section 513(e) allows a special exclusion from UBI for the income earned by a hospital providing the types of services listed in Section 501(e) to another hospital that has facilities to serve fewer than 100 patients, provided the price for such services is rendered at cost plus a "reasonable amount of return on the capital goods used" in providing the service.

The IRS has considered "related services" being rendered by a Section 501(c)(6) tourist and convention organization for the local government. Their memo discusses a broad range of services provided to businesses planning conventions in the city (which the EO was organized to benefit) and finds them related activity. Commissions received from hotels in return for referring groups and conventions for reservations, however, were deemed unrelated.[36]

---

[35] Section 512(b)(3).
[36] Tech. Adv. Mem. 9032005.

(C) HEALTH-CARE PROVIDERS

The sharing of assets, personnel, and services in order to reduce costs for three related exempt and one nonexempt organizations was sanctioned by the IRS.[37] The issue arose in connection with a reorganization of a nursing home. Transactions were proposed to be conducted at arm's length, with charges to be made at fair market value. The Service ruled that the sharing of assets and rendering of services was substantially related to the exempt purposes and would not result in unrelated business income.

The provision of health care services by hospitals, homes for the aged, and other organizations has long been considered to "promote health" and serve a charitable purpose.[38] There is no mention in the Regulations that service provision be free or at low cost to be considered charitable. Although the cases on this issue involve an organization's underlying qualification as a §501(c)(3) organization, the distinction is relevant in deciding whether certain types of health care services are a related or unrelated activity. New types of health care organizations, such as integrated delivery systems that include physicians' clinics, have been approved for exempt status in recent years. The evolution of government policy in the health care area may affect this question, so the reader should be alert for changes.

Health maintenance organizations (HMOs) have not readily been approved by the IRS as tax-exempt organizations because of the peripheral services, including insurance, that they provide in addition to traditional patient care. Certain types of services are considered as unrelated business activity, and the cases are instructive. For example, an HMO that did not itself provide health care services, but instead provided the service of promoting subscribership and arranging necessary health care—by reference an unrelated activity—was found not to be exempt. The HMO, *Geisinger Health Plan*, argued unsuccessfully that it was a "feeder organization."[39]

(D) SALE OF NAME

Sale of the *use of the organization's name* normally is accomplished by a licensing contract permitting use of the EO's intangible property—its name—with the compensation constituting royalty income that is excluded from UBI under concepts discussed in Section 27.20(e) of this chapter. In the IRS view, such arrangements usually constitute commercial exploitation of an exempt asset. Since issuing Rev. Rul. 81-178 (1981–2 C.B. 135), the IRS has been trying to tax EOs on payments for the use of their own and their members' names in connection with insurance programs, affinity credit cards, and other commercial marketing schemes. Note that a sale of the EO's name by transferring ownership

---

[37] Priv. Ltr. Rul. 9411043.

[38] Rev. Rul. 56-185, 1956-1 C.B. 202; Rev. Rul. 69-545, 1969-2 C.B. 117; *Eastern Kentucky Welfare Rights Organization v. Simon*, 506 F.2d 1278, 1287 (D.C. Cir. 1974), Priv. Ltr. Rul. 9535023.

[39] *Geisinger Health Plan v. Commissioner*, 100 T.C. No. 26 (May 3, 1993), *on remand*, 985 F.2d 1210 (3d Cir. 1993), *rev'g* T.C. Memo 1991-649. See also *Sound Health Association v. Commissioner*, 71 T.C. 158 (1978), for an example of an HMO sanctioned as an exempt organization. See also Priv. Ltr. Ruls. 9204033 and 9232003 for other examples of HMO service provider decisions.

of the name itself, rather than use of the name, represents a capital asset transaction and is characterized as a capital gain rather than a royalty.[40]

To add flavor to the problem, in April 1990, the IRS reversed its position that a "royalty arrangement" licensing an EO's name, logo, and mailing list to an insurance agent (to promote life insurance to its membership) didn't produce UBI for the exempt.[41] Because of the extensive involvement (active, not passive) of the exempt in servicing the membership lists, Section 513(h)(1)(B)'s narrow exemption of mailing lists, and the agency theory (discussed below), the IRS ruled the supposed "royalty arrangement" produced UBI. The American Bar Association lost a similar battle in 1986, although their case was made more complicated by an arrangement whereby their members made substantial donations of the program profits.[42]

Where the sale of the organization's name or logo is accompanied by any additional requirements on the part of the EO, such as servicing the mailing list as discussed above or endorsing a product or performing any other services for the purchaser, the IRS has made it very clear they consider such arrangements to produce unrelated income. Also suspect would be contracts where the "royalty" amount paid for use of the name is tied to the number of times it is used in solicitations, all of which are mailed to the separately purchased mailing list of the EO.

Affinity card revenues are in the same category as far as the IRS is concerned and do not qualify for the "royalty" exception. When first ruling on affinity cards, the IRS allowed royalty exclusion for a fraternal order's card income.[43] By 1988, they had reversed the initial position.[44] While use of the EO's name and logo alone can produce royalty income, the credit card arrangements often depend on an accompanying sale of the organization's mailing list and, in some cases, endorsements and promotion by the EO in its publications and member/donor correspondence. The IRS therefore again applies an "agency-type" theory to deem that the EO itself, rather than the intermediary organization, performed valuable services that produced unrelated income. Some organizations try to avoid this problem by bifurcating the royalty and mailing list aspects of the contract. The IRS has commented that "they are probably going to see them as one transaction, in reality, one contract, and apply UBIT."

Licensing the organization's name and logo for the promotion of five cash/risk management funds was ruled by the IRS to result in nontaxable royalty income payments to the EO. The license agreement provided that the EO would receive a percentage of the business generated. The agreement specifically stated that the EO would provide no services to the licensee, and the ruling stated that it appeared the parties had followed that provision of the contract.[45] Thus, a passive endorsement of the funds was

---

[40] Rev. Rul. 60-226, 1960-1 C.B. 26; see also Priv. Ltr. Rul. 9319044. When a university assigned the use of its name to a hospital joint venture, the IRS said the substantial services and control over hospital operations retained by the school caused the payments attributable to the license to be taxable UBI, not excludable royalty income.

[41] Priv. Ltr. Rul. 9029047.

[42] *United States v. American Bar Endowment*, 477 U.S. 105 (1986).

[43] Priv. Ltr. Rul. 8747066.

[44] Priv. Ltr. Rul. 8823109.

[45] Priv. Ltr. Rul. 9404003.

not considered the provision of active services that would cause the royalty to be re-classified as service income.

(E) ADVERTISING

Sale of advertising in an otherwise exempt publication is almost always considered unre-lated business income by the IRS. The basic theory is that the advertisements promote the interest of the individual advertiser and cannot therefore be related to the charitable purposes of the organization. The following examples are indicative:

- The American College of Physicians was unsuccessful in arguing with the IRS that the drug company ads in their health journal published for physicians educated the doctors. The College argued that the ads provided the reader with a comprehensive and systematic presentation of goods and services needed in the profession and informed physicians about new drug discoveries; but the court disagreed.[46]
- A college newspaper training program for journalism students enrolled in an advertising course, however, produced related income.[47]
- Institutional or sponsor ads produce UBI if they are presented in a commercial fashion with a business logo, product description, or other sales information. Only where sponsors are listed without typical advertising copy can the money given for the listing be considered a donation. Different sizes for different amounts of money may not cause the ad to be classified as commercial.[48]
- Despite classification of ad revenues as UBI, the formula for calculating the taxable UBI yields surprising results, however, enabling some ad sale programs to escape tax. (A more thorough discussion of advertising and the formula appears later in the chapter.)

(F) SPONSORSHIPS

Corporate sponsorships of a wide variety of events—golf tournaments, fun runs, football bowl games, public television, art exhibitions and so on—are a favorite form of corpo-rate support for exempt organizations. The appeal of wide public exposure for sponsor-ing worthy causes and cultural programs has gained extensive popularity. *The Wall Street Journal* ran a series of articles during 1991 discussing the extent of such support and why it made good business sense.

Under examination and in a heavily edited Private Letter Ruling 9147007, the IRS said the Cotton Bowl's payments from Mobil Oil Company were taxable, essentially be-cause the Cotton Bowl was rendering services for Mobil. Substantial benefit in the form of advertising was given to Mobil and such revenue was business income, not a contri-bution. The IRS announced in early 1992 that "Tax exempt organizations can publicly ac-

---

[46] *American College of Physicians vs. United States,* 457 U.S. 836 (1986).

[47] Treas. Reg. 1.513-1(d)(4)(iv) Example 5.

[48] *Fraternal Order of Police, Illinois State Troopers Lodge No. 41 v. Commissioner,* 833 F.2d 717 (7th Cir. 1987), *aff'g* 87 T.C. 747 (1986); Priv. Ltr. Rul. 8640007.

knowledge donors for their contributions, but if the organizations conduct advertising for donors, the payments are taxable income, not tax exempt contributions."

After an outcry from the exempt community, and in the face of proposed legislative changes, the IRS in 1993 issued proposed regulations concerning the character of sponsorship payments to tax-exempt organizations.[49] The proposals clearly reflect an IRS policy decision not to be responsible for hampering an exempt's need to raise private support. The primary goal of the regulation is to distinguish between commercial advertising and benevolent payments. Some commentators suggest the rules are too lenient; others suggest more detailed definitions of the terms. A representative of a museum suggests the guidelines are actually too broad and allow sponsors to demand types of recognition beyond what they customarily are willing to give.

The proposed regulations delineate sponsorship revenue as either an advertisement that is selling or promoting a product or an acknowledgment to express thanks to a supporter. The rules do not apply to sales of advertising in EO periodicals nor to qualified convention and trade show activities. Specifically with respect to sponsorship of the activities of an exempt organization, the regulation says:

> [a]dvertising means any message or other programming material which is broadcast or otherwise transmitted, published, displayed or distributed in exchange for any remuneration, and which promotes or markets any company, services, facility or product. Advertising includes any activity that promotes or markets any company, services, facility or product. Advertising does not include an acknowledgment.

> Acknowledgments are mere recognition of sponsorship payments. Acknowledgments may include the following, provided that the effect is identification of the sponsor rather than promotion of the sponsor's products, services or facilities: sponsor logos and slogans that do not contain comparative or qualitative descriptions of the sponsor's products, services, facilities or company; sponsor locations and telephone numbers; value-neutral descriptions, including displays or visual depictions of a sponsor's product-line or services; and sponsor brand or trade names and product or service listings. Logos or slogans that are an established part of a sponsor's identity are not considered to contain comparative or qualitative descriptions.

> Messages or other programming material that include the following constitute advertising: qualitative or cooperative language; price information or other indications of savings or value associated with a product or service; a call to action; an endorsement; or an inducement to buy, sell, rent or lease the sponsor's product or service. Distribution of a sponsor's product by the sponsor or the exempt organization to the general public at the sponsored event, whether for free or for remuneration, is not considered an inducement to buy, sell, rent or lease the sponsor's product or service for purposes of this regulation. If any activities, messages or programming material constitute advertising with respect to a sponsorship payment, then all related activities, messages or programming material that might otherwise be acknowledgements are considered advertising.

The proposals are much more lenient than expected by the exempt community and are very helpful in providing specific guidelines. Happily for many organizations, making

---

[49] Prop. Reg. §1.513-4, entitled "Certain Sponsorship Not Unrelated Trade or Business." A public hearing on the proposals was held July 8, 1993.

facilities, services, or other privileges available to sponsors—front row seats, dinner with the golf pro, or a reception with major donors—is permitted and "does not affect the determination of whether a sponsorship payment is advertising income." It is promotion of the sponsor's product by reflecting prices, comparisons, and other praises of the sort found in commercial advertisements that will cause the transaction to result in UBI.

Contingent sponsorship payments, however, retain their commercial taint. When the "gift" or sponsorship is contingent, by contract or otherwise, upon factors such as attendance at an event or broadcast ratings, the payment is deemed advertising. A sponsorship dependent upon an event actually taking place does not, in and of itself, mean that the payment is advertising.

The proposals contain eight examples that can be studied for additional guidance for organizations anticipating solicitation of sponsorships. Very importantly, the examples indicate that sponsorship payments in excess of the fair market value of the "advertising" can be excluded from UBI when the excess can be clearly demonstrated. Also significantly, amounts treated as advertising are still eligible to be excluded under other UBI rules, such as for ads sold by volunteers or an activity irregularly carried on.

The proposals add expense allocation examples for calculating the tax on such revenues. The first new example allocates expenses of a college bowl game among the related and unrelated revenues from the game when the sponsorship is treated as an acknowledgment rather than advertising. The bowl game example is expanded by adding unrelated leasing of the college's stadium during the year.[50] Allocation formulas for photographic museum advertising revenue for promoting a sponsor's photographic products are also given.[51]

Golf tournaments have presented a number of other issues not clearly answered by the proposed regulations. What if the sponsorship agreement includes endorsement of specific types of shoes, apparel, or clubs, or personal appearances by stars?[52] In connection with 1993 examinations of colleges and universities, IRS agents reportedly applied the sponsorship regulations to find that scoreboard advertising escapes UBI classification.[53]

As of September 1996, the proposed regs were still not finalized. There was strong criticism from the exempt community for the "tainting rule" found in the last sentence of the quoted proposal. When the sponsorship package contains both acknowledgements and advertising materials, all of the revenue will be treated as UBI. The IRS has encouraged exempts to follow the proposals and has stated that any changes made to the proposed regulations would be applied prospectively.[54]

(G) MEMBER SERVICES

Services to members will be scrutinized carefully by IRS. Note especially the following:

- Sale of legal forms by a bar association, billing and credit services for members, and testing fees have all been argued with decisions for and

---

[50] *Id.*, Example 3.

[51] *Id.*, Example 4.

[52] Priv. Ltr. Ruls. 8321094, 8303078, and 8411006.

[53] "*Are Universities Winning the Battle Against UBIT?*," Paul Streckfus, 9 *The Exempt Organization Tax Review* 509 (No. 3, Mar. 1994).

[54] Comments of Marcus Owens in an April 20, 1993 speech at Georgetown University, *supra* n.0.2.

against the organizations. EOs considering this type of income-producing activity should research this question thoroughly.[55]

- Free bus service provided to a particular shopping center versus a downtown area of a city was ruled to produce unrelated income for a chamber of commerce.
- The American Academy of Family Physicians' information clearing house for physician placement fostered the "appropriate distribution of physicians to provide health care for the nation." The court found that this stated objective advanced the organization's exempt purposes so that the fees charged to access the information were related income.[56]Member services should contribute to accomplishing the organization's overall mission versus benefiting its individual constituents.

The question to watch for is whether services rendered to members constitute private inurement or private benefit for the members versus the general public or the profession (for a business league).

(H)   INSURANCE

Group insurance programs have been a subject of active litigation among trade unions, business leagues, and the IRS, with the IRS prevailing in classifying revenues produced in an internally managed insurance program for members as UBI.[57] Instead of conducting the insurance program directly, creative EOs have instead licensed their membership lists to insurance providers in return for what they hope will be nontaxable royalty income. Similar to the factors considered in affinity card rulings and other mailing list licensing cases, the issue is to what extent the EO renders personal services in connection with the arrangement. Fees for services rendered do not qualify for the passive "royalty" exception discussed at Section 27.20(e) of this chapter.

A business league serving the public health community provided the criteria the IRS is currently using to evaluate such programs.[58] The following facts led the IRS to conclude that the EO provided valuable services, causing the payments to be classified as taxable UBI rather than royalties excluded by §512(b)(2):

- The company acts as the EO's agent and under contract agrees to choose suitable policies for the EO's members, review and market the program to members, and perform administrative services such as preparation of all solicitation materials, seeking enrollments, and handling the premium collections.
- EO agrees to endorse the program and allow the insurance agent to use its logo, name, and membership list to promote the program to its members.

---

[55] *San Antonio Bar Association v. United States*, 80-2 U.S.T.C. § 9594 (W.D. Tex. 1980).
[56] *American Academy of Family Physicians v. U.S.*, __ F. Supp. __ (W.D. Mo. 1995).
[57] *Louisiana Credit Union League v. United States*, 693 F.2d 525 (5th Cir. 1982); *Texas Farm Bureau v. United States*, 93-1 U.S.T.C. ¶ 50, 257 (C.D. Tex. 1993), *rev'd*, 95/USTC (5th Cir. June 1, 1995).
[58] Priv. Ltr. Rul. 9316045.

- EO retains the right to approve the form and content of mailings to its members, endorse the plan, and advise its members of its availability, and include plan information in new member packets.

The IRS felt that the EO's involvement was direct and extensive and represented the rendering of valuable personal services to the insurance company, so that the so-called licensing payments did not qualify as royalty income. Thus, the IRS is continuing to advance the arguments it used against the Disabled American Veterans, as discussed in Section 27.20(e) of this chapter.

Careful structuring of the contractual arrangements for such plans can allow the revenues to be bifurcated, resulting in some unrelated taxable income and some nontaxable royalty. Such an agreement would separate the requirements and compensation regarding services to be rendered. Terms for payments due for use of the organization's name should be clearly identified as royalty payments made strictly for use of intangible property, without regard to the service requirements. At best, two separate agreements could be reached to prove that the obligation to pay royalties is dissociated from services required to be performed.

Taxability of insurance program profits is also an unsolved issue for certain categories of exempt organizations. A *Report to the Congress on Fraternal Benefit Societies* was issued by the Treasury Department in response to a Tax Reform Act of 1986 mandate. Insurance policies issued by these §501(c)(8) EOs were found to serve the same markets as those served by commercial insurers. The content, pricing, and market for the insurance are very similar to those of large mutual insurers. The report generally concluded that such societies, if taxed, should be treated as mutual insurance companies. Those societies with minor insurance activity and major charitable and fraternal purposes would be allowed to retain tax exemption, but must report insurance activity as unrelated business income under §501(m).

(I) REAL ESTATE

Real estate development projects can be characterized as related (low-income or elderly housing), as a trade or business (subdivision, debt-financed, rental, hotel), as an investment (unindebted rental), or sometimes as a combination of all three.

Any EO anticipating such a program should study Private Letter Ruling 8950072 in which the IRS outlines the UBI consequences of four different methods of developing a piece of raw land owned by an exempt. Leasing or selling raw land unquestionably produced no UBI because of the passive income modifications. Completion of the preliminary development work of obtaining permits and approval prior to the property's sale did not convert the sale into a business transaction. But total development of the property prior to the sale converts the property into a business asset and produces UBI.

Development of an apartment building and parking garage as a part of an urban renewal effort is a related business for an organization whose purpose it is to combat community deterioration. The organization operates to assist the city by encouraging revitalization of its downtown area. While the activity would result in UBI if conducted for investment, in this case the activity served the EO's exempt purposes.[59]

---

[59] Priv. Ltr. Rul. 9308033.

A Catholic religious order received IRS sanction for a UBI exclusion of gain earned in a "one-time" liquidation of vacant land that had been used as part of its exempt facility. The order proposed to develop the land into 75+ residential lots to raise needed operational funds. The order obtained the permits, subdivided the land, and made the minimum physical improvements necessary to sell the lots, but an independent broker was to market and sell the lots. As explained in Section 27.12(b) of this chapter, the issue was whether the order was selling property "held for sale to customers in the ordinary course of a trade or business." The fact that the order took the steps necessary to prepare the land for sale and maintained control over the development process did not constitute active business activity.[60]

(J) AGENCY THEORY

An *agency theory* may be applied to look through certain arrangements. To avoid UBI classification for potentially unrelated activities listed above, an organization might engage an independent party to conduct the activity in return for a royalty or a rental payment. Inherently "passive" activities for which compensation is paid in the form of rent or royalty are not subject to UBIT, even if the activity is deemed unrelated. The question is, however, whether the IRS can look through the transactions and attribute the activity of the independent party back to the organization, as they did in the following example.

The National Collegiate Athletic Association (NCAA) hires an unrelated commercial publishing company to produce its tournament programs. NCAA gives the publisher a "free hand" in soliciting the advertisements, designing the copy, and distributing the programs, in return for a percentage of the advertising and direct sales revenues. Because they have little or no involvement in the activity, the NCAA treats the income as a passive and irregularly carried on activity not subject to the unrelated business income tax. There is no argument that selling the program itself produces related income; nor is there any question that the advertising income is unrelated. The tournament lasts only three weeks.

The issue considered by the Tax Court[61] was whether the NCAA had sufficiently disengaged itself under the contract. Did it sell the right to use its name or did it engage in the activity itself? The Tax Court adopted an "agency" theory, stipulating that because the publisher acted as the NCAA's agent, the activity was totally attributable to the NCAA. The Tenth Circuit Court agreed with the Tax Court but reversed the decision (because the activity was irregularly carried on and not in competition with business); the agency theory was not disputed. The IRS disagrees with the decision.

Another athletic tournament-sponsoring organization also failed the agency test. The independently hired promoter's efforts during a 15-month ad campaign were attributed to the organization.[62] The agency theory was escaped, however, by an organization who turned over the publication of its monthly journal to a commercial company, retaining one-third of the net revenues from subscriptions and reprints. All advertising income, two-thirds of the circulation revenues, and all the risk of publication expenses were

---

[60] Priv. Ltr. Rul. 9337027.
[61] *National Collegiate Athletic Association v. Commissioner*, 90-2 U.S.T.C. § 50513 (10th Cir. 1990), *rev'd*, 92 T.C. No. 27 (1989). See also Priv. Ltr. Rul. 9137002.
[62] Tech. Adv. Mem. 8932004.

borne by the company. So, the IRS decided, under the circumstances, that the company was acting on its own behalf, not as agent for the charity. No advertising revenue was allocated to the charity.[63]

The IRS once again rejected an organization's argument that revenues received from a publisher hired to produce its journal was a royalty. Despite a contract providing for royalties, the IRS found that the EO's role was hardly passive. Editorial materials were all written by the EO's members, advertising was sold in the EO's name, receipts were made out using the EO's name, and essentially the EO was deemed to be conducting the activity itself.[64]

Earnings of an ostensibly independent for-profit subsidiary may also be allocated back to the nonprofit parent using the agency theory. The subject's business is treated as separate only if it is managed at arm's length without the parent taking part in daily operations.[65]

27.9   The Exceptions

Despite their literal inclusion in the "unrelated" prong of the UBI rules, certain types of revenue-raising activities are not subject to UBIT presumably because they are not businesslike and do not compete with commercial businesses.[66] Charitable Section 501(c)(3)s qualify for all of the following exceptions. Certain exceptions do not apply to non-501(c)(3) organizations, as noted under the particular exception.

(A)   VOLUNTEERS

Any business where substantially all the work is performed without compensation is excluded from UBI. "Substantially" means at least 80 to 85 percent of the total work performed, measured normally by the total hours worked. A paid manager or executive, administrative personnel, and all sorts of support staff can operate the business if most of the work is performed by volunteers.

In most cases the number of hours worked, rather than relative value of the work, is used to measure the 85 percent test. This means that the value of volunteer time need not necessarily be quantified for comparison to monetary compensation paid. In the case of a group of volunteer singing doctors, the value of the doctors' time was considered. Because the doctors were the stars of the records producing the income, their time was counted by the court at a premium and allowed to offset administrative personnel whose time was paid.[67]

Expense reimbursements, in-kind benefits, and prizes are not necessarily treated as compensation unless they are compensatory in nature. Particularly where the expenses enable the volunteers to work longer hours and serve the convenience of the EO, the payments need not be counted in measuring this exception. Where food, lodging, and

---

[63] Tech. Adv. Mem. 9023003.

[64] Priv. Ltr. Rul. 9309002; also see Priv. Ltr. Rul. 9306030.

[65] The factors necessary to prove that the subsidiary's operation is separate are discussed in detail in Chapter 22 of author's tax planning and compliance book.

[66] Section 513(a).

[67] *Greene County Medical Society Foundation v. United States*, 345 F. Supp. 900 (W.D. Mo. 1972).

total sustenance were furnished to sustain members of a religious group, the members working for the group's businesses were not treated as volunteers.[68]

(B) DONATED GOODS

The selling of merchandise, substantially all of which is received as gifts or contributions, is not subject to the UBIT. Thrift and resale shops selling donated goods do not report UBI on donated goods they sell. A shop selling goods on consignment as well as donated goods would have to distinguish between the two types of goods. UBI would be earned for the consigned goods, but might escape tax if the shop is run by volunteers.

(C) BINGO GAMES

Bingo games not conducted in violation of any state or local law are excluded. Section 513(f) defines bingo as any game of bingo of a type in which usually (1) wagers are placed, (2) winners are determined, and (3) distribution of prizes or other property is made, in the presence of all persons placing wagers in such game.

The Regulations expand the definition by explicitly saying:

> A bingo game is a game of chance played with cards that are generally printed with five rows of five squares each. Participants place markers over randomly called numbers on the cards in an attempt to form a preselected pattern such as a horizontal, vertical, or diagonal line, or all four corners. The first participant to form the preselected pattern wins the game. Any other game of chance, including but not limited to, keno, dice, cards, and lotteries, is not bingo [and will create UBI].[69]

Pull-tabs and other forms of "instant bingo" are not bingo in the IRS's opinion and produce unrelated business income despite the fact that such variations of the bingo game are so classified by the state bingo authority. During 1990, the IRS aggressively examined EOs in the Southwest District and assessed tax on any bingo variations not strictly meeting the Code and Regulation definitions.

(D) PUBLIC ENTERTAINMENT ACTIVITIES

Public entertainment is defined as traditionally conducted at fairs or expositions promoting agricultural and educational purposes (including but not limited to animals or products and equipment) and does not produce UBI for Section 501(c)(3), (4), or (5) organizations. Section 513(d)(2) requires that the event be held in conjunction with an international, national, state, regional, or local fair or be in accordance with provisions of state law that permits such a fair.

(E) QUALIFIED CONVENTIONS AND TRADE SHOWS

A convention and trade show is one intended to attract persons in an industry generally (without regard to membership in the sponsoring organization), as well as members of

---

[68] *Shiloh Youth Revival Centers v. Commissioner*, 88 T.C. 579 (1987).
[69] Treas. Reg. § 1.513-5.

the public, to the show for the purpose of displaying industry products or stimulating interest in and demand for industry products or services, or educating persons engaged in the industry in the development of new products and services or new rules and regulations affecting the industry. A "qualified" show is one conducted by Section 501(c)(3), (4), (5), or (6) organizations in conjunction with an international, national, state, regional, or local convention, annual meeting, or show. Exhibitors are permitted to sell products or services and the organization can charge for the display space.

(F) INDIAN TRIBES

Income earned by a federally recognized Indian tribe from the conduct of an unincorporated business or a corporation incorporated under the Indian Reorganization Act of 1934 (IRA) is not subject to federal income tax.[70] A corporation formed instead under the laws of the state in which the tribe is located, however, would be subject to tax even though it is owned and controlled by an Indian tribe or members of a tribe. The basis of this distinction lies in the definition of an Indian tribe. Section 1 of the Internal Revenue Code subjects individuals, trusts, and estates to tax; Section 11 taxes corporations. A tribe is not such a taxable entity; a separately incorporated business would be.[71] In 1981 the IRS ruled that a properly established Indian tribal corporation (under the IRA) had the same tax status as an Indian tribe as it regarded activities carried on within the boundaries of the reservation.[72] This restriction to on-reservation activity was reconsidered and removed in the 1994 ruling. The ruling says that because an Indian tribe is not a taxable entity, any income earned by it—on or off the reservation—is not taxable for federal income taxes. It does not affect the application of other federal taxes, such as employment and excise taxes (including excise taxes on wagering), to Indian tribes or tribal corporations.

27.10   Exceptions for 501(c)(3)s and Veteran Posts Only

(A)   LOW-COST ARTICLES

Gift premiums costing (not fair market value) the organization no more than $6.70 (during 1996—indexed annually for inflation) and distributed with no obligation to purchase in connection with the solicitations of contributions are not treated as a sale of the gift premium. The gift must be part of a fund-raising campaign.

The recipient of the premium must not request or consent to receive the premium. Literature requesting a donation must accompany the premium and a statement that the recipient may keep the low-cost article regardless of whether a charitable donation is made. If the donation is less than $33.50 (during 1996—indexed annually), the fair market value of the premium reduces the deductible portion of the donor's gift.[73]

---

[70] Rev. Rul. 94-16, 1994-1 C.B. 19.
[71] Rev. Rul. 67-284, 1967-2 C.B. 55, 58.
[72] Rev. Rul. 81-295, 1981-2 C.B. 15, relying on *Mescalero Apache Tribe v. Jones*, 411 U.S. 145, 157 (1973).
[73] Rev. Proc. 90-12 (Feb. 1990), updated annually.

(B) MAILING LISTS

A business involving the exchange or renting of mailing lists between two organizations eligible to receive charitable donations under Section 170(c)(2) or (3) is excluded from UBI classification. In other words, a charitable organization exempt under Section 501(c)(3) and veteran organizations qualify for this special treatment added by Congress in 1986.[74] Sale or exchange of mailing lists by all other types of 501(c) organizations may create UBI.

A social welfare organization exempt under §501(c)(4) is not eligible for the special exception of §513(h) that permits (c)(3)s to exchange lists tax-free. In a 1995 letter ruling, the IRS reminded a (c)(4) organization of this rule and declared that such exchanges of mailing lists did not serve the organization's exempt purposes. The (c)(4) asked if the exchange could qualify as a like-kind property exchange not reportable as a capital gain under §1031. With no specific authority cited, the IRS also determined that the fair rental value of the lists was subject to UBIT as personal property rental of a dual-use asset, with costs and expenses allocated thereto on a factual basis.[75] One could argue that a list exchange typifies an exploited exempt activity (Section 27.14(f)) or a license that produces a royalty (Section 27.20(e)).

27.11 *501(c)(3)s Only Exceptions*

(A) CONVENIENCE

A cafeteria, bookstore, residence, or similar facility used in the EO's programs and operated for the convenience of patients, visitors, employees, or students is specifically excepted from UBI classification by Section 513(a)(2) for 501(c)(3) organizations only. Presumably, it benefits hospital patients to have family and friends visiting or staying with them in the hospital, and the cafeteria facilitates the visits. Museum visitors can spend more time viewing art if they can stop to rest their feet and have a cup of coffee or tea. Parking lots for the exclusive use of participants in an exempt organization's activities also produce related income.

When the cafe, shop, dorm, or parking lot is also open to the general public, the revenue produced by public use is unrelated income. Some commentators suggest the whole facility becomes subject to UBIT, particularly where the facility has an entrance to a public street. At best, the income from a facility used by both qualified visitors and the disinterested public off the street is fragmented. The taxable and nontaxable revenues are identified and tabulated and the net taxable portion is calculated under the dual use rules discussed later under "Calculating the Taxable Income."

Where the unrelated income produced is rental income, there is still a possible escape route from application of the UBIT. The technical question then becomes whether the lot rentals are excludable UBI under the "Passive Income Modifications."

The IRS admits it has issued unclear and conflicting positions on the matter. Their memo states unequivocally that revenue from direct lot operation never produces rent,

---

[74] Section 513(h).
[75] Priv. Ltr. Rul. 9502009.

ACCOUNTING, FINANCE, AND LEGAL ISSUES

and refers to the Regulations.[76] Only where the lot is operated by an independent party under a lease arrangement in which the organization performs no services can the revenue be classified as passive rental income excludable from UBI.

27.12   Passive Income Modifications

Income earned from passive investment activities is not included in UBI unless the underlying property is subject to debt. Social clubs, voluntary employee benefit associations, supplemental unemployment plans, and veterans' groups are taxed on such income. Types of passive income excluded from UBI under Section 512(b) include "all dividends, interest, royalties, rents, payments with respect to security loans, and annuities, and all deductions connected with such income." It is important to note from the outset that passive income of a sort not specifically listed is not necessarily modified or excluded from UBI.

(A)   DIVIDENDS AND INTEREST

Dividends and interest are paid on amounts invested in savings accounts, certificates of deposit, money market accounts, bonds, loans, preferred or common stocks, and payments in respect to security loans and annuities, along with any allocable deductions.

- In 1978, the general exclusion of interest and dividends was expanded to include the words "payments in respect of security loans." Since then, there has been uncertainty regarding sophisticated techniques such as "strips," interest rate swaps, and currency hedges. After two Private Letter Rulings were issued in 1991, Proposed Regulations were announced in September 1991, to recognize that such investments were "ordinary and routine" and to make it clear that income earned from such transactions in security portfolios would be considered as investment income for Section 512 purposes.[77] The Omnibus Budget Reduction Act of 1993 amended §512 to provide that gain and loss received from unexercised options on securities and real estate, as well as loan commitment fee forfeitures, are excluded from the UBIT.
- Such securities acquired with indebtedness are swept back into UBI by Section 514, and an EO must be careful to use new money to acquire each element of investment in its portfolio. A recent Tax Court case provides a good example. A pension fund, stuck with five-year certificates of deposit in 1979 when the interest rates shot up over five points, negotiated a plan to purchase new CDs using its old CDs as collateral, thereby escaping an early withdrawal penalty and receiving a higher rate of interest. The court found that, despite the fact that the transaction was not abusive, it fell squarely within the literal definition of a debt-financed asset purchase. The CD switch was not a "payment in respect of a security loan" within the meaning of Section 512(b)(1). Such a loan involves allowing a broker to use the EO's

---

[76] Gen. Couns. Mem. 39825.
[77] Prop. Reg. §§ 1.509(a)-3, 1.512(b)-1, and 53.4940-1.

674

securities in return for a fee, not a loan against which the securities are used as collateral. Thus, the fund's original CD produced "modified" or nontaxable income and the new higher-rate CD acquired with the loan proceeds was held to be taxable as unrelated debt-financed income.[78]

(B) CAPITAL GAINS

Gains from the sale, exchange, or other disposition of property generally do not produce unrelated business income. As a rule, the normal income tax rules of Sections 1221 and 1231 for identifying capital, versus ordinary income, property apply to identify property covered by this exception.

- Gains on lapse or termination of covered and uncovered operations, if written as a part of investment activity, are not taxable according to Section 512(b)(5), added to the Code in 1976.
- Sales of stock in trade or other inventory-type property or property held for sale to customers in the ordinary course of trade or business do produce UBI.
- Timber standing on real estate owned by the exempt organization can be treated as a capital asset under Section 613(b) if the organization retains an economic interest in the timber. The somewhat complicated rules must be studied for EOs owning such property to assure such treatment. Percentage depletion may apply, and specific rules for allocating the cost basis of the underlying property between the real estate and the timber are provided.[79]
- A gain from sale of real estate used by a social club to perform its exempt function(s) is not classed as UBI to the extent the proceeds are reinvested one year before or three years after the date of the sale.[80] It is property "used in regular club activities" that qualifies for special treatment. Thus clubs and the IRS argue about the meaning of the words as discussed below.
- Harvesting pine timber to preserve the usefulness of a club's property as a wildlife habitat was found to further advance the club's exempt purposes. The club, created in 1870, owned a five-square-mile fish and game preserve and historic clubhouse building adjacent to public land areas maintained in a natural state. The club, beginning in 1983, engaged professional foresters to plan timber harvesting to improve the habitat for wild game and to control gypsy moths. Sale of the timber pursuant to the plans did not create unrelated business income. Additionally, sale of the club shares and subsequent merger into a newly created supporting organization benefiting an environmental education organization exempt under §501(c)(3) did not create nonmember income. The acquiring organization planned to operate the

---

[78] *Kern County Electrical Pension Fund v. Commissioner*, 96 T.C. No. 41 (1991).
[79] Reg. §1.613-2 Priv. Ltr. Rul. 9242028 discusses a private foundation's sale of timber and concludes that the timber sale produces capital gain income not subject to the UBIT and further that the arrangement did not represent a "business enterprise" subject to the excess business holdings rules.
[80] IRC §512(a)(3)(D). Priv. Ltr. Rul. 9307004 says it is insufficient that the club bought the land with the intention of using it for club activities. Actual use is required.

facility to benefit the general public and eventually expected the state to acquire the property.[81]

- Short-term capital gain from a short sale of publicly traded stock through a broker was ruled not to create unrelated business income. Although a short sale technically creates an obligation for the purchaser to pay for any loss that may occur on covering the short position, this possible loss is not treated as acquisition indebtedness (see Section 27.17 of this chapter).[82]

Because social clubs often own valuable and desirable real estate, particularly country clubs and old-line city clubs, this exception can be very important. Note that when the property is considered as nonexempt function, the club must treat the revenue as nonmember revenue and also faces the possibility of failing a so-called "35/15 test" necessary to maintain ongoing exemption. Before the test was provided in 1976, a number of interesting cases used a slightly different, but instructive, standard for evaluating the relatedness of a piece of real estate. Continued exemption for the club was the issue.

A Florida club sold a portion of its property to participate in a land price boom and distributed the proceeds to the members. The court noted that the sale was a "violent departure" from the club's normal behavior and not merely incidental to the regular functions of the club. Because financial gain was the aim, the court revoked the club's exemption.[83]

Property contiguous to the club and held for possible future expansion, or simply protecting the club from the suburbs, is also not used directly, according to the IRS. In its opinion, which has been sustained by certain courts, only property in actual, direct, continuous, and regular use for social and recreational purposes qualifies. Similarly, a golf club was taxed on gain from selling off road frontage. The land was originally acquired with the expectation that it would be used for club facilities, but in actuality it was not.[84]

Use of vacant land containing no physical improvements for jogging, picnics, kiteflying contests, and other outdoor activities seemed to the Eleventh Circuit Court to constitute direct use by club members. The court said, "It is certainly conceivable that joggers derive as much pleasure and recreation from the pastime as golfers do from their rounds on the links."[85]

A "buffer tract," containing a steep incline and heavily wooded with thick undergrowth, however, was found not to be used directly in exempt functions. Even though it served to isolate the club from the surrounding developed area and roads, its physical condition indicated it was not devoted to exempt activity. Proceeds from granting a permanent easement for passage and use produced UBI.[86]

The normal income tax rules of Sections 1221 and 1231 for identifying capital, versus ordinary income, property apply to identify an exempt organization's property eli-

---

[81] Priv. Ltr. Rul. 9535051.

[82] Rev. Rul. 95-8, 1995-14 I.R.B. 1.

[83] *Juniper Hunting Club v. Commissioner*, 28 B.T.A. 525 (1933).

[84] *Framingham Country Club v. United States*, 659 F. Supp. 650 (D.C. Mass. 1987); Priv. Ltr. Rul. 9307003.

[85] *Atlanta Athletic Club v. Commissioner*, 93-1 U.S.T.C. ¶ 50,051 (10th Cir.), *rev'g* T.C.M. 1991-83, 61 T.C.M. 2011, Dec. 47,195(M).

[86] Tech. Adv. Memo. 9225001.

gible to be treated as nontaxable under the capital gain modification. Other code sections apply to timber sales and the sale of land owned by a social club.

(C) RENTALS

Rentals are excluded, except:

- Personal property rentals are taxable unless they are rented incidentally (not more than 10 percent of rent) with real property.
- Net profit (versus gross revenue) interests produce UBI.
- Where substantial services are rendered, such as the rental of a theater complete with staff, the rental will not be considered passive.

Sharecrop arrangements for farm land owned by exempt organizations may or may not be treated as excludable from UBI under the rent exception, depending on whether the terms indicate that the charity is a joint venturer participating in the framing operations or is simply renting the land to a tenant farmer. How the rent is calculated is determinative. Two recent cases illustrate the factors used to evaluate the question:[87]

- The exempt organization is not involved in the day-to-day operation of the farm; it simply provides the land and buildings.
- The EO bears no risk of loss from accidents.
- The EO is not required to contribute to any losses from the operation, but only pays an agreed portion of the operating expenses (in this case 50%).
- The rent is equal to a fixed percentage of the gross sale of the crop or a fixed amount, not a percentage of net profits.[88]

Parking lot rental presents a similar situation. Rental of the bare real estate to another party that operates the lot clearly produces passive rental income. If the EO provides some services to the operator, UBI taint may occur. The regulations speak of "services rendered . . . primarily for the convenience and other than those usually or customarily rendered in connection with the rental of rooms or other space for occupancy only." Providing maid service, but not trash hauling, in renting a room is the example provided.[89] Regarding a parking lot, where the EO itself has no relationship or responsibility to the parkers, passive rental should occur. In a recent letter ruling, an EO landowner received nontaxable rental income when it required the lessee to maintain the lot and its access and egress areas, including snow removal, signs, barriers, patching, painting of space markings, designation of persons who can park in the lease area, and policing the area.[90] Operation of a parking lot for the benefit of employees and persons participating in an exempt organization's functions, rather than disinterested persons,

---

[87] *Trust U/W Emily Oblinger v. Commissioner.*, 100 T.C. No. 9 (Feb. 23, 1993); *Harlan E. Moore Charitable Trust v. U.S.*, 812 F. Supp. 130 (C.D. Ill. 1993) *aff'd*, 93-2 USTC ¶ 50,601 (7th Cir.). Similarly see *Independent Order of Odd Fellows v. U.S.*, No. 4-90-CV-60552 (S.D. Iowa 1993); and *White's Iowa Manual Labor Institute v. Commissioner*, T.C. Memo 1993-364.

[88] IRC §512(b)(3)(A)(ii).

[89] Reg. §1.512(b)-1(c)(5).

[90] Priv. Ltr. Rul. 9301024.

may be a related activity.[91] Note that the parking rate structure was proposed to be "not consistent with commercially operated for-profit facilities in the same metropolitan area and reflected the EO's desire to provide a necessary service to the public."

(D) ROYALTIES

Royalties are excluded from unrelated business taxable income, whether measured by production or by the gross or taxable income from the property licensed in return for the royalty payment. Oil and gas working interest income, even if calculated like a royalty, is not modified or excluded from UBI. Similarly, when personal services are rendered in connection with property licensed in return for a royalty, the portion of the payment attributable to the services must be extracted from the passive and nontaxable royalty payment and treated as active business income. See Section 27.20(e) of this chapter for more discussion.

(E) SUBSIDIARY PAYMENTS

Controlled subsidiary payments for interest, rents, royalties, or annuities, however, are includable in UBI. Control exists when one organization owns stock possessing at least 80 percent of the total combined voting power of all classes of stock entitled to vote and at least 80 percent of all other classes of stock of another organization (exempt or nonexempt). A nonstock organization measures control by quantifying its interlocking directors. If at least 80 percent of the directors of one organization are members of the second organization or have the right to appoint or control the board of the second, control exists according to the Regulations.

That portion of a controlled organization's income which would have been taxed as UBI to the parent EO if the income had been earned by it is includable (whether or not regularly carried on). Thus, payments from a subsidiary corporation conducting a related activity would qualify as a modification and not be UBI.

Rents paid by a second-tier subsidiary were nontaxable and not subject to inclusion under §512(b)(13).[92] The IRS agreed that the section contains no attribution or indirect ownership requirement that would treat the parent as controlling its subsidiary's subsidiary. Because the parent did not have direct control of the subsidiary, its rental payments were not subject to UBI. As a caveat to organizations availing themselves of this important admission by the IRS, the ruling stated that it was predicated on the fact that the arrangement had economic substance and was not intended to avoid tax.

An association of golf clubs was similarly permitted to create a tier of subsidiaries to operate a public golf course. Land owned by the association was contributed to the first subsidiary, which was established to independently own the land and insulate the association from liability. That first subsidiary then created its own subsidiary to actually operate the course. Rentals paid by the first subsidiary to the association were treated as passive nontaxable unrelated income.[93]

---

[91] Priv. Ltr. Rul. 9401031.
[92] Priv. Ltr. Rul. 9338003.
[93] Priv. Ltr. Rul. 9506046.

(F) RESEARCH

Research income is not taxable if the research is performed for the United States, its agencies, or a state or political subdivision thereof by any EO. In addition:

- A college, university, or hospital can exclude all research income from private or governmental contractors.
- An EO performing fundamental research, the results of which are freely available to the general public, can also exclude all research income.

It is important to distinguish between "scientific research" that is treated as related income and "testing" that is considered a commercial and unrelated enterprise.

27.13 *Calculating the Taxable Income*

Gross unrelated business income, minus expenses and exemption (listed below), is reported on Form 990-T and subject to tax. As long as the percentage of revenues from UBI is modest in relation to the organization's overall revenues, the only problem UBIT presents is the reduction in profit because of the income tax paid. Tax planning of the sort practiced by a good businessperson is in order. Maximizing deductions to calculate the income is important. The income tax sections of the Internal Revenue Code of 1986 govern, and the same concepts apply, including:

- *Tax rates.* The income tax is calculated using the normal tables for all taxpayers: Section 1(e) for trusts or Section 11 for corporations. For controlled groups of exempt organizations (also including 80-percent-owned for-profit subsidiaries), the corporate tax bracket must be calculated on a consolidated basis under the rules of Section 1561.
- *Alternative minimum tax.* Accelerated depreciation, percentage depletion, and other similar tax benefits are subject to the alternative minimum tax just as for-profit taxpayers.
- *"Ordinary and necessary" criteria.* Deductions claimed against the unrelated income must be "ordinary and necessary" to conducting the activity and must meet the other standards of Section 162 for business deductions. Ordinary means common and accepted for the type of business operated; necessary means helpful and appropriate, not indispensable. The activity for which the expenditure is incurred must also be operated with profit motive.[94]
- *Profit motive.* To be deductible, an expenditure must also be paid for the production of income, or in a business operated for the purpose of making a profit. Section 183 specifically prohibits the deduction of "hobby losses," or those activities losing money for more than two years out of every five. The IRS will challenge the deduction for UBI purposes of any expenditures not paid for the purposes of producing the profit.[95]

---

[94] Treas. Reg. 1.512(a)-1(a).
[95] *Iowa State University of Science and Technology v. United States*, 500 F.2d 508 (Ct. Cl. 1974); *Commissioner v. Groetzinger*, 480 U.S. 23 (1987), Treas. Reg. § 1.513-1(4)(d)(iii).

- *Depreciation.* Equipment, buildings, vehicles, furniture, and other properties that have a useful life to the business are deductible theoretically over their life. As a simple example, one-third of the total cost of a computer that is expected to be obsolete in three years would be deductible during each year the computer is used in the business, under a system called "depreciation." Unfortunately, Congress uses these calculation rates and methods as political and economic tools, and the Code proscribes rates and methods that are not so simple. Sections 167, 168, and 179 apply and must be studied to properly calculate allowable deductions for depreciation.
- *Inventory.* If the EO keeps an inventory of items for sale, such as books, drugs, or merchandise of any sort, it must use the inventory methods to deduct the cost of such goods. The concept is one of matching the cost of the goods sold with its sales proceeds. If the EO buys ten widgets for sale and, as of the end of a year, only five have been sold, the cost of the five is deductible and the remaining five are "capitalized" as an asset to be deducted when in fact they are sold. Again, the system is far more complicated than this simple example and an accountant should be consulted to ensure use of proper reporting and tabulation methods. Sections 263A and 471–474 apply.
- *Capital and nondeductibles.* A host of nondeductible items contained in Sections 261 to 280H might apply to disallow deductions either by total disallowance or required capitalization of permanent assets. Again, all the rules applicable to for-profit businesses apply, such as the luxury automobile limits, travel and entertainment substantiation requirements, and 50 percent disallowance for meals.
- *Dividend deduction.* The dividends received deduction provided by Sections 243 to 245 for taxable nonexempt corporations is not allowed. As a general rule, a corporation is allowed to exclude 70 percent of the dividends it receives on its investments; exempts are not. This rule only presents a problem for dividends received from investments that are debt-financed. Most dividends received by exempts are excluded from the UBI under the "Modifications" previously discussed.

27.14   *Specific Categories of Deductible Costs*

As a general rule, there are two categories of expenses allowed as deductions for purposes of calculating UBIT: direct and dual use expenses. No portion of the organization's basic operating expense theoretically is deductible against UBI because of the exploitation rules discussed below. However, where there is an ongoing plan to produce UBI and such revenue is part of the justification affording a particular exempt activity, allocation of overhead may be permitted, although technically challenging.

(A)   DIRECTLY RELATED

Those expenses attributable solely to the production of unrelated gross income are fully deductible. According to the IRS, a "proximate and primary relationship" between the expense and the activity is the standard for full deduction. Proximate means near, close, or immediate. A "but for" test can be applied by asking the question, "Would the expense be incurred if the unrelated activity was not carried on?"[96]

(B)   DUALLY USED FACILITIES OR PERSONNEL

A portion of the cost of so-called "dual use," or shared, employees and facilities, is deductible. An allocation between the two types of activities is made on "a reasonable basis." The only example given in the Regulations allocates 10 percent of an EO president's salary to an unrelated business activity to which he or she devotes 10 percent of his or her time. Where actual time records are maintained to evidence effort devoted to related versus unrelated activities, deduction of the applicable personal costs is ensured. In the IRS *Manual*, examining agents are instructed that any reasonable method resulting in identifying a relationship of the expenses to revenue produced is acceptable. There is no particular approved method that must be followed.[97]

Absent time records, an allocation based on relative gross income produced might be used if the exempt activity reaps income. Take, for example, a museum bookstore that sells both related and unrelated items. Sales in this case could be used as the allocation base. Where an income-producing activity is carried out alongside one that is not producing revenue, time records must be maintained.

Where a portion of the building is devoted totally to unrelated activity, building costs, including utilities, insurance, depreciation of the cost, interest on mortgage, and maintenance, are allocated based on total square footage of the building used for the UBI activity. Where UBI space is shared with related space, again a reasonable method is used. For a publication project, the lineage devoted to advertising could be calculated for its relationship to the total publication.

Taxpayers and the IRS have argued about allocation methods, and there are differences of opinion. An EO with this question should be sure to determine the current situation. For hospitals, the Medicare cost allocations methods "usually fail to accurately reflect UBI," in the IRS's opinion.[98]

(C)   DIRECT VS. INDIRECT EXPENSES

A subset of the expense allocation problem is the application of different methods for direct and indirect expenses. Direct expenses are those that increase proportionately with the usage of a facility or the volume of activity; they are also called variable. The number of persons attending an event influences the number of ushers or security guards needed, and represents a direct cost; in other words, the cost is attributable to that specific use that would not have been incurred except for the particular event.

Indirect costs, on the other hand, are incurred without regard to usage or frequency of participation and are usually called the fixed expenses of the organization. Building costs are an example. The presumption is that the organization's underlying building costs, for example, do not vary with usage.

---

[96] *Supra* note 42.
[97] *Exempt Organization Examination Guidelines Handbook*, Section 720(7) of Internal Revenue Manual 7(10)69.
[98] Gen. Couns. Mem. 39,843.

(D) FORMULA DENOMINATOR QUESTION

The denominator of the fraction used to calculate costs allocable to UBI is significant in reducing or increasing allowable deductions. The question must be considered in view of the exploitation rules, and the point is again whether the EO would conduct the related activity without the unrelated revenue stream. Arguably, no fixed costs of an exempt institution should be allocated to UBI, but to date the courts have chosen to allow allocation among both the exempt and nonexempt functions that benefit from building use.

In allocating fixed facility costs, the courts haven't agreed on whether the total number of hours a facility is used versus the total number of hours in the year is the appropriate denominator. To anyone grasping mathematics, it is easy to see each factor yields vastly different results. Watch for new legislation or Regulations; more complicated and varied formulas have been proposed.

- The Second Circuit of the federal courts[99] in a college football stadium case allowed:

$$\frac{\text{number of hours or days used for unrelated purposes}}{\text{total number of hours or days in USE}}$$

- The IRS argues that fixed costs were to be allocated by:

$$\frac{\text{number of hours or days used for unrelated purposes}}{\text{total number of hours of days in YEAR}}$$

(E) GROSS-TO-GROSS METHOD

The gross-to-gross method of cost allocation is applied where costs bear a relationship to the revenue produced from exempt and nonexempt factors. For example, where students and members are charged one fee and nonmembers and nonstudents are charged another (usually higher) fee, an allocation using the total revenue from each different category would not be reflective of the true cost to produce the revenue. A proration based on the overall number of individuals in each group might better reflect reality and ostensibly be more accurate. This type of formula is often used in calculating allocations for social clubs or publications serving all participants at the same price.

(F) EXPLOITATION

When income is produced by a fundamentally exempt activity, such as ads sold for a member publication or a student bookstore that sells pajamas, unrelated income from the activity is said to "exploit" the exempt function. Two special rules apply to limit the

---

[99] *Rensselaer Polytechnic Institute v. Commissioner*, 732 F.2d 1058 (2d Cir. 1984), *aff'd* 79 T.C. 967 (1982).

amount of expenses that may be deductible against such income in calculating the unrelated business income tax.[100] The basic rule says expenses, depreciation, and similar items attributable to the conduct of the exempt activities are not deductible. The regulations explain that such expenses do not have the necessary proximate and primary relationships to the UBI and therefore are not directly connected—a basic requirement for deduction, as explained above in Section 27.14(a).

A very important exception to the rule, however, permits allocation of expenses if the activity has a commercial counterpart. The regulations say "Where the exempt activity exploited by the business is a type of activity normally conducted by taxable organizations in pursuance of such business," expenses can be allocated and deducted in calculating UBI. The regulations use advertising as an example of a "normal business." There have been virtually no cases or rulings defining the meaning of the terms.

Secondly, no loss from an exploited activity can be used to offset other UBI. The proposed sponsorship regulations permit allocation of expenses to taxable sponsorship revenue by adding a new example.

(G) CHARITABLE DEDUCTION

Up to 10 percent of an exempt corporation's UBI and 100 percent of a charitable trust's UBI is deductible for contributions paid to a charitable organization. The deduction is not allowed for internal project expenditures of the organization itself. Excess contributions are eligible for the normal five-year carryover allowed for-profit tax-payers. Social clubs, voluntary employee business associations, unemployment benefit trusts, and group legal service plans can take a 100 percent deduction for direct charitable gifts and "qualified set asides" for charitable purposes.

(H) ADMINISTRATIVE OVERHEAD

It bears separate note that a portion of the organization's administrative expenses may be deductible against UBI and substantially reduces the tax burden from unrelated activity. Adequate proof of the allocation methods and escape of the exploitation rule discussed above is important to support an EO's overhead deduction against UBI.

(I) $1,000 EXEMPTION

A specific exemption of $1,000 is allowed.

27.15 Accounting Method Considerations

(A) IN-KIND GIFTS

Donated goods and services properly recorded under accounting principles promulgated by the Accounting Principles Board (FASB #117) should be booked and deducted.

---

[100] Reg. § 1.512(a)-1(d).

(B)   DOCUMENTATION

To correctly calculate the EO's expenses that are allocable to UBI, documentation is critical. Time records, expense identification, departmental approval systems, and similar internal control techniques will allow the organization to compute maximum allowable deductions against UBI. Particularly for staff time allocations and administrative expense items, such as printing and supplies, capturing the information is simple once documentation methods are installed.

(C)   ACCRUAL METHOD

If the EO's gross income from UBI exceeds $5 million annually, the accrual method of accounting must be used. If an inventory of goods and products for sale is maintained and is a "material" income-producing factor, the accrual method must be utilized.

(D)   NET OPERATING LOSSES

A loss realized in operating an unrelated business in one year may be carried back for 3 years and forward for 15 years, for offset against another year's operating income. Gains and losses for different types of UBI earned within any single EO are netted against profits from the various business activities of the organization, including passive income from indebted investment property. Tax years in which no UBI activity is realized are counted in calculating the number of years for permissible carryovers. Conversely, net operating losses are not reduced by related income.

   A social club cannot offset losses on serving nonmembers against income from its other investments, according to the Supreme Court, which sided with the IRS in the *Portland Golf Club* case decided in 1990.[101] There has been a conflict of decisions in U.S. Circuit Courts for several years, and clubs claiming such losses must now consider filing amended returns to report tax resulting from the loss disallowance.

   It is extremely important for an EO to file Form 990T despite the fact that it incurs a loss. Reporting the loss allows for carryback or carryover of the loss to offset past or future income. An election is available to carry losses forward and forgo any carryback in situations where the EO has not previously earned UBI.

27.16   Estimated Tax

Income tax liability for UBI is payable in advance during the year, as the income is earned, similar to for-profit businesses and individuals.

27.17   Debt-Financed Income

The *modifications* exempting passive investment income from the UBIT, such as dividends and interest, do not apply to the extent the investment is made with borrowed

---

[101] *Portland Golf Club v. Commissioner*, 90-1 U.S.T.C. § 50,332 (Sup. Ct. 1990); *Iowa State University of Science and Technology v. United States*, 500 F.2d (Ct. Cl. 1974); *Commissioner v. Groetzinger, supra* note 6.

funds. Debt-financed property is defined by Section 514 as including property held for the production of income that was acquired with borrowed funds and has a balance of acquisition indebtedness attributable to it during the year. The classic examples are a margin account held against the EO's endowment funds or a mortgage financing a rental building purchase.

Although investment of a pension fund is admittedly inherent in its exempt purposes, debt-financed investments made by such a fund (or most other exempt organizations) are not inherent in a fund's purposes, according to §514(c)(4).[102] Similarly, the Southwest Texas Electric Cooperative's purchase of Treasury Notes with Rural Electrification Administration loan proceeds represented a debt-financed investment. The loan proceeds were required to be used to pay construction costs. The cooperative's cash flow, however, allowed it to pay part of the construction costs with operating funds. To take advantage of a more than 4 percent spread in the REA loan and prevailing Treasury Note rates, the cooperative deliberately "drew down" on the REA loan. The Tax Court agreed with the IRS that the interest income was taxable debt-financed income.[103]

(A) PROPERTIES EXCLUDED FROM DEBT-FINANCED RULES

Real or other tangible or intangible property used 85 percent or more of the time when it is actually devoted to such purpose, and used directly in the EO's exempt or related activities, is exempt from these rules. If a university borrows money and builds an office tower for its projected staff needs over a 20-year period, and if less than 85 percent of the building is used by its staff and net profit is earned, the non-university-use portion of the building income is taxable as UBI.

- Income included in UBI for some other reason, such as hotel room rentals or a 100 percent owned subsidiary's royalties, is specifically excluded by the Code and is not counted twice because the property is debt-financed. Conversely, an indebted property used in an unrelated activity that is excluded from UBIT because it is managed by volunteers, is for the convenience of members, or is a facility for sale of donated goods, is not treated as unrelated debt-financed property.[104]
- Future-use land (not including buildings) acquired and held for use by an EO within 10 years (churches get 15 years) from the date it is acquired, and located in the neighborhood in which the EO carries out a project, is exempt from this provision. This exception applies until the plans are abandoned; after five years, the organization's plan for use must be "reasonably certain."[105]
- A "life estate" does not constitute a debt. Where some other individual or organization is entitled to income from the property for life or another period of time, a remainder interest in the property is not considered to be indebted.

---

[102] *Elliot Knitwear Profit Sharing Plan v. Commissioner*, 71 T.C. 765 (1979), *aff'd*, 614 F.2d 347 (3rd Cir. 1980).

[103] *South Texas Electric Cooperative, Inc. v. Commissioner*, 95-2 U.S.T.C. ¶ 50,565 (5th Cir. 1995), *aff'd*, 68 TCM 285, Dec. 50, 008 (M).

[104] IRC §514(b)(1)(B) & (C).

[105] IRC §514(b)(3)(A)–(E).

- Debt placed on property by a donor will be attributed to the organization where the EO assumes and agrees to pay all or part of the debt OR makes any payments on the equity.

  Property that is encumbered and subject to existing debt at the time it is received by bequest or devise is not treated as acquisition indebted-property for 10 years from its acquisition, if there is no assumption or payment on the debt by the exempt.

- Gifted property is similarly excluded if the donee placed the mortgage on the property over 5 years prior to gift and had owned the property over 5 years unless there is an assumption or payment by the EO on the mortgage.

- A property used in unrelated activities of an EO, the income of which is excepted from UBI because it is run by volunteers, for the convenience of members, or sale of donated goods, can be indebted and still not be subject to this classification.

- Research property producing income otherwise excluded from the UBIT also is not subject to the acquisition indebtedness taint.

- Indebted property producing no recurrent annual income, but held to produce appreciation in underlying value, or capital gain, is subject to this rule.[106] A look-back rule prevents deliberate payoff prior to sale to avoid the tax. The portion of the taxable gain is calculated using the highest amount of indebtedness during the twelve months preceding the sale as the numerator.[107]

- Tax status of the tenant or user is not determinative. Rental of an indebted medical office building used by staff physicians can be related to a hospital's purposes.[108] Although their restoration served a charitable purpose, the rental of restored historic properties to private tenants was deemed not to serve an exempt purpose where the properties were not open to the public.[109] Regulations suggest that all facts and circumstances of property usage will be considered.

- The proportion-of-use test applied to identify property used for exempt and nonexempt purposes can be based on a comparison of the number of days used for exempt purposes with the total time the property is used, or on the basis of square footage used for each, or relative costs.[110]

- Federal funding provided or insured by the Federal Housing Administration, if used to finance purchase, construction, or rehabilitation of residential property for low-income persons, is excluded.

- Charitable gift annuities issued as the sole consideration in exchange for property worth more than 90 percent of value of the annuity is not considered acquisition indebtedness. The annuity must be payable over the life (not for a minimum or maximum number of payments) of one or two persons alive at the time. The annuity must not be measured by the property's (or any other property's) income.

---

[106] Reg. §1.514(b)-1(a).
[107] Reg. §1.514(a)-1(a)(1)(v).
[108] Rev. Rul. 69-464, 19969-2 C.B. 132; Tech. Adv. Memo. 8906003.
[109] Rev. Rul. 77-47, 1977-1 C.B. 156; Tech. Adv. Mem. 9017003.
[110] Reg. §1.514(b)-1(b)(ii), §1.512(b)-1(b)(iii) Example 2; Priv. Ltr. Ruls. 8030105 and 8145087.

• Schools and their supporting organizations, certain pension trusts, and 501(c)(25) title holding companies may have a special exception for indebted real property. If the property is purchased in a partnership with for-profit investors, profit- and loss-sharing ratios must have substantial economic effect and not violate the disproportionate allocation rules.[111]

(B) WHAT IS "ACQUISITION INDEBTEDNESS?"

Acquisition indebtedness is the unpaid amount of any debt incurred to purchase or improve property or any debt "reasonably foreseen" at the time of acquisition which would not have been incurred otherwise.

• Securities purchases on margin are debt-financed; payments for loan of securities already owned are not.
• The formula for calculation of income subject to tax is:

$$\text{income from property} \times \frac{\text{average acquisition indebtedness}}{\text{average adjusted basis}}$$

The average acquisition indebtedness equals the arithmetic average of each month or partial month of the tax year. The average adjusted basis is similarly calculated, and only straight-line depreciation is allowed.

(C) CALCULATION OF TAXABLE PORTION

Only that portion of the net income of debt-financed property attributable to the debt is classified as UBI. Each property subject to debt is calculated separately with the resulting net income or loss netted to arrive at the portion includable in UBI. Expenses directly connected with the property are deducted from gross revenues in the same proportion.

The capital gain or loss formula is different in one respect: highest amount of indebtedness during the year preceding sales is used as the numerator.

27.18 Planning Ideas

The first rule in reducing UBIT is to keep good records. The accounting system must support the desired allocation of deductions for personnel and facilities with time records, expense usage reports, auto logs, documentation reports, and so on. Aggressive avoidance of the "exploitation rule" must be backed up with proof.

Minutes of meetings of the board of directors or trustees should reflect discussion of relatedness of any project claimed to accomplish an exempt purpose where it could appear the activity is unrelated. For example, contracts and other documents concerning activities the organization wants to prove are related to its exempt purposes should contain appropriate language to reflect the project's exempt purposes.

---

[111] IRC §168(h)(6), 514(c)(9), and 704(b)(2).

PART IV   ACCOUNTING, FINANCE, AND LEGAL ISSUES

An organization's original purposes can be expanded and redefined to broaden the scope of activities or to justify some proposed activity as related. Such altered or expanded purpose can be reported to the IRS to justify the relatedness of a new activity.

Where dual-use facilities can be partly debt-financed and partly paid for, the EO could purposefully buy the nontaxable exempt function property with debt and buy the unrelated part of the facility with cash available. Or, separate notes could be executed with the taxable and unrelated property's debt being paid off first.

If loss of exemption is a strong possibility because of the extent and amount of unrelated business activity planned, a separate for-profit organization can be formed to shield the EO from a possible loss of exemption due to excessive business activity.

27.19 *Special Interest Topic—Museums*

Museum gift shop sales and related income-producing activities are governed by the "fragmentation" and "exploitation" rules discussed earlier. Since 1973, when it published a ruling concern greeting cards,[112] the IRS has formally agreed that items printed with reproductions of images in a museum's collection are educational, related to the exempt purposes, and their sale produces UBI. The ruling expressed two different reasons: (1) the cards stimulated and enhanced the public awareness, interest in, and appreciation of art; and (2) a self-advertising theory stating that a "broader segment of the public may be encouraged to visit the museum itself to share in its educational functions and programs as a result of seeing the cards."

Another 1973 ruling[113] explored the fragmentation rule and expanded its outlook to trinkets and actual copies of objects and distinguished items. The IRS felt that educational merit could be gained from utilitarian items with souvenir value. Since that time, it has been clearly established that a museum shop often contains both related and unrelated items and the museum must keep exacting records to identify the two.

(A)   IDENTIFYING RELATED AND UNRELATED OBJECTS

After the IRS and museums argued for 10 years about the relatedness of a wide variety of objects old, four exhaustive private rulings were issued in 1983.[114] The primary concern for a museum is to identify the "relatedness" of each object sold in its shops and segregate any unrelated sales. The connection between the item sold and achievement of the museum's exempt purpose is evidenced by the facts and circumstances of each object and the policy of the curatorial department in identifying, labeling, and categorizing objects on public view.

IRS rulings direct the *"facts and circumstances"* of each object to be examined, to prove the objects being sold have educational value, and list the following factors to consider in designating an item:

- "Interpretive material" describing artistic, cultural, or historical relationship to the museum's collection or exhibits.

---

[112] Rev. Rul. 73-104, 1973-1 C.B. 263.
[113] Rev. Rul. 73-105, 1973-1 C.B. 265.
[114] Priv. Ltr. Rul. 8303013, 8326003, 8236008, and 9328009, updated in 9550003.

688

- Nature, scope, and motivation for the sales activity.
- Are sales solely for production of income or are they an activity intended to enhance visitor awareness of art?
- Curatorial supervision in choosing related items.
- Reproductions of objects in the particular museum or other collections, including prints, slides, posters, post or greeting cards, are generally exempt.
- Adaptations, including imprinted utilitarian objects such as dishes, ashtrays, and clothing, must be accompanied by interpretive materials and must depict objects or identify an exhibition. Objects printed with logos were deemed unrelated.
- Souvenirs and convenience items are generally unrelated unless imprinted with reproductions or promoting a particular event or exhibition. Souvenirs promoting the town in which the museum is located are not considered related to the museum's purposes.
- Toys and other teaching items for children are deemed inherently educational and therefore deemed related in IRS rulings.

(B)   ORIGINAL WORKS OF ART

Original works of art created by living artists and sold by museums are considered unrelated by the IRS. "It is inconsistent with the purpose of exhibiting art for the public benefit to deprive [the] public the opportunity of viewing the art by selling it to an individual." This policy can apply as well to deceased artists.

- A cooperative art gallery established to encourage individual "emerging artists" was not allowed to qualify as an exempt organization because, in the IRS's opinion, the interests of the general public were not served by promoting the careers of individual artists. The art sales served no exempt purpose and constituted unrelated business income. Because the organization was supported entirely by unrelated business income from the sales of art of the artists, it was not exempt.[115]
- A community art center located in an isolated area with no commercial galleries obtained exemption and the Tax Court decided its sales of original art were related to exempt purposes. The decision was based on the fact that no other cultural center existed in the county, the art sales were not the center's sole source of support, and a complex of other activities were conducted.[116]
- An unrelated gallery managed by volunteers and/or selling donated works of art produces unrelated income but the income is not taxable, because of exceptions. Exempt status depends on whether the gallery is a substantial part of the EO's activities.

(C)   STUDY TOURS

Museums and other types of exempt organizations sponsor study tours as promotional, educational, and fund-raising tools. The issue is whether such tours compete with travel

---

[115] Priv. Ltr. Rul. 8032028.
[116] *Goldsboro Art League, Inc. v. Commissioner*, 75 T.C. 337 (1980).

agents and commercial tour guides and thus produce UBI. The crux of the matter, according to the IRS, is the intent of the tour-sponsoring organization. When the IRS judges the relatedness of a tour, it considers the difference between "serendipitous acquisition of knowledge" and a deliberate intent to educate.[117] A study tour led by professionals and qualifying for university credit qualifies as related to a museum's educational purposes. Generally, the IRS looks carefully and will scrutinize:

- The "bona fide" educational methodology of the tour, including the professional status of leaders and the educational content of the program. The amount of advance preparation, such as reading lists, can be a factor. The actual amount of time spent in formal classes, mandatory participation in the lectures, or opportunity for university credit are other attributes evidencing the educational nature of a tour.[118]
- Conversely, the amount of recreational time allowed to participants, the resort-taint of the places the tour visits, and holiday scheduling will suggest predominantly personal pleasure purposes and cause the tour to not qualify as educational.[119]

Not only the profit from the tour itself, but the "additional donation" requested as an organizational gift by all participants in a travel tour program, may be classed as unrelated income if the tour is not considered as educational.[120]

27.20 Special Interest Topic—Publishing

EO publications present two very different exposures to trouble: the unrelated income tax and potential revocation of exemption. As discussed earlier, the most universal problem is that publication advertising sales create UBIT in most cases. A less common, but more dangerous, situation occurs where the underlying exemption is challenged because the publication itself is a business.

(A) ADVERTISING

Revenue received from the sale of advertising in an otherwise exempt publication is considered business income by the IRS, and is taxed unless:

- The publication schedule or ad sale activity is irregularly carried on.
- The advertising is sold by volunteers.
- The advertising activity is related to one of the organization's underlying exempt purposes, such as ads sold by college students or trainees.

---

[117] Remarks of Marc Owens, Director of IRS Exempt Organization Division, Non-Profits in Travel Conference, on March 9, 1995.
[118] Rev. Rul. 70-534, 1970-2 C.B. 113.
[119] Rev. Rul. 77-366, 1977-2 C.B. 192.
[120] Tech. Adv. Mem. 9027003.

- The ads do not contain commercial material, appear essentially as a listing without significant distinction among those listed, and represent acknowledgement of contributors or sponsors.

The IRS has continually taken the position that advertising sold using the EO's name is unrelated activity despite the creative contracts attributing the activity to an independent commercial firm. See agency theory discussion at 27.8(j).[121]

(B)   READERSHIP VS. AD LINEAGE COSTS

Even if ad revenue is classified as UBI, the tax consequence is limited by the portion of the readership and editorial costs allowed as deductions against the ad revenue. The important question is what portion of the expense of producing and distributing the publication can be allocated against the revenue.[122] It is helpful first to study the *Calculation of Taxable Portion of Advertising Revenue*, a worksheet reflecting the order in which readership and editorial costs versus advertising costs are allocated. See Section 27.21.

What the formula accomplishes is to prorate deductions in arriving at taxable advertising income. Publication costs are first divided into two categories: direct advertising and readership. Because readership costs are exempt function costs, under the "exploitation rule" discussed later they theoretically shouldn't be deductible at all against the UBI income. In a limited exception, the Regulations allow readership costs, if any, in excess of readership income to be deducted against advertising income. In other words, advertising revenues can be offset with a readership loss. Arriving at a readership loss, however, means the publication's underlying production costs must be more than its revenues.

(C)   CIRCULATION INCOME

The term *circulation income* means the income attributable to the production, distribution, or circulation of a periodical (other than advertising revenue) including sale of reprints and back issues.[123] Where members receive an EO's publication as a part of their basic membership fee, a portion of the member dues is allocated to circulation income. Other types of member income, such as educational program fees or convention registration, are not allocated.[124] Where the publication is given free to members but sold to nonmembers, a portion of the members' dues is allocated to readership revenue. The IRS formulas require that an allocation of a hypothetical portion of the dues be made as described in the calculation.

1. Free copies given to nonmembers are subject to controversy with IRS (check latest decisions).

---

[21] Rev. Rul. 73-424, 1973-2 C.B. 190 and Tech. Adv. Mem. 9222001.
[122] Treas. Reg. § 1.512(a)-1(f)(6).
[123] Reg. § 1.512(a)-r(f)(3)(iii).
[124] Tech. Adv. Memo. 9204007.

2. If the EO has more than one publication, the IRS and the courts have disagreed on the denominator of the fraction for calculation of allocable exempt function costs.[125]

In Priv. Ltr. Rul. 9402005, the IRS provided some useful criteria for deciding what constitutes a "periodical." The definition is important because that portion of membership dues allocated to published periodicals is treated as taxable unrelated income. An educational organization devoted to the study of reproduction distributed a variety of publications, some of which were deemed periodicals and others of which were not. A quarterly newsletter and annual meeting programs distributed to members were periodicals for the following reasons:

- Each was published at regular recurring intervals.
- The right to receive the publication was associated with membership or similar status in the organization for which dues, fees, or other charges were received (even though nonmembers may also).
- Each contained editorial materials related to the accomplishment of the organization's exempt purposes; in this case, publicizing scientific developments in the field, technical articles, and reports of annual meeting.
- The newsletter was part of an ongoing series, with each issue indicating its relation to prior or future issues; it contained a regular feature column, president's message, and reports of organizational meetings and activities.
- With respect to the advertising portion of the publications, the purpose was the production of income.
- Each issue of a periodical indicated a relation with prior or subsequent issues.

Postgraduate training course brochures, however, were not classified as periodicals to which membership income was allocable, because they instead contained only the following:

- Materials describing the location and hotel facilities where the course would be conducted.
- Course, faculty, and schedule listings.
- No title, table of contents, or editorial staff listing, articles, columns, or other editorial features.

(D)   COMMERCIAL PUBLICATION PROGRAMS

The overall publication program can be considered a commercial venture, despite its educational content. Distinguishing characteristics, according to the IRS, are found by examining the EO's management decisions.

---

[125] *North Carolina Citizens for Business and Industry v. United States*, 89-2 U.S.T.C. § 9507 (Cl. Ct. 1989).

The characteristics deemed commercial by the IRS include:

- *Presence of substantial profits.* Accumulation of profits over a number of years evidences a commercial purpose. The mere presence of profits, by itself, will not bar exemption,[126] but other factors will be considered. Among the questions asked would be: for what purpose are profits being accumulated? Do the reserves represent a savings account for future expansion plans?
- *Pricing methods.* The method of pricing books or magazines sold yields significant evidence of commercial taint. Pricing at or below an amount calculated to cover costs shows nonprofit motive. Pricing below comparable commercial publications is not required but certainly can evidence an intention to encourage readership and educate, rather than to produce a profit.
- *Other factors.* Other factors can show commerciality:
  - Aggressive commercial practices resembling those undertaken by commercial publishers;[127]
  - Substantial salaries or royalties paid to individuals;
  - Distribution by commercial licensers, such as "est."
- *Nonprofit publications.* By contrast, nonprofit and noncommercial publications:[128]
  - Rely on volunteers and/or modest wages;
  - Sell some books/magazines that are unprofitable;
  - Prepare and choose materials according to educational methods, not commercial appeal;
  - Donate part of press run to other EOs or members;
  - Balance deficit budgets with contributions.

(E) THE ROYALTY DILEMMA

It is the IRS's opinion that Section 512(b)(2), which say royalty income is not unrelated business income, does not apply to certain types of "royalties," including particularly those received in return for the sale of an organization's mailing list and the EO's name or logo.[129] While agreeing that mailing lists are intangible property the use of which produces royalty income, the IRS argues that royalties are inherently passive. In the IRS view, when the royalty income is produced in an active, commercial manner in competition with tax-paying businesses, it is contrary to the underlying scheme of the UBIT to allow such royalties to escape taxation.

Among the UBIT changes proposed by the House Oversight Committee (discussed in the next section), royalties received for licensing property created by the EO, or prop-

---

[126] *Scripture Press Foundation v. United States,* 285 F.2d 800 (Ct. Cl. 1961), *cert. denied,* 368 U.S. 985 (1982).

[127] *American Institute for Economic Research v. United States,* 302 F.2d 934 (Ct. Cl. 1962).

[128] *Presbyterian and Reformed Publishing Co. v. Commissioner,* 70 T.C. 1070, 1087, 1083 (1982).

[129] Gen. Couns. Mem. 39827 (Aug. 20, 1990); Priv. Ltr. Rul. 9029047.

erty involving substantial services and costs on the part of the EO, would be subject to UBIT—a rule the IRS is essentially now applying without statutory authority. After its success in the DAV case discussed below, the IRS may turn its "active" argument to other types of licensing arrangements as it pursues its UBI Compliance Program. The issue is very unsettled and the details of the history may be useful.

Unfortunately, the term "royalties" is not defined under the code or Regulations concerning unrelated income. In response to objections by large charities whom the IRS was subjecting to UBIT on their list revenues, Section 513(h)(1)(B) was added to provide special exception only for organizations eligible to receive charitable contributions, primarily 501(c)(3)s, to exclude from UBI any mailing list sales and exchanges with other similar organizations. By reference, mailing list sales by all other categories of tax-exempts would be includable in UBI.

In an interesting case, the Sixth Circuit Court[130] in July 1991 reversed the Tax Court and said the Disabled American Veterans (DAV)'s mailing list revenues were taxable unrelated business income. DAV (a 501(c)(4) organization) was arguing in the courts to escape tax deficiencies of over $4 million based on $279 million of revenue. The IRS partly based its position on the active business principle, contending that the level of active business involvement in servicing the list rental activity prevented the revenue from being classified as passive and, thereby, excludable from the UBIT.

The DAV admitted the revenue was from an unrelated business activity. There was no argument that DAV managed the activity in a businesslike manner. Among the stipulations were the fact that DAV had several personnel working full-time to keep the list current (not a volunteer operation), placed conditions on the name usage, required advanced approval of the client copy, had a complicated rate structure printed and widely circulated on rate cards, and belonged to Direct Mail Marketing Association (DMMA), a trade association composed of organizations using direct mail techniques in their operations.

The DAV argued that the revenue was a royalty excepted from UBI. The Tax Court had decided that it was up to Congress to cause "active" royalties to be taxed when the Code plainly says all royalties are excluded. They found nothing in the policy of the statute to offer any basis for characterizing royalties earned by a tax-exempt organization differently from royalties earned by a commercial organization. This issue is of particular interest in the scientific and medical fields, where considerable sums are earned from royalties paid for the licensing of patented devices and methods.

The DAV case is complicated by the fact that the Court of Claims had already decided in 1981 that DAV's mailing list sale income was taxable (it specifically declined to decide about exchanges). What the Sixth Circuit decided in overruling the Tax Court was that DAV was collaterally estopped by the 1981 decision from bringing the argument again to court, not that mailing lists sales were necessarily taxable. Thus, although the DAV lost on a technicality, the Tax Court decision still stands as to sales and no decision has ever been made about list changes.

[130] *Disabled American Veterans v. Commissioner, rev'd*, 91-2 U.S.T.C. § 50,336 (6th Cir. 1991), 94 T.C. 60 (1990).

What appear from the facts to be the Interscholastic League also failed in its effort to turn advertising revenues in to royalties. Under the licensing agreements with sporting goods manufacturers and insurance providers, the league was required to perform services and provide free advertising for the commercial concerns.[131]

The Tax Court once again ruled that it could find no evidence that Congress intended to limit the royalty exception to passively held or investment properties.[132] The Sierra Club's unrelated business income received as a royalty from the sale of its mailing list was found to be excluded from tax, as discussed in Section 27.12(d) of this chapter. The court's reasoning was based upon three factors: (1) a donor list is intangible property; (2) the income was paid in return for licensing the intangible; and (3) a royalty is a payment for the use of intangible property.

The victory was by no means perfect. Essentially the court ruled that making the lists available on a "one-time per transaction" basis was an excludable royalty paid for use of the lists. The court reserved for future decision the taxability of any payments for "the physical medium." The court agreed to consider whether the club provided and charged for valuable services in providing its mailing lists to users.

A hearing was scheduled to gather more facts and allow the judge to issue a summary judgment—look for further developments. Questions to be answered include:

- Were there separate charges dependent upon the manner in which the lists were furnished (on magnetic tape or preprinted labels)?
- Should special services, such as computer sorting by type of donor, zip code, or age of name, be treated as a taxable service rendered?

The court did not suggest and the club (possibly momentarily) won the battle of allocation consideration to the work involved in analyzing, coding, and otherwise servicing the list to keep it up to date.

During 1995, the IRS continued to hold steadfastly to its position that the royalty exception is not applicable to income received from the use of membership lists in a credit card solicitation program.[133] In a 59-page private ruling considering more than 10 plus issues, the IRS comprehensively addressed the affinity card question, additionally reviewed publication advertising in connection with a convention and trade show, and even discussed the possible application of the Section 6113 disclosure rules.

---

[131] Tech. Adv. Memo. 9211004.

[132] *Sierra Club, Inc. v. Commissioner*, TCM 47751(M) Dec. 49025 (M) (1993).

In 1994, the Tax Court (*Sierra Club, Inc. v. Commissioner*, 103 T.C. No. 17) again ruled in favor of the Sierra Club. The sole issue in question was whether the club was in the business of selling financial services that could produce unrelated business income. The court found no intention on the part of the club to form a joint venture to share in a "mutual proprietary interest in net profits," nor did it bear any risk or loss or expense. The fact that the club was required to solicit members and keep records of their names and addresses did not, in the court's eyes, indicate that the club had control over the financial institution's actions for such actions to be imputed to the club. This decision, commonly referred to as *Sierra II*, was upheld by the Ninth Circuit in July, 1996, as it regards the sale of mailing list. The affinity card issue was remanded to the Tax Court.

[133] Priv. Ltr. Rul. 9509002.

27.21   *Calculation of Taxable Portion of Advertising Revenue*

(A)   BASIC FORMULA

$A - B - (C - D) = $ Net taxable advertising income or loss

where $A = $ Gross sales of advertising
      $B = $ Direct costs of advertising
    $C - D = $ Readership costs in excess of readership revenue

(B)   DEFINITIONS

$B = $ Direct costs of advertising:
     Occupancy, supplies, and other administrative expense $ _____
     Commissions or salary costs for ad salespeople   _____
     Clerical or management salary cost directly allocable   _____
     Artwork, photography, color separations, etc.   _____
     Portion of printing, typesetting, mailing, and other direct publication
     costs allocable in the ratio of total lineage in the publication to ad lineage   _____
                                                       $ _____

$C = $ Readership costs
     Occupancy, supplies, and other administrative expense   _____
     Editors, writers, and salary for editorial content   _____
     Travel, photos, other direct editorial expenses   _____
     Portion of printing, typesetting, mailing, and other direct publication
     costs allocable in ratio of total lineage in publication to editorial lineage
     (in general, all direct publication costs not allocable to advertising lineage)   _____
                                                       $ _____

$D = $ Readership (or circulation) revenues:
     If publication sold to all for a fixed price, then readership revenue
     equals total subscription sales.   _____

or

     If 20% of total circulation is from paid nonmember subscriptions, then
     price charged to nonmembers times number of issues circulated to
     members plus nonmember revenue equals readership revenues.   _____

or

     If members receiving publication pay a higher membership fee,
     readership revenue equals excess dues times number of members
     receiving publication, plus nonmember revenue.   _____

or

     If more than 80% of issues distributed to members free, readership
     revenue is the membership receipts times the ratio of publication costs
     over the total exempt activities cost including the publication costs.   _____

Suggested Readings

Blazek, Jody. 1996. *Financial Planning for Nonprofit Organizations*. New York: Wiley.

Blazek, Jody. 1993. *Tax and Financial Planning for Tax Exempt Organizations: Forms, Checklists, Procedures*, 2nd ed. New York: Wiley.

Desiderio, R. J. and Taylor, S. A. 1988. *Planning Tax-Exempt Organizations*. New York: Shepard's/McGraw-Hill.

Gross, M. J., Jr., Warshauer, W., Jr., and Larkin, R. F. 1995. *Financial and Accounting Guide for Not-for-Profit Organizations*, 5th ed. New York: Wiley.

Hill, Frances R. and Kirschten, Barbara L. 1994. *Federal and State Taxation of Exempt Organizations*. Boston: Warren, Gorham & Lamont.

Hopkins, Bruce. 1992. *the Law of Tax-Exempt Organizations*, 6th ed. New York: Wiley.

_____ . 1989. *Starting and Managing a Nonprofit Organization—A Legal Guide*. New York: Wiley.

_____ . 1992. *Charity, Advocacy, and the Law*. New York: Wiley.

_____ . 1991. *The Law of Fund-Raising*. New York: Wiley.

New York University Conferences on Tax Planning for 501(c)(3) Organizations. Annual. New York: Matthew Bender. Published annually.

Oleck, Howard L. 1992. *Nonprofit Corporations, Organizations, and Associations*, 5th ed. Englewood Cliffs, NJ: Prentice-Hall.

U.S. Department of the Treasury, Internal Revenue Service. Annual. *Exempt Organizations Continuing Professional Education Technical Instruction Programs*. Washington, DC: (Available from IRS Reading Room, Washington, DC.)

_____ . *Exempt Organizations Handbook*. 1992. IR Manual 7751. Washington, DC:

_____ . *The Exempt Organization Tax Review, Tax Analysts*. Arlington, VA. Monthly journal.

_____ . *The Journal of Taxation of Exempt Organizations*. New York: Warren, Gorham & Lamont. Quarterly journal.

_____ . *The Nonprofit Counsel*. New York: Wiley. Monthly journal.

_____ . *Private Foundations Handbook*. 1992. IR Manual 7752. Washington, DC.

United Way of America. 1989. *Accounting and Financial Reporting, A Guide for United Ways and Not-for-Profit Organizations*, rev. 2d ed. Alexandria, VA: United Way Institute.

28 ▼ Resource Conservation Strategies and Techniques

SARA H. SKOLNICK, BBA, CAE
System Science Consultants

28.1 Introduction

This *Handbook* is an invaluable guide for understanding, organizing, and operating a nonprofit organization. Each chapter has been written by one or two people who not only have achieved their expertise through formal education, but also have honed their skills and intuition in the school of hard knocks. They have given you the rules and then told you how the game is played. Further, they have included extensive references to open the window even wider, leading the manager or volunteer leader toward answers to his or her questions and often suggesting what the questions should be.

    If you have jumped first to this chapter, it's probably because a crisis has occurred or is on the horizon. The chapters on total quality management and strategic planning will help to organize and manage the nonprofit in a way that, by its nature, will conserve resources and encourage wise spending. The human resources and employee compensation and benefits sections will provide guidance in helping staff to fully participate and contribute to the culture and activity of the nonprofit. The financial management and legal sections help with development of policies and procedures to address fundamental financial and fiduciary responsibilities. But it is seldom our lot to start from scratch, with plenty of time to research, plan, and organize in a methodical way, first laying the groundwork, then building the organization function by function and program by program. The realization that "something has to be done," or "we've got to get this thing under control" is more likely the challenge to be faced. This *Handbook* is designed to help us do it right. This chapter is designed to help save money, materials, and other resources—first in the short term to allow time for planning and reorganization, and later (when good habits are entrenched) to help the nonprofit continue to be conservative when new operating procedures are in place.

(A) CHANGE AS A CATALYST

John Naisbitt predicted in *Megatrends 2000* (1990) that the changes in fundamental worldwide social, economic, political, and technological structures in the 1980s would continue apace. Of his 10 "millennial megatrends," 5 rapidly changing areas—global economy, free-market socialism, privatization of the welfare state, women in leadership positions, and the increasing influence of the individual—are impacting the nonprofit world. Change stirs the pot and moves us ahead: this is a good thing. Change upsets routine and disturbs carefully laid plans: this is not so good, unless the reaction to control the change is prompt and appropriate.

(B) DEFINITIONS

To be sure that we are clear about the meaning of our terms, a few definitions are in order.

(i) Conservation
Webster's New World Dictionary says that *conservation* means protection from loss or waste. Quite simply, this is one of the principal responsibilities of managers of nonprofit organizations, in the sense that, as stewards of other's funds, we are called upon to be especially vigilant and careful.

(ii) Resources
Webster's definition of *resources* is more complex. Resources are anything that "lie ready for use." Resources can be money, property of any kind, people, skills, talents, programs such as regularly held technical or professional meetings, certification programs, scholarship programs, even reputation and goodwill.

(iii) Conservatism
Webster's defines *conservatism* as the philosophy which embraces protection of the status quo and resistance to change. When *conservatism* is used here, we mean that we intend to maintain the status quo and resist change.

The principal emphasis of this chapter is *conservation of funds*, or money, but other resources are also considered. The mindset developed during a major conservation effort will carry over into all areas of the nonprofit's activity.

(C) A CAUTIONARY NOTE

As ideas are put forward, tried, and built upon, as they will be, care must be taken to thread a fine line between unreasonable conservatism and conservation. Change is inevitable and is to be welcomed for the growth potential it brings. But change must be explored, controlled, and adapted to. During the adaptation process, conservative practices help to make the most out of scarce resources.

The second caution is to remember that it takes money to make money, and appropriate spending is even more important than eliminating spending. As is discussed later, a short moratorium on all unnecessary spending is a useful technique for quick financial restabilization, but investment in opportunities for revenue generation should be carefully analyzed for the potential long-term payoff.

28.2 *Strategic Planning and Conservation*

Every nonprofit organization should be "conservative" in the sense that it makes the most of every dollar it brings in. By its charter, an association has a mission and a purpose that set it apart from the for-profit world. The Congress of the United States has recognized, historically, that nonprofit organizations provide certain services to the community better than private industry and better than government. This recognition takes the form of exemption from taxes on the revenue a nonprofit takes in, reduced postal rates, an opportunity for a hearing before Congress as the representative of a special interest group, and a number of other relaxations of the rules that govern commerce on national, state, and local levels.

Nonprofits that lose sight of their special privileges and begin to take advantage of the trust of their members or the public do so at great risk. Their nonprofit status can be lost; their membership can abandon the organization; their sources of revenue can dry up. Profligacy and luxury have no place in the nonprofit modus operandi.

This does not mean that the furniture all has to be secondhand, or that staff has to account for every paper clip. It means that a conservative attitude must permeate the organization from the top down. The volunteer leadership should set the example by not demanding expensive support or recompense for every cent spent on their activities. Volunteers should be volunteers in the true sense of the word; that means, to serve of one's own free will, without expectation of remuneration. Staffs who see members giving of their time and talent to an organization they believe in will quickly come to appreciate their own special role.

(A) ROLE OF THE GOVERNING BOARD

The governing board owes the organization and the staff sound leadership, recognition of its legal and fiduciary obligations, sound planning, clear instructions, hiring of a competent chief operating executive, and reasonable expectations. The governing board should not expect luxurious accommodation or personal service of any kind. Its members should stand as an example of the highest standards of volunteerism. They should develop and nurture an attitude of trust between themselves and the chief executive. The governing board should foster clear paths of communication between and among themselves, the membership at large, the staff, and the public they serve.

(B) ROLE OF THE CHIEF OPERATING EXECUTIVE

The chief operating executive, frequently called the Executive Director in associations, has dual responsibility. He or she is responsible to the Board for sound management of the association, and is also responsible for the staff members who work for him and look to him or her for leadership. While a "slash and burn" policy might save money in the short term and impress the Board with big savings, the long-term impact might not be profitable. Layoffs, salary cuts, loss of benefits, and other measures of taking the savings out of the human resources may have a devastating effect on those who remain, with loss of confidence, insecurity, and much time wasted worrying about who is going next. So, to avoid such problems, the Executive Director should look to the staff to create and develop the needed solutions. The Executive Director must be a motivator, a team builder, and a morale booster, and must trust his or her people and encourage and teach them to know the organization, to understand the problem, and to do the right thing.

(C) ROLE OF THE STAFF

Under the leadership of the chief operating executive, the staff should make themselves aware of the mission, goals, and objectives of the organization. They should develop a conservative attitude in the conduct of their duties and accept the responsibility that goes with acting on behalf of others. Staff should be watchful and look out for ways to do the job better, to save resources, and, even more importantly, to come up with new, creative ideas. In an atmosphere of trust and cooperation, staff members can be the first line of defense against waste and in the vanguard of opportunity for growth and development of new programs and services.

The staff has the responsibility to implement the plans developed by the governing board. They should fill the role of critic and analyst in the planning stages, but, once the final plan is accepted, it is their job to make it work.

The staff also has the responsibility to grow professionally, taking advantage of the knowledge and skills of their peers and the opportunities and services available to them through the professional association management organizations.

28.3 *Crisis Cost Control*

Every organization, at some time in its development, will experience a tight cash flow situation. Sometimes the causative factors can be predicted, and sometimes they cannot. Some of the predictable causes are:

- Annual dues billing, when most of the funds come in at the same time, leaving a relatively dry period 8 to 10 months later.
- A grant or contract runs out, leading to a predictable slimming down.

- Market trends move downward—the association will follow the declining curve by a few months to a few years, depending on how much money is in the pipeline. Whether the decline is steep or shallow will depend to a large degree on the attitude of the members and their level of confidence in the rate of recovery.

Some unpredictable causes of tight cash flow are related to both revenue and expenses, such as:

Revenue:

- A meeting is cancelled (no registration or exhibit money).
- A meeting turns out to be poorly attended, leading to larger than anticipated hotel bills and smaller than anticipated revenues.
- Publication of a book is delayed (no sales).
- An education series turns out to be less popular than expected (reduced income).
- A big advertiser pulls out of your periodical (lost revenue).
- A large invoice for attendance at your annual meeting is delayed (or lost) when a company declares Chapter 11 bankruptcy.

Expenses:

- A meeting scheduled for a hotel or convention center has to be cancelled (penalties have to be paid for the cancellation).
- Your computer network crashes, resulting in big repair bills.
- Your large printer dies and must be replaced right away.
- The compressor on your heat pump burns out and must be replaced.
- Your accountant gets sick and forgets to tell you he hasn't filed your annual tax return, resulting in a big penalty from the IRS.

The cash problem must be faced promptly and methodically to gain immediate benefits. Exhibit 28.1 is an outline of the method for addressing crisis cost control.

(A) PROBLEM DEFINITION

The natural reaction to many problems faced by nonprofits is that this is just another difficulty in the normal course of events and will balance out in a few months. It is important to analyze each situation carefully and assess the costs currently and in the coming months, including indirect costs or loss of revenue later. If payment of bills is delayed, finance charges may be incurred. Funds may not be available to make a necessary purchase, leading to further loss of revenue or increased costs again when a sale has to be passed by. Financial impact of more than two months duration should be considered serious enough to start crisis cost control. Quick, prudent action will usually avoid more expensive action later on.

(B) INITIAL STRATEGY DEVELOPMENT

The situation must be faced and strategy leading to a solution developed. In a small organization, the results will be quicker, more fair, and more long-lasting if the entire staff

EXHIBIT 28.1 Method for Addressing Crisis Cost Control

1. Define the problem
   a. What is the nature of the crisis?
   b. What is the immediate cost?
   c. What is the future cost?
   d. What was the cause of the crisis?

2. Assign responsibility for implementing the cost control program
   a. Who will develop the strategy?
   b. Who will implement the procedures?
   c. Who will resolve conflict?
   d. Who will make final decisions?
   e. What is the chain of authority between paid staff and the volunteer leadership?

3. Get the staff involved
   a. Select a planning team, composed of individuals who have the respect of others.
   b. Ask for volunteers whenever possible.
   c. Keep staff informed.
   d. Motivate and reward staff for success.

4. Develop initial strategy
   a. Refer to Chapters 8–10 of this *Handbook* for guidelines for the planning team.
   b. Devise short-term, intermediate-term, and long-term strategies.
   c. Set short-term, intermediate-term, and long-term goals.

5. Establish a reporting plan

6. Establish review and evaluation schedules
   a. Oversight on continuing basis.
   b. Review of cash flow at least weekly.
   c. Evaluation of efficacy of strategy monthly.
   d. Overall evaluation quarterly.

7. Implement the plan

8. Evaluate results

9. Adjust strategy as needed

10. Apply lessons learned to long-term goals and procedures

is involved in the discussion and development of a crisis plan. The senior staff can decide among themselves on who is going to lead the process, or the executive director or president might appoint someone. Whichever way is chosen, that individual must have the full faith and confidence of the director. Work should then begin on determining what immediate steps to take and how the overall strategy will be developed.

(C) STAFF INVOLVEMENT

The staff should be gathered together and informed of the situation. They should be informed that layoffs will be absolutely the last resort, and that the success of their joint efforts will go a long way toward assuring that layoffs will not be necessary.

Staff reluctance to do things differently, or to cut back on spending authority, can be overcome by offering rewards for successful reductions. Some possible rewards include money (always welcome), a half-day off, verbal recognition at staff meetings, a small gift or trophy, a letter of recognition for the personnel folder, or recognition in the organization's newsletter or magazine.

(D) REPORTING SCHEDULE

Part of the crisis cost control plan should be a clearly defined schedule for keeping track of the savings and reporting to the chief operating executive and the board. The cost control team might want to meet once a week at first to discuss the strategies, the results, and the impact of implementing the strategies. It is important to keep the program fresh and ready for adjustments and new ideas. Some actions will be effective for only a limited time and should be terminated when they no longer net savings without damage.

(E) EVALUATION OF RESULTS

Weekly cash flow statements, prompt monthly balance sheets, and lists of accounts payable and accounts receivable will be the basis for evaluation of the success of the cost control campaign. Staff members should be asked to give regular written assessments of their contribution to the effort, with suggestions for improvements or changes to the plan. Prepare a written summary of results so that all involved can have a visual picture of how they are doing.

28.4   Cost-Cutting Ideas

(A) SHORT-TERM IDEAS

A number of actions can be taken right away which will show immediate results and provide time for working on the more complex actions which will take longer to implement. The first thing to do is review all the bills and the petty cash records for the past three months. Divide them into Office Expenses, Program Expenses, and Human Resources Expenses. Office expenses will be the easiest place to find savings, so attack that area first. Program expenses, which are more complex, come next. Temporary or part-time human resources are next, with adjustments affecting full-time staff last.

   Look at the nonessentials first, then analyze the essentials to see if reductions are possible. Every office can find some creative ways to reduce costs right away. Staff members should be involved to think of them and implement them, with rewards of some type for the biggest saving of the week, or the most creative idea. Following are some ideas that have been successful for some organizations:

- *Declare a three-month moratorium on purchase of office supplies.* The one person responsible for approving all expenditures can make an exception if absolutely necessary, but that person should be very tough. Challenge staff to look for all the squirreled-away supplies, and see how far you can make them go. Clean out and straighten up desk drawers, supply cabinets, and closets. The bottoms of file drawers are great places to find paper clips.
- *Cancel the plant service.* Love plants? Each person interested can take care of what they like and enjoy. If no one wants to care for them at the office, they may want to buy them and take them home.
- *Perform routine building maintenance yourself.* Find a staff member who is knowledgeable and will be the first line for advice before a service person is called. This person may be willing to make minor repairs.

- *Use fax instead of overnight mail delivery or first-class mail whenever possible.* Postage for local mail is usually higher than the cost per call for the fax.
- *Use fax instead of long-distance telephone calls when possible.* Also use evening fax transmission when possible. Rates are frequently cheaper at night.
- *Cut telephone costs.* See Exhibit 28.2.
- *Review equipment maintenance policies and determine if you can do as well on time-and-materials basis.* This works well with relatively new equipment and equipment that has proven to be reliable and in need of little service. Fax machines frequently fall into this category, as do electric typewriters. Electronic typewriters, unfortunately, do not.
- *Review shipping and delivery services to be sure you are getting the best prices.* Continue to monitor shipping and delivery and take quality into consideration. Lost packages can cost more than a few cents more per shipment. Also check into delivery categories that might be less expensive and still meet your requirements. Don't skimp on insurance for valuable packages, though. One loss can wipe out your savings for a year or more.
- *Recycle supplies.* See Exhibit 28.3 for ideas.
- *Look into electronic processing* if credit card payments are accepted (a monthly fee will be charged). Negotiate a lower rate with the bank. You should be able to save several hundreds of dollars over a year's time. This service should be reviewed annually. Rates change frequently.
- *Mail smarter.* Use the smallest envelope possible for first-class mail, as a general practice. Call your local postmaster for information on training to save on bulk mail, barcoding mailing lists, and service categories that meet your needs at least cost.
- *Inventory furniture and equipment* and dispose of, through sale or donation, anything that is no longer useful. You may be paying personal property taxes on items no longer in use.
- *Collect your accounts receivable.* Keep after them on a regular basis.

EXHIBIT 28.2 Cutting Telephone and Electronic Communication Costs

1. Establish an immediate response policy to requests coming in long distance, thus reducing long-distance callbacks.
2. Switch from a local to a regional telephone carrier.
3. Have staff members log long-distance phone calls for a month to establish where the most calls are occurring, and reduce if possible.
4. Use voice mail for messages.
5. Analyze telephone, voice mail, and e-mail service. Determine the costs to send and receive e-mail messages outside of the provider's system. Sometimes these costs are alarming, but not easy to determine in advance. The cost for access to the Internet is a big variable, and has to be considered based on the type and duration of use. Use the information from several month's bills to understand what your actual costs are. Discuss any questions with your current service provider to see if there is any way to reduce the bills. Also use your analysis to compare with other service providers.
6. Use printed phone directories rather than telephone company information calls.

EXHIBIT 28.3 Reusable Supplies

Paper clips from cleaned-out files

Incorrectly addressed envelopes (put a label over incorrect address)

File folders

Use paper printed on one side for:
- Running drafts (be sure your printer will tolerate this)
- Cutting up for memo boxes
- Running reports or memos that will only be faxed
- Shredding for use as packing material instead of using purchased fillers

Save cartons for use in reshipping. Flatten them if storage is a problem.

Computer disks—old stored files might be consolidated and extra disks reused.

- *Make daily deposits to the bank.* Consider lockbox service if a large number of checks comes in every day.
- If you own your building, and real estate values have dropped in your area, consider requesting a *review of the tax assessment.* Some association management companies will do the paperwork for a percentage of the saving. Be sure to check this one with your lawyer first.
- *Review vendor selection.* Shop around for the entrepreneur or small business trying to build a clientele, such as for certificate generation, ribbons, graphics, poster making, meeting management, and so on. The cost should be lower.

(B) PROGRAM COST-CUTTING IDEAS

The association's programs are its services to members, and therefore are usually major sources of revenue, but there are ample opportunities for savings. Meetings, publications, training, and certification programs all are in big spending categories. Standard procedures for purchasing, use of outside services, mailing, and hiring should apply across the board. The opportunity may exist to review less effective programs and eliminate or revise them. However, ways should be found to continue programs that members expect. Exhibit 28.4 is a list of program cost control ideas.

Printing costs are usually one of the larger elements of program budgets. There are many ways to reduce them. Use of word processing to prepare such one-time-use items as evaluation sheets, tickets, on-site programs, attendance lists, and agendas can create savings, especially if they are copied in-house. Of course, appearance should not be overlooked, but use of colored or 'designer' paper can improve the cosmetics. Using standard formats for many of the printing preparation tasks can also shorten the time spent on layouts.

Requiring three bids for any printing job over $500 is good practice. Printers have different capabilities and costs can vary tremendously. Add new vendors to your list on a regular basis to allow for better selection.

Meeting planning is a functional specialty in itself, and having a good professional meeting planner on your staff is a must if your programs include conferences, symposia, meetings, or workshops. Hotels and meeting facilities are in the business to make money, and want you to help them do it. By the same token, they help you run successful programs. A sound relationship will be of benefit to both organizations, with the

EXHIBIT 28.4 Ideas for Program Cost Control

1. Prioritize your programs and identify your core and noncore programs. See if any noncore programs can be downsized or eliminated.

2. Redesign mailings to cost less to mail.

3. Review program bulletin printing specifications to assure maximum impact at minimum cost.

4. Work with hotel and meeting facilities to reduce costs for meetings. Market meetings often enough and far enough in advance to be sure room blocks are met, thus saving meeting room costs. Take advantage of complimentary rooms for staff and other incentives frequently offered by hotels as inducements.

5. Negotiate package deals with several meetings at the same facility and have some fees reduced.

6. Work with travel agents to negotiate reduced air fares for attendees, and thus for staff members as well. Try to negotiate no-cost tickets for meeting planners.

7. Trade services you need, such as copy service, videotaping, and audiotaping, for free exhibit space at meetings.

8. Use conference calls instead of travelling for some meeting planning.

9. Review staff travel and expense policies. Eliminate room service, movies, and set maximum reimbursements for on-site meals.

10. Provide lighter, less expensive meals at meetings. (Many folks prefer this these days.)

11. Use cash bars at conferences and meetings. (This reduces legal exposure as well.)

hotel helping you handle exhibit service companies, security guard services, audio services, catering, transportation, entertainment, and all the many activities that go to make up a good meeting.

Convention and Visitors Bureaus are good sources of information and sometimes can provide services such as taking care of hotel reservations (housing), setting up entertainment opportunities, and providing extra staff at your meeting. Meeting management companies (third-party vendors) are available to take over the complete meeting planning function, and some return revenue derived from discounts on hotel rooms and air fares. Limited staff can then concentrate on the meeting program, making sure all of the details are carefully tended to. Consistently good professional programs generate a good reputation and will be a stable source of income. Small associations will have to shop around for companies that are compatible with their culture, and that can be counted on to treat their members with the same consideration they would. Many people attending meetings and conferences are grateful to be able to make all of their arrangements with one phone call: registration for the meeting, hotel reservations, air reservations, and car rentals. Companies offering this service may be found in the telephone yellow pages under "Convention Services," or by a visit to the local library reference section.

Whether you use a service provider or do all of the work yourself, you should start with establishing procedures for negotiating contracts, guaranteeing meals, and setting room blocks. These procedures will help the meeting planner negotiate with potential vendors, letting them know that there are specific spending limits and quality requirements. Look for discounts and reduced fee opportunities; this is not a game for the bashful. Lots of negotiating room exists!

(C) HUMAN RESOURCES COST-CUTTING IDEAS

Although the involuntary termination of staff members is something to be avoided under most circumstances, sometimes it becomes necessary. Sensitive and helpful treatment of anyone so eliminated will go a long way toward maintaining the morale of the remaining staff. Before the point is reached, there are a number of actions that can be taken to reduce personnel-related costs. Exhibit 28.5 is a list of human resources cost-cutting ideas.

Many of the ideas on that list will be more palatable to the staff if they are a part of the cost-cutting endeavor and they can see that their contributions are significant and appreciated. If position elimination becomes necessary, it may be possible to take advantage of a voluntary departure to redistribute tasks, change job descriptions, and spread one position among several others. It also is sometimes possible to hire a new person for a less demanding position and at a lower salary.

A manager is well advised to keep his or her ears open to what staff members are saying and also to their casual comments. An unsuspected resource for organizational talent may be identified, a person who can take a complex, unwieldy program and structure it so it runs smoothly with time, materials, and tempers saved. Often, duties can be

---

EXHIBIT 28.5 Ideas for Savings Through Human Resources

1. Maximize the productivity of staff. Help them work smarter.
2. Offer employees a half-day or full day off without pay once a month.
3. Increase deductions on employee health insurance (if paying 100%), or get bids from other carriers to be sure you are doing the best you can.
4. Use student interns to fill in with training-level projects.
5. Hire a temporary employee for a busy period rather than increasing the permanent staff.
6. Get volunteers to come in to help with routine (and sometimes more complex) programs. They are waiting to be asked. Retirees are often knowledgeable experts in specialized fields and their contributions are frequently mutually beneficial— you get competent assistance and they have the satisfaction of being needed and useful.
7. Contract out functions such as payroll and bulk mailing.
8. Analyze daily routines and eliminate repetitive or unnecessary tasks.
9. Use direct deposit of payroll checks. This saves time signing individual checks and staff members going to the bank.
10. Reduce some positions to less than full-time.
11. Advertise for new hires through carefully designed newspaper ads rather than using an agency.
12. Substitute compensatory time for overtime; be careful to follow the rules.
13. Reduce paid holidays.
14. Close the office on Fridays during the slow season; reduce air conditioning, heating, lights, and equipment use.

---

shifted among staff members, with everyone satisfied. A good leader can develop a win–win situation by asking staff members what they like about their jobs, what they would like to be doing two or three years hence, and what they really don't enjoy doing. In such an atmosphere, problem areas can be identified and better resources, both human and procedural, can be applied where they are most needed. An interested, involved, empowered staff is the very best medicine for recovering from a financial crisis and moving on in a new environment.

28.5 Cost Control Policies for the Long Term

Associations are more likely to run into cost control problems than for-profit businesses because their activity is usually basic office work. For-profit businesses are often in manufacturing or sales, where unit costs must be determined or the business will quickly fail. Professional managers have done extensive work in developing measurement, analysis, and evaluation techniques that will identify high-cost areas and lead to concentration of effort to control and reduce costs. The *Financial Management Handbook for Associations*, published by the Chamber of Commerce of the United States (1984), describes the problem: "Office expenses are not generally expressed in terms of unit costs since the end product of the office is 'consumed' internally. Consequently, office expenses have escaped the rigorous scrutiny that is standard practice in the manufacturing plant."

The office worker frequently sets his or her own pace and even determines what work is done. Universal standards have not been developed and therefore are not available to the office manager or association executive to enforce, with the exception of controls for repetitive clerical tasks. Such tasks are not the problem for most associations. Inefficiencies exist through unnecessary work being done and work that should be done being neglected. The problem is compounded when a worker does an outstanding job in most areas of what is expected, meriting praise and encouragement. On the other hand, the neglected tasks remain, perhaps not realized or given lower priority.

The association manager is not completely without resources in addressing staff productivity as part of the long-term cost control plan. Following the strategic planning process, position descriptions should be updated to reflect what each person is doing. Each position should then be evaluated and the job descriptions rewritten to include the responsibilities necessary to implement the strategic plan. Salary ranges should be set for each position and performance standards established. Provided with the resulting information, the manager will see more clearly what changes should be made in the staff composition and what training will be necessary.

Performance standards and measurement techniques are discussed in the Chamber of Commerce *Financial Management Handbook* and may be of value. A number of job evaluation methods and systems are discussed in *Handbook of Business Problem Solving* (Albert, 1980).

Other basic elements to be considered and reviewed for adequacy and efficiency include the level of automation available for the performance of tasks, the office location and layout, and procedures for accomplishing such normal business activities as purchasing, accounts receivable collection, and inventory control.

(A) BUDGETS

Chapter 25 in this *Handbook* is an excellent introduction to budgeting, explaining several methods and citing their advantages and disadvantages. Faced with the task of reinventing an organization's budgeting process—which is no small endeavor—the old adage that "the best way to begin is to begin at the beginning" is sound advice. Because budgeting is basic to every activity of an association, samples appear throughout this *Handbook*, and can be used to develop a suitable version. Preparation of an operating budget should come first, followed by a cash budget showing revenue and expense projections throughout the year. Finally, a capital budget will be needed to keep track of the physical assets and provide for their replacement as they wear out or become obsolete.

Staff members should be asked to write budgets for the tasks for which they are responsible. This will not only spread out the work and yield detailed information for the manager to use in the overall budget, but will also help staff to obtain a clearer picture of possible cost savings available to them. Some months, even a year or more, will be spent preparing, reviewing, and revising these budgets. Volunteer committees can frequently be called upon to help with this effort, using expertise available in their businesses as well as their own experience.

The governing board will finally be called upon to approve the finished product, which will have been designed to meet the goals and objectives the board established. At that time, board members must be fully informed of the costs involved and should know what their role will be in generating sufficient revenue to fulfill the mission of the organization.

(B) REPORTING

The chief operating executive will participate with the finance committee or other financial oversight entity in setting a schedule of reports. The schedule will probably have at least three tiers, with staff reporting to their supervisors. Supervisors or department heads report to the chief operating executive, who in turn reports to the finance committee. A good finance committee will assist with developing the format of the reports so that they will get a true and useful picture of the financial situation on a continuing basis.

It is not unreasonable to require a weekly cash flow report, especially if vigorous cost control efforts are underway. Monthly balance sheets and statements of income and expenses should be prepared, as well as a comprehensive annual financial report. An excellent source of formats for these reports is *Financial and Accounting for Nonprofit Organizations* (Gross and Warshauer, 1983).

(C) EVALUATION

Time should be taken to evaluate all of the data relating to costs and finances and to assess the cost control program. Neither difficulties nor successes should be allowed to overshadow the other, as there are bound to be different levels and quality according to the situation. Those who are implementing the program need encouragement and recognition for their efforts. The human element may be the single most important part of the program. Without motivation, spirits wane and morale sags. An enthusiastic cadre of energetic "combatants" is the best force for achieving the economies and efficiencies sought.

The schedule for evaluation should be set with time periods far enough apart for results to be measurable, but not so far apart that the momentum is lost. A good way to develop a visual picture of what is being accomplished is to draw up charts so comparisons with previous periods can be easily seen. Quarterly evaluation sessions for the first year are not too often, and will allow for small adjustments in the program. When cost control procedures are in place and a part of the normal routine of the office, yearly evaluation should be sufficient.

(D) PROCEDURES

Written procedures are a desirable asset that can result from the work done to bring costs under control in the organization. Staff members can be asked to write up the procedures they are following to accomplish the requirements of the program and the tasks listed in their job descriptions. These can be refined and adjusted by supervisors and managers to reflect the preferred work methods. These procedures can be collected and organized into a manual which will serve as a reference book for managers and a source of material for new employee orientation. Written procedures also can be used in performance evaluations for employees, as well as reference material for program evaluations, management audits, and other administrative tasks.

28.6 Ideas for Revenue Enhancement

A natural accompaniment to cost control is revenue enhancement. Because the problem to be faced is shortage of funds (usually cash), increasing income will help to alleviate the problem. Sometimes a crisis can stir things up and expose areas where a little effort will make a sizeable impact.

The first consideration should be to make the most of what resources you already have. If a supply of emblematics is sitting in the supply room, organize them and price them fairly (including actual cost, full shipping costs, and handling costs that take into account all of the activity that goes into purchasing, selling, shipping, and invoicing). Make up a one-half or full-page ad with a clear description of each, the price, and simple ordering instructions, preferably with an order form, a fax number, and credit card payment opportunity. Make copies to provide on request, and publish the ad in every publication on a regular basis. Sales will materialize.

Proceedings of technical or professional meetings can be priced, listed, and marketed. Journal articles can be batched, reprinted, marketed, and sold. Printing services that use computer scanning techniques can frequently provide a basic supply of books (usually softcover) and then reprint almost on demand. A complete listing should be published regularly. Again, the ad will be cheap to prepare with word processing, and the return will astound you.

Programs should be marketed early to increase attendance or participation. Magazines with calendar listings appropriate to your organization should be utilized to the maximum degree.

EXHIBIT 28.6　Ideas for Revenue Enhancement

1. Accept credit card payments. Negotiate with as many credit card companies as practical to maximize convenience.
2. Rent out excess office space; rent use of conference room.
3. Increase sales of advertising space in journals or newsletters.
4. Ask individuals or companies your members work for to sponsor coffee breaks, luncheons, or receptions at your meetings.
5. Have companies sponsor an issue of your newsletter in exchange for a news article about their organization.
6. If a large purchase is necessary, develop a member-loan program, paying interest higher than savings accounts and lower than a bank loan. (Remember, though, you have to pay them back, but you can pay up early if funds become available.)
7. Run a membership campaign with prizes for recruiting.
8. Use lists of nonmembers in your interest area to market both membership and meeting attendance.
9. Price programs so that nonmembers wishing to attend will join.
10. Develop a special category of membership, perhaps called "Sustaining Members," who agree to contribute $100 each above dues each year. Provide special benefits and recognition for them in your publication and at the annual meeting.
11. Find new advertising opportunities, such as a business card page in your journal, magazine, membership directory, or newsletter.
12. Develop a scheduled fund-raising program among members (or the public, if you are a charity). Devise several different types of programs to appeal to a broad range of interests, such as scholarship loans, a special recognition category for those with discretionary funds, building fund, building upgrade fund, outreach program, annual fund drive. Then stick to your schedule.

Exhibit 28.6 is a list of areas for revenue enhancement. An open mind to new services desired by the members and the association's public is the best approach. Ask them what they want whenever an opportunity arrives to do a survey. Comparing notes with others in similar organizations frequently turns up an idea that should be pursued.

A final suggestion is to explore opportunities for unrelated business income. Some members of every group have no other access to group rates for life or health insurance. Some people like the idea of using a credit card with the organization's logo. Group rates for delivery service are available, as are rental car discounts, travel programs, and even long-distance telephone discounts. Most of these programs yield a modest royalty for the organization, and if carefully arranged and managed will not result in taxable income for the association. A reputable certified public accounting firm, experienced in nonprofit association work, should be consulted to protect the nonprofit status.

Suggested Readings

Albert, Kenneth J., ed. 1980. *Handbook of Business Problem Solving*. New York: McGraw-Hill.

Bennis, Warren and Goldsmith, Joan. 1994. *Learning to Lead*. New York: Addison-Wesley.

Buchholz, Steve and Roth, Thomas. 1987. *Creating the High-Performance Team*. New York: Wiley.

Chamber of Commerce of the United States, Association Department. Third printing 1984. *Financial Management Handbook for Associations*. Washington, DC: Author.

Gross, Malvern J. Jr., and Warshauer, William Jr. 1983. *Financial and Accounting Guide for Nonprofit Organizations*, rev. 3rd ed. New York: Wiley.

Loomba, N. Paul. 1978. *Management—A Quantitative Perspective*. New York: Macmillan.

Naisbitt, John and Aburdene, Patricia. 1990. *Megatrends 2000*, New York: William Morrow.

Roderer, Phyllis and Sabo, Sandra. 1994. *Human Resource Management in Associations*. Washington, DC: American Society of Association Executives.

29 Law and Taxation

BRUCE **R.** **H**OPKINS, JD, LLM

Polsinelli, White, Vardeman & Shalton

Nonprofit organizations in the United States are regulated at both the federal and state levels of government. The purpose of this chapter is to summarize this body of law, which largely is federal tax law.[1]

Each segment of this chapter is followed by a brief checklist, enabling an organization to review its status under and compliance with this body of law. An organization may wish to photocopy these checklists, complete them, and keep the information as part of its minutebook or other organization document file.

29.1 Nonprofit Organizations: The Legal Definition

United States society is comprised of three sectors. In one sector are the federal, state, and local governments. For-profit entities comprise the business sector. Nonprofit organizations constitute the third of these sectors, which is often referred to as the "independent sector" or the "voluntary sector."

The concept, in the law, of a *nonprofit* organization is best understood through a comparison with a for-profit organization.

In many respects, the characteristics of these two categories of organizations are identical: both require a legal form, have a board of directors and officers, pay compensation, face essentially the same expenses, are able to receive a profit, make investments, and produce goods and services.

However, a for-profit organization has owners—those who hold the equity in the enterprise, such as stockholders of a corporation. The for-profit organization is operated for the benefit of its owners; the profits of the enterprise are passed through to them, perhaps as the payment of dividends on shares of stock. This is what is meant by the term *for-profit* organization; it is one that is intended to generate a profit for its owners. The transfer of the profits from the organization to its owners is the inurement of net earnings to the owners.

Like the for-profit organization, then, a nonprofit organization is able to generate a profit. Unlike the for-profit organization, however, a nonprofit entity generally is not permitted to distribute its profits (net earnings) to those who control and/or financially support it. A nonprofit organization usually does not have any owners (equity holders). Consequently, the private inurement doctrine is the substantive dividing line that differentiates, for law purposes, between nonprofit organizations and for-profit organizations. (The private inurement doctrine is discussed further in Section 29.7.)

A *tax-exempt* organization is a subset of nonprofit organizations; that is, not all nonprofit organizations qualify as tax-exempt organizations. The concept of a nonprofit organization usually is a matter of state law, while the concept of a tax-exempt organization is principally a matter of the federal tax law. Nonetheless, nearly all of the states have some law pertaining to one or more tax exemptions.

[1] This body of law is summarized in detail in Hopkins, *The Law of Tax-Exempt Organizations*, 6th ed. (New York: John Wiley & Sons, Inc. 1992, annual supplements).

29.2 Role of State Law

The rules concerning the creation of nonprofit organizations are essentially a subject for state laws. A few nonprofit organizations are chartered by the U.S. Congress, but nearly all are formed under state law. A nonprofit organization must be created in one of three forms: a corporation, an unincorporated association, or a trust. The document by which these organizations are established is the *articles of organization*.

Today, most nonprofit organizations are established as corporations. This is the case because of the limitation on personal liability that the corporate form generally provides and because of the substantial body of law that defines the operations and duties of the organization and its directors and officers.[2] A corporation is formed by filing a set of articles of incorporation; the document containing its rules of operation is generally termed the *bylaws*. (See Exhibit 29.1.)

An unincorporated association is formed by the execution of a constitution. Again, its rules of operation are contained in bylaws. A trust is created by the execution of a trust agreement or a declaration of trust. A trust can, but infrequently does, have bylaws.

A nonprofit organization's articles of organization and/or operational rules should contain provisions addressing the organization's structure and administration. These elements include the origin and composition of the board of directors (or board of trustees), the origin and types of officers, whether there is a membership, and the nature of the organization's committees. (See Exhibit 29.2.)

EXHIBIT 29.1 Checklist for Incorporation

Form of organization:

_____ Corporation

_____ Unincorporated association

_____ Trust

_____ Other

Types of articles of organization:

_____ Articles of incorporation

_____ Constitution

_____ Declaration of trust

_____ Trust agreement

Date organization formed _____

Place organization formed _____

Date(s) of amendment of articles _____

Date operational rules (e.g., bylaws) formed _____

Date(s) of amendment of rules _____

---

[2] This body of law is summarized in Hopkins, *The Legal Answer Book for Nonprofit Organizations*, particularly Chapter 2 (New York: John Wiley & Sons, Inc. 1996).

EXHIBIT 29.2 Checklist for Articles of Incorporation

Fiscal year _____

Membership   Yes _____   No _____

    If yes, annual meeting date _____

    Notice requirement _____

Chapters   Yes _____   No _____

Affiliated organizations _____

Board of directors (or trustees):

    Origin _____

    Number _____

    Quorum _____

    Voting power _____

    Terms of office _____

    Annual meeting date _____

    Notice requirement _____

Officers:

    Origin _____

        Titles:

        _____ President

        _____ Vice President

        _____ Treasurer

        _____ Secretary

        _____ Other _____

        _____ Other _____

    Terms of office _____

Committees:

    _____ Executive

    _____ Nominating

    _____ Development (or Advancement)

    _____ Finance

    _____ Long-range Planning

    _____ Other

Registered agent _____

State law also addresses matters such as the extent of personal liability for the directors and officers of nonprofit organizations, the deductibility of charitable contributions (under state law), the imposition of or exemption from several taxes (such as income, sales, use, and property taxes), and the extent to which fund raising by the organization is regulated.[3] (See Exhibit 29.3.)

---

[3] The federal and state law concerning regulation of fund-raising is summarized in detail in Hopkins, *The Law of Fund-Raising*, 2d ed. (New York: John Wiley & Sons, Inc. 1996).

EXHIBIT 29.3 Checklist for Liability and Tax Concerns

Does organization have officers' and directors' liability insurance?	Yes _____	No _____
Is organization eligible to receive contributions that are deductible under state law?	Yes _____	No _____
Is organization exempt from state taxation?		
Income tax	Yes _____	No _____
Sales tax	Yes _____	No _____
Use tax	Yes _____	No _____
Tangible personal property tax	Yes _____	No _____
Intangible personal property tax	Yes _____	No _____
Real property tax	Yes _____	No _____
Other taxes: _____		

EXHIBIT 29.4 Checklist for Reporting Requirements

State annual report due _____

State in which organization is qualified to "do business"_____

Registered agent(s) in other state(s) _____

State law may require an annual report. If an organization has operations (is *doing business*) in a state other than the one in which it is based, it must comply with the corporate and other laws of that state. This situation can arise where the organization has an office and/or conducts programs in the other state (as to which it is a *foreign* organization). Some states regard the maintenance of a banking account or fund raising in the state as sufficient nexus to constitute doing business in the jurisdiction. (See Exhibit 29.4.)

29.3 Federal Taxation System

Generally, every person is subject to income taxation. The term *person* includes individuals and entities (corporations, unincorporated associations, trusts, partnerships, and estates).

Some organizations are exempt from federal and state income taxation; these are known, as noted, as *tax-exempt organizations*. The categories of organizations that are eligible for tax exemption include those that are charitable, educational, scientific, and religious, as defined under the law framed by Internal Revenue Code section ("IRC §") 501(c)(3).

Charitable organizations include those that have the following purposes:

- Relief of the poor and distressed or of the underprivileged.
- Advancement of religion.
- Advancement of education.

- Advancement of science.
- Lessening the burdens of government.
- Community beautification and maintenance.
- Promotion of health.
- Promotion of social welfare.
- Promotion of the arts.

Educational organizations include:

- Formal educational institutions, such as schools, colleges, universities, and museums.
- Organizations that instruct individuals for the purpose of improving or developing their capabilities.
- Instruction of the public on subjects useful to the individual and beneficial to the community.

The concept of education does not include propagandizing, which is the propagation of particular ideas or doctrines without presentation of them in any reasonably objective or balanced manner. The Internal Revenue Service (IRS) utilizes a *methodology test* to differentiate between educational activities and propagandizing.

Scientific organizations include:

- Research organizations.
- Publishing organizations.

Religious organizations include:

- Churches.
- Conventions and associations of churches.
- Integrated auxiliaries of churches.
- Religious orders.

However, tax-exempt organizations include organizations other than those that are charitable and the like. Other types of organizations that are exempt from federal income taxation include:

- Title-holding organizations (IRC § 501(c)(2))
- Social welfare organizations (IRC § 501(c)(4)).
- Labor organizations (IRC § 501(c)(5)).
- Professional, business, and trade associations (IRC § 501(c)(6)).
- Social clubs (IRC § 501(c)(7)).
- Fraternal organizations (IRC § 501(c)(8) and (10)).
- Employee benefit funds (IRC §§ 501(c)(9), (17), and (21)).
- Veterans' organizations (IRC § 501(c)(19)).
- Farmers' cooperatives (IRC § 521).
- Political organizations (IRC § 527).
- Homeowners' associations (IRC § 528).

The concept of *tax exemption* does not necessarily mean a total exemption from taxes. Thus, nearly all forms of tax-exempt organizations are taxable on their unrelated business income.

Public charities can become taxed if they engage in an excessive amount of lobbying activity or in any political campaign activity. The taxes on lobbying expenditures, which are technically cast as *excise* taxes, can also be imposed on the directors and officers of these organizations.

Private foundations are taxed on their net investment income. Private foundations (and others) can also be taxed, again in the form of excise taxation, if they engage in self-dealing with disqualified persons, fail to make adequate grants and other distributions for charitable purposes, have excess business holdings, make jeopardizing investments, or make various forms of taxable expenditures (such as lobbying or political expenditures, or certain grants to individuals).

29.4 Applying for Recognition of Tax Exemption

To be exempt from federal income taxation, a nonprofit organization must fit within at least one of the categories of tax-exempt organizations (see Section 29.3). Once this classification is achieved, and assuming it is maintained, the organization generally is tax-exempt by operation of law.

However, two categories of nonprofit organizations, to be tax-exempt, are required to have their tax exemption *recognized* by the IRS. These categories of organizations are subject to this "notice" requirement:

- Charitable, educational, scientific, religious, and like organizations.
- Certain employee benefit funds.

The other types of nonprofit organizations may apply for recognition of tax-exempt status if they wish. Charitable and like organizations make application for recognition of tax-exempt status on IRS Form 1023. Nearly all other nonprofit organizations make this application on Form 1024. Farmers' cooperatives and like associations apply by means of Form 1028.

(A) CONTENTS OF APPLICATION

When a nonprofit organization seeks to be recognized as a tax-exempt charitable or like organization, it also seeks to be classified as a charitable organization for purposes of the income, estate, and gift tax charitable deductions. Moreover, if the organization has a basis for avoiding classification as a *private foundation*, it makes this claim as part of this filing. All three of these statuses are retroactive to the date the organization was formed if the application is filed within 15 months (and, where an extension is necessary, up to 27 months) of the end of the month in which the organization was created. (See Exhibit 29.5.)

(B) EXCEPTIONS

Certain organizations are exempt from the general rule of mandatory application for recognition of tax-exempt status. These organizations are churches, associations and con-

EXHIBIT 29.5 Checklist for Application

Is organization tax-exempt under federal law?	Yes _____	No _____
If yes, IRC §: _____		
Has organization received IRS recognition of tax exemption?	Yes _____	No _____
If yes, date of determination letter _____		
Descriptive IRC section	IRC § 501(c) (_____)	
Other IRC section	IRC § _____	

ventions of churches, integrated auxiliaries of churches, and charitable and like organizations (other than private foundations) the gross receipts of which do not normally exceed $5,000.

29.5 Organizational Test

Most forms of tax-exempt organizations must meet an *organizational test*. This test is a set of rules containing certain requirements as to the contents of the document by which the organization was created. As noted above, this document will be articles of incorporation, a constitution, a trust agreement, or a declaration of trust. The organizational test requirements are the most refined in the case of charitable, educational, scientific, religious, and like organizations.

The organizational test for charitable and like organizations requires that the articles of organization limit the organization's purposes to one or more exempt purposes and do not expressly empower it to engage (other than insubstantially) in activities that are not in furtherance of exempt purposes. These articles of organization may not authorize the organization to devote a substantial part of its activities to legislative purposes or any of its activities to political campaign purposes. Moreover, these articles of organization must provide that, upon dissolution or liquidation, the organization's assets and net income will be distributed for exempt purposes.

Additional requirements are imposed for the governing instruments of supporting organizations and private foundations.

29.6 Operational Test

Most forms of tax-exempt organizations must meet an *operational test*. This test is a set of rules containing certain requirements as to the nature of the activities in which the organization can engage. Basically, the operational test requires that a tax-exempt organization engage primarily in exempt purposes. The operational test requirements are the most refined in the case of charitable, educational, scientific, religious, and like organizations.

The operational test for charitable and like organizations, because it focuses on the activities of these organizations in relation to their stated purposes, embraces the proscriptions on private inurement, substantial legislative activities, and political campaign activities. Organizations of this nature that engage in excessive lobbying activities or any political campaign activities are considered *action organizations* and, for that reason alone, cannot qualify as tax-exempt charitable organizations.

The federal tax law provides that a nonprofit organization, to be tax-exempt as a charitable or like organization, must be organized and operated *exclusively* for exempt purposes. The courts have converted the term *exclusively* to the term *primarily*, with the Supreme Court stating that the presence of a single nonexempt purpose, if substantial in nature, will destroy the exemption regardless of the number or importance of truly exempt purposes. The term must be interpreted in this manner, if only to accommodate the existence of some unrelated business activity (see Chapter 27).

29.7   *Private Inurement Doctrine*

A nonprofit organization, to be tax-exempt as a charitable, educational, scientific, religious, or like organization, must be organized and operated so that no part of its net earnings inures to the benefit of any private shareholder or individual. This is known as the *private inurement doctrine*. This doctrine also applies with respect to other categories of tax-exempt organizations.

The concept of private inurement is broad and wide-ranging. Essentially, the doctrine forbids ways of causing the income or assets of a tax-exempt organization (that is subject to it) to flow away from the organization and to one or more persons who are related to the organization (*insiders*) for nonexempt purposes. The Office of Chief Counsel of the IRS has stated the doctrine quite bluntly: "The inurement prohibition serves to prevent anyone in a position to do so from siphoning off any of a charity's income or assets for personal use."

The essence of this concept is to ensure that a tax-exempt organization is serving a public interest and not a private interest. That is, to be tax-exempt, it is necessary for an organization subject to the doctrine to establish that it is not organized and operated for the benefit of private interests such as designated individuals, the creator of the organization or his or her family, shareholders of the organization, persons controlled (directly or indirectly) by such private interests, or any other persons having a personal and private interest in the activities of the organization.

In determining the presence of any proscribed private inurement, the law looks to the ultimate purpose of the organization. If the basic purpose of the organization subject to the doctrine is to benefit individuals in their private capacity, then it cannot be tax-exempt even though exempt activities are also performed. Conversely, incidental benefits to private individuals, such as those that are generated by reason of the organization's program activities, will usually not defeat the exemption if the organization otherwise qualifies under the appropriate exemption provision.

The IRS and the courts have recognized a variety of forms of private inurement. These include:

- Excessive or unreasonable compensation (the most common form of private inurement).
- Unreasonable or unfair rental arrangements.
- Unreasonable or unfair lending arrangements.
- Provision of services to persons in their private capacity.
- Certain assumptions of liability.

- Certain sales of assets to insiders.
- Certain participation in partnerships.
- Certain percentage payment arrangements.
- Varieties of tax avoidance schemes.

There is a separate but analogous body of law termed the *private benefit* doctrine. This doctrine is a derivative of the operational test and is potentially applicable with respect to all persons, including those who are not insiders. Thus, it is broader than the private inurement doctrine and, in many respects, subsumes that doctrine. The private benefit doctrine essentially prevents a charitable or like organization from benefiting private interests in any way, other than to an insubstantial extent.

More specific rules are applicable to private foundations in the form of prohibitions on self-dealing. (See Exhibit 29.6.)

29.8 *Legislative Activities Limitation*

For many types of nonprofit organizations, considerations as to whether to engage in lobbying are paramount. Often, what ultimately is at stake is their federal income tax exemption. That is, for some entities, too much lobbying can mean payment of a tax or even loss of exempt status.

Nonprofit organizations, to qualify as charitable or like organizations, are subject to a rule of federal tax law, which is that no substantial part of the activities of the organization may constitute carrying on propaganda, or otherwise attempting to influence legislation.

The term *legislation* is broadly construed, and includes bills, resolutions, appropriations measures, treaties, and Senate consideration of presidential nominations. The term *propaganda* is discussed in Section 29.6, in the context of educational activities.

Legislative activities—or lobbying—are of two types. One is *direct lobbying*, which includes the presentation of testimony at public hearings held by legislative committees, correspondence and meetings with legislators and their staffs, and publication of documents advocating specific legislative action. The other is *grass-roots lobbying*, which consists of appeals to the general public, or segments of the general public, to contact legislators or take other specific action as regards legislative matters.

As to the meaning of the term *substantial* in this context, there are two sets of rules. One is the *substantial part test*, which is a vague requirement limiting allowable lobbying (both direct and grass-roots) to insubstantial lobbying. Insubstantiality in this setting can be measured in terms of expenditures, time, or influence. However, the IRS—supported by the courts—refuses to be constrained by any specific formula. A charitable or like organization that exceeds the bounds of insubstantiality is considered an action organization (see above) and may lose its tax-exempt status as a result.

EXHIBIT 29.6 Checklist for Self-Dealing

Has the organization identified its insiders?	Yes _____	No _____
If yes, identify them _____		
Is organization engaging in transactions with these persons?	Yes _____	No _____

For organizations that are governed by the substantial part test, some legislative activities are excluded from the concept of lobbying. These include responding to a request from a committee of a legislature to testify on a technical matter and engaging in nonpartisan analysis, study, and research.

Organizations that are under the substantial part test and lose their tax-exempt status because of excessive lobbying are subject to an excise tax in the amount of 5 percent of the excessive lobbying expenditures. A like tax may be imposed on the directors and officers of an organization who agreed to the making of the excess lobbying expenditures, unless the agreement was not willful and was due to reasonable cause.

The other set of rules, which is the *expenditure test*, must be affirmatively elected by eligible public charitable and like organizations. These rules measure allowable lobbying in terms of percentages of total expenditures (other than certain fund-raising expenses). Direct lobbying expenditures may be up to 20 percent of the first $500,000 of expenditures, 15 percent of the next $500,000, 10 percent of the next $500,000, and 5 percent of the balance, with no more than $1 million expended for lobbying in any one year. These percentages are measured over a four-year average. Maximum allowable expenditures for grass-roots lobbying are 25 percent of the allowable expenditures for direct lobbying.

This test exempts a wide range of legislative efforts from the concept of lobbying. These are:

- Making available the results of nonpartisan analysis, study, or research.
- Providing technical advice or assistance to a governmental body or legislative committee in response to a written request.
- Communications to a legislative body with respect to a possible decision by that body that might affect the existence of the organization, its powers and duties, its tax-exempt status, or the deduction of contributions to it.
- Communications between the organization and its members with respect to legislation of direct interest to it and them.
- Routine communications with government officials or employees.
- Examinations of broad social, economic, and similar problems, even if the problems are of the type with which government would be expected to deal ultimately.

An organization that exceeds the lobbying expenses tolerated by the expenditure test is subject to a 25 percent excise tax on the excess lobbying expenditures. Where the lobbying expenditures exceed 150 percent of allowable lobbying outlays, the organization may lose its tax-exempt status.

Private foundations (see below) are essentially prohibited from engaging in any lobbying activities.

Most other categories of tax-exempt organizations—such as social welfare organizations, membership associations, and veterans' organizations—may freely lobby without concern as to their tax-exempt status. Indeed, the primary purpose of some exempt organizations is lobbying; this is primarily the case with social welfare organizations and some membership entities. However, there usually is no business expense deduction for the costs of lobbying; legislative efforts by business and professional associations can cause a portion of the members' dues to be nondeductible.

Where a charitable organization wishes to engage in a substantial amount of lobbying, it may be advisable to place the activity in a tax-exempt social welfare organization. (See Exhibit 29.7.)

EXHIBIT 29.7 Checklist on Lobbying

Does organization engage in lobbying	Yes _____	No _____
Percentage of funds or time devoted to lobbying _____		
Has expenditure test been elected?	Yes _____	No _____
Does organization utilize related lobbying entity?	Yes _____	No _____

29.9 Political Campaign Activities Limitation

Nonprofit organizations, to qualify as charitable or like organizations, are subject to a rule of federal tax law, which is that they must not participate in, or intervene in (including the publishing or distributing of statements) any political campaign on behalf of (or in opposition to) any candidate for public office.

This prohibition is deemed by the IRS to be absolute, that is, not underlain with an insubstantiality threshold (as is the case with respect to the lobbying rules as discussed earlier). However, recent court opinions suggest that there is some form of a de minimis standard in this context. In general, this rule of federal tax law is considerably undefined, although it is clear that public charities may not make political campaign contributions or endorse political candidates.

The political campaign activities prohibition embodies four elements, all of which must be present for the limitation to become operative. These elements are:

- A charitable or like organization may not *participate* or *intervene* in a political campaign.
- The political activity that is involved is a *political campaign.*
- The campaign must be with respect to an individual who is a *candidate.*
- The individual must be a candidate for a *public office.*

A charitable or like organization may not establish and maintain a *political action committee* to engage in political campaign activities.

There are a variety of activities that may be considered political but are not political campaign activities. These activities include lobbying, action on behalf of or in opposition to the confirmation of presidential nominees, litigation, boycotts, demonstrations, strikes, and picketing. However, tax-exempt organizations may not engage in activities that promote violence, other forms of law-breaking, or other activities that are contrary to public policy.

A tax-exempt organization (other than a political organization) that engages in the type of political activity embraced by attempts to influence the selection, nomination, election, or appointment of any individual to any federal, state, or local public office will not lose its tax exemption but will become subject to a 35 percent tax. This tax is imposed on the lesser of the organization's political expenditures or its net investment income.

Charitable and like organizations that lose their tax-exempt status because of political campaign activities are subject to an initial excise tax in the amount of 10 percent of the political campaign expenditures and perhaps an additional 100 percent tax. Like taxes, in the amounts of 2½ and 50 percent, may be imposed on the directors and officers of an organization who agreed to the making of the political campaign expenditures, unless the agreement was not willful and was due to reasonable cause.

The IRS has the authority, in the case of a flagrant violation of this prohibition against the making of political expenditures, to immediately terminate the organization's tax year and assess the tax(es). If the organization flagrantly persists in the participation or intervention in political campaign activity, the IRS may commence an action in federal court to enjoin the organization from making further political expenditures.

Private foundations are essentially prohibited from engaging in political campaign activities.

Most other categories of tax-exempt organizations—such as social welfare organizations, membership associations, and veterans' organizations—do not directly engage in political campaign activities but utilize political action committees for that purpose. Political activity is the exempt function of these committees. By the use of them, the parent organizations can avoid payment of the tax on political activities. (See Exhibit 29.8.)

29.10   Public Charities and Private Foundations

The federal tax law differentiates between charitable, educational, scientific, religious, and like organizations that are *public* and those that are *private*. The latter type of organization is termed a *private foundation*. Since there is no advantage to being a private foundation, charitable and like organizations usually strive to be classified as public entities. The private foundation distinction does not apply with respect to any other categories of tax-exempt organizations.

The law does not define what a private foundation is; it defines what it is not. Generically, however, a private foundation essentially is a charitable or like organization that is funded from one source (usually, an individual, family, or corporation), that receives its ongoing funding from investment income (rather than a consistent flow of charitable contributions), and that makes grants for charitable purposes to other persons rather than conduct its own programs.

In defining what a private foundation is not, the federal tax law presumes that all charitable and like organizations are private foundations. It is, therefore, the responsibility of the organization to (if it can) rebut this presumption by showing that it is a public organization.

(A)   PUBLIC CHARITIES

There are four basic categories of public charitable organizations:

- Institutions, such as churches, universities, colleges, schools, hospitals, and certain medical research organizations.
- Organizations that are publicly supported, because the support is substantially in the form of contributions and grants (*donative* charities).

EXHIBIT 29.8 Checklist on Political Activities

Does organization engage in political campaign activities?	Yes _____	No _____
Does organization have a political action committee?	Yes _____	No _____
Does organization engage in any advocacy activities?	Yes _____	No _____

- Organizations that are publicly supported, because the support is substantially in the form of contributions, grants, and revenue from the performance of exempt functions (*service provider* charities).
- Organizations that are organized and operated exclusively for the benefit of, to perform the functions of, or to carry out the purposes of one or more public organizations (*supporting organizations*).

The donative publicly supported charity is one that receives at least one-third of its support directly or indirectly from the public. This support ratio is measured over a four-year period. Support from any discrete source is public support to the extent it does not exceed 2 percent of the entity's total support over the measuring period. Certain related persons are considered single sources of support for this purpose. Support from other donative charities is considered public support for this purpose, without limitation. A *facts and circumstances test* allows for qualified charitable organizations to be considered donative publicly supported charities where the public support ratio is as low as 10 percent; this test is often used by museums, libraries, and other heavily endowed charities.

The service provider publicly supported charity is one that receives at least one-third of its support from the public. This support ratio is measured over a four-year period. Support must come from permitted sources, which cannot be disqualified persons. Thus, large gifts or grants may not count as public support (if they are derived from substantial contributors). Relatively small amounts of fee-for-service revenue can constitute public support. These entities cannot receive more than one-third of their support as investment income.

A supporting organization is a charitable entity that would be a private foundation but for this exception. A supporting organization must support or benefit one or more public charities; an eligible supported organization must be a donative publicly supported charity or a service provider publicly supported charity. Support may be provided as grants or by the conduct of programs that advance the supported organization's purposes. There are several allowable relationships between these organizations, with a common one being a parent-subsidiary model. A supporting organization may not be controlled by disqualified persons (other than its directors and officers). Tax-exempt social welfare organizations, labor unions and like entities, and business and professional associations may maintain supporting organizations.

(B) PRIVATE FOUNDATION RULES

Organizations that are classified as private foundations are subject to a battery of rules and requirements:

- A private foundation must, at all times, know the identity of persons who have special relationships to it (such as directors, officers, and their family members, and major (*substantial*) contributors); these persons are termed *disqualified persons.*
- A private foundation may not engage in acts of *self-dealing* (such as sales, rental, or lending transactions, or the payment of excessive compensation) with one or more disqualified persons.

- A private foundation must annually pay out, in the form of grants for charitable purposes (termed *qualifying distributions*), an amount equal to at least 5 percent of its investment assets (termed *minimum investment return*).
- A private foundation may not hold more than 20 percent (sometimes 35 percent) of an active interest in a commercial business (with impermissible interests termed *excess business holdings*).
- A private foundation may not invest its income or assets in speculative investments (termed *jeopardizing investments*).
- A private foundation may not make expenditures for purposes that are noncharitable, lobbying, or political, nor make grants to individuals or organizations that are not public charities without complying with certain rules (termed *taxable expenditures*).
- Private foundations that make grants to organizations other than public charities must exercise *expenditure responsibility* with respect to the grants.
- A private foundation generally must pay a 2 percent tax on its net investment income.
- A private foundation must file an annual information return (see Section 29.11) that is more complex than that required of other charitable and like organizations.
- Contributions to private foundations may be less deductible than contributions to public charities.

There are some organizations that are not "standard" private foundations and thus are treated differently under the federal tax law. A private foundation that conducts its own programs is a *private operating foundation*; it is treated in certain ways as a public charity. Private foundations that are exempt from the investment income tax and that can receive grants that do not require expenditure responsibility are *exempt operating foundations*. Foundations that are supportive of governmental colleges and universities are regarded as public charities, as are community foundations. A *conduit* private foundation is one that makes qualifying distributions, which are treated as distributions out of its assets, in an amount equal to 100 percent of all contributions received in the year involved.

A private foundation may convert to one of the four forms of public charities. To do this, it must terminate its private foundation status, following one of a variety of procedures.

As noted, a charitable organization is classified as a public or private charity as part of the process of applying for recognition of tax-exempt status. An organization that qualifies as an institutional public charity or a supporting organization is categorized as a nonprivate foundation by a *definitive ruling* from the IRS. If an organization is seeking to be categorized as one of the two types of publicly supported charities, and it has been in existence for at least one full tax year, it may acquire nonprivate foundation status by means of a definitive ruling; otherwise, it will receive an *advance ruling* for a period during which it obtains the requisite public support (if it can), with that ruling subsequently ripening into a definitive ruling. This intermediate period is the *advance ruling period*. (See Exhibit 29.9.)

EXHIBIT 29.9 Checklist for Private Foundations

If IRC § 501(c)(3) organization:

    Public _____ Private _____

If public IRC § 501(c)(3) organization:

    Church _____

    University _____

    College _____

    School _____

    Hospital _____

    Medical research organization _____

    Donative publicly supported charity _____

    Fee-based publicly supported charity _____

    Supporting organization _____

    Other _____

    Date ruling issued _____

If private IRC § 501(c)(3) organization:

    Standard private foundation _____

    Private operating foundation _____

    Exempt operating foundation _____

    Other _____

    Date ruling issued _____

If publicly supported organization:

    Date advance ruling period (if any) ends/ended _____

    Date definitive ruling (if there is one) issued _____

If supporting organization:

    Name(s) of supported organization(s) _____

    Nature of relationship _____

    Date definitive ruling issued _____

29.11 Filing Requirements

Nearly every organization that is exempt from federal income taxation must file an annual information return. This return is one of the following:

- Most tax-exempt organizations—Form 990.
- Small (see below) tax-exempt organizations—Form 990EZ.
- Private foundations—Form 990-PF.
- Black lung benefit trusts—Form 990-BL.

The annual return for political organizations is Form 1120-POL and for homeowners' associations is Form 1120-H.

The annual information return filed by tax-exempt organizations must include the following items:

- The organization's gross revenue (such as contributions, grants, program service revenue, and investment income) for the year.
- Its disbursements during the year for program services.
- Its management and fund-raising expenses for the year.
- A balance sheet showing its assets, liabilities, and net worth.
- The total of the contributions received by it during the year, and the names and addresses of all substantial contributors.
- The names and addresses of its directors, officers, and key employees.
- The compensation and other payments made during the year to each of its managers and key employees.
- Information concerning lobbying and political campaign activities.
- Information with respect to direct or indirect transfers to, and other direct or indirect transactions and relationships with, other tax-exempt organizations (other than charitable and like organizations, and political organizations).

(A) FORM 990

The annual information return that is required to be filed by most tax-exempt organizations is Form 990. The general contents of this return are stated in the preceding paragraph. In addition, an organization must describe its *program service accomplishments*. Expenses must be reported on a functional basis, that is, allocated to program, management, and fund raising. Revenue-producing activities must be detailed. Business activities must be categorized using various codes.

A tax-exempt organization must report certain other information, including:

- Taxable subsidiaries.
- Changes made in the organizing or governing instruments.
- Receipt of unrelated income (see below).
- Ownership of an interest in a partnership.
- Liquidations, dissolutions, terminations, or substantial contractions.
- Relationships with other organizations.
- Receipt of nondeductible gifts.
- Requests to see an annual information return or application for recognition of tax exemption.
- A reconciliation of revenue and expenses as shown on the audited financial statement.

In addition to filing the annual information return, a charitable or like organization must file an accompanying schedule containing additional information. This is Schedule A of Form 990.

Schedule A is the document by which charitable and like organizations report on the compensation of the five highest paid employees, the compensation of the five highest paid persons for professional services, eligibility for nonprivate foundation status, and on information regarding transfers, transactions, and relationships with other organizations.

Charitable organizations that elected the expenditure test with respect to their lobbying activities must report their lobbying expenses, including those over the four-year averaging period. Organizations that have not made this election, and thus remain subject to the substantial part test, are subject to other reporting requirements.

(B) FORM 990EZ

The annual information return for smaller tax-exempt organizations is the two-page Form 990EZ. This return may be used by tax-exempt organizations that have gross receipts of less than $100,000 and total assets of less than $250,000 at the end of the reporting year.

An organization can use this annual information return in any year in which it meets these two criteria, even though it was, and/or is, required to file a Form 990 in other years. Form 990EZ cannot be filed by private foundations. A charitable or like organization filing a Form 990EZ must also file a Schedule A (see Section 29.11).

(C) FORM 990-PF

Private foundations must file an annual information return. This return is on Form 990-PF.

On this return, private foundations must report their revenue and expenses, assets and liabilities, fund balances, and information about trustees, directors, officers, other foundation managers, highly paid employees, and contractors. Private foundations must report on qualifying distributions, calculation of the minimum investment return, computation of the distributable amount, undistributed income, and grant programs and other activities.

A private foundation must calculate the tax on its investment income (unless it is an exempt operating foundation). A private foundation must provide certain information regarding foundation managers, loan and scholarship programs, grants and contributions paid during the year or approved for future payment, transfers, transactions, and relationships with other organizations, and compliance with the public inspection requirements.

In addition to reporting on its activities in general, like nearly all tax-exempt organizations, a private foundation must also report on any self-dealing transactions, failure to distribute income as required, excess business holdings, investments that jeopardize charitable purposes, taxable expenditures, political expenditures, and substantial contributions. Additional reporting requirements are applicable to private operating foundations.

(D) DUE DATES

The Form 990, 990EZ, or 990-PF is due on or before the fifteenth day of the fifth month following the close of the tax year. Thus, the return for a calendar-year organization should be filed by May 15 of each year. Extensions of time for filing can be obtained from the IRS.

The filing date for an annual information return may fall due while the organization's application for recognition of tax exemption is pending with the IRS. In that instance, the organization should nonetheless file the information return (rather than a tax return) and indicate on it that the application is pending.

(E) PENALTIES

Failure to file the appropriate information return, or failure to include any information required to be shown on the return (or failure to show the correct information), absent reasonable cause, can give rise to a $10 penalty for each day the failure continues, with a maximum penalty for any one return not to exceed the lesser of $5,000 or 5 percent of the gross receipts of the organization for one year. An additional penalty may be imposed, at the same rate and maximum of $5,000, on the individual(s) responsible for the failure to file, absent reasonable cause, where the return remains unfiled following demand for the return by the IRS. An addition to tax for failure to timely file a federal tax return may also be imposed.

(F) ESTIMATED TAX PAYMENTS

As noted, private foundations are required to pay an income tax on their investment income. This tax is paid on Form 990-PF. Form 990-W is used to compute a foundation's estimated tax liability; the tax must be paid four times a year. A foundation that does not pay the estimated tax when due may be charged an underpayment penalty for the period.

(G) EXCEPTIONS

Certain categories of organizations are excused from the filing of an annual information return with the IRS. These include:

- Churches, and associations, conventions, and integrated auxiliaries of churches.
- Religious orders.
- Organizations (other than private foundations) the gross receipts of which in each year are normally not more than $25,000.
- State entities and affiliated organizations.

29.12   Certain Disclosure Requirements

The annual information returns and application for recognition of tax exemption of an exempt organization must be made available during regular business hours for public inspection. This rule does not apply to private foundations; other requirements are imposed on these entities.

The penalty for failure to provide access to copies of the annual return is $10 per day, absent reasonable cause, with a maximum penalty per return of $5,000. The penalty for failure to provide access to copies of the exemption application, payable by the person failing to meet the requirements, is $10 per day, absent reasonable cause, without any limitation. Any person who willfully fails to comply with these inspection requirements is subject to a $1,000 penalty with respect to each return or application.

The application for recognition of tax exemption and any supporting documents filed by most tax-exempt organizations are open to public inspection at the National Office of the IRS.

EXHIBIT 29.10 Checklist for Filing IRS Form 990

Is organization required to file return with IRS?	Yes _____	No _____
If yes, identify form Form _____		
Date annual return due _____		
Is Form 990-T required?	Yes _____	No _____

A tax-exempt organization must pay a penalty if it fails to disclose that information or services it is offering are available without charge from the federal government. The penalty, which is applicable for each day on which the failure occurred, is the greater of $1,000 or 50 percent of the aggregate cost of the offers and solicitations that occurred on any day on which the failure occurred and with respect to which there was this type of failure.

A copy of a private foundation's annual information return must be made available to any citizen for inspection at the foundation's principal office during regular business hours for at least 180 days of its availability. Notice of the availability of this annual return must be published in a newspaper having general circulation in the county in which the principal office of the foundation is located. (Exhibit 29.11.)

29.13 Commerciality Doctrine

The Internal Revenue Code and the accompanying tax regulations contain rules concerning the eligibility of nonprofit organizations for tax-exempt status. The courts have engrafted onto these rules additional requirements for obtaining and maintaining exempt status. These rules include those of the *commerciality doctrine.*

In essence, the doctrine holds that a tax-exempt organization is engaged in a nonexempt (taxable) activity when that activity is conducted in a manner that is considered *commercial.* (To date, this doctrine has only been applied with respect to public charities.) If a tax-exempt organization engages in an activity that is comparable to the way a for-profit entity would conduct it, the exempt organization is operating in a commercial manner. If an activity is, or combinations of activities are, nonexempt in nature and substantial, the organization cannot be tax-exempt. Otherwise, the nonexempt activity is treated as an unrelated business (see Section 29.14).

There are several factors that can trigger application of the commerciality doctrine. They include:

EXHIBIT 29.11 Checklist on Disclosure Requirements

Does organization make its exemption application available to the public?	Yes _____	No _____
Does organization make its annual return available to the public?	Yes _____	No _____
Does organization make disclosure concerning information or services?	Yes _____	No _____
If private foundation, is return availability properly published?	Yes _____	No _____

- Sales of goods or services to the general public (this factor can raise a presumption that the activity is commercial).
- Operation in direct competition with for-profit organizations.
- Setting of prices using a formula that is common in the realm of commercial business.
- Sizable profit margins.
- Utilization of promotional materials and other forms of advertising to induce sales.
- Hours of operation similar to those in for-profit setting.
- Payment of employees and lack of use of volunteers.
- Charitable contributions not part of the revenue base.

Somewhat related to the commerciality doctrine is the *commensurate test*. This is a standard articulated by the IRS in 1964 and not vigorously applied until recently. The commensurate test is used to determine whether an exempt organization (particularly a charitable one) warrants ongoing tax-exempt status. This is done by comparing the amount of exempt activity in relation to the organization's available resources. (Exhibit 29.12.)

29.14   Unrelated Income Taxation

The unrelated business income rules are an integral part of the law of tax-exempt organizations. While discussed more fully in Chapter 27, a brief overview is warranted here.

(A)   OVERVIEW

Taxation of a tax-exempt organization's unrelated business income is based on the concept that the approach is a more effective and workable sanction for authentic enforcement of this aspect of the law than denial or revocation of exempt status. This body of law is fundamentally simple: The unrelated business income tax applies only to business income that arises from an activity—technically known as a *trade or business*—that is *unrelated* to the organization's tax-exempt purposes. The purpose of the unrelated business income tax is to place tax-exempt organization business activities on the same tax basis as the nonexempt business endeavors with which they compete.

The term *unrelated trade or business* means any trade or business, the conduct of which is not substantially related to the exercise or performance, by the tax-exempt organization carrying on the trade or business, of its exempt purpose or function. The conduct of a trade or business is not substantially related to an organization's tax-exempt

---

EXHIBIT 29.12 Checklist on Commerciality

Does organization have a for-profit counterpart?	Yes _____	No _____
Does organization operate in a commercial manner, using the above criteria?	Yes _____	No _____
Does organization satisfy the commensurate test?	Yes _____	No _____

purpose solely because the organization may need the income or because of the use the organization makes of the profits derived from the business.

Absent one or more exceptions, gross income of a tax-exempt organization subject to the tax on unrelated income—and most exempt organizations are—is includible in the computation of unrelated business taxable income if three factors are present:

- The income is from a *trade or business*.
- The trade or business is *regularly carried on*.
- The conduct of the business is not *substantially related* to the organization's performance of its tax-exempt purposes.

(B) TRADE OR BUSINESS

Generally, any activity that is carried on for the production of income from the sale of goods or the performance of services is a trade or business for purposes of the unrelated income tax. Some courts have added another criterion, which is that an activity, to be considered a business for tax purposes, must be conducted with a *profit motive*.

The IRS is empowered to fragment a tax-exempt organization's operations, run as an integrated whole, into its component parts in search of one or more unrelated businesses. This *fragmentation rule* enables the IRS to ferret out unrelated business activity that is conducted with, or as a part of, related business activity. The rule is intended to prevent exempt organizations from hiding unrelated business activities within a cluster of related ones.

(C) REGULARLY CARRIED ON

In determining whether a trade or business from which a particular amount of gross income is derived by a tax-exempt organization is regularly carried on, regard must be had to the frequency and continuity with which the activities that are productive of the income are conducted and the manner in which they are pursued. This requirement is applied in light of the purpose of the unrelated business income tax which, as noted, is to place tax-exempt organization business activities on the same tax basis as the non-exempt business endeavors with which they compete. Thus, specific business activities of a tax-exempt organization will ordinarily be deemed to be *regularly carried on* if they manifest a frequency and continuity and are pursued in a manner generally similar to comparable commercial activities of nonexempt organizations.

Where income-producing activities are of a kind normally conducted by nonexempt commercial organizations on a year-round basis, the conduct of the activities by a tax-exempt organization over a period of only a few weeks does not constitute the regular carrying on of a trade or business. Where income-producing activities are of a kind normally undertaken by nonexempt commercial organizations only on a seasonal basis, however, the conduct of the activities by a tax-exempt organization during a significant part of the season ordinarily constitutes the regular conduct of trade or business.

(D) SUBSTANTIALLY RELATED

Gross income derives from unrelated trade or business if the conduct of the trade or business that produces the income is not substantially related to the purposes for which tax exemption is granted. This requirement necessitates an examination of the relationship between the business activities that generate the particular income in question—the activities, that is, of producing or distributing the goods or performing the services involved—and the accomplishment of the organization's tax-exempt purposes.

Trade or business is related to tax-exempt purposes only where the conduct of the business activity has a causal relationship to the achievement of a tax-exempt purpose, and it is substantially related only if the causal relationship is a substantial one. Thus, for the conduct of a trade or business from which a particular amount of gross income is derived to be substantially related to the purposes for which tax exemption is granted, the production or distribution of the goods or the performance of the services from which the gross income is derived must contribute importantly to the accomplishment of these purposes. Where the production or distribution of the goods or the performance of the services does not contribute importantly to the accomplishment of the tax-exempt purposes of an organization, the income from the sale of the goods or the performance of the services is not derived from the conduct of related trade or business.

Whether activities productive of gross income contribute importantly to the accomplishment of any purpose for which an organization is granted tax exemption depends in each case upon the facts and circumstances involved.

In determining whether activities contribute importantly to the accomplishment of a tax-exempt purpose, the size and extent of the activities involved must be considered in relation to the nature and extent of the tax-exempt function that they purport to serve. Thus, where income is realized by a tax-exempt organization from activities that are related to the performance of its exempt functions but that are conducted on a larger scale than is reasonably necessary for performance of the functions, the gross income attributable to that portion of the activities in excess of the needs of tax-exempt functions constitutes gross income from the conduct of unrelated trade or business. This type of income is not derived from the production or distribution of goods or the performance of services that contribute importantly to the accomplishment of any tax-exempt purpose of the organization.

Ordinarily, gross income from the sale of products that result from the performance of tax-exempt functions does not constitute gross income from the conduct of unrelated business if the product is sold in substantially the same state it is in upon completion of the exempt functions. However, if a product resulting from a tax-exempt function is utilized or exploited in further business endeavors beyond that reasonably appropriate or necessary for disposition in the state it is in upon completion of tax-exempt functions, the gross income derived from these endeavors is from the conduct of unrelated business.

An asset or facility necessary to the conduct of tax-exempt functions and so used may also be utilized in a commercial manner. This is a *dual-use* arrangement. In these cases, the mere fact of the use of the asset or facility in exempt functions does not, by itself, make the income from the commercial endeavor gross income from related business. The test, instead, is whether the activities productive of the income in question contribute importantly to the accomplishment of tax-exempt purposes.

(E) EXCEPTIONS

Certain types of income or activities are exempt from taxation under these rules. These exemptions include:

- Interest, dividends, royalties, rents, annuities, and capital gains.

- Income derived from research for government.
- Income derived from research performed by a college, university, or hospital.
- Income derived from a business in which substantially all of the work is performed by volunteers.
- Income from a business conducted by a charitable or like organization primarily for the convenience of its members, students, patients, officers, or employees.
- Income from a business that is the sale of merchandise, substantially all of which has been received by the organization as contributions.
- Income from the conduct of entertainment at certain fairs and expositions.
- Income from the conduct of certain trade shows.
- Income from the provision of certain services to small tax-exempt hospitals.
- Income from the distribution of certain low-cost articles incidental to the solicitation of charitable contributions.
- Income from the exchange or rental of mailing lists with or to charitable organizations.

In computing a tax-exempt organization's unrelated business taxable income, there must be included with respect to each debt-financed property that is unrelated to the organization's exempt function—as an item of gross income derived from an unrelated trade or business—an amount of income from the property, subject to tax in the proportion in which the property is financed by the debt.

Unrelated business taxable income is reported to the IRS on Form 990-T. This tax must be paid on an estimated basis four times each year; the installments are calculated using Form 990-W. In computing taxable unrelated income, an organization can utilize all related deductions and is entitled to a specific deduction of $1,000. (See Exhibit 29.13.)

29.15 Combinations of Tax-Exempt and Nonexempt Organizations

One of the most striking and significant practices of contemporary tax-exempt organizations is the structuring of activities, which in an earlier era were or would have been in a single tax-exempt entity, so that they are undertaken by two or more related organizations, either tax-exempt or taxable.

EXHIBIT 29.13 Checklist on Unrelated Business Income

Does organization engage in any unrelated business activities?	Yes _____	No _____
If yes, identify activities _____		
Does organization rely on any exceptions from unrelated income taxation?	Yes _____	No _____
If yes, identify exceptions _____		
Does organization have unrelated debt-financed income?	Yes _____	No _____
Is organization paying related income tax on an estimated basis?	Yes _____	No _____
Is organization timely filing Form 990-T?	Yes _____	No _____

For example, there are several common categories of combinations of tax-exempt organizations. These include a tax-exempt organization that utilizes a tax-exempt title-holding organization, a tax-exempt charitable organization that has an affiliated tax-exempt social welfare organization that engages in substantial lobbying, a professional association with a related foundation, and a business association with a related political action committee. Another illustration of this type of bifurcation is the use of a supporting organization. Hospital systems generally represent the largest of the clusters of related tax-exempt organizations.

There are combinations of tax-exempt organizations and nonexempt organizations as well. Thus, tax-exempt organizations often utilize for-profit subsidiaries. Where this relationship is properly structured, the activities of the subsidiary will not be attributed to the parent tax-exempt organization for tax purposes. Revenues from the subsidiary to the parent tax-exempt organization may be taxable as unrelated business income, where a control test is satisfied. Where all of the entities are bona fide ones, revenues from a second-tier for-profit subsidiary (a subsidiary of the first-tier for-profit subsidiary) are not taxable to the exempt parent.

Another combination of exempt and nonexempt entities involves a partnership. However, it is the position of the IRS that a charitable or like organization will be denied or lose its federal income tax exemption if it participates as the, or a, general partner in a limited partnership, unless the principal purpose of the partnership is to further charitable purposes. Even where the partnership can so qualify, the exemption may be revoked if the charitable organization/general partner is not adequately insulated from the day-to-day management responsibilities of the partnership and/or if the limited partners are to receive an undue economic return.

A business which is unrelated to the purposes of a tax-exempt organization may be conducted by a partnership, which has the tax-exempt organization as a general or limited partner. The revenue from the partnership to the exempt organization is likely to be taxable, as the consequence of a *look-through rule*, which treats—for tax purposes—the business as if it were conducted directly by the exempt organization.

A tax-exempt organization may enter into a joint venture with a for-profit organization without adversely affecting its exempt status. The only situation where tax exemption would be revoked for participation in such a joint venture is likely to be where the primary purpose of the exempt organization is to participate in the venture and if the function of the venture is unrelated to the exempt purposes of the tax-exempt organization. (See Exhibit 29.14.)

EXHIBIT 29.14 Checklist on Partnerships

If organization has any of the following, identify:

Taxable subsidiary	_____
Participation in partnership as general partner	_____
Participation in partnership as limited partner	_____
Participation in joint venture	_____
Other affiliations with other exempt organizations	_____
Other affiliations with nonexempt organizations	_____

29.16   Other Legal Matters

There are a variety of other matters of law with which a nonprofit organization should be concerned. Some of these are referenced in Exhibit 29.15.

EXHIBIT 29.15 Checklist on Other Related Legal Matters

County tax exemption information _____

City tax exemption information _____

Tax returns due:

    State _____

    County _____

    City _____

    Other _____

Payroll taxes filings _____

Lobbying registration(s) (nontax):

    Federal _____

    State _____

Insurance information _____

Leases _____

Other contracts _____

Names and addresses of:

    Accountant

    Chief executive officer

    Chief financial officer

    Fund raiser[4]

(Continued)

---

[4] A separate checksheet in the fund-raising context is in James M. Greenfield's *The Fund-Raising Handbook*, Chapter 32 (New York: Wiley, 1997).

EXHIBIT 29.15 *(Continued)*

Lawyer

_____
_____
_____

Insurance representative

_____
_____
_____

President

_____
_____
_____

Registered agent(s)

_____
_____
_____

Suggested Readings

Blazek, Jody. 1993. *Tax Planning and Compliance for Tax-Exempt Organizations: Forms, Checklists, Procedures* 2nd ed. New York: Wiley.

Gross, Malvern J. Jr., Larkin, Richard F., Bruttomesso, Roger S., McNally, John J., Price Waterhouse LLP. 1995. *Financial and Accounting Guide for Not-for-Profit Organizations*, 5th ed. New York: Wiley.

Hopkins, Bruce R. 1996. *The Legal Answer Book for Nonprofit Organizations*. New York: Wiley.

_____ . 1992. *The Law of Tax-Exempt Organizations*, 6th ed. New York: Wiley.

_____ . 1993. *A Legal Guide to Starting and Managing a Nonprofit Organization*, 2d ed. New York: Wiley.

_____ . *The Nonprofit Counsel* (monthly newsletter). New York: Wiley.

Sanders, Michael I. 1994. *Partnerships & Joint Ventures Involving Tax-Exempt Organizations*. New York: Wiley.

Emerging Challenges to Tax-Exempt Status: Responding to a Challenge at the State or Local Level*

PAMELA J. LELAND, PhD
Seton Hall University

---

* **Author's Note:** Please forward any questions or new information regarding local or state cases to Dr. Pamela Leland, Center for Public Service, Seton Hall University, S. Orange, NJ 07079 or via internet: LELANDPA@LANMAIL.SHU.EDU.

A portion of the information in this chapter derives from a technical report, *Responding to a Property Tax Challenge: Lessons Learned in Pennsylvania*, written by the author and released by the Department of Public Administration, Marywood College, Scranton, PA in June 1994. Substantial portions of this technical report were published under the same title in *State Tax Notes*, October 3, 1994, at 927–940.

30.1 Introduction

Nonprofit-organization bashing has become a popular pastime. The media love a good scandal and, unfortunately, there has been sufficient fuel in recent years—from Jim Bakker and PTL to William Aramony at United Way and the recent New Era Foundation debacle. These incidents have coincided with growing concern over the increasing commercialism of the nonprofit sector, unethical and illegal fund-raising practices, and consumer/donor rights. The result had been increased scrutiny and increased regulation of nonprofit activity at the federal level.

Such incidents have also fueled efforts to examine charitable tax exemption at the state and local levels. Although many factors have contributed to this environment of nonprofit sector scrutiny, the concern over the legitimacy of exempt status for certain types of nonprofit organizations has been a significant component. Such concern has resulted in a growing number of direct challenges to exempt status throughout the country. Some states have initiated attempts to create an entire new tax structure; others have chosen to target the challenges toward specific classes of nonprofits or particular organizations.

This chapter attempts to provide the background necessary to understand these challenges to exempt status, as well as to provide the tools needed to successfully withstand such attacks at the state or local level. Being armed with this knowledge and these tools will be critical, because such challenges are, without a doubt, going to increase in the future. The tools suggested here are also consistent with the "Excellence Elements" of Effectiveness, Efficiency, and Environment essential for a *self-renewing* organization (as articulated by Connors in Chapter 1).

30.2 Clarifying Exempt Status: Federal Versus State Designations

Nonprofit tax exemption is not a simple issue. One of the many complicating factors is that designation as an exempt organization occurs at both the state and federal levels of government. In some cases these definitions are parallel; most often, however, the state designation is distinct from the federal designation.

When an organization's tax-exempt status is referred to, most people think of the federal tax code, I.R.C. § 501(c). Charitable nonprofit organizations are categorized as § 501(c)(3). This designation not only exempts the organization from paying federal corporate income taxes, but also provides a deduction benefit to the donor. Yet, in most cases, federal designation as an exempt (501(c)(3)) organization provides no benefit of exemption at the state or local level. Consider, for example, sales taxes. A national report on state sales tax exemption by Washington, D.C., attorney Janne Gallagher (1992) found that only 13 states granted sales tax exemption privileges according to, or referring to, the federal IRS designation. This means that in 37 states plus the District of Columbia, nonprofit organizations must meet additional or separate requirements to be considered exempt from sales taxes (see Exhibit 30.1).

Separate state processes also mean that there is no consistency among states in the kinds of nonprofit organizations granted exemption privileges or in the types of taxes from which an organization is freed. When one considers the many types of nonprofit charities (from schools to churches and synagogues to hospitals to museums to youth organizations) and the many different kinds of taxes (including sales taxes, school taxes,

---

EXHIBIT 30.1 States That Provide Sales Tax Exemption According to, or in Language Similar to, the Federal Tax Code, § 501(c)(3)

Colorado	New Jersey	Texas
Indiana	New Mexico	Vermont
Kentucky	New York	West Virginia
Maryland	Tennessee	Wisconsin
Massachusetts		

---

property taxes, business privilege taxes, and special use taxes), one begins to understand the potential variations. The significant conclusion here is that each state has its own rules, guidelines, and procedures; astute nonprofit administrators will determine exactly what does and does not apply within their particular jurisdiction.

30.3 Emerging State and Local Challenges to Exempt Status

(A) AN OVERVIEW

It seems that everyone knows of some organization that has had its exempt status questioned. Whether it is a local organization known only to a few, or a national organization known to everyone, such challenges appear to be becoming commonplace. Even high-status organizations are not immune. For example, in the summer of 1995 the American Association of Retired Persons (AARP) was required to appear before a Senate hearing to explain and defend its charitable status. But, in actuality, how prevalent are such challenges?

A determination of the extent of these challenges across the nation has not, to date, been made in any systematic way. What is available is anecdotal information gleaned from various periodicals and newsletters published by national associations or legal publishers. (A list of some of these sources of information is provided in Exhibit 30.2.) What we *can* learn from these newsletters is that dozens of states are involved in exemption-related issues. A recent newsletter from the National Council of Nonprofit Associations reviewed legislative activity in Arizona, Delaware, the District of Columbia, Florida, Iowa, Maine, Maryland, Michigan, Minnesota, Montana, Nebraska, New Hampshire, Ohio, Pennsylvania, and Washington.[1] Several of these reports concerned broad legislation that would (or could) significantly curtail exempt privileges (such as Florida, Maine, and Nebraska).

(B) EXPLAINING THE GROWTH IN THE NUMBER OF CHALLENGES

There is no single, definitive answer to why these challenges are occurring at this particular time. Several potential explanations can be offered and all likely contain some el-

---

[1] See the Spring 1995 issue of *State Tax Trends for Nonprofits*, published by the National Council of Nonprofit Associations.

EXHIBIT 30.2 Sources of Information on Challenges to Exempt Status

PERIODICALS
Chronicle of Philanthropy
Nonprofit Times

JOURNALS/NEWSLETTER

Journal of Tax Exempt Organizations
Faulkner and Gray
1110 Penn Plaza, New York, NY 10001
(212) 967-7000

The Nonprofit Counsel
John Wiley and Sons, Inc.
605 Third Ave., New York, NY 10158
(212) 850-6327

Nonprofit Issues
Montgomery, McCracken, Walker and Rhoads
Three Parkway, Philadelphia, PA 19102
(215) 665-7200

State Tax Trends for Nonprofits
National Council of Nonprofit Associations
1001 Connecticut Ave., NW, Suite 900
Washington, DC 20036
(202) 833-5740

Tax Monthly for Exempt Organizations
Harmon, Curran, Gallagher, and Spielberg
2001 S Street, NW, Suite 430
Washington, DC 20009
(202) 328-3500

---

ement of truth. Certainly one of the key explanations is the growing revenue needs of states and localities in the face of declining public sector resources, and the use of a challenge to exempt status as a means to generate additional local tax revenue.

Fiscal problems of local governments are well known. Cities and counties face a number of tough issues, including declining tax bases, corporate disinvestment, growing numbers of dependent populations, aging infrastructure, and increasing municipal costs. These rises in costs coincide with declining federal support. It would seem to be a logical response to attempt to derive some revenue from those properties currently paying nothing toward those municipal or county services, which are utilized on a daily basis. Also, a reality not to be denied is that much central city property is off the tax rolls. Medical centers, educational institutions, religious organizations, government buildings, social service agencies—all typically exempt—are often clustered in downtown, high-density areas and pay nothing toward the cost of running the local government. Although there are many potentially disastrous consequences to acting upon this belief (which are discussed in Section 30.6), the revenue needs of local units of government (including school districts) is a powerful explanation for the growth in the number of challenges to charitable exempt status.

A second factor is the increasing commercialism of nonprofit sector organizations. In the last 30 years, nonprofit organizations have become increasingly dependent on

public sector contracts, user fees, and services charges as sources of revenue. Private donations, for most nonprofit organizations, are a deceasing portion of organizational revenue. The national average is that less than one-fifth of organizational revenue comes
from private sources (individuals, corporations, or foundations), whereas government
dollars or user fees make up more than 80 percent (Salamon 1992). Critics of the nonprofit sector point to these statistics and question the "charitableness" of an organization
that receives the bulk of its revenue from a client or a third party.

Another dimension of commercialism is perceived competition with the for-profit
business sector. As nonprofit organizations have sought revenue stability, some have
moved into areas of activity that are considered to be the domain of the private sector.
For example, a hospital might decide to open a flower shop that competes with the
florist down the street, or a college might make its dining facilities available for community banquets and dinners, competing with a hotel conference center. Such revenue
is likely to be unrelated to the nonprofit mission and is, therefore, subject to federal income taxation. The criticism, however, is not that the nonprofit is not paying its taxes
*but that the nonprofit organization should not be conducting activities unrelated to its mission
at all.*

A third explanation for the growing challenges to exempt status is the perceived
"deviance" of the nonprofit sector (or at least some individuals and/or nonprofit organizations). Such perceptions are fueled by the kinds of scandals referred to in Section
30.1. As community leaders perceive that certain organizations or classes of nonprofit organizations are straying from their "charitable" nature, public examination and regulation may result. For example, in Pennsylvania, a high-profile case involving an Erie
medical center is commonly believed to be behind much of the initial activity by local
governments to challenge property tax–exempt status. In this case, the medical center
lost its exempt status because of a range of noncharitable activities, including ownership
of a lakeside marina. (Exempt status was eventually returned to the medical center
through a settlement which included divestiture of its for-profit subsidiary activities.)

Another perspective in attempting to understand these challenges to exempt status
is the proposition that these challenges are not really "new," but only the most recent in-
carnation. For example, concern over unrelated business activities of nonprofit organizations in the 1940s led to the UBIT rules of the 1950s. Criticism of foundations in the
1950s and 1960s resulted in the federal tax law changes of 1969. Though a compelling
proposition to explain changes to the federal tax structure, this explanation does not sufficiently explain the recent proliferation of these challenges at the local and state levels.
More likely is that a combination of local revenue needs, commercialism, and scandalous
behavior are the dominant factors.

30.4 *Pennsylvania: Visions of the Future?*

In discussing the growing challenges to exempt status which are occurring throughout
the country, Pennsylvania is a special case. For better or worse, Pennsylvania has become
a model for other states (such as Nebraska) and localities (such as Washington, D.C.) that
want to rethink the definition of, and privileges associated with, a public charity.

Using Pennsylvania as a case study in an attempt to understand these challenges in
greater depth is appropriate for several different reasons. First, challenges to exempt status have centered around the fundamental definition of *charity* and, more specifically,

the kind of organization that deserves the privilege of exemption. Second, challenges have been directed toward more than 1,000 nonprofit organizations across many jurisdictions throughout the state. No type of nonprofit has been immune and many organizations have, indeed, lost their exemptions. Third, and not insignificantly, research conducted within Pennsylvania reveals critical information in learning how to confront such a challenge (as discussed in Section 30.8).

(A) DEFINING A "PURELY PUBLIC CHARITY"

The Constitution of the Commonwealth of Pennsylvania allows organizations of "purely public charity" to be exempt, by statute, from taxation. The General County Assessment Law adopted in 1933 (P.L. 853, No. 155) delineated these conditions with the following language: "[H]ospitals, academies, associations of learning, benevolence, or charity . . . founded, endowed, and maintained by public or private charity" are exempt from "all county, city, borough, town, township, road, poor and school tax."

It was not until 1985, in a case related to sales tax exemption, that the Commonwealth Court (Pennsylvania's first-level appellate court) attempted to define a *purely public charity*. In *Hospitalization Utilization Project v. Commonwealth*, 507 Pa. 1, 487 A.2d 1306 (Pa. Commw. Ct. 1985), the court issued the following definition of a purely public charity. Note that all five criteria must be met in order to be considered a purely public charity:

1. Advances a charitable purpose
2. Donates or renders gratuitously a substantial portion of its services
3. Benefits a substantial and indefinite class of persons who are legitimate subjects of charity
4. Relieves government of some of its burdens
5. Operates entirely free from a private profit motive.

The problems arising from this definition of a charity (which is now commonly known as the HUP test) are not related to the criteria themselves. In fact, many individuals and groups have come out publicly in agreement with this conceptualization of nonprofit charity.

The problems relate to the application and interpretation of the criteria by various assessment boards and courts throughout the state. For example, a children's center that received United Way funding and state/federal day care subsidies was denied exempt status because only a handful of students were nonpaying and nonsubsidized. In this case, United Way dollars were not considered to be evidence of a charity. In another well-known case, the court ruled that showing a surplus meant that the organization did not operate "free from a private profit motive." (This ruling was later overturned on appeal.) A number of religious and nonreligious camps have lost exemptions because courts ruled that government has no burden to provide such services. Yet this ruling has not been consistently applied. For example in one county, more than 20 camps lost exempt status, but the Boy Scout camp retained exemption privileges. The list could go on.

(i) Legislative Solutions

There have been, and continue to be, efforts to create legislation to (1) clarify the five HUP criteria, and (2) create a state-level certification process for nonprofit charities. This certification process would "officially" designate a nonprofit organization as a purely public charity so that questions of local tax exemption would be eliminated. The advantage of state legislation is that it would create a uniform process in which all nonprofit charities would meet the same standards; the disadvantage is the creation of another bureaucratic, regulatory function at the sate level.

The first piece of Pennsylvania legislation, Senate Bill 877, was never fully considered by both houses of the state legislature and died at the end of the 1994 legislative session. A similar version, Senate Bill 355, was approved by the Senate in the summer of 1995 and sent on to the House Finance Committee. Likelihood of passage in 1996 remains an open question: state associations representing various local municipalities are against the bill; most groups in the nonprofit and religious community favor the legislation (in its current form).

(ii) Judicial Solutions

Even if passage occurs, a legislative solution in Pennsylvania may not be easily accomplished, for the simple reason that this is a *constitutional* issue. The state constitution provides the privilege of exemption for "purely public charities." Advocates have suggested that any legislation that might constrain these privileges could be challenged on constitutional grounds. Legislative responses are thus extremely vulnerable. These individuals and groups have been hopeful that the Pennsylvania Supreme Court would settle the issue once and for all.

As of June 1996, only one case related to charitable status had been heard by the Pennsylvania Supreme Court. In the *St. Margaret Seneca Place* case,[2] the court ruled in favor of the nonprofit organization, a nursing home outside Pittsburgh. While it offered some clarification of the five HUP criteria, it did not offer the sweeping interpretation that nonprofit advocates had hoped for. (See Exhibit 30.3 for a more detailed description of the *St. Margaret Seneca Place* case, including excerpts from the state supreme court decision.)

In the summer of 1994, a small, private liberal arts college in southwestern Pennsylvania, Washington and Jefferson College, lost its exempt status in the County Court of Common Pleas. The college appealed to the Commonwealth Court; the case was argued in March 1995. In September, the court delivered a 4–3 verdict reversing the lower court's decision and reinstating the college's exempt status. As of late 1995, appeal by the various taxing authorities was likely. Given the closeness of the decision, once again the nonprofit community is hopeful that the state supreme court will choose to hear the case and offer further clarity as to the five criteria named in the HUP case.

(B) EXTENT OF THE CHALLENGES

The growing number of challenges to charitable tax exemption at the local level has been a public issue for almost 10 years, since 1986, when the five HUP criteria were first used to deny property-tax-exempt status to the Pittsburgh YMCA. Yet, other than anecdotal information gleaned through newspapers or association newsletters, no systematic effort to determine the extent of these challenges occurred until the fall of 1994.[3]

---

[2] *St. Margaret Seneca Place v. Board of Property Assessment.*

[3] A more complete discussion of this research is to be published by the author in the forthcoming *Nonprofit Organizations as Public Actors* (tentative title), to be released by Jossey-Bass Publishers, San Francisco, CA.

EXHIBIT 30.3 The Case of St. Margaret Seneca Place, Allegheny County, PA

Currently the only case related to the five-point definition of a *charity* heard by the Pennsylvania Supreme Court

1. St. Margaret Seneca Place, a 180-bed nursing home in the Pittsburgh area, opened in April 1989.
2. The initial request for property tax exemption was denied by the Allegheny County Assessment Office. It was also denied on appeal to the Board of Assessment.
3. The Court of Common Pleas ruled that the nursing home was exempt because it met all five of the HUP criteria.
4. The various taxing authorities appealed to the Commonwealth Court (a three-member appeal court). This court determined that none of the five HUP criteria had been met. Within its decision, the Commonwealth Court concluded that the nursing home did not advance a charitable purpose because all of the residents paid for their care, either through Medicare, Medicaid, insurance, or private pay. Of no importance was the fact that reimbursements did not cover all costs. The court said that "when residents of a nursing home are required to pay the facility for their right to live there, the nursing home is not advancing a charitable purpose, but merely conducting business." It went further, citing the projected surplus in the third year of operation as evidence that the organization was not entirely free from a private profit motive.
5. St. Margaret Seneca Place appealed to the Pennsylvania Supreme Court. In April 1994, the supreme court reversed the Commonwealth Court's decision, determining that *all* of the criteria set forth in the HUP case had indeed been met. Important elements within the ruling included:
   - "The care of elderly residents who cannot pay their full costs serves a charitable purpose."
   - "The absence of indigent residents is certainly not, standing alone, enough to disqualify a nursing home from an exemption as a purely public charity."
   - "The decision to accept Medicaid payments to help defray the cost of care is perfectly consistent with a finding that the nursing home advances a charitable purpose."
   - "The requirement that an institution donate or render gratuitously a substantial portion of its services does not imply a requirement that the institution forgo available government payments which cover part of its costs, or that it provide wholly gratuitous services to some of its residents."
   - "The HUP test of whether an institutional has relieved the government of some of its burden does not require a finding that the institution has fully funded the care of some people who would otherwise be fully funded by government."
   - "[S]urplus revenue is not synonymous with private profit. . . ."

In this 1994 survey of Pennsylvania's 67 county assessment officers, it was found that some effort to generate taxes, payments, services in lieu of taxes, or voluntary contributions from nonprofit organizations had occurred in 37 counties. When one adds the five counties where it was indicated that such activities would be initiated in the near future, and the known activities in at least two of the nonresponding counties, one can conclude that these challenges to nonprofit tax exemption had taken place in *at least* two-thirds of Pennsylvania's counties. The good news was that, in most cases, fewer than 10 nonprofit organizations had been challenged; the bad news is that it was estimated that, across the state, more than 1,000 nonprofit organizations had been affected by these efforts. These included hospitals and nursing homes, colleges and universities, convents, senior housing programs, social service agencies, museums and historical societies, veterans associations, service clubs, youth organizations, and others.

(C)　FORMAL VERSUS INFORMAL CHALLENGES

One of the complicating factors in any attempt to determine the extent of these challenges is the informal nature of some challenges. For example: You, as an executive director of a nonprofit organization, are contacted by the local school district superintendent. She tells you, in so many words, that if your organization does not make a "voluntary contribution" to the school district, then they will "formally" challenge your exempt status with the county assessment office. At the direction of your board of directors, you give in to their demand and make a "donation" to the school district. You may even choose to formalize the arrangement with a legal agreement outlining your contribution for some defined period of time. All of this has occurred without any formal knowledge or involvement from the county government. Unless you or the school district chooses to go public with this agreement, how will anyone ever know?

These kinds of situations were uncovered in the 1994 research project referred to in the previous section. County assessment officers "knew" things or "had heard" about things in which they had no "formal" involvement. Such private agreements between individual taxing authorities and specific organizations are problematic for a number of reasons and are discussed extensively elsewhere.[4] For our purposes, it simply makes any kind of definitive conclusion as to the extent of such challenges to exempt status virtually impossible to calculate.

30.5　Responding to a Challenge

(A)　EVALUATING THE OPTIONS

Imagine this scenario: An executive director of a nonprofit organization is going through his mail. He opens the envelope from the county, wondering what the latest communiqué might be. Enclosed he finds a notification that as of the first day of the next fiscal year, his organization will be placed back on the property tax rolls. It is that simple. One day the organization is exempt; the next day it is not.

Or it might be a new organization (or an old organization with a new property) whose application for property-tax-exempt status is being denied. And do not forget that exemptions are not limited to property taxes. There are applications for sales tax exemptions, business privilege tax exemptions, or use tax exemptions which might be necessary. It is not uncommon for a nonprofit organization to be exempt from property and school district taxes, but to be liable for sales or business privilege taxes. Each state is different, with a tax structure that is differentially applied to various types of nonprofit corporations.

There are few options for those whose exempt status has been questioned or challenged. They are, quite simply: accept it, fight it, or negotiate some settlement. Each has

---

[4] *Ibid.*

advantages, each has disadvantages. The key is conducting a thoughtful analysis of the consequences of each option and making a decision based upon knowledge and reason.

(i) Accepting the Loss or Denial of Exempt Status

There are a couple of reasons why an organization might choose to accept the loss or denial of exempt status. First (and most common), the organization recognizes that it does not deserve exempt status at the local or state level (i.e., it acknowledges that it does not meet the particular local/state criteria). Remember that the loss of exempt status at the local or state level does not affect its federal tax status.

Second, an organization may decide that acceptance is the lesser of two financial evils. If, for example, an organization owns no property, and may only be liable for sales taxes (which is a small amount each year), the organization may decide that paying the sales taxes will cost a lot less than the legal costs incurred in fighting it. Very simply, it might be cheaper financially to simply pay the tax burden. *But a word of caution*: the choice to accept the loss or denial of exempt status for a purely financial reason should be weighed very carefully and only after a complete cost/benefit analysis has been conducted. Although the tax burden might be minimal at current organizational size and operations, future growth or a shift in an area of activity might significantly raise the tax burden. Though a future application for exempt status should be considered a stand-alone application, trying to explain or defend an application for exemption after you have historically acted as if you were in agreement with the previous denial of exemption, could be awkward and cumbersome (not to mention embarrassing!).

(ii) Fighting Back

For many organizations, the only perceived choice is to fight the loss or denial of exempt status. For some it is a matter of identity and honor: "How dare anyone question our charitable nature?" These organizations are likely to take it to the highest court if necessary. For example, one board of directors of a youth-serving organization in Pennsylvania was so incensed by the challenge that it ordered the executive director to wage a highly visible, public battle that included newspaper and radio interviews, trips to the state capitol, and mobilization of its hundreds of community volunteers.

For other nonprofit organizations, the level of the tax burden itself demands confrontation. Most nonprofit organizations, even larger ones, do not have sufficient revenue to pay property and other taxes on an ongoing basis. For these organizations, the financial risk of losing exempt status is greater than any legal costs incurred.

If an organization decides to wage a battle with the various taxing authorities, certain resources are required if there is any hope for success. First and most importantly, the board of directors must be clearly and unequivocally committed to the decision. This commitment translates into the provision of necessary financial and human resources. For the organization's staff, it translates into: time and energy on the part of the chief executive officer, finance officer, and other administrative staff; monies to pay attorneys' documentation and other paperwork activities; media involvement; presence at public hearings; and more. Such issues and strategies are detailed in Section 30.7.

(iii) Negotiating or Settling

A nonprofit organization's decision to negotiate some settlement with the taxing authority is typically driven by one of two reasons. First, the nonprofit organization may feel that, in the long run, the financial costs of fighting a lengthy court battle are too significant. Second, the nonprofit may be acting on some belief that, as a member of the community, the organization has a responsibility to contribute toward the cost of local services it utilizes on a regular basis.

Some aspects of this choice to negotiate a settlement require further discussion. First, for those who believe it is a matter of community citizenship to contribute to local government costs, the nonprofit organization might retain its exempt status and make these payments "voluntarily." In fact, the retention of exempt status is often critical to the settlement agreement. These payments are then "voluntary contributions" to the municipal coffers; they are, emphatically, *not* taxes. Likewise, these organizations are often selective in deciding to whom they choose to make these voluntary contributions. For example, they will make payments to the city or the county, but not the local school district.

A second point regarding the choice to settle is that a nonprofit organization may negotiate a lower rate of taxation while either losing or retaining its exempt status. If exempt status is returned to the organization, the tax becomes a "voluntary contribution"; it exempt status is lost, the tax is at a lower rate than for other taxable entities. For example, the exempt status of a healthcare organization in northwestern Pennsylvania was challenged in 1990. The county board of assessment ruled against the organization. This decision was confirmed in both the county court and the appellate court. The organization then went back to the local assessment board and cut a deal. For the return of its exempt status, it agreed to, among other things, make monetary contributions to a number of local taxing authorities. Another organization lost its exempt status in court, but an appeal to the assessment board resulted in a reduced payment level. The appeal did not result in a reinstatement of exempt status.

Not to be dismissed is the role that threats of ongoing challenges to exempt status may play in a decision to settle. Another example may prove helpful. In 1990, a Court of Common Pleas in southeastern Pennsylvania ruled in favor of a local hospital, saying that it met the five criteria of a purely public charity. Various units of local government (including the county) refused to accept the decision. However, rather than appealing the Common Pleas court decision, the county simply requested again, in the following fiscal year, that the hospital be placed on the tax rolls. At that point, the hospital chose to "settle." In exchange for no further challenges to its exempt status, the hospital agreed to build a borough fire station and provide a variety of community health and education services.

The decision to negotiate some settlement (whether the settlement involves voluntary contributions, services in lieu of taxes, or a lower tax rate) is often criticized by those who have chosen to fight the taxing authorities. These criticisms arise from the perceived larger implications of these settlements. Critics argue that these nonprofit organizations are giving in to a form of public sector blackmail and that the integrity of the entire charitable sector is being undermined. It is suggested, for example, that for every hospital that agrees to make a voluntary contribution, the legitimacy of charitable exemption for all hospitals grows weaker.

(B)   RESPONDING TO INFORMAL CHALLENGES

An *informal challenge* is one in which an individual taxing authority, such as a school district, contacts an organization privately without calling in the formal authority of the county assessment office. When faced with this type of challenge to exempt status, the choices available to a nonprofit organization are two: (1) agree to negotiate some settlement with the individual taxing body, or (2) refuse to negotiate. The pros and cons of negotiating a settlement were discussed previously. Put simply, by agreeing to negotiate a settlement, the organization is choosing to make some contribution to the taxing authority, while saving (potentially) lots of time and (hopefully) a bit of money. By refusing to negotiate, the nonprofit organization either hopes that the taxing authority is bluffing or believes that the organization is better served by going through a formal, public hearing.

30.6 Living with the Consequences: What Your Mother Never Told You

The potential impacts of a challenge to tax-exempt status on a nonprofit organization should not go unexamined. Although steps can be taken to minimize the negative consequences or even turn the process into an opportunity for growth and renewal, no organization will come through a challenge without being changed. Unfortunately, there is evidence to suggest that these changes are more often negative.[5] Research conducted on a small sample of Pennsylvania nonprofit organizations in the spring of 1994 found that clients and staff bear the greatest costs. (For a brief list of these potential outcomes, refer to Exhibit 30.4.)

It was found in this research process that organizations suffering the most were those whose board of directors were divided over how to respond; those without sufficient or appropriate documentation (and who, therefore, could not prove that they met the charitable test); and those without sufficient cash reserves. These organizations were likely to either lose exempt status or pursue a settlement of some sort. When faced with these unanticipated tax costs, these organizations had to do one of two things: cut programs or raise fees. One youth-serving organization closed one of its day care sections; another organization raised its membership fees. A third organization reduced the number of indigent clients in favor of private pay clients. Several of the organizations went immediately into deficit spending.

Even those organizations whose boards of directors were united in aggressively fighting to preserve the exempt status reported negative consequences. Chief executives reported that, in general, board members were more hesitant and less likely to take risks, always evaluating potential actions in terms of public perception. Though some may consider this community focus a positive component, the chief executives suggested that this wariness led to less innovation and a tendency toward the status quo. Simply put, board members acted as if they were frightened.

In the research process, the only organizations that did not appear to suffer negative consequences were those committed to making voluntary contributions as an indication of their membership and commitment to the community. Although only a small portion of the sample, these organizations suffered no financial consequences or altered board processes. This finding, however, makes sense: these organizations had adopted a policy and had planned agency budgets based on this policy. To be noted again, however,

---

[5] See Pamela J. Leland, *Responding to a Property Tax Challenge: Lessons Learned in Pennsylvania*, State Tax Notes, Oct. 3, 1994, at 927–940.

EXHIBIT 30.4 Potential Outcomes of a Challenge to Exempt Status

On organizational leadership:

1. Depending on size, type, and knowledge, the board of directors may experience excessive stress and dissension
2. Excessive workload for chief executive
3. Anxiety and turmoil among upper-level management staff

On organizational program and services:

1. Reduced level of service
2. Higher user fees
3. Change in client demographics
4. Less innovation and risk
5. Greater financial instability
6. Wasted human resources

---

is that these organizations were quite selective in which taxing authority received these "voluntary" contributions.

Although many of the outcomes found in the research were negative, there was evidence of the potential for positive change. Chief executives reported that organizational missions became clarified, board members were more active and invested, and communities and volunteers had rallied to their defense. Not surprisingly, these glimmers of hope were more often heard from chief executives whose organizations had successfully defended their exempt status. These organizations were also the ones who were prepared and ready. How to be prepared and ready is discussed in Section 30.7.

30.7 Responding in Strength: A Case for Being Prepared

Explanations for the increasing number of challenges to exempt status vary (see Section 30.3(b)). Whatever the cause, it is not likely that such challenges will taper off in the near future. As a recent editorial in *State Tax Trends for Nonprofits* said, "there is reason to think that the principle of tax exemption is being reexamined with a vigor that is unprecedented."[6] Given such a prediction, nonprofit organizations must be prepared to respond. Should the organization fight it out in court? Should a settlement be negotiated? Should the nonprofit accept the reality that it is no longer a charitable nonprofit and pay the taxes? There is no single, easy, or quick answer to these questions. There is, however, no excuse for not being prepared to answer them, and a number of things can be done to ensure that the best strategy is selected and the greatest possibility for success exists. Ultimately, each organization must determine for itself how to respond to such a challenge.

If an organization chooses to defend its exempt status, very simply, the nonprofit organization must be able to provide evidence that leaves no doubt as to the organization's

---

[6] *Editorial*, State Tax Trends for Nonprofits, Spring 1995, at 1.

charitable nature. (Remember, even a choice to negotiate a voluntary contribution is based upon the legitimacy of tax-exempt status.) The evidence needed to prove the legitimacy of exempt status can be generated through a process containing five components: education, planning, documentation, communication, and collaboration.

(A) EDUCATION

The first step in preparing an appropriate response to a challenge to tax-exempt status is to gather the knowledge to make the correct decision. Nonprofit organizations must educate themselves about this issue before a challenge is presented. Through training and discussion, both board and staff must understand the implications of the challenge for their own particular organization. For example, it is no longer enough to assume the mantle of "educational" or "healthcare" institution. Organizations must be able to articulate for themselves the reason their nonprofit healthcare organization is different from a for-profit healthcare organization. Another example might be: why is a nonprofit day-care facility deserving of an exemption when a for-profit is not?

This process of education is accomplished only through introspection, training, and dialogue. Boards of directors and staff must involve themselves in a broad-based conversation in which every member and group understands the issue and its implications. Through this dialogue, the following kinds of questions must be answered:

1. What has happened in our area regarding tax exemption and nonprofits? What efforts have the taxing authorities initiated? Which taxing bodies are actively involved?
2. Which organizations have been formally or informally challenged? How did they respond?
3. What decisions or outcomes have occurred thus far? Are any decisions pending or on appeal?
4. Why does our organization deserve continued exemption? What is our expressed rationale for tax-exempt status?
5. Is there consensus among the board and staff as to these issues?

(B) PLANNING

A natural outcome of knowledge is the ability to plan a response. As an organization's leaders understand the issues and their implications, decisions can be made as to appropriate strategies. The position of strength for a nonprofit organization is to be prepared for a challenge should one emerge. The goal in a planning process is to have necessary policies and procedures in place so that, if challenged, the normal difficulties associated with a tax challenge will not be exacerbated by indecision, bickering, and infighting among and between board and staff. To have the time to make reasoned, deliberate decisions is critical; planning allows for this.

Some of the planning questions to be answered include:

1. If challenged, what would we do? Would we negotiate? Would we go to court? Who would make this decision?
2. How is the board's position expressed? is there a policy or stated position?

3. Which board members would be involved on a day-to-day basis? At what point would the full board have to be consulted?
4. Which staff would be involved? Who would have direct responsibility for this issue?
5. What legal services would we need? What do we have available?
6. What financial resources would be needed? Where will these dollars come from?

(C) DOCUMENTATION

Critical to any organization's successful response to an exempt status challenge is the ability to provide both quantitative and qualitative information as to its charitable nature. It is not enough to simply say, "we serve poor people" or "we do good things for children." Everything an organization says about itself or its services must be proven.

The key aspect to this documentation is being able to meet the definition of a charity. Using the definition of *public charity* in Pennsylvania, the standards are as follows: (1) advances a charitable purpose; (2) donates or renders gratuitously a substantial portion of its services; (3) benefits a substantial and indefinite class of persons who are legitimate subjects of charity; (4) relieves government of some of its burden; and (5) operates entirely free from private profit motive. In attempting to meet the standards implied by this definition, some of the questions that must be answered include:

1. Who are our clients? Our constituency? How many do we serve?
2. Who uses our services? What are their ages and their incomes?
3. Who are our donors? How much money do they give us? How many donors?
4. Who are our volunteers? How much time do they give us? What is the dollar value of their time?
5. Are our services responsive to the needs of the community? How do we know this? What information can we provide to show that our organization is responsive to changing needs?
6. Who received which services? Who uses our various programs (for example, our community screenings, our educational programs, etc.)? What are their ages, race, income?
7. If fees are charged, how are levels of payment determined? Is anyone turned away for lack of resources?
8. What levels of subsidy are available? How many people are subsidized? Where do the subsidies come from?
9. What is our policy regarding "ability to pay"? How do we communicate these polices?
10. If local taxpayers are not the direct recipients of our services, how do they benefit?
11. How is local government relieved of a burden?
12. What does our budget say about us as an organization? How do we spend our money?
13. What kinds of financial practices are in place which result in the least amount of waste? How do we ensure efficient allocation of scarce resources?

(D) COMMUNICATION

Often there is a discrepancy between the community's perception of a nonprofit organization's fiscal health and its financial reality. Yet perception can be argued to be reality, in that what people believe to be true drives behavior and interactions. Therefore, effective communication between the nonprofit organization and its community is critical.

Questions to be considered include:

1. What messages do we, as an organization, communicate to the community?
2. Do our publications and advertising promote an image of inclusivity or exclusivity? How are we communicating, in written form, our charitable nature and mission?
3. Do we communicate issues of reduced fees, subsidies, scholarships? How would members of the community know of these policies?
4. If asked, would the community be able to express the benefits our presence offers? Would they agree that our organization deserves tax exemption? Would they agree that they are the direct or indirect recipients of our services and presence? How do we assess community perception?

(E) COLLABORATION

Research into the challenges to exempt status in Pennsylvania revealed a definite lack of collaboration among and between nonprofit organizations. This lack of collaboration is viewed as a weakness in potential responses to such challenges. There is tremendous power in the nonprofit sector; choosing to separate oneself from other nonprofit organizations because of some perceived uniqueness can be destructive to that power. This is not to argue that nonprofit organizations should create a single, unified response. Sharing of information and ideas and efforts to collaborate, however, can be positive for several reasons.

First, collaboration engenders a sense of community across diverse nonprofit organizations. Second, it empowers a group that could easily become fragmented and divisive. Third, it increases knowledge and experience of younger, smaller organizations. Fourth, it communicates to local units of government the strength that can be mustered should nonprofit organizations become united on issues. Fifth, it fosters creativity and innovation within the nonprofit sector. Finally, it creates a knowledge base about this issue. As mentioned before, much of what we know thus far about these challenges to property tax status is anecdotal. More good data is needed to create effective, responsible policy. The nonprofit sector should be proactive in the creation of this data, not reactive. Good information helps to ensure a position of power.

Questions to be considered include:

1. What issues unite us across fields of activity? Across dimensions of size and geography?
2. What do we as a sector gain through collaboration? What do we lose if we are divided?
3. In what kinds of activities, unrelated to tax exemption, might we collaborate?

4. How can we ensure the adoption of appropriate and effective legislation? What kinds of legislation will strengthen our position as nonprofit organizations?

5. Are there existing structures or organizations in which we can participate and join others on this issue?

(F)   CONCLUSIONS

Many nonprofit organizations will find the questions listed here difficult to answer. Some organizations may find that they are not currently in a position to answer them adequately. For these organizations, the process of self-examination and discussion becomes critical—not only as a means to improve existing services and operations but also as a means of preparation should exempt status be challenged. Yet any organization can benefit from this process of self-examination.

In considering how to respond to a property tax challenge, the most difficult part may be the removal of blinders and acknowledgment that, warranted or not, the status of your organization could be at risk. Many nonprofit executives are not interested in this issue until they are directly confronted with a tax bill. Chief executives are often surprised and dismayed by a challenge; they wonder how anyone could question their charitable status. Realizing that there are people and groups in your community who *do* question your charitable status can be a shock. For the smaller, more traditional charities, this may be especially true.

This hurdle must be overcome. Nonprofit organizations and their boards of directors must understand that, whether or not they are directly challenged, they will be affected. The manner in which all nonprofit organizations operate in the future will have to change as a result of these challenges.

To avoid the issue—to *not* plan a response—is the worst tactic an organization can choose. Through a process of discussion and education, planning, effective documentation, communication, and collaboration, a nonprofit organization can be well prepared for a challenge. It is these organizations that will be in a position of strength when questioned by a local unit of government. It is these organizations that will be successful in defending their exempt status.

30.8   Committing Ourselves to Ethical Practice

Nonprofit administrators serve multiple constituencies, from clients to funders to family members to elected officials to the community at large, and even to the staff themselves. Balancing the needs and demands of these various constituencies often presents unique challenges. Sometimes these needs exist in opposition to one another, raising issues of conflicting loyalties. In the following scenario, what would you do?

Many nonprofit organizations in your community have been challenged by the local school district (which is in desperate need of funds). You believe that your youth-serving organization is next on their hit list. Your board of directors is in full agreement that the organization should not only be prepared if challenged, but that the organization should fight as long as necessary to retain charitable status. They have instructed you to work closely with the agency's attorney to prepare appropriate documentation.

In reviewing your budgetary information, your attorney has raised a question about your "bad debt" budget line. You inform him that this line includes parents who miss or stop paying for the child care services they receive at the agency. He suggests that you rename the "bad debt" line in your budget to "charitable services/contributions." He believes that the ability to show on an annual budget sheet that the organization consistently provides "unfunded services" will really help in documenting that you are a charitable organization.

While you agree with the idea, this suggestion does not feel quite right. You, as the executive director, know that if parents miss too many payments, service is discontinued to the family. You also know that you work very hard to minimize the bad debt line and that this amount of money varies greatly from year to year. The attorney, however, thinks that "in this kind of war, you have to pull out all the stops." He believes you are being naive and has suggested (in a nice way, of course) that if you do not do as he suggests, he will make sure the board knows whose fault it is if the case is lost.

What do you do?

This scenario is based on a true story. How the executive director responded is not known. Clearly, she felt caught in a no-win situation.

Yet, in reality, several avenues were open to her. She obviously believed that the organization's charitable status was at risk because its revenue was so closely tied to client fees. One might, indeed, question the "charitableness" of an organization that discontinued needed services to low-income and at-risk families (who simply might need to take a break for a few months to pay other basic household expenses). Rather than blatant and intentional misrepresentation of agency activities, a better strategy would have been to locate funds to provide "free" services to such families. A better strategy would be to market and publicize this program so that the community was aware of its commitment to its families and how the agency stood with them through the bad times. A better strategy would be to plan to spend a portion of the annual budget on these needs, rather than calling such activities "bad debt" and attempting to minimize them. A better strategy would be to use such circumstances to ensure that the organization *deserved* its exempt privileges.

Obviously, an organization cannot provide free services to all its clients. But if part of your mission as a charitable institution is to "donate or render gratuitously a substantial portion of [your] services," and your services must "benefit a substantial and indefinite class of persons who are legitimate subjects of charity," then your organization had better be able to document such practices. Falsifying current practices in order to appear charitable is unethical (if not illegal). It is this kind of unethical practice which has contributed to the growing number of challenges to tax-exempt status. Administrators of nonprofit organizations are not only bound to professional standards of efficient and effective management practice, they are also bound to uphold the principles of community accountability and public trust. Anything less sacrifices the "other-serving" focus of charitable organizations and risks the loss of tax-exempt status.

Suggested Readings

Gallagher, Janne G. 1992. *Sales Tax Exemptions for Charitable, Educational and Religious Nonprofit Organizations* (Special Report from the Human Services Forum of the National Assembly and Independent Sector, Washington, DC, Sept.)

Leland, Pamela. Forthcoming. "The Extent of the Challenge to Property Tax Exemption in Pennsylvania: A Survey of 67 Counties." In Astrid Merget et al., ed., *Nonprofit Organizations as Public Actors*. San Francisco: Jossey-Bass.

Leland, Pamela. 1994. "Responding to a Property Tax Challenge: Lessons Learned in Pennsylvania." *State Tax Notes* (October 3): 927–940.

Salamon, Lester. 1992. *America's Nonprofit Sector: A Primer*. New York: The Foundation Center.

▼ Glossary

Abatement Generally, a diminution or decrease; in the nonprofit organization context, the relieving of a tax liability, for example the ability of the IRS to abate nearly all of the "excise taxes imposed upon private foundations."

Accessions Additions, both purchased and donated, to permanent collections held by museums, art galleries, historical societies, botanical gardens, libraries, and similar entities.

Account Individual record established for each category of asset, liability, fund balance, expense, or revenue.

Account Executive Individual within a professional organization assigned specific responsibility for service delivery to one or more clients.

Account Payable Debt or obligation due to suppliers or vendors for goods purchased or services rendered.

Account Receivable Money due to the organization from services rendered, donations or dues promised, grants awarded, loans made, or employee advances (not yet accounted for) due but not yet paid.

Accrual The accumulation and crediting of benefits to an employee by virtue of his or her participation in a compensation plan. Accrued benefits may be forfeited unless they are vested.

Accrual Method System of accounting for financial transactions according to when obligation to pay or receive actually occurs, rather than when cash is paid out or received (cash method). Preferred method for realistic reports.

Accrued Expense Obligation accumulating, not yet due and payable (such as rent due at end of year, salaries, property taxes, interest on mortgage), which is recorded currently (usually monthly) to assure accurate statement of debts.

Acknowledgment Answer, reply, or response expressing gratitude for a service or gift.

Acquisition Indebtedness Moneys borrowed to acquire or substantially improve a property, or before or after acquisition of property, debt that would not have been incurred "but for" acquisition.

Acquisition or Prospect Mailing Mailing to prospects designed to acquire new donors or members.

Act Bill passed by Congress or other legislative body.

Action Organization A 501(c)(3) organization whose purposes can only be accomplished through the passage of legislation.

Actuarial Equivalent Amount of equal present value. An amount to be received in the future is the actuarial equivalent of another if they have the same present value determined by using the same actuarial assumptions (such as rate of return and retirement age). See Present Value.

Actuary One who creates actuarial tables, including those used in the planned giving context in calculating income interests and remainder interests.

Ad Hoc "For this," referring to a specific purpose or situation. An ad hoc committee, for example, is a group created to accomplish a specific objective. When it is completed, the committee disbands.

Add-on Gift A gift in addition to a larger, main gift.

ADEA Age Discrimination in Employment Act, which prohibits discrimination in conditions or termination of employment because of age (protecting those over age 40). Mandatory retirement for employees eligible to receive pensions violates ADEA.

Advance Gifts Pledges or gifts confirmed in advance of a public announcement of a campaign.

Advance Ruling Tentative five-year IRS opinion issued in response to filing Form 1023 regarding charity organization's eligibility for tax exemption before operation has begun. Based upon information furnished, organization is "determined" to be a public charity.

Advisory Board (or Committee) (a) Group of leaders with specific expertise responsible for providing counsel and advice to public service organizations. Not normally invested with any specific legal authority. (b) Group of individuals, usually well-known, influential, or prominent, whose public support and endorsement supplies credibility.

Affirmative Action Process for assuring equal opportunity and nondiscrimination by an employer or program provider to ensure equal access to employment and program services.

Agency Exempt organization (EO) holding funds as custodian or fiscal agent for another exempt organization, such as the United Way.

AICPA American Institute of Certified Public Accountants.

Alphanumeric In printing, contraction of *alphabetic-numeric,* meaning a complete set of letters, numbers, numerals, punctuation marks, and related characters (e.g., period, plus sign, etc.); also called *alphameric.*

Anchor A synonym for *hyperlink.*

Annual Giving Fund-raising program which seeks repeatable gifts from donors throughout the year.

Annual Information Return IRS Form 990, return required to be filed by most "tax-exempt organizations" annually with the IRS.

Annual Report Yearly report, usually focused on financial or organizational conditions, compiled and published by the organization's leadership.

Annuity (a) Regular payment of a set amount of money for life or lives, or for a period of years, such as the annuity payable as the result of creation of a "charitable gift annuity" or a "charitable remainder trust." (b) Money or other property given to a philanthropic nonprofit organization on the condition that the organization contract to make periodic and fixed payments that terminate at a time specified by the donor or upon the death of the donor(s).

Annuity Trust See Charitable Remainder Annuity Trust.

Anonymous FTP Internet File Transfer Protocol tool which allows users to connect to a site, search available files, then download any file, document, or program without first establishing an account at that site.

ANSI The American National Standards Institute. A private sector, nonprofit coordinator and clearinghouse on national and international standards.

Application for Recognition of Exemption IRS Form 1023 or 1024, the form by which a "nonprofit organization" seeks recognition of tax-exempt status from the IRS.

Appreciation Market value increase of property over its original purchase price or tax basis; property the fair market value of which is greater than its cost basis.

Articles of Organization Also called Articles of Incorporation; the generic term for the document used to create a "nonprofit organization." Articles of incorporation in the case of a corporation; a constitution in the case of an unincorporated association; a trust agreement or declaration of trust in the case of a trust.

Asset Resource or measurable financial value owned by the organization—such as cash, investment securities, grants receivable, land, equipment, inventory, and collections.

Assignment Designation of specific responsibility for duties or actions in support of organizational objectives, including solicitation of prospective contributors (usually to volunteer).

Association An organization, usually nonprofit and tax-exempt, that has a membership of individuals and/or organizations.

Attributes Qualitative data capable of being counted for recording and analysis.

Audience (or Constituency) Persons selected to receive communications for a purpose.

Audience Composition Listing the people listening to a given program by categories such as age, sex, income, location, and so on; also called audience profile, percent composition, demographics, or profile.

Audiovisual Activities Organizations or functions responsible for the management of AV resources and for the provision of AV services and products. The term applies, but is not limited to, AV equipment, facilities, products, personnel, maintenance, supplies, acquisition, budget and other support functions when they support primary AV functions.

Audiovisual Production A unified presentation containing sound or visual imagery, or both, for conveying a message through a recorded medium or broadcast. The term may also apply to the process of combining or arranging any separate or combined audio or visual products in continuity, according to a plan or a script. A production is the end product of the production process.

Audit (a) Process whereby the IRS examines the records, files, and accounting documents of an organization, plus witnesses, to ensure compliance with internal revenue codes. (b) Examination of financial records by an independent CPA in accordance with procedures designed to ascertain the validity and accuracy of the financials and enable the CPA to render a formal opinion on the EO's status.

Audit Report CPA's report issued to express an opinion as to an organization's financial condition; can be unqualified, qualified, or disclaimed.

Audit Trail Link between original source documents or transactions and balances in accounting records and reports.

Authentication A security measure using the data encryption standard (DES), which verifies that the EDI transmission and message were not tampered with or altered.

Auxiliary Activity An activity providing a service that is not part of the basic program or services of the organization. A fee is normally not involved although a value may be calculated that is directly related to, although not necessarily equal to, the cost of the service.

Average Also called *mean*, the most commonly used term to express the centering of a distribution. Calculated by totaling the observed values and dividing by the number of observations.

Balance Sheet The financial statement, as of a particular date, of the EO's assets, liabilities, and fund balances.

Bar Code An electronic data collection technology using symbols to represent data.

Bargain Sale Property transaction to a "charitable" organization for less than its fair market value (FMV), thereby making the transaction part sale and part gift.

Bellwether Early gift in a campaign, which is intended to encourage other supporters to increase their levels of giving; a pace-setting gift.

Benchmarking See Competitive Benchmarking.

Benefactor A high-level contributor.

Beneficiary The person eligible for benefits or payments upon the death of a plan participant.

Benefit Charitable special event in which all proceeds beyond expenses are contributed to one or more causes or organizations.

Benefit Separation Separating a population into various groups based on the benefits they require or want, or the costs they wish to avoid.

Benevolent Synonym for "charitable." Broader in scope than "charitable" and not formally used in the federal tax law rules, although sometimes used in the context of state or local law.

Bequest Gift of personal property made through a will. Personal property donation received upon death pursuant to a will; real property is "devised."

Birthday Campaign A fund-raising effort focused on the anniversary date of an organization based on the rationale that the occasion will prompt special "birthday" contributions.

Bit Binary digit, the smallest component of information stored or transmitted by a computer business management system. Eight bits equal one byte.

Block Grant Financial assistance intended for a broad purpose—health, education, transportation—allowing implementing agencies considerable leeway in deciding how best to use the money. See Categorical Grant.

Board Development Process of defining the purpose and/or improving the effectiveness of the group of leaders charged with managing or advising a public service organization.

Board of Directors or Board of Trustees Two or more individuals serving as the governing body of an organization.

Bonus Lump-sum payment to an employee in recognition of some achievement. As a bonus is not added to the employee's base pay, some employers use this approach to limit compensation and taxation growth as well as to recognize achievement.

Boolean Logic System for searching and retrieving information from computers which uses and combines terms such as AND, OR, and NOT to help sort data.

BPS Bits per second, referring to the speed at which a particular modem can transmit data. To get an approximate idea of how many characters per second a modem is transmitting data, divide the BPS by 10.

Brainstorming Team decision-making tool; one of the easiest and most enjoyable approaches used to generate a variety of ideas without restricting their production or judging their merit during development.

Break in Service Year in which an employee is credited with no more than 500 hours of service. If an employee has such a break, he or she may lose credit for service before the break unless he or she returns to service and works another year. A qualified maternity or paternity leave may not be counted as a break in service but may be treated as a neutral year.

Bricks and Mortar Inclusive, slang term implying collectively all the physical plant needs of an organization, for example, the building. A bricks-and-mortar fund-raising campaign seeks contributions for the building as opposed to endowment, program, or operating funds.

Browser A World Wide Web client. An information retrieval tool.

Budget Financial plan of action for future periods.

Budget Authority Authority to enter into obligations which will result in immediate or future outlays involving federal funds. The basic form of budget authority is through appropriations. Budget authority may be classified by the period of availability (one-year, multiple-year, no-year).

Budget Surplus or Deficit The difference between budget receipts and outlays.

Budgeting Process of determining the allocation and expenditure of existing or potential financial resources of a specific period of time. The budget should be developed at the conclusion of the planning process where it represents the prioritized allocation of always limited financial resources to accomplish stated, quantifiable organizational objectives. The end product of the budgeting process serves as the primary guide for monitoring and controlling the financial activities of the organization.

Bulk Rate Mail Postage rates lower than First Class postage, including Second, Third, and Fourth Class postage.

Business Process A group of related activities that provide value to the customer.

Bylaws Organizational document containing its rules of operation.

Byte Eight bits, or the number of ones and zeros needed to express any alphanumeric character.

Cafeteria Plan Plan in which participants can choose from among two or more options consisting either of tax-qualified benefits or of a combination of cash and tax-qualified benefits.

Campaign Planned, carefully organized effort to raise funds for a nonprofit organization.

Campaign Costs Expenses essential to the planning and implementation of a campaign, or fund-raising effort, directly connected to budget projections.

Campaign Director Individual serving as the senior decision maker in a fund-raising campaign. Can be a member of a fund-raising firm or a professional staff member of the NPO. Also called *Campaign Manager*, *Resident Director*, or *Program Manager*.

Capital Additions Gifts, grants, bequests, investment income, and gains and losses on investments restricted either permanently or for a period of time by parties outside of the organization to endowment and loan funds. Capital additions also include similar resources restricted for fixed asset additions but only to the extent expended during the year.

Capital Asset Property held by an individual, not including inventory, depreciable property used in a business, certain literary or artistic compositions, and certain publications of the U.S. government.

Capital Campaign A fund-raising program designed and implemented to generate contributions to a charitable organization. Usually conducted for major projects or programs, such as a building, major item of equipment, or endowment fund. A fund-raising campaign focused on donations for capital as opposed to annual income.

Capital Expenditures Funds intended to be used to buy, build, improve, or rehabilitate physical facilities or equipment.

Capital Giving Programs   Programs which solicit larger gifts, usually in several installments over a period of three to five years, that are used to improve the asset position of a nonprofit organization. Capital gifts are usually restricted by use to the specific capital need identified when the solicitation occurs.

Capital Grant   Financial assistance intended for the purchase, construction, improvement or rehabilitation of physical facilities or equipment.

Case Statement   Document or text block setting out in detail the reasons an NPO needs or deserves financial support. Case statements usually document the organization's resources, services, present and future needs, and future plans.

Cash Contributions   Grantee's portion of project or program funds required by the grantor agency or organization. See In-Kind Contributions.

Catchment Area   The area from which the majority of an organization's customers are obtained.

Categorical Grant   Funds provided for a relatively well-defined "category" of activity in a particular programmatic area (e.g., drug abuse). Each categorical program usually contains a detailed set of regulations specifying the type of project or program, the recipients, and other stipulations on how the money can be used.

Cause-related Marketing   (a) Fund-raising approaches and techniques used to generate nongift revenues, involving "related" and/or "unrelated" activities. Term includes "charitable sales promotions" and other forms of "commercial coventures." (b) Cooperative arrangements between a company and another organization (e.g., nonprofit) in which the company promotes both its own product or service and the NPO "cause," often tying corporate donations to sales of the product or service.

CBO   (a) Congressional Budget Office. (b) Community-Based Organization.

CERN   The European Laboratory for Particle Physics. The originators of the HTTP and HTML concepts.

Certified Association Executive (CAE)   Credential granted by the American Society of Association Executives (ASAE).

Certified Fund-Raising Executive (CFRE)   Credential granted by the National Society of Fund Raising Executives to individuals based on an individual's tenure as a fund raiser (minimum of five years), education, service to the profession, performance as a fund raiser, and knowledge of the fund-raising field.

Certified Public Accountant   Licensed by one or more states to engage in the public practice of examining the financial affairs of entities and issuing opinions thereon.

CFC   Combined Federal Campaign.

Chairman/Chairperson of the Board   Individual selected (usually by the Board of Directors or Trustees) to serve as the leader of the board. Can be an "officer" position if so provided for in the Articles of Organization and/or Bylaws.

Challenge Gift   A substantial gift conditioned on other gifts (e.g., at a certain level or within a specified time), designed to stimulate additional fund-raising activity.

Charitable   A purpose, activity, or organization meeting applicable federal tax law requirements as having "charitable" objectives.

Charitable Contribution   A voluntary transfer or gift of money, property, or other assets of value to a nonprofit organization meeting qualifications established by the Internal Revenue Service which can be deducted by an individual or a corporation for income tax purposes. Transfers made with a reasonable expectation of financial return commensurate with the amount of the transfer are usually considered invalid as charitable contributions.

Charitable Contribution Deduction   A deduction allowed under applicable federal, state, or local laws for an amount of property or money transferred to a charitable organization.

Charitable Donation   Gift to a charitable organization qualifying for federal income tax deduction under IRC Section 170.

Charitable Gift Annuity   Revenue-generating approach for NPOs in which a donor transfers property or funds to a charitable organization in exchange for its agreeing to pay back a fixed amount annually to the donor (and/or survivor) for life. The approach is part charitable gift and part annuity.

Charitable Lead Trust   A trust used to facilitate the contribution of a "lead interest" or "income interest" to a charitable organization.

Charitable Organization   Organization created and operated for what the applicable law (federal tax law) regards as a charitable purpose. Nonprofit organization dedicated to and operating to pursue "charitable" purposes, as defined in IRC Section 170.

Charitable Remainder Annuity Trust   Financial assets irrevocably transferred to a trustee who pays the donor (or survivor) a predetermined amount at a minimum of 5 percent of the fair market value of the trust assets at the date the assets are transferred. Upon the death of the beneficiary (or survivor beneficiary, if specified), the charitable organization receives the remainder.

Charitable Remainder Unitrust   Money or securities or both, irrevocably transferred by agreement to a trustee (in many cases the charitable organization itself), who pays the donor (or survivor) income for life. Then, the remaining assets become the property of the specified charitable organization. The amount of annual payment to income beneficiary is dependent on the annually determined value of the trust's assets. See also Charitable Remainder Annuity Trust.

Charitable Sales Promotion   Essentially the same as a Commercial Coventure. See Cause-related Marketing.

Charitable Solicitation Acts   State laws regulating the process of soliciting contributions for charitable purposes.

Chart   Display of measurement data. Results are used to initiate corrective action.

Class Advocacy   Advocacy pertaining to an entire class of persons, often seen within a social movement whose goals include changing social service delivery systems and attitudes. Also called *cause, collective, corporate,* or *generic advocacy.*

Client   The software that allows users the ability to retrieve information from the Internet and World Wide Web. NCSA Mosaic is an example of client software.

Cliff Vesting   Schedule for vesting in which accrued benefits become nonforfeitable after a specified period of service, such as five years.

CODA   Cash Or Deferred (tax) Arrangement, as a 401(k) plan.

Coinsurance   Payment by employee for part of the benefit being provided. A common approach is for a health insurer to pay 80 percent of a health service while the employee pays the remaining 20 percent.

Cold List   A list, usually a direct mail list, that has not been previously tested for pull or currency.

Collection   Works of art, books, memorabilia, botanical or animal specimens, or similar items used for educational display or study.

Collections   Program used to obtain (usually small) sums from many people who are not particularly close to or aware of the specific organization. Employs such methods as setting out canisters at retail sales counters, "passing the hat," and house-to-house solicitation.

Commercial Activity conducted by a nonprofit organization in ways similar to those in which for-profit organizations conduct the same activity. The only federal law statutory limitations of this to date are the rules concerning "commercial type" insurance.

Commercial Coventure Arrangement between a for-profit organization and one or more charitable organizations, in which the for-profit entity agrees to make a contribution to the charitable entity, with the amount of the contribution determined by the volume of sales of products of services by the for-profit organization during a designated time period or a specified amount agreed to in advance. See Cause-related Marketing.

Commerciality The developing doctrine where an activity that is conducted in a "commercial" manner is deemed, for that reason alone, to be a nonexempt activity.

Commitment to Quality Value and process of assigning quality the major focus of all activity and effort in an organization. The continuous improvement of quality as perceived by customers in every aspect of the organization's business or services. It recognizes that everyone has a responsibility for quality, and to create an organizational environmental in which continuous improvement is "the way of doing business."

Common Barriers Any systemic impediments to routine continuous improvement activities.

Common Cause(s) of Variation Source of variation always present—part of the random variation intrinsic to the process itself. Origin can almost always be traced to a component of the system under the control of management.

Communication Mix Combination and apportionment of communication elements (e.g., public relations, publicity, advertising) used by an organization to convey its messages to the target market(s).

Communications Software A software program that controls computer hardware and modems and arranges for the transmission or reception of electronic data.

Community Relations Initiation and maintenance of communications and interaction with both the community at large and with specific constituencies toward effective relationships of benefit to the organization.

Competing Extension Grant Financial assistance to support a program or project beyond the funded period, based on successful competition against other projects. See Grant.

Competitive Benchmarking Systematic way of measuring the performance capabilities of other organizations and competitors; then developing plans to meet or exceed the levels or areas of competition.

Comprehensive Community Development Plan Detailed statement identifying current community conditions, needs, and major problems in a specific jurisdiction, including a comprehensive strategy for meeting needs and solving problems.

Concentrated Marketing Strategy Process of focusing efforts and resources on one target group, designing a marketing strategy specifically to reach that group.

Connect Time Period during which a user is signed onto an on-line service, bulletin board system, host computer, or Internet service provider.

Conservatorship Process of naming an individual to be responsible for an impaired person's property and/or the administration of his or her estate.

Consideration   An element of value in a financial transaction; something exchanged to receive something in return; both parties to a "contract" receive consideration.

Constancy of Purpose   Relentless pursuit of a clear objective; attitudes and behaviors demonstrating perseverance in spite of many impediments to reach a goal or objective. CoP establishes the common direction for all organization components, ensuring that all efforts contribute to achieving broad objectives which are relevant to the entire organization.

Constitution   See Articles of Organization.

Consultant   Someone providing services to an organization (usually for a fee) in a capacity other than that of "employee," such as a fund-raising consultant, training consultant, accountant, attorney; an independent contractor.

Consumer   Individual or organization who may use and/or benefit from technical assistance or other direct services rendered by an organization.

Continuous Replenishment   A business process wherein the supplier manages inventory levels at the customer using resale or consumption information transmitted electronically from the customer on a frequent basis.

Continuous Improvement Process (CIP)   Quality management which focuses on steadily improving quality through finding and correcting root sources of defects; improving all of the processes that determine the quality of the product. It means the continuous improvement of every requirement process, every design process, every development process, every manufacturing process, every quality assurance process, and paperwork and administrative processes.

Contract   (a) Group of promises or understandings between two or more persons or entities that creates, revises, or eliminates a legal relationship; a set of promises underlain by consideration. (b) A government agreement for services or work provided for agreed-upon conditions and payments.

Contribution   Transfer of money or property without expectation of material return. Gift of money or other property for which giver receives nothing in return; also called transfer without consideration, or donation.

Contribution Base   Amount equal to what is, in essence, an individual's adjusted gross income, used to compute the extent to which charitable contributions are deductible in a year.

Contributory Plan   One to which contributions are made in part or whole by participants rather than (or in addition to) their employer.

Control Charts   Charts using different forms of presentation—histograms, scatter diagrams, and so on—to illustrate processes and to reveal underlying patterns and relationships between variables. Used to track sources of variation which can then be more easily controlled or removed. See Graphic Tools.

Control Limit   Comparison line(s) or limits on a control chart (see Graphic Tools), used to judge the significance of variation in various subgroups. When variation exceeds a control limit, this is evidence that a special cause (see) may be affecting the process.

Coordination of Benefits   Procedure whereby two insurance companies share information to limit their individual liability for expenses. This may arise when spouses have insurance from different employers or when someone is covered by both Medicare and an employer-provided policy.

Core Technological Capability   The combination of an organization's information technology infrastructure and the knowledge and expertise of its people in using that technology to better manage their areas of responsibility.

Corporate Foundation   Nonprofit organization whose funds are provided by a profit-making corporation and whose primary activity is the making of grants. Usually very explicit regarding fields of interest, that is, to which support or funds will be provided.

Cost of Conformance   In general, the money spent to make sure that customer requirements are being met. It includes money spent on both prevention (prevent mistakes before they happen) and inspection appraisal (find the mistakes before delivery).

Cost of Lost Opportunity   Profit impact of lost revenues (for support in the case of nonprofit organizations) resulting from failure to meet customer requirements. If a company or organization loses business or support because of reputation for poor quality, it is losing revenue.

Cost of Nonconformance   In general, the money spent to fix products and services that don't meet customer requirements. This includes money spent when requirements are exceeded.

Cost of Quality   The "price of nonconformance," plus the "price of conformance". What an organization, division, or department is spending for overall quality. This term includes: cost of conformance, cost of nonconformance, and lost opportunity. Most estimates put the cost of quality at 15–20 percent of revenue for the average American company.

Coverage Test   Requirement that a plan benefit a minimum number or percentage of employees, with the aim of avoiding discrimination in favor of highly compensated employees.

Critical Mass   (a) A sufficient number of influential, powerful, knowledgeable leaders within an organization supporting a proposed change providing the impression of a growing, powerful movement carrying with a sense of momentum, a groundswell of interest and potency. (b) That point at which the primary means for moving information through a business process is electronic and human intervention is needed only for exceptions.

Critical Mass Marketing   The education of and marketing to both internal staff and trading partners as to the benefits to them of managing a business process electronically.

Cross-sectional Data or Study   Research data obtained from an entire population (or a representative sample) at a single point in time.

Current Services Estimates   Estimated budget authority and outlays for the upcoming fiscal year based on continuation of existing levels of service without policy changes. These estimates of budget authority and outlays, accompanied by the underlying economic and programmatic assumptions upon which they are based, are transmitted by the President to Congress when the budget is submitted.

Custodian Funds   Funds received and held by an organization as fiscal agent for others.

Customer   Individual or group that receives the output produced by the supplier. Customer may be either internal (within the company or organization) or external. The customer who is "next in line" and gets the output first is usually identified as the primary customer. Others who also get the output are sometimes referred to as secondary customers. The last customer in a chain of outputs is usually referred to as the end user. The direct benefactors of work output.

Customer Expectations   Features of services or products, performance, or functions identified by customers as needed, required, or desired. Customer expectations provide the basis for optimizing the design, nature, and attributes of a service or product. Customer expectations are measured in many ways, including: research and surveys, focus groups, audits, employee exchanges, joint problem solving, and customer service data analysis.

Customer Focus   Process of deliberate concentration on satisfying the needs and expectations of both internal and external customers as the foundation of all activity and improvements. Objectives include: increasing quality as defined by the customer; improving customer satisfaction; assuring customer feedback and input; and providing meaningful indicators of performance and improvement.

Customer Service   All supplementary services provided by an organization or group to meet customer needs (satisfy) and to counter competitors.

Customers   The direct benefactors of work output.

Data Element   The smallest meaningful piece of information in a business transaction. The data element may condense lengthy descriptive information into a short code. Equivalent to a "field" in a paper document or database, a series of data elements is used to build a data segment.

Deaccessions   Dispositions of items in collections held by museums, art galleries, botanical gardens, libraries, and similar organizations.

Declaration of Trust   Proclamation by a person of the existence of a trust; see Articles of Organization; compare Trust Agreement.

Declaratory Judgment   Declaration by the U.S. Tax Court, the U.S. Claims Court, or the U.S. District Court for the District of Columbia as to whether an organization is tax exempt as described in IRC SS 501(c)(3), a "charitable" organization (IRC SS 170(c)(2)), a "private foundation" or "public charity" (IRC SS 509), or a "private operating foundation" (IRC SS 4942(j)(3)) (IRC SS 7428).

Deductible   Expense amount that an employee must pay before other sources (insurance company or employer) assume liability for payment. Deductibles are seen as cost-saving measures by employers and insurance companies.

Deduction   An item (usually an expenditure) that is subtracted from adjusted gross income to arrive at taxable income, such as the "charitable contribution deduction."

Deeming   Process of determining the financial eligibility of an applicant for programmatic assistance through evaluation of income(s) and assets.

Deferred Capital Additions   Capital additions received or recorded before the related restrictions are met. See Capital Additions.

Deferred Compensation Plan   Program whereby employees of an organization are compensated for services rendered currently but the receipt of the compensation is deferred until a subsequent point in time (such as retirement).

Deferred Expenses   Expenditures paid ahead of time to be written off as an expense of current activities; also called *prepaid expense* and reported in the asset section of the balance sheet.

Deferred Giving Program   Program seeking funds which will come to the nonprofit organization after the death of the donor, such as a bequest or trust.

Deferred Revenue   Revenue booked as a liability because it has been received but is dedicated to future project(s).

Deferred Revenue and Support   Revenue or support received or recorded before it is earned, that is, before the conditions are met, in whole or in part, for which the revenue or support is received or is to be received.

Defined Benefit Plan   Pension plan that pays a specified benefit at retirement, often keyed to average salary over the last few years of employment and to years of service. Contributions to the plan vary according to the amount needed to provide the projected benefit. In this instance, the employer bears the risk, as he or she must set aside enough now to make the payments later.

Defined Contribution Plan Pension or profit-sharing plan to which the contributions are specified amounts and the participants have a right to receive benefits contingent on the accumulated value of the total contributions. In other words, the benefits may vary according to the investment expertise of the plan's trustee; the employee, therefore, bears the risk in this case.

Delivery System Combined and coordinated collective entity of services provided for clients.

Deming, Dr. W. Edwards Early quality guru—the first to introduce quality technology to Japan after World War II. The Deming Prize, for excellence in the application of statistical quality control, is named in his honor.

Deming Wheel See Plan-Do-Check-Act Cycle.

Demographic Segmentation Distinguishing or categorizing people based on demographic variables, such as income, age, sex, and religion.

Demonstration Project Activity or program designed and funded to demonstrate or determine the feasibility of new methods or approaches.

Denial Refusing to deliver services or program benefits to applications based on a determination of eligibility. Denial decisions are sometimes followed by a formal appeals process.

Dependent *Care assistance program plan* whereby the employer helps employees with services for dependents which the employee needs in order to earn a living. The employer may provide the needed services, pay the service provider directly, or reimburse the employee for the expenses incurred. If the employer gives the money to the employee, the funds are treated as regular compensation and the employee seeks tax relief under Internal Revenue Code Section 21 dependent care tax credit. If the employer provides or subsidizes the benefit, up to $5,000 per year may be excluded from gross income ($2,500 each for married individuals filing separately).

Depreciation Portion by which the cost of permanent assets, such as buildings or vehicles, declines (due to deterioration or obsolescence) over the accounting periods expected to benefit from its use; recorded as operational cost.

Depreciation Reserve Cumulative sum of depreciation written off (expensed) during the period assets are owned.

Designated Funds (a) Unrestricted monies set aside by the board of directors or trustees for specific purposes. (b) Funds set aside for specific purposes by action of the governing board. See Quasi-Endowment Funds.

Determination Letter Letter from the IRS "recognizing" the tax-exempt status of a "nonprofit organization." Opinion of the IRS concerning EO's tax exempt status. Primary evidence furnished to anyone seeking proof of organization's qualification.

Development Program A comprehensive program to manage several fund-raising activities, volunteer efforts, donor relations, and more that cultivates, solicits, and acknowledges charitable contributions.

Devise Gift of real property by means of a will.

Differentiated Marketing Strategy Developing different services or products and/or marketing or communications programs for each market segment the organization has elected to serve.

GLOSSARY

Direct Compensation Pay received in the form of cash or cash equivalents (generally, wages and salaries).

Direct Cost Expense specifically associated with and identifiable by program, project, or activity.

Direct Lobbying An attempt to influence the development of legislation by contact with legislators, their staffs, or staffs of legislative committees, such as by meetings, correspondence, and/or testimony at hearings (cf. Grass-roots Lobbying).

Direct Mail Package Components of a sales or solicitation program using the mails, including: mailing envelope, solicitation letter, brochure, response form, and business reply envelope.

Discrimination Favoring of highly compensated employees, owners, or officers by the operation or terms of a plan.

Disqualified Person Someone with a specified relationship to a plan, such as the fiduciary, the employer, and officers, directors, and highly compensated employees.

Distribution Universe or population from which observations are made, categorized, and formed into patterns. Based on the fact that anything measured repeatedly will achieve different results falling into statistically predictable patterns. The bell-shaped curve, for example, is an example of observations clustered in the center with fewer observations falling evenly on either side of the average.

Domain Name Unique name of a collection of computers connected to a network, such as the Internet. Domain names on the Internet typically end with a suffix indicating the type of site; for example, "com" indicates a commercial company, "edu" an educational institution, and "gov" stands for government.

Donor Acquisition Fund-raising program in which the emphasis is on the acquisition of new donors to a charitable organization; also known as "prospecting." See Donor Renewal.

Donor Renewal (a) Second phase of the direct mail solicitation, in which the objective is to ask prior donors to give again. (b) Fund-raising program in which the emphasis is on acquiring "contributions" from those who have previously given (the donor base) to a "charitable" organization.

Donor Upgrading Third phase of direct mail solicitation, in which the objective is to suggest an increase in the size of the donor's prior gift.

DP Disqualified person, as defined in IRC Section 4946.

Due Process Requirement that the government or other administrative agency act in a fair, nondiscriminatory manner, usually including the establishment of a hearing process, in which the individual or affected parties are given the opportunity to present evidence, cross-examine, and be represented by counsel.

Dues Amounts of money paid to join an organization and to receive membership services; where these services are "consideration" and the organization is a charitable one, the dues are not deductible as charitable contributions.

Earmarking Phraseology in a bill or other document accompanying a bill establishing a maximum or minimum level of funding for a specific purpose.

EDI Management Software Software that translates business data between internal formats and standard formats (such as ANSI X12 and UN/EDIFACT).

Educational Assistance Program Plan whereby an employer provides instruction for or pays educational expenses of an employee. The plan must be written and must not discriminate in favor of officers, owners, highly compensated employees, or their dependents.

Electioneering Process of intervening or otherwise participating in the campaign for or against the election of a candidate for public office.

Elective Rule In the context of "lobbying" activities by "public charities," the rule that enables qualifying "charitable" organizations to elect to come under certain standards for more mechanically determining allowable "lobbying" (IRC SS 501(h)).

Electronic Commerce Using electronic information technologies to improve business relationships between trading partners.

Electronic Data Interchange (EDI) The automated, electronic flow of business information between organizations without human intervention. This information is integrated with and flows into and out of the organizations' respective business management systems.

Electronic Funds Transfer The electronic transfer of funds and related payment information between banks or other financial institutions.

Electronic Mail (E-Mail) The movement of one or more electronic objects from a source to a target. Either source or target may be a person or a business management system.

Employee One who performs services for compensation and whose working conditions are set by the employer. Everyone who works for an organization, including owners and partners, full-time and part-time employees.

Employee Involvement Process through which people exercise increased control over their work to improve the effectiveness of their organizations. Teamwork involves leaders, managers, supervisors, and employees in improving product and service delivery, solving systemic problems, and correcting errors in all parts of work processes.

Encumbrance Binding contractual obligation committing the EO to purchase or acquire goods or services. Commitments in the form of orders, contracts, and similar items that will become payable when goods are delivered or services rendered.

End User Ultimate customer for an output. The end user for most organizational products is the external customer.

Endowment Accumulation of contributions not expended for program upon receipt, but instead held for investment, with the earnings available for program activities, either generally or as restricted by the donor. Legal restriction requiring that the principal sum donated be kept intact, with only its income being expended.

Entry Date Date on which an employee must be allowed to participate in a plan. The Internal Revenue Code requires that a tax-qualified plan admit an employee who has satisfied the age and length-of-service requirements no later than the earlier of these dates: (1) the first day of the first plan year beginning after the date on which the employee first satisfied the requirements; or (2) the date six months after the date on which the employee satisfied the requirements.

EO Exempt organization. A corporation, trust, or association qualifying for exemption from federal income tax and most state and local taxes.

ERISA Employee Retirement Income Security Act of 1974 (PL 93-403), the law that established the basic requirements for pension and welfare plans and allows uniform access to the federal court system for enforcement. ERISA covers pension and welfare plans, both of which must comply with provisions concerning reporting and disclosure, fiduciary responsibility, and enforcement. The former are also subject to detailed regulations concerning coverage, funding, and vesting. ERISA does not cover federal or state governmental plans for covering public workers, unemployment insurance, workers compensation, church plans, excess benefit plans, or plans maintained outside the United States.

ERISA Preemption   Explicit preemption by ERISA (in Section 514) of state laws concerning employee benefit plans, except those laws regulating insurance, banking, and securities.

Error Cause Removal   The system that identifies opportunities for removing or preventing error and hassle.

ESG   Executive Steering Group.

Estate   The property of an individual owned by him or her at death; federal tax law defines a "taxable estate" (IRC §§ 2051–2057).

Evaluation   Monitoring or assessing the extent to which a program or organization has met its goals and objectives.

Excess Benefit Plan   One that provides benefits beyond those in a tax-qualified plan and therefore is not covered by ERISA.

Excise Tax   In the "tax-exempt organizations" context, the sanctions sometimes used to enforce tax law prohibitions, for example, the "private foundation" rules and the "elective rule" in the "charitable" organizations "lobbying" field. Penalty taxes assessed for performance of prohibited acts by private foundations and public charities electing to lobby; found in IRC Sections 4940 through 4955.

Exclusion   In the tax context, an item of income that is excluded from the concept of "gross income," such as a scholarship (IRC SS I 1 7).

Exclusively   A charitable EO must be organized and operated exclusively for such purposes, but the presence of limited noncharitable activity is allowed. Thus, in this context the term means not solely but primarily.

Executive Committee   A subgroup of directors of an organization that has particular influence over the affairs of the organization, often empowered to act for the board of directors/trustees in the interim between regular meetings of the full board.

Executive Director   An employee of an organization who is assigned the principal responsibility for administering the organization; sometimes termed "*president*" or "*executive vice president*"; this may be an "*officer*" position.

Executive Order 12637   Established a governmentwide program to improve the quality, timeliness, and efficiency of services provided by the federal government. Issued by President Reagan in 1988.

Executive Perquisites (or Perks)   Special benefits made available to top managerial employees. These are becoming more and more likely to represent taxable income to the employee receiving them.

Executive Steering Group (ESG)   QM is being implemented in many organizations using a structure which includes the establishment of an Executive Steering Group (ESG) and a series of management- and functional-level Quality Management Boards (QMBs). The ESG creates a forum to bring together the users, the suppliers, and the policy makers to address and solve organizationwide problems.

Exempt Function Assets   Property or resources used by the EO in its projects and operations.

Exempt Function Revenue   Funds derived by a tax-exempt organization from the performance of an exempt function, such as revenue as tuition for education, ticket sales, or patient care.

Exempt PF   Private foundation eligible for special benefits because it is controlled by a public board and publicly supported.

Expendable Funds   Funds that are available to finance an organization's program and supporting services, including both unrestricted and restricted amounts. That portion of fund balances not already spent on fixed assets and available for use in satisfying obligations (except for endowment, pooled income, or permanently restricted funds).

Expenditure   Actual spending of money as distinguished from its appropriation. Money is appropriated by a legislative body; expenditures are disbursed by an executive branch of government. See Appropriation.

External Advocacy   Advocacy practiced by people employed outside and independent of a service delivery system.

Facilities Management   Directing and overseeing the legal, housekeeping, maintenance, and structural aspects of a building or other real estate; may also include architectural assistance, space utilization, or security.

Fair Hearing   Process in which an individual presents a complaint or appeals a decision (especially a decision to deny, suspend, or terminate benefits to which the individual believes she or he is entitled) which conforms to the due process and equal protection requirements of the Constitution with regard to:

- Right to adequacy of notices.
- Right to counsel or other representation.
- Right to hearing before an impartial hearing officer, body, or judge.
- Right to present evidence, subpoena witnesses, cross-examine witnesses, and have access to and use of records and documents.

FAQ   A file that contains Frequently Asked Questions and answers.

Federal Insurance Contributions Act (FICA)   Source of Social Security withholding requirements.

Feeder   Nonexempt trade or business operated for the benefit of an EO (IRC Section 502). An organization, not tax-exempt, that distributes all of its net income to a tax-exempt organization (IRC SS 502).

Fiduciary   One who is bound to look after the affairs of another using the same standards of care and prudence as he or she would use in attending to his or her own affairs, as in a trustee of a trust.

File Compression   Condenses computer data so that less is needed to represent the same information, thereby taking up less disk or file space, and transmitted in less time.

File Server   File-storage device on a local area network accessible to all users on the network.

Filer Commission   President's Commission on Private Philanthropy and Public Needs, chaired by John Filer of the Aetna Corporation in the mid-Seventies.

Financial Planning   Systematic process of assessing and matching an organization's monetary needs and actual or potential monetary resources.

Financial Statements   Basic financials for an EO are: (1) balance sheet (shows assets, liabilities, funds); (2) statement of activity (reports revenues, expenses, and changes in fund balances); (3) statement of cash flows (from operations, investing, and financing activities); (4) statement of functional revenues and expenses; and (5) notes and opinion (if issued by CPA).

Firewalls Special computers or programs that are installed on a network to prevent intruders from having access to protected data.

First-Tier Taxes See Initial Tax.

Fiscal Year The yearly accounting period, which begins October 1, and ends on the following September 30. The fiscal year is designated by the calendar year in which it ends, for example, FY 98 starts on October 1, 1997.

Fishbone Diagram Cause-and-effect diagram. See Graphic Tools.

Fixed Assets Assets acquired for permanent, long-term use, such as buildings or land (not used to pay for current operations or debts).

FMV Fair market value, or the price a willing buyer would pay a willing seller if neither is required to buy or sell and both have reasonable knowledge of all the necessary facts.

Focus-Group Interviews Method of obtaining qualitative information using a discussion with a small group broadly representative of the target market.

Focus on the Process Quality must be managed in, not inspected in. QM requires preventing defects through process improvement rather than discovering them through product inspection. Each process in an organization must be continuously improved to reduce variation, to conform to requirements, and to reduce waste, scrap, rework, and unnecessary resource expenditures.

Follow Along Regular communications with clients, their families, or service recipients, monitoring service(s) and progress. Also called *follow-up*.

Forfeiture Loss of benefits caused by leaving employment before all accrued benefits have been vested.

Forward Averaging Procedure of computing tax on a lump-sum distribution whereby the tax is determined as if the money were received over a period of years. This application of IRC Section 402(e) avoids combining the total distribution with the taxpayer's other income for a tax year, thereby lowering the overall effective tax rate.

Foundation See Private Foundation.

401(k) Plan See CODA; a profit-sharing or stock bonus plan wherein an employee may choose to be paid in cash or through having the funds placed in a trust under the plan. The 1986 Tax Reform Act said that tax-exempt organizations, as well as state and local governments, could no longer establish such plans, although any in existence before July 1986 could be continued. Can be offered again by private tax-exempts after Dec. 31, 1996.

403(b) Plan Tax-deferred annuity plan for retirement for employees of tax-exempt 501(c)(3) organizations. The same nondiscrimination rules apply here as to Section 401(a) plans, including minimum participation rules. In addition, a 403(b) plan can be considered discriminatory in terms of elective deferrals unless all employees have an opportunity to make the deferrals. (These deferrals are amounts shielded from current taxation through a salary reduction agreement.) An employee's annual deferral is generally limited to $9,500 (with some possible additions).

FTP File Transfer Protocol, a method of transferring files to and from remote computers.

Functional Accounting Departmental, category of service, or project classification for income and expense items, with financial reports reflecting revenues/costs by such classes of activity.

Functional Classification Classification of expenses that accumulates expenses according to the purpose for which costs are incurred. The primary functional classifications are program and supporting services.

Functional Group   A grouping of related transaction sets belonging to the same class. (For example, in a "PO" functional group there can be only purchase orders, purchase order acknowledgments, etc.)

Functional Reporting   Allocating expenses (and sometimes income) to various aspects of programs; as opposed to *natural expenses reporting.*

Fund   An accounting entity established to account for resources used for specific activities or objectives in accordance with special regulations, restrictions, or limitations.

Fund Accounting   Nonprofit accounting method that groups assets and liabilities by purpose to which they are dedicated. Fund balances are the equivalent of stockholders' equity, retained earnings, or capital accounts of a for-profit entity.

Fund Balance   Net worth, or what would be left if all assets were sold and debts paid; comparable to stockholders' or owners' equity.

Fund Group   Group of funds of similar character. For example, operating funds, endowment funds, and annuity and life income funds.

Fund Raiser   One who is employed (see Employee) or retained (see Consultant) to assist a nonprofit organization (usually a "charitable" one) in the raising of funds, conventionally in the form of "contributions" and "grants." May also be hired as a *"professional fund raiser"* or *"professional fund-raising counsel."*

Fund Raising   Process of soliciting private contributions from individuals, corporations, and foundations using written and/or verbal presentations; solicitation which culminates in securing financial resources for a nonprofit organization.

Fund-raising Expenses   Costs incurred as a direct result of generating contributions revenue for programs and activities of nonprofit organizations.

Fund Types

Endowment funds = subject to endowment restrictions.
Fixed assets fund = net amount of fixed assets (also called land, building, and equipment fund).
Restricted funds = received/held for particular project.
Custodial funds = held subject to instructions of donor.
Loan funds = held to make loans for exempt purposes.
Designated fund = earmarked by board for special purpose.
Unrestricted funds = assets available for any purpose.

Funding Ceiling   Upper limit of funding appropriation for a program.

Funds Held in Trust by Others   Resources held and administered, at the direction of the donor, by an outside trustee for the benefit of the organization.

GAAP   Generally accepted accounting principles, promulgated by the Accounting Standards Board of the AICPA.

General Partnership   Partnership where all of the partners are equally liable for satisfaction of the obligations of the partnership.

GIF   Graphics Interchange Format, an image file format.

Gopher   A text-based distributed information system developed at the University of Minnesota. Menu-driven, search-and-retrieve tool providing access to databases, text files, and other resources on the Internet.

Graded Vesting   Schedule whereby an increasing percentage of accrued benefits becomes vested, until 100 percent is reached.

Grant   (a) Financial assistance to enable implementation of a project or program based on an approved program, proposal, and budget. (b) Gift or donation received for either a restricted or unrestricted purpose.

Graphic Tools

- Flow Chart: A "picture of a process," diagram that displays the steps and activities in a process or system and how they interact. Used to promote understanding; to compare "actual" process with "ideal" process; to identify where measurements can be taken; and to differentiate between value-added steps and cost-added steps.
- Cause-and-Effect Diagram: A method for analyzing process dispersion whose purpose is to relate causes and effects. Known as the *Ishikawa Diagram* and the *fishbone diagram* (because the finished diagram resembles a fish skeleton), it is used to organize possible causes of variation, to identify categories and subcategories of "causes," to provide guidance for data collection, and to identify relationship of "positive" or "negative" effects.
- Pareto Chart: A vertical graph of categories in descending order of frequency. Used to provide a basis for selecting which "problem" to focus on initially, to prioritize, to indicate results of improvement efforts (baseline versus results of changes), to reduce data into meaningful information, and to provide clear employee feedback.
- Histogram: A bar graph showing distribution of data over a range of values. Used to simplify large data sets, to display amount of variation, to compare results with specifications, and to indicate the shape of a distribution.
- Scatter Diagram: A display of the relationship between two variables that have been collected in pairs. Used to indicate how changes in one variable are related to changes in another variable.
- Run Chart: A line graph that shows a variable plotted over time. Used to identify patterns of performance, trends, to show changes in process, and to compare different groups of data.
- Control Chart: A run chart with the addition of a center line and control limits; graphic representation of a process characteristic, consisting of plotted values of a selected statistic collected from that characteristic, plus one or two control limits. Basic uses include: determining if a process is in control; as an aid to achieving and maintaining statistical control, for example, when to adjust a process and when to leave it alone; or when a process is good enough that we should focus our improvement efforts and resources on more pressing needs.

Grass-roots Lobbying   An attempt to influence the legislative process by contacting the general public, or a segment of it, for the purpose of encouraging those individuals to contact the appropriate legislators; compare Direct Lobbying.

Gross Income   Except as otherwise provided in the IRC, all income from whatever source derived, including compensation for services (IRC SS 61(a)); gross income does not include "gifts" (IRC SS 102).

Group Technology   Organizing work on similar (family) groupings products around common processes to achieve optimum use of all resources and equipment, to minimize work and to achieve high-volume economies of scale even in low-volume situations.

Guidelines   Issued by agencies to clarify fine points of regulations, guidelines do not have the force of law, and may be changed at the discretion of the administering agency.

Hold Harmless Provisions   Provisions in the law governing some formula grants preventing, usually for a specified time period, any reduction in or loss of benefits to recipients caused by legislative developments or other causes.

Home Page   A top-level document of an organization or a document that a user frequently visits. By default browsers point to their own home pages. However, you can define anyone's home page as your home page. This document is usually displayed when you start a browser session. Often provides hyperlinks to other sites.

Hotlist   A user-defined list of preferred URLs to a given World Wide Web document.

H.R.   Number which identifies a bill originating in the U.S. House of Representatives.

HTML   HyperText Markup Language. The rules that govern the way we create documents to enable them to be read by a WWW browser. Most documents that are displayed by browsers are HTML documents. These documents are characterized by the .html or .htm file extension. For example: homepage.html or homepage.htm. HTML documents are essentially text documents that have tags embedded in them. These tags contain codes for text formatting, graphics, and hypertext links.

HTTP   HyperText Transport Protocol, the protocol used by the WWW servers.

Hyperlink   A connector in a given document to information within another document—jumps the user to different documents on the WWW. These links are usually represented by highlighted words or images. The user also has the option to underline these hyperlinks.

Hypermedia   Richly formatted documents containing a variety of information types, such as textual, image, movie, and audio. These information types are easily found through hyperlinks.

Identification Number   Number assigned to individuals and organizations by the IRS; also termed a Social Security number or an *"employer identification number"* and tax identification number (used even when the organization does not have any employees) (IRC SS 6109) to verify its tax-exempt status.

Impoundment   Any action or inaction by an employee of the United States that precludes the obligation or expenditure of budget authority provided by Congress.

Improvement   See Kaizen.

In-Kind Gifts   Donated services furnished without cash remuneration, due to the difficulty of assigning monetary value, are recorded if: (1) services are significant and integral to operations; (2) paid employee or contractor would be hired if the services were not donated; (3) the EO would continue the program without the volunteers; (4) duties provided are controlled by the EO; and (5) there is a clearly measurable basis for valuing services. Donated materials and facilities, if significant in amount, are recorded at fair market value.

In-line image   A graphic image that is displayed with an html document.

Income Interest   The right to receive all or some portion of the income from property for a stated period of time, either alone or with others.

Independent Audit   Financial evaluation process followed by a professional accountant to form an opinion as to the fairness of presentation of the financial statement for a specific period of time according to generally accepted accounting principles.

Independent Sector   The segment of U.S. society represented by nonprofit, principally "charitable," organizations; also known as the *"voluntary sector," "nonprofit sector," "third sector"* or *"private sector."*

Indirect Compensation   Pay received in the form of benefits or services.

Indirect Cost Rate   Ratio used to "fully cost" program services by calculating the proportionate share of indirect costs. Some funders limit the rate of reimbursement for such costs to a certain rate: total indirect costs divided by direct costs.

Indirect Costs   Costs not readily identifiable with a particular aspect of organizational operation (sometimes called overhead or administration). Examples: executive director salary, accounting department, and occupancy.

Information Technology Infrastructure   All the information technology used within an organization, including computers, networks, and software.

Initial Tax   Principally in the "private foundations" context, the "excise taxes" that are initially assessable in enforcement of the rules; also known as "first-tier" taxes.

Innovation Grant   Financial assistance provided to explore, evaluate, or develop new or experimental solutions to problems. See Grant.

Input   (a) Materials or information that a group needs to produce its outputs. In most cases, one group's input is another group's output. (b) What we obtain from others in order to perform our job tasks.

Inspection   Inspections, tests, and other planned evaluation used to determine whether outputs conform to customers' requirements; another term for *appraisal*.

Institution   Church, school, hospital, or medical research/education organization afforded special status as "public charity" regardless of sources of support. In the "tax-exempt organizations" context, entities such as churches, universities, colleges, schools, and hospitals; these entities are not "private foundations" (IRC SS 509(a)(1)) but hold certain tax-exempt privileges.

Integration   (a) Reduction of pension benefits or contributions to take into account Social Security benefits to which a participant is entitled. Some pension plans are designed to yield a retiree a certain amount when combined with Social Security. In such cases, the contribution or benefits will vary according to the amount being paid into or received from Social Security. (b) The process of moving data between computer systems and extracting that data from or entering it to respective business management systems without human intervention.

Interactive EDI   The on-line exchange and processing of single electronic documents or line item details in real time between trading partners.

Internal Controls   Accounting procedures and controls established to minimize the likelihood of misappropriation of assets or misstatements of accounts, while maximizing likelihood of detection, if it occurs.

Internal Revenue Code (IRC)   The statutory body of federal tax law developed by Congress and administered by the IRS; the current version of which is the Internal Revenue Code of 1986 (as amended).

Internal Revenue Service   The agency of the federal government whose responsibility includes regulating the activities of tax-exempt organizations (referred to as the "IRS"); a component of the Department of the Treasury.

Internet An international (noncommercial, self-governing) computer network that connects government, academic, and business institutions. The Internet is not an on-line service. Instead, it is a collection of tens of thousands of networks, on-line services, and single-user components.

Investment Pool Assets of several funds pooled or consolidated for investment purposes.

IRA Individual retirement account, a trust, insurance contract, or custodial account organized and created in the United States for the exclusive benefit of an individual and his or her beneficiaries. The limit on contributions for a tax year is $2,000, except for rollover contributions. An IRA may not be invested in insurance contracts or in "collectibles" (such as stamps or rare coins) and must provide for mandatory distributions. Under 408(c), employers and employee associations may establish IRAs for employees. Distributions from both types are taxable in the year paid.

IRS Internal Revenue Service.

ISDN Integrated Services Digital Network. Special connections using ordinary telephone lines to transmit digital (versus analog) signals.

Ishikawa Diagram See Graphic Tools.

Ishikawa, Kaoru Japanese quality guru who developed cause-and-effect analysis; the resulting charts are also known as Ishikawa diagrams or "fishbones." He is the author of *Guide to Quality Control*, a standard textbook in both Japanese and American companies.

J&S Joint-and-survivor annuity; one which, upon the participant's retirement, lasts for his or her lifetime and then provides an annuity for the lifetime of the surviving spouse.

Joint Venture An undertaking of two or more organizations and/or individuals for the accomplishment of a particular purpose; an arrangement closely akin to a "general partnership."

JPEG Joint Photographic Expert Group, a method of storing an image in digital format.

Just-in-Time (JIT) Production/Inventory Management Production process or system characterized by the arrival of materials or parts as they are needed for assembly, not maintained in inventories by the company or supplier. Kanban is a pull-demand method of inventory management in which parts or materials are delivered from a preceding stage in the process upon request (via a "kanban" card). JIT eliminates the waste of inventory, and the costs of carrying the inventory and of the space it occupies.

Kaizen Small improvements made in the status quo or standard operating procedures, as opposed to innovation which involves a drastic improvement in the status quo. Statistical methods applied to a process help determine sources of variation in the process, to improve average output, and to help eliminate root causes of variation. Zero defects is the constant goal, increasing customer satisfaction while simultaneously boosting profitability.

Kanban Signboards, cards, or chits used in a "pull" method of manufacturing, in which parts, materials, or components are delivered from a preceding station or stage upon request (sometimes after receiving a "kanban card"). As opposed to a "push" system in which work is performed at each individual station as parts or materials arrive and are retained as in-process inventory at each succeeding station. Advantage of the kanban is in keeping inventory as low as possible. Synonymous with just-in-time production systems. See Just-in-Time Production/Inventory Management.

Key Employee One who is an officer of the employer or who meets one of several ownership tests. "Key" and "highly compensated" are not synonymous.

Lapsed Donor Renewal Direct mail solicitation program whose objectives include asking prior (but not recent) donors to renew their interest in and support of the nonprofit, philanthropic organization.

Leased Employee Someone who is not an employee yet who provides services usually provided by an employee but does so under contract with a leasing organization and on basically a full-time basis for over a year.

Legal Remedies Protection, furtherance, or enforcement of the rights of a specific groups of citizens through such means as litigation, legal representation, negotiation, or intervention in judicial proceedings, on behalf of the designated group or category.

Legislation General rules of human conduct which are consciously and deliberately made by a legislative body; a declaration of general principles by a legislative body to be applied (usually prospectively) to all persons or general classes of persons.

Legislative Advocacy Type of advocacy whose objective is to affect changes in legislation, including activities ranging from testimony before legislative bodies, to outlining areas of concern to those agencies and organizations involved. See Lobbying.

Liability Obligation, debt, or claim on organization's assets.

Life Income Agreement An agreement whereby money or other property is given to an organization on the condition that the organization bind itself to pay periodically to the donor or other designated individual the income earned by the assets donated to the organization for the lifetime of the donor or of the designated individual, after which the principal becomes the property of the organization. See Charitable Remainder Unitrust.

Limited Partnership A partnership comprised of at least one "general partner" and at least one "limited partner," the latter being one whose liability for acts of the partnership is limited to the amount of investment.

Line Speed A measurement in bits (of information) per second (bps), or baud; relates to the speed at which a modem can pass data between computers.

Loaned Executives Paid leave for corporate employees who volunteer to work for a nonprofit organization for a period of time. Loaned executives remain on their company's payrolls and continue to be eligible for benefits.

Lobbying An activity usually associated with an attempt to influence a legislative process; generically, it means being in the lobby, so it can also mean attempts to influence the outcome of executive branch or regulatory agencies' decisions, or actions of a legislative branch that are not "legislation." Direct contact with members of legislative bodies to urge the introduction or passage of legislation. Grass-roots lobbying is urging the general public to lobby.

Local Area Network (LAN) A network connecting computers within a range of less than 1000 meters.

Long-Term Commitment/Constancy of Purpose Private and public sector experience in the United States and abroad shows that substantial gains come only after leadership makes a long-term commitment, usually five years or more, to improving quality. Long-term commitment includes establishing the vision, mission, and guiding principles of the organization.

Longitudinal Data or Study Research data or information gathered over time (e.g., periodic intervals) from the same sample or population. Provides the ability to monitor individual changes among members of the study.

Mailbox A storage point within a value-added network service for a specific user of that network. Messages are held until retrieved or forwarded to another mailbox.

Management Letter Report on any weaknesses in financial management and procedures, presented by independent CPAs at end of their audit or review.

Management Support Form of technical assistance to an individual or organization addressing both administrative and technical aspects of an agency's operations, using processes including: initial contact, diagnosis, assessment, agreement on intervention, implementation of intervention, evaluation, termination, and follow-up. See Technical Assistance.

Mandated Insurance Benefit One that a state requires be included in an insurance package or plan if the insurer is to operate within the state.

Mapping A process of diagramming what data is to be exchanged, how it is to be used, and what business management systems need it. Mapping is performed by the functional manager responsible for the business management system. Mapping is preliminary to developing an applications-link.

Market Definition Effort by the organization to determine and define which particular segment(s) of the market its operations, services, or products should be serving.

Market Niche Portion of a market in which demand exists for a product or service with specific attributes which distinguish it from other, competitive offerings.

Market Potential Calculation of maximum possible usage opportunities (if services) or sales (if products) in a defined territory for all providers of a product or service during a given period of time.

Market Segmentation Process and act of identifying submarkets or segments within a target market with similar characteristics (homogeneous).

Marketing Analysis, planning, and promotion of a program, service, or product to a targeted audience to achieve an organization's objectives.

Marketing Mix Basic ingredients in any marketing program which are most important in determining consumer decisions on whether or not to buy or use the product or service, for example, product (includes service as a product), price, distribution (or delivery system), and communication.

Marketing Planning Establishing objectives for marketing-related activities, followed by identifying and scheduling those steps necessary to achieve the objectives.

Match or Matching Proportion or percentage of allowable program costs not borne by the funding source. In many cases, the law, contract, or grant establishing a program also includes a percentage or formula relative to the total program budget which must be contributed from other sources.

Matching Gift The amount of a second gift to a nonprofit organization stimulated by an employee making the first gift.

Measurement (a) One of the four pillars of *Quality Management* strategy. The objective is to ensure that everyone in the organization use measurements in their day-to-day work. Measuring their outputs against customer requirements and using cost of quality estimates are two examples. Examination necessary to compare results to requirements. (b) Determining the value, amount, or degree of something—translating a characteristic into a symbol which can then be communicated and manipulated. Provides means to manage by facts, continuously improve while making improvements visible; used to make decisions, to track progress, and to determine success. Standardized rules for assigning numbers.

Messaging   The electronic transmission of electronic objects between parties.

MIME   Multiple Internet Mail Extensions, a standardized method of identifying files such that the first packet of information received by a client contains information about the type of file the server has sent. For example, text, audio, movie, postscript, word document.

Minimum Funding Standards   Guidelines for the minimum amount an employer must contribute to a plan to cover all liabilities and operating costs. Sections 301 to 306 of ERISA specify funding requirements for pension plans.

Minimum Vesting Standards   Requirements for the points at which benefits become nonforfeitable. Benefits derived from employee contributions are fully vested immediately. Employer contributions may meet one of three standards: (1) 100 percent vesting after five years (cliff vesting), (2) seven-year graded vesting, or (3) ten-year cliff vesting under multiemployer, collectively bargained plans.

MIR   Minimum investment return; 5 percent of PF assets, held for investment purposes and not dedicated to charitable purposes.

Mission   A brief statement that summarizes the organizations' reason for being, including: who we are, what we do, for whom we do it, and why.

Modem   A hardware device that converts digital (computer) data into audio (analog) tones for transmission over a telephone network. The process is reversed when receiving data. (MOdulator/DEModulator.)

Modifications   Term used in unrelated business tax context to describe the rules used to exclude certain forms of income, such as "passive income," from taxation (IRC SS 512(b)).

MPEG   Moving Pictures Experts Group, a method of storing movie files in digital format.

NCSA   The National Center for Supercomputing Applications. NCSA is located at the University of Illinois in Urbana-Champaign, Illinois.

Net Earnings   For nonprofit organizations, gross earnings less operating expenses; in for-profit organizations, net earnings are often passed along to owners (e.g., dividends paid to stockholders).

Net Investment in Plant   Total carrying values of all property, plant, equipment, and related liabilities, exclusive of those real properties that are held for investment.

Networking   Process of developing relationships or linkages between individuals or organizations through such means as exchanges of information and resources and/or coordination of activities or efforts.

Noise or Clutter   Communications (conflicting, counter, or unrelated) that distract from a message to members of a target audience.

NOL   Net operating loss.

Nominal Group Technique (NGT)   More structured approach to generating a list of options than either brainstorming or multivoting. Called "nominal" because the group restricts somewhat the interaction typical during team activity.

Noncompliance   Situations or instances in which projects or programs fail to comply with statutory regulations or other binding requirements governing the activity.

Nonprofit Organization   An agency or organization formed exclusively for public benefit purposes, for which tax-exempt privileges are granted.

Normal Retirement Age   The earlier of: (1) the age specified in the plan, or (2) the latest of (a) the participant's 65th birthday, (b) the fifth anniversary of plan participation, for someone who began participating within five years of the plan's stated normal retirement age, or (c) the tenth anniversary of someone's initial plan participation. Term does not refer to the age at which one falls asleep reading a benefits glossary.

Not-for-Profit Activities   Activities for which a business expense deduction is not available (IRC SS 183); often confused with "nonprofit" activities.

Obligations   Amounts of orders placed, contracts awarded, services rendered or other commitments made by federal agencies during a given period, which will require outlays during the same or some future period.

Officer   An individual who, by reason of an organization's "articles of organization" and/or "bylaws," or by law, is assigned certain duties in the operation of an organization.

OJT   On-the-job training. Learning provided by the supervisor at the work site. Usually limited to the knowledge and skills an employee must have to perform an assigned function or job.

Ombudsman   Person or position designated as a liaison to assist others in dealing effectively with an organization, institution, or governmental agency. One acting as counsel and advocate for another to rectify a grievance through investigation, intercession, and initiation of action on behalf of the complaining party.

On-line Service   Dialup service providing news, information, and discussion forums for users with modem-equipped PCs using the access software provided by the service.

Operational Definition   The defining of concepts and terms by specifying how they are measured.

Operational Plan   A detailed evaluation of an organization's internal operating procedures as they relate to business document processing and internal efficiencies. For example, as it relates to EDI, it serves as an operational focus for EDI to ensure implementation for maximum benefit/return while providing input for the strategic plan.

Operational Test   Rules applied (most frequently in the IRC SS 501(c)(3) context) to determine whether an organization's operations are such as to merit tax-exempt status for it. Also called *Organizational Test*.

Organizational Development   (a) Process of analyzing the formal and informal structures of an organization or agency, determining needs and problems, and designing a systematic plan for incorporating appropriate, feasible changes into the structures to increase the overall effectiveness of service delivery by the organization or one of its programs. (b) Bringing about organizational change in an orderly and meaningful way through what are termed "interventions."

Organizational Structure and Infrastructure   Definition of the relationships, roles, responsibilities, and capabilities within an organization.

Organizational Test   See Operational Test.

Outlays   Values of checks issued, interest accrued on the public debt, or other payments made, net of refunds and reimbursements.

Output   (a) Product or service produced by an individual or group and passed on to a customer. The customer for an output may be either internal (within the company) or external. In some functions, such as engineering, outputs are commonly referred to as *deliverables*. (b) Materials or services provided to others.

Pace-setting Gift   See Bellwether.

Paid Solicitor   See Solicitor.

Pareto Chart   See Graphic Tools.

Participant   Someone entitled to receive benefits under an ERISA plan. A former employee is a participant if he or she has been vested and has yet to receive all accrued benefits under a plan.

Participation   Taking part, or allowing one to take part in a plan. Generally, the maximum required waiting period is one year if the employer wants to retain tax qualification; an employer may allow employees to participate immediately. The usual minimum age requirement is 21, although tax-exempt educational institutions may use age 26.

Partnership   See General Partnership and Limited Partnership.

Passive Income   Income that is not generated from the active participation in a business, usually annuities, capital gain, dividends, interest, rents, and royalties.

PBGC   Pension Benefit Guarantee Corporation, an entity operated under the Department of Labor to administer pension plan insurance and termination provisions. The PBGC may terminate a plan experiencing financial difficulty; it might also assert claims against an employer filing for bankruptcy.

Pension Plan   One providing for definitely determinable retirement benefits over a period of years for participants or their beneficiaries. A tax-qualified plan must be in writing, be established by an employer, be communicated to employees, be a permanent rather than a temporary program, and must exist for the exclusive benefit of covered employees and their beneficiaries.

Person   An entity, either an organization (corporation, unincorporated association, trust, partnership, or estate) or an individual.

PF   Private foundation.

Pilot Project   Initial project designed and funded to serve as a model for similar projects meeting the same needs in other areas.

Plan-Do-Check-Act Cycle   Also called by Dr. W. Edwards Deming the "Shewhart Cycle" and known by the Japanese as the "Deming Wheel." The quality management approach, which includes:

- Planning for improvements.
- Making data-based decisions.
- Pursuing continuous improvement.
- Maintaining long-term perspective.
- Improving processes.
- Improving organizational systems.

PDCA includes the following phases:

- *Plan*: Plan a change or test. Carefully consider what should be done and how to identify key factors for success and how to measure the impact of improvement efforts.
- *Do*: Carry out the plan, preferably on a small scale.

- *Check*: Observe the effects of the change or test.
- *Act*: Act on what was learned. Reconsider, repeat the cycle with new knowledge.

Planning   Devising methods through which to achieve an objective. Detailed expression of an action program. Planning provides a map for all involved in or affected by the process of reaching an identified objective, enabling a coordinated, shared effort.

Pledge   Promise to contribute a certain amount to an EO, with specific timing and possibly a particular type of property (such as an art object pledged to be given upon death).

POF   Private operating foundation.

Policy Deployment   Developing and communicating guidance needed to coordinate and execute activity throughout an organization. Often achieves breakthroughs on major problems by focusing attention and resources on high-priority issues—aligning and converging efforts to achieve the organizational vision. Effective policy deployment assures the linkage of action and effort throughout the organization to achieve common goals and objectives while realizing optimal total performance.

Pooled Income Funds   A planned giving method in which money or securities are transferred by a donor to a charitable organization eligible for pooled income funds. The organization adds donor's funds to its pooled income fund which is maintained separate from other funds where the pooled gifts of many donors are invested together, with each donor receiving a pro rata share of earnings. Upon the death of the income beneficiary, the charitable organization subtracts assets from the fund equal to the donor's share and for use for charitable purposes. See Life Income Agreement.

Population   See Distribution.

PostScript   A page description language developed by Adobe Systems.

Poverty Level   Gross annual income considered to be below that necessary for self-support.

Present Value   Value in today's terms of money to be received in the future. Because money has a time value, a dollar today is not the same as a dollar received a year from now. Present-value calculations are used to translate future benefits or income to today's terms for ready comparison and to determine the amount of money one must put aside or invest to yield benefits of a certain amount in the future.

Prevention   Things done to keep mistakes from happening. An example is the time spent agreeing on requirements with the customer. Causing something not to happen or recur.

Price of Nonconformance   What it costs to do things wrong.

Primary Customer   See Customer.

Primary Demand   Current requirement (level of demand) from all sources for an entire product or service class.

Prime Sponsor   Agency, organization, or unit of government receiving funds for a particular program that can and/or does delegate some or all of its responsibilities in this program area to another agency, organization, or unit of government.

Prior Approval   Requirement in some programs (usually federal) that prior, written permission from an authorized official be obtained regarding actions resulting in the spending or obligation of funds, or the performance of certain specified activities under the sponsored program.

Private Foundation   A charitable organization that is usually funded from one source (an individual, family, or business), that makes grants for "charitable" purposes to nonprofit organizations (IRC § 509(a)); compare "private operating foundation." See Foundation. Charitable organization funded by small group of contributors, usually a family, or earning its income from endowment (not an "institution"). Subject to special rules prescribing its activities.

Private Inurement   (a) The doctrine, most prevalent in the IRC § 501(c)(3) context, that causes a "tax-exempt organization" to lose or be denied tax-exempt status where the organization is operated for the private gain of a "person," particularly insiders. (b) Economic gain or preference given to insiders; prohibited for EOs.

Private Operating Foundation   A foundation that operates one or more "charitable" programs (IRC SS 4942(j)(3)). Similar to a nonprofit organization, not a grant-making foundation. A PF that expends its resources to carry out its own projects, rather than granting funds to other organizations, as defined in IRC Section 4942(j)(3).

Problem-solving Process   A systematic, disciplined approach to identifying and solving work-related problems throughout an organization.

Process   A series of operations that result in a product or service. A set of conditions or causes that work together to produce a given result. Usually, a blending of machines, methods, material, people, and environment.

Process Action Teams   See QM.

Process Capability   A way of checking a work process to find out whether or not it will produce outputs that meet customer requirements.

Process Improvement   Any fact-based, analytical process that deliberately seeks systematic improvement in a work process focused on increasing customer satisfaction—a collection of people, equipment, and procedures organized to provide a service or product. The goal of process improvement is to increase quality and reduce time requirements and cost-improved efficiency.

Process Model   A conceptual tool to analyze any work activity. This tool helps break the job into component parts and establishes requirements for each part.

Process Proving   Testing a process using the same equipment, facilities, skills, suppliers, and resources as a full-scale run. It verifies that the process can meet the requirements and give continuing conformance.

Product   What is offered to prospective customers for their adoption, use, consumption, or acquisition; including services, physical goods, causes, and social behaviors.

Professional Solicitor   See Solicitor.

Profit Center   Unit within an organization having revenues and costs clearly identifiable and whose leadership is held accountable for controlling both sides of the income statement.

Program Development   Procedures involved in translating an idea into a functioning activity, project, or service, including: determining needs and how those needs will be met, setting objectives, outlining action steps, and designing the implementation.

Program Manager   See Campaign Director.

Program Services   Activities or projects accomplishing the purposes for which the EO was established.

Program Support   Form of technical assistance to a nonprofit organization or individual addressing the program or service activity aspects of an agency or organization's activities through a process including: initial contact, diagnosis and assessment, agreement upon intervention, implementation, evaluation, and follow-up. See Technical Assistance.

Project   Activity underwritten by a funding source, usually requiring matching contributions in specified amounts or percentages, permitting the funding office or organization to exercise judgment in project approval, the period of the project, the funding recipient, and the amount of the project funding.

Project Costs   Allowable costs incurred by a grantee or funding recipient while accomplishing the objectives of a program or project during the specified period.

Project Manager   An individual, usually a functional manager, assigned to organize the activities of a project team; as in the case of EDI, to electronically reengineer the business processes.

Project Team   A group of individuals, usually functional managers, responsible for gathering business information and performing implementation tasks as assigned by the project manager.

Proprietary Format   A message format specifically developed by a single company with the trading power to dictate its use by the company's trading partners.

Prospect Research   Fund-raising process of identifying and learning about prospective donors, the purpose of which is to help design and conduct solicitation successfully.

Prospecting   See Donor Acquisition.

Protocol   (a) A planned method of exchanging data over the Internet—assures that different network products can work together. (b) A set of rules governing information flow in an electronic communication system.

Provider   Individual or organization whose partial or main purpose is to assist other individuals or organizations in the resolution of identified issues through technical assistance.

Psychographic Segmentation   Separating the market into segments in terms of variables including interests, attitudes, values, life-styles, or personalities.

Public Charity   A charitable organization, usually an "institution" and thus not a "private foundation" (IRC SS 509(a)(1)). Federally tax-exempt organization meeting definitions of Section 509(a)(1) or 509(a)(2) and qualifying for favorable tax status afforded Section 501(c)(3) organizations.

Public Service Advertising   Advertising donated by the media or agencies.

Publicity   Special events or similar activities conducted to attract attention and focus, usually including the news media.

Publicly Supported Charity   A "charitable" organization is not a "private foundation" because it receives the requisite amount of financial support from the public (IRC SS 170(b)(A)(vi) and 509(a)(1) or IRC SS 509(a)(2)).

Qualified Plan   One that meets IRS requirements and therefore receives favorable tax treatment.

Qualifying Distributions   Grants, program service costs, or asset acquisitions of a PF that satisfy Section 4942 tests for annual charitable giving.

Quality   Generally defined as conformance to customer requirements.

Quality Dimensions   Quality of products or services is achieved by improving existing processes or through innovation in product, services, or processes. "The difficulty in defining quality," explained Dr. W. Edwards Deming, "is to translate future needs of the user into measurable characteristics, so that a product can be designed and turned out to give satisfaction at a price that the user will pay." The challenge for government organizations, with no market to capture, is to "deliver economically the service prescribed by law or regulation. The aim should be distinction in service. Continual improvement in government service would earn appreciation of the American public and would hold jobs in the service, and help industry to create more jobs." (Deming, W. E. 1986. *Out of the Crisis*, p. 6.) Quality has many dimensions, including: *accuracy, aesthetics, consistency, durability, ease of use, features, perception, performance, reliability, serviceability, timeliness,* and *uniformity.*

Quality Function Deployment (QFD) Any process designed to deploy "customer focus" throughout and across the organization to help ensure that every function is focused on satisfying the same fundamental set of requirements. Design approach using matrix charts to define customer requirements, focusing efforts on meeting customer requirements rather than simply manufacturing to a set of predefined specifications or offering services designed by intuition or other non–fact-based decision making processes.

Quality Improvement Team Group of individuals that runs the Quality Improvement Process. Part of a complete organization for promoting quality.

Quality Leadership Leadership is responsible for 100 percent of manufacturing or service provision processes. According to many quality experts at least 85 percent of the problems are systemic; fewer than 15 percent are attributable to some special cause or particular individual outside of the system. Because leadership and management controls the process, it is their responsibility to improve the system. Management defines the system and processes; employees work in them. Therefore only leaders can facilitate change. This change must be implemented from the top down. Leaders must drive out fear to promote innovation, risk taking, pride in workmanship, and continuous improvement. Top-level managers need to accept the challenge and take the lead in establishing the culture for quality. This leadership includes commitment and active involvement in both speech and action.

Quality Management Quality management has emerged as a fourth-generation management style, to replace the most commonly used management style of today, management by results. Quality management provides the method, often lacking in management by results, of continuously improving each and every process in an organization. This philosophy combines human resource management techniques and quantitative methods to focus on supplier internal processes and the customer.

Quality Management Boards (QMB) See TQL.

Quality Policy A management statement that communicates to everyone in a company where management stands on quality. A personal statement by an individual that commits him or her to doing the job right the first time.

Quantitative Methods Integrates statistical thinking and management actions to provide leaders and managers with the data necessary for fact-based decision making. We can no longer rely on instinct, intuition, or opinion to make those decisions that affect our internal organization, our customers, or our suppliers. Quantitative methods are used to: define processes, identify problems, indicate solutions, and monitor improvements.

Quasi-Endowment Funds Funds that the governing body of an organization, rather than a donor or other outside agency, has determined are to be retained and invested, with earnings to be used or reinvested for future use. The governing body has the right to decide at any time to expend the principal of such funds. See Designated Funds.

Quick Response   The use of electronic information technologies between retail trading partners to reduce purchase order lead times and finished goods inventory.

Range   Measure of variation in a set of data; calculated by subtracting the lowest value in the data set from the highest value in that same set.

REA   Retirement Equity Act of 1984, noteworthy for requiring that married vested participants retiring under a plan must receive joint and survivor benefits (rather than having the employee exhaust all benefits and the surviving spouse be left without income) unless both participant and spouse consent in writing to a different option.

Real-time EDI   The on-line exchange and processing of electronic business information between trading partners.

Recognition   The formal and informal acknowledgement of individual and group efforts.

Recognition and Reward   The objective is to use (and change where necessary) recognition systems to support the principles of continuous improvement.

Recognition of Tax Exemption   Process engaged in by the IRS or a state in determining that a "nonprofit organization" is a "tax-exempt, charitable organization."

Record Keeping   Design and implementation of a system to collect management or program information.

Regular Income Tax   Term used to describe the basic federal income tax, to distinguish it from the "alternative minimum tax."

Related Activity   A program activity in furtherance of the purposes of a "tax-exempt organization" (IRC SS 512).

Release Time   Time allowed away from work by many corporations to enable employees to perform community service work.

Remainder Interest   The element of an item of property that causes outright title of the property to pass to a person (usually a "charitable" one) after the "income interest" in the property has expired.

Requirement   (a) What the customer for a given output needs, wants, or expects that output to do. (b) What is expected in providing a product or service. The "it" in "do it right the first time."

Research   Critical and exhaustive investigation having as its aim and focus the discovery of new facts and their correct interpretation, or the revision of accepted conclusions, theories, or laws, in the light of newly discovered facts, or the practical applications of such new or revised conclusions, theories, or laws.

Research Project   Activity or program designed and funded to gain new knowledge or to evaluate current knowledge applied to new settings.

Resident Director   See Campaign Director.

Restricted Funds   Funds whose use is restricted by the donor for specific purposes as contrasted with funds which the organization may use for any purpose it chooses in keeping with its mission.

Restricted Gift   A "contribution," usually to a "charitable" organization, that is accompanied by documentation mandating that it be applied to a particular purpose of the organization, in keeping with its mission.

Return on Assets (ROA)   Ratio of profit (revenue minus cost) to assets. ROA is a widely used measure of a company's financial success.

Revenues   Gross increases in assets, gross decreases in liabilities, or a combination of both from delivering or producing goods, rendering services, or other earning activities of an organization during a period. For example, dues, sales of services, ticket sales, fees, interest, dividends, and rent.

RFC   Request for Comments. These are the agreed-upon standards by which all methods of communicating over the Internet are defined.

RFP   Request for Proposal.

Robust Design   Any approach which optimizes designs to minimize all problems; allows considerable variation in parameters of components with degrading performance. The objective is a design process which achieves the highest possible quality at lowest costs while focusing on the voice of the customer. Robust design approaches used in conjunction with other methods to reduce variation in the process can dramatically reduce manufacturing defects.

Root Cause   An original reason for nonconformance within a process. When removed or corrected, the nonconformance will be eliminated.

Run Chart   See Graphic Tools.

S.   Number (e.g., S. 3714) which identifies a bill originating in the U.S. Senate.

SC   Substantial contributor.

Scatter Diagram   See Graphic Tools.

Scrap   Outputs, either products or services, that fail to meet their customer's requirements.

Self-perpetuating Board   A "board of directors" that elect themselves to office, rather than by an outside source, for example, the organization's membership.

Server   A computer that serves information and software to the Internet community.

Service Project   Activity or program designed and funded to ensure the development, organization, establishment, provision, or expansion of services.

Set-Aside   Board designation or restriction of funds for specific future activity or asset acquisition.

SGML   Standard Generalized Markup Language is an international standard, an encoding scheme for creating textual information. HTML is a subset of SGML.

Shewhart Cycle   See Plan-Do-Check-Act Cycle.

Shewhart, Walter   Quality guru who developed quality control charts.

Simplified Employee Pension Plan (SEP)   Essentially an individual retirement account or annuity established by an employer, often under a model or prototype arrangement with a bank or other financial institution.

Six C's   The transitional stages involved in a cultural change. The Six C's are: *comprehension, commitment, competence, communication, correction*, and *continuance*.

SLIP/PPP   Serial Line Interface Protocol/Point-to-Point Protocol. Types of connections that allow users to connect their computer system to the Internet itself, rather than logging on through an Internet access provider's host computer. SLIP/PPP connections let users communicate directly with other computers on the network using TCP/IP connections.

SMTP   Simple Mail Transfer Protocol. Set of identified steps used by one Internet computer to connect to another computer to transmit a message to the next step.

Social Service Leave   Form of corporate paid release time for volunteering. Employees at any level may be granted a leave of up to one year to work for a nonprofit organization, remaining on the payroll during the leave period.

Solicitor   A "person" who is paid by a "charitable" organization to engage in the act of requesting "contributions" to the organization; also known as a *"paid solicitor"* or *"professional solicitor."*

SOP   Standard Operating Procedure(s). Established policies, directives, and rules for all major operations.

SPC   See Statistical Process Control.

Special Causes of Variation   Cause of variation characterized as intermittent, unstable, unpredictable; detected by point(s) beyond the control limits. See Total Quality Management.

Special Events   Activities used to draw attention to a nonprofit organization or to raise money, for example, dances, fashion shows, open houses, banquets, and so on. Often inefficient as money raisers, but an effective way to involve previously uninvolved supporters and to create wider "visibility" in the community.

Specification   Customer requirement translated into the most desirable terms.

Spending Authority   As defined by the budget act, a designation for borrowing authority, contract authority, and entitlement authority, for which the budget authority is not provided in advance by appropriation acts.

Split-Interest Trust   A trust that is established for the purpose of creating an "income interest" and a "remainder interest" in one or more items of property (IRC SS 4947).

Statistical Control   Condition of a process from which all special causes of variation have been removed, demonstrated by the absence of variation on a control chart beyond the control limits, and the absence of nonrandom trends or patterns within the control limits.

Statistical Process Control (SPC)   Tracking of variations in processes. Data is used to help identify sources of variation which can then be reduced. SPC is used within the broader concept of continuous improvement, including policy deployment and teamwork. SPC enables the control state of a process to be determined, necessary before special causes of variation can be identified and addressed, that is, to improve the capability of the process.

Stratification   Process of grouping and classifying data into groups and subgroups based on categories or characteristics.

Substantial   Measurement used with a variety of EO issues to test qualification, usually expressed as percentage. Amount is usually 85 percent or more but may vary from as little as 50 percent.

Summary Plan Description (SPD)   Summary of each plan that must be given to all participants and beneficiaries. It must be written in language which the average participant can understand while at the same time covering the plan's provisions.

Supplemental Appropriation   An act appropriating funds in addition to those in an annual appropriation act. Supplemental appropriations provide additional budget authority beyond original estimates for programs or activities (including new programs authorized after the date of the original appropriation act) for which the need for funds is too urgent to be postponed until enactment of the next regular appropriation act.

Supplier   Individual or group responsible for producing and delivering outputs to one or more customers.

Supplier Involvement   Deliberate engagement of suppliers as team members in the methods and processes of continuous improvement. This serves to continuously improve the quality of inputs; obtain dependable (best value) services and products; and establishes a win–win mutual benefit for all stakeholders, functioning as it does through teamwork, cooperation, and communication.

Supplier Partnership   No matter how much an internal process is improved, it is practically impossible to provide a quality product to a customer without the receipt of quality inputs. The output of a process, the product or a service, depends largely on the input, or the suppliers. Leaders must open the communication channels and establish a working partnership with the suppliers. Operational definitions of the quality product or service must be developed. These definitions must have quantitative measures and must be agreed to by both customer and supplier.

Suppliers Individuals or groups who provide inputs to you. Suppliers can be internal or external to an organization.

Support Donations, dues, or other property conveyed to EO without consideration; see also Contribution.

Support Constituency Individuals who have been, will be, or are affected by a nonprofit organization.

Support System Specific actions that can be planned before training and during training, job linkage, and follow-up to help maintain behavior and performance improvement.

Supporting Organization (a) A "charitable" organization that is not a "private foundation" because of its supportive relationship to one or more other organizations, with the supported organization or organizations usually the "institutions" or "publicly supported charities" (IRC SS 509(a)(3)). (b) Charitable EO operating to benefit one or more specified public charities, and controlled by or responsive to such charity (usually privately funded).

Supporting Services Sustaining activities auxiliary to operating activities, such as accounting or fund raising, also called management and general or administrative department. See also Program Services.

System Way of working toward a particular goal. For example, conformance to customer requirements. The most efficient system is prevention—avoiding mistakes by keeping them from happening. Another system, usually more costly, is to "fix it in the field." A series of steps taken to ensure that a stated goal is achieved.

Target Market Portion of the total market selected by the organization as the focus of its marketing, sales, or other efforts.

Tax-deferred Annuity One used to fund retirement plans of tax-exempt employers or their employees. See 403(b) plans.

Tax-Exempt Organization A "nonprofit organization" that is exempt from one or more of federal, state, and/or local taxes (IRC SS 501); also known as "tax-exempt entities."

Tax Preference Item An item, usually a deduction or credit, that enables a taxpayer to reduce taxable income for regular income tax purposes.

Taxable Income For individuals who elect to itemize deductions, "adjusted gross income" less itemized deductions and the personal exemptions; for individuals who do not itemize their deductions, "adjusted gross income" less the standard deduction and the personal exemptions (IRC SS 63).

TCP/IP Transmission Control Protocol/Internet Protocol, a set of rules that establish the method by which data is transmitted over the Internet between two computers.

Teamwork Coordinated effort and activity between several individuals in which each does a part, but with each subordinating personal prominence and individual recognition for the effectiveness and efficiency of the whole or entire effort.

Technical Assistance Nonfinancial aid to an individual or an organization which has resolution or organizational-related problems as its goal. The provision of technical assistance should be characterized by mutual problem identification, time-limited focus, and specific goal setting. Technical assistance is divided into *Management Support* and *Program Support*.

TEFRA Tax Equity and Fiscal Responsibility Act of 1982, regarded by some as the beginning of the trend toward nondiscrimination rules, as this applied nondiscrimination rules to group-term life insurance plans. When an employer pays the premium for more than $50,000 in group-term life insurance for an employee, the amount in excess of the premium for $50,000 of coverage is taxable income to the employee.

Term Endowment Fund that has all the characteristics of an endowment fund, except that at some future date or event it will no longer be required to be maintained as an endowment fund.

Testamentary Trust A trust created by a will.

TIFF Tagged Image File Format, a file format used for storing image files.

Title XX Federal social service program providing funds to states for social services such as family planning, foster care, day care, transportation for the elderly, and so on. Services can be provided by both public agencies and private organizations.

Top Heavy Giving disproportionately more benefits to key employees.

Total Quality Control See Total Quality Management or Total Quality Leadership.

Total Quality Management (TQM) or Total Quality Leadership (TQL) Term for broad approach to quality, extending past product quality and including virtually everything done by an organization for both internal and external customers. Continuous improvement is the goal toward measurable, more challenging quality targets. The application of quantitative methods and people to assess and improve: materials and services supplied to the organization; all significant processes within the organization; and meeting the needs of the customer, now and in the future.

Trade or Business An activity carried on for the production of income from the sale of goods or the performance of services (IRC SS 513(c)).

Trade Shows A function, usually of a "trade association," consisting of the exhibiting of products and services of interest to the association's membership, usually undertaken in conjunction with the association's annual membership convention.

Trading Partner A customer, supplier, service provider (such as banks, transportation carriers, etc.), or any other outside organization with which one exchanges information on a routine basis in order to conduct its business.

Transfer Movement of fund balances from one fund to another, usually because of an intended change in use of an asset.

Trust Agreement An agreement between two or more "persons" for the purpose of creating a trust; compare Declaration of Trust. See Articles of Organization.

UBI Unrelated business income.

UBIT Unrelated business income tax.

Unemployment Insurance Combined federal and state program (administered by each state) that is intended to provide financial security to jobless workers. Program is financed by an employer-paid tax on the first X dollars of each worker's pay; in a few states, a small employee contribution is required as well. Nonprofits may have the option of paying the tax (at a rate determined by employer age and experience) or of paying no tax but reimbursing the system for all unemployment benefits claimed. Such a choice can be made only once a year.

GLOSSARY

Unrelated Activity   An activity of a "tax-exempt organization" that is not undertaken in furtherance of the organization's tax-exempt purposes, other than most administrative, investment, and "fund-raising" activities (IRC SS 512).

Unrelated Business   Commercial activity that does not accomplish the exempt purposes of the EO which can be subject to income tax.

Unrestricted Funds   Funds that have no external restriction on their use or purpose, that is, funds that can be used for any purpose designated by the governing board, as distinguished from funds restricted externally for specific purposes. For example, for operations, planning, and endowment.

URL   Uniform Resource Locator, the address to a source of information. The URL contains four distinct parts, the protocol type, the machine name, the directory path and the filename. For example: http://www.ncsa.uiuc.edu/SDG/Software/Mosaic/NCSAMosaicHome.html.

Variable Cost   Expense that changes in direct relationship to changes in other activities, such as labor, supplies, parts, materials, or commissions.

Variation   Inevitable difference between individual outputs of a process, usually grouped into two major classes: *Common Causes* and *Special Causes*.

Vesting   Acquiring the right to receive benefits; reaching the point at which benefits become nonforfeitable.

Volunteer Management or Administration   Manner or system of managing the recruitment, screening, orientation, training, and supervision of the nonpaid staff of an organization.

WAIS   Wide Area Information Server, an Internet multimedia search-and-retrieve tool including more than 500 databases. WAIS (pronounced *ways*) allows users to look through the full text of a document.

Welfare Benefit Plan   Any plan or program to provide participants (and beneficiaries) with benefits for health care (medical, surgical, dental, hospital coverage), sickness, accidents, disability, death, unemployment, vacation, training, day care, educational assistance, or prepaid legal services.

Wide Area Network (WAN)   A network connecting computers and/or local area networks. It may extend over a wide geographical area up to being global.

Worker's Compensation   Employer-paid insurance program regulated by each state and designed to protect employees from financial loss as a consequence of a work-related injury or illness.

World Wide Web (WWW; W3; The Web)   A distributed hypertext-based information system conceived at CERN to provide its user community an easy way to access global information. The networkwide, menu-based program provides hyperlinks to a wide variety of information sources on the Internet.

Year of Service   Any 12-month period during which an employee has at least 1,000 hours of service.

Zero Defects   The attitude that all defects can be prevented and are unacceptable.

Index*

---

*References to footnotes are indicated by an "n" following the page number.